The Mississippi Valley Historical Review

VOLUME XXXIX

June, 1952 to March, 1953

Published Quarterly by the Mississippi Valley Historical Association

Contents of Volume XXXIX

ARTICLES

The Democratic Theme in American Historical Literature. By Merle Curti 3

Southern Ohio and the Union in 1863. By Eugene H. Roseboom 29

Rutherford B. Hayes, Educator. By Henry L. Swint . . 45

The Northern Great Plains: A Study in Canadian-American Regionalism. By Paul F. Sharp 61

The Immigrant Theme on the American Stage. By Carl Wittke 211

The Gaspee Affair: A Study of its Constitutional Significance. By William R. Leslie 233

Edward Channing's "Great Work" Twenty Years After. By John A. DeNovo 257

The Forty-Fifth Annual Meeting of the Mississippi Valley Historical Association. By Thomas LeDuc 275

The Secession Crisis and the Frontier: Washington Territory, 1860-1861. By Robert W. Johannsen 415

Watchers for the Second Coming: The Millenarian Tradition in America. By Ira V. Brown 441

Frederick Law Olmsted in the "Literary Republic." By Laura Wood Roper 459

Progressivism and Imperialism: The Progressive Movement and American Foreign Policy, 1898-1916. By William E. Leuchtenburg 483

Mercantile Education in the Ante-Bellum South. By Lewis E. Atherton 623

The Opposition of American Businessmen to Social Control During the "Gilded Age." By Chester McArthur Destler . 641

Frederic L. Paxson and his Approach to History. By Earl Pomeroy 673

Drang Nach Norden: The United States and the Riel Rebellion. By Donald F. Warner 693

NOTES AND DOCUMENTS

Origins of Immigration Restriction, 1882-1897: A Social Analysis. By John Higham 77

Imprisonment for Debt in America: Fact and Fiction. By Edwin T. Randall 89

Historians' Choice: Results of a Poll on Recently Published American History and Biography. By John Walton Caughey 289

The Parchment Peace: The Senate Defense of the Four-Power Treaty of the Washington Conference. By J. Chal Vinson 303

Ignatius Donnelly, James J. Hill, and Cleveland Administration Patronage. By Horace Samuel Merrill 505

Expedition to the Yellowstone River in 1873: Letters of a Young Cavalry Officer. Edited by George Frederick Howe . 519

Emerson, Thoreau, and John Brown. By Gilman M. Ostrander 713

Personal Accounts of the Albany Congress of 1754. Edited by Beverly McAnear 727

BOOK REVIEWS 103, 315, 535, 747

COMMUNICATIONS 163

HISTORICAL NEWS AND COMMENTS 165, 372, 590, 813

DIRECTORY OF CONTRIBUTORS . . 203, 403, 610, 820

The Democratic Theme in American Historical Literature

By Merle Curti

In recent years distinguished scholars have indicted much of the literature of American history in the decades since the first World War.[1] The indictment maintains that, in brief, historical writing has overemphasized or handled with undue sympathy liberal forces and factors in the national experience, and underemphasized those of a conservative nature. One historian has cried out against what he regards as unfair treatment of the so-called "robber barons" whom he sees as constructive architects of our mighty economy. Another has declared that in treating our wars critically historians failed to prepare youth spiritually for participation in World War II. Still another has deprecated a tendency to expose to the public view what he terms "pathological" aspects of the national past. Not all of these scholars have been explicit, but the indictment has often implied that these shortcomings are somehow closely related to the vogue of relativism and of so-called presentism or a tendency to see the past through the eyes of the present. The indictment is the more interesting in view of the fact that in 1919 a well-known historian concluded that the profession had been unable to see the American past with any sympathetic understanding of the democratic aspirations and struggles of the people.

The question whether historians have adequately understood the struggles of the plain people is certainly an important one. It is really, in one sense, the question whether they have dealt adequately with democracy in American history, considering the chief factor in democracy to be government of, by, and for the people. Democracy might be treated directly by historians; or it could be given

[1] This paper was presented as the presidential address at the forty-fifth annual meeting of the Mississippi Valley Historical Association in Chicago, Illinois, on April 17, 1952.

peripheral treatment, that is, the historian might report on events and developments which are aspects of a democratic process, and in so doing, would be indirectly dealing with democracy. In considering the democratic theme in American historiography, I shall first ask to what extent certain of our major historians have given central or peripheral treatment to the theme. In considering their contributions I shall keep in mind some questions bearing on ideas of relativism and of what is often called presentism. In what degree did the treatments of democracy by these historians reflect dominant or competing movements of thought in their time? Did those who questioned the view that objectivity, however desirable, is impossible to achieve, overemphasize the democratic theme? Did those who subscribed to the idea that history should be written with an awareness of current problems also overemphasize the democratic theme and also fail to appreciate conservatism? I cannot, of course, provide definitive or even full answers to all these questions. But I shall try to throw some light on them. And I would also like to suggest some of the tasks that remain to be done if we would have a clearer and better understanding of American democracy.

It would be pertinent to consider in some detail a large body of popular historical literature that began to appear in the middle of the last century, but I can only make brief reference to it. All but forgotten writers, such as John S. C. Abbott, Benson Lossing, James Parton, and John Barber, put forth hundreds of histories and biographies for young men, for heads of families and households, for "all people."[2] These writers professed devotion to accuracy and nonpartisanship. They also professed a utilitarian purpose — that of inculcating among the masses a veneration for the fathers and patriotic devotion to national unity. Their folk heroes were not, by and large, champions of democracy, that is, of the rights and interests of the plain people. In treating Shays' Rebellion, these writers failed to display an understanding of democratic grievances and handled the episode in a somewhat perfunctory manner. In discussing the adoption of the Constitution and the Jacksonian contributions to popular rule, these purveyors of history to the people

[2] For example, John W. Barber, *Incidents in American History; Being a Selection of the Most Important and Interesting Events Which Have Transpired Since the Discovery of America, to the Present Time* (3rd ed., New York, 1847), 180-81, 298; Benson J. Lossing, *Our Country. A Household History for All Readers, from the Discovery of America to the One Hundredth Anniversary of the Declaration of Independence*, 2 vols. (New York, 1875), II, 1149.

paid their respects not to the plain people but to their betters — to property, order, and authority. In general, the Federalist-Whig view of human nature and of society informed their writing. True, such abstractions as "liberty" and on occasion "democracy" met the eyes of the reader of these flamboyant pages. One of these writers did suggest that democratic theories developed into democratic practices when efforts were made to abridge rights.[3] And another, in the midst of the Civil War, interpreted our history in terms of a long conflict between aristocracy and democracy.[4] But in these popular histories democracy was not a main theme.

The limitations of these early popular histories lie in part in an excess of picturesque and dramatic incident, in an uncritical handling of materials, and in inadequate documentation. Even more, they suffer from a pervading presentism, or seeing the past through the eyes of the present. This accounts in part for the undue emotional patriotism of all these histories.

But I must chiefly concern myself now with certain historians whose writings still command the respect of the profession. Francis Parkman wrote of a period in our colonial history before the rise of modern democracy. His theme, of course, was the competition of France and England for the New World. And here and there, notably in *The Old Régime in Canada*, his pronounced antidemocratic bias was reflected.[5] He had no desire to play down his conviction about the dramatic and often decisive role of strong men. Nor could he conceal his patrician view of human nature nor his conviction of the superiority of the Anglo-Saxon "race" with its regard for individual initiative. Parkman realized, as did so many serious scholars in his day, that women are forever inferior to men in reasoning power! [6] He could therefore, in explaining why the Anglo-Saxon "race" was peculiarly fitted for self-government, re-

[3] Benson J. Lossing, *A History of the United States. For Families and Libraries* (New York, 1857), 207-208.

[4] John S. C. Abbott, *The History of the Civil War in America; Comprising a Full and Impartial Account . . . of Touching Scenes in the Field, the Camp, the Hospital, and the Cabin*, 2 vols. (Springfield, Mass., 1863-1866), I, preface, 17 ff.

[5] Francis Parkman, *The Old Régime in Canada* (Boston, 1874), 394-96.

[6] For Parkman's views on women, see "The Woman Question," *North American Review* (Boston, New York), CXXIX (October, 1879), 303-21. For his antidemocratic position, see "Aristocrats and Democrats," Boston *Daily Advertiser*, July 14, 1863; "The Tale of the 'Ripe Scholar,'" *Nation* (New York), IX (December 23, 1869), 558-60; and "The Failure of Universal Suffrage," *North American Review*, CXXVII (July-August, 1878), 1-20.

fer to it as "peculiarly masculine" in submitting "its action habitually to the guidance of reason" and in possessing "the judicial faculty of seeing both sides of a question."[7] But insofar as Parkman realized his conviction that the historian as historian should identify himself with the times he was writing about rather than his own, he succeeded, in his stirring, romantic, and colorful narrative, in holding his markedly antidemocratic bias to a minimum.

Other scholars who took a longer span of history for their bailiwick than Parkman likewise did not discuss democracy as such. Richard Hildreth was chiefly concerned with deflating the overblown filiopietism and patriotism that colored the work of so many of his contemporaries. His aim in *The History of the United States*, which he carried to 1821, was to tell the plain unvarnished truth. He did tell the truth as he saw it, but the narrative was varnished by the gloss of his own faiths. Paradoxically Hildreth championed such democratic values as religious freedom and antislavery on the one hand and all the aristocratic doctrines of Federalism on the other.[8] He was both radical and conservative. In reviewing the *History* Theodore Parker regretted that Hildreth's democratic leanings were so feebly reflected. But they were, even so, reflected. Indeed, Parker felt that it was because these values were present in spite of the author that the *History* was so distinguished an achievement.[9] In short, Hildreth determined to write objectively, but the *History* reflected competing movements of thought in his day.[10]

In carrying the story beyond the point at which Hildreth stopped, other historians also gave a peripheral rather than a central place to the democratic theme. Take James Schouler. This New Eng-

[7] Parkman, *Old Régime in Canada*, 397-98.

[8] This is explicit in much of Richard Hildreth, *The History of the United States of America*, 6 vols. (New York, 1875-1878). See, for example, II, 424-25.

[9] Donald E. Emerson, *Richard Hildreth* (Baltimore, 1946), 133-34; *Massachusetts Quarterly Review* (Boston), III (1850), 386-425.

[10] It is interesting to compare Hildreth's *History* with George Tucker, *The History of the United States, from Their Colonization to the End of the Twenty-Sixth Congress, in 1841*, 4 vols. (Philadelphia, 1856-1857). Although in some respects writing from a Jeffersonian view, Tucker, like Hildreth, expressed much admiration for Alexander Hamilton and George Washington, and declared that some of our "undiscriminatory ancestors, in their love of civil liberty, did not see that, for their sentiment to have any merit, it must be qualified by justice, order, and obedience to the laws. Liberty, in its largest sense, is the desire to do what we please; and it is this desire which animates the tyrant, the criminal, and, in short, every violator of the law." *Ibid.*, IV, 429.

land lawyer and Civil War veteran subscribed, as Hildreth had done, to ardent antislavery views. Unlike Hildreth, he accepted, in a mild form, the natural rights philosophy. These two tenets often affected his selection of materials, his emphases, and his judgments. He was no lover of the "fierce democracy" of Andrew Jackson but he nevertheless dealt sympathetically with the movement for universal suffrage.[11] He revered our Anglo-Saxon heritage but his faith in the natural rights philosophy led him to write sympathetically about immigrants. For, holding as he did the doctrine that men everywhere are created equal, he had to reject the idea that any one race could alone enjoy the blessings of freedom.[12] Schouler's devotion to popular rule is shown in his presidential address before the American Historical Association in 1897. On that occasion he called for a convention to draw up a new federal constitution designed to make government more responsible to majority will.[13] What president of any historical association in our own day of loyalty purges would dare propose to throw overboard the Constitution? On the other hand, Schouler, like Hildreth, paid proper respects to property rights when these did not operate in an exploitative fashion.

Or take the retired entrepreneur, James Ford Rhodes, who carried the story from 1850 into our own century. Rhodes was a middle-class critic of sudden or drastic social change, an advocate of property and educational qualifications for suffrage, and a warm admirer of John D. Rockefeller.[14] With such a social philosophy he naturally did not emphasize in the *History* the ingredients of democracy, with the exception of antislavery. In virtually ignoring the West and the rising industrial economy, each of which profoundly influenced democracy, Rhodes fell short of giving it adequate treatment. When he did discuss a topic directly related to

[11] James Schouler, *History of the United States of America under the Constitution*, 7 vols. (New York, 1880-1913), I, 404-405; III, 44-47.

[12] James Schouler, *Ideals of the Republic* (Boston, 1908), 28, 34-38, 173. See also the excellent discussion in Edward N. Saveth, *American Historians and European Immigrants, 1875-1925* (New York, 1948), 158-63.

[13] James Schouler, "A New Federal Convention," American Historical Association, *Annual Report*, 1897 (Washington, 1898), 22-34.

[14] James F. Rhodes, *History of the United States from the Compromise of 1850 to the End of the Roosevelt Administration*, 9 vols. (New York, 1928), III, 634; VIII, 34-35, 232; IX, 165-67. See also Mark A. DeWolfe Howe, *James Ford Rhodes, American Historian* (New York, 1929), 111-12; for views on the direct election of senators and the abilities of women, *ibid.*, 271, 333; and for explicit statements on democracy, *ibid.*, 139, 179, 329.

democracy, such as organized labor or the agrarian revolt, his treatment was highly biased.[15]

Or take Woodrow Wilson, perhaps the first president to make sustained and explicit use in state papers and public pronouncements of the term democracy in referring to the United States. Wilson paid little attention to democracy in his *History* — at least in the sense in which he used the word in later years. It is true that he gave ample consideration to constitutionalism, an essential element of democracy. But he was content merely to suggest that the frontier and industrialism had bearings on democracy.[16] And his unsympathetic treatment of labor, immigration, and Populism caused him no little embarrassment in his later political career.[17]

Again, take Edward Channing. He did, to be sure, deal with many topics related to democracy — the widening of the suffrage, the improvement in status of the underprivileged, and public education. But not until the fifth volume, published in 1921, does he refer explicitly to democracy either in the ideological or substantive sense. Then he confined the discussion to one note![18] If Channing had a central theme at all, it was the growth, not of democracy, but of nationalism. This he deeply appreciated despite the fun he had in demolishing pet hobbies of filiopietists.

All these historians, Schouler, Rhodes, Wilson in his prepolitical period, and Channing, accepted the doctrine that objectivity is not

[15] Rhodes, *History of the United States*, VIII, 46-49, 270-75, 385, 407, 425-27.

[16] For Woodrow Wilson's ideas about democracy as expressed in his formal writings in the fields of history and political science, see *The State. Elements of Historical and Practical Politics. A Sketch of Institutional History and Administration* (Boston, 1889), 603-609; and the thoughtful commentary on this book in Arthur S. Link, *Wilson:The Road to the White House* (Princeton, 1947), 21-22. See also Woodrow Wilson, *Division and Reunion, 1829-1889* (New York, 1893), 11-25, 111, 115-29, 161 ff.; *A History of the American People*, 5 vols. (New York, 1903), V, 82, 99, 127-42, 168, 186, 203, 300. Also illuminating is Wilson's article "Democracy in the United States, Character of," in *Harper's Encyclopædia of United States History From 458 A. D. to 1905*, 10 vols. (New York, 1905), III, 68-78. For Wilson's discussion of aspects of the history of democracy as developed in his essays and lectures, see Ray S. Baker and William E. Dodd (eds.), *The Public Papers of Woodrow Wilson*, 6 vols. (New York, 1925-1927), I, 396-415; and "The Course of American History" in *Mere Literature, and Other Essays* (Boston, 1896), 231-45. In addition to the valuable discussion in Link, see Harley Notter, *The Origins of the Foreign Policy of Woodrow Wilson* (Baltimore, 1937), 23, 40.

[17] New York *Times*, February 2, 1912, p. 12. See also Link, *Wilson: The Road to the White House*, 381, 388.

[18] Edward Channing, *A History of the United States*, 6 vols. (New York, 1905-1925), V, 377. For Channing's bias toward "radical elements" in 1798-1800, see *ibid.*, IV, 220; for his antipathy toward the "alien ideologies" of later immigrants, see *ibid.*, V, 71, 106.

only desirable but possible. None of these writers subscribed to the view that the past should be interpreted in terms of the present. None of them, however, even in their formal historical writings, succeeded in writing of the past without being influenced by the present. It is not hard to show how various schemes of thought entered into the writings of Schouler, Rhodes, Wilson, and Channing. If one rereads the histories of these men with the controversial issues of their day in mind, he cannot avoid the conclusion that what they wrote could hardly have given much comfort to the liberals and radicals of their time. They took sides, like others of their day.

If one stopped with these historians, one would have to accept the 1919 verdict of William E. Dodd. Writing to his friend Chief Justice Walter Clark, the Chicago historian observed: "You may well say, why can not historians see things from the people's point of view. I agree that most do not, that most historians, like most lawyers, are color blind." [19] In fact, however, Dodd was forgetting an important development in American historiography.

He was, for the moment, overlooking George Bancroft, the first of our major historians to make the democratic theme central in our early history. Bancroft subscribed to the natural rights philosophy. His view of human nature was a composite of the Enlightenment's faith in the universality of reason in all men and of Transcendentalism's faith in the divine intuitive quality of every mind. Bancroft was therefore compelled to make democracy, in the sense of the rightness of majority rule, central in his history.[20] Subscribing further to the Newtonian conception of an ordered universe governed by natural law, Bancroft assumed that the American achievement in self-government represented the implementation in human affairs of the "natural laws" of the universe. The rest of the world would, he was convinced, move toward the American example. Bancroft thus fused American democracy, in the political sense, with American nationalism. He was a presentist in that he wanted to justify American achievement to the American people

[19] William E. Dodd to Chief Justice Walter Clark, Chicago, June 7, 1919, William E. Dodd Papers (Manuscripts Division, Library of Congress), XIV.

[20] This is implicit in George Bancroft, *History of the United States of America, from the Discovery of the Continent*, 6 vols. (New York, 1884-1885), and beautifully explicit on many pages, as for example, IV, 5-6. It is worth noting that there is little difference between the democratic views Bancroft expressed in the *History* and those appearing in his addresses and private letters.

and to the rest of the world. He also believed that because he followed in his work the uniquely true dispensation about human nature and society, his *History* was thoroughly objective. Thus he did not take as unqualified praise Leopold von Ranke's remark that it was the best history yet written from the democratic point of view.[21]

We no longer accept the rational and divinely intuitive theory of human nature nor the natural rights philosophy — at least without qualifications. Nor the teleological conception of American nationalism. Thus we cannot approve the overweaning importance Bancroft gave to the early "achievement" of democracy. Modern scholars, reworking the period he surveyed, have corrected his overemphasis. We may here merely mention Charles McLean Andrews. He was an admirable example of an historian who achieved a high degree of the objectivity he believed desirable and who certainly reduced the influence of the present to a minimum. Writing shortly after the first World War, Andrews provided new evidence for the thesis that many historians both oversimplified and carried too far back into the colonial period the beginnings of democracy.[22]

Bancroft was not the only historian to give the democratic theme a central place in his history. Influenced no doubt by the current discussions of democracy and by the profound implications for democracy of the advance of corporate wealth, Henry Adams and Frederick Jackson Turner in quite different ways later gave the topic an important place in their historical writing. Both Adams and Turner were further influenced by certain emergent ideas in the natural science of their day — ideas which had a great appeal to thoughtful men of the time. The Darwinian theory of evolution was especially intriguing. It could be, and was, used in different ways by Adams and Turner and by other historians. And it provides an excellent example of the fact that movements of thought in a time and place, together with problems associated with the

[21] Mark A. DeWolfe Howe, *The Life and Letters of George Bancroft*, 2 vols. (New York, 1908), II, 183.

[22] Charles M. Andrews, *The Colonial Background of the American Revolution* (New Haven, 1924), 201; "Conservative Factors in Early Colonial History," *Authority and the Individual* (Cambridge, 1937), 156-69; and *The Colonial Period of American History*, 4 vols. (New Haven, 1934-1938), IV, 423-24 n. This was further developed by one of Andrews' students, Leonard W. Labaree, *Conservatism in Early American History* (New York, 1948).

economic, political, and social milieu, greatly influenced ways in which the democratic theme was interpreted.

Henry Adams was convinced that American experience in a peculiar way exemplified the laws of science. And since he was concerned with democracy in his own day and regarded it as the central issue in the first decades of the nineteenth century, it seemed to him clear that the laws of science could explain democratic development. "The more I write, the more confident I feel that before long a new school of history will rise which will leave us antiquated," he wrote to Francis Parkman. "Democracy," Adams continued, "is the only subject for history. I am satisfied that the purely mechanical development of the human mind in society must appear in a great democracy so clearly, for want of disturbing elements, that in another generation psychology, physiology, and history will join in proving man to have as fixed and necessary a development as that of a tree; and almost as unconscious."[23]

Adams, in the pages of his great *History*, assumed that the young democracy could not survive in a world of force and *real politik* unless, whatever its reluctance to do so, it took part in the struggle for existence. So he thought that it was strictly in the order of things that the United States should have become involved in the Napoleonic conflict, in spite of Thomas Jefferson's efforts to stay out. The war waged by the American democracy brought out the strongest qualities in that democracy: such were the terms of survival.[24] In domestic no less than in foreign affairs, Adams made the theory of evolution (adaptation, struggle, and survival) a central key: these doctrines explained the Jeffersonian shift from state rights to national power, the growing role of the executive, the inadequacy of the old ideas in the postwar world of 1816.[25]

But the mind of Henry Adams was too complex, his range of scientific interests too broad, to make Darwinism explain everything. He had become interested in the teachings of Lord William

[23] Harold D. Cater (comp.), *Henry Adams and His Friends. A Collection of His Unpublished Letters* (Boston, 1947), 133-34. The letter is dated December 21, 1884. See also Adams to Samuel J. Tilden, January 24, 1883, *ibid.*, 125-26; and Henry Adams, *History of the United States of America*, 9 vols. (New York, 1889-1891), I, 1, 5, 59-60.

[24] Adams, *History of the United States*, I, 162-63; II, 421-22; IV, 27, 33, 69, 74, 334; V, 234-36, 250; VI, 133-59; IX, 219-20. Mr. James Daffer, who is investigating the relation of Henry Adams to both science and democracy, has independently confirmed and carried further this interpretation.

[25] *Ibid.*, IX, 86, 104, 132, 226-27, 239.

T. Kelvin regarding physical energy in the universe. In passage after passage in the *History* Adams made energy or force, physiological, psychological, and mechanical, the key to what happened.[26] The historian concluded that the struggle for survival and the laws of thermodynamics in the years he surveyed gave some assurance for democracy in the period after 1818.[27] But only some. For he had discovered the painful shortcomings of the people. Even their most gifted leaders, including Jefferson, seemed helpless to direct the present, let alone the future. Indeed, they appeared "like grasshoppers kicking and gesticulating in the middle of the Mississippi River."[28] Moreover, Adams saw scientific law in recurring catastrophes which were presumably cyclical. From any point of view the *History* was a conscious, sustained, and intellectually sophisticated effort to make democracy the central theme of the period between 1800 and 1818. It testified to Adams' use of our discipline as an instrument for understanding present and future. And within the frame of assumptions suggested by his reactions, temperamental and intellectual, to currents of scientific thought, Adams achieved a marked degree of objectivity.

Adams in his earlier essays, and John Fiske[29] and Herbert Baxter Adams[30] later, emphasized the hereditary factor in the evolution of institutions and societies. Frederick Jackson Turner gave a different emphasis. In his view environmental factors were far more important than hereditary ones. The environmentalist view might seem to reduce the scope of individual freedom to create, and subject man to a fate conditioned if not determined by his physical

26 Ernest Samuels, *The Young Henry Adams* (Cambridge, 1948), 134-35; Henry Adams, *Democracy: An American Novel* (New York, 1880), 10; Adams, *History of the United States*, I, 116; II, 117; III, 56, 74, 196; VII, 407; VIII, 264; IX, 153, 192-93.

27 Adams, *History of the United States*, VI, 123; IX, 225-29.

28 Cater (comp.), *Henry Adams and His Friends*, 125-26.

29 John Fiske, *American Political Ideas Viewed from the Standpoint of Universal History* (New York, 1885), 5-6, 49, 94-95, 106-108, 135. For further illustrations of Fiske's views on democracy in American history, see *Essays, Historical and Literary*, 2 vols. in one (New York, 1907), I, 50-51, 115, 134, 146-48, 153-54, 166-67, 173-74, 222-23, 272-73, 301-306; *Old Virginia and Her Neighbors*, 2 vols. (Boston, 1897), II, 315-16, 395-97; *The Dutch and Quaker Colonies in America*, 2 vols. (Boston, 1899), II, 252 ff.; *The Beginnings of New England; or, The Puritan Theocracy in Its Relation to Civil and Religious Liberty* (Boston, 1889), 247-48.

30 W. Stull Holt (ed.), points out in *Historical Scholarship in the United States, 1876-1901: As Revealed in the Correspondence of Herbert B. Adams* (Baltimore, 1938), 16-17, that Adams, also a champion of the hereditary principle in his historical theory, was aware that the method of the Teutonic school, which influenced him, reinforced conservatism.

environment. But as Turner saw it, of course, the struggle of men with their environment, the constant beginning over again on new frontiers, developed a self-reliance and individualism, a not necessarily contradictory habit of neighborly cooperation, and an equalitarianism.[31] Turner was aware of the bearings of European democratic ideas and institutions on the course of American democracy; but he emphasized the American frontier environment in giving what he assumed to be a unique quality to democracy in the United States.

It is relevant to add that Turner was sympathetic to the idea that each generation must rewrite the history of the past in terms of its own vantage point and needs.[32] In 1917 he wrote to a former pupil that the historian had too largely held himself aloof from current struggles. The historian's special knowledge, he felt, might make his contributions to an emergency quite as important as those of the economist and the political scientist.[33] Thus on occasion Turner gave implied support to the contention that government controls must provide the equality of opportunity once provided by free lands.[34]

There is time to speak very briefly of the reactions to the theory of evolution of certain other historians of democracy. The generally neglected book that Bernard Moses wrote in 1898, *Democracy and Social Growth in America*, held that democracy was largely the result of material conditions that were transitory — free land and a simple rural society. Moses concluded that democracy as it developed in response to these conditions could not survive the new era of corporate wealth. If the government failed to control the monopolies, the old democracy was certainly done for; if it succeeded, the swollen government power necessary thereto likewise meant the end of a democracy that had evolved from transitory conditions.[35] The same year, 1898, Frederick A. Cleveland, a lawyer and political scientist who adopted the historical approach, published the

[31] Frederick J. Turner, *The Frontier in American History* (New York, 1920), 30-32, 54, 247, 249-51.

[32] Everett E. Edwards (comp.), *The Early Writings of Frederick Jackson Turner* (Madison, 1938), 52, 58; Turner, *Frontier in American History*, 323-24.

[33] Frederick J. Turner to Solon J. Buck, Washington, May 3, 1917, Papers of the National Board of Historical Service, Alphabetical by Authors A-B (Manuscripts Division, Library of Congress).

[34] Turner, *Frontier in American History*, 282-84, 319, 322.

[35] Bernard Moses, *Democracy and Social Growth in America* (New York, 1898), 1-35, 49.

first systematic historical account of democracy in which the concept was explicitly made the basis of the treatment. Cleveland viewed democratic, and indeed all institutions, in the light of the cooperative rather than the competitive factors in evolution.[36] Other writers utilized the concept, too.[37] But we must not dismiss this theme without reference to Charles A. Beard's essay, "The Evolution of Democracy." Published in 1919 this piece, one of the many that Beard devoted to the subject, dealt with the evolution of society from savagery and the corresponding development of the state. Beard traced the main aspects of the democratic victory over governmental institutions of kings and nobles and the adaptation of these to democratic purposes. He pointed to recent democratic forces which were working to subject to popular control all that the captains of industry had created — especially corporations.[38]

The new science not only called the attention of historians to evolutionary theory as a useful tool in their thinking. The implications of the scientific movement involved a more self-conscious effort to achieve objectivity by surmounting the limitations of class, religion, and politics. Further, natural science suggested to historians that all data, no matter how humble, may be important. Here was at least one justification for including in historical efforts all aspects of life, social, economic, and cultural as well as political and military.

The broadening conception of the past, to which new social issues contributed, explains John Bach McMaster's determination to make the people rather than political leaders the chief subject of his history. It was not clear, however, even at the end of the eighth volume, just what McMaster meant by democracy, which he talked about a good deal, or even what he meant by the people. For he seemed, like Bancroft, to conceive of the people in middle-class terms and to reject Hildreth's view of social and political groupings based on property. As Eric Goldman has pointed out, McMaster's *History* voted for William McKinley as Bancroft's had voted for Jackson.[39] Jefferson and Jackson are belittled, Ham-

[36] Frederick A. Cleveland, *The Growth of Democracy in the United States; or, The Evolution of Popular Co-operation in Government and Its Results* (Chicago, 1898).

[37] John S. Penman, *The Irresistible Movement of Democracy* (New York, 1923).

[38] Charles A. Beard, "The Evolution of Democracy: A Summary," in Frederick A. Cleveland and Joseph Schafer (eds.), *Democracy in Reconstruction* (Boston, 1919), Chap. XXIII, 486-91.

[39] Eric F. Goldman, *John Bach McMaster, American Historian* (Philadelphia, 1943), 143.

ilton, the bank, and the tariff, praised; and the pre-Constitutional inflationists are compared with the Greenbackers, those "mischievous schemers" whose money policy was labeled vicious and absurd.[40] It would be easy to point to other qualifications of McMaster's democracy. Though he praised many social gains,[41] what had been achieved represented in his eyes finality. There was neither need nor justification for carrying democracy further — especially in the economic sphere. In some degree, then, McMaster too, despite his attention to the people, was writing from the standpoint of his own position in society. His age, as he saw it, seemed to him superior to anything in the past. A certain "presentism" was also evident in his hope that the *History* would be "full of instruction" to the social agitators of the 1880's — that through it they might come to appreciate the great gains made under the peaceful evolution of popular rule.[42]

The decades preceding Dodd's 1919 indictment of historians for failing to see the past from the democratic point of view, also witnessed the marked impact on historical scholarship of the interrelated pragmatic philosophy and the progressive movement, broadly defined. Dodd seems to have overlooked — at least for the moment — certain historical writings that appeared in the decade prior to 1919, Albert Bushnell Hart's *National Ideals Historically Traced* (1907) for example. This inadequately appreciated book presented as a key to our democratic development the struggles that resulted in the improved status of disadvantaged persons — slaves, freedmen, women, immigrants, and industrial workers. It emphasized the role of public education in the democratic advance. It traced in a fashion quite acceptable to progressives the new devices to make democracy more efficient and more articulate. And it gave much the same weight to the frontier and the Industrial Revolution in the development of democratic movements as an historian today might give.[43]

40 John B. McMaster, *A History of the People of the United States, from the Revolution to the Civil War*, 8 vols. (New York, 1914), I, 201, 282, 476-77, 490; II, 51, 310; VI, 84.

41 John B. McMaster, *The Acquisition of Political, Social and Industrial Rights of Man in America* (Cleveland, 1903), 40, 59, 90-100, 110; *With the Fathers*; *Studies in the History of the United States* (New York, 1896), 239, 251-52.

42 McMaster, *History of the People of the United States*, II, 616-17; *With the Fathers*, 320.

43 Albert B. Hart, *National Ideals Historically Traced, 1607-1907* (1907), Albert B. Hart (ed.), *The American Nation: A History*, 28 vols. (New York, 1904-1918), XXVI.

The progressivism and pragmatism that illuminated Hart's study also helped historians to rediscover the significance of economic conflicts in the advance of democracy. Here Charles A. Beard was a pioneer. His realistic, pragmatic approach substituted for Bancroft's and McMaster's romantic and amorphous idea of "the people," and for the Marxist doctrine of the class struggle, the notion of a conflict of interest groups. This, Beard held, had marked an American society in which class lines were vague and mobile.[44] The conflict between group interests and its contribution to democratic advance also informed Thomas J. Wertenbaker's description of patrician-plebeian struggles in early Virginia.[45] And Arthur M. Schlesinger's *Colonial Merchants and the American Revolution*[46] was an especially important study in which the relation of democratic movements to economic interests and group conflicts was well documented. Among these writings, Beard's books on the Constitution and on Jeffersonian Democracy alone seem to have been regarded both by progressives and by conservatives as having an *ad hoc* or presentist bearing.

In indicting the historians for their color-blindness to the people's point of view Dodd must have excluded himself. His work as an historian of democracy has been studied by Wendell H. Stephenson. Like Beard, whose *Economic Interpretation of the Constitution* influenced him markedly, Dodd had shown sensitiveness to the role of group conflicts in American struggles for democracy.[47] Here we shall merely note that, partly in response to the agrarian revolt of the 1890's and its progressive heritage, partly as a result of his experiences in Germany and his studies of Jeffersonianism, Dodd had developed the idea that democracy in American experience meant, not merely political equality but also economic and social equality.[48] I must at least call attention to a remarkable essay,

44 Charles A. Beard, *An Economic Interpretation of the Constitution of the United States* (New York, 1913); *Economic Origins of Jeffersonian Democracy* (New York, 1915); and *The Economic Basis of Politics* (New York, 1922).

45 Thomas J. Wertenbaker, *Patrician and Plebeian in Virginia* (Charlottesville, 1910), 214-15. Cf. Richard B. Morris, *Government and Labor in Early America* (New York, 1946), 52-54.

46 Arthur M. Schlesinger, *The Colonial Merchants and the American Revolution, 1763-1776* (New York, 1918). See also Schlesinger's *New Viewpoints in American History* (New York, 1922), especially Chaps. III, V, VIII, IX.

47 Wendell H. Stephenson, "William E. Dodd: Historian of Democracy," will eventually appear in *Virginia Quarterly Review* (Charlottesville).

48 These ideas are to be found in many of Dodd's writings, especially *Expansion and Conflict* (Boston, 1915); and *The Old South; Struggles for Democracy* (New

"The struggle for Democracy in the United States." This appeared in 1918 in the *International Journal of Ethics*.[49] Here Dodd maintained that democracy had been an ideal rather than an actuality in American experience. This he ascribed to the influence of wealth, operating in a frame of ever greater concentration of power in the national government. He also showed how the great leaders of democracy had been forced to compromise with privilege by reason of war as well as by the pressure of property interests. Mrs. Wilson promised to read the essay to the President. Colonel Edward M. House enthusiastically approved it. So did Thomas Reed Powell and many others.[50] The essay was but one of the more or less self-conscious and systematic interpretations of democracy inspired by the crisis of the first World War.[51]

Another interpretation of democracy, likewise related to the challenge of Prussian militarism, came from the skillful pen of Dodd's colleague, Andrew C. McLaughlin. It was expressed, in the first instance, in the presidential address before the American Historical Association in 1914.[52] Analyzing American democracy, McLaughlin saw it in the first place as a composite actuality in which the constitutional convention and the political party were of special importance in realizing self-government. Like Beard and Dodd, McLaughlin called attention to the role of conflict in the advance of democratic actuality. He also viewed democracy, in the second place, as a composite ideal. To him this meant simply the belief that men should have a chance to realize their worth without being sifted by artificial theories of value.

In 1920 McLaughlin's *Steps in the Development of American Democracy* amplified the ideas in this address. This brilliant book traced the course of democracy and summed up its implications for the immediate future. It was a pioneer effort in making the demo-

York, 1937). The latter is interesting in the parallels it draws between the dangers of centralization and planning in the period after 1660 and similar tendencies in the New Deal.

49 William E. Dodd, "The Struggle for Democracy in the United States," *International Journal of Ethics* (Chicago), XXVIII (July, 1918), 465-84.

50 Mrs. Woodrow Wilson to Dodd, September 18, 1918, E. M. House to Dodd, July 24, 1918, Thomas R. Powell to Dodd, September 3, 1918, C. E. Ayers to Dodd, April 19, 1919, James R. Angell to Dodd, February 6, 1919, Dodd Papers, XIV.

51 Carl R. Fish, "American Democracy," *Minnesota History Bulletin* (St. Paul), III (February, 1920), 251-72, is, for example, a very thoughtful interpretation which weighs the contributions of the several sections to the democratic movement.

52 Andrew C. McLaughlin, "American History and American Democracy," *American Historical Review* (New York), XX (January, 1915), 255-76.

cratic theme the focus of our whole history. It was also notable for calling attention to the careless and contradictory ways in which Americans used the term "democracy." McLaughlin held that it was unhistorical to attribute to American democracy of the past anything theoretically involved in democracy in 1920. Eighteenth-century America, he noted, was democratic in comparison with the Europe of that time. It was not democratic in comparison with the Europe or the America of the first World War.[53]

It is worth noting that McLaughlin rejected presentism. And in a spirited correspondence with Dodd, McLaughlin took his colleague gently to task for reading too much of current economic conflict into his critical remarks on the framing and adoption of the Constitution, which McLaughlin regarded as an important step in the development of democracy. Dodd, he felt, was making the same mistake as Beard.[54] But note that Dodd, on his part, felt that McLaughlin was in the same camp with Beard in mistakenly holding that history should be written with an objective — in making it teach "too much." [55] What Dodd said of these historians he might well have said of himself. For he did not hesitate to make history teach lessons, though on this occasion he rejected such a purpose. I do not know whether Dodd ever explicitly accepted any definite doctrine of "relativism." I was, however, surprised to find that in the 1914 address McLaughlin clearly anticipated Beard in expressing the frame of reference concept: he frankly said that no historian could avoid being influenced by his background and experiences.[56] The point of all this is, of course, that historians tended to see in the work and position of their colleagues the same limitations that these in turn saw in them, regardless of whether or not presentism and relativism were explicitly avowed.

The treatment of the democratic theme in American historical literature since the first World War was, as in preceding periods, influenced by changing situations and by new movements of thought. Among the latter was concern with meanings of terms and especially with the relativism to which I have just referred. The

[53] Andrew C. McLaughlin, *Steps in the Development of American Democracy* (New York, 1920).

[54] McLaughlin to Dodd, February 11, July 19, 1918, Dodd Papers, XIV.

[55] Dodd to Carl Becker, May 21, 1932, Carl Becker Papers (Cornell University Library, Ithaca).

[56] McLaughlin, "American History and American Democracy," *American Historical Review*, XX (January, 1915), 258-59.

precedent of McLaughlin in defining the uses of the word democracy in terms of time, place, situation, and context generally was continued. It was not until 1939, however, that historians systematically probed the meanings attached to the term democracy in the past. In that year Charles and Mary Beard did so with telling effects.[57] From that time on few historians discussed democracy without some attention to definition.[58] This emphasis on greater precision has, I believe, increased the degree of objectivity historians have achieved. Yet some have maintained that the writing of history since the first World War has become, at least in the hands of leading historians, less objective than in earlier times. And they ascribe this to a growing acceptance of the relativist theory and a "presentism" stimulated by the crisis of depression and the war against totalitarianism.[59] Let us look, not of course at the whole body of historical writing in the past three decades, but at that considerable segment which has been more or less consciously concerned with the democratic theme, with the question in mind as to whether "presentism" has interfered with objectivity.

It is true that the mood of disillusionment following the first World War influenced interpretations of the past. It is also true that in many quarters there was uncritical complacency regarding our culture, and that this superficial optimism led some historians to search for distinctions between appearances and realities. This search helped give vitality to the Beards' *Rise of American Civilization*, the first really new synthesis of our national history since the prevailing one which had taken shape several decades before.[60] Vernon L. Parrington's *Main Currents of American Thought*, which appeared in the same year, 1927, identified democracy with the

57 Charles A. Beard and Mary R. Beard, *America in Midpassage*, 2 vols. (New York, 1939), II, Chap. XVII, 920-49. See also the admirable discussion of the meanings attached to the term "democracy" in Charles A. Beard, *The Republic; Conversations on Fundamentals* (New York, 1943), Chap. III, 27-41.

58 See, for example, Jeannette P. Nichols and James G. Randall (eds.), *Democracy in the Middle West, 1840-1940* (New York, 1941), xiv-xv.

59 For example, Samuel E. Morison, "Faith of a Historian," *American Historical Review*, LVI (January, 1951), 266-68; and James C. Malin, *Essays on Historiography* (Lawrence, Kan., 1946), Chap. IV, 109-68.

60 Charles A. Beard and Mary R. Beard, in *The Rise of American Civilization*, 2 vols. (New York, 1927), deal explicitly with conditions favoring democracy in the colonial period, the advance of democracy during the Revolution, the impact of the agricultural West on its development, Jeffersonian and Jacksonian Democracy, the relation of slavery and emancipation to it, the status of women, and the bearings of a machine civilization on it.

agrarian tradition, with American faith in an open universe, and with humane values. It also traced its "decline" before the advancing power of corporate wealth and centralized government.[61] The shortcomings of Parrington are not only obvious but have been so emphasized that we are in danger of forgetting his great contribution to an understanding of the democratic tradition.

The New Deal, evoked by the depression, brought an increased awareness of the problem of democracy in our history as progressivism earlier had done. Perhaps it inspired well-known historical writings with an undue presentism. Critics have levied such a charge at the author of the *Age of Jackson*, who explored the dynamics of power in the democratic process.[62] Alice Felt Tyler's useful synthesis, *Freedom's Ferment*, reflects a sympathy for an earlier phase of the democratic story that became accentuated in the 1930's.[63] Curtis Nettels in *The Roots of American Civilization* viewed colonial history as a struggle between large property owners and lesser folk for the control of political and economic institutions. Ralph Gabriel explored the history of democratic ideology, and argued that there is need in a time of relativist morals of a reassertion of certain values which he speaks of as absolute and as essential elements of the American democratic tradition.[64] Others emphasized the functional role of democratic ideas and forces in the history of American thought and put that history in a social setting which included tussles between competing interests and values.[65] The

[61] Vernon L. Parrington, *Main Currents in American Thought*; *An Interpretation of American Literature from the Beginnings to 1920*, 3 vols. (New York, 1927-1930). For a penetrating analysis of Parrington's handling of the democratic theme, see Arthur A. Ekirch, Jr., "Parrington and the Decline of American Liberalism," *American Quarterly* (Minneapolis, Philadelphia), III (Winter, 1951), 295-308.

[62] Arthur M. Schlesinger, Jr., "The Pattern of Democratic Change in the United States," Carl J. Friedrich, Arthur M. Schlesinger, Jr., and Alpheus T. Mason, *The Democratic Process: Lectures on the American Liberal Tradition* (New London, 1948).

[63] Alice F. Tyler, *Freedom's Ferment*; *Phases of American Social History to 1860* (Minneapolis, 1944).

[64] Ralph H. Gabriel, *The Course of American Democratic Thought*; *An Intellectual History since 1815* (New York, 1940); "Democracy: Retrospect and Prospect," *American Journal of Sociology* (Chicago), XLVIII (November, 1942), 411-18; and "Thomas Jefferson and Twentieth-Century Rationalism," *Virginia Quarterly Review*, XXVI (Summer, 1950), 321-35.

[65] Merle Curti, *The Social Ideas of American Educators* (New York, 1935); *Peace or War*; *The American Struggle, 1636-1936* (New York, 1936); and *The Growth of American Thought* (New York, 1943, 1951). Attention should also be called in this connection to the skillful development of this approach in Howard K. Beale, *A History of Freedom of Teaching in American Schools* (New York, 1941); and *Are Amer-*

writings of many of these historians suggested that a new chapter in the history of American democracy had begun in the late nineteenth century. The shift from an agrarian-frontier economy to an industrial one set the stage for a consequent shift from freedom to equality through government planning. No historian developed this theme more cogently than Avery Craven in *Democracy in American Life*.[66]

As if perhaps to put the history of their section into the democratic stream of thought accentuated by the New Deal, southern historians now found much more democracy in the history of their section than had been assumed. The newer school piled up evidence for this thesis.[67] That it was not altogether acceptable was suggested by the work of John Hope Franklin and Kenneth Stampp.[68] In the work of such young scholars was reflected a new concern with democracy in its humanistic and ethnic aspects. Much of what these postwar historians wrote was relative to new currents of thought. But if they were influenced by relativist theories they did not, I believe, champion these in their writings or at professional meetings. The effect of their work, certainly, was to raise further questions and to broaden our knowledge of American democracy. Their "presentism," if present, led them chiefly to call attention to additional data. No one would claim that all these newer contributions forever settled the problem of American democracy in our history. But it is a healthy thing, and conducive to finding out the truth about democracy in American life, that these varied points of view have been represented in research and writing.

The New Deal and its philosophies were, of course, the chief influences in the thirties. But during the late thirties and forties historians like everyone else became increasingly aware of the threat of totalitarianism, and aware too of the rapidly growing importance

ican Teachers Free? An Analysis of Restraints upon the Freedom of Teaching in American Schools (New York, 1936).

66 Avery O. Craven, *Democracy in American Life, A Historical View* (Chicago, 1941).

67 For example, Bell I. Wiley, *The Plain People of the Confederacy* (Baton Rouge, 1943); and *The Life of Johnny Reb, The Common Soldier of the Confederacy* (Indianapolis, 1943). See also Clement Eaton, *A History of the Old South* (New York, 1949); Fletcher M. Green, "Democracy in the Old South," *Journal of Southern History* (Baton Rouge, Lexington), XII (February, 1946), 3-23; and Frank L. Owsley, *Plain Folk of the Old South* (Baton Rouge, 1949).

68 John H. Franklin, *From Slavery to Freedom: A History of American Negroes* (New York, 1948); Kenneth Stampp, "The Historian and Southern Negro Slavery," *American Historical Review*, LVII (April, 1952), 123-45.

of the United States as a world power. This new awareness influenced historical writings, especially writings about democracy.

This is not to say that the relations of war and democracy were first explored in these decades. An important discussion of the theme had taken place, in fact, at the meeting of the American Historical Association in 1900. In the view of Professor S. M. Mcvane of Harvard, democracy, through its instruments the telegraph and the popular press, had made several nineteenth-century wars inevitable by interfering with the calm deliberation of statesmen. He was no doubt thinking about the recent Spanish-American conflict. John Bassett Moore disagreed, holding that war resulted chiefly from conflicts of national interest.[69] But in 1917 Mcvane's thesis was reinforced by George Blakeslee. The Clark historian held that throughout history the democracies had been quite as warlike as nondemocratic states. Blakeslee suggested that the answer to the quest for peace was not democracy, but federalism.[70] This issue was later exhaustively explored by Quincy Wright, a political scientist who used the historical method, and who concluded, though with many qualifications, that Blakeslee's position was essentially sound.[71] With the exception of Wright, these scholars wrote before "relativism" became an issue.

On the eve of the second World War, Frederick Logan Paxson brought out his history of our part in the first crusade to make the world safe for democracy. Himself a participant in the effort of historians to publicize democratic war aims but also a representative of the objective school of history, Paxson concluded, in the spirit of Blakeslee and Wright, that the historians had overemphasized the peaceful record of the democracies and the warlike record of the autocracies. At best historians had served democracy by picking out of the American story "validated events with which to construct the sort of picture that Americans wanted to believe; and that, believed, made firmer their willingness to carry out the war." Paxson further maintained that in the crusade the "imagination, manpower, and material strength of American democracy" was mobilized for the first time. To that part of the world which doubt-

[69] *American Historical Review*, V (April, 1900), 434-35.

[70] George H. Blakeslee, "Will Democracy Alone Make the World Safe: A Study of the History of the Foreign Relations of Democratic States," *Proceedings of the American Antiquarian Society* (Worcester), N. S., XXVII (1917), 358-74.

[71] Quincy Wright, *A Study of War*, 2 vols. (Chicago, 1942), II, 841.

ed whether democracy, lumbering and inefficient as it undoubtedly was, could be a suitable instrument for implementing national interest, Paxson was on the whole reassuring — more so than Henry Adams had been when in the 1880's he had discussed a comparable problem in an earlier test. When, continued Paxson, "emotion whittles the minority down to nearly nothing and makes citizens agree among themselves, even a democracy may act with speed, directness, efficiency, and weight." [72]

Yet Paxson also saw the weaknesses of democracy in military crises. For he pointed out that democracy, deprived of an effective challenge by a minority, degenerates into the rule of mob psychology against all dissenting elements. He was not surprised at the reactionary aftermath of the war — at the repression of democratic freedoms in a nationalistic hysteria. This he regarded as no less an authentic evidence of American democracy than the high, unified purposes that inspired common action during the struggle itself.

The ideological climate of the second World War was related both to that of the first crusade and the New Deal. Of note during the years of the contest with the fascist world was the tendency of American historical thought to redefine our democracy and to put it in the broader stream of western civilization. The tendency to relate American democracy to world currents was not entirely new, of course.[73] But it differed markedly from the view of Turner, whose influence on conceptions of American democratic development had been so pronounced.

In 1941, a year of many historical discussions of democracy, Carl Wittke noted that it was hard to define because it was a process never finished. Then he stated, in comprehensive form, the meaning democracy had come to have in many quarters: the conviction that human personality is the first and final reality, never to be used for purposes alien to itself; faith in the essential collective integrity and character of the masses of men and women; government by the consent of the governed, including as an imperative part of the process the functioning of free speech, free assembly, free elections; and a sustaining economic and social order, supplemented by as much government control as necessary to the end that everyone

[72] Frederic L. Paxson, *American Democracy and the World War*, 3 vols. (Boston, Berkeley, Los Angeles, 1936-1948), II, preface, 1-3, 48-49, 51, 453.

[73] See, for example, Herbert L. Osgood, *The American Colonies in the Seventeenth Century*, 3 vols. (New York, 1904-1907), II, 254 ff., 433 ff.

enjoy a fair and a reasonably unfettered chance in life.[74] This operational definition reflected the expansion and implementation of the democratic idea in the New Deal era and awareness of the importance in a democracy of protecting minority groups.

Others discussed American democracy within a broad context of values deemed universal at least in western civilization. Carl Becker, who in 1920 had published an interpretation of the American democratic experiment,[75] now in several writings gave the theme the broader treatment.[76] In related disciplines Ralph Barton Perry[77] and Perry Miller[78] accented the democratic aspects of New England Puritanism while locating these in the humanistic currents of the Renaissance. In a striking paper Arthur M. Schlesinger, Sr., pointed out that Americans had long recognized that the democratic movement transcends national boundaries. He further insisted that democracy could be understood only in terms of parallel movements elsewhere and of world perspective.[79] Of these historians, Carl Becker alone was an outspoken champion of the so-called relativist position in historiography though others in the group may have subscribed to it in some degree. Yet on the point at issue, the placing of American democracy in a world setting, all were in agreement — all were writing *in relation to* the needs of their times and of their country.

One important contributor to the historiography of American democracy did not entirely share this world orientation. It happened that he, like his friend Becker in the other camp, was a leading spokesman for the relativist position. It was not that Beard ignored the roots of many of our democratic ideas in other places and times.[80]

74 Carl F. Wittke, "The Evolution of Democracy," *Democracy is Different. . . . A Series of Lectures at Oberlin College* (New York, 1941), 1-2.

75 Carl L. Becker, *The United States; An Experiment in Democracy* (New York, 1920).

76 Carl L. Becker, *Modern Democracy* (New Haven, 1941); "What is Still Living in the Political Philosophy of Thomas Jefferson?," *American Historical Review*, XLVIII (July, 1943), 691-706; and the statement in Norman Cousins (ed.) *A Treasury of Democracy* (New York, 1942), 167-68.

77 Ralph B. Perry, *Puritanism and Democracy* (New York, 1944).

78 Perry Miller, *The New England Mind; The Seventeenth Century* (New York, 1939).

79 Arthur M. Schlesinger, "American and World History," in *Paths to the Present* (New York, 1949), 174-77.

80 This is clear in a great many of Beard's writings, including *The Rise of American Civilization*, written in collaboration with Mary R. Beard, and in *The Republic*. See also "The Evolution of Democracy: A Summary," Cleveland and Schafer (eds.), *Democracy in Reconstruction*, Chap. XXIII.

But his emphasis was, like that of Turner, on the uniquely American aspects of our democracy. In 1932 he had called attention to an important problem in reminding us that the history of democracy had been that of the conquest and adaptation of institutions already established by the privileged classes. In that democratic adaptation America had enjoyed the advantage of having had, at least in the national period, no feudal institutions, no established church, no military caste, no bureaucracy. It had on the other hand inherited and developed constitutional checks on power, many of which were sufficiently local to be close to the people. The country having been for the greater part of its history a nation of freehold farmers, Americans had acquired a daily experience in policy making. Whether the factory could provide comparable experiences and if not, what this fact meant for the general welfare, were questions that Beard raised but that no one could entirely answer.[81]

As the New Deal and the oncoming war concentrated power in the hands of the executive, Beard warned of the importance of preserving constitutional checks and balances. And he saw in the increasing reliance on military power and overseas activities further danger to American democracy.

Beard's later writings on foreign policy illustrated his own thesis that complete objectivity is impossible. But they raised a basic question. Have we so fully achieved democracy here that the defense of democracy is the same as national defense? This question involves others. Can democracy as Carl Wittke defined it survive in a world placing overwhelming emphasis on military measures? Does democracy need more critical and more informed implementation (both here and abroad) through economic and cultural as well as military means? Should historians, if they can muster the courage, try to help the American people to answer these questions?

This consideration of the democratic theme in American historiography suggests, I think, several things. First, the treatment of democracy in the American story has been for the most part peripheral rather than central — save in times of rapid change, sharp internal tension, or a heightened foreign challenge. Second, it is clear that the treatment of democracy in American experience reflected the reactions of historians to dominant and competing cur-

[81] Milburn L. Wilson, *Democracy Has Roots* (New York, 1939), preface. A. Whitney Griswold has challenged this thesis. See his *Farming and Democracy* (New York, 1948).

rents of thought about human nature, social relationships, and the place of America in the world at the time of writing. Third, there has been no consensus about either the meaning of American democracy or its origins and conditioning circumstances or the degree of importance it has had in our national experience. It is thus an open question whether or not the current confusion and uncertainty about democracy does not in some measure rest on our shoulders. For we have largely written and taught our history to our people and to the rest of the world.

This study also suggests that recent discussions of "objective versus relativistic" writing have been too heated. As the evidence here presented shows, I have been unable to find any historians whose work has not been influenced by dominant or competing movements of thought in their time or by the position they held in society. The degree of verisimilitude reached appears to have become somewhat greater in the historical writing about democracy since the progressive movement and the first World War — a period in which the democratic theme was given a greater and more realistic emphasis. I submit that scientific method, including the new scientific idea of relativism, has helped to bring this about by lessening the confidence of the historian in assuming he had achieved objectivity.

This survey also bears on the controversy between the advocates of history for its own sake and history for the sake of understanding the present. It has shown, in terms of craftsmanship, justification both for an awareness of the historian's responsibilities to the public and the dangers in mere presentism, whether the emphasis is one primarily critical of the *status quo* or primarily apologetic for it. I have not found evidence that historians who have subscribed to so-called relativism and so-called presentism have been more prone than others to overemphasize and glorify democratic elements in our history, and to undervalue and distort conservative ones. But I have found evidence to suggest that any position which calls for a return to the patriotic affirmations without due regard to our critical functions should give us pause. Any position that calls for suppressing "pathological" episodes in our past and for using our craft to support a currently held policy,[82] should give us pause.

[82] Conyers Read, "The Social Responsibilities of the Historian," *American Historical Review*, LV (January, 1950), 284.

Finally this report on my study of the writings on democracy may suggest certain questions that invite historical investigation. We need fuller and richer histories of American democracy. These future histories may, and should, approach the subject from various angles of vision and use varying methods. I have been, for example, seeking to test the validity of Turner's contention that the frontier was more democratic than older areas, by a more or less microscopic study of a carefully chosen Wisconsin place and period. In this investigation we have supplemented town, county, and state public records, newspapers, and private manuscripts by a quantitative analysis of the data in unpublished censuses. In this study we are asking questions of highly qualified authorities — of authorities so highly qualified as to inspire at least me with awe. We are asking these questions of International Business Machines! We hope their answers may throw some new light on relationships between economic status, political participation and leadership, and social and civic activities. We hope that our study will further clarify the relation between firstcomers or early settlers and later arrivals on the one hand and equality of economic opportunity on the other. And we hope that if our results are promising, similar case studies may be made for many frontier areas at many periods and, for comparative purposes, that similar studies may also be made of the longer settled areas.

Whether studies in the history of democracy in America be microscopic or broadly gauged, they should take into account the whole of the culture, of which the democratic idea and substance do not form the entirety. They must consider the problems of definition and meanings. Nor should such histories ignore efforts to state the traditional assumptions of democracy in a form acceptable to modern logic, psychology, cultural anthropology, and theories of knowledge. Such histories should be further informed by the writings about democracy by both American and foreign scholars in the fields of philosophy, education, religion, the other social sciences, and biology. And they should take into full account the relative importance at different times of indigenous and more far-reaching experiences and ideas in shaping democracy.

Such treatments of democracy will serve as warnings against crystallizing the history of American democracy into clichés and dogma for ideological warfare. Our American experience has been related to faith in an open universe, in man's ability to control rather than be controlled by the forces surrounding him, and democracy has been, not a finished accomplishment but a growing ideal and process. But recent developments suggest that a crystallization of democracy into fixed codes and clichés is not unthinkable.

I am thinking of such aspects of the cold war as loyalty purges and loyalty oaths, of the evidences of reluctance on the campuses to discuss "controversial" questions, and of the growing tendency to associate loyalty with conformity to the particular policies of the most articulate and influential groups. If official crystallization of the democratic faith should take place, perhaps by 1984, it would be impossible to explore any further the history of American democracy. At least we could not explore it freely as our fellow historians, including some of the pioneers of this Association, have explored it — and as I hope our younger colleagues may still want to explore it. But I for one have faith that the democratic theme will continue to be explored and written about in varied but scholarly ways, by historians who will continue to have not only the humility of scholars but the courage of patriots, and who because of this humility and this courage will keep on trying to rise above the pressures of their time and, just as they find it and see it, present in their writings the truth about the history of democracy.

Southern Ohio and the Union in 1863

By Eugene H. Roseboom

Historians have long regarded the Ohio Valley of the Old Northwest as the heartland of Copperheadism. This viewpoint has rested upon two major assumptions. The first is that this region was settled largely from the South. As a consequence, the people tended to reflect the customs, traditions, and prejudices of their southern forebears. They were not proslavery, for they did not want the peculiar institution extended north of the Ohio, but they were tolerant of it where it existed and intolerant of abolitionists who would destroy it with no regard for the consequences. Like their relatives and friends south of the Ohio, they were averse to having the free Negro as neighbor and economic competitor, and were susceptible to Peace Democratic propaganda warning of the dangers of a black influx into the North.

The other major explanation of the pull of Peace Democracy in this region is economic. Not merely kinship but southern markets were involved. Since pioneer days the Ohio-Mississippi outlet had been the vital artery of trade for the lower Northwest. Surplus produce and latterly the manufactures of the Ohio River cities flowed southward either for southern consumption or for export at New Orleans. While railroads in the 1850's reduced the dependence of the Ohio Valley upon this southern outlet for its exports, the volume of direct trade with the South was still increasing and the prosperity of the region was vitally affected by the outbreak of the Civil War. When the Union armies failed to reopen the Mississippi in the first two years of war, peace by compromise had a powerful appeal. According to peace propagandists, the two great obstacles in the way of a peaceful restoration of the Union were the Black Republicans — composed chiefly of abolitionists and profiteering eastern industrialists and financiers — and the secessionists of the South. The West should assert itself, repudiate the

Lincoln administration and the war, and mediate between the warring groups. To the Peace Democrats, drawn southward by ties of blood and markets, abolitionism was the greater villain.[1]

The converse of this familiar pattern is that the northern, or lake, sections of Ohio, Indiana, and Illinois were the staunch supporters of the war. Here resided the New England-New York strain with its antislavery sympathies and its devotion to the Republican party. Economic ties with the East by lake and railroad had strengthened this blood relationship. Consequently, the Old Northwest was the scene of bitter intrasectional struggle with the fate of the Union at stake. In the end the upper Northwest triumphed over the Peace Democracy of the Ohio Valley and the cause of the Union was sustained.

However accurately this simple geographical concept may seem to fit the situation in the cases of Indiana and Illinois, its validity for Ohio is open to serious question. Historians of the period have assumed a similarity of heritage and conditions up and down the Ohio Valley that are hardly borne out by the facts. Guilt by association — or proximity — seems to have been Ohio's portion. Such a conclusion constitutes a major error, for the Buckeye State cast nearly 44 per cent of the total popular vote of the three valley states in 1864 and cannot be dismissed merely as the exception that proves the rule.

The historian who did most to affix the stigma of Copperheadism on southern Ohio was Elbert H. Benton. In his study of the peace movement, much used by other writers, he asserted that the Peace Democrats decreased "in density of numbers as the distance northward from the Ohio River increased." Benton defined their Ohio center as "the area comprehended by a line drawn through Dayton, Hamilton, Chillicothe and Cincinnati."[2] Such a description is highly misleading, for it would leave out the Ohio River counties, if taken literally, but what Benton meant, obviously, was southwestern Ohio — some fourteen counties.

[1] Samuel Medary, editor of the Columbus *Crisis*, the most radical and perhaps the most influential peace organ, phrased it as follows, October 1, 1862: "Secessionism is not the *cause* of the war but the *effect* of Abolitionism. Abolitionism produced Secessionism, and the Secessionism was the *act* of war, not the cause. Had abolitionism been defeated, Secessionism would not have taken place, and war would never have occurred."

[2] Elbert J. Benton, "The Movement for Peace without a Victory during the Civil War," *Western Reserve Historical Society Collections, Publication No. 99* (Cleveland, 1918), 11.

Other historians, less specific and not so mathematical, still emphasize Copperheadism as an Ohio Valley phenomenon generally and do not exclude the state of Ohio from their conclusions. Some examples are Wood Gray, Henry C. Hubbart, and Wilfred E. Binkley.[3] Hubbart does concede that "even many southern and western counties" voted against Clement L. Vallandigham in 1863, but the implication is that they were clearly in the minority.[4]

One explanation of this failure to assess southern Ohio's sentiments more accurately is the attention focused on the Peace Democratic leadership in this area. Vallandigham of Dayton, George H. Pendleton, George E. Pugh, and Alexander Long of Cincinnati, and Samuel Medary of Columbus constitute a galaxy of nationally known figures.[5] This naturally has affixed the stamp of Copperheadism on their constituencies. Yet they were urban leaders from three of the state's four largest cities with strong delegate support in state conventions and the backing of important party newspapers. Their strength at the polls did not equal their influence in party councils. The case of Vallandigham is typical.

Vallandigham represented a wealthy, conservative, thickly populated congressional district, which had been almost evenly balanced between the two parties for many years. He was defeated twice before his victory of 1856, and even then apparently lost by a small margin on the face of the returns but was seated by the

[3] Wood Gray, *The Hidden Civil War; The Story of the Copperheads* (New York, 1942); Henry C. Hubbart, *The Older Middle West, 1840-1880* (New York, 1936); Wilfred E. Binkley, *American Political Parties* (New York, 1943), 264-67. Whitelaw Reid, *Ohio in the War; Her Statesmen, Generals and Soldiers*, 2 vols. (Columbus, 1893), I, 17, suggests a geographical concept of politics prior to the war but does not develop it later. George H. Porter, *Ohio Politics during the Civil War Period*, Columbia University *Studies in History, Economics and Public Law*, XL, No. 2 (New York, 1911), does not analyze the distribution of votes in wartime elections. The strength of Union sentiment in southern Ohio is suggested in Eugene H. Roseboom and Francis P. Weisenburger, *A History of Ohio* (New York, 1934), 275, 284; and in Eugene H. Roseboom, *The Civil War Era, 1850-1873* (1944), Carl Wittke (ed.), *History of the State of Ohio*, 6 vols. (Columbus, 1941-1944), IV, 409, but not analyzed. John L. Stipp, "Economic and Political Aspects of Western Copperheadism" (Ph.D. dissertation, Ohio State University, 1944), is in agreement with this article as to the geographical aspect of Copperheadism in Ohio but is more concerned with other aspects.

[4] Hubbart, *Older Middle West*, 216-17. The writer is in agreement with Hubbart's general viewpoints in much of this article but believes he has given inadequate consideration to Ohio's unique situation.

[5] Allen G. Thurman of Columbus and William Allen of Chillicothe are not so clearly identified with the peace element. Wood Gray, *Hidden Civil War*, 164, confuses former Senator Allen with a member of the House of the same name from western Ohio.

Democratic House after a contest.[6] He won in 1858 by 188 votes and in 1860 by 134. Defeated in 1862 by the addition of a Republican county to his district, he carried his old counties by a modest 657 votes in a year of sweeping Democratic successes and with the soldiers not yet permitted to vote. Three of the four counties in his district voted against him in his gubernatorial race the next year. Yet they are included in Benton's "stronghold" of Peace Democracy.

Alexander Long, a doctrinaire Calhounite, more extreme than Vallandigham, was elected from a normally Republican Cincinnati district in the overturn of 1862 by 131 votes after an initial defeat in 1860. The transfer of a Republican ward to the neighboring district by the gerrymander of 1862 accounted for his victory. He was not renominated in 1864 but his district voted Unionist by over three thousand votes. The more cautious Pendleton, more strongly entrenched in the other Cincinnati district, accepted the Democratic vice-presidential nomination in that year. This may have been a wise choice, for the district elected a Unionist by a larger margin than it had ever given Pendleton. George E. Pugh, formerly in the United States Senate, was the defeated candidate, his second defeat for office in two years. He had gone down with Vallandigham in 1863 when he had spearheaded the Democratic state campaign by running for lieutenant governor with the gubernatorial candidate in exile in Canada.

Samuel Medary confined his efforts to his peace organ, the *Crisis*, and helped keep Franklin County, containing the state capital, safely Democratic. But his own congressional district, represented by the moderate Samuel S. Cox for several years, turned Union Republican in 1864. Judged by its attitude toward the Peace Democratic leaders, southern Ohio did not display Copperhead leanings. Not one of the five men mentioned earlier was in public office when the war ended and their congressional districts had repudiated the peace viewpoint.

But stronger evidence of the strength of Union support in southern Ohio is found in the votes cast in the Brough-Vallandigham gubernatorial election of 1863. Here, more than in any other of the four wartime elections, the peace issue was of overshadowing im-

[6] Votes of Ohio congressional candidates are conveniently tabulated in Joseph P. Smith (ed.), *History of the Republican Party in Ohio*, 2 vols. (Chicago, 1898), I, *passim.*

portance. In the state election of 1861, the peace movement had few open adherents and the defeated Democratic candidate for governor, Hugh J. Jewett, was a supporter of the war. In 1862 the Democrats elected candidates for minor state offices and a majority of the members of Congress but deliberately played down the peace issue, preferring to emphasize arbitrary arrests, military failures, the Emancipation Proclamation, and the dangers of a Negro influx into Ohio. In the presidential election of 1864, General George B. McClellan's support of the war threw a wet blanket on the peace movement.[7] But in 1863 the nation's outstanding Peace Democrat headed the state ticket, and while the issue of civil liberties received much attention in the canvass, the peace element was in control of the party and Union supporters made the most of this fact. Certainly those Ohioans who voted for Vallandigham either were Peace Democrats or were willing to risk the consequences of putting an avowed advocate of peace in the statehouse at Columbus.[8] The most available yardstick of antiwar strength in Ohio is the Vallandigham vote of 1863.

The soldier vote, taken at the front, is a complicating factor in evaluating the results. There was a great deal of looseness in the operation of the system and some truth in Democratic charges that their newspapers and other propaganda sometimes failed to reach their destination.[9] Yet to ignore the military ballots altogether is to underestimate Unionist strength. Soldier hostility toward Copperheads was bitter and unrelenting. One Ohio soldier expressed a common sentiment when he wrote the following in a letter to a relative:

[7] Porter, *Ohio Politics during the Civil War Period*, *passim*; William J. Ulrich, "Ohio in the Election of 1862" (M.A. thesis, Ohio State University, 1948); William F. Zornow, "The Ohio Democrats and the 'Africanization' Issue in 1862," *Negro History Bulletin* (Washington), XI (June, 1948), 211-14; Elizabeth F. Yager, "The Presidential Campaign of 1864 in Ohio," *Ohio State Archaeological and Historical Quarterly* (Columbus), XXXIV (October, 1925), 548-80.

[8] After the election of 1863 Democratic newspapers debated the wisdom of Clement L. Vallandigham's nomination and the extent to which the peace issue was involved in the election. The Columbus *Crisis* and the Cincinnati *Enquirer* insisted that his vote was a peace vote, the Columbus *Ohio Statesman* and the Cleveland *Plain Dealer* disagreed but argued that his nomination was a mistake. The controversy shows that the peace issue was certainly before the voters, whether as an asset or a liability to the Democrats. See Porter, *Ohio Politics during the Civil War Period*, 184-85; Columbus *Crisis*, October 21, November 4, 1863; Cincinnati *Commercial*, October 22, 30, 1863; Millersburg *Holmes County Farmer*, October 22, 1863.

[9] William Young, "Soldier Voting in Ohio during the Civil War" (M.A. thesis, Ohio State University, 1948).

> Father writes to me and tells me not to vote for Vallandingham [*sic*]. now cousin do not you think the advice is unnecessary. do you think the soldiers will vote for a man that they hate worse than they do the rebels? without they are cowards? for we know that just such men as Vallandingham [*sic*] is keeping up this war and by keeping it up is causing all this misery. It makes me feel bad for a friend to tell me not to vote for a worse than rebel.[10]

A letter from a Democratic soldier, printed in the Columbus *Crisis*, is further proof of soldier feelings toward Vallandigham and the ineffectiveness of Democratic propaganda. He wrote to his father as follows: "It is useless to send more tickets. I stand nearly alone here, the defender of the patriot exile, Clement L. Vallandigham. There is a perfect furor of excitement against him, and others, who pretended to be good Democrats at Potomac Creek have yielded to the damnable pressure." [11]

A smaller proportion of soldiers voted than civilians, but it may be assumed that the votes cast did not materially misrepresent army sentiments, which were anti-Vallandigham rather than anti-Democratic. The vote of the regiments in the field was nearly 17 to 1 in favor of John Brough. In 1864 it was slightly more than 4 to 1 for Lincoln over McClellan. Because of a somewhat heavier military vote in southern than in northern Ohio in 1863, in proportion to population, the civilian vote has been given separately in the following analysis wherever it seemed to have special significance.

To determine the comparative strength of the Union (or Union Republican) and Democratic parties in northern and southern Ohio, the sections have to be defined. The National Road has been regarded as the traditional line of demarcation but it does not follow county boundaries and veers to the southwest after leaving Columbus. A more logical arrangement, based on canal-river trade

[10] Samuel C. Trescott to Cordelia Miller, October 17, 1863, Trescott Manuscripts (in possession of Mr. Morrell A. Miller of Columbus and used with his kind permission). Trescott was a private in Company C, 2nd Ohio Volunteer Cavalry. A letter, dated March 6, 1863, reveals that he participated in the attack upon the office of Medary's *Crisis*, carried out by soldiers of his regiment. He wrote: "It was a secesh paper and aided the rebels and as such should be put down." Other letters of May 10, 20, 1863, report Confederate prisoners and pickets as expressing the opinion that a Copperhead uprising in the North would bring about a southern victory. They had been reading northern peace newspapers, Trescott said.

[11] Youngstown *Mahoning Sentinel*, reprinted in Columbus *Crisis*, October 28, 1863. A soldier's letter in the Hillsboro *Highland News*, November 12, 1863, stated that there were only two Vallandigham supporters in his company. One received "a good whipping at Camp Dennison for hallowing for the traitor and then deserted." The other became "ashamed" and voted for the Union.

outlets, is to extend the northern boundary of Franklin County (containing the state capital) east and west to create two fairly equal divisions.[12] This places in the southern zone all the counties intersected by the National Road, plus Miami, Champaign, and Darke counties in western Ohio, which lie north of the road. Forty-nine counties make up the northern sector, thirty-nine the southern. The latter has a somewhat smaller area (due to the convolutions of the Ohio River) but had a slightly larger population in 1860.

A tabulation of the vote by counties in the election of 1863 shows that of the eighty-eight counties in Ohio, Vallandigham carried eleven in the northern half of the state, six in the southern half.[13] If only the civilian vote is considered, his total rises to twenty in the north and twelve in the south. In either case there is a heavy preponderance of Vallandigham counties to the northward. Only one county, Monroe, of his southern bloc, touched the Ohio River, though he was ahead in Brown before the soldier vote was added. In the southwestern area delineated by Benton as the center of Copperheadism, only two counties of the fourteen were Democratic, plus Brown, if one disregards the soldier vote. In fact, the core of Vallandigham's southern Ohio strength lay near the central part of the state and included the area directly south and east of Columbus — seven counties on the civilian vote, though four of these were lost when the soldier votes came in. Of the seven, Franklin and Licking were on the National Road, Fairfield, Pickaway, and Perry just south of it. This should dispose of the "density" theory — that the Peace Democracy decreased in strength in proportion to distance from the Ohio River. Actually the three counties located

12 This line follows roughly the divide between traditional trade outlets except in the northeast where several counties lie in the Youngstown-Pittsburgh zone of the Ohio Valley but are in other respects a part of northern Ohio. For canal traffic divisions, see Francis P. Weisenburger, *The Passing of the Frontier, 1825-1850* (1941), Wittke (ed.), *History of the State of Ohio*, III, 104.

13 The maps in Porter, *Ohio Politics during the Civil War Period*, opposite p. 183, and Roseboom, *Civil War Era* [422], (copied from Porter) are incorrect. Both authors wrongly assign Defiance County to the Union party and Licking and Brown to the Democrats. The last two were Democratic on the civilian vote but Unionist when the soldier vote came in. The case of Defiance is an egregious error, which the author of this article should have caught. Gray, *Hidden Civil War*, 152, also erroneously assigns Brown County to the Democrats. For votes by counties, see Secretary of State, *Annual Report, 1875* (Columbus, 1876), 144. *The Tribune Almanac and Political Register for 1864* (New York, 1864), 69, differs slightly from this in a few counties but the differences are unimportant, except that, by a printer's error, the civilian vote is given in the *Tribune Almanac* as the total vote for Brown County, which may explan the error above.

in the most southerly dip of the Ohio River — Gallia, Lawrence, and Scioto — were Unionist by majorities equaled only in the Western Reserve of the north. The first two led the counties of the south, voting for Brough by ratios of more than 3 to 1.

In addition to the geographical distribution of votes by counties, the Democratic totals in each half of the state should be compared. Of the 187,728 votes received by Vallandigham, 98,036, or 52.2 per cent, came from the southern sector, 89,692, or 47.8 per cent, from the northern. A small allowance should be made for the slightly larger population and total vote of the southern sector. To put it another way, in the northern counties the Democrats polled 38.4 per cent of the total vote, in the southern, 40.4 per cent. Both figures and percentages take on more significance when the vote of the Western Reserve is tabulated. The twelve counties of this strongly antislavery area cast less than one third of the northern Ohio total but provided two fifths of Brough's vote and two thirds of his plurality in this half of the state. The radicalism of the Reserve has helped to create a false impression of northern Ohio's Unionist sentiments. Outside these twelve counties, the Democrats had stronger and more widespread support than in the southern half of the state. Even with the Reserve included, the difference is not very pronounced.

One of the striking features of the election of 1863 is the resurgence of Union Republican strength after the near-debacle of the preceding year. In 1862 the Democrats captured fourteen of Ohio's nineteen seats in Congress and elected their candidate for secretary of state by 5,500 votes.[14] Southern Ohio was Democratic by nearly 13,000 votes, northern Ohio Unionist by 7,400. But if the vote of the Reserve's twelve counties is subtracted, the other thirty-seven northern counties had a Democratic margin of 9,600 votes. Outside the old abolitionist area, Ohio had reacted sharply against the Lincoln administration for reasons suggested earlier. As the military skies cleared in 1863 and Vallandigham's nomination brought the peace issue to the fore, a great Union revival set in. The increase in the Unionist vote, both numerically and in percentages, was greater in the southern counties than in the northern. More surprising, Vallandigham had 7,000 more votes in northern

[14] Secretary of State, *Annual Report, 1875,* p. 141. The congressional totals are sometimes used but offer complications. In the Toledo district, embracing eight counties, three candidates split the vote.

Ohio, including the Reserve, than the Democrats had polled in 1862; he dropped 3,700 under the vote of that year in southern Ohio, despite a great increase in the total vote. The southern sector showed that it had not voted for peace in the reaction of 1862.

In addition to these statistics, other types of evidence reveal little difference in the patriotic ardor of the two divisions of the state. Volunteering was not a matter of geography, and after the draft came into the picture, bounties and community pressure to escape the stigma of conscription make the numbers of enlistments no real measure of Union sentiments. Twenty-six counties filled their quotas with volunteers before the first draft of October, 1862.[15] Nineteen were in the southern sector, seven in the northern. Four of the nineteen were carried by Vallandigham, further proof of the difficulty of using such evidence. The people of the southern counties, nearer the fighting front, possibly showed more martial spirit but this is hardly proof of the weakness of the Peace Democracy among them. Butler County in the southwest was equally good at producing enlistments and Copperheads.

Likewise, violations of civil liberties might be due to overzealous patriots rather than to violent antiwar utterances of the victims. Eleven military arrests, reported by a committee of the legislature in 1863, were divided between the two parts of the state, six in the north, five in the south.[16] The more illegal destruction of Democratic newspaper offices and printing presses, bad in both sections, proves intensity of local feelings but not much else. Two instances of organized resistance to the draft may be cited, one in Noble County in the southeastern hills, the other, and more serious, in Holmes County in the northeast central section of the state. Neither was very formidable.[17]

If the Peace Democratic element was as definitely a minority group in southern Ohio as in the north,[18] what is the explanation?

[15] Tables in Reid, *Ohio in the War*, I, 77-78.

[16] Emilius O. Randall and Daniel J. Ryan, *History of Ohio*, 5 vols. (New York, 1912), IV, 186-87; Porter, *Ohio Politics during the Civil War Period*, 106-107. The cases of Edson B. Olds, a former member of Congress, and John W. Kees, editor of the Circleville *Watchman*, attracted the most attention. Both lived in southern Ohio. Hubbart cites ten instances in which newspapers or editors suffered from mob violence or official action. Six were in northern Ohio.

[17] Wayne Jordan, "The Hoskinsville Rebellion," *Ohio State Archaeological and Historical Quarterly*, XLVII (October, 1938), 319-54; Reid, *Ohio in the War*, I, 127-29. Hubbart, *Older Middle West*, 195, mentions five north central Ohio counties as the centers of opposition to the draft.

[18] Space does not permit an analysis of the intensity of peace sentiment within the

What about the concepts of southern origins of population, fears of Negro immigration after emancipation, and the pull of southern trade ties?

The first offers no problem. The explanation is a simple one. Only a minority of the people of southern Ohio had a southern heritage. The rest — or their immediate ancestors — came in large part from New England, the middle states, Germany, and the British Isles. Even in the early years of statehood the Pennsylvanians outnumbered the natives of every other state.[19] While such an element as the Scotch-Irish might display the same traits of character, whether from Pennsylvania or Virginia, it is a mistake to conclude that the diverse groups from the middle states always followed the political lead of the Southerners. Even the latter were not homogeneous.[20] Ohio's ethnic pattern was a complex one and two generations of statehood and the melting pot had reduced its political significance. Environment meant more than heredity, even though Yankees were difficult to assimilate.

But even in the area where the southern strain was strongest, the Virginia Military Tract, the Peace Democracy was not dominant. This part of Ohio, lying between the Scioto and Little Miami

Democratic party in the two sectors as shown by resolutions and votes of party conventions. Evidence seems to indicate that the extreme state-rights group, exemplified by Alexander Long and William M. Corry, was stronger in the south but it had slight influence in shaping the party's course. Vallandigham was defeated for delegate at large to the Democratic national convention because, in the state convention of 1864, southern Ohio Democrats refused him their solid support. He received 133⅔ to Rufus P. Ranney's 89⅓, which was insufficient to overcome Ranney's lead in the north, the latter's home section. Compiled from the Columbus *Crisis*, March 30, 1864.

19 William T. Utter, *The Frontier State, 1803-1825* (1942), Wittke (ed.), *History of the State of Ohio*, II, 393-94. Robert E. Chaddock's percentages of members of the legislature of southern birth in the 1820's averages 25 per cent. If this figure is used as the southern proportion of the native-born of 1860 and is added to the number of Ohioans born in the South, according to the census, the total is under half a million. If four fifths of these are allotted to the southern half of the state, approximately one third of that section was of southern ancestry, a liberal estimate. See Robert E. Chaddock, *Ohio before 1850; A Study of the Early Influence of Pennsylvania and Southern Populations in Ohio*, Columbia University *Studies in History, Economics and Public Law*, XXXI, No. 2 (New York, 1908), 44. Gray, *Hidden Civil War*, 21, estimates the number of Midwesterners of southern blood at 40 per cent, which would imply a far higher percentage for the Ohio Valley area.

20 John D. Barnhart, "Sources of Southern Migration into the Old Northwest," *Mississippi Valley Historical Review* (Cedar Rapids), XXII (June, 1935), 49-62; and "The Southern Element in the Leadership of the Old Northwest," *Journal of Southern History* (Baton Rouge), I (May, 1935), 186-97. The limited influence of southern heritage for the entire Middle West is demonstrated by Henry C. Hubbart in his article, "'Pro-Southern' Influences in the Free West, 1840-1865," *Mississippi Valley Historical Review*, XX (June, 1933), 45-62.

rivers, was more nearly a southern beachhead than any other part of the state. Originally reserved by Virginia to provide land bounties for Revolutionary War veterans, it was settled largely from Virginia and Kentucky. It has no geographical unity and the legislature ignored its boundaries in laying out counties, which adds to the problem of assaying its politics. However, it may be assumed that Virginians had no more regard for its limits than the lawmakers and that many moved across the rivers that were its boundaries. Consequently, we may include in its ethnic limits the counties that lie astride the Scioto and Little Miami, and limit it to the northward by the boundary of the southern sector suggested earlier.[21] The fifteen counties so included cast 46,658 votes for Brough, 31,701 for Vallandigham. The percentage for the Democratic candidate was 40.5 as compared with 40.4 per cent for all of southern Ohio and 39.4 for the state as a whole. This is certainly no indication of Copperhead preponderance and further refutes Benton's contention that the peace movement centered in this and adjacent areas.

The case of Highland County in the heart of the old Military Tract is very suggestive.[22] Its early settlers were of southern stock, chiefly from the Virginia and North Carolina uplands, who had little liking for slavery. In a few instances emancipated slaves were brought to the county and settled near their former masters. These firstcomers occupied the more desirable lands along the streams, prospered, intermarried with non-Southerners in many cases, and by 1860—in the second generation—displayed only a faint southern coloration in their politics. A later migration, drawn from the surplus rural population of Virginia and Kentucky and less averse to slavery, located in the less desirable hill sections of the county and still felt the pull of southern loyalties in the Civil War years. Yet even this county of predominantly southern ancestry had its minorities of Pennsylvanians, Germans (United Brethren and Dunkards), and Irish to complicate further the political picture. Conservative in its politics, Highland was Democratic in the pre-

21 If parts of counties are excluded, only eight entire counties would be left in the district, none of them (except Brown on the civilian vote) carried by Vallandigham. This would underrate Democratic strength, which was greater in the counties crossed by the Scioto River.

22 This analysis of Highland County is based on a seminar report by Victor Howard, a graduate student at Ohio State University, and on an examination of the Hillsboro *Highland News.*

war decade though Lincoln carried it over a divided opposition in 1860. In 1863 it reversed its Democratic majority of the preceding year and repudiated Vallandigham by over four hundred votes on the civilian returns alone. Southern solidarity was conspicuously lacking here.

Tied up with the kinship argument is the belief that fear of an African influx after emancipation did much to strengthen the case of the Copperheads. That this had a powerful appeal in southern Ohio and particularly in areas of southern settlement has been usually taken for granted. Democratic successes in 1862, following on the heels of the Emancipation Proclamation, would seem to bear this out. Yet in 1863 the potency of the Africanization argument is open to question. At least, paradoxically, it was ineffective where it should have had the most weight. Of the fourteen counties with the largest percentages of Negroes in their population — over 3 per cent — ten voted Unionist, and all were in the southern sector.[23] Of the four Democratic counties, two were in the south, two in the north. Most of the Vallandigham counties had few Negroes. In Highland County the four townships containing most of the county's Negroes voted Unionist. These were the centers of the older southern migration, long accustomed to Negroes in their midst. While not willing to accept the black man as a social equal, they tolerated his presence and made use of his labor. Such communities could withstand the anti-Negro barrage of the Democrats better than those who knew him only as pictured in hostile newspapers or, as the Irish did, as a labor competitor.

The last major explanation of southern Ohio's supposed Copperheadism — the closing of southern trade outlets — loses a good deal of its significance in view of the evidence already cited of the strength of Union sentiments in this area. Southern trade was important but its disruption could provide an incentive for fighting for its recovery as well as for peace.[24] Even Cincinnati, long mistakenly regarded as a southern outpost, was not so distressed by the war that its strong support of the Union could be translated into a peace-through-compromise stand.[25] Hamilton County voted

[23] Tabulated from tables in *Eighth Census, Population of The United States in 1860* (Washington, 1864).

[24] Albert L. Kohlemeier, *The Old Northwest as the Keystone of the Arch of American Federal Union* (Bloomington, Ind., 1938), 211.

[25] Charles R. Wilson, "Cincinnati a Southern Outpost in 1860-1861?" *Mississippi Valley Historical Review*, XXIV (March, 1938), 473-82. Gray's reference to Hamil-

Democratic by a small margin in 1862 in an election marked by a light vote. If the metropolis was voting for peace because of economic distress, the same logic applies to most of Ohio, north and south, except the Western Reserve, and to a large part of the North from New York to Iowa. In 1863, 64 per cent of Hamilton County's voters rejected Vallandigham. It is far more reasonable to assume that the hostile verdict of 1862 was antiadministration rather than propeace and that several factors, as suggested earlier, were involved.[26] Whatever potency the economic argument had was gone with the news of Vicksburg's fall. The Mississippi outlet had been won by fighting and southern Ohio was satisfied. War prosperity and the use of eastern trade outlets had already alleviated economic distress in any case. As to northern Ohio, the southern trade factor had little significance. Yet it had a large crop of Copperheads, whose presence requires explanation.

The most reasonable explanation for the wartime political behavior of both sections of Ohio lies in their political past. Traditions of party loyalty once established are not easily shaken. Space does not permit an analysis of the prewar pattern of political sectionalism in Ohio but at no time was the alignment a north-south one. Whigs and Democrats were fairly evenly distributed in both divisions of the state. The National Road was not a political boundary. While many conservative Whigs held aloof from the early Republican party in southern Ohio, by 1860 the larger part of them accepted the new communion and Lincoln carried both halves of the state.[27]

In the north, despite Republican inroads, the Democrats cast 47 per cent of the party's total vote in 1860,[28] though that section had a little less than half of the state's population. Vallandigham did a little better in 1863, securing 47.8 per cent of his total in the north. McClellan improved on this in 1864 by one tenth of one per cent.

The conclusion seems inescapable that the Peace Democrats of

ton County as "a peace stronghold during a large part of the war" may be a case of confusing the city of Hamilton, Butler County, with Hamilton County. Gray, *Hidden Civil War*, 84. Yet a recent writer has described Cincinnati as turning "her back on the state to watch Kentucky and guard her Southern markets." William B. Hesseltine, *Lincoln and the War Governors* (New York, 1948), 36.

[26] The Cincinnati *Commercial*, October 20, 1863, argued that the verdict of Ohio in both years was for a more vigorous prosecution of the war.

[27] Roseboom, *Civil War Era*, Chap. XII.

[28] This includes both Stephen A. Douglas and John C. Breckinridge votes.

Ohio were the old-line, hard-shell Democrats, strongest in the areas, whether in north or south, that were rock-ribbed Democratic. Southern ancestry and economic ties with the South had little to do with their stand. Generally they have been described as small farmers living on marginal lands in the hills and isolated valleys. There is much truth in this but it can be overdone. The map of the Old Northwest in Wood Gray's *Hidden Civil War* (p. 16), showing counties with per capita land valuations above and below the average for each state, has slight significance for Ohio.[29] Five of the twelve Vallandigham counties of southern Ohio (on the civilian vote) and nine of the twenty in the north were above the average for the state. Resentment against the draft, taxes, profiteers, emancipation, and federal power was not confined entirely to the poor.

These Copperheads have been pictured as agrarian liberals, resisting not merely the war and its attendant evils but struggling to check the rising might of railroads, banks, and industry. Their fulminations against the capitalistic East and all that came out of it have caused them to be heralded by some historians as the forerunners of later nineteenth-century agrarian reform movements. Vallandigham has been termed a "John the Baptist" of Populism and Bryanism.[30] Yet one may more logically reverse the picture and describe him and his Ohio following as archconservative individualists, looking backward to a happier agrarian, state-rights past, using the time-worn appeals of the Democrats of Jackson's day against banks, tariffs, and capitalists, and offering no solution for the nation's problems but "the Constitution as it is, the Union as it was, and the Negroes where they are." Such an interpretation gives the Peace Democrats much in common with the isolationists of a later day. Both were provincial-minded Americans, suspicious

[29] Part of the difficulty lies in attempting to use per capita land values in urban communities where the large population made for a low average. The counties containing Cincinnati, Cleveland, and Columbus were below the state average, yet were high in tax valuation. A better measure is the average value per acre. Such a map is in W. A. Lloyd, J. I. Falconer, and C. E. Thorne, *The Agriculture of Ohio*, Ohio Agricultural Experiment Station *Bulletin* No. 326 (Wooster, 1918), 200. The northwestern quarter of the state, settled last, was below the average value per acre of the state's lands and was largely Democratic. Elsewhere the pattern breaks down. An attempt at correlating votes and tax valuations by townships in a few counties produced perplexing results. In Franklin County (outside Columbus) Vallandigham carried ten of the sixteen townships, five of the six highest in taxable wealth and five of the seven lowest. In Columbus his heaviest vote came from the German wards. Compiled from Columbus *Crisis*, October 28, November 18, 1863.

[30] Binkley, *American Political Parties*, 265.

of the machinations of eastern capitalists, politicians, and newspapers. Both were antiwar and each had a personal devil, the one a Lincoln, the other a Roosevelt. And their respective spokesmen were middle-western sectionalists, Vallandigham and Colonel Robert R. McCormick.

Physical isolation helps explain this conservatism but it was more than a matter of lack of roads, canals, and railroads. There was the intellectual isolation that comes from reading one newspaper — or none. There was the social isolation set up by language barriers and the customs and protective clannishness that encased Germans and Irish. German support of the Peace Democratic movement deserves far more emphasis than it has received.[31] And there were religious fundamentalists who wanted preachers to preach the Bible only and not presume to apply it to social reforms — abolition in particular. Such motivations as these were not confined to any one part of the state.

Mercer County in western Ohio, just north of the sectional boundary defined in this article, is a good example of a Peace Democratic center. Settled largely after 1830 by a mixed population, it was still one of the smaller counties by 1860. Though it contained much good land, its growth was retarded by drainage difficulties and inadequate transportation facilities, for its only outlet was the Miami and Erie Canal which was frequently closed by low water. It had always voted Democratic and its one newspaper became a pronounced Peace Democratic organ. Almost two thirds of the county's vote went to Vallandigham, the highest percentage in the entire state. One township cast a unanimous Democratic vote. The most populous in the county, it had been settled largely by German Catholics, though in most of the other townships the Methodists were the leading denomination. The complexity of the pattern is evident.[32]

[31] An analysis of the votes in four Vallandigham counties, Franklin, Mercer, Holmes, and Crawford, revealed a rather significant correlation between numbers of Germans and Democratic strength. George L. Pry, a graduate student, examined Crawford County for the writer. Cincinnati's Germans were not typical of the group as a whole. They were strong Unionists.

[32] Lester J. DeFord, "Mercer County, Ohio, during the Civil War" (M.A. thesis, Ohio State University, 1948); Columbus *Crisis*, October 28, 1863. Three townships gave a total of 677 votes for Vallandigham, 20 votes for Brough. It must not be inferred that most Catholics were antiwar. The official *Catholic Telegraph* at Cincinnati was anti-Vallandigham and antislavery. See Cincinnati *Commercial*, October 22, 1863, quoting *Telegraph's* defense of its position, and *ibid.*, November 2, 1863, for speech of Archbishop John B. Purcell.

Whatever hypotheses one is prepared to accept as explanations of the Peace Democrats, at least the traditional view that the Ohio Valley was their stronghold can not apply to Ohio. Certainly, if the voters of the southern counties had played the role in 1863 that historians have generally assigned to them, Vallandigham would have been elected, with dire effects for the cause of the Union, or, possibly, have lost by such a narrow margin that a Democratic legislature might have come into power. Twice in this period in close elections (1857 and 1867) Republican governors won but the party lost the assembly. Since the governor had no veto power, a Democratic assembly with peace inclinations might have hamstrung the state's war effort. Even more important, the peace movement all over the North would have been immeasurably strengthened and Union morale dealt a devastating blow, if the election had been close. If Ohio saved the nation in 1863, as Lincoln put it in his telegram to victorious John Brough on election night, southern Ohio deserved a major share of the credit.

Rutherford B. Hayes, Educator

By Henry L. Swint

Rutherford B. Hayes,[1] called by a biographer "Statesman of Reunion," [2] was a man of varied interests. Known to many merely as the victor in the disputed election of 1876, to others as an advocate of civil service reform, and to others as "granny Hayes" the temperance president, Hayes was essentially a kind, humane, and generous man whose life epitomizes the virtues of middle-class nineteenth-century America. An advocate of temperance, he was no male Carrie Nation, and was willing to try hot lemonade and whisky as a cure for a stubborn cold — "It probably does help." [3] An energetic worker for penal reform, he was realistic enough to understand that progress often is more akin to the tortoise than to the greyhound. Opposed to slavery, he was no violent abolitionist, but fought gallantly in a war which he believed necessary for the preservation of the Union. Victorious in the nation's most bitterly contested presidential election, he conscientiously attempted to heal the sectional breach and to cultivate good feeling between the former antagonists. A prominent and active member of veterans' organizations, he was on friendly terms with many Confederate veterans and southern political leaders.

Although Hayes was interested in many reforms, his "hobby" and principal social interest was universal education.[4] For very definite reasons he considered education the most important "national concern" of his age, and devoted much of his time and energy to it, especially after his departure from the White House. Like Thomas Jefferson, he believed that democratic government

[1] This paper was read at a joint session of the Southern Historical Association and the Mississippi Valley Historical Association at Oklahoma City, April 20, 1950.

[2] H. J. Eckenrode, *Rutherford B. Hayes, Statesman of Reunion* (New York, 1930).

[3] Charles R. Williams (ed.), *Diary and Letters of Rutherford Birchard Hayes*, 5 vols. (Columbus, 1922-1926), IV, 642, March 23, 1891.

[4] Hayes to William H. Smith, June 22, 1885, Rutherford B. Hayes Manuscripts (Hayes Memorial, Spiegel Grove, Fremont, Ohio); Williams (ed.), *Diary and Letters*, III, 619, August 5, 1880; V, 36, November 27, 1891.

rests squarely on the intelligence and virtue of the people, and that free public schools are necessary in a republic. "Universal suffrage should rest upon universal education," he declared in his inaugural address. Men cannot be fitted for the duties of citizenship without free schools, and in the absence of free schools the people can be neither intelligent nor virtuous. His assertion that "peace, virtue, and social order prevail" and civil and religious liberties are "secure" wherever general education is found may seem a bit naïve to a later generation, hardened by the excesses perpetrated by highly trained men. To Hayes ignorance was the worst enemy of good government. Ignorant voters he considered "powder and ball for the demagogues." [5]

Specifically, Hayes saw in education the solution of a problem which he considered of the greatest importance — the proper distribution of wealth among the citizens of the republic. This was the most perplexing problem of the age, pregnant with awful possibilities for the future. It was not confined to America, however, but was vital in all "the civilized countries of the world." He feared an aristocracy built on wealth, and advocated the imposition of a severe inheritance tax, so that no individual could receive from inherited wealth an annual income of more than ten to twenty thousand dollars. Concentration of wealth in the hands of the few was endangering the republic, and all good citizens should attempt to stop the continuation of the trend. No man, he thought, should possess such vast power as that wielded by Cornelius Vanderbilt and similar industrial and financial chieftains. Indeed, he asked himself, "Shall the railroads govern the country, or shall the people govern the railroads? Shall the interest of the railroad kings be chiefly regarded, or shall the interest of the people be paramount?" [6]

It may seem a bit surprising to find this Republican President, even in an era of nascent reform, praising Henry George as a social prophet "strong" in his analysis of the "rottenness" of the American economic system, and advocating drastic changes in the legal

[5] *Letters and Messages of Rutherford B. Hayes* (Washington, 1881), 13. See also his message of December 6, 1880, to the third session of the Forty-sixth Congress, *ibid.*, 314-15; Hayes to an unidentified man, August 16, 1880, Williams (ed.), *Diary and Letters*, III, 620-21; *ibid.*, IV, 366, undated entry.

[6] Williams (ed.), *Diary and Letters*, III, 482, May 15, 1878; IV, 261, January 22, 1886; 261-62, January 24, 1886; 374, March 11, 1888; 551, March 1, 1890; 277, March 18, 1886; 277-78, March 20, 1886; 278, March 26, 1886; Hayes to Rev. R. M. Hatfield, March 22, 1889, p. 457.

status of corporations and in inheritance laws. It is perhaps even more surprising to find Hayes classing himself as a radical in thought and principle, although a conservative in method and conduct, praising E. W. Bemis' ideas on the power of the state to control economic activity in the public welfare, and challenging the contemporary faith that unrestrained competition necessarily means the survival of the fittest and best. The Darwinian struggle, said Hayes, often results in the accumulation of vast wealth by the unscrupulous.[7]

Hayes believed education the only solution to this vital problem. Apparently he feared that conflict between irresponsible and greedy men of wealth and the poverty-stricken, ignorant masses would inevitably bring about the collapse of the American system. Ignorant labor was always the tool of unscrupulous wealth, but educated and enlightened labor would be able to understand the problem of inequitable distribution and would take the necessary steps for its solution — "fully to know the evil is the first step towards reaching its eradication." Wealth, opportunity, power, and education are companions, and if education is limited to the wealthy few, plutocracy will result. The United States must, therefore, expand its educational system, for men must have equal educational opportunity as the surest way to guarantee to all an equal chance in the contest for property.[8]

Hayes considered the problem of education somewhat more acute in the South than in the relatively better educated North and East, for in the South it was complicated by the presence of great masses of Negroes, most of whom were illiterate. Now that the Negro was a citizen it was doubly important that he be educated — both for his own sake and for the health of democracy. Since universal education is the only safe foundation for universal suffrage, the Negro voter must be educated.[9]

The southern whites, for their part, must cease trying to drive the Negro and "*learn to lead.*" Indeed, while Hayes believed the South little worse off than New York, Chicago, or other northern cities with large uneducated masses, he felt that the education of

[7] *Ibid.*, IV, 354-55, December 4, 1887; 367, undated entry; 622, December 12, 1890.

[8] Hayes to William E. Dodge, February 1, 1887, *ibid.*, 309; 367, undated entry; 637, February 6, 1891; 354, December 4, 1887; 621, December 10, 1890; III, 482, May 15, 1878.

[9] Hayes to Guy M. Bryan, January 2, 1875, *ibid.*, III, 262-63.

the Negro was essential to "complete the victory" gained by the Union forces in the Civil War.[10] A glorious and holy war had been fought to "perpetuate the Union and to abolish slavery," and now the victory must be made complete by education, for "as long as any considerable numbers of our country men are uneducated, the citizenship of every American in every State is impaired . . . and . . . imperilled," he said in 1880.[11]

Because he believed the South too poor to support an adequate school system, Hayes advocated national aid to education. His inaugural address called for federal financial aid to education, and subsequent messages repeated the request in most emphatic terms. In his message of December, 1877, he expressed the hope that Congress would supplement state educational funds in all the states, not merely in the South, and in 1879 he asserted that Congress had "no more fundamental responsibility" than financial aid to education. The annual message of 1880 was even more positive. He was "firmly convinced" that public education was a problem of such primary concern to the entire country that the federal government should do anything which it could "fairly do" to promote it. He had no constitutional qualms. Indeed, when President Chester A. Arthur cautiously expressed approval of such federal aid as could "constitutionally" be extended, Hayes somewhat caustically observed that the federal government had found authority in the constitution to free the slaves and to give them the vote — surely it was within its power to fit the Negro for the proper exercise of the privilege which had now been given him. Education must be provided, through the states if possible, but by independent federal action if necessary.[12]

With this attitude Hayes naturally supported Henry W. Blair's proposal for federal aid to education, first introduced by the New Hampshire Senator in 1881. He frequently referred to the measure in his diary and letters, and actively attempted to gain support for it. In 1884 he wrote "daily" to various members of Congress urging them to use their influence in an effort to secure the passage of the Blair bill, and in 1886 he was still urging its adoption, some-

[10] Hayes to an unidentified man, August 16, 1880, *ibid.*, 620-21.

[11] Address to Ohio Soldiers' Reunion, Columbus, August 11, 1880, *Letters and Messages*, 304-306.

[12] *Ibid.*, 13, 97-98, 281, 305, 306, 315; James D. Richardson (comp.), *A Compilation of the Messages and Papers of the Presidents, 1789-1897*, 10 vols. (Washington, 1896-1899), VIII, 58; Williams (ed.), *Diary and Letters*, IV, 53, December 10, 1881.

what dogmatically asserting that there would be no general education in the South "for several generations" without national aid.[13] In his anxiety for the passage of the measure Hayes even proposed that the Board of Trustees of the Slater Fund, of which he was president, officially endorse the Blair bill, an action which had been taken by the Board of Trustees of the Peabody Fund in March, 1880.[14] Morris K. Jesup, treasurer of the Fund, strongly objected, however, and Hayes abandoned his proposal.[15]

Hayes decidedly favored industrial and technical education for both whites and Negroes. All children should be taught to use their hands, to respect labor, and to "have the spirit of labor." The essential dignity of labor should be the basic principle of any educational practice. The failure of the American school system to train every child in a vocation or trade he termed "a capital defect." He set a high value on industry, self-reliance, and thrift — "the virtues Dr. Franklin taught so well" — and believed that these virtues might best be inculcated by the study of the manual and technical arts and crafts. The southern Negro must be taught a trade, not because he was incapable of attaining a classical education, but because every citizen should develop skill of some practical value, and because only by so doing could the Negro accumulate property, an absolute necessity in a democracy as Hayes envisioned it. Nor did he contemplate training the Negro in the servile occupations, but as farmers, carpenters, architects, civil engineers, and mechanics.[16]

Such a philosophy inevitably placed Hayes in sympathy with the work of such men as Samuel Chapman Armstrong, founder of Hampton Institute. His work, said Hayes, "hits the nail on the head. It solves the whole negro problem." Armstrong he considered

[13] Williams (ed.), *Diary and Letters*, IV, 181, December 30, 1884; Hayes to Isaac H. Taylor, March 9, 1886, pp. 272-73; Hayes to J. M. Comly, March 27, 1886, p. 278; Hayes to Bryan, November 13, 1884, p. 176; Hayes to J. M. Sturtevant, March 21, 1888, pp. 377-78; Henry W. Blair to Hayes, May 2, 1884; John Eaton to Hayes, September 21, 1882; Hayes to William J. Davis, September 7, 1883; J. Warren Keifer to Hayes, January 7, 1885, Hayes Manuscripts.

[14] Peabody Education Fund, *Proceedings*, 6 vols. (Boston, Cambridge, 1875-1916), II, 265-301.

[15] Hayes to Daniel C. Gilman, March 31, 1886; Gilman to Hayes, April 6, 12, 17, 1889; Hayes to Gilman, April 14, 1886, Hayes Manuscripts.

[16] Williams (ed.), *Diary and Letters*, III, 482, May 19, 1878; IV, 76, May 7, 1882; 88, October 4, 1882; Hayes to S. T. Mitchell, February 23, 1886, p. 270; Hayes to an unidentified man, July 16, 1883, p. 122.

"next to Lincoln" as a friend and benefactor of the Negro.[17] The work of both the Slater and the Peabody funds had his enthusiastic support. He was nominated to the Board of Trustees of the Peabody Fund by a southern member in 1877 and was unanimously elected, a fact which gave him great satisfaction, for he considered the action proof that his pacific measures had been "approved by the entire country." He emphatically agreed with the thesis upon which George Peabody based his gift — a belief that the South, impoverished and depressed by war, would not be able, unaided, to provide adequate educational facilities for the youth of the section. Peabody's interest in moral and industrial education closely corresponded with his own.[18] The chairman of the Peabody Board, Robert C. Winthrop, was in agreement with his attitudes on education for the Negro and on national aid to education. There was, therefore, a congenial atmosphere on the Board, where Hayes was associated with such men as Winthrop, Morrison R. Waite, William M. Evarts, Alexander H. H. Stuart, and Barnas Sears, the able and active general agent of the Fund.

Hayes was especially interested in the normal school at Nashville. He felt that the Peabody Normal College, which had been in operation since 1875, should be developed into "a model," the ideal teacher-training institution, superior to any college of its type, and apparently he supported the school at every opportunity. By 1881 the Peabody Board had decided that the training of teachers was the foremost need of southern education, and Dr. Sears and the members of the Board proposed to develop at Nashville a fit monument to the donor.[19] After some difficulty, a cooperative agreement was reached with the state of Tennessee and the University of Nashville, and Hayes's dream of a model school seemed somewhat nearer realization.

In 1886 Hayes was appointed to the executive committee of the Peabody Board and in 1889 he became chairman of the Board's committee to study relations between Peabody Normal College and

[17] Hayes to Edward Everett Hale, January 5, 1892, *ibid.*, V, 46-47.

[18] Peabody Education Fund, *Proceedings*, II, 138-39; Williams (ed.), *Diary and Letters*, III, 444-45, October 7, 1877; J. L. M. Curry, *A Brief Sketch of George Peabody and a History of the Peabody Education Fund* (Cambridge, 1898), 20, 103. See also Daniel C. Gilman, "Thirty Years of the Peabody Education Fund," *Atlantic Monthly* (Boston), LXXIX (February, 1897), 163.

[19] Curry, *Brief Sketch of George Peabody*, 124; Williams (ed.), *Diary and Letters*, IV, 525, November 24, 1889; 601, October 8, 1890; Peabody Education Fund, *Proceedings*, III, 13, 341.

the University of Nashville and to take action on behalf of the Board in the interest of the College. Some members of the Board felt that the income from the Peabody Fund should be divided among the various state normal schools, but Hayes was strongly opposed to this policy of diffusion, and the special committee unanimously decided to strengthen the Normal College at Nashville. The committee believed the College to be "on the threshold of a great and noble future," which would demonstrate the wisdom of its founder.[20]

Hayes was one of the more influential and active members of the Peabody Board. Through the Board, and through his close relationship to J. L. M. Curry, he did much to mold and direct southern educational progress during the years 1877 to 1893. He was intimately acquainted with Curry, who became general agent of the Peabody Fund after Sears's death, and later, agent of both the Peabody and the Slater funds. The two men were especially close after Curry succeeded Atticus G. Haygood as agent of the Slater Fund, thus combining the work of the two agents. His keen interest in vocational and technical training and in the South, however, led Hayes to devote a large part of his time and energy to the Slater Fund after its establishment in 1882. He was chairman of the Board of Trustees of the Fund from its inception until his death, and his voluminous correspondence expressively demonstrates the interest which he felt in the subject and the important role which he played in the establishment and early operation of the Fund.

Apparently Hayes first learned of John F. Slater's intention to create a fund for the education of the Negro through meeting Rev. Leonard W. Bacon, a Congregational minister of Norwich, Connecticut, who called on him in October, 1881, with a letter of introduction from Chief Justice Morrison R. Waite, a member of the Peabody Board. Slater, a member of Bacon's congregation at Norwich, had requested Hayes to assist in setting up an endowment "to educate young men to teach the colored people of the South," the agency to operate somewhat like the Peabody Fund. Slater, perhaps on the advice of Bacon and Hayes, requested President Daniel C. Gilman of Johns Hopkins, President Theodore D.

[20] Peabody Education Fund, *Proceedings*, IV, 136-37, 232; Williams (ed.), *Diary and Letters*, IV, 513, October 3, 1889; 525, November 24, 1889; 601, October 8, 1890. Other members of the committee were Bishop H. B. Whipple, Governor James D. Porter of Tennessee, Samuel A. Green, and Randall L. Gibson.

Woolsey of Yale, William E. Dodge of New York, Justice Waite, Justice William Strong, Governor Alfred H. Colquitt of Georgia, Phillips Brooks, Bacon, and Hayes to serve as a Board of Trustees. Apparently Slater, on Bacon's suggestion, requested that Hayes act as president of the Board.[21]

During the intricate and prolonged negotiations by which the Slater Fund was set up, Bacon, as the principal aide and confidant of Slater, relied heavily on Hayes. He reported to him constantly, and in great detail. Slater had thrust great responsibility upon him, he said, and he felt the need of Hayes's counsel and assistance. In addition to Hayes, however, Bacon sought and received advice from some of the nation's most prominent political and legal figures. He discussed with Justice Waite, Senator George F. Hoar, Senator George F. Edmunds, and General Joseph R. Hawley the possibility of obtaining a congressional charter for the Slater Fund corporation, and frequently consulted other legal and professional leaders.[22]

After various suggestions had been adopted (such as eliminating the words "colored" and "Protestant" from the proposed charter) and at least eight, and probably ten, drafts had been prepared and discussed at length, a petition for a charter was filed in New York by Hayes, Waite, Brooks, Gilman, James P. Boyce, Dodge, Colquitt, John A. Stewart, Morris K. Jesup, and William A. Slater, son of the donor.[23] The charter passed through the legislature with little difficulty, although real estate was not exempted from taxation because of the opposition of Governor Alonzo B. Cornell. The object of the Fund, as stated by its founder, was the "uplifting of the lately emancipated population of the Southern States, and their posterity, by conferring on them the blessings of a Christian education." Slater also hoped to promote the training of Negro teachers. Neither principal nor interest could be used for the purchase of land or buildings.[24]

[21] Williams (ed.), *Diary and Letters*, IV, 42, October 9, 1881; Leonard W. Bacon to Hayes, November 1, 1881, Hayes Manuscripts. See statement of the Trustees that Slater consulted Hayes prior to the establishment of the Fund and that Slater chose Hayes as president of the Board at that time. Williams (ed.), *Diary and Letters*, V, 185. The evidence in Hayes's diary and in his correspondence with Bacon seems to contradict this assertion.

[22] Bacon to Hayes, November 16, 1881, Hayes Manuscripts.

[23] Williams (ed.), *Diary and Letters*, IV, 70, March 5, 1882. For details of the formulation of the charter, see Bacon to Hayes, October 26, November 1, 16, 26, 1881, January 18, February 6, March 4, 1882, Hayes Manuscripts.

[24] Bacon to Hayes, April 20, 1882, Announcement of the Board of Trustees, John

The first meeting of the trustees was held on May 18, 1882, at Jesup's office in New York City. Gilman was chosen secretary and Jesup treasurer. Jesup, Dodge, and Stewart were designated a finance committee, and Hayes, Colquitt, Boyce, Gilman, and Dodge an executive committee.[25] During the next few months the selection of an agent for the Slater Fund occupied much of Hayes's time. As early as February 6, 1882, Bacon had suggested Haygood, president of Emory College, Oxford, Georgia, as a possible choice, and by July it was apparent that Hayes had become convinced that Haygood was the logical man for the position. Hayes had kept in close contact with Curry, agent of the Peabody Fund, frequently asking his advice. He suggested to Curry that a Southerner should be retained as agent of the new organization and asked for his opinion of Haygood and Gustavus J. Orr, commissioner of education of Georgia, as well as for his advice on the general problems of the Fund. Curry urged Hayes to exercise great care in selecting an agent for the Slater Fund; an unwise choice would "be fatal," he warned. He hoped that the agents of the two Funds would cooperate in their important work, and expressed the opinion that both Haygood and Orr were able men.[26]

Several members of the Board, among them Boyce, Colquitt, Dodge, Gilman, and Waite, favored Haygood, to whom Bacon had already presented the matter. Haygood, despite his duties as president of Emory College, was extremely anxious to obtain the position. There was some doubt among the trustees whether Haygood could successfully act both as president of a struggling college (a position which involved administrative activity, financial responsibility, and teaching) and as agent for the new Fund, but Haygood confidently declared that he could "do the work — every part of it." Everyone who knew him understood, he said, that he could "do more work than the majority of men." [27]

F. Slater Fund (1882?), Hayes Manuscripts; *Documents Relating to the Origin and Work of the Slater Trustees, 1882 to 1894,* Slater Fund, Occasional Papers No. 1 (Baltimore, 1894), *passim.*

[25] Williams (ed.), *Diary and Letters,* IV, 76, May 18, 1882.

[26] Bacon to Hayes, February 6, 1882, Hayes Manuscripts; Hayes to Curry, April 20, July 5, 1882, Edwin A. Alderman and Armistead C. Gordon, *J. L. M. Curry, A Biography* (New York, 1911), 269, 270; Curry to Hayes, July 8, 17, 1882, Hayes Manuscripts.

[27] J. P. Boyce to Hayes, July 31, 1882; Alfred H. Colquitt to Hayes, July 12, 1882; William E. Dodge to Hayes, August 8, 1882; Gilman to Hayes, August 16, 1882; Morrison R. Waite to Hayes, July 22, 1882; Bacon to Will [Slater], September 29, 1882; Atticus G. Haygood to Bacon, January 25, 1882; Haygood to Hayes, October

Haygood's confidence and Hayes's endorsement apparently satisfied the members of the Board, for he was offered the position in October, 1882. He promptly accepted, thus adding additional responsibilities to an already full life. Haygood's influence extended into many fields and his remarkable career merits more thorough study than it has yet received. Educator, preacher, editor, author, and church official, he was one of the most active Southerners of his time. In his work as agent of the Slater Fund he traveled throughout the South, delivered innumerable addresses, and profoundly influenced not only the education of the Negro, but relations between the two races in the South. He kept in close contact with Hayes, who encouraged him when he was despondent, restrained him when his ebullience thrust him into difficulties, and mediated between him and Secretary Gilman and Treasurer Jesup when his impetuosity and impatience with sound business methods caused friction.

In 1884, for example, Hayes had to soothe Haygood's ruffled pride when Treasurer Jesup requested the agent to present detailed accounts of his expenditures. Haygood strongly objected, asserting that he was spending the money allocated by the Board in developing industrial education among the Negroes, and that no further explanation was necessary. Hayes defended Haygood, asserting that his report of the first year's effort was "most encouraging and satisfactory," but he saw some merit in the contention of the other trustees that Haygood should devote more time to Slater work. He agreed to "bring this forcibly" to Haygood's attention, which he did when the agent visited him late in October, 1884. Haygood

11, November 13, 1882, Hayes Manuscripts. For a widely different and dramatic account of the selection of Haygood as agent of the Slater Fund, see a statement by Luke G. Johnson, in Elam F. Dempsey, *Atticus Green Haygood* (Nashville, 1940), xvi. This account should be examined in the light of several facts. Haygood accepted the position of agent for the Slater Fund in October, 1882, almost two years before Slater's death. Moreover, Slater originally favored the appointment of a northern man as agent. See Bacon to Hayes, September 17, 1882, Hayes Manuscripts, in which Bacon reported that Slater's son William had assured him that his father's "prejudice in favor of a Northern man . . . has wholly abated," and that he did not wish to influence the Trustees in their selection of an agent. See also Haygood to Bacon, January 25, 1882, *ibid.*, in which Haygood, with characteristic detail, presented his qualifications for the post. The initiative in the matter seems to have come from Bacon, who was impressed by Haygood's statements on relations between the races in the South. Hayes also was acquainted with Haygood's writing, and he later stated that he considered Haygood a sincere and able man whose influence was a strong force for good. Williams (ed.), *Diary and Letters*, IV, 591, August 1, 1890; 608, October 23, 1890.

liked the idea, but felt that he could not abandon his work at Emory until the financial condition of the Georgia school had been improved. He had hoped to establish an industrial department there, but those few Southerners who had money were not sympathetic toward him because of his views on the Negro question, and it was necessary for him to seek funds elsewhere.[28]

In November, 1884, after further correspondence with Hayes, Haygood presented his problem to the aged and ill John F. Slater, who agreed to aid him in his financial drive for Emory College. Haygood then yielded to the wishes of the Slater Board, resigned as president of Emory College, and agreed to devote his time to the work of the Slater Fund for at least ten years, at an annual salary of $5,000 and an allowance of $1,000 for traveling expenses. He remained on the faculty of Emory as Professor Emeritus of Evidences of Christianity — a "purely honorary" post — and became president of the College's Board of Trustees. He felt that he was about to begin a work which would demand his full energies and attention for the remainder of his life.[29]

The new arrangement did not completely quiet Haygood's critics on the Slater Board, however, and Hayes, doubtless with some embarrassment, was again compelled to act as mediator between Haygood and Jesup. Hayes was completely "satisfied" with Haygood, and Haygood felt that he could not have done the work without Hayes's support. Hayes, said Haygood, was the only member of the Board who knew enough about the work to give advice. Jesup's insistence on detailed reports and accounts of expenditures was so annoying to Haygood that he protested violently, and his work probably suffered. He asserted that he wanted to do what the Board wished but found it difficult to do so, since "part of it don't know what it wants." He could not keep a diary, he said — "It would freeze up my soul." [30] Hayes advised him to keep calm, but by May, 1889, the situation had become so strained that an open break seemed inevitable. At its May meeting the Board agreed that Haygood must make two annual visits to each school receiving

[28] Williams (ed.), *Diary and Letters*, IV, 165, October 3, 1884; 166, October 4, 1884; 171, October 29, 1884; Haygood to Hayes, January 14, October 24, 1884, Hayes Manuscripts.

[29] Haygood to Hayes, November 3, December 6, 1884; Hayes to Gilman, November 11, 1884, Hayes Manuscripts.

[30] Hayes to Gilman, January 20, 1887; Haygood to Hayes, November 1, 1888, February 8, 1886, February 3, 1887, *ibid.*

funds from the Board; henceforth all expenditures were to be approved by Treasurer Jesup and Secretary Gilman; and the agent was to confer with the Board twice each year.[31] Haygood was indignant. This action made him "the Treasurer's travelling man" rather than the agent of the Board, he declared; it was "a Conductor's *schedule*" rather than an agent's work. He must not be annoyed by the necessity of keeping an itemized account for "a man like Mr. Jesup." [32]

In 1890 Haygood was elected to the episcopacy of the Methodist Episcopal Church, South. He had been elected in 1882, but had declined the position, saying that he must continue his work as president of Emory College. But when he was chosen a second time he accepted, asking Hayes that he be permitted to work as agent of the Slater Fund until May, 1891, in order that he might complete the work which he had already projected for the year.[33]

With the resignation of Haygood, Hayes again faced the problem of selecting an agent for the Slater Fund. There were numerous applicants and Treasurer Jesup strongly urged upon Hayes the appointment of the Commissioner of Education of New York State, a Republican. But Hayes, realizing far better than Jesup the delicacy of the agent's task, believed that the appointment of a man unfamiliar with the South and its people would be a serious mistake. The new agent must be well acquainted with the South and with the Negro and must be acceptable to Southerners. Hayes considered Curry, agent of the Peabody Fund, the best man for the position. Both Hayes and Haygood felt that Curry should have an assistant, who would be responsible for industrial training, and Gilman heartily agreed. The Board, said Gilman, should not be governed by too strong a desire to reduce expenses, but should feel free to take any action necessary to promote "the right kind of instruction" among the Negroes.[34]

Curry had been interested in the Slater Fund since its establishment, and had long been acquainted with Hayes. The two men had studied law at Harvard, where they lived in the same board-

31 Haygood to Hayes, November 7, 1887, November 1, 1888; Memorandum, Slater Board, May 15, 1889, *ibid.*

32 Haygood to Hayes, May 20, June 8, 1889, *ibid.*

33 Haygood to Hayes, June 2, September 17, 1890, *ibid.*

34 Hayes to Gilman, September 20, 30, October 10, 1890; Hayes [?] to Robert C. Winthrop, October 30, 1890; Gilman to Hayes, September 16, 22, 1890; Haygood to Hayes, October 3, November 10, 1890, *ibid.*

inghouse, and were "quite intimate." [35] In 1877 the newly elected president had offered Curry a post in his cabinet, and had asked his advice about other appointments. In ensuing months they had become even more closely associated and in 1880 Hayes had asked Curry to become a member of the Board of Visitors of the Military Academy and of the Naval Academy.[36]

Curry had also been very close to Barnas Sears, first agent of the Peabody Fund, who, long before his death in July, 1880, had selected Curry as his successor. With Hayes and Winthrop, president of the Peabody Board, urging his appointment, Curry was unanimously chosen agent of the Peabody Fund on February 3, 1881.[37] Hayes was highly pleased with Curry's "excellent" work as agent of the Peabody Fund. Consequently, when Haygood resigned his position with the Slater Fund to become a bishop, Hayes and perhaps other members of the Slater Board immediately considered Curry as a possible replacement. In the fall of 1890 Hayes proposed to Curry that he add the management of the Slater Fund to his already heavy responsibilities. Many of the members of both Boards thought the administration of both Funds by Curry a wise step, and at Hayes's suggestion Curry was elected to the Slater Board and appointed chairman of the Committee on Education, with duties similar to those of Haygood.[38]

The last phase of Hayes's educational work began with Curry's appointment as agent of the Slater Fund. Relations between the two men were quite close, and in 1891 Hayes joined Curry in a tour of the South. Hayes, ever the traveler, had visited that section in 1876, accompanied by his wife, and had been highly pleased by the reception which they received. After the close of his administration he traveled widely in attending the meetings of the two educational organizations of which he was a director, conferences on penal reform, educational rallies, and similar meetings, and in delivering many speeches before audiences in the East and Mid-

[35] Alderman and Gordon, *Curry*, 77. See also Jesse P. Rice, *J. L. M. Curry, Southerner, Statesman and Educator* (New York, 1949).

[36] Alderman and Gordon, *Curry*, 238, 248.

[37] *Ibid.*, 249, 253; Peabody Education Fund, *Proceedings*, II, 368.

[38] Hayes to Webb Hayes, October 6, 1881, Williams (ed.), *Diary and Letters*, IV, 38; Alderman and Gordon, *Curry*, 332-33; Curry to Hayes, November 15, 1890; Gilman to Hayes, September 22, December 22, 1890; William M. Evarts to Hayes, December 24, 1890, Hayes Manuscripts. Hayes made a "careful and prudent" speech nominating Curry, he said. Williams (ed.), *Diary and Letters*, IV, 610-11, October 27, 29, 31, 1890. See also Gilman's official announcement, December 30, 1890, Hayes Manuscripts.

west. At Nashville in 1889 Hayes spoke at a session of the National Prison Reform Association and participated in the conference of the Peabody Trustees with local educational figures that selected Tennessee's capital as the site of Peabody Normal.[39] As early as 1889 he planned an inspection of the South, during which he would visit Slater and Peabody schools and examine the educational systems of the various southern states. The Slater Board not only approved his plan, but formally requested that he make such a tour of inspection.[40]

Curry, as he began his work with the Slater Fund, felt that a tour of inspection of Slater schools in the South was necessary, and as a result of this mutual interest the two men agreed to take a "quiet" tour, as Hayes phrased it, avoiding publicity and formality as much as possible. Hayes and his son Rutherford joined Curry in Asheville, and the group visited Columbia, Orangeburg, New Orleans, Jackson, Memphis, and Nashville. Hayes thoroughly enjoyed the trip, finding it "laborious" but "full of gratification and interest." [41] Indeed, he was so pleased that he proposed to take a similar trip through the Southwest early in 1892. Curry believed that Hayes's visit to the Slater schools had been stimulating, timely, and very helpful. "You did a noble work," he wrote Hayes. "The influence will be permanently helpful. As a Southern man I thank you." [42]

Curry returned from his tour with Hayes thoroughly convinced of the wisdom of his policy of concentrating Slater grants in a few schools, even though this approach was precisely contrary to Haygood's theory of diffusion.[43] The available evidence does not justify any categorical statement on Hayes's attitude on the difference of

[39] Williams (ed.), *Diary and Letters*, IV, 524-25, November 18, 24, 1889.

[40] Memorandum, Slater Board, May 15, 1889; Gilman to Hayes, May 27, 1889, Hayes Manuscripts.

[41] Curry to Hayes, October 13, 19, 20, 1891; Hayes to Curry, October 17, 21, 1891; Curry to R. P. Hayes, October 18, 1891, Hayes Manuscripts; Hayes to Bryan, January 4, 1892, Williams (ed.), *Diary and Letters*, V, 45.

[42] Curry to Hayes, note, January 11, 1892, on Minutes of Meeting of the Educational Committee, Slater Board, December 23, 1891, Curry to Trustees, Slater Fund, January 14, 1892, Hayes Manuscripts.

[43] Curry to Hayes, November 27, 1891; Curry, Report to Trustees, Slater Fund, January 14, 1892; Curry to Hayes, note, January 11, 1892, on Minutes of Meeting of Educational Committee, Slater Board, December 23, 1891, Hayes Manuscripts; Haygood to Hayes, June 12, 1885, Curtis W. Garrison (ed.), "Slater Fund Beginnings: Letters from General Agent Atticus G. Haygood to Rutherford B. Hayes," *Journal of Southern History* (Baton Rouge, Lexington), V (May, 1939), 232-33.

opinion between the two agents, but since he had opposed the diffusion of the Peabody Fund, and since the Board adopted Curry's recommendations it seems probable that Hayes at least did not raise strong objection to the policy of concentration. After a meeting with Curry and officials of the denominations interested in southern education, held at Johns Hopkins University on March 3, 1892, he wrote in his diary: "Agreed perfectly with the doctors of divinity on the apportionment of our income." [44]

Although now seventy years of age, Hayes maintained a keen interest in education. Every good citizen must be active in supporting education, he asserted. "No step backwards is the motto of the hour," he wrote in February, 1892.[45] He kept in contact with educational activity throughout the country — at Ohio State University, at Cornell, Kenyon, Wooster, Cincinnati — continued his support of movements for penal reform and temperance and his activity in veterans affairs, Indian affairs, and politics, spoke frequently on a variety of subjects, and spent much time in reading. He was an omnivorous reader, finding pleasure in a great variety of literature — Tennyson, Walter Besant, Shakespeare, Dickens, William Morris, Alexander Brown, Tolstoy, Emerson, Pope, John Quincy Adams, Byron.

Throughout the period of his work with the Peabody and the Slater Funds, especially after the close of his administration, Hayes also was actively engaged in business. Yet he found time for a voluminous correspondence on a variety of subjects. As president of the Slater Board and a member of the Peabody Board, he was besieged by requests for information, assistance, and advice. Apparently few days failed to bring a request that he speak or write an article on some phase of education. Would he speak to the American Missionary Association, one of the oldest organizations active in freedmen's education? Would he deliver addresses at Berea College, the University of Michigan, Webb School (Bell Buckle, Tennessee), Johns Hopkins University, Kenyon College, Ohio State University? An endless stream of invitations poured into his study at Spiegel Grove, his home in Fremont, Ohio.

Requests for aid came in even greater volume and variety. Hayes was asked to give assistance to normal schools, industrial schools,

[44] Williams (ed.), *Diary and Letters,* V, 62, March 3, 1892.
[45] *Ibid., 55,* February 6, 1892.

orphans' homes, schools for Negro boys, schools for Negro girls, white youth, "poor whites." Applicants for teaching positions, government positions, and veterans' pensions sought his endorsement, students and would-be students requested aid and advice. Apparently Hayes gave each letter his personal attention, answering with characteristic grave courtesy, although he could be bitingly abrupt and sarcastic on occasion.

Hayes's strong faith in education was a reflection of his devotion to the basic principles of democracy as he understood it. Citizens in a democracy must be free, and freedom without knowledge could lead only to disaster. His humanitarianism and keen sympathy for his less fortunate fellows stimulated his interest in practical measures of social amelioration, including both education and prison reform. His insistence on universal public education and his attitude toward federal aid to education seem strikingly pertinent sixty years later, when federal aid is again being presented as the only solution to the problem of universal education in areas in which the children are many and the dollars few.

As a member of the Peabody and Slater boards, president of the Slater Board, a close friend and confidant of many members of both groups and of many of the leading educators of the time, and as friend and advisor to both Haygood and Curry, Hayes undoubtedly exercised great influence on education, especially in the South. Believing firmly in the value of technical and manual education for all, he naturally was more sympathetic toward the Hampton-Tuskegee idea than the Howard-Atlanta-Fisk philosophy. As a democrat Hayes strongly believed that all citizens should share in the rights as well as the responsibilities and duties of citizenship. Both Negroes and whites must be educated with this end in view, but not necessarily in mixed schools, he believed.[46] His advocacy of technical education, his strong endorsement of Samuel C. Armstrong, and his willingness to permit segregation are evidences of his sympathy for the former group, but he supported any cause which he considered beneficial to education and to the Negro. However influential he may have been, his unflagging support of education as a basic requisite for democracy places him in such distinguished company as Jefferson, Horace Mann, and Henry Barnard.

[46] Hayes to Bryan, January 2, 1875, Williams (ed.), *Diary and Letters*, III, 262-63.

The Northern Great Plains: A Study in Canadian-American Regionalism

By Paul F. Sharp

Regional rather than national studies of the Northern Great Plains promise a more complete understanding of our West. Such an approach supplements the national emphases which have dominated our research and helps us avoid the unfortunate tendency in western American history of emphasizing the sensational, the transitory, the erratic, and the pathological.

The Northern Great Plains comprises an area of 300,000 square miles, of which roughly one half lies in Canada. With its base resting on the Kansas-Nebraska line and its apex reaching the Park Belt of mid-Alberta and Saskatchewan, the region includes most of six western states and much of the three prairie provinces. Its eastern boundary is that indefinite zone of transition in which the ninety-eighth meridian has become the symbol of the changing characteristics that distinguish it from the prairies of the Middle West, while to the west the foothills of the Rockies form a major physiographical barrier.[1] The region is bisected by an international boundary which like so many political demarcations in the western hemisphere is of such recent origin that population movements and commerce have tended to ignore it and to conform to the geographical integrity of the region.

This northern grassland empire with its gently rolling plains, its rough, eroded areas, and its glacially created surfaces is as different in many vital ways from the southern High Plains, with which

[1] Oliver E. Baker, "Agricultural Regions of North America," *Economic Geography* (Worcester, Mass.), VII (October, 1931), 336; J. Sullivan Gibson, "Agriculture of the Southern High Plains," *ibid.*, VIII (July, 1932), 249; George A. Rogler and Leon C. Hurtt, "Where Elbowroom Is Ample," United States Department of Agriculture, *Grass, The Yearbook of Agriculture, 1948* (Washington, 1948), 477. The author gratefully acknowledges a grant-in-aid from the Social Science Research Council in preparing this article.

it is so often confused, as it is from the physiographic provinces that surround it. Differences in soil types and structures, rates of precipitation, evaporation, vegetation, surface features, and climate prevent within this region the uniformity characteristic of the true High Plains to the south.

Three areas of research seem especially fruitful. There is first an important area of economic, cultural, and political interdependence imposed upon the region by its geographical integrity that deserves further and more extensive investigation. Unless an international and regional analysis accompanies our national studies many facts pertinent for both peoples are ignored. Moreover, the universality of experiences common to explorers and settlers on both sides of the forty-ninth parallel passes unrecognized and these experiences are elevated to a uniqueness which they do not possess. Here on the northern plains the two great streams of Anglo-Saxon pioneering that had pushed across the continent reached their last West in the same environment. Frontiersmen of this northern plains country were fully aware of this community of interest.[2] The editor of the Fort Macleod *Gazette* spelled it out in the paper's first issue: "And to our American cousins in Montana: our brother frontiersmen over the way, whose boundary touches our own, and whose interests are so similar and allied to ours, to them we shall look for patronage . . . trusting that the *Gazette* may make one more of the many bonds and ties joining the two greatest countries in the world." [3]

A further theme for investigation is the comparative study of parallel developments in the two societies on the Northern Great Plains. This method has already been applied in the study of the persistent agrarian radicalism of the hard spring wheat belt.[4] With great profit the same technique could be applied to other regional

[2] Americans who moved into western Canada during the emigration to the prairie provinces at the turn of the century were impressed with this fact. S. T. St. John, who abandoned a promising career in the States to become a pioneer leader in Saskatchewan, observed in his unpublished reminiscences, "I have learned during my life, that the aims and aspirations of the two great branches of the English-speaking race on this continent are practically identical." S. T. St. John, "Pioneer Recollections," Saskatchewan Archives (Saskatoon), 4.

[3] Fort Macleod (Alberta) *Gazette*, July 1, 1882.

[4] Donald F. Warner, "The Farmers' Alliance and the Farmers' Union: An American-Canadian Parallelism," *Agricultural History* (Chicago, Baltimore), XXIII (January, 1949), 9-19; Paul F. Sharp, *The Agrarian Revolt in Western Canada: A Survey Showing American Parallels* (Minneapolis, 1948).

problems such as land use in an area of recurring drought, relations with eastern metropolitan centers, Plains Indians, law enforcement, role of investment in frontier communities, rise of Plains cities, transportation, and the growth of a Plains culture. Such studies would immeasurably enrich our comprehension of our own western problems. A recent examination of the political tactics of the Nonpartisan League in the American Northwest would have had wider application and the author's case would have been strengthened had the experience of the League in the Canadian Northwest been pointed out. There the League, though born of the same feeling of economic abuse and cradled in the same atmosphere of political radicalism, faced the problem of standing on its own feet as a third party, for without the American direct primaries the League could not invade the established parties. The author's conjecture that under such circumstances the League would have suffered "a short and inglorious existence" was true on the Canadian plains where the League sought power under different political structures.[5]

Differences which distinguished the two societies demand attention. Systematic, unbiased, and critical examination of these differences may focus a revealing light upon the hotly debated problems of the environmental influences of the Great Plains. Professor W. L. Morton's recent challenge to Canadian historians to examine the historical literature of the West in terms of "*conscious adaptation* at the margin of a living culture to an environment not to be denied, but with which terms may be made" is equally provocative to students of the American West.[6]

Similarity does not imply identity. Though poured into the same environment the two societies retained their separate cultural identities. Many extraregional relationships and many heritages from older societies were far too powerful to be affected by environment. Nationalism, the most pervasive influence in modern society, was unaffected by its movement into a plains environment and created Canadian plainsmen to the north and American plainsmen to the south. Each possessed loyalties reaching outside the region that prevented a complete identification of common problems. Thus

[5] Samuel P. Huntington, "The Election Tactics of the Nonpartisan League," *Mississippi Valley Historical Review* (Cedar Rapids), XXXVI (March, 1950), 632.
[6] W. L. Morton, "Marginal," *Manitoba Arts Review* (Winnipeg), V (Spring, 1946), 29.

nationalism achieved in a generation what nature had not accomplished in millenniums — it gave reality to a line which bisected a region of geographic and economic unity. It is a striking fact that Canadian historians have not been able to discover an "institutional fault line" along their ninety-eighth meridian, nor have they succumbed to the obsession of uniqueness in the western experience.

Regional unity in historical development is clearly evident in the story of the Indians who freely roamed the grasslands for so many centuries. Only in a regional setting can the historian follow the Indian in his search for buffalo or estimate the dreadful effects on Indian power of the northward and westward march of smallpox. National boundaries meant nothing in the northward progress of the horse from the Southern Plains or in the clash of the white man's civilization with Indian society. "The Indians north and south of the International boundary," wrote Commissioner Gilbert M. Sproat in 1878, "are one people, severed politically by an invisible line."[7]

Canadian treatment of the Plains Indians challenges comparison with the American. American precedent served as guide and warning and taught Canadians the importance of maintaining honest agents and of keeping good faith with the Indians.[8] Canadian policy was aided, moreover, by the absence of gold-crazed miners or land-hungry farmers until the Indians as wards of the state were adjusted to reservation life.

Responsibility for preserving order on the Canadian plains rested with the celebrated North West Mounted Police. Their success has traditionally been explained by the fact that the Plains Indians were impressed by the dignity and calculated showmanship of the force, by their discipline and semimilitary bearing, and by the high caliber of the carefully selected organization.

Equally important, but little known, were other factors. Highly important to the success of the Police was the fact that the men of the force were not Westerners who shared western views toward the Indian or who were indoctrinated in western mores. They were imported Easterners and Europeans whose attitudes closely resembled those of people in the American East.

[7] Canadian *Sessional Papers*, No. 10, 1878 (Ottawa, 1879), Special Appendix E, lxvii.

[8] "The experience of the United States shows that it is of great consequence that the confidence of the Indians in the good faith of the Government should not be shaken, and that Indian affairs should be honestly administered." *Ibid.*, xiii.

Further analysis suggests, moreover, that their problem was actually quite a different one from that facing American officials. The destruction of Indian power on the American plains made easier the task of reducing the Indian in Canada. The disappearance of the buffalo which occurred with dramatic rapidity after the completion of the Union Pacific railroad in 1869 was so complete on the northern plains by 1877 that Canadian officials were alarmed at the prospect of a "catastrophe." [9] By 1881 Police reports reveal that the Indian was starving[10] with the result, as Police Commissioner A. G. Irvine pointed out, that "he has to depend on the Government for assistance, being forced in so doing, to remain about the Police Posts, Indian agencies or other settlements." [11]

Unlike the American plains experience, this occurred before the rush of settlement onto the Canadian plains, thus giving Canadian Indians time to adjust to the new sedentary life before white settlement engulfed them. Canadian officials at the time were grateful for this difference. Commissioner Irvine summarized it in this manner:

> The experience of our neighbors to the South of the International boundary cannot be without its lesson to us. In their case the military had had no trouble with Indians until settlers appeared on the scene. The settlers, unaccustomed to the Indian manner and habits, do not make due allowances and exhibit the tact and patience necessary to successfully deal with Indians, and which is showed by an organized force kept under control.[12]

Yet another factor helped to keep Canadian Indians quiet. Against whom could they go on the warpath in the years before settlement? Commissioner L. W. Herchmer authoritatively believed that "the Indians could only retaliate on the Police themselves and on a few traders, quite able and only too ready to take care of themselves." [13] To the south retaliation was effective for it sought its toll among women and children. Thus conditions were so different due to lack of population pressure that an orderly, well-planned, and honorable Indian policy could be executed. Across the boundary, though in the same physical environment, the story was quite different.

[9] *Ibid.*, No. 11, 1877, xii.
[10] *Ibid.*, No. 3, Pt. II, 1881, p. 30.
[11] *Ibid.*, No. 18, Pt. III, 1882, p. 10.
[12] *Ibid.*, No. 3, Pt. II, 1881, p. 6.
[13] *Ibid.*, No. 28, 1888, p. 9.

Regional economic developments created strong ties of interdependence. American metropolitan centers viewed the Canadian-American Northwest as a vast hinterland to be developed. Chicago in the 1850's was the first American city to feel these ambitions. In part, of course, this was an expression of the Manifest Destiny that deceived many into the futile hope that this region was "maturing, like fruit in autumn, to fall into our expectant lap." [14]

To this well-known expansionist drive was also linked the belief that the region must inevitably be free territory. John L. Scripps, ardent spokesman for Chicago's interests in the northern plains, believed that "The blighting hoof of slavery shall never touch its green sward, but freedom of body and of mind shall there have its highest realization, and there shall American civilization achieve its noblest triumphs." [15]

Annexation, however, was but one manifestation of Chicago's concern for the region. Behind the nationalistic bombast and star-spangled oratory moved the dream of a great commercial empire stretching from the forty-sixth to the sixtieth parallel and reaching from the Great Lakes to the Rockies. Bold dreams fired their imaginations as Chicagoans surveyed the scene, for nature had made their "city the inevitable gateway to and from this country."[16] With this in mind, the Chicago *Daily Democratic Press* bitterly attacked the Hudson's Bay Company as "that great monopoly which now holds the Northwest in its grasp" and noisily urged that it be "driven out of existence" so that the "whole country [could] be thrown open to settlement." [17] Political ambitions undoubtedly prompted these sentiments but in the background were economic aspirations. As Scripps phrased it, the region "whether it becomes ours or not, must contribute to the greatness and wealth of our city through the coming centuries." [18]

Strategic position gave St. Paul similar dreams of a Northwest empire. For many years it was the center of an active interest in the Canadian prairies and at times a hotbed of annexation sentiment.[19] As early as 1858 the editor of the St. Paul *Advertiser* urged

[14] John L. Scripps, *The Undeveloped Northern Portion of the American Continent* (Chicago, 1856), [3].

[15] *Ibid.*, 19.

[16] *Ibid.*, 9.

[17] Chicago *Daily Democratic Press*, March 17, 1856.

[18] Scripps, *Undeveloped Northern Portion of the American Continent*, [3].

[19] John P. Pritchett, "The Origin of the So-called Fenian Raid on Manitoba in

his readers to realize that their city possessed a "practically inexhaustible" agricultural empire on the Canadian-American plains. "None of the states lying west of the Mississippi," he argued, "are backed up by similar resources. . . . Iowa looks out upon the *mauvaise terres* of Nebraska; Missouri has Kansas, but western Kansas is a sandy plain, which extends westward to the Rocky Mountains in the first installment of the Great American Desert." [20]

During the same years James W. Taylor began his eloquent and persistent agitation on behalf of the Saskatchewan country. The frequency of his pleas and the fervency of his crusade earned for him the title "Saskatchewan" Taylor. Taylor foresaw with prophetic insight the potential greatness of the economic empire that lay sleeping across the boundary. He believed, moreover, that American enterprise was destined to exploit the region and that St. Paul would become the center of that development. His grandiose schemes for railroad building planned to link the Minnesota capital and the Great Lakes to the Saskatchewan country. Hopes of a lifetime were summed up in the affirmation: "the Saskatchewan will be brought within our limits and within the grasp of our system of communications." [21]

Taylor's boldest scheme fitted the expansive railroad building era in which he lived, for it was no less than an international railroad spanning the continent from Montreal to the Pacific Coast. Widespread interest spurred Taylor to seek support for his plan from politicians and financiers on both sides of the boundary. Lieutenant Governor A. G. Archibald of Manitoba, anxious to secure railroads for his province, supported Taylor's program with the argument that such a railroad "passing several times from the territory of one nation to that of the other would . . . do much to connect the two countries commercially and develop . . . a strong feeling to promote a healthy commercial intercourse between the two countries." [22]

1871," *Canadian Historical Review* (Toronto), X (March, 1929), 23-42; Theodore C. Blegen, "James Wickes Taylor, A Biographical Sketch," *Minnesota History Bulletin* (St. Paul), I (November, 1915), 153-219.

[20] St. Paul *Advertiser*, March 20, 1858.

[21] *Ibid.*, February 28, 1857. For Taylor's railway schemes, see Walter Moberly to James W. Taylor, June 5, 1888, Taylor to Donald A. Smith, March 26, 1892, manuscript for article to New York *Times*, June 18, 1870, manuscript for article to Toronto *Globe*, May 18, 1870, James Wickes Taylor Papers (Minnesota Historical Society, St. Paul). See also Taylor to E. D. Litchfield, September 18, 1869, *ibid.*

[22] A. G. Archibald to Taylor, January 3, 1871, Taylor Papers.

"Saskatchewan" Taylor's ambitious dream was never realized as he had planned it. Yet for nearly fifty years St. Paul was the gateway to the region, handling its commerce, providing much of its capital, and planning its future. The Minnesota city impressed Canadian visitors with its close ties to their West and surprised them with the quantity of goods destined for the North West.[23] Businessmen testified to one visitor that the settlers of the Canadian West "are now, and have been in the past their best customers." [24]

Railroad building absorbed St. Paul's attention in the post-Civil War era. Jay Cooke pushed the Northern Pacific across the northern plains with ambitions to seize the commerce of the Canadian as well as the American West. American financial interests were determined to secure dominion over the region through the power of the railroad. As the New York *Tribune* patriotically phrased it, "The great northern thoroughfare across the American continent must be upon our soil. Nothing else can so assure our political and commercial dominance, and hasten the assimilating process through which British America will ultimately drop into our hand like a ripe pear." [25]

Jay Cooke's aspirations received powerful support. With Taylor, now American consular agent in Winnipeg, in his pay and instructed to use his great influence in the Manitoba legislative assembly,[26] and with Lieutenant Governor Archibald greatly interested in the project, Cooke played for international stakes.[27] To the builders of the Northern Pacific, the railroad "was an incident of North West development — a central agency in utilizing the empire of the North-West." [28] Financial interests in eastern Canada, however, were equally determined to keep this wealthy hinterland for their own exploitation. With the aid of the Dominion government they built the Canadian Pacific Railway and wrested complete control from their many American rivals.

[23] Peter Mitchell, *The West and North West: Notes of a Holiday Trip* (Montreal, 1880), 15.

[24] *Ibid.*

[25] New York *Daily Tribune*, January 20, 1864.

[26] Alexander Ramsey to Taylor, November 23, 1871, Taylor Papers. See also Jay Cooke to Taylor, January 18, 1871, *ibid.*

[27] Cooke to Taylor, April 27, 1871, *ibid.* Taylor wrote A. B. Nettleton of the Northern Pacific, "My relations with Gov. Archibald are very satisfactory. I shall be consulted with regard to the Railroad system of the North West British America and I am sanguine that it may be adjusted on an international basis, entirely with the interests of the Northern Pacific. I accept my consular office as a means to that end." Taylor to Nettleton, November 24, 1870, *ibid.*

[28] Nettleton to Taylor, July 7, 1871, *ibid.*

Desire for political annexation frequently accompanied commercial domination in the ambitions of St. Paul business interests before the building of the Canadian Pacific.[29] Confusion created by the Manitoba Rebellion under the messianic Louis Reil in 1869-1870 seemed to present the opportunity many annexationists had longed for. With destiny in their hands, however, they failed to give anything but oral support to the dissident groups. Oscar Malmros, from the Winnipeg consulate, pleaded in vain with Alexander Ramsey for funds to support the rebellion. "I am convinced," he wrote Ramsey in January, 1870, "that $100,000 would make the annexation movement a success." [30]

The enthusiasm of Minnesota politicians and businessmen for annexation was not shared by their eastern mentors. The builders of the Northern Pacific, for example, were convinced that commercial dominion could be achieved without the risks of annexation and refused to support their western friends. Taylor's private dispatches to Cooke were eagerly read by the officials of the railroad. When the so-called Fenian invasion was speedily crushed, the Northern Pacific high command was pleased. "We are much gratified," President A. B. Nettleton wrote Taylor, "at the prompt extinguishment of this new Fenian nuisance, and congratulate you on the prompt measure adopted by yourself to prevent a fresh cause of complaint on the part of our friends across the border." [31]

Projects to fish in the troubled waters of the Red River failed, but the dream of a "peaceful penetration" lingered for many years. With the Texas precedent in mind, some St. Paul citizens shared the futile hope of an "American emigration over the border which will settle the whole question peacefully." [32] Plans were maturing in Montreal and Ottawa, however, which were to settle the issue without the aid of the ambitious schemes of the city on the Mississippi.

29 Pritchett, "So-called Fenian Raid on Manitoba," *Canadian Historical Review*, X (March, 1929), 35; Taylor's manuscript for article in Toronto *Globe*, May 18, 1870, Taylor Papers.

30 Oscar Malmros to Ramsey, January 14, 1870, Alexander Ramsey Papers (Minnesota Historical Society, St. Paul).

31 Nettleton to Taylor, October 21, 1871, Taylor Papers. Eastern capitalists accepted Captain Wheaton's definition of the Fenian affair: "There is a lawless and turbulent element in the town of Pembina and they act or are under the influence of bad men who ought to know better than to view 'American' interests by their foolish cause." Captain Wheaton, 20th Infantry, U.S.A., to Taylor, October 12, 1870, *ibid.*

32 George L. Becker to Taylor, April 17, 1870, *ibid.*

Benton, Montana, was the last American city to dominate the commerce of the Canadian-American plains. Situated at the head of navigation on the Missouri River, Fort Benton was the gateway to the famous Whoop-up Trail that crossed Montana to reach Fort Macleod and Calgary. For a quarter of a century the trail was the main artery into the western plains, carrying thousands of tons of freight to supply government installations, North West Mounted Police posts, ranchers and beef for the reservation Indians. An illicit traffic in liquor moved up the trail in the years before the Mounties closed the whisky traders' forts at Whoop-up, Stand-Off, Spitzee, and Robber's Roost. With the collapse of this illicit traffic, however, a legitimate trade flourished as government contracts and private purchases were awarded to Benton companies.

I. G. Baker and Company of St. Louis and Benton dominated the trade, providing service as "bankers, freighters, Indian traders, steamboat operators, wholesale and retail dealers in general merchandise, and proprietors of . . . the bonded line from Eastern Canada to the North West Territories." [33] For over a decade the company supplied the Canadian plains, much to the disgust of patriotic Canadians who shared Captain Cecil E. Denny's feeling that "it always seemed the greatest pity that this amount of money should all go out of Canada . . . amounting to some millions of dollars, and that no Canadian or English firm had a finger in the pie." [34] Official reports frequently reflected a similar sentiment. Police Commissioner Irvine complained that "a large amount of money has been expended, in return for which there is little or nothing to show, our money is merely aiding to build up the town of Benton, U.S.A." [35]

Undoubtedly Benton profited greatly from its control of the northern trade. Goods valued at nearly $350,000 passed over the trail in 1882 to the three police posts at Fort Walsh, Fort Macleod, and Wood Mountain alone.[36] The total value of the trade is suggested by the estimate that 15,000 tons passed over the trail annually and that Canadian orders constituted 20 per cent of all the freight handled in Benton from 1875 to 1883.[37]

[33] W. B. MacDougall, *MacDougall's Guide to Manitoba and the North West* (Montreal, 1880).

[34] Cecil E. Denny, *The Riders of the Plains* (Calgary, 1905), 68.

[35] *Sessional Papers*, No. 18, Pt. III, 1882, p. 13.

[36] *Ibid.*, No. 23, Pt. III, 1883, p. 22.

[37] Gerald L. Berry, "Alberta-Montana Relationships" (M.A. thesis, University of Alberta, 1950), 35.

Benton's monopoly was destroyed by the Canadian Pacific Railway in 1883. Canadian plans to free their West from the economic control of American centers were realized as the railroad pushed westward.[38] Chicago, St. Paul, and Benton were virtually eliminated from the trade north of the forty-ninth parallel as Winnipeg emerged the key city of the Canadian West.

A countertheme to the American dream of a commercial empire that defied the international boundary was the Canadian hope that their West would serve as the breadbasket for an industrial United States. As early as 1880 the colorful Alexander Begg preached the doctrine that the United States was industrializing faster than its farmers could provide food for its proletariat. Industrial North America, therefore, would be forced to look to the wheat belt of the northern plains for its bread.[39] Thirty years later the hard-pressed grain growers of the Canadian West echoed the same argument in their vain efforts to secure entry to American markets through a reciprocity agreement.

Land use during the early years of settlement was strikingly similar on both sides of the forty-ninth parallel. Cattlemen were first to give agricultural value to the land in both areas, and ranching in southern Alberta and Saskatchewan was a northward extension of the Cattle Kingdom. Earlier American experience was applied as ranchers moved north into the luxuriant and unoccupied Canadian grassland. Cattle from American ranches stocked the ranges, practices dictated by American experience accompanied the expansion, and the South Western Stock Association adopted without significant change the rules of the Montana Stock Growers' Association.[40]

But ranching in Canada was not the image and transcript of the range cattle industry of the United States. Adjustments to environment in material culture were identical but Canadian ranching life was greatly influenced by its intimate ties with England. These ties clearly illustrate the strength of extraregional relationships, for

[38] The Fort Macleod *Gazette,* March 5, 1883, observed that "the line has been opened far enough to divert a good deal of the Montana trade to Winnipeg. Large quantities of flour and provisions are now purchased in Winnipeg . . . which were formerly bought in the American markets."

[39] *Canada North West: A Monthly Journal Devoted to the Settlement and Development of Manitoba and the North West,* I (January, 1880), 7.

[40] Fort Macleod *Gazette,* April 14, 1883. The extent of the dependence is suggested by the *Gazette's* notice on May 24, 1883, that "a special meeting is to be called to consider the round-up and other laws when received from Montana."

ranching in Alberta was a successful synthesis of "the customs and prejudices of Victorian England and those of the New West," or as Professor L. G. Thomas has so happily phrased it, "in such communities the body is American but the spirit is English." [41]

Material culture adjustments to Great Plains conditions are also demonstrated in the agricultural settlement that swept ranching off the plains and confined it to the Cypress Hills and foothills of the Rockies. Settlers from eastern Canada and Europe generally avoided the plains in favor of the humid Park Belt. American farmers, however, boldly pushed northward into the familiar environment. This rush of settlement was only a small wave of a general movement which sent thousands of middle western farmers into the subhumid plains region during the early years of this century.[42]

Settlement of the Canadian West marked the final phase of the occupation of agricultural North America. Armed with knowledge of "scientific" or "dry land" farming and equipped with tools and power denied to an earlier generation that had attacked the plains, this last great wave enthusiastically plowed under the buffalo grass and optimistically created a society on wheat.

Much of the optimism was based on fiction, even more of it was founded on misinformation. The rush of settlement coincided with a cycle of wet years that seemed to confirm the persistent belief that rain followed the plow.[43] Where adequate moisture failed to accompany cultivation, obliging rainmakers from the United States, experienced in the art and available for reasonable fees, promised to make the skies weep at will.[44]

Knowledge of dry farming techniques made possible the occupation of the northern plains, for it encouraged farmers to believe that through the application of scientific principles they could conquer the semiarid West. American experience contributed greatly to the opening of the Canadian "dry belt," since Yankee knowledge of dry farming antedated settlement of the Canadian West and

[41] L. G. Thomas, "The Ranching Period in Southern Alberta" (M.A. thesis, University of Alberta, 1935), 171, 137.

[42] Charles M. Harger, "The Revival in Western Land Values," *Review of Reviews* (New York), XXXV (January, 1907), 64.

[43] James Mavor, *Report to the Board of Trade on the North West of Canada with Special Reference to Wheat Production for Export* (London, 1904), 11. "The belief is prevalent in the semiarid region that mere cultivation diminishes aridity."

[44] Didsbury (Alberta) *Pioneer*, November 18, 1914.

preceded by many years Angus Mackay's discovery of the value of summer fallow at Indian Head in 1885. American settlers took the method with them as they moved north into Canada, for many were disciples of Hardy W. Campbell and Thomas Shaw. Some even returned to Campbell's experimental farms to study the latest refinements in dry farming methods.[45]

The most important individual contribution undoubtedly was that of Emil J. Meilicke, German-born ex-Populist state senator from Minnesota. Meilicke taught the Saskatchewan Valley Land Company the possibilities of the Regina plains and followed a policy of importing farmers into that region who possessed dry farming experience.[46] In Canada, as in the United States, dry farming became an effective propaganda tool in the hands of commercial companies interested in the sale and development of semiarid lands. In both countries it led to disaster for thousands of pathetically hopeful farmers who built their future on marginal lands.

Exchange of agricultural information was an important phase of the interdependence of the area. The earlier settlement of the American West dictated that the bulk of the knowledge flowed northward as settlers introduced the dugout for water storage, the chilled steel plow, the steam plow, and crops such as alfalfa, winter wheat, flax, and sugar beets. "Bonanza farming" also moved northward when W. R. Bell sold his interests in the Bell-Kelso farm in Kittson County, Minnesota, and applied the Dalrymple formula to vast acreages in the Qu'Appelle Valley.[47]

Experience on the American plains was highly valued by Canadian officials in their search for suitable settlers for the West. Their policy frankly recognized the physical integrity of the plains by placing a premium upon settlers who possessed farming experience in the neighboring states. Canadian Deputy Minister of Interior A. M. Burgess summarized the government's attitude: "They bring an experience of the climate and soil characteristics of the prairie region of the West, of the most approved methods of agriculture and of the care, breeding and feeding of farm animals, which it

[45] Canadian Pacific Railway pamphlet, *Western Canada* (n.p., n.d.), 58.

[46] Professor Arthur S. Morton believed that "the inevitable conclusion is that Emil Julius Meilicke, as a pioneer, did more to shape the development of the spacious plains between Saskatoon and Regina than any other individual." Emil J. Meilicke, *Leaves from the Life of a Pioneer* (Vancouver, 1948), 119.

[47] Emerson (Minn.) *International*, September 27, 1882.

takes the immigrant from Great Britain or continental Europe some years to acquire."[48]

American farmers benefited from this exchange, for discoveries on the Canadian plains also enriched American agriculture. The contributions of Dr. Charles Saunders and Seager Wheeler in the development of wheat strains for the northern climate were of international consequence.

Canadian immigration propaganda successfully convinced thousands of farmers in the United States that their future lay under the Union Jack. This migration is the only mass exodus of American citizens to another nation in recent years. As such, it commands attention, for their easy adjustment to Canadian institutions, their successful assimilation into Canadian life, and their rapid loss of American loyalty challenges our traditional emphasis upon the effectiveness of American nationalistic indoctrination. How deep really were the roots of American loyalty when, for the sake of cheap land, so many shed their nationality like their coats to become Canadians? Eastern Canadian and British writers deplored the invasion as the Americanization of the Canadian West but this fear proved an exaggeration as the expatriates with only a few exceptions became loyal Canadians. Canadian immigration officials refrained from discouraging these "nightmares of imperial disruption," for such fears stimulated emigration to Canada "to save the country to the flag."[49]

Other developments illustrate with equal force the unity of the region. The striking similarity in farmers' organizations and the persistent agrarian radicalism demonstrate the deep-seated community of interest of farmers on the plains. The northward march of the Farmers' Alliance, Society of Equity, Nonpartisan League, and Farmers' Union as well as the similar programs and creeds of western Progressivism in Canada and Populism in the United States are eloquent testimony of this fact.

Keen resentment against the colonial economy of the plains led to bitter, even pathological, sectionalism on both sides of the forty-

[48] *Sessional Papers*, No. 13, 1893, xviii. Ex-mayor Russell Wilson of Saskatoon believed that "these people who came into this country had an advantage over the Eastern Canadians, as they understood the production of the soil better, being much as in Minnesota and Dakota, and they had better implements to work with." *Narratives of Saskatoon, 1882-1912* (Saskatoon, 1927), 54.

[49] John W. Dafoe, "Western Canada: Its Resources and Possibilities," *Review of Reviews*, XXXV (June, 1907), 703.

ninth parallel. This particularism frequently expressed itself in extreme denunciations of the economic systems subordinating West to East. Such expressions confused some observers into believing that a unique western society was emerging in response to the environment. Actually this region was echoing the same resentment felt in all colonial economies whatever the physical environment. When the *Grain Growers' Guide* denounced Toronto as the "Babylon of Canada, where the Nebuchadnezzars of high finance live and move and have their being," it raised its voice in the traditional agrarian protest against dependence upon eastern capital and culture.[50]

Another phenomenon common to western society was a deeply rooted suspicion of European politics. Shielded by three thousand miles of ocean, protected by British sea power and the Monroe Doctrine, and absorbed in the development of the continental heartland, farmers on both sides of the boundary were often isolationist in sentiment. Western Canadian farmers, in spite of closer ties to Europe, were frequently as bitterly opposed to involvement in European disputes as their American cousins. They vigorously opposed cooperation in the Imperial naval rearmament program before World War I. "Canada has never needed any naval protection," argued the leading farm journal in western Canada, "does not need any now, and has not asked for any." [51] When the ominous crisis of August, 1914, settled darkly over Europe, newspapers reflected popular disinterest in a Balkan intrigue and denounced the use of war as wasteful and indecisive. Once Canada was engulfed by war, however, editors found a favorite theme in denouncing the isolationist spirit which seemed disinterested in the Empire's fate.[52]

Important differences marked the two societies that emerged on the northern plains. The rush of settlement into western Canada never outran organized government as it so frequently did in the American West. Moreover, it came in an age which imposed restraints through the use of modern technology that prevented a repetition of the Wild West atmosphere that characterized the

[50] *Grain Growers' Guide* (Winnipeg), X (October 17, 1917), 15.

[51] *Ibid.*, VI (July 23, 1913), 5.

[52] The Didsbury *Pioneer*, October 7, 1914, asked, "Is it because we are blessed to a certain extent in being a side eddy where the waters are calm and there is nothing extraordinary to upset the equilibrium . . . or is it because we are selfish?"

earlier settlement of the American plains. The Wild West of song and fiction simply did not exist on any scale in western Canada, though some Americans who contemplated migrating to the area seriously inquired of officials of the necessity of carrying weapons.

A repetition of the Mormon troubles that clouded the American story was impossible in Canada. Constitutional differences placed far greater powers in the hands of the central government under the Canadian confederation than in the American system. Litigation over water rights in the semiarid West was avoided in Canada by the denial of riparian rights, the rejection of the doctrine of appropriation, and the acceptance of the legal principle that water was the property of the Crown. American experience was a grim warning and Canadians turned to Australian precedent to escape American mistakes.[53]

Stronger ties with Europe through the Imperial relationship and a continuing immigration from the mother country provided a further source of difference. A conscious emphasis upon English culture reflected the recency of the transition and the immaturity of Canadian culture. On top of this, the frontier experience was too brief to have more than an ephemeral influence, and civilization in western Canada sprang up nearly full-grown, possessing a twentieth-century sophistication. Yet it was true that society on the northern plains, American and Canadian, was the heir of many cultures, the copy of none.

[53] *Sessional Papers,* No. 13, Pt. III, 1896, 31; C. S. Burchill, "The Origins of Canadian Irrigation Law," *Canadian Historical Review,* XXIX (December, 1948), 353-62.

Notes and Documents

Origins of Immigration Restriction, 1882-1897: A Social Analysis

By John Higham

At no period in American national history has immigration from Europe been so strongly encouraged and so fervently blessed as in the 1860's and early 1870's. During these years the federal government, two thirds of the states, and innumerable business organizations raided Europe's manpower.[1] Exuberant patriots rejoiced at the trans-Atlantic influx,[2] and few indeed opposed it. Yet a very few years saw a very great change. A campaign to reduce immigration replaced the campaign to increase it; friendliness turned into fright. Beginning with the law of 1882, which established federal supervision of immigration and excluded certain groups unable to support themselves, the restriction movement blossomed into a formidable and even violent crusade in the late eighties and nineties. It reached its crest in the winter of 1896-1897, when only the stubbornness of Grover Cleveland prevented the enactment of a drastic test to stop the entry of illiterates. Thereafter the drive subsided abruptly, but it left a legacy of tensions, policies, and ideas which a later generation abundantly exploited.

To explain the formative stage in the restriction of European

1 Merle Curti and Kendall Birr, "The Immigrant and the American Image in Europe, 1860-1914," *Mississippi Valley Historical Review* (Cedar Rapids), XXXVII (September, 1950), 204-11; Maurice G. Baxter, "Encouragement of Immigration to the Middle West during the Era of the Civil War," *Indiana Magazine of History* (Bloomington), XLVI (March, 1950), 25-38. A thorough compilation of federal and state legislation is contained in Reports of the Immigration Commission, "Immigration Legislation," *Senate Documents*, No. 758, 61 Cong., 3 Sess. Since the regulation of Chinese immigration was regarded at the time as a wholly different issue, it does not enter into the present discussion.

2 Kirk H. Porter (ed.), *National Party Platforms* (New York, 1924), 82-83; New York *Tribune Extra*, July 4, 1876, pp. 9, 38; William T. Harris, "On the Relation of Education to the Individual, to Society, and to the State," *Wisconsin Journal of Education* (Madison), IV (January, 1874), 1.

immigration, one might employ several methods. Most broadly, one might attempt a cultural approach, appraising the clash of native and immigrant folkways and illuminating the American experience by contrast with the traditions and behavior of other nations.[3] Most specifically, one might examine the tangled interlocking of particular events and ideas within the restriction movement. The second procedure could profitably direct attention to struggles for partisan political advantage, to the activities of important individuals, or to the appearance of new antiforeign concepts.[4] The present essay follows a course somewhere between these two general methods, less adventurous perhaps than the first, less precise than the second. The object here is to establish — in summary fashion — the connections between the nativist upsurge and certain large, concurrent changes in American society. This stressing of the functional context neither does justice to the weight of persistent traditions nor does it clarify the totality of immediate circumstance. But whatever may have been the cultural heritages behind immigration restriction, they were catalyzed by a new social situation. And whatever political maneuvers or intellectual ferment may have contributed, they worked within a framework of social change.

Of the general mutations in late nineteenth-century America, four had a special relevance to the rise of the restriction movement. The first of these to play a measurable part in the organized campaign was the development of a confused but many-pronged reform movement aimed at solving the problems of an urban, industrial society. A second transformation came with the so-called "new immigration," the flow of peasant and ghetto peoples from Italy, Austria-Hungary, the Balkans, and Russia, which began increasing rapidly in the early 1880's. Thirdly, the Roman Catholic Church experienced an unusual surge of strength and activity during the same years. Finally, the period from 1885 to 1897 was one of drastic social and economic dislocations — an epoch in which anger and misery raised a frightening challenge to the historic promise of a fluid society. Each of these factors entered into the making and

[3] Ralph Linton, "Nativistic Movements," *American Anthropologist* (Washington, New York, Lancaster, Menasha), XLV (April-June, 1943), 230-40; Elin Anderson, *We Americans: A Study of Cleavage in an American City* (Cambridge, 1937).

[4] Elmer C. Sandmeyer, *The Anti-Chinese Movement in California*, University of Illinois *Studies in the Social Sciences* (Urbana), XXIV (1939); Carl F. Wittke, *German-Americans and the World War (with Special Emphasis on Ohio's German-Language Press)* (Columbus, 1936).

shaping of the immigration restriction movement. In one aspect it was a reform effort, in another an expression of ethnic antipathy. In still another, it represented a response to anti-Catholic sentiment. And it was also a reaction to fears and frustrations generated by class conflict and economic collapse. None of these causes operated independently, but they had diverse and unequal impacts and deserve separate consideration.

The first general immigration law in 1882 demonstrated the early influence of humanitarian and reform impulses in launching the restriction movement. For many years relief agencies in eastern cities had been more or less constantly concerned at the strain which impoverished and disorganized immigrants imposed upon their own financial resources and upon the life of the community.[5] The charity groups had more philanthropic than reformist zeal, but many of them did hope for social improvement through public action. They began to lobby for federal supervision and regulation of immigration in 1876, after the Supreme Court forbade the states to collect an immigrant welfare fund from shipowners. Six years later the charity officials won their fight, although the statute was less restrictive than they had hoped it might be.[6]

The emergence of other groups with broader conceptions of social responsibility and a larger interest in public control quickened the restriction movement. To various types of reformers, restriction seemed a relatively easy and painless way of invoking national authority to combat corruption, squalor, and injustice. Was not the immigrant a demoralized tool of privilege? Edmund James said so as early as 1883,[7] and the progressive-minded economists who joined him in founding the American Economic Association offered a prize of $150 for the best essay on "The Evil Effects of Unre-

[5] L. L. Bernard and Jessie Bernard, *Origins of American Sociology: The Social Science Movement in the United States* (New York, 1943), 530-40; Edith Abbott, *Historical Aspects of the Immigration Problem; Select Documents* (Chicago, 1926), 345, 651-56.

[6] New York *Tribune*, January 19, 1878, p. 8, January 25, 1878, p. 1; *Proceedings of the Conference of Charities*, 1876 (Albany, 1876), 162-70; *Proceedings of the Eighth Annual Conference of Charities and Correction*, 1881 (Boston, 1881), 217-27; *Proceedings of the National Conference of Charities and Correction*, 1890 (Boston, 1890), 279; *Cong. Record*, 47 Cong., 1 Sess., 5106-13, 5415. For background, see Frank J. Bruno, *Trends in Social Work as Reflected in the Proceedings of the National Conference of Social Work, 1874-1946* (New York, 1948).

[7] John J. Lalor (ed.), *Cyclopaedia of Political Science, Political Economy, and of the Political History of the United States*, 3 vols. (Chicago, 1881-1884), II, 89-90.

stricted Immigration." [8] Following Josiah Strong, many spokesmen of the Social Gospel took a similar view.[9] The rising municipal reform movement felt a special alarm over the boss-ridden immigrant vote and produced in Abram S. Hewitt the most colorful nativist of the 1880's.[10]

While middle-class critics of laissez faire lent dignity to restrictionism, organized labor put pressure behind it. Through the Knights of Labor unionization was recovering in the early eighties from the debacle of the previous decade; but unemployment and immigration were increasing too. Vaguely class-conscious in outlook, the Knights held corporate wealth responsible for the tightening job market. Accordingly, they opened an assault, not on immigration itself, but on the importation of European labor by American employers.[11] This attack led to the second step in federal restriction, the contract labor law of 1885, which expressed the Knights' conviction that undesirable immigration was almost entirely provoked by scheming capitalists.[12] Other unions drew the same distinction between voluntary and induced immigration. For seven years after 1885 the principal labor spokesmen rebuffed all pleas for a general limitation on immigration. The American Federation of Labor rejected the literacy test as late as 1896.[13] They

[8] Richard T. Ely, "Scrapbook: American Economic Association, 1885-1906" (State Historical Society of Wisconsin, Madison), 27, 32.

[9] Josiah Strong, *Our Country: Its Possible Future and Its Present Crisis* (New York, 1885), 30-46; Samuel L. Loomis, *Modern Cities and Their Religious Problems* (New York, 1887), 67-100; William D. P. Bliss, *The Encyclopedia of Social Reform* (New York, 1897), 714; Wilbur F. Crafts, superintendent of the Reform Bureau, to Grover Cleveland, February 18, 1897, Grover Cleveland Papers (Manuscripts Division, Library of Congress).

[10] Allan Nevins, *Abram S. Hewitt: with Some Account of Peter Cooper* (New York, 1935), 512-16; *Nation* (New York), LII (April 16, 1891), 312; Charles E. Norton (ed.), *Orations and Addresses of George William Curtis*, 3 vols. (New York, 1894), III, 78-79. The degradation and misery of immigrant lives in tenement houses were first spread fully before the public by Jacob A. Riis, *How the Other Half Lives* (New York, 1890), but the conditions he described were not new. A quarter of a century before Riis wrote, the slum areas of some of the leading cities were already crowded with abject immigrant residents; yet their condition attracted little comment. It seems evident, therefore, that the restriction movement stemmed immediately from a rising concern over urban problems and only indirectly from an objective change in urban conditions. For descriptions of mid-century immigrant slums, see Oscar Handlin, *Boston's Immigrants, 1790-1865: A Study in Acculturation* (Cambridge, 1941), 93-127; Robert Ernst, *Immigrant Life in New York City, 1825-1863* (New York, 1949), 37-60.

[11] *Journal of United Labor* (Washington), X (September 26, 1889), 2; *Journal of the Knights of Labor* (Washington), XII (December 31, 1891), 1.

[12] *Cong. Record*, 48 Cong., 1 Sess., 5349; 2 Sess., 1785; Terence V. Powderly, *Thirty Years of Labor* (Columbus, 1889), 442-47.

[13] *Report of Proceedings of the Sixteenth Annual Convention of the American*

did so partly because of an idealistic belief in the international solidarity of the working class and partly because an extremely large proportion of union members were themselves foreign-born.[14] These factors limited the role of organized labor in the early restriction movement more than historians have usually believed.

Neither middle-class nor working-class reformers had a preponderant effect on the nativist crusade as a whole, but their attitudes point to another of its aspects. Very often the arguments for restriction as a technique of social improvement revealed a sharp contempt for the new immigration from southern and eastern Europe. Many reformers were also race-conscious. Indeed, the first concentrated attack on the new immigrants came from labor leaders during the campaign for the contract labor law. Since employers apparently introduced the first appreciable Slovakian and Italian settlements into the mining and industrial centers of western Pennsylvania in the early eighties, union officials concluded that this new immigration was an entirely unnatural one — a product of corporate greed. In this context hatred of the strange newcomers seemed very natural. Identifying southern Europeans with contract labor, the unions fell to reviling the people along with the system.[15] In the next few years this ethnic animosity infected a number of liberal intellectuals. The economist Edward Bemis concocted the idea of a literacy test in 1887 as a means of discriminating against southern and eastern Europeans.[16]

Federation of Labor, 1896 (Bloomington, Ill., 1905), 81-82; "Testimony Taken by the Select Committee of the House of Representatives to Inquire into the Alleged Violation of the Laws Prohibiting the Importation of Contract Laborers, Paupers, Convicts, and Other Classes," *House Miscellaneous Documents*, No. 572, 50 Cong., 1 Sess., 392, 399; "Report of the Select Committee on Immigration and Naturalization," *House Reports*, No. 3472, 51 Cong., 2 Sess., 706-709; Porter (ed.), *National Party Platforms*, 155. The Knights of Labor swung over to a general restrictionist position in 1892. *Proceedings of the General Assembly of the Knights of Labor*, 1892 (Philadelphia, 1892), 4, 86.

14 Powderly, *Thirty Years of Labor*, 429; Boston Central Labor Union to Cleveland, February 9, 1897, Cleveland Papers; *Report of Proceedings of the Seventeenth Annual Convention of the American Federation of Labor*, 1897 (Bloomington, Ill., 1905), 88-91; Isaac A. Hourwich, *Immigration and Labor; The Economic Aspects of European Immigration to the United States* (2nd ed., New York, 1922), 330-33, 552.

15 *Cong. Record*, 48 Cong., 1 Sess., 5349-50; "To Prohibit the Importation of Foreign Contract Labor into the United States," *House Reports*, No. 444, 48 Cong., 1 Sess., 8-9.

16 Edward W. Bemis, "Restriction of Immigration," *Andover Review* (Boston), IX (March 1888), 263. See also Richmond Mayo-Smith, *Emigration and Immigration; A Study in Social Science* (New York, 1890), 132-35; Riis, *How the Other Half Lives*, 27, 106-107; Arthur Mann, "Frank Parsons: The Professor as Crusader," *Mississippi Valley Historical Review*, XXXVII (December, 1950), 483.

By 1890 abhorrence of the new immigration was spreading to wider circles.[17] Exactly why many Americans singled out these peoples for special dislike is not entirely clear. For one thing, their very newness meant that they had fewer powerful friends and less influence than longer established groups; it also meant that they could provide a target for both the old immigration and the old stock. For another thing, the new immigrants submitted to particularly primitive living conditions — a fact which, in itself, affronted the competitive, material values of the period. Thus the Italians, who had a lower standard of living than any of the other prominent nationalities, also experienced more prejudice than any of the others.[18] Some West Coast nativists thought that the Italians were no less degraded than the Chinese.[19]

Whatever the reasons for the particular distrust of the new immigration, we should not overestimate this aspect of the late nineteenth-century restriction movement. Antipathy to southern and eastern Europeans did channel support to the plan for a literacy test, but that antipathy did not dominate the movement as a whole. If it had done so, one might expect to find a close correlation between the size of the new immigration and the intensity of xenophobia. The two trends arose simultaneously in the 1880's, but they soon parted company. From 1893 through 1895 immigration from southern and eastern Europe decreased sharply while the campaign for restriction surged ahead with increasing power. Not until the turn of the century did the new immigration begin to skyrocket, yet this was the very time when opposition died to a whisper.[20] Furthermore, restrictionists often showed little discrimination in

[17] Henry C. Lodge, "Lynch Law and Unrestricted Immigration," *North American Review* (Boston, New York), CLII (May, 1891), 611-12; *Public Opinion* (Washington), X (January 10, 1891), 325; Boston *Post*, April 14, 1891.

[18] *House Miscellaneous Documents*, No. 572, 50 Cong., 1 Sess., 208-14, 215-16; George J. Manson, "The 'Foreign Element' in New York City," *Harper's Weekly* (New York), XXXIV (October 18, 1890), 817. For another index to — and element in — the hatred of Italians, see the record of lynchings compiled in John B. Moore, *A Digest of International Law*, 8 vols. (Washington, 1906), VI, 837-49.

[19] "Chinese Immigration," *House Reports*, No. 4048, 51 Cong., 2 Sess., 1-5, 44, 55.

[20] United States Bureau of the Census, *Historical Statistics of the United States: 1789-1945* (Washington, 1949), 33-34. For evidence of the rise and fall of restriction sentiment, see n. 39 and n. 41. It should be noted, however, that a sudden surge of Italian immigration in 1896 contributed to the congressional passage of the literacy test in that year. Bliss, *Encyclopedia of Social Reform*, 714; New York *Tribune*, April 24, 1896, p. 3.

choosing adversaries. An extensive examination of congressional debates and hearings, magazine articles, newspaper editorials, and the publications of nativist and other organizations indicates that a general dislike of *all foreigners* was much more pervasive than the specific dislike of the new nationalities.[21] Actually, the new immigration stands out in hindsight more sharply than it did at the time. As late as 1900, 74 per cent of the European-born population of the United States derived from accustomed sources.[22] With vast numbers of old immigrants still conspicuous and partially unassimilated, antiforeignism prevailed over ethnic distinctions.

Clearly, other factors entered into the making of this generalized antiforeign sentiment. Some of it arose out of a third change in the American scene — a revival of religious conflict. With the meeting of the Third Plenary Council in 1884, the Roman Catholic Church in the United States entered upon one of its most vigorous decades, a period which brought twenty new dioceses, many parochial schools, the establishment of the Catholic University of America, and the appointment of the first Apostolic Delegate to the United States. Also, the Council's decrees strengthened the Catholic school policy and led to new pressure for state aid to parochial education.[23] These advances touched off a wave of Protestant hysteria. The few existing nativist societies expanded rapidly in the late eighties, and many new ones appeared.[24] Like similar Protestant groups in earlier periods, these organizations were antiforeign as well as anti-Catholic. Since the Roman hierarchy followed the leadership of the Vatican, anti-Catholic crusaders regarded the Church as alien and subversive. Since it recruited members chiefly from immigration, most religious nativists joined the restriction movement. Another connection between anti-Catholic and antiforeign fears arose out

21 Evidences of this indiscriminate restriction sentiment are too numerous to cite, but for examples see Rena M. Atchison, *Un-American Immigration: Its Present Effects and Future Perils* (Chicago, 1894); *Literary Digest* (New York), II (April 18, 1891), 693; Robert DeCourcy Ward, "Immigration Clippings, 1891-94" (Widener Library, Harvard University, Cambridge).

22 United States Bureau of the Census, *Historical Statistics*, 32. A leading proponent of the literacy test came mournfully to the same conclusion. Prescott F. Hall, "Present Status of Immigration Restriction," *Gunton's Magazine* (New York), XVIII (April, 1900), 308.

23 Gerald Shaughnessy, *Has the Immigrant Kept the Faith? A Study of Immigration and Catholic Growth in the United States, 1790-1920* (New York, 1925), 166; Daniel F. Reilly, *The School Controversy (1891-1893)* (Washington, 1943), 31-46.

24 Albert C. Stevens, *The Cyclopaedia of Fraternities* (New York, 1899), 290-327.

of the condition of municipal politics; in the eyes of alarmed Protestants the growing power of Irish Catholics in city government seemed an additional reason to slam the national gates. During this period Protestant agitators paid backhanded tribute to the importance of the Irish in ecclesiastical and political affairs by continuing to hurl more abuse at them than at any other nationality.[25] It is significant that the American Protective Association, which absorbed most of the other anti-Catholic societies in the early nineties, showed almost no interest in the new immigration and had little part in the campaign for the literacy test.

This fact in itself suggests that the impact of anti-Catholicism on the restriction movement was hardly decisive. The passion of midwestern Protestants, who armed to meet a rumored papal uprising in 1893, soon spent itself in empty fury. The immigration restriction bill introduced by William A. Linton, chief A.P.A. spokesman in Congress, never got out of committee.[26] The A.P.A. itself began to decline in 1894,[27] two years before the restriction movement reached its crest. Indeed, anti-Catholicism throughout this period lacked the respectability which it had previously enjoyed. No outstanding political leader identified himself with it, as Rutherford B. Hayes had done in 1875, and even many Protestant ministers urged a reduction of immigration without mentioning its denominational character.[28]

Xenophobia in late nineteenth-century America had a more potent source than religion or racism or reform. In its largest aspect it issued from a crisis in the whole American social order. From the mid-eighties to the mid-nineties a society already uneasy at the emergence of the first great trusts felt the shock of fierce industrial unrest. Americans had long believed that their land of mobility and opportunity was immune to the class conflicts of Europe. The railroad strikes of 1877 passed too quickly to do serious damage to

[25] *Ibid.; A. P. A. Magazine* (San Francisco), I (June, 1895), 89; Alvin P. Stauffer, Jr., "Anti-Catholicism in American Politics, 1865-1900" (Ph.D. dissertation, Harvard University, 1933), 18-19, 93-108.

[26] *A. P. A. Magazine,* I (July, 1895), 170; *Index to the Cong. Record,* 53 Cong., 3 Sess., H. R. 8774.

[27] Stauffer, "Anti-Catholicism in American Politics," 374-75.

[28] Charles R. Williams (ed.), *Diary and Letters of Rutherford Birchard Hayes,* 5 vols. (Columbus, 1922-1926), III, 274-90; Rev. B. W. Williams, "Our Attitude Toward Foreigners," *American Magazine of Civics* (New York), VIII (January, 1896), 65-66; *Public Opinion,* XIV (February 25, 1893), 585; XV (June 10, 1893), 222.

their faith. But the labor upheaval that began in 1885 ushered in a decade of massive and recurrent discontent. Alarmed at these new class antagonisms, unwilling to recognize them as indigenous, and unready to deal with them as such, many Americans surrendered to the conviction that they came from abroad. The equation between immigration and unrest seemed confirmed by the riot which occurred at Haymarket Square in Chicago in 1886. Coming as it did at the height of the huge eight-hour strikes, the bombing at Chicago struck panic from coast to coast over the threat of foreign-born anarchists. No other single incident did so much to provoke restriction sentiment. For years the memory of Haymarket and the dread of imported anarchy haunted the American consciousness. No general stereotype of the immigrant prevailed more widely than that of a lawless creature, given over to violence and disorder. Scores of conservative politicians, newspaper editors, educators, popular writers, and Protestant clergymen labeled the immigrant as peculiarly susceptible to anarchism.[29] Many blamed all of the major strikes of the period on foreign influence, and the composition of the trade unions gave specious credibility to the charge.[30]

In short, fears for social stability and the projection of those fears upon the immigrant became almost a common denominator of the restriction movement. Of all major restrictionist groups, only organized labor did not connect immigration with unrest; and even here a patrician organization like the Order of Railway Conductors, which favored cooperation with management, denounced immigration as the chief cause of current labor troubles.[31] Middle-class reformers saw the immigrant as both an author of revolution and an agent of reaction.[32] Opponents of Catholicism and of the

29 *Public Opinion*, I (May 15, 1886), 83-86; III (April 30, 1887), 49; XV (June 10, 1893), 222; clippings from Boston *Journal*, July, 1894, Ward, "Immigration Clippings," 31, 38; *Proceedings of the National Conference of Charities and Correction*, 1887 (Boston, 1887), 203-205; *The Poems of Thomas Bailey Aldrich*, 2 vols. (Boston, n.d.), II, 72; John H. Denison, "The Survival of the American Type," *Atlantic Monthly* (Boston), LXXV (January, 1895), 26.

30 T. N. Carver, "Immigration and the Labor Problem," *American Journal of Politics* (New York), III (July, 1893), 80-81; H. H. Boyesen, "Immigration," *National Perils and Opportunities* (New York, 1887), 67; National Educational Association, *Journal of Proceedings, and Addresses*, 1888 (Topeka, 1888), 145-47; *Public Opinion*, V (August 25, 1888), 432; XIII (August 6, 1892), 426.

31 *Railway Conductor's Monthly* (Elmira, Cedar Rapids), V (December, 1888), 613; *Railway Conductor* (Cedar Rapids), XI (April, 1894), 189.

32 *Publications of the Immigration Restriction League*, No. 1 (Boston, 1894); William H. Tolman, *Municipal Reform Movements in the United States* (New York,

new immigration often reacted in a similar way. The A.P.A. and other Protestant societies deplored the use of the strike and proposed antiforeign measures as a solution to class conflict.[33] The first full-length anti-Semitic tract written in the United States, the work of a Greek immigrant in 1888, described the strike as a peculiarly Jewish idea and John D. Rockefeller as a representative of the Jewish monopoly.[34] At a more august social level the fear of the foreign-bred discontent contributed powerfully to the mushroom growth of hereditary patriotic societies in the early nineties. Many of the new societies followed the lead of the Sons of the American Revolution in dedicating themselves to saving the country from insurrectionary immigrants.[35] The same concern contributed powerfully to a shift of business opinion toward a restrictionist position. By the late 1880's large numbers of American business leaders were turning to immigration restriction as a weapon against strikes, lawlessness, and other disorders.[36]

The specter of unrest would not have looked so frightening to Americans if they had preserved intact their old confidence in the capacity of their civilization to liberate men automatically from the restraints of fixed class and enforced poverty. But changes in American conditions seemed now to narrow the horizon of opportunity and compound the menace of discontent. The year after

1895), 103; Strong, *Our Country*, 43; Mayo-Smith, *Emigration and Immigration*, 88; Atchison, *Un-American Immigration, passim.*

[33] *A. P. A. Magazine*, I (July, 1895), 173-74; *American Standard* (San Francisco), I (May 25, 1889), 1; *Council Chat: A Journal Devoted to the Jr. O. U. A. M. and Kindred Orders* (Wilkes-Barre), I (November, 1890), 539.

[34] [Telemachus T. Timayenis], *The Original Mr. Jacobs: A Startling Exposé* (New York, 1888), 283-85, 295. This is the earliest indigenous book of this character in the Library of Congress, the New York Public Library, and the Jewish Theological Seminary of America. It is mentioned in Leonard A. Greenberg, "Some American Anti-Semitic Publications of the Late 19th Century," *Publications of the American Jewish Historical Society* (Philadelphia), XXXVII (1947), 421-25.

[35] *Proceedings of the Second Annual Congress of the Sons of the American Revolution*, 1891 (New York, n. d.), 8; *American Monthly Magazine* (Washington), XXVI (May, 1905), 407; Society of Colonial Wars, *Constitution and By-Laws, Membership* (New York, 1893), 53; *American Historical Register and Monthly Gazette of the Patriotic-Hereditary Societies of the United States of America* (Philadelphia), II (June, 1895), 1069.

[36] *Commercial and Financial Chronicle* (New York), LI (September 13, 1890), 316-17; *Bradstreet's: A Journal of Trade, Finance and Public Economy* (New York), XIII (June 5, 1886), 369; *Proceedings of the Twenty-First Annual Meeting of the National Board of Trade*, 1892 (Boston), 126-28, 272-73; Wisconsin Bureau of Labor and Industrial Statistics, *Second Biennial Report*, 1885-1886 (Madison, 1886), 416-21, 428-30.

Haymarket the agricultural frontier collapsed. Simultaneously, alarm over the dwindling of the public domain became widespread. Here was another reason for reducing immigration. As early as 1883 Henry George warned that the immigrant tide was becoming dangerous because the safety valve of western land was closing. After 1886 many newspapers expressed similar fears.[37] In the midst of more concrete troubles, western farmers shared in the general anxiety over pressure of immigration on the remaining land supply.[38] Then in 1893 economic distress spread throughout the whole country. In the next three years the contraction of employment and business activity added an urgency to the nation's claustrophobia. While restriction proposals as harsh as total prohibition received a hearing, an organized campaign for the literacy test developed.[39] To this plan Congress gave its first and overwhelming approval in 1896.[40]

Then suddenly the fears and frustrations of the Cleveland period dissolved, and the restriction crusade faded with them. Beginning in 1897 a tide of prosperity washed over the country's domestic troubles; soon the intoxication of war and imperialism added further impetus to the revival of national self-confidence. As the tensions of the nineties relaxed, much of the interest in restricting immigration disappeared.[41]

The downfall of nativism at the close of the century emphasizes again its function as an outlet for the baffled discontents of the preceding years. For the social historian those discontents supply the central key to the origins of immigration restriction. But surely

[37] Henry George, *Social Problems* (reprint, New York, 1886), 39-46, 161-62; *Public Opinion*, III (April 30, 1887), 50; III (May 14, 1887), 98-99; IX (May 24, 1890), 151; XXII (February 25, 1897), 231-32. See also John Swinton, *Striking for Life: Labor's Side of the Labor Question* (Philadelphia[?], 1894), 53-54.

[38] For an example, see Ed Brown to Henry Baldwin, February 13, 1888, Henry Baldwin Papers (Manuscript Division, New York Public Library). See also *Western Rural and American Stockman* (Chicago), XXX (April 23, 1892), 263.

[39] For symptoms of the quickening of the restriction movement by economic depression, see Office of Commissioner-General of Immigration, *Report of the Immigration Investigating Commission to the Honorable the Secretary of the Treasury* (Washington, 1895), 127-51; *Cong. Record*, 54 Cong., 1 Sess., 1028, 5421, 5425-26. The literacy test was first endorsed by a congressional committee in 1893. *Ibid.*, 52 Cong., 2 Sess., 901.

[40] *Cong. Record*, 54 Cong., 1 Sess., 5485; 2 Sess., 246.

[41] For indications of a sharp fall of interest in immigration, see Hall, "Present Status of Immigration Restriction," *Gunton's Magazine*, XVIII (April, 1900), 305-307; *Nation*, LXIX (October 19, 1899), 293-94; A. P. C. Griffin, *List of Books (with References to Periodicals) on Immigration* (Washington, 1907), 59-61.

this key will not unlock the whole problem. A balanced view will encompass the many-sidedness and complexity of the situation from which restriction arose. It grew in a climate of social crisis, but its roots extended into reform, into religion, and into immigration itself.

Imprisonment For Debt in America: Fact and Fiction

By Edwin T. Randall

Colonel Richard M. Johnson of Kentucky described for the Senate on February 16, 1824, the real or imagined misery of imprisoned debtors in America with sufficient eloquence to color the pages of history to this day. As the climax to his speech he provided "record evidence" which he said "might turn a Nero pale and make a Caligula shudder": Boston imprisoned 1,442 persons in 1820; 1,281 in the following year, and 769 in three quarters of the next. Of this total 430 were women. Boston, a community of 50,000,[1] was depicted as holding one neighbor in 50 behind prison bars for inability to pay debt, denying the prisoner opportunity to earn and robbing his family of productive enterprise. "Imagination shudders," Johnson exclaimed, "while she anticipates the result; and virtue, benevolence, and justice, weep and frown." [2]

Senator James Barbour of Virginia rallied to Johnson's support on the next day. He projected his colleague's record on a national basis to conclude that above 13,000 were imprisoned for debt throughout the land. He admitted, however, that among the 430 Boston women, "a proportion, and a large one, if you will, are the victims of vice." [3]

These early nineteenth-century exposés on imprisonment for debt have persisted unquestioned in the works of later historians. Describing the United States at the close of the eighteenth century, John B. McMaster says that "the laborer who fell from a scaffold or lay sick of a fever was sure to be seized by the sheriff the moment he recovered, and be carried to jail for the bill of a few dollars which had been run up during his illness at the huckster's or the tavern." [4] Discussing the economic ills at the close of the American

[1] According to the United States census, the population of Boston was 43,298 in 1820; 61,392 in 1830.

[2] *Annals of Congress*, 18 Cong., 1 Sess., 258 ff.

[3] *Ibid*., 279-80.

[4] John B. McMaster, *A History of the People of the United States . . .*, 8 vols. (New York, 1883-1913), I, 98.

Revolution, he writes: "It was then the fashion in New Hampshire, as indeed it was everywhere, to lock men up in jail the moment they were so unfortunate as to owe their fellows a sixpence or a shilling." The historian emulates Colonel Johnson in exploring the consequences of rigid law enforcement: "Had this law been rigorously executed in the autumn of 1785, it is probable that not far from two thirds of the community would have been in the prisons." [5]

A present-day historian informs his readers that in this period, "Everywhere men of all ages were lodged behind prison walls for inability to pay even trifling sums. In 1787, for example, ten men whose combined debts totaled only £24 were languishing in a New York prison without hope of release. Elsewhere the situation was equally bad." [6] He returns to this period to assert: "Thousands of unfortunate debtors lost everything, even their scanty household furnishings,[7] and the jails overflowed with prisoners confined for debt." [8]

In a discussion of the consequences of Thomas Jefferson's ill-fated embargo, McMaster creates a startling scene of closed business establishments and bulging debtors' prisons. "In the cities the jails were not large enough to hold the debtors. At New York during 1809 thirteen hundred were imprisoned for no other crime than being ruined by the embargo. A traveller who saw the city in this day of distress assures us that it looked like a town ravaged by pestilence." [9] This statement implies that the streets were deserted because their wonted strollers were confined to prisons. McMaster's account, a footnote indicates, was based upon the journal of John Lambert, early American traveler, but the reader will seek in vain for any mention of imprisonment for debt in it.

McMaster returns once more to this theme in tracing the reform movements which followed the War of 1812. "For the smallest debt possible to contract, though it were but a cent in value, the body of the debtor, whether man or woman, would be seized by the creditor and cast into jail. . . . poor wretches who owed a sixpence or a shilling . . . were dragged to prison by thousands." [10]

[5] *Ibid.*, 343.
[6] Harry J. Carman, *Social and Economic History of the United States*, 2 vols. (Boston, 1930-1934), I, 323.
[7] Exemptions of personal property by law should be noted.
[8] Carman, *Social and Economic History of the United States*, I, 339.
[9] McMaster, *History of the People of the United States*, III, 415.
[10] *Ibid.*, IV, 532-33.

Other myths have been promoted by twentieth-century writers. Frank T. Carlton in a *Yale Review* article based on fragments from popular periodicals and an incidental phrase in the fourth report of the Boston Prison Discipline Society, which estimated that in the United States 75,000 souls were put in chains for debt annually, added: "the jails at this period of our history seem to have been built and utilized chiefly for debtors instead of for criminals. In 1830, the ratio between the aggregate number of debtors and criminals confined in seventeen prisons located in the Northern and Eastern States was nearly five to one. Furthermore, a very large percentage of the debts for which persons were deprived of their liberty was small — under fifty dollars." [11]

Harry E. Barnes and Negley K. Teeters restate without examination the Boston Prison Discipline Society's estimate that 75,000 were imprisoned annually in this rich and prosperous land, and found further evidence for their conclusions in the daily newspapers.[12] Helen L. Sumner has found that "Many pitiful cases were cited by the press of the day. For example, the newspapers reported that in Boston a blind man, with a family dependent upon him, was imprisoned for a debt of $6; that in Providence, Rhode Island, a widow was imprisoned for a debt of 68 cents by the man to save whose property from fire her husband had lost his life, and that in Salem, Massachusetts, a man seventy-six years old, who had been wounded at the battle of Bunker Hill, was imprisoned for a 'debt of a few dollars'." She, too, picks up the Boston Prison Discipline Society's estimate that 75,000 were annually imprisoned, and adds that "In many places jails were overcrowded and in terribly insanitary condition, and in some States no provision was made for supplying even food to imprisoned debtors." [13]

Notes from the newspapers of 1788 in the *Annals of Albany* report a case in which "a rich and popular citizen" incarcerated an "humble artisan for inability to liquidate his rent," and thereby made him a charge upon the county and a defaulter to the rest of his creditors. The artisan's ingenuity captures attention and wins

[11] Frank T. Carlton, "Abolition of Imprisonment for Debt in the United States," *Yale Review* (New Haven), XVII (November, 1908), 339-40.

[12] Harry E. Barnes and Negley K. Teeters, *New Horizons in Criminology* (New York, 1943), 848.

[13] John R. Commons *et al.*, *History of Labour in the United States*, 4 vols. (New York, 1918-1935), I, 178 ff.

the reader's sympathy, for instead of wasting away in prison obscurity he set forth his plight in an advertisement:

> Whereas the subscriber (a master of shoemaking) is now confined in the City Hall, upper loft, for 20 pounds back rent which is owing to Gen. Schuyler; and as he is desirous of working for his living, and not to be chargeable to the good people of this city, he therefore humbly requests that such of the citizens and others, as are desirous of having well made shoes on the most reasonable terms, to favor him with their custom, and they may depend on being served on the shortest notice, and every favor shall be thankfully acknowledged by the public's humble servant, Thaddeus Lawrence.[14]

This is the image of imprisonment for debt bequeathed to us, but close study must raise the suspicion that it falsely depicts American life. The nation was not yet burdened by an embittered industrial population bound to the city at the mercy of uncertain day wages. Unrivaled forests and plains offered each man his own domain. Labor was in demand, the rewards exceptional. Population was sparsely distributed, police power insignificant. No overgrown government bureaucracy, as in prerevolutionary France, nor the vain distinctions of class, as in England and on the Continent, restricted the individual in the utilization of these natural resources or the development of his talents. American society had neither a fixed class of debtors nor creditors.

An examination of available facts necessitates a revision in the traditional view of imprisonment for debt. If it could be stated exactly what number of men were imprisoned year by year throughout the colonial period and the first fifty years of independence, the figures would throw no light on the system's cruelty. To measure that quality one must determine what the word meant with regard to debtors. Were they confined to a cell or prison yard? Or generally did they live and work in real freedom, although technically in custody, while their finances were untangled?

The definition of imprisonment is necessary by virtue of the universal custom of setting prison "bounds" for debtors. Colonel Johnson was not unaware of this, for he told the Senate, in a speech on January 15, 1823, that in many parts of New England the bounds were identical with the limits of the township or county, and that Michigan had extended them to the boundaries of the county.[15]

[14] Joel Munsell, *The Annals of Albany*, 10 vols. (Albany, 1850-1859), II, 206.
[15] *Annals of Congress*, 17 Cong., 2 Sess., 120.

Bounds varied from place to place and time to time, for state laws gave leeway to local officials in this practical matter.[16] Vermont at one period specified a maximum of four square miles;[17] New York once marked off five hundred acres,[18] but extended the bounds to several counties later on.[19]

Moreover, the drawing of bounds was not the only ameliorant. The honest insolvent was protected against imprisonment by state laws permitting bail, and by a right to take the "poor debtors' oath." How long, then, in common practice were honest men confined to the debtors' apartments of prisons because of inability to meet their obligations? American laws and reports of day-by-day experiences provide an answer.

Early in the colonial period laws for protection of the honest insolvent evolved. For example, in 1672 Connecticut provided that "no man should be kept in prison for debt, unless he had some estate he would not produce."[20] Traveler Hugh Jones reported from Virginia at the beginning of the eighteenth century: "Prisoners for debt are very rare, the creditors being there very merciful and the laws so favorable for debtors that some esteem them too indulgent."[21] Thomas Jefferson at the close of the century explained that "debtors unable to pay their debts and making a faithful delivery of their whole effects are released from confinement and their persons forever discharged from restraint from such previous debts."[22] The constancy of Virginia policy is further borne out by a letter, April 21, 1830, from John Reynolds, sheriff of Campbell County, who said: "In Virginia, debtors are seldom confined in Prison."[23] A modern writer has agreed that "imprisonment of debtors in Virginia, when practiced at all, was rather technical than

16 The laws of Connecticut granted the sheriff the power "to designate a certain reasonable space of ground, adjacent to each gaol, to be denominated the liberties thereof, and to alter the same as occasion may require." And it imposed on the sheriff the duty "to permit any person, who shall be in his custody, on civil process only, to go at large within the liberties of the prison so designated." *The Public Statute Laws of the State of Connecticut, as Revised and Enacted by the General Assembly, in May 1821 . . .* (Hartford, 1821), Title 42, sec. 8.

17 Boston Prison Discipline Society, *Fifth Annual Report* (Boston, 1880), 42.

18 *Ibid.*, 45.

19 *Cong. Debates*, 20 Cong., 1 Sess., 83.

20 *Public Statute Laws of the State of Connecticut . . . 1821*, Title 42, sec. 8.

21 Hugh Jones, *The Present State of Virginia* (New York, 1865), 30.

22 Thomas Jefferson, *Notes on the State of Virginia* (Philadelphia, 1825), 181.

23 Boston Prison Discipline Society, *Fifth Annual Report*, 48.

close. . . . Virginia had thus, before the Revolution, effectively nullified the English law of imprisonment for debt." [24]

George R. Minot, historian of Shays' Rebellion, does not designate imprisonment for debt as a cause of the unrest which followed the American Revolution. The Shays insurgents — at a moment when their situation was desperate and they were eager for public sympathy — did not assert that the jails were filled with debtors or condemn the basic system of imprisonment for debt. Instead, they denounced the expensive mode of collection, and warned that, along with the "great scarcity of cash, [it] will of necessity fill our gaols." [25] Further negative evidence on the public attitude toward the debt laws and their administration can be deduced from the action of a convention of fifty towns of the county of Hampshire, Massachusetts, held at Hatfield on August 22, 1785. The delegates voted seventeen "grievances and unnecessary burdens now lying upon the people" as "the sources of that discontent . . . throughout this Commonwealth," but debt imprisonment was not among them! [26]

The people and the states in the post-Revolutionary period were overburdened with debts public and private, confused over methods of raising taxes, distraught by depreciation of paper currency and scarcity of specie, offended by interest accruing to speculators in government securities and the expense of lawsuits growing out of affairs tangled by the long conflict. Questions of public finance were so important that Minot asserts: "Upon the right management, then, of the publick debt, the future tranquility of the Commonwealth greatly depended." [27] He further states:

> The scarcity of specie . . . furnished reluctant debtors with an apology for withholding their dues both from individuals and the publick. . . . Some indeed availed themselves of an advantage, which the laws of the country, for a long time put into their hands, and paid their creditors in depreciated currency; and some might have discharged their obligations in a more honourable manner. . . . Private contracts were first made to give place to the payment of publick taxes, from an idea that the scarcity of specie did not admit of the payment of both. The former therefore, were made payable in other property than money by . . . the Tender Act.[28]

[24] [Fairfax Harrison], "Imprisonment for Debt in Colonial Virginia," *Virginia Magazine of History and Biography* (Richmond), XXXV (January, 1927), 1-6.

[25] George R. Minot, *History of the Insurrections in Massachusetts* . . . (Boston, 1810), 82.

[26] *Ibid.*, 33 ff.

[27] *Ibid.*, 6.

[28] *Ibid.*, 13-14.

Throughout the first four decades of American independence, when the cumbersome debt laws were being revised or abandoned and bankruptcy laws were under discussion, responsible men argued, not that inhuman cruelty prevailed, but that leniency had been carried too far with respect to debtors. On January 15, 1799, James A. Bayard of Delaware said in a speech to the House:

> In most of the States there are insolvent laws, which . . . give all the advantages to the debtor, and none to the creditor. In the State of Pennsylvania, there is a law of this kind which goes to a great extent, and produces fraud without end. A man may be discharged from his debt in respect of his person without being an hour in jail. . . . by the laws of this wise State, (and certainly it is a wise one,) a man may hold property, be a rich man, and wallow in luxury, out of the reach of his creditor.[29]

A quarter of a century later Robert Y. Hayne of South Carolina compared the condition of debtors in the United States with those of other countries:

> Whatever may be said of the origin of the writ of *capias ad satisfaciendum*, or the theory on which it rests, it is certain that in modern times, and certainly in the happy land in which our lot has been cast, that process is, in practice, nothing more than the means of compelling a debtor to pay his debts — a debtor who, having the ability, is unwilling to comply with his obligations. We have heard of a question being agitated in other countries, as to the right of a creditor to the body of his debtor . . . for the purchase of the corpse, in order to honor it by the rights of a "Christian burial." . . . we have lately been shocked by an idle and shameful report of the arrest of a dead body, in one of the most moral, enlightened, and polished cities of this Union; but that report is known to be a mere fabrication. . . .
>
> Imprisonment for debt . . . "as a penalty for debt" . . . is almost unknown in the United States; there is not a State in the Union which has not provided by law for the release of debtors . . . ; and in respect to the courts of the United States, a similar provision has been made. . . . the existing laws do substantially provide . . . that a debtor shall only be imprisoned for the purpose of compelling him to surrender his property.[30]

Similarly, Senator William Smith of South Carolina on January 10, 1828, denied that the system was cruel and "a disgrace and stain upon our statute book. It might have been so in the dark ages," he continued, "But in the present age of charity and civilization, every one knows that no such thing exists. The several States have provided against it; and we talk of mere imaginary evils, when

[29] *Annals of Congress,* 5 Cong., 3 Sess., 2661-62.
[30] *Ibid.,* 18 Cong., 1 Sess., 485-86.

we speak of the cruelty of imprisonment under the present system."[31] Senator Samuel Bell of New Hampshire on January 18, 1828, said that "He was aware that persons whose sensibilities are easily excited by real or fictitious tales of distress, imagine that they see great oppression" in the existing laws. He assured his colleagues that "no practical evil had resulted from them, as now modified in the several States, so far as they had come under his observation."[32]

In New York the law, in its bare framework, permitted any adult or child, on appearing before a clerk of court, to name any member of the community in a process for debt. It required the clerk to issue the process, and the officer he summoned to imprison the accused. The prisoner — insofar as the basic law was concerned — might be held a year or more until his case came up for trial.[33] Thus, the possibility appeared to exist that an honest man might be held more than a year on a false claim born in the fancy of a child or the malice of an adult. However, the original law in New York, as elsewhere, was clothed in a patchwork of amendatory insolvency statutes designed to protect the honest man. Therefore, in order to understand the workings of the system we shall turn to contemporary testimony.

Two pamphlets[34] of the early nineteenth century throw considerable light on the actual functioning of the law. As the authors, Joseph D. Fay and Thomas Herttell, were crusaders for abolition of debt imprisonment, we may assume that they do not diminish the evils which they were eager to abolish. Both condemn imprisonment for debt on moral and legal grounds, but they do not reinforce their arguments with accounts of inhuman oppression and bulging jails. On the contrary, they reveal that the laws were so inefficient in collection that imprisonment had ceased. They say, however, that the laws' peculiarities were causing social and mercantile demoralization. "Imprisonment for debt is, now, at last," Fay acknowledges, "after a long course of progressive improvement, only allowed in a moderate and qualified degree; and an en-

[31] *Cong. Debates*, 20 Cong., 1 Sess., 41.

[32] *Ibid.*, 85.

[33] Joseph D. Fay [Howard, pseud.], *A Disquisition on Imprisonment for Debt, As the Practice Exists in the State of New-York* (New York, 1818), 5.

[34] *Ibid.*; Thomas Herttell, *Remarks on the Law of Imprisonment for Debt; Showing its Unconstitutionality, and Its Demoralizing Influence on the Community* (New York, 1823), 67 pp.

lightened age seems disposed to inquire for, and put in practice, every rational expedient that may safely render even that qualified degree less." [35] He further points out "That there are honest poor men is not to be doubted, and those who are honest will be found to deal honestly, and take up no credits they have not a moral certainty of discharging, and if sickness or other casualties distress them, their characters are known, and it is not often, if from such causes they happen to fall in arrear, that they are prosecuted or the helping-hand denied them." [36]

Both pamphlets assailed the laws on the ground, not that the jails were filled with honest men, but that the dishonest also were blessed by liberty. Said Fay:

> the dexterous knave now resorts to work himself through our insolvent laws, in spite of all the opposition that can be made by his creditors . . . and then turns to his business again, when the vexatious farce is over, with the capital he had before, and perhaps at the same stand, and even with precisely the same articles of merchandise, or traffick, or whatsoever may have been the commodities of his dealing. . . . Our existing laws for the prevention of the fraudulent concealment of property, by insolvent debtors, are lamentably deficient, and require radical correction. . . . They are operating to the serious demoralization of society. . . . Mercantile faith, once so strong and so auspicious to the mercantile character, is lamentably depreciated. . . .[37]

"So little do creditors now regard . . . [the laws]," Herttell explained, "as efficient means to coerce their debtors to make their payments, that, hopeless of success, they have for some time past, been gradually declining to seek or to expect to obtain justice through that channel; and thus the operation of the law of imprisonment for debt, and the counter operation of the insolvent laws, produce an effect nearly the same as if the whole were blotted out of existence." [38]

In sharp contrast to the traditional views about oppression of poor honest men, Fay condemned the New York law which permitted a man imprisoned for a debt under $25 to "be exonorated immediately, by a five minutes process, and simply swearing before a magistrate" that he was "not worth twelve dollars and fifty cents." Fay believed that this class was less entitled to special

[35] Fay, *Disquisition on Imprisonment for Debt*, 12-13.
[36] *Ibid.*, 41.
[37] *Ibid.*, 21-22.
[38] Herttell, *Remarks on the Law of Imprisonment for Debt*, 58.

favor under law than men who risked large amounts of capital in business and sometimes were rendered destitute by accidents which they could not foresee. Artisans and wage earners, he said, should have been able to gauge accurately what credits they could discharge.[39]

Fay and Herttell both condemned the patchwork of debt laws for the contradiction which they presented. "Our code as it now stands," Fay said, "is really . . . the most ludicrous contrivance legislation ever framed. One law allows the creditor to keep his debtor in prison . . . and then comes another law and lifts him out. . . . Laws that counteract so much their own purposes, can hardly be adjudged wise." [40] Herttell tells us that under the basic law the debtor and his family would have starved to death, but "that these dreadful consequences are averted by the insolvent laws" which were "predicated on the admission that it is wrong to keep an insolvent honest debtor imprisoned, and therefore provide for his *relief*. . . . If it is right to release them from prison, it was wrong to put them there before their guilt was ascertained." [41]

At another point Herttell said he understood that in times long past, law and custom had jailed alike the honest and the fraudulent, but by his own day (1823) the tables had been turned and the insolvent laws effected "the release of honest debtors, and fraudulent, indiscriminately" with the result that "creditors now, comparatively speaking, will imprison none." He asserted that "the insolvent laws narrow down the operation of the law for imprisonment for debt almost to a virtual repeal." [42]

The leniency of New York law as described in these pamphlets must have been known in other states. Senator Smith told his colleagues on January 17, 1828, that southern merchants sometimes went to New York for the purpose of being arrested and discharged under insolvency statutes. They were entitled to such benefits after ten days, and "The prison bounds of New York extend to the limits of the several counties," and so they could wash away their delinquency by an "imprisonment" which involved no actual confinement.[43]

[39] Fay, *Disquisition on Imprisonment for Debt,* 39, 40.
[40] *Ibid.,* 42.
[41] Herttell, *Remarks on the Law of Imprisonment for Debt,* 14.
[42] *Ibid.,* 47.
[43] *Cong. Debates,* 20 Cong., 1 Sess., 83.

The social demoralization resulting from such practice was noted by others than Fay and Herttell. Governor Matthew Harvey of New Hampshire, in a message to his legislature on June 4, 1830, called attention to the situation. However, he did not see men destroyed by foolish imprisonment, but forced into degrading circumstances in attainment and preservation of freedom: "the facilities for obtaining the poor debtor's oath are so great, that persons indebted, and possessing effects of small value, are induced to divest themselves of their property, so far that the amount remaining in possession shall not prevent the discharge provided by law, rather than to increase it by honest industry, with a view to the payment of debts. . . . The inevitable consequence is, a diminution of the quantity of labor, industry and economy; an accumulation of unnecessary cost; and an increase of poor and idle persons."[44] Governor Harvey also asserted that in New Hampshire, as in New York, "Imprisonment within the chartered limits of a town" had "little of real restraint about it," and through the extension of the "Jail yards to the extreme boundaries of the towns in which Prisons are situated . . . about *seven eighths* of all persons, committed to Prison for debt . . . have been discharged, on application to the commissioners of Jail delivery."[45]

Senator Levi Woodbury of New Hampshire explained to the Senate on January 18, 1828, that no imprisonment was permitted in his state except for a debt above $13.33, and every debtor could be discharged in fifteen days on a full and fair surrender of his property. In practice, the Senator pointed out, the surrender of property was usually made before the capias was served, so that "arrest" was a mere technicality involving no confinement whatsoever. When "he is in fact committed," said Senator Woodbury, "the detention continues only fifteen days, and has not, for many years, exceeded thirty days, unless the debtor wants further time to adjust his concerns."[46] But whatever the length of time, the debtor had the right of bail or the limit of the bounds. In North Carolina, according to a letter of Sheriff Joseph Medley, debt imprisonment was practically nonexistent, "as almost every man can give security for his appearance" in court. In Maine the debtor could take the oath without going to jail.[47]

44 Boston Prison Discipline Society, *Fifth Annual Report*, 63.
45 *Ibid.*
46 *Cong. Debates*, 20 Cong., 1 Sess., 90.
47 Boston Prison Discipline Society, *Fifth Annual Report*, 41.

This evidence contradicts the accounts which writers have presented through failure to analyze the abundant material in the Boston Prison Discipline Society reports. The founder and guiding genius of the Boston organization was Rev. Louis Dwight, who gathered, but did not himself digest, the great mass of information on this subject which the volumes contain. Imprisonment for debt was not mentioned in the first three reports of the Prison Society. However, in the fourth report (published in 1829 and devoted to the previous year) Dwight dropped the incidental remark that 75,000 unhappy men and women were imprisoned annually for failure to pay debt. This is the origin of the figure which has been accepted and repeated without investigation in book after book.

Even if it is an accurate estimate of the number of debt cases, it throws no light on the real operation of the laws for it does not disclose how long, on the average, debtors were confined to prisons or the bounds. But despite the worthlessness of the estimate, the fifth, sixth, and seventh reports of the Prison Society contain an enormous amount of instructive information. For example, statistics in the fifth report obtained by Dwight from 31 cities and towns from Maine to Maryland show 3,202 cases of imprisonment for debt. Of that number, 678 debtors were under arrest less than one day; only 527 were in technical custody more than thirty days; the remaining 1,997 were under "arrest" — whatever the word meant — between one and thirty days. An approximation of what "arrest" did mean may be obtained from other materials in the reports. In the seventh, Troy, New York, reported an average of 50 "on the limits," 3 only in close confinement, and New York gave the average on the limits as 400, in confinement 25.

Returning to the "record" which Johnson laid before the United States Senate, Senator James Lloyd of Massachusetts, alarmed at the indictment of his state which it constituted, appealed to Judge Peter O. Thacher of the municipal court of Boston, under whose jurisdiction management of the prisons fell, for enlightenment on the condition of Christian charity at home. Judge Thacher dispatched to Washington two reports from grand juries which had but recently inspected the prisons. The reports revealed that in August, 1823, there were but twenty debtors held in Boston, and in 1824 but twenty-two. Such was the measure of truth, said Senator Lloyd, borne by the "record" and "certain terrific stories now afloat," [48] stories about Massachusetts concocted by the representative of a faraway state which some years earlier had abolished imprisonment for debt.

Are the "pitiful cases" cited by the press of the day genuine? Was Helen L. Sumner's blind man with a dependent family locked up for a debt of $6.00? Was the Bunker Hill veteran at the age of seventy-six held in a cell for the crime of owing "a few dollars" which he was unable to pay?

No doubt these reports are true, but the significant information is lacking, which is why these particular debtors were denied the laws' generous provisions for bail, liberty of bounds, and the poor debtors' oath. It is obvious from the character of the insolvent laws and the testimony as to their practical applications, that these were unique, not ordinary cases. They illustrate the perils of using the press as a historical source, for the press seeks and expands the unusual; it does not always have the means and time, even if it nurtures the ambition, to gather all facts necessary to a faithful presentation of a situation. In the case of the shoemaker, Thaddeus Lawrence, whose story is preserved in the *Annals of Albany*, no attempt is made to explain his failure to benefit by the laws which set others free. Yet the newspaper notes give no indication that any other debtors were confined with him in the City Hall's "upper loft." He appears to have been a solitary prisoner.

Drunkenness played its part in debt imprisonment. We suspect this influence upon reading a letter from Sheriff I. S. Palmer of Madison County, New York, which stated that the number of debtors was more than twice as great in "haying and harvesting" as in winter.[49] And it comes into the open in a letter from Jailer Francis Armstrong, who told the Boston Prison Society: "Seldom have any been put to Jail but such as are intemperate; and not in one instance have any but transient persons been kept in close confinement, except when first committed, and while in a state of intoxication, and then only until they would get fairly sober." [50] Sailors, too, were sometimes jailed for failure to pay keepers of rooming houses.

It is true that societies were formed to alleviate the plight of jailed debtors. The important question, however, is what proportion

[48] *Annals of Congress,* 18 Cong., 1 Sess., 349.
[49] Boston Prison Discipline Society, *Seventh Annual Report* (Boston, 1832), 31.
[50] *Ibid.*

of the delinquents were so destitute of resources, character, and friends that bail was denied, or the liberties of the bounds refused.

Statements that between the Revolution and abolition of the system in the 1830's men were locked up "in jail the moment they were so unfortunate as to owe their fellows a sixpence or a shilling"; that rigorous enforcement would have carried off "two-thirds of the community" to jail; that "men of all ages were lodged behind prison walls for inability to pay even trifling sums"; that "the jails overflowed with prisoners," can not be reconciled with contemporary authority. According to Herttell, the "insolvent laws, hold out so many, and such powerful inducements to take the oaths . . . that they have become so frequent and so common, as to be regarded as but little more than mere matters of legal form. An honest man *can* take them, and a dishonest man *will* take them." [51]

The evidence is abundant that "imprisonment for debt" is a misnomer with regard to America — "arrest for debt" is more accurate. The system broke down as a means of collecting debt in a rapidly expanding commercial mode of life and disappeared in the 1830's.

[51] Herttell, *Remarks on the Law of Imprisonment for Debt*, 51.

Book Reviews

Virginia Venturer, A Historical Biography of William Claiborne, 1600-1677; The Story of The Merchant Venturers who Founded Virginia, and The War in the Chesapeake. By Nathaniel C. Hale. (Richmond: The Dietz Press, 1951. xvi + 340 pp. End maps, bibliography, and index. $5.00.)

William Claiborne, one of the foremost leaders in the founding of Virginia, came to the colony as a surveyor for the Virginia Company in 1621. In time he acquired numerous other offices: treasurer, chief commander of the military forces, councilor, secretary of state, and acting governor. He also acquired an extensive Indian trade and large tracts of land.

Mr. Hale's story emphasizes Claiborne's trading ventures and his struggle with Maryland over Kent Island and Indian trade. It is a story well worth telling. The author has treated his aggressive hero's controversies with the Calverts with judicial restraint. In fact, he has shown restraint beyond the call of duty when one considers the strange judicial activities of Captain Thomas Cornwallis, which resulted in the hanging of one of Claiborne's men as a pirate, the act of attainder against Claiborne, and the confiscation of Kent Island. However, the author does not fail to point out Claiborne's faults.

The chief adverse criticisms that may be made of the book are the unnecessary inflation of the facts at hand and too great a straining after popular appeal. These faults occur chiefly in the first part of the book, which should have been greatly condensed. The footnotes are few and inadequate. Both the footnotes and the bibliography need editing for proper form and consistency.

In the remaining portion of the book the author is on firmer ground. There is less speculative writing; the narrative is vivid; and the contents show a careful and understanding use of sources. Here the author discusses Indian wars, political strife within Virginia, fur trading in the upper Chesapeake, the founding of Maryland and the resulting conflict over Kent Island, the "thrusting out" of Sir John Harvey, Virginia under the Commonwealth, the Restoration of 1660, and Claiborne's activities as a Virginia planter.

Here and there Mr. Hale has woven into the story interesting accounts of life and politics in the new and expanding colony. He has not failed to recognize the remarkable continuity of political control from one crisis to another — a tribute to the reasonableness of those in authority, whether serving company, king, or parliament. It also proves the continuing traditions of the English Constitution, whether in England or America.

The format of the book is pleasing; the index is good; and the bibliography is extensive and well chosen.

College of William and Mary RICHARD L. MORTON

The Navigation Acts and the American Revolution. By Oliver M. Dickerson. (Philadelphia: University of Pennsylvania Press, 1951. xv + 344 pp. Tables, bibliography, and index. $6.00.)

After more than two decades of research in eighteenth-century commerce, Professor Dickerson here presents the results of his study in two complementary essays which formulate an ingenious and persuasive theory of Anglo-American relations in the Revolutionary period. Briefly his thesis holds that the Navigation Acts, far from being a disrupting force, were the "cement of empire." For over a hundred years the economic policy of regulation and development embodied in these acts was accepted by the colonies without serious opposition. Then after the peace of 1763 the policy changed qualitatively to one of exploitation. Now that the raw continent began to yield profits and "fortunes were in sight, the ruling clique in London saw an opportunity to push the colonials aside . . . and themselves take over the fortunes that were passing into the hands of leading American families" (p. 168). Americans protested, then resisted, and finally revolted.

This position, a refinement and amplification of the Beer thesis, has noteworthy strengths. In the first place, it is congruent with the utterances of colonial leaders who called for a return to 1763, that is, to the traditional navigation policy. In his analysis of American opinion Professor Dickerson finds no important dissatisfaction with the old colonial system. He judges that the "myth" of rebellion against mercantilism was a creation of the free trade followers of Adam Smith. Secondly, it satisfactorily answers the question how a system that had worked without dangerous friction for more than a century could suddenly disrupt the greatest colonial empire of the time. An entirely new policy instituted after 1763 brought protest against the hardships and property losses entailed on the colonists. The new policy was adumbrated by the Sugar Act of 1764, particularly the forty-odd sections "devoted to a revision of the customs and commerce regulations which amounted to a constitutional revolution in the relations of the colonies to the home country" (p. 179). Revenue provisions, elaborated in the Stamp Act and the Townshend Acts, were alone insufficient to provoke revolution, but interference with trade, customs racketeering, seizures of ships and cargoes on flimsy pretexts gradually undermined colonial loyalty and prepared the way for independence.

The formal development of the argument is above reproach but there are difficulties which could hardly have been avoided. Lawrence A. Harper has shown elsewhere the headaches awaiting the student who works with the intransigent and often treacherous statistics of the eighteenth century. In casting up the trade balance between Great Britain and the American colonies, the present author is obliged to select years when "normal" relations were upset (p. 43). The result is not completely satisfying. Occasionally a comparison or an assumption is not beyond reasonable doubt (pp. 41, 73). These imperfections are unavoidable and the criticisms concern details which do not materially affect the thesis. The second difficulty arises from the formulation of the problem which requires evidence that certain consequences did not follow from the operation of the Navigation Acts, namely widespread evasion and a body of antagonistic opinion. Negative proof is more difficult to adduce and the author's ingenuity in making his case (Chapters III and IV) is an illustration of the art of turning weakness into strength.

The Navigation Acts and the American Revolution is an able analysis of a controversial subject and for that reason, as well as for intrinsic qualities, is a major contribution to the literature on the period. Not the least among its merits are the clarity and force of the presentation. An impressive bibliography of contemporaneous writings which Professor Dickerson consulted in his research is a convenient check list for future students. The index leaves something to be desired.

Vanderbilt University AUBREY LAND

The Papers of Sir William Johnson. Prepared for publication by Milton W. Hamilton and Albert B. Corey. Vol. X. (Albany: The University of the State of New York, 1951. xiv + 998 pp. Illustrations. $5.00.)

This thick volume contains rich material out of which new history may be fashioned and old historical accounts corrected or strengthened. In a sense it is the second volume of the second series of the *Papers of Sir William Johnson*, eight volumes of which were drawn from the manuscripts that escaped the 1911 fire in the New York capitol and published between 1921 and 1933. With the aid of Richard E. Day's prefire *Calendar*, copies of many papers missing after the fire were found in other repositories and published in 1939 as a ninth volume (or *first* volume of the mythical "second series" paralleling, in point of chronology, parts of the first eight volumes). This is Volume X, which parallels materials in Volumes III and IV of the earlier *Johnson Papers*, supplementing (in fact almost doubling) the previous materials and covering the time span from September, 1758, through December, 1763.

Papers for this volume have been collected from the Public Record Office, London, the Canadian Archives, a half dozen or more American libraries, and a few private collections. The location of each item is indicated, and Dr. Milton W. Hamilton "has checked every item against the original." Only a few of the papers have been published hitherto.

The volume contains important and widely varied materials. After a useful "Chronology of Daniel Claus" (pp. ix-xiv), there are letters illuminating the English efforts to keep the Iroquois away from the French, minutes of conferences with Indians, frauds and attempted frauds in lands and in Indian trade, Indian affairs and western readjustments after the fall of the French power in Canada, materials relating to Pontiac's uprising, exchanges of letters with military and political leaders and with Indian agents. Taken together, these papers supply a mass of detail, some important, some "interesting," and some trivial, regarding a critical period in the struggle for control of North America. Imperial relations as well as Indian affairs are concerned, and much of tactics, trade, and human relations emerges from the papers. One suspects, also, that the public stature of Sir William Johnson is enlarged.

Such painstaking, high quality effort has been put into this volume that one pauses before offering adverse criticisms. Indeed, there are few that can be justifiably made. The book is a beautiful job of editing, printing, binding, and illustrating. Among the twelve illustrations, however, are some contemporary maps which, unfortunately, have been so reduced in size as to become virtually worthless. The editorial notes are limited almost entirely to the barest identification of persons and places, with occasional cross references to other volumes of the *Johnson Papers*. There appear to be very few errors. This reviewer felt that there were unnecessary repetitions in some instances (such as variations of the note on page 243, "Pani, a term regularly used to denote an Indian slave"). Fort St. Joseph has been inaccurately located (p. 545). In their enthusiasm to set forth every scrap of information the editors have printed some items omitted from previous volumes because of the papers' mutilated condition. Perhaps a few of these (especially on pp. 557, 607-608, 615) are so badly mutilated as to be valueless. These are paltry sins of commission which pale beside a great sin of omission — lack of an index. This volume and its predecessors total about ten thousand pages of published manuscript materials — and there are more promised. Can the users of these volumes count on a separate index volume when the series is complete?

University of Illinois RAYMOND P. STEARNS

George Washington: A Biography. By Douglas Southall Freeman. Vols. III-IV. (New York: Charles Scribner's Sons, 1951. Vol. III, *Planter and Patriot.* xxxviii + 600 pp. Illustrations, maps, and appendixes. Vol. IV, *Leader of the Revolution.* viii + 736 pp. Illustrations, maps, appendixes, bibliographical note, and index. $15.00.)

In these two volumes Mr. Freeman carries Washington from his return to Mount Vernon in January, 1759, after having resigned his military commission as a colonel with the British forces, to April 30, 1778, when, as commander-in-chief of the American army, he received the glad tidings that France had recognized the independence and had become an ally of the United States. These volumes, characteristic of the first two volumes of the biography, are detailed, thorough, and exhaustive — so detailed that they are tiresome reading. The author includes much of Virginia history that has little direct bearing on Washington. For instance Washington, while a member of the House of Burgesses, took no part in the Stamp Act controversy nor in the investigation of Speaker John Robinson's misuse of funds, yet Freeman devotes a chapter to each of these subjects. The organization is chronological rather than topical; some chapters are day by day accounts of Washington's doings, including trivial actions. Freeman's general introduction to Volume III constitutes an over-all synthesis of Washington's career for the period covered; it also gives the author's frame of reference together with explanations and interpretations essential for an understanding of the unity of the story. In so far as factual information is concerned this will be the definitive biography of Washington. Others may write to interpret, to popularize, or to emphasize a particular problem or point of view, but it is doubtful that anyone can add much to our knowledge of the facts of Washington's life.

Washington at Mount Vernon stands out in bold relief. Married to a rich widow, he wanted to retain his reputation and to gain the good opinion of his neighbors, but his ambition for wide acclaim was limited. Hence he devoted his attention to planting. Finding his soil unsuited to tobacco he shifted to wheat, established flour mills and marketed the product under his own name brand. He also engaged in commercial fishing. Even so, his expenditures for his household including furniture, clothes, a carriage and four, and entertainment kept him in debt to the London merchants and caused him no end of worry. He took an active interest in church affairs and served as vestryman and church warden. He was a justice of the peace, and was often called upon to act as guardian to wards and to settle the estates of deceased Virginia planters. But Washington's chief interest seems to have been the acquisition of lands. His zeal in purchasing and patenting lands would have won for a less respectable person the name of land-grabber. He acquired thousands and thousands of acres of choice western lands.

Washington the patriot is a less distinct figure. He served in the House of Burgesses for fifteen years but seemed to take his duties lightly. He was often late in attending the sessions and left before they were over. He served on committees but rarely took part in the debates of the House. He did not speak even on the important issue of the Stamp Act. But by listening to others speak and observing the work of the body, so Mr. Freeman concludes, Washington learned much of men and governmental practices that was to be of value to him in later years. By 1769 he had made up his mind on taxation of the colonists by England and declared that no man should scruple or hesitate to use arms as a last resort to resist the practice. He was active in the support of nonimportation but not of nonexportation. As he saw it, the colonists must sell abroad in order to pay their English debts.

Washington was a member of the First Continental Congress but took no part in either debate or committee. Nevertheless, he was positive on the right to resist encroachment on liberty. At first he did not believe that separation was either desirable or necessary but the Boston Port bill, according to Mr. Freeman, turned Washington "from faith in reconciliation to the belief that a struggle for independence might be the only recourse of a people determined to preserve the liberties they always had enjoyed as the inheritance of free born Englishmen." And in 1775 Washington declared that it was his "full intention to devote my life and my fortune in the cause we are engaged in, if need be."

In explaining Washington's election to command the American army in 1775, Mr. Freeman emphasizes Washington's spiritual qualities. Washington had had no military service for sixteen years, had never led an army, and had no experience with either artillery or cavalry. But somewhere along the line he had developed "patience, pity, understanding of men"; he possessed such traits of character as honesty, integrity, dignity, and sound judgment; and, not unimportant, he had the bearing of a soldier and the appearance of a leader. Furthermore, politics and sectionalism played their part. New Englanders were told that Washington's election was politically expedient because it would bring full southern support, and Southerners experienced sectional pride in the election. Sectionalism worked in reverse after Washington suffered defeat after defeat. John Adams, who had nominated Washington in 1775, favored a day of thanksgiving for General Horatio Gates's victory over Sir John Burgoyne in 1777 because it was "not immediately due to the Commander-in-Chief nor to Southern troops. If it had been, idolatry and adulation would have been unbounded."

The author pictures very clearly the difficulties Washington faced in building an army. Some of these were short-term enlistments, bounties and bounty jumping, inadequate supplies and equipment, lack of competent leaders, jealousy of subordinates, a poorly prepared hospital service, corruption and breakdown in the commissary, and lack of proper support from Congress.

Washington also experienced much difficulty in dealing with foreign officers appointed by Silas Deane, but the able Louis L. Duportail and the incomparable Lafayette won his heart. The author discourses at length on the Conway Cabal but fails to clear up the mystery. He does, however, clarify Washington's reaction to this plot. For once Washington, the demigod, displayed the frailties of a human being.

There is no question that the author's sympathies throughout the book are with Washington; nevertheless, the judgments are sound and judicious. Freeman recognizes Washington's weaknesses as well as his strength. And Washington's shortcomings, both positive and negative, were numerous. He had no skill in recruiting, devoted too much time to paper work, failed to exercise the full functions of a commander-in-chief, and operated without a proper intelligence service. He committed a serious blunder in sending Benedict Arnold's ill-equipped, poorly provisioned force over a difficult route to Canada. He conducted the White Plains campaign in a hit-or-miss way; he was confused and hesitant, and could not make up his mind. He "conducted the Brandywine operation as if he were in a daze." To offset these weaknesses Washington showed a realistic and correct sense of strategy in New England, conducted a masterly retreat across New Jersey, and won a brilliant victory at Princeton where luck aided him because of the pains he had taken in planning the attack. And Washington knew how to make an army out of a congeries of jealous contingents. He studied gunnery, learned what artillery could do, recognized the importance of a navy, and could discharge the business of an army with justice, diligence, and sound judgment. He won the respect of his officers and men by his integrity and devotion to the cause. Superior in nothing, he possessed in ample measure every quality demanded of a great army leader. He was no genius but a man of balanced parts, and he always made the best use of what he had.

University of North Carolina FLETCHER M. GREEN

Three Hundred Years American; The Epic of a Family from seventeenth-century New England to twentieth-century Midwest. By Alice F. and Bettina Jackson. (Madison: The State Historical Society of Wisconsin, 1951. xii + 368 pp. Illustrations, sources, and index. $4.00.)

Those who occasionally work in historical society libraries are acquainted with the practicing genealogist. She — for the genus consists mostly of females — comes early and stays late, patiently leafs through tomes, lists, and compilations, fingers a few collections of documents and learned journals, and departs with the happy knowledge that she has established another client's line. She produces only charts crammed with names and dates, bearing obscure numbers, and signifying little to historians.

The authors of this book, however, have many advantages over their unimaginative sister. The Misses Jackson have had the leisure and the means to pursue thoroughly their quarry, from Madison, Wisconsin, to New and eventually to Old England. Their interest has been higher because the elusive ancestors were their own. Moreover, they and their forebears share the particular type of upper middle-class standards found both in the Midlands and on the banks of the Charles. Industry, thrift, charity for the less fortunate, stamina in their own stringent times, genteel cultural tastes, propriety, occasional burning reform fever, and the commendable habit of saving heirlooms and family papers — these are their attributes.

Unfortunately, the authors found little trace of their paternal side. Thus they have had to lavish most of their attention on the offspring of Edward Jackson (a maternal ancestor, despite the name), who emigrated from London in 1639 and became a founder of Newton, Massachusetts. They find direct descent from General Michael Jackson, Revolutionary soldier on Washington's staff, and incidentally report him outweighing his commander by forty-three pounds one summer day in 1778. The ladies discover collateral relationship with the merchant and medical Jacksons of Boston and with the Oliver Wendell Holmeses. Likewise, the authors deal at length with the English Hobbins family, it being their mother's maiden name, and with other ancestors named Wright, Badger, and Russell. They give high place to their grandparents' migration in 1854 from Wednesbury, England, to Madison, and lovingly describe the developing Wisconsin scene.

The Misses Jackson call their account a "narrative genealogy." The charts are there, all seven of them, but clearly stated and minus the numerals. Vital statistics and short sketches of the personalities appear in the text. Family houses and portraits, the latter including a Copley, make up the well-reproduced illustrations. An adequate notation of books consulted, a finding list of heirlooms, and an exceptionally elaborate index will put the scholar in the authors' debt. Yet the same scholar will raise eyebrows at the frequent detailed conversations of long-gone persons, especially as the volume lacks footnotes, and he will quickly see that he may safely ignore the superficial introductions.

The historian will find the most useful grist for his small mill in the many quotations from informal letters, from Great-uncle Henry Wright's two-volume manuscript notebook, and from Grandmother Sarah Hobbins' twenty-five-year diary. He will also relish Miss Alice's and Miss Bettina's evident enjoyment of their quest, as told in a fifteen-page section, "How We Gathered Our Genealogical Data." After all, he, too, has delighted in research. He would be too unkind if he belittled the heroic nature of the Jackson family "epic"; yet he might not be too captious in wishing for either a Clarence Day lightness of touch or a John P. Marquand irony.

Oklahoma Agricultural and Mechanical College THEODORE L. AGNEW

A Documentary History of the Negro People in the United States. Edited by Herbert Aptheker. Preface by W. E. B. Du Bois. (New York: The Citadel Press, 1951. xvi + 942 pp. Index. $7.50.)

In *American Negro Slave Revolts*, Dr. Aptheker presented more evidence than any other historian for the fact that insurrections and plots were frequent throughout slavery. Unlike so many historians who continue to deal with the Negro as a passive factor in the determination of events, he has contributed to the growing literature upon the activist Negro. This approach, long sponsored by Dr. Carter Woodson and Dr. W. E. B. Du Bois, has also been taken up by the Marxists of whom the editor is obviously one.

The documents are selected from a large variety of sources, including the *Liberator*, pamphlets, journals, Negro newspapers, governmental records, and occasionally manuscript materials. The editor reminds us that William Lloyd Garrison's *Liberator* was to some extent a Negro organ; of its original 450 subscribers fully 400 were Negroes. Even in 1834, out of 2,300 subscribers, 1,700 were Negroes. Nineteenth-century Negro clubs and associations, some of which succeeded in gaining their demands through white abolitionist spokesmen, are here given their most adequate expression. Deprived of the franchise and often of the right to give court testimony, even in the North, the Negroes adapted their strategy for freedom to the realities of Jim Crow. Thus, Charles Sumner enters history as the champion of social equality in the Roberts Case, but the initiative and preparation for this contest came from Negro leaders.

Cultural history is excluded on the ground that excellent anthologies in this field already exist, but there is no real excuse for the omission of almost all social history that does not deal directly with slavery or civil rights. The militant Negro, particularly the most literate, completely dominates the selections, giving the reader the impression that only a handful of Negroes held conservative social, economic, and political views. As a result, the Negro intellectual elite, rather than the ordinary member of the race, is the subject of these pages. The exclusion of all documents by whites (save for the comments by the white editor) leads to awkward situations: Benjamin Banneker writes eloquently to Jefferson regarding race and slavery, but Jefferson is not permitted to reply (actually a significant letter too); and the significance of Roberts' letter in the Roberts Case is missed because the famous decision, necessarily by a white justice, is omitted. Finally, the book terminates at 1910, leaving a major gap that could have been filled in a volume of this generous size.

The underlying Marxist principle of selection is the familiar idea of the class struggle as the key to the racial conflict. To prove his point the editor has adopted economic explanations that do not meet the test of historical facts. Thus on page 750 he says of the 1890's: "This monopoly capitalism in these ten years also captured American agriculture in the West and in the South, launched an imperialist war against Spain, . . . and attempted to re-subjugate the Negro people." In his efforts to emphasize the class war, he even goes beyond Du Bois's mild criticism of philanthropy as inadequate by asserting that it "was a favorite device in the rulers' attempt to curb grass-roots Negro protest movements." He blames lynchings upon "monopoly capitalism." It is indeed unfortunate that so useful a project as this should be so badly marred, particularly in the final section, by partisan distortions and dubious principles of selection. Nevertheless, this volume will fill a necessary place until a better anthology is available.

Western Reserve University HARVEY WISH

Regionalism in America. Edited by Merrill Jensen. Foreword by Felix Frankfurter. (Madison: The University of Wisconsin Press, 1951. xvi + 425 pp. Maps and bibliographies. $6.50.)

A perfect testing ground for interdisciplinary research is afforded by the problem of regionalism or sectionalism in the United States. It has both historical and contemporary aspects, it figures in the thinking not only of social scientists but also of scholars in the arts and the humanities, and it affects the actual administration of government. The idea of bringing representatives of these various fields together to compare notes on the meaning and importance of regionalism was an exceedingly happy one. It was realized through a symposium held in 1949 at the University of Wisconsin under the auspices of its Committee on the Study of American Civilization, and the volume under review is the published result.

Of the fifteen papers contributed to the symposium, five are by historians (Fulmer Mood, Vernon Carstensen, Francis B. Simkins, John W. Caughey, and Lancaster Pollard), three by sociologists, two by specialists in literature and linguistics, two by students of the history of art and architecture, and three by men directly concerned with the administration of governmentally sponsored regional programs. Introductions to the various groups of papers have been furnished by five additional scholars, including the editor of the volume, Merrill Jensen. And Mr. Justice Frankfurter has written a general foreword. These twenty-one writers form a distinguished company, many of whom have achieved eminence by their contributions to the very subject under discussion. The resulting volume is important not only because it furnishes an up-to-date report of the conclusions about regionalism that have been reached in the various disciplines, but also because it constitutes the kind of comprehensive record upon which an evaluation of the regional approach itself is possible.

The volume itself does not culminate in such an evaluation, at least from the point of view of historiography. In the opening paper, it is true, Fulmer

Mood traces "The Origin, Evolution, and Application of the Sectional Concept, 1750-1900," and the story is briefly continued to the present by Vernon Carstensen. Professor Mood presents a mass of information (quite possibly too great a mass) concerning the early sectional classifications used by geographers, statisticians, and others, and he presents some illuminating excerpts from the unpublished correspondence of Frederick Jackson Turner. But the paper is a history of the development of regional (or sectional) interpretations, and of their culmination in Turner's work. It is in no sense a critique of the validity of such interpretations, which Professor Mood seems unhesitatingly to accept.

The one paper that subjects the regional concept to truly critical scrutiny is Louis Wirth's "The Limitations of Regionalism." This is an admirably astringent corrective to certain papers which convert regionalism into something resembling a gospel. But Mr. Wirth's contribution is sociological in approach, and contemporary in focus. There is room besides for a critique of the regional (or sectional) interpretation as applied to history. The remainder of this review is offered as a contribution to such a critique.

In the last analysis, there are two fundamentally different ways of looking at, and making use of, the idea of regionalism, and the two have never been sharply enough distinguished by historians. The first approach is taxonomic. When data are to be arranged by categories and compared systematically, the scheme of classification must exhaust the universe of things dealt with. In tabulating census figures by regions, or in subdividing the nation for administrative purposes, one must assign every part of the country to some particular region. Certain of these regions may be homogeneous in a multitude of different ways, while others may possess little real unity. But the latter may not be omitted for that reason. A scheme of classification with gaps is no scheme at all.

The other approach deals with regions that actually exist, in terms of certain specific criteria. If regionalism so defined is discovered to exist in one place, it does not follow that regionalism in the same sense must exist everywhere (or even anywhere) else. The Tennessee Valley, for example, may be taken as a region. Other regions of the same kind may or may not be found elsewhere. But there are certain to be large areas which belong to no region at all and manifest none of the characteristics of regionalism that are called for by the definition originally employed.

Historiography, it seems to me, has suffered more seriously than any other social science from confusion between these two ways of thinking. Regionalism or sectionalism (and the distinctions that can be made between the two terms do not concern us here) is a real and verifiable historic fact. It has occurred in many periods and places. An important task of the historian is to discover how this self-conscious regionalism has developed out of common interests and backgrounds, how it has been affected by pressures from without, and how it has worked itself out in programs of action. But the historian must be on guard against the fallacy of assuming that the existence of regionalism in one place implies its existence in another. The latter is a question of fact, to be determined on the basis of evidence not assumption. What is needed is evidence that regional consciousness did, in fact, exist, not evidence that factors were present which *ought* to have engendered such consciousness.

A few examples will illustrate the fallacy. New England has always possessed a strong regional self-consciousness. So also, though with more fluctuating boundaries, has the seaboard South. In between lies an area to which a name must be given in any scheme for subdividing the territory of the United States. The usual name is the Middle Atlantic states, or (in earlier times) the middle colonies. But has this ever been a region in the sense that New England or the South can be so described? Far too many historians, I believe, have treated it as such. But analogy, or the logic of classification, has impelled them to do so, *not* the primary sources. These, almost without exception, make it clear that the most distinctive fact about the middle states has been their diversity — in economic activity, in political institutions, in religion, in national origins, and even in language. Lying between two self-conscious regions, the middle states possessed the special quality of being nonregional. They made ties in all directions, and they engaged in intense rivalries among themselves, as the canal and railroad projects of New York, Philadelphia, and Baltimore bear witness. I myself was born in New York state, and I have known plenty of New Englanders and Southerners and Middle Westerners, but I have yet to meet an authentic "Middle-States-man" (a character for whom no one has ever felt it necessary to coin a usable name).

In discussing disputes involving sectionalism (to shift to the more common historical term) historians seem often to assume that if one party to a given conflict is a section, the other must be also. In the election of 1860, however, is it accurate to speak of the North as a section in the same sense in which one speaks of the lower South as one? In the 1890's the agrarian movement was sectional in character, but was the opposition a section or a class?

Two influential currents in American historiography have flowed from the work of Frederick Jackson Turner — the frontier interpretation, and the sectional and regional interpretation, of American history. The first no longer seems as universally valid as it once did. The second seems to me to suffer from the same fault of limited applicability. We need, of course, to study frontiers, sections, and regions as actual historic phenomena. But when we universalize these concepts — when we speak not of frontiers but of the frontier interpretation, and not of regions but of the regional interpretation —

we run the risk of imposing upon the historical evidence a set of preconceived ideas that may impede and warp objective inquiry.

University of Illinois ARTHUR E. BESTOR, JR.

South Dakota Historical Collections and Report. Vol. XXV, 1950. Compiled by the State Historical Society. (Pierre: South Dakota Historical Society, 1951. 481 pp. Illustrations, maps, and index. $4.50.)

Since the venerable Doane Robinson resigned as secretary of the South Dakota Historical Society some twenty-seven years ago, volumes in the *South Dakota Historical Collections* have varied greatly in quality. Generally speaking, the recent publications have not matched most of those turned out prior to 1925. The book under review is no exception, although it contains several good articles which will be of interest to both South Dakotans and to those outside of the state.

Nearly half of this volume is an account of "Early Explorations and Fur Trading in South Dakota" written by Donald D. Parker of South Dakota State College. The heart of Parker's story covers the years between 1790 and 1830. The activities of such familiar figures as Jean Baptiste Trudeau, Lewis and Clark, Manuel Lisa, Stephen H. Long, and many other figures are reviewed. Mr. Parker relies heavily upon the earlier works of Doane Robinson. In fact, there is little new material presented. But the work is valuable as a synthesis of the previously published writings.

The next fifty pages contain a study of "Trails to the Black Hills Gold Fields" by Hyman Palais. This is a phase of South Dakota history which has needed investigation and fills an important niche in western history. Mr. Palais has made a worthy contribution. The article locates and describes the main trails and wagon roads such as the Pierre-Black Hills, Deadwood-Cheyenne, Bismarck-Deadwood, and Medora-Deadwood. Legislation pertaining to wagon roads during the territorial period is summarized and some very valuable maps, prepared by editor Will G. Robinson, are included. The principal weakness of Mr. Palais' work is his failure to interpret his material and to show its importance by relating transportation developments to the economic life of the area.

The third article of major importance is by Norman Thomas and deals with the Hutterites in South Dakota during the period between 1874 and 1949. Although general in nature, the study will be of interest to both historians and sociologists. Mr. Thomas includes a valuable table which shows the past and present Hutterite colonies in South Dakota.

The rest of this volume is miscellany, including memoirs, an address on the Indian problem by Will G. Robinson, data on territorial and state legislators, and other material.

It is regrettable that this book is so seriously marred by typographical and other printing and editorial errors. They are too numerous to list. While one of the articles is entitled "The Last Bull Train into Rapid City in 1876," this appears on the running page headings as "The Last Bull into Rapid City in 1875"! Although the volume lacks a table of contents, a splendid index makes up for some of the other shortcomings.

University of Oklahoma GILBERT C. FITE

Men in Business; Essays in the History of Entrepreneurship. Edited by William Miller. Foreword by Arthur H. Cole. (Cambridge: Harvard University Press, 1952. ix + 350 pp. $5.00.)

There is little question that business has been a prodigious force in the making of the modern world. Bordering on so many social estates and skirting so many cultural currents, business history is no narrow specialty. Still, only a beginning has been made in understanding what business has actually done. The present work, by continually keeping enterprise in the foreground and by studying it in relation to the different societies in which it operated, furthers our understanding of business and indicates a real appreciation of its role as a major force in the development of our civilization.

Men in Business, sponsored by the Harvard Research Center in Entrepreneurial History and edited by William Miller, research fellow in Harvard University, is a collection of eleven well-written essays. Together, they raise such provocative questions as: To what extent does the entrepreneur mold the economic and social order? To what extent do cultural forces determine business policy? What are the social origins of the entrepreneurial class? While no attempt is made to answer such questions or to formulate general theories, each essay offers an illuminating case study of various aspects in entrepreneurial history. Differing in scope, subject matter, and emphasis, this volume suggests numerous potential and fruitful areas of inquiry.

As the editor explains, this work possesses both a unity (all of the essays deal with entrepreneurial history) and a diversity (each bears upon a different aspect of that history). Although the book concerns itself largely with the United States, the first three essays analyze some of the factors affecting entrepreneurship in France, Egypt, and Canada. The other essays are wholly concerned with America. Four deal with individual businessmen — John Stevens of Hoboken, an example of the nineteenth-century commercial capitalist at work; Henry Noble Day, a study in business failure; Frank Julian Sprague, the father of electric traction; and Henry Varnum Poor, best remembered as publisher of Poor's *Manual of the Railroads of the United States*. The others are broader in scope. One describes the role and function of the entrepreneur in New England between 1787 and 1816, another deals with the social origins of the entrepreneur in the 1870's. The business elite of the early twentieth century and capital accumulations in the life insurance business from the end of the Civil War to 1905 are treated in the other two essays.

A useful addition to the literature on business, this volume should appeal to all those interested in American social and economic history.

Carnegie Institute of Technology VINCENT P. CAROSSO

The Golden Age of the New Orleans Theater. By John S. Kendall. (Baton Rouge: Louisiana State University Press, 1952. viii + 624 pp. Illustrations, bibliographical note, and index. $8.00.)

A valuable addition to the history of the American stage has recently been made by the Louisiana State University Press in the publication of John S. Kendall's *The Golden Age of the New Orleans Theater*, an extended and exhaustive treatment of dramatic activities in the southern metropolis from 1791, when several French actors reached the city in their flight from a Negro insurrection on the island of Santo Domingo, until after the Civil War, when the great stock companies which had constituted the American theatrical system went down before the onslaughts of the touring companies. This volume fills, and fills well, one of the many gaps in the recorded story of our national theater and in the part it played in the cultural growth of the country. New Orleans was, during at least the first half of the nineteenth century, one of the most important theatrical centers in the United States. Its influence was effective from Mobile to Houston, and as far north as St. Louis and Cincinnati. It was a mecca for the great and the near-great of the profession, nearly every actor and actress of any consequence filling frequent and often lucrative engagements there. Its theaters were among the largest and handsomest in the country, and were managed through these years by men of vision, courage, and ability. Nevertheless, Mr. Kendall's work is the first full and comprehensive study of this subject to become available through publication.

Undertaking to cover a period of, roughly, a century in a city with the varied and complex dramatic activity of New Orleans, the author was confronted by a tremendously difficult task. History itself is seldom dull; historians frequently are, but not Mr. Kendall. His book is not the type to delight the casual reader, but it will assuredly please anyone seriously interested in the history of the stage. Since, however, it is the scholar for whom it is intended, it is regrettable that it is not more thoroughly documented. Footnotes, admittedly, have a way of being boring, but they greatly increase the value of a scholarly study. When the writer is no longer here, they remain to support his assertions, which, without them, are always in danger of being challenged. It is seldom that a book of such dimensions contains no errors, and this one is no exception, although they are not major ones. Yet, even granting this trivial weakness and also the inadequacy of the index, one can scarcely question the great value of this volume and fail to be grateful to the author who composed it with such affectionate care.

Washington University WILLIAM GLASGOW BRUCE CARSON

Doctors Under Three Flags. By Fannie Anderson. Foreword by Alfred H. Wittaker, M.D. (Detroit: Wayne University Press, 1951. x + 185 pp. Illustrations and bibliography. $3.50.)

Doctors Under Three Flags is a good example of how local medical history should be written. Mrs. Anderson's book convinces the reader that medicine as practiced in Detroit was not an isolated unit that developed apart from the cultural pattern of its era. The practice of medicine during the founding of Detroit was an empirical art but during the next 150 years it developed in many of its phases into an exact science. There was no local medical school and so the practitioners received their training elsewhere, reflecting world medicine as taught at Paris, London, and Edinburgh.

Mrs. Anderson appreciates the importance of discussing the entire social pattern, without a proper understanding of which no medical history is complete. Medicine is humanistic as well as scientific and is therefore a very important part of social history. The author not only discusses fully the surgeons and their background and training but also the patients the doctors had to treat. We are made fully aware of the patients' social environment, ignorance, superstitions, and poverty, and the mental outlook that characterizes those reared in the wilderness.

This study carries us through the beginnings of Detroit — from its founding until the time Michigan became a state. It is from such works as this, dealing with local medical history, that the broader social-medical history of medicine will be written.

Louisiana State University Medical Library W. D. POSTELL

Nursing in Ohio; A History. By James H. Rodabaugh and Mary Jane Rodabaugh. (Columbus: The Ohio State Nurses' Association, 1951. xiv + 273 pp. Illustrations, appendixes, sources, and index. $4.00.)

In this study the authors, a husband and wife team of trained historians, have told the story of the nurse in the history of Ohio. An important part of that story is the organization and growth of the Ohio State Nurses' Association, founded for the basic purpose of advancing the educational standards of the profession.

The pioneer in Ohio, as elsewhere, was frequently the victim of frontier hazards and epidemics abetted by lack of sanitation, stagnant water, insects, and an unbalanced diet. Treatment by available doctors was apt to be as severe as the illness itself. Nursing care became the lot of the able-bodied member of the family, a neighbor, or a practical nurse.

The rapid growth of settlements in Ohio by immigrants from eastern and southern states and from Europe emphasized the need for care of the ill. In 1821 the Commercial Hospital, now the Cincinnati General Hospital, became the first major hospital in the Old Northwest. Immigrants from Europe, bringing with them recollections of an older social order, sent back to their former homes for hospital personnel and nurses. The Sisters of Charity, originally from France, was one of the first religious nursing orders to come to Ohio, establishing St. John's Hospital in Cincinnati in 1852. Other religious orders followed.

The outbreak of the Civil War showed how inadequately prepared were the public and private agencies for the care of wounded and sick. The level of nursing for the soldiers was of the attendant type and a strong prejudice existed against women nurses. However, it was the courageous work of volunteer civilian relief organizations during the war that contributed most to the development of modern nursing. The war gave impetus to construction of hospitals and establishment of nursing schools in Ohio. By the end of the Spanish-American War, the Florence Nightingale system of nurse training had demonstrated nursing as a profession for women.

A movement toward state organization of nurses in Ohio grew out of nurse school alumnae and small local groups, and in 1904 the Ohio State Nurses' Association was founded. The work of the association has been a steady "struggle against prejudice and for humanity"; and for higher professional standards for the nurse.

The volume is balanced and well written. Dr. James H. Rodabaugh is editor of the *Ohio State Archaeological and Historical Quarterly*, and Mrs. Rodabaugh is managing editor of the *Ohio Nurses Review*.

Hayes Memorial Library WATT P. MARCHMAN

The Transportation Revolution, 1815-1860. By George Rogers Taylor. *The Economic History of the United States*, Vol. IV. (New York: Rinehart and Company, Inc., 1951. xvii + 490 pp. Illustrations, charts, figures, maps, tables, bibliography, appendixes, and index. $4.50.)

Few periods in American history are so thrillingly complex — and decidedly revolutionary — as that between 1815 and 1860. In *The Transportation Revolution*, Volume IV of Rinehart's nine-volume *Economic History of the United States*, Professor Taylor has attempted to tell the bulging story in 398 pages of text. There is scarcely room in that small compass to present adequately roads and bridges, canals, steamboats, and railroads in a critical era of their development, but the author includes also merchant capitalism, the merchant marine, the changing cost and speed of transportation and communication, domestic trade, foreign trade, manufacturing in the home and in the factory, working conditions, wage earners, banks and other financial institutions, money and prices and panics, government and economics, and a profile of the economic nation in 1860. Only agriculture, which is to be done in a separate volume, is omitted. While everyone will be impressed by the vast amount of material that makes up the book, not all readers will be convinced that the exciting drama of the beginning of the national economic structure is recounted with completeness and balance — a herculean task perhaps impossible to perform in the space available.

Economic history is never simple. And always there are those who would use a different approach from that which the author uses, whatever the period; they would omit that which is included and include that which is omitted. Moreover, they would give the author a basic understanding rather than the surface comprehension which, it seems, he demonstrates. Some will say that it was not transportation but markets that dominated economic progress between 1815 and 1860; others will have their particular themes to emphasize. Actually all are interdependent, and which is primary and which is secondary is often difficult to determine. The reviewing of economic histories may be well on the way to earning the title of the "dyspeptic science," but criticisms are of course in order when made in recognition of the fact that the critics suffer from the same human weaknesses that mark the authors. That I would quarrel with the title of the book under review is no indictment of the scholarship of Professor Taylor. I would, however, strongly disagree with the editors when they make the transportation revolution extend "far beyond these limits to embrace all the significant aspects of the nation's economic life during a period marked by changes of revolutionary magnitude." Roads, canals, railroads, and ships did affect the growth of factories and the progress of the wage earners, they did affect the financial investment structure, they did affect foreign and domestic commerce, and they did sometimes influence the attitude of government. On the other hand, factories and wage earners, financial and investment structures, foreign and domestic commerce, and the attitude of government in themselves inspired expansion in transportation facilities. Furthermore, the spread of a transportation system affected social and cultural institutions and habits no less drastically than the economic. Less than half the book is devoted directly to the transportation revolution; the theme is economic change.

The Transportation Revolution is not basically an original study. There is much that is new, but the volume is primarily a summation of printed materials. The consequence is that some of the chapters rest heavily on particular studies and reflect appreciably the viewpoints of the authors. Professor Taylor could profitably have used his obvious scholarship more generously in a careful examination of the abundance of source material concerning his period.

The greatest weaknesses of his volume are, in the opinion of this reviewer, omission and oversimplification. The appalling problems that accompanied economic development are too briefly stated; significant movements are seen only in part. Sectional transformations and sectional jealousies are indistinct. The cotton boats of southern rivers other than the Mississippi system are entirely missing. Canal building is portrayed as the traditional "mania," when actually it was only the desperate attempt of people to escape a galling economic situation, and the waterways were probably as carefully planned as were ever the railroads. New markets are little noted; the country store, the peddlers, the rise of the wholesaler, and the growth of new urban outlets are largely overlooked. The transformation by which the long-established river cities were by 1860 being stripped of their glory by the rising lake metropolises is not clearly depicted, and there is no hint of the fact that in spite of the marvelous economic progress that was being made the nation was drifting into a bloody war.

But the foregoing are more suggestions as to a few of the things one reader would like to find than criticisms of the book. Professor Taylor has done a workmanlike job, and he has packed a remarkable amount of information into the space available. He speaks out with candor when necessary, and he readily admits the complexities and uncertainties of his subject. The small number of errors attest to the industry of the author. The bibliography is an exhaustive one, although some of the old books and articles included might perhaps better have been left to their dust; a brief sketch of the major source materials and their locations would have added to its usefulness. The volume, notwithstanding its misleading title, will take its place as an outstanding survey of economic developments between 1815 and 1860. The illustrations are interesting, the index is adequate, and the charts, graphs, and tables are numerous enough to please the most demanding.

Temple University James A. Barnes

Impressions Respecting New Orleans. By Benjamin Henry Boneval Latrobe. *Diary & Sketches, 1818-1820*. Edited with an introduction and notes by Samuel Wilson, Jr. (New York: Columbia University Press, 1951. xxiv + 196 pp. Illustrations, appendixes, and index. $8.75.)

Benjamin Latrobe is best known as an architect and especially as one who played an important part in the early Greek revival in America, but he was in fact a person of many interests and accomplishments, a playright, a linguist, a civil engineer, and a speculator to his undoing. Born in England of American parentage, he was educated in Germany. He set up as a civil engineer and architect in London, but in 1796 he came to America, where he soon became acquainted with the leading men of his day. In 1803 President Jefferson appointed him surveyor of the public buildings of the United States.

He not only planned the completion of the Capitol in Washington but he was also the architect of many buildings in Virginia, Maryland, and Pennsylvania. After the destruction of the White House and Capitol by the British in the War of 1812, he was appointed by President Madison to reconstruct them.

His connections with architectural developments in Louisiana came in 1804 when he was authorized to construct a lighthouse at the mouth of the Mississippi River, which was never done according to his plans. His first structure in the state was the customhouse in New Orleans, and doubtless the first Greek revival building in that city. In 1811 Latrobe, with the aid of his son Henry, secured a contract from the city council to construct a water works. On the death of Henry of yellow fever in 1817, Latrobe went to New Orleans to carry out the contract. Thus did he come into personal contact with New Orleans, which led to his writings relating to his voyage from Baltimore, his residence there, his return to New York, and his final voyage down the Mississippi. He died in New Orleans of yellow fever in 1820.

He kept his diaries in eight booklets, one of which has disappeared. The others are published complete here for the first time (an abridged edition having come out in 1905). These manuscripts are much more than diaries, for in them Latrobe gives play to his philosophical observations, called forth by some comment on New Orleans, but otherwise unrelated to the Louisiana scene. He made excursions into such subjects as virtue and vice, the Indians as our red brethren, French tragedy and rhyme, and waxworks versus sculpture as representations of human beings.

But by far the greatest value of these diaries is in Latrobe's penetrating account of society in New Orleans, the classes of the population, slaves and their treatment, and the religious situation with special emphasis on Catholic services and Sunday observances, cemeteries and burials, architectural characteristics of New Orleans buildings, markets and peddlers, mosquitoes and yellow fever, and so on. No better picture of the exotic and unusual and the sordid and filthy can be had anywhere. Latrobe wrote with remarkable objectivity. Mr. Wilson, the editor, has written a scholarly introduction and contributed many footnotes, while the publishers have made of this book a work of art. And they have reproduced many of the ink sketches that accompanied Latrobe's manuscript and also several water colors and other illustrations which appeared in Latrobe's sketchbooks.

University of Georgia E. M. Coulter

Iturbide of Mexico. By William Spence Robertson. (Durham: Duke University Press, 1952. ix + 361 pp. End papers, illustrations, bibliography, and index. $6.00.)

Agustín de Iturbide, the unfortunate liberator and emperor of Mexico, has suffered in reputation at the pens of writers too easily deceived by diatribes of his political enemies. In a dispassionate effort to determine the truth, Professor Robertson has succeeded in providing the basis for a re-evaluation of Iturbide's meteoric career.

The future emperor, a Creole of excellent lineage, was completely identified with the conservative classes. Rebellion against the established order threatened the permanence of a system that held revered values. Iturbide, therefore, fought first as a royalist to defeat a revolutionary rabble; then, when liberalism loomed as a danger, he betrayed the royalist cause to champion revolution. As author of the Plan of Iguala, Iturbide reached the peak of his career. Conciliatory in contrast to his earlier ruthlessness, he brought to a successful conclusion a civil war that had cost so much treasure and blood. This work the Liberator climaxed with the Treaty of Córdova.

Iturbide's fatal error, the author shows clearly, was his failure properly to assess the Mexican desire for republican institutions. In the formation of the provisional government, in his dealings with Congress, in his acceptance of the crown, the revolutionist revealed a lack of finesse that was to bring him eventually before the firing squad. When exiled to Italy, Iturbide fell into the excusable error of exaggerating the danger from the European alliance. His trip to England and the subsequent voyage to Mexico were acts singularly lacking in foresight.

Many questions about Iturbide are not answered in this meticulously scholarly volume. They are questions that probably never can be answered since materials to make the man something more than a public figure are lacking. The conspiracies to bring Iturbide to the throne and then to restore his crown remain very obscure episodes. So much attention is devoted to details that only the reader already well informed about social, economic, and political conditions is able to place Iturbide in the Mexican scene.

Students learning the historian's art and technique of research could profit greatly from a careful study of this biography. Into it have gone the skills and knowledge acquired during a half century of fruitful scholarship. From archives and libraries in eight countries the author has assembled data with patience and persistence. The result is a definitive account of Iturbide's public career.

University of Mississippi HARRIS GAYLORD WARREN

Lafayette, Guest of the Nation; A Contemporary Account of the Triumphal Tour of General Lafayette Through the United States in 1824-1825 as Reported by the Local Newspapers, Vol. I. Compiled and edited by Edgar Ewing Brandon. (Oxford: Oxford Historical Press, 1950. 275 pp. Frontispiece and bibliography. $3.00.)

Lafayette's country-wide tour of America in 1824-1825 was a pageant commemorating national independence. Before quitting the United States he traveled over the Atlantic seaboard, crossed the South to New Orleans, regained the coast via the Ohio Valley and New England, spent some time around Washington, and lingered at intervals with Jefferson at Monticello. The trip was a continuous round of public celebration, official speeches, honorary banquets, old soldiers coming up to be recognized, with pickpockets sometimes working the crowd. The theme was national progress. There was a fine appropriateness in Lafayette's return after forty years to bear witness to the nation's achievements and its commitment to democratic principles.

The work under review consists of newspaper accounts of the tour of New York and New England, with some additions and annotations by the editor. Although the early pages arouse interest as a contemporary record, the remainder of the book adds little to first impressions. The same kind of receptions were held in every town, the same speeches were made, the same toasts proposed. Repetition of these details does not convey much except proof of their universality. The reports of Lafayette's progress and the functions he attended are surprisingly void of sociological implications or anything which would suggest the political issues of the day. A check of perhaps a dozen citations of New York and Boston newspapers reveals that the editor's selections are representative. Nothing was printed about Lafayette but the sort of thing he puts into the book. It would be too much to say that this will not have a certain value for scholars working in the period, but on the whole that value is limited.

The motive in publishing would therefore appear to be antiquarian rather than historical. This is further indicated by the fact that Lafayette's tour has already had rather ample treatment. The basic source is a two-volume work of Auguste Levasseur, who was secretary to Lafayette on the journey. Lafayette's day-to-day itinerary has been traced, on the basis of newspaper reports, by James Bennett Nolan, who also lists his main activities each day. Upon these works, besides numerous biographies and secondary accounts which deal with the outward facts of the journey, the editor of the present book imposes the newspaper accounts. An earlier contribution of considerable intrinsic interest was *A Pilgrimage of Liberty*, which reproduced press notices of Lafayette's travels in the southern and western states. The present volume does the same for New York and New England. It appears to be the first in a series intended to cover Lafayette's whole trip.

University of Maryland E. JAMES FERGUSON

The Political Theory of John C. Calhoun. By August O. Spain. (New York: Bookman Associates, 1951. 306 pp. Frontispiece, bibliography, and index. $3.50.)

Calhoun's career as statesman and theorist very nearly spanned the first half of the nineteenth century. He entered politics in 1807. In 1850 the small and simple republic created by men he knew personally had gone forever. Settlers had reached the Pacific; the foundations of an industrial society were already established; liberalization of the suffrage and increase in population had begun to create the conditions of a mass democracy. Calhoun witnessed these changes as a leader of his state, his section, and his country. His was a fine intelligence, and one is tempted to wish that he had devoted it to an analysis of the process by which constitutions framed in the eighteenth century were adapted to the United States of 1850. But to wish this is to ignore his limitations as a theorist and his greatness as a statesman. He was a keen observer of politics, and his writings reveal exceptional insight into the political practices of his era. But Calhoun's genius was that of a logician; he reasoned from first principles, and in the construction of his political philosophy he relied scarcely at all on knowledge gained from experience and observation.

Moreover, Calhoun was a statesman, and he concentrated unerringly on the overriding problem of his age. His philosophy was part of a great campaign to preserve the South as it was and the Union as he wished it to be. Thus was he led to the theory of concurrent majority. The problem was a difficult one: how could minority rights be secured in a government which represented a relatively permanent division between majority and minority. His answer was to give each major interest the power of self-protection through the exercise of a veto. The main premise upon which the doctrine rested, the self-interested nature of man, made it appear realistic. Yet it ended in a tissue of wishes. Its operative validity depended on constantly rational behavior, and on the precarious chance that a minority's possession of an absolute veto would lead to compromise rather than to intransigence. What a paradox that Calhoun, the most uncompromising figure of his generation, should have staked his hopes for the South and the Union on a doctrine of which the essence was forced compromise.

Professor Spain's study constitutes a convenient summary of the leading ideas in Calhoun's thought. These are presented clearly and concisely. The author's attempts at analysis and evaluation are less successful. Calhoun was undoubtedly a significant political thinker, but indiscriminate defense of virtually all his ideas does him no real credit. Nor does it increase our understanding of his thought to be told that, "Even though he accepted generally the American democratic doctrine, he made subtle exception of Negro slaves" (p. 257). His was a strange mind, severely logical, yet capable of entertaining many beliefs which seem patently irreconcilable — democracy and inequality in rights, freedom and slavery, justice and class exploitation. Professor Spain would have performed a great service had he explored these apparent conflicts with detachment. The theory of a man who believed so desperately and yet so magnificently that the Union might be saved by his own invention of a new idea deserves a sympathetic but rigorously critical examination which it has yet to receive.

Smith College CECELIA M. KENYON

Henry Charles Carey, Nineteenth-Century Sociologist. By Arnold W. Green. (Philadelphia: University of Pennsylvania Press, 1951. 218 pp. Bibliography and index. $4.00.)

Tradition has it that Henry C. Carey, the promoter of tariffs, was an economist with a one-track mind and a front man for reactionary industrial interests. The contention of this revisionist volume is that the traditional view, if not incorrect, is at least lopsided. True, Carey had a mania for upward revision of the tariff, but the author thinks this in itself did not make him a cynical manipulator for capitalist advantage. Carey claimed he was a reformer who cherished the interests of all classes, a useful rationalization, and the author thinks a sincere one. He also thinks, and this is the crux of the revision, that Carey was much more a sociologist than an economist, more concerned with the whole range of social relations than with conventional economic problems.

The heart of this book deals critically with the origins, content, validity, and influence of Carey's sociological theory. His social science was a patchwork, made up of the ideas of his father, Mathew Carey, the programs of the Philadelphia ironmongers, and the optimistic psychology of the age. He read the great masters of social theory, but only to borrow proofs, not to improve the foundations of his own system. He was thoroughly inconsistent, trying on the one hand to discover immutable social laws, and on the other to explain the dynamics of social change. As the author demonstrates, he often confused coincidence with causation: "If workers are leaving Pennsylvania to go West and old maids are having difficulty in finding husbands during a time when the Camden & Amboy Railroad holds a monopoly, then that monopoly is clearly at fault." Later generations of sociologists, impressed by the quantity of chaff in Carey's writings, ignored him. The author believes this was a mistake, for Carey was a pioneer in the use of the inductive method and of statistics, and long before Émile Durkheim he saw in the division of labor a useful key to the problems of social organization and social change.

On the debit side, the author has strained hard, and not always convincingly, to show that Carey was more than an economist and more than a spokesman for his class. Somehow the story always comes back to the tariff. The first chapter, intended as a background, is a catchall affair, lacking in direction and purpose. The author seems unaware that historians have many doubts about the safety-valve theory, and though he makes considerable use of Ralph Gabriel's *The Course of American Democratic Thought*, he never cites the title correctly.

Picayune matters aside, the virtues of this book outweigh its defects. The author does not claim too much for Carey, either as to the quality of his ideas or the extent of his influence. He does an excellent job of comparing and contrasting Carey's ideas with those of other leading sociologists, and even goes to the trouble of checking Carey's theories against the findings of historians — all to his subject's disadvantage. Unlike Carey, Mr. Green writes without dogmatism, and with a fine economy of words. This book is evidence of the fact that social science has come a long way since the days of Henry C. Carey.

University of Missouri IRVIN G. WYLLIE

Up the Missouri with Audubon; The Journal of Edward Harris. Edited and annotated by John Francis McDermott. (Norman: University of Oklahoma Press, 1951. xv + 222 pp. Illustrations, appendixes, map, and index. $3.75.)

In the summer of 1843 Edward Harris, a New Jersey gentleman-farmer and amateur ornithologist, accompanied John James Audubon, the celebrated naturalist, on a scientific expedition up the Missouri River as far as Fort Union near the mouth of Yellowstone. Harris kept a journal, which is here reprinted in its entirety for the first time.

The editor's introduction furnishes the background for the expedition and gives also a summary of the trip, with supplementary information drawn from the contemporary letters of both Harris and Audubon. The *Journal* begins with the departure of Harris from Philadelphia in March, 1843, and covers in chronological sequence the assembling of the party at St. Louis; the advance up the Missouri River; several hunting forays in the vicinity of the lower Yellowstone; and the return to St. Louis by mackinaw boat. Since the main purpose of the expedition was to study birds and the larger four-footed animals, much of the *Journal* is given over to notes on animals seen, identified, killed, and measured. But the journey up the Missouri was made through Indian country on a steamboat that was under the control of the American Fur Company, and the party spent two months at Fort Union as the guest of its superintendent. Consequently, the student of human as opposed to natural history will find much of interest regarding Indians, the fur trade, and the general character of the country. Obviously the buffalo was an object of great curiosity and Harris gave several long and vivid descriptions of buffalo hunts; he participated in some of them and expressed regret for his share in the wanton killing of these lumbering beasts.

The editorial notes are sufficiently full to provide a satisfactory identification of persons and things mentioned in the text. The illustrations, mainly reproductions of contemporary scenes, are appropriate and add to the interest of a well-printed and attractive book.

University of Colorado COLIN B. GOODYKOONTZ

Michigan Copper and Boston Dollars; An Economic History of the Michigan Copper Mining Industry. By William B. Gates, Jr. (Cambridge: Harvard University Press, 1951. xii + 301 pp. Illustrations, tables, charts, appendix, bibliography, and index. $5.00.)

Here is a concise, carefully drawn piece of business history which fulfills the promise of that field of scholarly investigation. It may be regarded as a worthy addition to the series of *Studies in Economic History*, published in cooperation with the Committee on Research in Economic History. The book deals with a major extractive industry — copper — and covers the full sweep of its development in Michigan from infancy, through growth and maturity, into decline and virtual exhaustion. The complete life cycle of such an operation, spanning approximately a century, gives the story a natural unity and a very real significance.

The strongest feature of Mr. Gates's book is its balanced and thorough organization. He is dealing with a highly complicated and technical subject, but he seems to be in command at all times. As the story unfolds he keeps close rein upon the many interrelated factors: capital sources, technology, management, prices, wages, transportation, market controls, profits, tariffs, labor relations, and community relations. He writes admittedly as an economist, and he holds economics in the forefront. Romance and human interest never carry the author away although they are not ignored.

This is, of course, a case study in the rise of American industrial capitalism. Many familiar elements appear: the prospector and the displaced workman or immigrant; risk capital and absentee control; the contest between technology and rising extractive costs; the struggle between old and new producers and the desperate effort to control the market; the disruptive effects of war, peace, and the business cycle; the sorry living conditions for laborers and their families; the company-run town; the disaffection of the working force and the pitched battle; the temporary triumph of paternalism and the ultimate achievement of collective bargaining. Mr. Gates tells it all — and with admirable restraint and balance. Perhaps a shade too much restraint for the social reformer or humanitarian, but the author sticks to his economics!

This book is hardly suited to that unknown quantity, the general reader. It is rather heavy with specialized language, and is hard going in spots even for the technically informed. A glossary of mining terms is mercifully provided, but the difficulty remains. The writing, notwithstanding the handicap imposed by the nature of the subject, is clear and forceful and well worth the effort. Documentation appears sound and sufficient; the reader who enjoys charts and tables will be pleased with the carefully prepared statistical appendix.

Michigan State College THOMAS H. GREER

On Good Ground; The Story of the Sisters of St. Joseph in St. Paul. By Sister Helen Angela Hurley. Foreword by William Busch. (Minneapolis: University of Minnesota Press, 1951. xiii + 312 pp. Illustrations, bibliography, and index. $3.75.)

This volume is obviously a labor of love, but it is also based upon sound historical training and painstaking research. It is furthermore refreshed by wit and acute observation which lift the book clearly above the general run of church histories. The immediate occasion for the book was the one hundredth anniversary of the coming of the Sisters of St. Joseph to St. Paul on November 3, 1851.

Drawing richly upon letters, diaries, church reports and records, newspapers, and other sources, the author presents a detailed but compellingly interesting account of the problems of establishment of Roman Catholic schools and hospitals on the Minnesota frontier. Backed by the diocesan clergy, especially Bishops Joseph Crètin and Thomas Grace and Archbishops John Ireland and Austin Dowling, supported financially in part by the Society for the Propagation of the Faith in France but chiefly from local and regional sources, and directed by remarkably able leaders, including three sisters of Archbishop Ireland, the Sisters of St. Joseph gradually built up an enviable record of service, primarily in the field of education but also in hospital service and in service to the poor. Incidental to the story but fully treated are the controversies as to religious education in St. Paul, the issue of nationalism which divided the church into Irish and German parishes and schools, and the dynamic work of Archbishop Ireland, called by a fellow archbishop the "consecrated blizzard of the Northwest." There are sidelights on individuals such as Ignatius Donnelly and James J. Hill, and throughout the volume one gets vivid impressions of the gradual changes of Minnesota and the upper Midwest region from pioneer days to the present.

The climax of the story is the creation of the College of St. Catherine in St. Paul, for which primary credit is given to Sister Seraphine Ireland, for thirty-nine years a provincial superior of her order, and to Sister Antonia McHugh, the first and long-time head of the College, who built up both the physical plant and the academic standards to the high level now achieved. The concluding chapter of the book, entitled "Women Who Know the Poor," is an account of convent life and a reminder by the author of the purpose of the Sisters of St. Joseph whose "little design" has indeed become an impressive one.

Carleton College CARLTON C. QUALEY

Mountains and Molehills, or Recollections of a Burnt Journal. By Frank Marryat. Reprinted in facsimile from the first American edition of 1855. Introduction and notes by Marguerite Eyer Wilbur. (Stanford: Stanford University Press, 1952. xxxi + 393 pp. Illustrations, appendix, and index. $5.00.)

When Frank Marryat arrived in California in 1850 he was only twenty-four, yet already the author of a travel book, *Borneo and the Indian Archipelago.* As writer and traveler he was emulating his more prolific father, and like many travel-writers he was perhaps more traveler than writer. His perspective was pronouncedly British; his attitude somewhat patronizing. He had much to say about the inconveniences of the raw frontier to which he came, yet these details were always set down in an uncomplaining, cheerful fashion as though to imply that such hardships by no means taxed his endurance.

Clearly Marryat was in, but not of, the Gold Rush. He recreated the mining scene at Murderer's Bar and he dwelt on the prospects for quartz mining, but nine tenths of his narrative was a travelogue discoursing on hunting, horsemanship, the habits of dress and diet among the Californians, their social and political practices, and his day-to-day experiences in the towns and the countryside of this improbable new state. Bayard Taylor's *Eldorado* is a more systematic travel report, and a more reliably graphic picture of life among the Argonauts is contained in Dame Shirley's *Letters.* Yet *Mountains and Molehills* holds rank as a minor classic on Gold Rush California. The current reissue is welcome, especially since the facsimile format retains the flavor and the somewhat grotesque illustrations of the 1855 printing. A few notes have been added and an introduction which is primarily biographical.

Los Angeles, California JOHN WALTON CAUGHEY

The Boston Y. M. C. A. and Community Need; A Century's Evolution, 1851-1951. By William B. Whiteside. (New York: Association Press, 1951. xii + 239 pp. Illustrations, bibliographical essay, and index. $3.00.)

This account of the Boston YMCA is a rewarding example of how what might seem a highly limited subject can acquire much wider historical significance. Though produced in close cooperation with the "Y" and apparently largely financed by it, the book is not, according to the author, an official history. His approach on the whole is sympathetic, but he does not hesitate to make critical judgments. More important is his deliberate effort to project the work against the social and economic developments of the past century in general as well as against local conditions in particular.

Thus Mr. Whiteside shows how the founding of the Boston YMCA in 1851 was an instance of cultural borrowing from English experience that at least two other cities on this continent duplicated almost simultaneously but independently. Its appearance in Boston resulted from a threefold situation: the urban pull upon young New England men who flocked into the city from rural areas in search of fame and fortune in the best Alger tradition, the evangelical zeal of the orthodox Protestant denominations which feared the effect of city life upon the moral character of these lads, not to mention the more subtly corrosive influence of Unitarianism, and the growing reliance upon voluntary associationalism to tackle such problems.

Especially interesting as a commentary on the social and intellectual history of the late nineteenth century is the manner in which by the late 1880's the "Y" lost its original emphasis upon prayer meetings, revivalistic methods, and an evangelical test for active membership (which was not entirely abandoned, however, until the 1930's), and turned to more secular features, especially the athletic program and later the educational activities which led to Northeastern University, until it became an important social agency facilitating adjustments to novel urban conditions. Perhaps less of a meaningful pattern emerges from the twentieth-century story, despite Mr. Whiteside's thesis that the YMCA's more recent task has been to create a better community feeling in a Boston sharply divided along national and religious lines. It may be that his comprehensive survey of an increasingly complex organization with numerous departments, as well as intricate links with other groups, is in itself equally revealing of trends in our contemporary society.

University of Pennsylvania WALLACE EVAN DAVIES

Guide to the Illinois Central Archives in the Newberry Library, 1851-1906. Compiled by Carolyn Curtis Mohr. (Chicago: The Newberry Library, 1951. xvi + 210 pp. Appendixes and index. Copies may be obtained free of charge from the Newberry Library.)

Carolyn Mohr has done a magnificent job in preparing this *Guide to the Illinois Central Archives* which now must rank with the Jackson and Curtis *Guide to the Burlington Archives* as among the best and most suggestive manuscript guides we have available. Here are described in welcome detail the 400,000 letters and other types of records which the Illinois Central Railroad with marked public spiritedness turned over to the Newberry Library for custody and investigation. A reading of the *Guide* alone provides much valuable information about railroad problems but more, it invites research into its different parts. Nothing can do more to reveal the enormous importance of railroads in American life or to set that story in its proper setting than the opening of such archives and the preparation of guides comparable to this one. One may hope that other railroads may either deposit their records in public agencies or, perhaps better, appoint trained archivists to arrange, classify, describe, and otherwise make available their historical records to students interested in settlement of new communities, transportation, agricultural and marketing problems, railroad rates, land policies, and social relations.

It would be a mistake to assume that the history of any railroad can be written entirely from its official archives. A project undertaken with any such idea would be sterile, uncritical, ill-balanced, and distorted. Railroad correspondence, broadly generalizing, does not often contain the critical examination of policies that one expects the present-day historian to make. Enthusiasm for a subject, a plethora of materials, and a pleasant atmosphere in which to work can sometimes lull a researcher into a mood in which he drops his usual reserve, his critical approach, and becomes an advocate, a defender. To provide a proper setting for a study of railroad problems one must also use congressional hearings, labor journals, national and local newspapers, especially those of the left-wing variety which were not subject to railroad influence through extensive advertising or other means as were many railroad journals, farm periodicals, and newspapers. Court records and extant manuscripts of those critical of railroad policies also need attention. Never has railroad history had as many devotees as today, but many accounts that are being published are superficial eulogies, overdramatized and uncritical. The use of company records such as the Burlington and Illinois Central have made available with their splendid guides properly offset by materials representative of the public interest should aid in correcting distortions, misconceptions, and misinformation about railroad history.

Cornell University PAUL W. GATES

A Guide to the Indian Tribes of Oklahoma. By Muriel H. Wright. (Norman: University of Oklahoma Press, 1951. xvii + 300 pp. Illustrations, maps, suggested readings, bibliography, and index. $5.00.)

This book is a compilation of the histories of the numerous Indian tribes of Oklahoma. Twenty-nine recognized tribes and thirty-eight small tribes and fragments no longer recognized separately, according to the author, are treated in alphabetical order, ordinarily with attention to name, linguistic grouping, present and former location, number, history, government and organization, and contemporary life and culture. In some cases, descriptions of the Indians are attempted and ceremonials and public dances are included.

The *Indian Tribes of Oklahoma* differs in several respects from the two-volume work edited by Frederick W. Hodge (*Handbook of American Indians North of Mexico*, 1910 and 1911), to which the author refers. There is a more consistent and systematic treatment in the present book (probably resulting from the single authorship); much greater detail on the Oklahoma experience of the Indians is given; and it is limited to Indian tribal groups instead of being an encyclopaedia of things Indian. Moreover, it is chiefly history, political history in the case of some groups, especially of the Cherokee. An anthropologist will find the book somewhat uncritical in anthropological matters.

Many of the estimates and counts of Indian population cannot be easily found elsewhere. However, in a number of cases it is not possible to tell to what degree of blood the figures refer; more serious, some estimates or counts appear exaggerated. A check of the total claimed for the Five Civilized Tribes against school enumeration figures suggests that the totals for the five (83,000) and for all tribes combined (100-120,000) as stated are much too high, at least for Indians of one fourth blood or more.

Only four tribes, Cheyenne, Arapaho, Iowa, and Kickapoo, are specifically stated to consist chiefly of full bloods. Probably the Kiowa should be included. However, the largest number of full bloods are probably Choctaw, Creek, and Cherokee. Significant differences between full bloods and mixed bloods in point of view, economic status, and geographical location are recognized in a number of tribes. The principal facts of the allotment of land can be pieced together from the various separate accounts and some comments on present ownership and use of land are included. The only important community property remaining is the oil and gas rights of the Osage. The relations of the Indians with their neighbors are reported to be generally harmonious and examples of achievements of individual Indians are given.

A Guide to the Indian Tribes of Oklahoma is Number 33 in the *Civilization of the American Indian* Series. It contains lists of suggested readings as well as bibliography and index. The five political maps, for three different periods, are very useful. Miss Wright, a granddaughter of a Choctaw chief, is research specialist in the Oklahoma Historical Society.

University of Nebraska LESLIE HEWES

Society and Thought in Modern America: A Social and Intellectual History of the American People from 1865. By Harvey Wish. *Society and Thought in America*, Vol. II. (New York: Longmans, Green and Company, 1952. xii+ 618 pp. Illustrations, bibliography, and index. $5.00.)

Covering the period from Reconstruction to the current "cold war," Harvey Wish concluded with this volume his survey of American social and intellectual development. Except for greater balance between the intellectual and the institutional, the plan of the book is similar to the first volume, *Society and Thought in Early America.*

Mr. Wish demonstrates familiarity with recent scholarship in this broad field. In addition to Charles A. Beard and Vernon L. Parrington, he acknowledges in the text and in the bibliography his debt to those who have preceded him, including Henry S. Commager, Merle Curti, and Ralph H. Gabriel.

Even more than Volume I, the second represents a significant attempt to bring together materials which the various disciplines can contribute to an understanding of American culture. In its scope lie its major difficulties. Selection and integration are primary problems in writing or in teaching social and intellectual history. The wide range of topics and personalities make the task of integration formidable. Likewise the seeming stress on "coverage" has left this reviewer with the feeling that he has "tasted" a wide variety of history but not really swallowed and digested it. Since this work is a survey, extensive analysis is not encountered frequently, though the author's conclusions and points of view are clear and when he does venture into analysis he is successful. In the literary chapters one might prefer more philosophical penetration and explanation, for the book is otherwise well designed as a text. On the other hand, the broad base which this book provides would make it possible to use class time and supplemental reading for deeper probing into a few of the suggested areas of study.

The breadth of the work can be seen in sampling the contents of the twenty-four chapters. We find here topics like "The South of Wade Hampton," "Urbanism and the Church," "The Labor Movement from Wendell Phillips to Samuel Gompers," "Invention and Urban Recreation," "Darwinism, Pragmatism, and Scientific Determinism," "Imperialism, Pacificism, and the War to End War," and "The Impact of Depression and War on the Social Structure." Most of the chapter titles include the names of particular individuals whose thoughts or actions are typical of what Mr. Wish is emphasizing. In some instances, however, the names in the chapter titles may be misleading; for instance, there is but one brief paragraph on Winslow Homer in the chapter entitled "Toward Realism in the Arts: Louis Sullivan and Winslow Homer (1865-1917)."

Despite the difficulty of integration and the stress on breadth without depth, there are several unifying themes which stand out clearly in Mr. Wish's work. The liberal, humanitarian approach of the author is apparent throughout; this can be seen particularly in his treatment of the unfortunate and the underprivileged, of minority groups and immigrants. The impact of science, industry, and urbanism on all phases of American culture is made crystal clear, but the "capacity of the human will and intelligence to transform the environment" is emphasized in an emphatically nondeterministic manner. The growth of concepts of social responsibility or collective individualism (from the self-centered individualism of earlier periods) is explained with clarity. Also characteristic of the book is its optimistic approach. Mr. Wish brings out the excesses in our cultural history, the manifestations of intolerance, extremism, and even fanaticism, but he sees "striking advances made in almost every direction," and he affirms his faith in the dynamic and progressive features of the total American culture.

The author concludes with evidence of the influence of American institutions and ideas abroad — even on the Soviet Union. His final beliefs that "chauvinism had made slight inroads," and that "the nation was growing measurably in intellectual maturity," may be doubted by the skeptics, but they indicate remnants of the optimism of the Enlightenment in an age when neo-orthodoxism seems to be growing in strength.

Colgate University MARVIN WACHMAN

Embattled Maiden; The Life of Anna Dickinson. By Giraud Chester. (New York: G. P. Putnam's Sons, 1951. xi + 307 pp. Illustrations, a note on sources, and index. $4.00.)

This is a pleasing biography, and in some ways a difficult subject to treat. Anna Dickinson had peculiar talents. She was a personality reminiscent, to a degree, of Adah Isaacs Menken, who was also involved in passing "sensations" and contact with notable and curious persons. Such lives as hers bear on "social history"; and treatment of them can on occasion be weak and unfocused — it certainly was in Allen Lesser's book on Menken, *Enchanting Rebel* (1947).

Mr. Chester has done better work: he has had, perhaps, better material. A twenty-one-year-old girl called to address Congress in 1864 on "Words for the Hour" deserves a second glance. She was credited by Republican leaders with having helped turn New Hampshire and Connecticut from the Democrats in state elections. As "America's Joan of Arc" during the 1864 elections, she was surely one of the great northern wartime orators. She spoke on all aspects of "universal freedom, universal suffrage, and universal justice," and during the 1860's and early 1870's, as "Queen of the Lyceum," faced record audiences on such subjects as free education, political equality, and anti-monopoly.

For all this, she was well paid and highly regarded. She lived well and generously, and without much understanding of her own success. Her rather calculated campaign for Horace Greeley in 1872 ended a period in her life, as well as that of her country. With the crash of 1873 the Lyceum felt less need for earnest young women whose oratory depended, in part, on a certain earnestness in public audiences. By that time, as Mr. Chester carefully discerns, Dickinson was out to shock her listeners into attention. Speaking on the evils of prostitution, she was, whether she realized it or not, on the entertainment circuit, not the educational. The next step was the theater. Her fame turned into controversial notoriety, her earning power was permanently reduced and rendered sporadic. There was one last blaze of public attention on the old model when she orated for the National Republican Committee in

1888. Then came a series of actions beginning in 1891, involving alleged insanity, sensational release from an asylum, and sensational suits against doctors, politicians, and newspapermen. The rest is silence, ending in 1932 when she died.

Mr. Chester sees her accurately, with discrimination, and with a sense of her living qualities. As he says, in a fine summing up: "with her sense of history and drama, Anna must have known that some day her story would be told and her career resurrected. . . . a story of a woman whom greatness had touched, but humility had passed by; a woman whose power of speech was sheer genius, whose failing was overweening pride. . . . Anna Dickinson's story . . . was a part of her nation's history."

Antioch College LOUIS FILLER

The Antislavery Origins of the Fourteenth Amendment. By Jacobus tenBroek. (Berkeley and Los Angeles: University of California Press, 1951. vi + 232 pp. Table of cases, source materials, and index. $3.00.)

Historians generally have ignored extrajudicial constitutional theory. Lawyers often have expressed mystification at the "curious draftsmanship" of the Fourteenth Amendment. Dr. tenBroek lays this ghost well. He shows that the privileges-immunities-due process-equal protection phraseology ranked as the abolitionists' trinity for thirty years before its employment by John A. Bingham and the Joint Committee in 1866.

A lawyer and specialist in constitutional law, Dr. tenBroek knows his Gilbert H. Barnes and Dwight L. Dumond and Clement Eaton and William S. Jenkins. He also builds on studies of early abolitionist constitutional doctrine which this reviewer published in the 1950 *Wisconsin Law Review*, pages 479-507, 610-61. With tenBroek's monograph these articles show that as early as 1834-1837 the Weld-Birney group spelled out a strongly nationalist constitutional theory based (1) on the concept of equal protection of the laws derived from Locke and the Declaration of Independence; (2) on the privileges and immunities of a paramount national citizenship. Abolitionists assumed such privileges and immunities to be guaranteed by the federal comity clause (Art. IV, Sec. 2) operating on and through antecedent natural rights. These same natural rights they also believed to be further secured by the bills of rights of *both* the state and federal constitutions, particularly by the due process clauses protecting "life," "liberty," and "property." Attacks on the Connecticut and Ohio "Black Laws" helped synthesize the trinity. Repetition in thousands of resolutions and meetings as incidents of the revival and petition campaigns made the core doctrine constitutional shorthand even before 1840.

Dr. tenBroek traces the growth of this theory from 1838 to 1866, and its metamorphosis from a natural rights system into a full-bodied system of constitutional rights and power. As the South proscribed discussion and (in the Pinckney Report, 1836) set up due process as a barrier to abolition in federal territory, lawyers like James G. Birney and Alvan Stewart quickly retorted in kind. Their answer to denied power was inherent power: the due process clause, and other *restraints* on powers of Congress, presently began to be regarded as *sources* of congressional power which might be employed to enforce civil rights nationally.

Dr. tenBroek's four sections cover "The Forging" of this doctrine; its "Dissemination" (chiefly by means of epitomes in the Liberty, Free Soil, and Republican platforms); "Consummation" in the Thirteenth Amendment; "Reconsummation" in the Fourteenth. The method throughout is analytical rather than narrative, and in 1866 the situation is treated largely by extrapolation.

Professor tenBroek's writing is clear and forceful, though some legal arguments require attentive reading, and a few notes lack supporting citations. Occasionally, phrases like "antislavery origins" and "a revolution in federalism" are employed ambiguously and as question-beggars. The excellent analysis of Bingham's speeches is most convincing.

Whether we accept his entire thesis or not, Dr. tenBroek's study makes immeasurably clearer why the Fourteenth Amendment outlawing race discrimination employed the triple, universally worded guarantee which made no reference to the freedmen or to race as such. That this was not only deliberate, but in the light of the backgrounds and premises a perfectly natural and logical — indeed admirable — solution, can no longer be questioned. Americans today have better reasons than ever to live up to their creed and eradicate race discrimination. That, in any event, is precisely what our Fourteenth Amendment is for.

Los Angeles County Law Library HOWARD JAY GRAHAM

The Swedish Theatre of Chicago, 1868-1950. By Henriette C. K. Naeseth. (Rock Island, Ill.: Augustana Historical Society and Augustana College Library, 1951. xvi + 390 pp. Illustrations, chronological tables, appendix, bibliography, and index. $3.00.)

This volume indicates two tendencies in American social and cultural history: a growing interest in the history of the early American theater and in the cultural contributions of immigrant groups to the development of the United States. The importance of the foreign-language theater as an institution serving the needs of the immigrant has been pointed out from time to time by historians. Although the German and French theaters in America have received considerable recognition, little attention has been paid to those of the smaller national groups. The Swedish theater in Chicago is an important and interesting development, and is, to some degree, representative of the foreign-language theater in America as a whole. It was never a professional theater, as its players were amateurs who did not follow the stage as a means of livelihood.

This history of the Swedish theater is developed chronologically. Beginning with a chapter pertaining to the general background, there are five others which cover successive periods from 1868 to 1950. Attention is paid to changes and trends in each of the periods. There is a chronological table of performances at the close of each chapter, and an additional supplement of group productions at the end of Chapter VI. The appendix lists plays, authors, theaters, halls, and casts of theatrical companies. The index is divided into three sections: persons, organizations, and subjects. Because of the position of the Swedish theater as a social institution, much material is included that is unavailable in ordinary theatrical annals. There are interesting details on the background and occupation of actors, on the attitudes and tastes of audiences, and on the friendly — or unfriendly — reaction of groups to the theater. Material is included on family activity, play analysis, evaluation of theatrical productions, and the work of actor-managers. The connection of the Chicago group with the theater in Sweden, and with the activities of other Swedish groups in America, is well brought out. There is a good bibliography, and the volume is based on sound historical research. A number of well-chosen illustrations adds to its attractiveness.

Students of the early western theater are familiar with the author's scholarly article, "The Early Theatre in Deadwood, 1869-1879," published in *American Literature*, November, 1938. The present work is another valuable contribution to the slowly growing list of studies dealing with the early American theater.

Southern Illinois University HAROLD E. BRIGGS

Hibernian Crusade, The Story of the Catholic Total Abstinence Union of America. By Sister Joan Bland. (Washington: The Catholic University of America Press, 1951. ix + 297 pp. Bibliography and index. $3.00.)

As a result of the heavy European immigration beginning in the 1840's, the American Catholic Church was for several decades practically a "foreign church" and the special target for the nativism of the latter half of the nineteenth century. Moreover, its most faithful members, the Irish, frequently brought discredit upon their church by their political activities and what Bishop John Ireland called their "native powerlessness . . . to resist alcohol." The Catholic temperance movement therefore can be explained on several grounds. One was the emphasis on a deeply religious ideal of self-denial, but another was the necessity to make Catholics more socially acceptable. "We are known as a religion of saloon keepers, of men who drink and who provide the means of drinking," commented another of the clergy who was disturbed by the particular nationality problems which embarrassed the reputation and the program of his church.

In her doctoral dissertation Sister Joan Bland has given us the story of the Catholic Total Abstinence Union from its inception to the triumph of national prohibition in 1918, with introductory chapters on the activities of Father Mathew, in Ireland and America. The C.T.A.U. held its first national convention in 1872, and from that point on the author summarizes its activities and leadership practically year by year. In addition to their main objective, national and local societies supported various auxiliary activities such as mutual insurance societies, temperance halls and recreation centers, literary and athletic clubs, and other programs primarily designed to raise the social and cultural level of the Irish-American group.

Obviously, the organization of foreign parishes for "temperance" proved difficult. German and Irish Catholics distrusted Puritan nativists, and regarded total abstinence, like the colonial blue laws, as a silly Protestant aberration. Another problem involved the extent to which Catholics could cooperate with Protestants in such organizations as the W.C.T.U. and the Anti-Saloon League. At best, such procedures received only halfhearted support from the hierarchy who emphasized prayer, the sacraments, and supernatural means of salvation, and looked with suspicion on mere humanitarian reforms or legislative programs initiated by radicals and "socialists." The Union was always under clerical leadership, but the attitude of local prelates varied widely. Many Catholics, moreover, believed it inconsistent to sell beer on Sunday at Catholic picnics and donate the profits to the church; to permit saloonkeepers to hold office in Catholic societies and Catholic papers to carry liquor advertisements; or to have Benedictine monks at Latrobe, Pennsylvania, make and sell lager beer with the consent of the Holy See. The Union itself never was committed officially to prohibition as a political or legislative issue, but some of its ablest leaders were prohibitionists. That the organization contributed to both the sobriety and the reputation of American Catholics seems clear, although how much credit should go to the Union itself is impossible to determine in view of the general rise of the Irish and other immigrants in the economic and social scale due to other causes.

Although more background material on the immigrant communities toward which the propaganda of the Union was primarily directed would have made the narrative more interesting reading, this study is a thorough and commendably objective piece of historical investigation of an organization and a movement which not only has significance for the history of Catholicism in the United States, but also has a bearing on the larger theme of nineteenth-century immigration.

Western Reserve University CARL WITTKE

"Marse Henry," A Biography of Henry Watterson. By Isaac F. Marcosson. Foreword by Arthur Krock. (New York: Dodd, Mead and Company, 1951. xviii + 269 pp. Illustrations and index. $4.00.)

Mr. Marcosson has written a very sketchy but readable biography of the man who for half a century controlled the destinies of the *Courier-Journal* and built it into one of the distinctive and influential newspapers of the country. The author follows the career of "Marse Henry" from his boyhood in the national capital, where he was a favorite with the Franklin Pierces, the Clement Clays, John Quincy Adams, and other famous people, through his Civil War experiences as editor of *The Rebel* and as a member of General Nathan B. Forrest's staff, to his still more colorful years as editor, traveler, gourmet, and confidant and critic of presidents. The anecdotes which the book abounds in are delightful, even though some of them are obviously based on legend.

The author was a close friend of his subject and he depicts him in these pages with a warmth, a realism, and an impartiality which is commendable. Watterson was a genial, hospitable, magnetic individual. He was a sentimentalist, yet a realist. He was a charming *bon vivant*, who had no superior as a convivial soul. Truly "he sparkled like the bubbles of the champagne he loved."

While Mr. Marcosson has brought to life a brilliant and lovable personality, it seems to this reviewer that he has done the famed editor a disservice in his failure to explain the many inconsistencies in his political views. Surely Watterson's placid acceptance of the Electoral Commission's report in 1876 needs some explanation in view of his previous plea for 100,000 men to march on Washington and demand the inauguration of Samuel J. Tilden. How can the author gloss over Watterson's support of the "sinister" William Goebel in the Kentucky gubernatorial election of 1899? And how can he leave unexplained Watterson's violent opposition to William Jennings Bryan in 1896, his support of him in 1900, his excoriation of him in 1904, his supporting him again in 1908, and finally denouncing him as "guilty of treachery or insanity" in his resolve to "rule or ruin the party to which he owes so much" (p. 181)? Truly, it is not an altogether admirable or honest "Marse Henry" who emerges from these pages. The author says Watterson was being "expedient" in his Bryan gyrations. This reviewer is not prepared to accept this view, but holds that if it is true it calls for more than the mild censure which the author gives.

The author does not agree with the conclusions of P. L. Haworth, the standard authority on the disputed election of 1876, nor does he list Haworth's book in his brief bibliography. He states that Grant had already captured Forts Henry and Donelson in the summer of 1861 (pp. 56-57). He has General Leonidas Polk "die so gallantly at Shiloh" instead of at Kenesaw Mountain more than two years later (p. 57).

Despite these criticisms the reviewer cannot conclude without a word of commendation for the valuable contribution which Mr. Marcosson has made to the field of American biography. This is the first full-length biography of Henry Watterson. The author has at least struck his plow in a virgin field even if the field needs deeper cultivation. There are no footnotes.

University of Kentucky A. D. KIRWAN

Origins of the New South, 1877-1913. By C. Vann Woodward. *A History of the South*, Vol. IX. (Baton Rouge: Louisiana State University Press and the Littlefield Fund for Southern History of the University of Texas, 1951. xi + 542 pp. Illustrations, critical essay on authorities, and index. $6.50.)

American historians can no longer take for granted the "New South." It was a slogan for Henry Grady and the Redeemers who were converted to the Yankee gospel of industrialism, and tried to make the South over in the image of a middle-class North. Why they never altogether succeeded, but at a bitter cost to the South insofar as they did, Professor Woodward explains in this extraordinarily rich history. For the first time he brings order out of the apparent confusion of southern history since Reconstruction.

Readers of his *Tom Watson* know what to expect of Professor Woodward. With critical detachment, he weighs what people did against what they said, and taking nothing for granted himself, he examines the shibboleths of conventional history with a true historian's skepticism. In this book not only the "New South," but all the clichés which have been coined to account for both its peculiar sectionalism and its national conformity — Reunion, Bourbon, White Supremacy, Poor White, Plantation System, Industrial Revolution, Democracy, Solid South, and even the uncapitalized stereotypes of poverty and progress — all the common coinage of historical thinking about the modern South is revalued. Prone to ask new questions and quick to scent fresh sources to answer them, whether in manuscript or newspaper collections, Professor Woodward fills every page with telling facts.

A brief review of so important a work can hardly do more than mention some of the significant revisions that the author has made in the traditional interpretation of southern history. Neither Confederates nor Radicals were so influential in shaping the modern South as the Redeemers. In the Compromise of 1877 they sought not only home rule but economic privileges. To explain their conservative alliance with the Republican North, Professor Woodward recapitulates the findings of his *Reunion and Reaction* (Boston, 1951), a revisionist monograph that may be compared for its implications with Charles A. Beard's work on the Constitution. The Redeemers were not all honorable men; the defalcations of many who held office show that corruption did not end with Reconstruction. The industrial revolution which they promoted, largely as agents for northern capitalism, went far beyond textiles and was not benevolent in character. In agriculture, although labor and capital were greatly changed, the plantation system did not break up. For a generation the southern people — white as well as colored — endured a numbing poverty, starved of education and of their share in the nation's prosperity until the present century.

The political consequence was agrarian revolt. As Alliancemen organized by C. W. Macune and Leonidas L. Polk, and then as Populists following Tom Watson and Ben Tillman, the southern farmers fought for power and prosperity. The forked road to reunion had led them to combine with the West. But their fundamental challenge to the new order was crushed in every state, not only by the cry of white supremacy but — perhaps more effectively by economic forces and adroit conservative opposition. Out of the political turmoil of the 1890's (which surely needs as much study as Reconstruction has had) emerged the Democracy of a white minority, allied again with the North in support of a colonial economy at the South. Progressive reformers like Braxton B. Comer, Hoke Smith, William Goebel, and James S. Hogg rose up earlier in the South than in the West. They succeeded, where Populists had failed, in reforming the worst abuses of privileged local government because their strength came from the new urban middle classes. They struggled for the relief of sectional discrimination and the improvement of social conditions. With their leadership the South regained its share of national power upon Woodrow Wilson's election to the presidency.

Perhaps the most remarkable chapters in this book (VI and XVI) are devoted to the southern mind and spirit. The tragic ambivalence which afflicted the South is exposed without any bias. For this work has a theme, not a thesis, and the author discovers it in the divided mind of a section that glossed the present with dreams of a dead past or a romantic future as economic forces pulled it into the Yankee pattern.

With deft compression and profound insight, in a sympathetic yet ironic style, Professor Woodward has here told the whole history of the South in its greatest transformation. No other section or period in our history has been more brilliantly treated. Every student of our recent past will grow wiser by reading this book, because it revises and enlarges our understanding of all sections and classes in this country. For these reasons this book will surely be recognized as one of the masterpieces of our historical literature.

New York City ROGER W. SHUGG

The Hermit Philosopher of Liendo. By I. K. Stephens. (Dallas: Southern Methodist University Press, 1951. x + 402 pp. Illustrations, bibliography, and index. $5.00.)

A certain couple who purchased and moved into an old plantation home in the Brazos Valley near Hempstead, Texas, in 1873 brought about much sharp comment and gossip. These newcomers seemed queer by any standard. They lived in "Liendo," the beautiful home built by the planter Leonard Groce two decades before; they rarely went beyond the boundaries of the plantation; and they apparently wished to have as little to do with their neighbors as possible. When it was necessary to introduce himself, the man gave his name as Doctor Montgomery; but he did not carry a medicine case and evidently was not interested in practicing medicine. When he was not tramping over the plantation hunting specimens, he was in the laboratory at Liendo, microscope in hand, examining the scum off swamp water or other earthy substances.

The woman seemed strange beyond comparison. Instead of running the home, as women were supposed to do, she left that to a German-speaking servant and spent her days riding over the plantation, dressed in bloomers, seeking to direct the operations of the hands; and for this task she was poorly qualified.

Edmund Duncan Montgomery was born in Edinburgh in 1835; but his early life was spent mainly on the Continent. He was trained in medicine by seven years study of the subject in the universities of Germany, meeting in his student days the beautiful and talented Elizabet Ney, soon to be recognized in her native land as an artist of first rank. He went to England to begin his medical career, but practice in London was hardly begun when an attack of tuberculosis forced him to go to the Island of Madeira for a prolonged rest. Later Elizabet Ney joined him there and they were married. The couple sojourned in Rome for awhile; then lived in Munich; and then for reasons not known hurried away to America in 1871. They resided some three years near Thomasville, Georgia, and finally located at Liendo, on the Brazos.

For some decade and a half this was the way of life of the Montgomerys; Edmund devoting himself to his science and philosophy and Elizabet running the plantation — which never prospered. Governor Oran M. Roberts visited Liendo, recognized the superior talent and training of these people, and later helped Elizabet end her self-imposed exile from the world of artists by securing contracts from the state for her to execute statues of its heroes and statesmen. She set up a studio in Austin (which is still preserved as an art museum) and became much better known in Texas than her scholarly husband.

For a while, Edmund gave up the life of a hermit to serve as county commissioner, chairman of the county Democratic committee, and to lend aid and encouragement to the infant state college for Negroes at Prairie View. However, he spent the first decade of the new century, the last decade of his life, much as he had spent the earlier years at Liendo, devoting most of his time to science and philosophy.

Edmund Montgomery never got beyond the twilight zone of success. If he could have remained at Saint Thomas Hospital in London, he might have become a distinguished doctor. There he had, furthermore, the best means of that day for carrying on experiments in the area of biology and might have become widely recognized as a scientist. He sought to learn the nature of the cell, and thereby explain the mystery of the origin and nature of life. Thus more and more his investigation and thought pertained to philosophy. If he had remained in Europe it seems likely that he would have attained better recognition by the philosophers of his day and might have influenced his contemporaries to a greater degree.

Notwithstanding his isolation, he was not unknown in the East and in Europe. Philosophical societies invited him to read papers at their meetings, but he always responded by sending in his paper to be read while he remained away from the gathering. Obviously this separation from fellow scholars was a handicap in several respects but it may account in part for the originality of his thinking. He contributed numerous articles of scientific and philosophical value to newspapers and learned journals in America, Germany, and England, and wrote and published three books.

As to the value of his philosophy, which Dr. Stephens sets forth as fully as possible in certain chapters, this reviewer is not qualified to judge; but that the hermit philosopher of Liendo was an original thinker of intellectual magnitude seems to be proved beyond a doubt. He attacked the point of view of contemporary scientists and philosophers alike, who, he contended, had not got beyond the "world machine" Newtonian concepts of the early eighteenth century. For these notions he would substitute his own explanation of life in terms of chemical processes, "living movements," that is, "the alternate expansion and contraction of protoplasm" (pp. 199 ff.).

The Hermit Philosopher of Liendo is evidently a labor of love by Dr. Stephens, representing years of gleaning, study, and painstaking effort. Ten illustrations add to the book's interest and attractiveness and a bibliography of twenty-one pages bears testimony to the author's workmanship.

Hardin-Simmons University RUPERT N. RICHARDSON

Brooks Adams, Constructive Conservative. By Thornton Anderson. (Ithaca: Cornell University Press, 1951. xiv + 250 pp. Frontispiece, bibliography, and index. $3.75.)

Although Henry was always the more famous of the brothers, Brooks Adams has long attracted a following of his own. His writings, particularly

The Law of Civilization and Decay, have had a devoted body of readers and deserve reconsideration in a period when we are inclined to give considerable thought to general theories of historical development. Mr. Anderson's work is the first extensive treatment of the subject; he has had access to papers hitherto denied to scholars; and he has drawn together some useful information.

But he has not supplied us with a satisfactory account of the man or of the man's ideas. This is not a biography but rather a chronological analysis of the main lines of Adams' thoughts, designed to demonstrate that he was a constructive conservative whose study of history brought him awareness of the dangers to modern society and who strove to define a theory of public administration to offset those dangers. Mr. Anderson develops his argument largely by summarizing Adams' most important works, often using lengthy quotations from the writings themselves.

In one sense, the author is critical of his subject. Anderson from time to time submits Adams' conclusions to comparison with the conclusions of modern psychologists or political scientists or geneticists. But there is a more important sense in which this book is totally uncritical; it takes for granted Adams' own account of the motivations, methods, and assumptions of his work. Thus Anderson never clarifies the single theme that runs through the ideas of Brooks Adams — the fear of a great international conspiracy, variously identified with Wall Street, the international bankers, and the Jews. Nor is there a convincing explanation of what conservatism meant to Adams; the definition on page 3 could be claimed by almost any American of 1900, from Eugene V. Debs to Mark Hanna.

To penetrate to the heart of these problems, it is necessary to move outside Adams' books and to consider the influence of his own situation on his writing. Adams was a dilettante who never subjected his ideas to the discipline of a profession or of any organized body of knowledge. Hence his disdain for the mere fact and his inclination to run off into glittering generalizations. Furthermore, Adams was a dilettante who was an *Adams*, who lived under the shadow of an illustrious father, grandfather, and great-grandfather, who was conscious of the obligations of his distinguished paternity and also of his own inability to fulfill those obligations. Finally, Adams could ascribe his own inadequacies to his society in which his own group had receded into a minority immobilized by the overwhelming numbers of men he counted foreign by race. Such considerations would throw light on the intellectual process by which a conservative democrat came to fear the "pliant masses," to judge universal military service "the first tinge of democracy" in modern America, and to aspire toward the concentration of all power in the hands of a single man "who really will protect the whole community."

Harvard University OSCAR HANDLIN

An Alaskan Gold Mine, The Story of No. 9 Above. By Leland H. Carlson. Foreword by Vilas Johnson, Nils William Olsson, and Conrad Bergendoff. (Evanston: Northwestern University Press, 1951. xii + 178 pp. Illustrations, appendixes, bibliography, and index. $3.50.)

The distinguishing feature of *The Story of No. 9 Above* is not that it was an Alaskan gold mine which was involved in litigation from 1902 to 1920, but that this litigation almost rent in twain the Swedish Evangelical Mission Covenant Church of America, and also adversely affected the fortunes of North Park College, Chicago. Professor Carlson states in his preface that he became interested in this Alaskan gold mine, No. 9 above Discovery claim on Anvil Creek in the Nome district of Alaska, when he was engaged in writing *A History of North Park College.*

"It soon became apparent that if I really wished to understand the history of the college and the life of its beloved president, David Nyvall, I would have to study the Alaskan background. It was Alaskan gold from Anvil Creek that made possible the erection of three buildings on the campus; it was Alaskan gold that caused bitter controversy and induced Nyvall to resign the college presidency in 1905."

No. 9 Above was an unlucky mine in the sense that its ownership was in question from the first. It was lucky because it produced $175,000 net by the end of the 1900 mining season. Mr. Carlson has carefully probed into the question of ownership and examined the various conflicting claims. The real problem was whether P. H. Anderson, a missionary of the Covenant Church, was the owner of the mine, or whether he held it as trustee either for an Eskimo boy, in whose name the claim had been staked, or for the mission station. Matters were complicated by the hostility existing between Anderson and N. O. Hultberg, another missionary, who had first discovered "pay dirt" on Anvil Creek in August, 1898. Anderson offered financial aid to North Park College, which was controlled by the Covenant Church. Both the church authorities and the college faculty were split on the question of Anderson's ownership. President Nyvall supported Anderson, but Professor Mellander opposed him.

The case was referred to the courts. The author has traced in detail the legal battles in Alaska, Illinois, Kansas, and in the Supreme Court of the United States. It is a long and tedious story which, however, throws real light on the interrelation of Alaskan gold mining and missionary activities. Mr. Carlson is to be commended for his careful and valuable research.

University of British Columbia WALTER N. SAGE

William Jay Gaynor, Mayor of New York. By Mortimer Smith. (Chicago: Henry Regnery Company, 1951. xiii + 192 pp. Illustrations, appendix, and index. $2.50.)

This lively and well-written account of the public life of one of New York City's most colorful mayors follows closely the interpretation presented in Louis Heaton Pink's *Gaynor* twenty years before. Few if any additional sources have been used and many interesting details have been omitted in the effort to compress the story. Yet as the earlier volume is not easily available, Mortimer Smith's brief yet competent portrayal of this brilliant but cantankerous figure will be read with pleasure and profit by many interested in the turbulent politics in the New York area during the early years of the century.

Unfortunately, most of the questions raised by Pink's more prodding study remain unanswered. As they are chiefly questions of personal motivation, the absence of documentary evidence is understandable, yet the result is to leave William J. Gaynor somewhat of an enigma still. Why did he undertake to prosecute Tilton? What was the extent of his involvement with McKane's machine before he waged his successful battle to destroy it? How could he reconcile his many highhanded actions as judge and later as mayor with his lofty views of democracy? No doubt the elusive answers to these and other questions will remain Gaynor's secrets, but his erratic character and the sharp biting quality of the many letters and remarks quoted here help to make this volume fascinating reading.

Rochester, New York BLAKE MCKELVEY

Harry Burns Hutchins and the University of Michigan. By Shirley W. Smith. (Ann Arbor: University of Michigan Press, 1951. xv + 329 pp. Illustrations and index. $4.50.)

An unusual and interesting development in the writing of university history in recent years has been the talented and scholarly contribution of nonacademic officers of the University of Michigan. Wilfred B. Shaw, long director of the Bureau of Alumni Relations, has written several historical books and articles and edited the several thorough and useful volumes of *The University of Michigan, an Encyclopedic Survey*, illustrating them with his own etchings. Now Shirley W. Smith, who retired in 1945 after many years as the University's vice-president and secretary in charge of business and finance, has written a biography of Michigan's fourth president.

Harry Burns Hutchins had the difficult assignment of being the successor of James Burrill Angell, who retired in 1909 at the age of eighty, after nearly thirty-eight years of service in which he had come to be venerated almost to the point of deification. The regents, after trying unsuccessfully to interest Woodrow Wilson, Charles Evans Hughes, and David Jayne Hill, finally reconciled themselves to the elevation of Hutchins, the former law dean and acting president. Hutchins was already sixty-two in 1909, and he accepted the presidency with the understanding that his term would be brief, but the war intervened and he did not retire until 1920. Shirley W. Smith, the son of a Michigan circuit judge, was a graduate of the University, and for a time an instructor in English. He became the University's chief financial officer shortly before Hutchins became president, and soon developed a warm admiration for him. Mr. Smith also developed a considerable reputation as a raconteur and toastmaster. All of these circumstances have entered into the style and the frame of reference in which this memoir is written. It is often adulatory and uncritical, and yet often pleasingly witty and urbane. Based partly on Hutchins' papers and other documentary sources, it is more largely based on the writer's own memory, and most of the copious notes at the end are anecdotal extensions of the text rather than documentations of it.

For those who are interested in the history and administration of American universities, the story told in this book raises several interesting questions. In the latter part of the nineteenth century Michigan ranked far above every other state university. But one must ask whether in the early twentieth century, in the last years under Angell and in the years under Hutchins, Michigan did not show unfortunate tendencies toward parochialism, complacency, self-admiration, inbreeding, and alumni-worship.

One of Mr. Smith's descriptions of Hutchins is especially apt: "He was like a good minister in his parish; not a great theologian, perhaps, but his parish knows his worth." Repeatedly Mr. Smith emphasizes with obvious approval President Hutchins' aversion and imperviousness to general ideas about educational theory. And though this reviewer will grant that such theories can sometimes be a nuisance and that educational faddism in particular can be a curse, he cannot help feeling that this book is an uncomfortably clear embodiment of that type of conservative and consciously "practical" administrative point of view which disregards the fact that ideas are the essence of a great university.

President Hutchins' favorite public address, which he often repeated before groups of his "Fellow Alumni," was called "Respect for the Law." During the same period President Charles R. Van Hise of the University of Wisconsin remarked in an address that "there is between the university and the reactionary an irrepressible conflict. We may cry peace but there will be no peace." It is interesting to notice that those were the years in which the national reputation of the University of Wisconsin rose like a rocket, while Michigan's, comparatively speaking, stood still.

University of California at Berkeley WALTON BEAN

The Political Career of Floyd B. Olson. By George H. Mayer. (Minneapolis: The University of Minnesota Press, 1951. 329 pp. Illustrations and index. $5.00.)

This analytical study of the most constructive and influential leader of the Farmer-Labor movement of the 1920's and 1930's is in many respects a model political biography. Dr. Mayer combines understanding appreciation with objective discrimination, enforced by a keen awareness of the ways of practical politics. The limitations of contemporary history are offset by the opportune collection of statements by representative participants checked with a considerable body of personal memoranda and correspondence. Candid photographs and cartoons help to vivify the narrative.

Floyd B. Olson was an anomaly among third-party standard-bearers. He was in no sense the conventional agitator, either of the idealistic or demagogic type. In temperament and reasoned conviction he was a progressive who could have been content in an old-line party reasonably responsive to the new order and receptive to new blood. As the author emphasizes, he was throughout a restless insurgent rather than a deliberate radical.

Balked by the regulars, he found an outlet for his unusually persuasive leadership in a left-wing combination that in a period of intensified protest entered the vacuum created by a decadent administration and a factious opposition. But as a practical politician he had no illusions regarding the uncertainty and impermanence of third-party ventures. He had no urge to champion lost causes and he was fearful of having his state following diffused and discredited in a nation-wide contest. At the same time, shrewdly enough, he endeavored to become his state's representative of the New Deal reforms. Throughout his career he sought deliberately and assiduously to build up a personal following apart from the interest groups that constituted the nominal organization.

The rivalries and vagaries of these interests brought increasing complications. As true a son of the sidewalks as Al Smith, Olson instinctively favored the junior partner of the expedient alliance of farmers and laborers. When he came fully to support the farmers in their disparate plight he needed no little briefing to avoid embarrassing and disastrous blunders.

Under pressure of internal dissension and unscrupulous attack from both the old camps, he was led more and more to compromising commitments to party rivals and to ultraradical proposals. Most regrettable, especially as the fatal malady came to weaken his fighting zeal, was the tendency to give way to the spoilsman and to ignore the petty grafter.

In spite of such errancies and deviations, Olson's public record as a whole ranks well above that of either the typical old-line politician or the narrow-gauge agitator by reason of two underlying principles which became the motivating guides for his public service: sincere and earnest humanitarian convictions and a recognition and appreciation of sound principles and practices of public administration — even to the utilization of academic experts.

The author is undoubtedly correct in his conclusion that Olson's fame has been enhanced by his premature death at the seeming height of his influence. He had the foresight to ride the flood tide of protest against the old order to notable political fortune, but signs of ebb were already evident and he had probably been carried too far from the old landmarks to secure future advancement in either of the two major parties.

Iowa State College EARLE D. ROSS

Franklin D. Roosevelt's Own Story, Told in his own words from his private and public papers. Selected by Donald Day. (Boston: Little, Brown and Company, 1951. 461 pp. Sources and index. $4.00.)

This is probably about the 2,000th biographical item to be published on Roosevelt since his name first began to have a mass appeal for the voting public and for the friendly and unfriendly journalists, advertising men, and other writers who saw in him another subject for a potboiler or serious literary contribution. Mr. Day's particular justification for going into print is to publish what he calls FDR's "political autobiography" — to provide "a chronological sampling," 1910 to 1945, of FDR's public pronouncements and recorded private comments and correspondence, and thus to let FDR "unfold his own social, economic, and political credo" (p. 5). Mr. Day calls this, furthermore, his own "confession" as a "convert" to FDR (pp. 3, 5). Apparently his project was also motivated by the additional masses of FDR papers at Hyde Park that were opened to students in 1950; yet more than 90 per cent of the items actually published in the present book were already accessible even before 1946, when the search rooms at Hyde Park were first opened to the public. In any case, Mr. Day surely must have been encouraged to sample those masses by the prospect of the splendid archival services that are offered there to all serious students, regardless of their political points of view, by the United States government. Indeed, a virtually complete roster of the Roosevelt Library staff, including the director and his secretary, constitutes the bulk of the acknowledgments, and the director was apparently prevailed on to read the entire manuscript (p. 442).

What unfolds is a chronological assemblage of about 650 documentary excerpts, chiefly from FDR's speeches, messages to Congress and to other bodies, and public letters to men and women used by FDR as "sounding boards." Perhaps less than 100 items are really "private" words spoken more or less confidentially at the time by FDR. Of them, 75 are quotations from a few of his many press conferences (FDR had about 1,200 such conferences, all of them completely recorded); and a dozen or two might be regarded as "private" letters (chiefly for the period 1910-1928). But nowhere in the book is there a single transcript or summary capturing any one of the tens of thousands of FDR's private conversations on public affairs which, more so than public pronouncements, dominated the working hours of his thirty-five years of public life.

Mr. Day's major sources were three, judging from his very brief bibliographical essay: (1) Judge Samuel I. Rosenman's monumental and politically significant thirteen-volume edition of FDR's "public" papers, 1928-1945; (2) Elliott Roosevelt's opportunistic and immature four-volume edition of "personal" items taken from his father's unofficial papers, 1882-1945 (which Mr. Day on page 4 regards as "spice"); and (3) the several massive archival collections themselves, 1882-1945, in the Roosevelt Library at Hyde Park. No acknowledgment, incidentally, is made of that Library's project for an objective, historically complete descriptive catalog of all known public statements by FDR, 1910-1945, under way since 1947 and now in draft form probably to about 1928. Nor, apparently, did Mr. Day make any attempt to probe the unrestricted parts of the several pertinent non-FDR collections, there and elsewhere, which surely must contain many significant bits of FDR's "own words" that did not get recorded in his own files. Mr. Day is, nevertheless, properly enthusiastic about the rich holdings and the high quality archival services at Hyde Park, but I think he is overly flattering to them, and to the inspiring countryside nearby, to say that the "only way to understand FDR completely" is to go to Hyde Park and read there "everything" that was written by and to FDR (p. 4). Not that Mr. Day subjected himself to such a physical and intellectual orgy, nor would one expect him to do so, were it not for the ambitious objectives stated elsewhere in his book and on its title page.

As to Mr. Day's methods of research and presentation on the 650 items that he did select, the end result is highly questionable to the professional archivist, historian, or editor, this reviewer believes. Thus, more than 60 per cent of the items (388 out of 650) are wholly unidentified and unevaluated, either in a heading or an editorial note, as to the circumstances, the place, the person, the institution, or the other context in which FDR was prompted to speak out. Similarly, most of the other 262 documents are only casually identified. In addition, Mr. Day fails to cite the physical location of a single item by even a routine file reference or a book page, and thus he surely guarantees frustration to any of the serious students to whom he says he is appealing (p. 5). Worse still, Mr. Day boasts that, by keeping each document anonymous (except for dating it), he has devised a "system" that keeps his book from being "weighted down by footnotes and citations" (p. 443); and on the next page he delivers the thoughtful reader to a meaningless hodgepodge of hundreds of unidentified dates that (if my memory of the collections in Hyde Park is correct) will surely defy the whole apparatus of the Roosevelt Library's catalogues and other finding tools. Finally, the index, which presumably is intended to rearrange the unrelieved chronology of the text by a topical, organizational, geographical, and personal-name approach at the back, is carelessly executed. For example, at least ten persons mentioned in FDR's letters (but with last name only) are omitted, presumably because it was easier to throw them out than to hunt up their full names. Similarly, under several of the country headings, certain page references are missing.

Such criticisms are not those of a crotchety archivist, legitimate as such would be. (In fact, some archivists, like some journalists and publishers, are too apologetic about footnotes, and too timid about discussing documentation problems with historian clients in their search rooms.) Rather, here are basic questions of historical method and historical evidence, and questions that could be expected as well from any reasonably critical lay reader who might inadvertently pick up this book in a library. Thus, only occasionally are the 650 items distinguished from each other according to their form, their type, and their original purpose. That is, in most cases it is impossible to tell from the editor's headings whether a given item is a speech, a formal message, an article in a magazine, a public letter, a private letter, or a recorded conversation. To cite a few typical problems of textual criticism, what are the allusions to the Plattsburg Commission (p. 24), the "death" of the navy (p. 26), the army "absorbing" the navy (p. 43), "W.J.B." (p. 30), and the "reserve oil lands" (p. 36), all between 1913 and 1918? Was Senator Frawley on duty in Albany or Washington in 1913 (p. 25)? Who in relation to FDR were the twenty or thirty addressees who are otherwise unidentified by the editor? Was FDR's analysis of the Republican party in May, 1919 (p. 49), a private or a public dissertation, and in what context? Is the item on natural resources, July 3, 1934 (p. 217), from an executive order, a contemporary comment on it, or a later justification of it? What, in at least thirty different documents, are the date and the circumstances of what the editor calls "later" comments by FDR on a given matter? Were FDR's several letters to cabinet members (e.g., pp. 184, 189, 231) and to other officials (pp. 157, 210), 1933-1934, confidential memos or "sounding-board" letters for public consumption? What are the documents that are headed, in the editor's characteristically parsimonious and elliptical style, "to Young Democratic Club" (e.g., p. 260) or "Consumers Advisory Board" (e.g., p. 181)? Is each one a memo to that organization, a speech before it, a private conference with it, a confidential comment about it, or a historical justification of it? Is FDR's message to four European countries, September, 1938 (p. 308), a sort of "Voice of America" item, or a secret appeal to their leaders, or something else? Is the item "from the Presidential yacht, Potomac," March, 1941 (p. 354), a speech, a radio dispatch, a two-way radio conversation, or a buckslip from ship to shore? FDR's remarks on Pearl Harbor, December 8, 1941 (p. 361), were probably made to Congress (judging from internal criticism), but they might have been part of a contemporary conversation with, say, General Marshall. Were FDR's remarks at the congressional reception, March 10, 1943 (p. 389), on or off the record?

With elementary canons of historical criticism and archival citation overlooked or ignored in such a compilation, with the so-called "new" stuff minute in proportion and hard to use, and with no particular "credo" emerging from it, the present volume is, in my opinion, an almost unusable item of Roosevelt literature and one that will be discarded as just another potboiler on the FDR theme.

Alexandria, Virginia MARTIN P. CLAUSSEN

Pacific Outpost; American Strategy in Guam and Micronesia. By Earl S. Pomeroy. (Stanford: Stanford University Press, 1951. xx + 198 pp. End maps, bibliography, and index. $5.00.)

Mr. Pomeroy has presented a detailed account of American policy in Guam from 1898 to 1947 and in so doing has surveyed the whole course of American naval strategy in the Pacific during those years. The story is one of good intentions never carried out, of sound strategic concepts never implemented. Guam was acquired in 1898 to serve as a coaling station between Hawaii and the Philippines. As a coaling station it was never developed, but the navy's ideas of the function of Guam soon went beyond the simple coaling station concept. In 1912 Commander Josiah S. McKean, apparently voicing "the prevailing trends of naval thought," was advocating the conversion of Guam into "a Pacific Gibraltar," a great advanced base covering Hawaii as Hawaii would cover the Pacific coast. Wilson's plan to free the Philippines and his reduction of emphasis on Asiatic policy in general were among the influences that retarded any such development. At the close of World War I the other islands of Micronesia were allowed to pass from German to Japanese control under mandate without serious opposition from the United States. Although in 1921 a joint army and navy board recommended that Guam be provided with fortifications "adequate to its defense against any force which could be brought against it," the navy acquiesced in the Washington Conference agreement not to fortify Guam because of a conviction that a proposal to fortify, as Admiral Sims put it, "could not get by the House of Representatives because the people do not understand the situation. . . . They are not taught as they should be." After expiration of the treaty prohibition, and as friction with Japan increased, the Hepburn Board of 1938 recommended a "fully equipped fleet base" at Guam, but only minor improvements, chiefly to facilitate the use of seaplanes, were actually advocated before Congress. Congress turned down even provisions for minor developments until March, 1941, when it appropriated $4,700,000 for harbor improvements. When the Japanese blow fell, Guam was defended by 365 marines and six light machine guns. Remembering the story of what befell the Philippines, one would guess that larger preparations would have resulted only in larger losses.

The experience of the Pacific War convinced the navy, and this time the public too, that all of Micronesia must be held firmly under United States control (though nominally under United Nations trusteeship), and enabled the navy to proceed with its long delayed plans for developing Guam and its neighboring islands into a major naval base. Coming at a time when the United States no longer faces a great naval power across the Pacific and when atomic weapons make heavy concentrations of men and machines of dubious value, these developments raise the question of whether the armed services are not, as on some other occasions, preparing for the last war instead of the next one. In a larger way the entire story, as Mr. Pomeroy intimates, suggests queries about "the capacity of a peace-loving people to plan their own material defenses and to adjust their relations with their neighbors."

University of Buffalo JULIUS W. PRATT

American Diplomacy, 1900-1950. By George F. Kennan. (Chicago: The University of Chicago Press, 1951. ix + 154 pp. $2.75.)

These essays come from the pen of one of the most distinguished of our professional diplomats, and one of the most disinterested of our public servants. They are beautifully written, and undeniably suggestive. But they are certainly not history. They are rather a series of laments at the course of American foreign policy in the last fifty years. In the essay on the Spanish-American War, Mr. Kennan suggests that the imperialism which followed it was a mistake; in the essay on the Open Door he suggests that this policy was really pretty futile; in dealing with America and the Orient he comes to the conclusion that we dealt in useful shibboleths rather than in the "power realities"; in discussing World War I he comes to the conclusion that we might have "refrained from moralistic slogans," "kept open our lines of negotiation to the enemy, declined to break up his empires and overthrow his political system," and exploited our bargaining power "with a view to bringing its full weight to bear at the crucial moments in order to achieve the termination of hostilities with a minimum prejudice to the future stability of the Continent" (p. 72). As he approaches the present his melancholy tends to deepen; he wonders whether the proper course for Western statesmen was not to embroil the totalitarian powers with one another; whether we might not (presumably by acquiescing in the Japanese ambitions in China) have avoided a clash with Japan; whether we did not deceive ourselves as to what we might accomplish in the great coalition of 1941-1945. And he is extremely unhappy in his chapter on "Diplomacy in the Modern World" with "the legalistic-moralistic approach to international problems," which he believes to be "closely identified with the concept of total war and total victory" (p. 101).

There is plenty of room for argument in this book, and it is undeniably true that it is not always serviceable to treat great issues of foreign policy in terms of principle. But there is, I think, a fundamental assumption in Mr. Kennan's work (a fundamental assumption natural to a professional diplomat) that is very questionable. This assumption is that diplomatic action is determined by cool and trained intelligence. In saying this I do not mean to deny that the makers of our foreign policy do not have considerable freedom of action, or that intelligence is not a desirable commodity. Let us have more of it, by all means. But let us not forget that in a democratic state the great tides of emotion and feeling will, in no small measure, determine the activities of statesmen. And, in addition, it is possible to challenge every one of Mr. Kennan's criticisms as criticisms from the land of might-have-been where historians — rightfully — fear to tread.

University of Rochester DEXTER PERKINS

American Crisis Diplomacy, The Quest for Collective Security, 1918-1952. By Richard W. Van Alstyne. Foreword by Graham H. Stuart. (Stanford: Stanford University Press, 1952. xiii + 165 pp. Index. $3.50.)

This penetrating volume is based upon the assumption that a clear presentation of facts is essential for the development of any comprehensive understanding of American foreign policy. The author never deviates from his avowed purpose of treating all issues from the viewpoint of experience, not theory. In his first two chapters, drawing upon material which appeared in his earlier work, *American Diplomacy in Action*, he carefully untangles the chief threads of American diplomacy in Europe and the Far East from the end of World War I until the close of World War II. In a superb analysis of the rise of the Far East as a crisis area he finds the inception of Pearl Harbor in a multiplicity of factors accumulating throughout the twentieth century since the Treaty of Portsmouth. His third and concluding chapter, significantly entitled "New Worlds, New Quarrels," is concerned with the changing fortunes of this nation's three postwar goals: a strong United Nations, a lasting friendship with Russia, and the elevation of a united Nationalist China to the rank of a policeman in the Far East. Through a series of excellent summaries of American objectives the author endeavors to defend his conviction that American policy since 1918 has not been without purpose.

Mr. Van Alstyne's emphasis on factual presentation must not be construed as an effort to avoid interpretation or to neglect the focusing of responsibility. His book is decidedly critical of isolationism and favors rather the balance of power principle as a guide to American policy. Conversely, it is quite uncritical of President Roosevelt's decisions during the period of preparation for war after 1939 and during the war itself. In his conclusion the writer disagrees with those who would bolster our commitments in the Far East and hasten our retreat from Europe. "Put in its simplest form," he cogently explains, "American foreign policy faces the paradox of two dangers: In Asia the danger is that it will meddle too much, in Europe that it will not meddle enough." Since much of the recent effort to define the conflict between the United States and Russia still encompasses the realm of theory rather than fact, the author understandably avoids the application of the same precise analyses to recent issues which he employs in his evaluation of the thirties. The confusion of the American experience precludes any effort on his part to propose a rational solution to the current dilemmas confronting American foreign policy.

In the author's ability to arrive at the heart of the great crises, to perceive what forces in Europe and Asia constituted the challenge to America, and to recognize the many domestic conflicts which have determined the American response rests the great merit of this slender volume. It gives repeated evidence of the author's wide exploration into the available documents as well as the diaries, memoirs, and reports of those men who shaped the American decisions. Its pertinence, style, and excellence recommend it not only to the scholar but to the general reader as well.

Iowa State College NORMAN A. GRAEBNER

The Caribbean Commission; Background of Cooperation in the West Indies. By Bernard L. Poole. (Columbia: University of South Carolina Press, 1951. xix + 303 pp. Illustrations, appendixes, bibliography, and index. $5.50.)

Here is a book it has been a pleasure to read and not an unpleasant task to review, for the author examined the essential material pertinent to his task, digested and organized it, and then set forth the consequent results in impeccable English.

The most significant and useful portion of the book is the first six chapters, which, logically enough, treat the "Background of Cooperation in the West Indies." In this section one will find good brief surveys of population constituents, social, economic, and political conditions up to about 1938 in the Caribbean possessions of Great Britain, the United States, France, and the Netherlands — possessions divided into fifteen administrative entities, embracing a fifth of a million square miles, sprawling in a 2,200-mile arc between the Bahamas and French Guiana, and inhabited by 6,000,000 heterogeneous people.

The next three chapters provide an account of the multiple welfare measures inaugurated in 1938, following three years of disorders and riots throughout the West Indies, and carried out with gratifying results during the succeeding decade. Having the greatest stake in the area, conservative Britain led the way in this welfare program, at least so far as definite administration was concerned. Fortunately, the United States and, a little later, France and the Netherlands followed suit.

The first administrative agency created to make effective the welfare program as conceived in London was the British West India Royal Commission (1938), an agency most of whose recommendations were enacted into legislation by the British parliament between 1940 and 1948. In 1942 the governments at London and Washington, stimulated by the exigencies of war and by the Tugwell-Marin success in Puerto Rico, created a new joint organization called the Anglo-American Caribbean Commission. This advisory body, which met seven times to the end of 1945, limited its activities to social and economic fields. Finally, in December, 1946, the French and Netherlands governments accepted invitations to become members of an expanded Caribbean Commission, and the four-power body succeeded the executive two-power commission of 1942.

In the concluding chapter the author sets forth a very sane appraisal of the work of the Caribbean Commission when he says it "is conducting a practical demonstration of international cooperation on a regional basis, with sufficient success to encourage the establishment of the South Pacific Commission as a similar regional arrangement" (pp. 254-55).

The painstaking author and the University of South Carolina Press have combined in producing a beautiful and useful book.

Ohio State University LAWRENCE F. HILL

Germany and American Neutrality, 1939-1941. By H. L. Trefousse. (New York: Bookman Associates, 1951. 247 pp. Illustrations, bibliography, and index. $3.75.)

This is a scholarly and objective study of German policy toward the United States from the invasion of Poland to the attack on Pearl Harbor. It treats only incidentally American diplomacy and non-American aspects of Germany's foreign affairs. The Reich's relations with Japan are considered near the end; but throughout attention is focused on Berlin, not on Washington or Tokyo.

After a somewhat inconclusive opening analysis of Hitler's ultimate aims, the author traces in five clear chapters the Führer's determined efforts to keep the United States neutral and the obstacles he encountered as this country gave increasing aid to his enemies. In each chapter Dr. Trefousse examines the general international situation; the propaganda directed across the Atlantic by the Nazis; the correlation between German arguments and those of the American isolationists and, finally, the opposition of Hitler's admirals to the restrictions he imposed upon their activity. This last topic is very well handled. The volume contains a conclusion, fifty-three pages of notes, and a helpful bibliography. Although occasional use has been made of the Roosevelt Papers at Hyde Park and other manuscripts, the narrative rests mainly on captured enemy documents, testimony from the trials of war criminals, Nazi propaganda publications, an extensive array of newspapers and periodicals (many of them in German), and an intelligent selection of printed works.

Dr. Trefousse contends that Hitler went to extreme lengths to keep the United States neutral. Eager to deal with his enemies singly, he sought through persuasion and pressure to insure American nonbelligerency until he had conquered Europe. Roosevelt, however, refused to be lulled or bullied into inaction and gradually stepped up assistance to Germany's foes. Yet even after lend-lease and the "shoot on sight" orders, the Führer tried to delay the inevitable until Russia had been knocked out or attacked from the rear by Japan.

It seems clear from this study that Germany did not instigate the raid on Pearl Harbor. Hitler did not even know of the move until it had been completed. To be sure, he had formally agreed on December 5, 1941, to come to Japan's aid no matter how that country got into the war, but he did so reluctantly and only to avoid losing his Far Eastern ally. The men in Tokyo parried all suggestions to aim their blow at Singapore or Siberia; in the end they consulted their own interests and not Germany's.

This unpretentious but workmanlike volume suggests that some of the energy now being spent on combing every nook and cranny of Roosevelt's mind and action might be more profitably directed to investigating how the American approach to war appeared to the diplomats in foreign capitals.

Northwestern University RICHARD W. LEOPOLD

The Army Air Forces in World War II. Edited by Wesley Frank Craven and James Lea Cate. Vol. III, *Europe: Argument to V-E Day January 1944 to May 1945.* (Chicago: University of Chicago Press, 1951. xxxix + 948 pp. Maps, charts, illustrations, and index. $8.50.)

The dominant theme of this volume is climax, as months of preparation, of experiment, often of disappointment, culminate in the shattering air offenses that contributed so vitally to the Allied reconquest of Europe.

All responsible strategists realized that the *Luftwaffe* would have to be rendered impotent before an Allied invasion of the continent could succeed. Despite the diversion of Allied bombing strength to attacks on "Secret Weapon" launching sites, tremendous blows were struck against air frames and components plants as well as against ball bearing production facilities. During the "Big Week" February 19, 1944, 3,300 bombers from the Eighth Air Force joined with 500 from the Fifteenth Air Force to drop 10,000 tons of bombs — a tonnage approximately equal to the whole first year of operations.

Defeat of the *Luftwaffe* was an indispensable prelude to "Overlord" — the great cross-channel movement and landing that will remain one of the greatest masterpieces of military history. On D-Day the United States Army Air Force alone dispatched 8,000 missions. Only three enemy fighters were sighted by covering forces during the whole first day of the landings — dramatic evidence to the degree to which Allied air supremacy had been established.

Even more spectacular was the isolation of the battlefield achieved by the remorseless attacks on bridges, railroad facilities, and motor transport. A German Combat Group took a week to cover 100 miles by rail; two Panzer units took as long to travel the last 200 miles to the front as had been required to cover 1,300 miles from Luow in Poland to Metz.

The account of air operations in Italy and in support of the invasion of southern France sustains the high level of scholarship and interest characteristic of the entire volume. The discussion of air operations in defense of the Anzio beachhead and in support of the attack on Cassino may well serve as textbook material in the development of air doctrine. The necessity for sustained interdiction operations to achieve isolation of a battle area was clearly demonstrated by the precarious situation on the Anzio front, where Field Marshall Albert Kesselring was able to concentrate enough force to prevent decisive expansion of the Allied beachhead. Experience in the Cassino attack showed conclusively that air bombardment, by the creation of bomb craters and reduction of buildings to heaps of rubble, can actually aid a tenacious defense, and the paramount necessity for immediate exploitation of air bombardment by attacking infantry was irrefutably demonstrated.

The technical skill of the historical craftsmen who have contributed chapters to this volume has been fully equal to the importance of the stories they have to tell. Chapter I ("Winter Bombing") and Chapter II ("Big Week") are models of critical historical writing, and the chapters on "Crossbow" (IV, XV) which deal with the Allied efforts to neutralize the German V-1 and V-2 attacks will rank among the most interesting of the entire series. The editors, as in previous volumes, have organized the material to insure the maximum of clarity and effectiveness, and all contributing authors are deserving of the highest praise.

Louisiana State University CHARLES EDWARD SMITH

They Fought With What They Had; The Story of the Army Air Forces in the Southwest Pacific, 1941-1942. By Walter D. Edmonds. Introduction by General George C. Kenney, USAF. (Boston: Little, Brown and Company, 1951. xxiii + 532 pp. Maps, appendix, list of sources, and index. $5.00.)

Early in 1945 Walter D. Edmonds, distinguished historical novelist, at the invitation of the Personnel Narratives Office of the Chief of the Air Staff, agreed to write an account of early air operations in the Southwest Pacific. This office, separately organized from the AAF Historical office, had as its objective the recording of air activities "from the point of view of the men in the field." In this, Mr. Edmonds' first volume, he has told the story through the evacuation of Java in March, 1942. A second volume will continue the narrative to a turning point of the Pacific war, the battle for Milne Bay, six months later.

The early days of the Pacific War offer splendid opportunity for a skillful writer. Here was a fight against heavy odds, waged under grim conditions by a handful of poorly equipped Americans fighting at times in conjunction with equally poorly equipped allies. Those who flew the planes were, in fact, so few that the combat experiences of each could be traced without overburdening the narrative. For documentation, Mr. Edmonds has drawn on the more or less official histories of participating units and on more than 140 interviews, many secured by the author himself.

But Mr. Edmonds has done more than piece together the experiences of fighting men. He has also provided detailed evidence for the thesis that our early defeats were the results of letting our defenses soften. Although there was some inertia and lack of foresight among the commanders in the Philippines, the author clearly shows that "it is absurd to lay the blame for the Philippines defeat to failures in judgment of any one or more of our commanding officers." The question is frequently asked: "Why were the bombers caught on the ground at Clark Field on 8 December 1941 when our commanders should have been alerted by the earlier attack on Pearl Harbor?" The answer is not that General Douglas MacArthur or any one else was caught unawares, but that there were not enough antiaircraft guns, pursuit aircraft, dispersal fields, and warning facilities adequately to protect the Philippine bases. The destruction there was to be repeated in the Southwest Pacific over and over again and for similar reasons throughout 1942. It would be easy to go astray in telling this story if sole reliance were upon personal interviews, but Mr. Edmonds had access to classified records, and he has made critical use of these as well as of published sources. Although it is occasionally possible to question his judgment in his evaluation of the sources (for example, the summary of activities of the Headquarters Far East Air Force and the testimony of Colonel A. H. Campbell, commander of the Aircraft Warning network in the Philippines), his evaluation is always carefully considered and alternatives recorded.

This volume covers the same general subject matter as the related chapters in *The AAF in World War II*, edited by James L. Cate and W. F. Craven. Whereas Cate and Craven stress global planning and organization equally with combat operations, Mr. Edmonds excels in telling the story of the men. He considers briefly theater organization and logistics, and his account of the precedent-establishing ABDA Command is excellent, but his comments understandably overlook to some extent the global problem.

The narrative is closely packed, yet always clear. The author writes with obvious sympathy toward the participants; yet he is cautious in evaluating claims and rarely pulls punches in pointing to failure. Most important perhaps, he has been meticulous in checking the accuracy of his detail.

This is a distinguished work both of writing and research.

Duke University RICHARD L. WATSON, JR.

Cross-Channel Attack. By Gordon A. Harrison. Foreword by Orlando Ward. Introduction by Hugh M. Cole. *United States Army in World War II: The European Theater of Operations.* (Washington: Office of the Chief of Military History, Department of the Army, 1951. xvii + 519 pp. Illustrations, charts, maps, appendixes, bibliography, and index. $5.25.)

This carefully planned and thoroughly documented volume covers the most complex military operation undertaken by the Western Allies in World War II. It tells how their armies crossed the water barrier between England and the Cotentin Peninsula with such force and deception and fought their way ashore with so much valor that the enemy's vaunted Atlantic Wall was broken and the stage was set for the reconquest of France. While no essentially new interpretation of events is presented in this volume, the whole story is told in full detail for the first time from an American point of view. Readers who want an informed "British" presentation of these events can find it in Chester Wilmot's *The Struggle For Europe* (London, 1952), pages 168-313. Mr. Harrison has had access to all American military records and a great many German documents.

In terms of emphasis the volume is weighted heavily in favor of the planning aspects of the operation, five chapters being devoted to the strategical and tactical planning and to operations preceding the landing. Two chapters are devoted to German plans, methods, and resources for opposing the landing, and only three chapters deal with the military operations from June 6 to July 1, 1944, when the Allied bridgehead was firmly established. This heavy emphasis on the planning stages of Overlord may be justified on the ground that Allied soldiers and statesmen differed more sharply over the concepts and implications of this operation than they did over any other during World

War II. It was, of course, the most important operation of the war as far as the defeat of Nazi Germany was concerned.

Mr. Harrison shows that a remarkable series of circumstances simplified the Allied problem of invading France. Hitler's campaigns in Russia had worn out many divisions; his policy of refusing to retreat was to tie down many more to indecisive areas. The command situation on the German side was hopelessly muddled. In the realm of doctrine and strategy the defense was crippled in advance by the quarrel between Gerd von Rundstedt and Erwin von Rommel over whether the beaches were to be defended in perimeter fashion or whether reliance should be placed on counterattacks by carefully husbanded mobile forces. Hitler's compromises made matters worse.

Not only did the Germans help the Allies in many ways, but preinvasion Allied air strikes at communications proved to be more effective than anticipated. The ability of the Maquis and French Forces of the Interior to tie down and delay the movement of German forces was a pleasant surprise. The ability of the Allied navies to neutralize German fortifications was proved early on D-Day except at Omaha Beach where the United States V Corps had a bloody time fighting its way ashore. The operation was much easier than anticipated, but not every participant in the landings of June 6 will share Mr. Harrison's opinion that the Allied "airborne landings had in fact achieved such complete tactical success that the seaborne infantry had little to do except walk ashore" — except at Omaha.

This is a fine addition to the series of volumes dealing with the operations of the United States army in the European theater of operations. The maps and illustrations are excellent.

University of Missouri H. A. DeWeerd

Communications

January 11, 1952

To the Managing Editor, *Mississippi Valley Historical Review*:

As one who has examined closely several phases of John Wesley Powell's many-sided life, I feel compelled to protest the notice of a Powell biography in the December issue of the *Review*. I mean Ray Allen Billington's review of the volume, *Powell of the Colorado*, written by William Culp Darrah.

One of my objections to Professor Billington's review is inspired by his over-all evaluation of this nineteenth-century explorer, scientist, and public administrator. He writes that "if Powell can be classified at all it must be as a promoter," while I believe that the man was a powerful thinker and had some original ideas in geology and land reclamation. I recognize that these opposite opinions lie in the realm of subjective interpretations; individuals can, with honor, disagree fundamentally. And a letter of this kind is not the ideal vehicle for arriving at a decision about so controversial a question. I would like, however, to refer you to my "Essay Review" of Mr. Darrah's volume in the March, 1952, issue of the *American Journal of Science*, which grants Major Powell greater stature than Professor Billington is willing to concede him.

The burden of my complaint rests on considerations which have, I feel, a more objective character and therefore evoke agreement at once or permit easy verification. There is the question of reliance upon source materials and here the reviewer makes his most serious mistake. He praises the "meticulous . . . research" of Mr. Darrah and emphasizes that "Every scrap of evidence has been exploited." How can Professor Billington say this when, as a matter of fact, the author scarcely touched the largest collection of Powell material — the records of the United States Geological Survey in the National Archives? In other words, he never looked at tens of thousands of letters received and sent by Director Powell between 1881 and 1894.

My second criticism of this review requires a brief discussion of Mr. Darrah's fact finding. His book is not without error in this respect. He has Powell entering Oberlin in 1858; at the same time he puts the young man teaching school at Hennepin, Illinois, and carrying on nature studies during the summer of that year. He writes that "Powell paid no heed to academic degrees" in the hiring of personnel for the United States Geological Survey, when the documents show the earnestness with which the Director sought men who not only were graduates of American colleges, but also had studied at German universities. And Mr. Darrah says that for periods of time up to two years the early survey did no paleontological research. Actually, beginning in 1879 — the year of establishment — when Clarence King, the first director, hired C. D. Walcott of the New York State Survey, this science was steadily prosecuted. I could multiply these examples several times.

I am not trying, however, to make a point against the Darrah volume. But I am critizing Professor Billington for neglecting to bring out, in some way, this weakness of factual reporting. By characterizing the volume as a "complete biography" and "a definitive study of Powell so long as Powell is remembered" he must give the unsuspecting reader the impression, not that Mr. Darrah has been somewhat careless about his facts, but that he has maintained the highest standards of accuracy.

I do not remember easily a letter to the editor of a professional journal which complained that a book review was too laudatory; usually it is the deprecatory comment which draws the fire of readers. But I think that the student of history should be as willing to speak up when the critical faculty is allowed to lie dormant as when it is overextended. Both situations are equally the breeding ground of historical error.

THOMAS G. MANNING
Washington, D. C.

January 31, 1952

To the Managing Editor, *Mississippi Valley Historical Review*:

Three points raised by Mr. Manning deserve comment. First, the question of whether Powell was a promoter or an eminent scientist involves subjective judgments which allow each student to cling to his own conclusions. The evidence presented by Mr. Darrah's biography and Major Powell's own writings has not convinced me that he ranks among the greater scientists of the nineteenth century; it has convinced me that he was an outstanding promoter. Second, Mr. Manning has performed a valuable service in his letter by calling attention to the Powell materials that he has unearthed while engaged in his own research on the history of the United States Geological Survey. Unless those letters are unusual indeed, however, they will not contribute as much to our understanding of Powell as did the diaries and letters uncovered by Mr. Darrah and others, and published by the Utah State Historical Society two years ago. Third, any reviewer is certain to note occasional errors in books under consideration. Some reviewers make it a practice to demonstrate their own learning by parading these errors before the public. It is my own belief that a reviewer should critically evaluate a book for the benefit of possible readers rather than display his own erudition. Mr. Darrah's biography is as accurate as most works of its kind; an occasional slip should not damn a book that will probably endure as the standard biography of Major Powell.

RAY A. BILLINGTON
San Marino, California

Historical News and Comments

Association Activities

The Mississippi Valley Historical Association, at its annual business meeting in Chicago, April 18, elected the following officers for 1952-1953: James L. Sellers, University of Nebraska, president; Fred Shannon, University of Illinois, vice-president; and Mrs. Clarence S. Paine, Lincoln, Nebraska, secretary-treasurer. Edward C. Kirkland, Bowdoin College, Bessie L. Pierce, University of Chicago, and Bell I. Wiley, Emory University, were elected members of the executive committee; and George L. Anderson, University of Kansas, and Carlton C. Qualey, Carleton College, were chosen members of the executive committee of the Teachers Section. Three new members were appointed to the *Review's* Board of Editors: Max Savelle, University of Washington; Richard W. Leopold, Northwestern University, and Roy M. Robbins, Butler University. Charles A. Barker of Johns Hopkins University was designated to fill the vacancy on the Pelzer Prize Committee.

The program committee for the 1953 annual meeting will have as its chairman George E. Mowry of the University of California at Los Angeles. The full personnel of this and other committees of the Association will be announced in the September number of the *Review*. The Association will assemble in Lexington, Kentucky, for its 1953 annual meeting.

Personals

The Norman Waite Harris Lectures were delivered at Northwestern University April 28-May 1 by Merle Curti of the University of Wisconsin. Choosing as a general theme "Prelude to Point IV," he developed as specific lectures "The Agriculturist Goes Abroad," "Transit and Microscope: Engineers and Doctors Export Their Knowhow," "Exporting the Techniques of Public Administration," and "The Educational Implications of the Prelude."

Robert F. Durden of Princeton University will join the Duke University history staff for 1952-1953 as instructor and Alexander DeConde of Whittier College as research associate. Frances Acomb will be on sabbatical leave during the first semester for research in London and Paris.

Roy F. Nichols, professor of history at the University of Pennsylvania, has been appointed dean of the graduate school.

Paul W. Gates, professor of history at Cornell University, delivered the Henry Wells Lawrence Lecture at Connecticut College on November 11, 1950.

H. Bailey Carroll, professor of history at the University of Texas and director of the Texas State Historical Association, has been elected a fellow of the Royal Geographical Society.

Charles E. Smith, chairman of the department of history at Louisiana State University, has been appointed dean of the university.

Chauncey S. Boucher, Abraham Lincoln Lecturer in American Civilization at Knox College since 1947, will retire this year. Dr. Boucher was president of the University of West Virginia and chancellor of the University of Nebraska. He has taught at several other leading American educational institutions, and, for ten years, was dean of the college of liberal arts and sciences at the University of Chicago.

Richard Hofstadter of Columbia University and Daniel J. Boorstin of the University of Chicago were lecturers on the Walgreen Foundation at the University of Chicago.

Oscar Handlin of Harvard University will teach in the University of Chicago summer quarter.

Henry H. Simms, professor of history at Ohio State University, will teach in the summer session at the University of Southern California.

R. Carlyle Buley, professor of history at Indiana University, has been honored with a life membership in the Ohio State Archaeological and Historical Society.

William R. Steckel of the department of history at the University of Wyoming will direct a conference on American Studies for teachers of American history in the high schools of Wyoming during the summer. David M. Potter, chairman of the department of American Studies at Yale University, will be the guest lecturer.

Among the historians participating in the eighth annual Institute of International Affairs of the University of Wyoming, scheduled for July 14 to August 15, 1952, will be Samuel Flagg Bemis, Sterling Professor of American Diplomatic History, Yale University, and Anatole G. Mazour, associate professor of Russian history, Stanford University. The Institute theme is "Inside Russia." Gale W. McGee, professor of American history at the University of Wyoming, is chairman of the Institute.

A symposium on "Twentieth Century Concepts of Man," held at the College of Wooster October 25-27, 1951, was participated in by Mark Van Doren, Columbia University, Chancellor Arthur H. Compton, Washington University, Reinhold Niebuhr, Union Theological Seminary, and Theodore M. Greene, Yale University. Merle Curti of the University of Wisconsin presented the point of view of an historian. Clayton S. Ellsworth, professor of history at the College of Wooster, will be on leave of absence during the academic year 1952-1953 to do research and writing in the field of American social history.

Howard R. Lamar of the Yale University history department will be a visiting lecturer at the State University of Iowa during the summer session of 1952.

At Queen's University, Kingston, Ontario, F. W. Gibson, formerly of the National Archives of Canada, has been appointed associate professor of history.

Albert V. House of Harpur College was elected the first secretary-treasurer of the American Studies Association of New York state which was organized at a meeting held on December 1, 1951, at Cornell University.

Dumas Malone, on leave from Columbia University, is working at the University of Virginia Library on the third volume of *Jefferson and His Time.*

Elisha P. Douglass, professor of history at Elon College, has been appointed assistant professor of American history at the University of North Carolina, beginning September 1, 1952. Loren C. MacKinney, professor of history at the University of North Carolina, delivered the inaugural lecture of the J. C. Trent Society of the History of Medicine at the Duke University medical school, February 19, 1952. Harold A. Bierck, Jr., of the University of North Carolina, has been elected secretary-treasurer of the Conference on Latin-American history of the American Historical Association.

Charles S. Sydnor of Duke University will teach in the Harvard University summer session; his colleague John S. Curtiss in the summer school at Stanford University.

Frank E. Vandiver, doctoral graduate of Tulane University, has been appointed instructor in history at Washington University, effective in September, 1952.

O. P. South retired from the history department of Alabama Polytechnic Institute at the end of the spring quarter, after eight years at Auburn and more than thirty years of service in state-supported schools of Alabama. James H. Grisham, who has been on leave for two years to work on the doctorate at the University of Texas, will resume teaching at Alabama Polytechnic Institute in the fall quarter, 1952.

Rodney C. Loehr, associate professor of history, University of Minnesota, who has been on leave in Germany, 1951-1952, serving with the Historical Division of the State Department, has been granted a year's extension by the Board of Regents and will not return to this country until summer, 1953.

Joseph C. Robert, professor of history and associate dean of the graduate school at Duke University, has been elected president of Coker College.

Selig Adler, associate professor of history and government at the University of Buffalo, is substituting in part for Glyndon G. Van Deusen, who is on leave of absence from the University of Rochester.

Worth Bailey, formerly resident historian at Mount Vernon for the Mount Vernon Ladies' Association of the Union, has been appointed director at Woodlawn, Lawrence Lewis' home in Fairfax County, Virginia, the first property acquired by the National Trust.

James A. Bear, Jr., recently on military leave for active duty as an infantry captain with the Marine Corps in Korea, has returned to his post as assistant archivist at the University of Virginia Library.

Thomas H. LeDuc of Oberlin College will be visiting lecturer in American history at the University of Colorado for the 1952 summer session.

Mitchell B. Garrett, senior professor of Modern European history at the University of North Carolina and author of popular textbooks on Modern Europe and scholarly works on the French Revolution, will retire in June, 1952, after twenty-four years of continuous service. Frank W. Klingberg, assistant professor of American history, will teach in the summer session of the University of California at Los Angeles. James E. King, assistant professor of European history, will spend the summer in Washington, D. C., engaged in research at the Library of Congress. Fletcher M. Green, Kenan Professor of History, will teach in the summer session of Duke University. Harold A. Bierck, associate professor of Latin-American history, participated in a round table on teaching problems in the field of Latin America, held in

Washington, D. C., April 1-2, 1952. The meeting was sponsored by the Department of Cultural Affairs, Pan American Union. Wendell H. Stephenson, professor of southern history at Tulane University, will teach in the summer session of the University of North Carolina.

Dwight L. Ling has been promoted to the rank of assistant professor at Centre College of Kentucky.

Glyndon G. Van Deusen of the University of Rochester, who has been on a Fulbright fellowship in New Zealand, is teaching at the March-April history session of the Salzburg Seminar in American Studies in Salzburg, Austria.

At the University of California, Los Angeles, Assistant Professor John Higham was on leave the past semester writing a history of American nativism, 1865-1925. For the year 1952-1953 Associate Professor Theodore Saloutos will be on sabbatical leave; Assistant Professor Jere C. King will take sabbatical leave in France to gather material for a historical biography of Leon Blum; and Associate Professor Raymond H. Fisher will have a sabbatical leave in residence to carry on studies and research in Modern European history.

Edgar Langsdorf has been appointed assistant secretary of the Kansas State Historical Society. He succeeds Nyle H. Miller who became secretary of the Society in October, 1951.

Louis B. Schmidt, professor of history at Iowa State College, will serve as visiting professor of economics in the second term of the summer session at the University of Arizona.

The President of the United States has appointed Professor Arthur M. Schlesinger of Harvard University a member of the National Historical Publications Commission, to replace George M. Elsey, whose term has expired.

Sanford W. Higginbotham, associate professor of history at the University of Mississippi, has returned to his academic duties after having served eighteen months with the Marines in Korea, Japan, and the United States. Wendell H. Stephenson, professor of southern history at Tulane University, delivered the third in the current series of Claiborne Lectures in History at the University of Mississippi on February 19. The Claiborne Lectures are sponsored by the Claiborne Historical Society and the department of history.

Herbert S. Deighton, a fellow and dean of Oxford University, England, in the United States as the recipient of a Fulbright-Whitney award, has been a visiting professor of history at Emory University for the winter quarter, 1952. During the first half of the summer session Walter B. Posey of Emory University will serve as visiting professor at West Virginia University, and Festus P. Summers of West Virginia University will serve in the same capacity at Emory. Joseph O. Baylen of New Mexico Highlands University will be visiting associate professor of history during the summer quarter, and Thomas J. Wertenbaker, emeritus professor of history at Princeton University, will serve as visiting professor for the winter quarter of 1953. Samuel R. Gammon, III, formerly of Princeton University and at present on duty with the United States army, has accepted an instructorship in history at Emory University for the academic year 1952-1953.

Ruth Scarborough of Shepherd College will teach at West Virginia University during the summer session.

The history department of the University of Michigan reports the promotion, in June, 1951, of Sidney Fine to the rank of assistant professor.

The executive committee of the Clements Library Associates announces that Luther H. Evans, librarian of Congress, has been appointed Randolph G. Adams Lecturer for 1952. He will deliver the first Randolph G. Adams Memorial Lecture in Ann Arbor on October 8, 1952. The Clements Library Associates and other friends of the late Dr. Adams established a memorial fund in 1951 for an annual lectureship.

Wilbur S. Shepperson has been promoted to assistant professor of history and political science at the University of Nevada.

Ray A. Billington, William Smith Mason Professor of American History at Northwestern University, has been elected a trustee of the Newberry Library, Chicago. Professor Billington has been on leave of absence for the winter and spring quarters and is working at the Huntington Library. He has been elected to serve as a representative of the American Historical Association on the Social Science Research Council. In January he was made a member of the Phi Beta Kappa Associates.

Richard W. Leopold of Northwestern University participated in the third conference of the Committee on American Civilization of the American Council of Learned Societies which met in Washington, April 25-26. Franklin Scott will be director of a summer seminar on Cultural Interchange, to be held at Northwestern University under the auspices of the Social Science Research Council, during July and August. Vincent P. Carosso of the Carnegie Institute of Technology will be a member of the faculty of the summer session.

Louis Gottschalk of the University of Chicago, Roy F. Nichols of the University of Pennsylvania, and John S. Curtiss of Duke University will join the summer school faculty at Stanford University.

Thomas J. Wertenbaker, professor emeritus at Princeton, served as visiting professor of history at the University of Delaware during the second semester.

J. Jean Hecht served as assistant professor of history at the University of Delaware for the past year, replacing John A. Munroe, who was on leave.

Merle Curti of the University of Wisconsin delivered two Charles Phelps Taft lectures this year at the University of Cincinnati.

Robert Reid, who has been on leave of absence from Baylor University while teaching at the American University in Beirut, Lebanon, will return to Baylor in September with promotion to the rank of assistant professor.

Thomas E. Downey, assistant professor in charge of the Latin-American history program at the University of Notre Dame, has taken leave of absence to serve in the State Department foreign service in Brazil.

At Indiana University John D. Barnhart, chairman of the history department, was on leave the second semester of 1951-1952. F. Lee Benns served as acting chairman. Edwin Cox, graduate student, taught during the second semester at Albright College, Reading, Pennsylvania. Ralph Morrow, graduate student, will teach the second part of the summer session at the University of Chattanooga. James F. Clarke, formerly of the State Department, has been appointed professor of history and director of the Institute of East European Affairs.

June 15, 1952, marked the retirement of Professor George Malcolm Stephenson of the department of history, University of Minnesota. He had been with the department since 1914, the year in which he finished his work for the doctorate at Harvard University. His undergraduate work was done at Augustana College, and in 1950 he was elected to membership in the college's chapter of Phi Beta Kappa. Professor Stephenson also holds a bachelor's degree from the University of Chicago (1906). In 1927-1928 he was granted a leave of absence, and a Guggenheim fellowship enabled him to spend the year in research in Sweden. In 1938 he was knighted by King Gustav V, and in the same year he was awarded an honorary doctorate of philosophy degree by the University of Uppsala. Professor Stephenson's publications include *A Political History of the Public Lands* (1917), *A History of American Immigration* (1926), *Religious Aspects of Swedish Immigration* (1932), *John Lind of Minnesota* (1936), *American History since 1865* (1938), *American History to 1865* (1940), and *The Puritan Heritage* (1952).

Orin G. Libby, former president of the Mississippi Valley Historical Association, died on March 29, 1952, aged eighty-seven. He received his bachelor's, master's, and doctor's degrees from the University of Wisconsin, the last in 1895. After serving as instructor in history at Wisconsin, he joined the faculty of the University of North Dakota in 1902, and continued there until retirement in 1945. Prior to 1920 he served as head of the history department; upon its division into American and European branches, he became head of the American department. His chief works were: *The Geographical Distribution of the Vote of the Thirteen States on the Federal Constitution, 1787-8* (1894); *The Arikara Narrative of the Campaign against the Hostile Dakotas, June, 1876* (1920); and sundry contributions to the *Annual Reports* of the American Historical Association, the *Collections* of the State Historical Society of Wisconsin, and the *Transactions* of the Wisconsin Academy of Sciences, Arts and Letters. The recently established manuscripts division of the University of North Dakota Library has been named the Orin G. Libby Historical Manuscripts Collection.

Randall V. Mills, assistant professor of English at the University of Oregon since 1938, died suddenly on January 25, 1952. In addition to his work in western American literature, he wrote on western folklore and western local and transportation history, publishing *Sternwheelers up the Columbia* (1947) and *Railroads Down the Valley* (1950). At the time of his death he was preparing a biography of Frances Fuller Victor. He was president and founder of the Oregon Folklore Society.

Andrew Fish, professor emeritus of history at the University of Oregon, died at Claremont, California, March 21, 1952. Born at Newcastle-on-Tyne in 1880, he was educated at the University of London, the University of Oregon, and Clark University, where he received the doctorate in 1923. He was a member of the history department at the University of Oregon from 1923 until his retirement in 1947; he taught at the University of Washington from 1947 to 1949, and at the University of Utah in 1950. He was president of the Pacific Coast Branch of the American Historical Association from 1943 to 1945. His writings were chiefly on historiographical topics.

Grants and Awards

A graduate student at the University of Washington, Robert W. Johannsen, received the Association's Pelzer Award for 1952. The subject of his essay: "The Secession Crisis and the Frontier: Washington Territory, 1860-1861."

C. Vann Woodward of Johns Hopkins University is the winner of the Bancroft prize in American history, awarded by Columbia University. The award was made for his book, *The Beginnings of the New South, 1877-1913*, the ninth volume of *A History of the South*, published by the Louisiana State University Press and the Littlefield Fund for Southern History at the University of Texas. The other Bancroft prize was awarded to Merlo J. Pusey for his biography, *Charles Evans Hughes*, published by the Macmillan Company.

Harvey Wish's *Society and Thought in Modern America* has been chosen as the American History Book Society selection for June. The author is professor of history at Western Reserve University; the publisher is Longmans, Green and Company.

Bessie Louise Pierce of the University of Chicago has been awarded a Newberry Fellowship in Midwestern Studies to aid in the completion of Volume III of her *History of Chicago*.

David M. Ellis, associate professor of history, Hamilton College, has been awarded a Ford Foundation Fellowship for 1952-1953.

Robert G. Athearn, assistant professor of history at the University of Colorado, has been awarded a grant-in-aid by the Social Science Research Council for a study on "General W. T. Sherman and the American West, 1865-1883."

John R. Hubbard, assistant professor of history at Tulane University, has been awarded an internship by the Joint Program for Internships in General Education. He will undertake his program at Yale University in 1952-1953.

James S. Ferguson of Millsaps College has been awarded a Ford Foundation Fellowship for study at Yale University during the academic year 1952-1953.

William R. Leslie of the University of Michigan has been awarded an American Council of Learned Societies Fellowship for the second semester of 1952-1953.

Irving Leonard of the University of Michigan spent the second semester as a lecturer at Oxford University on a Fulbright award. He also made a survey, for the American Council of Learned Societies, of area programs in English universities.

The second annual James Forrestal Fellowships in Naval History have been announced by the United States Naval Academy. The fellowships were established last year to encourage research in naval history as an aid to a better understanding of current and future problems of national defense. Further information may be obtained by writing to the Superintendent, United States Naval Academy, Annapolis, Maryland.

The Huntington Library, in pursuance of its policy of encouraging research in the humanities, particularly Anglo-American civilization from the sixteenth through the eighteenth centuries, recently announced the availability of a number of fellowships and grants-in-aid. Fellowships of the value of $4,000 each are awarded for twelve months, out of which the recipients are entitled to a month's vacation. A grant-in-aid is for a shorter period than a year. The purpose of the fellowships and grants-in-aid is to enable scholars to bring significant research to completion. No grants will be made for initial or exploratory researches. A supplemental grant of $25,000 from the Rockefeller Foundation to the Huntington Library and the allocation of a similar amount by its own trustees has enabled the Library to continue the study of the economic, cultural, and social development of the Southwest, that was begun in 1944, for another five-year period. Part of these two funds will be used for fellowships and grants-in-aid. Requests for further information and applications should be addressed to the Chairman of the Fellowship Committee, Huntington Library, San Marino 9, California. Application should be made not later than January 1 preceding the academic year for which a fellowship or grant-in-aid is desired. Appointments for 1952-1953 include the following historians: Edmund S. Morgan, professor of history, Brown University; Bell Irvin Wiley, professor of history, Emory University; Ralph P. Bieber, professor of American history, Washington University; A. P. Nasatir, professor of history, San Diego State College; Eugene Keith Chamberlin, assistant professor of history, Montana State University.

Historical Activities

With the aid of a recent foundation grant, the Center for Research on World Political Institutions in the Woodrow Wilson School of Public and International Affairs of Princeton University has undertaken a three-year interdisciplinary study of the history of political integration in modern times. The focus is one of trying to learn whether some of the conditions which caused or permitted the expansion of "community" in the recent past might exist at the present time. Dana G. Munro, director of the School, and Richard W. Van Wagenen, director of the Center, have announced the appointment of five historians as members of the group that will engage in the study. Maurice duP. Lee, formerly instructor in the department of history at Princeton, will analyze the unification of Italy. Francis L. Loewenheim, who recently finished his work for the doctorate at Columbia University, will study the unification of Germany. Martin Lichterman, formerly instructor in history at the Newark College of Rutgers University, will study the unification of the United States. Sidney E. Burrell, lecturer at Barnard College, from which he will take leave of absence for one year, will assume responsibility for a study of the England-Scotland case. On the assumption that at least two other quite different cases will shed some light on the problem of "expanding community," Raymond E. Lindgren, associate professor at Vanderbilt University, has been engaged to undertake a study of Norway-Sweden; Austria-Hungary is the other case which will be analyzed.

The annual meeting of the Pennsylvania Federation of Historical Societies was held on April 26, 1952, at Harrisburg. Featured speaker for the meeting was Richard P. McCormick, associate professor of history at Rutgers University and president of the New Jersey Historical Society.

A Newberry Library Conference on Indian Studies was held at the Library on March 29. Historians and ethnologists from various parts of the country met to discuss how each would profit from the study and use of the other's discipline. On April 5 the second Newberry Library Conference in American Studies took place. Some twenty-five invited scholars in various disciplines discussed a paper by Bernard Duffey of the English department of Michigan State College.

In place of the traditional annual address before the Virginia Historical Society, this year's meeting at the Battle Abbey in Richmond, on January 22, featured four papers on the colonial period in a broadcast "History Hour" presided over by Douglas S. Freeman. The speakers were Samuel M. Bemiss, on "Sir Walter Raleigh"; John M. Jennings, "Raleigh's Works"; Mrs. Philip W. Hiden, "English Background of the First Virginia Council"; and Francis L. Berkeley, Jr., "The General Assembly of 1619 — Its Historical Significance." Edmund Randolph Williams was re-elected president of the Society at the annual business meeting.

Under the auspices of the National Historical Publications Commission a committee has been formed in Virginia, with David J. Mays of Richmond as chairman, to consider plans for the publication of James Madison's Papers.

Other members of the committee are Lyman H. Butterfield, director of the Institute of Early American History and Culture, at Williamsburg, and Francis L. Berkeley, Jr., of the University of Virginia.

The University of Kentucky, through the University research facilities in cooperation with the National Historical Publications Commission, is undertaking the compilation and publication of the papers of Henry Clay. Letters both to and by Clay, other materials of which Clay was the author, and particularly significant items about him will be included. James F. Hopkins, professor of history at the University of Kentucky, will appreciate communications concerning the location of Clay materials.

The Collections of the McCormick Historical Association, formerly housed in their own building at 679 Rush Street, Chicago, from 1918 to 1949, have recently been given to the State Historical Society of Wisconsin. These Collections consist of more than a million manuscripts, some 20,000 printed items, and a number of museum objects, including models and full-size implements and machines which show the technical evolution of harvesting devices. There are also photographs, circulars, broadsides, and other types of illustrative materials. The manuscripts comprise the correspondence of Cyrus Hall McCormick, his family, friends and associates, 1790-1940; the letters, business papers, and accounts of the various McCormick Reaper companies in Chicago from 1847 to 1902, and a number of smaller collections, principally the papers of James D. Davidson and Colonel James McDowell of Rockbridge County, Virginia. Likewise there are papers of several iron furnaces, merchant account books, and various plantation records, chiefly of Virginia origin.

Among the printed items are an extensive file of agricultural periodicals, particularly strong in the ante-bellum period; selected publications of agricultural societies; bibliographies and genealogies; a varied group relating to American regional, state, and local history, with special emphasis upon Virginia and Illinois; almanacs and works on agriculture and mechanics. These are supplemented by mechanical and trade periodicals, publications of world expositions, and numerous catalogues of manufacturers of farm implements and machines. Patents and court cases relating to patents are well represented. Religious periodicals, newspapers, and a considerable body of pamphlets, circulars, and broadsides offer a cross section of civilization in the United States for more than one hundred years, running mainly from 1830 to 1940.

Those who are interested in the invention and evolution of the McCormick reaper and other forms of farm machinery, the life and varied activities of Cyrus Hall McCormick, together with the background of the society of the times in which he lived, the industrial and business development of the Mc-

Cormick companies, American history in general and agricultural history in particular, will find in these collections information of pertinence and value.

The McCormick records, moved to Madison, in October and November, 1951, are housed and have been arranged for service in the building of the State Historical Society. Officially these materials are designated as the McCormick Collection of the State Historical Society of Wisconsin. Dr. Herbert A. Kellar and Lucile Kellar, who assembled these materials and directed the administration of the McCormick Historical Association for many years in Chicago, will continue in charge of the records at Madison. Their titles are respectively coordinator and assistant coordinator of the McCormick Collection. The addition of the McCormick manuscripts to the State Historical Society of Wisconsin more than doubles its manuscript holdings and the printed items, illustrative materials, and museum objects supplement and strengthen those already in their possession.

The annual meeting of the Historical Society of New Mexico was held on January 23, 1952, in the Art Gallery, Museum of New Mexico, Santa Fe.

A project using a relatively new technique of chronicling history — by tape recording of individuals intimately concerned with important events and developments — was launched by the State Historical Society of Wisconsin in December, 1951. The oral history project, which will be tested on an experimental basis until July 1, 1952, will record the development of industry in Milwaukee, beginning with the tanneries. If the project is successful, the same technique will be used in other industries and fields.

The National Historical Publications Commission met on December 12, 1951. Among the important decisions arrived at were: to assume the responsibility for compiling the annual volumes of *Writings on American History* for publication as part of the *Annual Report* of the American Historical Association; and to undertake planning and preparatory work looking toward the editing and printing of comprehensive documentary publications of material pertaining to the ratification of the federal Constitution and the first ten amendments thereto, and the records of the first Congress under the Constitution. The Commission also discussed projects that are under consideration for the editing and publication by state agencies or institutions in Virginia, South Carolina, and Kentucky of the papers of James Madison, John C. Calhoun, and Henry Clay.

Stanford University's efforts to encourage studies of the United States in Japan will continue over the next five years. The program, carried out over the past two years by Stanford in cooperation with the University of Tokyo, will be extended through 1956 under a $160,000 grant appropriated by the

Rockefeller Foundation. The funds will cover expenses of both universities, provide scholarships annually for two Japanese to study in this country, and facilitate the building up at the University of Tokyo of a collection of the most important contemporary materials on America. George H. Knoles, professor of history at Stanford, will head the group of scholars who will go to Japan next summer.

The sixty-seventh annual meeting of the Ohio State Archaeological and Historical Society was held on April 4-5, 1952. R. Carlyle Buley, professor of history at Indiana University, spoke on "Writing a Pulitzer Prize-Winning History"; John S. Millis, president of Western Reserve University, on "The Impact of Science on the History of Ohio." Lowell Ragatz, Ohio State University, presided over a symposium of the Ohio Academy of History on the "American Studies Program in American Colleges and Universities." The discussion was led by Lyon N. Richardson, Western Reserve University. Linden F. Edwards presided at a meeting of the Committee on Medical History and Archives at which the following papers were given: "Dr. Jabez True, First Permanent Physician in the Ohio Country," by Gilbert F. Dodds; "High Lights of the History of Nursing in Ohio," by Mrs. James H. Rodabaugh; "Pathology in the Medical Colleges of Columbus," by Jonathan Forman; "History of Pharmacy in Ohio," by Bernard V. Christensen; "Albert M. Bleile, M.D.," by Norman Dohn; "The Oldest Medical College Hospital in the United States — St. Francis Hospital, Columbus, Ohio," by Linden F. Edwards; "Proposed Social Security for the Self-Employed," by Edwin C. Mills; and "Fairfield Medical School, an Ancestor of Ohio Medicine," by Howard Dittrick. At the close of the program a meeting was held to organize the Ohio Academy of Medical History to replace the Committee on Medical History and Archives.

At a session on Economic and Business History, Indiana History Conference, December 7, 1952, Joseph Baerncopf of George S. Olive Company, Indianapolis, presiding, papers were presented as follows: Doris M. Reed, curator, Indiana University Library, "Manuscript Collections Relating to Business History"; George M. Blackburn, Indiana War History Commission, "Published Writings on Indiana Economic and Business History Since 1900"; Lynn W. Turner, Indiana University, "Industrial History of World War II"; Bernard F. Trimpe, University of Tennessee, "Impact of History on Management: Stokely-Van Camp"; Leland L. Van Scoyoc, Bowling Green State University, Ohio, "History of the Monon Railroad."

The Alabama Historical Association held its fifth annual meeting on April 18-19, 1952, at Decatur. The following papers were read: "Railroads of the Confederate States," by Robert S. Henry, Association of American Railroads,

Washington, D. C.; "A Connecticut Yankee in Ante-Bellum Alabama," by William Pratt Dale, Howard College; "William R. King in Public Life," by Walter M. Jackson, superintendent of schools, Decatur; "The Alabama Republican Party in the Nineteenth Century," by Allen J. Going, University of Alabama; "An Appraisal of the Leading Alabama Congressmen in the First Wilson Administration," by Jack E. Kendrick, Alabama Polytechnic Institute; "Negro Colloquialisms in the Alabama Black Belt," by Hamner Cobbs, editor, the Greensboro *Watchman*; and "Madame Octavia Walton Le Vert: The South's most Famous Belle," by Caldwell Delaney, University Military School, Mobile.

In inaugurating the American History Research Center the State Historical Society of Wisconsin has launched what promises to be a major historical project. The idea of establishing the Center was proposed by the history department of the University of Wisconsin in October, 1950, and approved by the board of curators of the Society in November of that year. It was to be an organization to encourage the thorough and scholarly study of localized history in every part of the United States and in all aspects of history. During the past year the idea has moved closer to realization. An advisory council to assist the director in planning the work of the Center and in establishing standards for the Center's grants-in-aid program was chosen and came together twice during the year. Members of the council are: Theodore C. Blegen, University of Minnesota; Elmer Ellis, University of Missouri; William B. Hesseltine, University of Wisconsin; Edward C. Kirkland, Bowdoin College; Fulmer Mood, University of Texas; Richard H. Shryock, Johns Hopkins University; William C. Binkley, Vanderbilt University; Thomas D. Clark, University of Kentucky; John D. Hicks, University of California; John A. Krout, Columbia University; Frank L. Owsley, University of Alabama; Wendell H. Stephenson, Tulane University; John M. Caughey, University of California at Los Angeles; Charles M. Gates, University of Washington; Paul W. Gates, Cornell University; Richard P. McCormick, Rutgers University; Roy F. Nichols, University of Pennsylvania; and Clifford L. Lord, chairman, ex-officio, State Historical Society of Wisconsin. George M. Waller of Amherst College has been selected to head the Research Center.

Grants-in-aid will be made for research, for publication, or for both in the field of American localized history. Candidates must submit specific evidence of their ability to write good history of literary excellence. They must document their applications with evidence that, on the basis of work already performed, their project in all probability will increase significantly our understanding of how history is made in a democratic society and economy; result in amendment of current interpretations or widely accepted generalizations of American history; or augment to an important degree the available data for the interpretation of the American experiment, the significance of the individual, and the continuing diversity of the American scene at the localized level. Grants will be made both for research projects and for the publication of manuscripts meeting these requirements and judged by the Center to merit publication. There are no geographic, age, or academic restrictions limiting the eligibility of candidates. There are no limitations other than those mentioned above on the topics eligible for consideration. For further information applicants should address the Director, American History Research Center, State Historical Society of Wisconsin, Madison 6, Wisconsin.

Bibliographical Notices

The personal papers of the late William Howard Taft, including papers of his father, Alphonso Taft, and of other members of the Taft family, have recently been presented to the Library of Congress by the former President's children as a gift to the nation. Part of the papers have been in the Library since 1919, when the former President himself deposited them there. Until January 1, 1960, the papers may be consulted only with the permission of the Taft family, and such permission should be requested through the Chief of the Manuscripts Division. The group, which comprises over half a million pieces, furnishes a documentary record of Taft's long career as governor general of the Philippine Islands, secretary of war, president of the United States, Kent Professor of Law at Yale University, and finally chief justice of the United States.

Reprints of Ray A. Billington's "Guides to American History Manuscript Collections in Libraries of the United States" may be obtained from Peter Smith, Publisher, 321 Fifth Avenue, New York 16, N. Y. Price 50 cents. Peter Smith has also recently brought out a reprint of Ulrich B. Phillips' *American Negro Slavery*, which sells for $6.00.

The Canadian Library Association has recently issued a summary *Catalogue of Canadian Newspapers on Microfilm* listing the sixty-three titles which it has microfilmed to date. Its 1951 catalogue provides a preliminary union list for locating all Canadian newspapers on microfilm. These two catalogues may be had on request from the Microfilm Committee, Canadian Library Association, 46 Elgin Street, Room 49, Ottawa, Canada.

The Bobbs-Merrill Company has reprinted Bell I. Wiley's *The Life of Johnny Reb*. The price is $6.00.

Marion Dargan has brought out Part II of his *Guide to American Biography*. It covers the period from 1815 to 1933, listing the biographies by subject and providing short critical notes selected from reviews in leading periodicals. University of New Mexico Press is the publisher; the price is $3.50.

Joseph A. Borome is the author of a recent biography of the distinguished librarian *Charles Coffin Jewett.* Jewett's career as a librarian spanned the years 1841-1868, during which time he served Brown University, the Smithsonian Institution, and the Boston Public Library. Published in 1951 by the American Library Association, it sells for $3.50.

Students of the American Revolution will be interested in a new biography of Richard Price, who exerted no little influence upon the thought of the eighteenth century both in Europe and America. The author, Carl B. Cone, in his chapters on the American Revolution and the Constitution of the United States, expands upon events scarcely touched by earlier biographers of Price. The work is entitled *Torchbearer of Freedom; The Influence of Richard Price on Eighteenth Century Thought* (Lexington: The University of Kentucky Press, 1952. 209 pp. Illustrations, bibliographical note, and index. $3.75).

Master Plan U.S.A.; An Informal Report on America's Foreign Policy and the Men Who Make It, by John Fischer (New York: Harper & Brothers, 1951. 253 pp. $3.00), is an attempt to survey and explain the whole of American foreign policy today for the general reading public.

The Dietz Press, Richmond, Virginia has recently (1951) republished John Edward Caldwell's *A Tour Through Part of Virginia, in the Summer of 1808. Also, Some Account of the Islands of the Azores*, under the editorship of William M. E. Rachal (xxi + 61 pp. Index. $2.00). Caldwell's narrative was first published in Belfast in 1810 and has long been a rare book.

Volume XVIII of the University of Michigan *Publications in History and Political Science* is an examination of the problem of the *Presidential Succession* by Ruth C. Silva (Ann Arbor: University of Michigan Press, 1951. viii + 213 pp. Appendixes, bibliography, table of cases, and index. $3.00).

Volume XVI, No. 2, of the *Indiana Historical Society Publications* is the reminiscences of Oliver Johnson concerning life in early Marion County, entitled *A Home in the Woods* (Indianapolis: 1951. pp. 143-234. Frontispiece, map, and index. $1.00). The reminiscences are reported by Howard Johnson.

Virginia Wood is the author of a study that examines the interpretation and application of the due process clause of the Constitution during a critical period. The title of the work is *Due Process of Law, 1932-1949; The Supreme Court's Use of a Constitutional Tool* (Baton Rouge: Louisiana State University Press, 1951. ix + 436 pp. Chart of Supreme Court personnel, table of cases, and index. $6.00).

Herbert Butterfield in eight essays undertakes an examination of the meaning of history and its relationship to human motives. He discusses the role of the historian, Christianity as a factor in history, the Marxist interpretation of history, what he believes to be dangers in the study of history, and history as a branch of literature. The essays are published under the title, *History and Human Relations* (New York: The Macmillan Company, 1952. 254 pp. $3.50).

A recently published account of early settlement in the Far West by a pioneer settler is *Recollections of a Pioneer, 1830-1852: Rocky Mountains, New Mexico, California,* by Job Francis Dye (Los Angeles: Glen Dawson, 1951. 80 pp. $5.00).

Another in the growing number of historical studies of Catholic religious societies in the United States is Joseph W. Schmitz's *The Society of Mary in Texas* (San Antonio: The Naylor Company, 1951. x + 261 pp. Illustrations, appendixes, bibliography, and index. $3.75).

No. 36 of the *Preliminary Inventories* being issued by the National Archives has recently (1951) appeared. It is *Records of the Bureau of the First Assistant Postmaster General, 1789-1942* (v + 16 pp.), compiled by Frank J. Nivert and Arthur Hecht.

The Texas Folklore Society has brought out a new volume of southwestern folk tales from the Mexican people in South Texas. It is entitled *The Healer of Los Olmos,* edited by Wilson M. Hudson (Dallas: Southern Methodist University Press, 1951. ix + 139 pp. Illustrations and index. $3.75).

As part of the celebration of the University's centennial year the Northwestern University Press has published *A Pictorial History of Northwestern University*. The general editor of the volume is Franklin D. Scott. The price is $3.50.

Leaders of Men by Woodrow Wilson, edited by T. H. Vail Motter (Princeton: Princeton University Press, 1952. viii + 70 pp. Biographical notes. $2.00), is a previously unpublished essay on political philosophy given as a lecture by Wilson on several occasions in the 1890's.

Historians may find useful a compilation of *States' Laws on Race and Color* by Pauli Murray. It includes segregation laws, antimiscegenation statutes, digest of alien land laws, statutes regarding Indian, Japanese, and Chinese, and antidiscrimination laws of all of the states. The work was sponsored by the Woman's Division of Christian Service of the Methodist Church. It sells for $4.00.

Irving S. and Nell W. Kull are coauthors of *A Short Chronology of American History, 1492-1950* (New Brunswick: Rutgers University Press, 1952. 388 pp. Index. $6.50). Major emphasis has been given to social, economic, and political history. The field of cultural and intellectual history has been reserved for a supplementary volume.

The People of Louisiana, by T. Lynn Smith and Homer L. Hitt (Baton Rouge: Louisiana State University Press, 1952. 272 pp. Figures, tables, appendix, and index. $5.00), is an attempt to bring together the principal results derived from a series of population studies begun in 1932. Nearly every phase of population study has been given some attention.

A regional study of a subject of vital concern to the South is Charles S. Mangrum's *The Legal Status of the Tenant Farmer in the Southeast* (Chapel Hill: University of North Carolina Press, 1952. viii + 478 pp. Index. $7.50). This volume presents the law concerning landlord and tenant relationship as it has evolved in the eleven states which roughly represent the Old South.

A new edition of *Library and Reference Facilities in the Area of the District of Columbia* has been issued by the Library of Congress. This 153-page directory, prepared jointly by the Washington, D. C., chapter of the Special Libraries Association and the Library of Congress, describes the collections of 237 institutions, including federal libraries, in the Washington area. Copies of the directory are free to libraries and other interested institutions. Requests should be made to the Publications Section of the Library of Congress.

Recent Articles of General Interest

Abraham Lincoln Quarterly — June: "Lincoln and the Governance of Men," by J. G. Randall; "Isaac Harvey or Samuel Haddam," by Roy P. Basler.

September: "Lincoln and Civil Liberties," by Kenneth A. Bernard; "'Beef! Beef! Beef!' Lincoln and Judge Robertson," by Roy P. Basler.

December: "Boys in Blue," by Bell I. Wiley; "Lincoln and Governor Morgan: A Financial Footnote," by Robert G. Gunderson; "The Calvin Bates Fraud," by Lloyd A. Dunlap.

Agricultural History — January: "The Referendum Process in the Agricultural Adjustment Programs of the United States," by Robert E. Martin.

April: "A Livestock Specialist Looks at Agricultural History," by Edward N. Wentworth; "The Historical Background of Turner's Frontier Essay," by Lee Benson; "A Comparison of Railroad Land-Grant Policies," by William S. Greever.

July: "The Capron Mission and the Colonization of Hokkaido, 1868-1875," by John A. Harrison.

October: "Steam Power on the American Farm, 1830-1880," by Reynold M. Wik; "The Relation of the French Peasant Veterans of the American Revolution to the Fall of Feudalism in France, 1789-1792," by Forrest McDonald.

American Economic Review — June: "American Business Cycles, 1865-79," by Rendigs Fels.

American Historical Review — July: "Samuel J. Tilden: The Story of a Lost Opportunity," by Mark D. Hirsch; "Some Writings of Thomas Paine in Pennsylvania Newspapers," by Alfred O. Aldridge.

October: "Some Demagogues in American History," by Reinhard H. Luthin; "A Study in the Origins of Interstate Rendition: The Big Beaver Creek Murders," by William R. Leslie.

January: "Impressment in the Monroe-Pinkney Negotiation, 1806-1807," by Anthony Steel; "A Reappraisal of Charles A. Beard's *An Economic Interpretation of the Constitution of the United States*," by Robert E. Thomas; "The Elder Pitt and an American Department," by Charles R. Ritcheson.

April: "The Rise of American Intellectual History," by John Higham; "The *Roberts* Case: Source of the 'Separate but Equal' Doctrine," by Leonard W. Levy and Harlan B. Phillips.

American Jewish Archives — June: "Jewish Pioneering in American Social Welfare," by Abraham Cronbach; "A Jewish Peddler's Diary, 1842-1843," by Abram V. Goodman.

January: "The East-West Conflict in American Reform Judaism," by Martin B. Ryback.

American Political Science Review — June: "The Mutual Defense Assistance Program," by Robert H. Connery and Paul T. David.

December: "The British Labor Left and U. S. Foreign Policy," by Leon D. Epstein; "Where Paine Went Wrong," by Cecelia M. Kenyon.

Canadian Historical Review — June: "Commodore Chauncey's Attack on Kingston Harbour, November 10, 1812," by C. P. Stacey.

September: "Arnold Toynbee, Metahistorian," by Frank H. Underhill.

Catholic Historical Review — July: "Benedict XV, Wilson, Michaelis, and German Socialism," by John L. Snell.

East Tennessee Historical Society's Publications — No. 23 (1951): "James K. Polk's Wartime Expansionist Policy," by Norman A. Graebner.

Florida Historical Quarterly — April: "Fort Tonyn and The Campaign of 1778," by Ripley P. Bullen.

July: "The Seminole War: Its Background and Onset," by Mark F. Boyd.

October: "France to the Rescue: An Episode of the Florida Border, 1797," by Richard K. Murdoch.

January: "Education in St. Augustine 1821-1845," by Frank G. Lewis; "The Early Career of Edwin T. Jenckes: A Florida Pioneer of the 1830's," by Earl C. Tanner; "Arizona Apaches As 'Guests' in Florida," by Omega G. East and Albert C. Manucy.

Georgia Historical Quarterly — September: "Elijah Clarke and Anglo-American Designs on East Florida, 1797-1798," by Richard K. Murdoch.

Harvard Business Review — July: "Our Economic Policy in Asia," by Raymond W. Miller; "American Security: Lowest Common Denominator," by Eliot Janeway.

Historical Bulletin — May: "Bibliography of United States Church History, 1950," by E. R. Vollmar.

November: "Observations on Recent American Historiography," by William L. Lucey.

Indiana Magazine of History — December: "Mr. Lincoln Goes to Washington," by Paul Fatout; "Eugene V. Debs: Conservative Labor Editor," by David A. Shannon.

Journal of Economic History — Summer: "Government Engineering Aid to Railroads Before the Civil War," by Forest G. Hill.

Journal of Modern History — September: "American Cochineal in European Commerce, 1526-1625," by Raymond L. Lee.

December: "SHAEF — A Retrospect on Coalition Command," by Forrest C. Pogue; "Global Command: The Double Cross Bee Cee," by James L. Cate; "British Negotiations with American Meat Packers, 1915-1917: A Study of Belligerent Trade Controls," by Marion C. Siney.

Journal of Negro History — April: "The Present Status and Needs of Afro-american Research," by Melville J. Herskovits; "Teaching Negro History to Adults," by R. O. Johnson.

October: "The Problem of Slave Labor Supply at the Codrington

Plantations," by J. Harry Bennett, Jr.; " 'The Unconquered Champion,' " by Oscar Sherwin.

Journal of Politics — May: "Governmental Planning at Mid-Century," by Rexford G. Tugwell and Edward C. Banfield.

Journal of the Illinois Historical Society — Autumn: "Voice of the Volunteer of 1847," by Dayton W. Canaday.

Kansas Historical Quarterly — May: "Fighting Aguinaldo's Insurgents in the Philippines," by Todd L. Wagoner.

Maryland Historical Magazine — June: "Lincoln, Chase, and the Rev. Dr. Richard Fuller," by David F. Barbee.

September: "Maryland as a Source of Food Supplies During the American Revolution," by Harold T. Pinkett.

December: "Sidelights on American Science as Revealed in the Hyatt Autograph Collection," by Francis C. Haber.

Mennonite Quarterly Review — July: "The Mennonite Church in World War II, A Review and Evaluation," by Melvin Gingerich; "Relations Between the Russian Mennonites and the Friends During the Nineteenth Century," by Owen Gingerich.

Mid-America — October: "Tit for Tat: A Novel of Social Criticism," by George L. Phillips.

January: "William Parks, Benjamin Franklin, and a Problem in Colonial Deism," by Nicholas Joost.

New England Quarterly — June: "The American Civil War and Inevitability," by Pieter Geyl.

September: "The Transcendental Railroad," by G. Ferris Cronkhite.

December: "British Control of American Newspapers on the Eve of the Revolution," by O. M. Dickerson.

New Mexico Historical Review — October: "The Rough Riders," Part I, by Royal A. Prentice.

January: "The Rough Riders," Part II, by Royal A. Prentice.

Northwest Ohio Quarterly — Summer: "How Morrison R. Waite Came To Be Nominated Chief Justice of the United States," ed. by Mrs. Mathew S. Morgan.

Autumn: "How Andrew Jackson Settled the Ohio-Michigan Boundary Dispute of 1835," ed. by Randolph C. Downes.

Ohio State Archaeological and Historical Quarterly — July: "Local History — Foundation of Our Faith in Democracy," by S. K. Stevens.

October: "Materia Medica and Therapy Among the North American Forest Indians," by August C. Mahr.

January: "The Challenge of the Times to the Historian," by Carl Wittke.

Pacific Historical Review — August: "Materials for the History of Arctic America," by John E. Caswell.

Pennsylvania Magazine of History and Biography — January: "English Origins of American Politics," by Roy F. Nichols; "Shipwrecked in the West Indies, 1764," ed. by William W. Comfort.

Political Science Quarterly — June: "The Struggle for Land and the 'Irrepressible Conflict,'" by Paul W. Gates.

September: "Local Government Planning of Internal Improvements," by Carter Goodrich.

South Atlantic Quarterly — July: "The Attempt to Extend British Customs Controls over Intercolonial Commerce by Land," by O. M. Dickerson; "Nietzsche in America," by Ludwig Marcuse.

Southwestern Historical Quarterly — April: "The Rio Grande Boundary Dispute in American Diplomacy," by Donald W. Peters.

Tennessee Historical Quarterly — March: "Andrew Jackson as Seen by Foreigners," by John E. Burke.

West Virginia History — January: "Peter G. Van Winkle and Waitman T. Willey in the Impeachment Trial of Andrew Johnson," by R. W. Bayless; "Western Virginia's Contribution to the Adoption of the Federal Constitution," by Roy B. Cook.

William and Mary Quarterly — April: "Aaron Burr: Would-be Usurper," by John S. Pancake; "The Milliner's Mission in 1775," by L. H. Butterfield.

July: "The Molasses Act — A Source of Precedents," by Albert B. Southwick.

Wisconsin Magazine of History — Spring: "Changing Perspectives in Local History," by Richard H. Shryock.

Recent Articles Concerning the East

American-German Review — August: "Pennsylvania German Pioneers from Wertheim," by Don Yoder; "The Story of the Schoharie Germans," by Frederick A. Klemm; "Naturalization of German Settlers in Pennsylvania," by Grace M. Buchwalter.

Canadian Historical Review — December: "The Maine Press and the Aroostook War," by David Lowenthal.

Journal of Negro History — October: "Labor Competition and the New York Draft Riots of 1863," by Albon P. Man, Jr.

Mennonite Quarterly Review — April: "The Contribution of Christopher Dock to Contemporary Christian Teaching," by Karl Massanari; "Research on the Amish and Source Materials for the Study of the Amish," by John Umble.

New England Quarterly — March: "Emerson, Eliot, and the Elective System," by Hazen C. Carpenter; "Decline of the Great Awakening in New England," by Eugene E. White.

June: "Josiah Quincy: Reform Mayor of Boston," by Richard G. Hewlett; "Israel Mauduit," by Robert J. Taylor.

September: "Rise of the Democratic Party of Rhode Island," by Murray S. Stedman, Jr., and Susan W. Stedman; "The Military System of Plymouth Colony," by Douglas E. Leach.

New-York Historical Society Quarterly — April: "Thomas McIllworth," by Susan Sawitzky; "Three Early New England Rooms," by Joseph Downs; "Portraits in the Prentis Collection," by John M. Phillips; "Crèvecoeur and the First Franco-American Packet Line," by Léon Rey, trans. and ed. by Kent Forster.

July: "Gallatin Revisited, Anger in Indiana: Jean Badollet," Part II, by Wayne Andrews; "The Early Life and Work of Ezra Ames," Part I, by Theodore Bolton and Irwin F. Cortelyou; "The 801 Westchester County Freeholders of 1763," by E. Marie Becker.

October: "Santa Claus Visits the Hudson," by R. W. G. Vail; "Eliza Leslie: New York and West Point," by Ophia D. Smith; "John Mare (1739-c.1795) New York Artist," by Helen B. Smith; "The Perfect Pendant: André and Trumbull," by Theodore Sizer; "The Tragic End of Sir Danvers Osbourne, Bart.," by Wayne Andrews.

Pennsylvania Magazine of History and Biography — July: "Thomas Parke's Student Life in England and Scotland, 1771-1773," by Whitfield J. Bell, Jr.; "George Logan, Agrarian Democrat. A Survey of His Writings," by Frederick B. Tolles; "George R. Graham, Philadelphia Publisher," by J. Albert Robbins; "The Missing Diaries of George M. Dallas," by Roy F. Nichols.

October: "Sir Augustus in Pennsylvania," by Harry M. Tinkcom; "The Disgrace of John Kinsey, Quaker Politician, 1739-1750," by Edwin B. Bronner; "Notorious Tom Bell," by Brooks E. Kleber; "William

Tecumseh Sherman in 1850," by Roy F. Nichols; "After Gettysburg: Frederick Law Olmsted on the Escape of Lee," by Evelyn Page.

January: "Anna Dickinson, Mark Twain, and Bret Harte," by James H. Young; "A War on Philadelphia's Slums: Walter Vrooman and the Conference of Moral Workers, 1893," by Harlan B. Phillips; "Francis Hopkinson and the Grammarians," by Thomas P. Haviland; "Robert Waln, Jr.: Quaker Satirist and Historian," by William S. Hastings; "A Frontier Federalist and the War of 1812," by William A. Williams; "Daniel Coxe and The New Mediterranean Sea Company," by Albright G. Zimmerman.

William and Mary Quarterly — April: "The End of the World," by Perry Miller.

July: "Puritanism and Music in Colonial America," by Cyclone Covey; "Was Joseph Reed Disloyal?" by John F. Roche.

RECENT ARTICLES CONCERNING THE SOUTH

Agricultural History — April: "Noah B. Cloud's Activities on Behalf of Southern Agriculture," by Weymouth T. Jordan; "The Gulf Coast Rice Industry," by Edward H. Phillips.

July: "The Farmer in Post-Revolutionary Virginia, 1783-1789," by W. A. Low; "Agricultural Implements in North Carolina, 1783-1860," by Cornelius O. Cathey.

Alabama Historical Quarterly — Fall, 1947: "Vicksburg," by Wallace D. Malone; "The Life of Major General John H. Forney," by Annie Forney Daugette; "War Diary of Dr. Joseph Dill Alison of Carlowville, Alabama"; "The Family Sorrows of Jefferson Davis," by Arthur M. Shaw; " 'Pioneer' the First Submarine Boat," by Stanley C. Arthur; "John Gunther and His Family," by Carolyn T. Foreman; "Commercial Horticulture in Alabama 1900 to 1940," by Lyle Brown.

Winter: "Chronicles of the Canebrake, 1817-1860," by John W. DuBose.

American-German Review — April: "Late German Documents from the Organ Church," by Carl Hammer, Jr.; "Carl C. Brenner, A German American Landscapist," by Justus Bier.

August: "First German Church in New Orleans Celebrates 125th Birthday," by Martha M. Klein.

October: "Schuricht's Virginia-German Weekly," by Dieter Cunz; "Matthias Bartgis' Newspapers in Virginia," by Klaus G. Wust.

Arkansas Historical Quarterly — Spring: "Gerstaecker and the Konwells of White River Valley," trans. and ed. by Clarence Evans; "Some Reactions of Union Soldiers Stationed in the South During the Civil War," by Louise P. Olsen; "Albert Pike's First Experiences in Arkansas," by Walter L. Brown; "Medicine and Dentistry in Pioneer Arkansas," by Walter Moffatt; "The Springfield Wagon Company," by F. P. Rose.

Summer: "Story of an Early Settlement in Central Arkansas," ed. by Ted R. Worley; "Albert Pike: Citizen Speechmaker of Arkansas," by Virgil L. Baker; "Early Camp Meetings in Faulkner County, Arkansas," by Margaret A. Ross.

Autumn: "Journal of a Trip from Camden to Texas, 1849," by Orville W. Taylor.

Winter: "The Mountain Mind," by Mel H. Bolster; "Albert Pike, Arkansas Editor," by Walter L. Brown.

Bulletin of the History of Medicine — May-June: "The Founding of the New Orleans Marine Hospital," by William E. Rooney.

East Tennessee Historical Society's Publications — No. 23 (1951): "William Blount and the Establishment of the Southwest Territory, 1790-1791," by William H. Masterson; "Industry and Industrial Philosophy in Tennessee, 1850-1860," by Constantine S. Belissary; "The Nashville and Chattanooga Railroad, 1854-1872: Era of Transition," by Jesse Burt, Jr.

Filson Club History Quarterly — January: "The Kentucky Thoroughbred," by Sara S. Brown; "The Migration of Kentuckians Across the Ohio River," by John D. Barnhart; "Major Squire Turner, Lawyer, Statesman, and Economist," by Jonathan T. Dorris.

July: "The Kentucky Frontier in 1792," Part I, by Pratt Byrd.

October: "The Kentucky Frontier in 1792," Part II, by Pratt Byrd; "William Littel," by Robert S. Cotterill.

January: "Kentucky's Choctaw Academy, 1819-1842, A Commercial Enterprise," by Evelyn C. Adams; "Kentucky's Glamorous Shorthorn Age," by Lucien Beckner.

Florida Historical Quarterly — April: "The Battle of Marianna," by Mark F. Boyd; "Code Duello in Florida," by Herbert J. Doherty, Jr.

October: "Fort Pupo: A Spanish Frontier Outpost," by John M. Goggin; "Confederate Finance: A Documentary Study of a Proposal of David L. Yulee," by Arthur W. Thompson.

Georgia Historical Quarterly — June: "Historical Background of the Salzburger Emigration to Georgia," by Milton Rubincam; "The Camilla Riot," by Theodore B. Fitz Simons, Jr.; "Two Forsyth Letters," by Chase C. Mooney.

September: "An Isochronic Map of Georgia Settlement, 1750-1850," by Wilbur Zelinsky; "Carl Schurz's Letters from the South," ed. by Joseph H. Mahaffey.

December: "The Georgia-Tennessee Boundary Line," by E. Merton Coulter; "An Evaluation of Seventeen British Travellers to Ante-Bellum Georgia," by Jack K. Williams; "Two Poems from English Magazines on the Naming of Georgia," by Hennig Cohen.

Journal of Mississippi History — January: "Bethel Lodge and Palmer's Hall in Mississippi, 1849-1869," by Arthur P. Hudson; "Some Implications Arising from Robert J. Walker's Participation in Land Ventures," by Magdalen Eichert; "Dr. Monette's Observations on Emerald Mound," ed. by John L. Cotter.

April: "The Development of Mississippi Agriculture," by James H. McLendon; "Mississippi's Confederate Leaders After the War," by William B. Hesseltine and Larry Gara; "The Cornerstone of Old Fort Maurepas," by Margaret R. Caraway.

Journal of Negro History — April: "Negro Dissatisfaction with Republican Policy in the South, 1882-1884," by Vincent P. De Santis; "John B. Rayner — A Grass-Roots Leader," by Jack Abramowitz.

July: "Negroes and the Seminole War, 1817-1818," by Kenneth W. Porter; "Industrialism in Ante-Bellum Charleston," by Leonard P. Stavisky.

January: "Racial Historical Societies and The American Heritage," by Charles H. Wesley; "Slavery and the Martial South," by John H. Franklin.

Journal of Politics — May: "The Southern Politician — 1900 and 1950," by William G. Carleton.

Journal of Southern History — May: "George W. Cable's Beginnings as a Reformer," by Arlin Turner; "Thomas Corwin and the Election of 1848: A Study in Conservative Politics," by Norman A. Graebner; "Makeshifts of Confederate Ordnance," by Frank E. Vandiver; "The Woman Suffrage Movement in Texas," by A. Elizabeth Taylor; "A Southern Family on the Missouri Frontier: Letters from Independence, 1843-1855," ed. by W. Darrell Overdyke.

August: "A Southern Education for Southrons," by John S. Ezell; "Southern Attitudes Toward Immigration, 1865-1914," by Rowland T. Berthoff; "William Elliott, South Carolina Nonconformist," by Lewis P. Jones; "Letters from the Washington Peace Conference of 1861," ed. by Robert G. Gunderson.

November: "J. D. B. De Bow: Convolutions of a Slavery Expansionist," by Robert F. Durden; "The Penal Reform Movement in the South during the Progressive Era, 1890-1917," by Jane Zimmerman; "James K. Polk: Tennessee Politician," by Powell Moore; "Thomas Chalmers, the French Church of Scotland, and the South," ed. by George Shepperson.

Louisiana Historical Quarterly — January: "John McDonough: Man of Many Facets," by Arthur G. Nuhrah; "Veterans Versus Church-Wardens," by Simone de la Souchère Deléry.

April: "Charles Gayarré, A Biographical Sketch," by Grace King; "Some Inedited Gayarré Manuscripts," by Edward A. Parsons; "Tribunals of Criminal Jurisdiction in Ancient Rome," by Charles Gayarré; "Charles Gayarré, Louisiana's Literary Historian," by Wilford B. Yearns, Jr.; "An Evening with Gayarré," by Rudolph Matas.

Maryland Historical Magazine — June: "Edmund Pendleton on the Virginia Resolves," ed. by Edmund S. Morgan; "Comment on the Pendleton Letter," by Irving Brant; "Dr. Charles Carroll — Land Speculator, 1730-1755," by Raymond B. Clark, Jr.

September: "Thomas Gerard and His Sons-in-Law," by Edwin W. Beitzell; "Silas Warner's Journal," by George B. Scriven; "An Unpublished Letter of 'Parson' Weems," ed. by Alexander M. Saunders.

December: "More About the Nicholites," by Kenneth L. Carroll; "A Famous Maryland Prize Fight," by Paul Magriel.

North Carolina Historical Review — July: "Legal Education in North Carolina, 1820-1860," by Fannie M. Farmer; "David Crockett and North Carolina," by James A. Shackford; "The Professional Theater in Wilmington, 1870-1900," by Donald J. Rulfs; "The Editorial Experience of Joseph Gales, 1786-1794," by W. H. G. Armytage.

October: "David Caldwell and His Log College," by Aubrey L. Brooks; "The Poems of Paul Hamilton Hayne to Frances Christine Fisher," by Francis B. Dedmond; "Catawba Springs — Carolina's Spa," by Chalmers G. Davidson; "The Carolina Brigade Sent Against the Creek Indians in 1814," by John K. Mahon; "The Genesis of the Protestant Episcopal Diocese of North Carolina, 1701-1823," by Sarah McC. Lemmon; "The Professional Theater in Wilmington, 1900-1930," by Donald J. Rulfs.

Papers of the Albemarle County Historical Society — Vol. XI (1950-1951): "Parson John E. Massey, Relentless Readjuster," by Richard B. Doss; "James Gaven Field, Populist Candidate for the Vice-Presidency," by John H. Moore; "Thomas Mann Randolph, Piedmont Plowman," by William H. Gaines, Jr.; "Albemarle's Support of the Claims of James Monroe, 1828-1829," by Newton B. Jones.

Register of the Kentucky Historical Society — April: "The Shanks Family Massacre," by Thurman B. Rice; "The Governors of Kentucky," Part II, by Orlando Brown; "Kentucky is Born," by Elizabeth L. Hawthorne.

July: "Benjamin Bosworth Smith, Early Kentucky Clergyman," by Rev. W. Robert Insko; "John Fleming, Pioneer of Fleming County," by R. S. Cotterill; "The Governors of Kentucky," Part III, by Orlando Brown; "Kansas and Slavery in Two Lexington, Kentucky Newspapers — 1857," by Will D. Gilliam, Jr.; "The Colonial Northwest," by Willard R. Jillson.

October: "Some Early Church Experiences," by Howard E. Short; "Cassius M. Clay and Southern Abolitionism," by David L. Smiley; "The Governors of Kentucky," Part IV, by Orlando Brown.

January: "A Journal Remarks or Observations in a Voyage Down the Kentucky, Ohio, Mississippi Rivers &c.," by John G. Stuart; "Confederate Exiles in Canada, Last Letters of James Brown Clay, 1864, Montreal," ed. by Sarah A. Wallace.

South Atlantic Quarterly — July: "Virginia's Conservative Political Heritage," by Allen W. Moger.

South Carolina Historical Magazine — April: "A Southern Genteelist: Letters by Paul Hamilton Hayne to Julia C. R. Dorr," Part I, ed. by Charles Duffy; "Confederate Exiles in London, 1865-1870: The Wigfalls," Part I, ed. by Sarah A. Wallace.

July: "Ante-Bellum Milling in South Carolina," by Ernest M. Lander, Jr.; "The Journal of Robert Mills, 1828-1830," Part I, ed. by Hennig Cohen; "Confederate Exiles in London, 1865-1870: The Wigfalls," Part II, ed. by Sarah A. Wallace; "A Southern Genteelist: Letters by Paul Hamilton Hayne to Julia C. R. Dorr," Part II, ed. by Charles Duffy.

October: "Yellow Fever in Colonial Charleston," by John Duffy; "Confederate Exiles in London, 1865-1870: The Wigfalls," Part III, ed. by Sarah A. Wallace; "A Southern Genteelist: Letters by Paul Hamilton Hayne to Julia C. R. Dorr," Part III, ed. by Charles Duffy; "The Journal of Robert Mills, 1828-1830," Part II, ed. by Hennig Cohen.

January: "The Evacuation of Fort Moultrie, 1860," ed. by Frank F. White, Jr.; "A Southern Genteelist: Letters by Paul Hamilton Hayne to Julia C. R. Dorr," Part IV, ed. by Charles Duffy; "The Journal of Robert Mills, 1828-1830," Part III, ed. by Hennig Cohen.

Southwestern Historical Quarterly — April: "A Concise History of the University of Texas, 1883-1950," by W. J. Battle; "The Callahan Expedition, 1855," by Ernest C. Shearer; "General John Lapham Bullis, The Thunderbolt of the Texas Frontier," Part I, by Edward S. Wallace.

July: "The Historical Development of the Texas State Tax System," by E. T. Miller; "James O. Rice, Hero of the Battle on the San Gabriels," by William L. Mann; "The Magee-Gutierrez Expedition," by Harry McC. Henderson; "Life and Times in Albuquerque, Texas," by Roy S. Dunn; "General John Lapham Bullis, Thunderbolt of the Texas Frontier," Part II, by Edward S. Wallace.

Tennessee Historical Quarterly — March: "Robert Whyte, Agrarian, Lawyer, Jurist," by Enoch L. Mitchell; "James Hays Piper, a Sketch," by Curtis C. Davis.

June: "The Political Career of Adam Huntsman," by Chase C. Mooney; "The Early Nineteenth Century Missionaries in the Cherokee Country," by Henry T. Malone; "Summary of Tennessee Representation in Congress from 1845 to 1861," by Milton Henry.

Virginia Magazine of History and Biography — April: "Sir Samuel Argall," by Seymour V. Conner; "Wolf Trap: The Baptism of a Chesapeake Bay Shoal," by Alexander C. Brown.

July: "The Seaborne Trade of Virginia in Mid-Eighteenth Century: Port Hampton," by Francis C. Huntley.

October: "The Tuckahoe in New Virginia," by Willard F. Bliss; "A House Divided: The Civil War Letters of a Virginia Family," by W. G. Bean; "Railroad Practices and Policies in Virginia After the Civil War," by Allen W. Moger.

West Virginia History — July: "Nathan Goff — West Virginia Orator and Statesman," by Leonard M. Davis and James H. Henning; "McNiell Rangers: A Study in Confederate Guerrilla Warfare," by Simeon M. Bright.

October: "The Sandy Creek Expedition of 1756," by Otis K. Rice; "The Evolution of the State Geological Survey," by Paul H. Price; "Mercer Academy: A Brief History Thereof, 1819-1862," by Elizabeth W. Williams.

January: "When, Where and Why the Mason-Dixon Line was Drawn," by Harvey W. Harmer; "The Early History of Marshall Academy, 1837-1850," by Robert Toole; "West Virginia and the Tariff, 1865-1885," by Gerald W. Smith.

William and Mary Quarterly — April: "Music in Wachovia, 1753-1800," by Mauer Mauer; "Inflation in Revolutionary Maryland," by Elizabeth Cometti; "The Battle of Baltimore Illustrated," by Wilbur H. Hunter, Jr.

Recent Articles Concerning the Old Northwest

Agricultural History — October: "The Swamp Land Act and Wet Land Utilization in Illinois, 1850-1890," by Margaret B. Bogue.

American-German Review — October: "Some Cincinnati German Societies a Century Ago," by Wilbur D. Jones.

Bulletin of the Historical and Philosophical Society of Ohio — April: "Ohio Through French Eyes, 1849-1864," by David Lindsey; "A Paralyzed City," by Alvin F. Harlow; "Cincinnati Reminiscences of Lincoln," by Michael G. Heintz; "Isaiah Rogers in Cincinnati," by Denys P. Myers; "The Lane Seminary Rebellion," by Walter R. Keagy.

July: "A Perplexing Problem of History," by Roy G. Fitzgerald; "The Cincinnati Art Club," by Ernest B. Haswell; "Mary Ann Furnace, Industrial Community of Early Central Ohio," by Edward Noyes.

October: "James G. Birney's Anti-Slavery Activities in Cincinnati," by Betty L. Fladeland; "Frederick Eckstein, The Father of Cincinnati Art," by Ophia D. Smith; "Richard Allison, Surgeon to the Legion," by Virginius C. Hall; "Some of the Personalities and Problems of Supply Affecting the Indian Campaign of 1792-1794," by Carl A. Brettschneider.

January: "Ned Buntline," by Ernest I. Miller; "New Foundations: Cincinnati Concert Life, 1826-1830," by Harry R. Stevens.

Indiana Magazine of History — March: "William Maclure, 1763-1840: A British Interpretation," by W. H. G. Armytage; "Early American Geologists and the Oil Industry," by F. Garvin Davenport; "Settlements in Northwestern Indiana, 1830-1860," by Leon M. Gordon, II; "Letters of William H. Harrison to Thomas Worthington, 1799-1813," ed. by John D. Barnhart.

June: "Historical Background of the Restrictions Against State Debt in the Indiana Constitution of 1851," by Donald F. Carmony; "The Documentary Basis for LaSalle's Supposed Discovery of the Ohio River," by Frances Krauskopf; "Mail Service in Indiana Territory," by Howard H. Peckham; "The Race Issue in Indiana Politics during the Civil War," by Emma L. Thornbrough.

September: "Some Projects in Midwest Cultural History," by John T. Flanagan; "The Literature of Slavery: A Re-Evaluation," by Chase C. Mooney.

December: "The Indiana Scene in the 1840's," by Roger H. Van Bolt; "Roots of the Principle of Separation of Powers in the Indiana Constitution," by Darwin N. Kelley.

Journal of the Illinois State Historical Society — Summer: "Lincoln Rebukes a Senator," by Harlan H. Horner; "Yankee Land Agent in Illinois," by Larry Gara; "The Pikes Peak Gold Rush," by Wayne C. Temple; "The Civil War Comes to 'Egypt,'" by Jasper W. Cross.

Autumn: "Robert Todd Lincoln and a Family Friendship," by Charles

V. Darrin; "Books for the Boys in Blue," by Carrol H. Quenzel; "Hard Times in Illinois in 1870," by John H. Hauberg.

Winter: "The Cherokee Cross Egypt," by Scerial Thompson; "The America First Committee," by Wayne S. Cole; "Health Measures in Early Springfield," by Helen Van C. Blankmeyer; "Captain Benjamin Godfrey, The Prairie Prophet," by B. W. Denison; "Lewis B. Parsons: Mover of Armies and Railroad Builder," by Harry E. Pratt.

Michigan History — June: "Cadillac and the Founding of Detroit," by M. Mansfield Stimson; "Detroit Biographies: Robert Rogers," by Milo M. Quaife; "The 225th Anniversary: A Detroit Profile of 1926," by Sidney Glazer; "Alexander Winchell; Michigan Scientist and Educator," by F. Garvin Davenport; "The Michigan Logging Wheels," by Roy M. Overpack.

September: "Michigan's Writing Men," by Arnold Mulder; "Phillip Hone in Michigan," by Mentor L. Williams; "Michigan's Contribution to the Development of the Diesel Engine Industry," by James R. Irwin; "The Speeding Tempo of Urbanization," by Willis H. Miller; "John McDonnell and the Ransoming of American Captives After the River Basin Massacre," by Vernon L. Beal; "The United Hebrew Schools," by Allen A. Warsen.

December: "Horses and Horse Racing in Kalamazoo," by Leon W. Miller; "The Harbor at Lugington," by Frances C. Hanna; "The Natural Science Department of the Michigan State Normal College," by Jessie Phelps; " 'Good-Time' Laws Come to the Michigan State Prison, 1857-61," by Harold M. Helfman; "Postal Service in Michigan Territory," by Ralph R. Tingley; "A Voice in the Wilderness: Henry George in Detroit," by Elwood P. Lawrence; "The Changing Pattern of Personnel in the Michigan Legislature: 1887-1947," by Charles W. Shull and Louis J. McGuinness.

Northwest Ohio Quarterly — Winter: "Midwestern: Pioneer Life in Northern Ohio," Part I, by Alfred V. Churchill; "An American Art Student Abroad, Selections from the Letters of Karl Kappes, 1883-85," ed. by Randolph C. Downes; "Young Jim, The Ottawa's Last Hope," ed. by Robert F. Bauman; "The Stage Career of John Howard Payne, Author of 'Home, Sweet Home,' " by Vedder M. Gilbert.

Spring: "The Faurot Failure at Lima," by Harvey S. Ford; " 'Easy Payments' Among the Ottawa Indians," by J. W. Cunningham; "When 'A' Was For 'Amateur,' " by Marion S. Revett; "Midwestern: The Founding of Oberlin," Part II, by Alfred V. Churchill.

Summer: "The Practice of Medicine in Toledo at the Beginning of the Twentieth Century," by Nathan W. Brown; "The Old Stage Door," by

Marion S. Revett; "Midwestern: The Founding of Oberlin," Part III, by Alfred V. Churchill; " 'Social Security' — 1827 Style," by J. W. Cunningham; "The War of 1812 in Northwestern Ohio: The Year of Victory," by W. M. Heflinger; "Midwestern: Early Oberlin Personalities," Part IV, by Alfred V. Churchill.

Winter: "The Last Ottawa," ed. by Robert F. Bauman; "Fifty Years of Toledo Art," by J. Arthur MacLean; "Midwestern: New England Backgrounds," Part V, by Alfred V. Churchill.

Ohio State Archaeological and Historical Quarterly — July: "Edwin M. Stanton at Kenyon," by Wyman W. Parker; "Mark Twain's Hadleyburg," by Guy A. Caldwell; "Presbyterians in the Ohio Temperance Movement of the 1850's," by Donald K. Garrell; "Benjamin C. Howard and the 'Toledo War': Some Letters of a Federal Commissioner," by William D. Hoyt, Jr.

October: "Development of the Teaching of Physiology in Ohio," by C. I. Reed; "The Cincinnati Bible War, 1869-1870," by Harold M. Helfman.

January: "Ohio's Constitutional Convention of 1912," by Landon Warner; "Early Ohio Camp Meetings, 1801-1816," by Charles A. Johnson; "John H. Klippart, Secretary of the Ohio State Board of Agriculture, 1856-1878," by John F. Cunningham; "Charles Tinker's Journal: A Trip to California in 1849," ed. by Eugene H. Roseboom.

Wisconsin Magazine of History — Spring: "The Development of the Office of County Clerk in Wisconsin," by Lorentz H. Adolfson.

Summer: "James Duane Doty: Mephistopheles in Wisconsin," by Alice E. Smith; "Eben E. Rexford, 1848-1916," by Walter A. Olen; "Milwaukee-Downer College Rediscovers Its Past," by Grace N. Kieckhefer; "John V. Robbins, Pioneer Agriculturist," by Charles L. Hill.

Autumn: "J. J. Case: Some Experiences of an Early Wisconsin Industrialist," by Reynold M. Wik; "Early Rivalry Among Wisconsin Cities for Railroads," by Herbert W. Rice; "Jeremiah Curtin, Traveler, Linguist, Ethnologist," by Frederic Heath; "La Follette and the Election of 1900: A Half-Century Reappraisal," by Robert S. Maxwell; "The Wisconsin Milk Strikes," by Herbert Jacobs; "British Conquest of the Old Northwest," by John H. Krenkel.

Winter: "Labor in Wisconsin History," by Edwin E. Witte; "Timothy O. Howe, Stalwart Republican," by William H. Russell; " 'Brick' Pomeroy: Copperhead and Curmudgeon," by Frank Klement; "Down from the Ivory Tower: Paul Samuel Reinsch, Minister to China," by Alan E. Kent.

Recent Articles Concerning the Trans-Mississippi West

Agricultural History — January: "The Land Mortgage Company in the Early Plains States," by Allan G. Bogue.

October: "Smith Wildman Brookhart of Iowa: Insurgent Agrarian Politician," by Reinhard H. Luthin; "The Horse in New Spain and the Borderlands," by Robert M. Denhardt.

American-German Review — April: "The Private Papers of Carl Schurz," by Arthur R. Hogue; "Carl Schurz stürzt sich in die Politik," by Joachim Maass.

Annals of Iowa — July: "Farm Tenancy in Iowa," by Earle D. Ross; "Immigrants Trying Experiences," by N. Tjernagel.

October: "Indians Repelled in Kossuth," by Ambrose A. Call; "The Webster County Bar," compiled by Maude Lauderdale.

Annals of Wyoming — January: "Wyoming's Civilian Defense in World War II," by T. A. Larson.

Bulletin of the Missouri Historical Society — July: "The Cover-Attention Cavalry!" by Mrs. Dana O. Jensen; "The Garden Theater," by Gene Ellinger; "Missouri Potters and Their Wares," by Charles Van Ravenswaay.

October: "Missouri Prize-Fighting in the 1860's," by Paul Magriel; "Ezekiel Williams of Boon's Lick," by Frederick E. Voelker; "How Goes the Harding Fever?" by John F. McDermott.

January: "William Mackwitz, Wood Engraver."

Catholic Historical Review — July: "Peter C. Yorke and the A.P.A. in San Francisco," by Joseph S. Busher.

January: "The California Chronicle of Francis Sadoc Vilarrasa, O.P., 1850-1874," by Paul M. Starrs.

Chronicles of Oklahoma — Spring: "Jeremiah Hubbard, Friends Missionary Among the Indians," by Ezra Brainerd; "William Penn Adair," by Cherrie A. Moore.

Autumn: "Wheelock Mission," by Lona E. Miller.

Colorado Magazine — July: "Colorado Festivals," by Therese S. Westermeier; "Alfred E. Mathews, Western Artist," by Isadore Mathews; "Seventy-Five Years of Rodeo in Colorado," Part III, by Clifford P. Westermeier.

October: "Federal Relations With the Colorado Utes, 1861-1865," by James W. Covington; "Colorado Woman's College — The Colorado

Vassar," by June E. Carothers; "The Greenback Party in Colorado," by Richard C. Welty.

January: "Fort Davy Crockett, Its Fur Men and Visitors," by LeRoy R. Hafen; "John Franklin Shafroth, Reform Governor of Colorado, 1909-1913," by E. K. MacColl; "Ho for the Reservation; Settlement of the Western Slope," by Lois Borland.

Iowa Journal of History — April: "Diseases and Doctors in Pioneer Iowa," by William J. Petersen; "'Book Farming' in Iowa, 1840-1870," by Mildred Throne.

July: "The Cummins-Cannon Controversy of 1909," by Waldo W. Braden.

October: "The Education of John A. Kasson," by Edward Younger.

January: "Local Aid to Railroads in Iowa," by Earl S. Beard; "Iowa Reactions to Wendell Phillips, 1867," by Waldo W. Braden.

Kansas Historical Quarterly — May: "The Letters of Joseph H. Trego, 1857-1864, Linn County Pioneer," Part I, ed. by Edgar Langsdorf; "The Kansas Senators and the Re-election of Lincoln," by William F. Zornow.

August: "The Pictorial Record of the Old West," Part XIII, by Robert Taft; "The Swedes in Kansas Before the Civil War," by Emory Lindquist; "The Letters of Joseph H. Trego, 1857-1864, Linn County Pioneer," Part II, ed. by Edgar Langsdorf.

November: "The Motives of Stephen A. Douglas in the Organization of Nebraska Territory: A Letter Dated December 17, 1853," by James C. Malin; "The Pictorial Record of the Old West," Part XIV, by Robert Taft; "The Letters of Joseph H. Trego, 1857-1864, Linn County Pioneer," Part III, ed. by Edgar Langsdorf.

Minnesota History — Summer: "The Sioux Treaties and the Traders," by Lucile M. Kane; "Frontier Vacation: Joseph Le Conte's Early Geological Excursion," ed. by June D. Holmquist; "The Early German Theater in Minnesota," Part I, by Hermann E. Rothfuss.

Autumn: "Prelude to Populism," by Donald F. Warner; "Pioneers in Iron Land," by Eva L. A. Richards; "Peter Rindisbacher, Swiss Artist," by Michel Benisovich and Anna M. Heilmaier; "The Early German Theater in Minnesota," Part II, by Hermann E. Rothfuss.

Missouri Historical Review — July: "The Anti-Horse Thief Association of Northeast Missouri," by Minnie M. Brashear; "A Clay Countian's Letters of 1834," ed. by William D. Hoyt, Jr.; "The Missouri Radicals and the Election of 1864," by William F. Zornow.

October: "The Pioneer's First Corn Crop," by Robert S. Withers.

January: "The German Theatre of Early Rural Missouri," by Elbert R. Bowen.

Nebraska History — June: "The Second Nebraska's 'Battle' of Chickamauga," by J. R. Johnson; "The Importance of Fences to the American Pioneer," by Mamie J. Meredith; "The Story of Mud Springs," by Paul Henderson.

September: "Charles G. Dawes and the Nebraska Freight Rate Fight," by John E. Pixton; "Robert W. Furnas as Omaha Indian Agent, 1864-1866," Part I, by Robert C. Farb; "Fifty Years a Country Publisher: A Reminiscence," by William H. Smith; "P. A. Rydberg's 'Report of a Botanical Exploration, Made in Western Nebraska in the Summer of 1891, as a Special Agent of the Department of Agriculture,' " ed. by Walter Kiener.

December: "The Correctness of the 1890 Census of Population for Nebraska Cities," by Edgar Z. Palmer; "Robert W. Furnas as Omaha Indian Agent, 1864-1866," Part II, by Robert C. Farb; "P. A. Rydberg's 'Report of a Botanical Exploration, Made in Western Nebraska in the Summer of 1891, as a Special Agent of the Department of Agriculture,' " Part II, ed. by Walter Kiener.

New Mexico Historical Review — July: "Washington Ellsworth Lindsey," Part I, by Ira C. Ihde; "Cristóbal De Oñate," by Agapito Rey; "Development of the Cattle Industry in Southern Arizona, 1870's and 80's," by J. J. Wagoner.

October: "Fort Union Memories," by Genevieve La Tourrette; "A Boy's Eye View of the Old Southwest," by James K. Hastings; "Washington Ellsworth Lindsey," Part II, by Ira C. Ihde.

January: "Ranching in New Mexico, 1886-90," by A. B. Wadleigh.

North Dakota History — January: "North Dakota Land Grants," by Harold A. Hagen.

April-July: "Old Fort Stevenson," by Ray H. Mattison; "North Dakota Land Grants," Part II, by Harold A. Hagen; "Military Trails in North Dakota," by Dana Wright.

October: "The Mystery of the Arikaras," Part I, by George E. Hyde; "Ukranians in North Dakota," by Wasyl Halich; "The State Flag of North Dakota," by Russell Reid.

Oregon Historical Quarterly — March: "Black Harris, Mountain Man, Teller of Tales," by Verne Bright; "History of Papermaking in the Pacific Northwest," Part I, by W. Claude Adams; "Clinton De Witt Smith, Secretary, Idaho Territory, 1864-1865," by Merle W. Wells.

June: "Contributions of Virginians in Oregon, 1850," by Harvey E.

Tobie; "History of Papermaking in the Pacific Northwest," Part II, by W. Claude Adams; "The St. Helens-Hillsborough Territorial Road," by George A. Nelson; "Senator Baker of Oregon," by Grant Conway; "Quivira, A Legendary City of the Northwest Coast," by Verne Bright.

September: "Extinguishing Indian Tribes on the Oregon Coast," by Jerry A. O'Callaghan; "History of Papermaking in the Pacific Northwest," Part III, by W. Claude Adams.

December: "The Pacific Northwest: A Regional Study," by Lancaster Pollard; "The Folklore and History of the 'Oregon Fever,'" by Verne Bright; "A Note on Bison History: A Few Were Saved," by F. J. Clifford.

Pacific Historical Review — August: "The Los Angeles and San Gabriel Valley Railroad," by Franklyn Hoyt.

May: "The Transcontinental Railroad and Mormon Economic Policy," by Leonard J. Arrington; "Futile Filibustering in Baja California, 1888-1890," by Andrew F. Rolle.

November: "Maritime Factors in the Oregon Compromise," by Norman A. Graebner; "The Health Seekers and Early Southern California Agriculture," by John E. Baur; "British Impressions of Western Railroad Service, 1869-1900," by Robert G. Athearn.

Pacific Northwest Quarterly — April: "The Victory of National Irrigation in the Yakima Valley, 1902-1906," by Calvin B. Coulter; "The Earnest Ladies: The Walla Walla Woman's Club and the Equal Suffrage League of 1886-1889," by Nelson A. Ault; "Angus McDonald, Frontier Fur Trader," by Albert J. Partoll.

July: "Mark Twain in the Northwest, 1895," by Ruth A. Burnet; "Reindeer in Alaska," trans. and ed. by Sverre Arestad; "Anglicanism Among the Indians of Washington Territory," by Thomas E. Jessett.

October: "Henry Yesler and the Founding of Seattle; A Prospectus for the Study of the Governments of the Pacific Northwest States in Their Regional Setting," by Herman J. Deutsch; "Pope and Talbot's Tugboat Fleet," by Helen M. Gibbs; "Peter Pond and the Overland Route to Cook's Inlet," ed. by Richard H. Dillon.

January: "The Trust Business in Washington," by Howard H. Preston; "A New La Vérendrye Theory," by John W. Smurr.

Palimpsest — May: "Congregational Christians in Iowa," by Frederick I. Kuhns.

July: "The Minneapolis and St. Louis Railway," by Frank P. Donovan, Jr.

November: "Boyhood in Iowa," by Herbert Hoover; "The Meaning of America," by Herbert Hoover.

December: "Frontier Journalism," by Thomas E. Tweito.

January: "The Burlington & Missouri River Railroad in Iowa," by Mildred Throne.

Scientific Monthly — January: "Man, the State of Nature, and Climax: As Illustrated by Some Problems of the North American Grassland," by James C. Malin.

RECENT ARTICLES CONCERNING CANADA

Agricultural History — July: "The Significance of Site in the Settlement of the American and Canadian West," by W. L. Morton.

American-German Review — February: "German Seigneur of a Canadian Manor," by J. I. Cooper.

Canadian Historical Review — June: "New Bruswick's Age of Harmony: The Administration of Sir John Harvey," by W. S. Macnutt; "The Knighting of Francis Hincks," by Colin R. Lovell; "Canada and Commonwealth Affairs," by D. J. McDougall.

September: "The Ninth Crusade," by Leopold Lamontagne; "Intercolonial Trade during the French Regime," by Allana G. Reid; "A Note on John Richardson's 'Digression Concerning Hearne's Route,'" by R. Glover; "Canada and Foreign Affairs," by F. H. Soward.

December: "French-Canadian Participation in the Government of Canada, 1775-1785," by M. Elizabeth Arthur; "Conflict of Loyalties: The Problem of Assimilating the Far Wests into the Canadian and Australian Federations," by K. A. Mackirdy; "A Chapter in the History of the Intercolonial Railway, 1864," by Peter B. Waite.

Mid-America — January: "Belmont's History of Brandy," trans. by Joseph P. Donnelly; "The Real Quebec Act," by Joseph E. King.

Ontario History — April: "Early Methodism in the Niagara Peninsula," by J. S. Moir; "The Birth of the Town of Dundas," by T. Roy Woodhouse.

July: "Elementary Education in Upper Canada, 1820-1840," by George W. Spragge; "Louis Roy: First Printer in Upper Canada," by William Colgate.

Pacific Historical Review — May: "Canada: The Neighbor to the North," by Walter N. Sage.

The Immigrant Theme on the American Stage

By Carl Wittke

The contact of successive immigrant waves with a New World environment is one of the central themes of American history, for the United States represents the experience of many peoples from many lands, speaking many tongues, in a republic with political unity and cultural diversity, and where there are other tests for a patriot than a man's accent, birthplace, or the color of his skin.

One of the still largely unexplored phases of the history of American immigration is the characterization of the immigrant for purposes of comic relief and dramatic entertainment on the American stage, and the emergence of certain immigrant stereotypes which still affect the thinking of many Americans about their fellow countrymen from other lands. Americans have not only been concerned about immigrants, but amused by their deviations from the standard American pattern. By 1850, when the American melting pot boiled over for the first time from the immigrant tide from Europe, the American stage began to exploit the peculiar and the ludicrous in the lives of the newcomers for purposes of public entertainment. Character actors and so-called "comics," in a time when theater standards were low and slapstick comedy popular, created certain easily recognizable stereotypes of nationality groups which the average American readily accepted as authentic because of his own daily associations with the people he saw on the stage.

Early American comedy had portrayed familiar native types, such as the frontiersman or the Negro, to provide comic relief in more serious plays, but by the latter half of the nineteenth century playwrights and actors shifted to the humor which they found in the lives of the foreign-born, and they have continued to exploit its possibilities to the present day, in theater, screen, and radio. In almost every case, the comedy of the situation depended largely upon dialect, racial speech characteristics, and the unusual customs, folk habits, and character traits which actors mimicked with greater or less authenticity. In these stage presentations, however crude, exaggerated, untrue, and even unjust they may have been, we have the beginnings of a certain realism in the American drama, for they were based on actual observation of life experiences.

Such immigrant caricatures suggest a close parallel with the Negro of the American minstrel show. A unique American institution which could have originated in no other country, minstrelsy had only moderate success when it was exported to Europe, for foreigners had no understanding of the peculiar conditions from which it developed. The sources of American minstrelsy were the singing and dancing of slaves in the Southland; and on the humor and pathos, and the peculiarities of dress, manner, and speech of the Negro, the white minstrel built his performance.

In adapting the Negro folk figure to the stage, a stage type of Negro was evolved for purposes of comic effect. The Negro of the minstrel jokebook tradition became a shiftless fellow with unusual weaknesses for chicken coops, watermelons, big words which he only partially understood, crap games, and razors used primarily for social purposes. The burnt cork performers "made up" with large mouths to reveal rows of shining white teeth and exaggerated grins, and dressed in outlandish and gaudy costumes. Their songs revealed "the white man in the woodpile" and many were composed by white men who had never seen a cottonfield.[1]

As the Negro came into his own after the Civil War, as a self-respecting and progressive citizen, he resented such ludicrous caricatures, which became steadily worse as the professional minstrel show tapered off into atrocious imitations by present-day amateurs, both male and female. Negro leaders felt that the stage Negro did immeasurable damage to race relations by creating an inaccurate and unjust stereotype of a whole people, and their resentment extends to such modern portrayals as "Amos and Andy."

In the late nineteenth century the minstrel show degenerated into a tired businessman's variety bill, and minstrel men began to clutter up their programs with sentimental Irish ballads and "Dutch" slapstick comedy. Dan Bryant, for example, one of the minstrel "greats," as early as the 1860's washed off the burnt cork and ap-

[1] See N. I. White, "The White Man in the Woodpile," *American Speech* (Baltimore), IV (February, 1929), 209-10.

peared with great success in *Handy Andy*, *Rory O'More*, and *The Irish Emigrant*. Johnny Allen, another popular minstrel, turned to low Dutch characters and advertised in the *Clipper* for engagements for his "Schneider, or, Dot House von der Rhine," and Joseph Murphy left the minstrel semicircle for such Irish plays as *Kerry Gow* and *Shawn Rhue*, and "Dutch, Irish and Ethiopian delineations of character."[2] As early as 1859 Bryant's minstrels featured songs like "MacFadden Fadden Trio," written by J. H. Unsworth, author of "eccentric specimens of Ethiopian Hibernicism."[3] In 1875 the Cincinnati *Enquirer* referred to D. L. Morris as " 'the black Dutchman' of the minstrel stage who was 'infinitely ludicrous in his murdering and misapplication of the Queen's English,' "[4] and Carncross' Minstrels, playing in Philadelphia in 1889, introduced the song, "Down Went McGinty," in a travesty known as *McGinty in Town*.[5]

The Irishman, "as an insistent figure" on the American stage, emerged in the 1850's when thousands of Irish arrived in the New Canaan with empty pockets but high hopes and were left stranded in the eastern port towns. For the most part they were marginal, unskilled laborers and were forced to live in tenements that were "human rookeries." The drink evil hounded the early Irish in America and saloons and gang politics were closely intertwined. Irish immigrant boardinghouses, closely allied with grogshops, were notorious for overcrowding and lack of cleanliness. When Paddy arrived, clad in caped and high-waisted coat, brimless *caubeen*, knee breeches, woolen stockings, and rusty brogues, he was herded by immigrant runners and "shoulder hitters" into the broken-down shacks of Irish "shanty towns." In the second generation this type of Irishman largely disappeared, and as Orestes A. Brownson predicted, "out from these narrow lanes, blind courts, dirty streets, damp cellars, and suffocating garrets" would come men and women whom the country would delight to own and honor.[6] The play-

[2] See George C. D. Odell, *Annals of the New York Stage* (New York, 1927 —), VII, 546-47; Robert Grau, *Forty Years Observation of Music and the Drama* (New York, 1909), 312; Michael B. Leavitt, *Fifty Years in Theatrical Management* (New York, 1912), 189; New York *Clipper*, March 11, May 27, 1871.

[3] *Porter's Spirit of the Times*, February 5, 1859.

[4] Carl Wittke, *Tambo and Bones, A History of the American Minstrel Stage* (Durham, 1930), 90.

[5] *Ibid.*, 108. See also for the American stage Negro and "Ethiopian Drama," Laurence Hutton, *Curiosities of the American Stage* (New York, 1891), 89-144; and Robert F. Roden, *Later American Plays, 1831-1900* (New York, 1900), 119-20.

[6] Boston *Pilot*, July 1, 1854.

wright and actor, however, found his material for the theater in the congested areas of the first generation Irish, and before the end of the 1850's the stage Irishman had become a full-grown giant of the American stage and threatened to dwarf all other types, including the Negro and the Yankee.

Scotch and Irish characters were seen on the American stage as elements in the melting pot as early as 1767, in a poor musical comedy known as *The Disappointment, or The Force of Credulity*,[7] and an able student of early American drama has found Irish characters in twenty-two American plays before 1828. Some already suggested the "disturbing presence" of the Irishman in the United States,[8] and Irish airs, jigs, reels, and brogue were not unknown before the flood of Irish came in the 1850's.[9]

Tyrone Power, famous portrayer of comic Irish characters on the English stage who made three tours of America to introduce comedies in the 1830's with Irish settings, dances, and songs, generally avoided the grosser caricatures of Irish character. *O'Flannigan and the Fairies, or a Midsummer Night's Dream, not Shakespeare's*, a musical fairy story in which Power appeared in 1837, was based on the Irish belief in fairies and preached a vigorous lesson in temperance, because the entire action turned out to be the creation of a wild Irishman's brain, fired with too much whisky.[10] During the 1840's the struggle for Irish freedom stimulated plays that were both historical and nationalistic. By 1850 a whole series of "Mose and Jake" plays portrayed the life of Bowery boys and city loafers in which "fightin' Mose," a broth of a "b'hoy" in red flannel fireman's shirt, chewed tobacco like a virtuoso, spoke in extravagant Irish speech, wore "soaplocks," and outraced all others "with the machine." "Mose" strongly suggested an Irish ancestry, and was the forerunner of the full-grown stage Irishman of the next decade.

[7] Margaret G. Mayorga, *A Short History of the American Drama; Commentaries on Plays Prior to 1920* (New York, 1932), 29. See also Perley I. Reed, *The Realistic Presentation of American Characters in Native American Plays Prior to Eighteen Seventy*, Ohio State University *Bulletin*, XXII, No. 26 (Columbus, 1918), 22.

[8] See Catherine Sturtevant, "A Study of the Dramatic Productions of Two Decades in Chicago, 1847-1857 and 1897-1907" (Ph.D. dissertation, University of Chicago, 1931), 34-37.

[9] Constance M. Rourke, *American Humor; A Study of the National Character* (New York, 1931), 78. See also Arthur H. Quinn, *A History of the American Drama from the Beginning to the Civil War* (New York, 1928), 375.

[10] Arthur H. Wilson, *A History of the Philadelphia Theatre, 1835 to 1855* (Philadelphia, 1935), 64-65; Oral S. Coad and Edwin Mims, Jr., *The American Stage*, Ralph H. Gabriel (ed.), *The Pageant of America*, 15 vols. (New Haven, 1925-1929), XIV, 163.

By the middle of the 1850's "Mose" had given way to the urban Irishman, who remained the standard character in the theater for nearly two generations.[11] Costumed in ragged and dirty clothes, he usually was portrayed as an impudent, pugnacious, and eloquent character who swung a wicked shillelah for the protection of widows, children, and Irish maidens about to be seduced, revealed an unquenchable hatred for "dirty peelers," otherwise known as policemen, and got off "Irish bulls" which became a part of American folk humor.

Playwrights like James Pilgrim, Samuel D. Johnson, John Brougham, and Dion Boucicault turned to mass production of farces and melodrama on Irish themes and characters; and outstanding actors like Barney Williams and John Drew introduced their plays to American theater audiences from the Atlantic to the Pacific.[12] A six months' tour of California netted Williams and his actress wife a profit of $40,000.[13] W. J. Florence toured the country as an early specialist in Irish comedy parts,[14] and in 1858 he joined the temperance league and gave "a series of lectures on that topic, with Hibernian illustrations."[15] The Irish skits of Mr. and Mrs. F. S. Chanfrau were presented to packed houses on New York's East Side before the Civil War.[16] Less well known, but comedians of considerable talent, were John T. Kelly, a star on Broadway in Irish vaudeville and musical comedy;[17] the Russell Brothers, famous for their "Irish Servant Girls" act;[18] and Barney Gilmore, an Irish singer and dancer of the Chauncey Olcott type, who did Hibernian specialties in vaudeville and melodrama.[19]

11 See Rourke, *American Humor*, 138-39, 141; Reed, *Realistic Presentation of American Characters in Native American Plays*, 120; Wilson, *History of the Philadelphia Theatre*, 80, 82-83; and Kenneth H. Dunshee, *As You Pass By* (New York, 1952).

12 See Quinn, *History of the American Drama from the Beginning to the Civil War*, 376-77; *Porter's Spirit of the Times*, April 11, 1857.

13 Edmond M. Gagey, *The San Francisco Stage, A History* (New York, 1950), 57.

14 Samuel P. Orth, *A History of Cleveland, Ohio*, 3 vols. (Chicago, 1910), I, 438. Irish plays presented in Cleveland from 1854 to the Civil War included, among others, *Irish Assurance, The Irish Doctor, The Irish Tutor, The Irish Immigrant, Brian O'Linn, Paddy the Piper, Irish Assurance and Yankee Modesty, The Irish Mormon, The Irish Huzzar, The Green Banner of Erin, Ireland and America*, and *The Lake of Killarney*. See William S. Dix, "The Theatre in Cleveland, 1854-1875" (Ph.D. dissertation, University of Chicago, 1946), 11, 26, 55, 70, 124, 129.

15 See *Porter's Spirit of the Times*, April 10, 1858; also June 27, 1857, and September 4, 1858.

16 *Ibid.*, February 5, 1859.

17 Leavitt, *Fifty Years in Theatrical Management*, 152.

18 New York *Tribune*, January 18, 1890.

19 Lewin A. Goff, "The Popular Priced Melodrama in America, 1890 to 1910, with

From a reading of the lines of these Irish specialists, one must conclude that their success depended primarily on their powers of mimicry, make-up, and dialect, for neither the plot nor the jokes seem funny by modern standards. In terms of box office receipts, however, Irish comedy was a paying proposition. The Florences earned more than $500 a week in Chicago in the 1850's, and stars like Barney Williams and John Drew presented Irish plays in the same city to houses which sometimes netted nearly $600 a night.[20] From the Civil War to World War I, the American variety stage exploited Irish and other foreign-born groups for comic effect with continuing financial success.[21] The Gold Rush made San Francisco "a theatrical suburb" of New York, and Chanfrau, Florence, and other Irish comedians played to large audiences in youthful California, where theaters were still close enough to saloons to permit the audience to drink before, during, and after the performance. Plays about Mose, the Irish firefighter from the Bowery, and other Irish-American comedy patterned largely on the performances of Barney Williams, were as popular on the Pacific coast as in the large eastern cities.[22]

The popularity of Irish songs which helped to reinforce certain features of the Irish stereotype began nearly a century ago. They ran the whole gamut from the comic to the sentimental and heroic. In recent decades some of the best have been written by Jewish tunesmiths of Tin Pan Alley. "Billy" Scanlan, singer and Irish dialect comedian, popularized "Peek-a-Boo" and "Moonlight on Killarney," [23] and the constantly expanding Irish repertoire not only gave Americans such timeless favorites as "My Wild Irish Rose," "Sweet Rosy O'Grady," and "My Isle of Dreams," but such forgotten leaders in the American hit parade as "There Never Was a Coward Where the Shamrock Grows."

Plays on Irish themes featuring Irish immigrant characters were

Its Origins and Development to 1890" (Ph.D. dissertation in Dramatic Arts, Western Reserve University, 1948), 176.

20 See Napier Wilt, "A History of the Two Rice Theatres in Chicago from 1847 to 1857," University of Chicago, *Abstracts of Theses, Humanistic Series,* IV (Chicago, 1926), 411-17.

21 See also Arthur H. Quinn, "The Perennial Humor of the American Stage," *Yale Review* (New Haven), N. S., XVI (April 1, 1927), 553-66; and Douglas Gilbert, *American Vaudeville, Its Life and Times* (New York, 1940), 397 *et seq.*, for vaudeville acts from 1880 to 1930.

22 Gagey, *San Francisco Stage,* 3, 13, 28, 118-19; *Porter's Spirit of the Times,* February 5, 1859.

23 Fred J. Beaman, *Pearls from Past Programs* (Boston, 1931), 24-27.

so numerous after 1850 that for forty years only the blackfaced minstrel could compete with the stage types from the land of brogue and "bulls." Many of these Irish plays which were extraordinarily successful at the box office had little merit as literary or dramatic productions, but two Irish-American playwrights, Dion Boucicault and John Brougham, ranked among the most prominent American dramatists of their time.

Boucicault came to New York in 1853. Although he used other themes, he achieved his greatest popularity as an interpreter of Irish characters. With the talented actress Agnes Robertson, his second wife, Boucicault toured the country for many years. He never hesitated to help himself generously to the work of others, although he revised and frequently improved what he borrowed. His *The Poor of New York*, for example, first played in 1857, and later reissued in several forms, as *The Poor of Liverpool* and *The Streets of London*, was based on *Les Pauvres de Paris*, which in turn had been presented in New York as *Fraud and Its Victims*. Boucicault copyrighted it as his own.[24] The play depicted the suffering in the metropolis from the Panic of 1857, and the New York *Herald* pointed out that the "only real local character [was] Dan, the firebug." The author and star was urged to take the play to Washington for the education of congressmen.[25] Boucicault's "The Colleen Bawn" (1860), dealing with Irish gentlefolk, had more than three thousand performances. *The Shaughraun* (1874), full of Irish *bonhomie*, was a more authentic portrayal of the Irish type. Boucicault wrote or adapted 124 plays, and thrilled his audiences with melodramatic effects for years, yet he lived long enough to see his own plays become old-fashioned.[26]

John Brougham spent fifty years on the stage and wrote about seventy-five plays, all of which have been forgotten. He made his debut at the Park Theatre in New York in 1842, and his reputation rested largely on his portrayal of comic Irish characters. Laurence Hutton thought he "deserves a colossal statue in [the] Pantheon" of American burlesque.[27] W. J. Florence starred as Tim O'Brien, an

[24] *The Poor of New York* is in *French's Standard Drama* (New York, n.d.), CLXXXIX.

[25] *Porter's Spirit of the Times*, December 19, 1857.

[26] See Jesse May Anderson, "Dion Boucicault: Man of the Theatre," University of Chicago, *Abstracts of Theses, Humanistic Series*, V (Chicago, 1928), 439-42; Kenneth R. Rossman, "The Irish in American Drama in the Mid-Nineteenth Century," *New York History* (Cooperstown), XXI (January, 1940), 39-53.

[27] Hutton, *Curiosities of the American Stage*, 204.

honest Irish laborer, in Brougham's *The Irish Emigrant*, a play which stressed the more bizarre features of Irish life.[28] Among his other notable plays were *Life in New York; or Tom and Jerry on a Visit*, *The Irish Yankee; or the Birthday of Freedom*, and a farce, *Take Care of Little Charley*, modeled on the French, *LaFille bien Garde*, in which Brougham played a funny Irishman.[29] By the close of the 1850's Irish farces, with their practical jokes, rough comedy, and absurd characters, had become "the most favorite class of modern dramatic entertainment," [30] and their simple, romantic plots usually were generously interspersed with Irish songs, jigs, and reels.[31]

A brief description of several Irish immigrant plays will indicate the character of these productions. They do not read well to the modern reader; they follow a standard pattern which permits virtue and honesty to triumph in the end, and their success apparently depended almost entirely on the character actors who performed in them.

Brougham's *The Irish Emigrant* told in two acts the simple story of a truckman and a poor, hungry, ragged Irish immigrant who found $5,000 but was too honest to keep the money.[32] James Pilgrim's *Shandy Maguire* dealt with oppression in Ireland, in which the revenue man and the landlord were the villains, the squire's worthless son lusted for the old miller's daughter, and the characters and the audience were reminded that "there are hearts across the big waters, in the New World, that have stretched forth a helping hand to poor Ireland, and will do it again." [33] The farce, *Brian O'Linn*, was specially written for Barney Williams, the hero of the play. Williams appeared in dark brown breeches, gray stockings, a frieze coat and red vest, and the cast included several Irishmen, a

28 *Porter's Spirit of the Times*, June 13, 1857.

29 *Ibid.*, December 4, 1858. See also Wilson, *Philadelphia Theatre*, 109.

30 *Porter's Spirit of the Times*, December 27, 1856.

31 The list of Irish plays runs into hundreds. In addition to those already mentioned, the 1850's produced Fitz James O'Brien's *The Gentleman from Ireland*, *The Irish American; or The Lost Keepsake* (anonymous); John Brougham's *The Irish Fortune Hunter* and *Irish Stew*; James Pilgrim's *Paddy the Piper*, *Shandy Maguire; or, The Bould Boy of the Mountain*, and *Robert Emmet, the Martyr of Irish Liberty*; Boucicault's *Andy Blake; or the Irish Diamond* and *The Irish Broom Maker*; and S. D. Johnson's *Brian O'Linn*. Some of these and other Irish plays can be conveniently found in *French's Standard Drama*, *French's Standard Plays*, *French's American Drama* (New York, n. d.), and *French's Minor Drama* (New York, n. d.).

32 *Dick's Standard Plays* (London, n. d.), No. 621.

33 *French's Standard Drama*, CCXLIII, 24.

Catholic priest, a British army officer, and women in Irish peasant dress. As the curtain rose Williams was seen in his mother's humble cottage, trimming his shillelah and singing an Irish love song. The dialogue was full of witticisms and extravagant Irish blarney, but the plot stumbled along through absurd and tumultuous scenes in which the hero made love to the girl Sheelah, and fought periodically with the police. The action is so preposterous that it strains both the patience and the credulity of the modern reader,[34] but the play was a great success.

Irish Assurance and Yankee Modesty was a comedy built around the desires of Pat, "the devil after the girls," and his amorous pursuit of a "tigress Yankee girl." [35] *Ireland and America*, another special creation for Barney Williams, opened with an Irish fair and a chorus, singing

> The flowers of all Europe
> Are the pretty girls of Paddy's land.

The villains were the excisemen, who interfered with the Irishman's harmless desire to distill "the mountain dew," and the hated redcoats whose captain was intent upon seducing the hero's (Jimmy Finnegan's) Peggy. While under the influence of liquor, Finnegan was impressed into military service by "kidnappers that crawl through the lanes and valleys of our beloved country." He escaped to "the home of the stranger — America," and Act III found him in New York, breathing "the free air of that glorious land of liberty," where after three years of honest toil he was doing pretty well financially. For melodramatic effect, the playwright contrived to have him meet his ancient enemy, the British captain, who had been expelled in disgrace from the army, and now was engaged in robbing new arrivals from Europe as a New York immigrant runner. The beloved Peggy arrived with her mother on an immigrant ship in time to fall into the clutches of the erstwhile captain, who steered her party to an immigrant boardinghouse where he planned to divest her of both her money and her virtue. Meantime, the hero, now a successful Irish-American businessman, had resolved that it was his duty to rescue his fellow countrymen from their unscrupulous exploiters. He donned his old clothes to visit the dens where Irishmen were being fleeced, and the outcome was inevitable. In a final scene, in an old house where the villain held Peggy under lock

[34] *French's American Drama*, LXIII.
[35] *Ibid.*, LXIV.

and key, there was a terrific fight, and after the hero had cracked a sufficient number of heads with his trusty shillelah, the girl rushed into his arms.[36]

The action of *A Day in New York* (1857) opened with immigrants landing at Castle Garden, and was likewise concerned with an Irishman's beautiful daughter, who was imprisoned by an immigrant runner in one of the Bowery's dens of iniquity.[37] Brougham's *The Irish Yankee; or the Birthday of Freedom*, sounded the patriotic, nationalistic note. Its characters included Washington, costumed as he was when he crossed the Delaware; Lord Howe, Israel Putnam, and the Irishman O'Donahoo, a name "with a real good potato flavor," dressed in pantaloons and entrusted with carrying a secret letter to the Commander in Chief. Before the play ended, the audience saw the Boston Tea Party and a tableau of Bunker Hill, and listened to "The Star Spangled Banner" (not yet written at the time of the Revolution). In the final scene,

> The soldier, tired of war's alarms
> Beat a retreat to beauty's arms.[38]

William Kelly's *The Harp Without a Crown, or Mountcashel's Fair Daughter* belonged in the same general category. It opened with the defeat of the Irish at the Battle of the Boyne, and dealt with the continuing struggle of Irishmen to maintain their liberty and their faith. It featured much marching, many flags, and hairbreadth escapes; the lines abounded with "achuslas" and "ashtore machrees," and the play ended with the dying hero kissing the green flag and sighing for Ireland with his last breath.[39] In *The Hills of Erin, or Ireland's Last Struggle* (1866) the hero's experiences took him from Libby Prison to all the "woes beyond the seas." [40]

Although Irish plays were still being produced throughout the 1870's, and many of the earlier favorites revived, their vogue began to decline in the 1880's. Bridget and Pat ceased to be major char-

[36] *French's Minor Drama*, LXXIII.

[37] *Porter's Spirit of the Times*, December 5, 1857.

[38] *French's American Drama*, LXXXVIII.

[39] William Kelly, *The Harp without a Crown, or Mountcashel's Fair Daughter* (New York, 1867).

[40] Odell, *Annals of the New York Stage*, VIII, 222. Professor McEvoy's "The Hibernians," or "Tour of Ireland," a panorama described as a grand pictorial and musical exhibition, which explained the inspiration of Irish poets and orators and the attachment of the Irish for the homeland and purported to give a correct portraiture of "auld Ireland," was shown to large audiences in New York, Boston, Montreal, and many other cities. New York *Clipper*, April 4, May 2, 1863.

acters, and were retained, if at all, primarily for comic relief, and Irish skits were confined largely to the shorter performances of the vaudeville stage. By 1900 Irish plays were still romantic, but less realistic; the actors no longer dressed in rags; and scenes of extreme poverty no longer symbolized the Irish stage character. The Irishman had become Americanized and with Americanization Irish caricatures had become less popular; yet vaudeville actors, until the movies dealt their craft a knockout blow, continued to portray Irishmen working on a scaffold, or carrying mortar on ladders, throwing bricks at each other, or falling into mortar boxes, and counted on rapid, crossfire conversation and a knockabout kind of rough humor, based on misunderstanding and violent argument, for their applause. Kelly and Ryan, a popular vaudeville team, billed as "The Bards of Tara," did their act as coal heavers with scoop shovels; and such vaudeville acts frequently began and ended with a song and dance and clever improvising about events and issues of the day.[41]

Harrigan and Hart, two of the most successful delineators of Irish character in theater history, deserve a final word of comment, for in their day they made a genuine contribution to the American stage. Both started in vaudeville and expanded their acts into full-length plays. During the decade of the 1870's Harrigan composed no less than eighty sketches, and his material gradually evolved from a song to a duet, dialogue, and full-length plays, including not only characterizations of the Irish, but of Negro, German, Italian, and Chinese immigrant types as well.[42]

Edward Harrigan was born in New York in 1845. The veteran actor and producer, Leavitt, recalled meeting him in Sacramento where he worked as a caulker before going on the stage. Harrigan met his partner, Tony Hart (Anthony Cannon) while the latter was playing in a variety theater in Chicago, and formed a partnership which lasted for several decades.[43] Harrigan wrote the songs, dialogues, and plots for their skits. Originally they ran only from thirty-five to forty minutes. His plays, chronicling the adventures of Dan Mulligan and the Mulligan Guards, and known as the "Mulligan Series," were realistic, good-natured portrayals of New

[41] See the original Pat Rooney's "Is that Mr. Riley," sung in the 1880's; and Bradford and Delaney's song about the Knights of Labor, Gilbert, *American Vaudeville*, 62-72.

[42] See Mayorga, *Short History of the American Drama*, 200.

[43] Leavitt, *Fifty Years in Theatrical Management*, 233, 309-10.

York Irish. Dan, a veteran of the Civil War, was irascible, intemperate, impulsive, but generous, loyal, and honest. His wife Cordelia, originally portrayed as a prudent, frugal, simple Irish woman, developed into a social climber, and *Cordelia's Aspirations* recounted her rise, fall, ruin, and return to the old grocery and boardinghouse, and to her Dan, for whom she had a genuine motherly affection. Harrigan's *Squatter Sovereignty* satirized the conflict for prestige between two clans in the social caste structure of New York's Irish Shantytown. Other plays in the series were built around the rivalry between Dan Mulligan and Gustav Lochmüller, the German butcher who was his competitor and the foil for his quick Irish humor. *The Mulligan Guard* burlesqued the outings, riots, and target practice of New York's volunteer militia companies; *The Mulligans and the Skidmores* contrasted Irish and Negro character; and *The Mulligan Guard Ball*, which ran for a hundred nights in New York, described the complications that arose when a Mulligan fell in love with a daughter of a Lochmüller. Mrs. Annie Yeamans, her daughter Jenny, and Tony Hart played the female roles in the Mulligan Series, and Harrigan's father-in-law, David Braham, wrote the songs and marches which the nation whistled and sang from the 1870's to the end of the century.[44]

Harrigan's inspiration was the local color of New York's immigrant communities. He wrote about the common people — and

> Murphy's tenement, in the First Ward near the dock,
> Where Ireland's represented by the Babies on Our Block.

His humor was clean and good-natured, his plots not without significance for American "social history" and the melting pot, and they were pleasantly relieved by tuneful and clever musical numbers. The characters included street cleaners, contractors, grocers, shyster lawyers, politicians, policemen, truckers, and washerwomen;[45] and the scenes, dives, shantytowns, the water front, the clothes stalls of the Jews, the German *Turnvereine*, picnics, barber shops, and the corner grocery. Few of Harrigan's plays were published. Their success depended almost wholly on their genial satire and

[44] See Grau, *Forty Years Observation of Music and the Drama*, 100, 201, 360; Hutton, *Curiosities of the American Stage*, 52; Arthur Hornblow, *A History of the Theatre in America*, 2 vols. (New York, 1919), II, 344-45; Arthur H. Quinn, *A History of the American Drama from the Civil War to the Present Day*, 2 vols. (New York, 1927), I, 82-96.

[45] Edward B. Marks, *They All Sang, from Tony Pastor to Rudy Vallée* (New York, 1934), 45-46.

comedy types. They lived on the stage, not in the library. *Reilly and the 400*, which opened in Harrigan's Theatre in December, 1890, was his last great success. In it he played an Irish pawnbroker, opposite Annie Yeamans, a society leader. The song hit of the show was "Maggie Murphy's Home," which contained the lines

> There's an organ in the parlor, to give the house a tone,
> And you're welcome every evening at Maggie Murphy's home.

The catchy "Danny By My Side," a tune from *The Last of the Hogans*, written in 1891, was a favorite of the late Jimmie Walker, and Al Smith sang it in 1933 at the celebration of the fiftieth anniversary of the Brooklyn Bridge.[46]

By that time American audiences had almost completely forgotten the Mulligans and the Lochmüllers, and the early immigrant communities which produced them, but no less a critic than William Dean Howells believed that Harrigan and Hart were unsurpassed in the fidelity and refined perception of their portrayals of American immigrant types, and that their sociological and psychological studies constituted true American art.[47]

After the Revolution a few Dutchmen with long pipes served as foils for Yankee wit in several American stories and plays, but with the exception of Rip Van Winkle, the early Dutch character was quickly forgotten.[48] The Pennsylvania "Dutchman" (German) who by the nineteenth century represented a petrification of an American colonial stock with practically no further contacts with Europe, was represented in an occasional play, such as *Son and Father, or the Dutch Redemptioner* (1830), and in the character of the patriotic Krout, in *Blanche of Brandywine*, but such stage roles were exceptional.[49] Only comparatively recently has there been renewed interest in the art, customs, and language of the Pennsylvania Germans. They have been the inspiration for the stories of Helen R. Martin and Elsie Singmaster, plays like *Erstwhile Susan* and *Papa Is All*, and radio skits of Pennsylvania German characters, somewhat after the fashion of "Lum and Abner"

46 *Ibid.*, 45-48.

47 See *Harper's New Monthly Magazine* (New York), LXXIII (July, 1886), 316; *Harper's Weekly* (New York), XL (October 10, 1896), 997-98; and *Harper's New Monthly Magazine*, LXXIX (July, 1889), 315-16. See also Isaac Goldberg, *Tin Pan Alley* (New York, 1930), 66-83.

48 Rourke, *American Humor*, 78.

49 Quinn, *History of the American Drama from the Beginning to the Civil War*, 275, 281.

from Pine Ridge. Such portrayals provoked the usual controversy about their accuracy and fairness, and the extent to which they stress only the queer and unattractive qualities of this extraordinary early German group.

The large German immigration of the nineteenth century was of a different kind and made "Dutch slapstick" a favorite of vaudeville audiences. *King Lager, or Ye Sons of Malt*, produced in 1857, indicated the inroads this exhilarating beverage already had made on the American palate.[50] By the 1870's variety bills featured Irish and "Dutch" acts and songs, whose comic effects depended largely upon the contrast between the nimble, quick-witted, coleric Irishman and the slow, phlegmatic, heavy-footed German. The actor, Lewis Mann, was a master of several German dialects, and Gus Williams, a German comedian for nearly half a century, is credited with introducing the first German dialect song, "Kaiser, don't you want to buy a dog." [51] German comedians generally made up with chin whiskers and padded stomachs, wore long vests, short pants, and bowler hats, and spoke German with an emphasis on the guttural "r," and used the "z" sound for "th." Henry L. Mencken's *The American Language* points out to what extent they influenced the average American's vocabulary.

Eddie Cantor did "Dutch" acts, as well as blackface and Jewish comedy, at the beginning of his notable career. Sam Bernard sang German songs in the New York Turner Hall and in a "Concert Hall" in the notorious "Five Points" area and on Coney Island for $2.50 a performance, before he became the stage's most popular German comedian.[52] Joseph K. Emmett was best known for his portrayals of "Fritz, Our German Cousin," and there were other Irish performers who excelled in so-called "Dutch" acts.[53] Gus

[50] Odell, *Annals of the New York Stage*, VII, 67; *Porter's Spirit of the Times*, October 17, 1857.

[51] Grau, *Forty Years Observation of Music and the Drama*, 225, 240-41. As an example of such songs, and as an indication of how much German-American audiences apparently understood, we may cite the idiotic lines about

"Give a listen to the Mocking Bird . . .
Die mocking bird ein grosser macher ist.
Vas macht die mocking bird? . . .
Es mox nix ous vas macht die mocking bird."

See Claude T. Martin, *Handbook for Adeline Addicts* (Cleveland, 1932), 54-55. For skits about German immigrants in vaudeville in the 1880's, see Odell, *Annals of the New York Stage*, XI, 544.

[52] Leavitt, *Fifty Years in Theatrical Management*, 529-30.

[53] Beaman, *Pearls from Past Programs*, 28-31; Gilbert, *American Vaudeville*, 74.

Williams twisted his lines into a ludicrous mixture of English and German in a skit of the 1880's, entitled "The German Senator." Vaudeville favorites, like Lizzie Wilson, introduced the "Schnitzelbank" song, still a midnight favorite of lager beer saloons, and in 1879 Mary Fiske's English Blondes, the forerunners of the modern burlesque show, featured a court scene, entitled "Dutch Justice," with Irish and German comedians doing pure slapstick.[54] John W. Ransome, a pioneer in American vaudeville, toured in the 1880's as a Dutch comic,[55] and later, as the German brewer in *The Prince of Pilsen*, made nationally famous the line "Vas you effer in Zinzinatti?"

In 1879 *The Emigrant Train, or Go West*, playing at Tony Pastor's in New York, combined Irish, Dutch, and Italian immigrant dialect comedians and four blackface performers in one play.[56] The next season produced "The Emigrants," with Baker and Farron and characters known as Ludwig Vinkelsteinhausenblauser and Christina Waldhauser.[57] Further proof of the low comedy of such performances may be gathered from the inane patter of Cliff Gordon, who played a stupid, kindly German as late as the early 1900's, and included the following in a monologue on the scarcity of money.

> Efferbody says there iss a shortness of money. Who shortened it? I didn't done it. Who has got all dis money? I ain't got it. . . . We neffer had dese things when people like George Lincoln and Abraham Washington vas superintendencing the gufferment.[58]

Like Harrigan and Hart in Irish comedy, Weber and Fields were without a peer in the "Dutch" dialect comedy of their day, and their knockabout, slapstick act was imitated by many lesser talents. Both had appeared earlier in blackface, and as Irish comics. Joseph Weber was a product of the New York Ghetto. His family came in steerage from Poland. Lew Fields was the son of a Polish Jewish tailor. The boys met on the sidewalks of the Bowery, and at the early age of nine made their debut as a blackface acrobatic song and dance team in the New York Turner Hall. Weber was five feet four, and dumpy; Fields was tall and thin, a good combination for

[54] Bernard Sobel, *Burleycue* (New York, 1931), 38.

[55] Gilbert, *American Vaudeville*, 4, 6. See also *ibid.*, 401, 403, 407, 409-10, for other "Dutch acts."

[56] Odell, *Annals of the New York Stage*, XI, 102.

[57] *Ibid.*, 387.

[58] Gilbert, *American Vaudeville*, 294.

a vaudeville act. Their German accents were easily acquired for both heard Yiddish at home. When they sang such songs as "Ireland for the Irish," their pronounced Semitic faces added greatly to the comic effect.

Weber and Fields abandoned blackface and Irish parts to concentrate on the German dialect comedy which carried them to fame and fortune. They had a standard technique which they used throughout their career. They came shouting and gesticulating out of the wings. They dressed at first in loud, checkered suits, later in dress clothes. They mangled the English language with German words and accents, pushed each other around, hooked each other with canes, kicked each other in their padded stomachs, and usually ended their act by kissing each other. Fields frequently sank a hatchet in Weber's head which was protected by a steel-plated wig, or kicked his partner with a shoe that exploded, and they had other crude tricks which sent their audiences into gales of laughter.

It is impossible to reproduce the acts with which they entertained the American public for decades. They might begin their patter with "I am delightfulness to meet you," followed by "Der disgust is all mine." On a somewhat higher artistic level were such skits as the quarrel of two Germans in a poolroom in Düsseldorf, in which Weber played the trusting little man and Fields the bully; or their burlesque of a German *Schützenfest* in which they fired, blindfolded and at all angles, at electric lights revolving back stage, and never missed. From this they went on to the clever travesties which made Weber and Fields's Music Hall famous, and produced such burlesques as *Quo Vass Is?* (*Quo Vadis*); *Barbara Fidgety* (*Barbara Frietchie*); *Sing Bad, the Tailor; The Stickiness of Gelatine* (*The Stubbornness of Geraldine*); *The Corn Curers*, a travesty of Guy De Maupassant's Franco-Prussian War story, "The Conquerors," in which the major of German Uhlans spoke with an Irish brogue and drank beer from a trick stein that refilled itself; *Cyranose de Bric-a-Brac* (*Cyrano de Bergerac*) and *Sapolio* for *Sappho.*[59] Some of their routine was pure slapstick, including the periodic smashing of the orchestra leader's violin, but much was remarkably clever burlesque and satire.[60]

The German immigration developed theaters of high quality of

[59] See Gagey, *San Francisco Stage*, 198; Mayorga, *Short History of the American Drama*, 208; Grau, *Forty Years Observation of Music and the Drama*, 192, 229.

[60] See especially Felix Iman, *Weber and Fields* (New York, 1924), *passim*.

its own where the best of the German classics were presented, but the language barrier shut out average Americans from an appreciation of the culture imported by the leaders of the German element, so different from the Weber and Fields stereotype, and that of other vaudevillians who had come up through the beer halls and dime museums. The continuing popularity of Jack Pearl's radio portrayal of Baron Munchhausen indicates that this earlier conception of the American "Dutchman" has not yet completely lost its attraction.[61]

Although occasional plays introduced Jewish characters and their old clothes and pawnshops at an earlier date, the Hebrew stereotype did not make its formal entry upon the American stage much before the turn of the century. In the 1850's, when Irish and German characters became popular, the Jewish element was still too small to attract much attention. The most prominent and successful actors from this group belong to the early twentieth century, and by that time Irish and German characters had lost much of their popularity. Many earlier Jewish performers did blackface and "Dutch" acts before turning to the portrayal of the Jew of the tenement districts.

Frank Bush, a blonde German, did some of the first stage representations of the "Hebrew Drummer" and the Jewish pawnbroker and was regarded in the 1890's as a great Jewish comic. His vaudeville acts combined humor and pathos, and depicted Jewish characters in grotesque make-ups, with derbies or plug hats pulled far down over their ears, long black coats, long tapering beards, large spectacles, and hands crossed in an obsequious gesture. Bush intended to give an honest imitation of the kindly, humorous, shrewd, and philosophical East Side Hebrew pawnbroker whom he knew from real life.[62] One of his songs dealt with "Solomon Moses," "a bully Sheeny man," and ended with the chorus,

[61] For German and French plays adapted to the American stage, and for a history of the German theater in the United States, see Quinn, *History of the American Drama from the Civil War to the Present,* I, 20-33; Quinn, *History of the American Drama from the Beginning to the Civil War,* 89-112; and Esther M. Olson, "The German Theatre in Chicago," *Deutsch-Amerikanische Geschichtsblätter, Jahrbuch der Deutschen Historischen Gesellschaft von Illinois* (Chicago, 1937), XXXIII, 68-123; Ralph Wood, "Geschichte des Deutschen Theaters von Cincinnati," *ibid.,* XXXII (1932), 411-522; Alfred H. Nolle, "The German Drama on the St. Louis Stage," *German-American Annals* (Philadelphia), XV, 28-65; and Fritz A. H. Leuchs, *The Early German Theatre in New York, 1840-1872* (New York, 1928).

[62] Marks, *They All Sang,* 14.

> Solomon, Solomon Moses,
> Hast du gesehen der clotheses?
> Hast du gesehen der kleiner Kinder?
> Und der sox iss in der vinder? [63]

and apparently theatergoers understood enough German and Yiddish to follow such musical gibberish.

The team of Bent and Leon in 1878 used a store front as a setting for a vaudeville act in which they sang "The Widow Rosenbaum," a parody on "The Widow Dunn," about "a hock shop" with three balls over the door, "Where the Sheeny politicians can be found." [64] Joe Welch specialized on the crestfallen, unhappy Jew; his brother Ben featured the fast-talking pushcart type, and Julian Rose made the monologue, "Levinsky at the Wedding," famous as an act and a recording.[65] Joseph Lateiner's play, *Emigration to America*, opened with a scene of Jewish persecution in Europe, and ended with a Jewish wedding in New York.[66] Jewish vaudeville acts became a feature of American burlesque shows, and have remained standard equipment for the strip-tease companies. As early as 1896 Charlie Burke achieved burlesque fame as an Irishman who did a Jew act and sang "Rachel Goldstein." [67] In melodrama "Levi" or "Solomon" usually were only minor characters in the plot.

David Warfield began with low comedy and East Side Jewish caricatures in San Francisco and New York before he was discovered for the legitimate stage by David Belasco. In his characterization of Simon Levi, in *The Auctioneer*, the stage Jew reached perhaps his highest and most sympathetic portrayal, yet Warfield's characterization merely represented the perfection of a role which he had begun to play in his early music hall days.[68] Israel Zangwill's *The Children of the Ghetto* was staged with great effect in 1900. More recent Jewish caricature, of the Abe Potash and Mauruss Perlmutter variety, and such characters as Mrs. Feitelbaum with her "Nize Baby" to whom the mother tells "a Ferry Tail from de Pite Piper of Hemilton," remain favorites with vaudeville, screen, and radio audiences. "The Goldbergs" and the Sam

63 Gilbert, *American Vaudeville*, 287-90.

64 *Ibid.*, 72-73.

65 *Ibid.*, 290-92.

66 Odell, *Annals of the New York Stage*, XIII, 313.

67 Sobel, *Burleycue*, 120-27. In some cities, like Cleveland, objections to the use of Jewish material led producers to eliminate it from their burlesque bills.

68 Gagey, *San Francisco Stage*, 194; Coad and Mims, *American Stage*, 307.

Levenson program are current favorites on television. Eddie Cantor, a product of New York's East Side slums, began his career as an entertainer with Yiddish and blackface acts and German and Irish comics, and like his contemporary, George Jessel, has never hesitated to draw comedy effects from the life of the American-Jewish community and to rely heavily on Jewish content for his humor. Much of current American public humor still is of Jewish origin. The nature of that humor can perhaps be explained in part by its philosophical overtones, and the fact that a people that suffered economic and social frustration for centuries took it out in making fun of each other, in a kind of verbal exhibitionism.[69]

America also has had its flood of Jewish popular songs which appeared some ten to twenty years after the high tide of Jewish immigration and helped develop and perpetuate the Jewish stereotype. Irving Berlin's "Yiddle on Your Fiddle" marked the beginning of a new interest in the Jewish type in American song literature, and it was followed by such so-called "Yid" songs as "Yiddische Rag," "Yiddische Eyes," "How's de Mamma," "At the Yiddish Ball," "Maxie, Don't Take a Taxie," Fannie Brice's renditions of "Second Hand Rose" and "It's Tough When Izzie Rosenstein Loves Genevieve Malone," and the less well-known "Rocky Rifkowitz, Tell Me Witz is Witz."[70]

Other immigrant groups have figured to a lesser degree on the American stage. French farce, popular at the turn of the century, supported the popular notion that "Frenchy" somehow suggested something naughty and relatively licentious. "Gus" Hill, a professional club swinger who turned to the variety stage, has been credited with inventing the characters of Alphonse and Gaston.[71] Beginning with *Our American Cousin*, in which Edward A. Sothern played Lord Dundreary hundreds of times throughout the United States, the stage Englishman has generally been represented as

[69] Eddie Cantor, *My Life Is in Your Hands* (New York, 1938), *passim*; also Nathan Ausubel, *A Treasury of Jewish Humor* (New York, 1951).

[70] See Marks, *They All Sang*, 174-76. When the craze for ragtime was at its height, we had the "Italian Rag," "Irish Rag," "Yiddische Rag," "Deutschen Rag," "Indian Rag," and finally, the "International Rag." An example of the good-natured comedy between immigrant types is the story of the Irish priest who found a Jewish soldier dying in the trenches, and asked him whether he believed in the Father, Son and Holy Ghost, to which the Jew replied, "I'm dying, and he asks me riddles." The story appeared in an American jokebook as early as the 1870's. See Iman, *Weber and Fields*, 275.

[71] Grau, *Forty Years Observation of Music and the Drama*, 274.

something of a vacuous, self-confident fop, a silly "English swell," with a strange sense of humor and long side whiskers which once were known in America as "Picadilly weepers." In addition, there was the English low comedian who usually was outlandishly dressed and spoke in broad cockney.

By the 1890's the Swede fared no better than his Irish and German predecessors, and there was a short vogue for ludicrous Swedish-American stage characters such as "Ole Olson," "Yon Yonson," and "Hans Hanson." [72] The song, "Ay Vant to Go Back to Sweden," was written in 1904, and the Swedish maid was introduced as a minor character in many plays. Arthur Donaldson, a Swedish immigrant boy who came to New York in 1882 as a lad of thirteen and worked as typographer and watchmaker, and acted in Swedish plays while learning English, became a star of musical comedy, light opera, and screen. At the turn of the century he was playing the name rolls in the Swedish dialect comedies, *Ole Olson* and *Yon Yonson*, in the Swedish theater in Chicago.[73] On the vaudeville stage the Swede usually was depicted as a person of rather slow and heavy mentality. Kathryn Forbes's "Mama's Bank Account," popular on the stage as "I Remember Mamma," dealt with a Norwegian-American family in California, whose folkways were those of the mid-nineteenth-century immigration.

Italian characters were introduced early for purposes of comic relief, in such plays as Augustin Daly's *Under the Gaslight*, whose cast included "an Italian organ grinder from Cork" named "Raffardi, neé Rafferty." Harrigan occasionally played Italian immigrant roles, and produced *The Italian Padrone*, or, *the Slaves of the Harp*.[74] The first decade of the twentieth century brought a flood of Italian "Mariuch" songs, such as "Mariuch, She Taka da Steamboat" and "Mariuch Makea-de-Hootch-a-ma-Cooch," [75] and Italian character actors still appear occasionally in burlesque shows. "Life with Luigi," the popular radio program glorifying America as a land of opportunity and free enterprise, not only describes the Italian Luigi's adventures with Pasquale and his marriageable

[72] See George M. Stephenson, *The Religious Aspects of Swedish Immigration* (Minneapolis, 1932), 417.

[73] Henriette C. K. Naeseth, *The Swedish Theatre of Chicago, 1868-1950* (Rock Island, 1951), 95. Miss Naeseth refers to a number of Swedish immigrant plays that were produced in Chicago.

[74] Odell, *Annals of the New York Stage*, X, 264; and IX, 465.

[75] Marks, *They All Sang*, 132.

daughter Rosa, but from time to time introduces other immigrant characters, such as Jews, Germans, and Swedes. The Eddie Cantor radio show introduced Parkyakarkus, purported to be a Greek caricature.

Finally, in the period when popular priced melodrama flourished, stereotypes of the foreign-born figured in many popular thrillers. The Hebrew usually represented a mercenary character who was the butt of many jokes, but seldom a villain, and he frequently blundered into saving the hero or heroine. Irish and German types were stupid, and dressed to be funny, but generally on the side of virtue. The "bad" foreign types, represented as the villain's henchmen, were the French, Chinese, or Italians. The Chinaman of melodrama was often cruel and almost always connected with either the opium or laundry business; the Italian was hired to do the bloody work; while the Frenchman was the well-dressed, debonair, and smooth lover, who plotted his villainy with more refinement. *Chinatown Charlie, the Opium Fiend* was written by Owen Davis who produced scores of melodramas and other plays about the Chinese, but the action was really more concerned with melodrama than with the Chinese.[76] Charles H. Hoyt wrote a comedy of manners entitled *A Trip to Chinatown*,[77] and in Francis Powers' *The First Born*, a story of San Francisco's Chinese quarter, one of the leading characters was a learned Chinese and another a Jewish peddler.[78] The Chinese caricature remains popular in murder mysteries, and in such radio portrayals as Fred Allen's Chinese detective.

Sociologists and social psychologists probably would have much to say about the "minority caricatures" described in this paper, and would account for them by "the ethnocentrism of the majority," and explain the inaccuracy of stage stereotypes of the foreign-born in terms of "ethnocentric" majority attitudes.[79] The historian must be content with a description of the phenomenon, and a few simple deductions. The popularity of immigrant types in the theater fol-

76 See Lewin A. Goff, "Popular Priced Melodrama in America, 1890 to 1910," 345-56, 290-94.

77 Gagey, *San Francisco Stage*, 196.

78 *Ibid.*, 175-76.

79 See, e.g., an excellent paper by Harold E. Adams, "Minority Caricatures on the American Stage," George P. Murdock (ed.), *Studies in the Science of Society* (New Haven, 1937), Chap. I, 1-27. See also Carl Wittke, "Melting-Pot Literature," *College English*, VII, No. 4 (January, 1946), 189-97.

lowed in rough chronological order the major waves of immigration to the United States, for the group must be large enough and still sufficiently unassimilated to invite caricature. In the 1880's much of the comedy of the variety theaters still was racial; today it is much less so. There has been almost no reference to Slavs in the theater, probably because they did not come until the whole American entertainment pattern had outgrown the crudity of its adolescent years. The complex and difficult Slavic languages may be another factor, for they do not lend themselves easily to borrowing and mutilation for comic stage effects. Harrigan, in 1908, made the additional suggestion "that only Irish and Anglo-Germanic peoples know how to laugh," and that Latins and Slavs "want to laugh not with you but at you," and represent an entirely different kind of humor.[80]

American audiences saw these inaccurate stage immigrant characters and heard these dialects so long that many accepted them as completely authentic, although character traits, overplayed for comic effect, obviously emphasize idiosyncracies and deviations from the general folk pattern. Though most of the humor and comedy was good-natured and kindly, the aim of each minority group as it rises in the American social and economic scale has been "to clean up the caricature." Resentment of stage stereotypes grows more pronounced as each group becomes more Americanized, and senses the difficulties of dislodging such misconceptions from the public mind. The Irish, German, and Jewish-American have been steadily moving out of caricature on the stage, and today are no longer the stilted stage comics of old, but diversified, complex personalities, like other Americans. Such productions as Israel Zangwill's *The Melting Pot* (1908) which described the United States as "God's Crucible," *The Gentile Wife* (1918), and *Abie's Irish Rose* (1922), which had its greatest popularity during the Ku Klux Klan frenzy of the 1920's, made moving and effective appeals for reconciliation and tolerance among diverse religious and national groups.[81] The older immigrant drama and stage stereotypes have now become historical documents of sorts, illustrating how the creative artist responds to the social milieu of which he is a part, and at the same time has some part in reshaping it.

80 Quoted in Gilbert, *American Vaudeville,* 111.

81 See also George S. Kaufman and Moss Hart, *The American Way* (New York, 1939), for the German-American problem in World War I.

The Gaspee Affair: A Study of Its Constitutional Significance

By William R. Leslie

The burning to the water line of his majesty's schooner *Gaspee* while she was lying hard aground on a sandspit in Rhode Island's Providence River has long been recognized as a singularly important event. Although it occurred on the night of June 9-10, 1772, nearly three years before Lexington and Concord, it was nevertheless of major significance in leading to the outbreak of war between the American colonies and the mother country. Indeed, perhaps the musket ball which wounded Lieutenant William Dudingston, commander of the *Gaspee*, was really an earlier "shot heard 'round the world." Certainly the *Gaspee's* demise marked the end of the period of calm which had prevailed since the repeal of the Townshend Acts and the beginning of the series of events that ultimately led to revolution. Moreover, the appointment of a royal commission to inquire into the destruction of the *Gaspee* together with the threat to carry the culprits to England for trial was the proximate cause of the formation of the intercolonial web of committees of correspondence, the activities of which led relentlessly to colonial union and finally to successful collaboration in resisting British rule.

As the burning of the *Gaspee* and succeeding related events thus began a progression of historical causes and effects, constitutional issues and their concomitant arguments arose to warm even more an already heated arena of political and legal debate. Americans, grown accustomed to voicing loud protests against parliamentary acts, responded immediately with needed improvisation against decisions and procedures stemming from king in council. Englishmen, inured now for nearly a century to legislative finality and habituated to the convenience of pressing through parliament bills to relieve private as well as public distress, faced a sizable and unusually serious and perplexing administrative problem. Basically, the difficulties centered around the question: what laws, English or American, might constitutionally, that is to say, legally or justifiably impinge upon the colonists who perpetrated the burning of the *Gaspee* and where properly sat the court which was to administer those laws.

The conflict of English and American laws and jurisdictions actually arose with respect to the *Gaspee* before she was burned. Dudingston had scarcely sailed the schooner into Narragansett Bay early in March, 1772, before he embarked upon a vigorous enforcement program "for the protection of the Trade, and to prevent smuggling." [1] Incidentally, it is not true, as a recent account has it,[2] that Dudingston's tactics were something new to Rhode Islanders. They had met similar measures in 1764 by firing upon a British man-of-war and again in 1769 by burning his majesty's sloop *Liberty*.[3] Now they protested to their elected governor, Joseph Wanton, that "no commander of any vessel had the right to use any authority in the body of the colony without previously applying to the governor, showing his warrant for doing so, and being sworn to a due exercise of his office" because this was the "common custom" of the colony.[4] Wanton adopted this view which he supported strongly in an exchange of letters with Dudingston. As a result a dispute arose as to whose authority was the greater which immediately attained the level of a first-rate quarrel.[5] The controversy was intensified when Dudingston sent for adjudication to Boston a sloop and twelve hogsheads of rum which he had seized in Kent County, Rhode Island. He thereby failed to comply with a recent act of parliament requiring such trials to be held where the seizure took place.[6] Using expediency as his excuse, he ex-

1 Admiral John Montagu to Philip Stephens, secretary to the admiralty, Boston, June 12, 1772, "Gaspee Documents," *Proceedings of the Rhode Island Historical Society, 1890-1891* (Providence, 1891), 81.

2 John C. Miller, *Origins of the American Revolution* (Boston, 1943), 326. Professor Miller not only consistently misspells William Dudingston's name but also cites as authority for some of his statements respecting the *Gaspee* and Dudingston Volume III of the Rhode Island colonial records. *Ibid.*, 325-27, 326 n. Volume III of this source contains no references to the *Gaspee* affair.

3 *Records of the Colony of Rhode Island and Providence Plantations, in New England*, 10 vols. (Providence, 1856-1865), VII, 57-59.

4 *Ibid.*, 60-61.

5 *Ibid.*, 61-64.

6 8 Geo. III, c. 22. The title of the act is: "An act for the more easy and effectual recovery of the penalties and forfeitures inflicted by the acts of parliament relating

plained: "There was only the alternative to send her, or remain in this harbor, and guard twelve hogsheads of rum; a bait, the inhabitants of this government would willingly put in my way, if that could fix the schooner. I was not, at the time, ignorant of the statute to the contrary."[7] For this he was later sued in a civil action in the superior court at East Greenwich, Rhode Island, by the owners of the sloop and rum. The jury awarded the plaintiffs a verdict of £295, damages and costs,[8] which was not reversed in spite of Dudingston's three appeals to higher courts.[9]

Supported in his quarrel with Governor Wanton by Admiral John Montagu, Dudingston's superior officer in New England,[10] there was no let up in his rigorous enforcement policy. He steadily became ever more offensive to the Rhode Islanders as he blustered and swore and mistreated those whom he policed. They accused him of "Stealing Sheep, Hogs, Poultry, &c. from the Farmers round the Bay, and cutting down their Fruit and other Trees for Fire-wood—in a Word, his Behavior was as piratical and provoking that Englishmen could not patiently bear it."[11] Nor was the *Gaspee* the only craft in the king's service obnoxious to the colonies. A story in the Newport paper on June 1, 1772, complained that there were seven "Board of Commissioners Cruisers . . . on this Coast, including the Beaver and Gaspee now in this Harbour. Poor New England!—The Spaniards, taking your Whale-men in the West Indies, and your (pretended) Friends taking and harassing your Trade on your own Coast, and even in your Harbours and little Coves and Creeks!!!"[12]

to the trade or revenues of the British colonies and plantations." It provides in part that after the first day of September, 1768, "all forfeitures and penalties . . . relating to the trade . . . of the British colonies . . . in America, may be prosecuted . . . in any court of vice-admiralty appointed . . . and which shall have jurisdiction within the colony . . . where the cause of such prosecution or suit shall have arisen." Pickering, XXVIII, 70-71.

7 Dudingston to Montagu, May 22, 1772, *Records of the Colony of Rhode Island*, VII, 64-66.

8 Newport *Mercury*, July 27, 1772; Providence *Gazette*, August 1, 1772. Dudingston was not the only one in his position to be sued by irate Rhode Islanders. Robert Keeler, commander of his majesty's ship *Mercury*, was sued in separate suits for an affair which occurred in September, 1772, by the captain, mate, and owner of the vessel Keeler had seized. The jury returned verdicts for the plaintiffs in every case. Providence *Gazette*, March 20, 1773.

9 Unsorted files of cases (State of Rhode Island Archives, Providence).

10 Montagu to Joseph Wanton, Boston, April 8, 1772, *Records of the Colony of Rhode Island*, VII, 62-63.

11 Providence *Gazette*, January 9, 1773.

12 Newport *Mercury*, June 1, 1772.

It was at this time of rising tempers and growing protests that the *Gaspee* on the afternoon of June 9, 1772, chased the sloop *Hannah*, a Providence packet, out of Newport harbor and up the Providence River, "crowding on all the Sail she could make." Tacking too far to port, "the People on board not being acquainted with the River, at Three o'Clock in the Afternoon, she ran on Namquit Point, near Pawtuxet. About Twelve at Night a great number of People in Boats boarded the Schooner, bound the Crew, and sent them ashore, after which they set fire to the Vessel, and destroyed her." [13] Dudingston was the only one wounded by musket and pistol fire, a "Ball passing through one of his Arms, and lodging in the lower Part of his Belly," [14] or, as another account has it, five inches below his navel.[15] "He was immediately taken to Pawtuxet," reported the Providence *Gazette*, "And we are told he is in a fair way to recover." [16] Recover he did. For losing his schooner, he was court-martialed, tried aboard his majesty's ship *Centaur* in Portsmouth harbor, and, on October 14, 1772, honorably acquitted.[17] All of this was faithfully reported in the Rhode Island press together with the story that Dudingston before his trial was "promoted to the rank of captain, by his Majesty's *express command*!" [18]

On June 11 Darius Sessions, deputy governor of Rhode Island, wrote to Wanton at Newport about the attack on the *Gaspee*. Enclosed in his letter were affidavits he had obtained from her crew to prove the diligence of the Rhode Island magistrates in investigating the attack because, said Sessions, "The dangerous tendency of this transaction, is too obvious, to pass over with the least ap-

[13] Providence *Gazette*, June 13, 1772. It seems that the *Gaspee* did not have aboard her regular pilot, one Daggett, who at the time of the *Gaspee's* ill-fated run was on board the *Beaver* sloop of war in Newport harbor. *Ibid.*

[14] *Records of the Colony of Rhode Island*, VII, 77-192, *passim*; "Gaspee Documents," *Proceedings of the Rhode Island Historical Society, 1890-1891*, pp. 80-92, *passim*; Providence *Gazette*, June 13, 1772.

[15] This statement dated August 29, 1839, was made by Ephraim Bowen who claimed to be the last survivor of the party that attacked and burned the *Gaspee*. Bowen said he was 86 years old in 1839. *Records of the Colony of Rhode Island*, VII, 68-73. See also the account given in 1826 by John Mawney who said he helped burn the *Gaspee* in the special capacity of attending physician and who claimed to have dressed Dudingston's wounds aboard the *Gaspee* before he was put ashore. *Ibid.*, 74-76.

[16] Providence *Gazette*, June 13, 1772.

[17] Public Record Office, Court Martials, No. 46, *Proceedings of the Rhode Island Historical Society, 1890-1891*, pp. 85-92, *passim*.

[18] Providence *Gazette*, January 16, 1773; Newport *Mercury*, January 18, 1773; *ibid.*, November 23, 1772.

pearance of neglect." His letter also urged Wanton to issue a proclamation with a large reward since it was the "prevailing opinion of the gentlemen in this quarter [Providence] that it be done."[19] Wanton issued the proclamation at once (June 12), offering one hundred pounds sterling for the "perpetrators of the villainy."[20] This was given wide publicity by the Rhode Island newspapers.[21] Wanton likewise was by no means modest in trying to impress Montagu as well as the Earl of Hillsborough, secretary of state for the colonies, with his assiduous industry as he wrote them of his efforts to "detect and bring to justice the perpetrators of this violent outrage," this "daring insult upon authority."[22] In short, it is easy to agree with an early compiler of a documentary history of the destruction of the *Gaspee*[23] that "Governor Wanton and the officers of the colony would have been satisfied that the authors of the mischief should remain undiscovered; although their duty required them to exhibit great zeal and loyalty on the occasion."[24]

Such zeal and loyalty taxed to the utmost the skill of Wanton and his fellow officials in trying to retain in their own hands both control and authority over all aspects of the *Gaspee* affair. For example, when Montagu raised the question of jurisdiction by asking whether or not the act was "committed on the high seas, or in the body of the county," Wanton rallied the legal forces of the colony to declare that the "admiralty hath no jurisdiction" because when destroyed the *Gaspee* lay aground in a narrow river, was thirty miles from sea, and was therefore within the rule that all ports and havens are *infra corpus comitatus*.[25] Similarly, when the navy under Montagu's command seized and held one Aaron Briggs, a mulatto servant who confessed to participating in the raid on the *Gaspee* and who thereby implicated some of the more prominent citizens of Providence, the colonial magistrates issued a warrant

19 *Records of the Colony of Rhode Island*, VII, 77-78.

20 For an excellent copy of Wanton's proclamation, see the collected papers relating to the *Gaspee* affair (State of Rhode Island Archives).

21 Providence *Gazette*, June 13, 1772, through July 4, 1772; Newport *Mercury*, June 15, 1772, through June 29, 1772.

22 Wanton to Montagu, Newport, June 12, 1772, *Records of the Colony of Rhode Island*, VII, 85; Wanton to Earl of Hillsborough, June 16, 1772, *ibid.*, 190-92.

23 William R. Staples, *The Documentary History of the Destruction of the Gaspee. Comp. for the Providence Journal* (Providence, 1845), 56 pp.

24 *Records of the Colony of Rhode Island*, VII, 92.

25 Montagu to Wanton, Boston, July 8, 1772, *ibid.*, 93; Wanton to Montagu, Newport, July 22, 1772, *ibid.*, 100-101.

for his arrest in an attempt to remove him from the custody of the admiralty to the safer custody of the local officials. But, according to the sheriff's return, when he served the warrant on Captain John Linzee of his majesty's ship *Beaver* aboard which Briggs was detained, Linzee refused to deliver up his prisoner. In this manner did the British navy flout the civil authority of Rhode Island. Then, for detaining his servant, Briggs's master arrested Linzee who was freed from jail only when Montagu went his bail. Finally, when Wanton and friends were unable to force the British to surrender Briggs to them they attempted to discredit his confession by procuring several affidavits to declare that Briggs had not been off Prudence Island for more than a year prior to July 2, 1772, and could not therefore have been a participant in the burning of the *Gaspee*![26]

These preliminary maneuvers between the Admiral and the Rhode Island magistracy to control the *Gaspee* affair merely heralded the more serious collision of laws and jurisdictions yet to come. And yet, as accounts of the burning of the ship reached England, the press there paid little attention.[27] In Providence, however, Joseph Sherwood and Henry Marchant, "late agent for this Colony" who had just returned from England, reported to the Providence *Gazette* that the affair "having been great exaggerated and misrepresented, the Ministry were incensed on the Occasion," but that with the arrival of dispatches from "his Honour the Governor, containing a true Representation of the Facts, the Clamour against the colony had abated, and was almost entirely subsided. . . . The Privy Council was summoned to meet, but when the last vessel sailed, it was not known whether a meeting had been held."[28]

The meeting of the privy council mentioned by Marchant and Sherwood did occur on August 20. Before then, however, Hillsborough, who held the offices of secretary of state for the colonies and president of the board of trade and foreign plantations, had

[26] *Ibid.*, 92-106, *passim.*

[27] Fred J. Hinkhouse, *The Preliminaries of the American Revolution as seen in the English Press, 1763-1775* (New York, 1926), 159. The embarrassment of the British government with respect to the *Gaspee* affair was said to result, according to the Canterbury *Kentish Gazette*, from the great influence of those English merchants who traded with America and who were more concerned with profits than with country. *Ibid.*, 80.

[28] Providence *Gazette*, September 26, 1772.

already determined upon a mode of dealing with the *Gaspee* incident. His plan was inspired apparently by Montagu's letters to him [29] and to the admiralty [30] which pictured in bitterly partisan words the burning of the *Gaspee* and the wounding of Dudingston. Basic to the plan was a recent act of parliament entitled "An act for the better securing and preserving his Majesty's dockyards, magazines, ships, ammunition and stores." It prescribed the death penalty for burning the king's ships and, most important, it authorized suspects to be brought to England for trial or to be tried in the place where the offense was committed "as his Majesty may deem most expedient . . . any law, usage, or custom notwithstanding." [31] Despite contrary conclusions,[32] this act was not one of parliamentary retaliation for the burning of the *Gaspee* on June 10, since it had received the royal assent on April 16, 1772.[33] Nevertheless, such a recent parliamentary act was subject to the charge that it was a new instance of interference with the internal affairs of the colonies — in this case, of explicitly uprooting the rights of the colonies resting upon long established usage, custom, and law. The crown did not rely upon this statute, however; instead, at the meeting of the privy council on August 20 Hillsborough's whole plan was canceled and all letters pertaining to it (which he had already sent through the admiralty) were recalled. At the same time it was agreed to issue a commission of inquiry with the charge of high treason (levying war against the king) as the basis for the investigation.[34] Offenders were thus to be brought to England to

[29] Montagu to Hillsborough, Boston, June 12, July 11, 1772, *Records of the Colony of Rhode Island*, VII, 89, 94-95.

[30] Montagu to Stephens, secretary to the admiralty, Boston, June 12, 30, July 11, 1772, *Proceedings of the Rhode Island Historical Society, 1890-1891*, pp. 81-83.

[31] 12 Geo. III, c. 24. The bill was ordered on March 23, 1772, and the same brought in and prepared by "Lord North, Mr. Ellis, Mr. Attorney General, Mr. Sollicitor General, and Sir Charles Whitworth." *Journals of the House of Commons*, XXXIII, 608.

[32] Sydney G. Fisher, *The Struggle for American Independence*, 2 vols. (Philadelphia, 1908), I, 152-53 n. Incidentally, it is an odd fact that Fisher was the author of a paper entitled "The Legendary and Myth-making Process in Histories of the American Revolution" (Philadelphia, 1912), *Proceedings of the American Philosophical Society* (Philadelphia), LI (April-June, 1912), 53-75.

[33] *Journals of the House of Commons*, XXXIII, 701. On the same day, royal assent was given an act for the more effectual proceeding against persons standing mute on their arraignments for felony or piracy which, unlike 12 Geo. III, c. 24, explicitly referred to America: "And be it further enacted, That the provisions of this act shall extend to his Majesty's colonies and plantations in *America*." 12 Geo. III, c. 20.

[34] E. Thurlow and A. C. Wedderburn to the Earl of Hillsborough, Lincoln's Inn,

be tried under an old statute of Henry VIII instead of under a new statute of George III.[35]

The bases for these decisions of the privy council can best be understood from the papers drawn up by John Pownall, secretary to the board of trade, in preparation for this meeting of the "King's Servants." Pownall had been directed "to attend the Attorney & Solicitor General & to communicate to them such Papers as he apprehends may be useful for their Information upon this Occasion." They consist of a ten-page report entitled "State of the Business of Rhode Island proposed to be considered on Thursday the 20th of August" together with twenty-six appendixes. Some of the appendixes directly support the statements in the report. Others are such "as tend to shew the controuling power which has been exercised by the Crown in different Instances over the Charter and proprietary Governments, & the Opinions of the Law Servants of the Crown touching the Exercise of such Power; as also a precedent of a proceeding in the Privy Council in 1702, in the Case of Bayard & Hutchins tried, convicted & condemned for High Treason in the Province of New York." [36]

The report itself deals with two problems: the first with the manner in which the accused were to be brought to England for trial. Since no precedent permitted prisoners in the plantations to be sent for by warrant unless their names were known and there was information upon oath against them, the usual way was for the secretary of state to write to the governor of the place where they were in custody to deliver them on board the king's ships, "the Lords of the Admiralty giving Orders for their being rec'd on board, & brought over in safe Custody." Also, since 1712, there was a "standing Instruction to all Governors, that no person should be sent prisoner to England without transmitted [*sic*] at the same time full proof of their Guilt."

August 10, 1772, *Gaspee* Papers (Rhode Island Historical Society, Providence); "Gaspee Papers, 1772-1773," *Publications of the Rhode Island Historical Society*, N. S. (Providence), VII (January, 1900), 239-40; Lord Dartmouth to Thomas Gage, Whitehall, September 4, 1772, Thomas Gage Papers (William L. Clements Library, Ann Arbor). This letter directs the return of the correspondence and instructions previously dispatched by Hillsborough through the admiralty.

[35] Dartmouth to Wanton, Whitehall, September 4, 1772, copy enclosed in Dartmouth to Gage, same date, Gage Papers; 35 Henry VIII, c. 2; Providence *Gazette*, July 30, 1774 (an article in this newspaper discusses the whole basis for the court of inquiry together with the governmental policy behind it).

[36] A. C. Wedderburn Papers (William L. Clements Library).

The second problem was "with regard to the prosecution of them in the Colony, either by special Commission or otherwise." There was, it seems, no "precedent of a special Commission of Oyer & Terminer issued under any Authority from hence, in Colonies where Courts of Judicature have already been established." And while there were "many Instances of Commissioners appointed to enquire into & report the State & Condition of Colonies . . . fallen into great Disorder & Confusion," a commission with authority to try and determine "ought to have the Sanction of an Act of Assembly there, or an Act of Parliament here."

These suggestions, discreetly deferential and adroitly tactful, seem to have determined the ministry's approach to the *Gaspee* affair. A commission was appointed, not to hear and determine but to "inquire into and report." All other powers and authority necessary for the inquiry were also granted, such as "to receive informations," to inquire by the examination of witnesses on oath together with the authority to administer such oaths, and to send for such persons, papers, and records that might be useful.[37] In addition to the royal commission there were royal instructions to the commission. It was to communicate to the civil officers and magistrates of Rhode Island such information touching the persons concerned in that daring attack upon "our authority and commission, to the end that they may be accordingly arrested and delivered to the custody of the commander in chief of our ships and vessels in North America, pursuant to such instructions as we have thought fit to give for that purpose."[38] Also, by royal proclamation, rewards of five hundred pounds were offered for capturing any persons who had attacked the *Gaspee* and of one thousand pounds and "our gracious pardon for his said offense" to an accomplice who would betray the leaders and those who shot Dudingston.[39] Finally, it was directed that any disturbance or violence among the colonists ob-

[37] *Gaspee* Papers (State of Rhode Island Archives); copy enclosed in Dartmouth to Gage, September 4, 1772, Gage Papers; printed in *Records of the Colony of Rhode Island*, VII, 108-10. The commission's date is September 2, 1772. *Ibid.*

[38] *Gaspee* Papers (State of Rhode Island Archives); copy enclosed in Dartmouth to Gage, September 4, 1772, Gage Papers; printed in *Records of the Colony of Rhode Island*, VII, 110-12. The date of the instructions is September 4, 1772. *Ibid.*

[39] *Gaspee* Papers (State of Rhode Island Archives), contain an excellent printed copy; transcribed copy enclosed in Dartmouth to Gage, September 4, 1772, Gage Papers; *Records of the Colony of Rhode Island*, VII, 107-108. The substance of the proclamation was accurately reported in the Rhode Island press. Providence *Gazette*, October 24, 1772; Newport *Mercury*, October 26, 1772.

structing the execution of this plan was to be met with military forces sent into the colony "for aiding the civil magistrates in suppressing any tumults or riots, and preserving the public peace." [40]

In late October, 1772, the Rhode Island press carried news of the privy council's actions. Identical accounts in the Providence *Gazette* and the Newport *Mercury* declared with little regard for the truth that a "commission of oyer and terminer has passed the great seal, authorizing and empowering the Governors of New-York and Connecticut, and others named therein, to try any person or persons that may be taken in consequence of the proclamation issued for apprehending any that were concerned in plundering and burning the Gaspee schooner." [41] As Pownall had pointed out in his report, a commission of oyer and terminer was quite different from one to inquire and report because it would require either an act of the Rhode Island assembly or an act of parliament. The newspaper accounts contained errors of omission, too. They seem deliberate. It will have been noticed that these first accounts of the privy council's actions failed to state not only that the governor of Rhode Island was a member of the commission but also that he was to head it, facts, if reported, which would have made the commission more palatable to the Rhode Islanders. And then there were the incidents connected with Lord Dartmouth's letter to Wanton in which the whole plan of the government was outlined and explained. All this was supposed to be kept secret but the "Governor communicated to his Assembly, who got it printed," so that it was published in the "Boston weekly paper" [42] and "spread industriously over all New England." [43] In defending his action, Wanton maintained that he was required by law to lay such matters before the colonial magistracy but Dartmouth rebuked him sharply by replying that although he "could not do otherwise than communicate the Substance of that Dispatch to the other parts of your Corporation, I refer it to your candour whether it was proper to give copies of it?" [44] Equally serious was the fact that the letter

[40] Dartmouth to Gage, Whitehall, September 4, 1772, and enclosures, Gage Papers. Lieutenant General Gage was directed to use his judgment as to numbers and distribution of troops that might be needed! *Ibid.*

[41] Providence *Gazette,* October 24, 1772; Newport *Mercury,* October 26, 1772.

[42] Boston *Massachusetts Spy,* December 31, 1772.

[43] Dan[iel] Horsmanden, chief justice of New York and member of the royal commission of inquiry, to Dartmouth, New York, February 20, 1773, *Records of the Colony of Rhode Island,* VII, 182-85.

[44] Dartmouth to Wanton, Whitehall, April 10, 1773, Collected Letters from 1731 to 1849 (State of Rhode Island Archives).

was edited before it was released to the New England papers. The statement that the offenders were to be brought to England for trial was italicized [45] and so that nothing favorable to the government might be printed the following was omitted:

> As on the one hand, His Majesty expects that all due respect be paid to His Royal Commissions and authority and every countenance and protection given to His Officers in the execution of their duty, so I am commanded to assure you that, on the other hand, His Majesty will not fail to punish with utmost severity, those who shall either wantonly or unnecessarily distress and obstruct the lawful commerce of His subjects in Rhode Island, or shall otherwise injure them in their persons or properties.[46]

Inaccurate and misleading newspaper stories also tended to obscure the real issues. For example, although correct accounts of the commission's authorization, purpose, and personnel together with a correct statement of the proclamation for apprehending those who attacked the *Gaspee* were published toward the end of November, 1772,[47] a month later the press carried stories that Rhode Island was to be invaded by land and sea under the command of Montagu who "is determined to lay Newport and Providence to ashes." [48] Another report declared there were designs "against some

45 Newport *Mercury*, January 11, 1773. The letter was copied from the Boston *Gazette*. On December 25, 1772, Darius Sessions, deputy governor of Rhode Island, Stephen Hopkins, chief justice of Rhode Island, John Brown, and Moses Brown wrote to Samuel Adams regarding the *Gaspee* affair and enclosed an "extract" from Dartmouth's letter to Wanton. The committee of correspondence of Boston in a letter to the committee of correspondence of Cambridge, dated December 29, 1772, sent the "extract" on to that town. The letter first appeared in the Boson *Massachusetts Spy*, December 31, 1772. Hence it may be not unreasonably concluded that the Rhode Islanders edited Dartmouth's letter and then sent it on its journey to the Boston and later to the entire colonial press in their letter to Samuel Adams. See Harry A. Cushing (ed.), *The Writings of Samuel Adams*, 2 vols. (New York, 1906), II, 389 n., 392-94.

46 Dartmouth to Wanton, Whitehall, September 4, 1772, Gage Papers. The only attempt to print the extract above scarcely helped the government's cause: "We hear Lord Dartmouth, Secr. of State for the American Department, in a letter concerning the Gaspee Schooner, has assured his Honour our Governor, that his Majesty will punish in the severest manner any of his servants who shall obstruct the legal trade or in any wise insult and abuse any of his Subjects of this Colony; so that 'tis hoped there will be no more unnecessary firing upon and terrifying the poor, honest, industrious Woodmen, and others who bring the necessaries of life to this Market; nor any more knocking down boatmen, throwing their wood overboard, and cutting down the best wood and timber on private gentlemen's estates; of which almost numberless have been the complaints within 18 months past; tho in justice to the present commanders *here*, we can say we have heard scarce any against them." Newport *Mercury*, January 4, 1773.

47 Providence *Gazette*, November 21, 1772; Newport *Mercury*, November 30, 1772.

48 Providence *Gazette*, December 26, 1772; Newport *Mercury*, December 21, 1772.

considerable number of persons in Providence, &c. who were informed against upon oath, and if taken would be tried, and executed without delay. The ships and troops . . . give dignity and security to the court, and afford a sufficient power to put its judgements into execution. Wo unto the land when the wicked reigneth." [49] By the time the commission actually met in Newport on January 5, 1773,[50] and notices of its official business were published,[51] the press became less abusive toward it. The attacks directed primarily at Montagu continued, however.[52] These studied insults in the press and the refusal of the people to acknowledge officially or otherwise Montagu's authority provoked a reprimand and order from Dartmouth to the governor and company of Rhode Island that "His Majesty's Ships of War . . . having an Admiral's Flag or broad Pennant hoisted, be saluted in such a manner as is usual in all other Parts of His Majesty's Dominions in America." [53]

In addition to carrying inaccurate and misleading stories respecting the *Gaspee* affair, the Rhode Island press rapidly developed arguments against the British government's course of action. John Carter, printer and publisher of the Providence *Gazette*, was radically antagonistic to "British aggression." His paper teemed with patriotic and animating exhortations. Equally radical was Solomon Southwick who printed and published the Newport *Mercury* always with a spirited attack upon British interference with American affairs that was quite consistent with his motto: "Undaunted by TYRANTS — we'll DIE or be FREE!" [54] In their arguments they used a prototype of the modern "agit-prop" (agitation-propaganda) device so familiar to the twentieth century as the basic technique of certain radical groups. A few of the many

[49] Newport *Mercury*, December 28, 1772.

[50] *Records of the Colony of Rhode Island*, VII, 120.

[51] Newport *Mercury*, January 11, 18, 1773.

[52] The Providence *Gazette*, May 8, 1773, reported under London dateline that Admiral Montagu was tarred and feathered on the expedition to Rhode Island and returned to Boston "in a very woful condition." Another said: "Never was a more farcical piece of mock power than that now exhibiting in this American world; an English Admiral with his flag . . . setting out in the dead of winter to vanquish the Rhode-Islanders! who, be assured, are very much diverted at the buffoonery of Punch, who goes over land to Rhode-Island, and is there to hoist his flag aboard one of the ships during the seige. God save great George our King." *Ibid.*, April 24, 1773; Newport *Mercury*, April 26, 1773.

[53] Dartmouth to the Governor and Company of Rhode Island, Whitehall, March 3, 1773, Collected Letters from 1731 to 1849 (State of Rhode Island Archives).

[54] See the appropriate articles in L. E. Rogers (ed.), *The Biographical Cyclopedia of Representative Men of Rhode Island*, 2 vols. (Providence, 1881).

examples must suffice. In spite of the fact that the Rhode Island magistracy did little to apprehend those who burned the *Gaspee*, the methods pursued by the British administration were declared to be much more serious than the burning itself.[55] The commission was labeled "this alarming Star-Chamber," a "court of inquisition, more horrid than that of Spain and Portugal." The colonies, it was reported, "loudly complain of the violence and vexations they suffer by measures more unjustifiable than highway robbery; and applied to the basest purposes, those of supporting *tyrants* and debauchees." The people were urged to "stand forth in the glorious cause of freedom, with a truly Roman spirit of liberty," because "ten thousand deaths, by the halter, or the axe, are infinitely preferable to a miserable life of slavery, in chains, under a pack of worse than Egyptian tyrants who, to gratify their master, the d**l, who is a tyrant, and the father of tyrants and of liars, will glory in making a sacrifice of you and your posterity." [56] The "Duty every Man owes to his Country" was declared to be "above all, to guard against the Introduction of *new and arbitrary Methods of Trial*." [57] The Boston massacre was recalled and the question asked, "What shall hinder a like scene of blood, rapine and slaughter, in the colony of Rhode Island. We have reason, with firm alliance in HIM who hateth oppression and tyranny, devoutly to exclaim, *How long* — O LORD — *How long*!" [58]

Accompanying the "agit-prop" type of argument were those more restrained and very much like those advanced by the opposition in parliament a few years earlier when Lords (December 15, 1768) and Commons (February 8, 1769) passed resolutions and an address to the king asking that those guilty of treason and misprision of treason in Massachusetts Bay be ferreted out "in order that Your Majesty may issue a special Commission for enquiring of, hearing, and determining, the said Offences within this Realm, pursuant to the Provisions of the Statute of the Thirty-fifth Year of the Reign of King *Henry* the Eight." [59] The ministry had contended that by "bringing over the culpable, they hoped to strike a greater terror than any trials could do in that country, where it

[55] Newport *Mercury*, December 28, 1772.

[56] Providence *Gazette*, December 26, 1772; Newport *Mercury*, December 21, 1772.

[57] Providence *Gazette*, April 24, 1773.

[58] *Ibid.*, December 26, 1772, dateline, Boston, December 21.

[59] *Journals of the House of Lords*, XXXII, 210; *Journals of the House of Commons*, XXXII, 186.

would be impossible to get a jury not involved in the same guilt." [60] The opposition countered with the argument that it was "a futile and arbitrary measure; the suddenness of a judgement might have a good effect; but to bring a man a thousand leagues would take some time; when he arrived, and heard what he was charged with, he then must have time to send to North America, for his witnesses. The inhumanity of bringing prisoners so far; the expences even an acquittal must subject them to, and the spirit of the trial by juries of neighbours entirely ruined by such a measure, were urged, and to address the King to do such an injustice must be found odd to the world" since the statute of Henry VIII was "contrary, in its utmost extent, to the spirit of our laws, and not very clearly in force now." [61] Such arguments the Rhode Island press used again and again throughout the winter of 1772-1773 with respect to the *Gaspee* affair.

Connected with these arguments and appearing at the same time though more infrequently was the printing of the Virginia resolves of May 16, 1769, which had been endorsed by the general assembly of Rhode Island on October 25, 1769. The resolves maintained that all trials for treason, crime, and so forth ought of right be held in the courts of the colony where the act had been committed and that sending a person beyond the seas to be tried took away the privilege of being tried by a jury from the vicinage as well as the liberty of summoning and producing witnesses. Much was made also of Massachusetts' protest against the commission given by Charles II in 1664 to Robert Carr and others to hear and determine all complaints and appeals in all causes. Added to these was the prominent printing of the Rhode Island law of March 1, 1663, that "no Freeman shall be taken, or imprisoned, or deprived of his Freehold, or Liberty, or free Custom, or be outlawed, or exiled, or otherwise destroyed, nor shall be passed upon, judged, or condemned, but by the lawful Judgment of his Peers, or by the Law of this Colony." [62] Here then were many ideas both old and new which had been expressed at one time or another in England and

[60] *The History, Debates, and Proceedings of both Houses of Parliament*, 7 vols. (London, 1792), V, 22.

[61] Thomas C. Hansard (comp.), *The Parliamentary History of England from the Earliest Period to the year 1803*, 36 vols. (London, 1806-1820), XVI, 507 ff.; *History, Debates, and Proceedings of both Houses of Parliament*, V, 22 ff.

[62] Providence *Gazette*, December 19, 1772, January 9, 1773; Newport *Mercury*, December 21, 1772, January 18, 1773.

which now when needed were found to be as freshly vigorous and appealing as if they had been flown across the Atlantic in vacuum-packed tins.

Another and perhaps unique example of the migration of English ideas to America occurred in connection with the *Gaspee* affair when John Carter advertised, revised or caused to be revised, published, and distributed a new edition of Henry Care's *English Liberties, or, The free-born Subject's Inheritance.* Care (1646-1688) was a political writer and journalist described in the *Dictionary of National Biography* as a pettifogger in breeding, a little despicable wretch considered to be a poor sniveling fellow because he wrote for the Roman Catholic party. His *English Liberties*, one of thirteen published works, was continued in 1719 as a fourth edition by William Nelson (1653-*ca.* 1720), a legal writer described in the *Dictionary of National Biography* as having great juridical knowledge but lacking in judgment and acumen besides being inaccurate and slovenly. In 1721 a fifth edition was published in Boston by J. Franklin. Carter's proposal to publish by subscription a sixth edition began to appear in his Providence *Gazette* on Saturday, November 7, 1772, and continued through Saturday, January 30, 1773. The advertisements for the book used up a whole column which was one third of a page or one twelfth of the four-page paper. When news of the Tea Act reached America, Carter again advertised his proposed sixth edition beginning on Saturday, July 24, 1773, and continuing through Saturday, September 18, 1773. After the enactment of the intolerable or obnoxious acts in the spring and early summer of 1774, Carter announced in the *Gazette* of August 20, 1774, that *English Liberties* "On Saturday next will be Published by the Printer hereof." On August 27 the paper carried the following notice: "To the Friends of Liberty and Useful Knowledge/ This Day is PUBLISHED, and to be sold by the Printer hereof/ ENGLISH LIBERTIES, or The free-born Subject's Inheritance."

The book was also advertised in each succeeding issue through December 24, 1774, and then intermittently through March 11, 1775, for a total of thirty-eight times from the appearance of the original proposal on November 7, 1772, through March 11, 1775. Undoubtedly this is something of a record. There are, moreover, six unnumbered pages at the back of the book containing the names of 465 subscribers for a total of 642 copies priced at one dollar each.[63] Incidentally, it is a fact showing an amazing correlation of the publishing history of this book with the events of the times that just as the advertisements for *English Liberties* ended, the Providence *Gazette* for March 18, 1775, carried for the first time a "Proposal for Printing by Subscription, an elegant Edition of the MANUAL EXERCISE, as ordered by His MAJESTY in MDCCLXIV, now adopted in Connecticut, Rhode-Island, Massachusetts-Bay, and New-York, Together with PLANS and *Explanations* of REVIEWS, *Field-Days*, &c. Also the various Positions of a SOLDIER under ARMS." And one month later almost to the day the wisdom of substituting for a law book a manual of arms was being tested at Lexington and Concord. The migration of English ideas to America indeed!

The fifth edition of *English Liberties* was the source of much of the argument against the commission of inquiry and against the carrying of persons accused to England for trial. Surprisingly enough, it seemed to rank in usefulness with respect to the *Gaspee* affair far ahead of such better known works as Sir Michael Foster's *Crown Law*, Sir Edward Coke's *Institutes*, and Sir William Blackstone's *Commentaries*.[64] Articles quoting directly from *English Liberties* and very little from other books appeared in many issues of the Providence *Gazette* but most notably and most extensively in the issues of October 31 and November 7, 1772, and January 2, 1773. The fundamental argument from this source may be summarized as follows: that "Tryal by Juries" was an essential felicity to all English subjects, a great jewel of liberty, "deservedly ranked amongst the choicest of our fundamental law, which whosoever shall go about craftily to *undermine*, or openly to *suppress*, and render only a Formality, does *Ipso Facto* attack the government, and brings in an Arbitrary Power, and is an Enemy and Traitor to his King and Country." Moreover, "no man's Life shall be touched for any Crime whatsoever, but upon being found guilty on two several Tryals. That is to say, *Twelve* or more to find the Bill of Indictment against him, and Twelve others to give Judgement

[63] The statement regarding the sixth edition of Henry Care's *English Liberties* in John E. Alden (ed.), *Rhode Island Imprints, 1727-1800* (New York, 1949), 214, contains too few facts adequately to suggest the importance of the book.

[64] See the article signed "Aristides" which quoted from all four of these books. Providence *Gazette*, October 31, 1772.

upon the general issue of *Not Guilty*." [65] Here then is a rare instance indeed for the late eighteenth century of including inquiry by grand jury under the generic term "trial by jury." Its aptness is of course obvious whether the royal commission of the *Gaspee* affair was merely to inquire and report or more completely to hear and determine.

When Carter's sixth edition of Care's *English Liberties* appeared it might be expected, since it was "corrected and improved," that it was substantially different from the fifth edition but this was not the case. True, there were added many forms for justices of the peace and there was omitted material on constables, church-wardens, overseers of the poor, surveyors of the highways, and the like, but there were only four additions of substantial significance. Each of them was a note added at the bottom of the page and, with the exception of citations from two cases, all were excerpts from Blackstone's *Commentaries*.

The first of the excerpts from Blackstone was gruesomely apropos for the perpetrators of the *Gaspee* incident because it described in detail the punishment inflicted on those convicted of high treason. It told how the offender was drawn to the gallows, hanged by the neck, cut down, and, while still alive, had his entrails removed and burnt, and finally how his head was cut off and his body divided into four parts to be thereafter at the disposal of the king. The other three excerpts from Blackstone reiterated the importance of the writ of habeas corpus (presumably unavailable to those shipped to England for trial), declared every tribunal erected for the decision of facts without the intervention of a jury to be a step toward establishing aristocracy, and insisted that all judges should rely strongly on the jury summoned from the vicinage and not try to "lead it by the nose" because a man cannot see by another's eye, nor hear by another's ear.[66] Thus, while only four additions of substantial significance were made in the American sixth edition of Care's *English Liberties*, they were arguments which were unusually clear, sharply to the point, and most uncompromising toward the government's administrative policy.

Supplementary as well as complementary to the arguments appearing in the press and in *English Liberties* was a sermon of in-

[65] The quotations in the newspapers were accurate. See pp. 200-203 in the fifth edition and pp. 212-16 in the sixth edition of Care's *English Liberties*.

[66] Care, *English Liberties* (6th ed.), 78 n., 183 n., 216 n., 233 n.

fluential value delivered by John Allen at the Second Baptist Church in Boston on Thanksgiving Day, December 3, 1772.[67] The sermon answered directly Lord Dartmouth's letter to Governor Wanton which was, much to the chagrin of its author, edited and published in Boston soon after Wanton had received it. According to Frederick Smyth, one of the commissioners in the *Gaspee* investigation, this "Seditious preacher harrangned [*sic*] his congregation, by means of which the alarm was effectually given, and the utmost horror excited in the minds of the people against the means intended to be taken by Government in the cause of Public Justice." [68] Published under the title *An Oration on the Beauties of Liberty, or the Essential Rights of the Americans*, it went to a fourth edition in Boston and to a third edition in New London in 1773. There was even a Wilmington edition of 1775.

The published sermon begins with a dedication to the Earl of Dartmouth containing the first of two arguments. The responsibility for the government's action in the *Gaspee* affair is recognized as the ministry's but, it is asserted, whether it is the king, ministry, or parliament none has the right to take any action because the "laws of America only are broke" and not any of the laws of England. Indeed, if any laws were broken, then the king and ministry broke them by sending the *Gaspee* to America which they had no more right to do than to send her to Brest. The king, having no hereditary, parliamentary, or conqueror's right to rule in America, "can have no more right over *America* than what the people have, by compact, invested him with." Since this investment of kingly power was basic American law then only American laws can be applied in the *Gaspee* affair.[69] Here the dedication ends.

The sermon begins right at the point where the dedication ends and without pause opens up the second argument. Many biblical passages are cited to prove that the king receives all his power and majesty from the people. The law exists for the people who are to be tried by it and by a jury of their own peers which is particularly the "*Charter Right* of the *Rhode-Islanders*, whereby the Governor of the province, the Judges of the Superior Court, the House of

[67] Providence *Gazette*, December 19, 1772.

[68] Frederick Smyth to Lord Dartmouth, New York, February 8, 1773, *Gaspee* Papers (Rhode Island Historical Society).

[69] *An Oration on the Beauties of Liberty, or the Essential Rights of the Americans* (3rd ed., Boston, 1773), xiv-xxii.

Representatives, are solemnly bound by *oath* to maintain, to rule, govern, decide cases, and determine ONLY by their own laws." Judges must have no salaries from the crown or they will become slaves of ministerial power. Moreover, "*it is not rebellion* to oppose any King, Ministry, or Governor, that destroys by any violence or authority whatever, the Rights of the People." And "FINALLY. Let all lovers of Liberty, truth and justice now unite as one man in recovering and finally establishing the Liberties of America: That the *American* Parliament may enjoy every power and privilege the *English* Parliament enjoy." [70]

The importance of these two arguments thus linked together is difficult to exaggerate not only because they were widely disseminated but also because only here is there to be found a complete resolution of the basic conflict of laws and jurisdictions inherent in the *Gaspee* affair. The result was obtained by the creation, in theory, of two separate and distinct juridical areas to which the respective laws of each were confined and outside of which were to have no force and effect. It was therefore a constitutional repugnance to carry offenders committing crimes in America to England to be tried according to the foreign laws there obtaining. It is noteworthy that the argument and conclusion produced here rivals that of another New Englander, Joseph Story, who established the modern Anglo-American doctrine of the conflict of laws by exalting the territorial exclusiveness of the laws of each state to absolute supremacy. Also, it is an interesting fact that both Allen and Story, although writing nearly sixty years apart, rested their conclusions ultimately not upon narrowly legal but upon broadly political concepts.[71]

Incidentally, in another pamphlet, Allen replied to Thomas Hutchison's well-known aphorism that no line could be drawn between the supreme authority of parliament and the total independence of the colonies. Here again Allen leaves no doubt that total independence did not mean to him total independence from the crown but instead total independence from parliament to be achieved by establishing a supreme American parliament.[72] Along

[70] *Ibid.*, 47-63.

[71] See William R. Leslie, "The Influence of Joseph Story's Theory of the Conflict of Laws on Constitutional Nationalism," *Mississippi Valley Historical Review* (Cedar Rapids), XXXV (September, 1948), 203-20, *passim.*

[72] See the essay entitled "To his Excellency the Governor of the Province of the Massachusetts-Bay," *The American Alarm, or the Bostonian Plea, For the Rights and*

with this specific rationalization in Allen's pamphlets was a general sentiment expressed in the press strongly favorable toward the "*Union of the Colonies* which is now taking place" because it "is big with the most important advantages to this continent." [73] In other words, the desire to gather information "particularly of the principles and authority on which was constituted a Court of Enquiry, held in Rhode Island" not only led to the establishment under Virginia's leadership of the interprovincial committees of correspondence but also provided a strong impetus to and merged with the growing aspiration for a union of the colonies equipped with a supreme American parliament totally independent of and, under the crown, coequal with the British parliament.[74]

In addition to the arguments which appeared in the Rhode Island press, in Care's *English Liberties*, and in Allen's pamphlets, was the stand taken by those who refused to appear before the king's commissioners when summoned to do so. Most prominent among these were George Brown, John Cole, and Daniel Hitchcock, all lawyers, who were cited to appear at Newport on January 20, 1773. At first they refused to make any answer at all to the summons because, they said, the commissioners were not a court vested with any legal powers and therefore even the least notice taken of their summons would be a partial acknowledgment of their jurisdiction. As lawyers, they thought that would be "an eternal Infamy on those, who ought to be acquainted with the Principles of the Constitution." They also declared that a power to command without being endued by legal sanction with the authority to execute the command was unknown in British law. Only the civil authority of Rhode Island, they maintained, had the legal right to inquire into the *Gaspee* affair.[75] And yet in spite of their taking initially so strong a position against the commission, these same men did on the very next day (January 20, 1773) write to the commission disclaiming any pertinent knowledge respecting the burning of the *Gaspee* but insisting they would swear on oath to such knowledge as they did possess only before the civil authority in Providence.[76] Then on

Liberties of the People. Humbly Addressed to the King and Council, and to the Constitutional Sons of Liberty in America (Boston, 1773), 2 ff.

73 Providence *Gazette*, June 12, 1773.

74 *Ibid.*, May 15, 22, June 5, 12, 1773; Newport *Mercury*, June 14, 1773.

75 John Cole, G. Brown, and Dan Hitchcock to Stephen Hopkins, East Greenwich, January 19, 1773, *Gaspee* Papers (Rhode Island Historical Society).

76 *Records of the Colony of Rhode Island*, VII, 155-58.

June 3 and 5, respectively, Cole and Brown actually appeared before the commission at Newport and made sworn statements.[77]

The consequence of Cole's appearance before the commissioners was immediate because his acquiescence in the jurisdiction of the court of inquiry was thought to be inconsistent with his recent appointment by the general assembly to the Rhode Island committee of correspondence. At the annual town meeting in Providence for the election of officers, June 7, 1773, a motion was made that the town instruct its representatives in the colonial assembly to displace Cole on the committee of correspondence because he had "in a very flagrant Manner, shamefully violated and betrayed the Faith and Confidence reposed in him by his Country, in yielding Obedience to a Mandate from the Commissioners of Enquiry at Newport, and answering them on Oath, thereby fully acknowledging their Jurisdiction, and endeavouring to counteract the laudable Design of the House in appointing said Committee." Although no vote was had on the motion, John Carter reported the incident in the Providence *Gazette*, taking the occasion to declare that Daniel Hitchcock and Arthur Fenner, clerk of the superior court, had done "themselves high Honour, in nobly refusing to pay [the court of inquiry] the least Regard. — These two Gentlemen are *not* of the Committee!"[78]

These slurring remarks with their obvious implications prompted Cole in retaliation to prefer to the grand jury of Providence county a bill of indictment charging Carter with a "false, scandalous and malicious Libel." Carter's countercharge accused Cole of an "extraordinary attempt to destroy the Liberty of the Press, a matter of great Expectations, and did not fail to alarm the Friends of Freedom; their apprehensions however soon subsided, the honest Jury having returned the Bill IGNORAMUS. The Grand Jury on this Occasion discharged their Duty in a Manner truly honourable to themselves."[79]

The extreme position taken by Carter, the "Friends of Freedom," and those who refused even the least acknowledgment of the jurisdiction of the court of inquiry was not dissimilar from that taken by very respectable persons in England at a later time. In 1850, for example, Oxford University refused to admit the legality of a

[77] *Ibid.*, 170, 172-73.
[78] Providence *Gazette*, June 12, July 19, 1773.
[79] *Ibid.*, June 26, July 3, 1773.

commission of inquiry appointed by the crown with respect to the state, discipline, studies, and revenues of the university and colleges of Oxford. In the ensuing controversy no less personages than Sir John Dodson, advocate general, Sir A. J. E. Cockburn, attorney general, and Sir W. P. Wood, solicitor general, agreed that commissioners appointed to hear and inquire into offenses without determining them was a course of proceeding unknown to and contrary to the law because, quoting Lord Coke, "a man may be unjustly accused by false evidence, and shall not have any remedy." [80]

That later law officers of the crown thus confirmed the earlier American objections to the Rhode Island commission of inquiry in 1773 has its chief significance, perhaps, in justifying at least in part the American appeal to arms to prevent any recurrence of such inquiries. It is true, of course, that the Rhode Island commission of inquiry was unable from January 5 to June 22, 1773, to obtain sufficient evidence respecting the burning of the *Gaspee* to support the arrest and detention for trial of a single person.[81] Also, the lords of the privy council when considering the Boston port bill refrained from signing warrants for apprehending principal American "Incendiaries" for trial and execution in England only "because the attorney and solicitor general were in doubt whether the evidence was sufficient to convict them." [82] Nevertheless, the purpose of the government was clear. As Lord Mansfield said, "Things will never be right until some of them are brought over." [83] The government, moreover, never had any doubt as to what was the proper jurisdiction for bringing American offenders to justice. As

[80] *Report of His Majesty's Commissioners to Inquire into the State, Discipline, Studies, and Revenues of the University and Colleges of Oxford* (London, 1852), XXII, No. 1482, Appendix, 25, 32, quoted in Hugh M. Clokie and J. William Robinson, *Royal Commissions of Inquiry: The Significance of Investigations in British Politics* (Stanford University and London, 1937), 84 n. Sir Edward Coke's argument with respect to oaths administered by any commission runs as follows: "An oath is so sacred, and so deeply concerneth the consciences of Christian men, as the same cannot be administered to any unless the same be allowed by the common law or by some Act of Parliament. It is called a corporal oath, because he toucheth with his hand some part of the holy Scripture." Edward Coke, *The Third Part of the Institutes of the Laws of England* (4th ed., London, 1669), 165.

[81] "The Report of the Commissioners, &c., to the King," *Records of the Colony of Rhode Island*, VII, 178-82.

[82] Peter O. Hutchinson (ed.), *The Diary and Letters of His Excellency Thomas Hutchinson*, 2 vols. (Boston, 1884, 1886), I, 183, 219; cf. Lewis Einstein, *Divided Loyalties: Americans in England during the War of Independence* (London, 1933), 142.

[83] Hutchinson (ed.), *Diary and Letters of His Excellency Thomas Hutchinson*, I, 219.

in the case of the *Gaspee* affair, they could be "indicted of High Treason either here or in Rhode Island." [84] Thus the government saw no actual conflict of laws or of jurisdictions beyond that which required merely an administrative decision. Indeed, only from the British point of view was this a simple problem requiring merely an administrative decision — a point of view which occasionally finds expression even today when it describes in a superficial way the thought and expression of the American problem during the revolutionary period as being exceedingly simple and its contemporary discussion as being very trite.[85] The British did not recognize the oneness of American territorial area and hence did not accept the idea of American territorial exclusiveness. Instead, the report submitted to the privy council on August 20, 1772, by John Pownall shows that the British acknowledged as valid a commission of oyer and terminer regardless of whether it was established by a colonial assembly or by parliament and that likewise they thought courts already erected were equally competent to try offenders regardless of whether the courts were in the colonies or in England. With the same simplicity the Pownall report pointed the way to and affirmed the validity of the commission of inquiry set up by the crown whose work, if successful, could only result in the transportation to England for trial those accused of participating in the *Gaspee* affair. This cut deep and wide into areas claimed by Americans to be their exclusive concern and so touched off fundamental constitutional arguments. Because of their simple approach to the problem, the British on the one hand failed to understand American legal and political, that is to say, constitutional formulae which were produced because the Americans on the other hand were so very cognizant of the fact that the British instead of solving had raised difficult problems of conflicts in both legal and jurisdictional spheres. At the same time, it was the simplicity of the British view that gave their legal and jurisdictional ideas great strength — a strength against which no American argument could, or, indeed, did prevail except the ulimate recourse to arms.

84 Thurlow and Wedderburn to the Earl of Hillsborough, Lincoln's Inn, August 10, 1772, *Gaspee* Papers (Rhode Island Historical Society). See also Wedderburn's comments in the parliamentary debate on the bill for the administration of justice in Massachusetts Bay. Hansard (comp.), *Parliamentary History of England,* XVII, 1206-1207.

85 Max Beloff (ed.), *The Debate on the American Revolution, 1761-1783* (London, 1949), 5 n.

Even though no American arguments short of war prevailed, they who discussed the *Gaspee* affair should be given much credit for seeing so clearly the realities of sharp conflicts of laws and jurisdictions. Their discussions produced constitutional formulae which were a very long step toward the creation of a federal system because there was evolved through argument the first prerequisite to such a system, namely, the theory of two mutually exclusive legal and jurisdictional spheres encompassing the same area. This conceptual image appeared in many forms, as we have seen, in the literature relating to the *Gaspee* affair, but its basic outline was always the same. Its significance is quite substantial because it emerged with unusual clarity no matter by whom or in what mode it was presented. The unusual clarity of the image has in turn a greater significance because of the fact that the image was finally clothed with juridical substance when the present American Constitution was adopted. The *Gaspee* affair, therefore, has a most important place in the conceptual development of the American constitutional system.

Edward Channing's "Great Work" Twenty Years After

By John A. DeNovo

Twenty years after his death Edward Channing seems assured of a niche in the historians' Hall of Fame as one of the giants of American historiography. The nature of his accomplishment deserves examination, for he did not father a "school" of history as did his illustrious Harvard colleague, Frederick Jackson Turner, nor did he develop an arresting interpretive approach to American history which helps to explain the respect paid the names of Charles Beard and Hermann E. von Holst. Channing's claim to eminence rests largely on his six-volume *History of the United States* which covers American history from its beginnings through the Civil War.[1] This monumental work is still of sufficient popularity that the publishers have kept it in print. The "Great Work," as the *History* came to be known in Channing's inner circle, may well be the last effort by one man to write a comprehensive general history of the United States. The sources and monographs to be digested are now so vast that an average lifetime does not seem sufficiently long for a scholar to make the attempt.

Channing gambled with fate by waiting until he was nearly fifty years old before he published the first volume of his general history, but the period of waiting was far from idle.[2] During his early years

[1] Edward Channing, *A History of the United States*, 6 vols. (New York, 1905-1925): I, *The Planting of a Nation in the New World, 1000-1660* (1905); II, *A Century of Colonial History, 1660-1760* (1908); III, *The American Revolution, 1761-1789* (1912); IV, *Federalists and Republicans, 1789-1815* (1917); V, *The Period of Transition, 1815-1848* (1921); VI, *The War for Southern Independence, 1849-1865* (1925). A seventh volume carrying the *History* to the end of the nineteenth century was not ready for the press at the time of Channing's death. The original plan called for an eighth volume on twentieth-century America.

[2] For a more elaborate account of Channing's ancestry, education, and early career, see two revealing sketches, one by his distinguished former student Samuel E. Morison, "Edward Channing: A Memoir," Massachusetts Historical Society *Proceedings* (Boston), LXIV (May, 1931), 250-84; the other by his friend George P. Winship, "Edward

of teaching he conducted enormous researches, occasionally publishing his findings,[3] and he oriented himself philosophically by considering the nature of history and the historian's function in society.[4] Thus he came to his great work thoroughly trained in the techniques it demanded and matured in his thought about the nature of the task he was undertaking.

In aiming to cover the entire sweep of American history, Channing realized clearly that he was attempting an ambitious project which no other historian had lived to complete. Since the years remaining to him might be short, he set about revising the pattern of his life by giving up practically all commitments that did not contribute to the goal he had set. He gave up church attendance, since Sundays were needed for work; he wrote few articles, and attended few meetings of scholarly societies; he turned down proffered exchange professorships and withdrew from Harvard administrative affairs; he consciously caused himself to be regarded as a "social liability" by hostesses and "organizers of good causes." Only by devoting himself wholeheartedly to the *History* was he able to carry it through the Civil War.[5]

The years of preparation had sufficed to crystallize his fundamental assumptions about American history. Some commentators, complaining that they miss an integrating theme in his *History* which might give it coherence and unity, have not found a current to guide them "through the labyrinth of detail" to some culmination.[6] If Channing's writing lacks a controlling theme it was certainly not because he lacked a personal conception as to the larger

Channing," Allen Johnson, Dumas Malone, and Harris E. Starr (eds.), *Dictionary of American Biography*, 21 vols. and index (New York, 1928-1944), XXI, 166-68.

[3] George W. Robinson (comp.), *Bibliography of Edward Channing* (Cambridge, 1932), contains a complete list of Channing's writings from the major volumes through short unsigned articles and comments which appeared in *Science* (Cambridge), Massachusetts Historical Society *Proceedings*, and elsewhere. There is an introduction by Lawrence S. Mayo.

[4] A concise formulation of his opinions on the nature of history and of the historian's task is found in Edward Channing, "The Present State of Historical Writing in America," American Antiquarian Society *Proceedings* (Worcester), N. S., XX (October, 1910), 427-34. This is one of three articles under the same heading. The others are by J. Franklin Jameson, *ibid.*, 408-19, and by John B. McMaster, *ibid.*, 420-26.

[5] Morison, "Edward Channing," Massachusetts Historical Society *Proceedings*, XLIV (May, 1931), 281-83; Winship, "Edward Channing," *Dictionary of American Biography*, XXI, 167.

[6] Ralph R. Fahrney, "Edward Channing," William T. Hutchinson (ed.), *The Marcus W. Jernegan Essays in American Historiography* (Chicago, 1937), 305, 312.

meaning of American history. He informs the reader in the preface "that the most important single fact in our development has been the victory of the forces of union over those of particularism."[7]

Furthermore, in his view of American history, Channing was avowedly influenced by the evolutionary climate of opinion of his day. The social scientists were applying their versions of Darwinian thought to the study and analysis of the social structure. Channing found himself carried into this current of thought as early as his undergraduate days "when evolution was the chief basis of intellectual discussion, when Henry Adams was trying to be thrilled by it and John Fiske was thrilling and shocking his audiences by it."[8]

Channing thus came to think of American history as an evolutionary development and wrote his history with this fundamental idea in mind. Again we turn to his preface where he tells us: "The guiding idea in the present work is to view the subject as the record of an evolution, and to trace the growth of the nation from the standpoint of that which preceded rather than from that which followed."[9]

Closely associated with the evolutionary concept of American development in Channing's writing is a belief in progress. The victory of the forces of union over those of particularism is an indication of this progress. Again he bares this belief when he sees "in the annals of the past the story of living forces, always struggling onward and upward toward that which is better and higher in human conception."[10]

Furthermore, an "Unseen Hand" seems to guide this progress.[11] Some "Higher Power" apparently destined the Anglo-Saxon peo-

[7] Channing, *History*, I, v-vi. He continues: "It is essential that the forces and institutions which have made for disunion should be treated at length and in a sympathetic spirit; but it is even more necessary that the forces and institutions which have made for union should be constantly borne in mind and brought to the attention of the reader, for it is the triumph of these which has determined the fate of the nation."

[8] Carl R. Fish, "Edward Channing, America's Historian," *Current History* (New York), XXXIII (March, 1931), 866-67.

[9] Channing, *History*, I, vi.

[10] *Ibid.*

[11] Channing was not a particularly religious man, although he had been reared as a Unitarian. See Morison, "Edward Channing," Massachusetts Historical Society *Proceedings*, LXIV (May, 1931), 281. It should be said that Channing was far too conscientious a historian to explain many historical episodes and movements solely in terms of Providence. The idea, however, appears in enough different places in his writing to treat it as one of the currents of interpretation underlying his writing.

ples for a mission in the world. At least, the implication is strong that this explains in part why the French and Spaniards were eased out of North America by the English.[12] Fate, or whatever name Channing would give to this deterministic force, used George III as a tool to further this upward progression by making use of his obstinancy to lead the American colonies to revolt from England.[13]

Once the new nation began to pursue its independent course, "destiny" again seemed to decree that it should expand across a continent. The Louisiana Purchase is the key to this growth, for without it "there would have been no Missouri Compromise, no Texas annexation, no Mexican War, no Oregon boundary!"[14] Again, when the conflict of the Civil War threatened to tear the nation asunder the forces of union again triumphed over those of localism, and this time the "God-inspired" Lincoln was the instrument by which the desirable result was achieved.[15] Sometimes Providence does not guide with a purposeful hand, however; then Channing calls the blind force "chance." It was chance that won for Jefferson the election of 1800, and that has decided many issues in war.[16]

His belief in progress appears to have been somewhat, but not entirely, shaken by the 1920's. In the years since he had begun to publish, the "Wonderful Century," as he called it, had joined the limbo of the past.[17] A terrible World War with attendant revolutions created doubts for him. To what was the industrial evolution of the world and of the United States, in particular, leading? When he delivered his presidential address before the American Historical Association in 1920, he took "An Historical Retrospect" in which he surveyed the century just past. He ended his remarks on a note of questioning:

> In all this, in the evolution of the greatest industrial society that the world

[12] Channing, *History*, I, 110; II, 142. The "Unseen Hand" appears in connection with the Quebec expedition of the American Revolution, *ibid.*, III, 226; and in connection with John Brown, *ibid.*, VI, 222.

[13] *Ibid.*, III, 30-31.

[14] *Ibid.*, IV, 335. Without the Louisiana Purchase "The Kansas-Nebraska Act would never have been passed and there would have been no struggle for Kansas! Indeed there would have been no War for Secession with its attendant orgies of Reconstruction. But the star of destiny otherwise determined, and it is not the function of history to question."

[15] *Ibid.*, VI, 255, 295.

[16] *Ibid.*, IV, 211, 525.

[17] *Ibid.*, V, 1.

has ever seen, have we gained or have we lost? Are men and women today happier and better off, politically, spiritually, mentally, morally, and physically, than our ancestors were in the days of James Monroe, John Quincy Adams, John C. Calhoun, Henry Clay, Daniel Webster, and Andrew Jackson?[18]

If taken alone, these ideas implicit in Channing's writing—his belief that the triumph of union was "the most important single fact in our development," his belief in an upward evolution guided by Providence—would give a distorted picture of his view of historical development. It will, therefore, be necessary to fill in the gaps by sketching his other attitudes which temper the impressions given so far.

Channing left much room in his scheme of American history for the interaction of conflicting interests, especially those of a political and economic nature.[19] Eternal compromise was the way in which these divergent desires were reconciled.[20] Similarly, the free will of men shaped developments at many points. One way in which men show their influence is through propaganda efforts by which they find it possible to influence their fellows to achieve certain results.[21]

Some individuals change the course of events. Prominent figures, Jefferson, for example, exert an influence on events, but are, at the same time, victims of chance.[22] Whatever Channing concluded was the place of historical figures, he was a master in evaluating them succinctly. Often a single, compressed sentence gives a perspicacious

[18] Edward Channing, "An Historical Retrospect," *American Historical Review* (New York), XXVI (January, 1921), 202.

[19] By the time Channing published his sixth volume (1925), his point of view showed signs of broadening, although his *History* is preponderantly political and economic. In 1925 he wrote: "A quarter of a century ago or a third of a century ago, it was customary to lay great stress on the influence of economic factors; now it is more often the case to emphasize the sociological or psychical change that is wrought by changed modes of living and by the general operation of economic factors. Possibly the best way to analyze problems of progress or of change in human outlook would be to combine all these various factors into one, for surely one's mode of living exercises a very important influence on one's mode of thinking." Channing, *History*, VI, 383.

[20] "But History proceeds by compromise, and the annals of America have furnished no exception to this rule." *Ibid.*, III, 497.

[21] "From the time of Peter the Hermit to Theodore Roosevelt and Woodrow Wilson, mankind has been ruled by the propagandist. Whether right or wrong, he has only to shout loudly enough or write virulently enough and public opinion sooner or later will turn in his favor." *Ibid.*, VI, 113.

[22] "Jefferson's misfortunes were partly due to himself, but they were more especially the result of circumstances over which he had or could have little control. His idealism and the actualities of American political life had no continuing points of contact." *Ibid.*, IV, 347.

insight into a man's place in American history. For example, William Penn "was an idealist whom chance placed at the head of a great business enterprise, and he experienced the fate that befalls the dreamer when he has to do with actualities";[23] and "James Monroe was one of those men of persistent mediocrity from whom useful and attractive Presidents have been made." [24] Sometimes his judgments seem unfair and overdrawn, as in the case of James I who "turned out to be one of those curiosities whom the laws of inheritance occasionally bring to the notice of mankind." [25]

Channing strove hard, not always with success, to consider individuals and movements in terms of their own times. He obviously did not like Queen Isabella, but he tried to consider her in the light of her age.[26] The persecution of witches and the cruel punishments typical of colonial times could not, he felt, be evaluated in terms of his own twentieth-century environment. Instead, he tried to show how they fit into the attitudes of the seventeenth and eighteenth centuries.[27] Yet a sympathetic approach did not mean to Channing that he must approve of individuals and movements he did not like. His *History* is not without its moral judgments, and it is not entirely clear to the reader whether he realized when he was betraying a bias. That he occasionally fell into the pitfalls he warned against is not surprising.

Channing's humility compels admiration for the man who spent a lifetime trying to portray the past truthfully and yet realized how imperfectly this could be done. It was only with trepidation that he launched his *History*, knowing as he did the immensity of

[23] *Ibid.*, II, 103.

[24] *Ibid.*, IV, 314.

[25] *Ibid.*, I, 140. See his laudatory comments on Alexander Hamilton, *ibid.*, IV, 66, 65-88 *passim.* Short evaluations of Captain William Kidd appear, *ibid.*, II, 270; also of Washington, *ibid.*, 559; IV, 33-34; of John Quincy Adams, *ibid.*, 552; and of John Brown, *ibid.*, VI, 221.

[26] "In bigotry and duplicity she outran the standard of her time; but the student must be prepared to see and not to be misled by what is unpleasant if he wishes to penetrate deeply into the doings of the men and women of the fifteenth and sixteenth centuries." *Ibid.*, I, 19.

[27] *Ibid.*, 249-50. See also *ibid.*, II, 392-93, 456; III, 571-72. "It is one of the easiest things in the world to judge a nation's actions, or the doings of individuals, by the standards of other times and the successes of other men. One of the commonest animadversions of students of American history is to set forth in darkest colors the inertness of the revolutionists, the inefficiency of congresses and the members thereof, and to conjecture as to what a Napoleon or a Frederick would have done in the place of Washington, Howe, or Clinton. These are matters beyond the historian's ken. He must take nations, congresses, and generals as he finds them." *Ibid.*, 223.

the materials, the subjective element involved, "and the opportunity for error." [28] As he came to knotty problems that his best efforts could not unravel, he commented that "Few things are harder to unravel or more easy to exaggerate than the interplay of institutional factors, and it is not easy to disentangle the institutions of one people from those of another." [29] The reader finds similar doubts in each of his volumes. "It is impossible for any man within the scope of a single lifetime to master even a tithe of this material, and yet, some of the most important papers are still almost inaccessible." [30] "So much always goes on under the surface that is unknown to contemporaries and to historians that in a case of this kind one is forced to descend from fact to deduction." [31]

Aside from the big ideas implicit in the work as a whole, Channing's *History* abounds in little glimpses of the man among the facts. Sometimes he generalizes from his facts. Sometimes he speaks out in his own person, commenting in a way not directly concerned with the subject matter. Again, the reader of the volumes sees the great teacher with the provocative suggestions for further research.

Occasionally Channing's generalizations make the reader raise his eyebrows. From the 1952 vantage point the explanation Channing gives for the drinking habits of the 1760's demonstrates a completely false logic: "In the absence of excitation through the medium of the opera and the drama, the automobile and the aeroplane, our ancestors sought to refresh their spirits and re-create their flagging energies by drinking enormous quantities of cider, beer, wine, and rum." [32] It is to be readily conceded that the canons as to what is good art or good literature are relative, but it is perhaps safe to say that Channing's literary tastes left something to be desired when he could conclude that "In short, this half-century [1800-1850] in the United States in poetry, in fiction, and in history stands apart, — it is without an equal since the days of Shakespeare, Francis Bacon, and John Milton." [33]

Examples of Channing's comments in his own person are numer-

[28] *Ibid.*, I, vii.

[29] *Ibid.*, 438.

[30] *Ibid.*, III, 25.

[31] *Ibid.*, IV, 560. Statements similar in tone are available, *ibid.*, II, 125; IV, 180, 196-97, 413; V, 305, 578; VI, 256-57, 273-78, 315, 365, 495, 584, 601.

[32] *Ibid.*, III, 91-92.

[33] *Ibid.*, V, 305.

ous. As a prelude to a consideration of the social ferment of the early nineteenth century, he notes the effect of the wars of the French Revolution and Napoleon. After granting that war is a frightful scourge, he tries to see the beneficent results growing out of it. The readjustments it forces in social relationships, in political affairs, and in the mental outlooks of nations lead "to new thoughts and groupings; and humanity leaps from one stage of civilization to another." [34]

Later in Volume V, when discussing the Panic of 1837, he mentions the poor harvest that played a part in bringing about the crisis. This leads him to reflections as to the scientific connection between sunspots and crop failures, together with the observation "that the crises of 1837 and 1857 synchronized with a maxima of sun spots." [35]

There is no way of measuring the influence which Channing's suggestive hints for further research may have had, but they show a mind alert on topics that would increase our knowledge. For example, a discussion of colonial commerce leads Channing into the observation that "A most interesting essay might be written on the education of the European palate for foreign foods and drinks, and especially on the part played by tea, coffee, sugar, and rum in molding the fate of races and of empires." [36] Later, he throws out the suggestion that the modern history of cotton remains to be written and that few commodities "have so greatly influenced modern life" as the cotton plant.[37]

[34] *Ibid.*, 2-3. The full quotation is as follows: "In itself, war is a frightful scourge; but in its effects it oftentimes has produced most beneficent results. Wars and revolutions lead to readjustments in social relations, in political affairs, and in the mental outlook of nations and of races. Ordinarily, our rules and regulations, our ordinances, and our laws are directed to the preservation of human life, to the protection of individual liberties, and to the conservation of property. In war, on the other hand, our design is to kill, to destroy, and to make existence painful to men and women on the other side of the boundary line. In such times, the mind breaks adrift from its everyday moorings and turns to thoughts and theories that in peaceful hours seemed fantastic and incapable of attainment. War leads to a loosening of the mind, to a breaking of associations, to new thoughts and groupings; and humanity leaps from one stage of civilization to another."

[35] *Ibid.*, 457. "It is not impossible that a dimunition of solar activity influences agricultural production and thus affects all human activities."

[36] *Ibid.*, II, 508-509.

[37] "Few things in this World have so greatly influenced modern life as the fibre of the upland cotton plant. The development of the demand for cotton goods throughout the world is one of the extraordinary phenomena of the nineteenth century." *Ibid.*, V, 407. Cotton "changed the whole course of economic and social existence in the South and, indeed, governed the course of history of the United

Channing's position on the leading controversies of American history can be illustrated by two examples dealing with different periods of time. The first illustration concerns his view of the colonial period, and the second concerns his view of the role played by the frontier in the nineteenth century.

Channing published his three volumes on the colonial period between 1905 and 1912. In them he strove to use the approach, still new at the time he wrote, that the colonies were integral parts of the British Empire.[38] He sought to avoid the traditional method of American historians who treated "the colonists as living a life somewhat apart from the rest of mankind."[39] His study of the Tudor and Stuart periods was excellent preparation for understanding the place of the American colonies as part of a larger whole. In 1660 "The colonists were still Englishmen in their feelings and prejudices, in their virtues and in their vices."[40] The next century saw a change, however, which Channing attributed largely to Restoration policies in England.[41] The distresses and controversies in the mother country during that period allowed the colonies to develop along the lines they chose without a great deal of interference by the crown.[42] During this century institutions in America were remodeled "to adapt them to the needs of growing communities living on the fringe of a wilderness."[43]

Thus, the colonies and England had drifted apart by the 1760's. "In all that constitutes nationality, two nations now owed alle-

States down to the year 1865." *Ibid.*, 121. For his observations on Eli Whitney's cotton gin, see *ibid.*, IV, 430-31.

38 Charles M. Andrews, Herbert L. Osgood, and George L. Beer are generally considered the leading early representatives of the imperial school of American historiography. Michael Kraus, *A History of American History* (New York, 1937), 438-52, includes Channing in this group. Andrews, in *The Colonial Period* (New York, 1912), wrote in his bibliographical note (p. 253) that "All things considered, the best account of the colonies prior to 1765 will be found in Edward Channing's *History of the United States* (vols. I-III, 1905-1912)."

39 Channing, *History*, I, v.

40 *Ibid.*, 537. "Human nature, in short, was much the same in Virginia and Massachusetts, in Maryland and Rhode Island, that it was in contemporary England. . . . Contact with the wilderness and freedom from the constitutional restraints which held down Englishmen in England had not yet brought to the surface the latent elasticity of the Germanic race, had not yet resulted in making the colonists Americans." *Ibid.*, 536-37.

41 *Ibid.*, 328.

42 *Ibid.*, 334. "Fifty years of freedom gave the English-American colonists their opportunities." *Ibid.*, 421.

43 *Ibid.*, II, 3. Constitutional changes in England after the Revolution of 1688-1689 contributed to the growing gap between her and the colonies. *Ibid.*, 219, 221-22.

giance to the British crown." [44] Channing rejected in his analysis the older point of view that George III and his advisers brought on the Revolution in the fifteen years after 1760; the die had been cast during the previous century.[45]

Throughout his analysis of the colonial period, Channing directed barbed shafts at British policy with its "sublime disregard of the wishes of the colonists and of conditions which necessarily prevail in frontier settlements." [46] The tone of some of his statements is a far cry from the temperate, sympathetic approach he advocated elsewhere.[47]

More controversial is Channing's interpretation of American development in the ante-bellum years of the nineteenth century, for he believed that the mobility of men and things made possible by improved transportation and communication go further in explaining American history than does the ephemeral frontier. He saw the key to the country's growth and institutional change in the improvement of transportation and communication which made possible the speedier "transmission of intelligence and of administrative orders from one part of the country to another." [48] The importance of this phenomenon goes beyond its effect on the growth of cities and the development of farming areas. Actually, as he saw it, "By making practicable the working together of human beings in larger units . . . [transportation] has conduced to the development of democracy and direct government." [49] Old associations changed as, for example, those between the employer and the employee. The executive arose, entrepreneurs banded together, and labor was "forced to act in larger and larger units." [50] Adding these ideas together leads to this conclusion: Channing thought he had found the mainspring of American development in the indus-

[44] *Ibid.*, 599. Also see *ibid.*, III, 12. For his conception of nationalism, see *ibid.*, V, 404-405.

[45] *Ibid.*, II, 219.

[46] *Ibid.*, 184.

[47] George III is treated harshly, *ibid.*, III, 30, where Channing wrote: "Permanent mental incapacity found him still firm in the belief that he was right and always had been, and all the rest of the world was wrong." A few pages earlier he had written: "The governing classes of the old country wished to exploit the American colonists for their own use and behoof; the Americans desired to work their lands and carry on their trade for themselves." *Ibid.*, 1-2.

[48] *Ibid.*, V, 3-4. Channing's tremendous interest in transportation can be traced, *ibid.*, III, 395 ff., 426; IV, 2-8; V, 1-2, 40, 556, 564; VI, 378 ff., 391-92.

[49] *Ibid.*, V, 33.

[50] *Ibid.*, 33-34.

trialization that began its crescendo during the early nineteenth century in the United States. He contrasted his interpretation with that of his Harvard colleague, Frederick Jackson Turner, who felt that the frontier furnished a more adequate explanation for the growth of American democracy.[51] It is best to let Channing speak for himself in words, quoted not for their crystal clear logic, but rather to show how summarily he sought to dispose of the frontier: "It is remarkable how evanescent has been the influence of these new [frontier] conditions, for the American people is now and has been for some years among the most conservative of the nations of the earth." [52]

In view of this apparent disdain for the West, called "Transappalachia" by Channing, it is surprising how much attention he gave to the frontier.[53] Perhaps the late Carl Russell Fish was correct when he said that Channing realized "the West was there" and it disturbed him a little.[54] He was suspicious of the frontier thesis, perhaps because he had not originated it.[55] At any rate, he made an effort to show that the East was not relegated to insignificance by "Transappalachia." [56] Indeed, Channing was surprisingly aware of sectional conflicts in American history from colonial times on. He fitted both state and sectional divergences into his pattern of the struggles between unity and particularism; between agrarianism and capitalism.[57] The treatment of these themes was original at that time and undoubtedly provoked further inquiry.[58]

[51] *Ibid.*, 3-4, n. 1, where he wrote: "For a radically different view of the main springs of our national development from that given in the text, see Frederick J. Turner's 'Contributions of the West to American Democracy' in the *Atlantic Monthly* for January, 1906; his *Rise of the New West . . .* ; and his *The Frontier in American History*." He refers to Turner more extensively in the bibliographical note, *ibid.*, 67, and n. 1. Another reference is *ibid.*, III, 32, n. 3.

[52] *Ibid.*, V, 66, n. 1.

[53] See *ibid.*, II, 496, for his treatment of the colonies as a frontier area. He explains his preference for the term "Transappalachia," *ibid.*, V, 44, n. 1. It was a defined area that did not vary, while the "West" was a constantly shifting position.

[54] Fish, "Edward Channing," *Current History*, XXXIII (March, 1931), 865.

[55] Morison, "Edward Channing," Massachusetts Historical Society *Proceedings*, LXIV (May, 1931), 279.

[56] A concrete illustration of a difference in interpretation by Channing and Turner is provided in the election of 1828. Space does not permit analysis of the difference here, but see Channing, *History*, V, 375-76, and Frederick J. Turner, *The United States, 1830-1850; The Nation and Its Sections* (New York, 1935), 30, 36, 37.

[57] Channing, *History*, III, 468; IV, 62-63, 74 ff., 154 ff., Chap. VIII, *passim*, 541, 543; V, 329, 405 ff., 446-47; VI, *passim*.

[58] Some of these ideas have been developed further by Charles A. Beard and Mary R. Beard, *The Rise of American Civilization*, 2 vols. (rev. ed., New York, 1933),

When we turn to the consideration of Channing's technique, we recognize first that he was a careful workman who seldom lost sight of the need for the rigorous application of historical method to his evidence.[59] It is enlightening to analyze briefly his tools and methods, his organizational technique, and his style.

The materials for the *History* show that Channing culled a great variety of original material as well as monographs, theses, and volumes compiled by other scholars. Their variety is their striking characteristic and affords a contrast to John B. McMaster's excessive use of newspapers. The parade of published state papers, diaries, contemporary records, manuscripts, statistical tables, in addition to the secondary works, that passed through the crucible of his mind, is staggering. The excellent bibliographical notes that follow each chapter, together with the copious footnote references, are quiet evidence of his patient, intelligent industry. They leave the reader with a renewed realization that all scholarship is cooperative. His students, colleagues, and other scholars come in for generous thanks as their assistance in enlightening particular episodes is acknowledged in footnotes.

Among his principal tools were his knowledge of foreign languages, his familiarity with statistics, and his geographical information. References in several foreign languages occur throughout the "Great Work." Whether or not he was a master of French, Spanish, Latin, German, Italian, and Norwegian cannot be stated with assurance, but the significant inference is that he did not ignore materials in languages other than English.[60] Similarly, we cannot say that Channing's use of statistics would measure up to the standards of the scientific statisticians of today, but he did use statistics to good advantage, particularly for his account of the nineteenth century, where census materials become more adequate.[61] By employ-

passim, and Arthur M. Schlesinger, Jr., *The Age of Jackson* (Boston, 1945), *passim,* but no evidence has been found to indicate that these scholars consciously derived their ideas from Channing.

59 Some critics disagree with this statement, but they are in the minority.

60 For citations to works in French, see Channing, *History,* I, 18, n. 2; II, 135, n. 1, 142, n. 1, 150, n. 2, 527, n. 1, 562, n. 1; III, 213, n. 3, 242, n. 2, 287, n. 1, 312, n. 1, 345, 408, n. 2; IV, 307, n. 2, 500, n. 1; V, 456, n. 1, 497. For references to materials in Spanish, see *ibid.,* I, Chap. I, *passim*; IV, 307, n. 1; V, 336, n. 3. German references are fewer, but see *ibid.,* II, 421; IV, 351, n. 2; V, 254, n. 1, 350, n. 1, 472, n. 2, 495, n. 1. Italian, Norwegian, and Latin references occur *ibid.,* I, Chap. I.

61 He was perfectly aware of the shortcomings of statistics when he wrote: "It is true, of course, that the science of statistics was in its infancy in those days, at least within the United States, but looking over the figures that are available and bearing

ing available figures with caution he could add to our understanding of commerce, population movements, battle casualties, finance, and the like.[62] Maps, especially contemporary examples, were also used to make the past more real. This appreciation of cartography probably owes much to the geographical articles he wrote in the 1880's and to the influence of Harvard's great cartographer and historian, Justin Winsor.

Maps and charts are an aid to understanding the influence of geography and climate, of which Channing was ever cognizant. Geography and climate, to him, often changed the particular growth of institutions and the course of wars. We have already seen his observations on the part cotton culture played in determining American history.[63]

Channing rarely lost sight of the basic principles taught in the historical methods classes. He was chronically suspicious of the recollections of old men and the reliability of contemporary observers.[64] Mason L. Weems reaped his contempt for the historical frauds he perpetrated on the American public.[65]

If we bear in mind this keen interest in methodology, it will help to understand a salient characteristic of Channing's writing — the never quite successful effort to solve the ever-present problem of organizing and weaving together his narrative. He was at his best in portraying episodes — particularly knotty problems requiring the technique of the historical detective.[66] A prime example of this technique of wrestling with the evidence, weighing it, and analyzing the possibilities by use of shrewd inference when positive evidence is lacking, can be seen in his article on the "Kentucky Resolutions of 1798." [67]

While his technique on particular problems is almost faultless, Channing did, however, have trouble in integrating the many complex topics that go together to make up American history in any given period. His arrangement of chapters within individual vol-

in mind their crudeness, one may reach a few conclusions that are probably not very far from a reality." *Ibid.*, VI, 34. Another "caution" appears *ibid.*, 377, n. 1.

62 For some examples, see *ibid.*, IV, 431-32; V, 219 ff., 383; VI, 204 ff., 430 ff., 438-39.

63 For other references on the influence of geography and climate, see *ibid.*, III, 280-81; VI, 445 ff.

64 *Ibid.*, I, 77; II, 572, n. 1; III, 55, n. 1; VI, 310, n. 2, 401, n. 2, and especially 485.

65 *Ibid.*, IV, 57; V, 278-79.

66 Fish, "Edward Channing," *Current History*, XXXIII (March, 1931), 866.

67 Edward Channing, "Kentucky Resolutions of 1798," *American Historical Review*, XX (January, 1915), 333-36.

umes is often confusing and does not seem to be directed by any particular logic of presentation. Within chapters he sometimes breaks off the discussion of a given topic to sandwich in other subjects not directed specifically to the main theme.[68]

The shortcomings of his organizational scheme may be partially explained by the method he used in writing the *History*. He had early developed writer's cramp, which made it necessary for him to dictate his work to his competent secretary, Miss Eva G. Moore, whom Channing "had rigidly trained to his requirements." [69] When he "was ready to write, he threw aside his notes and, with his mind saturated with the subject, walked about the study for two or three hours at a stretch, dictating the narrative 'directly to the typewriter.' This procedure was followed by many rereadings and rewritings of the manuscript. Citations were then inserted, all facts and quotations verified, and the narrative read aloud 'to get the swing and rhythm of the words and sentences.' " [70]

His style is usually clear and concise but seldom brilliant; a few expressions, such as "it fell out," become hackneyed through overuse. Literary allusions are rare, and figures of speech are scarcely to be found.[71] Channing's nearest approach to brilliance is in the volume summaries, in which he condensed the characteristics of each epoch when he had finished discussing it.[72] The style is frequently enlivened, however, by impish humor and veiled irony, as when he described Philip H. Sheridan's activities in the Shenandoah Valley in 1864 as leaving it "in such condition that a crow flying over it would have to carry his food with him." [73]

The foregoing analysis has brought out gaps and shortcomings in Channing that it will now be well to analyze further. The critics of Channing's work have sometimes been harsh in pointing out his faults, some of which have already been observed or implied.[74] No

68 Examples of poor transitions may be found in Channing, *History*, III, 408; V, 30-31.

69 Winship, "Edward Channing," *Dictionary of American Biography*, XXI, 167.

70 Fahrney, "Edward Channing," Hutchinson (ed.), *Marcus W. Jernegan Essays in American Historiography*, 309, based on a letter from Miss Eva G. Moore.

71 Channing, *History*, II, 457; III, 285; IV, 325, contain the three literary allusions noted. For a metaphor used to present the function of the Supreme Court, see *ibid.*, III, 508: "Always the court has gone on its way performing its gyroscopic function of keeping the ship of state steadily on her course."

72 *Ibid.*, I, 536-37; II, 598-99; III, 573; V, 614, for examples.

73 *Ibid.*, VI, 575. See also *ibid.*, I, 207; II, 441.

74 Space does not permit a full listing of the reviews and commentaries used. The

over-all evaluation of Channing's work can ignore these defects, yet discussion of them should not obscure the considerable merits of his courageous attempt as a few reviewers and commentators have allowed it to do. Dixon Ryan Fox, whose reviews of Channing's work were among the fairest, pointed out that the author of a general history is expected to do the impossible in presenting a balanced, just account with every influence that has affected American development given appropriate space, "historic characters all assessed," and all materials evaluated.[75]

The criticism of Channing most frequently encountered is that he exhibited an undying New England point of view. While this charge cannot be denied, it must be said that in the later volumes, particularly Volume V, he sought to give the West its due. His treatment of the ante-bellum South would probably not receive the unqualified approval of southern historians, but he tried to understand the South and succeeded better than those who preceded him in covering this ground in general histories. It is quite clear that he did not approve of southern institutions. While he refused to veil his dislike for slavery, he did not believe that disapproval of men or institutions precluded a reasonably accurate understanding of them. Some reviewers granted that the various sections received their proportionate attention, but one historian of "Transappalachia," perhaps oversensitive on the subject, remained caustic.[76]

The severest appraisers hesitate to challenge Channing's intellectual honesty or sincerity. He doubted the possibility of achieving complete objectivity, but that did not keep him from using the science of historical method in ascertaining his particular facts. Ralph Fahrney believed, "The extent to which Channing measured up to the most exacting standards of historical method will always be a bone of contention among his critics." [77] Yet if we accept the premise that historical method is the key chiefly to ascertaining particular facts and that history in the large has more of the elements

best single analysis of Channing is Fahrney, "Edward Channing," Hutchinson (ed.), *Marcus W. Jernegan Essays in American Historiography*, 294-312. Fahrney must be used with care because of his proneness to quote the unfavorable portions of reviews while ignoring the laudatory comments.

75 Dixon R. Fox's review of Volume V of the *History*, in *American Historical Review*, XXVII (April, 1922), 589-92.

76 See review of Volume V of the *History* by C. W. A. [Clarence W. Alvord?], *Mississippi Valley Historical Review*, VIII (March, 1922), 377-80.

77 Ralph R. Fahrney, "Edward Channing," *Mississippi Valley Historical Review*, XVIII (June, 1931), 53.

of an art, Channing's achievement in historical method ranks high, while he falls down in the art of synthesis and interpretation.

Few reviewers agree with the proportions and emphasis Channing's individualistic approach led him to use. Skimpy attention to certain movements, individuals, or administrations distorted the picture of the whole for many in the guild. A sympathetic reviewer dwelling on the disregard of traditional valuations and the unique personal touches that resulted wrote, "only a great historian could 'get away' with them." [78]

Another group of complaints may be generalized under the criticism that Channing's *History* is too largely political and military with no controlling theme to guide the reader through the maze of facts to some culmination.[79] It is doubtful whether some who carp at the lack of interpretation bothered to read Channing's prefatory remarks where he makes it clear that he sees the victory of the forces of unity over those of particularism as the most important trend in American history; that signified progress to him. That is the undercurrent which runs quietly through Channing's *History* for the reader who will cover the entire six volumes, but one might not catch its force by reading isolated chapters or even separate volumes.

More justified is the dissatisfaction voiced over the heavy emphasis on the political, for that is Channing's strongest suit. In his later volumes, notably five, he does devote a generous proportion of his space to social factors, such as education, art, and literature, but the pictures drawn are static with little analysis of cultures or civilizations in motion. Channing did not solve the problem of showing how man's total culture has shaped his society and ideas about the world and the universe. Yet he saw the problem rather clearly, and for that he has not been given due credit; rather the concentration has been on his failure to achieve a technique for attacking and presenting cultural history. The best intellectual efforts that students of American history have been able to bring to bear are just now beginning to solve the special difficulties which

[78] Samuel F. Bemis, "Professor Channing and the West," *Washington Historical Quarterly* (Seattle), XIV (January, 1923), 39. This is a review of Volume V of the *History*.

[79] Channing has been accused of indulging himself by excessive attention to ships and naval actions. This interest grew out of his great love of the sea. Sailing was his hobby, and his contemporaries reported him as being an excellent sailor. Morison, "Edward Channing," Massachusetts Historical Society *Proceedings*, LXIV (May, 1931), 257-58, 261-62.

such an attack entails. Channing's point of view broadened with the years although he was not conspicuously successful either in showing the influence of factors other than political and economic or in portraying the dynamic forces that operate to shape society.

Practically all reviewers have found more to praise in Channing than to criticize. The specialists in the eras covered in individual volumes usually have admitted that they found new facts together with stimulating original interpretations. The agreement is almost complete that his was a unique accomplishment of high quality.

Any attempt to assess the influence of a man like Channing can result in few facts and many speculations. Some of both are introduced here.

Many graduate students who left Channing's seminars became recognized American scholars, known in their own right for their contributions to American historiography. Four of the more prolific, representing several phases of American history, are Samuel Eliot Morison of Harvard, the late Evarts B. Greene of Columbia, the late Carl Russell Fish of Wisconsin, and Samuel Flagg Bemis of Yale. Exactly what Channing contributed to these men either by training or by inspiration defies precise evaluation. Yet, these men were his students, and they have paid tribute to him in memorial sketches and prefaces to their own publications.[80]

The number of scholars who have found provocative interpretations and suggestions for further research in Channing's volumes can never be determined.[81] The *History* has been widely read by

80 Fish, "Edward Channing," *Current History*, XXXIII (March, 1931), 862-67; Morison, "Edward Channing," Massachusetts Historical Society *Proceedings*, LXIV (May, 1931), 250-84; Samuel F. Bemis, *Jay's Treaty, A Study in Commerce and Diplomacy* (New York, 1923), ix, where the author thanks Channing, who "directed my attention to the subject of this study and has constantly guided me with his astonishing erudition and kindliness."

81 Wesley F. Craven, *Dissolution of the Virginia Company: The Failure of a Colonial Experiment* (New York, 1932), 21-22; Julius W. Pratt, *Expansionists of 1812* (New York, 1925), 11. See also Warren H. Goodman, "The Origins of the War of 1812: A Survey of Changing Interpretations," *Mississippi Valley Historical Review*, XXVIII (September, 1941), 178-79. A recent estimate of Volume VI of the *History* indicates that Channing was ahead of his time in his treatment of the causes of the Civil War. See Howard K. Beale, "What Historians Have Said About the Causes of the Civil War," *Theory and Practice in Historical Study: A Report of the Committee on Historiography*, Social Science Research Council, *Bulletin* 54 (New York, 1946), 53-92. On page 89 Beale writes: "And Edward Channing, provincial Bostonian and conservative as he was, emphasized in his ivory tower many of the economic motives and psychological factors generally not stressed until after he published his volume

teachers and students, and promises to be useful for a long time.[82] His influence has even extended to foreign countries, where his volumes are known to have been used by French and German scholars.[83] His early textbook, *The United States of America, 1765-1865*, was translated into French, German, Russian, and Japanese.[84] The Russian translation may have had its small part in "undermining the Czarist regime," according to Maxim Gorki, who "told Channing that . . . [it] was read aloud in revolutionary gatherings." [85]

Channing belongs to the small group of historians who have written multivolume general histories of the United States, and he came the closest to covering the whole chronological sweep from the age of discovery to his own day. Although no great interpretative theme served as the nucleus around which he hung his facts, many of his findings were new and have been useful to other scholars in forming new combinations. He worked as an historical detective specializing in episodes, and, while not without a New England point of view, his *History* wears well twenty years after his death. His "Great Work" remains one of the major accomplishments in the field of American historical writing.

[VI], and even then chiefly by historians with whom no one would have suspected Channing of agreeing."

82 A letter dated April 17, 1946, from Harry B. McCurdy of the Macmillan Company, which published the six-volume *History*, stated that it has "sold steadily over the years in moderate amounts. The record in this respect has been most satisfactory considering that these books have been used largely for graduate and reference purposes." This letter gives the approximate number of copies printed:

Volume I	14,400	Volume III	13,200	Volume V	9,450
Volume II	12,500	Volume IV	10,950	Volume VI	8,600

For the progressive decline the writer ventures no explanation.

83 As a sample, see Ernest Lavisse and Alfred Rambaud (eds.), *Histoire générale du IVe Siècle à nos jours*, 12 vols. (3rd ed., Paris, 1925), VIII, 1032; IX, 1037; and Georg Friederici, *Der charakter der Entdeckung und Eroberung Amerikas durch die Europaër: Einleitung zur Geschichte der Besiedlung Amerikas durch die Völker der Alten Welt*, 3 vols. (Stuttgart-Gotha, 1925-1936), I, 333; II, 269; III, 359, 361, 363.

84 *Harvard Class of 1878, Secretary's Report* (Cambridge, 1917), 13.

85 Morison, "Edward Channing," Massachusetts Historical Society *Proceedings*, LXIV (May, 1931), 271.

The Forty-fifth Annual Meeting of the Mississippi Valley Historical Association

By Thomas LeDuc

The forty-fifth annual meeting of the Mississippi Valley Historical Association, held on April 17, 18, and 19, drew to Chicago members from all parts of the nation. The whole attendance was estimated at 650 and a new record in registration was set.

A committee under the chairmanship of Paul M. Angle, director of the Chicago Historical Society, was persuaded to accept the burdensome responsibility of effecting local arrangements for the meeting. The success of the meeting and the enjoyment of members and guests reflected in large measure the careful planning and generous services of this committee.

The program committee, after exploring the sentiments of the profession, found insistent demands for broad coverage of the diverse topical, geographical, and chronological fields of research. It was thought impracticable, therefore, to attempt to focus the twenty-six sessions on any single theme. A serious effort was made, however, to organize as a coherent unit each group of papers.

The meeting opened on Wednesday evening with a special dinner at which scholarly specialists in railroad history and representatives of the industry joined to celebrate the tenth anniversary of the founding of the Lexington Group. In the decade of its existence this informal organization has made substantial contributions to the elevation of standards in the field of railroad history. It has not only acquainted scholars with each other, but also with railroad executives. Semiannual joint sessions, planned by the group, have been held with the two major historical associations. Guides and bibliographies have been issued. The purpose of the Group has been to promote the production of acceptable scholarship as against the inferior volumes produced by sentimentalists and other untrained or subjective writers.

Thomas C. Cochran of the University of Pennsylvania gave the address of the evening, an appraisal not only of the contributions of the Lexington Group, but also of the intrinsic problems in investigating and publishing railroad history. The principal obstacle is that of securing adequate support for serious projects in railroad history. Corporations have frequently subsidized the preparation and publication of superficial "histories," but few of them have sufficiently appreciated the value to the corporation of sound scholarship to appropriate funds adequate to sustain competent scholars for the extended periods essential to the completion of creditable work.

In addition to its anniversary dinner, the Lexington Group held its customary daytime joint session. Two of the papers explored that subject of perennial interest, the railroad land grants. Taking the Texas and Pacific Railroad, Ralph N. Traxler of the United States Air Force compared the value of the grants made to that road by the state of Texas and the United States. John B. Rae of the Massachusetts Institute of Technology appraised the significance to the Great Northern of the grant acquired from a predecessor line and pointed out that the Great Northern, which built to the Pacific without the aid of land grant, offers a useful case study in evaluating federal policy. A third paper by Charles W. Turner of Washington and Lee University turned attention to an eastern soft-coal road, the Chesapeake and Ohio, and described the efforts of the Van Sweringen brothers to improve its strategic position by extension and consolidation.

An innovation this year was a joint session with the new American Studies Association. The size and constancy of the audience testified to the success of the plan to devote the session to the meaning of pragmatism in American social thought. Carl Bode of the University of Maryland, president of the new organization, served as moderator. Ray Ginger of Western Reserve University showed how the concept of process was used by diverse figures in the period 1890-1930 as a principle for organizing their ideas, and suggested some of its defects as they employed it. In a close-knit paper George R. Geiger of Antioch College ran a "trial balance" on pragmatism in America. Recognizing that the base of any philosophical system is its epistemology, Geiger analyzed the decline of the traditional theory of knowledge as an index of the wide gains of the "scientific humanism" of John Dewey.

Another heavily attended session at the same hour contrasted the extent and significance of midwestern resistance to entering the first and second World Wars. Arthur S. Link of Northwestern University, from his extensive research in the Wilson era, asserted that the Midwest was decidedly antiwar even after the resumption of unrestricted submarine warfare in 1917 and declared that this body of opinion affected Wilson's calculations of political expediency in 1916 and contributed to his success in campaigning on an isolationist platform. Jeannette P. Nichols, in her paper on the period before Pearl Harbor, developed the theme that only a minority in the Midwest was isolationist, and that this minority assumed leadership of a national movement that succeeded only in retarding American rearmament and aid to England and Russia and in encouraging Hitler in a disastrous miscalculation of American power. Comment on the two papers was offered by Richard W. Van Alstyne of the University of Southern California and Herman Kahn of the Franklin D. Roosevelt Library.

In a session on the industrial revolution in the South, H. C. Nixon of Vanderbilt University identified those who "killed John Taylor of Caroline" in the late nineteenth century. The "New South" movement was not only an alliance between northern capitalists and ante-bellum leaders; it also expressed a fundamental revision of premises and attitudes. The supremacy of agriculture was repudiated and industrialism was praised as a way of life and not merely as a contribution to economic diversification. That this gospel was soon qualified was demonstrated by Gustavus G. Williamson of Baltimore in his analysis of the plight of the Piedmont textile business in the mid-1880's. Faith in the margin of profits conferred by low wages led to overdevelopment of plant capacity in the textile business. The shortage of current assets, pressure from the Knights of Labor, and ruthless competition in a glutted market led to a major crisis in 1886. In another significant analysis of the business entrepreneur of the South in this period, Jean E. Keith of the Historical Division of the Army Engineers reported on his investigations of the place of the Louisville and Nashville Railroad in the development of the coal and iron industry at Birmingham.

The strategy of traffic building dominated the policy of the corporation in the relinquishment of its mineral lands and in its paternalistic extension of economic incentives to prospective industrialists. Mr. Keith's paper was discussed by James F. Doster of the University of Alabama.

At a luncheon meeting on Thursday, Curtis P. Nettels of Cornell University read a paper on the English background of the American Revolution. The paper advanced the thesis that the ruling party after 1763, the King's Friends, "forced the American war in order to forestall a revolution in England." This interpretation was challenged by Bernhard Knollenberg of Chester, Connecticut, the designated commentator.

Something more than perfunctory acknowledgment of the significance to historians of recent advances in the ecological sciences was made in the session held Thursday afternoon under the chairmanship of James C. Malin of the University of Kansas, and devoted to the interpretation of the role of environmental factors in the occupation of the Great Plains. Glenn T. Trewartha, professor of geography at the University of Wisconsin, introduced his discussion of climate with a preface designed to liberate historians from the traditions of geographical determinism. Environment is not a strait jacket but a complex set of variable conditions, within whose fairly broad limits of tolerance man can live with greater or less success. Through the application of scientific analysis man can determine the optimum use to which an area can be put and adapt his practices accordingly. The physical earth is a passive agent and not the personal demon implied in the American myth of "conquering the wilderness." Following this preface Trewartha traced some of the recent advances in the science of climate and suggested the implications for areal studies. A companion paper was read by James Thorp of Earlham College and the United States Soil Survey, formerly chief soils correlator for the Great Plains. Thorp's paper dealt specifically with soils and physiography, but he emphasized the interaction of these factors with other variables, climate, surface and subsurface water, and geology. In introducing historians to information and points of view accessible only in specialized and recent literature, his synthesis was particularly notable in its emphasis on the concept of soil as a dynamic and changing force.

At a session on the military mind in America, George E. Mowry of the University of California, Los Angeles, introduced three speakers who have investigated the dynamic forces behind the establishment of permanent conscription. Richard C. Brown of the Armed Forces Institute defended the thesis that General Emory Upton was "the Army's Mahan" and showed how Upton's criticism of American recruitment policy had influenced twentieth-century military thinking. Donald N. Bigelow of Columbia University gave a sketch of the career of Colonel William C. Church, longtime editor of the authoritative *Army and Navy Journal*. Arthur A. Ekirch of American University showed how the idea of conscription crystallized as War Department doctrine, and how it was rejected by public opinion. He suggested that the triumph of permanent conscription in the face of public distrust was accomplished by the semantic device of calling the creation a "citizen" army rather than a "standing" army.

For its session on recent military history, the program committee decided early in its planning to concentrate on the cold war period prior to Pearl Harbor, and therefore selected papers that dealt with economic mobilization. William T. Hutchinson of the University of Chicago presided. A paper prepared by Irving B. Holley of Duke University was read by Bell I. Wiley of Emory University. The theme of this paper was that orderly economic mobilization was impeded by the operation of statutes that recognized no twilight zone between peace and war. Richard M. Leighton of the Office of Chief of Military History of the Department of the Army in a paper that was highly praised laid bare the division of opinion in 1941 over the relative priority of armament manufacture and troop training. Roosevelt and his civilian advisers believed that the crucial contribution eventually to be made by the United States would be in supplying matériel; the military insisted that the "arsenal of democracy" program was retarding the development of that American military power that would ultimately be needed to decide the victory. Louis Hunter of the Industrial College of the Armed Forces commented on the papers.

The operational effects of Reconstruction politics in two midwestern states were examined in a session presided over by Fred A. Shannon. The success of the Republicans in making Iowa a one-party state was traced by Leland L. Sage of Iowa State Teachers College. The Radicals were able not only to tag the Democrats as the party of treason but to build an effective machine that suppressed both factionalism and the threats of liberals and agrarians long after the war and Reconstruction issues had lost their potency. Harris L. Dante of Kent State University showed that the situation in Illinois differed sharply from that across the river in Iowa. While the Republicans were aided in maintaining power by the blunders and the reputation of the Democratic party, sentiment towards the agricultural South became more moderate and conciliatory at a much earlier date than has been generally supposed. Illinois came out of the war feeling cheated and resentful of economic policies imposed by the East. Class issues cut across party lines and diluted the vigor of the appeal of the bloody shirt. Kenneth M. Stampp of the University of California, Berkeley, commented on the two papers.

The annual dinner of the Association was held on Thursday evening. James L. Sellers of the University of Nebraska, vice-president, served as toastmaster and presented to the large audience Merle Curti of the University of Wisconsin, president of the Association. As Mr. Curti's presidential address was published in the June issue of the *Review*, no attempt to summarize it need be made here.

The section meetings held on Friday morning suggest the diversity of the interests of the members of the Association, and the difficulties of so scheduling the sessions as to accommodate the maximum number. At a meeting devoted to party politics in the middle period, at which John D. Barnhart of Indiana University presided, Richard P. McCormick of Rutgers University offered a paper entitled "The Jacksonian Riddle: New Jersey." Charles G. Sellers, Jr., of Princeton University attempted to answer the question, "Who Were the Southern Whigs?" Re-examining the Arthur C. Cole and Ulrich B. Phillips interpretations of the southern Whig party as an organization of planters with strong views on state rights, the speaker concluded that this particularism has been overemphasized. Except for John C. Calhoun and a small group who regarded state rights as the most important political issue, the southern people divided politically over much the same questions as northern voters, particularly banking and financial policy. The Whig party, built around a nucleus of National Republicans and state rights men, received its greatest accession of strength from business-minded Democrats who deserted Andrew Jackson on the Bank issue. The Whig party became increasingly an alliance of the propertied classes that by 1841 had shaken off the state rights adherents and stood almost solidly in support of the policies of Henry Clay. The third paper, "Thurlow Weed's Network: Whig Party Organization in 1840," synthesized the long study of that campaign by Robert G. Gunderson of Oberlin College. He attributed the success of the Whig machine in that year to its untiring competence in introducing nonrational devices effective in getting out the vote and in appealing to the voters' emotions. In the judgment of the speaker, the increase of the popular vote and the success at the polls refute the contention of historians who have claimed that party organizations were relatively undeveloped before the Civil War.

One of the original ambitions of the program committee was to arrange a series of papers to evaluate business history. It was gratifying, therefore, that the Economic History Association fixed upon this topic as the theme for its joint session held on Friday morning. Arranged by John G. B. Hutchins of Cornell University, and presided over by Thomas C. Cochran of the University of Pennsylvania, this meeting drew an audience of two hundred or more. Thomas R. Navin of Harvard University recognized that the term business history has no accepted, objective definition, but asserted that a specific intellectual discipline exists. He classified the investigators who use business records and ventured several differentiations. One group emphasizes the entrepreneurial function in economic activity and through its studies hopes to make a contribution to theoretical economics. The business school historians, on the other hand, concentrate their attention on business administration as a concept for approaching and organizing business history. Chester McA. Destler of Connecticut College, as a professional historian, appraised business history as recently produced by the several groups of writers and scholars. He cited conspicuous examples of successful production from every group but found that much business history is deficient in coverage and in theoretical background, and vague or reticent about the social implications of business policy. He felt, too, that the concept of business history introduced by the N. S. B. Gras group at Harvard University and defended by Mr. Navin, was too narrow. As a means of solving some of the scholarly problems and of raising ethical standards in respect to company domination, Mr. Destler urged the establishment of an interdisciplinary committee to formulate some practical standards. Comment on the two papers was offered by Harold F. Williamson of Northwestern University and Bennett H. Wall of the University of Kentucky.

The theme of cold war reappeared in a session chaired by Merrill Jensen of the University of Wisconsin and sharply focused on the era of the quasi war against France. Marshall Smelser of Notre Dame University, tracing the background of the crisis, showed the interplay of European developments and domestic politics, and emphasized the power of nonrational forces. James M. Smith of Cornell University read a paper on the use of a federal criminal law to punish critics of the John Adams administration, and took the position that the Republican victory in 1800 represented a repudiation of the British tradition that rulers are masters whose acts are not to be questioned. The contribution of William Vans Murray in resolving the cold war crisis was explored by Alexander DeConde of Whittier College. The traditional view that John Adams sacrificed party unity to the cause of avoiding a disastrous war was challenged. Murray's diaries and private letters indicate that he worked secretly and independently to effect a rapprochement with France.

The many members of the Association whose professional interests center in Latin-American studies expressed approval of the session on Mexico in the mid-nineteenth century, at which Rev. W. Eugene Shiels of Xavier University presided. Walter V. Scholes of the University of Missouri analyzed the conceptual framework of doctrinaire liberalism during the Reform period and found that the formula strongly resembled contemporary European liberalism. Richard B. McCornack of the Department of State and Dartmouth College reported on his investigation in Mexican archives of the relations of other Latin-American countries to Mexico during the French occupation. Governments and individuals made some efforts to aid the Mexican cause, but in the long run Pan-Americanism was more preached than practiced. Turning to the early Díaz period, David M. Pletcher of Knox College read a paper on Mexico as a site of American investment. The reluctance of American capital to enter Mexico was neutralized by astute propaganda and by the development of conditions in the United States that created an outward thrust of capital. The papers were discussed by Clinton H. Gardiner of Washington University, St. Louis, and by several members of the audience.

The annual business meeting of the Association was held following the luncheon on Friday. As the reports of the Secretary-Treasurer, Mrs. C. S. Paine, and of certain standing and special committees will appear elsewhere, they will go unrelated in this account. The business meeting happily closed in good time for the afternoon sessions to open at the appointed hour.

With memories of the successful 1951 session at Cincinnati, many members besought the program planners to arrange another session on immigration. Attendance at the 1952 session seems to have justified the decision. Each of the three papers introduced by Harvey Wish of Western Reserve University dealt with the influence of a single immigrant group on American labor. Rowland T. Berthoff of the Institute for Advanced Study appraised the contribution of the English immigrants. With their background of unionism they often organized and led new American unions and exerted a powerful force to preserve the craft pattern and to inhibit the growth of industrial unions or the introduction of political action. The Finns, on the other hand, were "inimitable Marxists" in the words of John I. Kolehmainen of the University of Minnesota. Jewish trade unions had a distinctive flavor according to Moses Rischin of Brooklyn College. Along with usual wage and hour objectives were blended a miscellany of cultural and ideological impulses. Henry David of Queens College and David Shannon of Teachers College, Columbia University, discussed the papers.

Owing to the illness of the late Everett E. Edwards, E. N. Wentworth of Chicago was asked to preside at the joint session with the Agricultural Historical Society, planned by Lewis Atherton of the University of Missouri. Malcolm C. McMillan of Alabama Polytechnic Institute discussed the improvement and the manufacture of the cotton gin from 1793 to 1860. Edward H. Phillips of the Rice Institute showed the role of the tariff not only on the production of rice but on the movement for Philippine independence and on changing tariff sentiment in the South. Glenn N. Sisk of the Georgia Institute of Technology turned his attention to the recent era in his study of progress in effecting greater diversity in the agriculture of the Alabama black prairie.

A session on the beginnings of federal conservation was presided over by Oliver W. Holmes of the National Archives. Whitney R. Cross of West Virginia University discussed the cardinal role of W. J. McGee as the theorist of the conservation movement at the opening of the twentieth century and suggested the significance of Darwinian concepts in his thinking. Samuel P. Hays of Cambridge, Massachusetts, traced the development during the Theodore Roosevelt administration of multiple-purpose river planning and saw in the concept and operation striking similarities to the more successful program of the New Deal. Stow S. Persons of the State University of Iowa and John M. Blum of the Massachusetts Institute of Technology served as the designated commentators.

A session at which Fletcher M. Green of the University of North Carolina served as chairman was devoted to discussion of the work of the revived National Historical Publications Commission. Philip M. Hamer, executive director of the agency, outlined the scope of its work. Responsibility for continued preparation and publication of the *Writings on American History* has been assumed and other bibliographical projects are under way. In its first preliminary report the Commission has supported the proposal of the President of the United States for the publication of the complete writings of American leaders. Paul W. Gates of Cornell University, the designated commentator, criticized the Commission's proposals on several grounds. He questioned the wisdom of exhaustive publication of the writings of individuals and pointed out that the papers projected are mainly those of politicians. He called attention to the utility of the *American State Papers* and recommended the organization of documentary publication around topics rather than persons.

Through the generous hospitality of the Guild of the Chicago Historical Society some two hundred members and guests attended a tea at the Society on Friday afternoon.

For the second successive year the national historical fraternity, Phi Alpha Theta, held a dinner in conjunction with the meeting of the Association. Thomas D. Clark of the University of Kentucky introduced the entertaining address of Jay Monaghan on Ned Buntline.

Present and prospective construction of dams along the upper Missouri River and its tributaries, by dooming the accessibility of Indian village sites, has hastened archaeological research to the point where it is perhaps no exaggeration to say that current excavation is almost entirely concentrated in that area. Under cooperative arrangements universities and state museums are working aggressively with federal agencies to explore these sites before inundation. In view of the significance of the work already completed, the program committee was highly fortunate in securing Waldo R. Wedel, curator of the Division of Archaeology of the United States National Museum, to present a synoptic view of present knowledge of "Prehistoric Peoples of the Great Plains." Wedel's own research for twenty-five years has ranged up the valley from Missouri to Montana; his acquaintance as an administrator with the work of the numerous cooperating parties fits him perhaps better than any other to interpret for the historian the present state of knowledge about pre-Columbian occupation of the plains. The response of the audience at this illustrated lecture seemed to confirm the committee's expectation that it would be welcomed by the membership.

The enjoyment of the Chicago meeting was greatly enhanced by the smoker held at the Germania Club on Friday evening, with Mr. Andrew McNally III of Rand McNally and Company as host. Some two hundred and fifty members attended this pleasant occasion.

In view of the general interest in the subject and the unsatisfactory state of the literature, the program committee felt fortunate that it was able to offer for a session on American policy in the Far East a single long paper by Fred H. Harrington of the University of Wisconsin. Almost two hundred persons jammed the Boulevard Room for this session. In a masterful synopsis the speaker traced the evolution of American interest through its several stages from the middle of the nineteenth century. In analyzing American policy he measured realistically the disparity between assertion and action and declared that between 1914 and 1945, despite the reiteration of the Open Door Policy, the United States was actually pursuing a policy of Europe first. Walter Johnson of the University of Chicago, who presided, presented the three designated commentators, Harold W. Bradley of the Claremont Graduate School, Earl S.

Pomeroy of the University of Oregon, and Richard N. Current of the University of Illinois.

At another session held Saturday morning, LeRoy R. Hafen of the Colorado State Historical Society introduced three speakers whose papers dealt with urban development in the Rocky Mountains. Lynn I. Perrigo of New Mexico Highlands University traced the development of municipal government at Boulder, Colorado, in the second decade of its history. Study reveals that the city acquired new functions in response to felt needs rather than in pursuit of any theoretical plan. Robert G. Athearn of the University of Colorado, in a paper as entertaining as it was informative, summarized the impressions of British travelers to Rocky Mountain towns. These visitors, nurtured on the folklore and the formal literature of the "wild west" tradition, were at once surprised and pleased to discover that the towns of the real West were aggressively and consciously imitating eastern cities. Civic pride and economic incentives discouraged promiscuous pistol packing and other advertised folkways of the mining frontier. The need for eastern capital was again emphasized by K. Ross Toole of the Historical Society of Montana in a brilliant and provocative paper entitled, "Butte: A Phase in the Westward Movement of Capital." The speaker described his work as a case study in the mechanics of the interplay between capital and local institutions to produce in Montana a kind of colonialism to the East.

The annual joint session with the Southern Historical Association was planned by William B. Hesseltine of the University of Wisconsin and presided over by T. Harry Williams of Louisiana State University. Larry Gara of the University of Wisconsin reevaluated the underground railroad and concluded that it was more important as a propaganda device than as an aid to fugitive slaves. Stanley L. Jones of the Chicago Division of the University of Illinois discussed the propaganda of John Wentworth in the Chicago *Democrat* and showed that the antisouthern sentiment of this Illinois politician was keyed to both the slavery issue and the waterways-improvement pork barrel. The third paper, by John F. Stover of Purdue University, showed how the financial difficulties of southern railroads in the 1870's facilitated the achievement of the antebellum ambition of the Illinois Central Railroad to forge an all-rail route from Chicago to New Orleans.

The Teachers' Section, under the chairmanship of Martha E. Layman of Michigan State College, arranged two sessions that proved rewarding to those who attended. As in other recent years, secondary school teachers in the area gave negligible support to these sessions. At the morning session Whitfield J. Bell of Dickinson College reported on an investigation of the coverage given science, medicine, and technology in college textbooks in United States history. He found that while writers had recognized the significance of these aspects of American culture, the treatment was usually neither knowledgeable nor extensive. The dynamic interplay of science and society has been neglected and, except for familiar inventions, the advance of science has usually been presented as a catalogue of names. In a companion paper Brook Hindle of New York University surveyed the present status in college curriculums of courses in the history of science. Some 752 courses are offered, but the content and emphasis vary widely. The approach of students in the humanities is altogether different from that of scientists. The basic handicap that retards adequate presentation is the inadequate background of teachers to treat each of the several fields intelligently. Scientists with the necessary technical knowledge often fail to establish meaningful relationships among the disciplines, and historians who might apply a cultural approach are frequently deficient in basic knowledge. In discussing the two papers, Richard H. Shryock of the Johns Hopkins University emphasized that the fundamental problem in both writing and teaching is the shortage of personnel trained to deal with the field. Satisfactory training is both lengthy and expensive and university programs in the history of science remain few and primitive.

The luncheon of the Teachers' Section on Saturday concluded the program of the forty-fifth annual meeting. Wilbur R. Jacobs of Santa Barbara College of the University of California spoke on Frederick Jackson Turner as a teacher and read portions of a stenographic transcript of a Turner classroom lecture. Mr. Jacobs, in examining the bases of Turner's success, emphasized his complete identification of teaching and research and his versatility in assimilating data from diverse and unusual sources. Turner's eclectic approach broadened and enriched his interpretations, but his effectiveness in communicating to students the contagion of curiosity and a durable zest for research rested in considerable measure on the value which he attached to the contributions of his apprentices.

The chairman of the program committee cannot close this summary report without acknowledging his great debt to the many persons who contributed to the success of the meeting. Not only those who appeared on the program but many others gave generously of their time and thought. Members of the profession responded to inquiries with thoughtful suggestions. The officers of the Association were endlessly helpful and the officers of the organizations meeting jointly were prompt as well as discriminating in arranging their sections. Above all, to the other members of the program committee goes credit for whatever merit the program had. Those who served on the committee were George M. Anderson, W. Frank Craven, Richard N. Current, Oscar Handlin, John Higham, Martha E. Layman, Howard H. Peckham, Paul F. Sharp, W. Eugene Shiels, S.J., and Herbert Weaver.

Notes and Documents

Historians' Choice: Results of a Poll on Recently Published American History and Biography

By John Walton Caughey

Ours being a competitive society, the question of what is the best is always arising. A few years ago Arthur M. Schlesinger worked out ratings on our presidents, with results that are still occasionally debated. In some fields, such as pole vaulting or radio listener appeal, there are methods of measurement that yield exact answers. In other categories, of which published history is one, the rankings cannot be so conclusive.

Nevertheless, from time to time there are attempts to identify the extraordinarily good histories and the best, and, more important, there is a constant effort to appraise the literature of history. This appraisal process operates in book reviews and review articles which assess contributions as they appear. In less hurried and more contemplative fashion it speaks through historiographical studies, critical bibliographies, and recommendations of readings. Still more subtly it finds expression as every historian weighs and rejects or adopts other historians' findings and interpretations. Consciously and unconsciously this eternal sifting goes on, with the end result that some books are more highly regarded than others, and that a still more select group is almost unanimously held in high esteem. The word may not be entirely precise, but these works are often thought of as the "best."

In addition to this workaday winnowing and evaluating carried on by the reading public, by self-appointed channelers of public opinion, and by the profession, there are periodic attempts to crystallize such judgments. In American history and biography the best publicized are the annual Pulitzer awards. For the past several years the *Saturday Review* has conducted a poll of its own, conceived in rebuttal. Then there are the Loubat prizes, the Bancroft awards, the Commonwealth Club medals, the Beveridge and Dunning awards, the Pacific Coast Branch awards, the Pelzer medals, and a number of other recognitions for outstanding merit. Most of these have eligibility restrictions as to age, status, residence, or topic, and the others sometimes disclaim an attempt to select the absolute best. For the public this disclaimer is ineffective. Unless a tie is announced, we are sufficiently sports minded to assume that the winner came in first.

The fact that the judges in the "open" contests — the Pulitzer, the *Saturday Review*, and the Bancroft — are unannounced, nonprofessional, or so few in number as not to be thoroughly representative, suggested that it might be instructive to take a sounding of the views of American historians as to the best works published recently in that field.

Accordingly, lists were prepared of favorably received books in American history and biography published in the last three decades. Such has been the volume of publishing in this period that these lists could have been made exceedingly long — in fact, into a labyrinth of few returns. Wisdom seemed to dictate a shorter ballot. With the Pulitzer winners, the review columns of the principal historical journals, and the bibliographies and book lists in several histories of the United States as guides, a roster of praised, prized, and recommended books was worked out. To make the lists representative, works were included on the colonial, early national, and more recent period; and on political, military, constitutional, diplomatic, economic, social, and cultural history. Works of exhaustive research were entered, along with others more praised for their interpretive quality. Some monographs of modest size were listed, along with publications of more massive proportions.

Year-by-year balloting was not requested, because in history writing as in other things there are lush years and lean years, and such a strait jacket would have artificialized the results. The assembled titles, set down in order of publication, were put in page-long groups, the histories arbitrarily divided midway in the period, with 59 titles offered for the years 1920-1935 and 64 for 1936-1950, and the 69 biography titles spread on a third sheet. Writing in of other titles was encouraged, and selection of the best ten, ten, and twenty in the three brackets was invited.

Together with a cover letter[1] explaining at least in part why the project was undertaken, these sheets were sent out to 125 American historians. In drawing up this panel the aim was to get an approximate cross section of the profession. Those included ranged from the Atlantic to the Pacific, from past presidents of the American Historical Association to fledgling Ph.D.'s. Specialists on every phase and period were put on the roster. There were historians who have emphasized teaching and others who have emphasized research and writing. The end result, though not a perfect sampling, is probably a reasonably valid cross section.

A few men begged off and others were not heard from, but of the 125 approached, 103 responded with marked ballots, a phenomenally high return. Several got colleagues or graduate seminars to collaborate on making out a return. Sixty-four participants made one or more write-in selections. The added nominations included 46 histories and 44 biographies, of which 35 and 24 respectively got only one such vote, while the other 11 and 20 got from 2 to 9 votes each. A number of these works, particularly those whose nomination was not seconded, probably would not have come near the winning circle even had they been on the mimeographed ballots. Others almost certainly would have fared better had they not been penalized by omission. Except that there is no way of knowing what the corrective factor should be, one might treble or quadruple the write-in tally to determine placement with those on the ballots. Instead,

[1] This letter read: ". . . it would be of real help to me if I could have a response from you to the questionnaire here enclosed.

"I have prepared lists of some of the better works in American history and biography published during the last three decades. Because meritorious works almost certainly have been omitted, provision is made for the writing in of additional titles.

"On the history sheets for 1920-35 and 1936-50, after writing in whatever additional titles you wish, please check the best twenty, ten on each sheet.

"On the biography list, after writing in such titles as you think wise, please check your selections of the best twenty.

"I shall not attempt to define 'best' other than to say that in this context it may well mean best for reference use or for reading or for both purposes. It may properly take into account such factors as accuracy of findings, contribution to knowledge, judicious interpretation in contrast to mere reporting, clarity and perhaps distinction in style, and a sufficient approach toward definitiveness that the work does not need to be redone immediately.

"I hope to get a large enough response so that there will be valid indication of which books by consensus deserve the historians' accolade. . . . Of course your participation and your ballot will be held confidential. I hope also that the results will prove helpful in other phases of the investigation of critical writing in history. . . . Any comments that you want to add about your selections, about the basis for such choices, or about the larger problem . . . will also be welcomed."

the write-in votes are reported separately. To have scored as a write-in is, I believe, a more honorable mention than the statistics indicate.

At the risk of laboring the obvious, perhaps it should be pointed out that this poll makes no pretense of being an honor roll of American historians. It did not ask for a vote on the men who have contributed most to the profession. It did not inquire which have done the most as teachers. Nor did it attempt to find out which historians stand out because of the whole corpus of their published works. It was not a ballot on men, but on individual books. Its principal significance is in the over-all character of the books given preference, and here it may be pointed out that if the higher scores in the write-in tally were promoted to the preferred group, the general character of that list would be little changed.

In the replies received, by all odds the most frequent comment was an anguished admission of books unread. Nonparticipation on grounds of insufficient familiarity with the books had highest incidence among nonteaching historians — administrators, archivists, librarians, and full-time researchers and writers. Since productive research is usually rather highly specialized, and demanding as well, it is easy to see how it interferes with general reading. Teaching may have the same effect, but I am inclined to believe that more characteristically it is a spur and, as hinted by remarks from nonteachers, a needed spur. Yet many who teach as well as research profess to have missed most of the books here involved.

Another recurrent note in the comments received was that it would have been more pleasurable to vote on the worst books. Furthermore, comments such as "Not really a history," "Good but pompous," "Not a unified book, but separate essays varying greatly in significance," "Excellent as to content, sadly deficient as to style," and "I don't like it, but admit its importance," were made about some books that scored well in the voting. In fact, if the original lists had been subjected first to a panel of censors some of the highest scorers would have been challenged.

The tabulation of ballots, and some of the comments as well, indicate considerably less doubt about choices among the books published fifteen to thirty years ago than among those that are more recent. In the histories, for example, five of the earlier works were picked by more than half of the participants; of the more recent works not one. The number and range of write-in votes were far greater for the second half of the period. Several participants commented on the superiority of the earlier histories. As to biography, however, the publications of 1936-1950 outdistanced the earlier ones by approximately two to one. It may be that the art of biography writing has greatly improved. It may be that biographies depreciate more rapidly than histories. Or it may be that, because they are a less complex form, they are susceptible of more rapid evaluation.

In the poll comprehensive, exhaustive, and many-worded works stood in high favor. A small book's chances of winning the historians' accolade were not nearly so good. Nevertheless, the best vote-getting record per word was that of J. Franklin Jameson's *The American Revolution Considered as a Social Movement.*

A correlation perhaps more significant is that of preference for books that have circulated widely. Sometimes it is asserted that history to be popular has to be watered down, dramatized, overwritten, or otherwise distorted. That the historians in this poll put their seal of approval on so many books that were best sellers or near best sellers is encouraging. It suggests that the great books in American history, at least a good many of them, sold well and are generally available to be read. The less comfortable explanation may, however, be the truth, that only those books which have gotten a good circulation have registered with professional historians and have qualified for their endorsement. Although it is something of a fiction to talk of good books that will not sell, a greater contrast between the popular and the professional selections might have been expected.

It might also have been expected that books published by university presses would fare well. A goodly fraction of historical writing uses this channel. Works so published bulk large in the review columns of our professional journals. In the March, 1951, issue of the *Mississippi Valley Historical Review*, for example, thirty-five of the sixty books reviewed have university press imprints. These books are usually scholarly. They are, many of them, histories for historians, or so it is often said. If that is correct, this should have been the poll for them. Yet of the thirty histories preferred in this tally only seven are university press publications and of the thirty biographies only two.

The choices registered clearly indicate that attention to the nation as a whole is almost a prerequisite. Histories of cities or of individual states are conspicuously absent, though some very good ones exist. There are books included which have a regional or a particularized frame of reference, but in almost every instance the history dealt with also had significant impact on the nation. The same is true of the biographies. Several of the lives are of Southerners, and one of the figures, William Allen White, was a Midwesterner. All, however, had vital interest and participation in the affairs of the nation as a whole.

Most of the biographies deal with political figures, especially presidents. Only one of the thirty biographies centers on a businessman, and only two deal with out-and-out intellectuals. Among the histories it is a bit different. Political history leads, but economic and social history are well represented, four out of thirty deal specifically with the West, another four focus on the South, and cultural-intellectual history is prominent, especially among the more recent works. This last tendency amounts to a trend.

The chronological pattern of subject matter is even more striking. Of the thirty histories ten cover most of the colonial and national periods, one is set in the seventeeth century, five are wholly or primarily in the eighteenth, eleven wholly or primarily in the nineteenth, and only Henry S. Commager's *The American Mind* is devoted chiefly to the twentieth. Of the thirty biographies the ones on Columbus and Kino are poised at the close of the fifteenth and seventeeth centuries, six lie in the eighteenth, four are in the twentieth, and no less than eighteen are of the nineteenth century.

This remarkable clustering of choices upon books dealing with the nineteenth century points up the fact that, however much these sixty books deserve reading, they do not constitute an ideal or balanced reading program in United States history. That was not the purpose and is not the result. There are, it would seem, phases of United States history where high quality works are lacking or where they lack recognition. Some of these neglected areas, according to this particular balloting, are in seventeenth-century history and biography, in business history and biography since John Jacob Astor, and in appraisal of the twentieth century.

As to authorship a sharp contrast is offered by the thirty chosen histories and the thirty biographies. Of the histories three were written by professors of American literature, two by lawyers, and all the rest by professional, orthodox historians. A dean or two may be detected in the lineup, but no one who could be called an amateur, an untrained, or a self-made historian. Volunteers of this latter description have made so many and such valuable contributions to American historical writing that inclusion of some of their works in the first thirty might have been expected.

Of the biographies, on the other hand, only half are by historians who are thoroughly in the profession. The rest are by journalists, poets, lawyers, philosophers, professors of romance languages, and the like. Biography is simpler. It may be less exacting. Or perhaps it is just that it exerts a greater appeal to miscellaneous scholars and writers who could also turn out first-class histories if they wanted to.

Except for one coauthor all these books were written by men. Half a dozen of the authors belong to the region west of the Mississippi, a slightly larger number to the South, eight or ten to the states north of the Ohio, and all the rest to the Middle Atlantic and New England states. Probably this was a predictable leadership for the northeastern quarter of the United States, though it goes beyond the degree of population concentration there. In view of the obvious importance of the United States to the world it is arresting that not one of the sixty preferred books was written by a foreigner.

On the theory that great achievement in history is usually the result of sustained application rather than sudden inspiration, it is often said that the first rule for attaining stature as a historian is to live to be at least eighty. Of these sixty applauded works, however, the median of author age at date of publication is forty-nine for the histories and forty-eight for the biographies. Judging by the prefaces, most of these books had been in gestation for a long time, four or five years at a minimum, and twenty to thirty at a maximum. A few were first books by their authors. The vast majority, however, came after trial flights and test runs on other topics. The moral of the statistics may be that some of us, perhaps without realizing it, have already passed the time for bringing out or for starting work on a magnum opus.

It is practically certain that no one who inspects these lists of most-voted-for histories and biographies will be in 100 per cent agreement. The scattering of the votes, the large number of solitary nominations, and the fact that the highest scoring represents selection by only about four out of five participants indicate that historians are individualists, that their tastes are personally pragmatic, and that historical criticism is not an exact science. Whence this skewness of judgment arose is a tantalizing question. Unfortunately for this purpose, many of the ballots were unidentified and all the participants were promised that their individual replies would be kept confidential. There are, however, some observations on voting behavior and the election returns that can be made. Some derive from the ballots themselves, others from the cover letters and annotations that accompanied them.

First of all, there appeared to be a rather general endeavor to make selections that would bring in the major epochs and most of the facets of American history. Along with surveys in the grand manner, there was purposeful choice of others in which virtuosity had been applied to a much more restricted subject. The general requirement seemed to be that the research should fit the necessities of the topic, but the harder and more complicated the task had been and the more it represented pioneer effort, the more credit was assigned. Contributions to knowledge, however, were sometimes passed over in favor of contributions to thought. Besides soundness and thoroughness of scholarship, there was a demand for significance of findings, constructive interpretation, and attractiveness of style. Several participants stated that in the end they cast votes for books written without grace, but did so with reluctance. Books that had gripped on first reading, that had proved useful and stimulating, were particularly favored.

Personal associations and interests naturally influenced selections. The complex of mentor, alma mater, and school of history noticeably conditioned responses. In many instances the individual's particular brand of provincialism — geographical, chronological, and topical — showed through in the choices made. On the basis of comments and identified ballots it is clear that colonial specialists chose more colonial works than the average, that apostles of cultural history showed a preference for studies in that field, that cow country works were best appreciated in the great open spaces, and that the Lewis and Clark biography got most of its votes in the Pacific Northwest.

Passing comments also forecast dissatisfaction with the high placement of some of these works. One of the favored titles is challenged on the score of being popularized to the point of unreliability, another for having too much the quality of an argumentative tract. One chosen book has recognizable merits, but may impress many as not so worthy as another book by the same author which did not score high enough for inclusion. Still another title, though unquestionably meritorious, will appear to many to be classified in the wrong category. Even more disconcerting is the experience of finding oneself almost alone in appreciating certain works. Is Angie Debo's *Prairie City* too localized to have nation-wide appeal? Is J. Frank Dobie's *The Longhorns* too far out on the margins of history? Is it because not many historians have read Dexter Perkins' *Hands Off* that only a few endorsed it on these ballots? With other titles substituted, these are sentiments that many participants could echo.

So could the unknown jurors who have made the Pulitzer selections over these past thirty years. In biography, it is true, ten of the first twelve historians' choices had Pulitzer awards. The other two were J. G. Randall's *Lincoln*, which no doubt fell afoul of the rule excluding the obvious subjects of Washington and Lincoln, and Dumas Malone's *Jefferson*, which came in a year when good biographies were especially plentiful. If biographies are good enough, the Pulitzer judges as well as the historians can pick them.

Down the remaining two thirds of the lists the correlation is much lower. Only four other biographies were hailed by both. In a few instances, it is true, the deviation may be due to the freedom in this poll to choose more than one publication of a given year, whereas the Pulitzer people could not. More striking is the fact that no fewer than nine of the Pulitzer biographies did not get a single vote from the 103 historians, and another four got only one to eight votes each. The implication is that in thirteen of the thirty years, or more than 40 per cent of the time, the Pulitzer biography awards have left American historians unenthusiastic and unimpressed.

In the historians' honor roll of histories Pulitzer winners are even less prominent. Only seven appear among the thirty chosen, and they do not crowd to the top as was true with the biographies. Five of the prize winners drew from one to eight votes out of a possible

103; nine got absolutely none. In other words, almost half of the Pulitzer selections are completely out of the running so far as this historians' poll is concerned. The gulf between the two appraisals is virtually a Grand Canyon. The two sets of judgments cannot both be right. The advantage of perspective and of over-all view lies with the present poll. Its "jury" is large enough to approximate a referendum of the profession.

This of course is not the first time that the Pulitzer awards have been subjected to criticism. Long ago the good headlines on this theme were invented and put to use: "Pulitzer Prize Boners," "Runs, Hits, and Errors," "Mutiny on a Bounty," and "Pooh Pooh Pulitzers." The only reason for joining this chorus is that, partly by default, these awards have taken on the stature of the American Sweepstakes. As such they have considerable impact. When this historians' yardstick is laid beside the Pulitzer tabulation, the result speaks for itself.

The present poll identifies a number of specific works which the profession evidently regards as of enduring merit. Its major usefulness, however, is not in the conferring of honors. The leaders in each division got the most votes as among the best works published in the nineteen-twenties, thirties, and forties. It does not necessarily follow that the work voted for by the largest number is also regarded by the majority as the best in its class. Too much significance should not be attached therefore to the exact rankings or even to the inclusion or omission of any particular book.

What is probably more valid is the nature of the choices as a whole; what sort of books these are, what types of subject matter, of treatment, of publication, and of authorship they evince; what clues they offer as to the generation's achievement in the study and writing of history; and what clues to the present status of historical criticism. Some deductions and observations have been offered about the kind of studies in which the results seem to have impressed the profession most favorably. Further scrutiny of the tabulations may yield additional insights.

This poll also has the cardinal intellectual virtue that its answers suggest other questions. One is the basic problem of just how the judgments of historians on the literature of history are formed, whence they are derived, and how they are communicated. A supplementary question concerns the extent to which these judgments have been expressed and made available in book reviews, review articles, critical bibliographies, and the other channels of critical writing. The present tabulations provide some opening gambits for investigations into these matters.

Preferred Works in American History, 1920-1935[2]

	votes
Main Currents in American Thought, by Vernon L. Parrington, 3 vols., 1927-1930	84
The Frontier in American History, by Frederick J. Turner, 1920	83
The Great Plains, by Walter P. Webb, 1931	66
The Rise of American Civilization, by Charles A. and Mary R. Beard, 4 vols., 1927-1942	58
The Colonial Period of American History, by Charles M. Andrews, 4 vols., 1934-1938	54
The Declaration of Independence, by Carl Becker, 1922	51
Life and Labor in the Old South, by Ulrich B. Phillips, 1929	50
A History of the United States, by Edward Channing, 6 vols., 1905-1925	40
The Maritime History of Massachusetts, by Samuel E. Morison, 1921	36
New Viewpoints in American History, by Arthur M. Schlesinger, 1922	32
The Populist Revolt, by John D. Hicks, 1931	30
The American Colonies in the Eighteenth Century, by Herbert L. Osgood, 4 vols., 1924-1925	28
The Supreme Court in United States History, by Charles Warren, 3 vols., 1922	27
The American Revolution Considered as a Social Movement, by J. Franklin Jameson, 1926	26
The Growth of the American Republic, by Samuel E. Morison and Henry S. Commager, 1930	23

[2] Votes ranging from six to nineteen were cast for the following titles which also appeared in the circulated lists. Here as on the ballots the listing is in the order of publication. *The Founding of New England*, by James T. Adams; *The Spanish Borderlands*, by Herbert E. Bolton; *The Causes of the War of Independence*, by Claude H. Van Tyne; *A History of the American Frontier*, by Frederic L. Paxson; *The Emergence of Modern America*, by Allan Nevins; *The Monroe Doctrine*, by Dexter Perkins; *The Spanish-American Frontier*, by Arthur P. Whitaker; *John Brown's Body*, by Stephen Vincent Benet; *The Organization and Administration of the Union Army*, by Fred A. Shannon; *The Tragic Era*, by Claude G. Bowers; *The Critical Year*, by Howard K. Beale; *The Age of Hate*, by George F. Milton; *Norwegian Migration to America*, by Theodore C. Blegen; *Outpost of Empire*, by Herbert E. Bolton; *King Cotton Diplomacy*, by Frank L. Owsley; *Atlas of the Historical Geography of the United States*, by Charles O. Paullin; *The Significance of Sections in American History*, by Frederick J. Turner; *History of Agriculture in the Southern United States to 1860*, 2 vols., by Lewis C. Gray; *The Rise of the City*, by Arthur M. Schlesinger; *The Illinois Central Railroad and Its Colonization Work*, by Paul W. Gates; *Manifest Destiny*, by Albert K. Weinberg; *A Constitutional History of the United States*, by Andrew C. McLaughlin.

Preferred Works in American History, 1936-1950 [3]

	votes
The Growth of American Thought, by Merle Curti, 1943	51
The British Empire before the American Revolution, by Lawrence H. Gipson, 7 vols., 1936-1949	45
Ordeal of the Union, by Allan Nevins, 2 vols., 1947	39
The Civil War and Reconstruction, by James G. Randall, 1937	35
The Atlantic Migration, by Marcus L. Hansen, 1940	35
The Age of Jackson, Arthur M. Schlesinger, Jr., 1945	35
The Economic Mind in American Civilization, by Joseph Dorfman, 3 vols., 1946-1949	35
The New England Mind, by Perry Miller, 1939	32
The Flowering of New England, by Van Wyck Brooks, 1936	29
The American Mind, by Henry S. Commager, 1950	28
The Road to Reunion, by Paul H. Buck, 1937	27
Free Speech in the United States, by Zechariah Chafee, 1941	23
The Coming of the Civil War, by Avery O. Craven, 1942	22
The Sod-House Frontier, by Everett N. Dick, 1938	21
We Who Built America, by Carl F. Wittke, 1939	21

[3] Votes ranging from six to nineteen were cast for the following titles which also appeared in the circulated lists. Here as on the ballots the listing is in the order of publication. *Expansionists of 1898*, by Julius W. Pratt; *The Old South*, by William E. Dodd; *Middletown in Transition*, by Robert S. and Helen M. Lynd; *The Protestant Crusade*, by Ray A. Billington; *Cities in the Wilderness*, by Carl Bridenbaugh; *The Rise of New York Port*, by Robert G. Albion; *The Triumph of American Capitalism*, by Louis M. Hacker; *The Articles of Confederation*, by Merrill Jensen; *The Continental Congress*, by Edmund C. Burnett; *American Journalism*, by Frank L. Mott; *Hands Off*, by Dexter Perkins; *The Hero in America*, by Dixon Wecter; *Mr. Dooley's America*, by Elmer Ellis; *American Renaissance*, by Francis O. Matthiessen; *Secret History of the American Revolution*, by Carl C. Van Doren; *The Age of Enterprise*, by Thomas C. Cochran and William Miller; *On Native Grounds*, by Alfred Kazin; *The Year of Decision*, by Bernard De Voto; *Social Darwinism in American Thought*, by Richard Hofstadter; *Puritanism and Democracy*, by Ralph B. Perry; *Freedom's Ferment*, by Alice F. Tyler; *Woodrow Wilson and the Great Betrayal*, by Thomas A. Bailey; *The Farmer's Last Frontier*, by Fred A. Shannon; *Government and Labor in Early America*, by Richard B. Morris; *The South during Reconstruction*, by E. Merton Coulter; *The Atlantic Frontier*, by Louis B. Wright; *Historical Geography of the United States*, by Ralph H. Brown; *The American Political Tradition and the Men Who Made It*, by Richard Hofstadter; *History of United States Naval Operations in World War II*, by Samuel E. Morison; *The Disruption of American Democracy*, by Roy F. Nichols; *The Development of Southern Sectionalism*, by Charles S. Sydnor; *A History of the Old South*, by Clement Eaton; *The Atlantic Civilization*, by Michael Kraus; *This Reckless Breed of Men*, by Robert G. Cleland; *The Road to Pearl Harbor*, by Herbert Feis; *Virgin Land*, by Henry Nash Smith.

Write-in choices of histories published 1920-1950, with two to nine votes each, were as follows. The listing is in order of publication. *The Anti-Slavery Impulse*, by Gilbert H. Barnes; *History of the Pacific Coast*, by John W. Caughey; *History of American Magazines*, by Frank L. Mott; *The Founding of American Civilization: The Middle Colonies*, by Thomas J. Wertenbaker; *California*, by John W. Caughey; *The Course of American Democratic Thought*, by Ralph H. Gabriel; *American*

Preferred American Biographies, 1920-1950 [4]

	votes
R. E. Lee, by Douglas S. Freeman, 4 vols., 1934-1935	83
Admiral of the Ocean Sea, by Samuel E. Morison, 2 vols., 1942	83
Lincoln the President, by James G. Randall, 2 vols., 1945	74
Theodore Roosevelt, by Henry F. Pringle, 1931	72
Jefferson and His Time, by Dumas Malone, 1948	71
Benjamin Franklin, by Carl Van Doren, 1938	67
Grover Cleveland, by Allan Nevins, 1932	62
Roosevelt and Hopkins, by Robert E. Sherwood, 1948	62
John Quincy Adams, by Samuel F. Bemis, 1949	60
Abraham Lincoln, by Albert J. Beveridge, 2 vols., 1928	49
Andrew Jackson, by Marquis James, 2 vols., 1933-1937	45
Abraham Lincoln, The War Years, by Carl Sandburg, 4 vols., 1939	45
Lee's Lieutenants, by Douglas S. Freeman, 3 vols., 1942-1944	43
John Hay, by Tyler Dennett, 1933	40
Elihu Root, by Philip C. Jessup, 2 vols., 1938	40
Hamilton Fish, by Allan Nevins, 1936	39
Tom Watson, Agrarian Rebel, by C. Vann Woodward, 1938	39
John C. Calhoun, by Charles M. Wiltse, 2 vols., 1944-1949	39
The Thought and Character of William James, by Ralph B. Perry, 1935	37
Lafayette, by Louis M. Gottschalk, 4 vols., 1935-1950	36
Young Washington, by Douglas S. Freeman, 2 vols., 1948	34
Eve of Conflict: Stephen A. Douglas and the Needless War, by George F. Milton, 1934	32
The Autobiography of William Allen White, 1946	32
Rim of Christendom, by Herbert E. Bolton, 1936	31
John Jacob Astor, by Kenneth W. Porter, 2 vols., 1931	30
Thorstein Veblen and His America, by Joseph Dorfman, 1934	30
Jefferson and Hamilton, by Claude G. Bowers, 1925	30
Thomas Jefferson, by Gilbert Chinard, 1929	27
Edmund Ruffin, by Avery O. Craven, 1932	25
Henry Clay, by Bernard Mayo, 1937	25

Democracy and the World War, by Frederic L. Paxson; *The Age of the Great Depression*, by Dixon Wecter; *The Confederate States of America*, by E. Merton Coulter; *The New Nation*, by Merrill Jensen; *Church and State in the United States*, by Anson P. Stokes.

[4] These biographies, also on the ballots, were selected by from six to twenty-three participants: *Lincoln*, by Nathaniel W. Stephenson; *Stephen F. Austin*, by Eugene C. Barker; *The Life of Sir William Osler*, by Harvey Cushing; *Increase Mather*, by Kenneth B. Murdock; *Benjamin Franklin*, by Bernard Fäy; *The Raven*, by Marquis James; *Daniel Webster*, by Claude M. Fuess; *Charles W. Eliot*, by Henry James; *Bret Harte*, by George R. Stewart; *Beveridge and the Progressive Era*, by Claude G. Bowers; *Carl Schurz*, by Claude M. Fuess; *Cyrus Hall McCormick*, by William T. Hutchinson; *John Jay*, by Frank Monaghan; *The Life of Washington Irving*, by Stanley T. Williams; *Jefferson in Power*, by Claude G. Bowers; *Pedlar's Progress*, by Odell Shepard; *The Big Four*, by Oscar Lewis; *George Washington*, by Nathaniel

W. Stephenson and Waldo H. Dunn; *The Irrepressible Democrat, Roger Williams,* by Samuel H. Brockunier; *John D. Rockefeller,* by Allan Nevins; *Jonathan Edwards,* by Ola E. Winslow; *Willard Gibbs,* by Muriel Rukeyser; *American Leonardo, A Life of Samuel F. B. Morse,* by Fred Carlton Mabee; *George Bancroft,* by Russell B. Nye; *Walt Whitman,* by Henry S. Canby; *"First with the Most" Forrest,* by Robert S. Henry; *Alexander Hamilton,* by Nathan Schachner; *Lewis & Clark,* by John Bakeless; *Forgotten First Citizen: John Bigelow,* by Margaret A. Clapp; *Pontiac and the Indian Uprising,* by Howard H. Peckham; *Lincoln's Herndon,* by David Donald.

Write-in choices of biographies published 1920-1950, with two to nine votes each, were as follows. The listing is in order of publication. *Autobiography of Lincoln Steffens; Sherman, Fighting Prophet,* by Lloyd Lewis; *Charles Goodnight,* by J. Evetts Haley; *Roger B. Taney,* by Carl B. Swisher; *Sam Adams,* by John C. Miller; *Theodore Parker,* by Henry S. Commager; *A Puritan in Babylon,* by William A. White; *The Life and Times of William Howard Taft,* by Henry F. Pringle; *James Madison,* by Irving Brant; *Paul Revere,* by Esther Forbes; *Pitchfork Ben Tillman,* by Francis B. Simkins; *Brandeis, A Free Man's Life,* by Alpheus T. Mason; *Hubert Howe Bancroft,* by John W. Caughey; *Jefferson,* by Marie Kimball; *Woodrow Wilson, The Road to the White House,* by Arthur S. Link; *Anson Jones,* by Herbert Gambrell; *On Active Service,* by Henry L. Stimson; *Coronado,* by Herbert E. Bolton; *Jonathan Edwards,* by Perry Miller; *The Life of Ralph Waldo Emerson,* by Ralph L. Rusk.

The Parchment Peace: The Senate Defense of the Four-Power Treaty of the Washington Conference

By J. Chal Vinson

The United States, reaffirming a long-standing tradition, declared itself for world peace at the Washington Conference of 1921-1922, and indicated the steps which it would take to achieve the ideal of world order. American participation in the quest for peace would not be channeled through the League of Nations or President Warren G. Harding's long promised, but still ephemeral, Association of Nations. Rather than adhering to a permanent organization, the United States now favored settling problems of international concern by special conferences, and it sought to insure world peace by means of naval disarmament and open diplomacy. The former step would greatly reduce the possibility of war, and the latter method would make possible the enforcement of peace by employing the moral force of world opinion to curb international lawlessness.

These decisions set the pattern of American policy for the next two decades. An understanding of the factors influencing these vital choices can be greatly broadened by a study of the debates in the United States Senate on the treaties of the Washington Conference. In these discussions the members of the Senate in their arguments for, and against, the treaties sought to establish the aims of foreign policy, and to declare the methods which they approved for achieving them. The Senate did not speak for itself alone, for the debates were conducted in full view of the public and with proper regard for the opinions of the voters. Thus, for those who approved the decisions made at the Washington Conference the debates served as an opportunity to state the basis of the new policy and to justify it.

The greater portion of the Senate debate was devoted to the

Four-Power Treaty. This agreement abrogated the Anglo-Japanese Alliance, bound the signatories — Great Britain, the United States, France, and Japan — to respect each other's possessions "in the region of the Pacific Ocean" for ten years, and to settle any mutual controversy by conference, if negotiations through regular diplomatic channels broke down.[1] This was the key treaty of the Washington Conference, for the American diplomats felt that without the abrogation of the Anglo-Japanese Alliance the American aims of naval disarmament and the open door in China would become impractical.[2] However, this significance was not generally recognized, and the Four-Power Treaty was accepted with indifference by a public which mistakenly believed that the limitation of navies was the foundation of the Conference agreement. Consequently, senators who opposed all of the Conference's work realized that this vital treaty with its limited public appeal was an ideal point for attack. They hoped that ignorance and apathy might be converted into distrust and disapproval by applying to the Four-Power Pact the shibboleths of entangling alliance and secret diplomacy which had helped condemn the League of Nations. With its defeat the Conference would fail.

Despite this opposition to the Washington Conference, there was almost complete agreement in the Senate on the ideal of American support for the cause of world peace, and much support for a limited policy of internationalism. With such unanimity regarding the general objective, the debate centered on the most desirable means of accomplishing this purpose. Even in this matter of methods there was little debate as to general lines of procedure. The majority agreed that no action should be taken which could not be fitted into the well-marked pattern of traditional foreign policy. The disagreements which led to debate grew out of this devotion to tradition. Did the treaties before the Senate violate or implement American ideals and traditions?

[1] *Papers Relating to the Foreign Relations of the United States*, 1922, 2 vols. (Washington, 1938), I, 336.

[2] On this matter Secretary of the Navy Edwin Denby declared: "As combinations involving the above powers would necessarily destroy the ratios herein established [by the terms of the Five-Power Treaty], this plan is predicated on the prohibition of alliances between any of the conferring nations and the abrogation of such alliances as may exist." Denby to Henry Cabot Lodge, n.d., Henry Cabot Lodge Papers (National Archives), Box 294 k-1, Navy Report on the Limitation of Naval Building. See also Henry Cabot Lodge, "Foreign Relations of the United States, 1921-1924," *Foreign Affairs* (New York), II (June 15, 1924), 528.

Those senators who favored the Four-Power Treaty set peace as the ultimate goal of American foreign policy. The treaty, they insisted, was a significant step toward this goal, and one that did not require the sacrifice of worth-while traditions or interests.

In describing the contribution which the treaty supposedly made to the cause of peace, its advocates were unrestrained in their praise, but hardly specific in their proof. Senator Lawrence Phipps, a typical advocate, asserted that the Washington Conference "has done more toward establishing a better understanding and friendly relationship among nations than any other single event in history." [3] No less restrained in his praise was Senator Samuel Shortridge who felt that heaven as well as earth was moved by the success of the meeting. "I love to think," he told the Senate, "that the very angels sang in joy over the work of that conference." [4]

Senate champions of the Four-Power Treaty constantly emphasized that it was important not only for its own provisions, but also because it was the keystone of the work of the Conference. The other treaties drawn at Washington were so closely interrelated with the Four-Power Pact that it would be impractical to pass them if it were defeated. Senator Henry Cabot Lodge, a spokesman for this theory, asserted: "the defeat of the four-power treaty would endanger the treaty for the limitation of naval armament, and the failure of the naval treaty would shock and startle the world and bitterly disappoint the American people. . . . The defeat of the four-power treaty would mean the failure of the conference." [5]

The consequences of this failure would be too awful for contemplation even by the same senators who had witnessed, without flinching, the failure of the League Covenant. If the treaties were defeated, Lodge solemnly warned, the United States would "sink back into a sullen solitude, a prey to dark suspicions, a hermit nation armed to the teeth and looking forward always to wars as inseparable from the existence of mankind upon the earth." [6] Senator Irvin Lenroot, who had opposed the League of Nations, warned the Senate that the nations were already suspicious of America's

[3] *Cong. Record,* 67 Cong., 2 Sess., 4321.

[4] *Ibid.,* 4238.

[5] *Ibid.,* 3552. Secretary of State Charles Evans Hughes wrote to Oscar W. Underwood that the failure of the treaty "would be nothing short of a national calamity." Hughes to Underwood, March 11, 1922, *Foreign Relations,* 1922, I, 48-50.

[6] *Cong. Record,* 67 Cong., 2 Sess., 3552.

good intentions, and would shun the United States if these treaties were defeated.[7]

With the Four-Power Treaty thus firmly identified with the cause of world peace, the senators who favored its passage set about the task of demonstrating that it was consistent with American ideals in foreign affairs. Senator Oscar Underwood associated the treaty with American traditions by reminding the Senate that "Our national policy has been for peace since the beginning of our Government," and the American people's "great desire is that the future peace of the world may remain unbroken." He substantiated his assertion by citing American interest in arbitration, case by case, from the founding of the Republic to the current moment. This traditional love of peace was unabated, he added, for "even then [during the World War], deep in the heart, the great American heart, the call of peace remained." The people vowed that "when this Great War is over there must be peace, the peace of understanding." Therefore, concluded Underwood, "the American people approve of this treaty, because it means peace."[8] Senator Lodge, who was given responsibility for guiding the treaty through the Senate, emphasized the importance of this new instrument for peace by painting a somber picture of the consequence of past wars: "The misery and the horrors of the Great War must never come again if we can do anything to stop it. . . . We who have passed through the valley of the shadow in these last years must leave nothing undone that we can do to save our children and our children's children from the awful calamity which we of this generation have been compelled to endure." He explained that the American delegation's principal purpose had been to make a practical contribution toward world peace without jeopardizing America's cherished ideals of independence and sovereignty. Again and again he asserted that the Four-Power Treaty met these conditions. Through it, the United States could foster the cause of world peace in perfect safety, since the treaty was "without alliances or penalties or the sanction of force lurking in the background."[9]

Despite this testimony the opposition senators wanted more

[7] *Ibid.*, 3847. For Charles E. Townsend's similar view, see *ibid.*, 4251.

[8] *Ibid.*, 3710-13. Underwood, the Democratic leader in the Senate, and Lodge, who held the same post on the Republican side, were members of the official American delegation to the Conference.

[9] *Ibid.*, 3552.

specific proof of the power of the treaty to secure these blessings without cost or sacrifice. To their demands, explanations were given, but for the most part they were exceedingly abstract. Senator Underwood quoted Prince Iyesato Tokugawa of Japan who had said: "We have arrived at a spirit of international cooperation, which is the new spirit of the new age, upon which we are launching new ships of peace." [10] Lodge and other supporters of the treaty placed much confidence in this indefinable "new spirit" and professed implicit faith in its effectiveness. One element of this "new spirit" was the development, on an international scale, of a moral power which could be employed to enforce the peace. Senator Phipps declared that the very fact that four powers had been willing to confer, and had enough confidence in each other to sign treaties, was evidence of the development of an effective moral force.[11] Senator Underwood agreed, and added that the promise of peace in the Four-Power Treaty stemmed from "the great power, of the moral influence of four great nations." [12] Senator Lodge conceded that this agreement was no stronger than the will and honor of the powers that signed it; however, he felt that this could provide a solid basis for building a peaceful world, and he pleaded with the Senate to "make the great experiment and appeal to the men and women of the nations to help us sustain it in spirit and in truth." [13]

Other senators who favored the treaty also attempted to demonstrate that moral force was a practical and powerful agent for enforcing peace. The most important achievement of the Conference was the discovery of the existence of this "world conscience," according to Senator Fordney McCumber.[14] Senator Arthur Capper believed that world public opinion was already developed to a point where it would be more effective in assuring justice in international affairs than armed preparedness.[15] Said yet another believer in the power of world public opinion, Senator Hiram John-

10 *Ibid.*, 3721.

11 *Ibid.*, 4321.

12 *Ibid.*, 4612.

13 *Foreign Relations*, 1922, I, 166.

14 *Cong. Record*, 67 Cong., 2 Sess., 3837.

15 *Ibid.*, 4087. Arthur Capper also quoted Warren G. Harding: " 'I once believed . . . in armed preparedness. I advocated it. But I have come now to believe there is better preparedness in a public mind and a world opinion made ready to grant justice precisely as it exacts it. And justice is better served in a conference of peace than in a conflict at arms'."

son, "Let this public opinion operate . . . and there would be no future wars. . . . Openness, frankness, the sunlight of publicity alone are required."[16]

The advocates, moreover, maintained that the treaties had strengthened the United States in the Far East. One proof of this assertion, they claimed, was that the Four-Power Treaty had abrogated the Anglo-Japanese Alliance, which had long been regarded as a menace to the policy of America in the Orient. Furthermore, the United States had been freed of the burden of fortifying its Pacific Islands. In the opinion of many senators, such fortifications were now unnecessary, because public opinion and moral force had supplanted battleships and shore batteries as the bulwark of the nation's policy. Senators Lodge and Underwood elaborated on the importance of this fact by pointing out that Congress and the people would not approve an appropriation for the fortification of United States possessions in the Pacific. These senators doubted that the military defense of the islands would be practical even if it were desirable. It had never been the policy of the United States to fortify the Philippine Islands and their approaches, or to build a navy large enough to make them secure.[17] All of these islands were small and trifling in value and population. Lodge said, "The Marshall Islands, I think, contain nothing. They are very trivial Islands." He had "been a good deal amused at the agony of apprehension which some persons have expressed in regard to Guam. . . . We have never fortified it, and nobody would vote to spend money in fortifying it." Neither would the Senate agree to fortify the Philippines, for "It would cost hundreds of millions of dollars . . . and probably take half a century to do it."[18] The moral force of the Four-Power Treaty, Lodge concluded, had rendered expensive fortifications unnecessary, and guaranteed to the Philippines a security never before enjoyed.[19]

The advocates of the treaty, having shown its advantages, also proceeded to prove that it had no disadvantages. In particular,

[16] *Ibid.*, 3775.

[17] *Ibid.*, 3711.

[18] *Ibid.*, 3551, 4682-83.

[19] Colonel Theodore Roosevelt, Jr., assistant secretary of the navy, sanctioned this opinion, declaring that America had gained in the agreement, because it had given up fortifications it would never complete for fortifications which Japan certainly would have completed. Harold and Margaret Sprout, *Toward a New Order of Sea Power; American Naval Policy and the World Scene, 1918-1922* (Princeton, 1940), 274.

they were anxious to clear it of any taint of alliance. The American fear of alliances was more marked, perhaps, at this time than it had ever been in history. This phobia was compounded of reverence for the precepts of George Washington and Thomas Jefferson, the desire for complete independence in the management of foreign affairs, and the fear that alliances would draw the United States into war.[20]

The sensitivity of the Senate in this respect was well known, and, before the debate had begun, the Senate had been given every possible official assurance, at each stage of development, that the Four-Power Treaty was not an alliance. This was first asserted by Senator Lodge in presenting the treaty to the Conference.[21] At the conclusion of the Conference the American delegation transmitted the treaty to the President with a definite statement to the effect that it contained no features of an alliance.[22] President Harding submitted it to the Senate with a detailed and emphatic denial of the existence of any commitment or alliance within its terms.[23]

20 This feeling was reflected in the results of a poll taken by the *Literary Digest* on the policy which the United States should adopt toward France. Editors of 228 magazines from a total of 273 favored military and financial aid to France in case of unprovoked outside aggression. Yet, only 66 editors favored guaranteeing such aid to France by alliance. Apparently a word meant more to these American editors than a policy. "What We Will Do If France Is Attacked Again," *Literary Digest* (New York), LXXI (December 31, 1921), 5-9.

21 "There is no provision for the use of force to carry out any of the terms of the agreement, and no military or naval sanction lurks anywhere in the background or under cover of these plain and direct clauses." *Foreign Relations*, 1922, I, 30-31; *Conference on the Limitation of Armament, Washington, November 12, 1921-February 6, 1922* (Washington, 1922), 162.

22 In addition to quoting Senator Lodge's statement, given above, the delegation declared: "When controversies arise of the character stated in the Article, the Powers merely agree to confer together concerning them. No Power binds itself to anything further; and any consents or agreements must be reached in accordance with its constitutional methods." *Foreign Relations*, 1922, I, 337.

23 Harding stated: "I am not unmindful, nor was the conference, of the sentiment in this Chamber against Old World entanglements. Those who made the treaties have left no doubt about their true import." Later in his address, he declared: "I can bring you every assurance that nothing in any of these treaties commits the United States, or any other power, to any kind of an alliance, entanglement, or involvement. It does not require us or any power to surrender a worth-while tradition."

"The four-power treaty contains no war commitment. . . . There is no commitment to armed force, no alliance, no written or moral obligation to join in defence, no expressed or implied commitment to arrive at any agreement except in accordance with our constitutional methods." In concluding, he reminded his listeners again: "The Senate's concern for freedom from entanglements, for preserved traditions, for maintained independence, was never once forgotten by the American Delegates." *Ibid.*, 301-302, 305.

The Senate Committee on Foreign Relations recommended its ratification provided the Senate would also adopt a reservation which specifically stated that the treaty was not an alliance.[24]

Notwithstanding all of this testimony, many senators remained skeptical. Secretary of State Charles Evans Hughes assured them, in a letter to Senator Underwood, that the United States specifically stated that it would not become a party to any sort of alliance before the other nations even came to Washington.[25] More proof was given in an official statement by Assistant Secretary of State Fred Morris Dearing to Senator Medill McCormick.[26]

As the debate continued many senators added the weight of their opinions to that of the authorities who had previously spoken. Senator Lodge, assuming the role of historian, declared that "When Washington spoke about a 'permanent alliance' he was not referring to a treaty with another power to settle specific questions"; nor did Jefferson in his warning against entangling alliance have such treaties in mind.[27] With this opinion Senator Underwood concurred. An alliance, said the Alabama Senator, bound the signatories to a definite course of action. Although this agreement provided for conferences, there was no "obligation that binds the signatory powers as to what shall be done when they meet at the conference table." [28]

This preoccupation with the exact nomenclature of the treaty was carried so far as to become ridiculous. Senators became so engrossed in semantic studies that they carried to the debate many dictionaries, encyclopedias, and treatises on international law. With the aid of these authorities they attempted, by careful definition, to prove that the term alliance was not applicable to the Four-Power Treaty. A leader in this phase of the debate was Senator

[24] The Four-Power Treaty was understood to contain "no commitment to armed force, no alliance, no obligation to join in any defense." *Cong. Record*, 67 Cong., 2 Sess., 4496.

[25] Hughes declared that the Anglo-Japanese Alliance had been discussed long before the Conference met. The United States government had in these negotiations "clearly stated that this Government could enter into no alliance or make any commitment to the use of arms or which would impose any sort of obligation as to its decisions in future contingencies." *Foreign Relations*, 1922, I, 49.

[26] This brief asserted that "the parties do not bind themselves to pursue a policy for maintaining the *status quo*, they only declare their firm resolution to that end. Further, the parties do not engage themselves to uphold the *status quo*, but only to communicate with one another, in case the *status quo* is threatened." *Ibid.*, 51.

[27] *Cong. Record*, 67 Cong., 2 Sess., 3551.

[28] *Ibid.*, 3714.

Frank Willis who concluded, after reference to the *Century Dictionary*, the *Encyclopaedia Britannica*, John Bouvier's *Law Dictionary*, Henry Campbell Black's *Law Dictionary*, and Lassa F. L. Oppenheim's work on *International Law*, that an alliance was a contract between two nations for the purpose of aggression or defense.[29] This definition cleared the Four-Power Treaty; it was not a contract, and it was not designed for aggression or defense.

Senator Selden P. Spenser complained, after this exhibition, that Willis did not seem to be able to divest his mind of the implication "that there is something in the word 'alliance' that breeds war, or that means trouble, or that has the idea of force." Spenser also failed to see what difference it made whether one called the Four-Power Treaty an agreement to confer, or an alliance to confer.[30] In any event not all alliances were evil. "Marriage," said Spenser, "is the most familiar instance of 'an alliance.' Surely the Senator does not think that marriage is 'offensive and defensive' or is objectionable simply because it is called an 'alliance'." To this argument Willis answered with what was to the mind of a number of senators unescapable logic. He "would not vote for a treaty that took this country into an alliance. The American people decided that matter pretty fully a few months ago." [31] Willis attempted to give further proof that quibbling about the word alliance was worth while. He cited the fact that recently a senator had declared the treaty to be, in a broad sense, an alliance. This assertion had been sufficient to cause a flood of telegrams to Willis directing him to vote against "the four-power treaty and all such obnoxious alliances." [32] Therefore, he concluded that while actually there might not be a great deal of difference between an agreement and an alliance, to the American people there was a very definite and vital difference. To them, an alliance implied a threat to the peace and independence of the United States.[33]

The advocates of the treaty having "proved" that it was not an alliance in name, now sought to prove that it was not one in fact. The people had demanded peace without obligation, and the Senate majority was determined to claim that virtue for the Four-Power

29 *Ibid.*, 4005-4006.
30 *Ibid.*, 4009. See also Johnson's similar view, *ibid.*, 4013.
31 *Ibid.*, 3911.
32 *Ibid.*, 4004.
33 *Ibid.*, 4006.

Treaty. They maintained that the real danger in the treaty could be measured by the degree to which it obligated America. Here the debate turned on the interpretation of Article II: "If the said rights are threatened by the aggressive action of any other Power, the High Contracting Parties shall communicate with one another fully and frankly in order to arrive at an understanding as to the most efficient measures to be taken, jointly or separately, to meet the exigencies of the particular situation." [34] The rights referred to, they emphasized, were limited to the "insular possessions and insular dominions in the region of the Pacific Ocean," and American obligations in this area were not extensive. A typical exposition of this factor by protreaty senators was Lodge's assertion that it "involves the United States in no obligation except to meet with the other signatories and consult in case of any controversy arising or in case of aggression by some outside power not a signatory. I repeat that I think the obligation to meet and consult is the only obligation existing in this treaty." [35] Senator Willis agreed with Lodge. "As I understand this document, we are not bound to any action at all. . . . This conference is held, and the matter is talked over, and then we do whatever we please, so far as the terms of this treaty are concerned." [36] Other members of the majority party frequently reiterated that Article II contained no obligation except the obligation to communicate fully and frankly with the other signatory powers.[37] Senator Lenroot maintained that the United States would not violate the agreement by failing to put into action the decisions of a conference. Actually, this country did not agree to do anything, and consequently could not be guilty of an act of bad faith if it did nothing. Action was not implicit in the agreement.[38]

This effort to free the United States of any trace of responsibility for maintaining peace was climaxed with Senator Underwood's pragmatic analysis. He declared that in all probability there would be no obligations to discharge, because it was most unlikely that the treaty provisions for maintaining peace would ever be called into active use. Furthermore, continued the Senator, the signatory powers

[34] *Foreign Relations*, 1922, II, 25.
[35] *Cong. Record*, 67 Cong., 2 Sess., 3551-52.
[36] *Ibid.*, 4007. For Lawrence Phipps's similar view, see *ibid.*, 4321.
[37] *Ibid.*, 4321.
[38] *Ibid.*, 3616.

were the only nations with sufficient military strength to menace the peace of the Pacific. No other nation would be able to rival, within the ten-year life of the treaty, the might of the nations adhering to it.[39] Hence, even if the treaty did, in some unforeseen way, obligate the United States in theory, this country would never be called upon to honor the obligation in practice.

Thus, the case in favor of the Four-Power Treaty was completed. The treaty was not an alliance, and did not bind the United States to any sort of obligation; but, at the same time, it guaranteed the Philippines, abrogated the Anglo-Japanese Alliance, and was an answer to the "great heart throb of the American people, who are almost unanimous in their cry for Peace! Peace!"[40] Finally, the success or failure of the Washington Conference, which carried the hopes of civilization, was bound up with the passage or defeat of the Four-Power Treaty.

The Four-Power Treaty was adopted in the Senate by a vote of 67 to 27.[41] All the Republican members of the Senate, except the leading irreconcilables, William E. Borah, Hiram Johnson, Joseph I. France, and Robert M. La Follette, voted for it, and together with twelve Democrats they formed the majority. Of greater significance than the vote in revealing the mind of the Senate was the ballot on the Brandegee amendment,[42] which was framed to free the treaty of any taint of alliance. So anxious was the Senate to make its position on this point unmistakable, it approved the amendment by a vote of 91 to 2.[43]

The significance of the Senate's case for the treaty lies in the fact that the leaders and people of a great nation in all solemnity could take refuge in so fragile a fortress as the Four-Power Treaty. This they did, not so much because they believed in this agreement, but because they wanted to believe in it. The nation, confused in its policy, torn between isolation and world leadership, drawn between the inexorable demands of world security and the innate desire for normalcy, wanted to believe that faith without works would meet

39 *Ibid.*, 3711, 3412, 3719. For Harry S. New's similar view, see *ibid.*, 3412.

40 *Ibid.*, 1 Sess., 1678.

41 *Ibid.*, 2 Sess., 4497.

42 "The United States understands that under the statement in the preamble or under the terms of this treaty there is no commitment to armed force, no alliance, no obligation to join in any defense." *Ibid.*, 3496.

43 *Ibid.*, 4496.

any threat to its peace. It hoped that signatures could insure security. This was the parchment peace — a momentous precedent for the formation of American foreign policy during the decade and a half to follow.

Book Reviews

Lost America; The Story of Iron-Age Civilization Prior to Columbus. By Arlington H. Mallery with the assistance of Mary Roberts Harrison. Illustrations by Paula Mallery. Introduction by Matthew W. Stirling. (Washington: The Overlook Company, 1951. xviii + 238 pp. Illustrations, maps, charts, index, and appendix. $4.50.)

The north Atlantic seems to have been a busy seaway for five hundred years before Columbus. First to cross was not the Norseman Leif Ericsson in 1000, but the Irish, who in their "golden age" established a colony south of the St. Lawrence, and maintained it against all comers, including the Norse. The climate was warmer in those days, and permitted a settlement of treeless Greenland that found a ready trade in the timber of Labrador and Newfoundland (Vinland). From Vinland to Virginia and from Rhode Island to Ohio and Minnesota the Viking-Irish influence spread with its iron furnaces and grain sheds, its dialects, rune stones, and long houses. And then the Black Death, originating in flea-infested rats, crossed the Atlantic and concentrated with deadly effect on the more densely settled white villages. With this decimation died the pre-Columbian iron age, but not the new Iroquoian civilization derived in part from the Norsemen, and not the Algonquian derived in part from the Irish.

The reader will find his incredulity tempered by Mallery's documentation. Indeed, his use of source material is a challenge to historians whose documentary horizons are bounded by libraries. Taking the Icelandic, Greenland, and Norwegian sagas as bases, he has checked them against ancient charts, land risings and fallings, and the habits of skilled navigators. Taking to the sea, as Samuel E. Morison did in his well-known study of Columbus, he has found his way along the Viking trail to discover the stone ruins of the island shelters of the Norse timber cutters on the coast of northern Labrador, to the fragments of stone tools, iron nails, rivets, and long houses among the rubble of the raised beaches of northern Newfoundland where Leif the Lucky and his successors found their base. Old Icelandic, Norse, and Danish charts have been checked against the ocean currents, winds, fogs, landmarks, and hydrographic soundings to reveal the early trade routes. He has probed the Scandinavian, Celtic, Iroquoian, and Algonquian languages and compiled long lists of "loan words" used by the red men, although he admits certain dissimilarities, in grammar, for example. He has called in the metallurgist, and has shown with copious photographs and diagrams the similarity of iron furnace construction in pre-Columbian America, Scandinavia, and Germany. Chemical analysis shows that the low-grade American iron derived from bog ore is of the same quality as Scandinavian and German iron, and could not have been produced in America by English or French iron masters. The same can be said of the discovery in American sites of cladded (primitively welded) axes.

Some of Mallery's evidence is unconvincing. The similarity of Norse and Iroquoian collective landholding systems is not sufficiently demonstrated to prove relationship. The same is true of his comparison of their memorial services for the dead, and of the matriarchal customs. Philologists, ethnologists, cartographers, climatologists, and other technicians may find other flaws. But it is highly doubtful that the core of Mallery's demonstration will be weakened. All will agree with him when he writes that he and his associates have but scratched the surface of the mass of material awaiting examination.

University of Toledo RANDOLPH C. DOWNES

Behold Virginia: The Fifth Crown. Being the Trials, Adventures & Disasters of the First Families of Virginia, the rise of the Grandees, & the eventual Triumph of the Common & Uncommon Sort in the Revolution. By George F. Willison. (New York: Harcourt, Brace and Company, 1951. xii + 422 pp. Bibliography and index. $4.75.)

In his *Behold Virginia*, George F. Willison has written with charm and, at times, with uncommon insight. The first 261 of the 373 pages of text give a graphic account of the heartbreaking sufferings of the early colonists in Virginia, and of the tragic errors of the leaders of the Virginia Company. Many writers have glamorized this period to the neglect of its more grim and sordid aspects. Only 31 pages are devoted to the Virginia of the eighteenth century. Such modern historians as W. Frank Craven, Thomas J. Wertenbaker, and Charles M. Andrews have brought a proper balance, in their descriptions, to the story.

On the other hand, Mr. Willison has erred on the seamy side, both with innuendo and gusto. The reader beholds an untrue impression of Virginia, an image distorted by a warped mirror. Motives and men are for the most part evil until the reader comes to the generation of the Revolution, when suddenly by some miracle — or hocus-pocus — there "came as brilliant a generation or two of leaders as any society or comparable area ever produced." As examples of this warping of the mirror: the author, by a neat association in the text of the Bridewell women with the women sent over as wives for the colonists and by use of "doubtless" and "it appears," tends to produce the impression that most of the latter were depraved; in order to picture Captain Christopher Newport as a complete fool he gave a vivid imaginary account, drawn from inferences, of the Captain's unsuccessful start to Virginia in 1606; in order to make more lusty Robert Beverley's description in his *History* (1705) of the hospitable Indian custom of providing damsels for their important overnight guests, which appears on page 189 in Louis B. Wright's edition, Mr. Willison adds within the same quotation, after ellipsis marks, "Their Women are generally beautiful, possessing an uncommon delicacy of Shape and Feature [Features]," a quotation from page 159 — thirty pages before.

Throughout the work there are broad generalizations without firm bases and numerous small errors of fact. Quotations are not documented. A fundamental lack of knowledge and understanding of Virginia, especially after 1730 (see p. 352), explains why Mr. Willison considered that colony "a most unlikely seed-bed for great leaders, revolutionary thinkers, and passionate democrats," and why he was surprised to find himself in error.

College of William and Mary RICHARD L. MORTON

The Colonial Records of South Carolina: The Journal of the Commons House of Assembly, September 12, 1739-March 26, 1741. Edited by J. H. Easterby. (Columbia: The Historical Commission of South Carolina, 1952. xi + 613 pp. Illustration and index. $12.50.)

This is the second volume to appear in the current series. It maintains the high editorial standards set by the first volume (some notion of the editorial problems may be gleaned from the "Explanation of the Index," pp. 569-71), and its contents are a reminder that the journals of the House constitute a revealing commentary on the complex life of a diverse people. Whether the topic is a bill "for appropriating the Duty on Rum imported into George Town, towards building the said Parish Church and Parsonage House," the improvement of transportation, the administration of justice, the collection of "Warlike Stores," or the receipt of petitions, legislative journals are perhaps the most important single source for the history of the colony. The intended publication of the Council journals will substantially supplement the House journals.

The period covered by this volume (which represents only about one half of the journal of this particular Assembly) was a time of troubles. So great were the dangers from within and without that a long-standing dispute between the two houses over the method of amending money bills was adjourned, temporarily it was thought, but the compromise was renewed "and tacitly observed throughout the remainder of the colonial period." As Professor Easterby remarks, "It may well be regarded as the most significant constitutional step taken by this Assembly." Such a step would have been taken only for urgent reasons. As the Council put it, "there never was greater occasion for the Unanimity of both Houses, in providing for the Defense of the Province, than at this critical Juncture, when we have great Reasons to expect an Invasion from the Spaniards by Sea, and (if France in Case of War should act in Concert with Spain) from the French also by Land, who have now an Army on Foot behind us; and when we have already felt the unhappy Effects of an Insurrection of our Slaves within our Selves (an intestine Enemy the most dreadful of Enemies) which we have just Grounds to imagine will be repeated; and also at a Time when the Public Credit (without which no Government can subsist) is in Danger of being lost."

Among the "Series of Calamities and Misfortunes" was the most serious slave insurrection experienced by the colony. More than a score of whites were killed, and twice as many slaves executed. This insurrection led to an "Act for the better ordering and governing of Negroes and other Slaves" which formed the basis of the slave code as long as slavery existed in South Carolina. For months after the insurrection the journal was filled with references to it: the establishment of a patrol, rewards for slaves and Indians who aided in suppressing the insurrection ("When Services of this Nature are distinguished, and a suitable Reward bestowed in a public Manner, it may have a good Effect, as to encourage many others to follow such Examples"), and the settlement of public expenses arising from the tragedy. One slave, the "Negro July," was given "his Freedom, and a Present of a Suit of Clothes, Shirt, Hat, a Pair of Stockings, and a Pair of Shoes." July was appraised at £1,000 and his owner compensated accordingly. It was recommended that the clothes distributed as rewards "be made with blue Strouds, faced up with Red, and trimmed with brass Buttons."

Not all dangers were internal. The "great Preparations" made by the Spanish "for a powerful Descent" on the provinces of South Carolina and Georgia, together with the "Proclamation . . ., promising Freedom and other Encouragement to all Slaves that should desert," caused the Assembly to vote generous assistance to Oglethorpe for an expedition against St. Augustine. The investigation and liquidation of the expedition's failure gave the House much concern, as the pages of this volume attest.

The importance of this publication for the historian is beyond doubt. A reader of this *Journal* is likely to be impressed by the effectiveness, thoroughness, even precision, with which the Assembly worked, and to conclude that representative government extended much further in colonial South Carolina than is commonly believed.

Duke University ROBERT H. WOODY

Observations in Lower California. By Johann Jakob Baegert, S.J. Translated from the original German, with an introduction and notes, by M. M. Brandenburg and Carl L. Baumann. (Berkeley and Los Angeles: University of California Press, 1952. xx + 218 pp. Illustrations, maps, appendixes, and index. $5.00.)

Johann Jakob Baegert, Alsatian Jesuit, came to Lower California as a missionary in 1751, rose to be superior of the California missions, and was forced to leave when the Jesuits were expelled in 1767. Here in this "God-Forsaken" country, where eight German and four Spanish missionaries labored, where half that number of missionaries would have sufficed for the spiritual ministrations of the Indians if the great number of dialects had been less, Father Baegert labored as a labor of love. Upon his return to Europe, Father Baegert wrote his account of the California peninsula to satisfy curiosity about that area and to refute falsehoods and defamations of some writers. His work, published in 1771 and revised in 1772, included illustrations and Father Consag's map. The translation under review is the first complete English translation from the German original, although an abridged edition in English was published in the 1860's and a very good, complete translation was published in Mexico in 1942 (with which the writer has compared the one under review).

This well-edited work includes a translator's "Introduction" containing some material on the private life of Father Baegert and his family and the circumstances of writing the book and his own "Introduction." The main body of the text is divided into three parts. Part I, containing nine chapters, deals primarily with the geographical characteristics, the climate, and the products of Lower California, giving details of its location, size, rainfall, trees, fish, animals, pearl fisheries, and mines. Part II, containing ten chapters, deals with the inhabitants of California: their appearance, customs, habits, food, lodging, and missions. The second part is by far the most important and interesting portion of the volume. Father Baegert was intimately acquainted with the Indians; he completely mastered the Guaicuran Indian language, about which he gives many details, including translations of the Lord's Prayer and the Creed in that language and the conjugation of the infinitive "to play."

Part III, containing ten chapters, provides an interesting account of the establishment, the extensions, and the administration of the missions and the missionaries' work among the Indians. Chapter IX, containing some questions directed to Protestants, is superfluous and should have been omitted. Father Baegert does not tell us much about the reasons for the expulsion of the Jesuits but he does give an account of their expulsion and of the arrival of Gaspar de Portolá.

Two appendixes concern false reports about California and the missionaries. In addition the volume contains an alphabetical list of Jesuits in Lower California during the period 1697-1767. The notes of the translators are illuminating and especially helpful in identifying men and books referred to by Father Baegert. A good index and nine illustrations complete the makeup of the book. The pictures are chiefly of missions and one wonders why Baegert's illustrations of a California man and woman are omitted. From its toponymy the map included in the volume appears to be French in origin, but no comparison was made with Father Consag's map which was included in the original.

Father Baegert's observations on the topography, the climate, and the flora and fauna of Lower California along with his descriptions of political, social, and economic life of the aborigines provide significant insight into the region.

San Diego State College A. P. Nasatir

The Private Life of George Washington. By Francis Rufus Bellamy. (New York: Thomas Y. Crowell Company, 1951. v + 409 pp. Bibliography and index. $5.00.)

This new biography covers the public life only slightly less fully than the private life of Washington. Consistent with the title, however, there is more than the customary emphasis on his father, Captain Augustine Washington, and consideration is directed to the rare affection between George and his brother Lawrence.

Many years ago the present reviewer called attention to the obvious hostility between George and his mother. The present study goes more fully into this relationship and finds Mary Ball a particularly selfish and demanding woman, jealous of the time given by George to his country and the world, at what she conceived to be her own expense. The author notes the evident sense of inferiority felt by Mary Ball to her predecessor, Jane Butler Washington. Certainly Mary was not happy in the aristocratic surroundings at Mount Vernon, and she consistently avoided the place. Her death was a relief to Washington, but he survived her by approximately ten years, perhaps too short a time for complete emancipation.

The author stresses somewhat excessively the friendship between George Washington and Sally Cary, wife of his neighbor, George William Fairfax. This friendship has been, of course, well known to previous biographers. It has been credited as one of the civilizing influences, converting a rawboned country boy into a highly polished gentleman. Considering that the friendship survived many years of separation and continued into the old age of George and Sally, there has been conjecture as to how deeply stirred were the emotions. Sally has won a biography by her kinsman, Miles Cary. A modern representative of the Fairfax family has purchased the publishing rights to prevent quotation from its pages. But no previous writer has been so certain that the affair was a full-fledged romance, though even here George is not accused of adultery with the wife of a dear friend.

There is some internal evidence that the author, not unlike Rupert Hughes whom he quotes admiringly, came to scoff but remained to pray. Enthusiasm certainly mounts, but possibly that is inevitable with the increasing greatness of the subject. A fine account is given of the richest of Washington's friendships, that with Lafayette. There is not even a hint of sympathy for the Conway Cabal, championed so eagerly by Bernhard Knollenberg.

Noticeable, too, is the author's gradual acceptance of Martha as a true wife, notwithstanding her possibly excessive preoccupation with her Custis children and grandchildren. As Sally receded, the quiet Martha filled increasingly her husband's life. To many it will be of interest that Martha's daughter Patty reached testamentary age and designated Washington as her heir.

Of textual errors there are few. Some confusion attends the initials of G. W. P. Custis. The Washington estate was $532,000, not $630,000 (p. 138). Louis Philippe was King of the French, not of France (p. 380). Purely as a matter of taste, one marvels that the author of a book so superior to Woodrow Wilson's *George Washington* should quote approvingly from that mediocre work.

It is good that the first and greatest of Americans still inspires competent biographers.

Purdue University LOUIS MARTIN SEARS

George Washington and American Independence. By Curtis P. Nettels. (Boston: Little, Brown and Company, 1951. 338 pp. Illustrations, bibliography, and index. $5.00.)

That the leaders of the Continental army, the very personification of rebellion, should have found it necessary in the process of waging war against the king's troops to perform many acts which made independence more probable, might well be taken as a foregone conclusion. That their political ideology would keep pace with their military acts and make them among the foremost of those who favored independence is obviously reasonable. Most influential of all the Continental officers was Washington. To protect his men who were taken prisoner of war he had to insist on belligerent rights. To check espionage he had to reorient the concept of treason. To offset, in some degree at least, the British control of the sea he had to create an embryo navy. All these were for the colonists untrodden paths, and they converged in independence. Yet this significant phase of the American Revolution has never thoroughly been explored prior to the writing of the solid volume under consideration. The informed student will henceforth view the twelve months preceding independence with fuller knowledge and deeper understanding.

This study discusses the elements in Washington's background which predisposed him to independence but the reader is given little impression of any evolution in his attitude. It seems almost as if the author were so convinced of the rightness of independence and of the soundness of Washington's views that he is unable to envisage a time at which the idea of independence might have been unacceptable to Washington. Part of the background seems hardly valid. Washington presumably abandoned the culture of tobacco at Mount

Vernon less because of his difficulties in disposing of it in the London market, than because the land was unsuited to that crop. He continued to produce tobacco on the Custis estates. In any case, in diversifying his economy he was following the pattern of other progressive planters of his day.

There is no suggestion here as to when Washington first expressed the view that it might be necessary to resist British policies by force of arms, and the transition of his thoughts from those of armed resistance to independence is obscured. The transition was indeed a gradual one, and before the conviction had been reached that independence was a necessity, many actions had been taken which in one way or another implied independence. Yet there would seem to be confusion in imputing to Washington a design to impel Canada to independence when she was urged in September, 1775, to join in a permanent union with the other colonies, for Washington by his own word did not himself become convinced of the necessity of independence until the following month. Again, when Washington urged strong measures against the Loyalists, called for a redefinition of treason, and in many other ways took measures which in fact brought independence closer, was he acting with this objective in view, or was he taking necessary measures for the prosecution of the war which incidentally had this effect? The author wisely leaves the reader in some doubt.

Nettels suggests Washington's respect for the civil power, though he does not seem to go into this matter sufficiently deeply. If he was in fact trying to force upon Congress the most important political decision that it could possibly make, then his endurance of a galling measure of congressional interference in military matters would appear to stand in some need of explanation.

In scholarship and in exposition this study is not unworthy of the author of the best account of American colonial and revolutionary history ever to be placed between two covers. Its spirit seems open to challenge. The account of the British background is somewhat extraneous and entirely too dour. Public morality was indeed at a nadir, but constructive forces were at work which are here ignored. The difficulties of the imperial problems confronting the ministry, in the solution of which they might well have expected a greater measure of colonial cooperation, are accorded scant recognition. The emphasis is on the ugly and sinister. All in all, this seems too isolationist and Anglophobe, though he who makes such a charge exposes himself to the countercharge of being imperialistic and Anglophile. It is easy to wander from the middle way.

University of Pennsylvania LEONIDAS DODSON

Letters from America, 1773 to 1780; Being the letters of a Scots officer, Sir James Murray, to his home during the War of American Independence. Edited by Eric Robson. (New York: Barnes & Noble, Inc., [1951]. xxvi + 90 pp. Frontispiece, authorities, and index. $3.00.)

Sir James Murray was a young captain in the 57th Regiment. He served with General Henry Clinton during the futile attack upon Charleston, South Carolina, in 1776. He accompanied the defeated forces to New York, participated in the campaigns about that city, the capture of Philadelphia, the retreat across New Jersey, and some minor skirmishes. In 1779 he bought a commission as major in the 4th Regiment and was sent to the West Indies. His military career after the Revolution was important. He was a member of the House of Commons and secretary at war, 1807-1809.

There are twenty-four letters, of which only seventeen are from America. The first five were written from various places on the Continent and in Scotland and Ireland. They contain no important information and there is no apparent reason for their inclusion under the title *Letters from America.* The sixth and seventh were written on the eve of departure for America. While they are not from America, they are important because they reveal a boastful spirit of hostility. He promised his sister he would shoot "seven Americans a week — not women or children" — and advocated enslaving Americans and giving their property to the victors.

The eighth and ninth letters were written from near Charleston, and are full of interesting details of that mismanaged affair. The next ten letters are from New York and Philadelphia. These contain some interesting incidents of the campaigns in 1776, 1777, and 1778, including the very heavy contributions exacted of junior officers to pay for the elaborate farewell party given General William Howe in Philadelphia, May 18, 1778. The next three are from St. Lucia in the West Indies and the last three are from St. Johns in the same region. There is very little information of any importance in them.

The introduction gives full biographical details of the life of Sir James Murray and his work. The letters have been carefully edited and the footnotes carefully identify every individual mentioned or referred to. This small book should be of more value to students of English history than to American history scholars.

Greeley, Colorado O. M. DICKERSON

Henry Hamilton and George Rogers Clark in the American Revolution with the Unpublished Journal of Lieut. Gov. Henry Hamilton. Edited by John D. Barnhart. (Crawfordsville, Ind.: R. E. Banta, 1951. 244 pp. Frontispiece, bibliography, and index. $5.00.)

Professor Barnhart has performed a distinct service in presenting the journal of Henry Hamilton in published form. It is a significant documentary source not only in the history of the American Revolution but also in the history of the region which became the Northwest Territory. It is of real importance to the study of British administration in Canada, especially in the interior region between the Mississippi, the Ohio, and the Great Lakes; it is valuable too to the study of the Indians of the region.

The journal reveals many details in the transporting of a small military unit from Detroit to Vincennes. It describes the preparations for the expedition, the rigors of the journey, the weather, some geographical features, the contacts, councils, and feasts with Indians, the customs and habits of the Indians, the Europeans who were met along the way and at Vincennes, Hamilton's two-month management of Vincennes and Fort Sackville, the capture of the British forces by Clark, Hamilton's journey to Virginia as a prisoner of war, and his reception and treatment in Williamsburg. The period covered by the journal is from August 6, 1778, to June 16, 1779.

In an able introduction as long as the journal Professor Barnhart presents a biographical sketch of Hamilton, a career army officer who became lieutenant governor of Detroit in 1775, lieutenant governor of Quebec in 1782, governor *ad interim* of Canada in 1784, governor of Bermuda in 1787, and governor of Dominica in 1794 or 1795. Professor Barnhart argues an excellent case for a more important position in history for Hamilton than he has been allotted, and he attempts, with considerable success, to remove the odium attached to Hamilton's (the "Hair-Buyer General's") character in American history.

One of the significant disclosures in Professor Barnhart's introductory section is the confusion that reigned in the British administration of Canada from the office of the secretary of state in charge of the colonies to the lieutenant governors. The editor's researches tend to prove the lack of understanding of the West on the part of the home office and the governors — in this case Guy Carleton and Frederick Haldimand. Administrative weakness is evident in Hamilton's campaign against Clark and contributed to the surprise and capture of the British forces. Another study now under way reveals that British administration in the Great Lakes region continued to be weak and confused after the Revolution through the period of the Indian wars of the 1790's.

Voluminous footnotes, an essay on sources, and an adequate index conclude this volume. One criticism this writer would suggest is that the inclusion of the meat of parts of the journal and related footnotes in the introductory chapters is unnecessary.

The volume is dedicated to James Alton James, the author of the best biography of George Rogers Clark.

Ohio State Archaeological and Historical Society JAMES H. RODABAUGH

Storm Over Savannah; The Story of Count d'Estaing and the Siege of the Town in 1779. By Alexander A. Lawrence. (Athens: The University of Georgia Press, 1951. x + 220 pp. Illustrations, appendix, bibliography, and index. $3.50.)

The many lawyers who have made contributions to our knowledge of American history have been graciously received into the fold by professionally trained historians. If Alexander A. Lawrence, lawyer of Savannah, has not already been welcomed by the guild, he should be. Author of *James Moore Wayne, Southern Unionist,* he now gives to us a fine study of the unsuccessful Franco-American siege of Savannah in 1779.

There is no lack of volumes dealing with the military history of the War of Independence, and the siege of Savannah has often been briefly described. It has not, however, received the attention it deserves, partly because historians of northern background have commonly neglected the southern phases of that war. Mr. Alexander makes it clear that there was much at stake in the bloody fighting at Savannah. The British had captured the town in the closing days of 1778 and had thus acquired a base for major operations in Georgia and South Carolina. When Count d'Estaing, with a French fleet and several regiments of French troops, came to the coasts of the Old Thirteen in the fall of the following year, he joined forces with the American General Benjamin Lincoln and undertook with him to force the surrender of the British garrison at Savannah under General Augustine Prevost. Had they been successful, the later British offensive carried on by Sir Henry Clinton and Lord Cornwallis in the South would at least have been weakened. As it happened, the besiegers suffered more than the besieged, and a final desperate attempt to storm the town was beaten off, the allies incurring heavy losses. The British retained their base.

Mr. Alexander searched extensively for neglected documents and found many, especially in the French archives. He tells the story in detail and with scholarly accuracy. His judgments are judicious. Moreover, his narrative is fluent and colorful. Mr. Alexander has written a model monograph.

University of Nebraska John Richard Alden

Letters of Benjamin Rush. 2 vols. Edited by L. H. Butterfield. *Memoirs of the American Philosophical Society*, Vol. XXX, Pts. 1-2. (Princeton: Princeton University Press, 1951. lxxxvii + 1295 pp. Illustrations, appendixes, and index. $15.00.)

With the appearance of this handsome work, two men emerge as indispensable figures in the study of the American Revolution. The first is Benjamin Rush — gifted, compulsive, original, his pen touched with genius and his mind with aching. The second is Lyman H. Butterfield, who has contrived through his skill as an editor to fill these volumes with the people, the issues, the tensions and spirit of an age.

Editing is a confining task, full of tiny, vexatious problems. It is easy to write a note on Elias Boudinot, or Rufus King; but what can be said of a "Dr. Taylor of St. Kitts," or how can anyone be sure of the authorship of the "Centinel Letters"? And what of Citizen Robert, of whom nothing is known except that he turned up in Philadelphia in 1793, having journeyed from the Philippine Islands? Mr. Butterfield has solved more of such questions than any editor can reasonably be asked to do. Only on rare occasions must he confess that a name has not been identified; and when he does, it is fairly certain the identity will never be known. His sprightly, illuminating notes give only a suggestion of the vast amounts of sources of all kinds he must have poured through, sources covering an immense range of subjects.

He even locates quotations from literary works, sacred and profane, which Rush read and cited, long before writers had at hand the dictionaries of thoughts and sentiments which make our references today a simple matter for others to track down.

These notes are the essential part of presenting a manuscript. The reader cannot know the full value of a letter to Thomas Eddy on prison reform unless he is informed that Eddy was the "Howard of America," who had just written his book on New York's jail; nor can he read any letter with understanding and satisfaction unless the allusions are as real to him as they were to the writer, and the reader.

There are big problems in editing, too — selection, organization, presentation, problems of scholarship that precede the work. Ours has come to be a significant era of editorial projects in historical study, and this work is one of its principal achievements. Not so large as Julian P. Boyd's great *Jefferson* (on which Butterfield was formerly chief assistant) nor Edmund C. Burnett's *Continental Congress*, nor Clarence E. Carter's *Territorial Papers*, it is nevertheless a model of procedure, and the more difficult, perhaps, because Rush so often takes Mr. Butterfield into regions hitherto unknown to historians.

The introduction is modest and brief; it describes the curious history of Rush's manuscripts, and gives some account of the Doctor himself. Then follows an essay on "Scope and Method," which must be studied from now on by everyone undertaking an editorial task. The index contains a surprising invention, which others should use. Under "Rush, Benjamin," appears a full analytical index of the two volumes, and in addition a chronological list of the Doctor's writings published and unpublished — the only accurate bibliography of Rush's works to be found anywhere.

Three appendixes deal with special issues: the feud between Rush and

William Cobbett, Adams' appointment of Rush to a federal office, and an important discussion of the Doctor's relation with Washington. In this, Mr. Butterfield produces the best (though certainly it will not be the last) word on the so-called Conway Cabal. He observes quite justly that John C. Fitzpatrick's lurid passages on this nonexistent episode have set history back more than a century, are gross caricatures, even libel. I wish teachers, novelists, and textbook makers would discern this; they alas! are still gaping at a ridiculous fiction and calling it truth.

Model of editorial skill the work may be, but is Benjamin Rush worth it? To be the greatest single individual in the history of American medicine is one thing; to be a major figure in literature and civic life is quite another. But in Rush, Mr. Butterfield has made a surprising, important discovery. There was no part of his age which his vigorous, acquisitive mind did not touch, and scarcely an issue which his trenchant pen neglected. The religion, politics, medicine, morality, welfare, and humanism of his generation were his intense concern. "To spend and be spent for the Good of Mankind is what I chiefly aim at," he said. He was no rationalist of the Enlightenment; life was a heated romance, science a way to do good, belief a conditioned reaction of the viscera. Rush crusaded, campaigned, trumpeted his causes; he indulged in great angers, and in self-pity. Sometimes he was ridiculous, but he was never dull. Men loved or detested him; he wore his virtue on his sleeve, and therefore made enemies. He could be a formidable enemy himself.

But of all the men of his time, none left a more appealing record. Mr. Butterfield has selected the best of this vivid corpus of a warm-hearted man's travels through life, and the American revolutionist becomes the more understandable, as well as the more attractive, for his labors.

Philadelphia J. H. POWELL

The Old Dominion and Napoleon Bonaparte; A Study in American Opinion. By Joseph I. Shulim. (New York: Columbia University Press, 1952. 332 pp. Bibliography and index. $4.50.)

This analysis of Virginia public opinion concerning Napoleon as expressed chiefly in the newspapers concentrates on the period 1799-1809. An introductory chapter on "The Old Dominion in Transition" sketches political, economic, and cultural conditions during the last decade of the eighteenth century, showing the cleavage between the agrarian interests, predominantly Republican, and the rising commercial class which was Federalist in sympathy. In discussing the planters who maintained social and political control from colonial days, in spite of economic reverses suffered during and after the American Revolution, Mr. Shulim seems to measure the degree of aristocracy in deprecatory terms of "their lives of luxury," the growing popularity of dueling, and the existence of Negro slavery. He admits, however, that they "had their saving graces." He points out that the planters maintained political domination based upon their control of local government, but his statement that "the electorate was relatively small" (p. 42) is ambiguous. Relative to what? To the total population, unquestionably, but not to the size of the electorate in most other states, for the property qualification was very low in Virginia. Since many illiterate persons undoubtedly voted, the indirect influence of the newspapers upon public opinion must have been considerable through the spoken word of those who read them.

Through the controversy between the Jeffersonian Republicans who persisted in their optimism as to the outcome of the French Revolution, and the Federalists who supported conservative Britain for the security of America's future, Mr. Shulim provides the background for the reaction of Virginians to Napoleon's aggressive rise to power. It could be asserted, in the light of Mr. Shulim's survey of Virginia opinion to 1809, that the Federalists were more consistently pro-British and anti-French than the Republicans were the opposite. The latter might argue that Napoleon, a product of the Revolution, had cut short the instability of the French Directory in the *coup d'etat* by which he became first consul. But it is clear from the author's array of testimony from letters of Republican politicians and newspaper articles that the Napoleonic regime was increasingly hard to justify; at length Napoleon I, crowned emperor, was condemned as "the Betrayer." In Mr. Shulim's analysis of the cross currents of Virginia opinion on Jefferson's foreign policy the purchase of Louisiana stands forth again as his greatest accomplishment. The calculated risks were higher than most Virginians and Americans realized; the compelling alternative of alliance with Great Britain, if France occupied the province, was not generally recognized. How Jefferson's realistic course of action in the game of power politics contributed to the split in his own party is well demonstrated in the arguments pro and con while the future of Louisiana remained in doubt and afterwards when the Republican Quids coalesced into an opposing faction. Likewise the reader derives a renewed appreciation of the tremendous antagonism which the President's persistent policy of peace provoked throughout the rest of his administration, whether the Federalists were clamoring for war against Napoleon, or Republicans for another fight with perfidious Albion.

The author's conclusions are conveniently summarized in the last chapter. They are somewhat obscured throughout the body of the book by strict adherence to chronology which requires him to quote alternately Republican and Federalist opinions on a succession of issues, major and minor, somewhat to the bewilderment of the reader. Such synthesis as he offers is for the most part obscured by his detailed analysis; and one looks in vain for a clear-cut exposition of the newspaper press as the most important vehicle of news and opinion, or a unified interpretation of the significant role of the editors and their papers during this period.

Institute of Early American History and Culture — Lester J. Cappon

Nuttall's Travels into the Old Northwest; An Unpublished 1810 Diary. Edited by Jeannette E. Graustein. *Chronica Botanica*, Vol. XIV, No. ½. (Waltham, Mass.: The Chronica Botanica Company, 1951. vii + 88 pp. Illustrations, maps, and appendixes. $3.00.)

The author of an unpublished 1810 diary of travels into the Old Northwest, Thomas Nuttall, was born at Long Preston, England, on January 5, 1786. At twelve he became fatherless, and two years later became apprenticed printer to his uncle, Jonas Nuttall, at Blackburn and later at Liverpool. By eager and ambitious study during his seven years of apprenticeship, Thomas added to the meager education received earlier at the parish school. By 1804 opportunities for learning had been cultivated so vigorously as to jeopardize his health. Consequently, a vacation at his old home was arranged. Here he joined John Windsor, a youth of Settle, in botanical trips throughout the region. Ere long Thomas became so interested in plant life as to dedicate himself to the goddess of "Flora," in "whose service he was destined soon to leave his native land," and to become one of the outstanding collectors of new species of North American plants.

After a rough voyage across the Atlantic from Liverpool in the *Halcyon*, Nuttall reached Philadelphia on April 23, 1808. "Once on land he plunged into his self-appointed life work of mastering the flora of North America." Soon he made the acquaintance of Benjamin Smith Barton, professor of materia medica, natural history, and botany at the University of Pennsylvania. Barton immediately recognized the keen taxonomic judgment of this young, vigorous Englishman and gave him constant access to his house and the benefit of his botanical books.

Several collecting expeditions were made in the East before Nuttall began his journey to the Old Northwest in 1810. In the spring of that year, April 12, he left Philadelphia by stagecoach for Pittsburgh. From the latter city the young botanist continued the trip northward on foot, arriving at Erie on May 30, where he hoped to take a boat to Detroit. Unsuccessful in obtaining a vessel, the traveler proceeded again on foot, entering the Painesville region of Ohio June 5. Here he noted the density of the population and the fact that the inhabitants were for the most part New Englanders. The Englishman then progressed toward Sandusky along the shore of Lake Erie until he reached the Huron River where he took a boat to Detroit, remaining in that city approximately a month. On July 29 this young scientist paddled on towards Michilimackinac in a birch bark canoe with Aaron Greeley, the surveyor of Michigan Territory, arriving on August 12. By August 26 Nuttall was in La Baye on the lower Fox River near its outlet at Green Bay. This place he left on September 9 and spent the winter in St. Louis.

While the greater portion of the 1810 diary is devoted to the flora noticed by Nuttall on his journey from the East to the Old Northwest, some mention is also made of the fauna, minerals, and people — especially the Indians and their villages.

Dr. Graustein is to be commended for her excellent care in editing *Nuttall's Travels into the Old Northwest.* This work should be of interest to both historians and botanists.

Indiana University ELFRIEDA LANG

The Larkin Papers; Personal, Business, and Official Correspondence of Thomas Oliver Larkin, Merchant and United States Consul in California. Vol. I, *1822-1842.* Edited by George P. Hammond. (Berkeley and Los Angeles: University of California Press for the Bancroft Library, 1951. xxxi + 352 pp. Frontispiece. $10.00.)

This volume initiates a set of ten which will transcribe the Bancroft Library's file of correspondence accumulated by Thomas O. Larkin. A Yankee who had spent several unrewarding years in North Carolina, Larkin arrived in Monterey in 1832, opened a store, and soon became the foremost merchant in California. In 1843 he received an appointment as United States consul. Later he was Polk's secret agent. After the conquest he was a member of the state constitutional convention, a town founder at Benicia, and a real-estate owner in San Francisco, where he died in 1858. In the commercial as well as the political annexation of California he played a leading role. A documentary study centered on him thus has a high potential for informing about California's transition from a Mexican province to an American state.

Partly because there is such a preponderance of in-letters, the papers of this first installment do not bring Larkin alive. They suggest a canny, enterprising trader who had and deserved the confidence of his neighbors and the provincial authorities. They are far more revealing on the life around him, the trading contacts with Hawaii and Spanish America, the complications in business by barter, and the simplicity of the scene as instanced in the need to send six-year-old boys to Hawaii for their first schooling. These papers touch on many striking events, such as the Graham affair, the visit of the Pacific Exploring Expedition, the gold discovery near Los Angeles, and the seizure of Monterey by Commodore A. C. Jones. Often, however, the touch is merely in passing. The more satisfactory illumination is of the day-to-day conduct of Larkin's and California's business.

A structural limitation of *The Larkin Papers* is that they print merely the single-archive file, with no drawing on other holdings. In later volumes the official dispatches will be based on the Washington originals rather than on the Bancroft Library drafts. As compared to the *Jefferson Papers*, therefore, many threads are left dangling. A more serious defect is that the letters are not edited. Correspondents are not identified, allusions are not explained, and no references are offered to other materials that would round out what these documents have to say. The complete expert, if there is such a person, will not miss such aids, but the more casual reader would certainly have profited and the scholar would have been greatly assisted. Sumptuous printing in royal octavo and with few words to the page makes the set costly in price and in shelf space. It seems designed primarily for the collector. Nevertheless, publication of *The Larkin Papers* is an event in California historiography. Through these books readers will get a more circumstantial picture of mid-nineteenth-century California, and because of them a new stream of researchers will probably trek to the Bancroft Library to examine the original documents.

Los Angeles, California JOHN WALTON CAUGHEY

The First Military Escort on the Santa Fe Trail, 1829; From the Journal and Reports of Major Bennet Riley and Lieutenant Philip St. George Cooke. By Otis E. Young. *American Trail Series*, Vol. VII. (Glendale: The Arthur H. Clark Company, 1952. 222 pp. Illustrations, documents, bibliography, and index. $7.50.)

We are treated here to a microscopic examination of a military expedition westward from Fort Leavenworth to the Arkansas River in 1829, dispatched by President Andrew Jackson to lend aid and comfort to Santa Fe traders. By students and enthusiasts of western Americana this will without cavil be considered "a valuable addition" to a rapidly growing shelf of competently edited journals of exploration and emigration. To others it might seem that the really significant aspects of the case did not demand book-length treatment.

This concerns the march of the 6th United States Infantry under Major Bennet Riley to accompany the traders to the Mexican boundary, there to kill time for several months while the merchants prospered in Santa Fe, then to escort the merchants homeward. All of the real excitement is confined to the waiting period, when Kiowas and Comanches raided the troops rather gingerly, albeit with some success in soldiers scalped and animals stampeded. Since the expedition was required to live off the land, the buffaloes had a bad time of it that summer.

The editor brings out quite convincingly the fact that two major lessons in plainscraft were learned during this affair, much to the profit of later traders, emigrants, and soldiers. First, Charles Bent borrowed a brace of government oxen, which demonstrated superior qualities as transportation media under semiarid conditions. Second, the desultory skirmishing with the Indians made it clear that the best infantry in the world (which the 6th Infantry at the time probably was not) could make little impression against mounted Indian warriors. Aside from these demonstrations, the book is useful as a meticulous study of the army of the period operating under field conditions.

Despite the thinness of the subject, Mr. Young manages to avoid dullness by an excellent brand of writing, which includes a judicious sprinkling of dry humor (quite appropriate for the climate in question). One of the oxen which received a broadside from the stone age artillery was not simply injured or even riddled with arrows. He was "tolerably well perforated." In general, this reviewer feels that the subject has been "tolerably well ventilated."

National Park Service, Omaha MERRILL J. MATTES

Cape Horn to the Pacific; The Rise and Decline of an Ocean Highway. By Raymond A. Rydell. (Berkeley and Los Angeles: University of California Press, 1952. ix + 213 pp. Bibliography and index. $4.00.)

Whether through the Strait of Magellan or around Cape Horn, the westward passage around the tip of South America has always been one of the most trying and dangerous of voyages. Magellan on his memorable trip took thirty-eight days to beat his way through the strait and at that he fared little worse than many others who since then have attempted to navigate this tortuous passage. Even the route through the Strait of Le Maire and around Cape Horn, later followed by most vessels, might take well over a month in this region where contrary winds blew with gale velocity, great ground swells rolled in from the Pacific, and bitter cold, icebergs, and lee shores compounded the difficulties and perils of the voyage. Yet until after the Civil War this remained a main route to the American frontier in the Pacific.

It is this passage to the Pacific which provides the connective thread for the essays which Raymond A. Rydell brings together in his *Cape Horn to the Pacific*. His investigations indicate, he believes, "the intimate relationship between the development and westward expansion of the United States and American utilization of the Cape Horn route to the Pacific." The book consists of a series of historical essays, most of which are economic in emphasis. Among the topics treated are: "The Old China Trade," "Hides and Tallow," "The Whaling Industry," "The Forty-Niners," and "The Clipper Ship Era." Less exclusively economic are two essays: "Missionary Enterprise" and "The United States Navy." Each chapter presents a brief and therefore highly selective summary of the material available. Though adding little that is new either in content or in interpretation, the book is interestingly and competently written and provides a welcome addition to the literature.

The use of the Cape Horn passage as the point of reference for the essays provides a unique though perhaps not a very significant device for studying the American frontier in the Pacific. Other routes to that area, as the author notes, also played an important part even in the early days, and the specific relevance of the Horn route to such developments as whaling and missionary activity in the Pacific is not entirely clear. Nevertheless, the references to the Horn route in each chapter are always interesting and involve surprisingly little repetition. There is a good outline map of the Cape Horn area but none for the other Pacific regions extensively dealt with.

Amherst College GEORGE ROGERS TAYLOR

Seeing the Elephant; Letters of R. R. Taylor, Forty-Niner. Edited by John Walton Caughey. (Los Angeles: The Ward Ritchie Press, 1951. xv + 107 pp. Illustrations. $7.50.)

The oft-told California gold rush story is repeated here. But "coming from the fluent pen of a sensitive observer" (p. ix), the Taylor letters offer new information and interesting detail. They well reflect the feelings of the gold-seekers and their quickly changing psychological reactions to events.

Before contracting the gold fever Taylor had been employed as editor of a weekly newspaper and as an inspector in the customhouse in Boston. At the age of twenty-six he set sail to seek his fortune in the new El Dorado. The letters, addressed to his wife, were written en route to and in California, May, 1849, to April, 1850.

Half the space is devoted to the descriptions penned en route — New York to New Orleans, to Chagres, to Panama, to San Francisco. The remainder covers experiences at San Francisco and in the mines. "We are determined," he writes, "to see the entire 'elephant' from the end of his trunk to the tip of his tail" (p. 47). Most of his time was spent as storekeeper rather than as miner.

An excellent summary of the contents of the letters and a brief narrative of Taylor's trip and experiences are presented in Dr. Caughey's introduction. Little editing of the letters was necessary. The volume is handsomely printed and is well illustrated with interesting contemporary sketches.

State Historical Society of Colorado L. R. HAFEN

Heavens on Earth; Utopian Communities in America, 1680-1880. By Mark Holloway. (New York: Library Publishers, 1951. 240 pp. Illustrations, map, bibliographical note, and index. $4.75.)

From the seventeenth century to the present, experimental communities have played a role — always picturesque and at times significant — in American social history. The elements of social idealism, of sectarian zeal, and of sheer eccentricity have been so mingled in these communitarian ventures that to write a balanced narrative of their history through most of three centuries is no simple assignment. Mark Holloway, a British writer, has done so with considerable success in this brief volume addressed to the general reader. He exploits, as the popular writer is bound to do, the picturesqueness of his material, but he does not lose sight of the essential seriousness of purpose that underlay the movement. Chronologically, also, Mr. Holloway's sense of proportion is good. He allots a hundred pages to the religious sects of the colonial period and the early nineteenth century, and another hundred to the major experiments that were launched between 1825 and 1850: New Harmony, Brook Farm, the Fourierist phalanxes, the Oneida Community, and the Icarian colonies. He properly relegates the experiments of later date to a single chapter.

What Mr. Holloway presents is a readable synthesis of the information provided by the older secondary works on the subject. His is not, in any sense, a work of scholarship based upon original sources. The author cites no manuscripts or contemporary newspapers, his references to communitarian periodicals are quite incidental, and he subjects the published accounts of contemporaries to no serious critical examination. Recent scholarship is hardly represented, for the brief bibliographical note lists only two titles later than 1908.

As a consequence the book can throw no new light upon the significance of the communitarian movement in the United States. Its value is purely narrative. In broad outline this narrative is reliable enough, but in detail its accuracy is no greater than the accuracy of the secondary works on which it rests. And this foundation is far from sound. Most of the secondary works of half a century ago on the subject are compounded of fragmentary evidence, hearsay, *ex parte* testimony, and hasty observation. They contain valuable raw material for the critical historian, but hardly tested and verified conclusions for the use of the synthesizer.

A foreign writer can often illumine American history by throwing light upon it from a new direction. In this respect the present book is peculiarly disappointing. Mr. Holloway's treatment of historical background is perfunctory at best. Though many of the ideas which he writes about have entered into the process of socialization occurring in his own country, he makes no serious attempt to link American communitarianism with the social thought that developed simultaneously in Britain and on the Continent.

University of Illinois ARTHUR E. BESTOR, JR.

Rift in the Democracy. By James C. N. Paul. (Philadelphia: University of Pennsylvania Press, 1951. xiv + 200 pp. Bibliography, and index. $4.00.)

With "painstaking assistance" from Professor Jeter A. Isley of Princeton and financial aid from the Princeton history department's William DuBois Sheldon Fund, James C. N. Paul, Washington attorney and clerk for Chief Justice F. M. Vinson, has written an excellent account of the contest for the Democratic presidential nomination in 1844. The author's central thesis is that the acceptance by the Democratic party of the demand for Texas annexation was the "Trojan horse" of the Democracy that produced "rift" in 1844 and disruption in 1860. Although Polk was nominated as a compromise candidate, personal enmities and a deep ideological antipathy had been engendered and his nomination did not, and could not, heal the wounds that had been opened. The story of the years after 1844 the author leaves to others; he is content to point out that during this period the party "became a mere organizational framework within which sectional interests bickered and appeased each other," until finally in 1860 further compromise became impossible. His purpose in this volume is to analyze the conflicting forces in the contest for the nomination in 1844 which he views as the beginning of this period of decomposition.

The main outline of this story, the defeat of former President Martin Van Buren by the Texas annexationists and the nomination of James K. Polk in his stead, is not new, but the intrigues and manipulations of Robert J. Walker, Thomas Ritchie, Gideon Pillow, and Samuel Laughlin which were so important in bringing about this result are portrayed with dramatic realism not often found in historical writing. He has made extensive use of the abundant manuscript materials for this period; and from the correspondence of both national and local political figures he has combed significant details which he has pieced together into an absorbing tale. Most readers will find some detailed interpretations to which they will take exception — some may feel that Pillow's influence at Baltimore was not so significant as it is made to appear, while others may think that Romulus Saunders' part is overdrawn — but few will take serious issue with the author's major points. It may be that the reader is not sufficiently apprised of the varied interests within the Democratic party from its outset and is consequently led to believe that prior to the struggle in 1844 the party was a harmonious unit. The volume is, however, an excellent close-up of how things happen and of the men who bring them about. It will be read with interest and profit.

University of California, Los Angeles BRAINERD DYER

Bluejackets with Perry in Japan; A Day-by-Day Account Kept By Master's Mate John R. C. Lewis and Cabin Boy William B. Allen. Edited with an Introduction by Henry F. Graff. (New York: The New York Public Library, 1952. 181 pp. Illustrations and appendixes. $3.00.)

With the centennial of the so-called Perry Expedition to Japan in the offing, the editing and combined publication of two more journals describing some of those events is particularly welcome. One of these is the log of John Redman Coxe Lewis, master's mate on the sloop-of-war *Macedonian*; the other is the "Memorandum of A Cruise to China and Japan in the U.S. sloop of war *Vandalia* during the years 1853, 1854" by William B. Allen. These accounts add little to other firsthand reports, but short descriptions are given concerning the Liu Ch'iu Islands, the American landing at Kanagawa on March 8, 1854, the geography and natural history of Japan, the sermon of the Rev. George Jones off Kanagawa on April 9, the Bonin Islands, and the environs of Shimoda and Hakodate.

With a few exceptions, too miscellaneous to mention in a brief review, the editing has been carefully done, identifications being particularly numerous. The outstanding feature of this treatment is the interesting and useful seventy-page introduction which emphasizes the sources from which Americans learned about Japan prior to 1853. The editor has made a selection and evaluation of those accounts which had most influence upon American readers.

There is reason to suppose that other diaries of the Perry Expedition to Japan will appear from time to time. The only other valuable and unpublished manuscript of this sort known to the reviewer, however, is the journal of Lieutenant George H. Preble in the Massachusetts Historical Society. It is the longest and one of the more valuable journals of the expedition and has been abridged and edited as a master's thesis at the Claremont Graduate School by Mr. Jack C. Wooton.

Fletcher School of Law and Diplomacy ALLAN B. COLE

The Mysteries of Ohio's Underground Railroads. By Wilbur Henry Siebert. (Columbus: Long's College Book Company, 1951. xxix + 330 pp. Illustrations, maps, and index. $5.00.)

Professor Siebert published his monumental work, *The Underground Railroad from Slavery to Freedom*, in 1898. Since that time it has been an indispensable book in the field. The present study has added much information that was not presented in the earlier volume. The material, in the main, was obtained in personal interviews during the years 1889 to 1896 from participants in, and eyewitnesses to, the activities of the underground railroad in Ohio. Many people with whom the author talked had actually driven wagons at night from station to station. The fugitive slaves appeared at the ports along the Ohio River — Cincinnati, Ripley, Portsmouth, Athens, and a dozen others. The stations were well marked so that the escaping slave with the correct information had little trouble finding friends to help him in his flight to Lake Erie and Canada. The work of the Quakers, Wesleyan Methodists, and Scotch Covenanters stands out clearly.

The Fugitive Slave Law of 1850 greatly stimulated activity along every route of the underground railroad. This law brought the evils of slavery home to more people than anything that had ever occurred. Rapidly expanding railroad transportation from the Ohio River northward, as well as more steamboats on Lake Erie, made escape easier for the Negro slave and pursuit more difficult. The fugitives went forward in larger numbers. The slaveholders, as well as the law enforcement officers, are made to appear somewhat ridiculous in their efforts to track down and recover lost property. The names of the many humanitarians who defied federal and state laws to give help to the lowly black on his way to freedom have been preserved for future generations.

A lively style is maintained throughout the book. The very complete maps enhance its value. The index could have been more detailed.

Miami University, Oxford, Ohio FRED B. JOYNER

Lincoln and His Generals. By T. Harry Williams. (New York: Alfred A. Knopf, 1952. viii + 363 + iv pp. Illustrations, bibliography, and index. $4.00.)

This volume, as its title suggests, is a study of Abraham Lincoln's relations to his generals throughout the Civil War. Of necessity it deals with campaigns and battles, with heavy emphasis on the affairs of the Army of the Potomac. Most of the volume is given over to an analysis and criticism of strategy and tactics. This, however, serves as a background for the more important discussion of personalities and the interplay of man on man. The central theme of the work thus becomes the emergence of Lincoln as a military mind and of the general whom he had all along been seeking, Ulysses S. Grant.

Two major contentions develop in the study: first, that Lincoln was the greatest general produced by the North, and second, that Grant was a greater general than Robert E. Lee. Neither of these contentions is new. Colin R. Ballard, in 1926, offered the first in a brief monograph, now republished, entitled *The Military Genius of Abraham Lincoln: An Essay*, and Major General J. F. C. Fuller set forth the second, in 1933, in his *Grant & Lee, A Study in Personality and Generalship*. The latter, moreover, contended as does Mr. Williams that the American Civil War was the first modern war on all counts.

The notable things about Mr. Williams' book are its excellent style, its fair and balanced treatment of men and events, its insight into personalities, and its firm grasp of military materials. As to his major contentions, it need only be said that he makes the most of them. Whether he presents a completely convincing case is another matter. To begin with, he is favored by the growing disposition to glorify Lincoln and to transform him into an Olympian figure. The public is willing to accept as sound fact almost any claim or assertion made in his favor. To discover that he was a military genius is, therefore, only a logical step in the growth of the Lincoln myth. This trend should suggest to the scholar unusual care and plenty of moderation in judgment. On these grounds a slight modification of all-out claims should be made.

It can hardly be denied that Lincoln's understanding of military matters grew as did the man himself in the four bitter years of trial and responsibility. He would have been a decidedly weak individual had this not been the case. That he acquired some sound ideas of what was necessary to win the war is equally clear. It took little of genius, however, to understand that the Mississippi waterway had to be kept open. That was a western essential that had played no small part in bringing that section enthusiastically into the war. Nor does it indicate an inborn military ability to have realized after two years of defeat that it was more important to destroy Lee's army than just to capture the city of Richmond. Civilian minds, not hampered by old-fashioned military rules, early grasped that fact. Nor should it be overlooked that Lincoln had at his call the best military minds of the day and that he talked problems over with them as they came and went through the years and he remained to profit by their trials and errors. Henry W. Halleck was there at his side, his brain to be picked and his judgments to be weighed long after he had ceased to play a dominant role.

It is also clear from Mr. Williams' own narrative that Lincoln was wrong more often than he was right in military affairs. His choice of generals was faulty until he found Grant. He opposed Sherman's march to the sea; he would have pushed George H. Thomas to action sooner than proved wise; he pulled McClellan back from the James where he should have remained. In fact, he blundered along with the rest, learning as he went, but with the advantage of not bearing direct responsibility and not being "dismissed" when he made mistakes.

As to Grant's superiority, that contention rests entirely on the charge of Lee's lack of interest in "global" strategy. Yet, as Mr. Williams admits, Grant's plans for an all-out general drive were faulty until he came under Lincoln's influence. If Lincoln is the genius, then Grant deserves less of credit. The character of his position, a new one created for his benefit, required him to view all fronts. That was his job, not his genius. George G. Meade commanded the army with which he associated; Grant was more or less free to take the wider responsibility. Lee, on the other hand, served under a West Point graduate as the Confederate president, Jefferson Davis, took over the "global" side of things; Lee, of necessity, commanded the Army of

Northern Virginia. How well he did his job compared with how well Grant did his is a matter of opinion and bias and little else.

These comments, however, are made in the name of caution, not criticism. Mr. Williams has written too good a book to be judged by the almost universal tendency to give Lincoln and Grant the benefit of all doubts.

University of Chicago AVERY CRAVEN

Foreigners in the Union Army and Navy. By Ella Lonn. (Baton Rouge: Louisiana State University Press, 1951. viii + 725 pp. Frontispiece, appendixes, bibliography, and index. $8.50.)

This splendid study is a companion volume to an earlier publication, *Foreigners in the Confederacy*. In both books the author explodes the oft- repeated myth that the one hundred per cent Anglo-Saxon South was defeated by overwhelming hordes of foreign hirelings. Her conclusions are undoubtedly upsetting to the racialist's interpretation of the Civil War. The earlier work proved that "tens of thousands" (p. 220) of foreign-born helped to fill the ranks of the Confederate army. The present volume reveals on the other hand that the foreign element in the Union forces amounted to "between one fourth and one fifth of the total number of enlistments — nearer one fifth" (p. 582), a smaller figure than has often been assumed. More important is the assertion that soldiers of foreign birth did not bear more than "their share of the burden of fighting" (p. 585).

To stress these highlights is to distort unwittingly the true character of the book. For one thing an effort was made to avoid the pitfalls of a specialized study by placing the subject in its historical context. In this respect the writer was successful except in some of her accounts of military operations, a failing of which she was aware. To do full justice to the military contributions of foreigners would perhaps, as she claims, require volumes. Still within the limits of a book not a military history, there was room for improvement in the description of various engagements. Minor errors of omission and commission could have been avoided. For the sake of clarity identification of divisions, corps, and armies to which certain companies and regiments were attached should have been more precise. Some of the mistakes in fact are to be found in the reason given for the concentration of Lee's forces at Sharpsburg and the establishment of the blockade. These shortcomings are not typical of the book nor even of those sections which have been criticized. The clear exposition of the role played by the ill-fated Eleventh Corps at Chancellorsville is both well balanced and fair.

Several chapters are particularly noteworthy. In one, the reasons for the enthusiastic response of the foreign-born to the call to arms are examined. Contrary to certain traditional accounts, the mercenary motive was only one of many, some of which were perhaps more important, such as ideals of freedom, a sense of responsible citizenship, and a feeling of gratitude toward the adopted land. An analysis of the familiar charge that the Union government connived to recruit soldiers in foreign countries is made in the chapter, "Eager Volunteers and War Immigration," and results in an exoneration of official conduct. While Secretary Seward encouraged immigration, he carefully observed the "bounds of international law" (p. 435). Foreign recruiting and the abuses connected with it resulted from the activities of some private agents who hoped to "make a neat profit for themselves on the bounties" (p. 434).

Many more enlightening interpretations are revealed in this exhaustive treatise on an important subject. Tentative though some of them may be, they were reached only after weighing available evidence.

Lafayette College EDWIN B. CODDINGTON

The Life of Billy Yank, The Common Soldier of the Union. By Bell Irvin Wiley. (Indianapolis: The Bobbs-Merrill Company, 1952. 454 pp. Illustrations, bibliography, and index. $6.00.)

The historian of Johnny Reb, himself of Confederate forebears but who sometimes fraternized with Yanks in *The Life of Johnny Reb*, has now crossed the picket lines — with some trepidation at first, he says — and after settling himself in the camps of the invader, has written the social history of the "Damyank," inappropriately termed "Billy Yank." But if a Rebel historian had to write this book, it is only fair that it should be reviewed by a descendant of a loyal Union family whose representative at first Bull Run was in the forefront of the retiring Yanks.

The reviewer is happy to state that the author not only has no sectional bias but is almost too sympathetic toward his subject, making every allowance for misdeeds and carefully balancing evil with good. Frequently his letter writers condemn themselves out of their own mouths. Especially amusing are the comments of semiliterate Union soldiers about the ignorance and backwardness of the South, its slatternly, snuff-dipping women, and its shiftless males.

The author, using quotations liberally to fortify his conclusions, covers every aspect of Yank soldiering — recruiting, training, the test of battle, reaction to the South and the Negro, health conditions, diversions and recreations, the operation of military law, food, moral conditions, morale, composition of the army, and attitudes toward the enemy.

Yank and Reb were surprisingly alike, though the former was more literate and more intellectual, more politically minded, more practical, less emotionally religious, less inclined to humor and imagination, and less deeply concerned about the war. In one respect only did this reviewer desire more light. While stating that the Union soldier displayed more interest in politics than

Johnny Reb, the author has little to say about political attitudes, party propaganda, soldier voting, and soldier opinions on issues, except to quote criticisms of politicians in general and to cite examples of widespread hostility to emancipation. Possibly the Yank, like soldiers in other wars, was more articulate about matters of more immediate concern.

While some aspects of Union soldier life have been covered by other writers, the whole picture is presented here for the first time, based upon much original research in both cultivated and neglected fields. A bibliographical essay describes materials consulted by the author but the seventy-three pages of notes, placed at the end of the book, are better evidence of the remarkable thoroughness of the research. Northern newspapers, except for selected samplings, were not examined, though some journals of occupied areas and various regimental newspapers were used. Much soldier material is concealed in the hundreds of small-town northern newspapers but the arduous research involved in consulting them and the greater value of the vast soldier output of letters and diaries probably justify the author's sampling method. The book is illustrated with some well-chosen photographs and drawings of camp life and army types. This truly excellent volume will be enjoyed not only by historical scholars but even more by that larger number — of whom the reviewer is one — who have carried a rifle, griped at the brass, and crinkled their nostrils at the odors of an outdoor latrine.

Ohio State University EUGENE H. ROSEBOOM

Ploughshares Into Swords: Josiah Gorgas and Confederate Ordnance. By Frank E. Vandiver. (Austin: University of Texas Press, 1952. xiv + 349 pp. Frontispiece, bibliography, and index. $5.00.)

Students of the Civil War period will rejoice in this detailed study of General Josiah Gorgas and Confederate ordnance. The author has done his research thoroughly, using as sources not only the usual printed records and the manuscripts in the National Archives, such as the records of the Adjutant General's office and Confederate records, which contain many important Gorgas letters, but he has also pursued material in many states and abroad. From the Burton Papers in Connecticut to the Governor of the Bahamas Letters in Government House at Nassau; from the Governor John Milton Letter Book at St. Augustine, Florida, to the Charles W. Ramsdell Note Files at Austin, Texas, Dr. Vandiver sought information concerning the General. More important, it appears that he has located all the Gorgas manuscripts that have survived, including four diaries kept by Gorgas himself.

The book bears an intriguing and appropriate title, *Ploughshares Into Swords*, and several of the chapters are distinguished by clever headings. At only one point would the reviewer quarrel with the choice of titles: for Chapter XIX she would substitute, "I Am Not Yet Old, and the World is Open to Me," a quotation from a letter to Gorgas' wife, as more suggestive of the spirit with which he met the collapse of the Confederacy. The proportions of the volume are good: the author assigns four chapters to the General's years before the Civil War, three to his postwar years, and the remaining fifteen chapters to the significant period of the Confederacy.

Dr. Vandiver has shown a good grasp of his subject by dealing with the many aspects of General Gorgas' problems: establishing the line of demarcation between Confederate and state authority; providing armaments and ammunition by blockade-running and by domestic manufacture; securing lead, copper, and sulphur; fixing the wage scale for laborers in his organization; and attempting to solve the other intricate problems of logistics.

Despite all the technical discussion of Gorgas' work and problems, there emerges a clear picture of the head of the Ordnance Bureau, his personality and character, his devotion to duty — not obscured by devotion to his family —, and even an impression of his appearance. A particularly clear picture of Gorgas is presented as he celebrated his forty-fifth birthday, which occurred at the height of his career during the war. The writer has shown considerable imagination, incorporating at times a bit from a general source into a specific situation, and he seems to be able to inject himself into Gorgas' thought processes.

Attention may be called to some lapses in conventional form, for example, in the use of and in the failure to use *ibid.* To readers accustomed to the more conventional abbreviations it is a bit difficult to recognize *The War of the Rebellion: A Compilation of the Official Records of the Union and Confederate Armies* and *Official Records of the Union and Confederate Navies in the War of the Rebellion* under the abbreviations of *ORA* and *ORN*.

The University of Texas Press may be congratulated on producing a book of good proportions, well printed, and bound in Confederate gray. This color has almost become standard since Professor A. J. Hanna set the fashion a few years ago, though the use of red for the top seems out of harmony with the Confederate gray and white.

Goucher College ELLA LONN

A Pictorial History of the Confederacy. By Lamont Buchanan. (New York: Crown Publishers, Inc., 1951. 288 pp. Illustrations and index. $5.00.)

That an effort should be made in the face of great difficulties to produce a work of this kind is additional evidence of that undying interest manifested in such a variety of ways in the Civil War period. In the collection are posters, broadsides, engravings, lithographs, and photographs. Some of the productions are not very realistic, a fact which suggests the shortcomings of the lithographic art in the South in the 1860's. The effect of war upon photographic supplies and the destruction of many pictures help to explain some unavoidable gaps in this type of study.

Since the *Pictorial History* covers the years from the active beginnings of the secession movement until the collapse of the Confederacy, it presents a variety of materials. There are photographs, many very good, of the most prominent civil and military leaders of the South; posters designed to produce encouragement at home and resentment of the enemy; reproductions that depict the courage of the soldier and the carnage of war; and scenes that suggest the gloom of defeat.

Any pictorial history is of greater or lesser significance in terms of the proportion of integration with narrative material. In justice to the author, let it be said that he states in the preface that "this book is not a history book. It is not a 'scholar's' lengthy reference work." Had there been, however, some analysis of the interplay of forces in the Confederacy, of the difficult problems that pressed for solution, and often proved insoluble, the volume would be more worth while. There is narrative material, presented usually in chronological fashion, which serves to suggest the import of the pictorial representation, and suggests it adequately, the reviewer feels, as far as the layman is concerned. Occasionally, though, the narrative leaves something to be desired in the way of clarity. This minor criticism is illustrated by the statements that, with four tickets in the field in 1860, "the resulting national vote was purely sectional" (p. 16), and "Benjamin was wealthy and had made his wealth by virtue of the system which the South represented" (p. 73).

A Pictorial History of the Confederacy represents much time and effort on the part of the author, and its numerous and varied illustrations should prove interesting and entertaining to layman and scholar alike.

Ohio State University HENRY H. SIMMS

Private John Allen, Gentleman — Statesman — Sage — Prophet. By Claude Gentry. (Baldwyn, Miss.: The Author, 1951. xviii + 189 pp. Illustrations. $3.50.)

One discovers from the forty segments of this book that John M. Allen was born in 1846; that he served as a spy and scout during the Civil War; that he studied law under L. Q. C. Lamar at the University of Mississippi; that he practiced at Tupelo from 1870 until 1885; that he "kept Congress awake" for the next sixteen years; that he was an egotist possessed of much common sense and full of good-natured, needling wit; and that he lived the last sixteen years of his life in relative leisure — enjoying and adding to his reputation as a raconteur.

But one does not discover a coherent, balanced discussion of the career of this private-congressman-humorist. The book consists primarily of quotations from Allen's speeches; if the speech was on "cheese," there must be a segment entitled "Cheese." There is no evident effort to study the man and his ideas, to trace out principles and ideals to which he subscribed, or even to present enough chronology and sequence to enable the reader to make analyses for himself. Insufficient evidence is presented to justify the assertion that Allen was an "able statesman" endowed with great prescience, and certainly it would be difficult to prove that he was always "found on the right side of any question." The author seems to have been blinded by hero worship.

Superficiality is compounded with bad writing and misinformation: "There was not one bill bearing his name passed by Congress during his time there but he was instrumental in passing or defeating many bills, measures important to the nation, many of them he helped defeat would have been detrimental to the welfare of the country, if they had been passed, many he helped pass were helpful" (p. xvii)! Was "cowboys" one of the great games of the 1840's and 1850's (p. 2)? Was the horse and buggy rig the "only mode of travel" in the rural sections at that time (p. 2)? Did *each* roustabout *carry* a 500-pound bale of cotton *up* the gang-plank (p. 3)? Just what was Allen's age in 1862 (pp. 1, 5, and sketch between pp. 15 and 16)? Is it 125 miles from Tupelo to Memphis (p. 3) or 60 miles from Tupelo to Corinth (p. 5)? Was the Civil War "re-fought practically every day in Congress" in 1885 (p. 17)?

The book is entertaining, but it is bad biography and even worse history. Allen deserves better treatment.

Indiana University CHASE C. MOONEY

North America. By Anthony Trollope. Edited, with an introduction, notes, and new materials, by Donald Smalley and Bradford Allen Booth. (New York: Alfred A. Knopf, 1951. xxxvii + 555 + viii pp. Illustrations, appendixes, bibliography, and index. $6.00.)

Anthony Trollope's announced intention in writing *North America* was to fulfill a literary ambition of writing a book about the United States. In so doing it was his wish to describe to the best of his ability what to him was an exciting, if disconcerting, social and political experiment. He came to the United States to write his book at a critical time in the progress of that experiment. He came with sympathies entirely northern to write a book for English consumption when English feeling was pro-southern and American feeling was anti-English.

When Trollope came to the United States in 1862 to fulfill his ambition, the war was proceeding uncertainly, the new President was still an unknown quantity, and the federal government was beset with war scandals. Herein lies one of the intrinsic values of the book, the presentation of the point of view of a sympathetic Englishman when the northern cause was in peril both at home and abroad. Trollope had no hesitancy in speaking his mind to both Americans and to his fellow citizens on the need for a greater tolerance of other men's views.

North America was written primarily for English readers and for English readers with a very general notion of how American institutions operated. Eager to present a clear and lucid explanation of American practices, particularly where they related to the political scene, he drew frequent analogies with English practices and employed English terminology. In the original edition Trollope included the texts of the Declaration of Independence, the Articles of Confederation, and the Constitution. The editors of this new edition have wisely omitted these more obvious items.

One of Trollope's primary concerns and one which gave him considerable unhappiness was the causes of the war. Again and again as he made his way across the northern states he returned to the conflict to analyze, ruminate, speculate, and prognosticate. In spite of his wish to see the problem clearly, his conclusions and predictions are those of a novelist rather than one schooled in political theory or economics.

On his journey Trollope visited only the northern states and southern Canada. He went as far west as St. Louis and as far north as St. Paul. He visited army camps, institutions, public monuments, and other points of interest. He spent uncounted hours in hotel lobbies, on trains, and in public places chatting with American travelers. He commented freely, and at times petulantly, about American hotels, eating habits, education, newspapers, the war scandals, children, American women, trains and transportation facilities, the postal system, and the cities which he visited. As he knew that his work would be read on this side of the Atlantic as well as in England and as he knew that many of his comments would not be received favorably by Americans, the book has an apologetic tone. When he censured or spoke unfavorably about an American practice or institution, he hastened to add conciliatory remarks. Of the cities that he visited, Boston and Baltimore were his favorites; New York and Washington he found uncongenial.

Much of what Trollope said had been said before. He added little that was new or fresh in his observations. The value of the book rests in its eyewitness account of the northern states at a critical period in American history.

The editors have contributed a provocative introduction and an excellent bibliography. The text has been edited with care, copiously annotated and illustrated with prints from contemporary sources. The new edition is a handsome companion volume to the edition of Frances Milton Trollope's *The Domestic Manners of the Americans* which Alfred Knopf published in 1949 under the editorship of Mr. Smalley.

Western Reserve University RUSSELL A. GRIFFIN

Trail Driving Days. Text by Dee Brown. Picture research by Martin F. Schmitt. (New York: Charles Scribner's Sons, 1952. xxii + 264 pp. Illustrations and bibliography. $7.50.)

This is a big book; its over-all measurements are twelve by eight and a half inches. Its 8 chapters and 229 illustrations present a colorful panorama of the life of the range cattle area during most of the latter half of the nineteenth century. The text interestingly describes the work and lifeways of the "men who made the Cow Country." These include not only the great figures of the industry but also the lean, brown men who drove the herds up the long trails from Texas to the northern plains, joined in the roundups, and did most of the rough, and sometimes dangerous, work of the average cowhand.

Considerable attention is also given to the deeds, or misdeeds, of other picturesque characters: the county sheriffs, town marshals of such places as Abilene and Dodge City, outlaws, rustlers, buffalo hunters, gamblers, and the few women, good or bad, who helped to make up the pattern of society in this part of the West when it was truly wild. There are accounts of feuds and range wars, of the part played by the British and Continentals in this great pastoral drama, and of the tragic winter of 1886-1887 and its results.

Interesting as is the text, it is the illustrations which make the book a unique contribution to the literature of the West. There are approximately twenty pages of pictures following each of the eight chapters of text. Most of these are from photographs and the task of collecting them must have been an enormous one. The bibliography, while made up almost entirely of secondary accounts, is extensive, consisting of some five hundred titles. This is a beautiful book which contains the greatest collection of pictures of the Cow Country ever assembled in a single volume. Everyone interested in western history should read and own it.

University of Oklahoma EDWARD EVERETT DALE

Steamboats in the Timber. By Ruby El Hult. (Caldwell: The Caxton Printers, Ltd., 1952. 209 pp. Illustrations, map, appendix, and index. $4.00.)

It may come as news to many that the state of Idaho has a maritime history of its own. Between 1880 and 1940 steamboats plied the waters of Lake Coeur d' Alene and some of its tributaries — steamboats operating quite truly "in the timber" — and at its peak steamboating here was more extensive than on any other inland body of water west of the Great Lakes. The boats carried supplies to Fort Coeur d' Alene, ore from gold, silver, and lead mines, lumber from the forests and fish from the rivers, mail and freight to settlers along the lake shore and the river banks, produce to market, and, finally, honeymooners and sightseers. A historian might undertake a serious economic study of this activity. Miss Hult has written instead an entertaining, anecdotal story, which her publishers have wrapped up attractively with numerous apt illustrations and a good map. Her sources are the files of the Coeur d' Alene *Press*, especially a reminiscent "anniversary" issue of the paper, the oral recollections of steamboatmen and "other assorted old-timers," published memoirs, local histories, and popular accounts of certain phases of her subject, such as Stewart Holbrook's *Holy Old Mackinaw*.

University of Illinois RICHARD N. CURRENT

Legend into History: The Custer Mystery; An Analytical Study of the Battle of the Little Big Horn. By Charles Kuhlman. (Harrisburg: The Stackpole Company, 1951. xxi + 250 pp. Illustrations, maps, appendixes, bibliography, and index. $5.00.)

One of the intriguing mysteries of American military history is the "Custer Massacre" on the Little Big Horn in southern Montana in 1876. Despite the publication of a number of volumes, both reminiscences and sturdier works attempting to assess blame for that debacle, the question has remained one of partisan conflict between the Custer adherents and detractors. While judicious textbook writers have generally sidestepped the issue of passing judgment on Custer's competence, perhaps more people have been willing to believe that "Old Glory Hunter" rode recklessly to his own destruction.

Dr. Kuhlman chooses to ride right into the middle of this ancient controversy and to lay down a thesis that Custer behaved in a reasonable way as he led his troops on that broad reconnaissance from Rosebud Creek to the Little Big Horn. He does not pretend to offer new evidence, though he is familiar with all the published materials. However, he does bring to this knowledge of the debacle a microscopic understanding of the battle area and a willingness to test what a man did or said against that backdrop at the time when he was in action. This reasoning is packed both topically and chronologically within the ten chapters, and covers in great detail the events of that fateful third week in June, 1876.

Basic in Dr. Kuhlman's thesis are these propositions: Custer could not have known of the Indian concentration until it was too late to adopt a battle plan; his decision to turn right and go ahead of the other commands was correct in that the purpose was to make a flank attack upon the main body; that up to the time when he gave his last recorded order and rode off into legend, he had reason to expect reinforcements from Weir Point. All of this sets up a tight case to prove that Custer was no wild man who followed a premonition to his death.

It would be idle to assume that this book will put the matter to rest, but for those who live outside the Custer controversy it will stand as a reasonable case. The book leaves the impression that to argue with the author requires a correlation of geography and minute evidence which most readers do not have.

Wisconsin State College, River Falls WALKER D. WYMAN

American Conservatism in the Age of Enterprise; A Study of William Graham Sumner, Stephen J. Field, and Andrew Carnegie. By Robert Green McCloskey. (Cambridge: Harvard University Press, 1951. xi + 193 pp. Index. $3.25.)

This pungent volume is keen in ideological analysis but is inadequately oriented in the historical background and literature of the subject. The author's sins of omission and commission might be viewed with more charity did he not press so frankly the drastic devaluation of history implied in Voltaire's cynical definition and Carl Becker's relativism (p. 7). The book's chief contribution inheres in the sharp focus to which it brings existing knowledge of conservative trends of thought during the "Gilded Age." Mr. McCloskey depicts brilliantly how neoconservatism succeeded then in turning traditional democratic values, concepts, and ethics upside down, and substituted for them a brutal materialism, an elitist creed, and a laissez-faire system chiefly beneficial to business buccaneers. The analysis of Sumner's antidemocratic thought and of the dualism in the judicial dissents and decisions of Justice Field is most effective; that of Carnegie's writings is suggestive but more superficial.

The implications of the new conservatism for popular sovereignty, for government regulation of business, are well developed. Much if not all of this was discovered earlier by Charles A. Beard, Ralph Gabriel, Carl Brent Swisher, Richard Hofstadter, John D. Hicks, and Burton J. Hendrick. Mr. McCloskey is unacquainted with Benjamin R. Twiss's brilliant monograph which discloses the decisive influence exerted by Thomas M. Cooley upon conservative juristic theory and constitutional interpretation. Carnegie's doctrine of stewardship is not related to the Second Great Awakening, from which it probably sprang, and the steel magnate's sophistication is not weighed in the balance with the almost naïve essays and books that he distributed to influence minds unacquainted with the schools of philosophy (Positivism, Social Darwinism, etc.) from which he derived the real self-justification that Mr. McCloskey thinks he disclosed in *Triumphant Democracy*.

For all the verbal pyrotechnics of this interesting treatise, its author exhibits a naïveté all his own. Only this and ignorance of the business realities of the epoch he discusses can explain a readiness to accept as "sincere" a railroad tycoon's assertion that "national honor" was besmirched by a law requiring certain subsidized Pacific railroads to pay their bonded indebtedness (p. 17). The thought of the men studied can hardly be generalized into that of their entire era. Henry D. Lloyd, Richard T. Ely, Henry George,

Washington Gladden, Jane Addams, and Frances E. Willard kept alive and refocused upon the realities of the urban-industrial age the humane tradition, moral standards, and hierarchy of values of the traditional democratic creed in a manner that created the social dynamics of another great democratic revival during the same decades in which the neoconservatism of Sumner, Field, and Carniege was in the ascendant. Oliver Wendell Holmes's pragmatic jurisprudence originated in the same era.

Connecticut College CHESTER MCARTHUR DESTLER

Boss Ruef's San Francisco; The Story of the Union Labor Party, Big Business, and the Graft Prosecution. By Walton Bean. (Berkeley and Los Angeles: University of California Press, 1952. xii + 345 pp. Illustrations, bibliography, and index. $5.00.)

The story of Boss Ruef is a history of urban government early in the twentieth century. It was a period marked by manipulation of voters, irresponsible public administration, urban and industrial expansion with opportunities for private profit at public expense, business leaders willing to pay corruptly for favors and franchises, and insistent reformers hoping to slay corruption with one blow. Professor Bean's story is full of entertainment, human-interest drama, and implicit questions concerning democratic government and boss rule. This book is a factual narrative burdened with no thesis respecting corruption, civic virtue, or methods of reform. The lessons are for the reader to determine for himself. The author is aware of the national scene and of the larger importance of national figures who move through the story of Boss Ruef's San Francisco. Professor Bean's high level of writing ability, skill of organization, and detailed research have realized the potentialities of his subject.

At the turn of the century municipal politics posed the question whether American democracy, nurtured in an agrarian society, could survive in an urban and industrial environment. The nation's cities wallowed in maladministration and corruption but few matched the record that was established in San Francisco under Boss Ruef's manipulations. Abraham Ruef was a brilliant lawyer who started his public career as a reformer, became entranced by local politics, and played the game for all it was worth in personal power and dollars. Probably no less corrupt than the famous bosses of the late nineteenth century, he had the distinct historical advantage of possessing an interesting personality. Ruef fastened himself upon the local Union Labor party, having recognized the potential power of a party which might command the votes of the laboring people. By accident this third party came into full control of San Francisco's government in advance of Ruef's calculations and with a set of pliable officers, including an orchestra leader as mayor. Even with weak, amateur, and greedy lieutenants, Boss Ruef proceeded to construct an exchange for selling the favors of the city government at more than bargain-counter rates. Ruef had no shortage of eager customers for telephone and street railway franchises and aids to real-estate promotions. In accord with the sentiments of progressivism, a group of indignant citizens led by Fremont Older, of the famous San Francisco *Bulletin*, and Rudolph Spreckels set out to clean up the city. They had the encouragement of President Theodore Roosevelt and Lincoln Steffens, and the very aggressive aid of Francis J. Heney and William J. Burns. These reformers were doggedly determined at all costs to make an example of San Francisco, and prove that the source of corruption lay in aggressive Big Business more than it did in irresponsible government. The graft prosecutions were lurid and long-lived and they brought to light such a mass of malfeasance as to dull the public's sense of outrage. While the thieves fell out, the reformers differed as to their own ambitions. The prosecutions failed to secure conviction of any "higher-up" among the leaders of business and produced only one pitable victim, Abe Ruef. The prosecutions laid bare a record of municipal corruption which should have provided an object lesson for every public officer since tempted to forget his duty. Though Ruef was not crude, his errors were avoidable and the techniques used by him have been refined.

University of California, Davis JAMES H. SHIDELER

The California Progressives. By George E. Mowry. *Chronicles of California.* (Berkeley and Los Angeles: University of California Press, 1951. xi + 349 pp. Illustrations, bibliography, and index. $6.00.)

It is just forty years since the Progressive movement neared its crescendo in the election of 1912. Most of its leaders are gone, and the generation that it inspired in their youth is passing from power. Time has brought great changes also in the historical evaluations of the movement. From the autobiographies of Progressive leaders who saw in their programs the eternal salvation of mankind, through the disillusion implicit in books like John Chamberlin's *Farewell to Reform,* most of the writing suffered from distorting emotional overtones. Now Professor Mowry, although writing with an avowed liberal bias, has produced a lucid and remarkably objective analysis of one of the most important segments of progressivism.

In an earlier book Mowry examined a great national figure, Theodore Roosevelt. In this one he has made a definitive study of one of the most successful groups of state Progressive leaders. California in the early 1900's suffered from the essential factors which goaded Progressives to revolt. The Southern Pacific Railroad had a stranglehold upon the economy and government of the state; a corrupt machine based on union labor votes and doing business with the large corporate interests controlled San Francisco.

Frank Norris in *The Octopus* dramatized the struggle of the wheat farmers against the railroad, but it was not the agrarian interests that led the Progressive revolt, although they undoubtedly furnished votes for it. Rather, as Mowry demonstrates with quantities of evidence, its force was supplied by the young middle-class business and professional men — most of them rather well-to-do men who earlier had voted for McKinley. Their aim was to destroy the political power of monopoly in the state, whether corporate monopoly (the railroad), or labor monopoly (the San Francisco Union Labor party). They differed in their attitude toward labor from rather militant anti-unionism to merely a mild desire to prevent unions from perpetuating a corrupt city machine. Hiram Johnson, who was rather friendly, could muster the San Francisco labor vote. But the voting backbone of progressivism was the middle class.

With meticulous care, Professor Mowry lays bare the anatomy of the California Progressive movement. It involves not only the struggle of a class for power, but also the clash of rival Progressive politicians with varying ideas and ambitions. Their intricate maneuvering sometimes resulted in disaster for the movement as a whole. Johnson, who dominated the scene, was frequently egocentric and irrascible. As governor he led in the enactment of an array of reform measures, then chose to go no further. Rather he wished to use his wide following in the state to promote his national political ambitions. In 1916 this inevitably made difficulties for the Republican presidential nominee, Charles Evans Hughes. But Professor Mowry demonstrates that the failure of Hughes to carry California was due to more than Johnson's pique or some minor political accident. Too many California voters simply did not like Hughes, his party, and its program. At the same time they sent Johnson to the Senate, where he soon lost almost every vestige of progressivism. Most middle-class voters, like Johnson, had wished to see the enactment of only a limited group of reforms, and by the 1920's they were absorbed in other matters.

What happened in California had parallels and variants in many other states. That is what gives this brilliant study especial significance.

University of Illinois FRANK FREIDEL

The Private Papers of Senator Vandenberg. Edited by Arthur H. Vandenberg, Jr., with the collaboration of Joe Alex Morris. (Boston: Houghton Mifflin Company, 1952. xxii + 599 pp. Illustrations, notes, and index. $5.00.)

Arthur Vandenberg was an extremely significant figure in public life and particularly in American foreign policy in the years from 1943 to 1950. When his illness made it impossible for him to continue his activities, President Truman wrote to him in 1950: "You just don't realize what a vacuum there has been in the Senate and in the operation of our foreign policy since you left. . . . It is very seldom that men really become statesmen while they are yet alive, in the minds of the people and their associates. As you well know, I have always held you in that category."

Collected in this book are excerpts from the diaries, correspondence, and speeches of Senator Vandenberg. The editors, in addition to making the selections, have supplied explanatory material connecting the excerpts. The first excerpt begins in September, 1939, and the last is dated March 6, 1951. The material dealing with the "isolationist" phase of Vandenberg's career is highly condensed. The book really concentrates on the years from 1943 to 1951. As a result, his "isolationist" period is not sufficiently full to furnish the reader with enough information completely to understand the shift in thinking in his later career.

Of great value to the historian is the material dealing with (1) executive-congressional relations in foreign policy formation; (2) the development of, and vicissitudes of, a nonpartisan foreign policy; (3) the building of the United Nations; (4) the growth of a firm policy toward the Soviet Union; (5) Vandenberg's views on such personalities as Presidents Roosevelt and Truman, James Byrnes, Edward R. Stettinius, Jr., General Marshall, and Robert Taft.

Although the editors may well have left out much valuable material, this nevertheless is a frank and honest book. They fortunately have not been uncritical of the Senator nor have they fallen into the error of apologizing for his "isolationist" attitude. Furthermore, they have retained material which, from the standpoint of avoiding partisan political criticism of their editing, might have been deleted. In discussing the debates on the Marshall Plan, Vandenberg wrote (p. 501): "I get so damned sick of that little band of GOP isolationists who are always in the way that I could scream," or writing in 1947 (p. 379): "Evidently I am to have some degree of trouble with Bob Taft. So be it! The world is full of tragedy; but there is no tragedy greater than that we have to have a presidential election next year in the U.S.A. That must be what's biting Robert."

Although the editors include material on Vandenberg's ability from 1943 to 1950 to anticipate foreign policy developments, to overcome political obstacles in the Senate, and, as a result, to translate policy into law, this significant contribution of the Senator is not as fully developed as one might like. It was in this area, rather than in the creation of policy, that Vandenberg after all made his major contribution. Occasionally, too, the editors failed to supply needed explanatory material, but, in spite of these occasional gaps, they have prepared one of the better memoirs of the war and postwar years.

University of Chicago WALTER JOHNSON

The Mennonite Church in the Second World War. By Guy Franklin Hershberger. Foreword by Harold S. Bender. (Scottdale, Pa.: Mennonite Publishing House, 1951. 308 pp. Index. $3.50.)

Because of their belief in nonresistance the members of the Mennonite Church found the Second World War a period of unusual activity. This book, sponsored by the Peace Problems Committee of the church, traces a difficult period in the history of this religious organization.

The author gives an account of the variety of alternative services rendered by conscientious Mennonites and especially those who were subject to military service. Civilian Public Service was performed in soil conservation work, forestry (including fire fighting), agriculture, dairy herd testing, hospital and other health service, in human guinea pig experimentation, and similar activities. Foreign service was closed to draftees by act of Congress after some of the young men were as far away as Africa on their way to fields of work. Mennonites not subject to the draft, however, were able to enter upon foreign relief, rehabilitation, and refugee activities some of which had been begun before the United States entered the war.

The relief, rehabilitation, and refugee work was carried on in more than a score of countries and regions. On reading this account, one is impressed by the evidence that when doctors, dentists, nurses, and other professional and nonprofessional workers were called for, there were always volunteers ready to assume the responsibilities. Some of the personnel were loaned to agencies such as UNRRA and CRALOG while others worked cooperatively with LARA and similar organizations. The majority of Mennonites worked directly under the supervision of the Mennonite Central Committee of Akron, Pennsylvania. On the list of places where these volunteers worked one finds such strange names as Tczew, Cerbere, Lavercantiere, Torre Pellice, Itacurubi, Vigan, Nasielsk, Camino, Aibonito, and Jaszarokszallas. No doubt many a parent learned much new geography during the period.

While this world service was being performed, Mennonites of different countries and different backgrounds learned to work together. Also many of them learned that voluntary service need not be limited to the time of actual warfare. For those who would know about this experience of 66,000 Mennonites this book is required reading.

Western Reserve University JACOB C. MEYER

Canada and the United States; Some Aspects of Their Historical Relations. By Hugh Ll. Keenleyside and Gerald S. Brown. Introduction by W. P. M. Kennedy. Revised and enlarged edition. (New York: Alfred A. Knopf, 1952. xxvi + 406 + xii pp. Maps, tables, charts, bibliography, and index. $6.00.)

The extreme cordiality of official Canadian-American relations recently and the absence of any significant military operations along the border for a hundred and fifty years have led many people on both sides of the frontier to assume that this friendliness has been a permanent feature of relations between the two countries. This is the "unguarded frontier" beloved of orators and politicians. The facts, as this study reveals, have rarely coincided with this popular concept. Messrs. Keenleyside and Brown have taken great pains to show how relations between the two countries have often been far from amicable. The spirit of Canadian suspicion and resentment is by no means dead and finds expression today even in such an impeccable publication as the *Report of the Royal Commission on National Development in Arts, Letters, and Sciences in Canada.*

This book gives a clear and concise description of the course of Canadian-American relations from the invasion of 1776 down to the present. Originally published in 1929, it has been completely revised in the light of recent researches and embodies a good deal of material which has become available since the original publication. It is written in a pleasant and readable style which enhances the value of the account. The authors are concerned not only with the settlement of diplomatic disputes over boundaries, fishing rights, and interference in the domestic affairs of the other country but also with commercial relations and the extent and character of immigration between the two countries. Particularly valuable are the sections dealing with the effect of Canadian-American relations in shaping Canadian opinion toward the United States. They emphasize the importance of such events as the coming of the Loyalists, Canadian fear of manifest destiny, and American moral righteousness in World War I in creating a considerable body of public opinion in Canada hostile to the United States. The importance of the personal friendship between Mackenzie King and Franklin Roosevelt in mitigating this attitude and promoting more cordial relations is stressed. Moreover, throughout the book the authors maintain an impartial and judicious attitude which is in refreshing contrast to the usual Canadian or American discussions of this topic.

While there are no footnote references in the text, there is a small but useful selective bibliography of additional works. The presence of a number of tables and charts dealing with immigration and economic conditions is also helpful.

Australian National University WILLIAM K. ROLPH

Foreign Relations of the United States: Diplomatic Papers, 1934. Vols. I and II. (Washington: United States Government Printing Office, 1951. Vol. I: *General, The British Commonwealth.* xcvi + 1031 pp. $3.75. Vol. II: *Europe, Near East, Africa.* xcv + 1002 pp. $3.75.)

In Europe, as in the Far East, 1934 was a year of relative quiet for American foreign policy. The disarmament discussions at Geneva were allowed to run their unhappy course; the early end of naval ratios was accepted; the badly snarled issue of defaulted war debts remained unsolved; and the quest for international supervision of the arms traffic got nowhere. Ominous portents appeared in many quarters of the horizon; but American diplomacy continued in well-established and familiar channels, with no disposition to face up to the growing totalitarian challenge.

The organization of the volumes for 1934 follows the pattern set for 1932. There will be five in all. The first is devoted largely to problems the multilateral nature of which do not permit treatment under individual country headings. The World Disarmament Conference claims 216 pages (in contrast to the 574 for 1932 and the 335 for 1933). The discussions preliminary to the London Naval Conference of 1935 occupy another 210. Some papers bearing on this last topic were contained in *Foreign Relations of the United States: Japan, 1931-1941* (2 vols., 1943) and are not reprinted here. Other general subjects receiving less space are the protests of foreign governments against the procedures of the Nye Committee; the attempt to gain Senate approval for the Arms Traffic Convention of 1926; the European negotiations for an Eastern Locarno Pact of Mutual Guarantee; and the conversations on the application of the Johnson Act and the future of war debt payments.

The last fifth of Volume I is given over to negotiations with individual members of the British Commonwealth. In the second volume the arrangement is alphabetically by nations under the two major headings of Europe and of the Near East and Africa. Germany, where Hitler was consolidating his power, rightly receives the greatest number of pages; but there are useful, briefer extracts on the Dollfuss regime in Austria, the German minorities in Czechoslovakia, and Italy's stand during the Wal Wal incident which preceded the invasion of Ethiopia. Volume III, dealing with the Far East, has already been reviewed in these pages (XXXVIII, 138-39). The fourth and fifth will be concerned with the American republics. Controversies with Russia have been mostly omitted; they will be contained in a separate publication covering our relations with the Soviet Union from 1933 to 1939.

In perusing these documents today, one is struck by the extreme caution with which American diplomats moved on the European scene eighteen years ago. Even the most innocuous public statements were then watered down lest they be interpreted abroad as implying "aid against an aggressor" or at home as "an intervention in European political affairs" (II, 21). One is also reminded of the pervasive character of the war debt problem and the way in which it complicated other issues. From these pages emerges the almost forgotten figure of Norman Davis, a biography of whom is now overdue. The glimpses of Hitler, Mussolini, Yamamoto, and the disorganized Sudeten

Germans suggest how much time still remained before Munich and Pearl Harbor.

As noted before, this series does not provide as much material on the domestic forces that shaped American diplomacy as it does on conditions abroad. In these volumes there is some data on senatorial attitudes and alignments upon the Arms Traffic Convention and the St. Lawrence Waterway project but none at all, for example, on the bill liberating the Philippines or the plan to join the World Court. The planning and discussion within the State Department go undocumented, not because of editorial omissions but because that type of record apparently does not exist. It is to be hoped that that vital information will be obtained when the private papers and diaries of key statesmen become available.

Northwestern University RICHARD W. LEOPOLD

Documents on American Foreign Relations. Vol. XII, *January 1-December 31, 1950*. Edited by Raymond Dennett and Robert K. Turner. (Princeton: Princeton University Press for World Peace Foundation, 1951. xxvi + 702 pp. Index. $6.00.)

This book is far more than the title implies. It is not simply a collection of documents but rather a selection of documents chosen to illustrate the development of important phases of American foreign policy during the year 1950. These phases, including such topics as the conduct of foreign relations, economic development, and national defense, have been a standard part of the earlier volumes in this series. However, the growing role of the United States in world affairs has made it necessary to depart from the earlier organization in several ways. Chapter V, "International Peace and Security," has been expanded to include important developments in the organization of regional security agencies. In the last four chapters, which deal with the major geographical areas, special sections treating regional political problems have been added. The present volume also differs from earlier ones in that it devotes a separate chapter to Europe and a new chapter on the Middle East and Africa.

As a consequence of this elaborate organization, the various parts of the work are related to each other. At the same time its value for reference is enhanced as the material is easily and quickly located. The standard organization over the years makes all twelve volumes a unit, and cross-index references to earlier volumes increase the usefulness of the series. An index for the current volume is almost superfluous, although a good one is provided.

Those who predict that modern civilization will crush itself under a profusion of printed matter may find ample substantiation in the hundreds of documents relating to foreign policy issued by the government in 1950. In view of this inundation of information the winnowing work of *Documents on*

American Foreign Policy, wisely conceived and skillfully executed, is of great value to all persons concerned with current American foreign policy.

University of Georgia J. CHAL VINSON

The United States and the Far East, 1945-1951. By Harold M. Vinacke. Published under the auspices of the American Institute of Pacific Relations, Inc. (Stanford: Stanford University Press, 1952. vi + 144 pp. Index. $3.00.)

This book is an Institute of Pacific Relations publication and carries a brief preface by W. L. Holland, the executive vice-chairman of that organization. It is an adequate, but not penetrating summary of United States Far Eastern policies from 1945 to the summer of 1951. A seven-page chapter on the issues in Southeast Asia (Indonesia not included), is followed by chapters on China, Korea, and Japan. For his information respecting China, Mr. Vinacke has dipped liberally into the White Paper of 1949. China, he recognizes, was truly a "problem country" during the war, with two rival governments contending against each other; but official American policy proceeded on the established fiction that there was only one government, the Nationalist, and that this government would be a partner of the United States in the years to come. The chapter continues with an accurate summary of events until the expulsion of the Nationalists from the mainland, but it makes no attempt to get below the surface. The Chennault-Stilwell feud receives no mention, nor is there a reference to the fifty-page Wedemeyer Report of 1947, which the Truman administration suppressed for nearly two years.

The author maintains a severely neutral attitude toward American policies elsewhere in the Far East, as well as in China, but he recognizes the fatal weakness of basing policy on hypotheses or assumptions that are not supported by facts. An honest effort by the Department of State in 1949 to reexamine its policies, he points out, was defeated by the partisan attacks which followed the publication of the White Paper. The book is to be recommended as a sound, though too brief work of reference. It contains a good summary of the opposing points of view of Douglas MacArthur and the Joint Chiefs, and it warns in conclusion that mere cessation of hostilities in Korea will not bring peace to the Far East.

University of Southern California RICHARD W. VAN ALSTYNE

The Irony of American History. By Reinhold Niebuhr. (New York: Charles Scribner's Sons, 1952. xi + 174 pp. $2.50.)

Reinhold Niebuhr's successive books make increasingly clear how deeply a historical consciousness informs the outlook of Protestant neo-orthodoxy in the United States. Although this little volume is essentially a tract for the times, it reaches out boldly along two historical planes. To illuminate the moral and ideological difficulties surrounding America's foreign policy, it draws from the American past the persistent traditions which seem to endanger the present task. And to provide a ground for criticizing and controlling those traditions, it offers a Christian interpretation of the nature of history itself.

The center of Dr. Niebuhr's concern lies in the cold war. He warns that we may fail to sustain the present policy of cooperative, restrained, indefinitely prolonged resistance to world communism because many of our ideals tempt us to overestimate our abilities. Indeed, the present situation is full of "irony" (in Dr. Niebuhr's special sense of the term) because our ideals have become incongruous with reality and thus partial illusions. Optimistic illusions about human nature, although inherent in "modern liberal culture," have achieved special emphasis in the course of American history. From Puritan and Jeffersonian sources arose a belief that America — released from the evils of Europe — was making a new beginning for mankind. In foreign affairs the Americans became convinced of their unique innocence and of their messianic destiny to regenerate the world. Domestically, Puritan, Jeffersonian, and other influences inflated "bourgeois" materialism by equating prosperity, virtue, and happiness. Now, these pretensions to strength have become sources of weakness.

A final chapter suggests that ironic incongruities between human pretensions and human possibilities comprise the principal element in all history from a Christian point of view. Man's fate is ironic more often than tragic because men who recognize their excessive pretensions have the power to diminish them. So we are advised to have patience, to temper our expectations, and to combine resolution with contrition.

This conception of irony — freighted with unfamiliar meanings and dependent on certain conditions in the observer as well as the situation — adds little to the philosophy of history which Dr. Niebuhr has expounded before. It does, however, give a wide field for his love of paradox. More important, it indicates the special function of history in his system of thought. Religiously orthodox and politically liberal, he finds history a realm of mingled achievements and defeats. As such, it mediates between a theology which emphasizes man's failures and a pragmatic politics which endorses his strivings.

University of California, Los Angeles JOHN HIGHAM

The Policy Sciences; Recent Developments in Scope and Method. Edited by Daniel Lerner and Harold D. Lasswell. With the editorial collaboration of Harold H. Fisher, Ernest R. Hilgard, Saul K. Padover, Ithiel de Sola Pool, and C. Easton Rothwell. Foreword by C. Easton Rothwell. (Stanford: Stanford University Press, 1951. xiv + 344 pp. Figures, tables, bibliography, and index. $7.50.)

The purpose of this book, as indicated by its title, is to urge the greater use of social science in forming public or private policy. The case is ably argued by leaders in applied social science such as Harold D. Lasswell, Paul F. Lazarsfeld, and Robert K. Merton. The most telling argument is that the new perspectives of social scientists lead to the restatement of practical problems in more comprehensive form. Americans with their empirical, rule-of-thumb traditions are inclined to be deficient in long-range planning and vision, and the contributors to this volume indicate a number of specific ways in which the "policy sciences" may be used to correct this national nearsightedness.

But for most historians the book will probably have a different major value. Here in brief compass, if 307 double column pages of small print may be so called, is a series of articles by some of the nation's leading social scientists outlining the new theoretical developments that appear to have the most importance for application to practical affairs. This is certainly what the scientifically inclined historian needs, for example: from Clyde Kluckholn or Margaret Meade, he can learn of recent anthropological ideas regarding culture; from Edward A. Shils, he can become acquainted with the great interest of sociologists in the primary group; or with George Katona, he can view the borderland between psychology and economics. Of special interest to the recent historian who deals with living people are the two essays on interview techniques by Herbert Hyman and Rensis Likert. The historian may also find clues to new research in the explanatory footnotes that accompany each essay. In addition, there is a 26-page bibliography of both books and articles, but the basis for the inclusion of items is not discussed and the alphabetical list seems more the result of chance citation in the chapters than design by the editors. A topical index would have been a useful addition to a volume aimed at readers from many disciplines.

On the whole, the book is an unusually well-integrated symposium and does credit to editors Lasswell and Lerner. It is probably inevitable that in a vast field like human behavior any collection of essays will center around the special interests of the editorial group. In the present volume the strong area is sociology. This is no doubt justified on the basis of practical achievements. But in a comprehensive survey demography, geography, and secular trend studies in economics and history also deserve space. One gets the impression that while history, with its emphasis on the complexity of cultural traditions, is usually included in any formal listing of social or "policy" sciences, its importance is readily forgotten in practice.

A criticism, less serious from the scholarly standpoint, is the advanced language and uncompromising style of most of the essays. For other social scientists this will be only a minor disadvantage, although even they may be intolerant of each other's special concepts, but I suspect that the business executive, the government administrator, the physical scientist, and perhaps the historian will find the going hard, and the urge to escape by closing the book correspondingly strong.

University of Pennsylvania THOMAS C. COCHRAN

The Rise and Progress of Negro Colleges in Georgia, 1865-1949. By Willard Range. (Athens: The University of Georgia Press, 1951. x + 254 pp. Appendix, bibliography, and index. $3.75.)

This study, made through the assistance of a Phelps-Stokes Fellowship by the Phelps-Stokes Fellowship Committee of the University of Georgia, was designed to present "a detailed picture" of the growth of the higher education of Negroes in Georgia out of complicated social, economic, and historical issues.

The first part of the book, "The Crusade," deals with those teachers and missionaries who came to the South after 1865 to help educate the recently emancipated Negroes. This section of the book, which should be read in connection with Henry L. Swint's *The Northern Teacher in the South, 1862-1870*, published by the Vanderbilt University Press in 1941, shows that the chief support of such educational activities came from numerous northern missionary societies and the Freedmen's Bureau. In these activities there was much emotionalism and, as the American Missionary Association stated the case as late as 1869, "the war with bullet and bayonet" was over but "the invasion of light and love" was coming into its own. In Georgia, as in most of the other southern states, these activities of some well-meaning but often misguided people were not too successful. Following that period, however, more realistically philanthropic men and women gave aid from which some modern colleges for Negroes developed in Georgia.

The second part of the book deals with the transition to the modern colleges for Negroes in the state, many of which, as already noted, had their genesis in philanthropic and missionary effort. In this section the author discusses the steady rise of the Negro college "from the rickety corn-cribs of Reconstruction and the days of the 'Blue-Backed Speller.' A promising system of universal education had spread over the entire state." But there was still uncertainty of purpose, and in the gubernatorial contest of 1906 between Clark Howell and Hoke Smith much political mud was slung on the "nigger" question, which culminated in a race riot in Atlanta. Higher education for Negroes was forced into confusion by a conflict of ideas on the subject. The movement for public secondary education in Georgia later stimulated secondary schools for Negroes which in turn served to stimulate interest in higher educational opportunities for that minority group. But throughout the study there is evidence of competition among the institutions for Negroes, as there seems to have been among those for white people. There is also evidence of substantial aid from philanthropic foundations and increasing interest by the state. Georgia slowly awakened to a realization that the higher education of Negroes was a responsibility of the state government.

Among the interesting chapters in the book is one which discusses the characteristics of the modern college for Negroes in Georgia. Between 1918 and 1948 efforts were made to standardize and certificate the Negro colleges. By 1932 there were more Negro college students in Atlanta than in any other city in the South except Washington, D. C., and "Georgia was a leading state in the higher learning of the black race." In this awakening appear the names of some prominent workers, both white and Negro, for the higher education of Negroes. But the author concludes that: "In the troubled years of the twentieth century no man could predict with accuracy the eventual fate of the colleges, of Negro higher education, or of civilization itself. But at last it seemed as if the dreams of the founding fathers of the Negro colleges of Georgia had achieved a provident fulfillment."

The book contains an excellent bibliography and is well documented from original sources.

University of North Carolina EDGAR W. KNIGHT

Yale College, An Educational History, 1871-1921. By George Wilson Pierson. *Yale: College and University, 1871-1937*, Vol. I. (New Haven: Yale University Press, 1952. xv + 773 pp. Illustrations, appendixes, bibliography, tables, and index. $6.00.)

In celebration of the 250th anniversary of its founding, Yale is issuing an authorized and subsidized history of the University since 1871, as interpreted by George W. Pierson, who for thirty years has been associated with Yale. The first volume treats the undergraduate college and touches on the other schools of the University only as conflicts of policy and power involved them with the college.

Mr. Pierson describes his book as an "educational" history. He has concentrated his attention on the evolution of the course of study, the politics of control, and the personalities of the faculty and administration. This, therefore, is not the miscellany of annals and anecdotes characteristic of most of the anniversary "histories" issued by colleges, but a serious and informed study of the formal enterprise at Yale. The author's industry, fairness, and masterful control of the voluminous materials are manifest equally in the text and in the two hundred pages of notes, appendixes, and bibliography.

This volume has great merit and will take its place as one of the important contributions to the history of higher education in the United States. But whether Mr. Pierson has laid bare the authentic Yale is at least questionable. He has traced the unending search of the faculty for that perfect curriculum that would not only divest some of the interests of an established oligopoly but also, by some magic, effect the introduction of respectable standards. Assuming, as one possible hypothesis, that formal instruction was an integral part of Yale, it would then seem that a history of the curriculum should go deeper than a mere shuffling of course labels. Mr. Pierson's analysis of the course of study is political rather than intellectual. With infinite patience he has recorded the sordid battles that attended the many revisions, but he deals with course titles as though they had some universal signification. It seems possible that a more exact definition of the intellectual content of the courses would have added greatly to the value of this study. Mr. Pierson has made the first adequate study of the issue of the elective system, comparing Yale's experience with that of other institutions. Had he made a similar comparison of the substance and philosophy of the individual courses, we might better understand why Yale students rejected intellectual values.

One's first reaction is to congratulate the author on his firm exclusion of the miscellany of overorganized student activities and his emphasis on the teaching. But was this the real Yale? From Pierson's own suggestions and allusions it is clear that study was a minor and incidental occupation of the students. They inhabited a world of clubs, cribs, cram schools, conformity, compulsory chapel, class loyalties, and Christian endeavor. Into this other Yale, Henry Seidel Canby has given us the sharp insights of *Alma Mater* (republished 1947 as Part II of *American Memoir*). And the Yale that was an organized perpetuation of the gang age in boys has had its appropriate literary expression in the sagas of Stover and Frank Merriwell. To its joyous sons Yale was not unlike the preparatory schools whence most of them had come. The college put great store by loyalty and officially sponsored the factitious unity of the college class. Some mystical value was attached to the experience of playing, worshiping, and reciting in the company of one's class for four years. The emphasis was on attitudes — loyalty, hero worship, and success worship — rather than on intellect. As Pierson says, "Yale cultivated the emotions, not the imagination. Recitations on texts or examinations on lectures being the method, inquiry was not in order: the College valued character above intellectual curiosity." Even to an experienced teacher the indifference of Yale students to the educational experience, as portrayed by Mr. Pierson, seems impressive. Did Yale recruit an especially insensitive body of students, or did it divert good raw material with a meretricious code and discourage it with didactic methods? The official structure of Yale is only a part of the total community and culture; the history of the whole is yet to be written.

Oberlin College THOMAS LEDUC

The Story of Texas A. and M. By George Sessions Perry. (New York: McGraw-Hill Book Company, Inc., 1951. xiv + 264 pp. Illustrations, appendixes, and index. $4.00.)

To those who have seen (and heard) the Texas Aggie cadets stand throughout an entire game and never cease yelling or singing for an instant the purpose of this book is difficult to justify. It was apparently written as an enthusiasm inspirer for Aggie graduates. Texas A. and M. alumni, however, need no artificial stimulus to maintain their "pep." In fact, their rivals feel (perhaps with envy) that the "Aggies" already overdo the inspiration phase of academic experience. But have it they do. An institution whose first offer of its presidency was to Jefferson Davis and which furnished more general officers during the last war than any other school except West Point does not need an exhorter, no matter how gifted, to inject the serum of optimism. Mr. Perry's efforts seem in this respect to be as superfluous as concern over the stock of wooden nutmegs in Connecticut.

While many Texas urbanites think of A. and M. primarily as the source of repairmen for their feline and canine property, that phase of its activity is minor compared to its production of engineers, agronomists, and livestock experts. The school's contribution to Texas economy is its glory. The eradication of tick fever is to its everlasting credit.

Mr. Perry, a successful novelist and not an A. and M. man, does not conceal some of the less favorable episodes of Aggieland. He mentions that one of its chaplains was removed for "owning a stud horse" (and that at an institution proud of its contributions to animal husbandry!), and that another functionary got into serious trouble with the president's wife over the quarantining of an infant for whooping cough. The proscriptions and liquidations at A. and M. have been inspired by its military emphasis, and have been based on *lese majesty* rather than on economic heresy and the possession of "immoral literature" as in the case of the great sister state institution. But liquidations — almost pograms — both schools have had, especially in the football coach category. These phenomena have been the curse of most western state institutions, and Texas has not lagged in furnishing her share.

During the session 1853-1854 Congress passed the Morrill Act to appropriate public lands for the purpose of encouraging agricultural education. On constitutional grounds President Pierce vetoed it. Under Lincoln the Republicans won continuing glory by passing a similar measure. At the time "scientific agriculture" was sneered at by "practical" farmers, and it still is in certain rustic quarters. Texas took advantage of the act, and A. and M.

was launched in the late 1860's. Success came in the 1890's with the administration of the heroic Sul Ross and social activities at least "perked up" when at a banquet in 1896 (the William Jennings Bryan year!) both champagne and "white wine" were served.

A. and M. has always led Texas schools in the custom of hazing. In 1913, when the thousand mark in registration had been reached, twenty-two cadets were rusticated, and later 466 "upper classmen" issued an ultimatum and decamped, "some two hundred" never to be reinstated. Of course a goat was sought for, and it proved to be the current president. No such petty flurries, however, could keep A. and M. from flourishing. Its immense student body and elaborate physical plant, as well as its rampant enthusiasm, are proof of this.

Considering its purpose this book is a success, and both from a literary and format standpoint it is a striking volume.

Southern Methodist University H. A. TREXLER

James Parton, The Father of Modern Biography. By Milton E. Flower. (Durham: Duke University Press, 1951. ix + 253 pp. Illustrations, bibliography, appendixes, and index. $4.50.)

James Parton wrote in 1888 that a biographer should tell the truth in simple, direct, and charitable language. Know your subject thoroughly, he said, and index available information fully; avoid eulogy and apology and hide no facts from your reading public. "Be short when the interest is small, and long when the interest is great."

The author of *James Parton* has written an unusually interesting story of "the father of modern biograpy" and has woven into it delightful vignettes of his time. Parton the professional journalist-historian was a reformer, an active agnostic, and a pioneer muckraker. He was not without weaknesses, but he was fearless and aggressive, a bold seeker of truth. His important biographies include the lives of Greeley, Burr, Jackson, Butler, Franklin, Jefferson, and Voltaire. This is a formidable list for a journalist-biographer in Parton's time. Parton wrote numerous short sketches of significant men and women for leading newspapers and magazines and contributed many articles on timely subjects. To limit the story of James Parton to 202 pages has been no easy task. The *Life of Andrew Jackson* is discussed in five pages. In an appendix Mr. Flower presents some valuable letters on Jackson written by William B. Lewis. It has been said that Parton's *Jackson* is thin in spots, but it must be remembered that Parton had no great libraries or manuscript collections at his command. In his researches he resorted to newspapers, published works, interviews with contemporaries of his subjects, a "few important documents," and whatever letters he could procure. Parton admired Greeley, Butler, and Voltaire. He considered his *Voltaire* his crowning achievement. Parton regretted the passing of such editors as Bryant, Greeley, Bennett, and Howells, which left the press to be taken over by "business." As a secondary theme, Mr. Flower has adequately presented Parton's wife, Sara Payson Willis, who wrote voluminously under the pseudonym of "Fanny Fern."

Some authorities may disagree with the statement that Parton was "America's first professional writer," or with the assertion that Marquis James has written the "definitive" biography of Jackson. Francis P. Blair, Sr., was not so much clay in Jackson's hands, as the author suggests. In the 1860's Blair was still planning to write a biography of Jackson. His son Montgomery did write some chapters for such a work, but his son Frank did not seriously consider such a project. Barrels of Jackson papers were in the elder Blair's possession, but he could not turn them over to Parton, because he had already obligated himself to George Bancroft (Chap. VI). The author has copious footnotes, an excellent bibliography, and an adequate index.

Miami University, Oxford, Ohio W. E. SMITH

The Papers and Addresses of William Preston Few, Late President of Duke University. Edited, with a Biographical Appreciation, by Robert H. Woody. (Durham: Duke University Press, 1951. xi + 369 pp. Illustrations. $5.00.)

William P. Few was the first president of Duke University. He served in that capacity from 1924 to 1940, after twenty-eight years of continuous association with Trinity College, its academic parent. While president of Trinity, he nurtured the already active interest of the Duke family in the small North Carolina college and contributed significantly to the plan for the Duke Endowment of 1924. As a result, the endowment of the school was increased from $450,000, its figure when Few became president of Trinity in 1910, to the millions that made possible the almost miraculous metamorphosis from college to university. In the promotion of facilities for higher education this was an achievement almost comparable to that of the institution's chief benefactors in the business world.

From the present collection of Few's addresses and papers together with the perceptive biographical essay by Robert H. Woody with which they are introduced, a portrait of the personality responsible for this accomplishment emerges with remarkable clarity. In an admittedly tentative "Biographical Appreciation" which extends to some 140 pages, Professor Woody focuses primarily upon Few's professional activities — as professor, dean, and president —, his efforts on behalf of the growth of the institution, his association with members of the Duke family — especially Benjamin N. Duke —, his educational philosophy, and the personal and physical qualities of the man. He recreates a real person. Proof of this is found in the consistency that prevails between the tone of the writings and the character of their author as Professor Woody describes him.

The papers have considerable intrinsic interest, but they also bear upon a broader question, raised by the implication of a recent work on southern history, regarding the influence of southern men of wealth over the colleges they endowed. Few's writings undoubtedly reflect unqualified admiration for members of the Duke family and a tendency to extol industrial accomplishment in the post-Civil War South. Yet his oft-expressed zeal for and dedication to the building of an institution that would serve mankind through education suggest that his capacity to inspire was more important than his tendency to conform in enlisting the continued benefactions that made the University possible.

Because of the bearing of its contents upon problems of this nature, as well as on such questions of general interest as the John Spencer Bassett case, it is a pity that the volume was not indexed to give it greater utility for reference purposes.

New York University BAYRD STILL

Fifty Years of The South Atlantic Quarterly. By William Baskerville Hamilton. (Durham: Duke University Press, 1952. viii + 397 pp. Index. $5.00.)

This distinguished career of *The South Atlantic Quarterly* is celebrated by the publication of this fiftieth-birthday volume. Here are presented a history of the review, by the editor of the volume, and thirty-four articles from its half-century file.

Professor Hamilton's historical sketch is admirable. It emphasizes, of course, the dramatic episode by which the *South Atlantic's* reputation as a liberal journal was established — Editor John S. Bassett's forthright article, "Stirring Up the Fires of Race Antipathy," followed by a strident demand for the author's dismissal from the Trinity faculty, and the ringing declaration of the Board of Trustees (which unanimously disagreed with some of Bassett's statements about the Negro problem) in favor of free speech and opinion. This makes a fine story, which is here told simply but with just pride.

Professor Hamilton tells something of the various editorships, but devotes most of his space to an informal topical analysis of the file. His praise is mixed with no little criticism; for example, he notes that "one of the announced intentions of the early editors was to foster literary activity in the South," but he finds that the *Quarterly* did little to encourage "one of the liveliest periods of ferment in the literary history of any people," namely, the southern literary activity at the turn of the century.

The papers chosen for inclusion in this volume are almost without exception of the best types of the review essay. There are two by Bassett — the controversial one on the Negro problem, and one entitled "The Task of the Critic" which was part of another controversy. Bassett wrote philosophically about the critic of things as they are as an editorial defense of William E. Dodd, then professor of history at Randolph-Macon College, whose paper entitled "Some Difficulties of the History Teacher in the South" (also reprinted in this volume) had aroused bitter recriminations.

The editor of this volume does not too much emphasize, however, the southern interests which represent only a part of the scope of this review. Despite its title, the *South Atlantic* has had from the first a pretty well-defined national outlook, and a considerable proportion of its contributors have been from the North and West.

This is an interesting and well-balanced book, full of good stuff. It is encouraging that such a fine journal as the *South Atlantic Quarterly* is able to celebrate a semicentennial. May it live to observe many more.

University of Missouri FRANK LUTHER MOTT

International Bibliography of Historical Sciences. Eighteenth Volume for 1949, including some publications of previous years. Edited by Dr. Jirina Sztachova and Dr. Adolf Sztacho for the International Committee of Historical Sciences. (Paris: Librairie Armand Colin, 1951. Pp. lii + 354.)

This important bibliography is now published with the assistance of UNESCO and under the patronage of the International Council for Philosophy and Humanistic Studies. All historians can scan its many sections with profit; however, American scholars primarily interested in the history of the United States will find few works unfamiliar to them. Their own writings are, nevertheless, here brought to the attention of scholars in distant lands. A perusal of the selections made for American history indicates good judgment on the part of the editors and American historians will find listed a number of foreign works that may not have come to their attention. These will be examined possibly less for scholarly contributions than for reflections of attitudes on the part of others who are analyzing our past and trying to understand us today.

The volume for 1949 has 6,540 entries — at least that is all the reviewer could find, although the editorial preface and information on a fore-leaf refer to some 6,700 items. This represents an increase when comparison is made with other volumes recently published, although the issue for 1932 (Vol. VII) reached similar limits. The use of smaller type, entirely adequate in every respect, keeps the latest volume within 348 pages, whereas that for 1932 required 528 pages, although its listings were approximately the same in number. Only works of major significance and importance are noted and no attempt is made to cover local history or the history of cities. Naturally many towns are represented in the indexes, and articles of general interest also offer much for the local historian. Some 145 pages are given to general history, the history of antiquity and the middle ages, and to the various auxiliary sciences; approximately the same amount of space is reserved for the years after 1500. Any bibliographer faces the problem of classification and knows that there are limits to multiplication of subheadings, but often a heading is forced to cover here more than should be expected of it. An example of this sort is found on pages 133-36 where, for the middle ages, the caption "Storia della civilità, della letteratura e della scuola" covers all in alphabetical order. Certainly the use of three separate headings would more readily facilitate the rapid use of articles of interest to a searcher in this special field. There is an index for authors and persons and a separate one for places. Both have proven to be accurate and adequate where tested. It is to be hoped that the future volumes in this series will receive the same careful, skillful attention that has been given this issue.

Northwestern University GRAY C. BOYCE

White House Profile; A Social History of the White House, Its Occupants and Its Festivities. By Bess Furman. (Indianapolis: The Bobbs-Merrill Company, Inc., 1951. 368 pp. Illustrations, bibliography, and index. $4.00.)

Late in March President Truman moved back into the White House. But it was not the same structure in which thirty-one other presidents had lived. Only the outer walls of Aquia Creek sandstone remained; within that stout masonry a new building, supported by a steel frame, had been erected. That the public approved of the expensive effort to save at least the shell of the old mansion was eloquent expression of its unique hold on the sentiments of the American people.

Bess Furman of the New York *Times*, who has covered the executive mansion for more than twenty years, has essayed a timely profile of the White House. She sketches not only the building, but its occupants, with emphasis on the ladies who have presided there. She places presidential social functions in political perspective. She deals with the changes made in the structure throughout the years and with its effect on those who have lived within its walls. She has written a book which makes clear the extent to which 1600 Pennsylvania Avenue has become the symbol of the presidency.

Any sentimental attachment to the wood and plaster of the old White House interior should be destroyed by the account of the recurrent remodeling that the ancient dwelling has endured. Most presidents have found alterations and redecorating a necessity. Under Grant the East Room resembled the main salon of a Long Island Sound steamer. The fastidious Arthur eliminated some of the worst furnishings, but had Louis Tiffany construct an opalescent glass screen to separate the foyer from the long corridor behind. Photographs of the foyer as decorated by Arthur and as renovated by Theodore Roosevelt can scarcely be recognized as of the same room. Certainly such violent fluctuations in *decor* should not be permitted again.

Miss Furman has written her book primarily from published reminiscences and correspondence and from secondary accounts. She also has exploited architectural and social records in the National Archives and has sought out men and women with White House memories. She has labored under a difficult assignment; it is no easy task to organize a narrative around the White House and the people who have lived in it. The necessity of weaving in the political and diplomatic background make the occasionally poor integration of her story almost inevitable.

Historians will find little here that is new, though they will appreciate the attempt to bring a great deal of scattered information into focus and will enjoy the inclusion of such appealing scenes as Representative William McKinley booming out "Blest Be the Tie that Binds" at Lucy Hayes's Sunday evening hymn sings. The author has accomplished her objective — a profile. This reviewer believes, however, that an additional book on the White House is desirable. Perhaps the sources do not permit it, but our historical literature would be richer for a more detailed study of the mansion as a record of American taste in architecture and interior decoration.

University of Cincinnati Oscar E. Anderson, Jr.

Skid Road; An Informal Portrait of Seattle. By Murray Morgan. (New York: The Viking Press, 1951. 280 pp. Index. $3.75.)

This is centennial year in Seattle and it is appropriate that notice should be taken of it in a book that tells something of the people and the events of its hundred-year history. The question is: what people and what events? Murray Morgan's feeling is that the founding fathers, the prominent business leaders and public men, the "respectable" people of Seattle have had books written about them already. This one is about the city below the skid road. Here, says Mr. Morgan, is Seattle from the bottom up.

It is a gusty, irreverent account that he offers us, for the author has scant regard for the local household gods. Writing with an eye for the boisterous (and the bawdy), and following the general motto, history is nothing if not amusing, he saunters through the annals of the city singling out the characters and the episodes which lend themselves to satire and good-humored raillery.

Lynchings, anti-Chinese demonstrations, prostitutes fleeing their houses of ill fame as the flames of the great fire reduced them to ashes, the boom of the Yukon gold rush, public officials in league with the underworld, labor unions staging a general strike and later making their boss virtual ruler of the city, the circus politics of the depression years — these pages from the past set the key for the greater part of the book. Mr. Morgan enjoys telling about them and, to judge from the sale the volume has had, people in Seattle and elsewhere enjoy reading about them.

Skid Road is good entertainment. It is perhaps inappropriate to ask whether it is good history; doubtless it is not intended to be. All scholarly apparatus is lacking and the reader is left either to take the story on the author's unsupported statement or to follow an unmarked trail through the sources as best he can. Nevertheless, since historical personages and events form the subject matter of the narrative, the author might well have given us some assurance of serious purpose. This is the more true because his indifference to the obligations of the historian and his propensity for satire in some measure disqualify him in matters requiring a judicious appraisal. It is unfortunate, in view of the fact that Seattle has no up-to-date, well-balanced, and thoughtful history, that the serious reader must be content for a while longer with accounts and characterizations that suffer either from filiopiety or, as in the present instance, from too single a preoccupation with the amusing foibles of the frontier city.

University of Washington CHARLES M. GATES

Harney County, Oregon, and Its Range Land. By George Francis Brimlow. (Portland: Binfords & Mort, 1951. 316 pp. Illustrations, appendix, bibliography, and index. $5.00.)

This volume is a colorful and dramatic history of one of Oregon's southwestern counties — the town of Burns being its county seat. The author, a staff member of the Billings, Montana, *Gazette*, received his undergraduate education at the Universities of Montana, Oregon, and California, and his master's degree at Oregon. Beginning with the days of the Indian and the fur trader, Mr. Brimlow deals with a succession of frontiers: the exploration of the region by General William Sibley Harney, the opening up of the region for settlement, the gold rush, reclamation, reservation life and the Indian's last stand in the Bannock War, the "feudal" range, roads and railroads, and finally, the maturing of society — governmental and civic development, educational and religious growth, and the development of resources.

While 220 pages are devoted to the pioneer story, only 60 pages are given to the period since 1900. Among other things, perhaps more attention could have been given to the federal range program since 1934.

The author's narrative style is well suited to depicting the everyday life of pioneer times. Generally the "old-timers" are allowed to speak for themselves, the art of interview being used in a manner which enlivens the style and quickens the interest. Too, the extensive use of newspapers enhances the popular appeal.

There is no documentation, but an appendix includes a bibliography of source materials arranged according to chapters. Several groups of photographs and a sketch map of the county are important aides to the book. All in all, the author has produced a lively "story" of Harney County, as told by those who settled and made it.

Butler University ROY MARVIN ROBBINS

Historical News and Comments

Association Activities

The Association has accepted an invitation from the University of Kentucky to hold its forty-sixth annual meeting in Lexington on May 7-9, 1953. Thomas D. Clark has been appointed chairman of the committee on local arrangements.

Other committee assignments, announced by James L. Sellers, president of the Association, are as follows. Membership committee: Howard H. Peckham, Indiana Historical Commission, chairman. Nominating committee: Fred C. Cole, Tulane University, chairman; Ray A. Billington, Northwestern University; and Thomas LeDuc, Oberlin College. Program committee: George E. Mowry, University of California at Los Angeles, chairman; Arthur E. Bestor, Jr., University of Illinois; Harold Bingham, University of Connecticut; Arthur A. Ekirch, American University; Oliver Holmes, National Archives; Beverly McAnear, Stanford University; Fulmer Mood, University of Texas; Richard Murdock, Carnegie Institute of Technology; Stow Persons, State University of Iowa; Earl S. Pomeroy, University of Oregon; James Rabun, Emory University; James H. Rodabaugh, Ohio State Archaeological and Historical Society; Alfred B. Sears, University of Oklahoma; David Shannon, Teachers College, Columbia University; George R. Taylor, Amherst College; and T. Harry Williams, Louisiana State University.

Fulmer Mood of the University of Texas will read a paper on "Settled Areas and Frontier Lines, 1625-1910; A Historical Revision" at the joint session of the Association and the American Historical Association in December. Robert E. Riegel of Dartmouth College will preside, and Ray A. Billington of Northwestern University, Paul W. Gates of Cornell University, and George W. Pierson of Yale University will lead the discussion. Howard K. Beale, University of Wisconsin, will address the dinner meeting of the Association on the subject of historical ethics.

This issue of the *Review* carries, in the "Notes and Documents" section, John W. Caughey's thought-provoking study, "Historians' Choice: Results of a Poll on Recently Published American History and Biography." A discussion of Dr. Caughey's study will be arranged for one of the sessions of the May, 1953, annual meeting of the Association.

At the expense of repetition, the following excerpt is quoted from the minutes of the executive committee: "The managing editor . . . proposed, with the approval of the editorial board, that members of the Association be requested to submit personal data sheets to the editorial office with a view to facilitating selection of book reviewers. The managing editor stressed the fact that many competent reviewers were being overlooked, and expressed the hope that a larger number of members would be invited to participate in this important function of the *Review*." Requests for personal data on competency in periods and areas of American history should reach members early this fall.

The Pelzer Prize Committee will be grateful if directors of graduate research will call the attention of their students to the award granted annually for the best article in United States history. The competition is open to candidates for advanced degrees in North American universities. Essays should not exceed six or seven thousand words in length; footnotes, assembled at the end of the text and double-spaced, should follow *Review* style. Significance of subject matter, literary craftsmanship, competence in the critical handling of evidence, and accuracy of statements, quotations, and citations are some of the factors that will be considered in judging the manuscripts. The winner of the contest will receive a medal, and his essay will be published in the December issue of the *Review*. Studies submitted for the 1953 competition must be in the office of the managing editor by January 15.

Personals

James E. Gillespie, professor of history at Pennsylvania State College, has retired. E-tu Zen Sun, recently visiting lecturer at Goucher College, has been appointed visiting lecturer in Far Eastern history. Edward C. Thaden of the University of Paris and Robert S. Cope of Thiel College have been appointed instructors in history.

James O. Wetterean has been promoted to associate professor and W. Taylor Putney to assistant professor of history at New York University.

Harold L. Fowler of the College of William and Mary taught in the summer session of the University of North Carolina.

Charles George of Pomona College will replace George E. Warner at Colorado College while the latter is on leave for 1952-1953. Samuel F. Bemis of Yale University was visiting professor for the summer session at Colorado College.

Paul S. Lietz has been appointed chairman of the history department of Loyola University, Chicago. He succeeds Father Joseph Roubik, S.J., who had been chairman since 1933.

Vanderbilt University has announced the promotion of Henry L. Swint and Dayton Phillips to the rank of professor of history, Paul H. Hardacre to associate professor, and Constantine G. Belissary to assistant professor. Dewey W. Grantham, Jr., of the Womans College of the University of North Carolina has joined the department as assistant professor of history.

At Mount Holyoke College, Viola F. Barnes, professor of history, retired in June, 1952, after 33 years service. Wilma Pugh has been promoted to associate professor and chairman of the department. Mary Benson of Milwaukee-Downer College has been appointed associate professor and David Leonard of the University of Michigan instructor in history.

Donald C. Gordon, assistant professor of history at the University of Maryland, has been granted sabbatical leave for the first semester of 1952-1953 to work in London on his study of Australian nationalism. Roland Stromberg, assistant professor, is being transferred to the University's European program for 1952-1953. J. Wesley Hoffmann, University of Tennessee, Joseph Baylen, New Mexico Highland University, and Marvin Wachman, Colgate University, have been appointed to the University's European program for 1952-1953. Verne Chatelain, Horace S. Merrill, and Herbert Crosman have returned to College Park from their European assignments.

Gordon Wright has been appointed for a three-year term as chairman of the history department at the University of Oregon; he will be a member of the faculty at the National War College from August to December. Edwin R. Bingham has been promoted to assistant professor. Stanley A. Spector has been appointed instructor in history to replace Paul S. Dull during the latter's sabbatical leave in Japan.

The history department of the University of Michigan has announced the following promotions: William R. Leslie to be associate professor, John W. Hall and Karl H. Reichenbach to be assistant professors. Betty L. Fladeland has been appointed assistant professor in Wells College. For the period from February, 1952, to February, 1953, John W. Hall is in charge of the Michigan Center for Japanese Studies in Okayama, Japan. During his absence, courses in Far Eastern history are being given by Ronald S. Anderson of the University of California. Summer session appointments at the University of Michigan for 1952 included the following: W. C. McDermott from the

University of Pennsylvania, E. S. Morgan from Brown University, P. W. Powell from the University of California at Santa Barbara, and W. M. Whitelaw from the American International College.

Will D. Gilliam, Jr., has been promoted to associate professor of history at the University of Kentucky. Carl B. Cone taught at the University of Missouri this summer. Clement Eaton and Shelby T. McCloy have returned to the University of Kentucky after a year's leave in Europe.

At Lehigh University, Raymond G. Cowherd has been promoted to associate professor of history. Lawrence H. Gipson, former head of the department of history and government, held the Harmsworth Professorship at Queen's College, Oxford University, during the academic year 1951-1952.

Edward F. Dow, head of the department of history and government at the University of Maine, will be on leave of absence for the fall semester to be the executive secretary of the Little Hoover Commission for the state of Maine. He will continue on leave of absence for the spring semester, 1953, to work on a research project in Maine government. Robert M. York has been promoted to professor of history and will be acting head of the department of history and government during the academic year 1952-1953. William Jeffrey and David W. Trafford have been promoted to associate professor of history; Herbert Wood and John Nolde to assistant professor.

Colin R. Lovell, who has resumed academic duties at the University of Southern California after a leave of absence on military service, has been promoted to the rank of associate professor. T. Walter Wallbank, professor of history, has returned from a year's appointment at Fuad University, Egypt, as a Fulbright professor. Russell L. Caldwell, associate professor of history, has resumed his teaching at the University after a semester's leave during which he directed and taught in the extension program set up at the Nellis Air Force Base at Las Vegas, Nevada. Tracy E. Strevey, dean of the College of Letters, Arts, and Sciences at the University of Southern California, served as visiting professor of history on the summer session staff of the University of Hawaii.

Frank T. Inouye of Ohio State University has been appointed assistant professor of history at the University of Hawaii, Hilo Center.

Fred J. Ericson of Michigan State Normal College and Ellsworth Carlson of Oberlin College were visiting professors in the summer session at the University of Nebraska. C. H. Oldfather has retired as dean of the College of

Arts and Sciences at the University of Nebraska and will devote his entire time to teaching in the department of history.

Chester McA. Destler, chairman of the department of history at Connecticut College, was visiting professor in the summer session at Cornell University.

Charles F. Mullett, professor of history at the University of Missouri, spent the summer in England gathering material for a book on nineteenth-century British historiography. David H. Pinkney held a summer research professorship from the University of Missouri for work on his history of Paris. Irvin G. Wyllie has been promoted to the rank of associate professor.

George A. Lensen has been promoted to the rank of assistant professor in the department of history at Florida State University.

Arthur P. Scott of the University of Chicago has returned from his Fulbright lectureship in Thailand.

Orville Yeager, doctoral candidate at the University of Oklahoma, has joined the department of history at Mississippi College.

Cornelius J. Brosnan has retired from the history department at the University of Idaho. For 1952-1953 he will be visiting professor of history at Whitworth College.

James C. Bonner of the Georgia State College for Women will serve as visiting professor during the fall quarter at Emory University. James Z. Rabun of Emory has been given a leave of absence to teach the first semester at the University of Illinois.

Gale W. McGee, professor of American history at the University of Wyoming, has been granted leave of absence for the academic year 1952-1953. He will serve as a Carnegie Fellow with the Council on Foreign Relations in New York City and will be working on the Soviet policy of the United States. His work at the University of Wyoming will be taken over during the year by Clifford P. Westermeier.

Louis B. Schmidt, professor of history at the Iowa State College, gave the Phi Beta Kappa address at the University of Arizona, May 12, 1952.

Professor William T. Laprade, who has been chairman of the history department at Duke University since 1938, retired from that post on September

1. He continues with his other duties. He has been succeeded by Charles S. Sydnor, who has also been appointed dean of the Graduate School of Arts and Sciences.

David W. Noble, who recently received his doctorate from the University of Wisconsin, has been appointed instructor in the department of history at the University of Minnesota.

Carlton Ames has been granted a leave of absence from his position at Wisconsin State College to accept an appointment with the State Department for the next two years. His duties at the College will be assumed by George R. Gilkey of Westminister College, Salt Lake City.

At Stanford University, Thomas A. Bailey has been made Margaret Byrne Professor of American History, and has been designated executive head of the department of history. John C. Miller, who has been named to the new Edgar E. Robinson chair in American History, has been granted leave for 1952-1953. Beverly McAnear of the New York State Teachers College at New Paltz will substitute for Professor Miller during his year of absence. Ralph H. Lutz retired from active teaching at the close of the summer quarter. He will continue research in the Hoover Institute and Library. H. Stuart Hughes of Harvard University will take over the fields handled by Professor Lutz. John J. Johnson has been granted leave of absence for one year to assume duties in the Department of State in Washington. During the autumn and winter quarters of next year, Rolland Rogers will have charge of the work in Latin American history. J. Fred Rippy of the University of Chicago will be visiting professor during the spring and summer quarters of 1953. Norman A. Graebner of Iowa State College will teach at Stanford on a one-year appointment as acting associate professor. Howard M. Ehrmann of the University of Michigan will be visiting professor in the summer of 1953. George H. Knoles spent the summer in Japan serving as chairman of the committee in charge of American Studies Seminar Program. Anatole G. Mazour lectured at the University of Wyoming during a portion of the summer in the Institute of International Affairs. He was promoted to the rank of professor in the spring. Wayne S. Vucinich taught at San Diego State College during the summer session. James B. Burnell of Cornell University, Howard Kaminsky of the University of Chicago, and John H. Trueman of Cornell University joined the staff as instructors. Walter M. Simon has been promoted to acting assistant professor.

Kansas State College announces the promotion of Verlin R. Easterling and Hazel M. Riggs to the rank of associate professor of history and Homer E.

Socolofsky to the rank of assistant professor of history. George D. Wilcoxon, Jr., has been granted sabbatical leave effective February 1, 1953; he will travel and pursue studies in Great Britain and western Europe.

Herbert A. Wisbey, Jr., of Monmouth Junior College has been appointed associate professor and head of the department of history and political science at Keuka College.

Ira C. Ihde has been promoted to the rank of professor of history at Eastern New Mexico University.

During the past summer Julius W. Pratt, Capen Professor of American History and dean of the Graduate School of Arts and Sciences at the University of Buffalo, gave a series of lectures and conducted a seminar at the Salsburg Seminar. Selig Adler, promoted to professor at the University of Buffalo, is on leave of absence to teach at the University of Rochester, 1952-1953. Wendell N. Calkins has been promoted to assistant professor of history.

Edwin A. Davis, professor of history at Louisiana State University, has been made head of the department. Robert B. Holtman, associate professor of history, will be on sabbatical leave during the 1952-1953 session.

Donald Danker, professor of history at York College, has been appointed archivist of the Nebraska State Historical Society.

At the University of Texas, J. Harry Bennett has been promoted to associate professor of history, and Edward L. Cannan has been promoted to assistant professor of history. A. R. Lewis, formerly of the University of South Carolina, and abroad on leave from the University of Texas during 1951-1952, will take up his duties as associate professor of history in September, 1952. S. S. McKay of Texas Technological College taught in the summer session.

Clarence L. Ver Steeg has been promoted to the rank of assistant professor in the department of history at Northwestern University. Richard W. Leopold has been granted leave of absence for the fall quarter, 1952, and the spring quarter, 1953, to continue research and writing in the field of American diplomatic history. Gordon H. McNeil, professor of history and chairman of the Division of Social Studies at Coe College, is visiting professor of European history at Northwestern University for the year 1952-1953.

The history department of Mississippi State College announces the promotion of Glover Moore to the rank of professor and James H. McLendon to the rank of associate professor.

At the University of Delaware, John A. Munroe has been named professor of history and chairman of the department, and David Bushnell has been promoted to assistant professor. Visiting professors on the summer school history faculty were: Delaware State Archivist Leon deValinger, Jr., and Walter L. Woodfill, assistant professor of history at Wesleyan University, Connecticut.

Thomas J. Pressly will resume his teaching at the University of Washington after a year's leave of absence on a Ford Fellowship. Robert A. Schoyen, doctoral graduate of the University of London, will replace Donald E. Emerson while the latter is on leave during 1952-1953, and John Cavarnor will substitute for Solomon Katz who is on leave. Ernst Levy, professor of history at the University of Washington, has been given the rank of emeritus professor.

The Library of Congress has announced that Roy F. Basler, executive secretary of the Abraham Lincoln Association in Springfield, Illinois, has been appointed chief of the General Reference and Bibliography Division of the Library. Howard F. Cline, assistant professor of history at Northwestern University, has been named director of the Hispanic Foundation of the Library of Congress.

Elizabeth Cometti and Charles H. Moffat of Marshall College have been made professors of history.

Captain Charles A. Johnson, on military leave from the University of Maryland, has been assigned to Headquarters, United States Air Forces in Europe, at Wiesbaden, Germany, as assistant chief of the Historical Division.

John T. Lanning of Duke University has been made chairman of the Conference on Latin American History of the American Historical Association and has been appointed a member of the committee on the Albert J. Beveridge Memorial Fund. Joseph C. Robert, associate dean of the graduate school, has been elected president of Coker College, Hartsville, South Carolina. John S. Curtiss taught in the summer session at Stanford University.

Donald E. Everett, doctoral graduate of Tulane University, Charles P. Roland, Office of the Chief of Military History, and Mario Rodriguez, University of California at Berkeley, have been appointed instructors in history at Tulane University.

F. J. Taylor, recent doctoral graduate of Tulane University has been appointed associate professor of history at Louisiana College.

Charles E. Smith, professor of history at Louisiana State University, has been appointed dean of the University.

Robert A. Kann, associate professor of history at Rutgers University, has joined the staff of the Center for Research on World Political Institutions at Princeton University for a part of the year 1952 in order to write the Austria-Hungary portion of the Center's study of political integration.

It is with profound regret that we chronicle the death, on May 1, 1952, of Everett E. Edwards, whose name had become synonymous with the development of agricultural history as a systematic field of study and research. A score of annotated bibliographies and twenty years of *Agricultural History* stand as a monument to his memory. His office in the Department of Agriculture became a clearinghouse of information, whether in research projects, the organization of college courses in agricultural history, or the activities of the Agricultural History Society.

Born at Waltham, Minnesota, February 12, 1900, Edwards graduated from Carleton College in 1921 and from Harvard University in 1924 with the master's degree. Meanwhile, he taught a year in the Grand Rapids, Minnesota, High School, and served as instructor in history at Northwestern University, 1923-1925. Summer session assignments at Miami University (1926), Catholic University of America (1936), the University of Missouri (1939), and the University of Minnesota (1947), together with instruction in agricultural history in the Graduate School of the Department of Agriculture and American University, were important interludes in a busy life. His enduring work was accomplished, however, in the Bureau of Agricultural Economics, Department of Agriculture, whose staff he joined in 1927. Less tangible than his contributions as editor and compiler, but nonetheless significant, were his kindly guidance and counsel for the hundreds of historians who sought to share his wisdom. Members of the Association will recall his quiet, genial personality, his sense of humor, and his genuine interest in historical scholarship.

On Tuesday, June 17, 1952, Dr. Raymond C. Werner, professor of history at the University of Illinois, died after a brief illness at the age of 59. Professor Werner was a member of the department for the past twenty-five years. He came to the University as an instructor in 1917 with a Ph.D. from the University of Iowa where he did his graduate work under Winfred T. Root.

At the University of Illinois Professor Werner's time and energy were divided among several fields of activity. He was above all a teacher and his first love was the elementary course in American history. His lectures in this course were so well organized, so enlivened with human interest, so marked with droll humor, and so clearly delivered that this course became one of the institutions of the University.

His first assignment after he took his bachelor's degree at the University of Wisconsin in 1915 was as clerk to the American Legation in Peking. Here he developed a life-long interest in Chinese language and history. At the University of Illinois he developed a course in the history of Eastern Asia which has continued for years to attract and interest students.

The third area of Professor Werner's achievement was his work with graduate students, particularly in connection with the writing of master's theses. During the years of his service at the University of Illinois he directed the writing of over a hundred master's theses. His patience and sympathetic understanding of student difficulties were almost monumental.

In addition to his concern for teaching Professor Werner was definitely interested in research, especially in the life of Joseph Galloway, a Philadelphia merchant of the Revolutionary period. Among Dr. Werner's publications in this area were the diary of Grace Growden Galloway and articles on Joseph Galloway, as a politician and an imperial statesman. The volume on French foundations of Illinois, 1680-1693, in the publications of the Illinois State Historical Library written in conjunction with Theodore C. Pease appeared in 1934. In more recent years Professor Werner was working on a translation with critical notes of Gottfried Duden's *Bericht Über Eine Reise Nach Nordamerika*. For the purpose of finishing this work and in the hope of investigating more closely the Galloway papers in Ireland, Professor Werner was granted a sabbatical leave for the first semester of 1952-1953. The department of history and the University of Illinois both suffer greatly from his untimely death. [F. C. Dietz]

Julian Pleasant Bretz, professor emeritus of American history at Cornell University, died on June 15, 1951. He was born in St. Joseph, Missouri, December 29, 1876, and had his undergraduate training at William Jewell College, from which he graduated in 1899. He gained the degree of doctor of philosophy at the University of Chicago in 1906; and, shortly after, he joined the faculty of Cornell University, where he rose rapidly to his professorship in 1910. He retired from teaching in 1944. Dr. Bretz had an active and distinguished career as a teacher; he took a leading part in the Cornell faculty, which he represented for a time on the Cornell Board of Trustees; he was twice a candidate for election to Congress, and, in his later years, helped to form the Labor Legislative Conference of the State of New York, of which he became president in 1947. His colleagues in the historical profession knew him as a sound reviewer, who contributed frequently to this *Review* and the *American Historical Review* during the period 1910-1945. They knew and admired his essays, "The Economic Background of the Liberty Party" and "Early Land Communications with the Lower Mississippi Valley." They elected him to the Council of the American Historical Association, 1933-1935. [F. G. Marcham]

Grants and Awards

Stanley S. Ross of the University of Nebraska has received a Henry L. and Grace Doherty Foundation Fellowship for the year 1952-1953 and will pursue research in Mexico City relative to the Carranza Revolution.

Lloyd E. Worner, associate professor of history at Colorado College, has been granted a Ford Foundation Faculty Fellowship for 1952-1953.

Edgar E. Robinson, Margaret Byrne Professor of American History at Stanford University, has been selected by the executors of the estate of J. Brooks B. Parker of Philadelphia to write an "unbiased appraisal" of Franklin Delano Roosevelt under a $25,000 grant from the Parker estate. The book, tentatively titled "Roosevelt and His Influence: A Contemporary Appraisal," will be published by J. B. Lippincott Company.

Bessie L. Pierce of the University of Chicago has been awarded a fellowship in Midwestern Studies by the Newberry Library of Chicago to assist in the completion of the third volume of her *A History of Chicago*.

Donald E. Emerson, assistant professor of history at the University of Washington, has received a Ford Fellowship for the academic year 1952-1953. Solomon Katz, professor of history, will spend the year 1952-1953 in Europe, having received both a Guggenheim and a Fulbright appointment. He will be engaged in research in Paris and Athens.

George Howatt, instructor in the department of history and government, Lehigh University, has been awarded a Fulbright grant to Australia for 1952-1953. His project will consist of evaluating Australian experience with preferential voting and the Hare system of proportional representation.

Richard L. Morton and Bruce T. McCully of the College of William and Mary received grants for research for the summer from Richmond Area University Center and the College.

Raymond S. Ginger, assistant professor of economics at Western Reserve University, is the recipient of the Business History Fellowship for the academic year 1952-1953. This fellowship, awarded by the Business Historical Society, carries a stipend of $4,000 and enables an advanced scholar, usually the holder of a doctor's degree in history, to spend a year of study and research at the Harvard Graduate School of Business Administration. The recipient of the fellowship is permitted free use of his time while at Harvard to pursue whatever aspects of the history of business he may choose.

Arthur P. Whitaker spent the summer in Argentina, Chile, and Uruguay under a grant from the Doherty Foundation, gathering material for a volume on those countries in the American Foreign Policy Library edited by Sumner Welles and published by the Harvard University Press.

Henry L. Swint of Vanderbilt University has been awarded a Ford Foundation Fellowship for 1952-1953. Alexander Marchant spent the summer in Brazil on a grant-in-aid from the Social Science Research Council for a study of the relations between the United States and Brazil.

A. Hunter Dupree, assistant professor of history at Texas Technological College, has been appointed a research fellow of the Gray Herbarium of Harvard University and awarded a research grant by the American Academy of Arts and Sciences to work on a biography of Asa Gray.

Quirinus Breen of the University of Oregon will be on leave during 1952-1953 to study humanist literature in Italy under a Fulbright grant.

Ira V. Brown, assistant professor of history at Pennsylvania State College, has been awarded a faculty fellowship by the Fund for the Advancement of Education.

William R. Leslie of the University of Michigan has been appointed to an American Council of Learned Societies Fellowship for the second semester of 1952-1953. Gerald S. Brown has received a special research grant from the Institute of Early American History and Culture which he will use in support of a proposed study of British politics and administration in the American Revolution.

Avery O. Craven, Pitt Professor of American History at Cambridge University, was awarded the degree of Doctor of Humane Letters at the May, 1952, commencement of Tulane University.

Alan Simpson of the University of Chicago was awarded a $1,000 prize for excellence in teaching.

J. Russell Major has been granted a two-year leave of absence from Emory University to do research in France, Spain, and Italy. In 1952-1953 he will work under a Fulbright award and in 1953-1954 under a Guggenheim Fellowship.

E. Merton Coulter, professor of history at the University of Georgia, received an honorary LL.D. degree at the June commencement, University of North Carolina.

Edward Lurie, Hearst Fellow in History at Northwestern University, has been awarded an American Council of Learned Societies Fellowship to carry on research in the field of American intellectual history, primarily in the field of the history of science. Franklin D. Scott has received an appointment from the Social Science Research Council for a year's research work in Norway and Sweden. George T. Romani has been awarded a research fellowship by the Committee on International Exchange of Persons and will spend a year of research in Italy.

The following members of the history staff at Washington and Lee University received Carnegie Corporation grants-in-aid for research in 1951: William G. Bean, Ollinger Crenshaw, William A. Jenks, Allen W. Moger, and Charles W. Turner. Similar grants were also made in 1952 to William A. Jenks and Allen W. Moger.

Frank L. Klement, assistant professor of American history at Marquette University, has been granted a Ford Foundation Fellowship for 1952-1953 for the purpose of pursuing research in the period of the Civil War.

William R. Braisted, assistant professor of history at the University of Texas, has received a Ford Foundation Fellowship to pursue Far Eastern studies at Harvard University.

The University of Delaware awarded grants for summer research to the following members of its history department: John A. Munroe, Walter Kirchner, and David Bushnell. Assistant Professor Bushnell also received a grant from the Social Science Research Council for study at Columbia.

John C. Miller, professor of history at Stanford University, has been awarded a Fulbright grant to do research in Holland, England, and France. Charles D. O'Malley received a Guggenheim grant for research in England,

Belgium, Italy, and France during the summer. Thomas C. Smith of Stanford is in Japan on a grant from the Social Science Research Council.

Louis Filler, associate professor of American civilization at Antioch College, has been awarded a Faculty Study Fellowship of the American Council of Learned Societies and a grant-in-aid from the Social Science Research Council.

Three members of the history department of the Woman's College of the University of North Carolina, Greensboro, have received fellowships from the Ford Foundation Fund for the next year. They are as follows: Richard Bardolph, associate professor of history; Lenore R. O'Boyle, assistant professor of history; and Eugene E. Pfaff, professor of history.

Edward A. Guerrant of Davidson College has received a Ford Foundation Fellowship and will spend the next year studying and writing at the University of Southern California.

William K. Rolph of Tulane University has been awarded a three-year research fellowship by the Australian National University. William J. Griffith spent the summer in research in Guatemala on a grant from the Middle American Research Institute.

The Institute of Early American History and Culture, Williamsburg, Virginia, announces the following awards of grants-in-aid for 1952-1953 made at its annual Council meeting in May, 1952: Leslie V. Brock, College of Idaho, The Currency of the American Colonies, 1700-1775; Gerald S. Brown, University of Michigan, British Politics and Administration in the American Revolution; William L. Sachse, University of Wisconsin, Americans in Britain before the Revolution; James Morton Smith, Cornell University, The Virginia and Kentucky Resolutions and other Opposition to the Alien and Sedition Laws; and Marion R. G. Tinking, California State Department of Education, Edition of the Writings of William Byrd, II.

Historical Activities

The personal papers of the late Charles Evans Hughes have been presented to the Library of Congress by Mrs. Charles Evans Hughes, Jr. The collection, which contains more than 20,000 items, was used by Merlo Pusey in preparing his Pulitzer Prize biography of the former Chief Justice. The papers include letters of Hughes's student days at Colgate (then Madison) and at Brown University; material relating to the beginnings of his public career, especially to his exposure of corruption in the 1905 gas and insurance investigations, when he was counsel for the New York legislature; sidelight documentation on the presidential campaign of 1916; and correspondence and other papers concerned with his career as secretary of state under Presidents Harding and Coolidge and as chief justice of the United States. Other papers in the collection relate to his membership on the Permanent Court of Arbitration at The Hague, his attendance as United States representative at various Latin American conferences, and his brief service as judge of the Permanent Court of International Justice. The Hughes papers may be used only with the permission of the family, to be requested through the Chief of the Manuscripts Division.

Cordell Hull, former secretary of state, has presented his private papers to the Library of Congress. This gift consists of approximately 33,000 documents dating from about 1910 to 1950 and covering the major part of his public career. The Rockefeller Foundation has provided a grant for the arrangement and professional indexing of these important papers, and it is hoped that the work, which is already underway, will be completed within a year.

To honor the memory of the Chilean scholar José Toribio Medina (1852-1930) on the hundredth anniversary of his birth, the Pan American Union has organized a three-day series of events known as the Medina Centennial Celebration, scheduled to take place in Washington November 6-8 of this year. The Library of Congress and the Embassy of Chile to the United States are actively collaborating with this important program, which is enjoying the enthusiastic sponsorship of twenty-seven state, national, and international organizations.

The Institute of the History of Medicine of the Johns Hopkins University announces the continuation of its fellowships in the history of medicine and of the natural sciences. One purpose of these awards, which provide from $2,000 to $3,000 in each case, is to supplement the training of young scholars who may have become interested in the history or sociology of science. Those who hold the Ph.D., or who have at least completed residence work for this degree, are eligible to apply. Inquiries relating to 1953-1954 should be made of the Director, 1900 East Monument Street, Baltimore 5, Maryland, preferably before December 15, 1952.

The spring Upper Midwest History Conference was held at St. John's University on April 24. Lawrence Steefel of the University of Minnesota presided. A paper entitled "The Creation and Antecedents of the First Catholic Diocese of the Old West" was read by J. Herman Schauinger of St. Thomas College. Comments were made by A. C. Krey of the University of Minnesota and Rev. Vincent Tegeder of St. John's University.

At a recent meeting in New York a group of historians launched a new organization — the Conference on British Studies. Harold Hulme of New York University was elected president of the group. The Conference feels that there is an urgent need for a journal devoted exclusively to the publication of articles in medieval and modern English history and British Empire history. But because of the difficulties involved in starting such a journal, they wish to gain some idea of the probable number of subscribers before proceeding with their plans. They would, therefore, appreciate postal cards from all interested in such a journal. Cards should be mailed, with the sender's address, to Samuel C. McCulloch, Department of History, Rutgers University, New Brunswick, New Jersey.

The Ontario Historical Society held its annual meeting on June 19-21 at the University of Western Ontario. Louis B. Duff of Welland addressed the banquet meeting on the subject "Canada, Yesterday and To-Day," and R. A. Preston of R. M. C., Kingston, presented an illustrated address entitled "What Happened to Kingston's 1812 Warships." At the several sessions papers were presented by Fred Hamil of Detroit, Victor Lauriston of Chatham, Sheriff Cameron of St. Thomas, Orlo Miller, Fred Landon, and J. J. Talman of London.

The American Philosophical Society announces that it has funds available for grants for expenses to individuals engaged in research in the social sciences and the humanities. The Society's Committee on Research meets five times a year — in October, December, February, April, and June. An application may be made at any time and will be considered at the next meeting of the committee if received a month in advance. Information concerning grants and application forms may be obtained from the Executive Office of the Society, 104 South Fifth Street, Philadelphia 6, Pennsylvania.

The Stebbins Prize in Arkansas History, amounting to $100 in cash, will be awarded yearly at the spring meeting of the Arkansas Historical Association for the best documented manuscript of not more than 5,000 words in the field of Arkansas history. To be eligible for the 1953 award, manuscripts must be received by the selection committee on or prior to February 15, 1953. Members of the committee are Orville W. Taylor, chairman, Little Rock Junior College, Fred H. Harrington, University of Wisconsin, and J. V. Frederick, College of the Ozarks. All correspondence should be addressed to

Orville W. Taylor, Little Rock Junior College, Asher Avenue Station, Little Rock, Arkansas.

The annual meeting of the Arkansas Historical Association was held April 10-11 at Little Rock. Ten papers on a variety of Arkansas historical subjects were presented. Thomas D. Clark of the University of Kentucky gave two addresses before luncheon and dinner meetings: "A Reconsideration of Frontier Social History" and "Local History — A Community Asset." Claude A. Rankin, commissioner of State Lands of Arkansas, was elected president of the Association, succeeding J. H. Atkinson of Little Rock Junior College.

The seventh annual competition for the Albert J. Beveridge Memorial Fellowship of the American Historical Association for the best original manuscript in American history closed on June 1, 1952. Established in 1945, the fellowship has a cash value of $1,000 and also provides for free publication in the Beveridge series. Honorable mention may also be awarded to one or more additional manuscripts, and this award, too, carries with it free publication in the Beveridge series. "American history" is interpreted as including the history of the United States, Canada, and Latin America. All correspondence, including requests for further information and forms of application, should be addressed to Dorothy Burne Goebel, Department of History, Hunter College, 695 Park Avenue, New York 21, New York.

The American Council of Learned Societies has announced for the academic year 1952-1953 a program of awards for individuals to be designated ACLS Scholars, to be carefully chosen from teachers in the humanities temporarily displaced from college and university faculties as a result of the defense emergency. The announcement states that "each candidate will be required to present a plan for study or research which offers promise of relating his humanistic knowledge to the persistent problems of mankind and of developing his skill in communicating these interpretations to this generation." Individual candidates may apply for the scholarships or academic institutions may nominate candidates. Further information and application forms may be obtained from the Secretary for ACLS Scholars, American Council of Learned Societies, 1219 Sixteenth Street, N. W., Washington 6, D. C.

Mrs. Woodrow Wilson has presented some 10,000 papers to be added to the Library of Congress's Woodrow Wilson Collection. Besides correspondence, there are also memoranda, notes and drafts for college lectures and addresses, many early manuscripts of books and articles, and a large group of such memorabilia as medals, diplomas, and illuminated scrolls. Much of the correspondence was written in 1910, a period that was previously rather poorly documented in the Library's Wilson Collection.

The 1952 annual meeting of the Economic History Association will be held at Oberlin College, September 12-13. The program has been planned by a committee under the chairmanship of John G. B. Hutchins of Cornell University. Local arrangements and reservations will be made by a committee headed by Thomas LeDuc of Oberlin College.

The Nebraska State Historical Society conducted archaeological investigations in the Fort Randall Reservoir Area, South Dakota, last summer as a part of the federal-state cooperative program for the salvage of cultural materials from areas to be inundated as a result of the construction of reservoirs in the Missouri River Basin. The investigations are being supported in part by a grant from the National Park Service.

The personal papers of the late Harold L. Ickes have been presented by Mrs. Ickes to the Library of Congress as a gift to the nation. They cover the period from about 1907 to 1951 and include correspondence, articles, and speeches of the former Secretary of the Interior. At present the use of the material is restricted.

The Institute of Early American History and Culture at Williamsburg, Virginia, announces an annual prize of $500 for a published book in the field of early American history and culture. This field embraces all phases of American history to about 1815, including the borderlands of the British North American colonies and the British colonies in the West Indies to 1776. There is no limitation on the type of work eligible (monographic, documentary, bibliographical) or on its place of publication, but it must be in English. The first award will be made in May, 1953, for a book published during 1952. Books to be considered for the prize may be submitted to the Director, Institute of Early American History and Culture, Box 1298, Williamsburg, Virginia, at any time after this announcement is made, but cannot be considered if submitted later than January 15, 1953. The Institute reserves the right to withhold the prize in any year if no book submitted attains the standard of excellence desired.

Multilithed copies of the paper read by Philip M. Hamer, executive director of the National Historical Publications Commission, at the Chicago meeting of the Mississippi Valley Historical Association are available at the National Archives Building, Washington 25, D. C. The paper outlines new developments in the Commission's program, to which are appended the comments of Paul W. Gates and others.

REPORT OF THE SECRETARY-TREASURER FOR THE YEAR 1951-1952

By Mrs. Clarence S. Paine

The mid-year meeting of the Association[1] was held in New York City December 28-30, 1951, in conjunction with the annual meeting of the American Historical Association. Merle Curti, president of the Association, served as toastmaster at the dinner meeting on December 28, and Wendell H. Stephenson of Tulane University gave an address on "William E. Dodd, Historian of Democracy." Richard W. Leopold, Northwestern University, presided at a joint session of the two associations on the afternoon of December 29 at which the central theme was "Pressure Groups and American Foreign Policy." Two papers, "The Navy League of the United States," by Armin Rappaport of the University of California at Berkeley, and "War or Peace; America First Committee Strategy, 1940-1941," by Wayne S. Cole of the University of Arkansas, were discussed by James L. Sellers, University of Nebraska, and Walter Johnson, University of Chicago.

The executive committee assembled after the dinner meeting with the following members present: William C. Binkley, chairman, Ralph P. Bieber, Fred C. Cole, Merle Curti, Herbert A. Kellar, Jeannette P. Nichols, William J. Petersen, Carl Coke Rister, James L. Sellers, the managing editor, and the secretary-treasurer. The financial report for the period from April 1 to November 30 was approved. Reports were presented by the chairmen of standing committees: Ray A. Billington, for the nominating committee; Thomas LeDuc, for the program committee; Martha E. Layman, for the Teachers' Section program; Paul M. Angle, for the committee on local arrangements, and J. Monaghan, for the membership committee.

James L. Sellers, chairman of a committee to open and count the ballots on the change of the Association's name, made the following report: "Professor Thomas LeDuc, Robert Richmond, and I were at the home of the secretary on three different occasions for the opening and counting of the ballots. The ballots were sorted, rechecked, and carefully counted: 246 affirmative votes and 530 negative votes at our last counting November 14 is an accurate report of the returns. The ballots with one exception were signed by members; the exception bore a return address." The report was approved and the secretary was directed to preserve the ballots until after the April meeting.

The following report from Gordon C. Baldwin, acting for Everett N. Dick, chairman of the committee to cooperate with the National Park Service, was read by the secretary and placed on file: "There has been very little action

[1] This is a condensation of Mrs. Paine's annual report read at the Chicago meeting of the Association, April 18, 1952, the minutes of the executive committee, and the minutes of the annual business meeting.

by the committee since the April meeting. However, we do have the following accomplishments to report. Mr. Steven Hoekman, graduate student at the University of South Dakota, has completed his master's thesis on old Fort Sully, and Adrian Dunn, also of the University of South Dakota, has completed his master's thesis on old Fort Berthold. James K. Beakey of Montana State University is writing a thesis on the history of the Canyon Ferry Reservoir. These are projects sponsored by the Mississippi Valley Historical Association in cooperation with the National Park Service. We have corresponded with Professors Herbert S. Schell and Elwyn B. Robinson of the University of South Dakota and the University of North Dakota, respectively, regarding the possibility of interesting graduate students in doing research on historic sites related to reservoir areas in the Dakotas. A list of research topics in which we are particularly interested was submitted. While these gentlemen have been very cooperative in the matter, they have been unsuccessful in their efforts to interest students in these subjects, largely because of the paucity of graduate students at these schools. The program of the annual meeting in Chicago will include a paper by Dr. Waldo R. Wedel of the Smithsonian Institution on the subject 'Prehistoric Peoples of the Great Plains.' "

Philip M. Hamer presented a request for cooperation with the National Historical Publications Commission in its program for the publication of the papers of American leaders. Herbert A. Kellar proposed that the Association cooperate more closely with the American Association for State and Local History. After some discussion it was voted that Mr. Kellar explore the possibility of such cooperation and report at a later meeting.

A letter from the managing editor, resigning his position as of March, 1953, and expressing his thanks to the committee and to the board of editors for loyal support, was read by the chairman of the executive committee. A subcommittee consisting of William C. Binkley, Merle Curti, and Fred C. Cole was appointed to work out some plan by which the managing editor could continue in the office. No solution was found and the matter was left open until the April meeting.

The executive committee assembled for three sessions at the Chicago meeting of the Association, the first on the evening of April 16. The following members were present: Binkley, chairman, Harold W. Bradley, Cole, Curti, Dwight L. Dumond, Kellar, George H. Knoles, Reginald C. McGrane, George E. Mowry, Nichols, Petersen, Sellers, the managing editor, and the secretary-treasurer. Reports were made by the chairmen of the program, nominating (by Charles A. Barker in the absence of the chairman), and local arrangements committees. Upon the recommendation of Grace Lee Nute, chairman of the Alvord Memorial Commission, Theodore C. Blegen, Carlton

C. Qualey, and Theodore Saloutos were reappointed members of the Commission for terms of three years. Dr. Nute submitted the following annual report:

> The Commission's work this year has been largely that of publicizing *Military Life in Dakota* and starting final editorial work on "Ho! For the Goldfields." Approximately one third of *Military Life* stock has been shipped. Of the original 1,500 copies, 1,058 remain. Total money received is $1,694.58, with $145.22 in accounts receivable. Six mailings of publicity material have been made, totaling approximately 12,000 pieces, at a cost of $332.93, or twenty-two cents per unit. Miscellaneous costs have been $145.32.
>
> Reviews were very slow in appearing. Except for the excellent review in the New York *Times* of June 24, most of the important reviews waited until autumn or winter. They were excellent when they appeared, but their slowness in arrival held up purchases for months. . . . A by-product of this publicity for *Military Life* was a sudden spurt in orders for the first volume put out by the Commission, *Documents Relating to Northwest Missions*. In the month of March there were nine orders for that book. Only 151 copies of the edition remain. . . .
>
> The committee reminds you that your Commission operates on a revolving fund and that the sale of every volume should not only pay for its own publication but should also add to the original fund. Under these circumstances we shall be prevented from publishing our proposed next volume, "Ho! For the Goldfields," until many more copies of the current volume have been sold. The detailed accounting of our funds is comprised within the report of the Association's secretary-treasurer.
>
> It is expected that it will be another year before the next volume can go to press. Final revisions are now being made in accordance with the specifications of the general editor with the expectation that the book can be reduced to one of 500 pages without impairing its value. Although no publisher for the volume has been chosen it is hoped that the University of Oklahoma Press may issue it as they did the current volume in which instance the quality of the work was outstanding and the cost economical to say the least.
>
> This report cannot be closed without an expression from the Alvord Memorial Commission commending to the Association the Minnesota Historical Society and especially Miss Lucile Kane for their assistance in the distribution of books as they were received from the press. The Society has used its staff and facilities for the packing, shipping, and bookkeeping essential to the distribution.

Fred Cole made the following report regarding the effort to lighten the work of the managing editor: "Tulane University will continue to support the *Review* for such a period as the Mississippi Valley Historical Association and Tulane feel appropriate. In order that relief may be given to Dr. Stephenson and continuity in the editorial staff may be assured we shall look for an associate editor at the associate or full professor level to be added to the history staff. It is our hope that we can find some person who will have a sincere interest in helping with the *MVHR* in addition to being a highly competent historian. Funds for this purpose have been tentatively approved by the President of the University, and thus if the Association approves this proposal I believe a satisfactory arrangement for the next few years can be worked out. When such a person is found I shall resign as associate editor of the *Review*. We shall continue, however, to keep an assistant editor who will devote half time to the work of the *Review*. At a later date when Dr. Stephenson concludes that he should be relieved of direct responsibility for the *Review* it is our hope that the person who has worked with him as associate editor can step into the position as managing editor. This will be, of course, subject to the approval of the executive committee of the Association."

This generous offer on the part of Tulane University was discussed by the executive committee and it was voted to accept the proposal presented by Dean Cole on behalf of Tulane University concerning the editorship of the *MVHR*. Be it further resolved, that the executive committee, or a subcommittee of the executive committee, continue during the ensuing year to investigate means of providing Tulane University with some financial relief attendant upon the implementation of the proposal for the editorship of the *Review*.

Upon Mr. Kellar's suggestion it was voted that a committee of two be appointed to work in conjunction with a similar committee of the American Historical Association to promote cooperation with the American Association for State and Local History.

In the matter of increased postal rates now in effect on second class matter and bulk mailings of third class material, it was voted that the president and the secretary consult with postal authorities in an effort to have the Association, now an "authorized non-profit organization" on the records of the Collector of Internal Revenue, exempted from increased postal rates.

The committee to study discrimination as it relates to the Association (Carl Wittke, chairman, Theodore C. Blegen, Thomas D. Clark, Colin B. Goodykoontz, and Fletcher M. Green) presented the following report:

> Membership in the Mississippi Valley Historical Association is open to anyone interested in its activities and objectives, and willing to abide by the constitution and by-laws of the Association.
>
> All members are entitled to receive the *Mississippi Valley Historical Review* and to participate in the annual convention and other meetings and activities of the Association.

The executive committee of the Association shall recommend to the Association, as a meeting place for its annual spring convention, only such localities or institutions where all members of the Association will be permitted to participate in all official sessions, including luncheon and dinner meetings which are part of the official program.

After considerable discussion the executive committee resolved that a further study of the issues arising from the danger of discrimination within the Association is required, and that to provide for such continued study it instructs the president either to reassign to the existing special committee or to a new committee at his discretion the responsibility for a study of the problems and ramifications involved in all types of discrimination within the Association, to make recommendations designed so far as possible to eliminate all types of discrimination, and to present these recommendations to the executive committee not later than the annual meeting of April, 1953; and that this action and the reasons for it be reported to the business meeting of the Association.

The executive committee met again on the evening of April 17, following the annual dinner. The following members attended: Binkley, chairman, Bradley, Cole, Curti, Dumond, Kellar, Knoles, McGrane, Mowry, Nichols, Clarence S. Paine, Petersen, Sellers, the managing editor, and the secretary-treasurer. Thomas D. Clark and A. D. Kirwan of the University of Kentucky invited the Association to meet in Lexington in 1953, and assured the executive committee of the absence of discrimination in that city. The committee accepted the invitation with appreciation for the thoughtfulness of the Lexington members.

Upon the recommendation of the managing editor, Richard W. Leopold of Northwestern University, Roy M. Robbins of Butler University, and Max Savelle of the University of Washington were elected members of the board of editors for terms of three years; and Charles A. Barker of Johns Hopkins University was elected to the Pelzer Prize Committee for a term of four years. The managing editor also proposed, with the approval of the editorial board, that members of the Association be requested to submit personal data sheets to the editorial office with a view to facilitating selection of book reviewers. The managing editor stressed the fact that many competent reviewers were being overlooked, and expressed the hope that a larger number of members would be invited to participate in this important function of the *Review*. The executive committee authorized an appropriation to pay the cost of circularizing the membership in September, 1952.

The business meeting of the Association was called to order by President Curti after the luncheon on April 18. The secretary-treasurer's financial statement, audited by a committee headed by Reginald C. McGrane, was approved. The secretary-treasurer also summarized the Association's activities for the past year: its joint sessions with the American Historical Association on December 28, 1951; the work of special committees to count the ballots on changing the name of the Association, to study discrimination as it relates to the organization, and to work with the National Historical Publications Commission in its program of publishing the papers of American leaders; the publication of Volume III of the cumulative index to the *Review*; and the appearance of the Alvord Memorial Commission's *Military Life in Dakota; The Journal of Philippe Régis de Trobriand.*

Announcement was made of the appointment of Thomas C. Cochran, University of Pennsylvania, to represent the Association at the Philadelphia meeting of the National Council for Historic Sites and Buildings, October 29-30, 1951; of Donald W. Beatty, University of Minnesota, as a member of the Pan American Institute of History and Geography advisory committee; and of Paul Chibas, Havana, Cuba, to attend the Fifth Interamerican Congress of Municipal History in Ciudad Trujillo, Dominican Republic, April 24.

Thirteen members of the Association died during the year: Julian P. Bretz, Ithaca, New York; Robert B. Brown, Ann Arbor, Michigan; Arthur H. Clark, Sr., Glendale, California; Charles G. Dawes, Chicago, a life member and for many years a contributor to the guaranty fund; Clifford C. Dunlap, Chicago; Cad A. Foster, Oconomowoc, Wisconsin; Louis Koontz, Los Angeles; Lloyd D. Miller, New Orleans; Mark Morton, West Chicago, a life member and contributor for many years to the guaranty fund; Thomas F. O'Connor, St. Louis; Esmond Phelps, New Orleans; Nelson V. Russell, Waukesha, Wisconsin; and W. D. Stimple, Blacksburg, Virginia. Merle Curti became a life member. A total of 234 student members includes 140 who have enrolled during the year.

Two invitations for the 1954 meeting of the Association have been received and placed on file: one, presented by Frank L. Klement to meet in Milwaukee, sponsored by Marquette University, Milwaukee-Downer College, the Milwaukee Extension Division of the University of Wisconsin, and various civic organizations; the other, presented by Clifford L. Lord, director of the State Historical Society of Wisconsin, to meet in Madison to assist in the centennial celebration in honor of Lyman Copeland Draper.

The Association voted to support the proposal of the State Historical Society of Wisconsin to promote the issuing of a memorial stamp in honor of Lyman Copeland Draper.

The following report of the committee to cooperate with the National Park Service in the Missouri Valley Project was presented by the chairman, Everett N. Dick, and approved:

1. The committee to cooperate with the National Park Service in the survey, recording, and salvage of historic sites in reservoir areas within Region Two of the National Park Service, held its annual meeting on April 17. We are pleased to report progress in the program. During the past year three collaborative research projects have been completed on sites to be destroyed by inundation, and two new projects have been inaugurated.

2. The committee makes the following recommendations: (a) that we continue to encourage graduate students to undertake special studies of historic sites threatened by dam construction; (b) that the National Park Service be requested to submit annually to faculties of graduate colleges a list of research projects made urgent by the schedule of dam completions; and (c) that the Association sponsor the study of documentary research materials available to scholars in the Region Two Office of the National Park Service at Omaha.

Jay Monaghan, chairman of the membership committee, presented a lively and interesting report, and offered the following condensation for the minutes. A vote of thanks was extended to Mr. Monaghan for his long service on the committee.

The chairman of your committee on membership wishes to report that he has followed the previous practice of dividing the United States into twelve zones of approximately equal population — with the exception of Zone 12, the northeastern states. A leader was appointed for each zone and each was asked to take part in a friendly contest for new members.

Our secretary has furnished me periodically the number of new members recruited in each zone. I have incorporated this information in letters to all committeemen in order to keep them informed on their places in the contest. It was hoped that this occasional letter might remind the members of their obligations and stimulate their activities.

In December, 1951, Theodore Paullin's Zone 12 headed the list. Frederick I. Olson's Zone 5 stood second, and Lewis Atherton, with Kansas, Oklahoma, and Missouri, ranked third. This rating has changed: Paullin still holds the lead, and Olson the second place. Madison Kuhn, with Michigan and Indiana, has stepped ahead of Atherton for the third place. This consistent increase in membership in the Northeast is a gratifying trend in our Association's growth.

Most of the committeemen entered enthusiastically into this friendly competition. We owe special thanks to Arthur C. Cole who, though not a member of the committee, has sent in over fifty memberships from Zone 12.

The number of new members for the year is 257. In closing, I wish to thank the secretary for her hearty cooperation in our activities.

LeRoy Hafen, acting for Carl Coke Rister, chairman of the committee to cooperate with the National Historical Publications Commission, presented the following report which was approved by the Association:

The preliminary report of the National Historical Publications Commission included the names of 62 persons whose contributions to American life and whose preserved and available papers were such as would seem to warrant the publication of the papers of those persons.

In the opinion of a number of historians the list should be supplemented. Accordingly the Mississippi Valley Historical Association appointed a committee to advise with the Commission.

Lists of persons have been submitted by the individual members of your committee. These proposals, assembled by Dr. Rister, will be studied and criticized by the committee members, and the joint judgment and recommendations will then be submitted to the executive committee of the Mississippi Valley Historical Association.

The following report by O. Fritiof Ander, chairman of the joint committee of the American Historical Association and the Mississippi Valley Historical Association on the census, was approved by the Association:

At the last annual meeting of the Association I reported that a preliminary meeting of the Committee on the Census had been planned for April 20 at Cincinnati. Present at this meeting were Oscar Handlin, Frank L. Owsley, Carl Wittke, and the chairman. Theodore C. Blegen could not attend. The United States Bureau of the Census was represented by its director, Roy V. Peel, and two assistant directors. The director urged members of the committee to view the Bureau's activities as broader than the taking of the population census. It conducted inquiries into the fields of housing, agriculture, manufacturing, business, governments, and foreign trade, and on this basis the committee did not need to confine its recommendations to a given field.

At this preliminary meeting the committee expressed an interest in special tabulations from the 1950 census, special tabulations from past censuses and especially the 1850 census, and historical studies of internal migration. Conrad Tauber, assistant director of the Bureau of the Census, gave a brief report on the census monograph program. The members of the committee seemed most interested in special tabulations and studies of past censuses on which many suggestions were read by the chairman from excerpts of letters written by historians and sociologists.

Three members of the committee — Edward C. Kirkland (a replacement for Owsley, who had resigned), Handlin, and the chairman — met for a first regular meeting in Washington, D. C., on October 26 with representatives from the Bureau of the Census and the Bureau of Naturalization. Here it became evident that due to the limited resources of the Bureau of the Census retabulations of data from earlier censuses or studies of these in relationship to other materials could not be undertaken unless the committee succeeded in finding funds from private sources for such purposes. The representatives of the Bureau of the Census urged the committee to turn its attention to special monographic topics growing out of the 1950 census in order that these might provide materials of greater usefulness to future historians. The members of the committee were not ready to make definite suggestions with the result that the chairman appointed a subcommittee consisting of Handlin and Kirkland to study the problem of monograph topics in consultation with representatives of the Bureau of the Census.

The chairman has been a little impatient with the progress of the work of the committee, but he has been assured by Guy Stanton Ford and the director of the Bureau of the Census as well as others that an important foundation has been laid for a closer cooperation of historians and the Bureau of the Census of a nature which should be important to every one concerned. It should also be mentioned that the committee has been enlarged by the appointment of Bayrd Still to its membership.

Harold W. Bradley reported the action of the executive committee on the subject of "discrimination" and stated that the "executive committee believes a further study of the issues arising from the danger of discrimination within the Association is required, and that to provide for such continued study it instructs the president either to reassign to the existing special committee or to a new committee at his discretion the responsibility for a study of the problems and ramifications involved in all types of discrimination within the Association, to make recommendations designed so far as possible to eliminate all types of discrimination, and to present these recommendations to the executive committee not later than the annual meeting of April, 1953; and that this action and the reasons for it be reported to the business meeting of the Association."

Jeannette P. Nichols presented the following resolutions which were unanimously adopted by the Association:

Whereas: The most crucial issues of our times involving the security of the nation are in the field of international relations, and

Whereas: Wise policies cannot be devised and pursued for national security in a free society without the guidance and support of an enlightened public opinion, and

Whereas: For the formation of such informed opinion it is essential that the government take the public into its confidence by supplying official information honestly and frankly both as to current policies and historical policy developments to the fullest extent possible,

Be It Therefore Resolved by the Mississippi Valley Historical Association:

1. That the Association approves the widest possible dissemination by the Department of State of objective, factual information on current foreign policy through its publication program and other channels of communication, and

2. That the Association deplores the fact that the official public record of American foreign policy presented in *Foreign Relations of the United States* has been allowed to drop farther and farther behind, and that the Association urges that every effort be made to speed up the publication of this series, and

3. That the Association also urges continued support for the publication of *Documents on German Foreign Policy* and calls attention to the importance of making both this series and that of *Foreign Relations of the United States* available to the public as soon as possible through the war period so that historical writing on the origin and conduct of the war may be based on authentic information, and

4. That the secretary of the Association be directed to bring these resolutions to the attention of the Department of State and the appropriate committees of Congress.

The following resolution in regard to the *Territorial Papers* was adopted:

Whereas: The *Territorial Papers* project in the National Archives, under the able editorship of Clarence E. Carter, has through the years contributed greatly to the general understanding of American history and has proved to be of particular value to members of this Association,

Be It Therefore Resolved by the Mississippi Valley Historical Association:

1. That the Association herewith registers its appreciation of this monumental undertaking and strongly urges continued support of it, and

2. That the secretary of the Association be directed to bring these resolutions to the attention of the General Services Administration, the National Archives, and the appropriate committees of Congress.

Charles A. Barker, for the committee on nominations, reported the following officers and members of the executive committee and moved that they be elected: president: James L. Sellers, University of Nebraska; vice-president: Fred A. Shannon, University of Illinois; secretary-treasurer: Mrs. Clarence S. Paine; members of the executive committee: Edward C. Kirkland, Bowdoin College, Bessie Louise Pierce, University of Chicago, and Bell I. Wiley, Emory University; members of the executive committee of the Teachers'

Section: George L. Anderson, University of Kansas, and Carlton C. Qualey, Carleton College. The motion was seconded and as there were no other nominations the members were declared elected.

James Rabun of Emory University proposed the following amendment to Article IV of the constitution. The proposal will lie over for consideration at the 1953 annual meeting.

To substitute for sentence *one* of paragraph *two* of Article IV the following:

The president, vice-president, and secretary-treasurer shall be elected at the annual meeting each year from nominations made by the nominating committee and presented to the membership by mail by March 1 each year and from any further nominations presented to the chairman of the nominating committee not later than one day before the annual business meeting by petition sponsored by not fewer than twenty voting members of the Association.

To add after paragraph *two* of Article IV the following:

The three members of the executive committee to be chosen each year shall be chosen by ballot of the membership of the Association from at least two nominations for each executive committee membership made by the nominating committee on a ballot to be presented by mail to each member of the Association not later than March 1 of each year.

There shall be five members of the nominating committee, each member to hold office for two years. On alternate years two members and three members respectively shall be chosen by the voting members from at least two nominations for each committee membership made by the nominating committee on a ballot to be presented by mail to each member of the Association not later than March 1 of each year.

Ballots for members of the executive committee and the nominating committee must be in the hands of the chairman of the nominating committee one week before the annual business meeting of the Association at which the results of the balloting shall be announced.

Jeannette P. Nichols, chairman of the committee on resolutions, offered the following resolutions which received the unanimous vote of the Association:

Whereas: Certain kind and hard-working persons, by their assiduous labors have provided the membership of the Mississippi Valley Historical Association, at their 1952 convention, with much intellectual and gastronomic stimulus,

Be It Therefore Resolved: That the Association express its very warm appreciation to Thomas LeDuc and his cohorts of the program committee; to Paul M. Angle and his associates of the local arrangements committee;

and to the hospitable Chicago Historical Society and Rand McNally and Company.

Whereas: The *Mississippi Valley Historical Review* has been the recipient of much generous and understanding support from Tulane University, and

Whereas: The University is now increasing its aid yet more generously,

Be It Therefore Resolved by the Mississippi Valley Historical Association: That the Association hereby expresses its very special appreciation of this continuing and expanding sponsorship.

The executive committee assembled for a third session after adjournment of the business meeting. The following members were present: Binkley, Bradley, Dumond, Kellar, Edward C. Kirkland, Nichols, Paine, Petersen, Bessie L. Pierce, Sellers, Fred A. Shannon, the managing editor, and the secretary-treasurer. The first order of business was the election of a chairman to succeed Dr. Binkley whose term as a member of the executive committee had expired. Thanks and appreciation for his long and valued service as chairman were voted by the committee. Dwight L. Dumond was elected chairman of the executive committee.

O. Fritiof Ander appeared before the committee to request that the Association send greetings to John H. Hauberg, philanthropist and local historian, who would be honored by the Rock Island County Historical Society at its annual dinner on May 28. Mr. Hauberg founded the Society, served as president and as a member of the board of directors of the Illinois State Historical Society, and entertained the members of the Mississippi Valley Historical Association at its Rock Island meeting in 1948. The committee voted to send greetings, on behalf of the Association, to Mr. Hauberg.

Statement of Cash Receipts and Disbursements for the Year Ending March 31, 1952

Cash on deposit in National Bank of Commerce,
Lincoln, Nebraska, April 1, 1951:

Checking account	$10,505.21	
Savings account — Alvord Memorial Commission	316.79	$10,822.00

Receipts:

Alvord Memorial Commission	$ 2,043.61
Library dues	3,936.00
Sustaining memberships	5,936.64
New memberships	1,185.50
Life memberships	100.00

Registration fees		431.00	
Book sales		537.26	
Interest		450.00	
Advertising		1,293.25	
Donations		3,000.00	
Royalties		14.03	18,927.29
			$29,749.29
Disbursements:			
Expenses of Alvord Memorial Commission	$	314.43	
Expenses of Alvord Memorial Commission paid by Mississippi Valley Historical Association		3,616.47	
Reimbursement to Alvord Memorial Commission of interest which had been deposited in the checking account of Mississippi Valley Historical Association		12.50	
Clerical expense		3,100.00	
Office expense		13.80	
Postage and express		238.91	
Miscellaneous printing		1,022.28	
Travel		261.58	
Legal and professional service		131.34	
Publications		12,938.42	
Miscellaneous expense		109.61	21,759.34
Cash on hand and on deposit:			
On hand — Alvord Memorial Commission	$	20.52	
On deposit in National Bank of Commerce, Lincoln, Nebraska, March 31, 1952			
Checking account	$5,943.98		
Savings account	2,025.45	7,969.43	$ 7,989.95

The Secession Crisis and the Frontier: Washington Territory, 1860-1861

By Robert W. Johannsen

While a tremendous volume of scholarly historical work has been done on the Civil War period,[1] there exists no adequate treatment of the role played by the Pacific Northwest during that time.[2] Sparsely populated and isolated from the East by poor transportation and communication as well as by two thousand miles of prairies, deserts, and mountain peaks, this frontier region nevertheless felt a strong interest in national affairs and expressed a vital concern over the sectional crises that finally culminated in the Civil War. At its outbreak the area, known for many years as the Oregon Country, was divided politically into two major units: Oregon, which had been admitted to statehood in 1859, and Washington Territory, including what is now Idaho and parts of western Montana. A study of the reaction of the settlers of Washington Territory to the secession crisis of 1860-1861 illustrates not only the significance and character of national politics on the level of frontier politics but also the strong connecting tie that existed between the frontiersmen of the Pacific Northwest and the national government during one of the most crucial periods of American history.

In 1860 Washington Territory, with an area almost three times that of New England, had a population of only 11,594 people. The backgrounds of the settlers were varied, a large proportion of them originating in areas that had just emerged from a frontier stage. The census returns of that year indicate that nearly half of the native-born population in the territory had been born in ten

[1] This article received the Mississippi Valley Historical Association's Pelzer Award for 1952.

[2] A recent study, Kenneth M. Stampp, *And the War Came; The North and the Secession Crisis, 1860-1861* (Baton Rouge, 1950), largely ignores the Far West. This paper is a section of a projected study of the relationship between the Pacific Northwest and the nation during the Civil War and Reconstruction periods.

states of the middle and upper Mississippi Valley and that a large number had emigrated from slaveholding states of the upper and deep South.[3] Seven years earlier the area had been split off from the Territory of Oregon and given separate territorial status. From the first territorial election in 1854, the Democratic party had held undisputed sway over local politics. Although the territory had been created under a Whig president, the appointment of officers was left to his Democratic successor. From then until after the outbreak of the Civil War, the territorial patronage was closely controlled by the Democratic party. Not only did the appointed officers serve as a connecting link between the national and local party organizations but they built up around them a strong political machine, known locally as the "Olympia clique." The Republican party had a small beginning in the 1856 election and was considerably strengthened in following years by the demise of the local Whig party. It never was a match for the Democratic organization, however, which polled over 60 per cent of the total vote cast for the territorial delegate in the two elections preceding 1860.[4] Although the nature of the territorial system itself necessarily demanded an extension of federal power, sentiment in favor of the sovereign local state was strong among members of both parties in Washington Territory, a Jeffersonian ideal that persisted elsewhere on this far Northwest frontier.[5]

Almost from the very beginning of the territorial period, the settlers manifested an active interest in national politics, even though as a territory the region had neither a voice in national affairs nor a vote in national elections. The great distance which lay between the Pacific Northwest and the centers of political activity in the East, the sparse population, and the limited economy of the territory made many national issues abstract. The local political parties, however, followed the alignments of their national counterparts.

Although the extension and protection of slavery in the territories

[3] *Eighth Census, Population of the United States in 1860* (Washington, 1864), 580-85. Persons born in Oregon and the territories were excluded in the writer's tabulation because in 1860 they were probably under voting age.

[4] For a summary of political activity in Washington Territory in the years prior to the Civil War, see Robert W. Johannsen, "National Issues and Local Politics in Washington Territory, 1857-1861," *Pacific Northwest Quarterly* (Seattle), XLII (January, 1951), 3-31.

[5] Dorothy O. Johansen, "A Tentative Appraisal of Territorial Government in Oregon," *Pacific Historical Review* (Berkeley and Los Angeles), XVIII (November, 1949), 497-98.

was the dominant national issue during the fifties, it was of little practical significance in the far Northwest. Some slaves, however, were brought into the Pacific Northwest by settlers from southern states, settling for the most part in Oregon where the principle of slavery extension was argued more bitterly.[6] North of the Columbia River some minor excitement regarding slavery was recorded in the fall of 1860 when a young slave boy held by James Tilton, Washington Territory's surveyor general, escaped to Victoria where he was aided by British authorities. Tilton's protest was forwarded to the secretary of state in Washington, D. C., but no action was ever taken on his behalf. One Puget Sound newspaper, in reporting the matter, remarked, "Our proximity to the British Possessions on this Coast afford the same facilities to an underground railroad that the Canadas do on the Atlantic." [7] This incident, however, was the exception rather than the rule. Slavery was unimportant as a local issue in Washington Territory, although territorial politicians were often forced to discuss it because of their connection with the national party organizations. The leading Democratic newspaper in Washington Territory refused to admit that the issue had a practical bearing in the territory, maintaining that it had "long since been settled by latitude and climate." [8] At the same time the paper followed the national party organization by espousing the proslavery cause.

The year preceding the outbreak of hostilities between the North and the South in 1861 was a period of extreme significance to national politics. The long and bitter struggle between the sections was climaxed by the threatened destruction of the Union. Southern demands for a slave code and for federal protection of slavery in

[6] See D. G. Hill, "The Negro as a Political and Social Issue in the Oregon Country," *Journal of Negro History* (Lancaster, Washington), XXXIII (April, 1948), 130-45; Fred Lockley, "Some Documentary Records of Slavery in Oregon," *Oregon Historical Quarterly* (Salem, Portland), XVII (June, 1916), 107-15. In 1857 the people of Oregon Territory adopted a state constitution, at the same time rejecting slavery by a vote of 7,727 to 2,645. The following year, however, the Oregon territorial legislature debated a bill which would protect the institution of slavery in the territory. The bill passed the council but failed to reach a vote in the house of representatives. In February, 1859, Oregon was admitted as a free state. Charles H. Carey, *A General History of Oregon Prior to 1861*, 2 vols. (Portland, 1935-1936), II, 511, 519.

[7] James Tilton to Henry M. McGill, September 30, 1860, Letters and Documents Relating to the Offices of Governor and Secretary of Washington Territory, 1860-1864, Pacific Northwest Collection (University of Washington Library, Seattle); Steilacoom *Puget Sound Herald*, October 5, 1860.

[8] Olympia *Pioneer and Democrat*, January 18, 1861.

the territories brought matters swiftly to a head. The Democratic party, which had ruled the nation in the interest of its southern wing, found itself threatened by a new and relatively untried political party based on an issue that could only be sectional in its appeal. One southern state early in the year gave notice that its relationship with the national government would be seriously questioned should the approaching presidential election result in a Republican victory. On March 2, 1860, the Olympia *Pioneer and Democrat*, Washington Territory's "official" Democratic party organ and oldest newspaper, indicated that a feeling of anxiety and tension had penetrated to the far Northwest frontier.

> There never was a period in the history of this country when we were at peace or free from party excitement, in which there was manifested such absorbing interest in National affairs as at the present time. It pervades all classes and conditions of society. . . . It is the firm settled conviction of the public mind that we are approaching, nay, have reached a crisis in political affairs, compared with which all former ones were as gentle gales to the destroying whirlwind.[9]

A year earlier a pioneer settler of the Pacific Northwest wrote an old political friend in Illinois, unaware of the role his correspondent would soon play, "things are terribly mussed up every where politically & morally & no human Eye can see the results that will follow or foretell the consequences. We can only hope for the best." [10] Expressing an attitude of detachment that was soon to be lost, one territorial editor described the confusion and excitement that characterized national politics: "The slavery question is the all absorbing question of debate, and the way political matters are now mixed up at the East, it is an impossibility to tell which of the now existing political parties are the most Union loving and patriotic, or which are the most fool-hardy and headstrong." [11] Despite isolation from the rest of the nation, the settlers of Washington Territory anxiously watched the political, sectional storm.

Because of its status as a territory, Washington was not formally represented in the national presidential nominating conventions scheduled for 1860. The territorial Democrats, however, had an indirect representation at the national convention in Charleston in

[9] *Ibid.*, March 2, 1860.

[10] Anson G. Henry to Abraham Lincoln, February 16, 1859, Robert Todd Lincoln Collection, Lincoln Papers (microcopy in University of Washington Library of originals in the Library of Congress).

[11] Port Townsend *Register*, February 1, 1860.

the person of Isaac I. Stevens, Washington's delegate in Congress, former governor of the territory, and leader of the local Democracy. The state of Oregon was allotted six delegates for the Charleston meeting, but only two of those chosen actually attended. The other four votes were delegated by proxy and exercised by various individuals, among them Stevens.[12] The delegation was in full accord with the wishes of the Democratic party in the Pacific Northwest that the name of Joseph Lane, Oregon's popular senator, be placed at the top of the national ticket.[13] Throughout the convention proceedings the Northwest delegation acted with the administration, or southern, wing of the party. When the debate over the adoption of a platform resulted in the disruption of the convention, the rival wings of the party each scheduled a meeting in Baltimore for the middle of June. Stevens, assuming the leadership of the Oregon delegation, appeared in the Douglas convention but later withdrew. Joining with the Southerners he participated in nominating John C. Breckinridge and Lane on a strong proslavery platform.[14]

The nominations were received with jubilation by many Democrats in Washington Territory. When the news arrived enthusiastic citizens of Olympia, the territorial capital, fired sixty guns to celebrate the occasion. The *Pioneer and Democrat*, with a preoccupation for party regularity, at first cast a few doubts on the legality of the convention that nominated Breckinridge. These doubts were soon dismissed with the observation that, even if only "eleven" (*sic*) states were represented in the convention, the delegates represented people "who entertain views upon the question of slavery similar to those we hold to."[15] The optimism of territorial Democrats was heightened even more by the results of the local territorial

[12] The two members of the Oregon delegation who appeared in person at Charleston were John K. Lamerick, formerly a brigadier general in the Oregon militia, and Lansing Stout, Oregon's congressman in Washington, D. C. Lamerick later entered the Confederate army. Other delegates who held proxies were A. P. Dennison, an Indian agent in Oregon; Justus Steinberger, agent of the Pacific Mail Steamship Company; and R. B. Metcalf, a former Indian agent in Oregon Territory.

[13] As early as March 2, 1860, the Olympia *Pioneer and Democrat* had raised the name of Joseph Lane to the masthead of the paper as its choice for president. Lane, a staunch proslavery, administration Democrat, later wrote: "One thing, however, is certain, that is Douglas cannot nor will not be nominated, or if he should be the south will bring out a candidate and run him with the certainty of giving him the entire south. We are in a muss, and I can hardly see how we can get out with whole bones, but we will see." Lane to Matthew P. Deady, May 13, 1860, Joseph Lane Papers (Oregon Historical Society Library, Portland).

[14] Carey, *General History of Oregon*, II, 766-68.

[15] Olympia *Pioneer and Democrat*, July 27, 1860.

election in July, 1860, when twenty-four Democrats and nine Republicans were returned to the territorial legislature. In a confident tone that was shortly to be reversed by circumstances the Democratic organ declared, "The democracy were never before so united." [16]

Territorial interest in the national election was further enhanced by the appointment of Stevens as chairman of the Democratic National Executive Committee, the official Breckinridge and Lane organization. Since 1852, when he actively campaigned for Franklin Pierce, Stevens had been highly regarded by Democratic party leaders. Appointed governor of Washington Territory the following year, he was instrumental in perfecting the organization of the territorial Democratic party. In 1857 and again in 1859 he was elected territorial delegate. During his terms in Congress he kept in close connection with the Buchanan administration. When the party split over the Kansas issue, Stevens remained loyal to the administration wing. During the summer of 1860, when the threat of disunion became increasingly great, Stevens believed that the election of Breckinridge was the only alternative to an open break between the North and the South. From his headquarters in the national capital, he worked diligently throughout the summer, writing campaign pamphlets, making addresses, and conferring with leading Democrats.

The optimism of some territorial Democrats and the confidence of the Democratic organ were hardly justified. The Democratic party in the territory, like the national party, was not at this time united. Since 1856 a local split centered around the arbitrary actions of Governor Stevens during an Indian war along Puget Sound. It assumed larger significance as early as February, 1859. In an address to the voters of the territory, the Democratic Central Committee for Washington Territory announced:

> For near one year — since the unfortunate difference between President Buchanan and Senator Douglas on the Kansas question, there had evidently been a steady and fixed determination on the part of the *outs*, claiming to belong to the democracy [the anti-Stevens Democrats], to ignore the present administration, create a Douglas movement, and construct a party here whose issue with the democracy would be placed upon the ground of differance [*sic*] that existed between the President and that Senator at the last session of Congress.[17]

[16] *Ibid.*, July 20, 1860.
[17] *Ibid.*, February 18, 1859.

In spite of efforts to heal or ignore the breach, the Douglas, or anti-Stevens, wing gained strength.

Some Democrats in Washington Territory were quite disturbed at the disruption of their party on the national level. As the presidential election approached, the conviction grew that no candidate would receive a majority of the electoral vote, thereby throwing the decision into the House of Representatives.[18] Upon hearing of the split in the national party, one Island County Democrat observed, "This is a pretty *kettle of fish* indeed God only knows how it will come out my impression that it will go to the House of Rep — where Breckenridge [*sic*] has the best chance of any of them." [19] William M. Morrow, postmaster at Oakland and a leading Democrat of Sawamish (Mason) County, hoped that Breckinridge would be elected "if not by the people Surely the House will not Falter in such a trying imergency [*sic*]." In a letter to Stevens he predicted that the national Democracy would find itself in the minority following the election, "But their Principles if adhered to strictly must cause them to gather strength & finally Be stronger than ever." [20] Earlier, Stevens had been warned that "Democracy is . . . in the north fast narrowing down to Douglasism." [21] On the day of the election Winfield Scott Ebey noted in his diary, "If the People have made a choice, which is probable, that Choice has undoubtedly fallen on Lincoln. If not then the Election goes to the House of Rep & Breckenridge [*sic*] has the best Show I have a *faint* hope that Lincoln may be defeated — Yet I scarcely allow myself to believe Such can be the fact." [22]

Republicans in the territory were jubilant over the national turn of events. Two newspapers were founded in 1860 to provide the

18 It was the belief at the time that if Congress were called upon to elect the president, Lane would emerge victorious. For the basis of this belief, see Roy F. Nichols, *The Disruption of American Democracy* (New York, 1948), 341.

19 Winfield Scott Ebey Diary, No. 6, p. 334 (July 23, 1860), Pacific Northwest Collection. Ebey, an early settler on Whidby Island, took an active part in Island County politics during this period.

20 William M. Morrow to Isaac I. Stevens, October 10, 1860, Isaac I. Stevens Papers, Pacific Northwest Collection. Stephen A. Douglas' party, Morrow thought, would "Swallow up the Republican party as well as all the Jag ends of all parties & perhaps will be the very life & soul of a Douglass [*sic*] Democratic Party."

21 Edward J. Allen to Stevens, June 11, 1859, *ibid.*

22 Ebey Diary, No. 6, p. 373 (November 6, 1860). Ebey had earlier recorded a rumor that Douglas was contemplating withdrawal from the presidential race. "If such Should be done the Douglas Strength will be given to Col Bell & will probably Defeat Lincoln I hope it may be done." *Ibid.*, 370 (October 28, 1860).

new party with a medium for expression. The Olympia *Washington Standard* announced its determination to "do battle for the advancement of free territory, free labor, free speech, and free men." The first issues were devoted to the presidential election. In spite of the fact that Washington Territory had no vote in this election, the editor felt that the area had a vital interest in its outcome. The United States Supreme Court had, according to the paper, declared Washington a slave territory when it ruled on the Dred Scott case. "We have long entertained the opinion that Washington Territory was Republican at heart," the editor continued rather naïvely, that a large majority of the territorial electorate opposed the proslavery tenets of the Democratic party and regarded with horror the Democratic efforts to make slavery national and freedom sectional. That the territorial elections disproved these assertions did not seem to deter his enthusiasm. The northern states, he predicted, would vote for Lincoln while those of the South would support Bell. The paper was confident that "a day of brightness is about to dawn on our Territory which must dispel the dark shadows of locofocoism [rule by Democratic officeholders] under which it has been so long blighted and withered." [23] With the election of Lincoln the newly founded Port Townsend *North-West* looked forward to "a new era, in which a prosperity unparalleled shall commence with our people, justice and fitness filling our offices of trust, bribery, extortion and corruption hiding its hideous deformity, we trust, *forever*." [24]

On November 23, 1860, news of Lincoln's election in the *Pioneer and Democrat* dashed Ebey's "faint" hope. Elsewhere in the Northwest the voting revealed the relative strength of political parties in the region. A divided Democratic party in Oregon gave the state to Lincoln, who won by a bare 264 votes over Breckinridge, his nearest competitor. It is significant that Oregon was one of the two free states that gave Breckinridge a larger vote than Douglas.

The national triumph of a political party dedicated to the restriction of slavery was a victory only remotely felt by the Republicans on the far Northwest frontier. Of much more immediacy was the prospect that their party would henceforth control the territorial patronage. One Puget Sound newspaper complained

[23] Olympia *Washington Standard*, November 17, 1860. The politics of the *Standard* were, according to Ebey, "as mild as Dishwater." Ebey Diary, No. 6, p. 385 (December 4, 1860).

[24] Port Townsend *North-West*, November 1, 1860.

that no presidential administration could be worse than that of Buchanan as far as the territorial appointments were concerned.[25] It was charged that "the odor of disunion is *rank* among the old office holders!"[26] Richard D. Gholson, the Buchanan-appointed governor of the territory, had left Olympia early in 1860 for his home in Kentucky where he campaigned for Breckinridge and later urged the secession of his native state. A month before Lincoln's inauguration he tendered his resignation to the secretary of state, "unwilling even for a day to hold office under a (so called) 'Republican' President."[27] Local Republicans, indicating a complete lack of understanding of the territorial system, confidently expected that they would be called upon to assume the territorial administration. Even before Lincoln's election a New York lawyer wrote to one of his friends, an aspiring officeholder, "Now is the time to revolutionize Wash Terr & get rid of the clique that has ruled it for years & you are the man to do it."[28] In an effort to expedite Lincoln's task of filling the territorial offices and to reward deserving local politicans, a group of Republicans met at Olympia in December, 1860, agreed that only residents of the territory should be appointed, and drew up a tentative list of officers, giving first preference, of course, to those who were present.[29] One of the group admitted, "the darling idea of my heart, [is] to make this Territory, ultimately a Republican State."[30]

Democratic leaders in the territory were undaunted in the face of the national defeat of their party. Before the election of Lincoln was locally known, William Winlock Miller, former superintendent of Indian Affairs under Buchanan and a leading administration Democrat in the territory, cautioned Stevens that "we must keep up the Organization of the Democratic party and fight on and fight always."[31] A few days later Miller sent Stevens a few "honest

25 Steilacoom *Puget Sound Herald*, December 20, 1860.

26 Hugh A. Goldsborough to Montgomery Blair, May 20, 1861, Lincoln Papers.

27 Richard D. Gholson to Jeremiah S. Black, February 14, 1861, U. S. Department of State, Territorial Papers, Washington Series (microcopy in Pacific Northwest Collection of originals in the National Archives).

28 Dexter Hawkins to Bion F. Kendall, June 26, 1860, Bion F. Kendall Papers (Oregon Historical Society Library).

29 Olympia *Overland Press*, December 15, 1862.

30 Elwood Evans to William D. Kelley, July 29, 1861, U. S. Department of State, General Records, Appointment Papers, Applications and Recommendations (microcopy in Pacific Northwest Collection of originals in the National Archives).

31 William W. Miller to Stevens, November 18, 1860, Stevens Papers. Miller later became prominent in territorial politics as a War Democrat. In 1863 he was

words" regarding the future of the party in the territory. Lamenting the party's loss in the national election, Miller was confident that the Democracy would be able to retain political possession of Washington Territory. "A few faint-hearted Democrats, it is true," he wrote, "will follow off after the victorious camp, but these will be more than counterbalanced by the Democratic increase in the interior of the Territory. This winter we shall do all we can to harmonize the party and I think we shall succeed." [32] Ebey reconciled himself to the "bad news" and thought that the excitement following Lincoln's election, particularly in the South, would soon blow over.[33] The principal Democratic organ in the territory confidently looked forward to a reunion of the warring elements within the party. Lincoln's victory over the divided Democrats would serve to unite the party for future contests; Democrats, according to the paper, should profit from the past in order to be victorious in the future.[34] The Democratic leaders, however, did not reckon with the events, both national and local, that followed on the heels of the presidential election. The first blow was struck against Democratic confidence when the territorial legislature convened at Olympia in early December. The lower house was immediately organized by a coalition of Douglas Democrats and Republicans while the council remained true to the administration wing of the party by only the slightest margin.[35]

The greatest shock to Democratic hopes for party unity came during the critical months following Lincoln's election when news of the impending disruption of the Union reached the Northwest frontier. The settlers of Washington Territory were unprepared for the secession of South Carolina and the probability that the Gulf states would follow her example. Assuming that the Union would be preserved, Stevens emphasized the role of the Far West in the national crisis, through the medium of a public letter from Wash-

described as "the best specimen of a Union Democrat of the Andy Johnson stamp, we have in this territory." Anson G. Henry to Abraham Lincoln, November 18, 1863, Lincoln Papers.

[32] Miller to Stevens, November 29, 1860, Stevens Papers. Miller had reference to the great influx of miners, most of whom were Democrats, into the eastern portions of Washington Territory, the area soon to be included in Idaho Territory. For the full story of the significance of this movement, see Merle W. Wells, "The Creation of the Territory of Idaho," *Pacific Northwest Quarterly*, XL (July, 1949), 106-23.

[33] Ebey Diary, No. 6, p. 378 (November 18, 1860), 386 (December 5, 1860).

[34] Olympia *Pioneer and Democrat*, November 30, 1860.

[35] Miller to Stevens, December 6, 1860, Stevens Papers.

ington. The distance which separated his constituents from both the area of political activity in the East and from the issues which were precipitating the crisis, would, he hoped, give the region the character of a balance wheel between the warring sections.

> The action of the people in the Pacific States and Territories will be watched here with the deepest interest. It is felt that the great west is entitled to a potential voice in counsels affecting the integrity and future of the confederacy, and the hope is cherished that the position you occupy as neutrals — it may be as an arbiter — in the irritating contest between north and south, will enable you to exercise a beneficial influence upon both sections; on one hand checking aggression, and on the other restraining rashness, and so helping to extricate the Union from a danger which no rational man can contemplate without a shudder.[36]

Washington's territorial settlers, with few exceptions, followed Stevens' lead and assumed a position of compromise and reconciliation, without regard to party affiliation.

During the winter months, while secession was being hotly debated in the southern states, both political parties in the territory strongly denounced the actions of the southern fire-eaters, " a few hot-headed, reckless men," according to one newspaper.[37] As in the border states to the east, the territorial population tended to avoid the extreme positions of northern abolitionists and southern secessionists, although John Bell, the presidential candidate of the middle ground, had received almost no support in the election. One newspaper observed that "we are so remote from the sectional hostilities; so free from domestic disturbance, that we can speak of it more in sorrow than in anger." [38] Following the election the leading territorial Republican paper attempted to reassure the South that slavery was not in danger there. "No portion of the Union need fear that . . . [Lincoln] will violate their constitutional rights," the paper added. "And while he does this he will ever bear in mind that this country is designed for the white race." The greatest enemies of the Republican party were the "desperate and unprincipled" abolitionists of the North, although the northern

[36] [Stevens] to the Editor, November 28, 1860, Olympia *Pioneer and Democrat*, January 11, 1861. This is the first of a series of letters written by Stevens to his constituents and published in the "official" Democratic newspaper over the name "Jefferson." Although the original of this letter has not been preserved in the Stevens Papers, the remaining letters in the series are to be found in that collection.

[37] Port Townsend *North-West*, December 27, 1860.

[38] Olympia *Pioneer and Democrat*, January 4, 1861. There is no evidence that John Bell received any support in Washington Territory. In Oregon he polled only 183 out of a total of over 14,000 votes.

Democrats were censured for exciting the South with the false charge that the Republican administration favored abolition.[39] Confidence was expressed in the power of compromise, and so was the hope that latent Unionist sentiment in the South would soon express itself. "The true conservative element, both North and South," the editor wrote, "have before this saved the Union, and we have an abiding confidence that it will again be safely appealed to." [40]

The Democratic press was even more rabid in its denunciation of secession and disunion. Although the territorial Democratic party organization had supported the Breckinridge ticket, it did not countenance disunion as an alternative to defeat at the polls.[41] The *Pioneer and Democrat*, strongly in favor of Breckinridge a few months earlier, now recognized "no disunionist as a fellow partisan." Deploring the actions of South Carolina and the discussions of a Southern Confederacy, the paper also placed its hope in the conservative men in the South. When and if this element should speak out, "we hope to hear . . . of a strong reaction in favor of the Union." [42] When the report was circulated that Lane favored the right of secession, the paper was quick to assure the rest of the country that "this doctrine is not the reflex of public opinion on this Coast, but will be heartily condemned." Such a view "finds no echo in our principles or actions." [43] In a later issue the editor added, "No matter what sectional troubles exist in the States, we have nothing to complain, either of wrong or oppression." [44] A

[39] Olympia *Washington Standard*, November 30, 1860. These statements from the Republican press indicate an underlying anti-Negro bias in the Pacific Northwest that may be traced as far back as the original provisional government in 1843. This feeling reappeared in political campaigns throughout and after the war.

[40] *Ibid.*, December 8, 1860.

[41] This was by no means unique. The John C. Breckinridge vote was a Union vote in many parts of the border and upper South states. Breckinridge himself disavowed secession. See James G. Randall, *The Civil War and Reconstruction* (Boston, 1937), 256, 318-19.

[42] Olympia *Pioneer and Democrat*, December 7, 1860.

[43] *Ibid.*, December 28, 1860. On December 19 Lane delivered a lengthy speech in the United States Senate regarding his position in the crisis. "I belong to that portion of the people of this country . . . [who] will not march . . . to invade the soil of the gallant State of South Carolina when she may withdraw from a Confederacy that has refused her that equality to which she is entitled, as a member of the Union, under the Constitution. . . . I am not a disunionist. I am for the right, and I would have it in the Union; and if it cannot be obtained there, I would go out of the Union, and have that out of the Union that I could not obtain in it, though I was entitled to it." *Cong. Globe*, 36 Cong., 2 Sess., 143-44.

[44] Olympia *Pioneer and Democrat*, January 4, 1861.

Democratic newspaper in Port Townsend echoed the sentiments of a large majority of party members in the territory, denouncing the secession movement as

> a mere pettish gasconade that betrays a great deal of weakness, and we sincerely hope that better councils will prevail in the Southern convention which they are to hold preparatory to a more organized concert of action. . . . Whilst we regret the election to the Presidency of one whose principles are aggressive of Southern rights, we maintain that it is the patriotic duty of every good citizen to stand by that preference which the Nation has expressed conformably to the provisions of the Constitution. We, therefore, disavow any sympathy with those who place themselves in the attitude of Rebels against the powers that be.[45]

Later, after the news of South Carolina's secession had reached Washington Territory, the same paper hinted that strong measures should be taken to restore that state to the Union. Branding the southern movement as "blustering bragadocia [*sic*]," the editor declared that "the pretensions of South Carolina . . . to a distinct National recognition, are absurd and untenable, and the duty, it seems to us, of the Federal Executive is to compel her position *in statu quo*."[46]

As the disruption of the Union became an accomplished fact, some persons on the Pacific coast revived the idea of a Pacific Republic as an independent nation west of the Rocky Mountains. The idea had its inception with the first American settlement on the coast. Although the movement centered in California, it received some support in the Pacific Northwest. As early as 1855 it was reported that there was some talk in Washington Territory favoring the formation of a new republic in order "to bring nearer home to the people on the Pacific the powers of government, to secure independence, to cut off overland connection, and to make the new Republic the depot of Asiatic trade."[47] During the early months of 1861 rumors were again circulated in Washington Territory that groups of men stood ready to assume control of the governmental machinery should the Union fall to pieces. One Republican newspaper reported:

> It has long been understood that a secret, sworn society of armed men,

[45] Port Townsend *Register*, December 5, 1860.
[46] *Ibid.*, January 30, 1861.
[47] Olympia *Pioneer and Democrat*, April 14, 1855. For a summary of the movement during its entire period, see Joseph Ellison, "Designs for a Pacific Republic, 1843-1862," *Oregon Historical Quarterly*, XXXI (December, 1930), 319-42.

> numbering several thousands, existed on the shores of the Pacific, whose sole aim was to possess the arms, treasure and fortifications of the Federal Government, levy taxes *a la* South Carolina, and subjugate, by force and arms, such of the people as had the temerity to demur to their attempt at coercive control.[48]

Earlier the same paper gave expression to the rumor that certain citizens of the territory had already received their commissions in the new government but that the "precise time of their entering upon the discharge of their self-imposed duties" remained uncertain.[49] These alarms proved unfounded. Sentiment in the territory was strong against breaking away from the parent government. The official Democratic organ declared, "Our duty is plain — the path is straight — go with the North and West, or the confederacy formed by them." At the same time, however, the party withheld all sympathy for the North on the slavery question and came close to expressing a policy of neutrality for the Northwest. Since the slavery issue was not one of vital interest to the area, the paper could see no reason for discussing it, "nor for our involving ourselves in the terrible and angry excitement of the States." [50] The movement for a Pacific Republic was denounced as "useless, idle treasonable nonsense" and many practical arguments were offered against it. An independent government for such a large area and small population not only would lead to a ruinous taxation but also would increase the problem of adequate protection from the Indians.[51] In spite of tirades against the scheme, however, the door seems never to have been shut tightly against such a possibility. In February the Steilacoom *Puget Sound Herald*, a conservative Republican paper, suggested, "if we cannot have the Union, unbroken, by all means let us have the Great Northwest. Nothing less will satisfy us, and nothing less should satisfy the people of Washington Territory." [52] Two weeks later, while repudiating the

48 Port Townsend *North-West*, March 7, 1861.

49 *Ibid.*, February 28, 1861.

50 Olympia *Pioneer and Democrat*, January 18, 1861. A more extreme form of this same attitude prevailed in Oregon, where, during the early years of the war, the governor declared and attempted to maintain a policy of neutrality. A stanch proslavery Democrat, he even spurned Lincoln's requests for troops and refused to recruit men for the President's "wicked and unnatural war upon the South." See Robert W. Johannsen, "John Whiteaker, Governor of Oregon, 1858-1862," *Reed College Bulletin* (Portland), XXVI (January, 1948), 63-87.

51 Olympia *Pioneer and Democrat*, January 4, 1861; Olympia *Washington Standard*, January 12, 1861.

52 Steilacoom *Puget Sound Herald*, February 28, 1861.

idea for a Pacific Republic, the *Pioneer and Democrat* reported, rather contradictorily, "Before this, as an absolute necessity, a provisional government of our own would be preferred, as something more substantial, more just, and better adapted to our present situation." [53]

Washington Territory, however, declared for the Union, at the same time urging that some basis for compromise be found. To give formal expression to this sentiment, the territorial legislature debated through the winter a series of resolutions "expressive of our attachment to the national Union, and pledging Washington for the parent government." Toward the end of the session, which was described by a participant as one of "marked excitement," the resolutions were passed with but one dissenting vote.[54] Later a mass meeting was scheduled for March 14 at the capitol in Olympia for all who loved the Union and were opposed to a Pacific Republic. "A large and enthusiastic" crowd gathered, elected a president and seventeen vice-presidents, six secretaries and a committee on resolutions, including men drawn from all parties. Four resolutions were approved by the meeting, deploring the efforts to break up the Union, repudiating the attempts to establish a Pacific confederacy, proposing an amicable settlement of all grievances between the North and the South, and declaring the attachment of Washington Territory to the Union. It was hoped that these "evidences of our loyalty may not be without their weight, as they plainly show that we appreciate with warm gratitude, the care of our government." [55]

By the end of January, 1861, six southern states had withdrawn from the Union and a convention was scheduled for early February to organize a southern confederacy. In spite of these developments the early months of 1861 witnessed a deluge of compromise plans both in Congress and in the public journals designed to restore harmony between the sections. The vital question of union or disunion transcended party lines. In Washington Territory, as in the border states to the east, both the Democratic and Republican parties advocated saving the Union by compromise. "The true doctrine," it

[53] Olympia *Pioneer and Democrat,* March 15, 1861.

[54] Augustus Ripley Burbank Diary, 198 (February 7, 1861), (microcopy in Pacific Northwest Collection of original in Library of Congress); Territory of Washington *House Journal,* 1860-1861 (Olympia, 1861), 387; Territory of Washington *Council Journal,* 1860-1861 (Olympia, 1861), 310-11.

[55] Olympia *Washington Standard,* March 2, 16, 1861; Olympia *Pioneer and Democrat,* March 15, 1861.

was suggested, "is now to reconcile existing differences, and to allay the terrible revolution through which our country is passing; any measures of that kind, no matter where it comes, whether from Bell, Breckenridge [*sic*], Douglas or Seward, should be carefully and patriotically considered. — The question should not be, 'who presented this?' but 'what is it?' "[56] In his charge to the grand jury of the second judicial district, territorial Chief Justice Obadiah B. McFadden, a strong Democrat, expressed confidence that "conciliation, harmony and concession, may yet save our beloved country from the perils which are impending over her." He urged everyone to cultivate a spirit of conciliation, "to restore that spirit of harmony, brotherly affection and public confidence."[57] As early as January, 1861, the *Pioneer and Democrat* urged that a convention of all the states be summoned to settle the differences between them, that representatives fresh from the people be called together, instead of allowing the "insane red republican" views of such politicians as Senators Benjamin F. Wade and Alfred Iverson to hold sway.[58] The *Washington Standard*, spokesman for the Republican party in the territory, repeated its earlier stand in favor of compromise. The paper advocated the instant repeal of all personal liberty laws in the northern states and a strict rendition of fugitive slaves as a first step in bringing the hostile sections back together. The editor expressed the belief that the North "will not hesitate to evince their true patriotism by all just and appropriate compromises or concessions."[59] A month later the paper's view remained unchanged. Two alternatives faced the United States: compromise or anarchy and despotism. It was conceded that the southern people were as earnest and sincere in their convictions as the northern people. It should be everyone's aim, therefore, both North and South, to seek the perpetuation of the Union by compromise. "The time has arrived," the editor urged, "when concessions *must* be made to hold this fabric together."[60]

[56] Olympia *Pioneer and Democrat*, February 22, 1861.

[57] *Ibid.*, March 15, 1861. One year later Obadiah B. McFadden was described by the governor of the territory in a letter to President Lincoln as "a Bucannon [*sic*] Breckenridge [*sic*] Democrat . . . an open mouthed reviler of yourself & your friends, & a bitter opponent of every act of your administration." William Pickering to Lincoln, August 10, 1862, U. S. Department of State, General Records, Appointment Papers, Applications and Recommendations.

[58] Olympia *Pioneer and Democrat*, January 25, 1861.

[59] Olympia *Washington Standard*, February 16, 1861.

[60] *Ibid.*, March 23, 1861. The Republican press in Washington Territory strongly

Sentiment in the territory favoring compromise was further bolstered by the views and observations of the territorial delegate. Stevens was present on the floor of Congress during the months of the "secession winter" and was a witness to the heated discussions that accompanied this national crisis. In addition, he maintained a close connection with President Buchanan, and is said to have influenced, on more than one occasion, the policies of the President.[61] Because of his high position in the Democratic organization and his activities during the presidential election, Stevens was able to speak and converse freely with both northern and southern leaders. In a series of letters to the editor of the *Pioneer and Democrat*, he apprised his constituents of developments in the national capital. Stevens felt that the grievances of the South were in no way imaginary and that their demands for redress were not unreasonable. He did think, however, that these grievances should be redressed by constitutional means. Since the Republican party did not acquire a majority in Congress in spite of Lincoln's election, he doubted the necessity of secession.[62] The only way to reconcile the two sections, Stevens thought, lay through a convention of all the states, a "reconstruction" of the national government, rather than through coercion. If the latter were resorted to he foresaw only the direst consequences, "a strife of subjugation, where the conquered states will become provinces, to be ruled by the military arm."[63]

Although opinion in the territory was united in favor of the need for compromise, there were few positive suggestions as to how this compromise was to be achieved. The settlers in the Northwest seemed unable to grasp the seriousness of the situation; their exhor-

favored a settlement of the national crisis by compromise in spite of the fact that the national leader of the party was steadfastly opposed to any form of compromise, denouncing it in no uncertain terms in a speech at Cooper Institute in New York on February 27. See John G. Nicolay and John Hay (eds.), *Complete Works of Abraham Lincoln*, 12 vols. (New York, 1905), V, 327.

61 Philip G. Auchampaugh, "James Buchanan and Some Far Western Leaders, 1860-1861," *Pacific Historical Review*, XII (June, 1943), 170.

62 Stevens to the Editor, November 28, 1860, Olympia *Pioneer and Democrat*, January 11, 1861. See n. 12.

63 Stevens to the Editor of the Olympia *Pioneer and Democrat*, December 24, 1860, Stevens Papers. Although Stevens was strongly in favor of the preservation of the Union, he does not seem to have overlooked the fact that some arrangement might be made for a peaceful separation of the two sections. In one letter he wrote, "a Convention of all the states can alone meet the issue and settle it satisfactorily. . . . If it cannot cement or re-establish the present government, it may possibly arrange the terms of peace and good will between its several parts." Stevens to the Editor of the Olympia *Pioneer and Democrat*, December 10, 1860, *ibid*.

tations in favor of compromise, although sincere and motivated by patriotic desires, were largely unrealistic in view of the demands of the two hostile sections.

One of the most publicized of the compromise plans, and the one which probably came closest to success, was presented by John J. Crittenden, veteran senator from Kentucky. Many northern Democrats urged the adoption of his plan, and in Washington Territory the Democratic press eagerly took up the cry for the compromise proposals. One paper optimistically asserted that the territory as a whole heartily favored the compromise.

> We feel safely justified in pledging the warm support of the people of Washington Territory for Crittenden's compromise resolutions, so far as our expression of opinion is concerned. Although we have no voice in national affairs, yet we are allowed the privilege of expressing our warm and earnest devotion to the Union, and its preservation by a just and honorable compromise.[64]

Republicans in the territory ignored this plan that would write slavery into the Constitution.

The question of slavery remained throughout this period subordinate to the preservation of the Union. Members of both parties in the territory held little sympathy for the abolitionists; the emancipation of Negroes was not advocated as an urgent necessity. One newspaper charged that it was false and wicked philanthropy "to pit the emancipation of a Negro against the stability of the great North American Republic."[65] The Republican press consistently accused the Democrats of spreading lies to the effect that the Lincoln administration favored Negro emancipation.[66] It was recognized by one paper, however, that persistency in disunion on the part of the South might lead to the abolition of slavery before 1870.[67] Opinion remained, throughout most of the war, opposed to emancipation. The Radical wing of the Republican party never gained a foothold in territorial politics, although many efforts were made, particularly by some of the federal officeholders, to drive Washington Territory into the Radical camp.[68]

[64] Olympia *Pioneer and Democrat*, March 8, 1861.

[65] Port Townsend *Register*, February 27, 1861.

[66] Olympia *Washington Standard*, November 30, 1860; Steilacoom *Puget Sound Herald*, August 22, 1861.

[67] Port Townsend *North-West*, March 14, 1861.

[68] Henry to William H. Wallace, December 6, 1863, William H. Wallace Papers, Pacific Northwest Collection; Henry to Benjamin F. James, February 6, 1864, Lincoln Papers.

As the possibility of a peaceful restoration of the Union diminished, the party organs in the territory drifted into more extreme positions. Stevens himself became discouraged as the states of the lower South continued to withdraw from the Union and as all attempts at reconciliation failed in Congress. "The public mind," he wrote, "cannot possibly seize and seasonably adjust itself to the times. Our public men, many of them, cannot or will not." The destiny of the nation had been placed in the hands of Congress, where "men must give up pride of opinion to prevent the shedding of fratricidal blood." [69] In the territory the Republican *Washington Standard*, in announcing the inauguration of President Lincoln, suggested coercion for the first time as a possible means for bringing the disaffected states back into the fold. "*The Union must be preserved*," the editor maintained, "and if necessary, at the point of the bayonet." In the same issue a report that a northern lady had been tarred and feathered in Alabama provided an opportunity for an outburst of invective: "Talk of compromise with these fiends! Much as we desire peace with the Southern States, we say, if the perpetrators of the above fiendish outrage are a fair representation of the whole, No compromise but extermination, no peace till the stain be washed from our national fame with their blood." [70]

At the same time the Democratic organ briefly turned toward a "let-them-go-in-peace" attitude. Although the paper consistently maintained that the South had acted wrongly in not giving Lincoln a chance and that the only hope for a reconciliation lay in "compromise and reconstruction," it nevertheless favored "peace at all events, if to be had honorably, — even if by acknowledging the Confederated States — not as a matter of principle — but one of policy and necessity." [71] The patience of this frontier editor had grown thin. Early in March he expressed annoyance at the preoccupation of Congress with the national crisis at the expense of legislation for the territories. "If we could only get rid of the slavery question we could have our quota of legislation. The discussion of it has kept us back ten years. The Pacific coast all this time have been standing respectfully outside the doors of Congress, hat in hand, waiting for them to get done with their 'irrepressible

69 Stevens to the Editor of the Olympia *Pioneer and Democrat*, January 10, 1861, Stevens Papers.

70 Olympia *Washington Standard*, March 30, 1861.

71 Olympia *Pioneer and Democrat*, April 5, 26, 1861.

conflict.' "[72] The news of the attack on Fort Sumter shattered the hopes for a peaceful settlement and the Democratic party turned to a support of the administration in its war effort.[73]

The national issues that were bitterly debated during these months had considerable effect on the territorial political organizations, with local parties following closely the pattern set by their national counterparts. The year 1861 was important to the voters of Washington Territory. Stevens' term as delegate would expire with the adjournment of Congress in March; his office was the most important position to be filled. With confidence reinforced by the national success of their party, Republicans were certain that the election would bring victory to their party for the first time since the territory was organized. At the same time Democrats worked desperately to close the split in their party in order to present a united front to the voters. Their efforts, however, proved fruitless. The breach between the Douglas and administration Democrats became more closely identified with the old Stevens — anti-Stevens split, especially after it was learned that Stevens was to head the Breckinridge organization. In one last attempt to bring the warring factions together, the Democratic Central Committee issued an appeal for unity late in January, 1861. The committee urged territorial Democrats to ignore "issues that have no practical importance in this Territory" and to look only to "those paramount principles that in the past have elevated our common country." [74] The Democratic convention was scheduled to meet at Vancouver on May 13, where the appeal for unity was sabotaged by both national events and local prejudices.

As the convention approached, speculation mounted as to who would secure the party nomination for the office of delegate.

[72] *Ibid.*, March 8, 1861. Three years later a citizen of Steilacoom wrote: "I don't believe Congress will pay much attention to a few thousand people so far away, and out of the great trouble that now afflicts the land, while they have so much weightier things to attend to there. I expect to see this rebellion put down before I can expect much for this Territory or any other one from Congress." J. H. Munson to Wallace, January 28, 1864, Wallace Papers.

[73] The attack on Fort Sumter did not discourage all the peace hopes in the territory. Ebey looked forward to the meeting of Congress in July. Indicating a failure to grasp the true import of the situation in the East, he wrote, "By that time the Public Mind will have Calmed a good Deal I think the Northern States will see the utter folly & madness of attempting to reduce the South to Submission & the matter will be settled peaceably." Ebey Diary, No. 6, p. 438 (May 4, 1861). Just how the matter could be settled peaceably short of disunion Ebey did not clarify.

[74] Olympia *Pioneer and Democrat*, January 25, 1861.

Stevens returned to Olympia in April with the intention of becoming a candidate for re-election. He looked "grave and careworn, for he had taken deeply to heart the troubles between the north and south." [75] Soon after his arrival he delivered an address in which he not only denied the right of secession but also declared that the election of a Republican president was not sufficient cause for seceding. He held the Republican party responsible for disunion, however; the only salvation, he said, was through a reunited Democratic party.[76] Stevens soon learned that the tide had turned against him. As early as January the anti-Stevens members of the legislature had pushed through a resolution censuring the delegate for his participation in the national election.[77] Many persons questioned his loyalty and emphasized his leadership in the Breckinridge organization, in the course of which he had become intimately associated with many secession leaders.[78] When the nominating convention opened, Stevens withdrew his name as a candidate, partly in an attempt to restore harmony to the party and partly because he had determined to offer his services to the Union army. With the attack on Fort Sumter he gave up his former conviction that the nation could be saved by mutual compromise and made the full swing to a policy of coercion. In offering his services to the secretary of war, he declared himself in favor of "conquering a peace"— "this secession movement must be put down with an iron hand." [79] Discouraged by the failure of the efforts to reach a compromise, he wrote, "The policy of conciliation to which I adhered as long as it presented the least hope has not only been exhausted, but it has been contemptuously rejected by the South. The war ought to be prosecuted with the utmost vigor." [80]

75 Hubert H. Bancroft, *History of Washington, Idaho, and Montana, 1845-1889* (San Francisco, 1890), 206.

76 Olympia *Pioneer and Democrat*, May 10, 1861.

77 Territory of Washington *House Journal*, 1860-1861, pp. 337-38.

78 A typical accusation against Stevens was that of the Portland *Morning Oregonian*, February 28, 1861: "If the South has a more faithful dirt-eater than Stevens, we don't know where to find him."

79 Stevens to James W. Nesmith, May 22, 1861, Stevens to Brigadier General Joseph G. Totten, June 19, 1861, Stevens Papers.

80 Stevens to Nesmith, May 22, 1861, *ibid.* Stevens' offer of his services at first met with a cold response, ostensibly because of his past politics and his friendship with many of the southern leaders. He was finally given command of a New York regiment. After participation in campaigns in northern Virginia and along the South Carolina coast, Stevens, a major general and division commander, was killed while leading his troops in the battle of Second Manassas in 1862.

The Democratic nominating convention was beset with difficulties from the very first. By ruling out proxies, control of the meeting was seized by the anti-Stevens or Douglas wing. A majority over the Breckinridge Democrats was maintained, however, only by expelling one delegate, ruling out another proxy delegate, and shifting four votes from a Stevens county to one of the new counties created out of the mining region which as yet existed only on paper.[81] After bitter debates between the two factions, the convention nominated Selucius Garfielde, a former administration Democrat who, it was later said, "varied his politics according to the winds of fortune." [82] Resolutions reaffirming the principle of popular sovereignty and approving any amendments to the Constitution which would "clarify" the status of slavery were passed. The convention further declared that "the constitutional right of secession is a contradiction in terms," that Washington Territory stood "for the Union, the whole Union." A minority report from the resolutions committee discountenanced armed aggression against the South.[83] Although it was reported that "secession gabblers" could be found in the crowd, an undoubted Union sentiment prevailed on the convention floor.[84]

The Stevens, or Breckinridge, wing of the party, though it had lost its leader, refused to give up its organization. The highhanded manner in which the convention had been conducted by the Douglas Democrats determined them to refuse support to Garfielde.[85] After the convention had disbanded they presented Edward Lander, former chief justice of the territory, as an independent candidate for the delegateship, on a nebulous platform of "Our Country, the Union, the Constitution, Peace . . . The Union — It Must Be Preserved." [86]

The Republicans also met in convention late in May. With a

[81] Portland *Morning Oregonian*, May 17, 1861.

[82] Bancroft, *History of Washington, Idaho, and Montana*, 280, n. 33. Selucius Garfielde found it convenient during subsequent years to leave the Democratic party and join the Republican ranks.

[83] Olympia *Pioneer and Democrat*, May 24, 1861.

[84] Portland *Morning Oregonian*, May 15, 17, 1861.

[85] Even the Republican *Oregonian*, May 17, 1861, criticized the actions of the Douglas wing in the convention: "With the most undignified tenacity, they keep their names before a Convention which virtually rejects them, and endeavor to thrust themselves into a position which a majority of their own party does not award to them."

[86] Port Townsend *Register*, May 29, 1861.

minimum of debate they nominated William H. Wallace, a perennial candidate for the delegateship, who had just been appointed territorial governor by President Lincoln. The Republican platform simply endorsed the sentiments expressed in Lincoln's inaugural address and declared the preservation of the Union to be the "first of all patriotic duties." [87]

The election followed the pattern of the national presidential election. Wallace, the Republican candidate, was elected; although he received fewer votes than the two Democratic candidates combined, he won by 309 votes over Garfielde, his nearest competitor.[88]

During the summer months of 1861, as news of military preparations and armed clashes in the East arrived on the Pacific coast, efforts were made by some of the newspapers to take stock of the situation, in some cases to find answers to the question of why this catastrophe had descended on the land. In an editorial entitled "The True Cause of Secession," one of the older Republican papers declared: "it is *not* the agitation of the slavery question which has brought the present trouble upon the country, but simply the loss of power consequent upon the increase of free over slave States. Had there been *no* agitation of this question, the result would have been the same, precisely." The same result would have followed, the paper suggested, if Douglas or Breckinridge had been elected president.[89] Later one editor attempted to answer the question "What are we fighting for?" The war was not one for or against a sectional president or for slavery or abolition. Rather it was a war between the forces of democracy and those of aristocracy, to be fought "for the privilege of another Century's trial of a purely Democratic form of Government." If the abolition of slavery should result from the war "it is because the labor-owning oligarchists have, like the dog in the fable, dropped their pieces of flesh to grasp the shadow of 'rights of minorities to govern.' " [90]

Whatever the answers, whatever the reasons that lay behind the civil strife, the great majority of the settlers in Washington Territory recognized that their place was on the side of the Union. In

[87] Olympia *Washington Standard*, May 25, 1861.

[88] The total vote was Wallace, 1,585; Garfielde, 1,276; and Edward Lander, 747. Election Returns, 1861, Washington Territory (microcopy in Pacific Northwest Collection of originals in Washington State Archives).

[89] Steilacoom *Puget Sound Herald*, August 15, 1861.

[90] Port Townsend *North-West*, October 26, November 2, 1861.

one of its last issues the *Pioneer and Democrat* gave good expression to the attitude of these settlers:

> The question now is not one of slavery in the Territories, but a struggle to maintain the existence of the government itself as an escape from anarchy and despotism. . . . Much as we have deplored war, much as we have counseled peace and compromise, much as the two great parties of the North have differed in the past, now that war has been formerly [*sic*] inaugurated by the Confederate States, there remains but one course for the patriot: to stand by the Government. . . . The voice of our people is unanimous for the Government. What is to be the result no one can foresee, but that the North will maintain itself as a unit there can be no doubt. . . . There would seem no solution at present but by the sword.[91]

When Acting Governor Henry M. McGill, a Buchanan appointee but a strong supporter of the Union, answered Lincoln's call for state troops by ordering the territorial militia to be organized and held in readiness,[92] only a few "sympathizers" in McGill's own party criticized the move.

Although Washington Territory remained devoted to the Union cause throughout the war, it was by no means united in support of the Republican administration. The Democratic majority in the territory was not overcome, in spite of the Republican victory in 1861, until after the war had closed. The Democratic split persisted, however, but in a slightly different form. Although the majority of the party favored a vigorous prosecution of the war against the South, a small minority remained firm in the conviction that peace should be negotiated with the Confederate States. The situation was accurately summed up by one prominent War Democrat: "We intend to keep up the Organization of the party. . . . the party will support the war, but we will support the administration in nothing else. . . . Some of our once friends want to make a peace party of the democratic party here. But that will never do. Patriotism and policy both forbid it. To go for a dishonorable peace is no better than to be an open secessionist."[93] The "peace" Democrats gained sufficient support in the territorial legislature of 1861-1862 to enable them to defeat a series of Union resolutions. In 1863 the Democratic party elected George E. Cole to the dele-

[91] Olympia *Pioneer and Democrat*, May 17, 1861.

[92] *The War of the Rebellion: A Compilation of the Official Records of the Union and Confederate Armies*, 130 vols. (Washington, 1880-1901), Ser. I, Vol. L, Pt. I, 489; Olympia *Washington Standard*, August 24, 1861.

[93] Miller to Stevens, October 11, 1861, Stevens Papers.

gateship. Republicans contented themselves during the war years with internal quarrels and dissensions over the territorial patronage. The Democratic party was probably strengthened by the Republican preoccupation with office. One worried Republican cautioned Lincoln to make territorial appointments with extreme care and intimated that affairs in Washington Territory might be of larger significance. Although the territory "may not be very important in a political point of view," he wrote, its sentiment "may greatly influence for good or evil the pending important Election in Oregon." [94]

Despite the remoteness of Washington Territory from the theater of war, the national events of 1860-1861 which plunged the nation into civil strife provided the issues upon which the party battles in the territory were fought. The political events in this frontier area during the months of the secession crisis recapitulated, on a small scale, the national situation of a few months earlier. In the election in the summer of 1861, the territorial Republicans, although casting a minority of the total vote, nevertheless elected their candidate to the territorial delegateship. The split in the Democratic ranks which made this possible, although originating from purely local causes, had early assumed the form of the national Douglas-Breckinridge split. In their reaction to the events of the secession crisis, the settlers of Washington Territory largely followed the same patterns as in other areas of the Union. As in large portions of the South, the Breckinridge party was the dominant political organization in the territory. Not only did the Pacific Northwest consistently support the southern point of view in the early stages of the crisis, but the region also contributed two of its most prominent political leaders, Joseph Lane and Isaac I. Stevens, to the southern cause. Unlike the South, however, the Breckinridge party in Washington Territory was not a disunion party. As was generally the case in the border states, both political parties in the territory adopted a conservative attitude and strongly supported a settlement of the conflict by compromise and mutual concession. As in most areas of the North during these crucial months, the settlers of the territory failed to appreciate the real seriousness of the sectional struggle. There was a strong tendency to minimize the secession threat and to anticipate a Unionist reaction in the

[94] Henry to Lincoln, February 3, 1862, Lincoln Papers.

South that would thwart the hopes of the disunionists. Thus there existed in Washington Territory elements of all positions in the secession crisis, curiously mixed and modified by characteristic frontier conditions. Perhaps its very status as a frontier, with its strong dependence upon the national government and the nationalism that resulted from this dependence, caused Washington Territory to remain loyal to the cause of the Union. Because the area remained under territorial organization, it was barred from playing an effective role in the sectional conflict; it was, however, a part of the Union and, as such, vitally concerned with the issues that threatened to disrupt it.

Watchers for the Second Coming: The Millenarian Tradition in America

By Ira V. Brown

Among the most neglected of recurrent themes in the history of American thought is the complex of ideas encompassed in the term "millenarianism."[1] While many historians have some superficial acquaintance with the story of the Millerites and their notorious "ascension robes," relatively few have shown much appreciation of the antiquity, the persistence, and the prevalence of the millennial expectations associated particularly with William Miller and the period of the 1840's. Innumerable and multifarious though its particular forms have been, millennial theology in general has forecast the future transformation of the world by divine intervention and the establishment of the Kingdom of God on earth. The usual interpretation has been that this state of peace and blessedness will last a thousand years — the millennium — and will be followed by the final judgment. Adherents of this doctrine have differed over the question of whether the second advent of Christ is to precede or to follow the millennium, thus dividing themselves into premillennialists and postmillennialists. A more basic issue has been whether the Kingdom of God is to come by gradual stages and through human instrumentalities or in consequence of cataclysmic action by the Almighty.[2]

Millenarianism is an excellent example of America's cultural debt to the Old World, for while it has probably had its widest popularity and influence on this continent, its roots must be traced far back into the early days of the Hebrew-Christian tradition. The

[1] Ralph H. Gabriel gives it very brief attention in *The Course of American Democratic Thought; An Intellectual History since 1815* (New York, 1940), 34-37, as does Arthur M. Schlesinger in *Paths to the Present* (New York, 1949), 259-62.

[2] See Kenneth S. Latourette, "The Christian Understanding of History," *American Historical Review* (New York), LIV (January, 1949), 262-63.

peoples of the ancient Near East tended to depreciate the significance of human effort and to trust almost exclusively in special supernatural intervention for the eventual conquest of evil. The notion of a bitter struggle between the powers of darkness and of light, culminating in the final triumph of righteousness through the appearance of a Saviour, was an important element in Zoroastrianism.[3] It may have been from the Persians that the Jews borrowed some of the eschatology incorporated in the Bible. Hebrew leaders in the period of the Exile, most notably the prophet Daniel, forecast a miraculous deliverance of their people, the destruction of the kingdoms of this world, and the establishment of a glorious everlasting dominion of the saints. Daniel's vision of the four beasts, representing four monarchies, the last beast having ten horns, and their replacement by the everlasting kingdom of "the most High," has been especially influential on apocalyptic interpretation throughout the centuries.

The Gospels have much to say regarding the coming Kingdom, but nowhere is it recorded that Jesus attributed to it a thousand-year duration. And various sayings of Christ as recorded in the Gospels lend support to contradictory views regarding the realization of this kingdom. Some, like the parables of the mustard seed and the leaven (Matthew 13:31-33), suggest that it is to grow gradually by natural processes. Others, like those in Matthew 24 and 25, imply cataclysmic events centering about the second advent of Christ himself.

Millenarianism was very strong in primitive Christianity. It is reflected in the Epistles of St. Paul and in the famous Revelation of St. John the Divine. The return of Christ was expected momentarily, and confidence in the overthrow of the Roman Empire and the triumph of God's chosen few was an inspiration to the early Christians in the face of terrible persecutions. The historian Edward Gibbon attributed much of the success of Christianity to the millennial hope.[4] This faith found its most striking expression in the Apocalypse of John which, together with the book of Daniel,

[3] Shirley J. Case, *The Millennial Hope; A Phase of War-Time Thinking* (Chicago, 1918), 18-28. Especially valuable on the Biblical background of millenarianism, this work attacks the fundamentalist interpretation of prophecies based on the proof-text method and emphasizes the modernist idea that all Scripture must be understood in its historical context.

[4] Edward Gibbon, *The Decline and Fall of the Roman Empire*, 2 vols. (Modern Library ed., New York, 1932), I, 402-404.

has been the mainstay of millenarian calculations ever since. In the 20th chapter of this remarkable work, full of melodrama and Oriental imagery, it was forecast that Rome — variously referred to in the New Testament as "Antichrist," "Babylon," the "beast," and the "man of sin" — would be destroyed, and that those who had died for the faith would rise to reign with Christ on earth for a thousand years. At the end of this period Satan would be unbound for a brief time, only to be finally conquered and cast into a lake of fire. Then would come the general resurrection of the dead and the last judgment. The righteous would enter upon a life of eternal blessedness, the wicked would be condemned to eternal torment, and the whole cosmos would assume a new incorruptible status to endure throughout eternity.[5]

Millenarian conviction has usually prevailed most strongly among oppressed minority groups. When the Christian church acquired protection and respectability in the Roman world, the doctrine lost much of its appeal. With the cessation of persecution and the conversion of the secular powers to Christianity, there was no point in looking forward to a time of earthly triumph over the foes of the faith. The Greek church repudiated chiliasm early and kept Revelation out of its canon. St. Augustine was the decisive influence in the transformation of Roman theology. It was he who first ventured to teach, early in the fifth century, that the Catholic Church was the Kingdom of God and that it had been established during the initial ministry of Jesus. Thus the millenarianism of the early Christians was banished from official theology.[6]

But the idea would not die. At various periods in the Middle Ages there were outbreaks of millenarianism, in defiance of the tenets of the Church. Joachim of Flores, an Italian monk, inaugurated one of the most notable of such movements in the twelfth century, predicting that the present order would end in 1260 when the reign of Christ in a new "Age of the Spirit" would commence. Among the events preceding this consummation would be the appearance of Antichrist, whom Joachim saw as the Holy Roman Emperor.[7] Some of his followers concluded that the Papacy itself

[5] Case, *Millennial Hope*, 190-93.
[6] *Ibid.*, 179-83.
[7] G. G. Coulton, *From St. Francis to Dante; Translations from the Chronicle of the Franciscan Salimbene (1221-1288)* (2nd ed., London, 1907), 150 ff. A convenient introduction to Joachimism may be found in Karl Löwith, *Meaning in History; The Theological Implications of the Philosophy of History* (Chicago, 1949), 145-59.

was the Antichrist which, according to Revelation, must be destroyed prior to the millennium. This view carried over into the Reformation and survives among Adventist groups to the present day.

In the sixteenth century, when the authority of the Catholic Church broke down, apocalyptic interpretations of infinite variety sprang up with almost every new Protestant group. A bibliography of works written about the prophecies in the Reformation period would be a lengthy one, and there would be little value in studying in detail the variations among the many ingenious commentaries on Daniel, Matthew, the Epistles, and the Revelation. But it is worth noting, as one recent student of the intellectual history of that period has concluded, that this interest was "not a mere jigsaw puzzle, not a fantastic occupation of the lunatic fringe in theology, and must not be confused with the wilder fantasies of the Anabaptists." Rather it was "a deadly serious business which concerned Lutheran, Calvinist, and Anglican of every variety." [8] During this period the prophecies came to supply a philosophy of history for millions of Protestants. Chronicles were combed for fulfillments of predictions in the sacred books, and charts were made of the time remaining. Sir Isaac Newton was an avid student of prophecy; his *Observations upon the Prophecies of Daniel and the Apocalypse*, written about 1700, shows that even a man of science at that time could be seriously interested in the Scriptural forecasts of the future.[9] Sometimes apocalyptic teaching gave rise to radical action, as in the case of the Fifth Monarchy Men. This fanatical sect in England at the time of the Commonwealth concluded that the fifth kingdom foretold by Daniel was near at hand and prepared to introduce it by rebelling against English authority.[10]

Millenarianism was part of the cultural baggage which the Puritans brought from England to America in the seventeenth century. Examination of the writings of colonial religious leaders

[8] Ernest L. Tuveson, *Millennium and Utopia: A Study in the Background of the Idea of Progress* (Berkeley, 1949), 29. On the basis of careful study of three English philosophers of the seventeenth century (Joseph Mede, Henry More, and Thomas Burnet), Tuveson undertakes to show how the apocalyptic interpretation of history was converted from a harbinger of decay into a guarantor of progress. These thinkers, anticipating the dominant trend in Protestantism after the eighteenth century, came to the conclusion that the millennium was to be achieved gradually.

[9] Louis T. More, *Isaac Newton, A Biography* (New York, 1934), 621-28.

[10] Champlin Burrage, "The Fifth Monarchy Insurrections," *English Historical Review* (London), XXV (October, 1910), 722-47.

shows that analysis of the prophetic Scriptures was a significant element in the intellectual life of early New England. It is a striking commentary on the tendency of historians to read the assumptions and interests of their own day into the thought of past generations that this strand in the fabric of American thought has been so generally ignored by modern scholars.[11] The millennial concept has, of course, relatively little importance in the thinking of our intellectual leaders today, and this may account for its neglect by historians.

Some of the earliest works printed in the American colonies were expositions of the prophecies. Among these were several books by the Reverend John Cotton, who gave weekly lectures on the book of Revelation in Boston during the winter of 1639-1640, and wrote three treatises on the same subject: *The Churches Resurrection, or the Opening of the Fift and Sixt Verses of the 20th Chap. of the Revelation* (1642), *The Powring out of the Seven Vials: or an Exposition of the 16. Chapter of the Revelation with an Application of it to Our Times* (1642), and *An Exposition upon the Thirteenth Chapter of the Revelation* (1655). Cotton believed that the millennium would commence after the destruction of Antichrist, which he equated with the Papacy. About the same time Thomas Shepard, pastor in Cambridge, wrote *The Parable of the Ten Virgins Opened and Applied* (1660), an elaborate work dealing with the certainty of Christ's second coming to earth and the duty of church members to be ever watchful for this event.

The first systematic exposition of Daniel to appear in the colonies was written by Ephraim Huit, pastor at Windsor, Connecticut, and was published in 1644. Thomas Parker, minister at Newberry, Massachusetts, soon followed with *The Visions and Prophecies of Daniel Expounded* (1646), which forecast the end of the world about 1859. William Aspinwall, deacon in the Boston church and a member of the General Court of Massachusetts, contributed *A Brief Description of the Fifth Monarchy, or Kingdome That Shortly Is to Come into the World* (1653). Attempting to give a "hint of the time," Aspinwall suggested that it should not be later than 1673, by which time the "ten horns, or kings, which are

[11] An exception is Perry Miller, "The End of the World," *William and Mary Quarterly* (Williamsburg), Ser. III, Vol. VIII (April, 1951), 171-91, which treats particularly the apocalyptic thought of the seventeenth century.

the strength of the beast" (the fourth monarchy) should be broken. But "as for the precise yeare, I dare not determine." [12]

Increase Mather, whom Professor Kenneth Murdock has called "the foremost American Puritan," made an important contribution to millennial theology with his *The Mystery of Israel's Salvation, Explained and Applyed* (1669). Mather held that the millennium of the Apocalypse was still to come, that the second advent would be preceded by the conversion of the Jews, that it would be followed by a glorious earthly kingdom, and that all this might be expected to take place before another thousand years had passed. "Such a book," Professor Murdock has written, "lighting up vague passages of Scripture by learned interpretation, had for Puritans the same spell held for us by a sound explanation of a fundamental scientific fact directly affecting our lives." [13] In *A Discourse concerning Faith and Fervency in Prayer, and the Glorious Kingdom of the Lord Jesus Christ, on Earth, Now Approaching* (1710), Mather contended that the 1260 years of rule allotted to the Antichrist were "almost finished" and noted that "distressing Troubles and Confusions among the Nations" were mentioned as a sign that the Lord's Kingdom was near. "Is it not so this very day?" [14] Cotton Mather, son of Increase and famous as the author of *Magnalia Christi Americana*, also had a lively consciousness of the approaching end: "I am verily perswaded, *The Judge is at the Door*; I do without any hesitation venture to say, *The Great Day of the Lord is Near, it is Near, and it hastens Greatly.* O That our Minds May be as deeply Engaged in Thinking on the Second coming of our Lord, as the Saints of old were in thinking on His First." [15]

The preface to Increase Mather's *Mystery of Israel's Salvation* was written by John Davenport, who had helped to found New Haven and had later become a pastor in Boston. One of the most

[12] LeRoy E. Froom, *The Prophetic Faith of Our Fathers; The Historical Development of Prophetic Interpretation*, 3 vols. published (Washington, 1946-), III, 88. This Seventh Day Adventist work, while essentially polemical rather than historical, supplies a useful guide to the jungle of literature on the prophecies. The first two volumes deal with the period through the Reformation, the third carries the study up to William Miller, and the fourth will trace the history of modern Adventist thought.

[13] Kenneth B. Murdock, *Increase Mather* (Cambridge, 1925), 94.

[14] Increase Mather, *A Discourse concerning Faith and Fervency in Prayer, and the Glorious Kingdom of the Lord Jesus Christ on Earth, Now Approaching* (Boston, 1710), 96, 98.

[15] Quoted in Froom, *Prophetic Faith*, III, 151.

prominent chiliasts of colonial New England, Davenport emphasized the timeliness of prophetic studies: "Neither let anyone be offended with the seeming *Novelism* which is in these notions. . . . new discoveries of old truth ought not to be branded with the odious name of *Novel opinions*." [16] An early historian of the New Haven colony reported that belief in a literal resurrection of the saints to reign with Christ on earth for a thousand years following his second advent was a prevalent one in colonial New England, and that New Haven settlers expected their city to be the seat of the millennial kingdom, believing "that Christ would come in person and live with them a thousand years." [17]

Probably the most dramatic and most widely read literary expression of the adventist expectations of early New England is found in Michael Wigglesworth's famous poem, *The Day of Doom* (1662):

> For at midnight brake forth a Light,
> which turn'd the night to day,
> And speedily an hideous cry
> did all the world dismay.
> Sinners awake, their hearts do ake,
> trembling their loynes surprizeth;
> Amaz'd with fear, by what they hear,
> each one of them ariseth.
> They rush from Beds with giddy heads,
> and to their windows run,
> Viewing this light which shines more bright
> than doth the Noon-day Sun.
> Straightway appears (they see't with tears)
> the Son of God most dread;
> Who with his Train comes on amain
> To Judge both Quick and Dead.[18]

During the eighteenth century postmillennialism got a strong foothold in American Protestantism. This fact may be a reflection of the idea of progress developing during that period. The theory that the millennium would be achieved gradually through the universal triumph of the Gospel and the conversion of all nations and that it would be followed by the return of Christ for final judgment

[16] Quoted in Murdock, *Increase Mather*, 94.

[17] Edward R. Lambert, *History of the Colony of New Haven* (New Haven, 1838), 50.

[18] Michael Wigglesworth, *The Day of Doom, or a Poetical Description of the Great and Last Judgment*, ed. by Kenneth B. Murdock (New York, 1929), 10.

is associated particularly with the English theologian Daniel Whitby (1638-1726), whose *Paraphrase and Commentary on the New Testament* set forth this view.[19] In America it was popularized by Jonathan Edwards and his disciples Joseph Bellamy and Samuel Hopkins. Edwards was convinced that the prophecies of the last times were being fulfilled and considered the Great Awakening a prelude to the millennium. It was rumored that Edwards often said that the millennium had already begun, and that it began at Northampton.[20]

Unusual natural phenomena have often been interpreted as fulfillments of prophecy. Thus, for instance, a comet strengthened the Millerite cause in 1843. Thus also New England's famous "Dark Day," May 19, 1780, was seen in some circles as a harbinger of the end. Samuel Gatchel, deacon of the Second Congregational Church of Marblehead, regarded it as the darkening of the sun which according to Joel 3:15 was to precede "the day of the Lord" and argued that New England was to be the center of the New Jerusalem. Gatchel forecast that "Jesus Christ will in a small time take to himself his great power, and reign King of Nations as he now reigns King of Saints." [21]

Among the manifold effects of the French Revolution on the Western World was the stimulation of new interest in millennial speculation, both in Europe and America. The earth-shaking events of that period, seen in the light of pious study of the Bible, supplied ample evidence for the devout (and the fancifully inclined) of the approaching end of the age. Joseph Priestley, the distinguished scientist and theologian, contributed to this interpretation. Shortly before he migrated from England to Pennsylvania in 1794, Priestley delivered a sermon contending that the events of his time ap-

19 Froom, *Prophetic Faith*, II, 649-55.

20 Perry Miller, *Jonathan Edwards* (New York, 1949), 318. Edwards set forth his millennial theories in *An Humble Attempt to Promote Explicit Agreement and Visible Union of God's People, in Extraordinary Prayer for the Revival of Religion, and the Advancement of Christ's Kingdom on Earth, pursuant to Scripture Promises, and Prophecies concerning the Last Time* (Boston, 1747).

21 Samuel Gatchel, *The Signs of the Times: or Some Expositions and Remarks on Sundry Texts of Scripture, Relative to the Remarkable Phenomenon, or Dark-Day, Which Appeared in New-England on the Nineteenth of May, 1780: by Which It Appears That New-England Is the Place that the Prophet Joel Calls Zion and Jerusalem* (Danvers, Mass., 1781), 15. Scientists conjectured the cause of the darkness, like that which covered much of northeastern United States on September 24, 1950, to have been western forest fires. See James T. Adams and R. V. Coleman (eds.), *Dictionary of American History*, 5 vols. and index (New York, 1940), II, 110.

peared to be foreshadowing the second advent. Published under the title *The Present State of Europe Compared with the Antient Prophecies*, this address is replete with quotations from Daniel, the Gospels, Paul's Epistles, and the Revelation with reference to the approaching millennium. "Though the Saviour could not fix the time of his second coming, or the commencement of his proper kingdom," Priestley wrote, "he sufficiently forewarned his disciples of the signs of its approach, and of some circumstances that will immediately precede it, to which it certainly behooves us to be attentive." [22] Priestley thought three signs of the times were especially significant: the preaching of the Gospel to all nations, the great prevalence of infidelity, and the undermining of Catholic ("Antichristian") power by the French revolutionaries.

Interest in the prophecies during the period of the French Revolution was especially strong among the religious conservatives who fostered the second Great Awakening which swept the United States in those years. Among these may be mentioned Yale's famous president, Timothy Dwight, who has been called "the most conspicuous man in New England" and "the leading academic man in the United States" at that time.[23] Dwight chose the Apocalypse as the theme for his Fourth of July sermon in 1798, relating the prophecies of John to the suppression of the Catholic Church in France. The wondrous contemporary events persuaded him that "the advent of Christ is at least at our doors." [24] "Almost all judicious commentators have agreed," he announced in a later sermon, "that the Millennium, in the full and perfect sense, will begin at a period, not far from the year 2000." [25] It should be noted, however, that President Dwight expected the millennium to be realized gradually and through human instrumentalities. It was to be accomplished "not by *miracles*, but by means." [26]

[22] Joseph Priestley, *The Present State of Europe Compared with the Antient Prophecies* (London, 1794), 20. It should be noted that eighteenth-century Unitarians, among whom Priestley was outstanding, unlike the Deists and unlike modern Unitarians, did not question the authenticity of Scripture. See Herbert M. Morais, *Deism in Eighteenth Century America* (New York, 1934), 165-66.

[23] Dixon R. Fox, *Ideas in Motion* (New York, 1935), 111-12.

[24] Timothy Dwight, *The Duty of Americans, at the Present Crisis, Illustrated in a Discourse, Preached on the Fourth of July, 1798 at the Request of the Citizens of New Haven* (New Haven, 1798), 31.

[25] Timothy Dwight, *Sermon, Delivered in Boston, September 16, 1813, before the American Board of Commissioners for Foreign Missions* (Boston, 1813), 25-26.

[26] *Ibid.*, 19-20. See also Charles E. Cuningham, *Timothy Dwight, 1752-1817* (New York, 1942), 335-37.

Another New Haven divine had the audacity to fix an exact and imminent date for the Lord's return. This was the Reverend David Austin, who graduated from Yale in 1779 and studied theology under Joseph Bellamy. While pastor at Elizabethtown, New Jersey, he published in 1794 *The Millennium; or, the Thousand Years of Prosperity, Promised to the Church of God, in the Old Testament and the New, Shortly to Commence* — "shortly" being May 15, 1796. An excited congregation joined him in awaiting the event in church, but as the day wore on and nothing unusual happened he finally arose and preached from the text, "My Lord delayeth his coming." Though admitting that he had made a mistake in calculations, he did not lose his faith and returned to New Haven to build houses and wharfs for the Jews, whom he expected to gather there en route to meet the Messiah in the Holy Land.[27] "Mr. Austin was perfectly rational," President Dwight remarked, "upon every subject except the Millennium." [28]

Millenarianism was a dynamic force behind the inauguration of the foreign missions movement early in the nineteenth century.[29] A committee of the American Board of Commissioners for Foreign Missions, headed by the Reverend Jedidiah Morse, announced in 1811:

> For some time before the Messiah came a light to lighten the Gentiles and the glory of his people Israel, an expectation extensively prevailed, that a glorious luminary was about to arise, and an important change to commence. Prophecies to this effect were on record, and the providence of God strikingly indicated their approaching fulfillment. Something very similar to all this is manifest in the present age. If the Messiah was then the Desire of all nations, his millennial reign is no less so now.[30]

The Papal and Mohammedan impostures, Morse believed, had both been established in 606 A.D., and their overthrow could be expected 1260 years later, or about 1866. Then would come the millennium. His own times, he felt, bore many of the marks of the last days.[31] Similar calculations were made by Ethan Smith in his popular

[27] Harris E. Starr, "David Austin," Allen Johnson, Dumas Malone, and Harris E. Starr (eds.), *Dictionary of American Biography*, 21 vols. and index (New York, 1928-1944), I, 432.

[28] Quoted in Leon Howard, *The Connecticut Wits* (Chicago, 1943), 388.

[29] Oliver W. Elsbree, "The Rise of the Missionary Spirit in New England, 1790-1815," *New England Quarterly* (Baltimore, Portland), I (July, 1928), 318.

[30] "An Address to the Christian Public," *Panoplist, and Missionary Magazine United* (Boston), IV (November, 1811), 244.

[31] Jedidiah Morse, *Signs of the Times* (Charlestown, Mass., 1810), 22, 34.

Dissertation on the Prophecies relative to Antichrist and the Last Times (1811). Smith wrote: "Whether the above calculations will prove to be correct, or not, it is agreed I believe by all, that we are drawing near to the close of the wicked ages of the world; and that the Millennium cannot be far distant."[32]

Millenarianism was an important ingredient in nineteenth-century revivalism. It inspired revivalists, promoted conversions, and was itself fomented by evangelical fervor. Among the unusual psychological manifestations associated with the Great Revival of 1800 were trances and visions in which unlettered individuals freely predicted the time of the end of the world and the ushering in of the millennium.[33] Revivalism in general and belief in the imminent second advent in particular also reinforced many of the reform movements of the nineteenth century. The temperance crusade, abolitionism, Utopian experiments, anti-Masonry — these and others thrived on millennial expectation.[34] This connection is illustrated in a statement made by Mark Hopkins, the president of Williams College, to the American Board of Commissioners for Foreign Missions in 1845:

> Sooner or later, in one way or another, . . . the time must come, when the evils which now provoke the vengeance of heaven and curse humanity shall come to an end. . . . Wars, and intemperance, and licentiousness, and fraud, and slavery, and all oppression shall cease . . . through the transforming influence of Christianity; there shall be a society as perfect as we can conceive of in the present state when the Kingdom of God shall be set up, and his will shall be done on earth.[35]

It seems clear that millenarian faith in one form or another was entirely respectable socially and intellectually well into the nineteenth century. America's leading clergymen and college presidents subscribed to such doctrines. As Dr. Eliphalet Nott of Union College put it in 1806: "Christians are now, perhaps generally, united in the opinion that the Messiah is yet to reign a thousand years on

[32] Ethan Smith, *A Dissertation on the Prophecies* (Charlestown, Mass., 1811), 104.

[33] Peter Cartwright, *Autobiography* (New York, 1856), 51-52.

[34] This fact is well illustrated in David M. Ludlum, *Social Ferment in Vermont, 1791-1850* (New York, 1939), 69-70, 109-10, 156, 238. See also Whitney R. Cross, *The Burned-over District; The Social and Intellectual History of Enthusiastic Religion in Western New York, 1800-1850* (Ithaca, 1950), 165, 224.

[35] Mark Hopkins, *Essays and Discourses* (1847), 442-43, quoted in Gabriel, *Course of American Democratic Thought*, 36.

the earth."[36] With the new developments in geology and biology and in the higher criticism of the Bible, belief in adventism was gradually abandoned in academic circles. But it continued to have a very real hold among the less-educated elements of the population, most of whom have not yet been reached with the results of modern Biblical scholarship. Dixon Ryan Fox argued the thesis in his highly suggestive essay on "Refuse Ideas and their Disposal" that the dropping of ideas from one social and cultural level of the population to another is a striking feature of intellectual history: "The cast-off garments of the intellectuals of one age are found, albeit soiled and ragged, on the backs of the ignorant many in the next."[37] Thus Scriptural literalism, for instance, not only as to the prophecies but in most other respects, has in the past century largely dropped out of the higher strata.

While being abandoned by the leaders of orthodoxy, millenarianism found its most spectacular expressions in the founding of a variety of new religious sects based on a conviction of the imminence of the second advent. Among the earliest of these was the Shaker Society, known more properly as the Millennial Church or the United Society of Believers in Christ's Second Appearing, organized about the time of the Revolution. "Mother Ann" Lee, the founder, was believed to be the second — this time feminine — embodiment of the divine spirit in human flesh.[38] For her followers, then, the millennium had already begun; they lived in a new dispensation characterized by community of property, equality of the sexes, celibacy, nonresistance, and the simple life. By the 1830's they had established about twenty settlements in seven states with a membership of more than five thousand.[39] The Oneida Perfectionists, led by John Humphrey Noyes, also believed that the millennium was immediately attainable. Professor Arthur E. Bestor has concluded that most of the communitarian sects held chiliastic beliefs of one variety or another. Members of the Harmony Society, for instance, led by George Rapp, believed that the Kingdom of God was near at hand and that life in their society

[36] Quoted in Fox, *Ideas in Motion,* 112.

[37] *Ibid.,* 102.

[38] Shaker theology is set forth in Benjamin S. Youngs, *The Testimony of Christ's Second Appearing* (Lebanon, Ohio, 1808). See especially pp. 8-10, 435-36.

[39] See Edward F. Dow, *A Portrait of the Millennial Church of Shakers* (Orono, Me., 1931); Marguerite F. Melcher, *The Shaker Adventure* (Princeton, 1941).

was the best preparation for it. Even the rationalistic Robert Owen viewed communitarianism as a step toward realization of heaven on earth, and the word "millennium" is recurrent in Owen's writings during the period of his sponsorship of New Harmony, built on property vacated by the Rappites.[40]

The power of early Mormonism was based on the millennial hope. Many of the Latter Day Saints saw in Joseph Smith's new revelation conclusive evidence of the impending arrival of Christ. They sprang to his cause hoping to stand at the right hand of the Lord in the new day. Smith himself was infected with millennial enthusiasm and promised his apostles that they would see the Saviour come and reign upon earth with great power and glory. Although he "never officially forecast the exact year of the Second Advent, he once ventured to suggest that 'even fifty-six years would wind up the scene'."[41] The Mormon articles of faith still declare: "We believe in the literal gathering of Israel and in the restoration of the Ten Tribes; that Zion will be built upon this [the American] continent; that Christ will reign personally upon the earth; and that the earth will be renewed and receive its paradisiacal glory."[42]

No discussion of the millennial tradition, of course, would be complete without reference to the contribution made by William Miller. This humble product of the New England frontier of the late eighteenth century, after service in the War of 1812 and youthful experimentation with deism, became an ardent student of the prophecies and on the basis chiefly of Daniel's visions came to the conclusion that the second advent would occur about the year 1843. Miller's arithmetic was founded on an old and common supposition by prophetic interpreters that a "day" in the prophecies is to be construed as a year. The keystone in Miller's logical structure was Daniel 8:14: "Unto two thousand and three hundred days; then shall the sanctuary be cleansed." This was interpreted to mean that the earth would be purged of its evil twenty-three hundred years

40 Arthur E. Bestor, Jr., *Backwoods Utopias: The Sectarian and Owenite Phases of Communitarian Socialism in America, 1663-1829* (Philadelphia, 1950), 6, 91.

41 Joseph Smith and Heman C. Smith, *History of the Church of Jesus Christ of Latter Day Saints*, 3 vols. (Lamoni, Iowa, 1897-1908), II, 182, quoted in Fawn M. Brodie, *No Man Knows My History; the Life of Joseph Smith, the Mormon Prophet* (New York, 1945), 101-102.

42 *Ibid.*, 278.

after the time of Daniel's prophecy, which Miller concluded had been made in 457 B.C.[43]

Persuaded by friends and neighbors after several years that his message was too important to be kept quiet, Miller began cautiously to preach it in Baptist and Methodist churches near his home at Low Hampton, New York. His reputation probably would have remained purely local had he not visited Boston in 1839 and made the acquaintance of a master organizer, the Reverend Joshua V. Himes. The latter converted the movement into a great crusade, implemented through an army of revivalists, immense camp meetings, and journals such as the *Signs of the Times* (Boston), the *Midnight Cry* (New York), and the *Alarm* (Philadelphia). A special hymn book entitled *The Millennial Harp* was published. Throughout New England and New York and in lesser degree to other parts of the country the movement spread like wildfire, attracting thousands of converts.

Tradition has it that as the "last days" approached, many of the Millerites ran riot, went crazy, committed suicide, gave up their jobs and their property, made white robes, and gathered in cemeteries or on hilltops to await the Lord at the appointed time.[44] Uncritical acceptance of family legends and careless use of contemporary newspapers by later writers, including the renowned John Bach McMaster, have fastened this picture of the "deluded" Millerites securely in the minds of scholars and the public. Some recent studies, however, have concluded that most of these tales, especially those regarding "ascension robes," are not based on fact. The present writer's examination of the treatment of Millerism in Boston newspapers of the period revealed no convincing reports to authenticate them.[45] Professor Whitney R. Cross, after a thorough study of New York's "burned-over district," where Millerism was especially strong, announced: "Nor does any scrap of genuine evidence substantiate the myth of the ascension robes." [46] Dr. David

[43] William Miller, *Evidence from Scripture and History of the Second Coming of Christ, about the Year 1843* (Troy, 1836), contains a full exposition of his theory.

[44] These allegations are developed most fully in Clara E. Sears, *Days of Delusion* (Boston, 1924). They also figure prominently in such popular works as Meade Minnigerode, *The Fabulous Forties* (New York, 1924), 3-5; Carl Carmer, *Listen for a Lonesome Drum* (New York, 1936), 134-37.

[45] Ira V. Brown, "The Millerites and the Boston Press," *New England Quarterly*, XVI (December, 1943), 592-614.

[46] Cross, *Burned-over District*, 306.

M. Ludlum's book on social ferment in Vermont, a third great center of Millerism, leaves the same impression.[47] It seems beyond serious question that the great bulk of the Millerites gathered during the presumed "last hours" at their accustomed places of meeting, holding services and praying for themselves and their unregenerate contemporaries.[48]

While many of the disappointed abandoned the movement, many others adopted the theory that a heavenly sanctuary had been cleansed and that Christ's return to earth was only being delayed. Withdrawing or excluded from the churches of which they had been members, the Millerites organized congregations of their own which were loosely united in 1845 and from which are descended the Seventh-Day Adventist, the Advent Christian, and several smaller churches of our own times.[49]

The last great sectarian manifestation of the millennial tradition was the society known as Jehovah's Witnesses, originated in 1872 by Charles Taze Russell of Pittsburgh. This Congregational layman, after going through a period of infidelity as William Miller had done, "stumbled upon Adventism." Russell was the author of a flood of millennialist tracts and articles, of which *The Divine Plan of the Ages* is said to have reached a circulation of almost five million copies. In 1884 Zion's Watch Tower Society was organized to promote his teachings. Upon "Pastor" Russell's death on a lecture tour in 1916, leadership passed to "Judge" Joseph F. Rutherford, who was responsible for the adoption in 1931 of the name Jehovah's Witnesses.[50] A hundred thousand persons from sixty-odd nations attended their international assembly in Yankee Stadium in the summer of 1950.[51]

The central tenet among the Witnesses' confusing and somewhat

[47] Ludlum, *Social Ferment in Vermont*, 250-60.

[48] The outstanding Adventist study is Francis D. Nichol, *The Midnight Cry; A Defense of the Character and Conduct of William Miller and the Millerites, Who Mistakenly Believed that the Second Coming of Christ Would Take Place in the Year 1844* (Washington, 1944). Professor Everett Dick of Union College (Nebraska), well-known historian of the American frontier, is an Adventist and did his doctoral thesis, unpublished, at the University of Wisconsin on the Millerite movement. He also wrote the articles on Joshua V. Himes and William Miller for the *Dictionary of American Biography*, IX, 60-61; XII, 641-43.

[49] Elmer T. Clark, *The Small Sects in America* (rev. ed., New York and Nashville, 1949), 38-45.

[50] Herbert H. Stroup, *The Jehovah's Witnesses* (New York, 1945), 4-19.

[51] New York *Herald Tribune*, August 7, 1950.

contradictory doctrines is a highly literal belief in the imminence of Christ's kingdom, which they designate as the Theocracy. This reign began, they believe, with events taking place in heaven in 1914, but will not be complete until the forthcoming Battle of Armageddon, when Jehovah and Christ Jesus (understood as two separate individuals) will annihilate "Satan's organization," in which are included the leaders of all the orthodox churches as well as political rulers. During the ensuing thousand-year reign of Christ the dead will be resurrected bodily and will be given a chance to justify themselves. Those who repent in the millennial probation will have everlasting life in an earthly paradise.[52] "Not forever," said a recent issue of the society's magazine, the *Watchtower*, "will the Creator allow present distress and wickedness to continue on the earth. He has foreordained a definite time to bring the last vestiges of Satan's world to a violent end; and the remaining time is very short."[53]

The Witnesses' contention that national authorities are in league with Satan has led to their refusal to salute the flag. This intransigence, their claim to ministerial exemption from military service, and the efforts to limit distribution of their literature, have in recent years posed a number of striking constitutional issues involving American civil liberties. Much of the hostility to the Witnesses grows out of their strong anticlericalism, which takes an especially virulent form in the case of Catholicism. In this they typify the attitude of believers in the prophecies from the Reformation to the present day. Most of the early Protestant groups identified the Pope with the Antichrist to be destroyed at the second advent.[54]

More significant perhaps than these spectacular, and not inconsiderable, sects built specifically on apocalypticism is the strength of millenarian conviction among an indeterminate but unquestionably large number of orthodox Protestant church members.

[52] Charles S. Braden, *These Also Believe* (New York, 1949), 370-79. Chapter X, dealing with Jehovah's Witnesses, provides the best brief analysis of the movement. It gives an especially good statement of their doctrines.

[53] *Watchtower* (Brooklyn), LXXI (October 1, 1950), 368. This journal, which can be bought from street vendors in many communities, claims a circulation of over a million copies.

[54] Sister Mary Augustina (Ray), *American Opinion of Roman Catholicism in the Eighteenth Century* (New York, 1936), 22 ff. The imagery of the prophecies was prominently used in the orthodox Protestant crusade against Catholicism in the pre-Civil War years. See, for example, *Downfall of Babylon, or, The Triumph of Truth over Popery* (New York, Philadelphia), I, No. 1 (November 6, 1834), 3.

The two world wars and the Great Depression have given special impetus to premillennial teachings. Such doctrines offer to their adherents a "comprehensive, authoritative, and dramatic interpretation of the times" and provide a sense of security in a highly uncertain world.[55] Fundamentalists, ignoring or repudiating the new science and the historical criticism of the Bible, have made premillennialism a cardinal principle. The imminence of the advent—deduced from the signs of the times (such as "wars and rumors of wars," infidelity, immorality, and the return of the Jews to Palestine) — is a standard theme for latter-day evangelists. The success of such radio programs as the Old-Fashioned Revival Hour, broadcast nationwide, and numberless others reaching only local audiences, is based in part on exploitation of this doctrine. Among large denominations, the Baptists and the Presbyterians are especially permeated with premillennialists, both lay and clerical. For such lesser sects as the Free Methodists and the Nazarenes it is a central point of emphasis. One careful scholar has estimated that forty or more American sects, with a combined membership of over a million, today report premillennialism to be one of their key doctrines. Including fundamentalists who have not left their denominations, the number of its adherents is estimated at three or four million persons.[56] This is probably a conservative figure.

Even certain intellectual leaders, in some sections of the country at least, pay lip service to adventism. "What the United States does in the next five years will determine the kind of world we shall have for five hundred years," the President of Baylor University wrote recently, "— if the Lord delays his coming." [57]

It becomes evident, then, that "Millerism" was by no means the cultural aberration that it has usually been considered. It was but one of a number of extreme forms of a faith which was throughout much of history, and in some circles still is, wholly orthodox. In conclusion it might be noted that millenarianism has involved two distinct and somewhat paradoxical emphases. One is the idea of the imminent end of the world, a pessimistic view discouraging human efforts at reform. The other is the idea that paradise is to

[55] Robert W. McEwen, *Factors in the Modern Survival of Millennialism* (Chicago, 1936), 72.

[56] Clark, *Small Sects in America*, 34.

[57] *Southern Baptist Home Missions* (Atlanta), XX (February, 1949), cover. In colleges premillennialism is widely propagated through the Inter-Varsity Christian Fellowship.

prevail on the earth for a thousand years, an optimistic outlook in tune with "the American heritage of hope" and conducive to "progress." In this broader context millennial thought is related to "the mission of America" and other concepts outside the realm of religion.

Frederick Law Olmsted in the "Literary Republic"

By Laura Wood Roper

Frederick Law Olmsted, known best to later generations as America's greatest landscape architect, was something else to his Civil War contemporaries: a distinguished man of letters. His reputation and his influence, which were considerable both in England and the United States, rested principally upon three books which appeared between 1856 and 1860: *Journey in the Seaboard Slave States*, *Journey through Texas*, and *Journey in the Back Country*.[1] They were read with care and respect, and quoted widely. Typical of critical opinion was that of Charles Eliot Norton, who called them "the most important contribution to an exact acquaintance with the conditions and result of slavery in this country that have ever been published. They have permanent value, and will be chief material for our social history whenever it is written." [2]

Olmsted's circulation and his royalties were not commensurate with his reputation: his books made a pittance, and all together sold, probably, less than 25,000 from 1856 to the start of the Civil War. Although comparatively small, his public included editors, writers, scholars, scientists, politicians, intellectual leaders, shapers of public opinion. In synthesizing two subjects — travels and slavery — popular with serious readers, Olmsted produced works of sure if limited appeal. In synthesizing them brilliantly, he did more: he produced books of immediate influence on his most effective contemporaries, and classics which perfectly fulfilled Norton's prediction.

1 *A Journey in the Seaboard Slave States, With Remarks on Their Economy* (New York and London, 1856); *A Journey Through Texas; or, A Saddle-Trip on the Southwestern Frontier* (New York, London, and Edinburgh, 1857); *A Journey in the Back Country* (New York, 1860).

2 Sara Norton and M. A. De Wolfe Howe (eds.), *Letters of Charles Eliot Norton*, 2 vols. (Boston, 1913), I, 211.

The publishing history of these three books, and of the two-volume condensation of them, *The Cotton Kingdom*,[3] is an interesting and hitherto unknown episode in the annals of American letters.

"I have thoughts of going South this winter," the thirty-year-old Olmsted wrote a friend in October, 1852, "mainly with the idea that I could make a valuable book of observations on Southern Agriculture & general economy as affected by Slavery. . . . Matter of fact," he explained, "to come after the deluge of spoony fancy pictures now at its height shall be spent." [4]

Olmsted was an antislavery man of strong conviction, but temperate of outlook and unsympathetic to abolitionism. He could rightly say: "I am not a red hot Abolitionist . . . but am a moderate Free soiler — going to vote for Scott & would take in a fugitive slave & shoot a man that was likely to get him, on the whole I guess I represent fairly the average sentiment of good thinking men on our side. The way I look at it you will see in my 2^d^ vol. p. 106." [5]

Olmsted was a farmer; he was also, in a modest way, a writer. In 1850, on a visit to England, he had sent an eyewitness account of Sir Robert Peel's last appearance in parliament to the Hartford *Courant*.[6] He had contributed two notes and two articles to Andrew J. Downing's *Horticulturist*.[7] He had written *Walks and Talks of*

[3] *The Cotton Kingdom: A Traveller's Observations on Cotton and Slavery in the American Slave States*, 2 vols. (New York and London, 1861).

[4] Frederick Law Olmsted to Frederick J. Kingsbury, October 17, 1852, Frederick Law Olmsted Papers (Manuscripts Division, Library of Congress).

[5] *Ibid.* Olmsted referred to his *Walks and Talks of an American Farmer in England*, 2 vols. (New York, 1852). "Let us . . . never, either in brotherly love, national vanity, or subjection to insolence, fear to declare, that, in the misdirection of power by our slaveholders, they are false to the bases of our Union and blasphemous to the Father who, equally and with equal freedom, created all men. Would that they might see, too, that while they continue to manifest before the world, in their legislation upon it, no other than mean, sordid, short-sighted and barbarous purposes, they must complain, threaten, expostulate and compromise in vain. If we drive back the truth of God, we must expect ever-recurring, irrestrainable, irresistible *reaction*. The law of God in our hearts binds us in fidelity to the *principles* of the Constitution. They are not to be found in 'Abolitionism,' nor are they to be found — oh! remember it, brothers, and forgive these few words! — in *hopeless, dawnless, unredeeming* Slavery."

[6] This letter, in the Hartford *Courant*, July 25, 1850, was initialed "F." It has not previously been attributed to Olmsted; its authorship is established by a letter, John Hull Olmsted to Mary Olmsted, July 4 and 5, 1850, Olmsted Papers.

[7] "Queries on Sea-Coast Culture," *Horticulturist and Journal of Rural Art and Rural Taste* (Albany), II (August, 1847), 100; "The People's Park at Birkenhead, near Liverpool," *ibid.*, VI (May, 1851), 224-28; "A Note on the True Soldat Laboureur Pear," *ibid.*, VII (January, 1852), 14-15; "Apple Orchards in England," *ibid.*, VII

an American Farmer in England, a book in the popular travel *genre*, and had known the gratification of critical approval. Finally, he was on familiar terms with such literary figures as George William Curtis, Miss Anne Charlotte Lynch, Charles Loring Brace, Harriet Beecher Stowe, and his publisher George Palmer Putnam, whose informal Tuesday evening receptions he attended along with William Cullen Bryant, Parke Godwin, Bayard Taylor, Katherine P. Wormeley, and George Ripley.[8]

Olmsted's opportunity to go South came about when Henry J. Raymond, cofounder and editor of the one-year-old New York *Times*, consulted Olmsted's intimate, Brace,[9] about engaging a man to travel in the slave states and report to the paper on "the influence of Slavery, as a mode of employing labor, on the development of the general resources of the South." [10] On Brace's recommendation, Raymond invited Olmsted to apply. Their interview, a model of dispatch, took only five minutes. Raymond asked Olmsted his opinion neither on slavery nor on any other subject, proposed that he confine his reports to facts that fell within his personal observation, and told him that he need not feel constrained by the editorial position of the *Times*. Olmsted accepted the job at once.[11]

On December 11, 1852, he set forth on his classic tour of observation. The few private letters that survive from this journey suggest that he found his assignment difficult. "I cannot see my way out of Virginia," he complained to Brace. "It takes more time to write and study than I anticipated. More a great deal than to observe." [12]

Evidently Olmsted had arranged that Brace should get his letters into final shape for the *Times*. Brace, busy organizing his own life work, the Children's Aid Society, seems not to have acted to Olmsted's satisfaction. "The devil take you for leaving it all to Raymond," Olmsted wrote angrily early in February. "My letters are not fit to be used that way. . . . [Raymond] will be confoundedly dissappointed [*sic*] if he thinks they will and I'm afraid

(December, 1852), 549-52. The second article, signed "Wayfarer," is identifiable by comparison with Olmsted, *Walks and Talks of an American Farmer in England*, I, Chap. VIII; Olmsted to Kingsbury, August 5, 1851, Olmsted Papers.

8 George H. Putnam, *A Memoir of George Palmer Putnam, Together with a Record of the Publishing House Founded by Him*, 2 vols. (New York, 1903), I, 361.

9 Olmsted to Letitia Brace, January 22, 1892, Olmsted Papers.

10 New York *Times*, February 13, 1854.

11 *Ibid.*

12 Olmsted to Charles Loring Brace, December 22, 1852, Olmsted Papers.

will refuse them when he comes to read them."[13] Even so, he was thinking of a second trip for the *Times*, "to take in the frontier and S. W. Slave States."[14]

Raymond clearly was not disappointed. When Olmsted's first letter appeared, on February 16, 1853, Raymond introduced his correspondent with a flourish as "an intelligent gentleman, of decided ability, large experience, practical habits of action and speculation, known already to the world by his published works."[15] This editorial send-off gave Olmsted fresh anxiety: it was so "handsome" he feared he could not live up to it.[16]

He was, in fact, plagued by difficulties — particularly Southerners' reticence toward a Northerner, and lack of time. From Louisiana he wrote Brace: "You can't imagine how hard it is to get hold of a conversable man — and when you find [one] he will talk about anything else but Slavery. . . . They are jealous of observation of things that would tell against slavery."[17] To another friend he wrote that, though he had been entertained with cordial friendliness in a few southern homes, on the whole he had seen little of southern society or domestic life. "I go over too much ground and too hastily for that. . . . I have been able no more than to glance at the outside of things — occasionally getting peeps through accidental openings."[18]

Notwithstanding obstacles Olmsted furnished the *Times* with a series of fifty articles (misnumbered forty-eight) signed "Yeoman,"[19] all but one or two of which were based on this first trip. They ran, prominently displayed, from February 16, 1853, to February 13, 1854, and totaled about 120,000 words. Some appeared while Olmsted was still in Alabama or Louisiana; others he wrote from notes after his return to his Staten Island farm in the spring; and the last five or six he did, partly from notes of his first trip and partly from current observation,[20] after November 10,

13 Olmsted to Brace, February 8, 1853, *ibid.* This and all subsequent "Brace" letters are to or from Charles Loring Brace.

14 Olmsted to Brace, February 8, 1853, *ibid.*

15 New York *Times*, February 16, 1853.

16 Olmsted to Brace, February 23, 1853, Olmsted Papers.

17 Olmsted to Brace, February 23, 1853, *ibid.*

18 Olmsted to Kingsbury, February 26, 1853, *ibid.*

19 "Yeoman's" identity was no great secret. Olmsted's friends knew it at the time, and Olmsted announced it himself in *Slave States*.

20 New York *Times*, January 12, 1854; Olmsted to Brace, December 1, 1853, Olmsted Papers.

1853, when, accompanied by his brother Dr. John Hull Olmsted, he set off on his second trip for the *Times*.

Raymond, introducing this first series, stressed Olmsted's freedom from preconceived ideas on slave economy: not slavery's moral character or political relations but "its bearing upon the industry, the material interests, and the general progress of the Southern States, will be made the object of his special study. . . . upon this subject his opinions remain to be formed according to the facts he may meet." The letters, Raymond added, were intended "to contribute somewhat to that general and reliable public knowledge of the actual condition and character of the Southern States, upon which the public sentiment concerning them ought to rest." [21]

The southern press, however, accepted at face value neither this declaration of motive nor Olmsted's conciliatory statement that he hoped to show the North that it was only in the justice, good sense, and Christian feeling of the people of the South that the evils of slavery were to be ended.[22] Shortly after the series began, the Savannah *Republican* declared editorially that, since neither a Northerner nor a Southerner could be unprejudiced about slavery, neither was qualified to discuss it. Accusing the *Times* of sending a spy into the South, it demanded: "Why not . . . let us alone? Why not attend to your own business and relieve the misery at your own doors? . . . *It is not*," it concluded in italics, "*in the power of the North either to abolish Slavery or to hasten or postpone its extinction. . . . The South alone can give the negro freedom*, *and the extinction of the institution*, *if ever accomplished*, *will be the deliberate and well-matured act of the South as a whole*." [23]

The *Times* replied that the *Republican* apparently wished to preclude any discussion of slavery whatever, and that the great evil was not that it had been discussed, but that it had not been factually and reasonably discussed. Agreeing that only the South could end it, the *Times* reiterated that one purpose of Olmsted's letters was so to convince the North.[24]

Other southern papers took hostile note of the letters.[25] By the time Olmsted reached home in the spring, however, Raymond told

[21] New York *Times*, February 16, 1853.
[22] *Ibid.*
[23] Savannah *Republican*, February 22, 1853.
[24] New York *Times*, March 9, 1853.
[25] *Ibid.*, February 13, 1854.

him that "the papers had done talking of them because they were afraid to touch them." [26]

Not all southern reaction was suspicious or hostile. The New Orleans *Delta*, defending Olmsted from the charge of dishonesty and unfairness, called him "prejudiced, but manly and honest." [27] "A Native Southerner," upholding slavery on economic and moral grounds in the *Times*, expressed pleasure in "Yeoman's" "candor and intelligence," and said that his letters were acceptable to unbiased Southerners, though it was clear he was looking at things "through a pair of sharp Northern eyes." [28]

Although disappointed in the condition of the southern people, both citizen and slave, and resentful of the southern press's insinuations of venality,[29] Olmsted nevertheless tried scrupulously to be just in his reports. He asked his father to make notes of all "doubtful assertions, . . . errors of fact or calculation . . . etc., that I may have the advantage of them in revising." [30] He instructed Brace to modify an article containing a hasty and too harsh judgment;[31] and he invited southern readers to correct him if he misstated facts or misinterpreted public sentiment.[32]

Further, genuine appreciation of the difficulties that faced the South in connection with slavery led him into such expressions of sympathy that, Raymond said, the abolition press accused him of conducting a whitewash.[33] Some of his remarks were in effect versions of the very arguments with which Southerners retorted to antislavery agitation, and even recalled the Savannah *Republican's* editorial. He urged the North to realize that slavery was a matter beyond its control, to correct the injustices of its own labor system, and to abandon denunciation and exciting appeals — in which case, he thought, "hosts" of talented and selfless men would arise in Vir-

[26] Olmsted to John Olmsted, n.d. [spring, 1853], Olmsted Papers.

[27] Undated clipping, *ibid.* The writer has not access to *Delta* files and has not been able to date this clipping. It was quoted in the New York *Times*, January 28, 1856, in an advertisement for *Slave States*.

[28] New York *Times*, June 6, 1853. "A Native Southerner" is identified in Olmsted to John Olmsted, June 16, 1853, Olmsted Papers, as "the Reverend Mr. Lipscombe, an Alabamian." This was probably Andrew Adgate Lipscombe, 1816-1890, Methodist minister, educator, and writer.

[29] New York *Times*, February 13, 1854.

[30] Olmsted to John Olmsted, January 10, 1853, Olmsted Papers.

[31] Olmsted to Brace, February 8, 1853, *ibid.*

[32] New York *Times*, July 8, 1853.

[33] *Ibid.*, February 13, 1854.

ginia at least to attack the problem.[34] Contrasting the physical well-being of free and slave laborers, he reminded his readers that no slave ever killed its child in cool calculation of saving money by it, like English free women, nor froze to death for lack of shelter and fuel, like free men in Boston.[35] He offered without comment a résumé of one standard southern defense of slavery: that the Negro race was an inferior one expressly designed by Providence for servitude.[36]

Even his last letter, which cogently presented the conclusion that slavery was economically ruinous and morally indefensible, was softened. Wrong as slavery was, Olmsted said, slaveholding itself was not necessarily evil: the term "property" conveys the idea of stewardship over things which God has placed, under the state, in our hands. "I am willing, for the present, to look upon the relation of the master and the negro as that of stewardship, and am willing that the law should allow the master a reasonable use of the labor of the negro, as the wages of his stewardship."

As to the duty of the North in regard to slavery, it was to discuss it and to work for its ultimate disappearance — but not by direct action, which would in his opinion justify the South in leaving the Union. Olmsted's basic conservatism was implicit in the policy he recommended to the North: to make "the best possible use of free labor, by demonstrating that the condition of the laborer is *not* necessarily a servile one; that the occupation of the laborer does *not* necessarily prevent a high intellectual and moral development. . . .

"Yet mainly, the North must demolish the bulwarks of this stronghold of evil by demonstrating that the negro is endowed with the natural capacities to make a good use of the blessing of freedom; by letting the negro have a fair chance to prove his own case, to prove himself a man entitled to the inalienable rights of man. Let all who do not think Slavery right, or who do not desire to assist in perpetuating it, whether right or wrong, demand first of their own minds, and then of their neighbors, FAIR PLAY FOR THE NEGRO." [37]

Thus, somewhat surprisingly, Olmsted ended his first series of letters with a ringing admonition, not to the South, but to the North.

[34] *Ibid.*, March 30, 1853.
[35] *Ibid.*, April 8, 1853.
[36] *Ibid.*, November 26, 1853.
[37] *Ibid.*, February 13, 1854.

On the publication of the last letter Raymond editorially hailed the series as "the best report that has ever been made, of the industrial condition and prospects of the Southern section of the Union."[38] By that time Olmsted had already been gone some weeks on his second trip as *Times* correspondent.

Starting November 10, 1853, he went to Texas, and returned the following summer, probably late in July or in August. His great discovery on this excursion was the Texas Germans; he had not known about their substantial colonies in and near San Antonio,[39] and he was almost rapturous about them. Just before his second series began, the *Times* ran an editorial, "The Germans in Texas," based on "recent files of papers and private letters from Western Texas," which told that these Germans rejected slavery, worked better and cheaper than slaves, and were, by example and influence, "at least in Texas, uprooting the system more than all the ranting attacks of Abolitionists for the last twenty years."[40] It is a safe guess that the documents were, in fact, sent by Olmsted.

The second series, comprising thirteen numbered letters and two extras — "The Nebraska Question in Texas" and "Indian Troubles on the Texas Frontiers — Inefficiency of Measures for their Suppression" — amounted to about 30,000 words. It ran from March 6, 1854, to the following June 7, ending abruptly and without editorial comment. In an editorial on June 14 Raymond also published, unsigned, a letter from Olmsted on "Filibusterism and Other Matters in Mississippi."[41]

Olmsted's total pay from the *Times* for his two series of letters came to $720; he collected the last installment of it shortly before the end of the year.[42] Despite the modesty of this financial reward, the reception of his articles encouraged him to proceed with the book he had had in mind from the first. So, on his return from Texas, he devoted himself, with the approval of his brother and other advisers, to developing his first series of letters into *A Journey in the Seaboard Slave States*.[43]

A painstaking writer, he was subject to spells of discouragement.

38 *Ibid.*

39 Olmsted, *Journey Through Texas*, 132.

40 New York *Times*, March 3, 1854.

41 *Ibid.*, June 14, 1854; John Hull Olmsted to John Olmsted, June 15, 1854, Olmsted Papers.

42 Olmsted to John Olmsted, December 31, 1854, Olmsted Papers.

43 John Hull Olmsted to John Olmsted, June 15, 1854, *ibid.*

At the year's end he wrote his father: "In the last six weeks I have only finished thirty six pages . . . and I have calculated I shall have to write 1500 and I fear I shall not get done till so long past the events talked about, it will have lost all interest." [44]

The conscientiousness of his approach, too, delayed him. "Lately I have been studying Virginia history to follow down the influence of the aristocracy and slavery on the condition of the state etc. I have still one more chapter to write upon it to bring the sketch down to our own times." [45] His brother regarded the historical sketch as "a work of supererogation," [46] but Olmsted valued it so highly that, even when the beginning of the book was being printed and about fifty pages at the end remained to be written, he spent a good deal of time retouching it.[47]

Working assiduously on his book,[48] Olmsted had almost no time for social life, but he had time to develop the scheme which was to put him directly in the midst of that literary life to which he aspired: during the spring he made arrangements to join the partnership of Dix & Edwards,[49] publishers of *Putnam's Magazine*, lately purchased from George Palmer Putnam, and of the American edition of Dickens' *Household Words*. Leaving his reluctant brother in charge of his farm, Olmsted moved to the city in April, 1855,[50] and entered upon his brief, unfortunate publishing career.

His new duties during the next few months did not prevent him from working on the book, but they obstructed its progress.[51] The greatest obstacle the book encountered, however, was financial. Olmsted had arranged with Dix & Edwards, who were just branching out into the book-publishing business, that he was to own the book, paying the firm a percentage on its sales for bringing it out.[52] Usually, when an author owned his book, he paid all the expenses of publication, either advancing the money to the publisher to meet them, or being personally liable for them; in Olmsted's case this arrangement was altered to the extent that Dix & Edwards were to pay the publishing costs, charging Olmsted interest on the amount

[44] Olmsted to John Olmsted, December 31, 1854, *ibid.*
[45] *Ibid.*
[46] John Hull Olmsted to John Olmsted, December 14, 1854, *ibid.*
[47] Olmsted to John Olmsted, November 8, 1855, *ibid.*
[48] John Hull Olmsted to John Olmsted, December 14, 1854, *ibid.*
[49] John Hull Olmsted to John Olmsted, March 9, 1855, *ibid.*
[50] Olmsted to John Olmsted, April 1, 1855, *ibid.*
[51] Olmsted to John Olmsted, November 8, 1855, *ibid.*
[52] *Ibid.*

they advanced.[53] Then, in November, Arthur T. Edwards, one of Olmsted's partners, told him that the firm was too short of capital to dare publish *A Journey in the Seaboard Slave States.* Edwards wanted Olmsted to ask his father to pay the notes Dix & Edwards would have to give the printer, and to take the firm's notes for whatever he had to advance. By the time the Dix & Edwards notes to John Olmsted matured, Edwards thought, *Slave States* would have made up its costs by its sales.[54]

Frederick had already asked his father to advance $1,000 for publishing expenses and accept as security his property in his book.[55] John Olmsted had evidently hesitated over this proposal, and Frederick was chagrined at having to approach him with the second. "I am ashamed of myself, exceedingly ashamed of myself, to be so sufferring [*sic*] as I am with these cursed business responsibilities," he wrote bitterly.[56]

The intellectual and social side of the literary life, however, provided conpensations. In the spring Olmsted had gone to Boston to meet Henry Wadsworth Longfellow at Asa Gray's, and on to Concord and Andover to see Ralph Waldo Emerson and Mrs. Stowe.[57] For James Russell Lowell, an acquaintance of several years' standing, he had given a breakfast which was attended by George William Curtis, Charles A. Dana, Parke Godwin, "and others of the generation of serious literary men of somewhat earnest semi-political disposition antagonistic to the growing war spirit of the slave states." [58] Now he concluded his begging letter to his father: "I dined tonight with the Press Club at the Astor House. I was elected a member at the last meeting — cost $4.00 a month. Grand blow out; Thackeray, present and taken ill with chills — About 34 literary gentlemen present, including Washington Irving, who sat opposite me." [59]

John Olmsted seems to have yielded reluctantly to his son's second appeal. Then Frederick, who all his adult life had continually borrowed from this patient and generous man, was taken with qualms and offered to let him off. "I don't doubt that I could easily

53 Olmsted to John Olmsted, "8/9 Friday" [before November 8, 1855], *ibid.*
54 Olmsted to John Olmsted, November 23, 1855, *ibid.*
55 Olmsted to John Olmsted, "8/9 Friday" [before November 8, 1855], *ibid.*
56 Olmsted to John Olmsted, November 23, 1855, *ibid.*
57 Olmsted to John Olmsted, March 13, 1855, *ibid.*
58 Olmsted to Frederick Law Olmsted (son), August 15, 1891, *ibid.*
59 Olmsted to John Olmsted, November 23, 1855, *ibid.*

make such an arrangement as I proposed to you with someone here — Barney,[60] or Judge Emerson [61] and Dudley Field — for there can be little doubt that the book will pay eventually 20 prct over cost of publication I should think." [62]

There was a personal loan, however, for which Olmsted did not hesitate to ask his father. "There is a sort of literary republic," he explained, "which it is not merely pleasant and gratifying to my ambition to be recognized in, but also profitable. It would, for example, if I am so recognized & considered, be easy for me, in case of the non success of this partnership, to get employment in the newspaper offices or other literary enterprises at good wages. . . . To take & keep a position as a recognized literateur, as a man of influence in literary matters, I need at the time of the publication of my book to be able to spend a little more than I like to draw out of our partnership bank, and I hate as Edwards expects of me, to be running in debt to tailors & cobblers & cooks." [63]

When Olmsted drew up an agreement in the firm's name with his father, Edwards objected that it sounded as if John Olmsted were doing the firm a favor in advancing it money for the publication of *Slave States*, whereas the firm had no responsibility for the book and was merely commissioned to sell it.[64] After this reminder Olmsted presumably completed arrangements with his father. In any case, the book was published on January 16, 1856.[65]

Before publication Olmsted found more things to worry about: the bulk of the book, which threatened to run to two volumes and became "a goblin of botheration," and its proposed price, $2.50, "enough I apprehend to ruin a great circulation." [66] The book was, in the end, squeezed into one fat volume and the price set at $1.25. "It will require a sale of 3000 to pay cost at this, but . . . it will be easier to sell 3000 at 1.25 than 2000 at 1.50. A sale of 6000 will give me $800 over all expenses including publishers toll, & advertising. . . . The present commercial indications seem to me dis-

60 Probably Hiram Barney, a prominent Republican who became collector of the Port of New York.

61 William Emerson, a brother of Ralph Waldo Emerson, and a neighbor of Olmsted on Staten Island.

62 Olmsted to John Olmsted, December 9, 1855, Olmsted Papers.

63 *Ibid.*

64 Arthur T. Edwards to Olmsted, December 12, 1855, *ibid.*

65 Copyright statement, n.d., *ibid.*

66 Olmsted to John Olmsted, November 8, 1855, *ibid.*

couraging — the only order is one from Hartford for 12 copies." [67]

The first printing of 2,000 was followed at the end of March by one of 1,000 and by another of 2,000 on April 30. Their production cost, exclusive of advertising, was $2,906.71, and at the time Olmsted received his first statement 3,202 had been sold, bringing in $2,401.50.[68] Two hundred copies were set aside for editors, and Olmsted handed out his other free copies sparingly. It was only after long hesitation that he sent one to his old neighbor Mrs. Lydia Huntley Sigourney, and to the politically important James Dixon of Hartford.[69]

As expected, the book sold slowly at first.[70] By February 4 it had had no sale at all in a market overcrowded with slavery,[71] and at the end of May John Hull Olmsted suspected that the last 2,000 copies printed were still on hand.[72] In the two months preceding July 18, 1856, Dix & Edwards sold not a single copy.[73]

About the book's merit, Olmsted had never felt anxiety. "Reputation or notoriety it cannot fail to give me — not perhaps friendship but respect I think. . . . The style of the heavier parts of the book will, I think, be considered good." [74] George Ripley, who saw it in sheets, confirmed Olmsted's opinion. "He could not predict a commercial success for the book," Olmsted wrote his father, "but its literary success was undoubted. Ripley is the best judge in America." [75]

Critics, except in the South, upheld Ripley's prophecy. The fact that Olmsted had examined slavery from an economic, not a humanitarian standpoint, gave an interesting twist to his observations, and the northern press generally received *Slave States* with approval amounting to enthusiasm.[76] Even the abolitionists, as a rule

[67] Olmsted to John Olmsted, January 31, 1856, *ibid.*

[68] Copyright statement, n.d., *ibid.*

[69] Olmsted to John Olmsted, January 31, 1856, *ibid.*

[70] New editions were published by Mason Brothers in 1859 and 1861, and it was reissued by G. P. Putnam's Sons in 1904.

[71] Olmsted to Edward Everett Hale, February 4, 1856, New England Emigrant Aid Society Papers (Kansas State Historical Society, Topeka).

[72] John Hull Olmsted to Olmsted, May 28, 1856, Olmsted Papers.

[73] John Hull Olmsted to Olmsted, July 10-18, 1856, *ibid.*

[74] Olmsted to John Olmsted, November 8, 1855, *ibid.*

[75] Olmsted to John Olmsted, January 15, 1856, *ibid.*

[76] New York *Times*, March 29, 1856; New York *Tribune*, March 15, 1856; New York *Evening Post*, April 8, 1856; Boston *Transcript*, February 4, 1856; Portland (Me.) *Transcript and Eclectic*, February 16, 1856; Worcester *National Aegis*, February 13, 1856; Providence *Journal*, February 20, 1856.

contemptuous of gradualist suggestions, were cordial. John Greenleaf Whittier, to whom Olmsted sent advance sheets, wrote warm encouragement;[77] and both the *National Era* and William Lloyd Garrison's *Liberator* recommended it heartily.[78] Asa Gray sent a copy, "an admirable volume," to Sir William Hooker and mentioned that the writer was "a young friend of ours." [79] The *Christian Examiner* and *Putnam's* praised it [80] and the *North American Review* predicted that it would prove of permanent interest.[81] Mrs. Stowe, reviewing it in the *Independent*, called it "the most thorough *exposé* of the economical view of this subject which has ever appeared" [82] and wrote Olmsted that she "never saw a book calculated to do more good with less friction." [83]

The Baltimore *Sun*, in a brief notice, conceded that Olmsted was fair-minded and his book informative,[84] but articulate southern reaction, on the whole, was hostile — perhaps more intemperate than Olmsted had anticipated. He had expected at least a respectful hearing in the South, "for while I strike right & left and strike hard, I do so respectfully and with the grace of sincerity." [85]

Southern irritation was understandable. Although Olmsted had originally intended to make "a book almost exclusively of simple *observation* with little theorizing or sermonizing," [86] the very nature of his observations involved him in analysis and conclusions. Furthermore, reflection, study, and political events had stiffened his attitude during the two years that had elapsed between the original observations and the final writing: thus those olive branches he had offered the South throughout the first series of letters — the admonitions to the North to correct the evils of its own labor system, the presentation of proslavery arguments, the warnings that emancipation must come in the South's good time and on the South's initiative — were absent from the book. Instead, the two long

[77] Olmsted to John Olmsted, January 31, 1856, Olmsted Papers.

[78] Washington *National Era*, May 1, 1856; Boston *Liberator*, May 23, 1856.

[79] Jane Loring Gray (ed.), *Letters of Asa Gray*, 2 vols. (Boston, 1893), II, 41.

[80] *Christian Examiner* (Boston), LX (May, 1856), 453-55; "Olmsted's *Seaboard Slave States*," *Putnam's Monthly Magazine* (New York), VII (February, 1856), 218.

[81] *North American Review* (Boston), LXXXIII (July, 1856), 278-79. This review was written by Edward Everett Hale.

[82] "Anti-Slavery Literature," *Independent* (New York), VIII (February 21, 1856), 57.

[83] Olmsted to John Olmsted, January 31, 1856, Olmsted Papers.

[84] Baltimore *Sun*, February 27, 1856.

[85] Olmsted to John Olmsted, November 8, 1855, Olmsted Papers.

[86] John Hull Olmsted to John Olmsted, June 15, 1854, *ibid.*

chapters on the history and economy of Virginia suggested, among other things, that the slavocracy, far from intending to rid the state of the incubus of slavery, now positively intended to retain it.[87]

The *Southern Literary Messenger*, without noticing *Slave States* directly, complained that "the literary workshops of the North are even now resounding with the noisy and fanatical labors of those who, with Mrs. Stowe as their model, are forging calumnies, and hammering falsehood into semblance of truth," and laid upon southern writers the duty of producing proslavery works "for the maintenance of our position, and our justification before the world." [88]

The impact of the work in England must have been particularly exasperating to the South. The august London *Times*, which in those days reviewed no more than a hundred books a year, spent three columns recommending it to its readers as a book that would afford them "new light on the working of the slave system in retarding the legitimate progress of the South." [89] *Household Words*, the *Saturday Review*, and the *Examiner* all reviewed the book cordially,[90] and even the *Athenaeum*, which had the reputation of being "unusually severe on American authors," [91] offered Olmsted rather condescending congratulations.[92] The *Daily News's* glowing article on it took two installments.[93] "I suppose it is written by Miss Martineau," Olmsted wrote. "It is in the highest degree complimentary." [94]

Fraser's Magazine used *Slave States*, with Josiah Quincy's *Nature and Power of the Slave States*,[95] as the point of departure for an article that summarized the steps in the development of the

87 Olmsted, *Journey in the Seaboard Slave States*, 298-99.

88 W. R. A., "The Duty of Southern Authors," *Southern Literary Messenger* (Richmond), XXIII (October, 1856), 241-47.

89 London *Times*, November 1, 1856.

90 "Slaves and Their Masters," *Household Words* (London), XIV (August 23, 1856), 133-38; "Olmsted's Slave States," *Saturday Review of Politics, Literature, Science, and Art* (London), II (November 15, 1856), 645-47; London *Examiner*, July 20, 1856.

91 Boston *Transcript*, January 12, 1857.

92 *Athenaeum* (London), No. 1496 (June 28, 1856), 805-806.

93 London *Daily News*, July 19, 21, 1856.

94 Olmsted to "Dear Sisters," July 19, 1856, Olmsted Papers. The Paris *Constitutionnel*, November 15, 1856, unreservedly recommended *Slave States* to the particular attention of those who made a serious study of the great questions of social economy.

95 Josiah Quincy, *Address Illustrative of the Nature and Power of the Slave States, and the Duties of the Free States* (Boston, 1856).

slavocracy's power and urged the election of John C. Frémont.[96] When this was followed by the *Edinburgh Review's* "Political Crisis in the United States," based on *Slave States* and a half dozen other current books,[97] both *Russell's Magazine* and the *Southern Literary Messenger* went on the offensive. They not only took issue with the content of the article but denounced its writer, claiming that, although it purported to be written by an Englishman, it was actually the work of an American.[98] It was indeed: the writer was, as the *Messenger* suspected, William Henry Hurlbert,[99] an associate of Olmsted's on *Putnam's*; and Olmsted himself had been entrusted with the delivery of the manuscript to the *Edinburgh Review*.[100]

Olmsted's moderate proposal for the gradual and compensated extinction of slavery came to be more widely considered in the serious English periodicals than the suggestions of any other student of the subject.[101] Altogether, the appearance of *Slave States* made Olmsted what he wanted to be: "a recognized literateur, a man of influence in literary matters." Troublesome as its production had been, financially unrewarding as it proved, it nevertheless won him a prominent place in the "literary republic." *Texas* was to strengthen it.

Texas was a far less difficult accomplishment than *Slave States* — for Frederick: his brother John wrote it.

In December, 1855, while Olmsted was embroiled with other problems, John had begun work on it.[102] He had little enthusiasm

96 "What Are the United States Coming To?" *Fraser's Magazine* (London), LIV (July, 1856), 611-22.

97 Charles Sumner, *Recent Speeches and Addresses* (Boston, 1856); *Essays on the American Constitution, from the "Mercury"* (Charleston, S. C., 1856); Harriet Beecher Stowe, *Dred: A Tale of the Great Dismal Swamp* (London, 1856); Parke Godwin, *Political Essays* (New York, 1856); Harriet Martineau, *A History of American Compromises; Reprinted, with Additions, from the Daily News* (London, 1856); Quincy, *Address Illustrative of the Nature and Power of the Slave States.*

98 "The Edinburg Reviewer Reviewed," *Russell's Magazine* (Charleston), I (April, 1856), 1-14; "The Edinburgh Review on the Political Crisis in the U. S., October 1856," *Southern Literary Messenger*, XXIV (January, 1857), 23-32.

99 G. W. Skinner of Longmans Green and Company, Ltd., London, to Laura Wood Roper, January 30, 1950.

100 Olmsted to John Olmsted, February 28, 1856, Olmsted Papers.

101 Allan Nevins, *The Emergence of Lincoln*, 2 vols. (New York, 1950), II, 136.

102 John Hull Olmsted to Bertha Olmsted, December 18-24, 1855, Olmsted Papers. Frederick and John were not only brothers but such devoted friends that each seems to have regarded his own interests and duties as practically interchangeable with his brother's.

for the job: his health was miserable, he did not think the book would sell.[103] By July, however, he had picked up heart and wrote his brother, who in February had gone abroad on business: "Probably will be all ready by the time you arrive & want a preface & a final chapter from you." [104] The next month he sent Olmsted a preface which Olmsted reworked without being able to improve it.[105]

Dix & Edwards' affairs kept Olmsted abroad till late in the year. Although he felt that he was organizing their foreign business with some success,[106] he was greatly exercised by alarming though vague reports from home on the financial management of the firm.[107] His social life, however, diverted him from his anxieties. Among his associates were Mark Lemon, Tom Taylor, Henry Mayhew, and John Leech, all of *Punch*, the publishers Bradbury and Evans, William Henry Wills, assistant editor of *Household Words* and an intimate of Dickens, the sculptor William Wetmore Storey, and Thackeray, who entertained him at dinner.[108] As a writer, Olmsted had arrived.

When he returned from England toward the end of 1856, he found *Texas* well advanced. Although anxious to escape from the partnership, and to spend more time writing (Raymond wanted him to go to Kansas, Dana considered sending him to Utah, and he thought himself of going to Jamaica to study the results of emancipation),[109] he continued to use the firm as his publishers. His contract for *Texas* provided that they should, after reimbursing themselves for the cost of production, pay him a 12½ per cent royalty.[110]

Texas was published in mid-January, 1857, and, since no advertising was charged against it, quickly paid for itself. On Feb-

[103] John Hull Olmsted to Olmsted, May 28, 1856, *ibid.*

[104] John Hull Olmsted to Olmsted, July 29, 1856, *ibid.*

[105] John Olmsted to John Hull Olmsted, August 8, 1856, *ibid.* It is not clear whether this preface was "A Letter to a Southern Friend," signed by Frederick, at the beginning of *Texas*, or the introduction of the American editor, always attributed to Frederick, of Thomas H. Gladstone's *Englishman in Kansas* (New York, 1856), the American edition of which appeared several months after *Texas*.

[106] Olmsted to "Dear Sisters," July 19, 1856, Olmsted Papers.

[107] John Hull Olmsted to Olmsted, July 27, 1856, J. A. Dix to Olmsted, July 29, 1856, Dix to Olmsted, n.d. (received September 4, 1856), *ibid.*

[108] Gordon N. Ray (ed.), *Letters and Private Papers of William Makepeace Thackeray*, 4 vols. (Cambridge, 1945-1946), III, 116 n.

[109] Olmsted to Edwards, December 25, 1856 (draft), Olmsted Papers.

[110] Memorandum of Agreement between Dix & Edwards and Olmsted, January 12, 1857, *ibid.*

ruary 17 Olmsted told his brother that he could soon expect $200, in accordance with the arrangement suggested by John,[111] that the actual writer receive two thirds of the profits of the book. "Seaboard being charged with advertising . . . bears yet a debt of $600. If we go on I think you may calculate to receive $400 for Texas in the year." [112] By mid-February the first printing of 2,500 was almost exhausted and the publishers were fretting over the nonarrival of paper for the second.[113]

Like *Slave States*, *Texas* was well received in the North,[114] although the proslavery New York *Commercial* said it was cleverly tailored to maintain its author's views.[115]

In the South, as before, it was a different matter. Middleton & McMaster, bookdealers of Mobile, having innocently ordered a dozen copies, begged to return seven, protesting that they had had no idea it was abolitionist in sentiment and that "there is considerable objection made here." [116] *De Bow's Review*, while relying on it for some of the data for the lead article on Texas in its August issue, spitefully assailed Olmsted himself.[117]

An extravagant personal attack came, too, from Daniel R. Hundley who, in his *Social Relations in Our Southern States*,[118] took the opportunity to castigate Olmsted — not, however, by name. Instead, he denounced "a certain literary Peripatetic of New York, who has been in the habit of taking a jaunt through some portions of the South every few years and afterward putting in book-form an account of what he saw and heard";[119] and he lamented that there were "so many lying, sneaking, cowardly knaves,

111 John Hull Olmsted to Olmsted, November 10, 1856, *ibid.*

112 Postscript by Olmsted added to letter from Mary A. Parker to John Hull Olmsted, February 17, 1857, *ibid.*

113 Olmsted to John Hull Olmsted, February 16, 1857, *ibid.* A second edition of *Texas* was brought out by Mason Brothers in 1859, and there were two German editions: that of C. B. Lorch, Leipzig, 1857, and of G. Senf, Leipzig, 1865.

114 *Texas* was well reviewed in New York *Times*, February 24, 1857; *Morning Courier and New York Enquirer*, February 9, 1857; New York *Daily Tribune* and *Weekly Tribune*, February 16, 1857; New York *Evening Post*, March 3, 1857; Philadelphia *North American and United States Gazette*, January 25, 1857; Boston *Transcript*, January 29, 1857. See also "Olmsted's Texas Journey," *Putnam's Monthly Magazine*, IX (March, 1857), 274-82; *Christian Examiner*, LXII (May, 1857), 465-68.

115 Postscript by Olmsted added to letter from Mary A. Parker to John Hull Olmsted, February 17, 1857, Olmsted Papers.

116 Middleton & McMaster to Olmsted, May 6, 1857, *ibid.*

117 "Texas," *De Bow's Review* (New Orleans), XXIII (August, 1857), 113-31.

118 Daniel R. Hundley, *Social Relations in Our Southern States* (New York, 1860).

119 *Ibid.*, 207.

foot-padding it all through the Southern States, endeavoring by every devilish machination to kindle servile insurrection, and writing calumnious letters to Northern newspapers, oftentimes defaming the characters of the unsuspecting patrons, at whose hospitable boards their miserable carcasses are each day filled with abundance of every species of good cheer." [120] The presumption is almost inescapable that the New York "literary Peripatetic" was Olmsted; the heinous charges may be dismissed as hyperbole.

The use made of *Texas* was not calculated to mollify proslavery opinion. Olmsted and the New England Emigrant Aid Society, with the aid of sympathetic newspapers, used it in a quiet, systematic way to promote immigration, not only from the North but from England and Germany, to western Texas, in a futile effort to stimulate a free-soil movement there.[121]

If this maneuver escaped alert southern observation, English response to *Texas* probably did not. *Household Words* drew on it for an article in praise of the Texas Germans.[122] The London *Times* gave it almost four columns.[123] The *Westminster Review* used it, with other current books,[124] as the basis of a radical pronorthern article.[125] The *New Quarterly Review* recommended it [126] and the *Athenaeum* dropped its severity toward American writers long enough to say warmly of Olmsted: "He has not only right on his side, but ever-blessed reason also, with happy common-sense enabling him to support both." [127]

"If we go on . . . ," Olmsted had written ominously to his brother. Business at the time was generally bad; Dix & Edwards was in poor shape — "[George W.] Curtis publications and mine are I think the only books in the concern worth a dollar" [128] — and failure seemed likely. It finally overtook Miller & Curtis, successor

[120] *Ibid.*, 216.

[121] Laura Wood Roper, "Frederick Law Olmsted and the Western Texas Free Soil Movement," *American Historical Review* (New York), LVI (October, 1950), 58-64.

[122] "Germans in Texas," *Household Words*, XV (April 25, 1857), 393-97.

[123] London *Times*, October 22, 1857.

[124] Martineau, *History of American Compromises*; William Chambers, *Slavery and Colour* (London and New York, 1857).

[125] "'Manifest Destiny' of the American Union," *Westminster Review* (London), XII (July, 1857), 137-76.

[126] *New Quarterly Review* (London), VI (1857), 153-54.

[127] *Athenaeum*, No. 1535 (March 28, 1857), 399-401.

[128] Olmsted to John Olmsted, February 7-17, 1857, Olmsted Papers.

firm to Dix & Edwards, on August 6, 1857.[129] Trying to salvage some profit from his books, Olmsted asked the publishers of the new *Atlantic Monthly*, Phillips, Sampson & Company of Boston, to issue new editions, but they replied that they had bought some of Miller & Curtis' stock for thirty-five and forty cents, that other dealers had done the same, and that retailers were well stocked with Olmstediana.[130] Altogether, it was a disheartening experience for a man of letters, especially for one at work on his third volume.

Olmsted had begun *Journey in the Back Country* as early as February, 1857.[131] In the following months the book was pushed into the background by other events — the firm's failure, his brother's death, and his own entrance into his new profession of landscape architecture — but he planned to finish it when he could, "the labor already expended on it being too much to let slide."[132] Eleven installments, all but the last of which later appeared in the book, ran in the New York *Tribune* as "The Southerner at Home," unsigned and without special notice, from June 3 to September 25, 1857.[133] It was not, however, until April, 1860, that *Back Country* was finally in production.[134] Olmsted's publisher this time was Mason Brothers who, the previous year, had brought out a new edition of *Slave States* on which the author made all of $52.[135] On his new book he was going to make nothing whatever: he assigned his 12½ per cent royalty to Francis George Shaw, father-in-law of Curtis and a heavy loser in the Miller & Curtis failure, and received from Shaw a receipt for $500, the value as estimated by Shaw and Judge Emerson of Olmsted's rights in the book.[136]

Certainly literary life was not financially rewarding to Olmsted; his influence, however, was exerting itself more widely, and more forcibly for his continued moderation in the climate of accelerating crisis. He still opposed immediate abolition, still favored the continued subjection of the Negroes in the South to the whites,[137] still

129 George William Curtis to Olmsted, August 6, 1857, *ibid.*

130 Phillips, Sampson & Company to Olmsted, November 13, 1857, *ibid.*

131 Olmsted to John Olmsted, February 7-17, 1857, *ibid.*

132 Olmsted to John Olmsted, January 14, 1858, *ibid.*

133 The writer is indebted to Mr. Walter Oswald of Princeton, New Jersey, for calling her attention to this little-known fact.

134 Mason Brothers to Olmsted, April 27, 1860, Olmsted Papers.

135 Olmsted to John Olmsted, February 6, 1860, *ibid.*

136 Francis George Shaw to Olmsted, May 22, 1860; and Memorandum of Agreement between Olmsted and Mason Brothers, July 19, 1860, *ibid.*

137 Olmsted, *Journey in the Back Country*, vii.

believed in gradual, compensated emancipation,[138] still wrote in a composed, reasonable tone.

Curtis described *Back Country* as "the heaviest blow (being true and moderate) that has yet been dealt at the system. It shows conclusively what a blight it is, but at the same time how difficult and distant the remedy seems to be." [139] Henry Whitney Bellows, the popular Unitarian minister, wrote Olmsted: "It cannot but have a marked influence on public opinion." [140] Charles Darwin, who described himself as a close student of Olmsted,[141] called it "an admirable picture of man and slavery in the Southern States." [142] Friedrich Kapp, sending Olmsted the first bound copy of his new book on slavery,[143] which he had dedicated to Olmsted, said: "I copied the conclusion from you." [144] Lowell thought that no more valuable contribution to American history had been made than *Back Country* and the preceding volumes.[145] Norton epitomized critical reaction by declaring that Olmsted's three books were classics which would "constitute chief materials of our social history." Newspaper notices generally were favorable, though not as numerous as for the previous books.[146]

Again the South could take little satisfaction in English response. The *Westminster Review*, discussing the political situation in the United States, compared *Back Country* and Hinton R. Helper's *Impending Crisis*,[147] to the detriment of Helper whose extravagant suggestions and violent tone contrasted unpleasantly with Olmsted's dispassion.[148] The *Athenaeum* and the *Saturday Review* both

138 *Ibid.*, ix.

139 Edward Cary, *George William Curtis* (New York, 1894), 137.

140 Henry W. Bellows to Olmsted, November 3, 1860, Olmsted Papers.

141 Francis Darwin (ed.), *Life and Letters of Charles Darwin*, 2 vols. (New York, 1888), II, 116.

142 *Ibid.*, 152.

143 *Geschichte der sklaverei in den Vereinigten Staaten von Amerika* (New York, 1860). Friedrich Kapp, 1824-1884, was a German lawyer, publicist, and historian who lived in New York from 1850 to 1870. In the front rank of the new Republican party, he used his great influence with the New York Germans to unite them in support of the Union. He had been a friend of Olmsted for about seven years.

144 Kapp to Olmsted, October 19, 1860, Olmsted Papers.

145 *Atlantic Monthly* (Boston), VI (November, 1860), 635-36.

146 New York *Tribune*, July 25, 1860; New York *Evening Post*, July 20, 27, 1860; New York *Times*, October 12, 1860; Boston *Transcript*, August 1, 1860. See also *Christian Examiner*, LXIX (September, 1860), 301-303.

147 Hinton R. Helper, *The Impending Crisis of the South: How To Meet It* (New York, 1857).

148 "American Slavery: The Impending Crisis," *Westminster Review*, N. S., XIX (January, 1861), 152-71.

treated *Back Country* with rare enthusiasm.[149] The *Times* concluded from it that the South would be ill-advised to attempt secession, and suggested that "a new edition of the whole series would be an addition to our economic science, as well as a help to a better knowledge of the difficulties of our American kinsmen." [150]

Altogether, the demand in England for *Back Country* was so encouraging that Sampson Low, Son & Company of London sent Olmsted a number of favorable notices and proposed a new edition of the three volumes in condensed form.[151]

Despite its critical acclaim, *Back Country* did not enjoy a great sale in the United States: it went through only one edition and was not reissued until 1907, when G. P. Putnam's Sons brought out a new one. Mason Brothers, who had expected something better than a *succès d'estime*,[152] were discouraged and, advising Olmsted on the Sampson Low proposition, wrote him what is surely one of the most dispirited letters in publishing annals: "We have told you but you cannot appreciate how perfectly 'in the dumps' we publishers feel just now. Everything disappoints us, one book after another. . . . Just now we have confidence in nothing and wish to undertake nothing." The proposal, however, involved no risk to Olmsted beyond the loss of his time; Mason Brothers, since Sampson Low offered to ship them the plates free, could pay him 12½ per cent royalty; and the book would probably sell well here "if anything will sell." They therefore half-heartedly advised him to go ahead with the condensation. "But really," they concluded bleakly, "you cannot understand how little like entering into new projects we feel just now." [153]

Olmsted accepted Sampson Low's proposal. Months before he had decided that war was inescapable;[154] a recent serious injury disqualified him for active combat; his most immediate usefulness lay in extending the antislavery influence of his books both in England and the United States. Fully occupied in directing the creation of Central Park, he had no time himself for the necessary editing, so he arranged with Daniel Reeves Goodloe, abolitionist

149 "A Journey in the Back Country," *Saturday Review*, X (October 20, 1860), 486-88; "The American Question," *Athenaeum*, No. 1767 (September 7, 1861), 307-308.

150 London *Times*, December 8, 1860.

151 Sampson Low, Son & Company to Olmsted, January 16, 1861, Olmsted Papers.

152 Mason Brothers to Olmsted, January 29, 1861, *ibid*.

153 *Ibid*.

154 Olmsted to Brace, December 8, 1860, *ibid*.

editor of the *National Era*, to do the work for half the royalties.[155]

Goodloe made a number of editorial suggestions, no material one of which Olmsted accepted.[156] The condensation went rapidly, with only one serious hitch: Olmsted could not get access to the yet unpublished 1860 census returns and had to rely, as in his earlier books, on the 1850 returns.[157] By the end of June, 1861, the complete manuscript was in the hands of the English printer,[158] and the English edition was ready in October.

On receiving the plates, Mason Brothers' spirits cautiously rose. ". . . *it is selling well* in advance of publication. They think two editions will be called for," Olmsted wrote his wife.[159] The book was published here on November 7[160] and the first edition, at $2.00, sold out as predicted; a second, carrying a few minor corrections, was printed in 1862.

Cotton Kingdom was evolved principally by deleting sections of the original books, mostly of *Texas*; by effecting a certain amount of condensation and transposition; and by adding a new introduction. The most conspicuous omission was the account of the free labor communities of the Texas Germans. (Presumably this was deleted because they were atypical of southern society.) Altogether, no change in tone or temper distinguishes the body of *Cotton Kingdom* from its three sources.

The introduction, however, shows how far time and events had carried Olmsted since the first series of letters in 1853. The letters were written before Kansas-Nebraska; the introduction was written after Sumter. Critical years of history lay between, and had just climaxed in a desperate crisis. During them Olmsted's mind had gradually been made ready for it, and he met it uncompromisingly. He stated that the North could make no peace with the South as a foreign power; North or South had to be subjugated, North or South had to be forcibly compelled to accept the other's policy on union and slavery. For the rest, the introduction was the now familiar economic indictment of the slave labor system, with the pointed implication that because of it the South was weaker and less well equipped for war than either she or her friends supposed.

155 Olmsted to John Olmsted, March 22, 1861, *ibid.*
156 D. R. Goodloe to Olmsted, February 23, 24, March 8, 19, 1861, *ibid.*
157 Olmsted, *Cotton Kingdom,* I, 8 n.
158 Sampson Low, Son & Company to Olmsted, June 29, 1861, Olmsted Papers.
159 Olmsted to Mary Cleveland Olmsted, October 25, 1861, *ibid.*
160 New York *Tribune,* November 7, 1861.

Lowell, impressed by "the compactness and the quiet power of the introduction to the new volumes," wrote Olmsted: "I have learned more about the South from your books than from all others put together, & I value them the more that an American who can be patient & accurate is so rare a phenomenon. . . . An American who can write without partizanship, & especially on Slavery, is still rarer." [161] Charles Sumner called *Cotton Kingdom* "a positive contribution to civilization." [162]

Significantly, Olmsted dedicated it — and it was the only one of his southern books which he did dedicate — to John Stuart Mill. Significantly, too, it was after *Cotton Kingdom's* publication that Mill, who acknowledged his reliance on "the calm and dispassionate Mr. Olmsted," [163] wrote his article on "The Contest in America" for *Fraser's Magazine*, denouncing the southern cause as a bald effort to perpetuate a villainous institution, denying the legality of secession, and warning that, in case of a southern victory, England would have to fight the Confederacy within five years.[164] Shortly after *Cotton Kingdom*, John E. Cairnes's *Slave Power* appeared; dedicated, by an interesting coincidence, to Mill, it also relied heavily on Olmsted's books.[165]

The *Westminster Review* said that Olmsted's new work was of the highest importance "as a means of estimating not the proximate but the ultimate fate of Southern society." [166] The *Saturday Review*, facing about, dismissed it as a clever piece of special pleading designed to sway English opinion, and offered as a corrective the assertion that not in a northern but in a southern victory lay the best chance for the improvement of the slaves' condition.[167] The *Athenaeum* expressed its belief that Olmsted deserved the confidence of European readers, but thought *Cotton Kingdom* did not contain enough new material to justify so bulky a work.[168]

Cotton Kingdom, reviewed in the United States favorably but

161 J. R. Lowell to Olmsted, January 25, 1862, *ibid.*

162 Charles Sumner to Olmsted, December 28, 1861, *ibid.*

163 J. S. Mill, "The Contest in America," *Fraser's Magazine*, LXV (February, 1862), 258-68.

164 *Ibid.*

165 John E. Cairnes, *The Slave Power: Its Character, Career, and Probable Designs: Being an Attempt to Explain the Real Issues Involved in the American Contest* (London, 1862).

166 *Westminster Review*, N. S., XXI (January, 1862), 257.

167 "Olmsted's Southern States," *Saturday Review*, XII (November 2, 1861), 460.

168 *Athenaeum*, No. 1772 (October 12, 1861), 474-76.

not as widely as Olmsted's other books,[169] did little to relieve Mason Brothers' doldrums. In September, 1862, the firm failed. As they went down, however, they protected Olmsted's interests and earned his sympathy and gratitude. "They said they hope to pay me in full," he wrote his wife, "— about $100 due. They have managed to keep my plates & copyright out of the sale on the ground that as they had no contract with me they were my property . . . as they were evidently trying to secure all they could for me . . . & hope to start anew & retain my clientship, I left the whole business in their hands. They seemed to be honest, frank, efficient, unfortunate and ill-used by their special partner who ravages them maliciously and vindictively."[170]

Mason Brothers did go back into business, but they never again published Olmsted, although they paid him a royalty, $179.95, as late as 1866.[171] By that time he was fully committed to the profession of landscape architecture, and no longer thought of himself as a writer. His reputation as one, nevertheless, persisted. Years later Richard Watson Gilder, editor of the *Century*, heard a rumor that Olmsted contemplated a new book on the South,[172] and on running it to earth was disappointed to find it false.[173] Even later, in 1891, the aged John Murray Forbes, on rereading *Cotton Kingdom*, was so impressed and delighted that he proposed reissuing it,[174] but Olmsted dissuaded him. Although the book would somewhat counteract the mischievous tendency in recent literature to romanticize falsely the prewar slave states, Olmsted told Forbes, no commercial demand existed to justify its republication.[175] There was no turning back for Olmsted to his youthful career as man of letters, but the place he had earned in the literary republic was a permanent one.

[169] New York *Times*, December 11, 1861; Philadelphia *North American*, November 16, 1861; New York *Tribune*, November 8, 1861; Washington *National Intelligencer*, December 23, 1861.

[170] Olmsted to Mary Cleveland Olmsted, September 13, 1862, Olmsted Papers.

[171] Mason Brothers to Olmsted, December 31, 1866, *ibid.*

[172] Richard W. Gilder to Olmsted, November 19, 1881, *ibid.*

[173] Gilder to Olmsted, December 9, 1881, *ibid.*

[174] John M. Forbes to Olmsted, July 1, 19, 1891, *ibid.*

[175] Olmsted to Forbes, July 2, 1891, *ibid.*

Progressivism and Imperialism: The Progressive Movement and American Foreign Policy, 1898-1916

By William E. Leuchtenburg

No distinction is more revered by the American historian than that between domestic and foreign affairs and in few periods of our history has that distinction been more religiously observed than in the Progressive era. The Theodore Roosevelt who fought the trusts, defied the special interests, and stood at Armageddon to battle for the Lord, and the Theodore Roosevelt who preached jingoism and "took" Panama have been divorced on grounds of incompatibility.[1]

The leaders of the Progressive movement, we are given to understand, welcomed Roosevelt's aid in fighting the railway kings and the coal barons, but dissented vigorously from his imperialism and chauvinism. The Progressives were deeply disturbed by Roosevelt's racism, and even more by such episodes as the acquisition of the Canal Zone, but accepted his leadership because of his avowed hostility to corporation control of American life. George Norris' biographer represents the prevailing attitude in asserting that "Western progressives . . . had never adhered to the big-stick doctrines of Roosevelt."[2]

The thesis of this article is that the Progressives, contrary to the orthodox accounts, did not oppose imperialism but, with few exceptions, ardently supported the imperialist surge or, at the very least, proved agreeably acquiescent. The majority of the Progressive members of Congress voted for increased naval expenditures and for Caribbean adventures in imperialism. At no time did the

[1] Insofar as any link has been made between the domestic and foreign aspects of the Progressive period, it has been to present a tableau of Theodore Roosevelt, the warrior, brandishing a big stick at American corporations on the one hand and foreign potentates on the other.

[2] Alfred Lief, *Democracy's Norris* (New York, 1939), 155.

Republican insurgents in the Taft administration take issue with Dollar Diplomacy, even when the Progressives were searching for campaign issues in 1912. Not until after the 1912 elections did they concern themselves actively with foreign affairs and then it was not to combat imperialism but to urge the use of American force in Mexico and an increase in armaments. By 1916 the Progressive party had forsaken its program of domestic reform to condemn the foreign policy of the Wilson administration, and a fondness for a "strong" foreign policy was an important cause of the death of the party. Moreover, the ideological content and the motivation of imperialism and progressivism had much in common, a relationship made explicit in the writings of Herbert Croly.

Senator Albert J. Beveridge of Indiana epitomized the two interlocking forces, although his imperialistic views were unquestionably more fervently held than those of the average Progressive. One of the most eloquent orators of the period, he made the keynote speech at the Progressive convention of 1912 in Chicago. Beveridge's fame as an orator started with his declamatory avowal of American imperialism in the Spanish-American War, and he maintained this enthusiasm for imperialism throughout the Progressive era. " 'The opposition tells us we ought not to rule a people without their consent. I answer, the rule of liberty, that all just governments derive their authority from the consent of the governed, applies only to those who are capable of self-government'," he told an enthusiastic Indianapolis meeting in 1898.

> The proposition of the opposition makes the Declaration of Independence preposterous, like the reading of Job's lamentations would be at a wedding, or an Altgeld speech on the Fourth of July. . . . Cuba not contiguous? Porto Rico not contiguous? The Philippines not contiguous? Our navy will make them contiguous! . . . Dewey and Sampson and Schley have made them contiguous, and American speed, American guns, American heart and brain and nerve will keep them contiguous forever.[3]

No member of the Senate in the first decade of this century contributed more to the Progressive movement than Senator Beveridge. He sponsored the bill for federal meat inspection and carried the fight against the bitter opposition of the slaughterhouses. He fought a long, courageous, abortive campaign to end child labor in America. In the 1910 campaign in Indiana he urged federal con-

[3] Claude G. Bowers, *Beveridge and the Progressive Era* (Boston, 1932), 73-76.

trol of railways, the eight-hour day, and the regulation of capitalization. It was Beveridge who managed the insurgent revolt against the Payne-Aldrich tariff. He walked out of the Republican party with the Progressives in 1912, and he fought against the drift toward reconciliation after the election, even accepting the hopeless assignment of Progressive candidate for the Senate in 1914.

Yet his faith in America's imperialist mission continued to be just as strong as his belief in economic reform, and Beveridge's imperialism ultimately proved his undoing as a Progressive. Many of the reforms dearest to Beveridge, which the Republican party had opposed and Roosevelt had shunned, were pushed through Congress by Woodrow Wilson, and Beveridge could have little quarrel with the President's domestic program, but by 1914 he was bitterly opposed to him. Wilson should have recognized Huerta, for Mexico needed a strong man, and the repeal of the Panama tolls was a "fatal blunder." "The Progressive Party in Congress will be solid against the repeal."[4] In 1916 he lashed into Wilson for refusing to use arms to support American investments in China, for his proposal to withdraw from the Philippines, and, strangely, for not increasing the tariff to meet new European competition. Beveridge, faced with the necessity to choose between progressivism and imperialism for the first time, chose the latter. By 1920 he was crying out against " 'Organized labor's assault on American institutions!' " interspersing speeches against the League of Nations with demands for the repeal of the excess profits tax. Inflation was caused by the draining of money to Europe through foreign propaganda and the unreasonable demands of labor unions for higher wages.[5] Once more Beveridge's views on domestic and foreign policy had merged, and this new outlook persisted until his death.

At the outbreak of the Spanish-American War few men saw any conflict between social reform and democratic striving at home and the new imperialist mission; indeed, the war seemed nothing so much as an extension of democracy to new parts of the world, and few political figures exceeded the enthusiasm of William Jennings Bryan for the Spanish war.[6] As the war continued and its conse-

4 *Ibid.*, 448.
5 *Ibid.*, 511-12.
6 Merle Curti, *Bryan and World Peace*, Smith College *Studies in History* (Northampton), XVI, Nos. 3-4 (1931), 117 ff.

quences were realized, as the dream of *Cuba libre* gave way to the realities of Aguinaldo's insurrection, a few of the Progressives, like Hazen Pingree and Jane Addams, joined the anti-imperialist forces, but, first and last, it was the conservatives who bore the burden of the anti-imperialist campaign.

In late March, 1899, William Allen White explained the Emporia *Gazette's* support of the war. "'Only Anglo-Saxons can govern themselves. . . . It is the Anglo-Saxon's manifest destiny to go forth as a world conqueror'," [7] he observed. Years later he wrote of this time:

> And we in Emporia, and "Our Charley" in Washington, thought we were free to spout and jower and jangle about the atrocities of the "brute Weyler" without in the slightest affecting the reality of our lives. We were as little boys making snoots across the fence, throwing rocks into the next yard, but innocent of the fact that we were starting wars that would last far into the next century, threaten all that we loved and wreck much that we cherished.[8]

"Though I hate war *per se*," wrote Elizabeth Cady Stanton, "I am glad that it has come in this instance. I would like to see Spain . . . swept from the face of the earth." [9]

A few of the Progressives, and many of the older generation of radicals like Henry Demarest Lloyd, joined forces with the anti-imperialists, but it was conservative Republicans like Thomas B. Reed, Democrats like Grover Cleveland and Bryan, frequently for partisan ends, businessmen like Andrew Carnegie, and Mugwumps like Carl Schurz who provided the bulk of the leadership. "The Republicans who joined the anti-imperialist movement were, almost without exception, Republicans of the older generation. . . . The anti-imperialists made great efforts to attract labor support, but, on the whole, were unsuccessful." [10] The one important political figure who persistently linked the fight for progressivism with

[7] Walter Johnson, *William Allen White's America* (New York, 1947), 111.

[8] *The Autobiography of William Allen White* (New York, 1946), 305-306.

[9] Merle Curti, *Peace or War: The American Struggle, 1636-1936* (New York, 1936), 171.

[10] Fred H. Harrington, "The Anti-Imperialist Movement in the United States, 1898-1900," *Mississippi Valley Historical Review* (Cedar Rapids), XXII (September, 1935), 218-19. See also Fred H. Harrington, "Literary Aspects of American Anti-Imperialism, 1898-1902," *New England Quarterly* (Baltimore, Portland), X (December, 1937), 650-67. The support given by organized labor to various imperialist ventures may be traced in John C. Appel, "The Relationship of American Labor to United States Imperialism, 1895-1905" (Ph.D. dissertation, University of Wisconsin, 1950).

the struggle against imperialism was the ineffective Silver Republican, Senator Richard Pettigrew of South Dakota, and he was retired from office in 1900, partly because of his anti-imperialist views.[11]

Theodore Roosevelt's accession to the presidency brought the new imperialist movement to full flower, and, in all of his foreign ventures, in Santo Domingo, Panama, the Far East, in building a greater American fleet, Roosevelt had the support of a majority of the Progressives. "I confess that the half-hearted criticism I hear of the way of the administration with Panama provokes in me a desire to laugh," Jacob Riis noted. "I am not a jingo; but when some things happen I just have to get up and cheer. The way our modern American diplomacy goes about things is one of them."[12] Gifford Pinchot warmly admired Roosevelt's policy in Panama,[13] while Oscar Straus, the Progressive candidate for governor of New York in 1912, helped prepare the dubious legal defense of Roosevelt's course with Panama, with his concept of a " 'covenant running with the land'." As John Bassett Moore observed cynically to Straus, it was "indifferently, a question of the 'covenant running with the land' or a question of the 'covenant running (*away!*) with the land'!"[14] When Bryan negotiated a treaty of indemnity and apology with Colombia, the Progressives were outraged. The Colombians, said Senator Joseph L. Bristow heatedly, were "a lot of blackmailers." As for the contention that Roosevelt had acted immorally in Panama, "there could be no greater slander pronounced against the Government and nothing more unjust, and in my opinion it borders on treason."[15] The final word on the Progressive position on Panama was had by George Norris over forty years later, when he ruefully observed:

[11] Cf. Richard Pettigrew, *Imperial Washington* (Chicago, 1922); William G. Carleton, "Isolationism and the Middle West," *Mississippi Valley Historical Review*, XXXIII (December, 1946), 379. Even Senator Pettigrew favored war with Spain, "because I believe it will put us on a silver basis." Arthur W. Dunn, *From Harrison to Harding . . . 1888-1921*, 2 vols. (New York, 1922), I, 232. There was a close tie, in fact, between the jingoes and the silverites. Julius W. Pratt, *Expansionists of 1898* (Baltimore, 1936), 242 ff.

[12] Jacob A. Riis, *Theodore Roosevelt, The Citizen* (New York, 1903), 384, 385.

[13] Cf. Gifford Pinchot, *Breaking New Ground* (New York, 1947).

[14] Oscar S. Straus, *Under Four Administrations; From Cleveland to Taft* (Boston, 1922), 175, 176.

[15] New York *Times*, October 14, 1914, p. 10; Claudius O. Johnson, *Borah of Idaho* (New York, 1936), 191 ff.

> Often those years I followed him [Roosevelt] when I had some doubts as to the righteousness of his course. . . . Yet he built the Panama Canal after other governments and a great corporation had spent a vast amount of money and had failed in their efforts. He threw his heart into the construction of this waterway, whose long useful service has caused the struggle for it to be forgotten; but during its progress the means by which the Panama Canal was accomplished in some respects seem doubtful to me. *I followed him step by step in that fight.* Doubts assailed me at the time, and I have since reached the conclusion that our government's decision to establish the new republic of Panama, which in reality prevented Colombia from defending her own territory with her army, was open to argument.[16]

The Progressives were scarcely less cooperative in promoting American hegemony in the Caribbean and defending Roosevelt's big stick diplomacy there. On the Platt amendment Senators Beveridge and Jonathan P. Dolliver voted with the majority, and the Silver Republicans, Pettigrew and Henry M. Teller, cast the only dissenting Republican votes.[17] Roosevelt's action in taking over the customhouse of the Dominican Republic received the approval of Senators Beveridge, Moses E. Clapp, Dolliver, and Robert M. La Follette, with not a single Progressive senator voting against the treaty.[18] By March, 1907, Charles Joseph Bonaparte, who prosecuted the trusts under Roosevelt and was to be a bitter foe of George W. Perkins in 1916, could sound a popular note in praising the President's skill in "promoting the peace of Central America, in staying civil strife in Cuba, in discouraging rebellion in Santo Domingo."[19]

Bonaparte also shared with a great many Progressives Roosevelt's enthusiasm for a big navy, a viewpoint of inestimable advantage for a secretary of the navy. When Roosevelt appointed him to this post in 1905, Bonaparte assured him: "It is perhaps proper to say, in this connection, that I am in hearty sympathy with your frequently expressed views as to the importance and, indeed, necessity of a very strong and very efficient Navy to the United States."[20] The antinavy bloc in Congress was led not by the Progressives but

[16] *Fighting Liberal; The Autobiography of George W. Norris* (New York, 1945), 145-47 (italics supplied).

[17] *Cong. Record*, 56 Cong., 2 Sess., 3151-52.

[18] *Ibid.*, 59 Cong., 2 Sess., 3917.

[19] Charles J. Bonaparte, "Two Years of a Government That Does Things," *Outlook* (New York), LXXXV (March 16, 1907), 600.

[20] Joseph B. Bishop, *Charles Joseph Bonaparte* (New York, 1922), 100.

by the conservative Eugene Hale in the Senate and the conservative Theodore Burton in the House, and their main supporters were likewise conservatives.[21]

The first uprising of the insurgents against Nelson W. Aldrich occurred not over the Payne-Aldrich tariff, but on behalf of Roosevelt's request for four new battleships in 1908 against the outspoken opposition of the Old Guard. Led by Senator Beveridge, two fifths of the Republicans deserted Aldrich in a debate featuring repeated attacks on the leadership of the Old Guard. The debate, which ended in a compromise on two battleships, badly shook Aldrich's domination of the Senate. "The Senate oligarchy is in a bad way," reported the *Saturday Evening Post*. "It is tottery and wobbly at the knees. Its members do not know just what it was that hit them, but they do know that they have been hit hard." [22] On the final vote on the Piles amendment for four battleships, which was defeated 50 to 23, Beveridge, William E. Borah, and Jonathan Bourne voted with the big navy minority against Aldrich, W. Murray Crane, Thomas C. Platt, and other Old Guard leaders. Senator Weldon B. Heyburn expressed the general sentiment of the debate in observing: "I care nothing for the poetic idea of turning swords into plowshares and spears into pruning hooks. This is a business proposition." On this occasion two of the Progressives, Clapp and Joseph M. Dixon, voted against navalism, and Clapp launched a brilliant, bitter attack on Beveridge for raising false issues "that the public might be prejudiced." [23]

The degree to which the majority of the Progressives were bound to Roosevelt's foreign policy is indicated in a letter of Brand Whitlock's:

> I have your note asking me if I could help you with a letter against wasting $32,000,000 on two more useless battleships. I am not sure that anything I can say on that subject will be of any use in stopping the construction of battleships; if it would I would say a great deal, for, of course, it is all but a part of the vast and amazing superstition of war. . . . I suppose that as long as there are some nations in the world who want to go to war, and so long as there are commercial interests that will keep up revolutions in Mexico and Central and South America, we shall need a navy and army to do police duty and keep the peace in this hemisphere,

[21] Curti, *Peace or War*, 220.
[22] *Saturday Evening Post* (Philadelphia), CLXXX (May 23, 1908), 18-19.
[23] *Cong. Record*, 60 Cong., 1 Sess., 5291, 5284, 5274.

for which, under the Monroe Doctrine, I suppose we are responsible; but I know of no reason for going beyond this need.[24]

Whitlock was an intelligent, eloquent critic of Roosevelt's foreign policy who once observed that "Thayer can see the megalomania which afflicted Garibaldi but cannot see it when the same symptoms are repeated in Roosevelt."[25] Yet even the hostile Whitlock accepted reluctantly the obligations of "police duty" and the Monroe Doctrine, and from these premises much could follow.

In March, 1909, Theodore Roosevelt gave way to his heir apparent, William Howard Taft, and for the next four years the Progressives were confronted by the phenomenon of Dollar Diplomacy. Philander C. Knox, who had prosecuted the Northern Securities case, directed the new Caribbean policy, while Willard D. Straight, who in 1914 was to found the *New Republic* "to explore and develop and apply the ideas which had been advertised by Theodore Roosevelt when he was the leader of the Progressive party,"[26] fostered Dollar Diplomacy in the Orient. The liberal character of Straight's Oriental diplomacy, which attempted to force American capital to go into China where it did not care to enter, rests on the nice distinction between territorial integrity and economic hegemony, and the dubious assumption that the investments of Edward H. Harriman, who allegedly asserted he could buy Congress and, if need be, the judiciary, would be more beneficial to the Chinese people than French and Russian capital. Ultimately Straight ended up attempting to raise a foreign loan to crush the Chinese revolution, on the assumption that what China needed was a dictator. The British and Germans were unsympathetic, and Straight was forced to allow the Chinese people to determine their own political destiny.[27]

From the days of the Payne-Aldrich tariff dispute, the rift between the insurgents and Taft grew wider, and Taft was beleaguered by a Progressive bloc which at times opposed him on purely ideological grounds, on occasion out of personal spite, but at no

[24] Brand Whitlock to General Isaac R. Sherwood, February 26, 1913, Allan Nevins (ed.), *The Letters and Journal of Brand Whitlock*, 2 vols. (New York, 1936), I, 158-59.

[25] Whitlock to Albert J. Nock, June 14, 1916, *ibid.*, 195.

[26] Walter Lippmann, "Notes for a Biography," *New Republic* (New York), LXIII (July 16, 1930), 250.

[27] Herbert Croly, *Willard Straight* (New York, 1924), 422 ff.

time because of disagreement with Taft's Dollar Diplomacy. While the Progressives were meeting in Chicago in 1912 to establish their third party, Taft was landing American marines in Nicaragua, but no word of condemnation for Taft's foreign policy appears in the Progressive platform of 1912. Instead, the platform stated:

> It is imperative to the welfare of our people that we enlarge and extend our foreign commerce. In every way possible our federal government should co-operate in this important matter. Germany's policy of co-operation between government and business has in comparatively few years made that nation a leading competitor for the commerce of the world. . . . The Panama Canal, built and paid for by the American people, must be used primarily for their benefit. . . . American ships engaged in coastwise trade shall pay no tolls.

Roosevelt's speech to the Progressive convention called for building a larger navy,[28] and Frank Munsey assured his readers that "The new Progressive party believes in a navy that will insure peace, that will give us a rightful position among the powers of the world, and that will make the Monroe Doctrine an actuality." [29]

The two issues of foreign policy which did affect the Progressive bolt of 1912 were the arbitration treaties and Taft's Mexican policy, both of which earned the ire of Theodore Roosevelt, and with Taft's prosecution of United States Steel, brought about the final break between Roosevelt and Taft. "Describing the treaties as an outrage, born of some very 'sloppy thinking,' Roosevelt furiously set about to destroy them. He wrote innumerable letters to [Henry Cabot] Lodge, chairman of the Senate Foreign Relations Committee, corresponded with [Elihu] Root, and indirectly reached [Albert B.] Cummins and Borah." [30] In a series of articles in the *Outlook*, starting on May 20, 1911, Roosevelt lashed out at the arbitration treaties with thinly veiled references to Taft. We should not indulge in "amiable sentimentality"; it is "our duty not to indulge in shams, not to make believe we are getting peace by some patent contrivance which sensible men ought to know cannot work"; "to speak of it as silly comes far short of saying what should be said." [31] When the treaties reached the Senate floor, the Pro-

28 Chicago *Record-Herald*, August 7, 1912, p. 5.

29 Frank A. Munsey, "The New Progressive Party — What It Is and Why It Is," *Munsey's Magazine* (New York), XLVII (August, 1912), 678.

30 George E. Mowry, *Theodore Roosevelt and the Progressive Movement* (Madison, 1946), 187 ff.

31 See particularly Theodore Roosevelt, "The Peace of Righteousness," *Outlook*, XCIX (September 9, 1911), 66 ff.

gressive forces were divided, Borah, Bourne, Bristow, and Cummins voting for the crippling amendment to exclude from arbitration questions affecting the admission of aliens to the United States or any question involving the Monroe Doctrine, while Clapp and John D. Works voted against it, a courageous act on the part of Senator Works, who came from the alien-conscious state of California.[32] Roosevelt denounced as "flabby" Taft's firm action in refusing to intervene on behalf of American oil interests in Mexico.[33] "Of all the misconduct of the Administration," Roosevelt concluded, "no misconduct had been greater than that relating to foreign affairs."[34]

The campaign of 1912 offered the Progressives another excellent opportunity to attack Taft's Dollar Diplomacy, but they were strangely silent. Scarcely had the election returns of November, 1912, been counted, however, than they began their attack on Woodrow Wilson and a movement started within the Progressive party to return to the Republican fold at almost any price. The Progressives were embarrassed by Wilson's commendable record in domestic affairs, and as Wilson drove through one reform after another in 1913 it became clear that their only choice was between joining forces with Wilson or maintaining their party organization intact with a more radical approach to domestic problems; there were no grounds for choosing the Republicans over the Wilson administration. Instead, they chose to fight it out with the administration on foreign policy. For the first time in the history of the Progressive movement foreign affairs determined the line of direction, and by 1916 the Progressives were completely absorbed with foreign policy issues and their movement was moribund.

On July 11, 1914, Roosevelt announced the new direction of the party when he resigned as contributing editor to the *Outlook* to devote his time to opposing the Wilson administration for its foreign policy which had "meant the abandonment of the interest and honor of America."[35] In later years Roosevelt indicated that his violent turn against the administration was over Wilson's indifference to the plight of Belgium, but in September, 1914,

32 *Cong. Record*, 62 Cong., 2 Sess., 2954-55.

33 Mowry, *Theodore Roosevelt and the Progressive Movement*, 307.

34 *Ibid.*, 187 ff.

35 *Outlook*, CVII (July 11, 1914), 569.

Roosevelt was urging American neutrality with respect to Belgium. "Of course it would be folly to jump into the gulf ourselves to no good purpose; and very probably nothing that we could have done would have helped Belgium." [36] The main grievances of Roosevelt and the Progressives with Wilson were originally not over the European war at all, but over the treaty of apology and indemnity with Colombia, Bryan's cooling off treaties, and the "mushy amiability" of Wilson in withdrawing from Mexico and agreeing to arbitration by the ABC powers.[37]

Borah announced a "last ditch" fight against Wilson's bill to repeal the Panama Canal tolls, and on the vote for final passage, Borah, Bristow, Clapp, Cummins, La Follette, Miles Poindexter, and Works all voted in opposition, with only Asle J. Gronna and Norris voting with the Wilson administration.[38] Mexico was an even hotter issue. In March, 1915, Walter A. Johnson, New York state chairman of the Progressive party, asserted in an interview in the New York *Sun* that Wilson, instead of following the policy of "watchful waiting" in Mexico, should follow the sterling example of Theodore Roosevelt in the Perdicaris case in Morocco by sending warships and issuing an ultimatum.[39] A few months later Dr. H. Nelson Jackson, chairman of the Progressive party of Vermont, issued a statement to the Burlington *Free Press*:

> While hundreds of Americans were being murdered, their wives and daughters outraged, their property destroyed, and have received no protection from our spineless, psalm-singing administration, thousands of our citizens thought that President Wilson was locked in his study praying and planning for peace and good will to this beloved country of ours, but in the past few weeks they suddenly realized that his time had been taken up otherwise, with courting. . . . Oh! God give us a leader that will keep our country in the exalted position made possible by such leaders as Washington and Abraham Lincoln and that will make Americans feel no matter where they go, no matter where they invest their capital, that they,

36 Theodore Roosevelt, "The World War: Its Tragedies and Its Lessons," *ibid.*, CVIII (September 23, 1914), 169-78.

37 New York *Times*, June 25, 1914, p. 2.

38 *Cong. Record*, 63 Cong., 2 Sess., 10247-48. This is not to say that the Wilson administration was free from imperialist manifestations. Indeed, the degree to which Woodrow Wilson was involved with American imperialist aspirations makes the attitude of the Progressives all the more remarkable. The relation of the New Freedom to American foreign policy merits further study, but it necessarily lies outside the scope of this short paper.

39 *Progressive Opinion* (New York), I (March 27, 1915), 7.

their families, and their properties will be respected and protected, and above all that our dear flag will be honored among all nations.[40]

In December, 1914, the Progressives issued a statement completely omitting the progressive planks of the 1912 platform and concentrating on demands for a higher protective tariff, a far cry from the insurgency of 1909 and a clear bid for amalgamation with the Republican party. By the fall of 1915 domestic issues had almost completely disappeared from the Progressive program, and the one issue that was hammered home in Progressive publications and meetings was the need for military preparedness. On September 25, 1915, Victor Murdock, the Kansas radical who was chairman of the National Committee of the Progressive party, wrote Walter Johnson:

> I was greatly gratified to find this view [the necessity for maintaining the Progressive party] confirmed at a dinner given by Mr. Perkins to me at the Manhattan Hotel here on Wednesday evening. . . . There was straight-out, complete candor in the addresses made by all of them, and an absence of boast and fustian. They were in favor of holding the line, facing forward and throwing themselves into the campaign of 1916 with uncompromising aggression, behind a ticket and platform which will challenge the sense and patriotism of the nation.
>
> The strong notes sounded were for military and economic preparedness. The men present favored insuring peace for the nation by placing us in a position to command respect and for an adjustment of the tariff under the Progressive plan of a tariff commission to meet the abnormal selling campaign by Europe which will follow inevitably the cessation of hostilities abroad.[41]

Not only had foreign policy become a key issue, but it had been linked by now with the need for high tariff walls, a prophecy of the economic policy of Warren G. Harding and Herbert Hoover.

In December Chairman Murdock issued a statement emphasizing the main points of the Progressive party program:

> The Progressive Party proposes to bring, first of all, a constructive program for business ills, the proposal of a sane protective tariff policy and a demand for social justice and for straight-out preparedness both on the military side and the industrial and economic sides. The Progressive Party's policy of 1912 for a tariff commission with broad powers has already the endorsement of the whole country and must be enacted into law if the industrial invasion from Europe after the war is to be forestalled.[42]

40 *Ibid.*, II (January, 1916), 3.
41 *Ibid.*, II (October 2, 1915), 2.
42 *Ibid.*, II (December 4, 1915), 3.

On January 11, 1916, the Progressive National Committee, meeting in Chicago, issued a statement, adopted unanimously, condemning the Wilson administration for its failure "to deal adequately with National honor and industrial welfare."

> The Wilson administration has repudiated the faith of our forefathers which made the American flag the sufficient protection of an American citizen around the world. It has suffered American men, women and children to be slaughtered in Mexico and on the high seas, American property to be destroyed and American liberty to travel and trade to be subject to the arbitrary and lawless coercion of foreign belligerents. . . . We need a reawakening of our elder Americanism, of our belief in those things that our country and our flag stands for.

At their national convention in 1916 the Progressive party, which had had only a few sentences on foreign policy in its 1912 platform, devoted almost its entire platform to preparedness, Americanism, and the excoriation of the Wilson program on Mexico and the European war. The Progressives demanded a regular army of 250,000 men, compulsory universal military training, and "a navy restored to at least second rank in battle efficiency." When Roosevelt refused the nomination, the party turned to Charles E. Hughes, who Roosevelt told them stood for "clean-cut, straightout Americanism," and the party decided to support him, because only he could "serve the two vital causes of Americanism and Preparedness." [43]

For many it was a hard choice. The Republican platform of 1916, as the *New Republic* observed, was a "stupidly, defiantly and cynically reactionary document." "The Republican party of 1916 does not differ in any essential respect from that portion of the party which nominated Mr. Taft. . . . They have revised none of their professed principles; they have dismissed none of their objectionable leaders; they have not by a single act or declaration betrayed a leaning towards liberalism, such as would make an honest Progressive welcome reunion." [44] When Raymond Robins of Illinois, chairman of the national convention, heard Roosevelt tell him that "Mr. Hughes would answer the preparedness, Americanism and progressive demands of our party," Robins dissented. On June 26, at a meeting of the Progressive National Committee,

[43] Progressive Party, National Committee, *The Progressive Party; Its Record From January to July, 1916* (New York, n. d.), 6 ff.

[44] *New Republic*, VII (June 17, 1916), 160.

Robins announced: "At this hour, if I had to vote or declare my sentiments, I should declare for Woodrow Wilson and vote for him."

Robins sounded out the other Progressive leaders. Hiram W. Johnson, Gifford Pinchot, and James R. Garfield all told him that the only hope was to go back to the Republican party and support Hughes, Pinchot explaining it was necessary because of "this national crisis." Soon Robins was announcing his support of Hughes, in part because "we must develop a national mind that will comprehend our social, industrial and military unpreparedness. It must appreciate the domestic injury and national danger that lies in our lack of a definite foreign policy." He further asserted his warm support of compulsory military training, the Oriental Exclusion acts, and "our obligations under the Monroe Doctrine."[45]

In the campaign of 1916 the Progressive party frankly announced its abandonment of its earlier political ideals. On June 26, 1916, the National Committee, after listing recent important gains in progressive legislation, which it termed "national advance," observed that the war had brought

> an issue deeper than national advance, the issue of national unity and the nation's existence, of Americanism and of Preparedness. The Progressive Platform of 1916, therefore, placed foremost as our immediate need preparedness in arms, industry and spirit. . . . The Progressive National Committee recognizes that such are now the issues that immediately confront the country and *looks only to the duty that arises therefrom.*[46]

The Republican and Progressive platforms of 1916 were almost identical, except that Lodge could not get the Republicans to accept the provision for universal service.[47] Partly out of political desperation, partly out of loyalty to Roosevelt, in large part because of their views on foreign affairs, the mass of the Progressives supported Hughes, although the Republicans made no pretense of progressivism and Wilson had enacted much of the Progressive platform. The 1916 campaign was the last presidential election the Progressive party entered; imperialism and militarism had replaced the old liberal formulas of protest, and within a year the party was dead.

[45] Progressive Party, National Committee, *Progressive Party; Its Record From January to July, 1916*, pp. 102 ff.

[46] *Ibid.*, 112 ff.

[47] Mowry, *Theodore Roosevelt and the Progressive Movement*, 348.

How does one account for the wide divergence between Progressive principle and practice, between a concern for democratic processes at home and a disregard of them abroad, for antagonism to financial empires in America and encouragement of them overseas, for the destruction of American progressivism in the interest of imperialism, militarism, and Americanism?

In the first place, many Progressives were able to convince themselves that there was no conflict at all, that their domestic and foreign policies were two sides of the same coin. The Spanish-American War was not merely a struggle to bring freedom to Cuba and end Spanish tyranny but a crusade for principle against the greed of Wall Street interests opposed to the war. "Cuba is free and she thanks President Roosevelt for her freedom," wrote Jacob Riis. "But for his insistence that the nation's honor was bound up in the completion of the work his Rough-Riders began at Las Guasimas and on San Juan Hill, a cold conspiracy of business greed would have left her in the lurch, to fall by and by reluctantly into our arms, bankrupt and helpless, while the sneer of the cynics that we were plucking that plum for ourselves would have been justified." [48] "We will have this war for the freedom of Cuba in spite of the timidity of the commercial interests," Roosevelt told a Gridiron dinner.[49] We must save the "wretched Cubans" from Spain, Roosevelt averred, and then noted, "It would be a splendid thing for the Navy, too." [50]

Compulsory military training was likewise a phase of progressivism. "The proposed continental army is utterly undemocratic; it denies to the patriotic man of small means the chance to train which it gives to his well-to-do brother," Roosevelt asserted.[51] Compulsory universal military training, agreed Raymond Robins, "will do more in one generation to break down class and section prejudice, develop disciplined, vigorous and efficient citizenship, and to unify the diverse groups of our national life in a vital Americanism than all other forces combined." As opposed to this Progressive program, Robins added, the Democrats, in opposing universal training, offer only "a state-dominated militia with its

[48] Riis, *Theodore Roosevelt, The Citizen*, 383.

[49] Arthur W. Dunn, *Gridiron Nights* (New York, 1915), 70 ff.

[50] Theodore Roosevelt to Henry C. Lodge, August 3, 1897, Henry C. Lodge (ed.), *Selections from the Correspondence of Theodore Roosevelt and Henry Cabot Lodge, 1884-1918*, 2 vols. (New York, 1925), I, 268.

[51] *Progressive Opinion*, II (December 4, 1915), 6.

menace of shiftless incompetence, spoils politics and organized snobbery as a national defense force, at a time of world peril." [52]

Secondly, it is impossible to understand the acquiescence of many Progressives in the imperialist movement without realizing the remarkable hold that Theodore Roosevelt had on his followers. Norris' testimony that "often those years I followed him when I had some doubts as to the righteousness of his course" is not an isolated instance. To many American liberals "Roosevelt was . . . [by 1912] something more than a revered political leader. He was gradually becoming a minor deity." [53] Years later, William Allen White described his first meeting with Roosevelt:

> I met Theodore Roosevelt. He sounded in my heart the first trumpet call of the new time that was to be. . . . I had never known such a man as he, and never shall again. He overcame me. And in the hour or two we spent that day at lunch, and in a walk down F Street, he poured into my heart such visions, such ideals, such hopes, such a new attitude toward life and patriotism and the meaning of things, as I had never dreamed men had.[54]

Even after Roosevelt had deserted the Progressives and helped disrupt the movement, even after he had had the obtuseness to suggest Lodge as the standardbearer, Harold Ickes could see only George Perkins as the Iago of the movement and had no harsh words for Roosevelt.[55]

Thirdly, the attitude of the Progressives toward the American Negro made them more receptive to American imperialism. They readily accepted the notion that the little brown brother was a ward of the United States, not fit for self-government, because they regarded the southern Negro as a ward when they did not think of him as a corrupt politician attempting to sell his vote to the highest bidder at Republican conventions. The Progressive party plan with respect to the Negro, wrote Roosevelt, was "to try for the gradual re-enfranchisement of the worthy colored man of the South by frankly giving the leadership of our movement to the wisest and justest white men of the South." [56] Despite the fact that the Negro

[52] Progressive Party, National Committee, *Progressive Party; Its Record From January to July, 1916*, pp. 121 ff.

[53] Mowry, *Theodore Roosevelt and the Progressive Movement*, 243.

[54] *Autobiography of William Allen White*, 297.

[55] Harold L. Ickes, "Who Killed the Progressive Party?" *American Historical Review* (New York), XLVI (January, 1941), 306-37.

[56] Theodore Roosevelt, "The Progressives and the Colored Man," *Outlook*, CI (August 24, 1912), 911.

vote in Maryland was credited with giving Roosevelt his margin of victory over Taft in the 1912 primaries, he persisted in his aim to make the Progressive party a lily white party in the South, with Senator Dixon, his national campaign manager, publicly disavowing a Progressive organization in South Carolina because of its Negro membership and the convention refusing to seat any southern Negro delegates, despite the dissent of Jane Addams.[57] W. A. D. Venerable, head of the Colored Men's National Progressive Association, denounced the Progressive party for holding the Negro unfit for suffrage in the South, and, immediately after the convention, his organization announced for Wilson in the 1912 elections.[58]

Nor was this policy limited to the Progressive party. At the American Socialist Congress in 1910, over a third of the delegates, led by Victor Berger, favored legislation against Asiatic immigration. Ernest Untermann, the Socialist candidate for governor of Idaho, asserted: "The question as to what race shall dominate the globe must be met as surely as the question of what class shall own the world. We should neglect our duty to the coming generation of Aryan peoples if we did not do everything in our power, even today, to insure the final race victory of our own people." Both Robert Hunter of the National Executive Committee of the Socialist party and Adolph Germer of the Miners' Union attacked foreign and Negro labor as hostile to unionism, and Untermann stated, " '*we should be false to our Socialist agitation if we insisted first on doing away with the race prejudice*'."[59]

Hostility toward and contempt for Oriental labor, in particular, was an avowed part of the Progressive campaign of 1912, a legacy of its trade union support and the sectional attitudes of the west coast which made an unsympathetic attitude toward Oriental nations a concomitant part of the outlook of many Progressives. The *Progressive Bulletin*, the official organ of the party, attacked Wilson in 1912 because he "prefers Chinese immigrants to white," and inquired whether "the Chinese are more desirable immigrants

[57] "Official Minutes of the (Provisional) Progressive National Committee," Theodore Roosevelt Collection (Widener Library, Harvard University, Cambridge); George E. Mowry, "The South and the Progressive Lily White Party of 1912," *Journal of Southern History* (Baton Rouge, Lexington), VI (May, 1940), 237-47.

[58] Chicago *Record-Herald*, August 6, 1912, p. 1; August 9, 1912, p. 2. See also the attack on the action of the convention in "No Square Deal," *Independent* (New York), LXXIII (August 15, 1912), 391-93.

[59] William E. Walling, *Progressivism—And After* (New York, 1914), 377-81.

than the white people who dig our ground?" The first two points listed on Roosevelt's "labor record" in the 1912 campaign were "renewing the Chinese Exclusion Act and extending its provisions to the island territory of the United States," and "prohibiting the employment of Mongolian labor on irrigation works." [60] Nor did the Progressives always view southern European labor with favor. "These hearty 'hunkies' and 'dagoes' feel that they are working to make America rich and that their services should be appreciated, but are they?" asked the leading Progressive magazine on the west coast. "Are they not rather displacing the American of forty-five to fifty, when otherwise, he would work on until sixty without showing the white feather?" [61]

Most important, imperialism and progressivism flourished together because they were both expressions of the same philosophy of government, a tendency to judge any action not by the means employed but by the results achieved, a worship of definitive action for action's sake, as John Dewey has pointed out,[62] and an almost religious faith in the democratic mission of America. The results of the Spanish-American War were heartily approved not merely because the war freed subject peoples from tyranny, but because, since the United States was the land of free institutions, any extension of its domain was *per se* an extension of freedom and democracy. It was an age that admired results, that was not too concerned with fine distinctions and nice theories. The Progressives, quite apart from sharing in the general excitement of middle-class America in the rise of the United States as a world power and the sense of identity with the nation which imperialism afforded in a time of national stress, admired anyone who could clean up the slaughterhouses or link two great oceans, who could get a job done without months of tedious debate and deference to legal precedents.

The Progressives believed in the Hamiltonian concept of positive government, of a national government directing the destinies of the nation at home and abroad. They had little but contempt for

[60] *Progressive Bulletin* (New York), I (September 16, 1912), 5. At the same time, however, the *Bulletin* attacked the nativism of the Republican party.

[61] *California Outlook* (Los Angeles and San Francisco), XII (February 10, 1912), 5. William Allen White recalled that "of course, I read the popular pseudo-sciences of the day, such as 'Anglo-Saxon Superiority,' by Edmond Demolins." *Autobiography of William Allen White*, 326.

[62] John Dewey, *Characters and Events*, 2 vols. (New York, 1929), I, 91.

the strict construction of the Constitution by conservative judges, who would restrict the power of the national government to act against social evils and to extend the blessings of democracy to less favored lands. The real enemy was particularism, state rights, limited government, which would mean the reign of plutocracy at home and a narrow, isolationist concept of national destiny abroad, which would deny the democratic mission of America and leave the brown peoples pawns of dynastic wars and colonial exploitation.

No writer better demonstrates the close link between progressivism and imperialism, with the concept of the Hamiltonian state and the democratic mission, than Herbert Croly, whose *The Promise of American Life* (1909) influenced the Progressive movement more profoundly than any other work. Roosevelt was more deeply moved by Croly's book than by anything he had read since the early Alfred T. Mahan. A few months after his return from Africa, Roosevelt was preaching the "New Nationalism" of Croly in his Osawatomie address and the war against the Old Guard was on in earnest.

"The American nation, just in so far as it believes in its nationality and is ready to become more of a nation, must assume a more definite and a more responsible place in the international system," wrote Croly. ". . . In spite of 'old-fashioned democratic' scruples and prejudices, the will to play that part for all it was worth would constitute a beneficial and a necessary stimulus to the better realization of the Promise of our domestic life."[63] We should shun the Jefferson administration's policy of basing "its international policy not upon the firm ground of national interest, but on the treacherous sands of international democratic propagandism."[64]

The first task of a truly national foreign policy was to develop hemispheric solidarity, and Croly left no doubt of what he meant by "a stable American international system."

> In all probability no American international system will ever be established without the forcible pacification of one or more centers of disorder. . . . In short, any international American political system might have to undertake a task in states like Venezuela, similar to that which the United States is now performing in Cuba. . . . The United States has already made an effective beginning in this great work, both by the pacification of Cuba

[63] Herbert Croly, *The Promise of American Life* (New York, 1909), 289.
[64] *Ibid.*, 290.

and by the attempt to introduce a little order into the affairs of the turbulent Central American republics.[65]

Our work was greatly simplified by the fact that the political condition of Mexico, under the dictatorship of Diaz, had "become more stable and more wholesome," and "any recrudescence of revolutionary upheavals in Mexico would enormously increase the difficulties and perils of the attempt." [66]

The Spanish-American War was a great boon to the American people for it ushered in the Progressive era.

> Not until the end of the Spanish War was a condition of public feeling created, which made it possible to revive Hamiltonianism. That war and its resulting policy of extra-territorial expansion, so far from hindering the process of domestic amelioration, availed, from the sheer force of the national aspirations it aroused, to give a tremendous impulse to the work of national reform . . . and it indirectly helped to place in the Presidential chair the man who, as I have said, represented both the national idea and the spirit of reform. The sincere and intelligent combination of those two ideas is bound to issue in the Hamiltonian practice of constructive national legislation.[67]

Bryan's campaign of 1900, on the other hand, Croly continued, was composed of two disastrous mistakes. "In seeking to prevent his countrymen from asserting their national interest beyond their own continent, he was also opposing in effect the resolute assertion of the national interest in domestic affairs. He stamped himself, that is, as an anti-nationalist, and his anti-nationalism has disqualified him for effective leadership of the party of reform." [68]

Far from being isolated movements, our international mission and our domestic reform program were interlocking forces, and frequently one and the same thing, Croly concluded, for "it is entirely possible that hereafter the United States will be forced into the adoption of a really national domestic policy because of the dangers and duties incurred through her relations with foreign countries." [69]

As Felix Frankfurter observed, "Unlike almost all American prewar writers on politics (with the notable exception of Captain

[65] *Ibid.*, 302-303.
[66] *Ibid.*, 301, 303.
[67] *Ibid.*, 169.
[68] *Ibid.*, 157.
[69] *Ibid.*, 310.

Mahan, because of his special interest in navalism) Croly saw the American situation with its international implications." [70] He did more than that. He provided an intelligible rationale for the union of progressivism and imperialism, ordering the apparently unrelated events of the Roosevelt administration into a coherent political system and contending that imperial ventures were an important phase of the new religion of national reform, steps toward the fulfillment of the promise of American life.

The attitude of the Progressives toward imperialism explains much about the basic character of the Progressive movement. Despite the evangelical aura about the 1912 convention, the movement was not an attempt to remold the world anew, to discard the old system for a new society. The Progressives were completely a part of American life, accepting the traditional values and ideals, cherishing the aspirations of middle-class America, including the new sense of delight in the rise of the United States as a world power. Although a few leaders like Jane Addams saw the movement as an aspect of a broad humanitarian philosophy, the most influential spokesmen thought not in terms of universals but of providing remedies for certain specific political abuses and economic ills. Insofar as they thought in more general terms, they were concerned less with the rights of *all* men, with universal brotherhood, than with the promise of *American* life. They were interested not only in a more equitable division of the pie but in a larger pie to divide, and consequently saw nothing incongruous in supporting American investments abroad in the interest of expanded markets while condemning the same businesses at home for excessive profits and substandard wages. The same group of men who could tear the Republican party asunder because of a discriminatory tariff in 1909 could outdo the Old Guard in arguing for protectionism in 1916 when they feared foreign goods would undercut the home market.

In the final analysis the Progressive movement suffered from a contradiction between humanistic values and nationalist aspirations, which, if not inherent, had certainly beset other democracies from the time of the wars of the French Revolution. In arguing for a positive national government, the followers of Croly ulti-

[70] Felix Frankfurter, "Herbert Croly and American Political Opinion," *New Republic*, LXIII (July 16, 1930), 248.

mately lost sight of the distinction between the state as an instrument and the state as an end. The consequences were not only the endorsement of an imperialistic foreign policy but the death of the Progressive party in the interest of their nationalist zeal.

Notes and Documents

Ignatius Donnelly, James J. Hill, and Cleveland Administration Patronage

By Horace Samuel Merrill

The election of Grover Cleveland to the presidency in 1884 evoked an uncommon scramble for patronage, for the long-suffering Democratic party had finally defeated the long-serving Republican party. During the postelection weeks and months, the policy Cleveland employed in distributing the patronage largely determined the nature of the ruling power in the government. He could make choices from among civil service reformers, political bosses, free traders, antimonopolists, and business tycoons, all of whom expected recognition for themselves or their interests.

As it turned out, public interest was inadequately served. There was no abrupt break with past deficiencies as excessive political expediency and conservatism blighted any hope for substantial reform. Cleveland struck down both civil service crusaders and pleaders for economic reform. Some hesitant gestures were made to appease the civil service element which had given him valuable support in the election, but there was very little recognition that the merit principle in public office should be extended to include meritorious non-Democrats.[1] More important, although less publicized, was Cleveland's political decapitation, by use of the patronage, of those Democrats who were not in good standing with

[1] The policy followed for ridding the postal service of Republican fourth-class postmasters was to remove them for partisan activity. In a "confidential circular" to several Democratic congressmen, Postmaster General William F. Vilas stated: "I will require no more proof" of partisanship than the "affirmation of knowledge on the part of a Representative or Senator that the Postmaster has been an active" partisan. William F. Vilas to Henry B. Payne, April 28, 1885, Vilas to Thomas W. Cobb, April 29, 1885, Vilas to Benton J. Hall, May 6, 1885, Vilas to James B. Weaver, May 6, 1885, Vilas to J. H. Murphy, May 6, 1885, and to others between April 28 and May 6, 1885, Postmaster General Letterbooks (National Archives, Washington).

wealthy party supporters or local and state bosses. Politicians who had worked for Cleveland in the campaign, but who were champions of unhappy wage earners or distraught antimonopolist farmers, found no positions awaiting them in the new administration. Shortly after the 1884 election one antimonopolist who suspected such discrimination wrote to Minnesota's Ignatius Donnelly: "Cleveland is elected, . . . yet I do not look for much relief for the masses, for the same monopolies that run the Republican party run the Democratic party." [2]

Cooperation with political "bossism" and economic monopoly were nationwide in scope, but the most striking illustration appeared in Minnesota. In that state Donnelly, James J. Hill, Patrick H. Kelly, and Michael Doran provided a show that revealed more than mere bickering over patronage. Through them the nature of the Democratic party in the Cleveland era was made clear. The patronage contest in Minnesota was between intrepid antimonopolist Donnelly, on the one hand, and a "triumvirate" consisting of party bosses Kelly and Doran and railroad magnate Hill. Donnelly sought the minor federal job of surveyor general for Minnesota and control of some of the federal patronage in the state; the triumvirate wished to exclude Donnelly from any power whatsoever in the Democratic party. In the bitter, protracted contest which followed, Donnelly entertained the public with colorful outbursts of invective, Kelly and Doran openly and unabashedly employed boss tactics, and Hill attempted to leave the impression that he was in no way involved in the sordid game, while actually exerting the full force of his tremendous influence.

This contest was the culmination of a long series of clashes between ambitious, colorful Donnelly and the politically and financially entrenched Democratic leaders of Minnesota. In this particular engagement Donnelly based his claim to Democratic recognition upon his services to the party, especially in the 1884 campaign. He soft-pedaled his role prior to 1884, because he could not claim to have been a consistent Democratic supporter. During the Civil War he was elected to Congress as a Republican, but in 1868, because of a party split in his district, he failed to be reelected. In 1870 he bid unsuccessfully for return to Congress, this

[2] J. E. Fullerton to Ignatius Donnelly, November 27, 1884, Ignatius Donnelly Papers (Library of the State Historical Society of Minnesota, St. Paul).

time as an independent with Democratic party endorsement. Soon thereafter he became a Granger spokesman, with a substantial following among farm voters. As a Granger, however, Donnelly maintained a vague and tenuous alliance with the Democracy, the two using each other whenever it appeared that their united efforts might unseat the Republicans.[3]

In 1884 the Donnelly-Democratic union appeared to be closer than usual, or so Donnelly seems to have believed. That year Donnelly sought election to Congress, with the endorsement of both the Democratic district convention and a "Peoples" convention representing antimonopolist farmers. He also received token financial aid from the state Democratic organization. In the campaign Donnelly lambasted the railroad and flour mill monopolists of Minnesota and the high tariff monopolists everywhere.[4] In the voting Donnelly and the entire Democratic ticket in traditionally Republican Minnesota went down to defeat. Yet Donnelly himself ran far ahead of the ticket and almost defeated Congressman Horace B. Strait. In the previous election Strait had won by a majority of 8,850; in the 1884 contest his margin was reduced to a mere 850 votes.[5] So spectacular a performance would seem to make Donnelly the leading Democrat of Minnesota. A few days after the election Donnelly received a letter from his wife stating that "Cleveland will be obliged to give you patronage."[6] Donnelly felt the same way.

The Kelly-Doran-Hill triumvirate also expected to receive substantial reward for services rendered the national Democratic party. Its claim rested primarily upon its help in preventing radical capture of the national party organization. Ever since 1868, when New York's conservative Samuel J. Tilden, August Belmont, and Horatio Seymour had captured the national Democratic nominating convention, Empire State conservatives had controlled the national party. Their dominant position depended to a large degree on satellite state machines in the hinterland. Obviously there was

[3] William W. Folwell, *A History of Minnesota*, 4 vols. (St. Paul, 1921-1930), III, 16, 49, 118; *H. P. Hall's Observations; Being More or Less a History of Political Contests in Minnesota from 1849 to 1904* (St. Paul, 1904), 143-52, 229-30; John D. Hicks, "The Political Career of Ignatius Donnelly," *Mississippi Valley Historical Review* (Cedar Rapids), VIII (June-September, 1921), 80-106.

[4] St. Paul *Pioneer Press*, November 3, 1884.

[5] *Ibid.*, April 19, 1885.

[6] Mrs. Katherine Donnelly to Donnelly, November 8, 1884, Donnelly Papers.

little likelihood of conservative Democratic victories at the polls in the normally Republican Middle West, but that was of relative unimportance. The chief consideration was to insure conservative control of Democratic national nominating conventions and the national party committee. It would be folly to allow Grangers, Greenbackers, or laborites to be delegates and committeemen. Their votes would be dangerous.

The Minnesota triumvirate carried out its assignment of helping to insulate the national party from the prairie winds of radicalism. Moreover, it contributed financially to the cause. The 1884 national campaign committee informed Cleveland that Kelly and Hill had each contributed $5,000.[7] Hill, in addition, after consulting with corporate attorney Tilden, instructed his railroad officials in Minnesota and other states to work for Cleveland's election.[8]

Within Minnesota the state Democracy functioned as if it were the national Democracy in miniature. Kelly, Doran, and Hill enjoyed the game of politics and the economic advantages that came with it. The triumvirate had acquired its influence in Minnesota politics by using boss tactics and money, rather than by bidding for popular support in the state as a whole. Kelly, Doran, and Hill knew that as conservative businessmen they had nothing to offer the predominantly agrarian Minnesota voters that would draw the farmers away from their habitual Republicanism. Chance might bring a Democratic victory, but the triumvirate looked upon that as incidental to their more personally gainful role of protecting business interests from the antimonopolist politicians.

In carrying out this policy of minority rule, the triumvirate relied heavily on control of the St. Paul Democratic organization. The skeleton Democratic organizations out in the state were merely adjuncts of the large, disciplined, and financially superior St. Paul party core. Triumvirate overlordship of the St. Paul, and hence the state, Democracy rested on several pillars of strength. The St. Paul Democracy was predominantly Irish-American; Kelly and Doran were Irish-born citizens of St. Paul. Hill employed many

7 "Contributions to the Campaign Fund of the National Democratic Committee, 1884," February 5, 1885, Grover Cleveland Papers (Manuscripts Division, Library of Congress).

8 Joseph G. Pyle, *The Life of James J. Hill*, 2 vols. (Garden City, 1917), I, 426; Matthew Josephson, *The Politicos, 1865-1896* (New York, 1938), 362.

Irish-Americans on his railroad. The triumvirate also had money for party contributions. Doran was a successful commission merchant and banker. Kelly was a successful wholesale groceryman.[9] Hill, of course, possessed even greater wealth. Kelly and Doran, moreover, were energetic and skillful political managers. Doran had served for several terms in the upper branch of the state legislature, where he stood out as an able leader. The Republican Minneapolis *Tribune* reported, January 4, 1885, that Doran "was decidedly the leader of his party in the last senate."[10] He was also chairman of the Democratic state central committee. Kelly was even more prominent in the party. He had never held a public office, but he had risen to membership on the national party committee. A few weeks after the 1884 election, the Republican St. Paul *Pioneer Press* informed the state Democracy that it should be grateful to Kelly, for he had paid the party bills, more than once checked its "blundering imbecility," and "powerfully helped to maintain" its organization.[11]

The Minnesota triumvirate was indeed formidable. Nevertheless, it had an Achilles heel. It was not prepared for the 1884 national victory at the polls. With that victory came the obligation to fulfill promises — both implicit and actual. The conservatives had made an implied promise to their rural constituents, which in the event of the usual Democratic defeat would not require fulfillment. They had permitted rural voters and leaders to believe that a Democratic victory would be an antimonopoly victory. That was a convenient way to retain the loyalty of the rural Democratic party leaders and even pick up a few farmer votes. In the 1884 election, however, the Democrats experienced both a victory and a significant near-victory. Cleveland had triumphed, and hence there were federal jobs to be passed around. Donnelly had almost captured a seat in Congress, and hence he was in the forefront of claimants for patronage. To deny Donnelly a place would be an obvious repudiation of a political obligation. To reward Donnelly fairly would endanger conservative control of the Democratic party.

When the 1884 election outcome became apparent, the victors

9 Warren Upham and Rose B. Dunlap (comps.), *Minnesota Biographies, Minnesota Historical Collections* (St. Paul), XIV (1912), 183, 395.

10 Minneapolis *Tribune*, January 4, 1885.

11 St. Paul *Pioneer Press*, December 15, 1884.

began to spar for patronage. Kelly thought it would be a fine thing for Donnelly to get an appointment that would take him far from Minnesota. The night after the election, Kelly remarked to Donnelly, "pick out any foreign mission you please and you shall have it." [12] But Donnelly had other ideas. He did not want a foreign post, and he did not want his reward to come through Kelly. Donnelly's inordinate ambition led him to believe that he could get a satisfactory appointment without Kelly's help and that he could also obtain places for other Minnesotans. The position he sought for himself was the surveyor generalship for Minnesota. The salary was only $2,000, but the job held additional possibilities. Successful entrepreneur and politician William D. Washburn had once held the position. Donnelly may have believed that was one of the ways to acquire knowledge on how to become wealthy. Perhaps Donnelly, whose own real estate ventures had ended in failure with the advent of the panic of 1857, was anxious to reacquaint himself with land speculation opportunities. There were also patronage opportunities in the surveyor generalship, for there would be subordinates to appoint.

Donnelly's first move was an attempt to attract the attention of Cleveland. He wrote to the President-elect on November 17, suggesting that in the inaugural address "you dwell with especial force . . . upon the necessity for a law to prevent the importation of foreign workmen under labor contracts." Donnelly explained that there were "white cooleys" working for sixty cents per day in Hocking Valley, Ohio. He believed that a statement on this subject from the President would "demonstrate that you are upon the side of working people and [it would] greatly strengthen the Democracy with the vast labor force of the country." [13] He did not mention his other favorite issues, the tariff or the railroads. Donnelly approached Cleveland with caution.

In his bid for administration favor, Donnelly cultivated his already friendly relations with Wisconsin's William F. Vilas, who was high on the list of Cleveland favorites. It was rumored that Vilas would be chosen as the western representative in Cleveland's cabinet, either as secretary of the interior or as postmaster general. Vilas had never held an important public office, but he was the

[12] *Ibid.*, April 26, 1885.

[13] Donnelly to Grover Cleveland, November 17, 1884, Cleveland Papers.

leader of the Wisconsin Democracy. More significant, for years he had been in close alliance with the powerful New York conservative group that had elevated Cleveland to national prominence.[14] A Vilas bandwagon had developed, and Donnelly wished to be among the first to jump aboard.

Donnelly and Vilas were not well acquainted, but they knew each other as low tariff advocates and as effective orators. They had managed during the election to cooperate and to overlook, for the time being, the fact that Donnelly was an enemy of railroad monopoly and Vilas was a practicing railroad attorney. They had exchanged friendly politenesses. Donnelly received word from a St. Paul friend: "I went to Hudson [Wisconsin] Monday to hear Vilas. . . . He says you made for *us* in 1872 by speech [*sic*] 300 votes at Madison by 'actual count.' He thinks you the most effective speaker on the hustings he ever heard. He is a judge." [15] In the same week, Vilas wired to Donnelly requesting that he address an election eve Democratic rally in Madison.[16] Donnelly was unable to go, but after the election he offered his help in obtaining for Vilas the cabinet position.[17] Vilas expressed his thanks, and his regrets that Donnelly had met with defeat at the polls, adding that he had hoped that among the Minnesota Democratic candidates, Donnelly, "at least, would have been elected." [18]

Donnelly's aid to Vilas was in the form of a letter to Cleveland, signed by him and the other defeated Democratic congressional candidates of the state. The petitioners praised Vilas and urged his appointment to the cabinet.[19] Vilas, in turn, showed his appreciation by writing a very friendly letter to Donnelly reporting on a mid-December conversation between Cleveland and himself. The new President, wrote Vilas, "will be a fair exponent of the general views expressed [by Donnelly] in that most capital speech at the St. Paul jollification." That particular address, celebrating the

14 Vilas' role in the Democracy was later well summarized in the Chicago *Chronicle*, July 8, 1895.

15 John B. Brisbin to Donnelly, October 22, 1884, Donnelly Papers.

16 Vilas to Donnelly (telegram), October 22, 1884, *ibid.*

17 Donnelly to Vilas, November 19, 1884, William F. Vilas Papers (Library of the State Historical Society of Wisconsin, Madison).

18 Vilas to Donnelly, November 22, 1884, Donnelly Papers.

19 Donnelly and Minnesota Democratic nominees for Congress to Cleveland, November 27, 1884, Cleveland Papers, copies in Vilas Papers and Donnelly Papers.

Cleveland victory, Vilas added, was "sound . . . manly, . . . wise, eloquent, witty, skillful."[20]

Soon thereafter Vilas became more cautious in his relationship with Donnelly, for the Wisconsin leader discovered that close identity with Donnelly could be a political liability. The powerful anti-Donnelly triumvirate had selected Vilas as its candidate for Cleveland's cabinet.[21] Early in January, 1885, Vilas was a guest in Kelly's home. The two men held friendly conversations with leading St. Paul and Minneapolis citizens. Donnelly was not included.[22] In February Kelly went to New York, where he did what he could to advance Vilas' candidacy.[23]

When the Cleveland administration, including Vilas as postmaster general, assumed office, Donnelly was on hand in Washington to collect his reward. He also planned to build up his fences with a few postmasterships for some of his Minnesota friends. In anticipation, these friends had even helped finance Donnelly's trip to the national capital.[24] If Donnelly had any doubts about the success of his mission, he did not express them in his letters to his Minnesota followers. From Washington he informed one would-be Minnesota postmaster, "my relations to Mr. Vilas are such that there will be, I think, no doubt of your appointment." Donnelly stated that his own affair would be terminated in a few days, but that he would remain in Washington until he had his friend's case acted upon. Perhaps the recipient of that letter was pleased; perhaps he would have been more pleased had the letter not included a request for fifty dollars to help defray Donnelly's extended stay in Washington.[25] Mrs. Donnelly's letters to her husband reflected somewhat less optimism. When she learned that her husband had been entertained in Vilas' home, she tersely wrote that she hoped he had worn his "dress suit for dinner" when a guest of the "elegant Vilas."[26] She wrote with some bitterness that "it looks to me as if

20 Vilas to Donnelly, December 13, 1884, Donnelly Papers.

21 Patrick H. Kelly to Vilas, December 30, 1884, Vilas Papers.

22 Vilas' diary, items dated January 30, February 2, 1885, *ibid.*; Minneapolis *Tribune*, February 1, 1885; Madison (Wis.) *Democrat*, February 3, 1885.

23 Alexander Barclay (Kelly's secretary) to Vilas, February 20, 24, 1885, Vilas Papers.

24 Donnelly to G. E. McAllister, March 16, 1885, William P. Christensen to Donnelly, March 23, 1885, P. H. Rahilly to Donnelly, May 8, 1885, Donnelly Papers; St. Paul *Pioneer Press*, May 17, 1885.

25 Donnelly to McAllister, March 16, 1885, Donnelly Papers.

26 Mrs. Donnelly to Donnelly, March 14, 1885, *ibid.*

there is always to be a railroad or millers ring in some shape standing in the way and choking you off." [27]

There were influences in Washington that were indeed choking off Donnelly's progress. The triumvirate was not idle. Friends of Donnelly believed that Hill went to great lengths to defeat the Minnesota antimonopolist, even bringing "influences from New York to bear on the President." [28] Kelly was in Washington, where he was in close touch with Vilas.[29] The triumvirate even received unsolicited aid from influential Democratic Congressman Samuel J. Randall of Pennsylvania. Protectionist Randall did not approve of Donnelly's tariff views.[30] As a result of these factors, Donnelly left Washington empty-handed. Kelly, however, as he boarded the train in Washington, happily told reporters, "I got all I wanted." [31]

Donnelly, swallowing his pride, then asked Kelly to aid him in obtaining the surveyor generalship. Kelly replied, April 2, 1885:

> I regret I cannot comply with your request for a letter to [Secretary of Interior Lucius Q. C.] Lamar.
>
> Having consulted with the leading Democrats of our state, I find that your appointment as Surveyor General, would bring about more disaffection and trouble than I care to encounter.
>
> For the sake of peace and quiet in our party here, I trust you may be induced to withdraw your application for the position.
>
> I will be glad to assist you in obtaining a mission abroad should you desire it.[32]

The incensed Donnelly underlined with red pencil the final sentence of the letter and wrote at the bottom: "How can a man be worthy of a mission abroad and not worthy of a little place at home?" Then he sent the letter on to President Cleveland.[33]

After refusing to accede to Donnelly's request, Kelly blandly informed the public that he and Doran had complete command of federal patronage in Minnesota. On April 15, shortly after his triumphant return from Washington, he and Doran reported on the patronage situation to a gathering of the state Democratic committee and other party leaders. This group passed, unanimously, a

27 Mrs. Donnelly to Donnelly, March 11, 1885, *ibid.*
28 Rahilly to Donnelly, May 29, 1886, *ibid.*
29 St. Paul *Pioneer Press*, March 8, 1885.
30 *Ibid.*, March 18, 1885; Minneapolis *Tribune*, March 23, 1885.
31 St. Paul *Pioneer Press*, March 11, 1885.
32 Kelly to Donnelly, April 2, 1885, Cleveland Papers.
33 *Ibid.*

resolution by which Kelly and Doran were "authorized to act for the Democrats of Minnesota in endorsing and transmitting to Washington applications for appointments to federal positions." It stated further that applications for local offices must be made to Kelly and Doran, and requested "the presiding heads of the [federal] departments to recognize no other endorsement from this state." [34]

Republican newspapers professed to be shocked at this method of patronage distribution. The St. Paul *Pioneer Press* referred to the new set-up as the "Kelly-Doran office-broking agency." [35] The Minneapolis *Tribune* called Kelly and Doran the "proconsuls for the province of Minnesota." The *Tribune* also thought it "worthy of remark" that it was "the first time in American history in which the state central committee of a great party has formally recognized and sanctioned 'boss' dispensers of federal patronage in their state." [36]

The irate Donnelly reacted to this patronage brokerage by launching a campaign to dislodge Kelly, Doran, and Hill from control of the state Democracy. In an attempt to discredit the triumvirate with the national leadership, Donnelly complained to Vilas,[37] to Cleveland, and to everybody else who would listen. To Cleveland, who did not bother to acknowledge the communications, Donnelly forwarded anti-Kelly and Doran newspaper clippings and letters he had received. He informed Cleveland that "I am so firm in my own honesty and my popularity with the Democrats of the Northwest that I would be glad if you would send some reliable agent to Minnesota to enquire as to the facts." [38] When the Kelly-Doran-Hill trio promoted William M. Campbell for the office of United States marshal for Minnesota, Donnelly wrote to Cleveland that "Campbell is a noted lobbyist working every winter in the interest of the Rail Road Companies in their efforts to corrupt legislation by buying up members of the State Legislature, and thus prevent remedial legislation demanded by the people." [39] The outcome was Cleveland's endorsement of Campbell.[40]

[34] St. Paul *Globe*, April 15, 1885; Minneapolis *Tribune*, April 17, 1885.
[35] St. Paul *Pioneer Press*, April 22, 1885.
[36] Minneapolis *Tribune*, April 17, 1885.
[37] Donnelly to Vilas, April 23, 1885, Donnelly Papers.
[38] Donnelly to Cleveland, May 1, 1885, Cleveland Papers.
[39] Donnelly to Cleveland, November 3, 1885, *ibid.* See also Donnelly to Cleveland, October 21, December 3, 1885, *ibid.*
[40] St. Paul *Pioneer Press*, February 18, 1886.

On the Minnesota front Donnelly concentrated on trying to convince the public that Hill was the real power in the state Democracy, and hence the chief obstacle to Donnelly's advancement and to the furtherance of Donnelly's political-economic program. Donnelly told a reporter that "Michael Doran and Patrick H. Kelly are simply the mouthpieces of Jim Hill. Jim is the *deus ex machina*, the colored gentleman under the woodpile: the new leader of the reformed Democracy of Minnesota. Jim don't approve of my granger legislation in the past, or my granger proclivities in the present, or my granger possibilities in the future." [41]

Proof, however, of Hill's political activities did not reach the public. The St. Paul and Minneapolis papers carefully avoided stating categorically that Hill was, or was not, involved in Democratic politics. They all reported Donnelly's outbursts, but always within quotation marks. The Democratic St. Paul *Globe* dodged the issue. The Republican Minneapolis *Tribune* took for granted that its readers knew of Hill's connection with the Democracy, and then went on to report additional "rumors" regarding its nature. When a St. Paul *Pioneer Press* reporter sought an interview with Hill on the Donnelly issue, the railroad president "sent out word from the inner recesses of his sanctum that he did not care to say anything in relation to the matter." The reporter then called on Doran, who said: "'Mr. Hill isn't in politics.'" [42] One of the few items to reach the papers, aside from Donnelly's charges, that seemed to contradict Doran's statement also appeared in the *Pioneer Press*: "P. H. Kelly, J. J. Hill and Michael Doran were in close confab in the private office of the latter yesterday afternoon." When they emerged from the conference, a reporter tried to interview the trio, "but they looked so 'big with the fate of nations and of men,' his tongue clove to the roof of his mouth." [43]

The *Tribune* noticed that its sister Republican paper, the *Pioneer Press*, wrote almost tenderly about the triumvirate, while heaping abuse upon Donnelly. It connected this lack of impartiality with the rumor being circulated that Hill had purchased a quarter interest in the *Pioneer Press*.[44] Indeed, the *Pioneer Press* did reserve its choice epithets for Donnelly, referring to him as a "pestiferous

[41] *Ibid.*, April 19, 1885.
[42] *Ibid.*, April 21, 1885.
[43] *Ibid.*, August 18, 1885.
[44] Minneapolis *Tribune*, April 20, 21, 1885.

little demagogue," one who "was never known to tell the truth," and as having a "reputation as a writer of entertaining fiction." At the same time that paper reported that it "feels almost" like coming to the defense of Kelly, for "there is a good deal of lying inspired by Donnelly and other jealous aspirants for the position of 'boss.' " It praised Doran, stating that although it was difficult to get a promise of support from him, once he gave his word he would stick to it in the face of any pressure.[45] The *Tribune*, for its part, finally printed a long editorial in which it charged that the *Pioneer Press* was a tool of Bosses Kelly and Doran, "through their silent partner." [46]

Positive evidence that Hill was deeply involved in Democratic politics did exist, but it was not accessible. The Democratic inner circle did not want Grangers and wage earners to know that Hill had contributed financially to the 1884 Democratic campaign and that he had ordered his subordinate railroad officials to work for Cleveland's election. Neither was it revealed that Hill wrote patronage letters to Cleveland's private secretary, Daniel S. Lamont. Hill left routine patronage matters to Kelly and Doran, but occassionally he took a hand.[47] On one occasion, when Kelly and Doran wrote to Cleveland urging the appointment of Campbell to the marshalship position, and William Crooks to the surveyor generalship, a note from Hill was enclosed. Addressed to Kelly and Doran, it stated: "Your secy has just shown me your letter to the President every word of which has my full endorsement and if you desire I will sign the letter with you but bearing in mind the fact that I have already written in behalf of these two gentlemen it might be considered too urgent." [48]

Donnelly, meanwhile, not content with confining his protests to letters to Cleveland and statements to newspaper reporters, carried his fight to the people. On July 1, 1886, in the St. Paul Pfeifer Hotel, Donnelly participated in an antitriumvirate Democratic conference, consisting of 123 party members from all parts of the state. They passed a resolution attacking bossism in the state

[45] St. Paul *Pioneer Press*, November 2, 1884, April 19, May 16, 1885.

[46] Undated clipping from Minneapolis *Tribune*, sent by Donnelly to Cleveland, October 21, 1885, Cleveland Papers.

[47] James J. Hill to Daniel S. Lamont, May 5, 10, August 8, 1888, Daniel S. Lamont Papers (Manuscripts Division, Library of Congress).

[48] Hill to Kelly and Michael Doran, August 1, 1885, enclosed with Kelly and Doran to Cleveland, August 1, 1885, Cleveland Papers.

organization and applauded when Donnelly summarized the issue: "shall the Democratic party of Minnesota be run in the interest of Jim Hill or in the interest of the people?"[49]

Another and more effective medium Donnelly utilized in his campaign was the nonpartisan Farmers' Alliance. This antimonopoly movement was spreading rapidly in the western states, and Minnesota was no exception. Donnelly spoke at many large Alliance meetings.[50] Upon returning from one of these extended speaking tours in 1886, he reported that he had found farmers disposed to cooperate with any political party that would help them fight the railroads. " 'If the Democratic party sends Kelly, Doran, and Jim Hill to back seats,' said Donnelly, 'and takes strong ground against watered stocks and wheat rings, a combined ticket can be made of Democrats, alliance men and workingmen that will sweep the state.' "[51]

As the economic depression of the nineties deepened,[52] it became increasingly apparent that conservatism was losing its hold on the Democratic party, both nationally and in agrarian states like Minnesota. Finally, in 1896, the conservatives were pushed aside on the national stage to make room for William Jennings Bryan as the Democratic presidential candidate. The conservatives had to relinquish their control in Minnesota as the state convention endorsed the free silver crusade. Donnelly at last found a Democratic party with which he could cooperate. His Populist party, the Democratic party, and a Silver Republican rump organization combined forces in a vain effort to defeat the regular Republicans.[53]

It would be a long time, however, before the farmers and laborers could have confidence in the Minnesota Democracy. In 1896, despite the Democracy's endorsement of Bryanism, many free-silver supporters preferred to follow the Populist or Republican banners. The voters saw, and during the ensuing years they continued to see, that conservatism and machine politics continued to be the real core of the Minnesota Democracy. The Democracy

49 St. Paul *Globe*, July 2, 1886.

50 St. Paul *Pioneer Press*, March 19, 1886.

51 St. Paul *Globe*, July 11, 1886.

52 During this period Hill wrote lengthy reports to Cleveland on the economic plight of the West. See Hill to Cleveland, April 4, June 15, July 4, 1893, May 5, 1894, Cleveland Papers.

53 Folwell, *History of Minnesota*, III, 220-21.

might endorse reforms, but experience showed that once in power, conservatism and bossism prevailed. The overwhelming majority of voters continued to have more trust in the Republican organization and in third parties.

Expedition to the Yellowstone River in 1873: Letters of a Young Cavalry Officer

Edited by George Frederick Howe

Surveys to establish the route of the Northern Pacific Railroad between Bismarck and Bozeman were undertaken in 1872 and 1873. This portion of the right of way crossed an area inhabited by hostile Sioux tribes and had to be surveyed under substantial military protection. In 1872 one party started eastward on July 27 from Fort Ellis, near Bozeman, escorted by a force of about 400 cavalry and infantry,[1] while a second group made preliminary surveys westward from Fort Rice, near Bismarck, protected by almost 600 infantry, one 12-pounder, and two Gatling guns.[2] The two parties were expected to meet near the junction of the Yellowstone and Powder rivers. The eastern force arrived there on August 18. After a battle at Pryor's Fork on August 14 against a large number of Sioux, the smaller western party turned back when it had continued only as far as Pompey's Pillar. The group from Fort Rice surveyed the route eastward, somewhat harried by Indians, and reached the station on October 15. In effect, the Indians had seriously hampered the project and become correspondingly emboldened.

A second survey during the summer of 1873 was provided with much greater military protection. Nineteen companies of infantry were assembled at Fort Rice from four different regiments stationed along the line of the upper Missouri. The Seventh Cavalry, which

[1] Under command of Major E. M. Baker, 2nd Cavalry. See Report of Major General Winfield S. Hancock, CG, Department of Dakota, October 3, 1872, *Report of the Secretary of War*, 1872 (Washington, 1872), I, 39-41. The *Report* is in *House Executive Documents*, No. 1, Pt. II, 42 Cong., 3 Sess.

[2] Report of the expedition to the Yellowstone, Colonel David S. Stanley to Assistant Adjutant General, Department of Dakota, St. Paul, Minnesota, October 28, 1872, War Department Records, National Archives, No. 3512 (AGO) 1872. His party consisted of 33 officers, 553 enlisted men, and over 150 armed teamsters, escorting a surveying party of 47. The expedition was threatened by one eloquent Indian who identified himself as Sitting Bull.

had been scattered at southern stations following its earlier service against the Cheyennes, was reassembled to join the expedition to the Yellowstone River. The ten companies moved by railroad to Camp Sturgis near Yankton during the early spring, and thence by stages (Forts Randall, Thompson, and Sully) along the Missouri River to Fort Rice.[3] At successive points along the river the cavalry column met an accompanying steamboat which carried forage, stores, and, among its passengers, the wives of some of the officers. Three other steamboats later supported the combined cavalry-infantry force, beyond Fort Rice.[4]

One of the young officers of the Seventh Cavalry on the expedition of 1873 was Second Lieutenant Charles W. Larned, then three years out of the United States Military Academy and soon destined to return to it as an instructor. As a correspondent of the Chicago *Inter-Ocean*, he published some letters in that paper; a much more numerous series to his mother is now in the possession of a son, Major Paul Larned, United States army, retired. Selections from this correspondence illuminate the military aspects of the expedition of 1873, the life of the young officer, the lot of the officers' wives, and the roles of various men who were destined only three years later to perish in the famous "Last Stand" on the Little Big Horn.[5] Larned's letters reveal considerable literary craftsmanship, as well as an interest in good literature.

[3] A vivacious account of this part of the journey forms part of the recollections of Brigadier General George A. Custer's widow, Elizabeth B. Custer, "*Boots and Saddles*"; *or Life in Dakota with General Custer* (New York, 1885). She rode with the regiment.

[4] One of the engineers in 1873, later chief engineer of the Northern Pacific Railroad, was Thomas L. Rosser, a former Confederate cavalry commander, whose career was somewhat intertwined with that of Custer from the time when both were cadets at West Point, just prior to the outbreak of the Civil War. See Joseph M. Hanson, "Thomas Lafayette Rosser," Allen Johnson, Dumas Malone, and Harris E. Starr (eds.), *Dictionary of American Biography*, 21 vols. and index (New York, 1928-1944), XVI, 181-82.

[5] The story of the Yellowstone expeditions of 1872 and 1873 is available in published accounts of Custer's career: Mrs. Custer, "*Boots and Saddles*"; Frederick Whittaker, *A Complete Life of Gen. George A. Custer* (New York, 1876), 479-500; and Frederick S. Dellenbaugh, *George Armstrong Custer* (New York, 1917), 148-63; in Eugene V. Smalley, *History of the Northern Pacific Railroad* (New York, 1883); and in reports to William T. Sherman, general of the army, from the Military Division of the Missouri, *Report of the Secretary of War*, 1872, I, 39-41; *ibid.*, 1873 (Washington, 1873), I, 40-41. The *Report* for 1873 is in *House Executive Documents*, No. 1, Pt. II, 43 Cong., 1 Sess. A search in the National Archives for Colonel Stanley's official report for 1872 was successful, but for 1873 only supplementary reports on the geography of the area and on army administrative matters were discovered.

Camp at Yankton, Apr 12, 1873

You will not blame me, I am sure, for having allowed a day to slip by since my last without a letter, when I tell you that my desk with my furniture has been boxed all day awaiting our change of camp. I told you that the five companies under [Major Joseph G.] Tilford [6] had arrived while I was writing. The same day I mailed the letter [Lieutenant Colonel George A.] Custer [7] came with the remaining four troops. His arrival was the signal for an entire change of location, so that ever since, the whole command has been hard at work taking down tents and moving bag and baggage to the new site — about half a mile from our temporary location.

We are now regularly encamped — ten companies in all, and the regular routine of military discipline established. My tent is an admirable one and a model of comfort and neatness. Bed on one side, chest at the end, table and desk in the corner, washstand at foot of bed, trunk opposite and a bit of carpet on the ground to complete the picture of luxury. As I write the wind, which, it seems, never ceases here, shakes my habitation to its "foundations", and flares the candle in a highly unsatisfactory manner; but all its efforts to distort my equanimity are fruitless, on the principle that familiarity breeds contempt. The climate is fast making an aboriginal of me, both as regards complexion and health, so that I am not disposed to be captious with its eccentricities however annoying.

More of the ladies than I supposed, from reports at Louisville, are here, huddled together in the slovenly outrage they call a hotel, and bewailing the impossibility of going elsewhere. Mrs. Hart, Benteen, McIntosh, Gibson, Yates, Calhoun, Custer and Godfrey [8] comprise the circle, all, as I told you, brought by pecuniary necessity, except, perhaps, Mrs. Custer and all in the agony of uncertainty as to their next move. The last plan suggested is to storm Fort Rice in a body, take to tents, throw themselves on the charity of the government and the "ins" at that post, and scramble through the summer in the best manner possible. The officers, however, smile grimly at the project and say nothing. Yates is going to send his family to St. Paul, he tells me. The wiser or more fortunate few, as Smith, De Rudio,[9] and myself, congratulate themselves daily on their foresight and good fortune, and watch the commotion complacently. The little hotel! is crammed to suffocation and grows fat and greasy from the substance of its comfortless guests, absorbed at first class rates. The officers, however, who are independent of them and

6 Captain, 3rd Cavalry, 1861; major, 7th Cavalry, 1867; lieutenant colonel, 7th Cavalry, 1883.

7 Custer, after attaining the grade of major general of volunteers on April 15, 1865, was mustered out of the volunteer service, having been brevetted major general for his service in northern Virginia. He became lieutenant colonel, 7th Cavalry, on July 28, 1866, and was much of the time thereafter in actual command of the regiment.

8 These ladies were the wives, respectively, of Captains Verling K. Hart and Frederick W. Benteen, First Lieutenants Donald McIntosh and Francis M. Gibson, Captain George W. Yates, First Lieutenant James Calhoun, Custer, and First Lieutenant Edward S. Godfrey.

9 Second Lieutenant Charles C. De Rudio.

can run their camp messes at the first symptom of extortion, are accommodated with day rates at times as reasonable as the first are reverse. . . .

Camp at Yankton
April 12th, 1873

. . . Today has been rainy and disagreeable. We have settled into camp life and await the first news of our movements with impatience. The ladies are still uncertain and uncomfortable. Those who would go to St. Paul or elsewhere, as Mrs. Yates, have no one to escort them and have to submit to bed bugs and anxiety until something turns up. A circular order has just passed around camp confining the officers very strictly to its limits after tomorrow. How the married men will like that is not a question of much uncertainty.

My day is pretty well divided between reveille, morning stables, retreat, tattoo and meals. The latter I shall take at the hotel so long as Custer will permit as I can live much more cheaply there than in a private mess of our own — about $22.00 per month. Craycroft, Hodgson, Braden, Godfrey, Hale and Col. Thompson [10] are among those with us whom you used to know. Very little changed any of them and all very friendly to me. Calhoun, Custer's brother-in-law, is adjutant of the cavalry. . . .

Camp Sturgis, Yankton DA
April 19th, 1873

. . . We have all settled back again into our old camp and everything is running smoothly once more.[11] Weather delightful and snow rapidly disappearing. The character of the soil is so spongy that water stands on it but a very short time, and the constant breeze dries the surface very rapidly. The first morning after the storm was bright, but cold and windy. I left my stable and rode out alone over the prairie to camp. The scene was anything but inspiriting, desolation and silence being the only inhabitants of our lively little cloth village. The white tents [were] half buried in snow with here and there a gap in the line where the wind had proved too strong for guy rope and tent pegs. A few men who had straggled or been sent back from town were busy digging their effects out of the drifts, or shoveling the snow out of the interior of the tents, where it had generally attained the height of four or five feet.

I found my own things perfectly safe and dry, and my tent, strange to say, entirely free of snow. After establishing a guard I returned to the city and hotel and found everybody generally demoralized. Before evening, however, the men were mostly gathered together, marched out to camp and set at the

10 Second Lieutenants William T. Craycroft, Benjamin H. Hodgson, and Charles Braden, Captains Owen Hale and William Thompson. Thompson had been a colonel of volunteers in 1864.

11 An extremely heavy wind from the Northwest brought a blizzard from April 13 to 16 which buried tents under five to six feet of snow, and drove men and horses to shelter in Yankton. Mrs. Custer, "*Boots and Saddles,*" 20-29, gives her recollections of this storm.

work I have described. Our company was particularly fortunate in having less snow in the company street than any of the other troops, and in a short time the tents and picket line were clear and ready for men and horses. Thursday afternoon, the horses were brought in, and by yesterday evening everything had assumed its former appearance. The damage done to stock and men is not nearly so great as any one would naturally have anticipated who experienced the fury of the storm. Cases of frozen members were quite plentiful and here and there used up a horse, but happily no loss of life. Our escape from severer consequence is solely due to the comparative moderation of the temperature. Ten degrees lower, few if any of those left in camp could have escaped. I never cease to be thankful that I did not bring you with me when I think of the discomforts. . . .

. . . Our squadron mess will be started tomorrow. It consists of four officers, MacIntosh, Yates, Wallace [12] and myself. As I have the management of it, I run it as economically as I choose.

. . . .

The only thing that troubles me is the fear that Custer will force us to buy horses. He has already sent an order around directing that all officers desiring to purchase horses shall make their application by Monday morning. I am afraid that some time on the march he will spring a trap similar to the one that caught most of the officers napping during the Kansas Campaign, and forced them to buy horses at ruinous prices. . . .

Custer is not making himself at all agreeable to the officers of his command. He keeps himself aloof and spends his time in excogitating annoying, vexatious, and useless orders which visit us like the swarm of evils from Pandora's box, small, numberless, and disagreeable. However, we are enjoying ourselves hugely. . . .

Camp Sturgis, Yankton
April 25th, 1873

. . . .

Last night we attended the ball given in our honor by the citizens of Yankton. It was a homespun affair, but given and received in the same spirit of cordiality and kindness. It would have amused you, for a short time, to have seen the bumpkins and their sweethearts — the Touchstones and Audreys of this locality — shake the frost out of their heels to the enlivening accompaniment of our band. The army ladies were there in full force taking their last draught from the bowl of dissipation and festivity. I came home among the first, after paying my respects to the fair bluebloods of our own patrician circle.

. . . . . .

Camp Sturgis, Yankton, DA
April 30th, 1873

. . . .

Yesterday noon I marched off my tour of officer of the guard. The duty . . . consists lately of a mixture of that of a policeman and detective. He is

[12] Second Lieutenant George D. Wallace.

stationed in the city entirely out of camp, with orders to patrol the streets four times a day, visiting each time all the saloons and pothouses in the place, and arresting all soldiers found therein without a pass. You can imagine the pleasures of such occupation better than I can describe them. Yankton, like all frontier towns, is half composed of gambling halls "et id genus omne" and a midnight tour among them, clothed with an office not congenial to their frequenters and proprietors, is perhaps instructive but not amusing. However, I shall not again be called upon to perform that duty before leaving. Today the best part of daylight, before the storm came on, has been consumed in muster and inspection. The command presents a splendid appearance under arms and is in magnificent condition. Custer, however, wears the men out by ceaseless and unnecessary labor. The police of camp, stables twice a day, water call (involving a 5 mile ride) twice — mounted guard mounting (a guard of 65 men) drills twice, and dress parade composes an exhaustive routine. We all fear that such ill advised and useless impositions will result in large desertions when the command is paid off, as it will be tomorrow morning. Custer is not belying his reputation — which is that of a man selfishly indifferent to others, and ruthlessly determined to make himself conspicuous at all hazards.

We have just heard today to our great joy that Gen. [Samuel D.] Sturgis [13] is to be here this evening and that he will take command. For how long, no one knows; perhaps to Fort Rice — perhaps only for a few days — any time would be a relief. We have received the order from Dept. Hdqrs. organizing the expedition. (Gen. [Absalom] Baird [14] will get you a copy of it.) It does not vary in any particular from the information we have already received. Four battalions of Infantry — numbering some twenty companies in all — our ten companies of cavalry — two Rodman guns, and 75 scouts. In all, including teamsters, some twenty-five hundred men; to leave Fort Rice on the 12th or 15th of June.

. . . We still anticipate leaving here on the 5th, but can make no definite prophecies. Custer, I understand, is not sure that he will be able to arrange about forage so early, and we may linger three or four days after that date before starting. After the receipt of this you had better direct your letters to Fort Sully DA, where we stop for five days, until about the tenth of May, after which direct all to Fort Rice DA. I have received an order appointing me Judge Advocate of that inevitable court martial which follows me so closely. Terry [15] it seems has not forgotten me. There are ten of the officers of my regiment on the court. We sit at Sully. . . .

. . . .

[13] Samuel D. Sturgis was in 1873 colonel of the 7th Cavalry. He had been a brigadier general of volunteers, and had been brevetted major general for gallant and meritorious service. He did not remain with the expedition after it left Fort Rice.

[14] General Absalom Baird was in 1873 assistant inspector general with the permanent grade of lieutenant colonel. In 1864 he had been awarded the Medal of Honor for gallantry in action and was brevetted a major general.

[15] Brigadier General Alfred H. Terry then commanded the Department of Dakota in the Military Division of the Missouri.

Camp Sturgis, Yankton, DA
May 6th, 1873

. . . The order was . . . sent around today for a start at 12 m. tomorrow. Our allowance of baggage is quite comfortable, much better than we had anticipated. Each officer is allowed to carry one medium trunk. This will give me ample room for all the necessaries and many comforts. I have packed my trunk with all my substantials and transferred all the superfluities to the chest. I am provided with everything I can think of necessary for my physical well being and with a small dictionary and my Shakespeare in the bottom of my trunk shall not suffer mentally. Dick [16] rides in Capt. Yates' wagon and takes charge of the lunch together with my valise. There is a steamboat provided to carry forage, following on the river our march by land, and meeting us at different points whenever practicable. The ladies go on this boat together with the sick. Our first stopping place available for mail will be Fort Randall [17]— four days' march. The condition of the roads between may however delay us several days. From Randall you will hear from me with account of the march etc. etc.

Camp at Fort Sully, DA [18]
May 24, 1873

We camped about five miles from here all day yesterday changing our location this morning to within half a mile of the post. Our last march was a long and tedious one of over thirty miles and it is with no slight feeling of satisfaction that we welcome the prospect of a four or five days' rest.

Since leaving [Fort] Thompson [19] the march has not been characterized by anything unusual, except perhaps a day or two of clear weather. Some of the scenery on the way up has been very fine as we obtained occasional glimpses of the river from the high bluffs bordering it, but as a general rule the monotony of rolling treeless prairie has been uninterrupted.

. . . .

We have ascertained since our arrival some additional facts about the expedition. Gen. [David S.] Stanley [20] is here and has been unreserved in his conversation in reference to it. It seems then that from Rice we strike across to where his expedition terminated last year and make that our base of supplies; i.e. the mouth of Powder River. From there we separate in two detachments, one to go North and Northwest to where Baker had arrived at the time of his repulse, and the other to proceed to the South and Southwest as far as the Montana settlements. It is not expected that we will remain out longer than the 15th of October, leaving Powder River on or about that time for return. . . . Those with whom I have spoken and who were out last year anticipate no trouble whatever from the Indians. One assured me

16 A servant.
17 Situated on the Missouri River, near the Nebraska border.
18 On the Missouri River, near the mouth of the Cheyenne River.
19 In northern Dakota on the Missouri River at the Crow Creek Agency.
20 In 1873 Stanley was commanding officer of the 22nd Infantry.

that he would have no hesitation whatever in taking a hundred men and crossing the country from the Missouri to the Pacific. . . .

Fort Rice DA
June 11, 1873

We arrived here the day before yesterday, eleven days from [Fort] Sully — and no mail between. The last week's marching had been fine and enjoyable — pleasant camps and short tramps. We met two Indian camps on the road, one at Grand River Agency, and another some forty or fifty miles from here, comprised of nearly a hundred lodges under Two Bears, a Yankton Sioux. We have had no trouble with any of these gentlemen but have had our fill of their society. Tawdry cavalcades of the rascals, mounted on their little ponies, decked in comical assortments of skins and rags, tin plates, feathers, neckties, beads, earrings, and stove pipe hats, have thronged our camp semi occasionally affording gratification to a mutual but quickly satisfied curiosity.

The Court Martial at Sully was the source of endless annoyance and trouble to all concerned. Custer undertook to bully and insult that body at the start, and, finding that his efforts at control were powerless, did everything in his power to hector and annoy its members. The court has made an indignant protest against his assumption, the which as recorder I have written out and will forward to Dept. Hqrs. On our arrival here we found all of the infantry already in camp and waiting. Stanley [was here] with his staff, and [so was] all our baggage which had been left behind at Yankton for shipment. . . .

. . . .

We are all in a hubbub as yet waiting the arrival of [General] Terry, who is expected tomorrow, before deciding upon the day of departure or even the line of march. It seems that [General Philip H.] Sheridan was opposed to a separation at Powder River and in consequence the plan of campaign from that point is somewhat uncertain as yet. A large number of wagons — part of our train, is yet to arrive as well as 600 head of stock for our consumption.

The infantry officers I have met have not impressed me favorably. They appear to belong to a very inferior class of society. There will be, however, very little necessity for association as the two corps will be quite isolated. . . . The scientific corps has not arrived yet, but are expected tomorrow. They say Stanley has received more orders in regard to them than for all the rest of the expedition. Stanley seems to be very much liked and impressed me very favorably when I met him. Large, handsome and dignified. Since the establishment of the depot at the mouth of Powder River,[21] by means of steamboat communication, our facilities for mail will be very much increased. Boats will make several trips from there in all probability — backwards and forwards and in addition, trains with scouts will be sent back occasionally.

[21] Following a report by Major George A. Forsyth on his reconnaissance, a site was selected at that point. See Report of Lieutenant General Philip H. Sheridan, CG, Military Division of the Missouri, October 27, 1873, *Report of the Secretary of War*, 1873, I, 41.

The appearance of things here would seem to indicate a picnic on a grand scale. Three large steamboats lay at the wharf, soldiers, officers, Indians, scouts and guides throng about the post and keep up quite a metropolitan bustle and excitement. Two young English lords are to accompany us and have bought a wagon and team bodily to take them and their effects. . . .

Your wishes in regard to accompanying the ladies up would speedily change into congratulations at having escaped their experience. Only today Mrs. Yates and others were saying that you had acted so wisely in remaining. They have all been more or less sick, cooped up in the small cabin of a rear wheeled boat, living on the most atrocious of boat fare for 34 days. During that time they have succeeded in discovering each other's failings with astonishing distinctness, and, from all I hear, have made the atmosphere pretty warm. Add to this the difficulty of officers communicating with the boat after a hard day's march — forced to go sometimes two or three miles to where she lay, through the woods, and return late in the dark — losing thereby the best part of a much needed night's sleep, and there is but little remaining to make the trip desirable. Here the ladies are all adrift with the prospect of the command leaving in a few days. I never saw such confusion and uncertainty. No two of them think alike or seem to have any definite plan. They were all obliged to hustle off of the boat on its arrival, and seek accommodations on another whose stay is almost as uncertain as the first. Some talk of going back to Yankton and Sioux City, to St. Paul, to Indiana, and even to Canada. . . .

Ft. Rice June 17, 1873

Taps have just sung our evening lullaby and camp subsides into the drowsy silence of night. . . .

. . . .

We have had two or three intensely hot, dry, dusty days, relieved, however, by the blessing of cool nights. Terry reviewed us yesterday with the thermometer 96°. Whew! A detachment of 25 cavalry under De Rudio and 4 companies of Infantry left two days back for the [Missouri River] crossing,[22] to escort the Engineers from there, and meet us after our start some miles out. They reached [Fort] Lincoln about the time the rumor came to us that the Fort had been "bounced" by the reds. Today, a courier brings tiding that the detachment has been having a little brush with them. The Indians are showing by this their evident intention for the Summer, which will probably be to abandon us to our own sweet will and touch up the posts on the river which have thus been reduced by the expedition. They can do very little harm beyond picking off stragglers and stealing stock.

We are down to fighting trim. Small "pup tents" for the men and A tents for officers. My trunk and chest are packed with all superfluities and the campaign allowance confined to the limits of the valise and whatever I can smuggle into my bedsack. I shall have ample. I have had made for my

[22] Near Bismarck, protected in 1873 by Fort Abraham Lincoln.

bedding a long canvas bag, double thickness, drawing together at the top. In the bottom of this I place all the heavy clothing for the Fall return, including warm underclothing, socks, etc. My bedding is then rolled up and slipped in on top the bag, drawn together, buckled and strapped, forming a piece of furniture hard to equal for compactness and variety of uses. In the valise I can carry many conveniences and all the necessaries for the Summer. "Man needs far little etc." The mattress is boxed, and together with trunk, chest etc. stored under charge of an officer left behind in charge. . . .

. . . Terry said in a little speech he made us on the occasion of our call that this was the most interesting of all the Indian campaigns. What with English lords, scientists, and outsiders of every military description you would imagine it a big picnic. . . .

Camp on Heart River DA
June 25th, 1873

Here we are sixty miles from Rice in a delightful camp with a day's rest before us. We have had a pleasant and interesting march out with a fair proportion of rain and storm, but still altogether delightful. We make an imposing show on these rolling prairies — 1500 men, 250 teamsters, 40 scouts, 250 wagons, 800 horses, 600 head of cattle and 1500 mules;[23] too imposing, in fact, for the Indians who have not as yet put in an appearance. The marches have been short and somewhat tedious, on account of the difficulty of moving so large and heavy a train. The average will not exceed 8 miles a day, although some days we have exceeded it largely and on others fallen very much below that mark. The weather, as I have said, has not been uniformly pleasant but then the storms, although terrible and severe while they last, are only of hours instead of days duration. The thunder and lightning I have never seen equalled for intensity and grandeur. Fortunately, we have been in camp, with one exception, before their commencement. . . .

We find the country a perfect wilderness. Grass is the only vegetation with a few scattered trees along the creek and river bottoms. The prairie is broken by ravines and barren stony bluffs which cross and cut it in every direction. We have passed through hundreds of antelope that follow the column and trot curiously along its flanks. Hunters are out every day and keep our mess supplied with their meat which has become quite a drug on the market. The dogs catch the young and afford many an exciting chase. A very pretty young fawn came into my hands through their agency, which I brought into camp with the intention of raising. By evening, it was quite

[23] The trains for the Yellowstone expedition of 1873 "consisted of two hundred and two 6-mule teams, nine 4-mule teams for spring-wagons, two 6-mule teams for artillery, and some 12 riding-mules for wagon-masters. In addition, there were one 6-mule team, one 4-mule spring-wagon and team, and nine riding-horses provided for the use of the scientific party accompanying the expedition." They were assembled at Fort Abercrombie, Minnesota, in April and May, 1873. The teamsters were hired in St. Paul and Fort Leavenworth, Kansas. See report of Captain G. B. Dandy, assistant quartermaster at Fort Abraham Lincoln, *Report of the Secretary of War*, 1873, I, 112-13.

tame and docile, but the difficulties of finding proper nourishment and the want of means for its transportation induced me to let it go. Today, we struck the Heart river, a narrow, rapid stream that empties into the Missouri. . . . We found a lovely bottom quite well wooded for these latitudes, surrounded by high bluffs with a fine rich growth of grass for grazing. Here we have established ourselves for a day in order to send out scouting parties to find the Engineers and [escorting] detachment who left Lincoln a day or two before we started from Rice.

June 26th

This morning at 5 o'clock, Moylan was sent out with his troop for this purpose. He takes a day's rations and no wagons. Is to return by evening. Went over to the Infantry Camp to call on Jones, Grant, etc. Found that Stanley had about decided to divide the command as soon as we reached the Engineers, take five troops of cavalry and two battalions of Infantry (22nd and 17th) and move on ahead by rapid marches for the Yellowstone. He intends leaving Custer in command of the remaining 5 troops and two battalions who stay behind with the Engineers. If he does this we will reach the Yellowstone some 15 or 20 days before the rest, go into camp there, meet the boats, build the depot and have a pleasant time. I say *we*, because the cavalry has been divided into two wings — one under the command of Capt. Hart and the other under Benteen. Hart's wing contains Moylan, Tom Custer and all those related to the "royal family" whom Custer will of course retain with him. We are in Benteen's wing, comprising besides "F" troop, Hale's (K) with Godfrey and Aspinwall, Weston's (L) with Braden, McIntosh's (S) with Wallace, and Benteen's (H) with Gibson and De Rudio. De Rudio, you will remember, was sent, before we left Rice, to Lincoln with twenty-five men and two companies of Infantry to escort these same Engineers until they met us. It was on the day of their start that they had the skirmish with the Indians. This afternoon, about six, he suddenly made his appearance here. He had been sent from their camp yesterday afternoon to find us and after a ride of about 40 miles struck our trail at 10 o'clock this morning and followed us in. He reports that their column was struck two days ago by a furious hail storm while on the march, which stampeded all their horses and mules, upset and smashed the most of their wagons and demoralized them generally. They are camped about 25 miles to the northeast and are awaiting our arrival. The order comes around this evening that the whole of the cavalry will move on ahead and reach them tomorrow. It will take the Infantry and train two days to accomplish the distance. I sincerely hope that Stanley will carry out his idea of moving ahead to the Yellowstone and that we go with him. It will be infinitely pleasanter than poking along with the Engineers. There we will meet the boats, go into camp and have a long, refreshing rest.

. . . .

Fort Lincoln, D. T.
July 6, 1873

My telegram will have taken the edge off of your surprise, so you will expect this as a natural consequence of it. My lucky star must be near the Zenith to have brought about so happy a conjunction of circumstances as has brought me here at so fortuitous a time.

We had reached the crossing of the Heart River and had sent out a detachment to find the locality of the engineers, when De Rudio came in from them and brought accounts of their suffering from the hailstorm. Stanley ordered Custer ahead the next morning with the whole of the cavalry to reach Townsend and the engineers by night, if possible. We accordingly made a long march of it, bridged the Big Muddy and reached their camp an hour before sunset. Here we lay over a day expecting Stanley to come up in the meanwhile. The morning after Custer started off without him on his own hook. We had not gone more than 11 miles before a courier from Stanley brought a peremptory order for him to halt on the spot, and to send back one squadron as escort to a supply train to be sent to Lincoln for forage. We, as good luck would have it, received the order to leave in an hour, which we accordingly did retracing our steps and reaching Stanley at sundown 20 miles back on the Big Muddy exactly where we had crossed two days before. The river had risen ten feet and they found it impossible to cross with 250 heavy wagons. We camped on the opposite side and remained two days while a pontoon bridge was manufactured out of inverted wagon beds filled with kegs. On this structure they crossed in a night and a day. We accompanied them as far on the road to Custer at the old Engineer Camp and from there struck back with 60 wagons for Lincoln. As our train was empty we made the distance in two days and reached here on the 2d at 8 A.M., tired but glad to see once more anything in the semblance of a house.

. . . .

Camp on Yellowstone
July 21st, 1873

. . . Stanley, after joining the engineers who had started from Lincoln, at a point about 20 miles north of the Heart river and 45 miles from the Missouri, concluded to send back such a portion of his train as had become empty for new supplies and ordered a squadron to be detached from Custer to escort it. Col. Baker, Q. M. of the expedition, accompanied us and with young Dashiell and Dr. Ruyer, our surgeon, composed our little party. We left Stanley at 5 o'clock on the morning of July 3d and reached Lincoln at 8 o'clock a.m. July 4th, camping overnight at the crossing of the Heart about 10 miles from our destination. What occurred there you will sufficiently have gathered from my motley letter [of July 6]. . . .

. . . .

We left Lincoln with 53 wagons heavily loaded and have been exactly twelve days in making the journey here — 250 miles. Every morning saw us up at 3 o'clock and on the march by 5. Have averaged eleven hours in the saddle. Sometimes marched twelve and once it was fifteen. Our object was to reach Stanley as soon as possible and to accomplish this it was necessary to double up on his marches with a train as heavily loaded as his own. Continuous rains for the first week filled the creeks and ravines and rendered bridging and filling necessary every few miles. We expected to find Stanley encamped on the Little Missouri 140 miles from Lincoln waiting our arrival in case we did not reach him before. On the fourth day we rejoined [the] camp where we had left Custer and came suddenly on a small war party of 11 Sioux quite ignorant of our proximity. They were not long in the neighborhood, some business of a pressing and unexpected nature requiring their attention "over the hills and far away". This was on a small stream called the "Little Muddy" perhaps on your map. On the seventh day we began to approach what are called the "Mauvaises Terres" or Bad Lands. We found a note on the trail left by the Adjutant General informing us that Stanley had pushed on to the Yellowstone but had left a body of 100 infantry on the right bank of the Heart river near its source to await our arrival. This was good news as we had but ten days rations. The next day we crossed to the right bank of the Heart and began to keep a lookout for reinforcement. We marched all that day, however, without striking them and went into camp in a ravine by some rain pools. We had made about 24 miles and had ridden eleven hours and were well fatigued. Two hours before sunset four men were sent forward to find the infantry, if possible. They were to return, if unsuccessful, after ten or twelve miles. At dusk our pickets and one of the scouts reported a number of Indians on the horizon. This news made us anxious for the safety of the party sent forward to reconnoitre and I was accordingly ordered out with a detachment of 25 men to follow their trail and bring them back. This I did with some difficulty as the tremendous storm rendered it a very difficult task for two hours at a very rapid gait. I lost the trail several times and only recovered it again by the aid of the vivid and incessant lightning. . . .

The next day we made a long march and reached the infantry who were in an entrenched camp one day's march from the Little Missouri. This river we forded and for the two succeeding days marched through the bad lands. The description of these I must leave to a succeeding letter and more leisure, as Yates is impatiently waiting for me to finish this. It is sufficient to refer you to Doré's[24] "Inferno" for the present. Yesterday morning with the thermometer 103° in the shade we crawled over the bare bluffs that fringe the river and saw its welcome length trailing at our feet. There is a level flat two miles wide on each side rising into high bluffs.

We are encamped in the woods waiting the order to cross. Stanley farther back on the flat. We leave about 100 infantry in a stockade to guard the depot and cross within five days. Expect to be gone on the other side between 40 and 60 days. Are to follow down the river to Pompey's Pillar, return by

[24] Paul Gustave Doré (1833-1883), the famous illustrator of an edition of Dante's *Divine Comedy*.

the "Muscleshell" and hope to reach Lincoln by the middle or end of September.

[Camp on the Musselshell River
August 19, 1873]

Dr. John Hensinger, veterinary surgeon, Seventh Cavalry, and Mr. Balaran, sutler, were [on August 4] the two victims to a want of caution that our long immunity from attack had engendered.[25] They had left the train during the halt for the purpose of watering their horses, and on their way back skirting the foot of the bluffs in order to meet the column in its descent, quite unconscious of danger and the horrible fate awaiting them, were suddenly surprised by a party of three Sioux, who had secreted themselves in a ravine, and shot from behind with arrows.

General Custer in the morning had taken a squadron, A and B troops of the Seventh Cavalry, and moved rapidly ahead of the main body about four miles beyond the point at which this tragedy occurred. There, in a belt of woods, his escort had unsaddled, picketed their horses and were lying under the trees awaiting the arrival of the main body, when a shot from the pickets and their sudden appearance brought everyone to his feet. Quickly and quietly the horses were brought in and saddled, a dismounted detachment thrown out as skirmishers, while the remainder of the command moved in the direction of the attack. But three or four Indians were to be seen, galloping and gesticulating wildly in front of the column, which moved quickly forward at a trot. Hardly, however, had the flank arrived opposite a second belt of dense woods before a long line of Indians suddenly moved in regular order from their midst straight to the attack. They were all in full war costume, mounted on stalwart little ponies, and armed, as are all we have seen, with the best of Henry rifles. As rapidly as possible the command was dismounted and formed in skirmish line in front of the horses, but not a moment too soon, as the enemy came whooping and screeching down upon it. A square volley in their teeth cooled their ardor, and sent them flying back to a respectful distance. For three hours the fight was kept up, the Indians maintaining a perfect skirmish line throughout, and evincing for them a very extraordinary control and discipline. After this desultory fighting had become tiresome, the cavalry mounted suddenly and dashed forward at a charge, scattering their wary antagonists, who were not prepared for such a demonstration, in every direction. Our casualties were one man and three horses wounded. The loss of the enemy, estimated from those seen to fall, must have been something in the vicinity of ten in all, and five ponies.

For the next three days nothing was seen of our friendly neighbors in person, but abundant evidence of their camps, and the heavy trail of a retreating village, numbering, as our Indian scouts told us, in the neighbor-

[25] This letter was sent for publication in the Chicago *Inter-Ocean.* The Indian hostilities formed the subject of a report by Custer which was reprinted as an appendix in Mrs. Custer, "*Boots and Saddles,*" 280-90.

hood of eighty lodges. Each day General Custer, with two squadrons of cavalry, pushed on in advance, following rapidly on the trail.

It was not, however, until the evening of August 8 that he received orders from General Stanley to push on with the whole of the available cavalry force, make forced night marches, and overtake the village, if possible. . . .

At early dawn on the 10th our efforts to cross [the Tongue River] commenced, and it was not until 4 in the afternoon that they were reluctantly relinquished, after every expedient had been resorted to in vain. The current was too swift and fierce for our heavy cavalry. We therefore went into bivouac close to the river bank to await the arrival of the main body, and slept that night as only men in such condition can sleep. We hardly anticipated the lively awakening that awaited us. Just at daylight our slumbers were broken by a sharp volley of musketry from the opposite bank, accompanied by shouts and yells that brought us all to our feet in an instant. As far up the river as we could see, clouds of dust announced the approach of our slippery foes, while the rattling volleys from the opposite woods, and the "zip", "zip" of the balls about our ears told us that there were a few evil disposed persons close by.

For half an hour, while the balls flew high, we lay still without replying, but when the occasional quiver of a wounded horse told that the range was being acquired by them, the horses and men were moved back from the river edge to the foot of the bluffs, and there drawn up in line of battle to await developments. A detachment of sharpshooters was concealed in the woods, and soon sent back a sharp reply to the thickening compliments from the other side. Our scouts and the Indians were soon exchanging chaste complimentary remarks in choice Sioux — such as: "We're coming over to give you h — l;" "You'll see more Indians than you ever saw before in your life," and "Shoot, you son of a dog" from ours. Sure enough, over they came, as good as their word, above and below us, and in twenty minutes our scouts came tumbling down the bluffs head overheels, screeching: "Heap Indian come." Just at this moment General Custer rode up to the line, followed by a bright guidon, and made rapid disposition for the defense. Glad were we that the moment of action had arrived, and that we were to stand no longer quietly and grimly in line of battle to be shot at. One platoon of the first squadron on the left was moved rapidly up the bluffs, and thrown out in skirmish line on the summit, to hold the extreme left. The remainder of the squadron followed as quickly as it could be deployed, together with one troop of the Fourth Squadron.

On they came as before, 500 or 600 in number, screaming and yelling as usual, right onto the line before they saw it. At the same moment the regimental band, which had been stationed in a ravine just in rear, struck up "Garry Owen." The men set up a responsive shout, and a rattling volley swept the whole line.

The fight was short and sharp just here, the Indians rolling back after the first fire and shooting from a safer distance. In twenty minutes the squadrons were mounted and ordered to charge. Our evil-disposed friends tarried no longer, but fled incontinently before the pursuing squadrons. We chased them eight miles and over the river, only returning when the last Indian had gotten beyond our reach.

No less than a thousand warriors had surrounded us, and we could see on the opposite bluffs the scattered remnants galloping wildly to and fro. Just at the conclusion of the fight the infantry came up, and two shells from the Rodman guns completed the discomfiture of our demoralized foes. Our loss was one killed, Private Tuttle, E Troop, Seventh Cavalry, and three wounded. Among the latter, Lieutenant [Charles] Braden, Seventh Cavalry, while gallantly holding the extreme left, the hottest portion of the line, was shot through the thigh, crushing the bone badly.[26] Four horses were killed and eight or ten wounded, and deserve honorable mention, although non-combatants. Official estimates place the Indian loss at forty killed and wounded, and a large number of ponies.

The troops engaged consisted of the following companies of cavalry: A, Captain Moylan, Lieutenant Varnum; B, Lieutenants Tom Custer and Hodgson; E, Lieutenants McDougall and Aspinwall; F, Captain Yates and Lieutenant Larned; G, Lieutenants McIntosh and Wallace; K, Captain Hale, Lieutenant Godfrey; L, Lieutenants Weston and Braden; M, Captain French, Lieutenant Mathey.[27] A detachment of scouts under Lieutenant Brush, Seventeenth Infantry, were with us and did excellent service. Accompanying headquarters were Lieutenant Ketchum, Twenty-second infantry, Lieutenant Jones, Fourth Cavalry, and Lieutenant Calhoun, Seventh Cavalry.[28] Captain Hart, Seventh Cavalry, was second in command, and in charge of the left wing. We have seen but three or four small parties of half a dozen Sioux at a distance since the fight, and are at present encamped on the upper waters of the Musselshell, hoping to reach the crossing of the Yellowstone by the 10th of September. Until then, au revoir.

[26] Charles Braden was brought back 350 to 400 miles on a litter suspended from long poles between the front and rear axles of an old spring wagon. He survived, retired from the army on June 28, 1878, and was later brevetted first lieutenant for gallantry and meritorious service in the action at Tongue River.

[27] In addition to those previously identified, these were Second Lieutenant Charles A. Varnum, First Lieutenants Thomas W. Custer, Thomas M. McDougall, Edward G. Mathey, and Captain Thomas H. French.

[28] First Lieutenants Daniel H. Brush, Hiram H. Ketchum, and James H. Jones.

Book Reviews

English Discovery of America to 1585. By Franklin T. McCann. (New York: Columbia University Press, 1952. xiv + 246 pp. Bibliography and index. $3.50.)

By *English Discovery of America* Mr. McCann means intellectual awakening to the existence and possibilities of a new continent rather than voyages of discovery. Except for the shadowy John Cabot explorations and a few adventures into the frozen north, England's role in unveiling the Americas had not been particularly impressive up to 1585. Most readers will be surprised, moreover, at the slowness with which sixteenth-century Englishmen digested the vast amount of geographical information that the Iberian voyagers year by year were placing at their disposal. England did awaken at last, however, and the author feels that by 1585 the turning point had been reached and a "New World" concept had taken hold.

The title of this book naturally calls to mind Professor Eva Taylor's *Tudor Geography, 1485-1583*, published in 1930 and covering some of the same ground. Yet the two are altogether different in emphasis. Miss Taylor is an historical geographer, primarily concerned with the evolution of geographical science. McCann, on the other hand, shows how the everyday Englishman, who was neither scientist nor scholar, gradually had his notion of the earth changed, from the venerable medieval one to a notion which, with some reservations, can be called modern. The change was wrought partly by the innate curiosity of the Englishman, partly by translations of Spanish and Portuguese books that came his way, and mostly by the efforts of English propagandists, popularizers, and playwrights. Richard Eden, the predecessor of the Hakluyts as a colonization advocate, probably comes closer than anyone else to being the hero of the story.

The work is interesting from the introductory chapters on medieval geography, as understood by Englishmen, to the "grand finale," which is the author's analysis of the rousing Christopher Marlowe play, *Tamburlaine.* McCann takes this, and no doubt rightly, to be an incitement to English empire-building ambitions and a stimulus to go forth and conquer the Americas.

University of Illinois Charles E. Nowell

Soldiers, Indians and Silver; The Northward Advance of New Spain, 1550-1600. By Philip Wayne Powell. (Berkeley and Los Angeles: University of California Press, 1952. ix + 317 pp. Bibliography, maps, and index. $4.50.)

In the year 1546 word reached Mexico City that silver had been discovered in Zacatecas. Professor Powell begins at this point his discussion of some of the problems created by the opening of the mining frontier area in the latter half of the sixteenth century. The government's immediate task was to build and maintain roads, and then it had to evolve a policy which would effectively subdue the Indians, who were a constant threat to the orderly exploitation of the mines. The author discusses the development of this Indian policy from the time of Viceroy Mendoza down through the reigns of the later viceroys.

Viceroy Enriquez — who held conferences with learned men in order to be certain that war against the Chichimecas was legal — intensified the efforts at military conquest and made the first attempts to systematize the financing of the wars. Gradually there evolved, after two decades, the use of the presidio system. Finally, in the years 1590-1591, Spain achieved her goal of pacification. Powell notes that throughout the period under consideration events in the Caribbean, the Floridas, and the Philippines had a bearing on the war against the Indians since these areas too required supplies of military equipment. In discussing the wars and the evolution of the policies against the Chichimecas, the author also describes the Spanish soldiers and the Indian auxiliaries.

Two conclusions can be drawn from this excellent piece of research: (1) In New Spain a central government was necessary to provide protection on the frontier so that the frontier area could be allowed to develop its own institutions. (2) The sword was essentially a minor factor in subduing the Indians. Powell states: "After forty years of war, Spanish domination of the Gran Chichimeca of sixteenth-century Mexico was achieved, not by the sword but by a combination of diplomacy, purchase, and religious conversion."

University of Missouri WALTER V. SCHOLES

Cavalier in the Wilderness; The Story of the Explorer and Trader Louis Juchereau de St. Denis. By Ross Phares. (Baton Rouge: Louisiana State University Press, 1952. ix + 276 pp. Illustrations, bibliography, and index. $3.50.)

Cavalier in the Wilderness is the life story of Louis Juchereau de St. Denis, famous French agent at Natchitoches, Louisiana. In its wider aspects it is the story of Franco-Spanish rivalry for control of the Indian tribes along the Lower Mississippi and its tributaries and for possession of the Lower Gulf coast. The tale begins in 1700 at Biloxi, with the arrival of St. Denis under

Iberville's command. At Biloxi he found that the French settlement was flimsy and weak. Here, too, he met Bienville, with whom he was to be associated for a time, and he reveled in the stories told by these men around the fire and dreamed of adventure in this new land of opportunity.

Briefly, this book is divided into the following topics: (1) St. Denis' explorations from 1700-1707, most of which started from Fort St. John on the Mississippi. This was the time when he proved his adaptability to life on the frontier and his mastery of Indian psychology. (2) The period of Antoine Crozat, who had received a contract to develop Louisiana when St. Denis was sent to Mexico to strike up trade with the Spaniards. During his visit there he ingratiated himself not only with the officials of the border but also with those in Mexico City, and, on his return, married the commandant's granddaughter. Then, as a salaried Spanish official, he led the expedition sent to reoccupy East Texas in 1716. (3) St. Denis' second expedition to Mexico, and his imprisonment on suspicion of smuggling. (4) The war of 1719 between France and Spain, and its aftermath, when St. Denis was placed in charge of the French post at Natchitoches. (5) The rivalry between the Spaniards at Los Adaes and the French at Natchitoches, and the illicit trade between them, masterminded by St. Denis. (6) The eternal contest for control of the Indian tribes, at which St. Denis was the acknowledged master.

Phares' book is a good, popular account of a complicated scheme of international rivalry and intrigue. The story is told without specific references to authority, except for a short bibliography, and is apparently not intended for the scholar. Throughout the narrative St. Denis emerges as the hero. The author is obviously very proud of this frontiersman, his achievements, and his besting of the Spaniards. In fact, the story borders on hero worship.

The book is nicely designed and printed, has several illustrations and an index, but no map. There are but few typographical errors, the only one of consequence being a change in date on page 186.

The Bancroft Library,
University of California, Berkeley GEORGE P. HAMMOND

St. Michael's, Charleston, 1751-1951. By George W. Williams. Foreword by DeWolf Perry. (Columbia: University of South Carolina Press, 1951. ix + 375 pp. Illustrations, appendixes, bibliography, and name index. $5.00.)

In 1751 communicants of the Church of England living in Charleston, South Carolina, secured from the Assembly a permit to erect a church to be called St. Michael's. Nine commissioners important in the civil, military, and economic life of the province were designated to proceed to the task. In this group were Charles Pinckney, chief justice between 1752 and 1753, William Bull, lieutenant governor from 1759 to 1775, Andrew Rutledge, an important retail merchant, and Gabriel Manigault, one of America's richest men. Financial support for the proposed building was a problem and retarded the plans of the commission. Little by little, however, the church began to take form and after eleven years it was completed at a cost of $45,000.

The book was written to commemorate the bicentennial celebration of the founding of this historic church. The original building, with some changes and alterations, has withstood the ravages of time, the Civil War, a cyclone in 1885, an earthquake in 1886, and a tornado in 1939. Her magnificent spire rises above the city and daily serves as a reminder of a glorious past and an influential present. Important families have sat in her pews, men of distinction have constituted her vestries, and influential rectors, such as the noted Bishops Theodore Dehon and Nathaniel Bowen, have graced her pulpit. The number of communicants has risen slowly but steadily during the past half century, and today the membership is the largest in the two hundred years of existence.

Seldom has an individual church received a lengthier treatment in a more attractively printed book. The story of St. Michael's past is told in great detail. Lovers of the region will delight in the descriptions of the structure, its furnishings, and its equipment. People who are intensely interested in this church will not grow weary from reading the seventy-five-page chapter on "The Bells and the Clock." Other readers less interested will find the book unduly wordy and filled with lengthy quotations chiefly taken from the fifteen volumes of the minutes of the vestry, without which record the book would have been well-nigh impossible. An appendix, compiled from statistical data, presents in table form the long history of the church. Twenty-seven pages of illustrations and endpapers enhance immeasurably the value and the beauty of the book.

Agnes Scott College and *Emory University* WALTER B. POSEY

The Papers of Henry Bouquet. Vol. II, *The Forbes Expedition.* Edited by S. K. Stevens, Donald H. Kent, and Autumn L. Leonard. (Harrisburg: The Pennsylvania Historical and Museum Commission, 1951. xxxiii + 704 pp. Illustrations, bibliography, and index. $7.00.)

This volume is a tribute to the work of the Pennsylvania Historical and Museum Commission under the direction of Dr. Stevens. It manifests a thorough search extending over many years for documents, and also careful, scholarly editing. All the aids desired by the reader are supplied by the editors — foreword, chronological list of documents, translations as well as the original text of those letters which Bouquet wrote in French, illustrations, bibliography, chronological list of events, footnotes, and index. Included are the letters to and from Bouquet, June 1 — December 1, 1758, and his Orderly Book, June 17 — September 15, 1758. The search in repositories and private collections in the United States, Canada, and Great Britain yielded also relevant petitions, journals of Indian conferences, speeches, memoranda, and the like. All found have been included. The editors need, therefore, not fear that their work will fail to stand up through the years because of an attack such as a reviewer made of the current publication of Theodore Roosevelt's letters on the basis of publishing only selected items. Besides military affairs, these documents also supply information about Indian trails, Indian chiefs, traders' routes, geographical factors in road building, Pennsylvania, Maryland, and Virginia soldiers — including Washington in particular — farmers, businessmen, and political leaders.

Bouquet found durable satisfaction in the art and practice of war. A Swiss by birth, he had served as an officer in the armies of Holland and Sardinia before becoming lieutenant colonel of the Royal American Infantry Regiment, formed in the colonies in 1756. He was a cultured, educated, professional soldier who spent much time between his European commands studying tactics and strategy, and also mathematics and science as related to war. To characterize him as a "soldier-of-fortune," as is done in the foreword, gives a wrong estimate of the man. One of the few British officers who were able to adapt themselves to frontier fighting, Bouquet drilled his men in open order combat and mobility of action. His great ability as an organizer and strategist, illustrated in many documents in this volume, manifested itself when the illness of General John Forbes caused much of the responsibility for the capture of Fort Duquesne to fall upon him as second in command. His rare patience and tact overcame the delays of the colonists. The major problems faced were collecting and transporting supplies, building forts and supply centers on the way, and cutting through Pennsylvania the great highway known as Forbes Road. Their solution resulted in the evacuation by the small French force of Fort Duquesne without a major battle. Victory depended upon the ability to supply an overwhelming force of 7,000 men and to secure it against surprise attack.

Great as was Bouquet's contribution to the winning of the French and Indian War on the Ohio frontier, the foreword overstates it: "without the abilities of Henry Bouquet, the history of Pennsylvania — even the history of North America — might have taken a different turn." The decisive military events which enabled the first great British Empire to be built took place upon the seven seas and in many other far-flung land theaters as well. Had Forbes's expedition been routed like Edward Braddock's and campaigns elsewhere won as they were, the results would have been the same. The inevitable westward movement of the Anglo-Saxon would have proceeded in much the same way, save for a delay of a few years. The British started colonizing in 1607 and the French in 1608, but by 1750 the population of the British colonies was approximately 1,200,000, and of the French only 80,000.

However, for the upper Ohio country and the frontiers of Pennsylvania and Virginia, the period was most critical. After Braddock's defeat Indian and French attacks carried the tomahawk and torch to log cabins and forced the English pioneer settler's frontier line to recoil. English influence among the Ohio tribes was at its nadir. Only an overwhelming force, well led, well organized, and well supplied, could guarantee a complete reversal in this theater of conflict and make its contribution to winning the global war and the duel for empire.

Ohio University A. T. VOLWILER

Women Camp Followers of the American Revolution. By Walter Hart Blumenthal. (Philadelphia: George S. MacManus Company, 1952. 104 pp. Foreword, appendix, and bibliography. $3.75.)

The title of this book alerts the interest, of readers with a certain turn of mind at least, but turns out to be mostly a collection of notes with here and there a warm tribute to the services of the women who accompanied both the British and American armies during the American Revolution. The first chapter is called "British Women on the Ration"; the second and final chapter is titled (perhaps unfortunately) "American Camp Women Under Washington." An appendix includes reports of the British Commissary in 1777 listing the number of men, women, and children to whom rations were being issued. A report of May lists 23,601 men, 2,776 women, and 1,904 children. The figures may not be exact but they give some notion of the personnel of an eighteenth-century army.

On the whole the author seems to think that women camp followers of the British army were not as virtuous as they might have been, although there were many wives included among them. On the other hand, he inclines to the view, and the patriotic bias is understandable, that the women followers of American armies were of a nobler variety. However, his citations to Washington's various orders relating to women with his army do not indicate that Washington had an equally high opinion of them.

The book is based on fairly wide reading in published sources and in some manuscripts, but it is essentially a collection of notes. Perhaps, given the fact that women and children camp followers of eighteeth-century armies were taken for granted, an adequate account could not be produced without far more work than has gone into this book. But it could have been better written. Only occasionally is there a flash of light. For example, in writing of troubles with women who went back and forth between Philadelphia and the camp at Valley Forge in the spring of 1778, the author quotes what were obviously futile orders by Washington to his officers in an effort to keep the soldiers from wandering outside the camp to meet such women, and then concludes: "Perhaps it was too much to expect these men to remain quiet, with Spring whispering its harbinger, and a Republic to be sired."

University of Wisconsin MERRILL JENSEN

Rag, Tag and Bobtail; The Story of The Continental Army, 1775-1783. By Lynn Montross. Maps and end papers by Alice Wesche. (New York: Harper and Brothers Publishers, 1952. 519 pp. Illustrations, maps, appendix, sources, and index. $5.00.)

This new military history of the Revolution serves to demonstrate again that the thousands of books and articles devoted to the War for Independence have not withered it as a vital theme for historical writing nor staled its infinite variety for a reading public. Although adding little to our knowledge of the conflict, the book presents in readable form a great deal of human interest material drawn from soldiers' diaries and journals, much of which has been so buried in old and obscure publications as to be practically forgotten. The narrative is well balanced, factually accurate, and adequately illustrated with maps and topographical mock-ups.

But Mr. Montross's volume has shortcomings in other respects. In an apparent attempt to garnish his story to what he imagines to be the popular taste, he has overloaded it with long quotations which might better have been compressed and worked into the text, and he has used too frequently stylistic devices like inductive leads and whimsical chapter headings which occasionally confuse the reader and hinder the flow of the narrative. As a result his account, while often vivid, becomes somewhat kaleidoscopic and sometimes loses its focus on the main course of events. It lacks the terse, compressed narrative style of Willard M. Wallace's *Appeal to Arms*, another popular history of the Revolution published last year.

From the historical point of view, a certain amount of special pleading for Horatio Gates at the expense of Benedict Arnold and Philip Schuyler merits more severe criticism. Certainly military reputations are often supported by the slenderest of evidence, often mere judgment after the fact of victory or defeat, and it is quite possible therefore that prevailing estimates of the three generals in question need revision. Nevertheless, Mr. Montross is something less than impartial when without citing his evidence he dismisses as legend the brilliant ruse by which Arnold has been credited with forcing Barry St. Leger to raise the siege of Fort Stanwix, and when he ignores John Burgoyne's statement that the American victory at Bemis Heights which made Saratoga inevitable was the work of Arnold. As regards Camden, Mr. Montross gives scant attention to the tactical blunders which led to Gates's defeat. He quotes Nathanael Greene to the effect that Gates was "unfortunate but not blameable," but does not mention that Greene questioned whether the battle should have been fought at all, considering the unfavorable circumstances facing the Americans.

One might also question Montross's interpretation of the Conway Cabal as evidence of a widespread ideological conflict in the army between great landowners of aristocratic tastes and Yankees of democratic persuasions. Although there are similar judgments throughout the work which invite challenge, yet with due allowance for criticism on historical and stylistic levels, *Rag, Tag and Bobtail* is useful as a kind of sociomilitary history of the Revolutionary War and certainly merits the attention of professional historians.

University of North Carolina ELISHA P. DOUGLASS

George Washington in American Literature, 1775-1865. By William Alfred Bryan. (New York: Columbia University Press, 1952. xii + 280 pp. Appendix, bibliography, and index. $4.00.)

The publication of William Alfred Bryan's study of George Washington as a theme in American literature has an unusual pathos because of the author's death just after its completion in 1950. The work was to have been presented as a doctoral dissertation at Duke University.

Since the sources for such an investigation, as Professor Bryan remarks, are "staggering" in quantity, he wisely contented himself with surveying "a very large sample" consisting primarily of books, but including also the files of the *Southern Literary Messenger*, the *North American Review*, and *Knickerbocker*, as well as other articles in magazines and newspapers. The bibliography lists more than two thousand primary sources, and the work as a whole is a highly useful bibliographical tool.

After an introductory chapter which sketches the main outlines of Washington's reputation down to 1865, Professor Bryan compiles references to the man by people who knew him firsthand as a means of throwing into relief "the specious, ethereal, Jovian Washington of the nineteenth century." The study of Washington in literature is divided according to genres: oratory (including sermons), biography, verse, drama, and fiction. This arrangement seems logical but it has the disadvantage of not bearing a close relation to the various aspects of the image of Washington. The chapter on verse, for example, is subdivided into sections in such a way as to obscure the chronological development of Washington's reputation. Other chapters, especially that on fiction, are better organized, and the general conclusions which the author draws are interesting despite the fact that no major writer dealt with Washington extensively. It is clear that Washington appealed to Americans primarily as evidence to all the world concerning "the type of man the new nation could produce." He became an austere allegorical figure representing national virtue. During the quarter century after his death the Federalist coloring of his fame tended to dampen the enthusiasm of Jeffersonians, but he was a national possession nevertheless, and with growing sectional tension his name could be invoked as a symbol of unity. Toward 1860 southern sectionalists tried to emphasize Washington the rebel, but this view did not prove widely acceptable.

Because of their stylistic conventions, oratory and verse could more readily use the severely abstract conception of Washington that was prevalent. James Fenimore Cooper's reverent treatment of the Commander in Chief in *The Spy* "was looked upon as lese majesty, for he showed Washington in lowly, undignified situations." Later novelists generally portrayed Washington as a ghostly presence having little or no part in the plot. Among pre-Civil War biographies, Professor Bryan considers Washington Irving's the best, but "it appeared too late in the period to have much influence on imaginative literature."

University of Minnesota HENRY NASH SMITH

Portraits and Miniatures by Charles Willson Peale. By Charles Coleman Sellers. American Philosophical Society *Transactions*, Vol. XLII, Pt. I. (Philadelphia: American Philosophical Society, 1952. 369 pp. Bibliography and illustrations. $5.00.)

The historian of the Revolutionary and early national periods will find in this ambitious and comprehensive volume invaluable insights and suggestions for his richer understanding of these years in the life of the American nation. The study of the fine arts as a tool for the grasp of historical data and, more specifically, the realization that American painting is an important segment of American history has been either neglected or simply tolerated by too many academic historians. However, there are signs that a group of scholars are discovering the significance of this kind of "knowledge" for our more complete awareness and grasp of the historical situation, and for these students Mr. Sellers' study will be appreciated and its implications incorporated into their thinking, teaching, and writing.

For the social, intellectual, and cultural historian, Mr. Sellers' discussion and illustrations will certainly be of interest. Thus the author indicates that some of the "occasions for a painting" were the prospect of death in the family, the established propriety of having the portraits of the husband and wife in the home, and the gift of a portrait as a token of friendship. But in addition to these paintings of a domestic and private nature, Charles W. Peale's many portraits of the leading military, political, scientific, intellectual, and artistic figures commemorate significant public service. And Mr. Sellers' account of Peale's experience in London with the "American School" of Benjamin West is illuminating. There the painter studied the Italian masters and there he learned that art is the imitation of nature, and, therefore, of God, according to the sixteenth-century Giovanni Paolo Lomazzo. This fitted Peale's practical approach to his art, which stressed sound draughtsmanship and "truth" rather than finish, and also his Deist philosophy. The painter's search for a cultural tradition and economic security, a quest which is equally familiar to American artists in our own time, is expressed in one of Peale's letters (dated 1772): "A good painter of either portrait or history must be well acquainted with the Grecian and Roman statues, to be able to draw them at pleasure by memory, and account for every beauty. . . . These are more than I shall ever have time or opportunity to know, but as I have variety of characters to paint I must . . . make these my antiques, and improve myself as well as I can while I am providing for my support."

That Peale had "variety of characters" to paint as a substitute for antiques is amply demonstrated by the 1,046 items under the alphabetical list of portraits. The author has attempted to identify each subject, to show the relationship of the subject and painter, and to narrate the history of the making of the picture. Along with the 451 excellent illustrations (several in color), these two sections reveal the private and public world of the late eighteenth and early nineteenth centuries in America in genuinely humanized terms. They give, in effect, still another dimension to the historian's understanding of the period.

University of Minnesota **Joseph J. Kwiat**

The Early Histories of St. Louis. Edited by John Francis McDermott. (St. Louis: St. Louis Historical Documents Foundation, 1952. xi + 163 pp. Illustrations and index. $4.00.)

This unusual collection of rare source materials will delight the scholar or student concerned with the history of St. Louis during its first fifty years. The editor states that his purpose is merely to make the included materials easily available. However, much history of value appears in the enlightening running comment which constitutes his introduction. This is attractively written, although the reviewer was forced to his dictionary upon encountering "fascicules" (p. 27). And the editor's quotation on the next page from an imaginative account of the founding of St. Louis, published in 1858, adds a neat touch of humor to lighten properly the weight of historiography in the introduction.

Of primary importance is the inclusion in this book of writings on early St. Louis by Auguste Chouteau, identified by the editor as the "co-founder" of the town (pp. 7, 30) and as "the most influential of its early historians" (p. 30). All other historical accounts of early St. Louis seem to derive from Auguste Chouteau's *Narrative.*

An effective brief introduction precedes each writer included, but the reviewer regrets that the editor did not deem it opportune to bulwark the history in the documents with detailed interpretative comment from his own rich scholarship. One excellent footnote to that end does occur on pages 55-56. The reviewer would have appreciated a similar approach to the historical views expressed by Wilson Primm on Lieutenant Governor Fernando de Leyba and the attack on St. Louis in 1780 (pp. 122-23, 125).

The mechanical features of this volume include an index, a set of interesting illustrations, a list of references for detailed reading, and a documented chronology for the early history of St. Louis containing useful brief bits of historical facts drawn from a considerable range of reliable sources. The book is well printed in a sturdy and attractive binding. Unimportant but rather amusing is the reference on page 16 to a "typograhical error."

Altogether, this study is a nice addition to the field of American historiography of basic source materials out of print and difficult to find.

Principia College FLOYD A. MCNEIL

Cathedrals in the Wilderness. By J. Herman Schauinger. (Milwaukee: Bruce Publishing Company, 1952. xiii + 334 pp. Illustrations, bibliography, and index. $4.00.)

The history of the Catholic Church in the Kentucky area has not been an altogether neglected field, yet like many of the other religious group histories this one has not been adequately treated. Among the earlier works were the two by Father Martin J. Spalding, *Sketches of the Early Catholic Missions in Kentucky* and *Sketches of the Life, Time and Character of the Rt. Rev. Benedict Joseph Flaget, First Bishop of Louisville.* In 1940 Sister Ramona Mattingly published her monograph, *The Catholic Church on the Kentucky Frontier*, and subsequently other volumes have appeared, including a recent biography of Father Charles Nerinckx which makes no contribution. In his study of the church, Mr. Shauinger makes pretty much a biographical approach to the subject. He deals especially with the work of Martin J. Spalding, Charles Nerinckx, and Benedict Joseph Flaget. He gives most attention to the work of Flaget.

Catholics appeared on the Kentucky frontier from the beginning. Mrs. William Coomes of Harrodsburg was Kentucky's earliest schoolteacher, and many settlers came from Maryland where they had been members of the church. The largest Catholic settlement was that in Nelson County about Bardstown. From this core the church spread out to other communities, and as the towns, especially Louisville, grew larger, the Catholic membership expanded. By the 1850's the Catholics were under fire by the ardent nativists who saw great harm coming to the country not so much because of the church, but because so many members were immigrants. In this instance anti-Catholic sentiment ran strong, but generally Kentucky has been hospitable and tolerant in its attitudes toward the Catholic Church.

Three orders have found Kentucky an attractive home. There are the silent Trappist at St. Gesthemane and the Sisters of Charity at Nazareth and the Sisters of Loretto at Loretto. Mr. Shauinger deals briefly with the background of the founding of these houses and relates their activities to the growth of the church. Like the Protestant church historians, this author practically drowns his reader in details. These details are not always so virulent within themselves, but they are given a church slant which possibly makes them almost as confusing to a Catholic as to the Protestant reader. The history of the Catholic Church in Kentucky is interesting, and if Mr. Shauinger had lived up to his good preface and his first two or three chapters, he would have contributed a book of more than passing importance. He saw the source materials, and his research appears to have been adequate at least and exhaustive at most.

The reviewer wishes that Mr. Shauinger might have spent more time relating the Catholic Church to its frontier social and economic backgrounds. In places he does discuss relationships with the Protestants, but he does not follow up the interesting leads that he suggests. Too, his statistics are often narrowly quantitative rather than comparatively qualitative. The reader gets a statistical view of the actual numbers of Catholics, but how did these compare with the members of other faiths? There is no lack of specific detail, and this book serves the useful purpose of detailing for the first time the specific movement to the West. It gives a clear picture of the difficulty the church had in organizing its congregations into stable groups and the hardships which the bishops had in supplying priests to frontier congregations. The comings and goings of the flock of ministers who came to Kentucky are all but overwhelming. The priestly career of that able and courageous leader, Benedict Flaget, is given the attention it deserves. The chapters are without headings, and the index inadequate.

University of Kentucky THOMAS D. CLARK

Instructions for Governing the Interior Provinces of New Spain, 1786. By Bernardo de Galvez. Translated and edited by Donald E. Worcester. Bibliographical note by George P. Hammond. (Berkeley: The Quivira Society; Albuquerque: University of New Mexico Press, 1951. xiii + 150 pp. Index, frontispiece.)

This publication adds another title to the list of source materials on the Spanish Borderlands available in English translation. In addition to its general interest the work will have particular appeal to historians of the Southwest because the Apache problem, dealt with at length in the Instructions, was inherited in almost identical form by the United States in the nineteenth century.

A basic assumption of the Galvez regulations is that the menace of

European rivals had been largely removed as a result of Spanish participation in two recent wars and that the chief remaining threat to the internal peace and security of the northern provinces of New Spain was the hostility of certain native tribes, notably the Apaches. The regulations laid down by the viceroy were therefore concerned primarily with the problem of Indian control.

Of particular significance is the fact that Galvez recognized the need which obliged the Indians to rob in order to eat, the desire to achieve the goals of liberty and idleness, and the poverty that engendered perverse inclinations as forces which drove native tribes to commit depredations upon the Spanish settlements (Article 45). The measures he prescribed were designed to ease the pressures which caused hostility (Article 42). The necessities of the Indians he proposed to supply by peaceful trade, but those nations which refused the Spanish offers of peace were to be relentlessly chastized until they either submitted to the Spanish terms or were exterminated.

Trade regulations were to be liberalized as they had been in Louisiana where the Spaniards adopted a modified form of the French system of Indian control through trade and periodic distributions of presents. In exchange for peltry the natives were to be supplied food, clothing, knives, trinkets, cattle, mules, and, in sharp contrast to earlier Spanish policy in the area, horses, firearms, ammunition, and intoxicants (Articles 62-65). These measures would, it was argued, reduce the Indians to greater dependence upon the Spaniards and predispose them to peaceful pursuits. Control of the frontier could then be maintained at a greatly reduced cost in money, destruction, and suffering.

The Apaches were to be the objects of special attention. Under the assumption that they would not yield to peaceful persuasion, their Indian friends and allies were to be won away until they could be dealt with in isolation. Their native enemies were to be incited against them, and the Spaniards, although instructed to dissimulate when they were too weak to punish and destroy, were ordered on all other occasions to wage relentless war until the Apaches were exterminated, or sued for peace and accepted the conditions of trade which the Spanish authorities were commanded always to offer.

The effectiveness of the program outlined by Galvez in his Instructions was never completely tested in practice. His death during an epidemic later in the same year brought about administrative changes in the Provincias Internas which prevented the execution of the plan on the scale which he had projected.

In making the document available to a wide audience the editor has performed a valuable service. The translation, however, is subject to criticism. The general reader will perhaps not find the free rendition objectionable, but those who insist on exactness will find frequent reason to disagree with the translator, and scholars who may wish to use the English version for precise fact will find numerous instances of mistaken interpretation of meaning (for example, Articles 3, 24, 61, 105, 144, and 179). This shortcoming is compensated in part, however, by the reproduction of the Spanish text with which the translation can be compared.

A well-written introduction places the Instructions in their historical context, and a selected bibliography amplifies the notes that accompany the text.

Tulane University WILLIAM J. GRIFFITH

Crisis in Freedom; The Alien and Sedition Acts. By John C. Miller. (Boston: Little, Brown and Company, 1951. 253 pp. Bibliography and index. $3.50.)

This is a history of the Alien and Sedition Acts of 1798 and of the prosecutions that took place under them. It is also a study of the opposing moods of two bodies of American public opinion, in the conflict between which these laws had their setting. More important still, it is a commentary upon the eternal dilemma presented by the effort to devise laws which may preserve order and limit licentiousness without destroying freedom and upon the significance of this particular "crisis in freedom" for the definition of the constitutional nature of the American union.

In the preparation of this history Professor Miller read extensively in the manuscript papers of the leading actors in the drama; he read, also, many contemporary newspapers, pamphlets, and memoirs. These materials he has used with evident care and critical accuracy. He writes well, in a style that is popular rather than technical; his narrative is descriptive rather than profoundly analytical. At the same time, throughout the book he editorializes upon the events he is describing as though he hoped to teach the modern American nation a moral lesson to be drawn from this tragic (Federalist) blunder of its youth.

The book surveys the moods of fear and conservative conviction that dominated the thinking and feeling of the Federalist rank and file in the moment of the cold war with France under the Directory that underlay the passage of the Naturalization Act, the Enemy Aliens Act, and the Sedition Act in the summer of 1798, then proceeds to narrate the story of the passage of those acts and the prosecutions under them. And it points up the fact that these acts, far from running counter to public opinion, had the clear support of the great majority of the press, of the rank and file of the Federalist party, and (probably) a substantial majority of the American people. If they constituted error, it was an error of the American people, not merely of a small, willful minority.

The Sedition Act was by far the most important in this series of laws;

practically all the prosecutions under the entire series were initiated under this one. In the hands of the Federalists, according to Professor Miller, this law became more of an instrument for maintaining the party's hold on government than a mechanism for the suppression of genuine sedition. Despite his obvious, even explicit, condemnation of the whole series, however, Professor Miller gives the Devil the benefit of the doubt, as it were; and he makes it clear that, however much the Federalists and their sympathetic judges might have used the laws to suppress political dissent, and did, they, and the nation at large — especially in the North — were in a considerable degree sincere in their genuine fear of Jacobinism, on the one hand, and in their conviction that the Federalists were the only part of American society who could preserve against internal subversion the precious republic lately founded, on the other.

The most satisfying part of the book, probably, is that part (Chapter V) in which the author discusses the Sedition Act (and, incidentally, the sedition laws of the states) in its relationship to the older common law. Did the federal government have the right, as some maintained (although even Justice Samuel Chase denied it) to prosecute for libel under the common law and without any statutory or constitutional provision of such power? The state-rights Jeffersonians bitterly denied it: give the federal government this power, they said, and the sovereignty of the states would disappear. To meet this objection the Federalists passed the Sedition Act as a statutory "re-affirmation" of a power they always assumed the federal government to have anyway. But they also thought of this law as "liberalizing" the common law, since it provided that malicious motivation must be shown; it accepted the truth of a publication as justification; and it provided that the juries and not the judges were to decide the law (as well as the fact) — all of which ran counter to the precedents and the practices of the common law. But the important point in the controversy was the question whether the federal courts had common law jurisdiction. The opposing positions of Jeffersonian Republicans and Federalists were entirely consistent with their respective "strict-construction" and "loose-construction" positions.

Beyond this, however, there were two other issues, both of profound importance to the subsequent development of the American way of life, involved in this first great "crisis in freedom" after the War of Independence. One of these was the issue of civil rights. For the Federalists, frankly distrustful of democracy and the depravity of the mob, and moved by an hysterical fear of all things "Jacobinical" and "democractical" — quite apart from their overpowering distaste for criticism — sought to preserve American freedom by severely limiting it. As Professor Miller says (p. 74): "In the Sedition Act, the United States government was in effect declaring war upon the ideas of the French Revolution. To protect the American way — as interpreted by the Federalists — the people were to be safeguarded against the dangerous opinions spreading over the world. . . . Moreover, the Sedition Act was an implied acknowledgment by the Federalists that force and coercion rather than reason and argument were to be the ultimate arbiters of political controversy in the United States."

That the Sedition Act did represent the authoritarian philosophy in government is amply shown by the prosecutions under it, and, in particular, by the judicial expressions of such Federalist judges as Samuel Chase. "There is nothing we should more dread than the licentiousness of the press," said Chase (p. 117); and, elsewhere, "If a man attempts to destroy the confidence of the people in their officers, their supreme magistrate, and their legislature, he effectually saps the foundation of the government" (pp. 86-87).

It is an ugly picture, this — the picture of a nation persecuting its own citizens simply for dissenting from the views of, and for criticizing, the party in power. It is impossible to escape the dramatic parallel between the Sedition Act of 1798 and the Internal Security Act (the McCarran Act) of 1950 (and all the "little McCarran Acts" passed in the states) and the circumstances that produced them. Nor does Professor Miller intend to evade it, or even to let the parallel present itself. For he does not hesitate to editorialize upon his history (pp. 232-33):

"Without doubt, liberty of speech and of the press lies at the heart of all liberty: 'where men cannot freely convey their thoughts to one another, no other liberty is secure.' In every society worthy to be called free there is an untrammeled play of public opinion; immunity from criticism is the privilege of no government officials; and the right of arguing about ideas is jealously guarded.

"This is the kind of society envisaged by the first amendment to the Constitution; freedom of speech and of the press is the first article of the Bill of Rights. The Federalists who were responsible for the enactment of the Sedition Act had little comprehension of this ideal; their thoughts ran in channels which lead not to freedom and democracy but an authoritarian slough of despond. . . .

"The issue, then and now, is the same: 'Whether the state can punish all words which have some tendency, however remote, to bring about acts in violation of law, or only words which directly incite to acts in violation of law.' "

In the larger sense this test of the democratic faith in the experience of 1798 might be regarded as one of the errors in the long trial-and-error effort to define the line between freedom and order. It might be argued, in extenuation, that the young republic, not yet sure of itself, nor, indeed, as yet committed to democracy in the modern sense, in these acts tried out a method of controlling treasonable dissent, and, having learned that you cannot preserve freedom by destroying it, had become more devoted than ever to the unqualified freedom intended under the first amendment to the Constitution. Unfortunately, the present recurrence of the same moods compels the conclusion that the young republic learned nothing, permanently, from its experience.

The second profoundly significant issue bound up with the history of the Alien and Sedition Acts involved the nature of the constitutional structure of the American union itself. For, actually, the debate over the Alien and Sedition Acts was quite largely a debate over the nature of the relationships between the states and the federative union. Supposing the federal Congress to be capable of passing a law that violated the Constitution, who was to declare it so? At that time the Supreme Court had not yet arrogated to itself that power. Was it the power and prerogative of the states to declare an act of Congress unconstitutional? Madison and Jefferson, in the Virginia and Kentucky Resolutions, argued that it was. Such a doctrine, if accepted, would have made the American Union effectively a federal rather than a national union. The Federalists, naturally enough, argued contrarywise, although it was not until John Marshall read the Supreme Court's decision on Marbury *v.* Madison that the Federalists could offer any very clear alternative to the constitutional doctrines of the Virginia and the Kentucky Resolutions.

The prospect, that appeared about 1800, that the Jeffersonians on coming into power might turn the Sedition Act against its Federalist authors, and that they very probably might do it in the state rather than in federal courts, inclined many Federalists to welcome the expiration of the law. But this prospect also called attention to the further dilemma presented by the probability of having federal law administered in state courts. Was such a thing possible? Actually, it was done in the case of these laws, in Virginia and elsewhere. This dilemma emphasized again the as yet inchoate status of the relationships between the states and the federal government — an inchoateness that was resolved only by the unequivocally federalistic decisions of John Marshall.

This can hardly be called a profound book (Professor Miller probably never intended to be). For it makes no real effort to present a thorough, penetrating, or exhaustive discussion of the great constitutional questions confronting the young nation and upon which it had not yet made up its mind, either the problem of the nature and the limitations of civil rights in a republic or that concerning the constitutional structure of the republic itself. Rather, it is a relatively "popular" — and convincing — descriptive and mildly polemical account of America's first "crisis in freedom." As such, it is to be devoutly hoped that many American citizens may read it, and that there may take place that rarest of all historical events, a lesson learned from history!

The professional historian, however, must still await a thoroughgoing analytical history of this particular "crisis in freedom."

University of Washington MAX SAVELLE

John Colter; His Years in the Rockies. By Burton Harris. (New York: Charles Scribner's Sons, 1952. xiii + 180 pp. Maps, bibliography, and index. $3.50.)

John Colter's stature as a legendary frontier hero is probably rivaled only by that of Daniel Boone who, in 1811, was his venerable neighbor at Charette, Missouri. Colter's achievements as a discoverer and his remarkable adventures incidental thereto have been widely publicized by scholars as well as romanticists. Colter's unique role in early western history has been well defined by Hiram M. Chittenden in his *American Fur Trade* and by Stallo Vinton in his *John Colter, Discoverer of Yellowstone Park.* However, the Harris book is the first full-blown account by one who is thoroughly familiar with the intricate geography of the country explored and who is also capable of distinguishing between facts and guesswork. It is a labor of love by a New York businessman who was born in Wyoming. Reliable source data on Colter are fairly skimpy, but the author makes intelligent use of every sliver of evidence and fills in the gaps by thoughtful speculation.

Colter's perambulations across and around the Rocky Mountains, beginning with his enlistment with the Lewis and Clark expedition in 1803 and ending with his disgusted departure from the Blackfoot-infested post at Three Forks in 1810, are followed carefully. His primary feat of exploring the headwaters of the Big Horn, Wind, Snake, and Yellowstone rivers is the crux of the discussion. The reviewer is gratified to find full confirmation by Harris of his interpretation of the historic "Colter's Hell" as an actual identifiable spot near Cody, Wyoming. Refutation of the popular belief that this was originally a vague term for the thermal wonders of Yellowstone Park was first expounded in print by the reviewer in the September, 1949, issue of the *Mississippi Valley Historical Review.*

The interpretation of Colter's general route describing a loop through present Shoshone National Forest, Grand Teton National Park, and Yellowstone National Park seems reasonable, but certain details will be hotly debated. Chief reliance for the theory of a side trip across the rugged Teton Mountains into Pierre's Hole is based on the "Colter Stone," an inscribed rock of dubious authenticity. The common belief repeated here that Indians were scared stiff by the Yellowstone geysers and avoided them is without foundation in known fact. Finally, even though Harris confesses that Colter in all probability did not visit the geysers of the Firehole Basin in the Yellowstone Park area, he includes descriptions of geysers in stories attributed to Colter by his fellow trappers. Geologists do not concede that the little thermal area near Cody, Wyoming, contained anything resembling Old Faithful.

On the whole, Harris is careful to distinguish between the occasional fact and the frequent conjecture. He cheerfully supplies all the missing details, including what went on in Colter's own mind, but he does not repeat the mistakes characteristic of Wyoming authorities such as Dee Linford, Charles G. Coutant, Nolie Mumey, and Hubert H. Bancroft who are prone to make positive assertions on matters that can only be conjectural. This is a fresh and solid contribution which is not likely to be superseded in our time.

National Park Service, Omaha MERRILL J. MATTES

David Thompson's Journals Relating to Montana and Adjacent Regions, 1808-1812. Transcribed from a photostatic copy of the original manuscripts and edited with an introduction by M. Catherine White. *Montana State University Studies*, Vol. I. (Missoula: Montana State University Press, 1950. clxi + 345 pp. Illustrations, maps, appendixes, bibliography, and index. $7.50.)

David Thompson, through his remarkable contribution to the geographical knowledge concerning North America, deserves to be ranked as one of the greatest geographers of all time. But until very recent years his name and work have been almost completely unknown.

Born in Westminster, England, in 1770, he was apprenticed to the Hudson's Bay Company at the age of fourteen for service in America. As fur trader, explorer, surveyor, and map maker, first for the Hudson's Bay Company and later for the North West Company, he traveled on foot, on horseback, or by canoe not less than 50,000 miles over the vast area from Hudson Bay to the Pacific Ocean. He explored the source of the Mississippi River and surveyed all the southern and part of the northern shores of Lake Superior. Crossing the Rocky Mountains for the first time in 1807, he ascended the Columbia River to Lake Windermere where he built Kootanae House, the first trading post on the Columbia River. During the next four years he surveyed that river throughout its entire course of over 1,100 miles. In 1809 he built Kullyspel House on Pend Oreille Lake, and Saleesh House in what is now northwestern Montana. These were the first trading posts west of the Rocky Mountains in the United States and the jumping-off-places for the extensive fur trade carried on by the British in the Oregon Territory during the next forty years.

In 1812 Thompson retired from active service in the fur trade and was commissioned by the North West Company to complete his large map of Canada. This map, measuring 10′3½″ x 6′6″ and including that portion of country from Hudson Bay to the Pacific Ocean, and from the Great Lakes and the Columbia on the south and northward to Lake Athabaska, was finished within two years. The accuracy of the work is truly amazing, considering the means at Thompson's disposal. From 1817 to 1827 he served as astronomer and surveyor for the British Boundary Commission, provided for in the Treaty of Ghent.

The original journals of David Thompson comprise thirty-nine volumes of manuscript and cover a period of more than sixty-five years, 1784-1850. Except for the records of the Lewis and Clark expedition, Thompson's journals for 1808-1812 are the earliest account of exploration and trade carried on by white men in western Montana, northern Idaho, and eastern Washington, the region now known as the Inland Empire. The parts of his journals relating to Idaho, Washington, and Oregon, including his journey down the Columbia River to Astoria in 1811, have been edited by Mr. T. C. Elliott and published in Washington and Oregon historical quarterlies. The parts relating to Montana, and covering a much longer period, now appear in print for the first time in the volume under consideration and constitute the one series previously missing from the published account of Thompson's activities in the western part of the United States.

The editor, with extraordinary industry, has transcribed the photostatic copy almost in its entirety and has endeavored to reproduce it as nearly as possible in its original form. An introduction of 157 pages gives practically all the available biographical information concerning David Thompson, along with the background of the fur trade in Canada and its westward expansion through the Hudson's Bay and North West companies. Copious footnotes, both for the introduction and the transcribed journal, give an extraordinary amount of supplementary material which will be of great value to research workers. The fifty-page index includes all persons, places, and terms, and complete subject entries. The edition is limited to 500 copies.

An occasional typographical error indicates the difficulties of editing and printing this kind of material but does not detract from the general excellence of the book.

Montana State University EDWARD EARL BENNETT

An Agricultural History of the Genesee Valley, 1790-1860. By Neil Adams McNall. (Philadelphia: University of Pennsylvania Press, 1952. xii + 276 pp. Maps, tables, bibliography, and index. $5.00.)

Somewhat more than a century ago, the Genesee Valley, comprising five counties in western New York with Rochester the major urban center, enjoyed the reputation of being one of the nation's outstanding farming areas. Flour milled from its wheat and bearing its name commanded premium prices and enjoyed an international reputation for quality. The valley's population was progressive and articulate; it was the home of one of the best and most influential agricultural journals of the 1830's and 1840's—the *Genesee Farmer*. Numerous travelers have left us their observations on the area.

This volume deals with the economic aspects of the development of agriculture in the Genesee. The narrative begins with earliest settlement, the alienation of the land by the state of Massachusetts to speculators in large blocks, and the exploitation of the land by purchasers and tenants in the pre-canal subsistence period, moves on with the commercial wheat cropping economy during the canal and early railroad periods, and carries into the movement towards diversification forced by soil depletion and western competition. As the author points out, the transformation of the valley "recapitulated the development of farming in much of the Northern United States."

The central thread in the story is the search for markets and the commercialization of agriculture. But the Genesee Valley is also of special interest in that it was the scene of some of the nation's earliest large landholding operations. The Holland Land Company and the Wadsworth family were among the most important and are given special attention since they provide an important contrast. For while the land company sold its holdings to settlers, the Wadsworths retained most of their acreage, successfully developing a system of tenant farming capitalistic rather than feudalistic in character. Scarcity of monetary capital resulted in slow sales by the land company and Professor McNall's chapter on the development of institutionalized land-mortgage credit by New York bankers is a major contribution to an obscure corner of agricultural history. The Wadsworth operations receive particular attention, not only in the management of their own farms, but in an excellent discussion of the evolution of their tenancy policies.

Manuscript papers of the Wadsworth family have been effectively utilized though the papers are very incomplete. The attempt to integrate the story of the Wadsworths with that of the valley generally, however, never quite succeeds. The narrative moves uneasily between the Holland Land Company, the Wadsworths, and the numerous forces and effects which make up the story. Other organizational deficiencies also mar the performance. Abrupt transitions are too frequent for pleasant reading; e.g., the chapter on livestock raising suddenly concludes with a description of farm housing; we are told of the impact of the railroad on a given point before we are warned that it has arrived.

If the volume thus requires greater exertion than even the professionally interested reader prefers or should be asked to give, it is nevertheless a most welcome addition to the small shelf of area and regional agricultural histories to which Professor McNall has made an important contribution.

Washington, D. C. CLARENCE H. DANHOF

Funk of Funk's Grove: Farmer, Legislator, and Cattle King of the Old Northwest, 1797-1865. By Helen M. Cavanagh. (Bloomington, Ill.: Pantagraph Printing Co., 1952. v + 208 pp. Illustrations, map, appendix, bibliography, and index. $3.50.)

The author of *Funk of Funk's Grove* evidently feels somewhat as did the ancient writer of the Book of Genesis who observes (6:4), "There were giants in the earth in those days." Few will challenge this estimate of the life, accomplishments, and public services of Isaac Funk recorded here for the first time in a full-length biography by Helen M. Cavanagh. Certainly no man contributed more to the economic development of central Illinois or to the extension of agricultural enterprise, chiefly the raising and feeding of livestock, than did Funk of Funk's Grove. His energy and foresight and, above all, his abundant faith in Illinois agriculture which carried him from humble beginnings to a position of wealth and prominence adds up to a remarkable success story. Miss Cavanagh has told it with dignity and restraint, nicely avoiding the temptation to applaud or moralize over her hero's achievements.

One will find in the volume a definite effort to relate the activities of the Funk family, and in particular those of Isaac Funk, to the social and economic climate prevailing in a rapidly developing frontier agricultural economy. If the Isaac Funk who emerges from these pages is something more of an institution than he is a flesh and blood person, the fault may not rest entirely with the author. Anyone who has ever attempted a biography will appreciate the handicap under which she has labored — the loss by fire of valuable personal papers and manuscript materials originally belonging to Isaac Funk. Also, readers will do well to remember that this mid-nineteenth-century farmer neither spoke, wrote, nor thought in terms of a twentieth-century biography. As a man of action Funk would seem to fit admirably a definition of "Western Men" whose characteristics were said to be "Determined energy, untiring perseverence, willingness to labor, practical business talent, devotion to accumulating money, and a keen attention to purely commercial literature" (p. 137).

There are a few particulars in which the book could have been improved. For example, in Chapters IV and V, which give a great deal of attention to early railroad building in Illinois, a map or two identifying the rail lines mentioned in the text would be most welcome. This reviewer is fully aware of the difficulty involved in avoiding confusion when dealing with the mass of local railroad projects arising in Illinois during the mid-century years. Perhaps a closer examination of the ever growing list of railroad archives rather than an exclusive dependence upon local newspapers for this information would have simplified matters.

Likewise, the book deserved more careful proofreading. Numerous small errors have crept in, but these minor shortcomings will subtract little from the debt of appreciation which those interested in midwestern history and agriculture will owe to the author of this compact little volume.

University of Illinois ROBERT M. SUTTON

The Texas Revolution. By William C. Binkley. (Baton Rouge: Louisiana State University Press, 1952. viii + 132 pp. $2.50.)

Only a scholar as familiar with the Texas Revolution as Professor Binkley could have written this slim volume; anyone else would have used four times the space to tell the same story. Writing against the rich background gained by a quarter century of study, he has produced four connected essays — originally delivered as the Walter Lynwood Fleming Lectures at Louisiana State University — which offer the best interpretation of the Texan struggle for independence yet to appear. His achievement is the more remarkable in that he makes no pretence of either offering new materials or writing the entire history of the revolution. Instead, his contribution is to draw new meaning from familiar monographic studies and to give logical order to a sequence of events that have remained chaotic in the hands of many earlier historians.

His interpretative ability is best shown in the first essay on the underlying causes of independence. Forever dispelling both the older myth of the slaveholders and the newer myth of the land speculators as principal revolutionists, he demonstrates that the struggle was "a manifestation of the Anglo-American frontier process being worked out under unusual conditions." Developing resistence, he concludes, "marked the culmination of hitherto diversified frontier interests into one general problem of securing a satisfactory adjustment to the changing conditions which accentuated the difference between the Texans and the rest of the Mexican Republic."

In a second essay tracing the steps leading to independence, Professor Binkley's principal contribution is to bring order to the confusion achieved by most writers who have examined the period between 1834 and 1836. A third chapter sketching the course of events immediately preceding hostilities emphasizes the confusion and division among Texans which found final expression at the Alamo and Goliad. At this stage, he believes, the revolution "was the product of the unplanned combination of a large number of unskilled participants whose conception and aims differed greatly." A final essay traces the emergence of a spirit of unity under the impact of these disasters until a constitution and independence could be achieved.

This stimulating volume deserves the attention of every student with sufficient background to appreciate the extent of Professor Binkley's knowledge and the astuteness of his interpretations.

Northwestern University RAY ALLEN BILLINGTON

Calhoun; Basic Documents. Edited by John M. Anderson. (State College, Pa.: Bald Eagle Press, 1952. 329 pp. $5.00.)

The Calhoun revival continues to flourish, the latest contribution being a kind of Calhoun sampler, edited by the chairman of the philosophy department of the Pennsylvania State College. The volume begins with an eighteen-page introduction summarizing Calhoun's ideas on "political unity and sectionalism," "the development of social structure," "power and principle," and "responsibility and freedom." Next comes the *Disquisition on Government*, the text of which is taken from Richard K. Crallé's standard edition of Calhoun's *Works* (6 vols., 1851-1856). Then follows a group of eleven speeches, ranging from 1811 to 1850, which "have been selected to show the development of Calhoun's thought from his early nationalism to his final views and to set the theoretical tenets of his thought in their matrix of practical politics" (pp. 328-29). The text of these speeches, with one exception, is from the published records of congressional debates, not from the *Works*. Throughout the book editorial apparatus is kept to a bare minimum, a total of two notes sufficing for the *Disquisition* and two more for all the speeches. This reprinting of Calhoun materials is justified (p. 5) on the ground that "his basic work on political theory has not been readily available to students since the publication of *A Disquisition on Government* in 1851." As a matter of fact, the *Disquisition* was republished in a photolithographic reproduction from the *Works* in 1947, and copies of the *Works* themselves are by no means rare in college and university libraries. Nevertheless, Professor Anderson has performed a useful service in bringing together, in one convenient and attractive volume, these intelligently selected documents. For historians, he would have performed an even more valuable service if he had provided a wholly new edition of the *Disquisition*, from the original manuscript, and if he had supplied a thorough annotation and commentary for both the essay and the speeches, to say nothing of an index.

University of Illinois RICHARD N. CURRENT

A Chronicle of Old Muskego; The Diary of Sören Bache, 1839-1847. Translated and edited by Clarence A. Clausen and Andreas Elviken. (Northfield, Minn.: Norwegian-American Historical Association, 1951. xxi + 237 pp. Appendix and index. $3.50.)

In the 1840's hundreds of Norwegian immigrants arriving at Milwaukee went first to the pioneer settlement near Lake Muskego, a short distance southwest of the lakeport. Here they received shelter, food, and information from those who had arrived earlier. Soon the tide of migration swept westward to new centers, but Muskego remained a living name among Norwegians. In considerable part responsible for the early prominence of Muskego in Norwegian immigration and settlement was Sören Bache, son of a wealthy lumber dealer and shipper of Drammen, Norway, who with a companion emigrated to America in 1839. After searching about for land in both Illinois and Wisconsin he settled at Muskego, returned to visit his father and relatives in Norway in 1842-1843, and sailed again for America to stay until 1847 when he returned permanently to his homeland for reasons not clearly given. The gifted young man kept a diary which gives a vivid picture of pioneer life in southeastern Wisconsin. Dean Theodore C. Blegen in his preface to this volume succinctly describes the diarist:

"Bache was endlessly curious about the pageant of America in the 1840s. He crossed and re-crossed the Atlantic, visited New York and Washington, climbed the Bunker Hill Monument, built a home in an ancient Indian mound, wandered about in the pioneer Wisconsin settlements, celebrated a Fourth of July in the infant city of Madison, took an interest in politics and in the War with Mexico, helped to launch the pioneer Norwegian newspaper in America, quarreled with and grumbled about the 'papistry' of pioneer Lutheran clergymen, thumbed over almanacs and gazeteers for information about the many states he visited, walked rough country roads, had a look at Niagara Falls, set forth theories about disease in the frontier communities, took note of Joseph Smith and the Mormons, and in general tossed into his diary, or 'Memorandum,' as he calls it, odd bits of information that he picked up from whatever source. Thus his record is both a diary and a collection of miscellaneous memoranda."

The very difficult job of transcribing, translating, and editing this important immigrant diary has been admirably done, especially by Professor Clarence A. Clausen who took over from the late Andreas Elviken. The diary has been broken up into fifteen chapters dealing with the departure from the homeland, the voyage, the settlement at Muskego, the return trip home in 1842-1843, and an astonishing variety of observations concerning life in the pioneer settlements and in cities visited by Bache on his journeys. Bache was an indefatigable traveler, and, unlike most of his fellow emigrants, he had the money to indulge his curiosity. A tendency to snobbishness grates on the reader's sensibilities at times, but his comments are generally clear and penetrating and he holds one's interest to the end. Professor Clausen's informing introduction and generous footnotes add much to the value of the volume. The managing editor of the Norwegian-American Historical Association, Dean Blegen, is to be congratulated upon another important publication in the field of American immigration.

Carleton College CARLTON C. QUALEY

The Texas Santa Fe Trail. By H. Bailey Carroll. (Canyon, Texas: Panhandle-Plains Historical Society, 1951. 201 pp. Illustrations, maps, appendix, bibliography, and index. $5.00.)

The major aim of this book is to trace in detail the route of the Texan Santa Fe expedition of 1841. It is not concerned especially with the origin or objects of that ill-fated venture, nor with the reasons for its failure, although these aspects of the undertaking are mentioned. No effort has been made to retell George W. Kendall's vivid *Narrative of the Texan Santa Fe Expedition*, although many excerpts from that classic of western adventure have been quoted along with others from Thomas Falconer's *Letters and Notes on the Texan-Santa Fe Expedition*. Use has been made of the other contemporary sources, especially the Gallagher-Hoyle Journal which is reproduced in the appendix. With all available records at hand, the author has gone over the entire route, matching narrative and diary against topography. He has taken counsel with men who are familiar with local history and geography. Detailed maps of the region, in so far as they are available, have been studied. The result is what may well be called a definitive route. In most instances the author can locate with assurance the river crossings, the camp sites, and even many of the gullies and breaks through which the party made its way. In a few places where such precision is impossible, because of uncertainties in the records or the character of the terrain, locations approximately correct have been suggested.

The journey was much longer and more difficult than had been anticipated. Instead of being welcomed as emissaries of a friendly neighbor who wanted to open up trading relations, the Texans were regarded as hostile invaders and treated accordingly. In retrospect it seems strange that they risked life and treasure on such meager geographical knowledge and so much political misinformation.

There may be some who will ask whether the determination of the exact route of this particular expedition was worth all the time and effort it required. Many scholars will answer quickly in the affirmative; certainly there will be no doubt in the minds of those who realize the importance of local history. And it may be noted here that Dr. Carroll is one of those who have helped arouse a great and intelligent interest in the local history of the Lone Star State through the Junior Historian movement. Not all students of history share this interest, and, as the author says, quoting a remark attributed to Abraham Lincoln, "For a person who likes this type of book, this is a good example of the type of book which he likes."

There are four maps showing the route as reconstructed from Austin to Laguna Colorado in New Mexico. These maps show county lines and rivers, but only a few of the present towns, even though many references are made to them in the text; the curious reader who is not familiar with the towns along the route must refer to a current atlas. The bibliography bears witness to the thoroughness of the study.

University of Colorado COLIN B. GOODYKOONTZ

The March of Empire; Frontier Defense in the Southwest, 1848-1860. By Averam B. Bender. (Lawrence: The University of Kansas Press, 1952. 323 pp. Illustrations, map, bibliography, and index. $5.00.)

The March of Empire is a notable addition to the history of the Southwest. Professor Bender has succeeded in welding a mass of material into a coherent account of the region, from the Treaty of Guadalupe Hidalgo to the opening of the American Civil War. The story is well balanced, readable, and usually accurate. It answers questions that the student of western history wants to have explained, and gives fresh, vital information on frontier leaders. Some passages are little masterpieces of narrative — as, for example, the story of Stephen W. Kearney's expedition to Santa Fe and California. For the general reader, interested in a good story about real people, this account is excellent; for the student of history who has some acquaintance with Kearney and his associates, it is fascinating.

The chapters on "Western River Surveys" and "Explorations for Defense" are well done. Snag pulling on the Red River, exploration and improvement of the Texas rivers, and the thorough exploration of the Colorado of the West are the high points in the account of river surveys. The career of Captain Randolph B. Marcy as an explorer is presented with interesting detail.

The sketch of John Coffee Hays, Texas Ranger, "a true frontiersman and typical Indian fighter," is unforgettable. Commander of the Rangers at the age of twenty-three, Hays marked out a trail from Texas to Santa Fe, led punitive expeditions against Paiutes and other Indians, was held in awe by outlaws from the Gulf to the upper waters of the Brazos, Red, and Colorado rivers, and in countless ways "had a most remarkable control over men." In person "Colonel Jack" was a "small, modest, and retiring frontiersman, who thought much and spoke little." After his service in Texas he went to California, where he was sheriff of San Francisco and in 1853 surveyor general of the state.

The Mormon migration and the place of the Mormons in frontier development are treated adequately and fairly. The Indian tribes of the Southwest, constituting a large element in the struggle over United States expansion, appear repeatedly throughout the book, in various aspects of war and peacetime activity. The author does not demonstrate the same sure grasp of Indian life that he shows in his accounts of trail finders and frontier law officers. There is some tendency to characterize Indian tribes as "thievish," "industrious," "intelligent," "treacherous," "cheerful," "bloodthirsty," "innocent," "unsavory," "brave," "thriftless," or "debased" without sufficient evidence.

White frontiersmen often applied such terms to various Indian bands, and perhaps by their use of adjectives contributed to popular confusion about the native Americans.

In spite of minor flaws, the book is generally well done. It has in it so much of the history of the Southwest, so attractively presented, that it cannot be neglected.

University of Oklahoma EDWIN C. MCREYNOLDS

Journal of an Expedition to the Mauvaises Terres and the Upper Missouri in 1850. By Thaddeus A. Culbertson. Edited by John Francis McDermott. Smithsonian Institution, Bureau of American Ethnology, *Bulletin* 147. (Washington: Government Printing Office, 1952. viii + 164 pp. Maps, appendixes, bibliography, and index. $.75.)

This interesting and valuable diary was written by Alexander Culbertson's younger brother, who had been commissioned by the Smithsonian Institution to collect natural history specimens while he accompanied his well-known brother on a summer trip.

The Culbertsons traveled by boat from St. Louis to Saint Joseph, thence by land along the Missouri to Fort Pierre. Here Thaddeus set off to collect fossil specimens in the *Mauvaises Terres* on the White River. An eleven-day trip of three hundred miles in the badlands yielded excellent specimens. Throughout the trip Culbertson assembled skeletons of the animals of the region, cured and stuffed skins, and carefully observed the bird life and botany of the region. The Indians of the area fascinated him and he observed them at close range. The young man traveled to the upper river on the *El Paso* which that year established a new distance record beyond the mouth of the Milk.

The diary is the best record of the subject we have for the year 1850. Culbertson was a theological student at Princeton University at the time, and the journal lacks many details a more experienced explorer might have included. He was well trained, however, and had broad scientific interests. His brother gave him invaluable aid, and the result is a vivid and thoughtful description of the Upper Missouri, its commerce, personalities, its Indians in considerable detail, the river forts, and especially its natural history.

The editor is to be commended for gathering scattered parts of the journal from the Missouri and Montana historical societies and meshing them smoothly with the scientific excerpts originally published by the Smithsonian Institution in 1850. Brief and helpful footnotes, contemporary maps, and additional Culbertson notes in an appendix make a satisfactory although brief documentary view of the Upper Missouri River in 1850.

Montana State College MERRILL G. BURLINGAME

Refugees of Revolution; The German Forty-Eighters in America. By Carl Wittke. (Philadelphia: University of Pennsylvania Press, 1952. ix + 384 pp. Index. $6.00.)

Probably no other immigrant group comparable in numbers has influenced the culture or the intellectual and political life of the United States as did the German "Forty-eighters" in the period of storm and stress from 1850 to 1875. "Like a stone thrown into still water," says their historian Carl Wittke, they "produced waves in the German-American pool high enough eventually to affect the entire American cultural pattern."

The Forty-eighters were not all or uniformly successful. They were a crotchety crew, as ready to try to reshape their new world as they had been to revolt against their old one. Lone-wolf Karl Heinzen's "unquenchable thirst for controversy" and his unfortunate genius for "making enemies unnecessarily" doomed him to a life of penury; but his *Pionier* was a paper of character and distinction. Many fumbled for a while, as "Latin farmers" or otherwise, or as Carl Schurz did in real estate, before finding secure footing, often in the professions for which they had been trained before migration. Usually they clung tenaciously to their love of music, the theater, "literary" activities, and convivial gatherings. The lyceum platform, the teaching and medical professions, orchestras and choral societies, and local militia organizations were strengthened by their coming.

Gregarious and "German" though they were, with the persistent national pride characteristic of immigrant groups, most of the Forty-eighters were arrant individualists. They wrangled among themselves and criticized their neighbors — not always tactfully. No two were quite alike, even in this. Yet it is possible to generalize about them. They were generally anticlerical, and inveterate enemies of Puritan "blue laws" for Sabbath observance. They hated both slavery and nativism, and needed persuasion by Schurz and others to bring enough of them into the Republican party in 1860 to help materially to elect Lincoln. Like other Americans they fought for the Union or for their states or section in the War Between the States, but more of them for the North than for the South because more had found homes there. With Schurz again their most vocal spokesman, they advocated civil service and sound money after the war, and gloried in the strength of the new Germany politically unified under Prussian leadership by their old enemy Bismarck.

It is largely as individuals — hundreds of them — that Dr. Wittke writes about them, with an encyclopedic wealth of biographical detail, and with the genial sympathy and tolerant understanding of long and intimate acquaintance. As they made places for themselves in the life of their second fatherland, they find their places in this friendly book. Here are the outstanding medical men, founders of hospitals, medical schools, and journals: Doctors

Abraham Jacobi and Ernst Krackowitzer of New York (both Jewish), Hans Kudlich of Hoboken, Heinrich Tiedemann of Philadelphia, Hermann Kiefer of Detroit, Ernst Schmidt of Chicago, and many others; Civil War soldiers such as Franz Sigel, Ludwig Blenker, Schurz, and whole companies and regiments of "other ranks" unnamed; political reporter and war correspondent Henry Villard, turned railway entrepreneur and associate of Thomas Edison in the Edison General Electric Company; Heinrich Steinweg, the Steinway piano maker; Schurz, senator and secretary of interior, independent in politics and ultimately anti-imperialist; and a host of others.

To those others whose names are not recorded, the author gives perhaps his highest praise: "Their lives blended harmoniously with the great American stream, and they found both freedom and economic opportunity in the Republic which gave them their new start in life."

University of Wisconsin CHESTER V. EASUM

Abraham Lincoln; A Biography. By Benjamin P. Thomas. (New York: Alfred A. Knopf, 1952. xiv + 548 + xii pp. Illustrations, maps, bibliography, and index. $5.75.)

Dr. Thomas is unusually well qualified to write a biography of Lincoln. He has done research of the highest quality in special fields, he has written a definitive book on Lincoln biography, and he has lived with the materials of the Robert Todd Lincoln Papers since these were opened to the public. He has made excellent use of these and other original sources in this book. He has ably demonstrated his qualifications in this readable and authoritative volume.

By choice the author held himself to a single volume, thus accepting severe restrictions. Background material is necessarily brief. References to contemporaries, whether of high or of minor importance, are rigidly compressed. There could be but little historical exposition. Nevertheless the scale of the work is unexceptionable: 129 pages take Lincoln through Congress, 95 pages cover the "return" to politics and the candidacies for the Senate, and 296 pages are devoted to the period of the presidency. Within these limitations, and on this scale, Dr. Thomas has written a chronicle of the Lincoln story which may be expected to become the standard single-volume biography.

Readers will disagree with some of the author's decisions and will question certain features of the book. In the reviewer's judgment, the chapters on Lincoln's early life are too conventional. Yet here the author properly omits or revises many of the traditions, e.g., Thomas Lincoln is correctly presented as not shiftless, Mrs. Lincoln is delineated with sympathy and appreciation, and the Ann Rutledge tale is handled critically. However, the book continues the myth that Lincoln after his congressional term retired from politics, to emerge when the Kansas-Nebraska Act repealed the Missouri Compromise. He was, in fact, never out of politics, and the Kansas-Nebraska Act was the occasion for Lincoln to rehabilitate himself and to run for office on the slavery issue.

There is ground for more serious criticism. Not only are Lincoln's contemporaries but briefly treated; they play hardly more than supporting roles. Thus Douglas appears to have served no more useful purpose than Lincoln's opposite. Surely he deserves more than this. In the narrative of the presidency the war eclipses all else — hardly anything is said of Lincoln's administration as economic developments are involved. The Homestead Act is noted, the National Banking Act is mentioned as an instance of Salmon P. Chase's "financial wizardry" but with no recognition of its part in the emergence of the new industrialism, and the Contract Labor Law, the Morrill tariff, and the Morrill Act are not so much as mentioned. The reader of this book will be assured that Lincoln saved the Union, but he will not learn what kind of a Union Lincoln's party leaders were creating. Dr. Thomas touches lightly — much too lightly — what William B. Hesseltine so devastatingly demonstrated in his *Lincoln and the War Governors.* It appears to have been the War Department which was decisive in the election of 1864. The result is that while Dr. Thomas has given us an excellent chronicle of Lincoln's life he does not "explain" him; to the reader of this book Lincoln is still an enigma.

Presumably the publisher, not Dr. Thomas, is responsible for the illustrations being few and mediocre. Quite properly the book is undocumented; the author has supplied a well-selected and thoroughly comprehensive bibliographical note.

University of Illinois,
Chicago Undergraduate Division DONALD W. RIDDLE

Doctors in Blue; The Medical History of the Union Army in the Civil War. By George Worthington Adams. (New York: Henry Schuman, 1952. xii + 253 pp. Illustrations, sources, appendix, and index. $4.00.)

Doctors in Blue is of genuine merit. It is based on extensive source materials such as surgeons' reports, inspectors' observations, soldiers' narratives, and others. The book contains an excellent bibliography but no footnotes. Much statistical information, however, is recorded throughout the study on such subjects as the many and varied diseases that were contracted by the Union soldiers and the methods of treatment. "Medical Department statistics show an annual average of 2,435 cases of sickness per thousand among white troops [Colored, 3,299]. The annual average death rate from disease was 53.4 per thousand [Colored, 143.4]. There is reason to believe that large numbers of men failed to 'report sick' unless they were seriously ill, and that the mortality was greater than the records indicate because of the thousands of discharged soldiers who died at home" (pp. 222-23, 239).

Behind the sickness and mortality statistics lay ignorance, inexperience, inefficiency, and carelessness. On the other hand, great strides were made in medical science. The result of "the War experience was a preparation of both the medical mind and the public mind for the great era of sanitary reform" (p. 229).

The eleven chapter headings reveal the nature of this study: "The Medical Confusions of 1861," "Reformers *vs.* Regulars," "The . . . Army Surgeons," "Beginnings of an Ambulance System," "Improvement in Field Tactics," "Wartime Surgery," "Operations and Infections," "The General Hospitals," "Nurses, Staffs and Convalescents," "Army Sanitation and Hygiene," and "Diseases and Treatments."

The book is well written, interesting, carefully balanced, and scholarly. It contains illustrations, engravings, and pictures of northern hospitals. It must be considered one of the essential books of the Civil War period. In fact, it is the best single volume on the medical history of the Union army during the Civil War.

Lehigh University GEORGE D. HARMON

Business in the Gilded Age; The Conservatives' Balance Sheet. By Edward C. Kirkland. (Madison: University of Wisconsin Press, 1952. 59 pp $1.50.)

This thin little booklet of fifty-nine pages, with the ambitious title *Business in the Gilded Age; The Conservatives' Balance Sheet*, is made up of three lectures delivered at the University of Wisconsin during the second semester of the academic year 1950-1951 under the Kemper K. Knapp Bequest. Mr. Knapp left to Wisconsin a fund with the request that a part of the income be "used to cultivate in the student body ideals of honesty, sincerity, earnestness, tolerance, and social and political obligations." In addition to setting up scholarships and fellowships, those individuals charged with the administration of the income have wisely "sponsored from time to time lectures, conferences, and visiting professorships in the belief that extracurricular lectures on appropriate subjects by outstanding men representing various points of view would appeal to the imagination of our students and might help to awaken in the student body a sharper understanding of the privileges and responsibilities which as citizens of this country and the world we have all inherited."

Professor Kirkland, economic historian of wide reputation, distinguished member of the Bowdoin College faculty, and one of the early visitors at Wisconsin under the Knapp benefaction, makes it plain in his introduction — though less obvious in his lectures — that he is concerned with rewriting some of the pages of the past. That the dramatic period between the Civil War and 1900 needs re-evaluation is hardly to be disputed by one who looks dispassionately at the great accomplishments of those years. Re-evaluation to me, however, must begin not with the question of whether "robber barons" is or is not a proper designation but with a re-examination of the basic forces that in three decades unrolled before us such a tremendous material panaroma. Did the rest of the world fall behind the United States in thirty short years because other nations did not possess men of greed and of corrupt hearts? I do not think so. Heretical as the viewpoint may seem, I am inclined to feel that the hard core of progress is to be found in whatever it was that in the face of difficulties and handicaps and even rottenness built pounding plants great and small and rushing railroads local and transcontinental and then made it possible for the people of the nation to buy the goods and use the trains and emerge at the turn of the century with wealth unmatched and with at least hopes for leisure and social justice. After that is explained one must, of course, explain why so much good was plagued with so much bad, why the manipulations so completely overshadowed the basic accomplishments, and what strange quirk in human minds brought forth so much evil that somehow seemed to strike so deep into the very fiber of strength — "robber barons" might then be understood in its real meaning.

No one could be expected to present a definitive story of business even in any single one of its many phases in fewer than threescore pages. The greatest weakness, however, of this particular undertaking, at least to this reviewer, is that the presentation is neither general nor specific; it neither sets the stage in whole nor gives an act complete. Basically it is made up of the observations of a twentieth-century scholar on the observations of three individuals of the Gilded Age: Charles Francis Adams, Jr., Edwin L. Godkin, and Andrew Carnegie. There is not even a thumbnail sketch of business or of the Gilded Age, and the balance sheet is limited to a brief peroration that seems to reflect a deep nostalgia for "the good old days." Does Mr. Kirkland imply in that peroration that the success of the great men of the golden age of American industry was a direct result of their comprehension of and their obeisance to "first principles and fundamental laws"? Does he mean to say by indirection that the complexities of the modern world and its puzzling problems would disappear if we but returned to sanity? It may possibly be that the two ages, however closely related, have their own peculiar generative forces and their own peculiar frivolities. These questions and exceptions notwithstanding, all readers must admit that Mr. Kirkland's lectures, though seeming to lack his usual force and direction, are studded with keen comments, and all historians will be looking forward to the completed study.

Temple University JAMES A. BARNES

Norwegian-American Studies and Records, Vols. XVI-XVII. (Northfield, Minn.: Norwegian-American Historical Association, 1950, 1952. Vol. XVI: vii + 218 pp. $2.50; Vol. XVII: vii + 185 pp. $2.50.)

These volumes, under the vigorous and able editorship of Theodore C. Blegen, continue to demonstrate the high standards of scholarship of this *Studies and Records* series. The first volume (of the two under review), the publication of which marked a quarter century of activity of the Norwegian-American Historical Association, is devoted exclusively to papers and documents dealing with the Pacific coast, one of the last of America's frontiers. The completion of the first rail connections to California by means of the Union and Central Pacific lines in 1869 meant closer contact on the part of Norwegians of the Middle West with the small groups of Scandinavians in the San Francisco region and elsewhere. It also meant greatly facilitated travel for those looking for a place of settlement more favorable than parts of the Middle West. Later, the completion of more northerly transcontinental railroads to the Pacific Northwest stimulated much Scandinavian migration to that area.

In 1870 the Norwegian Lutheran Synod, sensing an opportunity to extend its work in the West, put the Reverend Christian Hvistendahl in charge of a mission in San Francisco, and he organized Scandinavian elements living there into a chucrch, of which he was pastor until 1875. The eccentric A. E. Fridrichsen at about the same time started work with a Scandinavian congregation in Portland, Oregon. Communications from these pioneer religious leaders, as reported in the Norwegian-language press of the Middle West, form the basis for an extended discussion of Hvistendahl's career by Kenneth Bjork of St. Olaf College and of Fridrichsen's activities by Nora O. Solum, also of St. Olaf College.

Sverre Arestad of the University of Washington edits an early account by O. B. Iverson of the beginning of a Norwegian settlement in the Puget Sound region. C. A. Clausen of St. Olaf College translates and edits a series of letters written by Norwegians after 1896 from the gold fields of the Klondike and Alaska. Carl L. Lokke of the National Archives in turn uses diaries and other materials to give information regarding an expedition led by his grandfather to the Klondike and beyond.

In the second volume Einar Haugen of the University of Wisconsin gives an interesting discussion of the struggle over the use of the Norwegian language in American educational, religious, and social life. Oystein Ore of Yale analyzes parts of a Norwegian play of 1839 that reveals significant attitudes of the time toward emigration to America. Professor Bjork assembles much information regarding "Norwegian Gold Seekers in the Rockies." Franklin D. Scott of Northwestern University discusses the influence of Soren Jaabaek, a Norwegian journalist and poet who viewed emigration with sympathy and understanding. Gerald H. Thorson of Augsburg College, Minneapolis, gives an interesting account of the beginnings of Norwegian-American literature. Finally, Franklin D. Scott discusses the accomplishments of the Norwegian-American Historical Association, and Theodore C. Blegen looks with enthusiasm upon the prospects for a second twenty-five years.

Each volume contains a valuable bibliography of recent publications in the field of Norwegian-American history compiled by Jacob Hodnefield.

Ohio State University FRANCIS P. WEISENBURGER

Henry Adams: Scientific Historian. By William H. Jordy. (New Haven: Yale University Press, 1952. xv + 327 pp. Appendix, bibliography, and index. $5.00.)

This book falls substantially into two sections. The first is a close and illuminating analysis of Adams' *History of the United States of America during the Administrations of Jefferson and Madison* and adds another voice to the chorus of praise the work has elicited since its publication. Once again it establishes that Adams has made a contribution of the first order to American history. In the second section the author trains his guns on the "scientific" project of Adams which has never ceased to disturb and mystify his fellow historians since, if brought to a successful termination, it would have written finis to history as practiced since Herodotus by smothering it in the embrace of the natural sciences. The works which Adams published in pursuit of this dream are "The Tendency of History," "The Rule of Phase Applied to History," *A Letter to American Teachers of History*, and the concluding chapters of *The Education of Henry Adams* devoted to the wonders of the dynamo. This is the novel and decisive portion of the book. We are informed that the idea of the subjection of history to the sciences, and more particularly to physics, did not take root in Adams' mind until his inborn pessimism gained such indisputable mastery over him that he lost his zest for life. When he then yielded to the fascination the natural sciences had for him from early manhood, he focused his attention on the second law of thermodynamics, which with its assertion of the steady decline of available natural energy fell in perfectly with his ageing state of mind. What Jordy then sets forth with unanswerable fullness of detail is that in elaborating his argument Adams drew only on authorities which favored his position and blandly ignored all contrary opinion. What is worse, he misunderstood or even perhaps consciously mispresented some of the scientists he summoned as witnesses. The case of Willard Gibbs is particularly glaring. It was from Gibbs that Adams took over the concept of phase; but, says his critic, "it would be difficult to imagine how Adams could have distorted Gibbs's phase rule more completely" (p. 169). Even more destructive of Adams' standing as a scientist is that, having rested his argument on the unchallengeable "truth" of the second law of thermodynamics, he should have failed to mention that Gibbs, by rejecting its universality, swept the whole flimsy construction of the would-be scientist into the dustbin. With mounting indignation at Adams' amateurish procedure, Jordy charges him with glibness and flippancy and concludes with stigmatizing the total effort to transform history into a natural science as unprofitable wasteland. In short, the "scientific" works of Adams are left the shambles every historian suspected them to have been before Jordy subjected them to a professional autopsy. How it happened that a man of undoubted genius should have fallen into this colossal aberration is a riddle of personality which the author glances at but refuses to plumb because it is buried in impenetrable subconscious depths. Succinctly recapitulated, this book declares that Adams, the historian, continues to shine with undiminished luster but that Adams, the quasi scientist, has crumbled to dust and ashes.

Michigan City, Indiana FERDINAND SCHEVILL

Erwin Frink Smith; A Story of North American Plant Pathology. By Andrew Denny Rodgers, III. (Philadelphia: American Philosophical Society, 1952. x + 675 pp. Illustrations and index. $5.00.)

Though as a graduating senior Erwin Frink Smith was highly recommended as a "man of character and worth [with] a natural taste for agriculture and a desire to study problems of practical utility such as plant diseases," he did not go to the University of Georgia. Instead he joined the newly organized United States Department of Agriculture laboratory of plant pathology, at first sharing the quarters of the department's artist in the old government building on the Mall. From 1886, when funds were small, books few, and only the simplest of microscopes at hand, Smith's professional life spans the growth of phytopathology as a science. A quarter of a century later sees its instruments focused on cancer research, which he launched, on viruses and antibiotics.

Rodgers began chronicling American botany in 1940 with his biography of William S. Sullivant. Six other books have followed, on John Torrey (1942), Asa Gray (1944), John M. Coulter (1944), Liberty Hyde Bailey (1949), Bernhard E. Fernow (1951), and now Smith, — totalling 3,178 pages, a notable publication record! This biography of botanist Smith and his retinue — for this is not the portrait of *a* man — recounts valorous struggles with politics in universities, government officials "drest in a little brief authority," and disputatious colleagues who resisted as with a kind of antibiotic any notion that bacteria might live in plants. Rodgers has written a factual story of "good work accomplished," in a style plodding and humorless, with exceedingly fine and honest detail. Stories of how the use of copper sulphate and lime checked the Peronospora grape disease, or the leaf disease of coffee transplanted the coffee growing industry from Java and the Indian Ocean shores to America, or how the tobacco mosaic virus was detected, are tales never dwelt on long enough to develop a mycelium in our minds before they are sterilized by another injection of names and phrases. Yet indisputably this biography makes available historical fact from abundant sources that might have been lost.

Smith's great contribution was the relation of crown gall of plants to human cancer. He found heredity an insufficient explanation for cancer, remarking that "heredity furnished the canvas but could not paint the picture." For "forty years he devoted his life's services to the broad field of pathology," and at seventy planned five projects including a translation of Heredia's sonnets, an autobiography, and the completion of his Carnegie monograph. Three years later death stopped his schedule, but the diseases and Smith's zeal to study and combat them live on.

Tulane University JOSEPH EWAN

Essays Honoring Lawrence C. Wroth. (Portland, Me.: The Anthoensen Press, 1951. xxi + 515 pp. Frontispiece and index. $25.00.)

The editorial committee of this *Festschrift*, under the chairmanship of Mr. Frederick R. Goff, followed the simple rules which make such books at once a contribution to a subject and a testimonial to the worth of the man they honor. Out of the wide circle of friends and admirers of Mr. Wroth, they limited the contributors to those who could write in his own field of Americana before 1801; they chose people, for the most part able, who reflected in their several interests Mr. Wroth's own mixture, unusual in these days, of bibliographer, book collector, historian, and librarian. As a result nearly every essay in the volume says something of importance to some specialist or other. The historian may not consider that the dating of the first printing of the Maryland charter as 1635 rather than 1632 or the possibility that Goddard printed a broadside and a playbill before the announcement of his press is of particular moment, but to the collector such information is more important than that the Gulf Stream was first studied, simultaneously, by Benjamin Franklin and William De Brahm.

Of the twenty-five essays in the book, nine consist largely of lists of books or of persons, seven describe single books or a few only, two deal with special collections, and seven can be classified as historical. For the historian the essays in the first category are of greater value than those in the last. The longest, sixty pages instead of the average of twenty, is also the most useful, both for historians and collectors, being a list of one hundred maps of America published in Great Britain between 1600 and 1850, with careful bibliographical descriptions by Henry Stevens and Roland Tree. A bibliography of American booksellers' catalogues, by Clarence S. Brigham, opens wider the door to a class of source material which historians have not fully utilized, while Richard S. Hill's list of eighty-five American parodies of the tune of "To Anacreon in Heaven," the melody of "The Star Spangled Banner," shows its popularity as a vehicle for the expression of patriotic sentiment.

Fittingly enough, there are essays on John Carter Brown, on the Brown family of Providence and Brown University, on John Carter Brown's purchase from Henry Stevens, in 1846, of Hispanic-American books from the Ternaux collection, and a bibliography, nineteen pages in length, of Mr. Wroth's own writings.

Newberry Library STANLEY PARGELLIS

Charles Waddell Chesnutt, Pioneer of the Color Line. By Helen M. Chesnutt. (Chapel Hill: The University of North Carolina Press, 1952. viii + 324 pp. Index. $5.00.)

This is an intimate account of the life of this country's first notable Negro novelist by his daughter. We are given all the facts about Chesnutt's private and literary life except why he was so fair-skinned that he could have joined the white race. There is nothing dramatic to tell because Chesnutt always lived a well-protected life in the bosom of a loving family. He was industrious, sober, and justified in the high value he put upon his own moral worth. His daughter's book is hardly more than a stringing together of his letters and addresses without the elimination of repetition and of data not called for by the chapter headings. No attempt is made to appraise Chesnutt's literary achievements — to explain his partial success as a writer and why he did not make for himself a lasting place in American literature. But the reader can draw conclusions from the data which are faithfully presented here.

Chesnutt as a man was able to get ahead in the world. He was determined to overcome the handicaps of caste of the little North Carolina city in which he was reared. Doubtless he was the most energetic person in Fayetteville in the 1880's. He learned all he could acquire in the Negro schools and then studied privately English literature, Latin, Greek, music, and stenography. He was rewarded with the best teaching position Fayetteville offered a Negro. Not satisfied with his southern environment, he moved to the North where he became a professional stenographer and a professional author. There he became prosperous enough to have a big house and a servant, to travel extensively, and to send his children to Smith and Harvard colleges. He won the friendship of literary people and his stories and novels were produced by important publishers.

This ambitious Negro was not the great pioneer in depicting his race he hoped to be. His abandonment of the region he sought to portray damaged his originality as a novelist. He had too much education for a colored man of his day not possessed of unlimited abilities. His education made him too genteel to tolerate the crudities of Negro life. His education made him didactic and humorless because he could not get rid of its democratic clichés. He pictured the South with the intolerances of an abolitionist. His literary advisers were Walter Hines Page and George Washington Cable, southern exiles turned preachers. William Dean Howells told him that there was "more justice than mercy" in one of his novels. Chesnutt lacked the cunning patience of Booker T. Washington. He was not human enough to follow after Mark Twain's *Puddin'head Wilson* and Lafcadio Hearn's Louisiana tales. He was only a pamphleteer repeating, from a comfortable northern exile, the progressive cant of his day.

Longwood College, Farmville, Virginia FRANCIS B. SIMKINS

Addresses and State Papers of James Stephen Hogg. Edited and with a biographical sketch by Robert C. Cotner. Foreword by Eugene C. Barker. (Austin: University of Texas Press, 1951. xi + 579 pp. Illustrations, appendixes, and index. $6.00.)

Few men have influenced the course of Texas history more than James S. Hogg, and this volume of his addresses and state papers, reissued to mark the one-hundredth anniversary of his birth, is a fitting memorial of his public service. The present work is a great improvement over the edition of Hogg's *Speeches and State Papers* that Judge C. W. Raines prepared in 1905; its editor, Professor Cotner of the University of Texas, has in process a full-length biography of Hogg. In addition to a short biographical sketch, this volume contains his most important extant speeches and official papers, arranged in chronological order for the period from 1886 to 1905. The editor and publisher have done a competent job; the editorial notes are interesting and appropriate, the text is free from typographical errors, and the bookmaking is excellent. A representative selection from Hogg's personal correspondence would have enhanced the value and the attractiveness of this collection. Although this would probably have required two volumes, the result might well have been as good as the two-volume edition of *The Papers of Walter Clark*.

Hogg became an important political figure in the late 1880's when he served four years as the state's attorney general. In this position he forced the dissolution of the powerful Texas Traffic Association, moved vigorously against illegal fire and insurance companies, rewrote the state's ineffective antitrust laws, and initiated successful suits for the recovery of a large amount of land unlawfully held by railroads. By 1890 he was the obvious choice to lead the reform element of his party in its demand for more effective regulation of the big corporations. He was elected governor in 1890 and during the next four years drove through the legislature measures providing for the creation of a strong railroad commission, the regulation of railroad securities, and the prevention of land monopolies. He continued until his death in 1906 to crusade for real state supervision of business organizations, whose unrestrained activities he had long felt posed a great threat to democratic government. Hogg was not a radical and he resisted the encroachment by the federal government into what he believed to be the field of state powers. But this much-maligned man had few equals during this period as a consistent and courageous champion of the regulation of big business by the state. The progressivism of a later Texas governor, Thomas M. Campbell, rested in no small part on the work of James S. Hogg.

Vanderbilt University DEWEY W. GRANTHAM, JR.

Far Corner, A Personal View of the Pacific Northwest. By Stewart H. Holbrook. (New York: The Macmillan Company, 1952. viii + 270 pp. Index. $3.75.)

Covered-wagon migrants to the American Far West appear to have felt strong compulsions to write of their experiences. Most of these California and Oregon-bound pioneers were not what we would call highly literate and well informed, but they nevertheless took pen in hand and made jottings in diary books, wrote pieces for eastern newspapers, and composed guides for the brethren following in their wake. There were also those who, after years of residence on the frontier, produced what might be classed as memoirs or recollections. Stewart H. Holbrook's *Far Corner* is the latter type, a combination of personal recollections of his thirty years residence in the Pacific Northwest and assorted historical paraphernalia. This book is more than welcome because, in a way, it constitutes a type of writing rarely done in this day and age.

There has prevailed in the West the belief that personal experiences of the postcovered-wagon era could not possibly be of much historical interest and significance. Quantitatively, at least, the published personal items pertaining to the earlier period far outnumber those relating to the postfrontier era. Whatever the cause of this modern temerity may be, Mr. Holbrook, for one, has had the courage to relate some of his own rich experiences and observations in British Columbia, Washington, Oregon, and to a less degree Idaho. He tells his story against a backdrop which portrays not only the Pacific Northwest as the author has experienced it, but also in the light of the region's historical past. The reader of this book will have the vicarious experience of traveling with Mr. Holbrook in and out of the niches of the *Far Corner* and enjoying the author's interesting historical accounts bearing upon the places visited.

Mr. Holbrook has here done that which he does best; he uncovers unusual people, events, and things given scant, if any, attention by other writers about the region. Such subheadings as "The Longest Bar," "The Legend of Rawhide," "The Edens of Erewhon," and "Opal the Understanding Heart" are among those which entice and entertain the reader.

An entire chapter is devoted to the "Whitman Saved Oregon" myth. Mr. Holbrook's review of this theme is good in that he attempts to separate fact from fiction. In his determined effort to free his readers of the fiction surrounding Marcus Whitman, Mr. Holbrook fails to extricate himself and his audience from one of these myths when he writes (p. 192) that "Dr. Whitman, his wife, and some fifty of his people at the mission were set upon by Indians and massacred." The number slaughtered, including the Whitmans, is understood to be fourteen, not in excess of fifty. In presenting this exaggerated figure, he weakens his case against the mythmakers at Vanport who had "the dead stacked like cordwood."

University College, London University OSCAR OSBURN WINTHER

Mount Rushmore. By Gilbert C. Fite. (Norman: University of Oklahoma Press, 1952. xiv + 272 pp. Illustrations, maps, chronology, bibliography, and index. $3.75.)

As the reviewer leisurely followed this saga of the "carving" of the heads of Washington, Lincoln, Jefferson, and Theodore Roosevelt in the granite of the Black Hills, he came to feel that the author must have begun his task in somewhat the following mood. "As a professional historian I recognize certain standards and obligations. In addition, there is an obligation to the approximately one million Americans who yearly peer up at the colossal figures from the platform in front of viking Borglum's old studio. To them, Mount Rushmore — and its history — is a part of the public domain." It was a dilemma that will be familiar to writers of the *Rivers* and the *Lakes* series. Though his resultant popular touches and flashbacks occasionally appear a little forced, Dr. Fite has generally succeeded in combining these techniques with accuracy and discernment. His job will not have to be redone for this generation.

Essentially this is a dependable history of the financial, personal, and administrative problems of the creation of the four figures. Therein lies one weakness of the book. For despite scattered technical analyses and excellent pictures, events in Gutzon Borglum's studio, in Rapid City, and in Washington often become more real than the slow emergence of the four heads in their Black Hills environment.

"Only history," Dr. Fite observes with caution and honesty, "can determine Mount Rushmore's true significance." The figures have not been hailed as "great art" by experts in such matters. They are, however, striking likenesses in the tradition of romantic naturalism and are confidently identified by tourists. Opinions differ as to how well the artist has captured the character and personality of his subjects, but it is certain that visitors see in them many of the characteristics of the four leaders. That these symbols will materially aid in preventing the United States from departing from the pattern they collectively represent is highly doubtful in view of the facility with which new cultures capture and transform the symbols of the old. One thing is certain, the monument is "a damn big thing." And, as the author points out, the citizens of some hundred thousand years hence can not doubt that "a civilization which had carved a mountain into heroic likenesses of four men was one of power, audacity, and importance."

University of South Dakota CEDRIC CUMMINS

United States Army in the World War, 1917-1919, Vols. V-X. Edited by Historical Division, Department of the Army. (Washington: Government Printing Office, 1948. Vol. V, iv + 693 pp. $3.50; Vol. VI, iii + 563 pp. $3.00; Vol. VII, ii + 921 pp. $4.75; Vol. VIII, iv + 324 pp. $2.75; Vol. IX, v + 598 pp. $3.50; Vol. X, v + 1240 pp. $6.00. Maps and photographs.)

These volumes form the second installment of a seventeen-volume collection, designed to present the most significant documents on the operations and history of the American army in France, 1917-1919. The first four volumes, which were reviewed in this journal for June, 1950 (XXXVII, 160-61), covered organization, policies, training, and operations to early July, 1918. The volumes in the present set, actually printed in 1949 and 1950, deal with operations on the Champagne-Marne, Aisne-Marne fronts (Vol. V); the Oise-Aisne, Ypres-Lys, and the token force at Vittorio Veneto (Vol. VI); the Somme (Vol. VII); St. Mihiel (Vol. VIII); the Meuse-Argonne (Vol. IX, with planning and the renewed argument over an Americn army in Vol. VIII); and the armistice and occupation problems to July, 1919 (Vol. X).

The material on each operation has a brief introduction, but footnote comment is restricted. English, French, and German documents are included, the last two in either contemporary or editorial translations. The military historian may find this collection a useful introduction to the subject; the common reader will garner at odd moments engaging revelations on the higher levels. Sir Douglas Haig, for instance, blurts out that the American army "had suffered a great deal on account of its ignorance of modern warfare" (X, 20, October 25, 1918) — though Haig may not have been an expert in the subject himself. Nevertheless this material rarely gets down to the regimental or lower level for any length of time; as those who have worked in military history well know, the corps or army picture of an operation is not always accurate.

The volume on the armistice and postarmistice period, though very lengthy, will generally be found the most interesting and not without contemporary value. Reports from German sources show the desperate effort of the high command to hold the front in October and so gain better armistice terms; after the armistice they stress French vindictiveness and harp on the necessity of keeping Germany strong to combat bolshevism. The American army discovers French machinations in Luxemburg, in Alsace-Lorraine, in German factories, in efforts to get American troops to rebuild France; the resulting expressions of surprise, irritation, and horror at the intermixture of political and military action remind the reviewer of our IV Corps reports in Italy during 1945 concerning the French occupation of certain Italian frontier districts. Like the ancient Roman conquerors of Greece, American generals tend to uphold the internal and external stability of the individual European states and to oppose aggrandizement even by their allies. Like Rome's supporters, France and Belgium discovered that our generals could be distressingly stubborn, and had to refer major decisions back to distant political authorities. Demobilization, economic reparations, feeding the defeated, friction with the local population over wine and women — these and numerous other problems arose in 1918-1919 as they did in 1945-1946.

The criticisms on the editorial work of this set which I made in my earlier review remain sadly true for these volumes. Typographical errors are all too common; documents are repeated, at times within a few pages (X, 547 and 556, 549 and 553); the tables of contents are not sufficiently full to compensate for the absence of indexes.

University of Illinois CHESTER G. STARR, JR.

Peace in Their Time; The Origins of the Kellogg-Briand Pact. By Robert H. Ferrell. (New Haven: Yale University Press, 1952. x + 293 pp. Note on sources and index. $4.00.)

In a highly creditable first book, Dr. Ferrell has given new depth and fuller meaning to what may seem a familiar subject. In many ways his is a model study. He writes with verve and distinction. The tone is excellent. The twin pitfalls of special pleading and cynical second guessing, especially dangerous in this case, have been avoided. The author is eminently fair to all concerned, yet he can detect humor, irony, and sham when they are present. The book is broadly conceived. Its story is placed in a world setting with European forces receiving as much attention as American and with domestic pressures being related to diplomatic maneuvering. Finally, Dr. Ferrell has made extensive use of the personal papers of the participants and thus has escaped the besetting sin of most political studies of the 1920's. He has found these manuscripts in eight different repositories and in private hands. The diary of Assistant Secretary of State William R. Castle was particularly valuable.

The first five of eighteen chapters set the stage. These sixty-five pages sketch the mood of 1918, the various peace advocates on both sides of the ocean, and France's unending quest for allies. Chapters VI through XI, some hundred pages long, skillfully trace the tortuous negotiations. Numbers XII and XIII discuss the various modifications, qualifications, considerations, and interpretations that evolved during the talks, and their effect upon the meaning of the finished treaty is carefully appraised. The next sixty pages describe, often amusingly, the formal signing in Paris, the debate in the Senate, and the official ratification and proclamation. A perceptive conclusion underscores the "appallingly naïve" popular American approach to international affairs in the 1920's. In the United States the professional diplomat proved to be wiser, if less ambitious, than the professional pacifist. Salmon O. Levinson, whose role has hitherto been exaggerated by the extensive manuscript collection he left behind, is properly cut down to size in these pages.

This may not be the last book on the subject, but it should be. To be true, neither the French nor British archives have been opened; and the Kellogg Papers (the one important group the author apparently failed to uncover), while not now usable, will soon be available in the Minnesota Historical Society. But it is difficult to believe that such fresh data will materially alter the picture here given. Much more useful than another volume on the origins of the pact would be a study of its subsequent role in American diplomacy. Since Dr. Ferrell recognizes on the last page the need for such a history, this reviewer hopes that he will undertake it.

Northwestern University RICHARD W. LEOPOLD

Roosevelt and Daniels, A Friendship in Politics. Edited with an introduction by Carroll Kilpatrick. (Chapel Hill: The University of North Carolina Press, 1952. xvi + 226 pp. Index. $3.50.)

This volume consists of the letters between Franklin D. Roosevelt and Josephus Daniels during their long period of friendship which began in 1912 and ended only with Roosevelt's death in 1945. Few political friendships in recent history compare with that of Roosevelt and Daniels in length of time or warmth of relationship. Roosevelt was only thirty years old while Daniels had already reached fifty when they first met in Baltimore at the Democratic National Convention of 1912. This difference in age was not without its influence upon their relationship, for while young Roosevelt had more than his share of the self-confidence and ambition desirable in youth, Daniels had acquired the tolerance and wisdom which a varied experience can, but too infrequently, brings. But there were other differences which might have destroyed a promising political friendship. Daniels was a small-town southern editor, an ardent dry, a critic of economic power and urban sophistication, whereas Roosevelt, child of wealth, was a product of Groton and Harvard and a social sophisticate. Nevertheless, before he had completed his service as assistant secretary during Daniels secretaryship of the navy, 1913-1921, Roosevelt had learned to respect the kindliness, tolerance, and integrity of Daniels. The latter, on his part, learned too that much good could come out of the urban East.

From the beginning of his service in the Navy Department, Roosevelt was impatient of delays. Like his cousin Theodore, in an earlier period, he generally insisted on immediate action on his particular projects and in like manner easily acquired an exaggerated idea of his own importance. As early as August 5, 1914, just after the outbreak of World War I, Roosevelt wrote his wife Eleanor, "Alive and very well and keen about everything. I am *running* the real work, although Josephus is here! He is bewildered by it all, very sweet but very sad!" Nevertheless, Daniels was able to survive Roosevelt's ebullience. The young Assistant Secretary made an important contribution to the prosecution of the war, particularly in his part in the decision to close the North Sea and the English Channel to German submarines by means of a mine barrage, albeit he chose to send his proposal direct to Wilson despite Daniels' own support of the project.

Roosevelt and Daniels saw each other infrequently in the long, lean Democratic years from 1921 to 1932. Although the letters during that period are not numerous, to this reviewer they are the most interesting and give a good picture of the division in the Democratic party between the South and the East in the years 1924-1928.

The years of Daniels' ambassadorship to Mexico, 1933-1942, contain a considerable number of letters, but unfortunately they add little to what Daniels has already told in his *Shirt-Sleeve Diplomat*. Indeed, the same criticism may be made of the entire volume. Most of the important information has already appeared elsewhere, either in the two Daniels volumes on the *Wilson Era* or in *F. D. R., His Personal Letters, 1905-1928*. Also on points on which one might hope for information, such as Roosevelt's attempt to purge Senators Walter F. George and Millard E. Tydings in 1938, there were apparently no letters. Nevertheless, there are scattered throughout the exchanges revealing tidbits that portray the personalities of these two men and their views on many public questions. Kilpatrick's brief introduction is an interesting analysis of the relationship between these two dissimilar, friendly men both of whom were engaged for so long in making and keeping the country Democratic and in making the Democratic party a liberal and progressive force.

University of North Carolina J. CARLYLE SITTERSON

Back Door to War; The Roosevelt Foreign Policy, 1933-1941. By Charles Callan Tansill. (Chicago: Henry Regnery Company, 1952. xxi + 690 pp. Bibliography and index. $6.50.)

In this long book Professor Tansill sweeps a wide horizon of American foreign policy. He starts with the year 1899, rather than 1933 as the title indicates, and touches the principal events down to Pearl Harbor in American relations with the Far East and Europe. The work is based on an impressive bibliography of printed and unprinted original source material, books, newspapers, and periodicals. Judging from the footnotes, Professor Tansill had complete access to Department of State records which he refers to as manuscripts, *confidential* manuscripts, and *strictly confidential* manuscripts. The whole work bears the imprint of extensive and laborious investigation.

A large part of the work is a factual and unadorned narrative of events, but on the parts that cover the major decisions of American policy, Professor Tansill has placed the heavy weight of his personal views. He begins with the assertion that "the main objective in American foreign policy since 1900 has been the preservation of the British Empire," and ends with the inquiry whether "the preservation of the British Empire" was worth the "blood, sweat, and tears" of the Americans who lost their lives in the Second World War. It is remarkable, however, that in all the expanse of coverage throughout some 650 pages, he does not feel a necessity or discover an opportunity to present even one piece of exact evidence to warrant the assertion or justify the inquiry.

Professor Tansill presents other interesting opinions. He believes that Woodrow Wilson was "a so-called statesman" who spiked his drink with the "hard liquor of deceit" and promised peace while he wove at Versailles the "web of war." He believes that the "pseudo-statesmen" at Versailles imposed chains of slavery on Germany which Hitler and the men hanged at Nürnberg should not have been condemned for trying to break. He thinks that the invasion of China by Japan was a "national imperative" of self-defense which the United States should have recognized. He pictures Japan as being willing to conciliate China and the United States by withdrawing all her troops from Chinese soil and restoring China to full territorial and political sovereignty. But China and the United States, victims of Russian intrigue, were unwilling to accept the peaceful overtures of Japan. The wrong people, he thinks, were tried by the Far East Military Tribunal. Appeasement of Italy was a "golden opportunity" which Secretary Cordell Hull missed because he "would rather be right than save the world by a touch of realism." President Franklin D. Roosevelt's Quarantine Speech was a "big herring" drawn across the "noisome trail" of Justice Hugo L. Black. Former students of Professor William E. Dodd will be surprised to learn that he possessed "a second-rate mind that had mastered merely the dubious fundamentals of how to get ahead in the historical profession." These opinions, and many others like them, would not mar Professor Tansill's work if he presented adequate evidence to sustain them or the full context of events out of which they might be selected. Unfortunately, these saving elements are not present.

Most historians like to think that amidst the furor of polemical writing on contemporary politics and recent events they are able, through their training and discipline, to stand a little above the din and to examine and appraise complicated and conflicting data to the end of finding truth however elusive it may be. This requires patience, a degree of serenity, all the detachment possible, and a firm, unyielding devotion to the purposes of historical investigation. It is to be regretted that these are not the distinguishing characteristics of Professor Tansill's work, and equally to be regretted that so much effort should result in so little advantage. The book is unredeemed by humor, art, or insight. To read it and to write about it are unrewarding tasks.

Tufts College and the Fletcher
School of Law and Diplomacy RUHL BARTLETT

Conscripted City; Norfolk in World War II. By Marvin W. Schlegel. Foreword by S. H. Ferebee. (Norfolk: Norfolk War History Commission, 1951. xi + 396 pp. Illustrations and index. $3.00.)

Dr. Schlegel's interesting volume on Norfolk is a significant addition to his writings on World War II history. While the "Conscripted City" was in many respects more harassed by wartime problems than most American cities, students of urban history and of social history generally will find this detailed and graphic account both suggestive and revealing. The care with which the daily papers have been used, as well as official and other contemporary records, and the skill with which the story has been reconstructed, almost month by month, enable the reader to relive many trying wartime experiences.

The task outlined in the foreword by S. H. Ferebee, chairman of the Norfolk War History Commission, to produce a book "which pictures Norfolk's ugly aspects alongside its noble ones," has been ably performed. Clearly revealed are the conservatism and hesitation of community leaders when faced by expanding wartime needs, their jealousy of and reliance on state and federal initiative and funds, the bungling confusion of much of this outside leadership, the indecision and chicanery which delayed efforts to safeguard health, supply adequate housing, and provide a wholesome social environment for the many thousands of war workers and service men who literally piled into Norfolk in the early years of the war. The occasional glimpses supplied by the author of the restricted and degraded positions into which Norfolk's Negroes were forced add to the sordid character of the story, yet a spirit of patriotic determination to survive persists and wins in the end.

The final burst of triumph with which the book ends is, however, the national triumph of arms, to which Norfolk no doubt contributed more in home-front sacrifices than most American communities, yet the success with which Dr. Schlegel has recounted the city's wartime experiences makes one hope that he will round out this intimate and graphic story in a complementary volume which will follow some of the hard fought issues of the community at war through to their peacetime settlement.

While a detailed account of Norfolk's own contributions to the armed services was deliberately omitted, a listing of the city's Gold Star honor roll concludes the book.

Rochester, New York BLAKE MCKELVEY

Closing the Ring. By Winston S. Churchill. *The Second World War*, Vol. V. (Boston: Houghton Mifflin Company, 1951. xvi + 749 pp. Facsimile, maps, diagrams, appendixes, and index. $6.00.)

The fifth volume of Mr. Churchill's memorable series deals with that period between the wresting of the initiative from the Axis by the United Nations on all fronts and the launching of the final crushing offensive against Germany. The U-boats are mastered; the transparency of Japan's ability to hold Asia is apparent; Russia's massive attacks are everywhere successful in the East; the *Luftwaffe's* doom is sealed; and Mussolini's strident lunacy vanishes from the Palazzo Venezia. Gone, then, is the threnody of near defeat; yet to come is the paean of "Overlord."

The central military theme is the Italian campaign, and actions which since have become legendary pass under review: Sicily, Salerno, Anzio, Monte Cassino, and the capture of Rome. For this "Third Front" Churchill assumes full responsibility. He makes his case to the historian that his insistence that the vast Allied accumulation of men and materiél in the Mediterranean not stand idle while only Russians fought Germans in no sense negated his wholehearted support of the cross-Channel invasion. His preference for striking north from the Adriatic through Istria rather than through the south of France never implied that either action should be more than an appendage of "Overlord." The Anzio landing was his idea; for it he and his colleagues fought the United States chiefs of staff; and he is as quick to praise the German Field Marshal Albert Kesselring as he is to blame the American field commander, General John P. Lucas, that "125,000 men with 23,000 vehicles, all so painfully landed to carry them, . . . only got twelve miles." And in the breakthrough to Rome it was General Harold Alexander who drew his praise and General Mark Clark his odium for not closing the German escape route at Valmontone. Perhaps never before has the vital importance of logistics been so dramatically presented as in the landing craft controversy. Through it all runs Churchill's demand that the British effort in the Mediterranean be given its just recognition.

The transition to the offensive by the Allies is reflected in the first meeting of the Big Three at Teheran, the arrangement for which was a "diplomatic curiosity." This was not a conference conditioned by the urgency for self-preservation. Stalin was given a definitive promise on the opening of the Second Front, and the participants looked beyond military victory to the political realignment of Europe. "Yalta" and "Potsdam" were anticipated in the Russian pledge to enter the war against Japan and in the discussions of the future of Poland and Germany. Churchill left the meeting content with the military arrangements and acknowledging that the political survey was "very preliminary." He was too sanguine, however, in his claim of procuring a mitigation for Finland *vis a vis* the Soviet Union. That Stalin accepted Petsamo for Hangö is academic before the fact that Russia procured Porkkala, only ten miles *west* of Helsinki.

An absorbing chapter deals with the preparation of Britain's defenses beginning in the spring of 1943 against German rockets and pilotless aircraft. British determination was illustrated by Air Marshal Arthur T. Harris' injunction to his bomber crews that the attack on Peenemünde would be repeated nightly until successful regardless of casualties. Thus was Hitler's secret weapon rendered ineffective.

Churchill's candid treatment of individuals continues unrestrained. He minces no words on Chiang Kai-shek and the incredibly obdurate Charles de Gaulle. He captures the savagery of the Tito-Mihailovic struggle in Yugoslavia. He corrects General Dwight D. Eisenhower's version of his attitude toward "Overlord." Most interesting is his undisguised admiration of Mussolini, "the Italian lawgiver" who Churchill assumes saved Italy from Bolshevism and was overthrown only because he misjudged Britain's staying power. Revealing is the Prime Minister's obituary to the fallen tyrant: "His great roads will remain a monument to his personal power and long reign." The same might be written of Caesar — and was of Ozymandias.

Yale University JOHN R. HUBBARD

Behind the Wall Street Curtain. By Edward Dies. (Washington: Public Affairs Press, 1952. 153 pp. $2.75.)

This slim volume, the work of a Chicago businessman who has done some venturing into academic fields, is both a history and a plea.

The history is the story of Wall Street, from its beginnings in the 1600's to the present time, told in brief chapters. Space in the book is proportioned to the importance of the Street in the national life; consequently, most of the volume concerns the late nineteenth and early twentieth centuries. Mr. Dies has not been concerned with new facts. Instead he presents easily available materials in a swift, colorful form, shaping them into buttressing for his plea.

The plea emerges ever more plainly as the book goes on until, in the final chapters, it completely takes over. Mr. Dies is indignant at "the howling crowd of New Deal-left-wingers" and the "nimble tabloid thinkers with leftish leanings" who, he believes, have made the nation suspicious of Wall Street. The Street, he urges everyone to recognize, may have had its "notorious" periods, but these are now done. Moreover, during the total history of the country, Wall Street has been the heart of American free enterprise and free enterprise is what distinguishes "democracy" from "Communism, or statism." He is especially anxious to underline that the modern Wall Street, "as a symbol of freedom of trade by free men," is more American than the "wanton government waste and devastating taxation" of the New Deal and Fair Deal.

Historians of modern American conservatism will find *Behind the Wall Street Curtain* a useful genre document. Historians who agree with Mr. Dies's interpretation will no doubt agree with Mr. Dies's interpretation.

Princeton University ERIC F. GOLDMAN

The Uprooted; The Epic Story of the Great Migrations that Made the American People. By Oscar Handlin. (Boston: Little, Brown and Company, 1951. 310 pp. $4.00.)

It is not surprising that *The Uprooted* was a Pulitzer prize book in its year. It is, as the publisher's blurb confesses, history with a difference. The difference is found principally in the sympathy and depth of feeling with which the author, son of an immigrant, writes about the hardships of migration and the series of shocks sustained in the process by those who migrated. It is rather of the strains and stresses of migration upon the spirit of the immigrant that Dr. Handlin writes than of the contribution of the foreign-born to American society.

There are other differences. Although Dr. Handlin does not confine his attention exclusively to any one group or period, he writes principally of the European peasant, traditionally established member of a settled and patterned rural village community, for whom for economic reasons home no longer had a place. He came to the United States, therefore, to better his condition; but having survived the gruesome hardships of the migration, he found only too often that he had lost his status, with little improvement in his condition. He remained an alien, and his children also found status difficult to attain though less difficult than he.

In his genuine concern over the travails of those for whom survival was the only triumph and assurance of heaven for themselves and acceptance for their children the only surviving hope, the author seems to the reviewer to have underwritten somewhat the story of the successful, leaving it to others such as Carl Wittke to stress what the immigrant brought to the United States in addition to a plentiful supply of cheap labor without bargaining power.

The intensity of the author's sympathy for those of whom he writes leads him often to lapse into the present tense as if one of them were soliloquizing. The device is effective, though sometimes more disconcerting than consistent use of the simple past tense would have been. Carelessness or a new English usage is indicated here and there by sentences such as "The children had each their task, . . ." and "Grandparents, aunts and uncles . . . found a place and a job." The merits of the book, however, are real and substantial. The faults are only freckles.

University of Wisconsin CHESTER V. EASUM

A History of the American Theatre, 1700-1950. By Glenn Hughes. (New York: Samuel French, 1951. ix + 562 pp. Illustrations, bibliography, and index. $5.00.)

A History of the American Theatre is not intended to supplant Arthur Hobson Quinn's *A History of the American Drama*; rather it is an attempt to consolidate old and new material on theatrical history into one compact and readable volume. Professor Quinn's work is centered upon dramatic literature; Professor Hughes takes the entire theater for his province — its buildings, managers, actors, plays, playwrights, and critics; its human, animal, and mechanical competitors; its beginnings, its conquest of the "frontier," its "happy days," and its current contraction and threatened extinction. His purpose, Professor Hughes says, is merely to assist the American people in taking stock of their theater in a time when such stocktaking is necessary. For this purpose the book is admirable.

But the book is also a history, and here its limitations become evident. Inevitably, Professor Hughes faced the problem of footnoting; he solves it (satisfactorily for the general reader) by eliminating footnotes entirely. A second problem, that of organization, he solves by instituting a rigid chronological arrangement for his chapters; but within the earlier chapters he deviates from chronology, sometimes disconcertingly, to follow a geographical pattern. Gradually, as New York becomes more and more important as a theatrical center, this device is dropped, but now the mass of material has become so great that Professor Hughes resorts often to groupings of theatrical personalities and to mere season-by-season lists of "highlights." The material in its highly condensed state has, obviously, become too much for assimilation; and evidences of indigestion become apparent in the numerous repetitions. The reader is told, for example, on pages 133, 246, 265, and 266 that the parents of John, Lionel, and Ethel Barrymore were Georgiana Drew and Maurice Barrymore.

One of the great strengths of Professor Hughes's *History* lies in the use he makes of the work of regional historians. One can only wish that he had relied more heavily on these "patient annalists," for by doing so he might have avoided at least one major error that mars the book: following the autobiography of Noah M. Ludlow, Professor Hughes perpetuates the story that New Orleans witnessed its first professional theatrical performance in English in 1817. Ludlow's work is notoriously unreliable. Further, this error has been corrected twice: in 1939 by Roger P. McCutcheon ("The First English Plays in New Orleans," *American Literature*, XI, 183-99), and in 1945 by Miss Nelle Smither ("A History of the English Theatre at New Orleans, 1806-1842," *Louisiana Historical Quarterly*, XXVIII, 85-274, 361-572).

Despite these flaws, Mr. Hughes's *History* remains an interesting book, particularly valuable to those who wish only a concise and sweeping view of the history of the American theater. It is not, however, a definitive work. The real history of the American theater must wait until all the "patient annalists" have completed their tasks.

Tulane University JOSEPH P. ROPPOLO

News and These United States. By Edith Merwin Bartow. (New York: Funk & Wagnalls Company, 1952. viii + 292 pp. Illustrations, bibliography, and index. $5.00.)

Two impressions present themselves forcibly to the historian who reads Edith M. Bartow's *News and These United States*. First, she has industriously studied the nation's newspaper files. Her primary source material includes liberal descriptions of and excerpts from a broad cross-section of the press from the beginnings down to 1900. Secondly, an inadequate knowledge of history causes a misinterpretation of some of her research findings and leads to some curious misstatements of fact. For instance, we read (p. 127): "In Florida, just purchased from Spain, Andrew Jackson's Kentucky and Tennessee sharpshooters were in hot pursuit of the inhospitable Creeks and Seminoles." Jackson's raid preceded the purchase. On page 147 there is a reference to the Albany *Argus* of September 30, 1828, followed by the statement: "abuse, not only of the Whigs but of disgruntled party 'slivers' was liberally included and Old Hickory lost this election to John Quincy Adams." Jackson won in 1828. Perhaps the strangest scrambling of facts is a paragraph on page 203: "Newspaper headlines . . . editorialized with: 'Grand

and Glorious News!!! "Atlanta Ours, Fairly Won" Says General Sherman.' Then George Washington Smalley made history by riding through the night to telegraph his newspaper of the defeat of Lee at Antietam. The operator insisted on sending the news to Washington, and the exhausted reporter set out for New York writing for the *Tribune* his story so soon followed by the dramatic THE END LEE SURRENDERS." It actually was Antietam, in 1862, that Smalley reported, with the difficulty here described.

But the liberal sprinkling of historical errors and the misspelling of several names does not obscure the fact that descriptions of the content and format of newspapers are better here than in any other study of journalistic backgrounds. Earlier press histories have revolved too heavily around biographical detail of great editors, with too little description of their papers, their operating methods, or the social and economic background against which they worked. This study, liberally sprinkled with quoted excerpts from the files, stands out in this respect. Moreover, where other writers have concentrated on the large city press, especially New York, this author is particularly good in dealing with frontier movements and early printers and journalists on the west coast.

The story ends about 1900. Concluding chapters present some of the author's views, generalized, about what she believes the contemporary press, especially that of the small towns, should be, but there is no specific twentieth-century detail. The literary style throughout is marked by cumbersome and confusing sentences and poor continuity in paragraph structure.

Pennsylvania State College FREDERICK B. MARBUT

A Two-Party South? By Alexander Heard. Foreword by York Willbern. (Chapel Hill: The University of North Carolina Press, 1952. xviii + 334 pp. Figures, tables, appendixes, and index. $4.75.)

The obstacles to the establishment of a two-party system in the South seem almost insuperable after reading Mr. Heard's thorough and brilliantly written analysis of them. Had the author prefaced his book with a chapter on the historical causes for the creation of the solid, Democratic South, any reader heretofore hopeful of a Republican renaissance must have turned his face to the wall and given up the political ghost. Republican Reconstruction created the solid South and the folk memory of this ordeal combined with an inferior and often obnoxious type of Republican leadership up to the present time has made it all too easy for southern politicians to keep the South Democratic.

The Democratic obstructions in the path of Republican advance, as presented by Mr. Heard, may be described as "defense in depth." The Democrats ironically stole the Republican Reconstruction rules book and edited and enlarged it. They practically disfranchised the Negro or rendered his vote and that of his fellow white Republicans futile by Democratic control of the registration and election boards and the entire election machinery. In such states as Tennessee, Kentucky, North Carolina, and Virginia, where there are strong Republican areas, the Democrats have with complete cynicism disfranchised these areas by the most incredible gerrymanders — that is by splitting a Republican stronghold and attaching the fragments to larger Democratic districts.

The leadership of the Republican party both North and South has also placed stumbling blocks in the way of strengthening the southern wing. Little money has been expended on the southern Republicans by the national leaders who prefer to use their cash in the large pivotal states of the North. The southern Republican leaders until recently have borne the stench of "carpetbagger" or "scalawag" and have had very little power to attract voters. Nor have they wanted to strengthen their party in the South, but preferred to be a sort of social club that would divide the political pie when their party won a national election. This attitude was brought out in the recent Republican nominating convention, in which the Taft delegates from the South represented only themselves and showed bitter hostility toward gaining Democratic support for their party in the South. The Eisenhower delegates were apparently concerned with creating a real party in the South, though the movement may prove to be only a "flash in the pan."

The author is of the opinion, despite the many obstacles to a two-party system in the South, that there are certain forces at work that will bring about such an end. One is the southern state rights or "Dixiecrat" movement, which may eventually carry many conservative Democrats into the Republican party. Another, of course, is the "middle of the road" attitude of the bulk of southern Democrats as expressed through Senator Richard Russell. The mass influx of the Negro voters into the Democratic party, particularly if these new Democrats vote over a long time as a bloc, could well cause a great mass of southern white Democrats to align themselves with the Republican party. Finally, the author is of the opinion that the rapid change in the economic and social structure of the South will bring about mass realignments, so that a vigorous two-party system will evolve in the South.

The reviewer would like to add another ingredient for change to those of Mr. Heard's scholarly and provocative study — the Republican party would gain several million voters in the South overnight if it changed its name and ran Jefferson and Lincoln alternately for president rather than putting Lincoln up every four years.

University of Alabama FRANK L. OWSLEY

The Negro and the Communist Party. By Wilson Record. (Chapel Hill: The University of North Carolina Press, 1951. x + 340 pp. Index. $3.50.)

Wilson Record has carefully and comprehensively delineated the story of the efforts of the Communist party to capture the American Negro. Record's presentation of the party's shifting tactics, its relationship to conventional Negro welfare organizations, and its influence upon the Negro community cannot be effectively challenged by competent and objective observers.

Negroes en masse have refused to follow the Communist Pied Piper. The rejection of communism does not mean that the Negro is complacent. Negroes are practical. They are pragmatists. Their culture is American. They believe in the American ideals. They desire, however, that these ideals be effectively implemented in the society as a whole. They also insist that these ideals be reflected in the role assigned them in the American society. The future of American Negroes is suspended in the context of the total development of the American society. Thus, Negroes realize that their "advancement in this country is contingent on identification with white groups around a set of common problems."

The desertion of Negroes from the Republican party for the New Deal in 1936 and their defection from the Fair Deal in a much smaller ratio than for the population as a whole attest the dissatisfaction of Negroes with the status quo. Further, the remarkable postwar increase in Negro voting in the South, and predominantly for New and Fair Deal social objectives, illustrates that Negroes desire basic change.

The investigations of Gunnar Myrdal, Valdimer O. Key, Samuel Lubell, and Alexander Heard provide further and convincing documentation for Record's conclusion that "Negroes would constitute a valuable resource for any authentic third party movement built around organized labor. To command the support of American workers — and of American Negroes — such a movement would have to be grounded in the native radical tradition. It would need more than a conglomeration of confused intellectuals, old-time pacifists, isolationists, and Communist hacks such as the Progressive Party represented. Negroes have played an important role in shaping the American radical tradition; they are by no means loath to participate in its extension. But their loyalty will not be won to a movement that uses the window dressing of such a tradition as a front for the expansion of world communism."

Howard University EMMETT E. DORSEY

Historical News and Comments

Association Activities

The membership committee of the Association has been enlarged so as to have a representative in each state. His job in this year's campaign is to make sure that every instructor and professor in history and political science departments of all the colleges of his state receive an invitation to join the Association. Small colleges have sometimes been overlooked, and this minute canvassing will bring the Association to the attention of every eligible person serving on a college faculty. University history departments will be approached to interest their graduate students in membership.

Personals

Frederick I. Kuhns, formerly research associate of the State Historical Society of Iowa, has accepted a position as professor of Bible at Rocky Mountain College.

Robert A. Rutland, doctoral candidate at Vanderbilt University, has joined the staff of the State Historical Society of Iowa as research associate.

At Indiana University, John C. Andressohn has been promoted to professor of history. John J. Murray, associate professor of history, has resumed his teaching duties after a year's absence as a Fulbright scholar in the Netherlands. Arthur R. Hogue, associate professor of history, was among the one hundred American scholars invited to tour Germany as a guest of the Bonn Republic from November 10 to December 10. Ralph E. Morrow, graduate student, taught at the University of Chattanooga in the summer session.

James H. Rodabaugh has been appointed head of the division of history and science of the Ohio State Archaeological and Historical Society.

Charles F. Delzell, doctoral graduate of Stanford University, has been appointed assistant professor of history at Vanderbilt University.

Harold M. Hyman has joined the faculty of Earlham College as assistant professor of history.

At Saint Louis University, Edward R. Vollmar, S.J., has been named editor of the University's *Historical Bulletin*. He has also undertaken the task of completing the bibliography for American Catholic history begun by the late Thomas F. O'Connor, and during the past summer toured the Old Southwest collecting data for this project. Jasper W. Cross was promoted to associate professor of history upon his return from a year's leave of absence. Lowrie J. Daly, S.J., has also returned from an eighteen-month leave of absence during which he organized and supervised the University's project of filming the materials of the Vatican Library. Martin F. Hastings, S.J., who has completed his doctoral program at the University of California at Berkeley, has been made instructor in history.

Dorothy E. Wyatt, formerly professor of history at Goucher College, has been named dean of women at William and Mary College.

Frederick H. Jackson has been promoted to assistant professor of history, division of general studies, at the University of Illinois.

John C. Cairns of the Woman's College of the University of North Carolina has been appointed lecturer in history at the University of Toronto.

Elon College announces the appointment of H. H. Cunningham, recent doctoral graduate of the University of North Carolina, as head of the history department.

Bert James Loewenberg, professor of American history at Sarah Lawrence College, is lecturing at Ruskin College, Oxford, during the first term of 1952-1953, and will lecture at the University of Jerusalem beginning in January, 1953.

J. C. Russell, chairman of the history department at the University of New Mexico, is spending the current academic year as a Fulbright lecturer at University College, Aberystwyth, Wales. In his absence Benjamin Sacks is acting chairman of the department.

C. Bickford O'Brien has been named acting chairman of the department of history and political science at the University of California at Davis. W. Sheridan Warrick, doctoral candidate at the University of Chicago, has been appointed acting instructor in history. Vernon J. Puryear is on sabbatical leave from July 1 until December 31.

Paul McCain of the history department of Brenau College was visiting professor at Western Carolina Teachers College during the first term of summer school.

Marvin R. Farley has been promoted to the rank of assistant professor of social sciences at Western Carolina Teachers College.

George B. Tindall has been appointed to the history department faculty of the Woman's College of the University of North Carolina.

Joel Colton has been promoted to assistant professor of history at Duke University.

Joseph F. Steelman has accepted a position at the Agricultural and Mechanical College of Texas.

The appointment of Rembert W. Patrick of the University of Florida history department to the post of associate editor of the *Florida Historical Quarterly* has been announced.

At the University of Virginia, Francis L. Berkeley, Jr., curator of manuscripts in the Alderman Library, is a 1952-1953 Fulbright scholar in the United Kingdom searching for manuscripts pertaining to colonial Virginia. During his absence Joseph C. Vance, doctoral candidate in history, has accepted a position as manuscripts assistant. Malcolm Lester of the Mercer University history department and Samuel Schroeter of the history department of King College have returned to complete their doctoral requirements. T. P. Hughes, doctoral candidate in history, has been appointed instructor of Engineering English. O. J. Hale, land commissioner of Bavaria, has returned to assume his duties as professor of European history. Thomas T. Hammond, on leave during 1951-1952 as a Ford scholar, has resumed his duties as assistant professor of Russian history. William L. Neumann, formerly of the University of Maryland, is substituting for Alan Hutchinson, assistant professor of Latin American history, who is on leave for research during the 1952-1953 session.

Jane Carson, formerly assistant in manuscripts at the University of Virginia, has accepted a position as assistant to the director at the Institute of Early American History and Culture.

Wesley Laing, doctoral candidate at the University of Virginia, has accepted a position as assistant professor of history at Longwood College.

Graham Roberts, formerly map assistant at the University of Virginia, has accepted a position as head librarian at Drake University.

Robert L. Scribner, professor of history at Oglethorpe University, has joined the staff of *Virginia Cavalcade*, a slick paper historical journal issued by the history division of the Virginia State Library.

Robert W. Richmond, former archivist on the library staff of the Nebraska State Historical Society, has accepted a similar position on the staff of the Kansas State Historical Society.

Roger Van Bolt, formerly historical research editor and director of the Illinois junior historian program of the Illinois State Historical Library, has been appointed historical research specialist at the Henry Ford Museum and Greenfield Village.

At the University of Arkansas, Hal Bridges and Wayne Cole have been promoted to assistant professorships in the department of history. James Hudson and Arthur P. Kautz have been added to the staff as instructors. Robert Reeser has returned to the department as associate professor. Boyd C. Shafer has been appointed chairman of the department.

Margaret Burr DesChamps has been appointed assistant professor of history at Agnes Scott College.

W. Magruder Drake, who has completed his residence requirements for the doctorate at the University of North Carolina, has been appointed instructor in the department of history at the University of Mississippi.

At the University of Oklahoma, Everett Edward Dale retired from active service July 1, 1952, but in his emeritus status will be available for consultation by graduate students while he pursues his personal research and writing. Professor Dale has been a member of the history staff for thirty-eight years and for half of them chairman of the department. His courses in the history of the West have been allocated to Donald Berthrong, doctoral graduate of the University of Wisconsin, and recently of the University of Kansas City. Gilbert C. Fite, associate professor of history, spent the summer in Washington, New York, and Palo Alto in research on a biography of George N. Peek. Morris L. Wardell, professor of history, and John S. Ezell, associate professor of history, spent the summer as educational consultants for the Stanolind Oil Company. Alfred B. Sears, chairman of the department, will spend the second semester in England.

At the University of Alabama, Frederick Cox, recently promoted to associate professor of European history, returned in July from a two-year sojourn in Egypt and the Near East where he had gone in 1950 on a Fulbright fellowship. Charles G. Summersell, professor of history, will return to the University in January, 1953, from a two-year tour of duty in the navy where he holds the rank of lieutenant commander.

James Z. Rabun of Emory University has been given a leave of absence to teach the first semester at the University of Wisconsin. The university was incorrectly identified in the September issue of the *Review.*

Edmund T. Peckham of Harvard University has been appointed instructor in history and political science at the Rice Institute.

Louis Bernard Schmidt, professor emeritus of history at Iowa State College, will lecture on American agricultural history at the annual meeting of the Agricultural Extension Service at the University of Arizona in December.

At Dartmouth College, John G. Gazley is on leave of absence for the first semester to teach at the National War College. Richard B. McCornack has returned to Dartmouth as assistant professor of history after eighteen months of service with the Department of State.

At the University of Texas, Professor Fulmer Mood has taken leave of absence to spend the year in California. Ralph W. Steen, professor of history at Texas Agricultural and Mechanical College, is serving as visiting professor in his place. Edward L. Cannan has returned from a year's leave in Italy where he went as a Fulbright scholar.

Francisco Aguilera, assistant director of the Hispanic Foundation of the Library of Congress, attended the first Ibero-American Congress of librarians, archivists, and copyright experts, which was held in Madrid, Spain, beginning October 20.

Weymouth T. Jordan of Florida State University has been appointed editor of the Florida State University *Studies.*

The University of Chattanooga has extended the leave of absence of Culver H. Smith for the year 1952-1953, and James W. Livingood will continue to serve as chairman of the history department in his absence. Professor Smith will continue his work in the University of Maryland overseas program.

Siegfried Rolland has been appointed assistant professor of social sciences at the University of Idaho.

William M. Dabney, assistant professor of history at the University of New Mexico, was on the visiting faculty at the University of Virginia during the summer session of 1952.

The University of Georgia announces the appointment of Robert G. McPherson as instructor in history and the promotion of Horace Montgomery to the rank of professor. C. Mildred Thompson, who retired from the University of Georgia history department in June, 1952, has been appointed adviser to students at the University in Exile, Strassburg, France.

The University of Notre Dame announces the promotion of Marshall T. Smelser to associate professor of history and the appointment of Richard Balfe as instructor. Vincent P. De Santis, who was recalled by the army during the year 1951-1952, has returned to the University. Thomas N. Brown has also returned after a year's leave of absence spent in research on the history of Irish immigration.

The following promotions have been announced by Purdue University: Walter O. Forster to associate professor of history and government, George H. Mayer to associate professor of history, and Robert J. Graf, Jr., and John F. Stover to assistant professorships in history.

James O. Wettereau of New York University has been promoted to associate professor of history.

Irvin G. Wyllie has been promoted to associate professor of history at the University of Missouri. David H. Pinkney, associate professor of history, will be on leave during the winter term.

F. W. Gibson, formerly of the Public Archives of Canada, has been appointed associate professor of history at Queen's University. Geoffrey Seed of the department of history at St. Andrews University has been appointed to the McLaughlin Lectureship in History for the 1952-1953 session.

J. Wesley Hoffmann, head of the department of history at the University of Tennessee, is on leave for the year 1952-1953 to teach in the University of Maryland program in Germany. During his absence Stanley J. Folmsbee is serving as acting head of the department. James E. Gillespie, retired from Pennsylvania State College, holds an appointment as acting professor of history.

At the University of North Dakota, John Parker, instructor in history, has returned to the University of Michigan to continue his doctoral program. Jerry DeWitt of Yale University and John Harnsberger of the University of Minnesota have been appointed instructors in history. George Lemmer, assistant professor of history, is on leave of absence for one year as Air Force historian at the Pentagon.

Professor Albert Hyma, who is on sabbatical leave from the University of Michigan, is spending the academic year in research in Europe.

The Pennsylvania State College announces the appointment of H. Trevor Colbourn of Johns Hopkins University as instructor in American history. Robert W. Green of the University of Iowa has been appointed instructor in European history.

At the University of Delaware, H. Clay Reed has been named chairman of the newly established university committee on American Studies. Walter L. Woodfill has been appointed assistant professor of history and John L. Beatty has been appointed instructor.

Thomas D. Clark of the University of Kentucky is on leave this semester on an educational mission for the Department of State in India and Pakistan. Rhea A. Taylor is on sabbatical leave for the year and is in Washington, D. C., doing research.

At the University of Kansas, James E. Seaver has been promoted to associate professor of history. George M. Beckmann, recent doctoral graduate of Stanford University, has been named assistant professor of history.

At the University of Illinois, Ernest C. Dawn has returned from military service in Washington and has been promoted to assistant professor of history. Frank Freidel has been promoted to associate professor and William J. Bouwsma to assistant professor of history. Theodore S. Hamerow, recent doctoral graduate of Yale University, and Samuel P. Hays, recent doctoral graduate of Harvard University, have joined the staff as instructors in history.

K. W. Swart, formerly of the University of Illinois, has accepted an assignment at Georgetown University.

Donald F. Tingley, recent doctoral graduate of the University of Illinois, has joined the staff of the Illinois State Historical Library as director of the junior historian program.

Edward H. Gibson, III, doctoral candidate at the University of North Carolina, is teaching in the department of history at Carson-Newman College. Lowell R. Tillett, assistant professor of history, is on leave of absence for the academic year to continue his graduate studies at the University of North Carolina.

Thomas M. Pitkin, formerly chief historian, Office of the Quartermaster General, has been appointed historian with the National Park Service with headquarters in Boston.

At the University of Rochester, Dexter Perkins, chairman of the department of history, will be on leave the second term of 1952-1953. He will lecture again at the Salzburg Seminar in American Studies, Salzburg, Austria, in March-April, 1953. Professor Perkins has been president of the Salzburg Seminar since 1950. Glyndon G. Van Deusen, professor of history, has resumed teaching after a year's leave on a Fulbright grant. In March and April he taught at the Salzburg Seminar and later toured Europe. He is now bringing to a conclusion his biography of Horace Greeley for which he was awarded the Albert J. Beveridge Prize.

William E. Leuchtenburg, formerly of Harvard University, has been named associate professor of history at Columbia University.

James M. Smith, formerly of Cornell University, has joined the department of history at Ohio State University.

William W. Sweet, professor of history at Southern Methodist University, is serving as visiting professor at Pomona College.

At Amherst College, Edwin C. Rozwenc has been promoted to professor of history and John B. Halsted named instructor in history.

At Harvard University, Alan Heimert, William R. Taylor, and James A. Early have been appointed teaching fellows in history and literature. Sidney Ahlstrom has been named instructor in history. Bernard Bailyn has been appointed research associate in history in the Graduate School of Education. Clifton Phillips has been named a teaching fellow in history.

Arthur Mann, Massachusetts Institute of Technology, has been promoted to assistant professor of history.

William A. Williams of the Ohio State University has been appointed assistant professor of history at the University of Oregon.

Gale W. McGee of the University of Wyoming is on a year's leave of absence to serve as a Carnegie research fellow with the Council on Foreign Relations in New York City.

Horace C. Peterson, professor of history at the University of Oklahoma and a member of the Mississippi Valley Historical Association for many years, died July 19, 1952. His death was the result of a severe cranial fracture sustained in a fall on the steps in Gittinger Hall. Born in Oskaloosa, Iowa, June 20, 1902, Peterson attended high schools in Pasadena, California. He received the bachelor's degree with honors from Pomona College in 1931, the master's in 1932, and the doctorate from Cornell University in 1935. He did extensive research at the Library of Congress, the Hoover War Library at Stanford, the Harkness Library at Yale, the Clark University War Library, and the British Museum. During 1935 he traveled extensively in Belgium, England, Germany, and France gathering information on war propaganda. Before joining the University of Oklahoma staff in 1936 as instructor in history, Peterson served as principal of Douglas Schools, Pebble Beach, California, and as instructor at Deep Springs Foundation, Deep Springs, in the same state. During World War II he served with military intelligence and as assistant military attaché in Rio de Janeiro, where he received the Order of the Baron of Rio Branco issued by the Brazilian government to members of the diplomatic corps. An outstanding author, Peterson in 1939 wrote *Propaganda for War*, a University of Oklahoma Press publication which was chosen by *Current History* as one of the ten most important books of the year. At the time of his death he had two books ready for publication — "A Study of Public Opinion in the United States during the First War" and "The Peace Conference Diary of Irvin Hoover."

Colleagues, friends, and former students of Professor Peterson announce the establishment of the Horace C. Peterson Memorial Scholarship in History at the University of Oklahoma. Any members of the Association who care to contribute may do so by writing to Alfred B. Sears, chairman of the history department at the University of Oklahoma. [Alfred B. Sears]

Frank Harmon Garver, 77, professor of history at the University of Southern California for nineteen years until his retirement in 1945, died at his home in Los Angeles on September 24. He had been in failing health for several years. Holding his master's and doctor's degrees from the University of Iowa, Dr. Garver taught at Morningside College, Iowa, and the State Normal College, Montana, before going to the University of Southern California in 1926. Past president of the Pacific Coast Branch of the American Historical Association, chairman of the Southern California history department for three years, and active in the various professional organizations, Dr. Carver was also a prolific contributor to scholarly periodicals and a former member of the editorial board of the *Mississippi Valley Historical Review*. During the two years prior to his death, he wrote an extensive series of newspaper articles on "The American Background." These are being assembled in book form by his colleagues as a memorial edition, and will be published early in 1953. [Donald W. Rowland]

Owen Cochran Coy, emeritus professor of California and Western United States history at the University of Southern California, died in Los Angeles on August 31, 1952. Born in Farragut, Iowa, on April 16, 1884, he received the Ph.B. degree at the College of the Pacific in 1907, the M.A. degree from Stanford University in 1909, and the Ph.D. degree from the University of California, Berkeley, in 1918. He became a leading authority in his field of specialization, California history. He served as secretary and director of the California Historical Survey Commission, 1915-1923, historian of the State Council of Defense, 1918-1919, state technical director of the Historical Records Survey, WPA, in 1936, and director and executive secretary of the California State Historical Association, acting in the last capacity until shortly before his retirement. Joining the staff of the history department of the University of Southern California in 1925, he remained there until his retirement in 1950. Dr. Coy was the author of many articles and books on California history, among them a *Guide to the County Archives of California* (1921), *Genesis of California Counties* (1923), *Gold Days* (1929), *The Humboldt Bay Region, 1850-1875* (1929), *The Great Trek* (1930), and *In the Diggings in 'Forty-nine* (1948). He also served in an editorial capacity on various publications, notably for the *Pictorial History of California* (1925), and for the *California History Nugget.* [Donald W. Rowland]

Grants and Awards

J. Allen Cabaniss, professor of history at the University of Mississippi, is on leave for the year with a grant from the Institute of Advanced Studies at Princeton University.

Thomas P. Abernethy, Julian Bishko, Edward Younger, and Alan Hutchinson held research grants from the University of Virginia Institute for Research in the Social Sciences during the summer of 1952.

Robert E. Quirk, instructor in history at Indiana University, spent the summer in research in Mexico City as the recipient of a Graduate School fellowship. Maurice G. Baxter, instructor in history, received a similar fellowship to enable him to complete his study on Orville Browning. Oscar O. Winther, professor of history and assistant dean of the Graduate School, is in England for the academic year studying the background of British migration into the Trans-Mississippi West. He has a Fulbright research grant and is affiliated with University College, University of London.

Three $4,000 postdoctoral fellowships in statistics are offered for 1953-1954 by the University of Chicago. The purpose of these fellowships, established under a grant from the Rockefeller Foundation and open to holders of the doctor's degree or its equivalent in research accomplishment, is to acquaint established research workers in the biological, physical, and social sciences with the crucial role of modern statistical analysis in the planning of experiments and other investigative programs, and in the analysis of empirical data. The closing date for applications is February 1, 1953; instructions for applying may be obtained from the Committee on Statistics, University of Chicago, Chicago 37.

The University of Notre Dame Committee on International Relations has received another grant of $65,000 from the Rockefeller Foundation for its program of research. During the three years the committee has been functioning, four volumes of studies have been published and five other volumes are nearing the publication stage. Besides these books, the committee has conducted several symposia and published several articles, chiefly in the *Review of Politics*. The chairman of the committee is Waldemar Gurian, and the other permanent members are Ferdinand A. Hermens, Stephen Kertesz, William O. Shanahan, and Matthew A. Fitzsimons.

Arthur P. Dudden, assistant professor of history at Bryn Mawr College, has received a grant from the American Philosophical Society toward a biographical study of the industrialist and reformer, Joseph Fels. Professor Dudden solicits information as to the whereabouts of letters, speeches, memoirs, or pamphlets pertinent to this study.

A. R. M. Lower of Queen's University has received an honorary doctorate from the University of British Columbia.

George M. Beckmann, University of Kansas, has received both Fulbright and Ford awards for a year of study in Japan.

Enno E. Kraehe, University of Kentucky, is on leave for the academic year on a Fulbright research grant in Vienna, Austria.

Walther Kirchner, University of Delaware, is on leave as a Fulbright research scholar at the University of Copenhagen.

The Social Science Research Council has announced the following fellowships and grants to be offered in 1953: research training fellowships, area research training fellowships, travel grants for area research, grants-in-aid of research, and faculty research fellowships. Research and area research training fellowships provide full maintenance and are designed to further the training of research workers in social science. The other awards are designed to aid scholars of established competence in the execution of their research, do not provide full maintenance, and are not available to students working for degrees. All awards are restricted to permanent residents of the United States or Canada. Faculty research fellowships are offered only in the United States. Applications, on forms provided by the Council, must be filed not later than January 5, 1953. Preliminary inquiries should be made and applications filed immediately. Inquiries, which should indicate age, academic status, vocational aims, the nature of the proposed training or research, and the type of assistance desired, should be addressed to the Social Science Research Council, 726 Jackson Place, N.W., Washington 6, D. C.

Richard C. Wade, assistant professor of history at the University of Rochester, is on leave for the academic year on a Social Science Research Council fellowship to pursue his study of "The Origins of Midwestern Urbanism, 1790-1830."

Edward Lurie, doctoral candidate at Northwestern University, has received an advanced graduate fellowship from the American Council of Learned Societies. He is presently studying at the Johns Hopkins University.

Four manuscripts have been received for the $1,000 annual David Clark Everest Prize in Wisconsin economic history. Judges of this year's entries are Edward C. Kirkland, Bowdoin College, Paul W. Gates, Cornell University, and Wendell H. Stephenson, Tulane University. The winner will be announced in January, 1953.

Earle D. Ross, professor of history at Iowa State College, was awarded the degree of Doctor of Humane Letters by Grinnell College at the June, 1952, commencement.

Historical Activities

The history staffs of the northern New England colleges, which have been meeting for a two-day session for some years, assembled at Dartmouth College on October 11 and 12; the general theme for the 1952 meeting was the Far Eastern situation and the place of courses on the Far East in the college curriculum.

Members of the Mississippi Historical Society met in Jackson on October 3, 1952, to reactivate the Society and to plan for the resumption of meetings after a forty-year lapse. An interim executive committee was selected to prepare for an annual meeting in the spring, to draft a revised constitution, and to direct a membership campaign. The members of the committee, serving also as subcommittee chairmen, are James W. Silver (chairman), University of Mississippi, program; Ross Moore, Millsaps College, local arrangements; Dawson A. Phelps, National Park Service, membership; John K. Bettersworth, Mississippi State College, editorial; Richard A. McLemore, Mississippi Southern College, special projects; William F. Winter, Mississippi House of Representatives, constitution; Frank Smith, United States House of Representatives, nominations; and Hunter Ross, National Park Service, publicity. Since the last annual meeting in 1911 and the cessation of publications in 1921, the only activity of the Society has been the publication of the *Journal of Mississippi History* which was established in 1939 by William D. McCain, director of the Mississippi Department of Archives and History. Dr. McCain, now on active duty as a lieutenant colonel with the army, expects to return in February, 1953.

"Votes for Women," an exhibit depicting the efforts of three generations of women to secure the franchise, was on display during October and November at the New-York Historical Society, New York City. The display included photographs of suffrage meetings and parades, colorful pennants, sashes and buttons, pro and antisuffrage literature, and pictures of leading suffragists.

The seventy-eighth annual convention of the Historical Society of Michigan was held at Petoskey on September 26, 27, and 28. One session of the meeting was devoted to Petoskey as part of its centennial celebration.

The annual Anglo-American Conference of Historians was held at the Institute of Historical Research in London on July 10, 11, and 12. Ten papers were read and a number of social gatherings held. A similar conference will be held on July 9, 10, and 11, 1953. Historians from North America who expect to be in England at that time are asked to communicate with the secretary of the Institute early in 1953 so that invitations may be sent to them.

The Nebraska State Historical Society held its seventy-fourth annual meeting in Lincoln on October 18. Marquis Childs was the principal speaker. During the day members toured the Society's new building, the exterior work on which was nearly completed.

A series of regional meetings in nineteen cities was sponsored by the State Historical Society of Wisconsin in September and October. Five executives of the Society, headed by Director Clifford Lord, toured the state in an effort to publicize the activities of the Society.

The first volume of a definitive catalog of the library of Thomas Jefferson has been published by the Library of Congress. Prepared by E. Millicent Sowerby of the staff of the reference department, the catalog will be in five volumes and will, when completed, give scholars an opportunity to map the bounds of Jefferson's vast knowledge and explore the sources that gave body and stimulus to his thought.

A new magazine venture of interest both in this country and abroad, *Perspectives U S A*, a quarterly in paper-bound book format, was launched in October by the Ford Foundation through its nonprofit organization, Intercultural Publications. Its primary object will be to give readers in other countries a representative picture of the intellectual and artistic life of the United States. The Viking Press will handle the bookstore distribution of *Perspectives* in America. The over-all director of the project and editor of the first issue is James Laughlin. A series of guest editors, including Malcolm Cowley, R. P. Blackmur, and Lionel Trilling, will select the contents of subsequent issues.

The University of Delaware and the Henry Francis duPont Winterthur Museum inaugurated this fall, with the support of the Rockefeller Foundation, a two-year graduate program leading to the master's degree in American Decorative Arts and Cultural History. The aims of the program are to encourage research in the art and culture of the United States from 1640 to 1840 and to train students for careers in museum and library work and in teaching. The courses taken at the University of Delaware are co-ordinated with laboratory work at the Winterthur Museum, which has remarkable collections of furniture, silver, pewter, pottery, glass, lighting fixtures, folk art, ceramics, fabrics, and floor coverings. Ten fellowships have been established which provide an annual stipend of $2,000 for two years. The degree program is limited to fellowship students, but courses at the University are open to any qualified student. Distinguished scholars in history and art who will visit the University for one week each in 1952-1953 are Theodor E. Mommsen and Thomas J. Wertenbaker, Princeton University; William S. Heckscher, University of Iowa; Wallace Notestein and John Marshall Phillips, Yale University; Edgar Wind, Smith College; W. C. Constable, Boston Museum of Fine Arts; Charles Nagel, Brooklyn Museum; Michael Kraus, City College of New York; Perry Miller, Harvard University; Louisa Dresser, Worcester Art Museum; and M. W. Thomas, Jr., Colonial Williamsburg. Inquiries should be addressed to Dean Carl J. Rees, University of Delaware, Newark, Delaware.

The Live Manuscripts Committee of the South Atlantic Modern Language Association seeks to encourage the living professional writer to help scholars, teachers, historians, and other qualified investigators in the search for understanding of our time through the work of our serious living writers. The committee asks the writer to deposit in a research institution — twenty-eight in the region are recommended — working materials from which the creative work grew: such as rough drafts, notebooks, journals, plans, records or tape if dictation was used, and letters. Preservation of working materials may be accomplished by outright gifts, loans, legacies, or in some other way which the writer proposes. Correspondence should be addressed to the chairman of the committee, John Bowen Hamilton, English Department, Georgia Institute of Technology, Atlanta.

The annual banquet of the East Tennessee Historical Society was held in Knoxville on October 4. Gregg Phifer, professor of speech at Florida State University, spoke on "Andrew Johnson's 'Swing Around the Circle,' 1866."

The Library of Congress has recently acquired some 11,000 papers of the late Owen Wister, among them the original drafts of many of his books, short stories, essays, and addresses, as well as his notebooks, journals, and correspondence; four volumes of the papers of Francis Baron Howard of Effingham (1643-1695), covering the period 1684-1688 which Lord Effingham spent in Virginia as governor of the province; 20,000 pieces of the personal papers of the late Gutzon Borglum, including material relating to his early years in European art schools, his association with the Progressive party, 1912-1916, his part in the Hughes aircraft investigation of 1918, and the controversy over the Confederate monument at Stone Mountain; some 15,000 personal papers, 1903-1950, of the late General H. H. Arnold, including correspondence files, diaries, photograph albums, scrapbooks, and manuscripts of speeches, statements, articles, and books; 20,000 additional Albert J. Beveridge pieces, among them early diaries, correspondence, materials relating to the Senator's addresses, and a large body of manuscript notes, memoranda, drafts, proofs, and other material accumulated in the preparation of his *John Marshall* and *Abraham Lincoln*; some 52,000 papers, 1916-1937, of Newton D. Baker, including correspondence and other materials relating to his career as secretary of war and his services on the Permanent Court of Arbitration at The Hague and on the Law Enforcement Commission.

The committee on the John Carroll Papers of the American Catholic Historical Association is searching for letters written by or to the Archbishop, or other documents of his authorship. Information should be addressed to Reverend Henry J. Browne, The Catholic University of America, Washington 17, D. C.

The annual meeting of the West Virginia Historical Society was held in Charleston on October 25. Speakers included Gerald W. Smith, instructor in history and political science at Marshall College, J. Merton England, associate professor of history at the University of Kentucky, and B. Floyd Flickinger, chairman of the department of political science at the University of Baltimore.

George L. Anderson, chairman of the department of history at the University of Kansas, and Nyle H. Miller, secretary of the Kansas State Historical Society, participated in a conference on the writing of local history held in cooperation with the Medicine Lodge Indian Peace Treaty Association at Medicine Lodge on October 10 and 11.

Julian Park, dean of the College of Arts and Sciences at the University of Buffalo, was the moderator of a round table discussion on the "Fall of France, 1940," at a meeting of the New York State Association of European Historians at Cornell University on October 17 and 18.

The autumn Upper Midwest History Conference was held at the University of Minnesota on October 17. Lawrence Steefel, professor of history at the University of Minnesota, presided. A paper entitled "The Influence of the United States in the Italian Migrations of the Twentieth Century" was read by George R. Gilkey of Wisconsin State College. Comments were made by Carlton Qualey, Carleton College, who is also chairman for the semiannual conferences for 1953. Walker D. Wyman was re-elected secretary.

A new monograph series for the publication of scholarly papers marks an expansion of the publishing program of the Public Affairs Press, Washington, D. C. The series has been established in recognition of the urgent need for publishing the findings of scholarship more promptly, effectively, and inexpensively than has hitherto been possible. The first publication is the *Historical Development of the American Flag* by William M. Markoe. Inquiries regarding papers believed suitable for inclusion in the new series should be addressed to the Editor, Annals of American Research, 2153 Florida Avenue, Washington 8, D. C.

Robert Taft, University of Kansas, was elected president of the Kansas State Historical Society at its seventy-seventh annual meeting held in Topeka on October 21. Features of the program included retiring president Will T. Beck's address entitled "Daniel Webster Wilder — He Implanted Erudition and Culture on Kansas Territorial Soil," and the first display of 300 photographs of Junction City scenes and people, 1895-1909, from the J. J. Pennell collection of the University of Kansas. Other officers of the Society elected were Angelo Scott, first vice-president; F. D. Farrell, second vice-president; Nyle H. Miller, secretary; and Mrs. Lela Barnes, treasurer.

R. Carlyle Buley, professor of history at Indiana University, was guest lecturer at the Ohio State Archaeological and Historical Society meeting on November 6. His subject was "Pioneer Ills and Doctors."

Bibliographical Notices

The University of Georgia Press has brought out a selection of Robert Preston Brooks's writings entitled *Georgia Studies*. The collection is edited by Gregor Sebba. The selection contains Professor Brooks's study, "The Agrarian Revolution in Georgia, 1865-1915," his "Howell Cobb and the Crisis of 1850," and a generous sampling of his work on historical subjects that has appeared in a variety of publishing media from 1911 to the present. The price is $3.50.

Lincoln in Marble and Bronze (New Brunswick, N. J.: Rutgers University Press, 1952. xiii + 353 pp. Illustrations and index. $7.50) is a study of the sixty-eight original heroic statues of Lincoln that have been erected from 1866 to 1949. The author, F. Lauriston Bullard, recounts the history of each statue — the movement for its erection, dedication ceremonies, something of the life and work of the sculptor, and the critical appraisal the works received.

Richard M. Dorson has published a group of folktales that he collected among the people of the Upper Peninsula of Michigan. They deal with a number of folk traditions from a variety of European stocks, regional groups, and American Indian tribes. The title of the collection is *Bloodstoppers & Bearwalkers* (Cambridge: Harvard University Press, 1952. 305 pp. Illustrations, appendix, and index. $5.00).

A bibliographical summary prepared for the guidance of scholars in the history of science has recently been issued by the Chronica Botanica Company. The compiler of this *Guide to the History of Science* (Waltham, Mass.: 1952. xvii + 316 pp. Index. $7.50), George Sarton, prefaces his guide to the sources with three lectures on the purpose and meaning of the history of science. The guide includes books, journals, and serials. It is organized according to special countries, special cultural groups, special sciences, and contains additional sections on institutes, museums, libraries, and international congresses.

The Comanches: Lords of the South Plains, by Ernest Wallace and E. Adamson Hoebel (Norman: University of Oklahoma Press, 1952. xiii + 381 pp. Illustrations, bibliography, and index. $5.00), is a presentation of the salient facts of Comanche history and culture in a manner calculated to attract the general reader as well as the anthropologist and the historian.

A recent monograph in the University of California's *English Studies* series is John Stafford's *The Literary Criticism of "Young America"* (Berkeley and Los Angeles: University of California Press, 1952. 154 pp. Bibliography and index. $2.00). It is, as its subtitle suggests, "a study in the relationship of politics and literature" for the period 1837-1850.

Another addition to the folklore of the cattle country is *Come An' Get It; The Story of the Old Cowboy Cook*, by Ramon F. Adams (Norman: University of Oklahoma Press, 1952. xi + 170 pp. Illustrations. $3.75). The author ranges from recipes for sourdough to his estimate of the influence of the cowpoke cook upon western life.

Art and Technics, by Lewis Mumford (New York: Columbia University Press, 1952. 162 pp. $2.50), is the title of Number 4 in the series, the *Bampton Lectures in America* delivered at Columbia University in 1951. In these lectures Mr. Mumford traces the conflict within man between the subjective artistic impulse and the objective "technical" impulse, illustrating his thesis from the history of painting, sculpture, architecture, engineering, and printing.

The failure of the military intervention of the United States in Siberia in 1918-1920 forms the subject of Clarence A. Manning's investigation entitled *The Siberian Fiasco* (New York: Library Publishers, 1952. 210 pp. Illustrations, bibliography, and index. $3.75).

Eleven additional *Preliminary Inventories* have been issued (1951-1952) by the National Archives: No. 31, *Records of the Petroleum Administration for War* (ix + 152 pp.), compiled by James R. Fuchs and Albert Whimpey; No. 36, *Records of the Bureau of the First Assistant Postmaster General, 1789-1942* (v + 16 pp.), compiled by Frank J. Nivert and Arthur Hecht; No. 37, *Records of the Office for Agricultural War Relations* (v + 19 pp.), compiled by Harold T. Pinkett; No. 38, *Climatological and Hydrological Records of the Weather Bureau* (v + 76 pp.), compiled by Harold T. Pinkett,

Helen T. Finneran, and Katherine H. Davidson; No. 39, *Records of the Hydrographic Office* (v + 17 pp.), compiled by Walter W. Weinstein; No. 40, *Records of the United States Mint at Philadelphia* (v + 38 pp.), compiled by Lyle J. Holverstott and Jean McNiece; No. 41, *Records of the Office of Inter-American Affairs* (v + 138 pp.), compiled by H. Stephen Helton; No. 42, *Records of the Senate Committee on Education and Labor: Subcommittee on Wartime Health and Education* (v + 11 pp.), compiled by George P. Perros; No. 43, *Records of the War Refugee Board* (v + 6 pp.), compiled by Henry T. Vlasek and Ira N. Kellog, Jr.; No. 44, *Records of the National Recovery Administration* (viii + 226 pp.), compiled by Homer L. Calkin, Meyer H. Fishbein, and Leo Pascal; No. 46, *Records of the Price Decontrol Board* (v + 4 pp.), compiled by James J. Fleischmann and Victor Gondos, Jr.

The National Archives has published, as Number 7 in its *Bulletin* series, *Historical Editing* by Clarence E. Carter (Washington: 1952. $.20). The author has distilled from his long experience as an editor some of the fundamental principles and practices of the craft of historical editing as they have evolved in recent years for the use of new apprentices.

A *Calendar of the Speeches and Other Published Statements of Franklin D. Roosevelt: 1910-1920*, compiled by Robert L. Jacoby (Hyde Park, N. Y.: Franklin D. Roosevelt Library, 1952. vii + 160 pp. Index. $1.25), now provides a combined list, abstract, and index to a hitherto scattered and virtually inaccessible group of papers.

Frederick B. Tolles has edited a diary kept by Lucretia Mott of her visit to England to attend the World Anti-Slavery Convention of 1840. The diary, entitled *Slavery and "The Woman Question,"* is published jointly by the Friends' Historical Association of Haverford, Pennsylvania, and the Friends' Historical Society of London (1952. 86 pp. Appendix and index. $1.00).

The Bobbs-Merrill Company has reprinted Holman Hamilton's *Zachary Taylor: Soldier of the Republic*, companion volume to his *Zachary Taylor: Soldier in the White House*. The price is $6.00.

Political Aspects of Slavery and the Civil War, a collection of seven articles on the period by George D. Harmon, has been published under the auspices of the department of history and government of Lehigh University. The articles have been previously published in historical journals. Only eighty copies of the book are for sale. Address: Head of the Department of History and Government, Lehigh University, Bethlehem, Pennsylvania. The price is $2.00.

A full-length study of Ernest Hemingway as artist, stylist, and craftsman, *Hemingway, The Writer as Artist*, by Carlos Baker (Princeton: Princeton University Press, 1952. xix + 322 pp. Check-list and index. $4.50), furnishes a systematic analysis of his work for the period 1920-1952.

In *Conquered Press* William J. Coughlin tells the story of General Douglas MacArthur's handling of the Japanese press and of American correspondents in occupied Japan. The book is published by Pacific Books, Palo Alto, California (1952. 165 pp. Appendixes, bibliography, and index. $3.00).

The "case" of Ezra Pound is taken up by Harold H. Watts in his *Ezra Pound and The Cantos* (Chicago: Henry Regnery Company, 1952. 132 pp. Index. $2.75). The author discovers in *The Cantos* Pound's relationship to American society, his relations to capitalism and fascism, and the fruits of his study of other cultures in pursuit of a "usable past."

Directory of Contributors

Robert W. Johanssen is a teaching fellow in American history and a doctoral candidate at the University of Washington.

Ira V. Brown is assistant professor of history at The Pennsylvania State College.

Laura Wood Roper of Washington, D. C., is presently engaged in writing a biography of Frederick Law Olmsted based on a (largely) hitherto unused manuscript collection.

William E. Leuchtenburg is associate professor of American history at Columbia University.

Horace Samuel Merrill is associate professor of American history at the University of Maryland.

George Frederick Howe is in the Department of the Interior, Washington, D. C., writing an administrative history of its defense agencies.

Mercantile Education in the Ante-Bellum South

By Lewis E. Atherton

Church and school received constant acclaim in nineteenth-century America as basic institutions. While their cultural and civilizing influences were recognized, promoters of towns, and others who chose to comment on the essentials of civilization, were quick to point out how real-estate values and the level of accomplishment in material things seemingly increased when associated with these agencies.

This justification of schools on practical grounds was characteristic of the ante-bellum southern mercantile class. Some facility in reading, writing, and arithmetic was essential for anyone entering the occupation, since these constituted everyday tools of the mercantile class. Business records and letters were written in longhand, although letter press devices enabled merchants to make copies of their correspondence and thus avoid additional labor. The prevalence of depreciated currency which might be rated in pounds, shillings, and pence, in Spanish monetary terminology, or in the American decimal system as late as 1850 required greater dexterity in figures than is ordinarily needed for similar transactions in the twentieth century. Such knowledge constituted minimum essentials even for the clerk, and men in charge of stores had to acquire a much broader range of information.

Beyond the three "R's," however, storekeepers were inclined to feel that formal schooling was wasteful and preferred to obtain additional training through apprenticeship and experience, as evidenced by the limited amount of formal training mentioned in mercantile biographies. Out of 234 of these examined by the writer in biographical encyclopedias,[1] 110 provided sufficient information

[1] The 234 biographies were compiled from biographical dictionaries, biographical volumes accompanying general state histories, and county histories for various south-

to judge the extent of formal training. Only 31 of these men possessed more than an elementary education gained in schools, a higher proportion probably than for the 124 who failed to state their educational preparation.

Although even more of the 234 failed to state exactly how they entered merchandising, it is significant that 69 mentioned having held clerkships in stores at an early age. Newspapers and business records indicate this to have been far below the percentage of storekeepers who started out as apprentices or clerks for older men. Boys preferred to indenture themselves to seaboard merchants, whose position in international trade provided a wealth of experience for the neophyte. William Taylor thus trained a number of young men in his mercantile house at Baltimore around the beginning of the nineteenth century and later started them out in branch establishments in New Orleans, a procedure which other Baltimore houses were also following.[2]

Applications for such appointments generally exceeded the supply. William Murrell, Statesburg, South Carolina, merchant, asked his Charleston agents in 1796 to find a place for a young man of his community. The difficulty in obtaining such an appointment became apparent when he tried to place his own son, whom he had given every advantage of a classical education for a youth of his years, in some Charleston house in 1801. Murrell hoped that the boy would enter one of the learned professions, but the attraction of merchandising proved too strong for him. Although salary was not an object in placing the boy in Charleston, no suitable place could be found for him, and the father had to start the son's mercantile training in his own country store at Statesburg.[3] Another youngster failed to obtain employment at Knoxville, Dandridge, or Greenville in 1834, and succeeded in finding a place in a chain of country stores operated by a Colonel Chunn of Asheville, North

ern states. Most of them were written in the post-Civil War period and in virtually all cases families paid to have the biographies published. While such material has limited value, it does provide information on the ordinary aspects of the lives considered.

[2] This is described in Lewis E. Atherton, "John McDonogh — New Orleans Mercantile Capitalist," *Journal of Southern History* (Baton Rouge, Lexington), VII (November, 1941), 451-81.

[3] William Murrell to Cantey, Henry and Company, May 24, 1796, Murrell to Edward Mortimer and Company, March 28, 1801, Murrell to J. and J. Hargraves, September 14, 1801, Murrell to William Marshall, October 5, 1801, Letter Book 1795-1812, William Murrell Collection, 1793-1851 (Duke University Library, Durham).

Carolina, at a salary of $75 a year and board only by borrowing a horse and rushing to interview the Colonel as soon as he heard of the opening.[4]

Boys who lacked the connections necessary to obtain a place in a large seaboard house readily accepted positions in interior stores. Here they might work for their board and a small salary, or none at all, for three or four years, after which they hoped to become a junior partner in the establishment of some older man or to be placed in charge of a branch store farther to the interior. In the interval they acquired a knowledge of bookkeeping, salesmanship, and goods.

This procedure was perhaps still the most popular form of training on the eve of the Civil War, although indentures were no longer drawn with the exactitude common at the beginning of the century. William C. Grasty's career demonstrates both the operation and the survival of the system. In 1836 he started as an employee of Royall Young and Company at a salary of $350 a year, board, and necessary clothing at cost.[5] In July, 1838, he settled with the firm, receiving $756.12. This represented his savings and perhaps some interest in a little over two years as a clerk. He was still under twenty-one, for his guardian had to sign the articles of agreement with the Mount Airy, Virginia, merchant from whom he bought on March 7, 1838, the store originally owned by his father.[6] Perhaps superior ability on his part accounted both for his own higher salary while learning the mercantile business and the ease with which he attracted apprentices to his small Mount Airy store. On January 1, 1847, Beverly B. Walker indentured himself to Grasty for a four-year period. Board and washing were to constitute the sole remuneration for the first year, with a salary of $20 added for the second year, $25 for the third, and $30 and one half the net proceeds from the Mount Airy post office for the fourth.[7]

Although many youngsters achieved their hopes of a junior partnership on the completion of their training, the system was not

[4] Frederick C. Welcker to Charles Welcker, August 2, 1834, Letters and Legal Papers of Colonel Charles F. Welcker, Tazewell, Tennessee, merchant, being chiefly his correspondence with his brothers George and Z. C., and his sons Henry, Benjamin, Frederick, Charles, and James, 1803-1880 (Lawson McGhee Library, Knoxville).

[5] Agreement April 9, 1836, William C. Grasty and John F. Rison Papers, 1800-1869 (Duke University Library).

[6] Settlement July 9, 1838, and contract March 7, 1838, *ibid.*

[7] William C. Grasty Journal, 1846-1847, p. 320, *ibid.*

without fault. Bad practices were perpetuated along with the good, and perhaps apprenticeship training has not received its proper evaluation as a factor in the retention of obsolete methods.

Merchandising itself provided a remarkably diverse and stimulating educational experience. Interior and country stores often served as post offices and thus gave the storekeeper access to all the newspapers that arrived in the community. The mails lacked the privacy of the modern day, and there was little objection to the perusal of a newspaper until its owner could ride in to claim it. In many cases the storekeeper-postmaster ordered magazines and papers in his own name for his customers and thus felt even freer to glance over the contents in his moments of leisure.[8]

General stores also commonly stocked books for sale. In smaller places this practice prevailed until the close of the period, and even in larger towns bookstores developed rather late in the process of specialization. The numerous lists of books in mercantile inventories and their sales recorded in daybooks have been overlooked by students of intellectual history in their efforts to determine the reading interests of ante-bellum America. Storekeepers were not averse to purchasing bargain lots of books without too much investigation of the contents, but many of their orders reflected fairly accurately the reading tastes of their customers. A certain uniformity of selection of books for general stores prevailed. Schoolbooks, along with dictionaries and almanacs, naturally were included. These were often supplemented by a wide range of English and classical literature, medical and religious works for daily reference, and histories and biographies.[9]

Most storekeepers perhaps limited their attention to the cursory examination of contents considered necessary to move such items in the normal course of trade, but some at least went beyond this preliminary duty of the successful businessman. George Paschal,

[8] Hugh Graham, storekeeper and postmaster at Tazewell, received a great variety of newspapers and magazines, such as the New York *Observer*, *American Protestant*, *Christian Observatory*, *Southern Literary Messenger*, *Puritan Recorder*, *London Quarterly Review*, *North British Review*, *Blackwood's Magazine*, *Putnam's Monthly*, New York *Journal of Commerce*, *Missionary Herald*, Baltimore *Weekly American*, and *Knickerbocker Magazine* in the late 1840's and early 1850's. Hugh Graham Papers, 1803-1886 (Lawson McGhee Library). Ordering these in his own name gave a storekeeper-postmaster a reputation as an obliging merchant. Since he could frank his own mail, his customers were saved the cost of postage necessary to send the order.

[9] For representative lists, see Lewis E. Atherton, *The Southern Country Store, 1800-1860* (Baton Rouge, 1949), 81-82.

who as a young man operated a store at Lexington, Georgia, had little formal academic training. His son later told how the father's inquiring mind had led him to study history and French literature, from which he emerged with a positive dislike for priests and kings. It is true that the father made a failure of merchandising, but failure typified as many storekeepers as did success.[10]

Joseph Anderson's diary of his career as a clerk and storekeeper in various small Tennessee towns about 1840 reveals the extent to which men of intellectual curiosity turned to the books on their shelves as welcome friends on days when business lagged. On one occasion he devoted part of the day to reading John L. Stephens' *Incidents of Travel in Greece, Turkey, Russia, and Poland* (1838), in spite of interruptions by customers during the afternoon. The impressions of the travel book still remained vividly in mind three weeks later when he complained about the amount of credit requested by customers in the current depression. Recalling the story of Russia, he commented that half the country population would be "as the serfs of Russia" unless times improved. On another occasion he was blessed again by the absence of customers, and after a hunt around the store found a copy of "Perkins' Travels in Egypt" which absorbed his attention immediately. In 1843 he was in charge of a country store at Eden's Ridge, where on quiet days he wrote poetry, trying to express his yearning for a "lovely form not divine." [11] More storekeepers contented themselves with pious maxims from Benjamin Franklin, it is true, but the availability of books in their stores provided opportunities which existed in few other occupations.

Still another educative force developed from the necessity for travel on the part of the successful storekeeper. Irregular and slow methods of communication and transportation, coupled with the unstandardized quality of merchandise, made at least yearly trips to the larger cities to purchase goods highly advisable. As a consequence, storekeepers became familiar with the larger eastern cities as well as the rural life of their own section, whereas the average citizen was denied frequent opportunity to witness at firsthand the great diversity in various parts of America. Daniel R. Hundley, in

10 George W. Paschal, *Ninety-four Years. Agnes Paschal* (Washington, 1871), Chap. IV.

11 Microfilm copy of Diary of Joseph Anderson, 1839-1843 (Vanderbilt University Library, Nashville).

discussing the dreams which drew "Young Hopeful" away from an agricultural life and into the field of merchandising, described the attraction of the idea of "making semi-annual visits to New-York or Philadelphia after goods; and coming in a carriage with servants in livery, to see the old homestead every Christmas; and having the seat of honor awarded him [Young Hopeful] on such occasions, while he makes the eyes of all to stare in awe and wonder at the marvellous yarns he spins out concerning the sights to be seen in the metropolis."[12]

Merchants were prone to complain of the discomforts and hardships involved in these long journeys, and many sincerely disliked the necessity of making such trips. Still, there was much to be seen and learned, a recompense to be appreciated more after the traveler was once again comfortably settled at home. John Coffee, who engaged in storekeeping with Andrew Jackson for a time in Tennessee and remained his lifelong friend and confidant, kept an account of his expenditures on an eastern buying trip in the nineteenth century. He prepared for the journey with some care, as evidenced by his inoculation for the kinepox. Personal purchases of items such as lockets, guitar strings, and telescopes occupied some of his time, and he also visited an exhibition of ventriloquism, the circus, Charles Willson Peale's famous Philadelphia Museum, and witnessed a performance by "the learned pig." Perhaps his purchases of "bugles" and "spangles" were for Andrew Jackson, as he seems to have transacted either personal business for the latter or to have made purchases for his store. On his way home he spent some five or six dollars at the Baltimore theater and recorded other small sums which seem to have gone for amusement.[13]

David Campbell, a merchant of Abingdon, Virginia, and later governor of the state, found part of his trip to the wholesale cities in 1821 very interesting. At Fredericksburg, where Campbell transferred to a new stage, he met the president of the University of North Carolina and an "eccentric gentleman" by the name of Dr. Warrell, who carried on a spirited intellectual discussion with him.

[12] Daniel R. Hundley, *Social Relations in Our Southern States* (New York, 1860), 103.

[13] Expense accounts, Robert Dyas Collection of the General John Coffee and Donelson Family Papers (Tennessee Historical Society, Nashville). One trip was made about 1803. So detailed and confusing are his accounts that it is possible the expenditures were for a series of trips east.

So heated did the other two passengers become in their remarks during the course of the journey that they finally insisted on Campbell settling an argument which had arisen. In his estimation both had "acted like children" in the matter, but even so he thoroughly enjoyed the stimulus of such company.[14]

A Tennessee merchant in 1830 was decidedly impressed by New York City, as a letter to his son revealed:

> I wish you were taking a walk with me here on Broadway to see what a city looks like every thing that I have before seen hardly deserves the name however so well charged a man or a dandy may be with self importance and his own conceit here he will be lost in the blaze of splendour and fashion and feel like he had just emerged into a new world in which he had everything to learn.[15]

Another merchant who visited Baltimore in 1836 refused to be awed by eastern cities. In his estimation Nashville possessed more impressive buildings, and a Presbyterian preacher whom he heard on Sunday morning lacked the fire and zeal of western exhorters. Visits to the Washington Monument and to Sunday afternoon services at the Catholic church at least escaped unfavorable comparisons with western counterparts. Philadelphia proved more interesting, but he was so busy buying goods that he retired to his comfortable room early each evening to sit before an open fire and calculate his daily purchases. By eleven at night he was ready to retire and turn his mind in the direction of God, his home, and his family. After his purchases were completed and while he was arranging transportation for his goods, he did take time to examine the local waterworks, a remarkable sight to him, and the local navy yard. The great number of charitable institutions which he observed on his trips around the city also appealed to him, and perhaps the fact that Quaker influences were credited locally with these achievements accounted for his visit, along with other country merchants, to a Quaker meeting on the Sabbath. All were greatly impressed by a speech of a fifty-year-old Quaker woman on that occasion.[16]

Younger storekeepers seemingly preferred greater excitement. A North Carolinian in 1848 wrote home from New York City that the theater seemed to be the main attraction at the time and that

14 David Campbell to Mary H. Campbell, December 16, 17, 1821, David Campbell Collection, 1773-1908 (Duke University Library).

15 Robert Allen to Dixon F. Allen, September 15, 1830, *ibid.*

16 David Campbell to Margaret Campbell, March 6, 21, April 1, 1836, *ibid.*

he had been prevented from attending by the pressure of business and a bad cold.[17] His letter indicated that he was accustomed to such recreation on most of his trips and that his brother, who had remained at home to look after the store, would be interested in knowing about New York amusements during the current season.

Another North Carolina merchant combined a trip in 1837 to the eastern cities to purchase goods with a honeymoon tour. On this occasion city hack drivers received liberal patronage, as the groom seems to have taken his bride to points of interest in each city visited. Niblo's Garden in New York City cost a dollar for admission to its wonders and the theater accounted for another six. Perhaps this explains a donation of only thirteen cents when the happy couple attended services at Saint Paul's Church. Included in the detailed expenditures were twelve cents for two glasses of ale and six and one fourth cents for a glass of beer.[18]

George W. F. Harper, who visited the larger cities regularly for goods in the late fifties, had the advantage of being able to make part of his journey from Lenoir, North Carolina, by rail. Although this improved method of transportation tempted him to write in his diary while traveling, he soon abandoned the effort with the comment "Higity jigity. Can't write." [19] For the excitement which merchants had found in the days of stagecoach travel, Harper could substitute the story of his train mangling an organ grinder on a trestle as it roared its way through Virginia.[20] Like so many of the earlier group, however, he wrote his beloved Ella that he attended church on Sunday morning, visited friends in the afternoon to escape from a crowded hotel, and spent his evenings by himself with her ambrotype for company.[21] Ella seems to have accompanied him on at least one trip since he wrote from Philadelphia on March 30, 1861, that approaching dissolution of the Union had created stagnant business conditions and that "you and Em" would have little trouble now in parading on Market Street.[22]

[17] R. A. Hamilton to C. E. and R. A. Hamilton, March 21, 1848, John Bullock Papers, 1760-1882 (University of North Carolina Library, Chapel Hill).

[18] Entries in Memorandum Book, Fall, 1836, and Spring, 1837, John W. and William A. Williams Papers, 1799-1919 (University of North Carolina Library).

[19] Entry March 13, 1859, in George W. F. Harper Diary, 1859-1860, George W. F. Harper Papers, 1838-1921 (University of North Carolina Library).

[20] Entry April, 1859, in Harper Diary, 1857-1859, *ibid.*

[21] George W. F. Harper to Ella Harper, March 18, 1860, *ibid.*

[22] George W. F. Harper to Ella Harper, March 30, 1861, *ibid.*

While storekeepers mentioned visits to the theater, southern mercantile letters uniformly failed to provide anything which would give support to the occasional charge made in business journals that clerks in wholesale houses frequently were expected to be prepared to initiate country customers into the vices of city iniquity.[23] The writer has looked in vain for positive evidence that western or southern storekeepers saw Mademoiselle Celeste at the New York City Bowery in 1835 in the "celebrated traditionary drama" *The Wept of Wish-Ton-Wish* and the melodrama *The French Spy, or the Wild Arab of the Desert*. Nor did they admit seeing the same actress in Philadelphia the following year in the same plays, to which she had added by that time a new grand opera dance entitled "La Preciosa" and a specialty labelled "The Wild Arab Dance."[24] Instead, they visited the local waterworks or remained in their hotel rooms to look at pictures of their wives. These semiannual or annual trips, often for a distance of 1,500 or 2,000 miles each way and lasting for as long as two months, did much to broaden the horizon of the storekeeper and to give him a clearer perception of his country than many of his customers could ever hope to have.

Apprenticeship and practical experience thus constituted the educational preparation of the overwhelming majority of storekeepers, and they were joined by many others in a common conviction that this provided the best possible training for merchandising. William Murrell's plan to transfer his son from the classics to an apprenticeship under a Charleston merchant immediately after the boy's decision to become a storekeeper reflected almost exactly the same reaction as that of a North Carolina lawyer in 1797. The latter's younger brother was attending the University of North Carolina at the time but had expressed a preference for a business career. A good knowledge of accounts and an "easy business hand" were essential, said the lawyer, and these could be perfected while the youngster was seeking a place in some mercantile house. The practical element received heavy emphasis in the lawyer's advice:

> If you study physic you must serve an apprenticeship in beating at the mortar and rolling up pills. If law, you must copy lengthy Bills, answers & you must set Richard Roe & John Doe (poor innocent names) to eject,

23 The Rev. Henry Dennison, "Commercial Ethics," *De Bow's Review* (New Orleans), XXVII (October, 1859), 444-53; see especially p. 447.

24 Advertisements in New York *Evening Post*, January 12, 1835; Philadelphia *Public Ledger*, September 12, 1836.

> assault, battle and misuse each other and then bring them to justice against their wills. If merchandise, you must sweep up the store house, weigh sugar, measure salt, write a great deal and stand constantly behind the counter for a long time before you would be able to earn your bread.[25]

There was no implication whatever that the youngster's cultural training might make him a more desirable or more successful merchant.

An Alabama paper in 1853 offered much the same advice in extracts copied from Edwin T. Freedley's *A Practical Treatise on Business*. Physical strength was considered more important than theoretical training: "Great care must, therefore, be taken that the health be not impaired in a strife for useless honors, that the feelings be not suffered to grow over-sensitive in recluse contemplation, nor the mind lose its spring and elasticity under a load of cumbersome and unpractical training." To escape these dreadful evils of formal, cultural training, the future merchant should be placed in the countinghouse following his elementary schooling. This constituted the businessman's "proper college," for there he would lose any conceits of formal education and would acquire truth, accuracy, and decision.[26]

Such smug sentiments in favor of "practical" training naturally evoked replies from disciples of the classics. One of the most amusing of these appeared in a Richmond, Virginia, paper in 1853, though it had been published originally in some other contemporary sheet. The editor introduced the subject by saying that the reprint of the letter represented the sentiments of a "cute" merchant, one of that class that thought of nothing in the whole world but trade. It supposedly represented the order, with reasons, of a merchant to the headmaster of a classical school to send a son home:

> Sir: My son's of 10th inst., came duly to hand, and cont's noted. Sorry to hear he has been stud'g Latin, etc. What's use? I never studied any such thing-nothing but Webster's Sp'g Book and Daboll's Arith'k and P'r Richard's Alm'k; yet got along well enough-made money; am Bank Direct'r, Memb., Chamb., Com., etc., etc. — Latin! better look into McCulloch-some use in that. Learn all about Dr. and Cr., cwt., cur'cy, exch.,

[25] Charles W. Harris to Robert Harris, November 27, 1797, Charles Wilson Harris Papers, 1777-1803 (University of North Carolina Library).

[26] Huntsville (Ala.) *Democrat*, November 3, 1853. This was Edwin T. Freedley, *A Practical Treatise on Business: on how to Get, Save, Spend, Give, Lend, and Bequeath Money: with an Inquiry into the Chances of Success and Causes of Failure in Business* (Philadelphia, 1852), 29. The newspaper quotation was not an exact reproduction of the phraseology in the book.

bank facil., md'ze, etc; that's the commodity of true knowledge — the best md'ze for count'g room — always in den'd — always available in market, when y'r Latin and y'r Greek wouldn't fetch a *soomarkee*, as my cap'ain says.

But to point: My son is now 14 yr's old-am in want of another clerk-must have finished his ed'n by *this* time, surely; would have let him staid another half year though, but for the Latin, and high rates of tuition at board'g sch'l. Please ship him on board Siftsure, with invoice and bill of lad'g of books, etc., consigned to Merx & Co., N. Y'k.

P.S. - Send bill, and will remit by return mail. Stocks rather heavy. Sho'd be glad to sell you a lot of damaged Java at 7 cts. per lb. - very cheap, and good enough for board'g sch'l. Please advise.[27]

This contest between the severely "practical" educator and the classicist brought into the open the two bodies of opinion which probably did most to retard pre-Civil War movements for formal commercial education. Certainly it contained little hope for those moving in that direction, and neither classical nor "practical" education alone received much attention from those who discussed such matters at length in public print.

Article after article in both *Hunt's Merchants' Magazine* and *De Bow's Review* in the 1840's and 1850's urged merchants to take a position in life commensurate with their wealth and economic power. They should realize what commerce had meant for civilization and should keep its historic position alive by endowing schools, libraries, and philanthropic institutions. Both recognized the need for formal education beyond the narrow limits of the countingroom, and both generally leaned in the direction of making this fit mercantile needs rather than narrow scholastic preparation. Although the movement proposed to draw from both cultural and professional elements of training, it pleased neither the narrow classicist, because it lessened his tenacious grasp on all formal education, nor the country storekeeper, because he suspected the value in any kind of advanced, formal training.

Hunt carried reports of speeches by men like former President John Tyler urging merchants to become philosophers and men of

[27] Richmond *Morning Mail*, August 6, 1853. John R. McCulloch, *A Dictionary, Practical, Theoretical, and Historical, of Commerce and Commercial Navigation* (London, 1832), had been introduced to the American commercial world in 1840 in an edition by Professor Henry Vethake of the University of Pennsylvania, and had received much acclaim. See review of the book in *Hunt's Merchants' Magazine* (New York), III (December, 1840), 531-32.

letters as well as purveyors of articles of commerce.[28] Ben Casseday, editor of the Louisville *Commercial Review*, argued in an article published in *Hunt's* in 1856 in favor of a liberal education as an excellent background for the professional training to follow.[29]

De Bow seemingly favored any training which would broaden the outlook of those intending to enter the mercantile occupation, but he stressed most of all statistical and commercial education for commercial men. In a long article in 1847 he stated the major tenets of his educational philosophy. He praised learning highly for itself and also the success of the classical approach in preparing men for the professions. The current educational theory of the period was also accepted in his remark that almost any kind of study would lead to a discipline of the mind and an enlarged capacity to act, but he departed radically from this school of thought when he suggested that a man should gain an additional advantage by devoting his attention to those subjects which were in line with his occupational needs after schooling had been ended.

From this point he labored the virtues of commerce and the need for training men especially for that occupation. Commercial men now had an opportunity to foster such formal training at the new University of Louisiana, and De Bow hoped they would endow a Professorship of Public Economy, Commerce, and Statistics. Such a man could elevate the standard of commercial character by enlarging and expanding the views of those preparing for the occupation, provide an opportunity for the education of youths who found nothing to their liking in the traditional curriculum, and through the necessary library give New Orleans a constant bureau of statistics.

In the theoretical aspects of the work this professor would be expected to handle material which in the modern college generally is grouped under the headings of economics and political science. Present-day college students in those fields would readily recognize such books as Adam Smith's *Wealth of Nations* and John Locke's *Essays on Government*, both of which De Bow cited in his list of works suitable for the chair which he hoped to see created. In the practical field, the professor would regale his students with statis-

[28] John Tyler, "The Merchant of the Past and the Present," *Hunt's Merchants' Magazine*, XXXIV (May, 1856), 542-48.

[29] Ben Casseday, "Dignity of the Mercantile Profession," *ibid.*, XXXV (July, 1856), 54-56.

tics of population and wealth in their relation to commerce, agriculture, and manufacturing.[30]

Maunsel White, New Orleans cotton factor and one of De Bow's firmest supporters, took the lead in raising money for the establishment of such a chair.[31] Under these conditions, and also because De Bow had fostered the idea, he was appointed to the professorship. In the August, 1849, issue of his *Review* he announced his plans for the "Commercial College at New Orleans," a department within the University of Louisiana. Classes would be organized to start the following November, and two courses of instruction would be given. One would consist of a series of twenty-five or thirty historical, economic, and general lectures planned with the idea of appealing to all interested in the mercantile occupation. A modest fee of ten dollars covered all costs for the course.

The regularly matriculated students would receive instruction in the whole field of commercial education in classes meeting three or four times each day. Writing, bookkeeping, commercial correspondence, accounts, account sales, invoices, general principles of commercial law, banking, insurance, partnerships, exchange, factorage, guarantee, brokerage, bankruptcy, wrecks, salvage, freights, privateering, marque and reprisal, quarantine, customhouse regulations, and sketches of prominent merchants were specifically mentioned as part of the subject matter. De Bow expected to have a tutor help him with this training which would cover a period of five months and cost only $50 for registration. An element of business college procedure crept in through his announcement that a deduction in rates would be made for those entering the course after it had started.[32]

De Bow's plans seem not to have advanced beyond delivery of the first of the general lectures, although he continued to use the title of professor on the front page of his magazine. In 1855 he stated that the lectures had been interrupted by an outbreak of cholera in New Orleans and had not been resumed following that trouble. His plans had obviously not gotten beyond the paper stage in the interval since 1849. The blame was assigned to such factors

30 James D. B. De Bow, "Commerce and Agricultural Subjects of University Instruction," *De Bow's Review*, III (June, 1847), 502-16.

31 [James D. B. De Bow], "A Professorship of Commerce," *ibid.*, VI (August, 1848), 110-13; see especially p. 111. A number of articles in De Bow's journal of this period discussed the development of plans for the professorship.

32 "Commercial College at New Orleans," *ibid.*, VII (August, 1849), 188.

as an unfavorable legislature, failure to complete the building in which courses were to be held, a slow administration, and the bungling of the endowment. Certainly this was sufficient evidence to support his conclusion: "*In short*, the *circumstances of the university were not auspicious for carrying out the purposes of the professorship.*"[33] De Bow was still hopeful of success, but he was to be disappointed.

The attraction of merchandising for ambitious southern boys and the limited number of openings under the apprenticeship system provided some encouragement to bookkeeping and writing schools, and these managed to survive in spite of the indifference, or even openly expressed contempt for formal business training. They displayed considerable ingenuity in adjusting to the contrary factors of limited commercial opportunities in a heavily agrarian economy and prevailing sentiment.

Occasionally a permanent resident of some community supplemented his regular income by giving lessons in penmanship or bookkeeping. Frederic Pigeon operated a small store at Opelousas, Louisiana, for a number of years in the 1850's but, judged on the basis of volume of advertising, his business never rivaled that of his wife, who conducted a local millinery store. Perhaps this accounted for Frederic's advertisement in 1856 that he would conduct classes in bookkeeping twice a week from eight to ten in the evening for the reasonable sum of five dollars a month.[34]

Most teachers followed the well-recognized pattern of circuit-riding preachers and lawyers, itinerant artisans, and peddlers, and moved from town to town in quest of students. Writing classes for young ladies often were organized as a means of supplementing the income gained from instructing those anxious to gain a foothold in the business world.[35] Moreover, it was quite common for these itinerant teachers to advertise the virtues of formal training and their own special preparation to teach commercial subjects. In 1829 J. C. Newnan ran a sizable notice in the Athens, Georgia, paper offering to instruct a few classes in penmanship for the modest fee of three dollars a month. Much of the advertisement consisted of copies of testimonials, including one from the president of the Uni-

33 "Subjects of University Instruction," *ibid.*, XIX (October, 1855), 431-37; quotation on p. 436.

34 Opelousas (La.) *Courier*, April 12, 1856.

35 Advertisement of Miller's Academy, Natchez *Southern Galaxy*, July 2, 1829.

versity of North Carolina to the effect that he was "a gentleman, a scholar, and an unrivalled penman." [36] A visiting teacher at Huntsville, Alabama, in 1848 attempted to pave the way for the opening of his "double entry and steam-boat bookkeeping school" by answering the criticisms currently in vogue. Those who argued against trying to learn a system of bookkeeping because no two merchants kept books alike, he said, failed to realize that these differences were only in the form and number of books employed. Others objected to formal schooling on the grounds that it gave the pupil no knowledge of goods, but a knowledge of accounts and a knowledge of goods were two different things. He would teach the former, and the latter could be obtained in actual experience. To parents and guardians whose sons and wards were anxious to achieve commercial success without "years of painful and laborious duties as subordinates," he promised to prepare candidates for lucrative bookkeeping jobs within six weeks and for only $50.[37]

The Dolbear family seems to have been the most successful of all these itinerant business teachers. With New Orleans as their headquarters, they visited smaller places throughout the South for over twenty years giving short courses. They called at Baton Rouge in 1832 for this purpose, at Montgomery in 1834, and at Huntsville in 1843 and again in 1856 — representative examples of their advertised visits during their long career.[38] Such trips generally were made during the summer when New Orleans was resting from the rigors of the business season.

While the Dolbears ordinarily did not attempt lavish advertisements, their long career in the business provided them with a wealth of material when they chose to assert their pre-eminence. The Huntsville, Alabama, paper in 1843 contained one of their notices which ran to three fourths of a column. They called attention to their book, the *Science of Practical Penmanship*, in which they reduced the art to a science, and also invited the public to call and

36 Athens (Ga.) *Athenian*, January 20, 1829.

37 Advertisement of T. H. Harris, Huntsville *Democrat*, April 10, 1848.

38 With the exception of the Montgomery, Alabama, visit of 1834, which is cited from a chronological chart in M. P. Blue, "A Brief History of Montgomery," in Beale and Phelan assisted by M. P. Blue, *City Directory and History of Montgomery, Alabama, with a Summary of Events in that History, Calendarically Arranged, Besides other Valuable and Useful Information* (Montgomery, 1878), this list is compiled from newspapers for the years cited: Baton Rouge *Gazette*, July 7, 1832; Huntsville *Democrat*, December 7, 1843, July 17, 1856.

examine the improvement of some two or three hundred men who had taken their courses at Nashville, living proof of their superiority in a field which they considered to be crowded with quacks. Then followed a list of twenty-five prominent men, headed by General Edmund P. Gaines, who had examined the work of Dolbear and pronounced it superior to all others. The indorsers were indorsed in turn by former President Andrew Jackson himself:

> Being requested by Messrs. Dolbear to state the standing of the gentlemen, signers to the within, I do so with much pleasure, being acquainted with most of them, and as far as I am acquainted with them, they are highly respectable and gentlemen of education and of high standing in society. Given at the Hermitage this 23d day of Oct. 1843. Andrew Jackson.

Included also was a letter from former President Martin Van Buren commending their book and a letter from Senator Thomas Hart Benton from Washington to J. W. Dolbear, in which he added his blessing in his usual pontifical style: "I . . . applaud your meritorious exertions to improve the chirography of the age." Letters from preachers, including a bishop, and state officials added to the impressiveness of the whole.[39] The real promotional efforts of Rufus Dolbear were to come with his attempt to create a great southern commercial school at New Orleans in the late fifties, however.

Both country and city boys had an opportunity to attend these itinerant commercial schools as they moved back and forth between large and small towns, but mercantile library associations benefited primarily those who were employed only in the larger trade centers. Hunt mentioned seven such organizations in an article in 1853,[40] only one of which was in the South, the Charleston Mercantile Library Association. Petersburg, Virginia, had started one by 1856,[41] and others probably existed in the South before the Civil War. Such organizations were maintained by contributions from older merchants and an annual payment of dues from all members. These associations possessed reading rooms where members could consult business volumes or materials of a lighter nature. Classes in bookkeeping, languages, and other subjects of interest often were held,

[39] Huntsville *Democrat,* December 7, 1843.

[40] "Mercantile Library Associations," *Hunt's Merchants' Magazine,* XXIX (October, 1853), 437-48.

[41] John Tyler addressed this organization in 1856. See Tyler, "Merchant of the Past and the Present," *ibid.*, XXIV (May, 1856), 542 n.

and some organizations also supported a yearly course of lectures.[42]

In the 1850's commercial teachers began to capitalize on the growing sectional hostility. The Southern Commercial College at Nashville in 1860 advertised its origin and its charter from the state legislature in the following manner: "The great importance of Southerners educating their children on Southern Soil, where they would be free from the contaminating influence of Northern fanatics, first led to the establishment of the above Institution and its subsequent charter in 1854." Its curriculum consisted of bookkeeping, commercial law and calculations, and penmanship, and it boasted of graduates from seven different southern states who were now engaged in banking, merchandising, or newspaper work.[43]

Rufus Dolbear thought he saw even greater possibilities in the troubled state of the nation. Under date of August 29, 1859, he asked all newspapers which favored "Practical Southern Education" to announce that subscriptions to the capital stock of Dolbear Commercial College were now open. Shares would be sold for $25 and could be applied on tuition at any time.[44] In 1860 he was advertising his college as operating under a charter from the state legislature, with a capital stock of $250,000 and a curriculum entitled to expand into the agricultural and mechanical fields. He listed the names of nine professors who presided over departments offering in addition to the traditional commercial subjects such things as classical and modern languages, and he obviously intended to expand into the fields of rhetoric and elocution. Dolbear asserted that his school was the oldest in the United States, a claim based on his teaching of commercial subjects in New Orleans since 1832, and that it was the only chartered commercial college in the Southwest.[45] War terminated his venture before it could be seen whether this man, probably the greatest promoter among the older itinerant teachers of commercial subjects, could realize his ambitious plans.

Southern attitudes toward mercantile education differed very little from those expressed by northern businessmen in the antebellum period, for constant contacts between the sections contrib-

42 "Mercantile Library Associations," *ibid.*, XXIX (October, 1853), 437-48.

43 L. P. Williams and Company, *Nashville City and Business Directory for 1860-61* (Nashville, 1860), contains a description of the school and also a full page advertisement on the last page.

44 Alexandria *Louisiana Democrat*, September 14, 1859.

45 New Orleans *Daily Crescent*, April 2, 1860.

uted to a similarity of outlook. In both areas merchants stressed the value of apprenticeship training and experience in preparing young men for business careers. Since classical training still dominated college curriculums in both sections of the country, boys were encouraged to forego college work unless they intended to enter one of the professions. In both North and South efforts were made in the last ante-bellum decade to find a new approach to mercantile training that would avoid siding either with the classicists or their opponents. This legacy of conflict in practice and tradition was passed on to the post-Civil War era for solution.

The Opposition of American Businessmen to Social Control During the "Gilded Age"

By Chester McArthur Destler

The demand that American business be subject to social control was the product of substantial fact rather than of doctrinaire imperatives during the "Gilded Age." Important segments of the community concluded then that the abuses perpetrated by business and its spoilsmen allies should not be borne. When competition did not provide a remedy the aggrieved elements voiced their disapproval of specific malpractices. In those cases where the pressure of public opinion proved ineffective a demand emerged that some type of government regulation or control be imposed upon the recalcitrant business organizations as a practicable means of securing relief, even though it was less attractive than a continued regime of untrammeled individualism.

The mobilization of public opinion was the joint task of the independent press, injured economic interests, and self-appointed leaders who sought to extend the empire of "Reform" from the humanitarian field to the structure of business and its relations to consumers and wage earners. Sporadic public protests, at times of great and prolonged intensity, were the result. These began with the demand that the offending concerns discontinue harmful business practices. Sometimes rugged individualists tried to implement public opinion by unilateral action. Such was the rawboned farmer on the Granger railroads in Illinois, Wisconsin, or Minnesota who presented the conductor with the legal fare in lieu of that demanded by the carrier's tariff and declined to pay the difference. The farmer's muscle and that of the Grangers who rallied to his side might secure him delivery to his destination despite the efforts of the entire train crew; but neither this muscular protest nor the cry of newspapers and farm periodicals succeeded in inducing the midwestern railroads on their own initiative to adopt schedules of uniform, moderate fares and freight rates during the era.[1]

Consumer protests and press campaigns against the buccaneering tactics and bad car service of municipal street railroads in such cities as Chicago were equally abortive. The demand for pure foods and drugs met a similar fate while the rising tide of criticism of the wasteful practices of lumbering firms was simply ignored as the forests melted swiftly.

The great entrepreneurs of the epoch were generally indifferent to public protests of this type. Judging from the statements of John D. Rockefeller, Jabez A. Bostwick, and John D. Archbold on the witness stand, such magnates preferred to attribute criticism of their methods to the interested motives of allegedly inefficient competitors. The possibility that the public had a legitimate interest in the methods of business and finance was ignored or brusquely shouldered aside by Jay Gould, the Rockefeller coterie, the Huntington group, the Phillip D. Armour interests, drug manufacturers, the Vanderbilts, and the like. Gould was singularly unperturbed by the publication of a scathing exposure of him and his methods in the *Atlantic Monthly* in July, 1882, by an article entitled "The Political Economy of Seventy-Three Million Dollars."[2] Other business executives, when indicted before the bar of public opinion, coolly denied indulging in criticized practices, as did the Standard Oil men regarding secret railroad rate favors from 1888 to 1906.[3]

Although William Cullen Bryant's New York *Evening Post* and Simon Sterne campaigned relentlessly against the orgy of "special legislation," whereby a horde of promoters, railroads, and utilities secured legal advantages at the expense of taxpayers, competitors, consumers, and state and local governments, this hardly retarded the flood of private bills that were brought up in each state legislative session in New York and Pennsylvania.[4]

[1] Solon J. Buck, *The Agrarian Crusade* (New Haven, 1920), Chap. IV; Robert E. Cushman, *The Independent Regulatory Commissions* (New York, 1941), 37-38.

[2] Henry D. Lloyd, "The Political Economy of Seventy-Three Million Dollars," *Atlantic Monthly* (Boston), L (July, 1882), 69-81.

[3] "Trusts," *House Reports*, No. 3112, 50 Cong., 1 Sess., *passim;* "The Standard Oil Trust," *ibid.*, *passim; Report of the Committee on General Laws on the Investigation Relative to Trusts, March 6, 1888, New York Senate Documents, 111th Session, No. 50* (Troy, 1888), *passim; Report of the Industrial Commission*, 19 vols. (Washington, 1900-1902), I, XIII, *Trusts and Industrial Combinations, passim.*

[4] New York *Evening Post*, April 17, 1869, and *passim*; John Foord, *The Life and*

Where business methods complained of were violating established law, the next step of aggrieved elements and an indignant public was to demand that the law be enforced against the recalcitrants. Prior to statutory enactments a shipper could, if he wished, carry his case to the courts and invoke the common law in a damage suit against a common carrier for discriminating against him. Scofield, Shurmer & Teagle of Cleveland sued the Lake Shore and Michigan Southern Railway Company and won an award of $5,000 (1885) because of damage inflicted upon this independent oil refining company by exclusive rebates paid to the Standard Oil. So far as the Rockefeller company was involved, the competitive advantage that it had enjoyed by virtue of this secret rate concession far outweighed the damages and the cost of the suit.[5]

Enforcement of statutory regulations might be sought by similar litigation, although in railroad cases there was the danger of incurring permanently the displeasure of the carrier affected. The offending business concern could, in any case, resort to all the delays that an unreformed legal system then tendered to the bitter-end defendant. As an example, the companies ignored the Minnesota Railroad Act of 1871, the first rate law of that state, and continued to collect their own rates which were higher, generally, than those ordained by the statute.

> One man only in the whole state invoked the law. He received a consignment of goods, and tendered the company the rate established by law and demanded the goods. The railway company refusing to deliver them, he commenced action in replevin. The action was commenced in June, 1871; in October the case was decided in the district court; in October, 1872, it was decided in the State Supreme Court; in October, 1876, just five years after the first trial, it was decided in his favor by the Supreme Court of the United States. The amount involved was forty-three cents.[6]

Antagonized by undesired regulatory legislation, business in-

Public Services of Simon Sterne (London, New York, 1903), 174-75 and *passim*; William A. Russ, Jr., "The Origin of the Ban on Special Legislation in the Constitution of 1873," *Pennsylvania History* (Philadelphia), XI (October, 1944), 260-75. Contrast with Charles Francis Adams, Jr., and Henry Adams, *Chapters of Erie, and Other Essays* (New York, 1886), 422. See also Simon Sterne, "Crude Methods of Legislation," *North American Review* (Boston, New York), CXXXVII (September, 1883), 158-71.

[5] 43 Ohio 571 (1885); Henry D. Lloyd, *Wealth Against Commonwealth* (New York, 1894), 69-70.

[6] Alpheus B. Stickney, *The Defects of the Interstate Commerce Law. An Address . . . at a Meeting of the Washington Economic Society, in Washington, D. C., February 3, 1905* (n.p., n.d.), 20.

terests might rally the bar to boycott its enforcement. In Illinois, when Mrs. Florence Kelley was appointed factory inspector by Governor John P. Altgeld, not a lawyer or prosecuting attorney would handle the violations that she quickly detected. It was necessary for her to study law, gain admittance to the bar, and try such cases herself.[7] Fearing the possibility of undesired regulatory legislation, it was possible at times for a powerful business interest to mobilize the press and public opinion in its behalf. When the Vest Committee invaded the bailiwick of the "Big Four" Meat Packers in 1889, it was subjected to unprecedented public hostility aroused in such manner, while it discovered quickly that the witnesses summond to testify were subjected to intimidation. The responsibility of the "Big Four" for this seemed indubitable to the committee.[8]

Defiance of investigating committees was a characteristic attitude of prominent businessmen during the "Gilded Age." All the "Big Four" Meat Packers' chief executives and their leading subordinates ignored the subpoenas of the Vest Committee when it was in Chicago. When the secretary of the Chicago Union-Stock-Yards Company was finally induced to testify in Washington, he declined to produce the stock book of this firm or tell who its stockholders were on the ground that his superiors and counsel had advised him not to do so.[9]

Cool effrontery in asserting a lack of memory on embarrassing details was a favorite tactic of Standard Oil magnates, when they were not claiming immunity from answering on the ground that to do so might incriminate them.[10] The insertion of a doctored or expurgated court record into the proceedings of an investigation was

[7] Florence Kelley, "I Go to Work," *Survey Graphic* (Concord, N. H.), XVIII (July 1, 1927), 271-74, 301; Jane Addams, *Twenty Years at Hull-House* (New York, 1910), 310-11; Chicago *Times*, May 4, June 6, 1894; Mrs. Florence Kelley to Mrs. Henry D. Lloyd, October 31, 1894, Henry D. Lloyd Papers (State Historical Society of Wisconsin, Madison).

[8] "Report of the Select Committee on the Transportation and Sale of Meat Products, May 1, 1890," *Senate Reports*, No. 829, 51 Cong., 1 Sess., 1, 4-5.

[9] *Ibid.*, 4-5; "Testimony Taken by the Select Committee of the United States Senate on the Transportation and Sale of Meat Products," *ibid.*, 483.

[10] *Report of the Special Committee on Railroads, Appointed under a Resolution of the Assembly to Investigate Alleged Abuses in the Management of Railroads Chartered by the State of New York* (Albany, 1879), 42; *Proceedings of the Special Committee on Railroads, Appointed under a Resolution of the Assembly to Investigate Alleged Abuses in the Management of Railroads Chartered by the State of New York*, 8 vols. (Albany, 1879), III, 2601-2710. The second work is cited hereafter as Hepburn Committee, *Proceedings*.

the achievement of Samuel C. T. Dodd, solicitor of the Standard Oil Trust and its affiliated companies, during the congressional inquiry into the trusts in 1888.[11] Impugning the motives of critics and opposing witnesses was a favorite device of this particular coterie. Archbold was notoriously persistent in charging that public complainants, competitors, or publicists were attempting business blackmail when they instituted litigation, attempted to refine and market petroleum products, or criticized the Standard Oil in public, respectively.[12] It is interesting that a recent apologist for the Rockefeller group has revived this unfounded accusation with respect to Charles B. Matthews of Buffalo.[13]

Such magnates, in general, flouted legislatures, courts, and the statute or common law whenever it suited their convenience or will to do so. The combination movement in railroading and industry, when it produced monopolistic status, was organized in defiance of the law by such promoters as the Morgan banking house, the Standard Oil men, Elbert H. Gary, Judge W. H. Moore, Charles R. Flint, Jr., and regional railroad groups. "Rockefeller was generally more than two jumps ahead of the law," as Thomas C. Cochran has remarked. Instead of admitting its guilt and correcting its methods after courts found against it, the Standard Oil and its executives uniformly insisted that the public accept its futile defense as the correct version of case after case and that they be permitted to continue to practice the illicit methods of which they had been found guilty. In fact, they continued to do so and succeeded in their defiance of the law until Theodore Roosevelt's "Big Stick" laid bare the continental proportions of their illicit operations, deprived them of the discriminatory complex of railroad rate and service upon which their monopoly was founded,[14] and initiated the suc-

11 "Standard Oil Trust," *House Reports*, No. 3112, 50 Cong., 1 Sess., 801-951.

12 Particularly in his testimony before the Industrial Commission, but earlier in the congressional investigation into the trusts in 1888.

13 Allan Nevins, "Communication," *American Historical Review* (New York), L (April, 1945), 684. For the truth of the matter, see Chester McArthur Destler, "A Commentary on the 'Communication' from Allan Nevins in the *American Historical Review*, April, 1945," mimeographed copy (Connecticut College, New London, April 15, 1945), 7-8; or *Bill of Exceptions, People of the State of New York vs. Everest et al., Court of Oyer and Terminer, Erie County, Feb. 1866* (Rochester, 1887), 282-86, 291.

14 *Report of the Commissioner of Corporations on the Transportation of Petroleum, May 2, 1906* (Washington, 1906), *passim*; Thomas C. Cochran and William Miller, *The Age of Enterprise, A Social History of Industrial America* (New York, 1942),

cessful suit for the dissolution of the Standard Oil "Trust" after it had assumed the guise of a New Jersey holding company.

In the vitally important matter of the inspection of illuminating oil the Standard Oil and its distributors resisted the enactment of inspection laws by the states in the interest of consumer safety. Once a law of this type was on the books the control of the state oil inspector was then sought. In Kentucky, Iowa, Minnesota, Nebraska, and Massachusetts it was obtained, for a while at least, by paying a salary to the inspector. This practice had the added advantage of enabling the company to affix his seal to oil that he did not see. In Massachusetts it was not discovered that this arrangement prevailed until after a series of disastrous fires. In view of this situation it is hardly surprising that independent chemists at Massachusetts Institute of Technology discovered that the illuminating oil involved flashed below the minimum legal standard, or that the state oil inspector should then have declared that it was above it.[15]

This intransigent attitude was characteristic of the railroad chief executives and their lieutenants from the days of the Erie Ring to the passage of the Hepburn Act. For the early part of this epoch all accept as valid the indictment that Charles Francis Adams, Jr., made of the railroads during the decade when he was the leading figure on the Massachusetts Board of Railroad Commissioners: "Corporations, owning and operating the highways of commerce, they claimed for themselves a species of immunity from the control of the law-making power. When laws were passed with a view to their regulation, they received them in a way which was at once arrogant and singularly injudicious. The officers entrusted with the execution of those laws they contemptuously ignored."[16]

When the Wisconsin "Potter" Law became effective in April, 1874, the president of a leading railroad in that state wrote to the governor that its board of directors, after having consulted counsel "'and after mature consideration, believed it their duty to disre-

144; Allan Nevins, *John D. Rockefeller, The Heroic Age of American Enterprise*, 2 vols. (New York, 1940), II, 555-84.

[15] "Standard Oil Trust," *House Reports*, No. 3112, 50 Cong., 1 Sess., 535; Lloyd, *Wealth Against Commonwealth*, 410-17 and notes.

[16] Charles F. Adams, Jr., *Railroads: Their Origin and Problems* (rev. ed., New York, 1878), 127. See also James F. Hudson, *The Railways and the Republic* (New York, 1886), 25-250, 345.

gard so much of said law as attempts arbitrarily to fix rates of compensation for freight and passengers.' "[17]

So persistent and widespread was this flouting of the law by the railroads that sixteen years later the president of the St. Paul Railroad could write: "This enormous business is now in the control of several hundred petty chieftains, who are practically independent sovereigns, exercising functions and prerogatives in defiance of the laws, and practically denying their amenability to the laws of the country."[18]

If this paper were restricted to the presentation of the verbal objections and opposition of leading businessmen to social control it would be brief indeed. Businessmen were seldom articulate in the expression of their views in a manner that would gratify the student of the history of ideas. At the beginning and toward the close of the "Bourbon" epoch, to be sure, both Cornelius Vanderbilt and J. Pierpont Morgan informed their attorneys that their function was not to tell them that the laws prohibited a certain type of business activity, but rather to devise means of attaining the desired end with a semblance of legality. The "Commodore" is reputed to have said, "Hain't I got the Power?" in a statement that prefaced his attorney's assignment with the assertion that no railroad could be operated in accord with the laws of New York. Sternly reprimanded by the elder Morgan, Elbert H. Gary was quick to inform him that there was "a way" of achieving what he wanted despite the laws of Illinois.[19]

Few magnates, whether the Napoleonic Jay Gould or the letter-writing Collis P. Huntington, were sufficiently articulate to voice a philosophy of defense and exposition of the merits of "rugged individualism" as practiced in the formative era of business combination. Andrew Carnegie appears to have made use of the ghost writer to help formulate conceptions that he had in mind. Inasmuch as men like Rockefeller found the Carnegie-Bridge-Spencer version of Social Darwinism a convenient justification of the methods of the architects of the trusts, this aspect of the intellectual history of American business merits some attention. So does the propagan-

[17] Alpheus B. Stickney, *The Railway Problem* (St. Paul, 1891), 101.

[18] *Ibid.*, 206. Cf. Robert E. Riegel, *The Story of the Western Railroads* (New York, 1926), 226-27.

[19] Ida M. Tarbell, *The Life of Elbert H. Gary; The Story of Steel* (New York, 1926), 81.

da of defense emitted by Samuel C. T. Dodd and other paid apologists of the Standard Oil. Equally important was the legal philosophy and system of constitutional interpretation developed by the attorneys of great business leaders in resistance to government regulation. Testimony given by business leaders under oath on this subject is another source of information of importance. Even more, we must examine what they did in organizing an effective opposition to government regulation. In the case of men like Huntington, Gould, Rockefeller, Armour, and various railroad magnates and their lieutenants, their actions are the acid test of their thought on the subject at hand.

So it is with the tenement house cigar manufacturers of New York City, the American Sugar Refining Company, the sweatshop clothing manufacturers, and the glass industry of Illinois. Especially is this true of the railroads where the demands of their attorneys in the courts were supplemented by important railway participation in politics. It is applicable to the Western Union, with emphasis; to the Standard Oil emphatically if we would discover the reason for the long immunity of that illicit combination from effective government action.

Andrew Carnegie enunciated the libertarian faith which businessmen invoked generally in opposition to government regulation or control. As an amateur "student of political economy" in a magazine article, "The Bugaboo of Trusts," published in 1889, he urged that *laissez faire* was the proper remedy for these combinations. Competition in an economy free from regulation was the certain remedy for monopoly, he declared, even in the railroad field:

> The people of America can smile at the efforts of all her railway magnates and of all her manufacturers to defeat the economic laws by Trusts or combinations, or pools, or "differentials," or anything of like character. Only let them hold firmly to the doctrine of free competition. Keep the field open. Freedom for all to engage in railroad building when and where capital desires subject to conditions open to all. Freedom for all to engage in any branch of manufacturing under like conditions.[20]

Forcibly put by the nation's greatest steel magnate, such views seemed to justify the Sherman Anti-Trust Act when it was placed upon the statute books the following year. Only so far as interven-

[20] Andrew Carnegie, "The Bugaboo of Trusts," *North American Review*, CXLVIII (February, 1889), 149. For a review of Carnegie's economic theory, see Ralph H. Gabriel, *The Course of American Democratic Thought* (New York, 1940), 150-53.

tion to prevent monopoly may be regarded as social control did Carnegie seem to sanction it.

Eleven years later, when the Standard Oil still stood intact despite economic, common, and statutory law, Carnegie added a "law of aggregation" to his economic doctrine. He stoutly maintained, nevertheless, that permanent monopolies were impossible in a free economy unless resting upon patents or control of raw materials as in the case (mistakenly asserted) of the Standard Oil. By that time, it should be observed, control of raw materials was an attribute of each successful steel combination. Legislation was unable to deal with this condition, Carnegie declared. It should be left to the operation of economic laws for correction. Investment of new capital in monopolized business fields would provide an automatic corrective for the trusts. Thus, to Carnegie at the "Turn of the Century" even the Sherman Act and state antimonopoly laws lacked efficacy, the virtue of common sense, and justification in economic laws.[21]

Much earlier Carnegie had discovered in Herbert Spencer's Social Darwinism release from the inhibitions which Calvinistic theology and fear of the supernatural had imposed upon him. The friendship that he formed with the engineer-philosopher illustrates the importance that the steel magnate placed upon the new doctrine of deterministic evolution, but only his *Autobiography* expresses in retrospect the sense of complete freedom and untrammeled optimism derived from it that inspired his entrepreneurship in the steel industry:

> Not only had I got rid of theology and the supernatural, but I had found the truth of evolution. "All is well since all grows better" became my motto, my true source of comfort. Man was not created with an instinct for his own degradation, but from the lower he had risen to the higher forms. Nor is there any conceivable end to his march to perfection. His face is turned to the light; he stands in the sun and looks upward.
>
> Humanity is an organism, inherently rejecting all that is deleterious, that is, wrong, and absorbing after trial what is beneficial, that is, right.[22]

It is hardly surprising that James H. Bridge, Carnegie's former literary assistant, should invoke the same creed in justifying the acts of the men who had built the Carnegie Steel Company. "It

[21] Andrew Carnegie, "Popular Illusions About Trusts," *Century Magazine* (New York), LX (May, 1900), 143-49.

[22] *Autobiography of Andrew Carnegie* (Boston, 1920), 339.

is a natural evolution," he wrote, "it must be remembered that in the fight for industrial life, as in that earlier struggle for physical existence, the victory is not to the gentle and the tender-hearted, but to the others. No great business has yet been built on the beatitudes; and it is not all cynicism that condenses a negative decalogue into a positive exhortation to be successful — 'somehow!' "[23]

Several years later, in his well-known anecdote on the perfection of the American Beauty rose, Rockefeller asserted, "The growth of a large business is merely a survival of the fittest."[24] It is pertinent to inquire here, however, into the extent to which the defenders of the Standard Oil invoked Social Darwinism or the doctrines of classical economics during the years when it was subject to continuing attack. This involves the moot point as to whether that giant organization actually sponsored a counterpropaganda of defense during the years prior to and subsequent to the adoption of the Sherman Act, since Allan Nevins asserts in his biography of the senior Rockefeller that its regular policy was that of silence under criticism.[25]

In 1888 the Standard Oil men were obliged to appear before investigating committees of the New York Senate and the national House of Representatives which were seeking information on the trusts. Following hard upon the revelations published by the Cullom Committee, it was clear that mounting indignation, unless forestalled, would procure antitrust legislation of a type not desired by the Rockefeller group.

After its members had testified before the New York Senate Committee, where they had been obliged to make public the Standard Oil Trust Agreement for the first time, Dodd made a formal argument in defense of business combinations. Some months later he published this, together with a "History of the Standard Oil," in a pamphlet entitled *Combinations: Their Uses and Abuses, with a History of the Standard Oil Trust*. The contents of this treatise must be regarded as the official defense of the Standard and of the emerging trusts that it fathered. It was supplemented the next year by speeches in which Dodd attacked the pending Sherman Anti-Trust Bill. These were circulated as pamphlets. Several years later

[23] James H. Bridge, *The Carnegie Millions and the Men Who Made Them; Being the Inside History of the Carnegie Steel Company* (London, 1903), vii, viii.

[24] William J. Ghent, *Our Benevolent Feudalism* (New York, 1902), 29.

[25] Nevins, *John D. Rockefeller*, II, 59, 339-40.

he published in the *Forum* a laudatory "Ten Years of the Standard Oil Trust," an article that redepicted it as a great public benefactor.[26]

What was the nature of Dodd's defense of combinations and of the Standard Oil? Part of it was legalistic, consisting of an attempt to narrow the definition of monopoly to the specific conferring by the government of some exclusive privilege upon a business firm. Combinations were not necessarily monopolistic, he urged. Each combination was necessary to the conduct of a modern business, where the large national and world market made huge aggregations of capital organized into corporations necessary. The unfettered right to combine would be the greatest blessing government could confer upon business, he stated. Then he quoted William Graham Sumner's "What the Social Classes Owe to Each Other" to clinch his argument that aggregated capital was " 'for the benefit of all.' " Those business methods were "correct and legal" that subserved "the greatest good of the greatest number." "To this end unrestricted competition is absolutely necessary and so is unrestricted combination."

Proper competition Dodd defined in a manner that included price-fixing agreements and excluded price cutting with a view to the extermination of competitors. After this statement, tongue in cheek surely in view of the traditional Standard Oil method of disposing of competition by means of local price cutting, Dodd asserted that combination had meant better prices for consumers. Any combination that diminished production costs, increased consumption, and "distanced competitors by selling at less prices" should be termed legal. Thus the Solicitor of the Standard Oil Trust voiced the early version of that distinction that has since come to be known as the "rule of reason."

As Dodd would have had the New York legislature and the Congress formulate it, "The use and legitimate effect of industrial combinations is *to furnish the public a larger supply of commodities at a smaller price*. The illegal purpose and effect of such combinations

26 See the following works by Samuel C. T. Dodd: *Combinations: Their Uses and Abuses, with a History of the Standard Oil Trust* (New York, 1888); *Shall All Business Co-operation be Rendered Criminal? . . . A Statement of Pending Legislation and Its Consequences* (n.p., n.d.); *Trusts; An Address before the Merchants Association of Boston, January 8, 1889* (n.p., n.d.); "Ten Years of the Standard Oil Trust," *Forum* (New York), XIII (May, 1892), 300-10.

is *to furnish the public a smaller supply with intent to unduly increase the price*." [27] Inasmuch as any combination would be obliged to increase production eventually to satisfy the rapidly growing national market, all that it would have to do to gain legal sanction, should the Dodd doctrine prevail, would be to establish in court this fact and show that it marketed its product at a price less than had prevailed at some date in the recent past.

Dodd promptly employed his peculiar definition of a proper combination to present the Standard Oil as a trust that was furthering the Benthamite "utility" that he had invoked as the purpose of all proper combinations. It is interesting to note, however, that he opposed the Interstate Commerce Commission's ruling that the railroads should charge uniform rates of all petroleum shippers on the ground that this violated the principle of "natural selection." Instead, freight rate uniformity would ensure that "The unfittest as well as the fittest survive." [28] In Dodd's eyes, apparently, an ability to wangle exclusive secret freight rate favors from the railroad by fair means or foul was an essential attribute of the "fittest" in the American business jungle of 1888.

Utilitarianism, economic Darwinism of the Sumner type, a definition of competition that opened the door to monopoly or at best monopolistic competition, plus unrestrained railroad freight rate discriminations were the strange ideological mélange that Dodd offered in defense of combinations in opposition to pending state and national antitrust legislation.

This series of publications might be regarded as a specific episode were it not for the fact that during these years the oil monopoly or its leading executives took under their wing a certain George Gunton. Formerly a radical labor leader and champion of the eight-hour day, this individual re-emerged into public view as the head of a School of Social Economics on Manhattan and editor of a supposedly learned journal, the *Social Economist*, that he renamed eventually *Gunton's Magazine*, which was secretly subsidized by the Standard Oil group. In the *Social Economist* its editor elaborated upon the Dodd thesis of the social beneficence of large-scale business combinations and applied to them repeatedly the test of cheapness of product that the Standard's Solicitor had invented.

[27] Dodd, *Combinations: Their Uses and Abuses*, 24.
[28] *Ibid.*, 35.

Gunton's contribution to the pro-Standard propaganda assumed the form of attacking all critics of it and kindred trusts as enemies of property and fomenters of dangerous unrest in a manner that displayed a Hamiltonian contempt for the masses.

Gunton attacked Henry D. Lloyd, for example, as a social revolutionary because of the exposures of Standard Oil business methods by *Wealth Against Commonwealth* in a review that was also distinguished by misrepresentation of the book's contents and by impugning the motives of the petroleum monopoly's competitors.[29] Another Standard Oil editor, Patrick C. Boyle of the Toledo *Commercial*, dealt such libelous blows at the officials of the city of Toledo, who had dared to open a natural gas pipe-line and distribution system in opposition to a Standard Oil subsidiary, that he was obliged to plead guilty in a criminal libel suit in Ohio.[30]

Dodd returned to the charge in a symposium on the trusts in the *Independent* on the day of William McKinley's inauguration in 1897. In a short piece entitled "The War Against Wealth," the Solicitor of the Standard rang the changes on Gunton's claim that the critics of the trusts were leaders in a rising popular "craze." All such individuals were leaders in "the warfare against capital which has been long in progress" in which the masses were aroused to frenzy by appeals to jealousy of "success and wealth." Then Dodd discharged a new weapon, which Standard men had employed on the witness stand ever since the highly embarrassing Buffalo criminal conspiracy case in 1885. This was the accusation that critical writers who attacked the trusts were engaging in a species of blackmail and even went so far allegedly as to notify directors of combinations that they would attack them publicly unless bought off.[31]

Since 1888 Dodd had spoken repeatedly in public on the same general theme. In 1889 he addressed the Boston Merchants' Asso-

29 George Gunton, "The Integrity of Economic Literature," *Social Economist* (New York), IX (July, 1895), 11-25; George Gunton, *Trusts and the Public* (New York, 1899), 44-60, 213-25, and *passim.*

30 Toledo *Commercial*, March 25, April 17, 1890; Clark Waggonner to Ralph H. Waggonner, April 16, 1890, Clark Waggonner Papers, Letterbooks, VIII (Toledo Public Library); Lloyd, *Wealth Against Commonwealth,* 325; statement of John H. Doyle, John D. Rockefeller Conversations with William O. Inglis, 1166L-Q, John D. Rockefeller Papers (by the courtesy of John D. Rockefeller, Jr., and Allan Nevins in whose possession this collection was when examined by the writer).

31 Samuel C. T. Dodd, "The War against Wealth," *Independent* (New York), XLIX (March 4, 1897), 267-68.

ciation in defense of combinations and the trusts, reviewing Great Britain's experience with anticorporate and anticombination legislation in an attempt to demonstrate the futility of American antitrust legislation. In 1898 he delivered a formal address at Syracuse University on "Aggregate Capital" in which he expanded upon his thesis of the social beneficence of combinations. In the interim, he asserted emphatically in the New York *Tribune* in 1890 that the state antitrust laws of the United States made all business "cooperation" illegal, and argued that English law and experience justified combinations.

Dodd republished all these, save his *Independent* piece, in a volume entitled *Trusts*. This appeared in time to combat the antitrust campaign of the Bryanite orators during the second McKinley-Bryan presidential contest. Several years later, after the combination movement had risen to unprecedented peaks of achievement, Dodd aided Charles R. Flint, Jr., a noted promoter of combinations, in the preparation of a cooperative volume entitled *The Trust: Its Book*. In this treatise which may have been intended for the eye of a president by accident, Flint elaborated upon the Darwinian justification of large combinations. Their existence, he declared, was proof of both "evolution" and the "survival of the fittest."[32]

In the meantime, the Solicitor of the Standard Oil had attempted without avail to establish the legality of the "Trust" in the Ohio courts. The Supreme Court of that state in a noted decision (State of Ohio *v.* Standard Oil Company) declared that the Standard Oil Trust was an agreement whose purpose was to create a monopoly in the petroleum industry with control of production and prices in such a manner as to destroy competition. Concentration of such an industry in a few hands, the court declared, was contrary to public policy which should be to multiply the numbers of independent enterprisers so as to cheapen prices to consumers by means of competition. In the light of this and a preceding New York court ruling, Dodd was obliged to recognize that judicial opposition had "ended this peculiar form of organization."

He appealed, however, to the entire legal profession in behalf of business combinations in a series of articles in the law journals.

[32] Charles R. Flint, Jr., *et al.*, *The Trust: Its Book* (New York, 1902), Chaps. I-III, V, and *passim*; Samuel C. T. Dodd, *Trusts* ([New York], 1900), *passim*.

The most important of these, "The Present Legal Status of Trusts," appeared in the *Harvard Law Review* in October, 1893. Admitting there that the trust was now illegal, he urged that the "Trust Problem" involved the legal status of all large business enterprises. He took the extreme position that all incorporation or large-scale business organization conferred some control over production and prices, some interference with the business of others, or entailed "engrossing" as forbidden by the common law. As a result, he argued, all officers of corporations or large enterprises were liable to criminal antitrust prosecutions in the United States. This was an attempted *reductio ad absurdum* developed in an attempt to discredit the score or more of state and territorial antitrust acts. He then taxed the Sherman Anti-Trust Act with lacking precise definition of what was meant by "restraint of trade," and "to monopolize," and with levying a blanket prohibition against doing a large business.

In Great Britain, *per contra*, parliament had recently repealed hundreds of statutes that prohibited the restraint of trade and had authorized the organization of joint-stock companies. The implications of this, Dodd declared, had been recognized recently by the House of Lords in Mogul Steamship Company *v.* McGregor. Although the Lords had been careful to state that legal combinations must be "for mere purposes of trade" in a manner for which capital could legitimately be employed apart from mere combination, and hence be another means of carrying on competition, Dodd deduced from this decision that it had legalized combinations in general irrespective of their effect upon the market and urged that United States courts follow this precedent.

After citing many state court and some federal court decisions adverse to combinations, trusts, and restraints of trade, Dodd was able to quote certain cases involving the Whisky Trust in which the federal courts had accepted the narrow thesis of his *Combinations* that monopoly existed only where exclusive privileges were possessed by a business.[33] He cited the opinions of other federal judges, also, who ruled that the Sherman Act did not prohibit mere "bigness," nor limit business acquisition of property in interstate commerce by legitimate methods even when this brought with it market

[33] S. D. Ohio, 52 Fed. 104 (1892), quoting Judge Jackson, *In re Greene*; Beale *v.* Chase, 31 Mich. 521 (1875).

control in a field of business, nor even prohibit an agreement among lumber manufacturers and dealers to raise prices where it did not absorb the entire lumber trade.

Monopoly in the more popular sense, if incidental to business growth or achieved by combination, would have been legalized generally if the courts had accepted the validity of the Dodd position. In this article, also, Dodd claimed that the history of large business enterprise demonstrated that it almost invariably cheapened the product. This made large business combinations both reasonable in law and a public benefit.

Hence "Big Business," or "monopoly" as the populace regarded it, was justifiable. It should be legalized as socially beneficent and as necessary to the conduct of business in a day of large markets even though it involve a substantial control of production and the market. In this manner, in technical form, the Solicitor of the Standard Oil presented to the American bar an early if not the initial plea for the adoption of the "rule of reason" in construing antitrust legislation.[34]

A month earlier he had published an article, "Peculiar Legislation," in the *Counsellor*. This made a biting attack on the Texas antitrust act of 1889 which had made any conspiracy in restraint of trade punishable with fine and imprisonment for ten years and listed a series of definitions of prohibited practices including price fixing by agreement. The Standard's chief counsel sought to discredit this measure by again resorting to the device of *reductio ad absurdum*. Strictly construed, he maintained, the Texas statute would prohibit a joint effort to invent a cotton picker. Didn't the Texas legislators foresee that their law would prohibit "all association and thereby paralyze business? Apparently not." Similar statutes of other states would prohibit doing business under ordinary partnership organization. In six of them it was a crime to reduce prices, Dodd declared. The Sherman Act, which he also designated as a notable piece of "Peculiar Legislation," even made criminal some contracts in restraint of trade that were not criminal or even void in common law and which "have been held to be reasonable

[34] Samuel C. T. Dodd, "The Present Legal Status of Trusts," *Harvard Law Review* (Cambridge), VII (October 25, 1893), 157-69. Among the common law decisions that Dodd cited, *ibid.*, 163, are: Diamond Match Company *v.* Roeber, 106 N. Y. 473 (1887), "anticompetitive contracts to avert personal ruin may be perfectly reasonable"; Horner *v.* Graves, 7 Bing. 735 (1831), "a party may legally purchase the trade and business of another for the very purpose of preventing competition."

and conducive to trade." So far as interstate trade was concerned, just where did "the attempt to monopolize begin?" "Is every attempt to enlarge a business an attempt to monopolize a part of the trade" and hence illegal in federal law? A statute creating a new crime should be so plain that the wayfaring man could comprehend it. "Blackstone claimed law to be the perfection of reason. There has been some peculiar legislation since Blackstone's day which casts some doubt upon the truth of his assertion." [35]

In this fivefold manner, by defensive litigation, in argument before a legislative committee, by appeals to the universities and to the general public, and in presumably learned but *ex parte* articles in the law journals, Dodd sought to persuade the American democracy and its governors that large-scale business combinations and monopoly should be regarded as reasonable and beneficial. If he carried the debate in favor of his Standard Oil superiors and their friends in similar organizations, legalization would follow as a matter of course, either by legislation or juridical action.

What relation this prolonged propaganda campaign bore to the immunity that the Standard Oil enjoyed from federal prosecution during the years when it was the best hated business organization in the country can now be envisaged. Was it related also to the prolonged inactivity of the federal Department of Justice with regard to the general enforcement of the Sherman Act?

The public was not entirely lulled into acquiescence by it. The gallery in the National Anti-Trust Conference of September, 1899, at Chicago booed George Gunton vigorously when he stepped upon the stage as a pretended, independent authority on the trusts to demand approval of them as "*bona fide* producers" and to claim for them the "liberty" which was the normal attribute of a competitive business system.[36] Perhaps some of the audience were aware of the ludricuously funny but entirely abortive secret attempt that Rockefeller, Dodd, and the Reverend Frederick T. Gates had made in 1896 to induce the Protestant Social Gospel clergy to become the public defenders of their allegedly enlightened and pure business methods.[37] It was not until nearly a decade later that the

35 Samuel C. T. Dodd, "Peculiar Legislation," *Counsellor* (New York), II (April, 1893), 195-97.

36 *Chicago Conference on Trusts . . . Held September 13th, 14th, 15th, 16th, 1899* (Chicago, 1900), 276-85; Gunton, *Trusts and the Public*, 226-38.

37 Rev. B. Fay Mills to Rev. Edward Everett Hale, April 21, 1896, Lloyd to Rev.

full nature of Gunton's relation to the Standard Oil was revealed. In the interim he published his collected essays, *Trusts and the Public*, and accepted a professorship of economics in the leading educational institution on Manhattan Island.[38]

The Dodd-Gunton-Flint protrust propaganda was clearly related to the "Gospel of Wealth" that received so wide a hearing during the "Gilded Age." A composite of the Social Darwinism of the day and the modified Calvinism of the second Great Awakening, which emphasized personal piety, philanthropy, and the stewardship of wealth, this "Gospel" stressed the importance of maintaining an individualist society distinguished by a maximum of "Liberty" and a minimum of government action in order to foster evolution by means of "natural selection" and the "survival of the fittest." Observance of the behavior maxims of this "Gospel," church and prayer-meeting attendance, the appearance of fidelity to the family, and generous philanthropies to the churches and educational institutions were so marked and so effective in molding the public attitude toward the business activities of the practitioners that the Reverend Washington Gladden felt obliged to preach on the subject of "Tainted Wealth." Even before Gladden preached on that theme, J. P. Morgan's noted attorney, Wayne MacVeagh, had privately urged a writer friend to expose the danger to the public mind and morals that was inherent in "restitution" disguised as large-scale philanthropy.[39]

What the railroad and oil magnates meant when they invoked the libertarian doctrines of the Manchester and Darwinian creeds was clear to the independent petroleum firms of Pennsylvania. After the Standard Oil gained control of the pipe-line network of the oil region, it resisted tenaciously and successfully the enactment of a proposed free pipe-line bill by the Pennsylvania legislature. Business freedom did not include toleration of long-distance pipe lines for crude and refined oil so far as the carriers were concerned, where they could prevent their construction. This the sponsors of the Tidewater Petroleum Company and the United States Pipe-

Washington Gladden and Edwin D. Mead, April 28, 1896, enclosures and ensuing correspondence, Josiah Strong to Lloyd, May 11, 1896, Lyman Abbott to Lloyd, May 19, 1896, Mills to Lloyd, May 7, 1896, Lloyd Papers.

38 Gunton, *Trusts and the Public*; Chicago *Sunday American*, January 14, 1906.

39 Wayne MacVeagh to Lloyd, April 28, 1902, Lloyd Papers; Gabriel, *Course of American Democratic Thought*, 143-60; Nevins, *John D. Rockefeller*, I, 538.

Line learned to their cost in the late seventies and mid-nineties, respectively.[40]

Did the railroad men or their spokesmen invoke the same doctrines that the Carnegie and Rockefeller groups found so useful? What their attitude was toward social control has already been indicated in part above. From the days of the first Granger law until the enactment of the Hepburn Bill, with several exceptions, this was generally that of a bitter-end opposition to government regulation in all its forms and a stony repudiation of public protests and customer criticism. Yet, what did the railroad men have to say when put on the witness stand in defense of this position? During the New York Hepburn Committee's investigation of 1879, William H. Vanderbilt not only exhibited a remarkably bad memory on the details of his enterprise but he went so far as to advise his questioners that the legislature was helpless to protect the New York Central and Hudson River Railroad from the incursions of the Standard Oil magnates: "they are very shrewd men; I don't believe that by any legislative enactment or anything else through any of the States or all of the States, you can keep such men down; you can't do it; they will be up on top all the time; you see if they are not . . . on top of everybody that comes in contact with them; too smart for me."[41]

As for a state railroad commission, Vanderbilt insisted that even the weak Massachusetts "advisory" type had been a failure. His general manager, James H. Rutter, declined repeatedly to divulge to the Hepburn Committee the New York Central's rate for shipment "of Standard oil now," and did so finally only in confidence. Samuel Goodman, assistant general freight agent of the same railroad in charge of its general freight business, volunteered his opinion to the committee that no railway could be carried on except by means of "the system of special rates" that was being so vigorously attacked before it by the merchants of New York and upstate.[42]

During these same hearings the committee questioned Albert Fink, organizer and executive of the Eastern Trunk Line Pool, at

[40] *A History of the Organization, Purposes and Transactions of the General Council of the Petroleum Producers' Unions and of the Suits and Prosecutions Instituted by it From 1878 to 1880* (Titusville, Pa., 1880), 9 and *passim*; Ida M. Tarbell, *History of the Standard Oil Company*, 2 vols. (New York, 1905), I, Chap. VI; II, Chaps. IX, XV.

[41] Hepburn Committee, *Proceedings*, II, 1669.

[42] *Ibid.*, I, 119, 197-98; III, 2549-51.

some length. Perhaps the most interesting part of his testimony that is relevant to the subject of this discussion was his stout assertion that a railway corporation stood in exactly the same relation to the public that a private business did. This denial of common carrier status, with all that it implied in resistance to effective regulation, made clear the attitude of the New York Central and Erie railroads toward social control.[43]

The argument made by Chauncey M. DePew in behalf of the New York Central at the conclusion of the Hepburn Committee's hearings is interesting for the reasons that he proffered in opposition to state regulation of the railroads of New York. DePew accused the New York Chamber of Commerce, which had sponsored the inquiry, of being "represented in a public capacity in a communistic spirit, seeking to destroy vested rights, seeking to pull down and to impair the value of other people's property in order to enhance the value of their own." To this charge of "communism" raised against wealthy New York merchants and the appeal to "vested rights" DePew added his prophecy that the establishment of a railroad commission "in the State of New York is and will be a source of tyranny and corruption." "To attack the New York Central Railroad Company, and attempt to put it by legislation upon a level with other companies that are run differently is to tax enterprise, business skill, business management, and business integrity for the benefit of corruption, and business idiocy." Oddly enough, DePew neglected to mention the six thousand secret special rate contracts in the interest of favored shippers then in force on the lines of his client. He concluded with this sweeping statement of the railroad's position on the issues at stake:

> The railroad companies admit very broad powers in the State; they deny its right to so legislate as to impair or destroy the value of the enterprise into which it has invited capital to invest. . . . we claim that the testimony proves that legislative interference invariably results in great loss and evil to the State and injustice or ruin to the roads. Competition, the laws of trade, the interests of owners, the pride of officers, the ever present force of public opinion, capable of practically acting upon the companies at all times through the Legislature, makes that commonwealth the most prosperous where the railroads are free from restrictive legislation or State interference in their management.[44]

[43] *Ibid.*, I, 557.

[44] *Ibid.*, IV, 3718-19, 3780, 3782; Hudson, *Railways and the Republic*, 362-63.

The New York Central's subsequent defeat of the Hepburn anti-discrimination railroad bill, and its opposition to the passage of the railroad commission bill when presented to the state legislature by the Hepburn Committee came as a matter of course.[45]

Several years later the New York Board of Trade's Committee on Fares and Freights propounded some questions to Leland Stanford, president of the Central Pacific Railroad. In reply that magnate cited the Declaration of Independence and remarked bluntly, "The essence of ownership is control." Railroad men should be left free to manage their properties as they saw fit.[46]

This was undoubtedly the objective of Collis P. Huntington, Stanford's associate, when he systematically corrupted both houses of Congress in the late seventies in order to block Tom Scott's Texas and Pacific scheme and prevent the United States government from collecting interest on the bonds it had loaned the Central Pacific as a second mortgage in aid of its construction. Huntington's letters to his lieutenant, David Colton, are still the best introduction of the scholar to the methods whereby the Central and Southern Pacific Railroad men bent national, state, and territorial governments to their will while they established their regional transportation monopoly and avoided effective regulation on all levels.[47]

East of the Rockies such magnates as William H. Vanderbilt and Jay Gould were alarmed by the support accorded the Reagan Bill in Congress. As they organized a series of regional railroad pools of which Albert Fink was the leading inventor and director, in order to prevent a recurrence of the disastrous rate wars of the late seventies, they drew Charles Francis Adams, Jr., into their service. Hardly had he been persuaded to be chairman of the Board of Arbitration of the Eastern Trunk Line Pool than he consented to speak in their behalf to the Commerce Committee of the national House of Representatives in opposition to the Reagan Bill. As a substitute for it Adams proposed that Congress legalize a national "federation" of railroads. When examined closely this was none other than a national railroad rate and traffic pool, which Fink had

[45] Foord, *Life and Public Services of Simon Sterne*, 19-23; Alexander C. Flick (ed.), *History of the State of New York*, 10 vols. (New York, 1933-1937), VIII, *Wealth and Commonwealth*, 236.

[46] Chicago *Daily Tribune*, January 24, 1881.

[47] *Ibid.*, December 27, 28, 1883; Stuart Daggett, *Chapters on the History of the Southern Pacific* (New York, 1922), *passim*.

recently proposed. It was to be administered by the railroads in their own and presumably the public interest, subject to arbitration of interrailroad disputes by a National Board of Railway Commissioners which should serve also as a statistical bureau.[48]

This scion of the Adams family invoked the Darwinian theory in a peculiar manner to justify his and Fink's proposed "federation." Competition in railroading as in business, Adams urged, led inexorably to combination with the resulting elimination of the weak. "The law of the survivorship of the fittest" would continue to operate in this fashion until "at last the one strongest — the one fittest to survive — will emerge itself from among the rest." "This, so far as our railroad system is concerned, seems to me to be that survival of the fittest which must result from indefinite, unregulated railroad competition." To avoid the final consequences of this law of competition and combination among the carriers they should be permitted to join voluntarily in such a federation under government auspices but with a minimum of restraint. For years to come Adams asserted that this was the proper solution for the lawless and antisocial management of the carriers which he had been among the first to denounce years earlier, first as a free-lance writer and then as a public official.[49]

When the public demand for national railroad regulation developed a dangerous strength, the carriers employed the political power that they had hitherto employed to render the state regulatory commissions ineffective and to place prorailroad men in the United States Senate. Early in January, 1884, the Chicago *Daily Tribune* editorialized:

> The Union Pacific Railroad has several Senators, the Northern Pacific has one, the Pennsylvania Railroad has two, Central Pacific has two, the Georgia Railroads have one, . . . the Chesapeake and Ohio has one. . . . Behind every one of half the portly and well-dressed members of the Senate can be seen the outlines of some corporation interested in getting or preventing legislation, or some syndicate that has invaluable contracts or patents to defend or push.[50]

[48] Chicago *Daily Tribune*, January 20, 1880; Charles F. Adams, Jr., *The Federation of the Railroad System. Argument . . . before the Committee of Commerce of the United States House of Representatives on the bills to regulate interstate railroad traffic* (Boston, 1880), 7-9 and *passim; Charles Francis Adams, 1835-1915; An Autobiography* (Boston, 1916), 191.

[49] Adams, *Federation of the Railroad System*, 7-9; Adams, *Railroads: Their Origin and Problems*, 200.

[50] Chicago *Daily Tribune*, January 10, 1884.

The following January and during the ensuing months Grover Cleveland's prospective elevation to the White House seemed to presage victory for the railroad regulation forces whose triumph the same paper predicted. Then, railroad magnates such as Jay Gould proceeded to supplant prorailroad-regulation Republican senators such as Nathaniel P. Hill of Colorado and, later, C. H. Van Wyck of Nebraska with more pliable men. This coup, which involved at least six senators, bore a probable relation to the vagueness of the powers of the Interstate Commerce Commission when it was finally established.[51]

The Adams-Fink program of legalized railroad pooling was the answer of the Vanderbilt group and its allies to the rising public demand for national railroad regulation when it came to a head before the Cullom Committee. A weak "advisory" commission of the Massachusetts type would be acceptable, if the public insisted, but Fink made it clear to the Cullom Committee that the only persons competent to handle the intricate problems of railroad management were the railroad managers. Now and then a railroad executive would declare, as did W. G. Raoul, president of the Central Railroad and Banking Company of Georgia, that either the government should accord "freedom of action" to the railroad owners "in conducting their business" or adopt a course of "State ownership." Rate regulation by a commission would be the equivalent of the latter in Raoul's opinion, as it was in that of James J. Hill.

[51] *Ibid.*, January 9, 14, 19, 22, 27-29, 31, February 2, 4, 5, 14, 1885, and *passim*: editorials, "State Affairs," and a special article on Jay Gould's distribution of stock in the Union Pacific Railroad among members of Congress and officers of the administration in an effort to defeat the pending Interstate Commerce Bill and a bill for settlement of government claims against the Union Pacific. See also Marie U. Harmer and James L. Sellers, "Charles H. Van Wyck — Soldier and Statesman," *Nebraska History Magazine* (Lincoln), XII (April — June, July — September, October — December, 1929), 83-128, 190-246, 322-73; Lloyd to Van Wyck, January 22, 1885, Jabez B. Watkins Papers (University of Kansas Library, Lawrence), by courtesy of Paul W. Gates. Some of the senators whose election was secured by the railroads and their allies in the Western Union and the Standard Oil were William M. Evarts of New York, John A. Logan of Illinois, Henry M. Teller of Colorado, Leland Stanford of California, John Coit Spooner of Wisconsin, all Republicans, and Henry B. Payne of Ohio, a Democrat. In the matter of a demand for a senatorial investigation into Payne's election, made by the Ohio legislature, it was Evarts (Gould's lawyer), Teller, who had been allegedly elected by funds supplied by the Western Union and Union Pacific, and Logan, whose election was secured after a three-months' contest under suspicious circumstances, who broke with their party, voted with the Democratic minority, and therefore prevented the formal inquiry that was urgently demanded by George F. Hoar, chairman of the Senate Committee on Elections. See also Albert H. Walker, *The Payne Bribery Case and the United States Senate* (Hartford, 1886).

An occasional businessman among the long list of merchants, chambers of commerce, produce markets, and industrialists who were demanding effective national railroad regulation would declare, as did E. C. Simmons, president of the Simmons Hardware Company of St. Louis, that the great size of the country made national regulation of the carriers not feasible or hold with several New York merchants that national rate fixing should be left to competition. Neither the Fink group, nor Raoul, nor Simmons were much concerned with the elimination of the discriminations in rates and services that had stimulated the powerful public demand for regulation. The banking house of J. P. Morgan supported their opposition to the Cullom Bill. That the Armour Meat Packing Company would urge the impracticability of prohibiting rebates by law and deny that they were wrong in principle to the Cullom Committee merely emphasizes the influence that decisive enjoyment could have on the views of a powerful business firm.[52]

The policy of the carriers *vis à vis* the inadequately empowered Interstate Commerce Commission after 1888 is well known. In the struggle that ensued, whose final phase was waged always in the federal courts after the Commission's decision went against the railroad or railroads concerned, it devolved upon the railroad attorneys to state the case for the carriers who were at the same time resisting local and state taxation. Led by such figures in the American Bar Association as Roscoe M. Conkling, John M. Carey, John Randolph Tucker, James Coolidge Carter, inspired by Thomas M. Cooley's publications although now in opposition to him as chairman of the Commission, they sought and won for all corporations the status of persons in the federal Constitution. They then won judicial protection for railroad corporations as persons from unrestrained legislative and regulatory commission rate fixing on the grounds that this violated the substantive, vested interest conception of "due process" that they had borrowed from Cooley. It was but a step from there to persuading the Supreme Court that final determination of the reasonableness of rates was the function of the courts. State railroad regulation was rendered at least partially

[52] "Report of the Senate Select Committee on Interstate Commerce," *Senate Reports*, No. 46, 49 Cong., 1 Sess., Pt. I, Appendix, 57-147; Pt. II, 89-124, 148-58, 206-344, 598-673; *Cong. Record*, 40 Cong., 1 Sess., 1011; Joseph G. Pyle, *The Life of James J. Hill*, 2 vols. (New York, 1917), II, 344; Frederick L. Allen, *The Great Pierpont Morgan* (New York, 1949), 59.

ineffective by the Minnesota Rate Case and Smyth *v.* Ames. In fifteen of sixteen cases involving the authority of the Interstate Commerce Commission the railroads won their cause before a Supreme Court whose membership had been replaced in large part by corporation attorneys since the Granger Cases.

In the same years the leadership of the American Bar Association, including certain highly placed federal judges, managed to divert the Sherman Anti-Trust Act from the great railroad and industrial combinations to employment as a weapon against the relatively weak labor movement of the day. Thus even a negative federal government intervention in business as a means of preserving the free enterprise system was rendered abortive until the days when a "Rough Rider" strode into the White House.[53]

Resort to the courts by businessmen as a means of defeating government regulation was successful also on the state level during the "Gilded Age." Again, the chief instruments and spokesmen of the firms concerned were the lawyers of the laissez-faire or, if you will, of the natural rights-historical school of jurisprudence. It was the "Prince of the American Bar," William M. Evarts, famous as Gould's lawyer, who persuaded the New York Court of Appeals to declare unconstitutional the Rooseveltian measure that prohibited cigar manufacturing in tenement houses on the ground that this law violated "due process," "the principle of competition," and especially "liberty of contract." It was the doctrine and precedent of this decision that encouraged the glass manufacturers and sweatshop garment makers of Illinois to organize the Illinois Manufacturers' Association to combat the Factory Act of 1893, take it to court, and carry the issue of its constitutionality up to the state Supreme Court in the case of Ritchie *v.* The People of Illinois. The judgment and theoretical grounds in this case were identical with those of *In re* Jacobs; and the exploited women and children of the garment and glass industries of Illinois went unprotected for

[53] Henry F. Pringle, *The Life and Times of William Howard Taft*, 2 vols. (New York, 1939), I, 102-105, 130-32; Benjamin R. Twiss, *Lawyers and the Constitution. How Laissez Faire Came to the Supreme Court* (Princeton, 1924), 189-90 and *passim*; Allen Johnson and William A. Robinson (eds.), *Readings in Recent American Constitutional History, 1876-1926* (New York, 1927), 78-82, 98-101; Donald B. Chidsey, *The Gentleman from New York: A Life of Roscoe Conkling* (New Haven, 1935), 368-70; Andrew C. McLaughlin, "The Court, the Corporation and Conkling," *American Historical Review*, XLVI (October, 1940), 45-62.

another dozen years until Jane Addams could muster her forces for another march on Springfield.[54]

Business opposition to government regulation was manifest in other ways. The railroads again serve as an illustration. Having determined to flout the Interstate Commerce Act and secure its nullification by the courts, the carriers took care to see that the Senate Interstate Commerce Committee in the future should contain a safe majority of prorailroad senators. This was done so skillfully that after the Maximum Rate Case Senator Cullom discovered to his dismay that the antirailroad regulation majority of his committee would not even permit him to report adversely to the Senate a bill that he had drafted to confer upon the Interstate Commerce Commission the rate-making power that he believed had been granted to it by the act that had brought it into being. Not until Theodore Roosevelt employed political dynamite was it possible to get an effective railroad regulation bill upon the floor of "The American House of Lords," as the Chicago *Tribune* had once dubbed the United States Senate.[55]

In the light of this and of similar success with state regulatory commissions, courts, and legislatures, we can now understand how the President of the St. Paul Railway could refer to his fellow railroad managers as "practically independent sovereigns." How complete and successful was their defiance of the law of the land was illustrated to contemporaries by the ever tightening anthracite coal combination, sponsored in its later phase by J. P. Morgan and Company.[56]

Like Alexander J. Cassatt of the Pennsylvania, A. B. Stickney believed that this was all wrong. Vigorously he championed effective national regulation of the railroads by a railroad department with power to make rates as a means of saving the carriers from the fatal financial consequences of their own mismanagement, the dictation of rates by now powerful elevator and industrial combina-

[54] Twiss, *Lawyers and the Constitution*, 99-108; Alfred H. Kelly, "A History of the Illinois Manufactures' Association" (Ph.D. dissertation, University of Chicago, 1938), 10-14; Illinois Bureau of Labor Statistics, *Eighth Biennial Report*, 1894 (Springfield, 1895), 464-67.

[55] Shelby M. Cullom, *Fifty Years of Public Service* (Chicago, 1911), 328-30; Chicago *Daily Tribune*, May 23, 1884.

[56] Eliot Jones, *The Anthracite Coal Combination in the United States* (Cambridge, 1914); Allen, *Great Pierpont Morgan*, 56-57; New York *World*, January 30, February 3, 1896; Boston *Herald*, January 6, 1901.

tions, and the effects of managerial lack of faith with all and sundry. Stickney's view of the illicit, amoral, treacherous system of railroad management then in vogue strongly supports that which Adams expressed before he donned the yoke of Vanderbilt and Gould.[57]

What, it may be asked, was the attitude of businessmen toward control in their own and the public interest by a voluntary organization composed of themselves? Such was the Chicago Board of Trade, chartered by Illinois in 1849 with the object of promoting "uniformity in the customs . . . of merchants; to inculcate principles of justice and honesty in trade; to facilitate the speedy adjustment of business disputes." For some years the Illinois courts held that this body had the power to discipline its members and enforce its regulations upon them.[58] This included not only the regulation of trading in grain and provisions on its board, but also certification of grain elevators for purposes of insurance and safety as "regular" or "irregular" and to determine the extent to which the grain elevator firms could trade in grain in the great mart. The membership of the Board of Trade, during the "Gilded Age," was composed of "legitimate" brokers or traders, the speculators or "illegitimate" traders who frequently sought to "corner" wheat, corn, oats, or pork, firms with a "bucket shop" liaison, and the grain elevator interest.

Some elevator companies were the beneficiaries of such exclusive secret rate and service favors from a railroad that enabled it to monopolize the incoming grain traffic on that carrier. The elevator firms long maintained a monopolistic organization on their own in which the Armour elevators held a central position. It is hardly surprising in view of these facts that the elevator combination was consistently opposed to effective regulation by the Board. Inasmuch as the Armour trading group were extremely prominent among the speculative traders and were frequent manufacturers of "corners," they led this group and the grain elevator interest in resisting the drafting and enforcement of more stringent rules.

These were the achievement of the reform party of legitimate traders who for some years were in the majority. They drafted

[57] Stickney, *Railway Problem*, 206, 211, and *passim*; Adams, *Railroads: Their Origin and Problems*, 124-27.

[58] Chicago *Daily Tribune*, December 24, 27, 1874.

repeated revisions of the rules to prevent bear raids and "corners" in an attempt to restrict transactions to an actual exchange of commodities. These efforts proved abortive, in part because the courts declined to back up the penalties the Board imposed upon recalcitrant members on the ground that it was a "voluntary association," in part because of the rapid increase in the power of the speculative group when prosperity returned in the early eighties. This faction procured, temporarily, the abolition of the anticorner rule. Although this was subsequently restored it was enforced with varying vigor.

After much agitation the reform element elected William Taylor Baker president in 1890 with a mandate to exterminate the "bucket shops" that had developed a far-flung system of gambling on future quotations on the big Board. After severing the secret connections between numerous members and the "bucket shops" by stringent measures, Baker and his party attempted to bring the grain elevators to book after exposing the unethical practices of this group. These involved trading in grain that the elevators were storing, issuing warehouse receipts in excess of the actual quantity of grain in storage, misgrading grain, and discriminating against unfavored merchants.

An appeal to the enlightened Judge M. F. Tuley secured enforcement of the rule that confined the elevators to performance of their function as public custodians of grain stored with them and prohibited them from trading in that commodity. This decision reversed that of Judge Elbridge Gary in the lower court.

Following this victory the Board in the mid-nineties classified all Armour elevators as "irregular" since they violated state law by transferring inspected grain from warehouse to warehouse without reinspection, and ruled that traders accepting warehouse receipts from the Armour interests did so at their own risk. The Central Elevator Company was declared "irregular" on the same grounds, while the Board insisted upon enforcing a state law of 1871 that prohibited elevators from mixing their own grain with that of their customers. The total effect of these measures was to deprive the Illinois Central, the Chicago, Burlington & Quincy, and the Chicago and Northwestern railroads of storage.

This precipitated a struggle between the reform and speculator-grain elevator party in which the latter won a decisive victory. The

Armours mustered their forces when brought to a formal trial before the Board, while on the markets they offered reparation to any injured customers. After winning a verdict of not guilty, although an associated firm was banned from the Board for twenty years, they forced that body to restore the "regular" rating of their elevators irrespective of continued use of an automatic conveyor system for moving grain between them without reinspection. Then Charles T. Yerkes, a leading speculator, repudiated his trading contracts when caught "short" and successfully defied the Board's order that he meet his contractual obligations.

The elevator men then took advantage of "Corporal" John R. Tanner's election to the governorship in 1896 to procure the repeal of the act of 1871, despite the Board's insistence that its prohibition against mixing elevator-owned grain with that of their customers be continued. When the reform party sought to secure adoption of a rule prohibiting the storing of grain owned by its proprietors or managers in any "regular" warehouse it was decisively defeated. As Armour's biographers state, "by the first week of July, 1897, the elevator men were masters of the situation and the Board of Trade declared 'regular' 80 per cent of the elevators that applied for such rating." The Baker party was thus decisively defeated by the Armour group. Stubborn opposition by powerful speculative and elevator interests had made effective regulation of grain storage and of trading in grains and provisions by the Board of Trade an impossibility, even though the Illinois Board of Warehouse and Railroad Commissioners was supposed to cooperate with it and the Board possessed the authority to declare "irregular" any elevator that violated any of its rules or any state law.[59]

All this will explain why, some fourteen years earlier, the chief of the editorial staff of the Chicago *Tribune*, recently its financial editor, demanded in a widely acclaimed article national regulation of the Chicago Board of Trade and other commodity exchanges as a means of preventing the speculative manipulation of the prices

[59] *Ibid.*, December 13, 16, 24, 27, 1874, January 1, 2, February 7, March 5, 10, 22, 27, 1875, November 14, 1877, September 28, 1879, March 27, November 24, 1880, November 22, December 19, 1884; Charles H. Baker, *Life and Character of William Taylor Baker* (New York, 1908), 111-47; Harper Leech and John C. Carroll, *Armour and His Times* (New York, 1938), 290-304; C. L. Hutchinson to Lloyd, [April 29, 1888], Lloyd to Hutchinson, May 2, 1888, Lloyd to M. A. O. Slaughter, September 6, 1896, Lloyd Papers.

of food.[60] To complete the record in this particular area of business activity we should clarify the attitude of the Chicago grain elevator firms toward regulation of their business by the state government. During the summer of 1896 nine of these concerns were found guilty by the Illinois Board of Warehouse and Railroad Commissioners of having traded in grain in defiance of state law. Instead of acquiescing in this ruling of the Commission the condemned elevator firms promptly took their cases to court.[61]

Effective regulation of business in the public interest was opposed on the local government level by public utility franchise groups who, in general, preferred to purchase franchises on their own terms from bipartisan "rings" of city councilors rather than accept undesired restrictions in behalf of the public as the price of doing business. The activities of the Yerkes traction interests in Chicago, the Widener-Elkins group in Philadelphia and elsewhere, and the granting of franchises on Manhattan during the years of "Boss" Richard Croker's supremacy are illustrative here.[62]

The attempt to prevent the marketing of diseased meat is a case in point. In Chicago, in the late seventies, an ordinance had been enacted that established a system of meat inspection with the object of discovering diseased meat, whether in butchershops, packing houses, or in the livestock held by cattle dealers. This meat processed or on the hoof was to be condemned, confiscated without compensation, and destroyed to prevent it from reaching the consumer. Early in October, 1879, the pressure of the affected business interests was sufficient to procure a modification of the meat inspection ordinance so as to authorize the sale at auction, with no safeguards for the consumer, of diseased meat. This was done despite the vigorous editorial opposition of the Chicago *Tribune* which then campaigned to procure a return to the earlier policy.[63]

60 Henry D. Lloyd, "Making Bread Dear," *North American Review*, CXXXVII (August, 1883), 118-36; Van Buren Denslow, "Board of Trade Morality," *ibid.*, CXXXVII (October, 1883), 372, 380-87; Charles Partridge to Lloyd, May 8, 1883, Lloyd Papers.

61 Leech and Carroll, *Armour and His Times*, 291.

62 R. R. Bowker, "The Piracy of Public Franchises," *Atlantic Monthly*, LXXXVIII (October, 1901), 463-79; George Schilling, "The Suppressed Parts of the Ninth Biennial Report of the Bureau of Labor Statistics of Illinois. Subject, 'Franchises,' 1896," *Social Forum* (Chicago), II (April, 1900), 97-158; Chicago *Chronicle*, October 25, 1895; "Report on Franchises, 1896," Illinois Bureau of Labor Statistics, *Ninth Biennial Report*, 1896 (Springfield, 1897), 78-79; Charles E. Russell, *Bare Hands and Stone Walls; Some Recollections of a Side-Line Reformer* (New York, 1933), 98-105.

63 Chicago *Daily Tribune*, October 10, 22, 27, 1879.

The same paper, the most influential journal of the trans-Allegheny region, conducted another vain campaign in behalf of an effective Pleuro-Pneumonia Bill that was before Congress in 1884. This measure would have provided a federal cattle inspection service to detect and destroy all cattle infected with this disease before they reached the packing houses. The Great Plains cattle barons favored the measure, but the midwestern stockyards companies and the "cattle eveners" who semimonopolized the shipment of livestock between Chicago and the North Atlantic coast mobilized a powerful lobby that induced Congress to emasculate the bill. Apparently the traffic of these carrier and mercantile interests was of such importance that in their eyes it held precedence above the welfare of consumers and cattle raisers. It was not until 1889 that European market protests induced the Chicago meat packers to consent to the enactment by Congress of a federal inspection bill that applied solely to exported live cattle and chilled beef in order to rehabilitate their reputation abroad.[64]

This powerful industrial interest was opposed, however, to effective regulation of itself in behalf of the American consumer. The Chicago *Tribune* and the New York Health Department campaigned vigorously against the marketing of adulterated margerine and poisoned or diseased meats during the early eighties. In a noted editorial, "Morals and Money," the *Tribune* plumped for a national pure food law to prevent such abuses. It followed this up in January, 1885, with an equally vigorous review of Dr. Cyrus Edson's investigation into the widespread poisoning and adulteration of foods. Thus the leading midwestern daily gave powerful support to the demand for regulation of the food and drug industries that was implicit in the pioneer investigations of Professor Charles Frederick Chandler and Dr. Edson, for which a national inspection service was a minimum remedy.[65] When N. K. Fairbank revealed to a congressional inquiry in February, 1888, that 40 per cent of the refined lard manufactured in Chicago was adulterated, he precipitated the Vest Committee investigation in behalf of the United States Senate into the processing and transportation of meat products. Phillip D. Armour's success in diverting this committee's

64 *Ibid.*, May 27, 1884; Leech and Carroll, *Armour and His Times*, 175; "Transportation and Sale of Meat Products," *Senate Reports*, No. 829, 51 Cong., 1 Sess., 40 and *passim*.

65 Chicago *Daily Tribune*, April 14, 1884, January 15, 1885.

attention to the railroads from the meat packing industry, when he finally consented to testify before this committee in Washington, D. C., is further evidence of the "Big Four's" resistance to social control in any form whatever in behalf of the domestic consumer.[66]

[66] "Transportation and Sale of Meat Products," *Senate Reports*, No. 829, 51 Cong., 1 Sess., 1, 4-6, 13, 33; Leech and Carroll, *Armour and His Times*, 172, 192-95.

Frederic L. Paxson and His Approach to History

By Earl Pomeroy

One of our major misfortunes as historians is that we do not have the record of how our professional procedures have developed, of how the patterns of our interpretation have been defined. It has been traditional, since Herbert B. Adams's time and Turner's, to speak of the seminar and the study as laboratories, and yet the laboratory processes have been incompletely recorded. The few who have written serviceable manuals of historical method have written chiefly in generalities, and most of those whose books guide us in substantive matters have not chosen to take time from their writing to tell specifically how they wrote. Edward Channing all but wrote his great work in his seminar; he left a manual for his undergraduates, but the picture is incomplete and reveals more how he weighed individual problems than how he wrote, or than how he established the synthesis that he presented in his lectures and in his textbook but not in his six-volume *History of the United States*. The case of Turner is still more in point. Perhaps no other historian has left his hypotheses and his procedure so much in view, or been the subject of so many historiographical essays. Yet there is little agreement not only in judgment among those who profess to weigh his conclusions but also in practice among those who profess to follow his method.

Frederic L. Paxson led and represented a generation of historians at Wisconsin, where he succeeded Turner in 1910, and another generation at California. He was a pioneer in two fields of American history, western and recent, and wrote the first surveys of them as well as a long series of special studies.[1] His influence as scholar

[1] When he came in 1901 to what he later called a "bench of history" at the College of Colorado, two thousand miles from the diplomatic materials that he used for his dissertation on *The Independence of the South American Republics* (Philadelphia,

and teacher would make his picture of the problems of American historians (or of his own problems) of especial interest if he had chosen to draw it as a whole. He did not, and even in his seminars he seldom philosophized at length; he talked of techniques and of specific problems and their meaning more than of validity in the abstract. He left, however, a record of his own approach to the problems of writing history in his book reviews, which with his articles are probably his most characteristic writings, and in a half-century's accumulation of notes that he used in writing his books, and that he might have used in writing other books.

Most men's notes are useless stuff to others, useless even to themselves with the passage of time, and useless especially because of chaotic arrangement. The notes that Paxson left are unique both in scope and in organization. They span his professional lifetime, from the years when he studied colonial history with Channing at Harvard and taught ancient and medieval history at the College of Colorado. Occasionally he noted down what he heard and saw as well as what he read, and sometimes what he said and did, although he also kept a diary in separate form. The three-by-five inch slips of thin paper eventually filled about eighty wooden file drawers. And he classified the notes day by day, under topical-chronological headings that eventually extended from 4639 B.C. to 1949, the year after his death.

The very orderliness of Paxson's notes may lead to erroneous impressions of what they were and how they were used, and of the mind that used them. Their superficial appearance is that of a kind of shelf list catalogue of American history, day by day, which they were not. Even the students in Paxson's seminar knew his file chiefly as a reflection of his remarkable memory for detail, as a wonderful apparatus into which he dropped his notes on their semi-

1903), he turned to local western studies, and from these to a preliminary synthesis of frontier history in *The Last American Frontier* (New York, 1910); in his *History of the American Frontier* (Boston, 1924), for which he won a Pulitzer prize, he extended the synthesis to proportions that became standard in the field. Meanwhile, in his two textbooks, *The New Nation* (Boston, 1925, 1927) and *Recent History of the United States* (Boston, 1921, 1929, 1937), though he wrote with the aid of series such as James Ford Rhodes's and Ellis P. Oberholtzer's, he sketched a framework beyond their dimensions both chronologically and topically, and based his story essentially on his own research. In his last published volumes, the trilogy *American Democracy and the World War* (Boston, Berkeley, 1936-1948), he continued with the recent themes that became his chief concern, analyzing the impact of crisis and reconstruction on the American system over the years 1913-1923.

nar reports, and that he consulted on disputed points.[2] The file was complex enough, and the task it represented was large enough, so that few of his sixty-five doctors, who watched the file grow in the seminar as part of the historical laboratory process, have maintained full files of their own. The difficulty of adopting his system appears the greater when one finds, for instance, that there are seven filing dates for the Santa Fe trail and trade, eight for Phineas T. Barnum, perhaps sixty for automobiles. The arrangement at first glance may seem consistent with the organization of John B. McMaster's earlier volumes, which gave an impression of reality if not of logic by crowding together events in approximately the order that they forced themselves on the attention of the people of the United States, and with no apologies (even in stylistic articulation) for sudden shifts and breaks in the picture.

Yet Paxson's purpose was analytical rather than annalistic. He arranged his notes as he did, in semichronological form, in part because he did not wish to commit himself in advance to a framework that might govern his interpretation or that might cease to make sense as the facts accumulated and as his interpretations changed. Events might appear in various logical relationships, but all events occurred in time and could be linked to points or pegs in the calendar more easily, and with more reservation of judgment, than to any other system of pegs. The chronological arrangement served to remind him of both the movement and the crowded contemporaneity of events. It helped him to reconstruct atmosphere; it gave unexpected clues to general attitudes; it sometimes suggested how an event suddenly rose or fell in the public notice through accidental association with other events. Events pushed each other into and out of the headlines; an earthquake obliterated not only houses but also a presidential message; Doctor Win the War succeeded Doctor New Deal. "It should never be forgotten," he reminded his readers, "that each episode depends as much upon the atmosphere in which it happens as upon those of its causes that run directly back into the past. Cross-purposes and

2 At Wisconsin a story used to circulate to the effect that he once reached for a drawer and stopped a student report with the challenge, "That isn't what Hicks said in 1915. That isn't what Osgood said in 1923. That isn't what Riegel said in 1926. Are you sure?" And when the student said that he was sure, and why, Paxson tore the old notes across, and dropped them into the wastebasket. The story does not square with Paxson's usual care in handling his notes, but in the telling it reflects the awe in which his students held him and his file.

traffic jams become in themselves new causes to complicate the story." [3]

The order of the notes is at once chronological and topical. Paxson's theory was that ordinarily a development, or a principal phase of it, could be identified with a specific point in time, origin, climax, institutionalization, or impact. Thus notes on Hiram Johnson appear under dates of January 3, 1911 (his inauguration as governor of California), April 2, 1917 (his induction as senator), and August 6, 1945 (his death); notes on automobiles in part under April 19, 1892 (Charles E. Duryea ran the first gasoline auto), March 4, 1902 (American Automobile Association), June 16, 1903 (Ford incorporated), September 16, 1908 (General Motors incorporated), October 31, 1913 (Lincoln Highway), July 11, 1916 (Federal Roads Act), August 3, 1923 (federal highway system), December 2, 1927 (the new Ford), and the dates of a series of automobile shows beginning with January 22, 1900. Notes on the formation of a president's cabinet appear under the date of the inauguration; on the personnel of the Supreme Court under the dates of nomination of chief justices. As notes accumulated, he filed them under new and subsidiary headings, with cross-references (on the index card) to related headings, which might be numerous and many years remote.

Offhand the breakdown of topics into many categories, attached sometimes to widely dispersed chronological pegs, may seem to have a disintegrating tendency, and a tendency inconsistent with the responsibility of interpretation. Actually Paxson's purpose in postponing arrangements according to causal hypotheses, in fixing his mind first on the verification of fact, was not to avoid interpretation but to prepare his mind (and perhaps his reader's mind) to receive a larger volume of evidence and to interpret it more soundly. He was impressed by the difference between written history and (though he did not use the phrase) what Charles A. Beard called "history as actuality"; he was impressed by the data available to the recent historian, and by the requirements that they impose.

[3] Frederic L. Paxson, *America at War, 1917-1918* (Boston, 1939), 1-2. In his *Postwar Years* (Berkeley, 1948), 70, Paxson reminded the reader that "the culture of America was . . . always at hand, and still at hand when for the moment the major attention was diverted to domestic affairs, to war, or to world affairs. The reader watched from day to day the proceedings in Paris but did not forget that the Kentucky Derby was to be run in May, or that the major baseball leagues would begin to play in April."

"When the great historian of the United States shall . . . sit down to his work," he copied from the New York *Times*, "he will be appalled at the mass of material with which he will have to deal. A marvelous literary digestion will be a previous condition of his success."[4] His system represented an attempt to bring together parts of the great mass that the modern historian faces, and that, he felt, the historian must face in a literal and personal sense, himself scanning and weighing the evidence. His cross-references linked the stages of a topic; the chronological breakdown and the cross-references together put the stages in their setting.

Newspaper materials satisfied the demands of Paxson's chronological classification scheme and his views of the scope of history and of historical materials; perhaps they suggested both. They contributed also to the mass of testimony, free from hindsight, that Paxson felt necessary to establish historical fact. He sometimes commented to his seminar on the ability of American newspaper reporters to winnow out the truth, especially in "continuing" stories, where there was occasion to restate and correct, meet rebuttal, pare out extraneous details, and forget the passions that may have colored the original statement. At all events notes on newspapers comprise the greater part of the Paxson note collection. He took them day by day, from about the time he went to Colorado in 1901, and he took them in increasing volume. By the thirties he was taking notes (and occasionally clippings) daily from three newspapers, less regularly from other newspapers, the *Congressional Record*, and a wide selection of magazines as well as from books. The volume of notes that he accumulated was large enough to support a substantial amount of writing, but before he wrote he went again to the sources and took a much larger number of notes. He thus followed, over a wider range of data than any one man could hope to use fully, the advice that he sometimes gave in reviews, that a historian should work fully through the background material. "That would be a prolonged task," he remarked in a review of J. C. Long's *Bryan, The Great Commoner* (1928), "involving weary years of turning newspaper pages and exploring local and in-themselves-unimportant political events. But without such a study . . . it is impossible to prepare a biography of great historical

[4] Editorial in New York *Times*, June 9, 1879, filed under date of September 10, 1884 (date of founding of American Historical Association), Paxson File (Bancroft Library, University of California, Berkeley).

importance."[5] The system worked well enough in Paxson's hands so that no one who knew him well could imagine that his years were weary or doubt that he turned the pages himself.

However large the mass of material, however deliberately mechanical the organization of the notes, research and writing in Paxson's view were deeply personal processes. The historian must stand above his data, neither imposing himself prematurely on them nor allowing them to master him. A note system, he told his students, should permit rearrangement and study of notes in different relationships "until the fact itself is brought out against the background in all its important details."[6] Paxson never used a research assistant, even though his work involved much checking and gathering of minutiae. "There is no reason why a writer should not use openly . . . the contributions of a corps of helpers," he said of James Ford Rhodes; "but the result of such historical method is unlikely to be volumes that reveal unity of historical construction or the ripe judgment and point of view that come only to the writer who has done his own selecting and discarding among the sources."[7] And the author must not merely articulate his sources; he must digest them. A long passage quoted or closely followed "remains an undigested bit of foreign matter." "Over quotation may mean under thought."[8]

The process of digestion was of necessity and by principle a personal or individual process. It was so personal that Paxson sometimes filed away notes registering his own reactions as events occurred, as

[5] Review of J. C. Long, *Bryan, The Great Commoner* (New York, 1928), *Mississippi Valley Historical Review* (Cedar Rapids), XV (September, 1928), 270.

[6] Note headed "notes," n.d., Paxson File, unclassified.

[7] Review of James Ford Rhodes, *History of the United States From Hayes to McKinley, 1877-1896* (New York, 1919), *American Historical Review* (New York), XXV (April, 1920), 525. Paxson sometimes filed notes handed in by students in the course of routine checks on their work (to about 1913), and he regularly took notes on students' oral seminar reports, but he apparently did not depend on such notes. On the other hand, he often went out of his way, in his own writings, to refer to related works by his students.

[8] Note, "*Quotations: make them* brief," n.d., unclassified, Paxson File, and note, "*Your sentences must be your own.*" "A long quotation burdens your text. The printer commonly puts it in a different type and indicates that it is a thing apart. The quotation will be most effective when it is brief and pertinent and may be amalgamated in your own paragraph. The more completely you understand your sources the more aptly & gracefully you will quote." "Do not take out of a secondary work a paragraph or its substance and incorporate it in your work. . . . Use it if you must, but restate it in your own terms, and make its form entirely yours. Give the footnote of course but remember that you must be the author."

how he voted.[9] And sometimes, reflecting on the significance of even minor trends, he filed what he thought of their relationships to the larger patterns of history, or embroidered a cross-reference with whimsy. "The cartoon personality," he noted, for example, "enters the U S about 1922. See the race for Cong in ChTrib in

[9] November 7, 1916: "I expect to vote for Woodrow Wilson

I

"He has proved a capacity to translate into statutes desires that have pervaded the American mind for many years, and to secure for these laws the approval of Congress. His congress has been not too wise and not too single hearted in its public devotion; but better cannot now be hoped from a Republican congress in either head or heart. Our President must be a leader to be a success. He must not be timid respecting the bounds of his sphere of influence. When things go wrong he will be held responsible; it is up to him to see that they go right. And Mr. Hughes has had no chance to prove this trait.

II

"He has revealed powers of insight and description, has seen the ideals of freedom, peace and independence that have run beneath our history, and has not hesitated to express them. He has been called visionary and doctrinaire, but they are our visions and our doctrines. If those of Mr. Hughes are different I do not want them in the W. H; if they are similar I have no certainty that Mr. Hughes can phrase them. And our president must be teacher as well as doer.

III

"He has given force to the . . . [word illegible] policies that I desire: a neutral America, with jealous regard for the rights of the peaceful world; a friendly neighbor not ready to profit by the adversity of a friend; a domestic program for the betterment of the individual life and the coordination of our national resources. If Mr. Hughes is truthful, he disapproves of these, and will change them if he can.

IV

"So I shall vote for Woodrow Wilson / done 11/7"

November 7, 1922: "Election day I am not voting to-day. There is no doubt as to the outcome; but there is no one up in Wis. that I can support with any comfort. I cannot vote the dem. ticket—it does not mean anything here. I stand in general program with the progressive group, and have mostly approved La Follette's aims in domestic legis. I cannot forgive his war stand, nor his present alliance with the wets. Therefore I stay out."

November 4, 1924: "I voted today the straight Republican ticket, except that I scratched the sheriff Daggett because I believe him to be a boot leg road house keeper, and substituted Burmeister, of whom I know little more, and who has the drawback of being alleged to be the KKK candidate.

"I voted for Coolidge, because I have no confidence in the Democratic party organization, although I think Davis a much superior man. I could not vote for Bob, although I agree with much of his economic policies, because he is extreme and unreasonable, and because there can be no sound fusion between grouchy farmers and the part of labor that votes politically. The *labor* vote, as labor, is socialist or socialistic.

"I voted for Blaine because he is in office, knows the job has the confidence of a majority, and is I think honest and courageous. I do not admire his administration, but I do not think a single democratic term, as Judge Lueck would have, would be any use. There is no real democratic party in Wis., and the conservative republicans have no single responsible and respectable leader."

1922. These figures become real; other papers run news stories about them; they are personified traits so clear that all can recognize them. Consider them as the growing folk lore that the papers are able to estab[lish] and compare with mediaeval acta sanctorum on the popular side; or fabliaux."[10] The cross-references themselves, though usually brief to an extreme, occasionally were little articulative essays. "The bad towns" of the West had their several filing dates, and under date of March 19, 1931 (when Governor Fredrick B. Balzar signed the Nevada gambling and six-weeks divorce bills), Paxson noted of "Reno, and the others," "Three naughty contemporaries in the civic picaresques were Deadwood, Leadville and Tombstone. The first passed towards respectability when Wild Bill was shot, 8.2.1876; the second incorporated, or at least organized, 1.14.78, immed[iately] produced HAW Tabor, who was a gaudy hero. The third, Tombstone, incorp 2.21.1881, was passing out of the era in which Wyatt Earp and the gunmen, good or bad, were the dominant figures."[11] None of these notes was ever used in his writing; probably they were taken with no thought of specific use, but out of absorption in the American scene.

The mass of Paxson's paper work may appear more clearly now than the zest with which he labored, but the essence of his method was in the spirit rather than in the product. He enjoyed the weighing and checking of evidence, even concerning relatively minor points; sometimes it seemed that he liked to remind himself on a small scale of the processes by which truth is preserved, obscured, and revealed. More than that, he enjoyed his larger search, his writings, his teaching, his profession. He was famous on campus for regular hours — nine to twelve, one to five; no work accumulated on his desk, and none was carried home. "Telephone me at eight o'clock," he used to say; "I shall be at breakfast." "There are two things to learn," he told a student: "one is to work, and the other is to play." Off campus there was no more delightful host or conversationalist or golf partner; at work none could do business more quickly. Those who knocked at his study found his "come in" always hearty, his attention undivided with no hint of regret at the interruption, his comment illuminating and to the core; but even a dull student sensed that work was being done, and that he must get

[10] N.d., filed under March 19, 1931, Paxson File.
[11] Paxson File.

on to his own with new momentum, and leave Paxson to his. One suspected that Paxson's love for his work may have tempted him to labor too long, and that he established a schedule to protect himself and the keenness of his mind, to keep himself from his desk instead of at it, as is some men's purpose.

One may only speculate on whether Paxson's note system significantly determined the kind of history that he wrote, and on the relationship of the system to his theory of history; that they were in harmony is clearer than which evoked the other. Certainly he did not attempt to divorce his method of filing from his method of writing, as he divorced work from recreation. In his last books, as in his notes, his filing dates stand out to those who look for them, and his bibliographical citations (somewhat as Lord Acton's) have been absorbed into the text: there are no footnotes. Further, in his later years his notes and his writings were more on political and military than on social and economic themes, and certainly most persons attempting a chronological file would find it easier to classify political than social data. Yet his notes on social and economic developments are many, his writings substantial.[12] He admitted "an indefensible interest in the unimportant items" of history, as when men stopped wearing shirts that button up the back and shoes with elastic in the sides, and why, and he also put the scraps together into patterns that fascinated his students. And as Paxson's political notes generally were separated more than the others — the classification was more complex — it seems unlikely that the problems of filing governed the directions of his interests. While he did not attempt to write down all that he thought and knew, apparently he was seldom if ever at a loss to find a place for a note. He filed away successive series of lecture notes, notes that he took on seminar reports, even notes on the scenery that he saw from a train. The range was as wide as his activities and interests as scholar, teacher, citizen of state and nation. He had a separate bibliographical file, kept in six scantily filled drawers in his coat closet, and it is obvious

12 Frederic L. Paxson, "The Cow Country," *American Historical Review*, XXII (October, 1916), 65-82; "The Rise of Sport," *Mississippi Valley Historical Review*, IV (September, 1917), 143-68; "Finance and the Frontier," James F. Willard and Colin B. Goodykoontz (eds.), *The Trans-Mississippi West . . .* (Boulder, 1930), 257-66; and "The Highway Movement, 1916-1935," *American Historical Review*, LI (January, 1946), 236-53. Some of the largest aggregations of notes pertain to transportation, not only railroads and highways but also western trails and bridge and tunnel systems.

that he used it little in later years. His author-title entries usually went into the main file, after the appropriate subject index cards. The file was so much a habit that it was no burden. He took it to Washington when he went into war service in 1917-1918; he kept his note pads always in his pocket. Yet there was never a question of who was master. While he took more notes as he grew older, they were more abbreviated, often more citations than notes in the usual sense; he depended more on his memory, which he developed in the daily work on his file. On the whole, his efficiency probably reduced the time required for taking and filing notes to the amount other historians spent in note-taking alone. What he wrote in his notes was brief, and yet specific enough so that he saved himself the job of searching at length for what he had read. His mind was free to reflect and appraise.

Some aspects of Paxson's note system and style, and some of his remarks, may suggest that he projected the canons of historical absolutism from the era of Leopold von Ranke into the era of Beard, that he was one of the last adherents to what Theodore Clarke Smith called "a noble dream." [13] His reviewers noted a quality of reticence, "a spirit of aloofness" that went beyond the balanced statement, beyond style. His written prose was rhythmical, muscular to an unusual degree, and yet always scrupulously removed from the causes he described and from the passions of the time in which he wrote. "Say what one may of historical philosophy," he wrote in 1926, "history is a matter of facts; and the establishment of facts, desiccated as they may be, is the chief function of the genuine historian." [14] He felt that the Beards had gone too far in making their facts "generally incidental to some conclusion that has pre-determined their selection and arrangement." [15] Their method of handling evidence *a priori* distressed him, though he rejoiced in other aspects of their work. "If one is chiefly to explain the present, he must understand it; and none of us does that," he wrote in a review of Louis M. Hacker and Benjamin B.

[13] Theodore C. Smith, "The Writing of American History in America, from 1884 to 1934," *American Historical Review*, XL (April, 1935), 449.

[14] Review of John B. Black, *The Art of History; A Study of Four Great Historians of the Eighteenth Century* (New York, 1926), *New York Herald Tribune Books*, December 12, 1926, p. 12.

[15] Review of Charles A. Beard and Mary R. Beard, *The Rise of American Civilization*, 2 vols. (New York, 1927), *Mississippi Valley Historical Review*, XIV (September, 1927), 233.

Kendrick's textbook in 1932. "If everything is to be brought to a focus at a date of publication, the forces of obsolescence must begin to operate at once, and the very timeliness of the work makes it shortly out of date."[16] "The *Verdict* of History," he scrawled on a note: "There is none — . . . Apart from verif of facts There is no verdict only onesided testimony."[17] Yet Paxson (as, indeed, Ranke and Beard themselves) subscribed to no extremist philosophy of history — merely to mention bias was neither to exorcise it nor to justify it. His own field of recent history was the real dark ages, he told his students, darkened by the suppression and the plethora of evidence, and darkened by the bias of the historian, who had been, of necessity, a participant in the history of which he wrote. He noted how John Hay had told John G. Nicolay that "we ought to write the history of those times like two everlasting angels who . . . don't care a twang of their harps about one side or the other,"[18] and how Hay, when he said that, had bent his mind to the specific wishes of Robert Todd Lincoln.[19] But any historian was biased, and if not by being a friend of Abraham Lincoln or a literary beneficiary of Robert Lincoln, or a contemporary of either, then simply by knowing what happened after the events he described. The curse of the historian is that he "cannot see the event as it was, knowing the outcome. He distorts the meaning of sources. He makes events eventful. He assumes that the right *knew* it was right."[20] On the other hand, knowing the hazards on the road, Paxson had no wish to immobilize himself before them. He reserved sharpest criticism for those who wrote disconnectedly, or in a vacuum, without theme or conclusion. He scorned the com-

16 Review of Louis M. Hacker and Benjamin B. Kendrick, *The United States Since 1865* (New York, 1932), *Annals of the American Academy of Political and Social Science* (Philadelphia), CLXI (May, 1932), 264-65. In his papers is a less favorable draft, marked not used. That the book would shortly be out of date seems confirmed by the drastic shift in point of view in the postwar edition. See John F. Gerstung, "Louis M. Hacker's Reappraisal of Recent American History," *Historian* (Albuquerque), XII (Spring, 1950), 140-66.

17 Note, n.d. (probably made during the 1920's), unsorted, Paxson File.

18 William R. Thayer, *The Life and Letters of John Hay*, 2 vols. (Boston, 1915), II, 33.

19 Notes of July 25, 1930, talk at Superior State Teachers College, Paxson File.

20 Note, "*The Curse of the Historian*," taken December 24, 1935, San Francisco Overland Limited, unclassified, *ibid.* Pronouns, articles, and punctuation added. The note goes on: "his picture of what did not happen cf H Adams and McMaster *His curse on the Indian* the history of the successful picks camp[aigne]rs who won ignores those who also ran yet human progress based on 'also rans' Can he escape it?"

piler — the writer of "scissors and paste history"; and he scorned the "pedestrian historian" who simply through lack of distinction escaped both the temptations of the fleshpots and the criticisms of the "witch-smellers": "few notice his existence, and his books are subject only to the hazards of time and dust, and the occasional venom of other historians as sterile as himself."[21] The obligation of a historian was to come to some conclusions on his subject as a whole, and to fit his segment of history "into the general social and political life of his period." Otherwise his "book is history of the most restricted type."[22] He should "give depth as well as detail to his picture of American life."[23] He must make an attempt at synthesis, however tentative and inexact.

Paxson wrote several unusually sharp reviews of books by McMaster, Rhodes, and Ellis P. Oberholtzer, historians whose methods have been compared with his own. McMaster's *Stephen Girard* (1918), he said, was a "series of anecdotes . . . without connection" and with little interpretation or analysis.[24] In Rhodes's last two volumes the facts rarely appeared "to have meaning or to be parts of a coherent structure."[25] "No simple theme, like that which dominated his great work, is apparent here. Mr. Rhodes has not seen any constructive unity in the years he covers. Instead of making a synthesis that would of itself lead the reader to a clearer understanding of American history . . . , he has developed his topics paragraph by paragraph, with often abrupt transition from theme to theme."[26] His failure in the final product followed, Paxson suggested, on his use of "his own by-products and the contributions of a corps of helpers."[27] Oberholtzer had succeeded in "his de-

[21] *New York Herald Tribune Books*, December 12, 1926, p. 12.

[22] Review of Harry E. Smith, *The United States Federal Internal Tax History from 1861 to 1871* (Boston, 1914), *Mississippi Valley Historical Review*, I (December, 1914), 459.

[23] Review of Brand Whitlock, *Forty Years of It* (New York, 1914), *ibid.*, I (September, 1914), 315.

[24] Review of John B. McMaster, *Life and Times of Stephen Girard: Mariner and Merchant*, 2 vols. (Philadelphia, 1918), *Mississippi Valley Historical Review*, VI (June, 1919), 120.

[25] Review of Rhodes, *History of the United States From Hayes to McKinley, 1877-1896*, *American Historical Review*, XXV (April, 1920), 525.

[26] Review of James Ford Rhodes, *The McKinley and Roosevelt Administrations, 1897-1909* (New York, 1922), *ibid.*, XXVIII (April, 1923), 566.

[27] Review of Rhodes, *History of the United States From Hayes to McKinley*, *ibid.*, XXV (April, 1920), 525. Rhodes concurred in at least part of this judgment. Writing to Paxson after the first review appeared, he said, "You are right, it seems to me, that the incorporation of monographs into a general history has its drawbacks.

tailed pictures of men and motives" but failed in his attempts to present "general principles." [28]

The problem of establishing relationships runs throughout Paxson's thought on social and economic history especially. He criticized alike those who, as Oberholtzer, left it out of their bindings and those who put it in their bindings but left it out of the organism of their history; he commended those who made honest attempts. McMaster's great contribution was in calling attention to economic and social themes;[29] Rhodes and Oberholtzer left their stories "one-sided and incomplete" in that they ignored economic factors. "The political history that was vital in the period 1840-1860 ceases to explain the United States after the civil war. And increasingly . . . the historian who would picture America and its motivation must broaden his canvas and increase his themes." [30] For all his concern over the Beards' biases, Paxson found *The Rise of American Civilization* "ripe, notable"; historians needed to know "that such a synthesis as this can actually exist." [31] "The cultural patterns of American life are brought into articulation with the course of American history more convincingly than any of the rest of us have been able to do it." [32] He wished that the Beards' articulation might have been still closer,[33] though he had little patience with others who, in his opinion, wrote out of less learning and failed in

Tempted by the high price paid for magazine articles and the wide circulation that they entailed I did make a number of studies of episodes which I purposed using in this volume. . . . As you intimate the dovetailing of them together hardly seem 'to be parts of a coherent structure.'" Rhodes to Paxson, May 15, 1920, attached to Paxson's copy of *From Hayes to McKinley*.

[28] Review of Ellis P. Oberholtzer, *A History of the United States Since the Civil War*, 5 vols. (New York, 1917-1937), II (1922), *Mississippi Valley Historical Review*, IX (December, 1922), 255.

[29] American Historical Association, *Annual Report*, 1932 (Washington, 1934), 55; Frederic L. Paxson, "The New American History," *Quarterly Review* (London), CCIII (January, 1915), 170, 181.

[30] Review of Oberholtzer, *History of the United States*, II, *Mississippi Valley Historical Review*, IX (December, 1922), 255.

[31] Review of Beard and Beard, *Rise of American Civilization*, *ibid.*, XIV (September, 1927), 233.

[32] Review of Charles A. and Mary R. Beard, *America in Midpassage* (New York, 1939), *Pacific Northwest Quarterly* (Seattle), XXXI (January, 1940), 10. In 1946 he spoke enthusiastically of Arthur M. Schlesinger, Jr., *The Age of Jackson* (New York, 1945), acknowledging only perfunctorily, when I asked him, that he did not accept the main thesis.

[33] "The chapters on the American intellect . . . are genuine and useful contributions even though the authors hardly know how to relate them to the grand mosaic that they have constructed." Review of Beard and Beard, *Rise of American Civilization*, *Mississippi Valley Historical Review*, XIV (September, 1927), 235.

their attempts to integrate "cultural status and the flow of history." [34] On the other hand, he regretted that Samuel Eliot Morison, in his *Oxford History of the United States, 1783-1917* (1927), had told (though in sparkling style) too much of diplomacy and of the Civil War, too little of economic and social developments; the proportions seemed to follow on "the antiquarian or the romantic point of view. . . . If this is what our English friends want from American history it is hardly worth while to gratify them." [35]

Paxson had a phenomenal knowledge of American political history, and he was impatient with the merely political; like Turner, he had a phenomenal knowledge of the detail of local history, and he looked beyond the accumulation of detail. "The present trend of Western history . . . ," he wrote in 1932, "is the uncovering of its local detail and the presentation in attractive form of its more human episodes. This is to be welcomed. But it must be remembered that the interpretation of its meaning still calls for more Turners to launch their hypotheses, and more followers to check the conclusions." [36] Turner, as he pointed out, was not a local historian, worthy though the name is. As soon as he had enough facts to warrant it, "he made his transition from the particular to the general." He sought not for masses of local detail but "for a motivation and a causation in American history. No investigation may properly be called Turnerian unless its goal is more than the description of a set of facts." [37] Paxson spoke informally along similar lines in 1940, after criticisms of Turner had suddenly appeared and multiplied:

> I am not much like Turner; but I believe that I am like him in that I am aware that in history you cannot prove an inference. You cannot prove causation, much as you crave to do it. You may present sequences of events, whose relationship suggests a link-up of cause and consequence;

[34] Review of Hacker and Kendrick, *United States Since 1865*, *Annals of the American Academy of Political and Social Science*, CLXI (May, 1932), 264-65.

[35] Review of Samuel E. Morison, *The Oxford History of the United States, 1783-1917* (London, 1927), *American Historical Review*, XXXIII (July, 1928), 891. Later, after Morison and Henry S. Commager had enlarged the scope of the *Oxford History* in their *Growth of the American Republic* (2nd ed., New York, 1937), Paxson praised it warmly, telling his seminar that its second volume was the best available on recent history, much better than his own textbook.

[36] Frederic L. Paxson, review article, "Western Outposts," *Yale Review* (New Haven), XXI (June, 1932), 829.

[37] Frederic L. Paxson, "A Generation of the Frontier Hypothesis, 1893-1932," *The Great Demobilization and Other Essays . . .* (Madison, 1941), 23-30, reprinted from the *Pacific Historical Review* (Glendale, Calif.), II (March, 1933), 34-51.

> you may carry on the inquiry for a lifetime without discovering other events inconsistent with the hypothesis which has caught your eye. But you can never get beyond a circumstantial case. . . .
>
> But we historians must have some guide in our thinking; some rational scheme to be tested until it falls; or we become mere antiquarians with nothing in our inventory but disconnected facts. Perhaps that is all we can hope to be. Yet we keep on inquiring and hoping, and it may be that so doing we slightly narrow the range of productive thought by placing limits beyond which all thought is profitless.[38]

Similarly, Paxson found McMaster's greatness in that "instead of limiting his task to the verification of fact he sought persistently for the mainsprings of conduct that lie behind the environment, the prejudices, and the passions of the common people."[39] His own objective, in writing his *History of the American Frontier*, was "not to write a history of the west — but one of the U. S. as it was influenced and moulded by the west. . . ."[40] Like Turner, he looked upon the frontier as a "quasi-laboratory of the social sciences," where the historian had a unique opportunity to push back the larger frontiers of truth even though his hypotheses were likely to remain hypotheses. "Our conclusions, if we have any, may well possess greater value in interpreting society off the frontier than in determining the meaning of the frontier itself."[41]

Thus Paxson was not content to limit historians to the immediate and the ascertainable. Historical truth must appear through something short of scientific method, and in something other than scientific form, linked and geared to the unassimilable mass of facts. There was no standard technique suited to all persons and purposes, in note-taking or in composition. "The ordinary methods of historical narrative are ineffective before a theme that is in its essentials descriptive," he wrote of Archer B. Hulbert's *Forty-Niners* (1931) in 1932. "In some respects the story of the trails can not be told until it is thrown into the form of epic poetry, or comes under the hand of the historical novelist."[42] " 'There are nine and

38 "A Footnote to the Safety-Valve," August 15, 1940, Paxson Papers (University of California Library, Berkeley).

39 Frederic L. Paxson, "Memorial to John Bach M'Master," American Historical Association, *Annual Report*, 1932, p. 55.

40 Note made August 15, 1921, filed at October 7, 1763, Paxson File. The rest of the note reads, "frontier always growing ever the same."

41 Paxson, "Finance and the Frontier," Willard and Goodykoontz (eds.), *Trans-Mississippi West*, 259-60.

42 Review of Archer B. Hulbert, *Forty-Niners: the Chronicle of the California Trail* (Boston, 1931), *American Historical Review*, XXXVII (April, 1932), 567.

sixty ways of constructing tribal lays, And-every-single-one-of-them-is-right.' "[43] He brushed aside the criticism that Walter P. Webb's *The Great Plains* was not scientific. He said, in reviewing it in 1931, that he did not know whether it was history or sociology, and the question was immaterial; it was one of the best books written on the West in many years.[44] If Webb had followed his critics' suggestions, "his book might easily be collecting dust . . . instead of being worth a critical examination." The "famous Miles O'Reilly fake about Grant and his whiskey" seemed in point. "If Webb's 'work of art' . . . 'was written in a state of suppressed emotion,' one may wish that more historians . . . might have a portion of that emotion and not suppress it."[45]

Paxson's style and his themes were not much like those that he defended in Webb and Hulbert, but his choice of themes reflected both conviction and circumstance. In accordance with his emphasis on unity in history, Paxson found the political framework, among other conventional frameworks, indispensable in telling a general story. Even under the most favorable circumstances it was difficult to bring "in fragments of culture-history and have them look as though they belonged in the places in which they are put." Like Carl Becker, he doubted the wisdom of the plan of the *History of American Life* series, which "excluded all those elements of history that may contribute a real and provable articulation to the narrative."[46]

As the pioneer textbook writer in two fields — frontier history and recent United States history — Paxson naturally was obliged to concern himself closely with the factual ribs of his story, though when it appeared his *Recent History* was unusual in its emphasis on social and economic factors. When he wrote his *History of the American Frontier*, no one had told the whole story; the material

[43] Review of Fred A. Shannon, *Critiques of Research in the Social Sciences*: III. *An Appraisal of Walter Prescott Webb's The Great Plains* . . . (New York, 1940), *Pacific Historical Review*, X (March, 1941), 91.

[44] Review of Walter P. Webb, *The Great Plains* (Boston, 1931), *American Historical Review*, XXXVII (January, 1932), 359-60.

[45] Review of Shannon, *Appraisal of Walter Prescott Webb's The Great Plains*, *Pacific Historical Review*, X (March, 1941), 91-92.

[46] Review of Allan Nevins, *The Emergence of Modern America, 1865-1878* (New York, 1927), *Mississippi Valley Historical Review*, XIV (March, 1928), 571. Cf. Carl L. Becker, "What is Historiography?" *American Historical Review*, XLIV (October, 1938), 23; and Charles A. Beard's review of another volume in the series, *ibid.*, XXXVIII (July, 1933), 779-80.

of western history was still chiefly romantic, local, cartographical, and antiquarian in its orientation. He gave it a national political setting in the book, and then turned his mind to other phases of the West. Herbert Bolton's students, he noted in 1933, had begun by emphasizing archival materials and colonial systems, and to great advantage; "but the next steps in the portrayal of the West . . . will have to deal with the experience of the individuals as units, and must uncover the simple occurrences of non-official life." [47]

In most of Paxson's later writings the political theme became still more prominent, and probably neither because of his method nor simply because his work was first in the field. His teachers had been essentially political historians, and many of his later contemporaries tended to be that also, "in an age when democracy is fighting for its life." [48] When the millennium is not imminent but Stalin is, as William T. Hutchinson has said,[49] then the most natural objects of historical inquiry are political processes, in the broadest sense. The crisis of democracy in a world threatened by militarism and dictatorship, and in a nation mobilized for war, preoccupied Paxson in the thirties and forties; this was the theme of his trilogy, *American Democracy and the World War* (1936-1948). He found the people turning ever more to government, and political processes a more significant inventory than before of the state of the nation, while less easily appraised. These last books were not only more political in theme but more restrained in style than some of his earlier writings, sometimes even cryptic in degree of understatement; some reviewers complained that interpretation was too cautious, too lightly advanced. Though some reviewers (as of any book) mistook his purpose and complained, in effect, that he did not write on some other topic, it may be that his style became too restrained for the general taste. It may be that in using his system he developed his mind and his knowledge of history to the point where he expected his readers to draw more inferences from the facts he selected than most modern readers are accustomed to doing, in this day of the predigested book. "Professor Paxson has the gift of

47 Review of *New Spain and the Anglo-American West. Historical Contributions Presented to Herbert Eugene Bolton* (Lancaster, Pa., 1932), *Pacific Historical Review*, II (June, 1933), 232-33.

48 John D. Hicks, *The American Nation, A History of the United States from 1865 to the Present* (Boston, 1941), v.

49 William T. Hutchinson, "The Significance of the Constitution of the United States in the Teaching of American History," *Historian*, XIII (Autumn, 1950), 12.

marching prose," one of the reviewers had said of his *History of the American Frontier*. His later style at times had less rhythm though more precision; his later books were less popular but may have been more suggestive, presented more novel theses than his early books. To a degree they were written, as he said of Turner's essays, for historians rather than for the crowd.[50] Meanwhile his lectures, reviews, and essays, and his informal remarks in class and seminar were always vigorous and richly suggestive. His lecture notes, revised from year to year, suggest that in later years he lectured more interpretatively, more topically, less in a chronological framework, which he left the textbooks to provide, giving his classes analysis and hypothesis and a sense of contact with living men and problems rather than narrative. His students had, as they listened, a sense of participating in his exploration of the past; knowing him, they felt that in his books he sometimes preferred to equip them further for the search rather than to press on them the views that he held when he wrote.

At the same time, Paxson by no means withdrew himself from the present, but rather studied it the more carefully, and considered the responsibility of the historian in a world at war. As a department chairman in two world wars, he experienced the impact of war on higher education, which he expected to describe in his history of American state universities.[51] He took notes chiefly on the current scene; his notes were bulky, carefully classified, and apparently meant to be used. He had inquired, in 1938, "whether American society, or any society, could win another 'peace' ";[52] he watched closely over the attempt. It was consistent with his view of the historian and teacher, and with his general good taste and his habit of reserve, that he publicly stated few personal opinions on matters such as party politics, though his interest in politics was close,[53] and

[50] Review of Frederick J. Turner, *The Significance of Sections in American History* (New York, 1932), *American Historical Review*, XXXVII (July, 1933), 773-74.

[51] After his retirement in 1947 the Carnegie Corporation of New York persuaded him to write a history of American state universities, which came to interest him intensely. At the end of a year he had written half of the book and sorted his last notes. He notified the university administration that he was unable to complete the job before leaving his study for the hospital where he died, October 24, 1948. The volume is being completed by one of his students, Professor Walton E. Bean of the University of California.

[52] Frederic L. Paxson, "The Great Demobilization," *American Historical Review*, XLIV (January, 1939), 251.

[53] His students read with interest his comment on Woodrow Wilson, in *The Pre-*

his judgments were definite. He was deeply conscious of the high civic mission of the historian in appraising the present, a mission too important to be filled in light or facile spirit. The United States, he told a group of teachers in 1942, was the "one greatest laboratory in which both . . . freedom and the implements of freedom have received their testing. . . . Armed with the story . . . , our on-coming citizens are better prepared to act in cast or chorus. When I consider my conviction that knowledge of the past is a prerequisite to sound performance in the present, in any present, I feel the solemn duty to bring the lessons of the past to the attention of today. . . . To sit in judgment upon all the past, and to reduce it to anything resembling an instructive doctrine will require us to risk all of the occupational hazards of the historians. We judge the past with safety only because it is past, and mostly dead." Interested parties would "struggle to control the conclusions which we teach, order us to their type of uniformity, and threaten us with dire disaster if we balk." And "we shall endanger the solvency of the craft we serve unless we serve the truth astutely and, like the aviator, never take our eyes from the instrument panel." [54]

Paxson developed his own instruments, the techniques that he used in his search for historical truth, so elaborately that some who did not know him may be more conscious of technique than of the larger search. Neither the published conclusions nor the laboratory equipment of a great teacher and scholar can adequately represent the inspiration of his teaching, the depth of his inquiry. And Paxson was so complex a thinker, so little disposed to commit himself to any simple formula in the interpretation of history and of the historian's task, that no one can adequately define his position for

war Years, 1913-1917 (Boston, 1936), 3: "He aspired consciously to a large career in politics (as who has not?). . ."

[54] Manuscript, n.d., Paxson Papers. A recent writer has called attention to a passage in Paxson's presidential address before the American Historical Association in 1938, in which he remarked that historians "needed Cheyney's warning . . . not to write in 1917 or 1918 what might be regretted in 1927 and 1928." Paxson, "Great Demobilization," *American Historical Review*, XLIV (January, 1939), 237; Herman Ausubel, *Historians and Their Craft: A Study of the Presidential Addresses of the American Historical Association, 1884-1945* (New York, 1950), 105. His counsel was, however, far from negative. He had gone into government service under George Creel in 1917, along with Guy Stanton Ford, Edward S. Corwin, and others, editing the *War Cyclopedia*. His article on "The American War Government, 1917-1918," published in 1920, brought twentieth-century history for the first time into the *American Historical Review*. Cf. his "American Mobilization in the United States for the War of 1917," *Historical Outlook* (Philadelphia), X (January, 1919), 37-50.

him, though one can see in his writings and in the unique resource of his notes something of how a conscientious historian wrestled with the problems of writing history over a lifetime. In his respect for larger historical truths, he often deliberately understated his conclusions, or advanced hypotheses more subtly than some others have done. Some of his colleagues have said much more of the theory of historical truth than he did. But none pursued the truth with greater keenness and devotion.

Drang Nach Norden: *The United States and the Riel Rebellion*

By Donald F. Warner

That Manifest Destiny has been one of the major forces in the making of the nation is well known to all historically conscious Americans. Too many, however, seem to regard it as an almost entirely westward and southwestward movement and neglect the fact that one of its major impulses was to drive to the north and engulf British America. Perhaps this phase of national acquisitiveness has been slighted because it failed and we often confuse importance with success. At all events, this flank thrust was one of the great dynamics of Canadian history and an important factor in our own.

The fruit which the northward-looking annexationists hoped to pluck was all British America; but it was that part lying between the Rockies and Lake Superior whose American destiny seemed most manifest in 1869-1870. Here geography had rolled the plains, furrowed the valleys, and piled the mountains on a north-south axis. Here the soil, the climate, and the socioeconomic potentials on both sides of the 49th parallel were so identical that the thin political line seemed a mockery. The American expansionists were convinced that nature and her forces would avenge this frustration of her great purpose, blot out the boundary, and make one nation of those living on both sides of it. As a catalytic agent for this natural process, one of the most vigorous and best organized annexation movements in our history arose soon after the Civil War with this region as its locus and its goal.

The roots of the story lie deeply embedded in the past. In 1670 Charles II of England bestowed upon the Hudson's Bay Company by charter the vast empire which drained into Hudson Bay and Hudson Strait. The company, largely concerned with peltry, did not develop its domain. In the 1860's only one real settlement existed there, Fort Garry at the junction of the Assiniboine and Red rivers. At first this colony was a closed corporation under the company which controlled its economy and its only communication with the outside world, the arduous water route to Hudson Bay. Gradually this tight grip relaxed. The rise of St. Paul as the entrepôt for the trade of the Northwest attracted from Fort Garry the long processions of Red River carts which creaked and shrilled their ungreased way across the lake and prairie regions. This easier approach supplanted the trade line through the bay, and the company's hold on the economic affairs of the colony slipped. Moreover, the government of the colony broke down when it tried to prevent the colonists from setting up a private trade in furs, via the cart trail and in violation of its charter monopoly. In attempting to smother this activity, government officials merely succeeded in fanning a blaze which they could not put out; their strongest efforts only advertised their futility. The government of the colony was broken beyond repair. What would replace it? [1]

It seemed likely that the answer would be the United States, which was casting its shadow over Fort Garry and the hinterland. The economic ties with the south were growing as those with British territories withered. American settlers had followed the trail to the colony and clustered about Fort Garry where, dynamic, restless, and aggressive, they became the yeast of political ferment. Thus the first fingers of the tide of the American frontier had crawled north of the 49th parallel, perhaps soon to be followed by a flood which would wash away British authority. Historically conscious British officials, perhaps painfully aware of a parallel between this situation and that which had existed earlier in Oregon when the same British company played King Canute to the same irresistible force, hastened to try to save the Northwest for the empire. The most logical means was Canadian purchase to forestall American occupation of the region and to encourage a Canadian counter-frontier which would dilute the American frontier. Moreover, if Canada were to become a great nation, it must have room to expand,

[1] There are numerous good accounts of the early history of the colony and of the Riel Rebellion. Those principally used as background for this article include Alexander Begg, *History of the North-West*, 3 vols. (Toronto, 1894-1895), I; George F. G. Stanley, *The Birth of Western Canada* (London, 1936); and Arthur S. Morton, *A History of the Canadian West to 1870-71* (London, 1939).

a West comparable to that of its neighbor.[2] Already the surplus population of what is now Ontario was spilling into Michigan, squeezed out of Canada by the cramping Laurentian Shield. As Canadians saw their frontier escaping over the line, they became anxious to obtain the Northwest.[3]

Mutual dislike between the Canadian government and the Hudson's Bay Company, however, threatened to prevent this acquisition until the growing fear of the United States ended their quibbling in the 1860's. The company, after some acrimonious negotiations,[4] agreed to sell its title to the Northwest for £300,000 and the right to retain certain blocks of land and to continue its trading activities, though not its monopoly. Canada accepted these terms and appointed a government for the new territory, which was named Manitoba.

But the prospect of incorporation into Canada alarmed many in the Red River district. Some of them, particularly the métis, were squatters who had no title to their land and feared that the new government would dispossess them. The people of the Red River also resented the fact that they had not been consulted during the negotiations but had been sold like serfs on a medieval manor. Politically they had hoped to become a self-governing province rather than a territory with an appointed administration. The French half-breeds also wished the same constitutional safeguards for their language and religion which their cousins in Quebec enjoyed.

These grievances should have been ameliorated. The government in Ottawa, however, ignored the audible rumblings from the west [5] and dispatched William McDougall, newly appointed lieutenant governor of Manitoba, to his post. In October, 1869, he reached the

[2] Halifax *British Colonist*, December 14, 1867.

[3] Reginald G. Trotter, *Canadian Federation, Its Origin and Achievement* . . . (Toronto, 1924), 222-25.

[4] The British government, through the Governor General, was constantly urging the need for haste upon the Canadians. Lord Monck to the Duke of Buckingham, October 19, 1867, G 573 A, Secret and Confidential Despatches, 1867-1870 (Public Archives of Canada, Ottawa). The course of negotiations may be followed in Canadian *Sessional Papers*, No. 5, Pt. V, 1865 (Ottawa, 1866); and in Ronald S. Longley, "Cartier and McDougall, Canadian Emissaries to London," *Canadian Historical Review* (Toronto), XXVI (March, 1945), 25-41.

[5] John S. Dennis to William McDougall, August 21, 1869, *Sessional Papers*, 1870, V, No. 506. See also Joseph Howe Papers, IX, 695-98 (Public Archives of Canada).

international boundary en route from St. Paul to Winnipeg. Here armed half-breeds met him and, over his astounded protests, turned him back. Discontent had flared into rebellion and the settlement was in the hands of the brilliant but unpredictable leader of the métis, Louis Riel. American annexationists prepared to take advantage of the cloud of uncertainty which hung over the future of western British America. As a basis for understanding the subsequent actions of these gentlemen, it is important to identify them and their several motives.

The *dramatis personae* of this production was a variegated assortment, ranging from the great financier of the Atlantic seaboard to the rough-bearded fur trader of the West. The eastern headquarters of the movement was in Washington where the annexationists were few but noisy. Their leader was Senator Alexander Ramsey of Minnesota who desired to acquire the Red River area because it was an important commercial adjunct to his state. Ramsey was seconded by Senators Zachariah Chandler and Jacob M. Howard of Michigan who represented the merchants of Detroit and saw in annexation of the British West the possibility of increasing Great Lakes trade important to their city. These senators expected the help of President Ulysses S. Grant, a persistent expansionist with no great sense of direction, and of Hamilton Fish, secretary of state. Fish was a nationalist, anxious to see his country grow but handicapped by a confining conscience. He wanted to obtain British North America, not by subterranean intrigue or compulsion, but with the consent of the imperial authorities and the desire of the people concerned.[6]

Near-by Philadelphia contributed an important expansionist, the enigmatic Jay Cooke whose money financed the movement. What Cooke hoped to gain — and he was a firm believer in *quid pro quo* — is not entirely clear but the evidence permits conjecture.[7] He was, at this time, assuming the promotion of the Northern Pacific Railroad. One possible route for it ran north of the border, but construction there might be politically difficult or impossible

[6] Richard W. Van Alstyne, "New Viewpoints in the Relations of Canada and the United States," *Canadian Historical Review*, XXV (June, 1944), 128; Charles P. Stacey, "The Military Aspect of Canada's Winning of the West, 1870-1885," *ibid.*, XXI (March, 1940), 7.

[7] Joseph A. Wheelock to Alexander Ramsey, April 7, 1870, Alexander Ramsey Papers (Minnesota Historical Society, St. Paul); Henrietta M. Larson, *Jay Cooke, Private Banker* (Cambridge, Mass., 1936), 335-38.

if the boundary continued to exist. On the other hand, if the road were built south of the line, the country north of it, in American hands, would be an important feeder area. Should Canada acquire this area, a Canadian railroad would be built and a Canadian tariff erected as an effective ceiling on the region tributary to the Northern Pacific.

Ramsey, Cooke, and the other eastern expansionists gave pecuniary and political support to the movement. For direct action they depended upon their western brethren, principally in Minnesota. That state, and particularly St. Paul, seemed to swarm with annexationists. The reasons were not far to seek. Manifest Destiny was a persistent force in such pioneer communities and here it was supercharged with strong economic interests. Foremost was the desire to retain and expand the trade with the Red River area, already valued at between one and two million dollars a year.[8] If Manitoba were absorbed into the Dominion, an east-west Canadian road would soon be built and would slash through this north-south commercial artery.[9] Besides, Minnesota railroads, other than the Northern Pacific, also hoped to profit from the annexation. The St. Paul & Pacific, for example, was building into Breckenridge, Minnesota, and hoped to bend its line northward at that point and continue up the Red River Valley to Winnipeg. To aid this enterprise the road was fishing for a federal land grant and its lobbyists in Congress were using the expansionist agitation for bait, arguing that the road would increase the pressure on the people of the British North-West to join the United States. They wished to keep the annexationist movement alive at least until they had obtained the desired grant.[10] These Minnesota expansionists had an able spokesman in Joseph A. Wheelock, editor of the St. Paul *Daily Press* who constantly and powerfully urged annexation and actively joined in the intrigues to get it.

But St. Paul was not the only center of annexationism in the

[8] St. Paul *Daily Press*, February 11, 1870; Alexandria (Minn.) *Post*, August 7, 1869; J. Fletcher Williams, *A History of the City of St. Paul, and of the County of Ramsey, Minnesota* (St. Paul, 1876), 304-306; W. G. Fonseca, "On the St. Paul Trail in the Sixties," Historical and Scientific Society of Manitoba, *Transactions* (Winnipeg), No. 56 (January, 1900).

[9] St. Paul *Daily Press*, February 3, 1870.

[10] George L. Becker to James W. Taylor, December 18, 1869, March 3, 1870, James Wickes Taylor Papers (Minnesota Historical Society); St. Paul *Daily Press*, May 19, 1870.

West, for another group was active at Pembina, Dakota Territory, where it was able to make its influence immediately felt in the Red River settlement. One of the principals here was Colonel Enos Stutsman, treasury agent at the customhouse and a wily politician [11] who became for a time a confidential adviser to Louis Riel. Also prominent was Joseph (Joe) Rolette, Jr., whose hirsute countenance peers frequently from the pages of Minnesota and Dakota history. The amiable Joe had his reasons for desiring annexation. He was a typical frontier product, the capitalist jack-of-all-trades, deeply involved in politics, land speculation, and the fur trade.[12] He knew that the Red River Valley soil was rich, that it would be settled more rapidly as American than as Canadian territory, and that, as the local land dealer, he would reap a rich harvest of profits if annexation came.[13]

The tentacles of the movement did not stop at Pembina but curled north into the Red River colony itself, and even into the inner circles of Riel's group. There were several small but active groups of annexationists in Fort Garry and Winnipeg. The most vocal was the clump of American settlers in the region, but they were not alone in their opinion. Some of the employees of the company were reported to be quietly urging that the colony join the United States rather than the Dominion. Their motive was emotional — they did not love the republic, but they did hate Canada. [14] Another group which took a similar stand was a handful of priests. This is surprising, for the Roman Catholic Church in Canada has always been an impregnable bulwark against annexation. These exceptions were priests born in France whose detestation of Britain overmatched their allegiance to the polity of their superiors.[15]

Finally, two individuals in the colony merit attention. The first was General Oscar Malmros, American consul in Winnipeg, who guided the métis rebels with one hand and held the other out

[11] George Bryce, *The Remarkable History of the Hudson's Bay Company* (New York, 1910), 463; Henry V. Arnold, *The History of Old Pembina, 1780-1872* (Larimore, N. D., 1917), 149-50.

[12] Arnold, *History of Old Pembina*, 142, 159; St. Paul *Daily Press*, July 19, 1870.

[13] See also John P. Pritchett, "Some Red River Fur-Trade Activities," *Minnesota History Bulletin* (St. Paul), V (May, 1924), 413-17; Clarence W. Rife, "Norman W. Kittson, A Fur Trader in Pembina," *ibid.*, VI (September, 1925), 234-35, 249-51.

[14] Taylor to Hamilton Fish, January 25, 1870, Taylor Papers.

[15] Bryce, *Remarkable History of the Hudson's Bay Company*, 463-64; Wheelock to Ramsey, April 7, 1870, Ramsey Papers.

to Washington to beg aid for them. The other was W. E. B. O'Donoghue, a mysterious adventurer, most of whose career is lost in the mists of obscurity. He was born in Ireland and migrated to the United States where he became a citizen. Like his kind, who seem instinctively to go where impending trouble stirs, he popped up in the Red River district shortly before the uprising. He eagerly joined Riel and rose rapidly to a position of prominence in the ranks of the rebellion. O'Donoghue's Irish origin and his American citizenship frame the motivation of his ardent, but not always wise, efforts to promote annexation.[16]

Even this brief description reveals the miscellaneous composition of the annexation movement in geography and motive. It remains to mention the human cement which bound together this conglomerate — James Wickes Taylor. Taylor, formerly state librarian of Ohio, was the greatest American authority on western British America and peddled his knowledge to advantage. During the period of the revolt the Department of State employed him as a secret agent to keep Fish posted on Red River affairs[17]; at the same time he was also serving as informant and publicist for Cooke and for George Becker, general manager of the St. Paul & Pacific. Taylor, however, was more than a hack for special interests. He believed sincerely in the mutual benefits and the ultimate inevitability of annexation. He knew all of the groups of expansionists, commuted between the centers of agitation, and became the liaison man for the movement. Its failure was not due to any lack of ability or effort on his part.[18]

Thus the annexation movement south of the line had many of the ingredients of success: leadership, money, and influence. It also had opportunity north of the line, for Riel had revolted against rule from Canada but seemed at first to know what he did not want rather than what he did want. The annexationists had a positive answer to this question. Moreover, their agitation had been going on quietly for some years, and the foundations of their work were laid.

16 I. Persons, "W. B. O'Donoghue" (Minnesota Historical Society).

17 Fish to Taylor, December 30, 1869, Instructions to Special Missions, 1852-1886 (National Archives).

18 For a description of his career, see the comprehensive article by Theodore C. Blegen, "James Wickes Taylor: A Biographical Sketch," *Minnesota History Bulletin*, I (November, 1915), 153-219.

Although the annexation movement began much earlier, it had slumbered for some years until Senator Ramsey abruptly reawakened it in December, 1867, by introducing a bill which would grant Canada practically a restoration of the recently terminated Reciprocity Treaty of 1854. This was no gift. In return, Canada must abandon to the United States all territory west of ninety degrees of longitude. The American government would pay the Hudson's Bay Company $6,000,000 for its rights, assume the debt of British Columbia up to $2,000,000, and subsidize the building of the Northern Pacific to Puget Sound.[19] The fact that Canada did not own one foot of this land was beside the point. She obviously had an option on the territory and Ramsey proposed to buy it up.

This bill did not pass but it spurred on the negotiations between Canada and the company, whose success caused no rejoicing in Ramsey's state. Instead, the Minnesota legislature adopted a resolution of protest and forwarded it to Congress. This document deplored the fact that the territories had been transferred to Canada without holding a plebiscite of the inhabitants, "An unwarrantable interference with the principle of self-government . . . [which] cannot be regarded with indifference by the people of the United States." The resolution added that "the cession of Northwest British America to the United States accompanied by the construction of a Northern Pacific Railroad should be regarded by Great Britain and Canada as satisfactory provisions of a treaty which shall remove all grounds of controversy between the respective countries."[20] In short, Minnesota proposed to trade the *Alabama* claims for western British America. Congress had this address printed but otherwise ignored the promptings from Minnesota.

The indifference of the federal government banked the fires of annexation in the West for a time. No further protests were heard and it seemed that the Dominion would quietly take possession of Manitoba on December 1, 1869. Manfully trying to conceal its disappointment, the St. Paul *Daily Pioneer* observed that "we do not know as we want Canada very bad . . . we had better become

[19] *Senate Miscellaneous Documents*, No. 4, 40 Cong., 2 Sess., 4. An earlier bill, introduced into the House by General Nathaniel P. Banks, provided for the annexation of British America with a payment of $10,000,000 to the company for its lands. Taylor drafted both bills. "Commercial Relations with British America," *House Executive Documents*, No. 128, 39 Cong., 1 Sess., 34.

[20] Minnesota *General Laws*, 10 Sess. (March, 1868).

reconstructed, secure our finances and see if we are able to take good care of what we have before assuming the charge of much more."[21]

A few rays of hope, however, were soon filtering through this gloom. One advocate of political union saw that the form of government which Canada was imposing on its new subjects was a "complete proconsulship"; he predicted that it would be "obnoxious" to the people of the Red River.[22] As this forecast was substantiated and the soon-to-be Manitobans grew restless, the American annexationists perked up. They were neither startled nor unprepared when the little settlement broke into revolt. Indeed it is quite possible that the expansionists in Pembina and Winnipeg gave Riel and Destiny a push forward by prodding the métis into this action.[23]

Whether or not they prompted the uprising, the annexationists knew an opportunity when they saw one and immediately swung into action. Early events in the West took a favorable turn for them. Having repulsed McDougall, Riel seized Fort Garry, center of the company's power, and thereby destroyed the only government in the colony.[24] A political vacuum was thus created and the annexationists, hoping that the United States could rush in to fill it, sought to exploit the uncertain situation to gain control of the revolt. Three of them began to exert their influence on Riel who, though no pliant tool, was willing to listen to advice. Colonel Stutsman was particularly active at this time, constantly commuting between Pembina and Fort Garry.[25] Between trips he acted as Riel's unofficial "consul" at the border, issuing or denying the passes necessary to cross the line. He also joined the other inhabitants of Pembina in the agreeable winter sport of baiting McDougall and compounding the misery of that frustrated functionary who had fled to the Dakota post after being turned back by the métis.

Malmros, who had no pent-up sense of responsibility as the representative of a friendly power, was nearly as active as Stutsman.

21 St. Paul *Daily Pioneer*, July 31, 1869.

22 Taylor to Ramsey, June 14, 1869, Taylor Papers.

23 Bryce, *Remarkable History of the Hudson's Bay Company*, 463.

24 As the history of the rebellion is well known, no attempt has been made to give more than the outline necessary to carry the annexation story.

25 St. Paul *Daily Pioneer*, January 1, 1870; Alexander Begg, *The Creation of Manitoba* . . . (Toronto, 1871), 84, 91, 199, 201, 215.

He had anticipated the uprising and, before it broke out, informed the Department of State that trouble threatened and that he would be glad to organize a force and seize the region for the United States when the time was ripe.[26] The meticulous and proper Fish probably approached apoplexy when he read this dispatch. If so, he recovered in time to veto Malmros's proposal sharply and lectured him sternly on the necessity of strict neutrality. The consul, obviously regarding his chief as a spoilsport, took these instructions lightheartedly. Within a short time he was reporting to a fellow worker in the annexation vineyard that he had "materially assisted in producing the present situation [of revolt] & prevented many mistakes on the part of the popular leaders." [27]

O'Donoghue, who carried more weight than either Malmros or Stutsman among the rebels, also worked constantly during this period to convert the uprising into an annexation movement. There is evidence that he and his associates exerted a strong influence on Riel and were largely responsible for such moves as the seizure of Fort Garry.

The annexationists thus had a dangerous grasp on the helm of the rebellion in its early months and, for a time, it appeared that they might steer the colony into the United States. McDougall unwittingly helped them on their course. Thwarted and embittered, he listened to foolish advice and issued a proclamation announcing his appointment as lieutenant governor and the transfer of the region to Canada. This pronouncement played into the hands of the American party. It set the Red River colony legally adrift by officially canceling the company's power but not providing a substitute for it since McDougall could not enter the territory. The confusion was completed when the government in Ottawa refused to accept the transfer of the territory from the company while the revolt persisted. Thus, by default, Riel was the *de facto* government and Riel seemed to be guided by the annexationists.

McDougall was not through playing the fool. He also commissioned one of his lieutenants to cross the border, rally all loyal men, and attack the rebels. His call to arms was a fiasco but nearly provoked a disastrous bloodletting. Such irresponsible action drove

26 Oscar Malmros to John C. B. Davis, September 11, 1869, Consular Despatches, Winnipeg, I (National Archives).

27 Malmros to Ramsey, January 6, 1870, Ramsey Papers.

many who had mistrusted Riel into support of the métis. For the time Canada stood repudiated in the Red River Valley.

This was the loud knock of opportunity and the annexationists hastened to answer it. Stutsman moved from Pembina to Fort Garry and clung to Riel's side, ready to press any advantage which might emerge from the cloud of uncertainty.[28] O'Donoghue, now the treasurer of the provisional government which Riel had established after McDougall's proclamation, joined Malmros and Stutsman in placing the young métis leader under a heavy bombardment of advice. But it was not enough to have Riel's ear; the annexationists also attempted to broaden their base of action by winning popular support when a means to do so offered. They bought a moribund local newspaper, the *Red River Pioneer*, for £550, an expenditure painless to all except the company from whose strong box it was seized,[29] rechristened it the *New Nation*, and placed it in the hands of Major Henry Robinson, an American-born annexationist.[30]

The leading article in the first edition starkly revealed its political orientation. Entitled "Annexation our 'Manifest Destiny,'" it argued that the colony should follow its purse strings into the United States rather than be tied by its heartstrings to the British Empire. The article stated the obvious fact that the republic was the principal market and means of communication for the Red River area and must remain so for years to come. A commercial tie with Canada was impossible across the tumbled sea of rock which intervened for seven hundred miles between Winnipeg and the nearest inhabited portions of Ontario. Editor Robinson also pointed out that union with the republic was the order of the day; movements for that purpose existed from the Maritime Provinces on the east to British Columbia on the west, and it was time that Manitoba joined the rest.[31]

The annexationists thus baldly bid for the prize. But the Canadian government, now shaken out of its complacency, was not going to let the game go by default. The Governor General of the Dominion issued a proclamation stating that the way was open for the

28 Begg, *Creation of Manitoba*, 195.
29 *Ibid.*
30 Taylor to Fish, January 27, 1870, Department of State, Special Agent, Red River Affairs (National Archives).
31 Fort Garry *New Nation*, January 14, 1870.

redress of the legitimate grievances of the Red River people. Three commissioners were appointed by Sir John A. Macdonald, the prime minister, and sent out with instructions to probe the disaffections and allay the fears of the Manitobans. This mission constituted a serious threat to the annexationists. If Canada met Manitoban demands, the chances for political union with the United States might shrivel. Riel's pro-American advisers apparently met this threat by persuading their leader to receive the commissioners coldly and to prevent them from establishing contact with the people of the colony by keeping them as house prisoners.[32]

The future thus hung in the balance early in January, 1870. Outwardly the annexationists occupied a strong position. Their leaders were close to Riel and were blaring their wares to the people in the *New Nation*. Riel had not declared for them, but his acceptance of their advice and his easy toleration of their open agitation seemed to speak for him. On the other hand, however, most of the people of the settlement seemed eager to learn the intentions of the government in Ottawa from the Canadian commissioners and to suspend their opposition to the Dominion if their grievances were redressed. If this were true, annexation would become only their last desperate resort and the ultimate destiny of the Red River colony would be decided by the wisdom and generosity of the Canadian government and not by the machinations of agitators.

While the annexationists at Fort Garry were making their strike for success, their colleagues in the United States had not been idle. In Minnesota, press, politicians, and merchants united to build up public interest in the acquisition of Manitoba. Ignatius Donnelly declared that "If the revolutionists of the Red River are encouraged and sustained by the avowed sympathy of the American people, we may . . . see the Stars and Stripes wave from Fort Garry, from the waters of Puget Sound, and along the shores of Vancouver." [33] The St. Paul Chamber of Commerce called a public meeting and loosed the same orator upon it. Donnelly spent an enjoyable evening twisting the lion's tail by urging the seizure of the British North-West to repay its former owners for their recent sympathies with the Confederate States. Public reactions indicated that this was a popular sentiment, and the press was not far behind. Both the St.

[32] Begg, *History of the North-West,* I, 439.

[33] Speech quoted at length in the St. Paul *Daily Pioneer,* November 24, 1869.

Paul *Daily Press* and the St. Paul *Daily Pioneer* clamored for Manitoba. The *Pioneer*, however, soon lost interest and sourly commented that annexation was impossible because the people of the Red River district did not want it.[34] This change of heart, which represented either an objective analysis of the situation or a congenital inability to agree with the rival *Press*, did not notably decrease the noise of the annexationists.

The eastern annexationists also worked earnestly. Ramsey, undeterred by the cold indifference to his earlier bill, again sought to stir the sluggish appetite of Congress for territory. He introduced a resolution calling on the President to submit all available information regarding the revolt. The motion passed, although the Senate showed no interest in it and several members remarked that the troubles were "none of our business." Ramsey hotly retorted that the future of Manitoba was of vital concern to Minnesota at least. The people of the Red River, he added, should decide their own future. If Manitoba and British Columbia expressed a desire to join the republic, the American government could buy Canada off by giving her commercial union.[35] President Grant soon submitted the desired information, but Congress ignored it.

The executive department was equally cool to the annexation project. As we have seen, Fish wanted to acquire Canada only with the consent of its inhabitants, and he had already rapped Malmros's knuckles for proposing unneutral action. The Consul, who had carefully concealed his subsequent actions from his chief, now tried to work on Fish through Ramsey. He informed the Senator that the métis desired union with the United States and would fight for it if they could get financial support. Success had a specific price — "$100,000 would make the annexation movement a success."[36] Ramsey was impressed and suggested to Fish that money from the secret service fund be used for that purpose. The Secretary brusquely refused to take part in such subterranean practices.[37] He did show a spark of interest, however, when Malmros directly informed him that many of the Hudson's Bay Company employees desired

[34] *Ibid.*, January 1, 5, 29, 1870.

[35] *Cong. Globe*, 41 Cong., 2 Sess., 3, 29-30, 932-34.

[36] Malmros to Ramsey, January 14, 1870, Ramsey Papers.

[37] Allan Nevins, *Hamilton Fish; The Inner History of the Grant Administration* (New York, 1936), 387. See also Stacey, "Military Aspect of Canada's Winning of the West," *Canadian Historical Review*, XXI (March, 1940), 8.

the union of the settlement with the United States and had urged it upon their superiors in London.[38] Here was an indication of annexationist sentiment in the colony itself. Fish promptly made inquiries in London to learn whether high company officials favored American acquisition of the North-West.[39] When he found that they did not,[40] he lost interest in the Red River colony.

Thus by January, 1870, success had evaded the annexationists and promised to become more elusive as time passed. The American government and public, except for Minnesotans, were largely indifferent, and the foundations of the movement in the colony itself were eroding. This disintegration soon accelerated. One of the commissioners from Canada, Donald A. Smith, finally secured Riel's reluctant permission to hold a public meeting and deliver the message of the government in Ottawa. He assured the people that Canada would give careful consideration to their grievances and rights. These tidings were welcomed by all classes except the American party. A convention was elected to draw up a list of rights to be sent to Ottawa for the consideration of the federal government. This list, as amended by Riel, asked such concessions as the admission of Manitoba as a province rather than a territory, confirmation of landholdings, protection for French rights, and a complete pardon for all who had been connected with the rebellion. In the selection of a committee to bear this list to Canada the annexationists were given a faint new hope. One of the delegates chosen was Alfred H. Scott, reputedly a member of the American party. If Scott were not an annexationist, he was soon to be keeping strange company.

These activities were, in all other respects, a heavy blow to the expansionists. An obdurate Canada might have driven the people of the Red River into the arms of the United States; a conciliatory Canada was tempering their hot wrath into warm affection. Moreover, Riel had now gained the support of nearly all elements of the population. His bold stand for Manitoban rights was winning a better deal for the entire population, white as well as métis.

Now, as the attitude of the whites towards Riel changed, so did his attitude towards the annexationists. What the young leader

38 Malmros to Davis, December 24, 1869, Consular Despatches, Winnipeg, I, 19.

39 Fish to John Motley, January 14, 1870, Diplomatic Instructions, Great Britain, XXII (National Archives).

40 Motley to Fish, February 2, 1870, *ibid.*, CI.

actually thought of them is something of a mystery and the conflicting reports of his contemporaries are no help in solving it. His previous toleration of their activities and acceptance of their counsel are susceptible of several explanations. Perhaps he was willing to see the colony join the United States if a majority of its inhabitants clearly desired to do so; the popular reception of the Canadian commissioners would dispel all doubt on this score. On the other hand, perhaps he tolerated their activities and teased their hopes because he needed the support of some element of the white population to give an appearance of interracial unity to his movement.[41] Whatever the reason for his previous attitude towards the annexationists, he now began to tighten the tether on them. The first to be brought up short was Major Robinson, editor of the *New Nation*, who had ranged far in the columns of his paper. Riel suddenly suppressed one edition and ruthlessly censored later ones in advance, tearing out all references to annexation. As a further token of his displeasure, he cast the unhappy Robinson into jail for a time.[42]

Another blow soon smote the annexationists. O'Donoghue, an uninhibited spirit, took it into his head to cut down the British flag which Riel had hoisted over Fort Garry, and substituted for it a flag of the rebellion, a concoction featuring shamrocks and fleurs-de-lis. Riel restored the Union Jack and bluntly warned O'Donoghue that his brains would be blown out if he again molested it. This episode abruptly ended O'Donoghue's usefulness to the American party.[43]

Meanwhile, Consul Malmros had likewise suffered in this attrition of leadership. This considerate official had enlivened his dispatches to Washington by the inclusion of some delightful but indiscreet characterizations of prominent Manitobans. Perhaps

41 Morton holds that Riel was British in fundamental loyalty. He played along with the annexationists so that, if the Canadian government proved obdurate and tried to crush his rebellion by force, he could appeal for American aid. Morton, *History of the Canadian West*, 896-97.

42 St. Paul *Daily Press*, April 22, 1870. The annexationists in the colony complained bitterly to an American visitor that Riel had pretended to favor them to get their support, then had turned upon them when they were no longer necessary. However, the same visitor reported that both O'Donoghue and Riel told him that they favored annexation but would be honor bound to take Manitoba into the Dominion if Sir John A. Macdonald met their terms. Nathaniel P. Langford to Taylor, June 12, 1870, Taylor Papers.

43 Henry Robinson to Davis, May 10, 1870, Consular Despatches, Winnipeg, I.

feeling that it would be criminal to hide this deathless prose unappreciated in the dust of a remote archive, the Department of State shared the gems with the world by publishing them. When Malmros learned this, he wrote a letter of despair to Ramsey, groaning that when the publications reached the Red River his position would become "untenable, impracticable and, in fact, intolerable." Having made this point fairly clear, he added that he intended to flee the colony that very night though he was ill, the climate was Arctic, and snow blocked the roads. This he did, not even pausing to send a formal letter of resignation to the Department of State.[44]

Battered by adversity, deprived of leadership, and frightened by the lowering hostility of Riel, the annexationists in the colony abruptly ceased their agitation.[45] But the expansionists in the United States continued to work in high gear and spirits and planned a bold stroke for success in the spring of 1870. Early in April, William Marshall, former governor of Minnesota and one of Cooke's associates, appeared in the Red River colony and there closeted himself with Riel for a long interview. Although no record of this meeting seems to have survived, other evidence indicates that Marshall promised financial and military aid to Riel if he would turn his revolt into an annexation movement.[46] Meanwhile, the three delegates bearing Manitoba's "List of Rights" to Canada had arrived in St. Paul. Scott soon found his way to Wheelock, and another mysterious meeting took place. The editor, rejoicing, wrote to Ramsey that the list contained demands which "are preposterous and extravagant to the last degree and were obviously devised, as I am assured they were [by Scott?] for the express purpose of being rejected." Should this occur, the shock of disappointment might well impel the Manitobans to seek the United States. Wheelock added that "without letting Scott into the secret of the movement on foot, I assured him . . . with emphasis that if the Red River people desired to keep Canada out . . . they could depend on the co-operation of powerful interests in the United States which stood ready to lend whatever material aid was necessary."

44 Malmros to Ramsey, March 15, 1870, Ramsey Papers.

45 Langford to Taylor, July 10, 1870, Taylor Papers.

46 Cooke had hoped to reach some tacit understanding with Riel. Larson, *Jay Cooke*, 338. Marshall's trip smacks strongly of a secret mission, for it was not mentioned in the press, which was printing every scrap of news and rumor which concerned the Red River. Over a month later his journey was casually and inconspicuously referred to. St. Paul *Daily Press*, May 14, 1870.

Wheelock concluded by saying that he had arranged for an interview between Scott and Cooke and by urging that Riel be supplied with "one or two batteries [of artillery] and men to work them." [47]

This letter is both promising and provocative. It reveals that the American annexationists had a specific plan of action; at the same time, it leaves several questions unanswered. Precisely what was "the movement on foot?" How did "the powerful interests in the United States" intend to get aid to the rebels, and what would be the attitude of the American government to such adventures? Scraps of evidence indicate that the annexationists mooted an armed expedition to aid Riel if he would divert his movement into the desired channels. Certainly the nation which had produced William Walker could spawn another "grey-eyed man of destiny" to lead filibusters to the north. But the planned coup was never delivered. Perhaps Riel rejected the suggestion of an armed expedition if, indeed, Marshall proposed it to him. Or the results of the Manitoban mission to Ottawa, to be recounted below, may have convinced the Cooke cabal that the project was hopeless. Whatever the reason, the American annexationists made no further move.

The game was also drawing to a losing conclusion in Washington, despite the efforts of Ramsey and Chandler. The latter introduced a resolution into the Senate in April, 1870, requesting the President to appoint two commissioners to negotiate with the people of Winnipeg for annexation to the United States.[48] The Senate debated the motion on April 22, and Chandler enlivened the occasion by hurling some verbal thunderbolts, charging that Canada was a nuisance which the United States must abate, and concluding with the assertion that "This continent is ours, and we may as well notify the world . . . that we will fight for our own if we must." [49]

This supreme effort evoked no response from Chandler's colleagues other than an "amused smile of recognition" of the fact that the Senator was riding a favorite hobbyhorse.[50] Even the British minister at Washington, who trembled at every will-o'-the-

[47] Wheelock to Ramsey, April 7, 1870, Ramsey Papers.

[48] *Cong. Globe*, 41 Cong., 2 Sess., 2887-88.

[49] *Ibid.*, 2888-89.

[50] Edward Thornton to the Earl of Clarendon, 167, April 25, 1870, Great Britain, Foreign Office, Ser. V, 1192 (photostatic copy in the Manuscripts Division, Library of Congress).

wisp threat to British possessions, realized that Chandler stood virtually alone in his desire to seize any part of British America by force.[51]

This indifference in Congress reflected the obvious fact that the annexation movement was moribund. It received its *coup de grâce* when the Canadian government accepted most of the demands in Manitoba's "List of Rights" and incorporated them in the Manitoba Act which was pushed through parliament. This bill admitted Manitoba as a province, confirmed existing land titles and occupations, reserved 1,400,000 acres of land for the half-breeds and their children, and established a separate school system. To pacify Ontario, furious at this coddling of French half-breed rebels,[52] an armed expedition was sent to confirm Canadian possession.

As this act conceded more than the people of the Red River had dared to hope, the proposed military expedition was now the only straw at which the annexationists could clutch. From the safety of his editorial chair, Wheelock hopefully urged the Red River people to resist this "armed invasion," slyly hinting that there were numerous places where it might be ambushed and reporting that Fenians were gathering near the border to go to the aid of Riel.[53] The Manitobans ignored these suggestions, and the paper bullets from St. Paul were the only ones fired at the expedition. It reached the Red River country late in August and found that Riel had discreetly departed from Fort Garry. The métis army quietly dispersed and Manitoba entered the Dominion as its fifth province.[54]

Thus the movement to add the British North-West to the United States ended its career. The reasons for its failure are several. Most obviously, it did not succeed because the people of the Red River settlement preferred Canada to the United States. The métis were hostile to annexation because it would spoil the chances of the Roman Catholic Church whose hierarchy hoped to make Manitoba into a new Quebec, peopled with the surplus population

[51] Thornton to Sir John Young, April 23, 1870, Ser. G, 147, No. 1417 (Public Archives of Canada).

[52] English Canadians were especially outraged because Riel had executed one Thomas Scott, an Ontario Orangeman. This unfortunate episode revived bitter race hatred in Canada and was largely responsible for the sending of the expedition.

[53] St. Paul *Daily Press*, May 18, 1870.

[54] For an account of an attempted annexation expedition from the United States a little later, see John P. Pritchett, "The Origin of the So-Called Fenian Raid on Manitoba in 1871," *Canadian Historical Review*, X (March, 1929), 23-42.

of that eastern province.[55] If Manitoba joined the United States, American settlers would swarm in and thwart this plan. Moreover, the American Constitution did not offer the special position and privileges which the Church and other French institutions enjoyed under the British North America Act. Hence the métis, the bulk of the population, were impervious to the attempted infiltration of the annexationists. The white population, aside from the exceptions noted, also opposed union with the republic. Some of them had recently come from Canada and were eager for political reunion with their former country. Most of the rest were from the British Isles and had brought with them both a love of their native land and an aversion to the United States.

Deep-seated and unremedied grievances against Canada and the imperial government might have upset the loyalties of both the métis and whites and driven them into the arms of the United States. The grievances, however, were of a nature which the Canadian government could remedy. When Macdonald was fully awakened to the danger of the situation and promised redress, resistance to Canada melted and washed away the hopes of the expansionists. It was thus evident that there was little real demand in the British North-West for annexation to the United States. This meant that American expansionists must either abandon their agitation or use force. As we have seen, some of them were willing to fight if there were a chance of success, but there was none. They were too few, their government was hostile, and the great majority of their countrymen were indifferent.

So the movement failed for lack of support. Despite this, it has importance for the historian. For one thing, it indicates that Manifest Destiny did not entirely die out with the Civil War and that the frontier continued to foster the expansionist spirit. Again, it shows a facet of the activities of the railroad builders, an extremely important group in this period. It was the money and influence of these men that made this one of the few annexation movements directed at British America which had organization and important material resources. Finally, the movement had significant effects on Canadian history. There seems little doubt that the agitation was at least partly responsible for the excellent terms by which

[55] Chester Martin, "Confederation and the West," Canadian Historical Association, *Annual Report*, 1927 (Ottawa, n.d.), 22; St. Paul *Daily Pioneer*, May 19, 1870.

Macdonald reconciled the Red River people to entering the Dominion. With the United States in the contest, even though unofficially, he bid high for the prize. Ironically, the annexation movement thus hastened what it was designed to prevent — the union of the British North-West with the Dominion of Canada.

Notes and Documents

Emerson, Thoreau, and John Brown

BY GILMAN M. OSTRANDER

The chief merit of Emerson's life, Wendell Phillips said, was that, having talked about heroism all his life, he recognized the hero when John Brown appeared. Emerson probably would have disagreed. His friend and biographer, James E. Cabot, suggests that he revised his opinion of Brown in later life.[1]

Thoreau, who died less than three years after Brown was executed, seems to have entertained no such later doubts. Emerson, speaking at Thoreau's funeral, mentioned John Brown as one of the men who had most influenced Thoreau in his last years.[2] Whatever their second thoughts may have been, both men, immediately following the Harpers Ferry raid, took a vigorous part in the defense of Brown, and by their eloquent assertions of his saintliness undoubtedly contributed much to the making of the Brown legend.

Emerson, at the time, was sure that history would echo their exalted opinion of Brown.[3] It has not done so. Brown's most recent biographers have shown that he was an embezzler, a murderer, a cattle thief, and an inveterate liar.[4] Something of the nature of Brown's fanaticism was shown by his leadership in the cold-blooded midnight murders of five proslavery men at Pottawatomie Creek, Kansas, in 1856. These murders were committed during the slavery controversy in Kansas Territory in an atmosphere of fear, hatred, confusion, and violence. Nevertheless the Pottawatomie massacre stands out, even in those turbulent times, as a fiendish atrocity. Brown's most sympathetic biographer in the twentieth century can

[1] James E. Cabot, *A Memoir of Ralph Waldo Emerson*, 2 vols. (Boston, 1887), II, 597.

[2] Franklin B. Sanborn, *The Life of Henry David Thoreau* (Boston, 1917), 383.

[3] Ralph Waldo Emerson, *Emerson's Works*, 12 vols. (Boston, 1904), XI, 208-209.

[4] Oswald G. Villard, *John Brown, 1800-1859; A Biography Fifty Years After* (Boston, 1910), 30-41; James C. Malin, *John Brown and the Legend of Fifty-Six* (Philadelphia, 1942), *passim*; Robert P. Warren, *John Brown, The Making of a Martyr* (New York, 1929), *passim*.

find no justification whatever for the deed.[5] It was in the year following this incident that Brown made the acquaintance of Emerson and Thoreau.

Emerson and Thoreau were important to the John Brown myth not only as character witnesses but also as the foremost proponents of the rationale by which Brown and his defenders justified his most hideous acts — that any atrocity is justified if the motives of the doer are pure. The operation of this "transcendental reasoning" is evident in a statement made by John T. Morse, Jr., following the exposure of Brown's leadership in the Pottawatomie massacre:

> We must separate Brown from what Brown did . . . the deed, considered solely in and by itself without getting color or character from the faith and purposes of the actors, was a series of brutal and cowardly murders. The world, however, is well agreed that John Brown was neither brutal, cowardly, nor murderous. He was one who virtuously committed a frightful atrocity, because he believed himself divinely inspired and ordered to do so. To acquit, even to respect him, it is only necessary to admit the sincerity of the belief; and this no one now questions.[6]

In January, 1857, John Brown presented himself to Thoreau and Emerson in Concord as a fighting leader of free-state resistance in Kansas Territory. He told of battles with proslavery Kansans. Two years later he returned to tell of slave-freeing raids on Missouri farms. It was on the basis of these accounts that Emerson and Thoreau marked him as a hero in a righteous cause.

As to the righteousness of the cause, Emerson had already stated his opinion. Speaking during the previous winter at a meeting to raise money for free-state Kansas, he said, "There is this peculiarity about the case of Kansas, that all the right is on one side." [7] At a time when the "bleeding Kansas" issue had excited Americans on both sides to bitter partisanship, Emerson pictured the struggle in simple, vivid terms. On the one hand there were peaceful northern settlers, on the other, "border ruffians." "We hear the screams of hunted wives and children," he said, "answered by the howl of the butchers."

Two days after the Pottawatomie massacre Emerson spoke in Concord Town Hall on Representative Preston Brooks's caning of

[5] Villard, *John Brown*, 187.

[6] "John Brown," *Atlantic Monthly* (Boston), LVII (February, 1886), 273, a review of Franklin B. Sanborn (ed.), *The Life and Letters of John Brown, Liberator of Kansas, and Martyr of Virginia* (Boston, 1885).

[7] *Emerson's Works*, XI, 197.

Senator Charles Sumner. In a burst of impassioned rhetoric, he explained the attack as a symptom of the barbarism of slavery,[8] unhampered by any knowledge of Brown's atrocity, committed in the name of freedom. News of the murders had been distorted or omitted in the eastern press.[9]

Emerson's attitude toward slavery has been thoroughly discussed by various writers.[10] In his early thirties he believed that the Negro was innately inferior to the white man, and that slavery was his natural lot.[11] It was not until 1844 that Emerson publicly repudiated this belief upon making "the proud discovery that the black race can contend with the white."[12] Even so, he still felt that emancipation would come of itself in the South in "a single noble wind of sentiment,"[13] and that abolitionist activity was unnecessary. Then in 1850, when the fugitive slave law involved Massachusetts citizens in the duty of restitution, Emerson rebelled to the extent of refusing to recognize the rights of the slaveholder within his state.[14] This position, reiterated in 1854,[15] was Emerson's most radical stand against slavery.[16] He might not have given Brown so sympathetic a hearing had he not thought of Brown's Kansas battleground in the black and white terms of the Republican press.

Thoreau appeared to have even less reason to approve of Brown's Kansas activities. The very actions Brown was to speak of during his first Concord visit had been denounced by Thoreau a year earlier. "For only absorbing employment prevails . . . and permanently occupies . . . free Kansas against all border ruffians," he wrote. "The attitude of resistance is one of weakness, inasmuch as it only faces an enemy; it has its back to all that is truly attractive."[17]

8 *Ibid.*, 191-92.

9 Malin, *John Brown and the Legend of Fifty-Six*, 89-116.

10 Cabot, *Memoir of Ralph Waldo Emerson*, II, 425-32, 574-98; Marjory M. Moody, "The Evolution of Emerson as an Abolitionist," *American Literature* (Durham), XVII (March, 1945), 1-21; Raymer McQuiston, *The Relation of Ralph Waldo Emerson to Public Affairs*, University of Kansas *Bulletin, Humanistic Series* (Lawrence), III, No. 1 (1923), 35-49.

11 Cabot, *Memoir of Ralph Waldo Emerson*, II, 428-30.

12 *Emerson's Works*, XI, 141.

13 *Ibid.*, 143.

14 Cabot, *Memoir of Ralph Waldo Emerson*, II, 578.

15 *Emerson's Works*, XI, 169-88.

16 Cabot, *Memoir of Ralph Waldo Emerson*, II, 588, 592-93, 595.

17 *The Writings of Henry David Thoreau*, 20 vols. (Walden ed., Boston, 1906), XV, 36.

Furthermore Thoreau, despite an abolitionist background, took no part in the abolitionist movement.[18] He wrote of the movement in terms of whimsical scorn, when he wrote of it at all.[19] His published writings reveal little interest in the question of Negro slavery. He did attack the fugitive slave law in one speech, "Slavery in Massachusetts," delivered in 1854.[20] In doing so, however, he specifically disclaimed concern, as a citizen of Massachusetts, in the question of slavery in Nebraska Territory.

His essay on "Civil Disobedience" was occasioned partly by the slavery question: refusal to pay taxes to support the extension of slave territory by force of arms against Mexico,[21] but the question of slavery is important to the essay only as a point of departure. He avoided the whole issue of abolition by force simply by stating that it was unnecessary, for "if *one* HONEST man, in this State of Massachusetts, *ceasing to hold slaves*, were actually to withdraw from this copartnership, and be locked up in the county jail therefor, it would be the abolition of slavery in America. For it matters not how small the beginning may seem to be: what is once well done is done forever." [22] It is this idea of the efficacy of passive resistance, not slavery nor the Mexican War, that is the central point of the essay. Obviously passive resistance cannot be reconciled with John Brown's act of moving to Kansas with the object — according to his own statement [23] — of fighting slaveholders and freeing slaves.

John Brown's Kansas activities violated Thoreau's precept of passive resistance, but this was only of secondary importance to Thoreau. He had previously refused to deny the righteousness of force in a good cause,[24] and his enthusiasm for Brown was founded on a conviction more fundamental to him than his belief in passive

[18] A thorough study of Thoreau's attitude toward the abolitionist movement is given in Henry S. Canby, *Thoreau* (Boston, 1939). An attempt to prove Thoreau was an abolitionist is made by Nick A. Ford, "Henry David Thoreau, Abolitionist," *New England Quarterly* (Baltimore, Portland), XIX (September, 1946), 359-71.

[19] *Writings of Henry David Thoreau*, VI, 260; Canby, *Thoreau*, 409-11.

[20] *Writings of Henry David Thoreau*, IV, 388-408.

[21] *Ibid.*, 356-87.

[22] *Ibid.*, 370.

[23] According to Professor Malin, land speculation, not antislavery activity, was Brown's primary motive in moving to Kansas Territory. Malin, *John Brown and the Legend of Fifty-Six*, 7-23.

[24] Raymond Adams, "Thoreau's Sources for 'Resistance to Civil Government,'" *Studies in Philology* (Chapel Hill), XLII (July, 1945), 649-50.

resistance or his opinions on the Kansas issue. This conviction is also expressed in "Civil Disobedience."

> I do not hesitate to say, that those who call themselves Abolitionists should at once effectually withdraw their support, both in person and property, from the government of Massachusetts, and not wait till they constitute a majority of one, before they suffer the right to prevail through them. I think that it is enough if they have God on their side without waiting for that other one. Moreover, any man more right than his neighbors constitutes a majority of one already.[25]

For Thoreau, convinced as he was of John Brown's righteousness, there could be no higher law to bind Brown than the private law of his own divinely inspired principles. It was on this fundamental "transcendental" belief that Emerson and Thoreau based their defense of John Brown. They believed that Brown was divinely guided in paths of lawlessness. Mystically obeying the higher law, he was justified in following a course which the ordinary citizen could not honorably follow.

The introspective transcendentalists were themselves far too aware of their own frailties to place themselves in this heroic class, and if one or the other occasionally did feel the need to break the human law at the call of a higher one, the act won him little respect from his fellows. In 1843 Bronson Alcott was jailed for refusing to pay his poll tax, in protest against slavery. Thoreau, at first approving of the gesture, soon complained that Alcott acted as if he had started a revolution.[26] Three years later, when Thoreau spent his night in jail under similar circumstances, Alcott recorded in his journal Emerson's comment that it was " 'mean and skulking, and in bad taste.' "[27]

Emerson's most lawless act was his statement of refusal to cooperate in enforcing the fugitive slave act. He apparently never experienced that intuitive compulsion of a higher law, which was so important a part of his philosophy.[28] On the contrary, he exalted his own law-abiding disposition:

> How much, preventing God, how much I owe
> To the defenses thou hast round me set;

[25] *Writings of Henry David Thoreau*, IV, 369.
[26] Canby, *Thoreau*, 233.
[27] *Ibid.*
[28] George E. Woodberry, *Ralph Waldo Emerson* (New York, 1907), 188-90; Yvor Winters, *In Defense of Reason* (New York, 1947), 279.

Example, custom, fear, occasion slow, —
These scorned bondmen were my parapet.
I dare not peep over this parapet
To gauge with glance the roaring gulf below,
The depths of sin to which I had descended,
Had not these me against myself defended.[29]

Thoreau wrote in "Civil Disobedience," "I came into this world not chiefly to make this a good place to live in, but to live in it, be it good or bad." [30]

The case of John Brown seemed different. In Brown the two transcendentalists saw a man who was, in Emerson's words, "without any mixture of self-indulgence or compromise," [31] a man morally able to count as Thoreau's "majority of one."

John Brown came to New England in January, 1857, a fugitive from justice, feared and hated by many of the free-state Kansas settlers for the private wars his murders had helped to instigate.[32] In New England almost nothing was known of his Kansas activities.[33] He arrived in Concord with a letter of introduction to Franklin B. Sanborn, then a young Concord schoolmaster.[34] As secretary of the Massachusetts State Kansas Committee, Sanborn introduced Brown to men who were eventually to finance the Harpers Ferry raid.[35] He also introduced Brown to his Concord neighbors, Thoreau and Emerson.

> I . . . took . . . [Brown] with me at noon, across the street, to dine at Mrs. Thoreau's table, where I was then dining daily . . . and at two o'clock I left Brown and Thoreau discussing Kansas affairs in Mrs. Thoreau's dining room. . . . Brown narrated in detail to Thoreau his most noted battle in Kansas — that of Black Jack, the June before, where, with nine men, he captured twenty-odd men. . . .[36]

While Thoreau and Brown sat thus conversing in the early afternoon

[29] *Emerson's Works*, IX, 343.
[30] *Writings of Henry David Thoreau*, IV, 368.
[31] *Emerson's Works*, XI, 217.
[32] Malin, *John Brown and the Legend of Fifty-Six*, 77, 590.
[33] *Ibid.*, 230.
[34] Franklin B. Sanborn, *Recollections of Seventy Years*, 2 vols. (Boston, 1900), I, 84.
[35] Villard, *John Brown*, 271.
[36] The exact details of the Battle of Black Jack are still unclear, but Brown apparently omitted from his account the fact that fifteen or sixteen free-state men were involved in addition to his own small command, and that larger reinforcements were moving in at the time of the surrender. Malin, *John Brown and the Legend of Fifty-Six*, 589-90.

of a short winter day, Emerson, who had returned from his Western lecture-tour, came up, as he often did, to call on Thoreau, and was introduced by him to John Brown. He invited Brown to his own house . . . the second night of this two-days' visit at Concord. . . . From the conversation at Thoreau's . . . and from the longer intercourse of Saturday night, when Brown was Emerson's guest, came to Emerson and Thoreau that intimate knowledge of Brown's character and general purpose which qualified them, in October, 1859, to make those addresses on his behalf which were the first response among American scholars to the heroism of the man. . . .[37]

Several days after this first meeting Emerson heard Brown speak in Concord and recorded in his journal:

Captain John Brown of Kansas gave a good account of himself in the Town Hall, last night. . . .

He believes on his own experience that one good, believing, strong-minded man is worth a hundred, nay, twenty thousand men without character, for a settler in a new country; and that the right men will give a permanent direction to the fortunes of a state.[38]

The following month Emerson asked that a small subscription he had made to the Lyceum be given to John Brown for the Kansas project,[39] and Thoreau wrote later in his journal, " 'I subscribed a trifle when he was here three years ago. I had so much confidence in the man — that he would do right.' " [40]

What Brown told the two men may be learned from reading their speeches about him, delivered after the Harpers Ferry raid.[41] Emerson and Thoreau had probably never heard of the Pottawatomie massacre, and Brown obviously made no direct mention of it. Even to so trusted a friend as Sanborn, who had heard of the incident, Brown denied having taken part in it.[42] He apparently spoke to them only of the skirmishes which were later played up as the vital factor in the success of the free Kansas movement. The details of his Kansas exploits were of secondary importance to Emerson and Thoreau, however. They were more impressed by his man-

[37] Sanborn, *Recollections of Seventy Years*, I, 103, 104-105.

[38] Edward W. Emerson and Waldo E. Forbes (eds.), *Journals of Ralph Waldo Emerson*, 10 vols. (Boston, 1909-1914), IX, 81-82.

[39] Ralph L. Rusk (ed.), *The Letters of Ralph Waldo Emerson*, 6 vols. (New York, 1939), V, 69.

[40] *Writings of Henry David Thoreau*, XVIII, 437.

[41] *Ibid.*, IV, 409-54; *Emerson's Works*, XI, 207-18. An account of the Concord funeral services for Brown, in which both took part, is given in James Redpath (ed.), *Echoes of Harper's Ferry* (Boston, 1860), 437-54.

[42] Malin, *John Brown and the Legend of Fifty-Six*, 349.

ner and motives than by his deeds. The way the self-righteous man of action impressed them is recorded in Thoreau's account of the first meeting.

> I noticed that he did not overstate anything, but spoke within bounds. I remember, particularly, how, in his speech here, he referred to what his family had suffered in Kansas, without ever giving the least vent to his pent-up fire. It was a volcano with an ordinary chimney-flue. . . .[43]
>
> When I expressed surprise that he could live in Kansas with a price set upon his head, and so large a number, including the authorities, exasperated against him, he accounted for it by saying, "It is perfectly well understood that I will not be taken. . . ." [44]
>
> Yet he did not attribute his success, foolishly, to "his star," or to any magic. He said, truly, that the reason why such greatly superior numbers quailed before him was, as one of his prisoners confessed, because they *lacked a cause*. . . .[45]

"For himself," Emerson said, "he is so transparent that all men see him through. He is a man to make friends wherever on earth courage and integrity are esteemed, the rarest of heroes, a pure idealist, with no by-ends of his own." [46]

In Brown they believed they had found "a transcendental saint." He was, Thoreau said, "a transcendentalist above all, a man of ideas and principles, — that was what distinguished him." [47] This was the basis for their enthusiasm for the man; it was also the basis, at least in part, for the crucial limitations of their understanding of him. While Brown used the same terms they used, he differed widely from them in his fields of experience and habits of thought. They appear sometimes to have been misled by the deceptive familiarity of his words. Emerson, who spoke out against slavery occasionally in masterful metaphor, almost certainly misunderstood the literal words of Brown:

> He believes in two articles — two instruments, shall I say? — the Golden Rule and the Declaration of Independence; and he used this expression in conversation here concerning them. "Better that a whole generation of men, women and children should pass away by a violent death, than that one word of either should be violated in this country." [48]

[43] *Writings of Henry David Thoreau*, IV, 413.
[44] *Ibid.*, 415.
[45] *Ibid.*, 416.
[46] *Emerson's Works*, XI, 208.
[47] *Writings of Henry David Thoreau*, IV, 413.
[48] *Emerson's Works*, XI, 208.

As Robert Penn Warren has pointed out,[49] this was a statement Emerson himself might conceivably have made. In his speech on the caning of Senator Sumner he declared that the whole population of South Carolina was as nothing compared with the solitary man that one member of that population had struck down. For Emerson the comparison was used to honor Sumner and disparage the southern slaveholder. When Brown used a similar comparison, Emerson must have assumed that Brown used it as an eloquent literary convention, not as a literal statement.

Thoreau seems to have been similarly misled by Brown's literal speech. From Brown's conversation he recalled:

> Also referring to the deeds of certain Border Ruffians, he said, rapidly paring away his speech, like an experienced soldier, keeping a reserve of force and meaning, "They had a perfect right to be hung." He was not in the least a rhetorician, was not talking to Buncombe or his constituents anywhere, had no need to invent anything, but to tell the simple truth, and communicate his own resolution. . . .[50]

Of this statement, Sanborn, who was present at the meeting, wrote, "Brown had in his mind then, no doubt, the five victims of his Pottawatomie executions."[51] If so, Thoreau underestimated that "reserve of force and meaning."

Sanborn gave a further instance of Thoreau's misinterpretation of the literal Brown. Speaking of Brown's trip to Europe, Thoreau said:

> There, as everywhere, he had his eyes about him and made many original observations. He said, for instance, that he saw why the soil of England was so rich, and that of Germany (I think it was) so poor. . . . It was because in England the peasantry live on the soil which they cultivate, but in Germany they are gathered into villages at night.[52]

The idea of the rewarding nature of a closer relationship between the peasant and his land would have appealed to Thoreau, the transcendental naturalist. Sanborn noted, however, that "What Brown said to me on this topic was, that this retiring from the fields to sleep in the villages, with their cattle and horses, was 'taking the natural manures away from the soil' in German and Belgian rural districts."[53]

[49] Warren, *John Brown, The Making of a Martyr*, 245-46.
[50] *Writings of Henry David Thoreau*, IV, 413-14.
[51] Sanborn, *Recollections of Seventy Years*, I, 112.
[52] *Writings of Henry David Thoreau*, IV, 410.
[53] Sanborn, *Recollections of Seventy Years*, I, 111.

The confusion was heightened by other resemblances to themselves which they saw in Brown. "He was by descent and birth a New England farmer, a man of great common sense, deliberate and practical as that class is, and tenfold more so," [54] said Thoreau. Emerson said, "He was happily a representative of the American Republic. Captain John Brown is a farmer, the fifth in descent from Peter Brown, who came to Plymouth in the Mayflower in 1620." [55] They admired the good New England stock from which Brown came. They also spoke highly of his New England Puritanism. This emphasis on Brown as a "fair specimen of the best stock of New England" is particularly heavy in Emerson's speeches. Thoreau, while he explained Brown in terms of New England virtues, soon found them too confining. For the grandeur of Brown's militant Puritanism, Thoreau found adequate precedent only in Cromwell.[56] It is hardly likely, however, that the conception Emerson and Thoreau had of John Brown was simply the result of a misunderstanding on their part. It appears from their accounts that Brown made a studied effort to present himself to them as the kind of hero they would be most apt to admire.

The thesis of Warren's biography is that Brown's great genius lay in rationalizing his actions to others. "One of the most significant keys to John Brown's career and character," Warren writes, is "his elaborate psychological mechanism for justification, which appeared regularly in terms of the thing which friends called Puritanism and enemies called fanaticism." [57] Certainly he justified himself to Emerson and Thoreau with striking success.

Of the reaction in Concord to the Harpers Ferry raid, Bronson Alcott wrote:

> When the tidings came that John Brown was captured, I was with Henry Thoreau at Emerson's house. It was startling to all of us. Thoreau spoke of it then much as he soon afterwards did publicly. . . . Emerson said little then; it seemed to be a painful subject to him. Some weeks after, when he had returned from Salem, where he made that much-quoted speech in praise of Brown . . . he said to me, with an air of relief, "We have had enough of this dreary business." [58]

[54] *Writings of Henry David Thoreau,* IV, 411.

[55] *Emerson's Works,* XI, 207. In this Emerson was mistaken. See Villard, *John Brown,* 10.

[56] *Writings of Henry David Thoreau,* IV, 412.

[57] Warren, *John Brown, The Making of a Martyr,* 446.

[58] Franklin B. Sanborn, *The Personality of Emerson* (Boston, 1903), 87-88.

A month after the raid and several weeks after Thoreau made his "Plea for Captain John Brown," Emerson gave his first speech on Brown at a meeting held in Boston for the relief of John Brown's family. On December 2, the day of Brown's execution, he joined Thoreau and Alcott in conducting services for Brown at Concord.[59] Two weeks later he was persuaded, much against his will, to give a speech on Brown in New York, but the date for the meeting was changed and he was unable to attend.[60] He thought the cause a good one, he wrote, but he felt that the person who was heading the New York meeting was not a very "judicious" man.

On January 6 Emerson brought the "dreary business" to an end with the address, "John Brown," delivered in Salem. In addition, in his mid-November lecture on "Courage," delivered in Boston, he made that eloquent judgment of Brown, which, in later years, he edited from the essay: "that new saint, than whom none purer or more brave was ever led by love of men into conflict and death,—the new saint awaiting his martyrdom, and who, if he shall suffer, will make the gallows glorious like the cross." [61]

Emerson's letters and entries in his journal reflect little of the exaltation of this statement. "We are all very well," he wrote a few days after Brown's capture, "in spite of the sad Harper's Ferry business, which interests us all who had Brown for our guest twice. And the story of 'bushels of letters' naturally alarmed some of his friends in Boston.[62] He is a true hero, but lost his head there." [63]

The defense of Brown was sober duty to Emerson, but it was naked joy to Thoreau. His friend William Ellery Channing wrote: "Thoreau worshipped a hero in a mortal disguise, under the shape of that homely son of justice. . . . his pulses thrilled and his hands involuntarily clenched together at the mention of Captain Brown." [64] At the news of Brown's capture Thoreau was on fire, arguing with his neighbors, giving speeches, writing in his journal,

[59] Redpath (ed.), *Echoes of Harper's Ferry*, 437-54.

[60] Rusk (ed.), *Letters of Ralph Waldo Emerson*, V, 183-84.

[61] Cabot, *Memoir of Ralph Waldo Emerson*, II, 597.

[62] Emerson referred to letters captured with Brown incriminating members of the "Secret Committee of Six," who helped to finance some of Brown's activities. The six were: Theodore Parker, Gerrit Smith, George L. Stearns, Thomas W. Higginson, Samuel G. Howe, and Sanborn. Sanborn, *Recollections of Seventy Years*, I, 155-56, 187.

[63] Rusk (ed.), *Letters of Ralph Waldo Emerson*, V, 178.

[64] William E. Channing, *Thoreau, the Poet-Naturalist, With Memorial Verses*, ed. by Franklin B. Sanborn (Boston, 1902), 262.

and instructing friends to round up people for him to address. In his journal he wrote, apparently after bitter arguments with his neighbors, all the cutting retorts he might have made. Then, armed with these and with his personal recollections of Brown, and with the statements of Brown's heroic behavior, which issued daily from the press, Thoreau gave notice to the people of Concord that he would address them on Sunday evening in the vestry of the Old Parish Church on the "character of Captain Brown, now in the clutches of the slaveholder." [65]

"The Republican Committee and the Abolitionist Committee sent him word that it was premature and not advisable," Emerson later remembered.[66] "He replied — 'I did not send to you for advice, but to announce that I am to speak,' " and to a full hall he delivered, on October 30 as promised, his "Plea for Captain John Brown," perhaps the first important public defense of the man delivered in the country. The "Plea" was repeated the same week at Worcester, and again before a large audience in Tremont Temple, Boston, the following Sunday.[67] In addition Thoreau spoke at the services held for Brown on the day of his execution, and in the following year wrote a Fourth of July speech on "The Last Days of John Brown," which was read for him at the site of Brown's former home.[68] Emerson's speeches on Brown were brief and funereal; Thoreau's "Plea" was long, sarcastic, and charged with invective against his Concord neighbors, the New Englander, the modern Christian, the newspapers, the Republicans, the Democrats, Massachusetts, and the Garrisonian abolitionists.

The line of defense taken by the two men, however, was basically the same. It was with Brown's character that they were concerned, for they assumed that if his character could be proved to be pure, it would follow that his actions must have been justified. They did not feel it necessary, therefore, to answer the charges that Brown led a band which invaded Virginia, captured a federal arsenal, and killed five people (including an unarmed free Negro, and the mayor of the town, also unarmed, who had recently purchased four slaves in order to free them).[69] "The question is not

[65] *Emerson's Works*, X, 356; *Writings of Henry David Thoreau*, VI, 358.
[66] *Emerson's Works*, X, 356.
[67] *Writings of Henry David Thoreau*, VI, 358-59.
[68] *Ibid.*, IV, xi.
[69] Villard, *John Brown*, 433, 441-42.

about the weapon, but the spirit in which you use it,"[70] said Thoreau, while Emerson proved Brown's integrity to his own satisfaction and asked, "Is that the kind of man the gallows is built for?"[71]

Facing the issue of the raid more squarely than did Emerson, Thoreau quoted witnesses to prove Brown's sanity and the well-planned nature of the raid. He then appeared to state specifically his approval of the raid.

> It was his peculiar doctrine that a man has a perfect right to interfere by force with the slaveholder, in order to rescue the slave. I agree with him. . . . I shall not be forward to think him mistaken in his method who quickest succeeds to liberate the slave. I speak for the slave when I say, that I prefer the philanthropy of Captain Brown to that philanthropy which neither shoots me nor liberates me. . . . I think that for once the Sharp's rifles and the revolvers were employed in a righteous cause. The tools were in the hands of one who could use them.[72]

This statement of approval is not as specific as it seems. It ignores the fact that Brown planned, not merely to free slaves, but to recruit a nation of slaves in an Appalachian fastness to fight the South.[73] In speaking for the slaves Thoreau ignores the fact that the slaves who were temporarily liberated by Brown were liberated against their will. His approval, furthermore, rests on the assumption, which was hardly warranted by the circumstances, that Brown launched the raid with some prospect of success. In short it is a statement of Thoreau's support for an entirely different kind of raid, the kind which Brown had made when he smuggled slaves out of Missouri into Canada.[74] It takes no account of the real aims of the Harpers Ferry raid or of the manner in which it was carried out.

Actually the details of the raid are no more important to Thoreau's defense of Brown than they are to Emerson's. The significance of Harpers Ferry for both men is stated precisely by Thoreau in his Fourth of July speech of the following year.

> Men have been hung in the South before for attempting to rescue slaves, and the North was not much stirred by it. Whence, then, this wonderful difference? We were not so sure of *their* devotion to principle. We made

[70] *Writings of Henry David Thoreau*, IV, 434.
[71] *Emerson's Works*, XI, 209.
[72] *Writings of Henry David Thoreau*, IV, 433-34.
[73] Villard, *John Brown*, 331-32.
[74] *Ibid.*, 368-73.

> a subtle distinction, forgot human laws, and did homage to an idea. The North, I mean the *living* North, was suddenly all transcendental. It went behind the human law, it went behind the apparent failure, and recognized eternal justice and glory. Commonly, men live according to a formula, and are satisfied if the order of law is observed, but in this instance they, to some extent, returned to original perceptions, and there was a slight revival of old religion.[75]

The Fourth of July speech was Thoreau's last service to the martyrdom of Brown. Thoreau died two and a half years after his execution. Emerson, who lived through another generation, mentioned Brown only once again in a way useful to his eulogists. The occasion was the funeral services held for Lincoln at Concord in 1865. Speaking of Lincoln's Gettysburg Address, Emerson said: It "will not easily be surpassed by words on any recorded occasion. This, and one other American speech, that of John Brown to the court that tried him, and a part of Kossuth's speech at Birmingham, can only be compared with each other, and with no fourth."[76] Slight as the contribution was, it served to link Brown's name with Lincoln from that point on in the writings of the Brown partisans.[77]

Other writers have served the Brown legend more diligently than did Emerson and Thoreau, but probably none has been more important to it. Emerson and Thoreau, more than anyone else, developed the transcendental argument which was the basis for the defense of Brown. In addition they contributed greatly to that glorification of Brown which has sturdily survived a half century of adverse re-examination, and their usefulness to the John Brown myth is by no means at an end. While the writings of other nineteenth-century Brown apologists, such as Sanborn and James Redpath, are no longer widely read, the eloquent praises of Emerson and Thoreau have been incorporated into the body of their country's great literature.

[75] *Writings of Henry David Thoreau,* IV, 443.

[76] *Emerson's Works,* XI, 255-61.

[77] Lincoln, a year after the Harpers Ferry raid, said that Brown could best be classed as a political assassin. Arthur B. Lapsley (ed.), *The Writings of Abraham Lincoln,* 8 vols. (New York, 1905-1906), V, 142.

Personal Accounts of the Albany Congress of 1754

EDITED BY BEVERLY MCANEAR

On September 18, 1753, the Lords of Trade instructed James DeLancey, lieutenant governor of New York, to arrange for a general treaty of the Six Nations and the continental British American colonies for the purpose of hearing the Indians' complaints and restoring their good will towards the English. This order resulted from the growing disaffection of the Indians and the rapid penetration of the Ohio Valley by the French. Both New York and Pennsylvania failed miserably to maintain their influence over the Six Nations and their allies in the Ohio Valley, and confusion was spread throughout the Southwest and Northwest by Virginian efforts to gain control of the Indians to the west of the Appalachians.[1]

On receipt of the instructions, DeLancey hastened to call the Congress to meet at Albany on June 14, 1754, upon the terms of the very general language of the royal command. By the middle of February, however, Governor William Shirley of Massachusetts was proposing to his fellow governors that the commissioners of the several colonies should receive powers to form a colonial union empowered to control Indian relations and to fix quotas for the expenses of defense and erection of forts within the Indians' country. To this proposal DeLancey demurred; he would agree only to a system of forts across the northern frontier, to be built and maintained at the expense of all the colonies. Unable to agree with each other, DeLancey and Shirley separately urged their respective plans upon their colleagues.[2]

[1] Lords of Trade to Sir Danvers Osborne, September 18, 1753, Edmund B. O'Callaghan *et al.* (eds.), *Documents Relative to the Colonial History of the State of New-York* . . ., 15 vols. (Albany, 1853-1887), VI, 800-801; Lawrence H. Gipson, *The British Empire before the American Revolution* . . ., 7 vols. published (Caldwell, New York, 1936-), V, 98-111.

[2] New York Council Minutes, December 10, 12, 1753, April 4, 1754, Public Record Office, Colonial Office 5: 1197 (Library of Congress film, Washington); [Samuel

When the delegates finally assembled at Albany, the conferees were concerned with the insistence of the New Yorkers that they retain a privileged position in dealing with the Indians. This theme, entangled with jealousies over boundary disputes, caused repeated conflicts between the New Yorkers and the representatives of Massachusetts. In this unhappy atmosphere the commissioners undertook to write a constitution for a colonial union and to pacify the Indians.[3]

Of the men assembled at Albany, only four seem to have made a contemporary chronicle of the events during the Congress. One of these memoirs was a report by Richard Peters, secretary of Pennsylvania, to Thomas Penn, one of the proprietors of the province.[4] Unfortunately the letter has been lost. Joel Munsell preserved a report that Benjamin Tasker of Maryland "wrote a very interesting account of the congress, which we remember to have seen some time since in the library of the late Gov. Lloyd at the Wye House, Talbot Co., Maryland."[5] This paper likewise cannot be located. A third narrative was written in the form of a diary by Theodore Atkinson, the leader of the New Hampshire delegation and secretary of that province. His bald and unpretentious entries give valuable information concerning the deliberations and likewise indicate Atkinson's tepid interest in the formulation of the plan of union.[6] A fourth statement is contained in a letter written by Thomas Pownall probably to the Earl of Halifax, president of the Lords of Trade. Pownall, the brother of the secretary of the Lords,

Hazard] (ed.), *Minutes of the Provincial Council of Pennsylvania . . .*, 10 vols. (Harrisburg, 1838-1852), V, 713-23; James DeLancey to W[illiam] Shirley, March 5, April 22, 1754, Massachusetts Archives, Colonial Correspondence (Massachusetts State House, Boston), IV, 442-44, 451; *Collections of the Connecticut Historical Society*, 24 vols. (New Haven, 1860-1932), XVI, 437-38, 441-42.

3 Gipson, *British Empire*, V, 117-19; [Thomas Pownall to Earl of Halifax?], New York, July 23, [17]54, Personal Manuscripts (Manuscripts Division, Library of Congress); New York Council Minutes, July 6, 8, 1754, Public Record Office, CO 5: 1199; Theodore Atkinson to Colonel [William] Brattle, Portsmouth, April 14, 1773 (Historical Society of Pennsylvania, Philadelphia); report of Massachusetts commissioners, October 25, 1754, Massachusetts Archives, Colonial Correspondence, IV, 459-64; William Smith, [Jr.], *The History of the Late Province of New-York . . .*, 2 vols. (New York, 1830), II, 225-26.

4 The letter was dated July 22, 1754.

5 Joel Munsell, *The Annals of Albany*, 10 vols. (Albany, 1850-1859), III, 157.

6 B[enning] Wentworth to Shirley, Portsmouth, June 7, 1754, Massachusetts Archives, Colonial Correspondence, V, 194-95; Clifford K. Shipton, *Biographical Sketches of Graduates of Harvard University . . .*, 8 vols. published (Cambridge, Boston, 1873-), VI, [221]-31.

had come to America as secretary of Sir Danvers Osborne, governor of New York and brother-in-law of Halifax. Unfortunately for Pownall, Osborne committed suicide almost immediately after his arrival in New York in 1753. Without employment, Pownall undertook to inform himself upon colonial conditions, reporting his conclusions informally to Halifax. Naturally he wished to attend so important a gathering as that at Albany. And since he was on intimate relations with Halifax and since Lieutenant Governor DeLancey was seeking to avert the appointment of a full governor who would supersede him, it is not surprising that DeLancey invited Pownall to attend the Congress as his guest. But there were colonials who were amazed to find that DeLancey caused a memorandum by Pownall, a mere "Stander-by," to be included within the official journal of the conference. The Congress concluded, Pownall hastened to report to his noble patron in one or two letters, only a portion of the first of which has been preserved.[7]

Printed below are the remnant of the Pownall letter and that portion of the Atkinson diary which deals with the Congress.[8] Both manuscripts are in the Manuscripts Division of the Library of Congress. The Atkinson diary was acquired by Peter Force, the great Washington publisher, collector, and compiler. It now is located among the Force Papers, a massive collection of tens of thousands of documents, of which many are transcriptions, many are originals, and few are carefully catalogued. The Pownall letter is to be found among the Personal Manuscripts. It is only an odd item, probably a stray from the long-dispersed files of the Earl of Halifax. Its condition — torn, mildewed, and incomplete — bears testimony to its parlous travel.

[Theodore Atkinson's] Memo Book of my journey as one of the Commissioners on Treaty with the Six nations of Indians, Viz., 1754.

[7] Leonard W. Labaree, "Thomas Pownall," Allen Johnson, Dumas Malone, and Harris E. Starr (eds.), *Dictionary of American Biography*, 21 vols. and index (New York, 1928-1944), XV, 161; Gipson, *British Empire*, V, 130-31; O'Callaghan *et al.* (eds.), *Documents Relative to the Colonial History of the State of New-York*, VI, 893-97; [Pownall to Halifax?], New York, July 23, [17]54; DeLancey to Archbishop of Canterbury, New York, October 15, 1753, William Smith Manuscripts, I, 4 (Archives of Protestant Episcopal Church, New-York Historical Society, New York).

[8] The Atkinson diary is entered in what originally was a pad of twenty-two small leaves of paper, loosely stitched together. It now is bound. There are daily entries from June 3 to July 19, 1754, for Atkinson made notes not only of the events of the Congress but also of the journey. However, nothing of interest occurred during the ride except that on the way to Albany the New Hampshire commissioners con-

Mond., [*June*] *17.* Coll Wendal[9] having Engaged Lodging in the Cyty for us,[10] we Crossd the ferry in the morning & went Directly to our Lodgins at one Lansinghs.[11] Lt Gov D[e]Lancy[12] Sent to Invite us to Dine with him wh[ich] we Did. Near Twenty Gentlemen Dined there; a Handsom Enter-[t]ainmt., good wine & Arrak Punch. After Dinner we Traversed the Town & returnd to our Lodging. Ye Govr & Several Gentleman Calld on us. I was Prevented Sleeping by the tooth Ach or Ague in my face which was Extream Painfull.

Tuesday, 18. The Connecticut Comissioners[13] who was the only ones that Dined with us yesterday Visited us & Desired to See *the Letter from the board of Trade to Govr Wentworth*[14] on the affair of the Interview.[15] We Shew it them & gave them a Copy of it. I could not go out this Day by reason of the Pain in my face. We Dined at home & after Dinner recd a Visit from the Philodelphia Comissioners.[16] The Govr Sent us word he Proposed a Conferranc or[?] meeting of the Comissioners from ye Several Governments & Desired we would attend at the Council Hall at 11 oClock

ferred with John Worthington of Massachusetts and Roger Wolcott, Sr., of Connecticut. Therefore, the writer has printed only the section dealing with Atkinson's stay in Albany. In transcribing both the diary and the letter, punctuation has been altered where necessary for intelligibility, and occasionally the writer has raised to a capital the first letter of the beginning word of a sentence.

9 Colonel Jacob Wendell was a Boston merchant, descended from an Albany family. He was a councilor of Massachusetts, 1734-1760, and a colonel of the Boston militia, 1736-1743. He had represented Massachusetts at the Albany Indian conference of 1751, but in 1754 had no official business at Albany. The New Hampshire commissioners had met him the day before while all were lost in the woods near Kinderhook. Atkinson, Diary, June 16, [1754]; Society of Colonial Wars in the State of New Hampshire, *Register . . . 1907* (n.p., 1907), 77.

10 The New Hampshire commissioners were Theodore Atkinson, Meshech Weare, Richard Wibird, and Henry Sherburne, Jr. O'Callaghan *et al.* (eds.), *Documents Relative to the Colonial History of the State of New-York*, VI, 853.

11 Possibly the house of Jacob J. Lansing. Claude G. Munsell, *The Lansing Family* (privately printed, 1916), 30; Joel Munsell (ed.), *Collections on the History of Albany . . .*, 4 vols. (Albany, 1865-1871), II, 30-31.

12 DeLancey was chief justice of the New York Supreme Court, 1733-1760, and lieutenant governor, 1753-1760. From 1753 to 1755 and again from 1757 to 1760 he acted as governor. C. W. Spencer, "James DeLancey," *Dictionary of American Biography*, V, 212-13.

13 William Pitkin, Roger Wolcott, Jr., and Elisha Williams. O'Callaghan *et al.* (eds.), *Documents Relative to the Colonial History of the State of New-York*, VI, 853.

14 Wentworth was governor of New Hampshire, 1742-1767. Isabel M. S. Whittier, "Benning Wentworth," *Dictionary of American Biography*, XIX, 653-54.

15 The letter ordered the governors of New Hampshire, Maryland, Virginia, Massachusetts, and Pennsylvania to send commissioners to treat with the Six Nations at a time and place to be fixed by the governor of New York. The Connecticut commissioners were ignorant of the content of this order, for they were present on an invitation issued by Lieutenant Governor DeLancey on his own responsibility. Gipson, *British Empire*, V, 111-[13].

16 John Penn, Richard Peters, Isaac Norris, and Benjamin Franklin. O'Callaghan *et al.* (eds.), *Documents Relative to the Colonial History of the State of New-York*, VI, 853.

on that affair. The Govr told us yesterday at Dinner that he had recd a Letter from the Interpreter [17] that had the Conducting the Indians to Town that they had Spent a . . . Day or Two in Condoling the Loss of a Sachem & Expected an other Day to be Spent on the Same Occasion when they got to the Next Tribe So that they Should not be in Town before Wednesday or Thursday. The Pain in my face so Extream I got no Sleep till Day & than very little refreshed by it.

Wednesday, 19. My face raged So almost all night that I got Little or no Sleep the whole night. About 10 oClock We returnd our Visit to the Comissioners of Connecticut & Pensilvania & went With the other Comser to Town Hall w[h]ere we found the Liut. Governr and 4 of the N. York Coun[c]il.[18] After Produceing our Several Comissn which the Govr. ordred the Deputy Secry [19] to read, they were Delivered us again & a Copy Left. The Governr that [then] Read a Paragraph *of his Majy Instructions relating to this Interview* [20] & Said that, as it was to Publich on All the Government Equally Concerned, He thot it might be adviseable for the Comissioners to meet Previous to the Indians Attendence & Consult & Conclude upon what he Should Say to them, that the Se[c]ry of the Province & the Comissrs for Indian affairs [21] Should give us their Attendence when required & Lay before us any former Treaty or give any Information they could. The Perticular Iddoms or Diction might be Left, as they were very Peculiar, to those that Should diliv[e]r the Same to the Indians &ca. *There was Some Inquiry weither any body was Comissionated from N York. But none was* & Concluded if the Govr Would be Present at every Consultation there would need none but if otherwise A Comission would be necessary. In reading the Several Comissions I observed that most of them began with the Stile of the Governrs, not the King, Philodelphia & ours only with the regal Stile and worded almost Exactly alike. We had *no Dispute abt Superiority* but was by the Govr Desired to walk in & *take Places as we thot Proper*. There was a Back Seet that the Se[creta]ry Sot in & 2 rows of Seets under it & four Each End which with a Seet In the front Enclosed a Large Table. *The Govr & his Council* Sot und[er] the Sery at the Table, *Massa* [22] & *New Hampr*

[17] Arent Stevens. Edmund B. O'Callaghan (ed.), *Calendar of Historical Manuscripts in the Office of the Secretary of State . . .*, 2 vols. (Albany, 1866), II, 616, 622.

[18] John Chambers, William Smith, Sr., Joseph Murray, and William Johnson. O'Callaghan *et al.* (eds.), *Documents Relative to the Colonial History of the State of New-York*, VI, 853.

[19] Goldsbrow Banyar. *Ibid.*

[20] Lords of Trade to Osborne, Whitehall, September 18, 1753. *Ibid.*, 854-56.

[21] The Commissioners for Indian Affairs for New York were a board which managed Indian diplomacy. At this time a full board would have numbered twenty-seven; actually business was managed by about ten Albany merchants interested in the Indian trade. By "secretary" Atkinson probably meant Peter Wraxall, the secretary to the Indian Commissioners. Edmund B. O'Callaghan (comp.), *Calendar of New York Colonial Commissions, 1680-1770* (New York, 1929), 36, 39-40.

[22] Samuel Welles, John Chandler, Oliver Partridge, John Worthington, and Thomas Hutchinson. Gipson, *British Empire*, V, 114 n.

opposite, *Philodelphia, road Island*[23] & *Mary Land*[24] at one End, *Connecticut* at the other. We adjournd till 5 oClock P. M. & ordres was given to have the Table removed in order that we might be all Accomodated in Setting round it without being behinde Each other. Accordingly about 5 oClock the Comissioners met again & Was Entertaind by Mr Wells of Boston with an Accot of the Vast Expence that Governmt had been at & yet how willing they Still were &ca. Here mentiond the Expedition now carrying [on] building forts &ca at Kennybeck.[25] Mr Peters from Pensilvania gave us a History of the Procedure of . . . that Government with the Indians above them, their Traders being Captivated &ca. These two narrations took up the greatest Parte of the afternoon So that nothing was Done Except the Nomination of one Comissionr from Each Governmt to Calculate & Draw up a Speech to be made to the Indians at opening the Interview with the Indians, which were Mesrs Tasker, Maryland; Moris [Norris], Philodelpha; Johnson, York; Williams, Connecticut; Howard, road Island; Wells, Boston; Atkinson, N Hampe. Thunder & rain abt one oClock.

20, Thursday. This Day was Chieffly Spent in calculateing the Speach to be made to the Indians by Lt Govr in the Name of his Majty at the Desire of the Several Governments. As yet but few of the Indians got in, about 20. Winde South & Some Sprinkling Showers & very hot.

Fryday, 21. The Comissioners met at the Town Hall & the Comittee appointed to make a Draft of the Speach to the 6 nations acquainted the Comissionrs that they were ready to make their report & [to] the Comissioners, & it . . . was thot Proper to Acquaint His Honr the Lt Govr thereof before the Same was read at the board. Accordingly Messrs Atkinson & [blank] were appointed by the Comissions to wait upon his Honr to Acquaint him that the Comittee were ready to report &ca, which being don his Honr asked if the Comissioners Expected or Desired he Should be Present. They answerd they Imagined that the message was Intended he should be Present if He thot Proper. He readally went to the Town Hall, took his Seat & the report was read. Some aditions being Proposed & the Indians not arived, it was ordred to Lay till the afternoon. Here arose A motion about the Seats the Comissioners were to take at the Interview and after Several Propositions, as that those Governments that had been Longest in attending the Treaty, heretofore those that been at the Largest Expence &ca, The Kings Governmts before the Charter Govts &ca, but at Last it was upon a motion of his Honrs *Determined that the Comissioners Should take Place according to the Situation of yr respective Governmts begining* either at the North or South. Finally

23 Stephen Hopkins and Martin Howard, Jr. *Ibid.*

24 Abraham Barnes and Benjamin Tasker, Jr. *Ibid.*

25 The Massachusetts commissioners had been instructed to accent the province's heavy contributions to defense in an effort to gain "some Reimbursement, or at lest to a more favourable future quota." "Heads of Instruction for the Comissioners . . . ," Massachusetts Archives, Colonial Correspondence, IV, 468-69.

'twas Determined *to begin at the North.*[26] New *Hampr then Claimd the first Seat, but, as the County of York was mo[re] no[r]therly, the Massa took Place.* This being the forenoons work, the Comissioners adjournd till afternoon. We N H. C. went to the flatts [27] & Dined with Coll Schulyer [28] & returnd in the even[i]ng. Nothng was Transacted by the Comisrs.[29] Several thunder Showers this afternoon, the wind Southerly.

Saturday, 22d. Had a Visit from the Massa, Connecticut & road Island to acqt us with what Passd in the afternoon yesterday in our absence & to Consult about appointing a Clerk &ca. Then we went to the Town Hall, Canvassed the Speach as the Comittee had Drafted it. Some objections arose Concerning Chieffly that it ought to be G[e]neral & only Salutary & that, if any one Perticular that related to one governmt only was Containd in it, that every thing that Each Govern had to Say to the Indians Should be also Incerted[?].[30] This being the minde of the Comissioners, Messrs Huchinson, Mr Peters & Coll Johnson was Desird to Alter the Speach Agreable to the Minde of the Comissioners as Declared, which being Don, it was again read & approved of & then the Sd Gentlemen were Desired to wait upon the L Govr [to] Shew it [to] him for his approbation. Then Adjournd till monday. Now about 200 Indians arrived. Several hard Showers with Thunder both forenoon & Afternoon. By Invitations we Dine with Coll Cuyler.[31] After Diner wait [walk?] up the hill on the Back of the Town to View the Indians &ca. It Clears up & the Wind about North West.

Sunday, 23d. The wind got in the night at North East & raind almost all night. Went to Church in y[e] forenoon. Heard Mr Peters [32]; in the Afternoon Mr Ogleby;[33] in the Evning Mr William,[34] a Minister from Connecticut, who Preach in the Duch Church. Dine this Day with the Governour; the Merriland Comissioners Also Dined with his Honr. The winde continued North Easterly & rain'd the whole Day.

26 The minutes credit DeLancey with this solution. O'Callaghan *et al.* (eds.), *Documents Relative to the Colonial History of the State of New-York*, VI, 859.

27 The farm of the Schuyler family, four miles north of Albany. George W. Schuyler, *Colonial New York . . .*, 2 vols. (New York, 1885), I, 154-56.

28 Philip Schuyler, one of the New York Indian commissioners. *Ibid.*, II, 158-59; O'Callaghan (ed.), *Calendar of Historical Manuscripts*, II, 638.

29 The other commissioners had spent the afternoon proposing amendments to the speech to the Indians. O'Callaghan *et al.* (eds.), *Documents Relative to the Colonial History of the State of New-York*, VI, 859.

30 One objection of the commissioners was to New York's insistence that the Indians be rebuked for interference with traders bound for Oswego. See below, June 25, 1754; O'Callaghan *et al.* (eds.), *Documents Relative to the Colonial History of the State of New-York*, VI, 858.

31 The reference may be to Cornelius Cuyler. Maud Churchill Nicoll, *The Earliest Cuylers in Holland and America . . .* (New York, 1912), 24.

32 Richard Peters, one of the Pennsylvania delegates.

33 John Ogilvie was rector of the Anglican Church in Albany, 1749-1760. Munsell (ed.), *Collections on the History of Albany*, I, 458.

34 Elisha Williams, one of the Connecticut delegates.

24th, Monday. It raind all night & this morning went to the Town Hall where the Comisrs met. A motion was made for the nominating a Clerk & many other and amongst which was one *wether the Council of York ought to Set or not without a Comission &ca.* They Spent the Greatest part of the forenoon & nothing finally don Except a nomination of Mr Raxwell [35] as Clerk. Coll Worthington & Mr Howard to Acquaint his Honr that the Comissrs were met &ca. His Honr told Them he could not Possibly attend, being So Surroinded with the Indains. Then Adjd till 3 oClock P M. The Lt Govr Met the Comissioners at the Town Hall & Acquaintd them that *Mr Raxwell was Sworne as Clerk.* Accordingly was ordred to take Such Minitts of the Comissioners attendanc & Transactions as Should be given him by the Deputy Secry who had Acted as Clerk & to Enter them regularly in a Book by Themselves &ct & to recive also the Copys of the Several Comissions &ca & file them regularly. This being Don, a motion was made *wether the building two forts for the Safety of the Six nations was not necessary,*[36] the Consideration of which was Deferrd till Some Steps might be taken *to Effect a Union of the Several Provinces & Collonies in America,* & a motion being at the Same time made that a Comittee might be appoint[ed] by the Commissioner[s] to Draft a Plan for Such a union, Mr *Hutchenson, Atkinson, Hopkins, Pinking* [*Pitkin*], *Smith, Franklin, Tasker were appointed to Draft a Plan* & Present it with all Imaginable Speed. Then adjd till tomorrow 11 oClock A M.

Tuesday, 25. Met in the Town Hall and, the Comittee not haveing a report ready or a [37] Plan for the union of the Provinces aforesd, Nothing was Don but adjd till 5 oClock P M, when his Honr Sent to the Commissioners the Speach Calculated by the Comissrs altred in Some Places with which the Comissrs agreed Except one Article relateing to the Indians of the Oneidas Interrupting the Albany Traders — Insisting upon the Benefit of Carrying the Traders goods Cross the Carryin Place & exacting great freight &ca, which being a Perticular thing that related to N York only was heretofore & now objected to till all the Governments that had any thing to Say to them Should Likewise have an opportunity, & Mr Peters & Mr Hutchenson appointed to wait upon his Honr to acquaint him thereof. The Rain that fell on Sunday &ca Caused Such a flood that water Encreased near about 14 foot in Perpindicular & welld over the Banks of the river, Drowned all the Corn & Grain &ca on the Inner[?] vale, Came into the Cyty & was in Some Places even with the Top Pallosaidoes, Drove near a Dozen Sloops from their moorings & Carryd Down Stream Eleven miles from Scenactada, only fill the river with rubbish & fleeted Of[f] many Piles of boards.

[35] Peter Wraxall. O'Callaghan *et al.* (eds.), *Documents Relative to the Colonial History of the State of New-York,* VI, 859.

[36] The motion was made by DeLancey and had been the basis upon which he had called the conference. *Ibid.,* 860; *Collections of the Connecticut Historical Society,* XVI, 437-38.

[37] Overwritten.

Wednesday, 26. Wrote Mrs Atkinson by Mrs Mcgregore &, the Indians not being ready to recive the Speech, the upper Castle of Mohawks not being yet come in & the Comittee of Union haveing not yet made their report, We rode out to View the Cohoos about 10 or 12 miles;[38] returnd in the afternoo[n]. Wind Southerly & Very Hot, the Corn & Grain not So much Damaged as was Imagined. The River fallen about Six feet. Fair & hot.[39]

Thursday, 27th. Met the Comissioners at the Town hall. Settled our minits in the Journal & had the Speach to be made to the Indians returnd from the Governr with his Alterations & our realterations &ca read & unanimously Agreed upon & Voted and Calculated an aditional Paragraph which was Left to the Governr to be Incerted or not as he Should think Proper, which was to tell them that the Comissioners & Sundry Tribes of Indians had been waiting near 14 Days to open the Congress & hoped the[y] would be more Punctual for the future. This was on Accot of Hindrich & the Cononjiro Indians not comeing in &ca.[40] Rainy weather all Day.

Fryday, 28th. Hindrich & the Indians of his Tribe arived & twas Thot best to make the Speach on the morrow, to which the Lt Governr Consented. The Comittee . . . Appointed for Drafting a *Plan for a Union of the Governmt &ca* Exhibited the Draft which was read a first & Secd Time & then Directed *that Each Colloney be Served with a Copy for their Perusal & Consideration.*[41] This took up the Greatest Part of the Day. Fair weather. Wind South.

Saturday, June 29. The Comissioners met as usual. Debated upon the Draft of a Scheme for a Union & Proposed & Voted (which had before been talked of) the Printing a Sermon Preached by Mr Peters at the Church on Sunday Last about 11 oClock.[42] The Governr Acquainted us that the Indians were ready to hear what we had to Say to them. We Accordingly went to the Place appointed, which was before the Govrs Door, where were about 10 rows of boards. Each row would hold abt 20 Indians. Opposite & between the Indains & the Govr House were Placed a row of Chairs, the Lt Govr & Council of New York Seated in the Center, at the Extream End on far right hand the Massa, next N H., then Connecticut, then the Govr &ca, next on the Left hand road Island, then Pensilvania, & on the Extream Maryland. The Govr read the Speach Paragraph by Paragraph which was Interpreted by the N York Interpreter. At the Delivery of Each belt they Signifyed

[38] The Cohoes are falls on the Mohawk River near its junction with the Hudson.

[39] The speech to the Indians was further debated at a meeting attended only by the New York, Massachusetts, Rhode Island, and Connecticut commissioners. O'Callaghan *et al.* (eds.), *Documents Relative to the Colonial History of the State of New-York,* VI, 861.

[40] For the full text of the speech, see *ibid.*, 861-63.

[41] This draft must be the so-called Weare plan, printed as "Meshech Weare's Plan for Colonial Union, 1754," *Bulletin of the New York Public Library . . .* (New York), I (June, 1897), 149-50.

[42] Apparently this sermon was never printed.

their understanding of Each Paragraph by a kind of universal Huzzah. When the great or Chain belt was Dil[i]vered on this occasion, they Signifyed their understanding or Consent by Such a Huzzah repeated Seven Times over for every Tribe. Thus finished the Speach. The Indians made a Long Pause & then Hendri[c]h rose & repe[a]ted the Substance of Speach & Said they would Consider of & answer it on monday. The Comissioners met In the afternoon &, it being mentioned that the Stockbridge or river Indians were in Town & had no notice taken of them nor were Invited, Ordred that Mr Wells & Mr Franklin wait on his Honr the Lit Govr to Acquaint him of the Circumstances & Desire that they may have Some Provissions &ca & that on monday the Comissioners would Consider further of them. Adjd till monday. Raind in the morning. Cleard up about 10 oClock. Wind Southerly.

Sunday, 30th June. Went to Church forenoon & afternoon, after which attended at Church w[h]ere the Mohawks were Calld to Prayers & the Service in their Langwage, which was Performed with the utmost Decency. Many of them had books & responded. One of them Sot the Psalm & one other made or repeated a Long Prayer &ca. Mr Ogleby Officiated as their Priest. He Preached the afternoon; Mr Peters the morning.

Monday, July 1. Attended the Comissrs in the Town Hall. The Comittee Appointed to Wait on the Governr in relation to the Stockbridge or river Indians made their report that his Honr thot it most Proper of those Indians to be Supported by the Massa as they Lived in that Governmt & were not Sent for to this Treaty by him.[43] Afterwards the Govr comeing to Council Said he would give orders for their Support but thot it reasonable that the Comissioners Should in Some Proportion reimburst the Cost &ca. The Comissioners reasumd the Debatd report of the Comittee in relation to the Union of the Several Colls & Debatd thereon the remainder of the forenoon as they did also in the Afternoon till Colld to hear the answer the Indians of the 6 nations had to make to the Speach made them on Saturday Last. When we all Attended w[h]ere the Indians being Placed as before, they Made their Answer in which they Expressed their heartyness in renewing all Covenants. *Lade the faults to the Englihs or reather N York Government whom they had had no Interview for 3 years; upbraded them with folly & Cowardise in neglecting their fortifications, in not takeing Crown point &ca,* burning their own fort at Sarratoge, in Letting the fire go out at albany which they Said Pointing to ye albany Commissioners for Indian affairs, and Extinguishing

[43] Massachusetts and Connecticut had been inducing Mohawks to settle at Stockbridge as civilized Christians. New York felt that this proselyting was merely refined kidnapping of its frontier defenders. Memorial of Martin Kellogg to Connecticut Assembly, 2 Thursday, October, 1750, May 9, 1751, committee report to Connecticut Assembly, [May], 1751, Connecticut State Archives, Indians (Connecticut State Library, Hartford), II, 64a, 67a, 68; *Collections of the Connecticut Historical Society,* XVI, 94-95; committee of New York Council to [George Clinton], July 19, 1751, (copy), Massachusetts Archives, Colonial Correspondence, IV, 136-39; Massachusetts Legislative Council Minutes, December 5, 1753, Colonial Office 5: 815.

the fire at Coll Johnsons Castle whom they Love & he Loves them & gave a belt to Govr Clinton *Desireing that all business between them & him might Pass thro Coll Johnsons hands*, but he, th[e] Govr, was Gon & they Supposed the belt was Drowned for they had heard nothi[n]g of it Since.[44] Fair Cool weather.

Tuesday, July 2d. Debated again on the Scheme for a Union and before the Comissioners broke up it was Put to Vote, every Comissioner Present, Viz., weither they were then ready to Put the Question that had been so Long & often in Debate, Viz., *weither an Act of Parliament was the only Expedient to Obtain Such a Union and it Past in affirmative to this Question; all yeas Except Connecticut.* Then the Sd *Question was Put* and this *Passt in the Affurmative; 3 from Connecticut & 2 from Pensilvania did not Vote for it.* In the afternoon the Govr Sot with the Comissionrs when . . . ye Indians Speach was read &c [illegible word].[45] A Comittee was Chosen to Calcule [calculate] Some thing to Say to the Indians in answer to what they had dilivered in their Speach Yesterday.[46]

Wednesday, July 3. We, the Comtee, Dil[i]vered to ye Comissioners a Drafts of a Spech to be made by the L Govr to the Indians, which was approved of, & what his Honr Proposed to Say to them in answer to what was Perticularly Said about the albany Comissrs for Indian affairs &ca being Added And approved, his Honr ordd the Indians to Attend at 6 oClock this afternoon, when, being all Seated as before, the Speach was d[elivere]d them by the Interpreter as was also *the News of Govr Shirly Eastern Voyage, Govr Wentworths Sending to Serch*[?] *a fort at Connecticut,* [illegible line of six words] the True State of the affa[i]rs at Philodelphia & Virginia with relation to what the Indians Said in their Speach about opening Paths without their Knowledge &t.[47] All the Comissioners & many Gentlemen dined by Invitation from the Mare & Corporation of the . . . City in the Town Hall. Had a great Dinner & wine &ca. Enough broke up about 6 to Speak to the Indians.[48] Were very merry. Fair Cool weather this Day.

44 The references to military events relate to efforts to take Canada and to defend the northern frontier from 1746 to 1748. In the course of these campaigns Governor Clinton took the control of Indian affairs out of the hands of the New York Indian commissioners and made Johnson the agent. Since Johnson had a considerable amount of money to spend on the savages, he was very popular. But political exigencies forced Clinton to restore the power of the commissioners in 1752, and Johnson then retired from the Indian service. *The Letters and Papers of Cadwallader Colden*, IV, *1748-1754, Collections of the New-York Historical Society* . . . , 75 vols. (New York, 1868-1942), LIII, 274-77; James Sullivan *et al.* (eds.), *The Papers of Sir William Johnson*, 9 vols. (Albany, 1921-1939), I, 383.

45 The speeches of Hendrick and Abraham, sachems of the upper castle of the Mohawks, are printed in O'Callaghan *et al.* (eds.), *Documents Relative to the Colonial History of the State of New-York*, VI, 869-71.

46 The membership of this committee was the same as that appointed on June 19 to draw up the first speech to the Indians. *Ibid.*, 871.

47 For text of speeches, see *ibid.*, 872-75.

48 Atkinson was not present at the conference with the Indians. *Ibid.*

Thursday, July 4th. Attended at the Town Hall where the Comissioners again Debated on Sundry Paragraphes of the Comittees report in relation to *a Union of the Collonies.* Agreed to Several, I think *every Comissioner Except the Connecticut Gentlemen who thot there was too great a Power* Lodged *in the President Genll* but were Still ready to assist in the main Designe. In the afternoon the Governr Sent us word that the Indians were ready to make their Last Speach or answer to what had been Laid to them. We accordingly attended & this Speech Detained us till Some time after Sunset. They were then Told by the Governr that they must be ready to receive the Kings Present Early on the morrow. Accordingly *we of N Hampr Imediatly retired & Concelled what & How to give what our Governmt had ord*[*ere*]*d to them.* This Day the Comissr from the Severall Collonies Invited the Governr & Council of York, the Mare & Corporation & Gentlemen of Albany, Strangers &ca to Dine in the Town Hall on the Morrow at 3 oClock that we might have Time to go thro the Comittees report for a Union if Possible before Dinner. Fair Cool Northerly Weather.

Fryday, July 5. Attendd the Comissionrs in the Town Hall. Spent the forenoon on ye Comittees report about a Union of the Several Provinces. Voted Several of the Perticulars. In the afternoon Attended the Comittee & made a Draft of a report to Lay before them of the Situation of our Country, Especially with regard to the Indians, ye Said Trade &ca. His Honr this afternoon also Dilivered the Kings Present to the Indians which was a good assortment & a great Quantity among which were 400 good guns, Some Extraordinary.[49] In the Ev[en]ing *Determined upon our Present &ca.* This Day the Comissioners joynd & Entertaind the Govr & Council of York, Mare & Corporation & officers & Gentlemen of the City at Diner in the Town Hall which Turnd out well. Fair Weather & not too hot. In the afternoon ye Govr made a Speach to the River & Scahacook Indians. Comissioners met as usual.

Saturday, 6. We waited for the Indians to come & recive our Present. Mr *Wibird* & I Tareyd for them. Mr W & *Sher*[burne] attended the Comissioners. About 10 oClock 2 Sachems of Each Tribe & Some few others Attended & we made a short Speach as on file; gave the Present to them & their Answer. They gave us the name of *Sosaquasowane* &ca.[50] See ye Speach & answer. *They told us to give them a Discription of our Province, Which we did. Hendrich Said he had been there.* Then told us they Percieved We was upon busines & Desired us not to wait on their Accot &ca. We Left them with wine &ca & went to the Hall. Debated Several Things. The Govr Informd us that the river Indians would not Speack with or have any thing to do with the Sactacooks. So was forced to Divide the Present & Permit them to answer our Speach the Govr made them yesterday Seperately. In their answer which the *river Indians made, the*[*y*] *Said Something about their Land* which was thot best to D[e]ferr till monday morning & make them

[49] For text of speeches, see *ibid.*, 875-77.

[50] Jeremy Belknap, *The History of New-Hampshire*, 3 vols. (Dover, 1812), II, 221 n., claimed that this name meant "again-a-dish-large."

Some Answer to. So *they Did not recieve their Present which was Parte of the Kings favr & a Contribution of the severall Governments.* So this Day Concluded. Fair; not uncomfortabol.

Sunday, 7. Heard Mr Peters in the forenoon, Mr Oglevy in the afternoon. Dined at my Lodgings. Drank Tea at the Mares. Spent the evning at Home.

Monday, 8th. We on Saturday at the 6 nations hint that *the[y] Expected Some thing as a Treat* when they united & gave a Name &ca. Bespoke *a Cow* which this morning was brot us Early. We sent for Hendrich; acquainted him thereof. He came & Liked her; Sent Some young fellows, Carryed her off & killd her in the camp. We went to the Town Hall, Settled the Speach, Debated upon the union report & the Comittee report upon the State of the English Colonies Indiam Trade &ca. In the afternoon *the Govr Settled a Dispute with Some of the Indians that was going off to Canada because they had no Share of the Present.* Made a Speach to the five nations, took our Leave of them which took us till abt 8 Clock P M. Fare Weather & Pritty hot.

Tuesday, 9. Finished the Interview with the Scatecooke & river Indians, *gave them their Present* from the King & the Comissioners & took our Leave of them. Went to the Town Hall & . . . *went thro the report of the Comtee on the affair of the Union Paragra[p]h by Paragraph & Voted them. Desired Mr Franklin to reduce them to regularity.* Dined at Mr Beekmans, a Young Gentlemen Late out of his Time with Coll Wendell. Began to think of going home & Prepareing therefor in the afternoon. Read *the report of the Comitte on the State of the Colonies* &ca Paragraph by Paragh. Made Some Little alterations & then his Honr put to the Comissionr & it Passd to be *Entred on the Jour[n]al* of the Comissioners.[51] Adjd about SunSet Till 9 oClock tomorrow. This Day fair & Prity Hott, not Imoderately.

Wednesday, 10. Began Early this morning. Set to Settle all our Accots in hopes of Getting over the ferry this afternoon but was Disapointed. Detaind by the Governr & Comissioners which Sot all Day *Consulting the report for an act of Parliament building forts in the Country &ca.*[52] Severe Shower & hard Thunder. Cleard up before night. W[i]nd South. Got all our Papers Copyd. Attended the Comittee at Coll Johnsons on the affair of *Building forts. Came to A Conclusion of the Number Necessary for the frontiers of all the Collonies.* Sot till 12 Coclock.

Thursday, 11. Attended the Comissioners & made our report relateing to forts &ca.[53] Debated the Same. Passd Several Votes. Broke up the Treaty. Dined & Crossd the ferry. . . .

51 This representation was a summary of French aggression and the state of Indian relations. It was written by Thomas Hutchinson. O'Callaghan *et al.* (eds.), *Documents Relative to the Colonial History of the State of New-York*, VI, 885-88.

52 This measure was again proposed by DeLancey. Though Atkinson does not say so, it was on this day that the commissioners agreed to submit the plan of union to the several provinces. *Ibid.*, 889-91.

53 The report stated in effect that action on the plan of union should be awaited before plans were made for the construction of forts as a joint venture. *Ibid.*, 892.

N. York, July 23, [17]54

My Lord:

I beg leave to acknowledge the honor in receiving your Lordship's letters of Recommendation, & hope You will not be offended at my frequent repetition of Thanks; For ye repeated instances of yr Lordships Favor & Kindness to me more than demand them: to retain & act under a right sense of so high an honor is to be carefull not to discredit it, it is my Duty so to act it shall be my Study. My heart is indeed full even to overflowing with gratitude towards Your Lordship, but were I not restrain'd by good manners from troubling your Lordship with my sentiments of it, I shou'd yet be silent being unwilling to debase them with those phrases (& there are no other) which ye insincerity of compliment & ceremony have usurped the Use of.

Since I troubled your Lordship with my last I have been up at Albany from whence I am just return'd. His Honor, ye Lt Governor [James DeLancey], invited me to go with him & made me his Guest. The observations that occurr'd to me on ye Indian Treaty & Indian Affairs on ye Conference held by the Comissioners of ye Provinces there mett to consider on some general Plan are what this letter waits upon yr Lordship to lay before You. I shall not presume to take your time with repeating such things as you may hear from ye Persons concernd & or will appear on ye Face of buisness but with such as your Lordship will hear only from a Stander-by as I am.

The First thing that occurr'd was ye Delay & Difficulties the Indians made before they came down. There are Many reasons given but I am told I may be positive the following are true. Their disinclination (particularly ye Mohawcks) to treat at all since Indian affairs have been taken out of the hands of Col. Johnson. But this Difficulty he removed by coming down himself & in the most freindly & respectfull manner joining with & assisting the Governor. Twas known that in their way down they held many Councils. The matters that occasion'd these are variously reported, I am taught to beleive the following: to settle their Conduct on these two points: viz., 1. what satisfaction they shou'd require & accept in regard to their Complaints. That the two Resolutions they came down with on this head were: To have nothing more to do with ye Albany Commissioners for indian affairs, & to have full & final satisfaction about their Lands before they began the treaty. 2dl. Twas [manuscript torn] on & supposing that at this meeting the[y] shoud be required *to strike out with ye Hatchet that is in their hands*, being conscious on one hand that their League & Alliance with ye English shou'd oblige them to do it if required & on ye other being really & in good earnest afraied of the French, & having no confidence or trust in any measures or promises we enter into & finding that by our measures we are neither able nor willing to defend them, they were sensible that such a declaration (drawing ye french upon them) must be ye ruin of them. Their Resolution therefore was to observe a neutrality &, if they were press'd by ye English (who themselves took no real & Actual Step) to declare, I am told they wd have spoke, according as they express it, *from ye Mouth & not from ye Heart.*

Accordingly in Relation to the first head. In ye Afternoon of ye Day in which ye Governor spoke ye General Speech to them, there came a Deputation of ye Five Nations to acquaint him (according to their method of expressing things) that, when they mett to consider of an Answer, they found something so heavy upon their Hearts they coud not speak till it was removed & therefore desired to conferr first with ye Governor in ye presence of the Provinces there mett about this matter, viz., their complaints, that nothing but Love & Union might appear in the Treaty. The Governor with the Assistance of the Council of N York held a private conference with them, I suppose upon ye supposal that matters relating to Lands &c in the Province of N York were under the Jurisdiction only of the Government of N York.[54]

There was a matter occurrd in the course of the Treaty which does not appear upon ye Face of it. When ye Great Chain or Covenant Belt was deliver'd to & receiv'd by ye Indians, the whole Five Nations, according to ye usual Custom, every Nation singly after one another, shou'd have sounded ye Yoheigh-igh. (This is ye Form by which in Treaty they express their solemn acceptance of ye Belt deliver'd & approbation of ye proposition made. If a Sportsman was to sound this Yo-heigh-eigh in ye same tone & manner as ye Huntsman sounds the *Hark Forward*, he woud exactly express ye sound.) Instead of that they sound[ed] but one great [?] Indiscriminate [?] Yo heigh-eigh till, being reminded that the other was expected of them, they afterward gave ye *Yo-heigh-eigh* according to ye usual Custom. Some say this was from mere forgetfullness: but that is very unlikely from them who are such strict observers of These forms. Therefore others say it was they had a mind to disguise that all ye Nations did not universally give their hearty assent to ye Covenant 'till they saw what redress they were likely to find & upon what terms they were likely to be for ye future. However from ye Assurances they receivd & from the Disposition they observ'd in all the Commissioners from ye several provinces mett there, they took confidence all wd be well & spoke freely from their heart in their first speech.[55] But being a little dissatisfyed with some matters, & having (as it was saied) receiv'd some private reasons to appear satisfyed with others, You will easily observe in the second[56] that all Sincerity & Reality is sunk into Political Farce & Compliment (In which for ye address & management of it These People, tho we are apt to think them savages & so on, do actually exceed ye Europeans): "The Power is ye Governors, he has a right to do as he will, 'tis ours to be satisfyed & we submit"—"Virginia has done well in engageing in ye Assistance of our Flesh & Blood against ye French"—"Pensylvania has done well in doing nothing, Onas is wise of head & knows his own time."—If this be not insincerity but has a meaning, I am told this is ye mean-

[54] The conference of June 27 and 28, 1754. *Ibid.*, 865-68.
[55] The conference of July 2, 1754. *Ibid.*, 868-71.
[56] The conference of July 5, 1754. *Ibid.*, 875-77.

ing: That ye Indians as they are now circumstanced wou'd be sorry to see a general War between ye English & French & are therefore glad that matters have been so conducted on ye Ohio, that ye Dispute wears ye face of a private quarrel only amongst neighbours about land & is not made a general quarrel, as it wou'd have been, had Pensylvania, making it a common Cause, engaged also. But I shoud think that the Paper of Col Johnson's,[57] where he mentions ye Sentiments of ye Indians in regard to ye Lands & settling on ye Ohio, woud help to explain this. However, this Matter is now settled by ye Purchase that the Pensylsanians have made.[58] There was one thing which Hendrick said when he was told that ye Half King has engaged in ye Schirmish with Major Washington, which shows in what Light ye Indians view these formal Treaties. He said, if it be a Fact that the Half-King be engaged in blood, 'tis of more consequence to ye English than twenty such Treaties.[59] — The Belt they gave when they made the proposition about Col Johnson was as rich & larg a Belt as that which they gave in answer to ye Covenant Belt. — 'Tis by ye worth of ye Belt they deliver with any propositio[n] that they woud have understood ye importance of it & their earnestness in it & yet this does not appear in the transcript of ye treaty. As to ye Interpreting, tis most extream bad; at best the Interpreter is a most extream stupid, ignorant & illeterate Person. And a Standerby may observe that at times there are things which do not alway on ye face of the Treaty appear in their true meaning. — Your Lordship may wonder at my speaking thus upon a point I must be ignorant of as I do not know ye Language. But, My Lord, Many of ye Indians know English. Many almost all ye Albany people speak Indian. I always gott some one, when I cou'd, that cou'd speak it to stand next me, & I am intimately acquainted with a Gentleman who speaks ye Language readily.

As to ye matter of ye French Trade between Albany & Canada, the offering it to consideration in point of the advantage or disadvantage it is to ye English Trade is a disguis'd view of it. Tis ye hurt it does the English Interest amongst ye Indian by enabling our Rivals in that trade to forego us with ye Western indians in general, & in particular maintains the Cacknuagas in ye French Interest, for they are their Carriers & Factors in this Trade. But if the matter was properly inquired into, many secrets in this Trade might be unveild, for ye Albany People are quarreling amongst Them-

[57] *Ibid.*, 897-99.

[58] In order to forestall the purchase of the Wyoming Valley from the Six Nations by the Connecticut company, at the Albany Congress the Pennsylvania proprietors purchased for £400 New York currency the land south of 41° 31′ between the Susquehannah River and the western bounary of Pennsylvania. Gipson, *British Empire,* V, 121-22.

[59] The Half-King performed this chore with a vengeance at the surprise of Jumonville's camp: "Sometime after [the French surrendered], the Indians came up. The Half-King took his Tomahawk and Splitt the head of the ffrench Captain, having first Asked if he was an Englishman And having been told that he was a ffrench Man, he then took out his Brains, and washed his hands with them, And then Scalped him." Testimony of John B. Shaw, South Carolina Council Minutes, September 6, 1754, Colonial Office 5: 471.

selves. The two Parties are ye Oswego Traders & ye Canada Traders (I forgot to mention that some of ye Albany Commissioners are ye principal Canada Traders). The Former are in ye Interest & have ye Interest of the Five-Nations, the latter of ye Cacknuaga's & other french Indians.[60] — Upon ye whole Issue of the Treaty the Indians are gone away much better satisfyed that cou'd have been expected &, as Mr. Weiser [61] told me, he did not expect to find them so good Englishmen as they proved in their inclinations to be. Yet their Satisfaction rests in a Confidence of the English being in Earnest in the Promises they have made them. If after this Solemn treaty they find themselves deceiv'd, They will be more alienated than ever. — All ye Provinces that were present at this Treaty brought very handsome & large Presents. It was once proposed amongst them that part of ye Money intended for ye Presents shou'd be expended in Carrying ye Presents up into the Country. How this Came to be dropp'd, I can not say nor do I care or think it just to indulge [in] Conjectures when they lye on ye accusing side. There come a few of each Nation down to Albany (of some not a dozen in all); the presents are divided equally amongst the nations. Those few, finding it difficult enough to carry their own share, find that part they shou'd take up with them for their nation too much for them, & there are alway people enough ready to ease them of this Burthen. Moreover, besides ye Temptation the People have of byeing these things of ye Indians for nothing, it interferes with the Interest of ye Indian Traders that ye Indians shoud be supplyed & furnish'd by any hands but their own. There is one article of the Presents, namely, ye Rum (ye Gunpowder too) (why shou'd not it be so with all ye rest) that is never deliver'd to them 'till they gett into their own Country. This indeed may keep them from comitting Riots & doing mischief on the way. But Rum they will have, so ye Traders & People bye their presents all the way as they pass for Rum, &, when an Indian is once sett agoing, he will sell even to his skin for a single Dram. There is indeed a Proclamation alway issued on this occasion against selling Rum to the Indians, but it is a poor ineffectual remedy never putt in Execution. The People bye out of their very mouths the Provisions that are given them, & You see them dead drunk, in the Face of Day, at their Doors. — These matters might easily be remedied. There are measures that wou'd do it. But ye Albany Interest is powerfull in the Assembly & Governors have never cared to disoblige them: This is the Key to many Matters, particularly in Indian affairs.

The Treaty being now [torn] following according to the best Account I can gett is ye present state of Indian affairs. The Indians, [who] never loved the French nor their politics & alway considerd Alli[ance] with them as

[60] Charles H. McIlwain (ed.), *An Abridgment of the Indian Affairs Contained in Four Folio Volumes, Transacted in the Colony of New York, from the Year 1678 to the Year 1751*, by Peter Wraxall (Cambridge, 1915), lxiv-lxxxiii.

[61] Johann Conrad Weiser was the Pennsylvania Indian agent or interpreter from 1731 to 1760. He therefore opposed the policies of William Johnson and the interests of New York. Carl Bridenbaugh, "Johann Conrad Weiser," *Dictionary of American Biography*, XIX, 614-15.

putting themselves under subjection to them, have therefore endeavord to avoid their alliance as far as they coud keep themselves out of their power & woud still if they were able to support themselves against them; but the French with one hand have a strong Party amongst the Indians themselves that wou'd betray ye nations over, & with ye other they hold the Hatchet over their heads, ye Fall of which the Indians dread as not able to award ye Blow. The Indians, unwilling to undergo ye Yoke of a French alliance yet dreading to defye their power, have acted hitherto a timid & double part. But if they coud hope for a real & effectual Support in our Measures, viz., that we woud strengthen & support ye English Party amongst them & engage in such a plan as they coud trust woud be sufficient to resist ye French, The English Party woud be strong enough to make all declare in our favour. They have held out hitherto in these hopes. This last Treaty has now given them a solemn promise of such & ye Issue of it will determine Indian affairs. The late unfortunate blow ye English receiv'd on ye Monongahela [62] comes seasonably to convince ye several Assemblies of the necessity of their doing something if it does not prove of bad consequence in our Indian affairs. Yet if instead of waiting for ye Assistance of others, N York had built a Fort or two in ye Indian Country & run up an armd Vessel on ye Lake Ontario, the French coud neither have subsisted w[h]ere they are nor have gott back, for the Indians, being secured, woud not have permitted them to pass thro' their Country, & they coud not have gott thro ye Lakes.

I had proposed troubling your Lordship with my Sentiments about ye Conference held at Albany & ye Plan & Representation that was the consequence of it. But since I began this Letter, Mr Franklin of Philadelphia, with whom I have ye pleasure to have created an Intimacy, call'd in upon me & has promised to send me from Philadelphia ye P[lan] [63] together with ye Reasons & [purpose?] [63] upon which it is form'd with ye best account he can give me of ye Effect & consequences it is likely to have. Desirous as I am to obey yr Lordships commands & to send You the best account I can of these matters, I think myself very happy that I shall be thus able to transmitt to your Lordship by ye next ship that sails from hence the best account that coud come from America.[64] F[r]om the best observation I cou'd make I am persuaded that the Commissioners here mett on this occasion came with hearty inclinations to serve the Crown & Country. They were all the Leading Men in their respective Provinces. What was their Opinion will be the Sense, in general, of the Provinces they represented. What appears in the Minutes was the Unanimous Opinion of all mett except N York & in some points Mr. Norris of Philadelphia & he only so far differr'd as ye Principles of ye Party he is at ye head of lead him to appear.[65] In these Minutes your

[62] The defeat of George Washington at Fort Necessity on July 4, 1754.

[63] Torn.

[64] This statement probably refers to Franklin's explanation of the plan of union, printed in Albert Henry Smyth (ed.), *The Writings of Benjamin Franklin*, 10 vols. (New York, 1905-1907), III, 203-26.

[65] The Quakers.

Lordship will see in real earnest & without disguise their Sentiments of the General Interest of this Country. And from ye Attention that is given to these matters in England, I know they will form their Opinion of ye Attention & Inclinations of the Ministry to American Affairs. I hope your Lordship will excuse ye Liberty I have taken In mentioning this; 'tis because I can observe that (however unjust & unreasonable it may be) they indulge themselves in a jealousy of their being neglected. The having Commissioners from other Provinces making inquisition into ye Conduct of N York felt very disgustfull to this Province. They were & are very angry but express their resentment only against Massachusets under ye Supposition that that Province made this Inquisition subservient to their private Interest in ye Line in Dispute. I do not know how it is, but there seems a Strong Jealousy in this Province against any Inquiries Such as a Traveller of any Curiosity woud make. [Then they] become suspicious. Even I, insignificant as I am, have & do Experience this, Whereas ye People in ye Other Colonies I am acquainted with take pleasure in informing me of every thing about their Country & Government.

May I take ye Liberty to trouble your Lordship with an Observation or two that occurrs to [me].[63] The consequence of this meeting will certainly be that some [torn] Patents will be broke. And that for the future Lands will be granted out in a very different manner from what they have been. If the Lands allready unpatented & those that thus revert to ye Crown shoud for ye future be patented to some Trustees &c who shoud be directed to portion out such Tracts in Farms to private Settlers in Fee at very low prizes, just enough to pay them for their tro[uble][66] & expence of the Patent, Such Tracts woud not only be settled immediatly, but it wou'd lower ye Price of Land thro' ye whole Country which woud be another means to settle it.

2 If in Consequence of this Scheme of Union & Representation it shoud be thought necessary to send over or raise here Troops to guard ye Frontiers &c, they must be upon a very different Establishment from what they have been hitherto or they will alway be as bad & useless as they are at present. Upon ye Establishment they are at present to drudge on in perpetual Servitude without being releived, & under a condition of Life severer than they see that of ye Negroes to be here, under a kind of Transportation for Life without hope or encouragement of Reward: to be thus serving for six pence pr Diem out of which ye Exchange defrauds them of —— pr cent. while they cou'd labour in a free service & have five times ye Price;[67] to feel themselves under these circumstances while They see all . . . round them, Foreigners & Beggars & even Convicts that have servd their time, nay some time even Negroes (made free) enjoying all ye Blessings & Fruits of Liberty, masters of Property, of themselves & their own Labour, Thriving & growing rich under the Protection of their Service. The Sense of this State alway has had

66 Stained.

67 It was customary in New York for the company commander to draw for the soldiers' pay in sterling but to pay the men off in depreciated New York currency. Thereby the paymaster kept the difference between New York and sterling money.

& always will have such an effect upon the Minds of Men That it is impossible for ye best officers in ye World to keep up a good Souldiery. All, ye good as well as bad, become drunken & besotted with Rum & are soon Invalids or worse. If there be some few of steadiness of Mind sufficient to bear up under this uncomefortable state & to resist ye bewitching & universal remedy of Rum, they will either desert or remain with a disposition more pernicious to the Service. The Case may be made very different in Europe, but this, My Lord, is a known Fact of all ye Troops that have been & are at this day on this Continent & e[ver] will be ye Case.[68]

[68] The last line and a half are illegible. The remaining pages of the letter are missing.

Book Reviews

The Lost Discovery; Uncovering the Track of the Vikings in America. By Frederick J. Pohl. (New York: W. W. Norton & Company, 1952. 346 pp. Illustrations, appendixes, bibliography, and index. $3.75.)

In 1898 an alleged runestone was discovered at Kensington, Minnesota. Certain writers, notably Hjalmar R. Holand, claimed it as an authentic record of a fourteenth-century Viking expedition. Holand's writings in particular have had some vogue in recent years. Much interest has also attached to the round stone tower at Newport in New England, which, it is claimed by Holand and others, served Viking settlers in a dual capacity as church and fortress. Old Norse artifacts in the form of a sword, an axe, and a metal bar were reportedly discovered in 1930 near Lake Nipigon in Ontario. These objects, together with other alleged runestones, mooring holes, iron furnaces, and weapons, have been cited as evidence of extensive pre-Columbian European activity in North America.

A majority of scholars have been either openly hostile or profoundly skeptical in their reactions to the claims of the Holand school. The recent report of the investigations of Professor Johannes Bröndsted, a Danish archeologist, agrees substantially with the views long held in the learned world. This report, in the preparation of which Bröndsted was assisted by two runologists and two philologists, brands the Kensington Stone as a forgery; similarly, it refuses to accept as genuinely runic the markings on numerous other stones. While admitting a striking resemblance between the Newport Tower and medieval Norse architecture, Bröndsted agrees with American archeologists that the structure was probably a lookout tower of seventeenth-century construction. As for the metal objects from Ontario, he acknowledges that these are indeed of late tenth-century Norwegian origin, but adds that there is no proof that they were not brought across the Atlantic in recent times and "planted" in American soil.

In fairness to Holand and his friends, it should be remarked that reputable scholars have come to their defense. His chief supporters, however, are a group of writers of varying backgrounds and abilities who share one vital quality — an unwavering faith in their cause. Their painstaking study of records and tireless search of evidence to support their exciting theories can be compared to the labors and self-sacrifice of consecrated missionaries. As a result of their writings, what was once largely the concern of a few foreign-language newspapers or the subject matter of a kind of regional folklore has now produced a flood of books that shows little indication of receding. For better or for worse and with or without academic blessing, the quest for the "lost discovery" continues.

Frederick J. Pohl's recent volume, *The Lost Discovery*; *Uncovering the Track of the Vikings in America*, should be viewed against the background of the writings of such men as Holand — both because of the book's content and because of the author's methodology. In one respect, however, it rests on firmer ground; eleven of its fifteen chapters are devoted to an original reading of such sources as the Icelandic *Flateyjarbók* and *Hauksbók*. Mr. Pohl's interpretation of these records is supported by extensive field work in New England. Concerning the voyages of Bjarni Herjulfsson and of Leif and Thorvald Ericson, his conclusions may be briefly stated: the *Flateyjarbók* is an accurate narrative when read with the eye of an experienced mariner rather than that of the landlubber scholar. Leif's Helluland is Newfoundland; Markland (meaning Forestland) is Nova Scotia. Vinland is located, not vaguely in southern New England, but in Nantucket Sound on Cape Cod. Leif, we are told, established his Shelters (or camp) on Follins Pond, a swelling of the Bass River. In this area Mr. Pohl discovered a number of alleged Viking mooring holes in the rocks along the water's edge. Leif's brother Thorvald, in a later expedition, led his men northward into Somes Sound on Mount Desert Island, Maine. There the first Norse encounter with Indians (Skraelings) took place, and there, too, Thorvald was laid to rest in the first Christian burial in America. In telling the story of Gudrid and her ambitious plan of settlement in America, Mr. Pohl reconciles the divergent accounts in *Flateyjarbók* and *Hauksbók*.

There the book might have ended but doesn't. The author retells Holand's story of the Paul Knutson voyage and the consequent writing on the Kensington Stone. It is Holand's belief, and apparently Mr. Pohl's too, that the Norsemen who disappeared from the Western Settlement in Greenland during the fourteenth century were living in southern New England at the time of this voyage; Knutson, in fact, is said to have journeyed from this settlement to Minnesota by way of Hudson Bay. Pohl accepts the Newport Tower as a Viking structure after demonstrating that its linear unit of construction was the Norse foot. The little-known Zeno narrative is also injected into the volume as the record of an Atlantic crossing in 1398 by a fleet under the command of Prince Henry Sinclair of Orkney. This expedition, the author maintains, landed at Asphalt, Nova Scotia. For good measure, the author tosses into an appendix an account of pre-Viking Irish discovery of America (Greenland) as well as a novel interpretation of "Pattee's Caves" in New Hampshire. The appendixes include, among other things, a surprisingly long chronological list of "Pre-Columbian Voyages in the Atlantic" and a summary of

"Theories as to Location of Leif Ericson's Vinland." The book also contains a "selected Bibliography" and a carefully prepared index.

Professor Bröndsted suggests the advisability of sponsoring a well-equipped and well-manned scientific expedition to investigate and if possible to settle once and for all the disputed question of Viking activity in America. In the meantime, a thoughtful social historian might profitably study the writings of Holand, Pohl, and others with the view to determining what it is in American life that makes able men of both New England and immigrant stock so sure of theories arrived at by insufficient documentation and tortured logic.

St. Olaf College KENNETH BJORK

American Beginnings; Highlights and Sidelights of the Birth of the New World. By Jarvis M. Morse. With an introduction by Luther Evans. (Washington: Public Affairs Press, 1952. ix + 260 pp. Index. $3.75.)

The present volume is devoted to a survey of contemporary accounts of the English colonies in America prior to the War of Independence. It is concerned not merely with the accounts themselves but with the circumstances under which they were produced, and with the men who produced them. It thus contains a series of biographical sketches, often of necessity tantalizingly brief and fragmentary, which nonetheless afford a measure of insight into the character of the early writers to whom we owe much of our knowledge of this country's beginnings. Taking advantage of the scope given him by his somewhat ambiguous title, the author does not confine himself to historians properly so-called. Descriptions of geography and ethnology, promotional literature, the polemics of controversy, all are germane to his task. Nor does he restrict his attention to books, even though he "has seldom descended to review of tracts shorter than five or six pages." The result is quite comprehensive; its wide sweep being in itself a tribute to Professor Morse's acquaintance with early Americana.

Chapters reflect a topical arrangement within a general chronological framework. Accounts of explorations are succeeded by those dealing with the early abortive attempts at colonization. Virginia's primacy is recognized in a separate chapter, and the author accords similar treatment to his native New England. The colonies, from Newfoundland to Georgia, are then surveyed with a sweep which bears the reader down the Atlantic coast, and then out to sea to embrace Bermuda and the West Indies. A chapter on the Indians acknowledges the superiority of Wraxall's account to Colden's, but surprisingly accords the former no further recognition. "Intrigue and Insurrection" may well be for many readers the most interesting of all. It is replete with the literature of internal controversy, with New England receiving more than twice as much attention as New York, Maryland, and Virginia combined. "The Great Puritans," "The Imperialists," who wrote of the colonies with more of a world view than did their contemporaries, and "The Provincial Chronicles," the efforts of the more conscious historians of the period, are then surveyed in turn. The author draws his various threads together in a concluding chapter.

Despite an occasional passage which might lead the casual or uninformed reader into minor misconception, this is a volume of substantial merit. Its admittedly uneven coverage, while partly occasioned by the incidence of the writings themselves, also reflects the author's own enthusiasms, and these enthusiasms are infectious. It will be read with pleasure as well as profit, and the expressed hope that some of its readers may be induced to look up the "ancients" will surely be realized.

University of Pennsylvania LEONIDAS DODSON

Colonial South Carolina; Two Contemporary Descriptions by Governor James Glen and Doctor George Milligen-Johnston. Edited by Chapman J. Milling. *South Caroliniana Sesquicentennial Series*, No. 1. (Columbia: University of South Carolina Press, 1951. xxii + 209 pp. Map and index. $4.00.)

South Carolina has lagged behind most states in the publication of her source materials relative to the colonial period. Serious students of her history have had to choose between pleasant, but expensive and time-consuming, sojourns in South Carolina, or dependence upon secondary works. Even the purchase of microfilms or low-cost photostats has been difficult or impossible, due to library restrictions or the lack of facilities. Thus the unique files of the pre-Revolutionary South Carolina newspapers in the Charleston Library Society have been available only to residents and visitors.

In recent years, however, has appeared the promise of better things. Under the editorship of J. H. Easterby, the Historical Commission of South Carolina has renewed publication of the *Colonial Records of South Carolina.* And now, under the general editorship of Robert L. Meriwether, a series entitled *South Caroliniana* has been begun, using some of the rare imprints and manuscripts from the collection of the South Caroliniana Library of the University of South Carolina.

Two facsimile pamphlets comprise Number 1 of the *South Caroliniana* series. An excellent introduction, by Chapman J. Milling, traces the careers of Governor James Glen (1743-1756), one of the most intelligent of South Carolina's royal governors, and of Dr. George Milligen-Johnston, a physician resident in South Carolina between 1749 and 1775.

Glen's *A Description of South Carolina* . . . (London, 1761), and Milligen-Johnston's *A Short Description of the Province of South Carolina* . . . (London, 1770), are reproduced from recently discovered copies which belonged to Dr. Milligen-Johnston himself. Both works benefit from their former owner, for the Doctor wrote a one-page manuscript "introduction" to Glen's work, inscribed several pages of "Additions" to his own *Description* covering the years 1763 to 1775, and offered other marginalia comments and corrections.

The pamphlet by Glen, originally written in answer to "Queries" of the Board of Trade, is the more comprehensive of the two works. But both of them touch upon nearly every important aspect of South Carolina with a general objectivity which is sometimes relieved by fleeting glimpses of their authors' pleasure or sorrow, hopes or despair at certain characteristics of the luxurious and fascinating culture they had come to know so well.

Roosevelt College of Chicago RICHARD J. HOOKER

Architecture and Town Planning in Colonial Connecticut. By Anthony N. B. Garvan. (New Haven: Yale University Press, 1951. xiv + 166 pp. Illustrations and index. $7.50.)

Connecticut contains many notable nineteenth-century and modern buildings, but surprisingly few important colonial structures. Fortunately the relatively meager pre-Revolutionary material has been thoroughly investigated and admirably published. Isham and Brown, Trowbridge and Andrews produced valuable studies, while the writings of John Frederick Kelly are models of their kind. Thus Anthony Garvan's handsome book is but the latest addition to a distinguished series.

The title is misleading. The author rarely mentions the eighteenth century, being concerned almost exclusively with the problems and achievements of the first few generations of settlers. Nor is his book a comprehensive study even of their architecture. It is rather a series of essays dealing with the immigrating population, the planning of towns, the laying out of rural areas, and some of the techniques and traditions which determined the forms of the early buildings.

By and large previous writings have been narrowly architectural, a series of detailed analyses of individual monuments. Mr. Garvan's essays provide a valuable background for them. He shows how the theories advanced by social historians can illuminate architecture. Particularly important is his knowledge of foreign source material. For example, one great difficulty for the student of our earliest buildings is the disappearance of most of the English structures comparable to those of our seventeenth century. Garvan has examined the manuscripts of English real estate surveys. He has discovered striking parallels between the settlement of the British colonies in North America and the contemporary occupation of Ulster. The new information he thus acquired enables him for the first time to define exactly the dependence of our buildings on those of the mother country.

In addition to these solid virtues the author's originality and perceptiveness give his book further significance. With a few keen observations he deftly destroys Isham and Kelly's evolutionary theory of colonial house design which has been all but universally accepted. Noting that the core of New Haven is oddly oriented, he suggests that the planner may have been faithfully following a prescription of Vitruvius guaranteed to protect a city from prevailing winds. Throughout, the traditional jargon of aesthetic analysis is altogether lacking. Yet here and there in the later chapters the author shyly reveals a fresh appreciation of the beauty of the buildings he is discussing. One can only regret that he was so reticent and so rarely permitted himself to express this sensitivity.

The book does seem incomplete. Garvan has made such stimulating contributions to the few topics he has discussed that one can only hope that someday he will take up many others. Until he has gratified them in this way his readers will be as greedy as they are grateful.

Fogg Museum, Cambridge, Massachusetts JOHN COOLIDGE

Gentlemen Freeholders; Political Practices in Washington's Virginia. By Charles S. Sydnor. (Chapel Hill: The University of North Carolina Press, 1952. ix + 180 pp. Appendixes, bibliographical note, and index. $3.50.)

It seems to be generally agreed among American historians that we have never had a group of leaders equal to those who dominated the scene during the Revolution and the early years of the republic. The fact that these men received their training in the aristocratic colonial school of politics may have caused some inquisitive souls to wonder why our more recent democracy has never been able to turn out a better product. But, as far as the reviewer is aware, Professor Sydnor is the first to devote serious attention to this problem.

In order to arrive at an answer, he has analyzed the political institutions of Virginia during the late colonial and early republican periods, going into detail as to the electorate, the elections, and the elect. Since the electorate was restricted to freeholders and leadership to the gentry, the system was a thoroughly aristocratic one. It had its origins in England, but had been modified in various ways by local conditions, and among the more important changes was the development of almost complete autonomy by the parish vestries and the county courts. This naturally put much power into the hands of the chosen few, yet the machinery worked smoothly and gave general satisfaction, owing largely to the sense of public responsibility felt by the governing class and the deference then due to "a man of pedigree." As Professor Sydnor so trenchantly points out, the author of the statement "that all men are created equal" had no faith whatever in the equal fitness of all men for political leadership.

Though the description of political practices is scholarly and authentic, one gets the impression that the picture changed but little as a result of the

Revolution. This is largely because so much more attention is paid to the lower house of the legislature than to the governor and Council. Actually, a new group of leaders took command when the movement for independence got under way and the colonial aristocracy never again exercised the influence which it had previously possessed. It is true that local government was carried on without much change and that the landed gentry still ruled, but it was no longer the closed corporation that it had been in former times. The author maintains that aristocracy and democracy are not antagonistic principles and that we might profit in some degree by the example of the Founding Fathers as to the process by which leaders should be trained and selected. Whether or not he approves of their insistence upon local autonomy is not clear. However, the volume is concerned primarily with facts rather than theories; it only suggests that we think about the significance of the facts.

We are indebted to the Institute of Early American History and Culture, under whose auspices this book was published, for yet another informative and provocative study.

University of Virginia THOMAS PERKINS ABERNETHY

Thomas Mifflin and the Politics of the American Revolution. By Kenneth R. Rossman. (Chapel Hill: The University of North Carolina Press, 1952. xii + 344 pp. Illustrations, bibliographical note, and index. $5.00.)

Although Thomas Mifflin is "only a secondary figure in a period studded by great men," it is remarkable that in the century and a half since his death he has not been made the subject of a comprehensive biography. His role on the national stage during the American Revolution, and later in Pennsylvania where for fifteen years he held a state office, and was chief executive of the state for nine consecutive years, would seem to entitle him to such consideration. Even now Mr. Rossman does not offer us a biography, but rather a study of Mifflin's part in the politics and intrigues of the American Revolution, and more than two decades of Pennsylvania state history. Stress therefore is laid on the times, their impact on Mifflin, and his relations to the men and movements of his day.

In twenty-three chapters of very uneven length — there are chapters of five and six pages, and others of twenty-four and twenty-seven — the author sketches Mifflin's military and political career. The first chapter quickly brings Mifflin to his first experience in officeholding; then we trace his career in the Continental army, review his conduct of the office of quartermaster general, and follow him through the years of uninterrupted holding of civil office till his death.

In his portrayal of Mifflin Mr. Rossman touches upon a number of topics, which, it must be admitted, have been treated more exhaustively by others. *Bring Out Your Dead*, by John H. Powell, is a more complete account of the yellow fever visitations of Philadelphia; *Pennsylvania in the American Revolution*, by Charles Lincoln, is a fuller treatment of the part played by the keystone state in the struggle for independence; *The Republicans and Democrats in Pennsylvania, 1790-1801*, by Harry M. Tinkcom, is a more detailed survey of the controversy over the revision of the state constitution. The merit of Mr. Rossman's volume lies in his centering the events and movements around a man who played an important part in them, and showing how they affected Mifflin, and how he, in turn, influenced them. This procedure has definite advantages, and the author has accomplished his purpose satisfactorily. No startling discoveries are recorded. An objective approach and a conservative attitude characterize this study; for example, after a detailed analysis of the Conway Cabal he sides with Edmund C. Burnett in regarding the episode as "one of the historical puzzles of the Revolution," rather than with the extreme view of Bernhard Knollenberg that the "so-called plot" was "a myth."

If, as is the reviewer's opinion, this book will be read by scholars rather than by the general public, why are the footnotes not placed at the bottom of the page for the convenience of the scholar? Exception might be taken to the use of such phrases as "a recent writer," or "a recent biographer," with no indication of identity; for such practice makes it impossible for the reader to evaluate the worth of the testimony. On page 130 reference is given to Allan Nevins' comment on the Continental Congress, while Burnett is denied such recognition. Assuredly in this instance Burnett's opinion is the more worth while. As the author admits, quotations abound in Chapter XIII, but it is a matter of opinion whether they are excessive in number. Now that Mr. Rossman has given us a thorough study of the times and their impact on Mifflin, we suggest that he give us a brief biography with emphasis on home life and friendships to combat the impression that Mifflin was just a soldier and civil official who won political battles and battles of wits but waged a losing fight for personal sobriety.

West Baden College CHARLES H. METZGER

Valley Forge; The Making of an Army. By Alfred Hoyt Bill. (New York: Harper & Brothers, 1952. xii + 259 pp. Bibliography and index. $3.50.)

This volume deals with Valley Forge, but it is really a history of the army under the personal direction of Washington during the years 1777-1778. The author believes that the achievements of that army and of its commander during that period have been insufficiently appreciated. He thinks that "The attack at Germantown, though it failed, did as much as Saratoga to convince the French King's ministers" that France should recognize the United States; that "Washington's accurate estimate of the country-wide situation and the marching and fighting of his army throughout the summer and early fall of 1777 . . . made the victory at Saratoga possible"; that "The heroic defense of the forts on the Delaware . . . was an indirect cause of Sir Henry Clinton's fatal tardiness in going to the assistance of Burgoyne." It will not surprise those familiar with the historiography of the American Revolution that Mr. Bill writes of the Conway Cabal as a fact, a "conspiracy."

There is very little that is new in the author's narrative, in his theses, in his evidence. Mr. Bill belongs to the "George-did-it" school of historians. He follows in the wake of John C. Fitzpatrick and the many writers who have exalted Washington and his seeming friends at the expense of his critics, including both members of Congress and military men. Is it worth while to point out that the evidence does not show Germantown influencing French policy in the same degree as Saratoga? Or that proof of a Conway conspiracy is lacking? The "George-did-it" school will pay no attention, will continue to ignore the findings of cool and competent scholars such as Edward Channing, Bernhard Knollenberg, and L. H. Butterfield. A fair estimate of the achievements of Washington and his army in 1777 and 1778 requires highest praise for both. Such an estimate does not require violent criticism of a Congress burdened with many troubles nor excessive depreciation of a Gates suffering from diarrhea and doing his not-so-horrible best.

Mr. Bill errs rather too frequently in matters of detail, notably in dealing with the British side of the war. However, he writes quite freshly, and his narrative is definitely readable.

University of Nebraska JOHN R. ALDEN

George Washington; A Biography. By Douglas Southall Freeman. Vol. V, *Victory with the Help of France*. (New York: Charles Scribner's Sons, 1952. xvi + 570 pp. Illustrations, maps, appendixes, bibliographical note, short-title index, and index. $7.50.)

Volume V of Freeman's life of Washington carries the General from the receipt of the news of the French alliance on April 30, 1778, to his one great military victory at Yorktown and his return to Mount Vernon on December 24, 1783. The central theme of the volume is the part played by the French-American alliance in the final defeat of the British forces in America. Washington himself declared "no event was ever received with more heartfelt joy" than the news that that alliance had been signed, and he often expressed the view that supremacy on the sea through the French navy was essential to success. Because of this view he refused to engage in an all-out contest with the enemy until that superiority was attained. Mr. Freeman is in complete accord with Washington's view; he says that "America never had a prospect of winning her independence by force of arms until her ally protected her waters and defeated or blockaded the fleet of Britain." But if the French fleet under de Grasse and artillery under Rochambeau assured final victory at Yorktown, the author recognizes Washington's contribution. He concludes,

"Washington had a final basis of victory the credit for which was primarily his own. That was the speed of his concentration."

Washington proved most adept in his relations with the French. He opposed an independent French campaign against Canada and was often disappointed in French delay in bringing up naval support, but he only once voiced criticism of French cooperation. De Grasse was difficult to deal with but Washington was on most cordial terms with Lafayette and Rochambeau.

Mr. Freeman emphasizes in Volume V, as he did in the preceding one, Washington's difficulties in maintaining an army. The winters of 1779-1780 and 1780-1781 were nearly as severe as that at Valley Forge. The men were naked, without shoes, shirts, stockings, hats, uniforms, and blankets; lacking in meat the troops had only unpalatable bread and, consequently, devoured every kind of horse feed except hay. Washington reported from Morristown that "more than half [the men] were naked and two thirds were starved." Under such conditions it is not surprising that Washington was faced by wholesale desertion and mutiny. At first he wavered between argument and force but finally decided upon resolute, even severe, means to suppress mutiny. He ordered Robert Howe to quell the mutiny by force and then "instantly execute a few of the most active and incendiary leaders." "Unless this dangerous spirit can be suppressed by force, there is an end to all subordination in the Army, and indeed to the Army itself." Washington was also bedeviled by pride, envy, and quarreling among his officers over rank and seniority. Since Mr. Freeman relies chiefly on Washington's reports on these problems he doubtless magnifies the difficulties.

The author brings new light to bear on the Newberg addresses and Washington's leave-taking from his army, both of which are dramatically played up. He also emphasizes Washington's views on strengthening the government. Writing to Alexander Hamilton on March 31, 1783, Washington said: "No man in the United States is, or can be more deeply impressed with the necessity of reform in our present Confederation than myself." The reform he thought necessary was to establish "An indissoluble Union of the States under one Federal Head," with supreme power in Congress to regulate and govern the general concerns of the republic, in a word a national government.

The present volume is excellent for a study of Washington's military career but it has certain limitations. Except for Washington's relations with the French, the General is pictured as an isolated figure with little regard for the many who were working with him. One gets only a partial picture of the war since Mr. Freeman excludes from the story those events with which Washington was not directly concerned. Thus the story of the war in the South is inadequately sketched.

The last twenty-odd pages review Washington's career as a strategist, tactician, leader of men, and army administrator. The author points out the

General's weaknesses as well as his strength, and accounts for his final victory. This section, a superb character analysis, ably supplements the two similar studies found in earlier volumes. Integrity, says Mr. Freeman, was the secret of Washington's strength.

University of North Carolina FLETCHER M. GREEN

Commentaries on the Constitution, 1790-1860. By Elizabeth Kelley Bauer. (New York: Columbia University Press, 1952. 400 pp. Bibliography and index. $4.75.)

According to the author, this work is a survey of the formal interpretation of the Constitution before the Civil War. It has been prepared from the historical standpoint as a contribution to the history of American political thought and occupies a position midway between the fields of history, political science, and law. In this study only "formal commentaries" are used, that is, those published in book form and "designed to be expository" even though controversial. Excluded are such materials as judicial decisions, acts of congress, presidential pronouncements, speeches, pamphlets, magazine and newspaper articles, and works of foreign observers like De Tocqueville and Martineau. The works of "Congressional spokesmen" like Webster and Calhoun as well as such "argumentative tracts" as the *Federalist Papers* likewise fall outside the main confines of the study.

An introduction of fifteen pages and two chapters comprise Part I. Part II contains three chapters of brief biographical sketches of thirteen writers classified as commentators of the "Middle States" (Wilson, Rawle, DuPonceau, Kent, Duer, Hoffmann), the "New England Nationalists" (Chipman, Dane, Story, Walker), and the "States Rights School of the South" (St. George and Henry St. George Tucker and John Taylor of Caroline). Part III has three chapters dealing respectively with the location of sovereignty, the compact theory as opposed to the supreme law theory, and "Story's *Commentaries on the Constitution*." The twenty-five pages of Part IV are entitled "The Uses of the Commentaries."

Obviously, this is by no means a definitive or exhaustive study. The author apparently has chosen to use the form of a scholarly monograph to write primarily for undergraduates in law and liberal arts to whom "the majority of the pre-Civil War commentators are unknown." As a bibliographical exercise, the study represents in book form scarcely more than a part of the preparation any serious graduate student should make before attacking a major constitutional problem in the pre-Civil War period. There are some interesting biographical data, however, which may be useful to the general historian. But by separating the biographical data of the commentators from her comments on their commentaries, the author has made careful reading of her book a difficult task. Indeed, whatever her intention, the writer seems to have compiled a reference book of sorts.

A remarkable aspect of the book is its "sampling." Seeming to inquire into the whole thought of none of the commentators, the author attempts to present the views of them all on two selected subjects, namely, the location of sovereignty and the nature of the Union. She also examines Story's *Commentaries on the Constitution* "in its entirety, to see what subjects were included." Nevertheless, the author chooses to emphasize "Story's basic theory of nationalism as it appears in his Commentaries."

This, of course, is no place to discuss the merits of sampling, either qualitative or quantitative, but at least it is noteworthy that the basis of Story's theory of constitutional nationalism is found primarily in his *Commentaries on the Conflict of Laws*. It is the author's comment on these commentaries that "Story touched on juridical concepts in the federal relations of the United States" (p. 156).

University of Michigan WILLIAM R. LESLIE

The Keystone in the Democratic Arch: Pennsylvania Politics, 1800-1816. By Sanford W. Higginbotham. (Harrisburg: Pennsylvania Historical and Museum Commission, 1952. x + 417 pp. Notes, illustrations, bibliography, and index. $3.00 cloth; $2.50 paper-bound.)

This important publication begins where Professor Harry M. Tinkcom's excellent study, *The Republicans and Federalists in Pennsylvania, 1789-1801*, ends. These two books give a complete coverage of Pennsylvania politics from 1789 to 1815.

The first chapter of the study under review carries the same title as that of the book. It opens with these words: "The Jeffersonian Republicans in Pennsylvania were firmly convinced that they had been largely responsible for the triumph of Thomas Jefferson and his party over the Federalists in 1800. Proud of their exploits, they boasted that their state was the '*key stone in the democratic arch*,' unmoved by all attempts to dislodge it. In the national political crises of the sixteen years which followed, events were amply to justify this claim" (p. 1).

The introductory chapter deals with farming and trading, the racial groups who made their home in the Keystone State, the rise of political parties, and the principles for which they stood locally and nationally.

The second chapter is chiefly concerned with the uniting of the Republican party in the state against the unwise measures passed by the Congress during the presidency of John Adams, such as the Alien and Sedition Acts and the tax on dwellings. The conduct of the troops in the suppression of Fries's Rebellion was so outrageous that the Republicans charged the Federalists with instituting a reign of terror. These political mistakes led to the downfall of the Federalists and to the triumph of the Republicans. "After the election of 1800 Federalism in the state declined precipitately; and within two years John Quincy Adams was to describe it as 'so completely palsied, that scarcely a trace of it is to be discovered except in here and there a newspaper edited by New England men' " (p. 25). The temporary incapacitated Federalist party weakened the compulsion for unity among the state Republicans, which in turn led to a number of local divisions within the party. This political disunity eventually precipitated a fight between the governor and the legislature.

Jefferson had his trouble with the federal courts; so did Governor Thomas McKean of Pennsylvania. McKean's problem, however, was different from that of the President, who wished to repeal the Judiciary Act of 1801 and to impeach certain federal judges. In Pennsylvania the members of the legislature rather than the Governor demanded reform and also the impeachment of at least one state judge. This political struggle was the beginning of a major break within the Republican party. A complete treatment of the state judicial reform efforts is to be found in Chapters III and IV.

The author clearly demonstrates in Chapter VII his understanding of the political and diplomatic issues involved in the election of 1808. The Federalists opposed Jefferson's Embargo Act, but the Republicans of the state supported it. The coalition of the Quids and Republicans assured the election of Madison to the presidency.

Chapters VIII and IX present the Olmsted case and the first administration of Governor Simon Snyder respectively. Chapter X is entitled, "Foreign Affairs, War and the Presidential Election: 1809-1812." The author reviews the causes of the War of 1812, the declaration of war, and the early phases of the military struggle. He does not, however, neglect the political situation in 1812. Madison was running for re-election against DeWitt Clinton. The former naturally defended his record, whereas the latter attacked the inept conduct of the war. Despite minor Republican defections, Pennsylvania voted for Madison; otherwise he would have lost the national election.

The chapter on "War, Politics, and Schisms" is excellent. Here internal strife and political discords are emphasized; but other questions are treated, such as federal loans, manufacturing, prices, war finance, and suspension of specie payments. The last two chapters deal with the Treaty of Ghent and Pennsylvania in retrospect.

The book is filled with valuable historical, political, and diplomatic information, secured primarily from original sources, state papers, and magazines. The study is well annotated, the bibliography is adequate, and the index is excellent. The book places Pennsylvania politics in its proper national perspective.

Lehigh University GEORGE D. HARMON

The Era of Good Feelings. By George Dangerfield. (New York: Harcourt, Brace and Company, 1952. xiv + 525 pp. Bibliography and index. $6.00.)

In this delightful volume Mr. Dangerfield has attempted a synthesis of that well-defined period of American history which begins with the Treaty of Ghent and ends with the inauguration of Andrew Jackson. It is a fascinating America that comprises the subject of this book, one that had at the conclusion of the War of 1812 suddenly turned its back on Europe and had fallen upon its own resources to enter an era of intense internal development. This momentous national decision produced a singular energy in politics and diplomacy, for both were geared to national growth and independence. The author analyzes many facets of this exuberance, building his panorama of the period around five chronological episodes — the diplomacy at Ghent, the Panic of 1819, the Missouri Compromise, the Monroe Doctrine, and the administration of John Quincy Adams. The narrative moves logically beyond events to personalities, for this was an age when the personal myth exceeded the institution in importance. Each of the significant characters such as Adams, Clay, Calhoun, Jackson, Monroe, Marshall, and Canning is introduced with a lucid and often amusing biographical sketch. Taken together these constitute a major contribution of the book. All is written, moreover, in an imaginative literary style seldom found in historical works.

Despite its general excellence, the book cannot escape all criticism. The author does not seem to exploit fully the possibilities presented by a remarkable organization that permits the coordination of the twin developments of nationalism and sectionalism. After disposing of Ghent, for example, he sees in the westward expansion into the Mississippi Valley the vehicle for describing the rise of agrarian nationalism. Under his deft handling the views of the West and its two leaders, Clay and Jackson, become crystal clear. Yet he analyzes neither the breaking of the home market in the Ohio Valley nor the geographical pattern of western politics. He treats a second phase of American sectionalism superbly in the Missouri Compromise. Here he evaluates the South and the beginnings of the southern defense of slavery. But as he moves on into Monroe's second administration and the shift to economic nationalism, he all but ignores the expansion of New England industry as an important aspect of sectional growth. Instead, he prefers to interpret these years in terms of British industrialism and the incipient free trade movement in England as reflected in the "New Toryism" of George Canning. Here as elsewhere he gives evidence of his own British heritage and his prior interest in British liberalism.

Any criticism of this work is overshadowed by its evident merits. The writer's reliance on source material has been ample if not extensive. If he has produced little new interpretation, it must be recalled that the monographic and biographical materials of this period are rich enough to preclude any great originality. Unquestionably he has gleaned what is most pertinent from these writings to produce a volume characterized by freshness and penetrating observation. Such qualifications, needless to say, make it a very worthwhile and useful volume.

Stanford University NORMAN A. GRAEBNER

The Territorial Papers of the United States. Compiled and edited by Clarence Edwin Carter. Vol. XVIII, *The Territory of Alabama, 1817-1819.* (Washington: United States Government Printing Office, 1952. xiii + 875 pp. Symbols and index. $5.50.)

Alabama began its territorial existence with a successful effort to retain its boundaries against an encroaching Mississippi and ended it with an unsuccessful attempt to extend them over western Florida. For the short two years between these two events the relevant documents are of such huge bulk that the editor of this volume has been compelled to omit great masses of them. The most conspicuous omissions (as in other volumes of this series) lie in the field of Indian affairs. The Creeks alone of the Indians had villages within the confines of the Territory and their recent indulgence in the delights of civil war had rendered them all but impotent to affect the burgeoning development of the land. The documents here published reveal that the Creek contribution to territorial history was limited to the exacting of exorbitant rates on the ferries they had been canny enough to retain in their own hands, and of engineering the demise of the Ft. Mitchell factory by giving their trade to their own licensed (and unlicensed) traders.

The reviewer has the impression (which he has not confirmed by actual count) that the bulk of the material included in this volume has to do with the survey and sale of public lands, of which, thanks to the grand larceny of the treaty at Ft. Jackson, Alabama largely consisted. Most of this is of a technical and highly prosaic nature but the few documents relating to the French Tombigbee settlers hint of far adventure. Throughout the territorial existence (as for long afterward) the land speculators were ever present and at times their machinations were so bold as to halt the sales altogether. There is, as there was bound to be, quite a bit of material on the Federal Road, the bottom of which seemed to be perennially falling out nothwithstanding the fact that it was apparently in a chronic state of relocation. The large number of documents relating to the mails reveals that this government service abundantly deserved the continual flow of maledictions so liberally bestowed upon it. As the Territory neared its end the shadows of the Panic of 1819 were falling upon it as upon the other portions of the United States. The deposit of land revenues in the territorial banks, notably those at St. Stephens and at Huntsville, had encouraged them in the loose banking practices demanded by the flush times; the danger of losing these revenues in the gathering hard times called down on the banks some very candid criticism from Treasury officials.

All in all this volume of *Territorial Papers* serves rather to confirm than to increase our knowledge of Alabama history. The fault does not lie with the compiler for it is not likely that any wider selection of material would have materially changed the picture. And, as in preceding volumes of the *Papers*, the editing is of such excellence as to make superfluous any criticism by the reviewer.

University of Georgia R. S. COTTERILL

The American Diaries of Richard Cobden. Edited, with an introduction and notes, by Elizabeth Hoon Cawley. (Princeton: Princeton University Press, 1952. xii + 233 pp. Bibliography and index. $4.00.)

The publication of Richard Cobden's diaries of his visits to America in 1835 and 1859 will be welcomed by those keenly interested in pre-Civil War America and in Cobden himself. To the general students of English and American history, they will be of less interest. Since Cobden never intended their publication, his entries are sketchy and random, and too often concerned with the externals of travel. Although he notes many fascinating facts and makes some shrewd observations, little of what he tells is new. The principal value of the diaries is the fullness and greater accuracy they give to existing interpretations of Cobden and of the American scene.

To John Morley's *Life of Richard Cobden*, for example, the diaries add little more than an emphasis on the personable side of Cobden. In the diaries he is not, as in the House of Commons and on the lecture platform, all logic, seriousness, and economics. His rollicking accounts of fellow passengers and his vivid descriptions of nature show him to be a man full of humor and poetic feeling. The diaries also show him to be a middle-class manufacturer, a fact which colored much of his view of America.

America, as Mrs. Cawley notes in her excellent introduction, pleased Cobden mightily. He shows none of De Tocqueville's doubts about America's social equality and none of Dickens' irritation with their passion for money. Instead Cobden praises the sobriety and good conduct of the lower classes, rejoices in the equal opportunity offered by a free education, and speaks well of their industry and enterprise. And his enthusiasm for American democracy was tempered only by his English and middle-class prejudice against the Irish proletariat of the large towns. But it was not the working of democracy as much as signs of economic progress which above all caught his observant eye. He recorded rents, prices, and wages with the care of a businessman surveying a field of investment. The economic historians will find the diaries rewarding — as will the social historians if they remember the limitations of Cobden's middle-class outlook. In passing through Cincinnati, for example,

Cobden noticed that this young city had twenty men each worth a half million, though during one month in New York he said nothing of its 70,000 paupers. Nor did he mention New York's unsanitary, overcrowded slums which shocked Dickens and which meant that New York's rate of mortality in 1859 was twice that of London. But these oversights reflect the limitations of the English middle-class reformer and not the conscious prejudices of Cobden. Within these limitations he was a judicious and accurate observer, and his praise of America in 1859 holds as true as does his prophecy of her future greatness. As an apostle of social equality, economic freedom, and democratic progress, he was well suited to comment on a country where such beliefs were being realized.

University of Washington DAVID ROBERTS

California Emigrant Letters. Edited by Walker D. Wyman. Illustrated by Helen Bryant Wyman. (New York: Bookman Associates, 1952. 177 pp. $3.00.)

This is a collection of letters relating to the overland emigration and life in the mines and towns of California in 1849 and 1850. Drawn from newspapers published in St. Louis and St. Joseph, it represents the sort of information available to those who stayed at home during the first two years of the gold rush. Attention is focused upon the overland route, and there are no letters representing travel by way of Cape Horn or the Isthmus.

The accounts are arranged in a series of general subject classifications which include reports on California before the beginning of the 1849 emigration, the outfitting of parties on the Missouri border, overland journeys in 1849 and in 1850, advice from 1849 emigrants to those at home, appraisals of California after 1850, mining methods, and life in the mines and towns of California. In order to further this topical organization, the editor has divided some of the letters, and parts of the same letter appear in different sections of the book. Material regarded as redundant or unimportant has been omitted entirely although in the text there is no indication as to where these excisions have been made.

The letters published have been drawn mainly from three sources. There are forty-four selections from the *Missouri Republican*, forty-six from the *Missouri Statesman*, forty-five from the St. Joseph *Adventure*, and one from the *Merchant's Magazine and Commercial Review*. In a number of instances, however, the letter originally appeared in another paper so that the range of sources is somewhat wider than might be thought. Still it would have been interesting to know what proportion of the California letters appearing in these newspapers have been reproduced here, and even more, a wider coverage of the press of the Mississippi Valley on this subject would have been valuable.

Mr. Wyman originally published this collection in four numbers of the California Historical Society's *Quarterly* in 1949, and it appears here virtually without change. There is a brief, general introduction, but no notes to identify persons and places or to explain events and references. One obvious slip is the placing of an 1849 letter in the category of the next year (pp. 98-99). The sketch map is useful only for the most general sort of identification of places. There is no index.

Although this book has limitations from the viewpoint of the serious student of western history, it was obviously intended for a wider audience. In view of this aim, it is a commendable presentation of colorful and informative materials on the overland emigration.

Naval War College JOHN HASKELL KEMBLE

White Columns in Georgia. By Medora Field Perkerson. (New York: Rinehart & Company, 1952. xv + 367 pp. Illustrations, bibliography, and index. $7.95.)

This is not a book about Georgia architecture as its title might seem to indicate. Rather it is a storybook about the state's white-columned, ante-bellum homes, "a delightful compendium of their history, legends, folklore and odd-doings." In its pages duels and murders occur; skeletons rattle; even ghosts walk.

Mrs. Perkerson has been thorough in gathering her data and acknowledges the help of scores of people who assisted her with that task. But the authoress does not quibble between fact and fable. If the legend connected with a house makes a better story than sober fact, tell it she does. But this is only to be expected in a section of our country where much tradition passes for authentic history. At any rate, the treatment results in a warm portrayal of the life lived in these classic mansions for, as she says, "old houses hold on to the people who have lived within their walls, and they hold on longest to those who have lived most vividly."

Mrs. Perkerson divides her subject matter into thirty-seven short chapters. In the first she sets the stage of what she calls the "Gone with the Wind Country" and tells us briefly how Georgia became what it is. Then she strikes out from Atlanta, following Sherman's route to the sea, upon a pilgrimage which takes her readers pretty much over the state.

One of the charms of the volume is the collection of 112 carefully selected photographs with which it is illustrated. These form an excellent setting for the stories which the authoress tells about these houses. Early in the journey she takes us to Burge plantation near Covington, then into the town to visit several houses. Next is Oxford with its legends and lore, Madison with its stalwart porticoes, Etonton and its ghosts, Milledgeville with its Doric and Ionic mansions, Waynesboro, Birdsville, and Sandersville, with a pause at

Lebanon plantation before we enter Savannah which, the authoress says "captured Sherman," who spared the city in order that it might "charm present-day visitors . . . with its lovely old houses which are considered crown jewels in the state's architectural heritage."

Next our journey takes us to the great plantations: Wormsloe, Hopeton, Altama, Kelvin Grove, West Point, Grove Point, King's Retreat, Sapelo, and others equally charming. There is a chapter about the graceful ladies who presided over these plantation homes, "a law unto themselves," and accounts of the three millionaires who have owned Sapelo.

Other jaunts take us to Cherokee Chief Joseph Vann's house at Spring Place; Chief John Martin's home near Chatsworth; Bullock Hall in Roswell; Thornwood, The Chieftain's and Oak Hill at Rome; Overlook, the Holt house, and Sidney Lanier's birthplace in Macon; Nutwood, The Oaks, Bellevue, and Hills and Dales in the LaGrange area; Montrose, Sand Hills, and the ante-bellum plantation house which now serves as the headquarters of the National Golf Club in Augusta; the Robert Toombs and the Colonel A. T. Colley homes in Washington; and the many glorious houses in the university city of Athens and at Marshallville, Thomasville, Albany, and Columbia.

The book is supplied with an ample bibliography and a thorough index.

University of Illinois REXFORD NEWCOMB

On Freedom's Altar; The Martyr Complex in the Abolition Movement. By Hazel Catherine Wolf. (Madison: University of Wisconsin Press, 1952. xii + 195 pp. Illustrations, bibliography, and index. $3.75.)

On Freedom's Altar summarizes the careers of the three abolitionists who gave their lives, and sketches the experiences of a score of others — including one woman — who suffered oppression from mobs or courts while espousing emancipationist doctrines between the early eighteenth century and the outbreak of Civil War. The three martyrs were Elijah Lovejoy, shot by a mob; Charles Turner Torrey, who died of tuberculosis in prison; and John Brown, hanged by the state of Virginia. Stress is placed on the episodes of maltreatment, the sense of exultation with which those who were persecuted responded to their suffering, and the conscious exploitation by the abolitionists of the identity between their cruelly treated members and the martyrs of the Christian tradition. The moral fervor to sustain the nineteenth-century abolitionist when faced by peril was rooted in both evangelical Christianity and the natural rights philosophy of the Enlightenment.

Winning new recruits for the cause is suggested as the personal motivation of the abolitionist martyr. Less altruistic considerations, such as the desire for esteem from his fellows and the expectation of salvation in heaven, certainly were also at work. The analysis of the martyr complex among abolitionists could have gained in insight had the author applied techniques used fruitfully in conceptual studies of martyrdom in the early Christian era, such as the work of Donald W. Riddle.

The final chapter, concerning the Civil War, describes the manner in which Elmer Ellsworth, "Parson" Brownlow, the Massachusetts troops who were killed while marching through Baltimore, Union soldiers in Confederate prisons, and Lincoln were viewed by Northerners as martyrs to the cause of saving the Union. A shift of emphasis thus occurs from the preceding discussion of martyrdom in behalf of the slave. The earlier theme might well have received continued stress. For the abolitionists viewed Generals Frémont and Hunter as martyrs when rebuked by Lincoln for their premature emancipationist gestures, and abolition oratory accentuated the heroic sacrifice of slaves in aiding Union troops. Freedom for the slave, not the preservation of the Union, remained the more fundamental cause for which abolitionists would honor those who died in battle. Abolitionists eulogized the assassinated Lincoln as the emancipator and pleaded for continued attention to the problem of justice for the freedman.

Newspapers, tracts, printed letters, and biographies (only one manuscript collection is cited) provide the sources for Miss Wolf's well-written narrative.

Emory University JAMES HARVEY YOUNG

Benjamin Harrison, Hoosier Warrior, 1833-1865. By Harry J. Sievers. Introduction by Hilton U. Brown. (Chicago: Henry Regnery Company, 1952. xxi + 344 pp. Illustrations, bibliography, and index. $5.00.)

Two quotations from letters may aid one to form an estimate of the young warrior who emerges from these pages. In recommending Harrison for promotion to a brigadier generalship for his part in the Atlanta campaign, Thomas Hooker wrote, "Colonel Harrison is an officer of superior abilities and of great professional and personal worth." Just before this campaign began Harrison himself wrote his wife, "So in our national life, this sad time of death shall yet yield its fruit in a purer, higher and surer national life."

In this first of a projected two-volume life, Mr. Sievers attempts to show what forces helped form the character of the later president. His own father, John Scott Harrison, was a remarkable man and had far more influence in shaping his character than the shadow of a grandfather. Long hours of study added to a natural brilliance made the time spent at Farmers' College and Miami University profitable. Deeply religious and formally received into the Presbyterian fold while still in college, he was undecided for a time between a career in the law or the ministry. He turned to the law and was admitted to the Ohio bar. After his marriage (before he was twenty), he moved to Indianapolis.

The six years of practice before the war were filled with the usual hardships of the young attorney before he entered a lucrative partnership. During this period he joined the new Republican party in time to campaign for Frémont. His own family was shocked; his father was a Whig congressman who followed the Native American party and wrote his son long letters concerning the wickedness of the Republicans. His brother wrote from Kansas in the same vein. However, by the outbreak of the war Benjamin had become a respectable figure in the Indiana Republican party, having served as city attorney and as secretary of the state Republican Central Committee. In 1860 he was elected reporter of the Indiana Supreme Court.

In 1862, at the urgent request of Governor Oliver P. Morton, he raised a regiment and was made its colonel. The 70th Indiana was sent to Kentucky and then to Tennessee, spending most of its time on guard duty, but the civilian colonel made it into a well-drilled unit. In the spring of 1864, assigned to the forces under Sherman and Thomas, it had its real experience of war and gave an excellent account of itself in the Atlanta campaign. Harrison was also in the final campaign against Hood. Near the end of the war he was brevetted brigadier at the age of thirty-two.

This biography may well become the definitive life of Harrison. Harry Sievers was commissioned by the Arthur Jordan Foundation of Indianapolis to write it and has spent three years so far on it. He has had access to papers hitherto unavailable to historians and so may be able to change the estimate of the stature of Harrison in the nation's history. He has brought the Harrison life only to the threshold of maturity; the next volume will undoubtedly be a great deal longer. Then only can proper judgments be made of this biography and of the life of Harrison as a whole; now only qualifications may be made. The book is very well illustrated, but the maps are hard to read.

College of St. Thomas J. HERMAN SCHAUINGER

Ersatz in the Confederacy. By Mary Elizabeth Massey. (Columbia: University of South Carolina Press, 1952. xii + 233 pp. Illustrations, bibliography, and index. $5.00.)

Although there may be some turnings over in Confederate graves at the foreign word in the title of Miss Massey's book, the scholarly world may rest assured that the famed makeshifts of the Confederate era have now been properly dealt with. Unfortunately, the name of this book is a bit misleading, for in her preface the author announces that she is really concerned with the vast problem of "shortages," a word for which ersatz is an ersatz synonym.

Miss Massey begins her study with an examination of the genesis of these shortages and the governmental policies designed to deal with them. Then, in separate chapters she discusses deprivations and makeshifts in food and drink, clothing, housing and household goods, drugs and medicine, and "the little things of life." One chapter considers the hardships occasioned by inadequate transportation facilities and the lack of industrial and agricultural equipment.

A final chapter, entitled "The Balance Sheet," assays some of the effects of wartime shortages on the South — increased industrialization, for example. One is somewhat troubled by the absence of evidence that southern makeshifting resulted in any strides forward in science, medicine, and the applied arts such as often come out of the privations of war and blockade. Perhaps the scientific mind of the South, like that of the entire country at that time, was still somewhat immature. At any rate, it appears that most Southerners were mere alchemists haphazardly trying to turn baser things into ersatz.

It is regrettable that Miss Massey's study, which was obviously an excellent doctoral dissertation, has undergone some transmigrations of body apparently designed to curry favor with antiquarians and daughters of this-and-that. As a result, several portions of the text have been heavily colored with patches of postdissertational purple. The designers at the University of South Carolina Press have not, however, entered fully into the spirit of the thing. The nine photographs of ersatz items, arranged either in cases or on uneasy mesdames, are inferior in both composition and lighting, and the typography of the book suffers occasional lapses.

There will doubtless be critics who will be moved by the several minor shortcomings of this book to dismiss the whole thing as trivial. Perhaps the modern how-to-do-it magazine, which has made a fetish of ersatzing, has jaundiced the eye. There will also be some grumbling to the effect that Confederate scholarship, which has lately spent much time explaining the South's defeat in terms of shortages of everything from salt to manpower, has now begun to suffer a topical shortage and is scraping the bottom of its barrel. Nevertheless, Miss Massey's book bids fair to survive the critics. While its contribution to scholarship is not phenomenal, the study is a substantial effort and it has been done with commendable thoroughness.

Mississippi State College JOHN K. BETTERSWORTH

The Railroads of the Confederacy. By Robert C. Black, III. (Chapel Hill: The University of North Carolina Press, 1952. xiv +360 pp. Illustrations, maps, appendix, bibliography, and index. $6.00.)

The Railroads of the Confederacy is a study by one who knows something about railroading. Southern railroads are measured in terms of the adequacy of the system rather than in the number of miles of track or in the number of trunk lines. The unevenly distributed tracks of poor construction and of different gauges impaired the system; and inadequate feeder lines, junction points, and sidings made conditions worse. An average railroad system possessed about 200 miles of track of rolled wrought iron, 235 wooden cars, and from 20 to 30 locomotives. The typical freight train consisted of 15 cars, with carload limits of 16,000 pounds each, pulled by an American 4-4-0 locomotive that moved along at 12 miles an hour and traveled for 50 to 60 miles on a cord of wood. Compared to the North, the South hardly had a system. It had only a mere "shadow of the main lines of the future."

Certain general weaknesses of southern economy are illustrated by the difficulties of the Confederate railroads. Mr. Black indicates that railroad building was financed before the war largely by state aid and credit from outside the South. No extraordinary stockpile of supplies existed when the war began and the manufacturing potential offered little prospect of meeting the needs of the Confederacy. It was believed in 1863 that if the necessities of the railroads could not be met their days were numbered. In another year the railroads were disintegrating. Their effectiveness, like that of other phases of the war effort, was hindered by labor shortages, conscription, inflation, speculation, cost-plus contracts, and military interference. The comparative industrial lag of the South is made even more striking by Mr. Black's consideration of railroads in relation to the military successes and failures from Manassas to Appomattox.

The Confederate States, however, "by no means made the best of what they had." Legislation authorizing the president to regulate and take control of the railroads was introduced in 1861, but it was not until 1863 that an adequate railroad bill was passed. This power Jefferson Davis failed to use until February, 1865, when time had run out. Railroad owners were "unwilling to make serious sacrifice of their personal interests" and "the Confederate Government was loath to enforce the kind of transportation policy the war effort demanded." The Confederacy had too little government coercion and not enough public cooperation.

The Railroads of the Confederacy is a superior historical monograph. Mr. Black has examined a technical subject with the understanding of an engineer. He has followed the conventional interpretations, ascribing southern failure to Jefferson Davis, state rights, and lack of industrial capacity. Despite a lengthy bibliography, the writings of Charles W. Ramsdell were not fully utilized (e.g., "The Confederate Government and the Railroads," *American Historical Review*, XXII, 794-818). The apparent failure to consult the *American Historical Review*, the *Mississippi Valley Historical Review*, or the *Southern Historical Society Papers* raises some doubts as to the degree of systematic research. The illustrations and the maps add to the pleasure and value of the book, but the effort to write colorfully is labored. Mr. Black has provided the historian with a valuable reference on an important phase of the Confederacy.

Teachers College of Connecticut HAROLD JAYNES BINGHAM

The Northern Railroads in the Civil War, 1861-1865. By Thomas Weber. (New York: King's Crown Press, Columbia University, 1952. xii + 318 pp. $4.00.)

The importance of railroads in the Civil War has long been recognized, both in special studies and in general literature. For the first time in American history railroads became of strategic importance in war, with many military operations oriented toward railroad transportation, and with the efficient northern military railroad control an important factor in federal success. Furthermore, the existence of strong northern railway systems made possible the development of civilian economy even as the army was being supplied; in fact, the North was even able to expand its railroad net significantly during the course of the war. Mr. Weber points out that railroad business increased during the war and that profits became larger in spite of higher costs of materials and labor. Much of this increase was actually a statistical delusion, since it was offset by the deterioration of equipment and by a generally higher price level, although Mr. Weber makes no effort to handle the difficult problem of how much of the gain, if any, was real.

This study of northern railroads during the Civil War is monographic in nature, with something over a quarter of the book devoted to footnotes, bibliography, and index; presumably it originated as a Ph. D. thesis under the direction of Professor Allan Nevins. It is highly factual and informative, written clearly but never excitingly. The exact limits of the study produce a little feeling of frustration and incompleteness. Certainly the western railroads were integral parts of the northern railroad network, but under the self-imposed limits of the study they are given but little treatment. Similarly, this reader at least keeps wondering what happened to the southern railroads. While in one sense an author can hardly be criticized for not doing what he did not set out to do, one can at least express a regret that the coverage was not a little larger.

Mr. Weber's research, as indicated in both footnotes and bibliography, is adequate, and he may well be right in citing ordinarily the original sources rather than secondary accounts, even when the material is contained in the latter. The one great lack is maps, which presumably have been omitted because of publishing costs; they would have increased immensely the usefulness of the narrative. Altogether the study is a praiseworthy piece of research, even though its use will be confined almost entirely to specialists in the field.

Dartmouth College ROBERT E. RIEGEL

Howells & Italy. By James L. Woodress, Jr. (Durham: Duke University Press, 1952. xi + 223 pp. Bibliography and index. $3.50.)

By preparing the *Lives and Speeches of Abraham Lincoln and Hannibal Hamlin*, young William Dean Howells earned a consulship for himself.

Campaign biographies are a notoriously low form of literature but Howells had less to be apologetic about for writing one than many another literary man, including Hawthorne when he published his pompous little book on Franklin Pierce. After Lincoln's inauguration Howells applied for the post at Rome. Upon learning that it would pay him only $500 a year, though, he decided to ask for Venice, which would yield double that amount. By September 7, 1861, he could write of Nicolay's telling him that his commission had been signed by the President, so that he could be on his way to Europe. Two months later Howells left for Venice and there he stayed during four fruitful years. He went there fresh from Columbus, Ohio, with a good deal of callowness still clinging to him. He returned to this country with a reputation as undoubtedly the most promising young man of American letters.

Using material from the National Archives and unpublished letters, among other sources, Professor Woodress has studied those years. The result is a considerably better than average monograph. The sheer bulk of Howells' writing — the Library of Congress printed catalogue, for instance, shows almost two hundred entries of separate books and reprints under his name — and the variety of his activities have combined, it may be guessed, to discourage anyone from attempting a full-dress biography. The last general study of him, by O. W. Firkins, appeared a generation ago. On the other hand, interest in Howells has clearly risen in recent years, and several dissertations, a good bibliography, and various articles have been written. The researches of Arms, Cady, Gibson, the Kirks, and Lutwack are among the testimonies to that fact.

The main question which Professor Woodress attacks is — as, given his premises, it should be — literary rather than biographical or historical: What effect did Howells' stay in Venice have on his writing?

Howells & Italy is divided into four substantial chapters. Only the first is primarily biographical. In it Howells' Italian stay is described with an amount of detail not before approached. Firkins' book (although this contrast is somewhat unfair) takes less than a page to cover this same biographical period. In his first chapter Professor Woodress lays the groundwork for his later analysis of the relation between Howells' writing and his Venetian experiences. The second chapter, entitled "Literary Apprentice," explains the genesis of two books, *Venetian Life* and *Italian Journeys*. "The most important product of Howells' Italian sojourn was *Venetian Life*, his first book after returning from Europe, and his first outstanding literary success" is the judgment of Professor Woodress. *Venetian Life* began as a series of travel letters that the new consul wrote, submitted to the *Atlantic Monthly* (which rejected them), and finally printed in the Boston *Advertiser*. Thereafter published in book form, *Venetian Life* received both wide and discriminating praise. *Italian Journeys* is an attempt to do something like *Venetian Life* for several other Italian cities.

In the third chapter Professor Woodress is mainly concerned with the impact of Italian literature on Howells and his service to it by way of his translations and critical writings, but he considers in addition some reflections of the literature in Howells' own work. Professor Woodress stresses the contribution of the Venetian dramatist Carlo Goldoni in turning Howells away from literary romanticism to realism. The fourth and final chapter leads naturally into a discussion of how Italian life showed itself in his realistic novels and sketches.

Clear in style and well thought out, *Howells & Italy* is an unusually satisfactory synthesis of the materials on the subject. To the social historian it offers an interesting example of the impression made by one culture upon the representative of another and far different one.

University of Maryland CARL BODE

The Katy Railroad and the Last Frontier. By V. V. Masterson. (Norman: University of Oklahoma Press, 1952. xvi + 312 pp. Illustrations, maps, bibliography, and index. $4.00.)

The building of railroads and the disappearance of the frontier went hand in hand. As the iron rails penetrated new territory great stretches of prairie country, hills, and valleys gave way to thriving settlements; towns and villages sprang up along the railways as though by magic. The Missouri-Kansas-Texas railroad, better known as the Katy, was the precursor of settlement. Along its right of way countless cities were born, trade and industry expanded, and cultural influences left their permanent impress. Victor V. Masterson, a member of the Katy public relations staff, gives an excellent account of this western railroad. But he does considerably more; he recreates a part of the social and economic history — a segment of the life on the last frontier.

Mr. Masterson skillfully traces the history of the Katy across four states (Missouri, Kansas, Oklahoma, and Texas) from a young fledgling until it emerges as "one of the most modern, up-to-date railroads in the nation." To arouse and sustain interest he builds his story around key characters. Giants of finance, railroad kings, and empire builders — good and bad — hold the reader's interest from beginning to end. Robert S. Stevens, dynamic general manager of the Katy, Judge Levi Parsons, financial wizard and visionary of a great railroad system, and big John Scullin, heavy-fisted boss of the Irish Brigade tracklayers are presented as heroes. Andrew Peirce, Jr., general manager of the old Atlantic and Pacific (the present Frisco), and Jay Gould, the "Mephistopheles of Wall Street," are portrayed in the guise of villains. Ethics played a minor role in the grandiose plans of the empire builders, and Masterson has the courage not to whitewash the Katy promoters and management.

The author is masterful in portraying the seamy side of life in frontier settlements. In Denison, Texas, for example, the reader sees "rat alley," with its gambling halls, hurdy-gurdy joints, lowest class saloons, cockfighting pits, variety houses, and deadly "dovecotes." Here, Rowdy Joe the muscle man, Cherokee Jake the cold killer, and Monte Jack the gambler of classic report hold sway until dethroned by Red Hall the fearless two-gun sheriff.

This is only a sample of the author's colorful, dramatic style, which seems to have been tailored especially for the general reader. The use of dialogue adds to the spirit and flavor of the narrative. Some historians may feel that the author overplayed his hand at times and achieved the melodramatic, as in the description of the simultaneous, dual bank holdup by the Dalton gang (pp. 257-60).

Mr. Masterson relied principally upon original company records. He also drew upon contemporary newspapers and secondary works, but seems to have overlooked government documents. Several shortcomings have been noted, but these are not serious; for example, the author states that Congressman Oakes Ames was "impeached" for his Union Pacific activities (pp. 216-17), instead of censured by the House. The book has forty-one short chapters, a number of which might have been effectively combined. However, the scholarship is sound; the style, despite its melodramatic flavor, is refreshing and recreates the spirit of the frontier. Pertinent illustrations, more than a dozen maps, a bibliography, and an index enhance the value of the book. *The Katy Railroad and the Last Frontier* is a valuable contribution to the history of the West.

Harris Teachers College A. B. BENDER

Good Old Summer Days; Newport, Narragansett Pier, Saratoga, Long Branch, Bar Harbor. By Richmond Barrett. Introduction by Mary Lasswell. (Boston: Houghton Mifflin Company, 1952. xiii + 338 pp. Illustrations and index. $3.50.)

If a professional historian ever undertakes a serious study of the American expatriate colony living in Paris throughout the first quarter of the twentieth century, he would do well to begin his work by reading Basil Woon's *The Paris That's Not in the Guide Books* (New York, Brentano's, 1926). This gossipy account presents a picture of the Ritz Bar, Ciro's, the casinos, the dressshops, the restaurants, and the hotels where the main characters of the colony lived their lives. To know Woon's book is to gain an amazing quantity of knowledge about the period, the place, and the people. So it is with Richmond Barrett's *Good Old Summer Days.*

Mr. Barrett has extracted the flavor of the great American summer resorts in the late nineteenth century and has presented it to his readers in highly palatable form. As one proceeds through the sections on Newport, Narragansett Pier, Saratoga, Long Branch, and Bar Harbor, he feels as though he were actually visiting those places in their years of glory. What is more significant, the reader becomes gradually aware of his gaining new perspective in appraising the "high society folk" of the period. Mrs. William Astor, the uncrowned queen, and Ward McAllister, her ingenious prime minister, emerge as believable figures, with measurable influence in American life. And the world in which they moved takes on a coloring, with relation to its European counterparts, less brash and impudent than it has seemed to most Americans of our modern day.

The insufficient integration of the material into the general history of the period is the usual weakness of this type of work — and *Good Old Summer Days* adheres to the familiar pattern. But the reviewer refrains from criticizing the volume in such terms, for he feels that it serves significant purposes while standing in its vacuum. To the general reader it offers social history in attractive form and plenty of entertainment. For the historian it paves the way to understanding an influential segment of American life in the late nineteenth century, and suggests a number of avenues to more detailed investigation.

From a literary point of view, the conclusion of the book is weak. We are suddenly in Bar Harbor — and we are suddenly closing a finished book. A section tying the various separate accounts together would have added much to the structure of the material. The index has small value, with its complete absence of subtopics.

Some members of the historical guild may hesitate to label this book "history." But they would be grateful for its help in exploring some of the phenomena with which they deal. As in the case of Basil Woon's "guidebook," Mr. Barrett has captured a flavor with skill and has passed it on with the stamp of authenticity.

Yale University ROLLIN G. OSTERWEIS

He Hanged Them High; An Authentic Account of the Fanatical Judge Who Hanged Eighty-Eight Men. By Homer Croy. (New York: Duell, Sloan and Pearce, 1952. viii + 278 pp. Illustrations, sources, and index. $4.00.)

Judge Isaac C. Parker presided over the United States Court for the Western District of Arkansas at Fort Smith from 1875 to 1896. He sentenced 172 persons to the gallows, and 88 were hanged. The court was unusual in its jurisdiction, independence, and amount of business. Parker's territory included western Arkansas and most of the present state of Oklahoma, and during the first sixteen years of his tenure no appeal to the Supreme Court of the United States was possible. The extraordinary number of cases docketed in the "Court of the Damned" is accounted for by the attraction the Indian country had for criminals plus Parker's zeal for law enforcement.

Formidable difficulties have faced biographers of the "hanging judge." A tornado destroyed Parker's personal papers. His twenty-one-year career, filled with hard work, monotonous routine, and singularly devoid of avocational activities and interests, was unpromising stuff for biography. That he was "the most extraordinary judge that the United States has ever known," as Mr. Croy contends, is hardly supported by this book. Parker did have an extraordinary zeal in sending men to the gallows, a zeal that led in the last five years of his tenure to thirty reversals in forty-six cases involving the death penalty appealed to the Supreme Court. The ironic fact is that such fame as Parker achieved sprang from public interest in the escapades of the hoodlums who were hauled into his court.

Mr. Croy has been aware of the difficulties of his subject. He has focused attention on the outlaws and marshals and on his interesting pursuit of information about them. He appears to have made slight use of the records of the court, but he actually found an outlaw who had been in Parker's court, interviewed him, and almost got shot for his trouble. After thirty-three pages wherein the author brings Parker from his birth in Ohio through a brief career at St. Joseph, Missouri, to Fort Smith, the bad men hold the center of the stage. The reader is more aware of Parker, his hangman, George Maledon, and the Supreme Court as directors and stage technicians than as actors. The exploits of Cherokee Bill, Belle Starr, Ned Christie, Texas Jack, and the Dalton boys are depicted in a sprightly, humorous, and usually objective manner. The desperadoes emerge neither as Robin Hoods nor as unfortunate victims of bad environment but simply as bad men — and women.

Arkansas State Teachers College TED R. WORLEY

Barbarians in Our Midst; A History of Chicago Crime and Politics. By Virgil W. Peterson. Foreword by Estes Kefauver. (Boston: Little, Brown and Company, 1952. x + 395 pp. Appendix and index. $4.50.)

In 1893 the British editor, William T. Stead, told a Chicago audience, "You are gigantic in your virtues and gigantic in your vices. I don't know in which you glory the most" (p. 64). It is to record these gigantic vices that Virgil W. Peterson has written *Barbarians in Our Midst.* The author was for twelve years an agent for the FBI and is now operating director of the Chicago Crime Commission. It is not surprising, therefore, that this study mainly comprises a series of dossiers of the leading figures in Chicago's underworld, their background, relations with one another, the kinds and extent of their rackets, and their political affiliations.

Paraded through these pages are the major and many minor racketeers: Mike McDonald, "Hinky Dink" Kenna, "Bathhouse" John Coughlin, Mont

Tennes, Jim Colosimo and John Torrio, the progenitors of the Capone syndicate, Al Capone and his successors, Frank Nitti and Tony Accardo.

The enterprises of the crime syndicate are catalogued and brought up to date in chapters summarizing the Kefauver Committee hearings. Mr. Peterson calls "unrealistic" the opinion that Al Capone was a product of prohibition. It was not liquor but gambling rackets which were the hard core of his organization's wealth and power.

Like his predecessors, Capone was the product of a deeply entrenched political system, an alliance of the underworld and politicians for mutual advantage. The author is outspoken in his criticism of political leaders; few are spared. The administrations of Carter H. Harrison, Sr., are described as an era of rare prosperity for professional gamesters; those of his son are criticized more than praised. The tawdry buffoonery and ineptitude of "Big Bill" Thompson's long regime are exposed. Anton J. Cermak is represented as even more nefarious than Thompson because of the machine he had built along Tammany Hall lines. Patrick A. Nash, Edward J. Kelly, and Jacob M. Arvey, heirs of the Cermak organization, are revealed for what they were and are — political opportunists. Despite respect for the present mayor, Martin H. Kennelly, as a man, Mr. Peterson's praise of him is grudging. Governor Adlai Stevenson is almost the only law-enforcement officer to escape criticism.

The ramifications of the Chicago criminal syndicates with the Illinois legislature and the federal attorney general's office are spread upon these pages; also the link with racketeers and political organizations in other areas — New York, Kansas City, New Orleans, Nevada, and the West Coast.

In documenting the history of such a lurid subject as organized crime, inevitably an author tends to sound like an evangelist preacher denouncing hell. Mr. Peterson does not escape this tendency. Furthermore, he is concerned mainly with a historical exposé rather than with an analysis of the sociological conditions which make the alliance of crime and politics flourish. He does reiterate the persistence of the tradition of violence which dates from the city's beginnings as a frontier town. He mentions such social mores as Chicagoans' secret pride in the wickedness of their city and their acquiescence in its bad reputation so long as business is good. Yet he does little more than suggest the social dislocations and political consequences caused by the enormous expansion of the city's population from 1880 to 1930 and its transient character in some of the worst districts.

How does Mr. Peterson propose to clean up the mess and separate crime from politics? He is convinced from the Nevada experience that legalized gambling is not the solution. Nor does he place much reliance in mechanical changes in government, though he believes the system of nominating judges might be improved and that the police civil service should be reformed to encourage appointment and promotion of men of merit. Rather it is the people themselves, he insists, who can solve the problem by direct community action and eternal vigilance. This is the price of free government.

Although there is no separate bibliography, the footnotes include the principal sources. An appendix lists the officers responsible for law enforcement in Chicago, 1833-1951, and the population figures, 1833-1950.

Kenyon College LANDON WARNER

The Letters of Theodore Roosevelt, Vols. V and VI. Elting E. Morison, editor, John M. Blum, associate editor, Alfred D. Chandler, Jr., assistant editor, Sylvia Rice, copy editor. (Cambridge: Harvard University Press, 1952. Vol. V: *The Big Stick, 1905-1907*. xxiv + 864 pp. Illustrations. Vol. VI: *The Big Stick, 1907-1909*. vi + 865-1715 pp. Illustrations, appendixes, and index. $20.00.)

With the appearance of the fifth and sixth volumes of *The Letters of Theodore Roosevelt*, Elting Morison and his associates bring their huge task of selecting and editing the pertinent correspondence of the "strenuous" President to the three-quarter mark; with two more volumes, on Roosevelt's post-presidential career, yet to be published. Again Mr. Morison has set the same high standard of editorial craftsmanship that characterized the previous volumes of the series. He has provided the reader with complete explanatory notes on all little-known personalities or terms that crop up in the Roosevelt letters; there is a day-by-day chronology of Roosevelt's activities; and the index is complete, well arranged, and convenient.

This two-volume set, subtitled *The Big Stick*, comprises the "Imperial Years" of Roosevelt's administration. From November, 1904, when he was elected to the presidency in his own right, until March, 1909, when he at last turned over the office to a successor of his own choosing, T. R. was the dominant personality on the American scene and his every action was of newsworthy importance. These were joyous and busy years. Roosevelt wrote soon after the 1908 election, "I have had the best time of any man of my age in the world. . . . I have enjoyed myself in the White House more than I have ever known any other President to enjoy himself" (p. 1387).

Yet the years of *The Big Stick* had their full share of difficult and critical problems for the President to solve. Nowhere is Roosevelt's consummate skill as a politician better exhibited than during the drawnout controversy with the Senate over railway rate making. Through his letters one can trace the infighting and tactical shifts that accompanied the passage of the Hepburn Act. It is fascinating to follow the action as Roosevelt repeatedly returned to a middle-of-the-road bill and eventually emerged with a substantial "half-loaf" despite the pressure of the extremists from both the left and the right. The letters dealing with meat inspection, the Pure Food and Drug Act, Indian affairs, public lands, forest reserves, Latin-American relations, the Algeciras Conference, and the ever touchy Japanese immigration problem are rich in new information and colorful side lights concerning these topics. The correspondence devoted to the organization and work of the Panama Canal Commission is especially interesting. To most students of American history the drama of the Panama Canal story ends in 1904. In many ways it had just begun, for the digging of the canal proved more difficult than the acquisition of the site (pp. 504-81). But despite his many activities, Roosevelt reserved a special place in his interest for the navy. Throughout the entire period of his presidency he exhibited constant concern for its well-being and acquired considerable expert knowledge of the needs of the fleet. Much of the improvement in firepower, armor, and design that were achieved before the first World War were due to T. R.'s constant prodding of both the senior officers and of Congress.

Equally interesting in these letters are the revelations about Roosevelt the man. Theodore Roosevelt, moralistic and dogmatic, emerges even more clearly here than before as the champion of the "Square Deal" and "substantial justice" for all. So positive was he of his opinions and judgments that all who disagreed with him tended to become "fools" or "scoundrels" or both (pp. 700, 925). That his sense of "substantial justice" took peculiar twists at times is illustrated by his reluctance to retreat from his stand on the Brownsville "incident." It is also shown, somewhat more amusingly, by his refusal to sign an order to release from prison a man who was guilty of passing Confederate money, in spite of a court decision that it was not counterfeit. The man "was in prison," he "ought" to be in prison, and he, Roosevelt, would not be a party to allowing him to get out (p. 910).

Theodore Roosevelt's progressivism became more articulate as the "Imperial Years" passed. His deep fear of the growth of the Socialist parties in America and abroad stimulated his desire for moderate, sound reform that would cut the ground from under their feet (p. 183). By 1908 he had evolved a more mature philosophy of regulation and control than was evident in his early "trust busting" days (p. 922) ; yet he mistrusted the extreme left of his own party. During his years in the White House his callers were much more likely to be men like Cannon, Aldrich, or Spooner rather than La Follette, Norris, or Cummins.

The some fifteen hundred letters that comprise *The Big Stick* were taken, according to the editor, from a mass of about twenty thousand letters that were written by Theodore Roosevelt during this four-year period. This represents an even more drastic culling than occurred in the previous volumes and is doubly regrettable as this is the most influential portion of Roosevelt's career. The editors have sought to mitigate this situation by including several penetrating essays based on the whole manuscript collection which elaborate three of the most important questions. Morison has contributed an excellent introduction which discusses at length Roosevelt's philosophical and psychological attributes; Alfred D. Chandler, Jr., has ably discussed the organization and administration of the Panama Canal Commission; and John M. Blum has added an essay on "Theodore Roosevelt and the Hepburn Act." In addition the editors have, in their explanatory notes, drawn on the unpublished letters for bits of added information concerning some unclear point. In some places, however, they have "over-edited" the manuscript in their efforts to answer all of the questions of the general reader. Such excursions into general history as the long note explaining the causes and course of the Panic of 1907 (p. 747) might have been omitted. The interpretive essays, excellent though they are, might more properly have appeared in a historical quarterly. The space thus saved would have made possible the inclusion of a considerable number of additional letters. These, however, are relatively minor criticisms. The series as published to date represents a major contribution to the literature of recent American history. *The Big Stick* is a welcome and valuable addition to this series.

Stephen F. Austin State College ROBERT S. MAXWELL

A Scholar in Action: Edwin F. Gay. By Herbert Heaton. (Cambridge: Harvard University Press, 1952. vi + 260 pp. $4.25.)

Of professors we have had few biographies. Perhaps the drought is about to be broken as graduate students, keening for thesis subjects, fall upon the full reservoirs of diaries and letters which professors have written and, archive-minded, have not thrown away, and transform these abundant materials into studies in intellectual history. The volume under review does not fall in that pattern. When the Friends of Edwin F. Gay collected a fund in his memory they diverted a portion of it to the preparation of this memoir. They were fortunate in securing as author a mature scholar whose reputation for literary craftsmanship is rightly unmatched in the guild of economic historians.

Perforce the book has limitations. The circumstances of its appearance mute controversies and differences of opinion by omitting the names of combatants and pass lightly over some academic strivings, fabulous in perhaps more ways than one. Gay himself imposed other limitations. The early chapters on a scholar's preparation, on the prewar career at Harvard with the first deanship of the Business School, on war work in Washington in statistical administrative capacities, and as Lamont's manager editor of the New York *Evening Post* all have their own dramatic integrity. Though we are aware of the false starts, the divided loyalties, the generous spending of energy and time, Gay's life, nevertheless, had in those years a succession of focuses. For one with so successful and useful a career the failure of the *Post* adventure was an ironic climax. Gay was then fifty-six.

The last two chapters fill the reader with as much distress as the years they chronicle must have occasionally filled Gay. Here is a catalogue of rushing about, "the eternal triangle" of Cambridge, New York, and Washington and the transcontinental journeys from the Huntington; of addresses and articles finished on the deadline and usually to his own dissatisfaction; of innumerable committee and board meetings; of scholarly enterprises conceived, organized, directed, and financed in fair times and in foul. Though the National Bureau for Economic Research and the Council on Foreign Relations were his most important achievements, Gay's secretary at one time counted his participation in twenty-eight organizations or permanent committees. It was not in these years that he wrote almost ecstatically, "I enjoy the hodgepodge immensely," but that he referred to his own career as "distracted and dislocated."

With skill and restraint this book lays bare the puzzle that was Edwin Gay. It tells us that he was a person of influence. Surely the evidence to that effect is undeniable. But scholars who never knew him may still wonder why a man who wrote so little was the dean of American economic historians and how he made Harvard the center of studies in that discipline. Perhaps the explanation lies in the fact that Gay's students knew his incompleteness incompletely. Largely unaware of their master's contradictory loyalties and dispersed energy, they caught his enthusiasm for perfection, the intense seriousness of his purpose, his relentless energy, and his conviction that though it takes "fifteen or twenty generations more of hard and painstaking work" the task of learning was worth while. As he talked even the long columns of merchant marine statistics spread on the blackboard in Harvard 6 were touched with flame.

Bowdoin College EDWARD C. KIRKLAND

Walter C. Woodward, Friend on the Frontier; A Biography. By Elizabeth H. Emerson. Preface by Errol T. Elliott. (Richmond, Ind.: Friends Book and Supply House, 1952. 316 pp. Bibliography. $2.00.)

Anyone whose knowledge of Quaker history was drawn entirely from books could be pardoned for concluding that the Society of Friends was an eccentric, radical, historically interesting, but now extinct sect, which had once flourished in England and on our Atlantic seaboard. The fact is, of course, that the Society of Friends is still a going concern (to use a Quaker term in its non-Quaker sense), that more than three fifths of its members live west of the Appalachians, and that present-day Quakerism in the Middle and Far West is not precisely what it was on the banks of the Delaware in William Penn's or John Woolman's time. It may be emotional, revivalistic, fundamentalist Quakerism in Oregon; rationalist, humanist, "social-gospel" Quakerism in Southern California; conservative, plain-bonnet, "thee-and-thou" Quakerism in Iowa; respectable, churchified, quasi-Methodist Quakerism in Indiana. The historians, with one or two exceptions, have served us ill in not giving us the story of this expansion and these changes.

Quakers and those who knew Walter C. Woodward (he held a Ph.D. in history from the University of California) will read Elizabeth Emerson's biography as a warm tribute to an able, well-loved Quaker leader. Historians can well read it for its illumination of American Quakerism in the Middle and Far West between 1880 and 1942.

Walter Woodward's family history recapitulated the westward movement of Quakerism. The first Woodward lived in Pennsylvania in the days of the Penns. Later Woodwards moved south to Carolina, west to Tennessee, north to Indiana. In 1880 Walter Woodward himself, aged two, was taken to the Willamette Valley in Oregon, to a Quaker community founded a few years before by a traveling Friend from Iowa. Young Walter Woodward grew up in this postfrontier community, attended Pacific Academy, a Quaker school (where he debated the question "Resolved, that more people have been destroyed by liquor than by war" with another Oregon Quaker boy, Herbert Hoover), and went "back east" to Earlham, the Quaker college in Indiana, for his bachelor's degree. In 1910 he left Oregon, Quakerism's farthest frontier, and moved permanently to Indiana, its heartland. During his mature years he occupied two strategic positions in the Society of Friends: general secretary of the Five Years Meeting, the national organization of "orthodox Gurneyite" Quakerism, and editor of the *American Friend*, its organ.

He had an irenic spirit and a facile pen, two indispensable qualifications for these posts. Not that he was ever a trimmer, all things to all men, or that he was a mere journalistic hack. He had theological opinions of his own — and they were too liberal for his old friends out in Oregon, who seceded from the Five Years Meeting in 1926. He had independent political opinions too — and they did not always please his predominantly Republican constituency: he supported Wilson and the League; he leaned towards La Follette in 1924; he could even see some good in the New Deal, though he had been a Hoover man from boyhood. But whether he was in agreement or dissent, Walter Woodward's relationship to American Quakerism, as Elizabeth Emerson presents it, is always illuminating to the student of recent religious history. It is more so because she presents it largely through the medium of his editorials in the *American Friend* — editorials which always had a luminous quality that raised them above the average level of religious journalism in the United States.

Despite the regrettable absence of an index and an occasional lapse into sentimentality, this book usefully fills part of a great gap in Quaker historiography.

Huntington Library FREDERICK B. TOLLES

The Wild Wheel. By Garet Garrett. (New York: Pantheon Books, 1952. 220 pp. $2.75.)

This is a small etching of an American industrialist. The motif is *laissez faire*, the subject is Henry Ford as the "divine mechanic . . . who thought with his hands."

From this portrait it appears that "the man with wheels in his head" was a paradoxical representative of *laissez faire* and industrial progress. Here was the great capitalist able to parlay an investment of $28,000 into hundreds of millions — who loathed Wall Street, believed in fiat money, and once favored government ownership of railroads and public utilities. His early renown for the five-dollar day (economy-by-largesse) was a cost-cutting scheme based on a reduction in real wages through speed-ups and layoffs. A profound mechanic and born tinkerer, Ford had a naïve faith in ignorance; so many dismissed experts joined the "Ford Alumni Association" that an inevitable paraphrase appeared — "Watch the Ford Officials Go By." Contrary to orthodox economic law he put price before cost, but he took much of the cost out of labor, suppliers, and distributors. Books disturbed his twenty-track mind and he thought history was bunk, but he developed an aching nostalgia for village industry and rustic life exemplified in Greenfield Village. The man whose greatest failing was in human relationships was indirectly responsible for the Ford Foundation, devoted to the welfare of mankind.

This slender volume is an impressionistic vignette. Its chief values are a sprightly style and effective shading based on the firsthand observations of Garet Garrett, who at seventy-four has been financial editor of leading New York papers and chief editorial writer for the *Saturday Evening Post*. It is an interesting composition which is neither history nor biography. For the complete canvas the reader is referred to the well-documented *Legend of Henry Ford* published in 1948 by Keith Sward, who is both a clinical psychologist and an economic historian.

Western Reserve University C. H. CRAMER

The Memoirs of Herbert Hoover. 2 vols. (New York: The Macmillan Company, 1952. *The Cabinet and the Presidency, 1920-1933*. xii + 405 pp. Illustrations, appendix, and index. $5.00. *The Great Depression, 1929-1941*. xv + 503 pp. Illustrations and index. $5.00.)

In the second and third installments of his memoirs, written largely during the years 1933 to 1936, Herbert Hoover provides us with an accounting of his period as secretary of commerce and president of the United States and with a highly critical appraisal of Franklin D. Roosevelt and the New Deal. The first of the volumes under review is concerned primarily with Hoover's activities as a member of the cabinets of Harding and Coolidge and with the problems of his own administration that were not directly related to the "great depression"; the second deals almost entirely with the depression.

Hoover's years as secretary of commerce were, as the former President declares, "happy years of constructive work." The services which his department rendered the business community were considerably expanded. New statistical publications were made available, trade associations were promoted, and suggestions were made with regard to the elimination of waste in industry. The Secretary's interests actually spilled over into the realm of other departments, and Hoover's own account indicates that there was some truth in the remark attributed to Coolidge circles that Hoover was the "Secretary of Commerce and Undersecretary of All Other Departments." He concerned himself with the commercial interests of farmers and with the development of the nation's water resources. It was he, we are informed, who, acting through Harding, persuaded the steel industry to abandon the twelve-hour day and who was responsible for the provision of the Board of Mediation in the Railway Labor Act of 1926.

As president, Hoover continued to foster the policies of "reconstruction and development" which he had championed as secretary of commerce. Problems of foreign affairs, and particularly the Manchurian crisis of 1931, secured their share of attention. But overshadowing all else was the depression, the "nightmare," Hoover tells us, of his presidency. Hoover puts forward once again his highly questionable thesis that although domestic causes produced a "recession" in the United States between October, 1929, and April, 1931, the depression itself was European in origin and did not begin in this country until after the European collapse in 1931; that, partly as a result of the Hoover policies, recovery was underway by July, 1932, but that the upward trend was reversed and the depression prolonged until World War II because of the election of Mr. Roosevelt and the New Deal's "attempt to collectivize the American system of life."

Mr. Hoover points to the part he played in securing a one-year moratorium on the payment of intergovernmental debts and the "standstill" agreement with respect to German short-term obligations, and in the convocation of the World Economic Conference of 1933 as evidence of his awareness of the European nature of the depression, but he inconsistently defends the Smoot-Hawley tariff, which can hardly be classified as a measure of enlightened internationalism. He points with particular pride to the high duties on agricultural products which the tariff imposed but does not tell us how these duties were to benefit farmers producing crops of which there was an exportable surplus. He implies that the "flexible provision" of the tariff was something new and important when in actuality it was, except for certain administrative features, merely a restatement of the similar and largely ineffective provision in the Fordney-McCumber tariff.

Mr. Hoover takes particular pains, and justly so, to demonstrate the falsity of the oft-repeated charges that he did nothing to cushion the shock of the depression or to spur the forces of recovery. Although he relied largely on the marshaling of voluntary efforts during the early months of the depression, he did ultimately invoke the powers of the government to cope with various aspects of the crisis, and in many of his actions and suggestions for action he anticipated the reforms of the New Deal. Hoover, however, as his memoirs suggest, was unable to make an all-out attack on the depression because of his insistence on balancing the budget despite a condition of deflation, his unwillingness to sanction a program of large-scale "nonproductive" (to use Hoover's term) public works, and his opposition to direct federal relief.

The harshest words in Mr. Hoover's two volumes are reserved for F.D.R. and the New Deal. Indeed, Mr. Hoover's estimate of the Roosevelt domestic policy is, in a sense, the counterpart of the Beard-Tansill evaluation of Roosevelt's foreign policy. He accuses Mr. Roosevelt of dissimulation during the 1932 campaign. He criticizes him for his failure to cooperate with his defeated rival during the interregnum between election and inauguration, but does not note here, as he did in his letter of February 20, 1933, to Senator David Reed, that had Roosevelt made the declarations requested of him, he would have committed himself to an acceptance of the Hoover program and to the abandonment of most of the New Deal. He charges further that Roosevelt, after first permitting the banking crisis to develop by refusing to cooperate with the outgoing administration, unnecessarily closed the nation's banks in a deliberate attempt to create a crisis atmosphere ("it was the American equivalent of the burning of the Reichstag") which would be conducive to the acceptance of New Deal reforms. As for the New Deal itself, it represented "an attempt to cross-breed Socialism, Fascism, and Free Enterprise." It must indeed be distressing to Mr. Hoover to see his party regain the White House committed to an acceptance of so many of the New Deal reforms.

If any one theme pervades Mr. Hoover's memoirs, it is that of the proper relationship of government to economic life. Mr. Hoover is certainly no advocate of *laissez faire*, and his ideas as to what constitutes a properly "regulated individualism" would no doubt have horrified William Graham Sumner. But Hoover is all too apt to characterize as socialistic or fascistic measures which go one step beyond what he considers the proper limits of state action. Thus he endorses federal regulation of the power industry and government construction of multipurpose dams of which power might be a byproduct but castigates as socialism and "degeneration" government construction of dams primarily designed to produce power and government distribution of this power. He approves government action to raise farm prices and to retire marginal agricultural land but condemns the McNary-Haugen Bill and the A.A.A. programs as fascism. As secretary of commerce he proposed the establishment of a government fund to liquidate surplus high-cost coal mines and to provide allowances during the period of readjustment to coal miners displaced as a result of this action, and yet he criticizes the Guffey Acts of 1935 and 1937 as outright fascism. Distinctions such as these conditioned Mr. Hoover's actions as secretary of commerce and as president, and they explain much of what is written in his memoirs.

University of Michigan SIDNEY FINE

Wendell Willkie, 1892-1944. By Mary Earhart Dillon. (Philadelphia: J. B. Lippincott Company, 1952. 378 pp. Bibliography and index. $4.00.)

In what the jacket blurb calls a "pioneering biography" the author portrays Wendell Willkie as a defender of free enterprise and as an internationalist, a believer in "One World." In doing this she makes no effort to suppress her own views — she finds very little to praise in the New Deal and has nothing but venom for New Dealers — and does not manage to give a fair account of other people's. Nowhere, for example, does she consider a public utility as affected with the public interest, nor is Commonwealth and Southern's battle with the government considered outside the framework of government interference with private industry. Multiple purpose river valley development, though the author is aware of it, is not seriously discussed. The entire background of this controversy is ignored: Muscle Shoals, municipal ownership, the Federal Trade Commission's investigation of the "Power Trust," Ontario Hydro, and the rest. Samuel Insull is dismissed as a "robber baron," though Willkie in a 1935 speech, not quoted by the author, referred to him as a "forceful, dynamic and attractive figure."

From business to politics the same theme prevails — Willkie defending free enterprise. During the 1940 campaign, as the author points out, he compromised these principles and accepted the New Deal almost entirely. In his Portland, Oregon, speech, not discussed in this volume, he even agreed not to oppose public power if the people of an area desired it. His mistakes, and they were considerable, both in the political and international fields, are ascribed chiefly to poor advisers or to lack of comprehension on his part. In this area the author does not spare Willkie criticism. She feels that he was far too gullible about communism, both in his interview with Stalin and in the Schneiderman case, but that he eventually became disillusioned and before his death was critical of the chances of achieving "One World." In this respect he was ahead of his opponent in 1940; this point of view allows the author an opportunity to get in a dig about Yalta.

One hundred and twenty pages are used to bring Willkie to the brink of his political career. The rest of the volume covers the events of the last five years of his life. The entire work is not marred by a single footnote. The author has relied upon a prodigious number of personal interviews, though not a single manuscript was examined. Newspapers, with the exception of the New York *Times* magazine section, were not consulted. The printed bibliography, while extensive — fourteen pages — includes such choice items as "Revue des Deux Mondes, La. 1829 to date," "Congressional Record: . . . 1874 to date," among others.

The volume is cluttered with minor factual errors. To cite but a few, Burton K. Wheeler in one place (p. 232) is listed as a Republican, in another (p. 253) as a Democrat. The New York *Times* is called an independent Democratic newspaper (p. 342). Power development at Boulder Dam is construed as a Democratic innovation (p. 42). Speaking of the 1940 campaign, the author says, "never, since the campaign of 1860, when the Southern Democrats flung the grossest libels against Abraham Lincoln, had American presidential politics sunk to such a low level" (p. 216).

Surely Wendell Willkie deserves better than this.

University of Maryland RICHARD LOWITT

Working with Roosevelt. By Samuel I. Rosenman. (New York: Harper & Brothers, 1952. xiv + 560 pp. Illustrations and index. $6.00.)

Judge Rosenman has added another memoir to the swelling list of volumes about Franklin D. Roosevelt. And this one, certainly, is entirely justifiable; it makes a unique contribution to our knowledge of F.D.R. and the modern American presidency. Probably no other person had such an intimate and continuous connection with Roosevelt's speechmaking during the fateful years 1928-1945. In addition, the author had the experience of compiling and editing the thirteen-volume *Public Papers and Addresses.* If a man can be understood through his verbal expressions, Judge Rosenman was surely in a position to understand his chief. An outstanding virtue of this book is the well-rounded picture it presents of F.D.R. Other memoir writers have written more fully of the President's view on some particular subject, such as labor, foreign affairs, or relations with the press. Judge Rosenman writes with a specialty in mind, too — speechmaking. But his specialty, more than any other, ties into the innumerable facets of Roosevelt's job, mind, and personality. His book therefore represents a continuum, both in time and subject matter, relative to Roosevelt.

The principal focus of the first chapter is the way in which Roosevelt's speeches and papers were prepared. We have heard of this subject before; but from the historian's point of view, Judge Rosenman becomes the key witness. His account is not only firsthand, but it is given dispassionately and with a ring of complete sincerity and honesty. The author here reveals, without conscious effort, the traits that must have endeared him to F.D.R. — craftsmanship, adaptability, modesty, and an even temper. There is a discernible quality in this book that clearly marks the author from the more volatile personalities which also surrounded the President — from a Moley, Corcoran, Hopkins, Ickes, or Wallace. He relates in painstaking detail how a major Roosevelt speech would be drafted — the preliminary work, the interchange of ideas, the casting and recasting, and the final insertions and alterations (plus Roosevelt's irrepressible ad libs!). It was a most interesting procedure, but Judge Rosenman insists that in spite of all the operations and hands involved, the speeches truly belong to F.D.R. He contributed the major ideas, refined or cast out what was returned to him, and sealed the finished product with his inimitable style of delivery. A good portion of the book is concerned with Roosevelt's method of writing and speaking, which after all were the chief instruments of his popular leadership. He had the superb dramatic sense, and he favored the short sentence, the homely example, rather than flowery oratory. He studiously avoided using statistics in his addresses and always tried to translate their meaning into a commonplace, concrete illustration. A good lesson in pedagogy, and the "Old Professor" knew how to teach!

The book throws new light on many significant events of the Roosevelt era: the genesis of the "Brain Trust," Roosevelt's decision to run for a third term, and his attitude toward Truman before the 1944 Democratic convention. No views are given on the Pearl Harbor issue, presumably because Judge Rosenman was not working closely with the President at that time. The author takes pains to demonstrate, however, that for at least two years leading up to Pearl Harbor, the President had been taking an aggressive stand, in speech and action, against the aggressors — and that he made no effort to conceal that fact from the American people. His program involved a calculated risk of involvement in war, and the people knew it.

Judge Rosenman, writing immediately from memory and aided later by documents and the advice of associates, admits that "This is a partisan book." Much of it is given to anecdotes and recollection of incidents which illuminate Roosevelt's personality — his flaws and his strong points — and above all, his humanity. In this he largely confirms what we have already read and heard from earlier sources, friendly and otherwise. The particular value of seeing such evidence in this book derives from the value of Judge Rosenman as a historical source. He is partisan, to be sure, but shrewd and scholarly in his observations — and he was *there*. What is the author's over-all estimate of F.D.R.? Judge Rosenman ranks him with our "greatest Presidents" — Washington, Jefferson, and Lincoln.

Michigan State College THOMAS H. GREER

Fleet Admiral King; A Naval Record. By Ernest J. King and Walter Muir Whitehill. (New York: W. W. Norton & Company, Inc., 1952. xv + 674 pp. Illustrations, charts, maps, and index. $6.75.)

For forty years Ernest King prepared himself for the supreme test. From 1901 to 1941 he moved through the grades from ensign to admiral; he saw service in battleships, destroyers, submarines, supply ships, and aircraft carriers, in Europe, Asia, and the Caribbean; he served in engineering, on the staff of the commander of the Atlantic fleet in World War I, on the General Board, in the Bureau of Navigation and as chief of the Bureau of Aeronautics; he taught at the Naval Academy and studied at the Naval War College where he worked on problems of Pacific strategy; and he commanded important units of the fleet. When the Japanese struck at Pearl Harbor, King was supervising convoy operations to Europe as commander of the Atlantic fleet. Within two weeks he was made Cominch, United States fleet, and three months later replaced Admiral Stark as chief of Naval Operations. No man in the United States navy was better equipped by training and experience to direct the global responsibilities of the navy in World War II; no man could have performed the job with greater success.

The first half of the book covers the apprenticeship; the second half deals with the stewardship. From 1941 to 1945 King ran the war at sea. As Cominch-CNO he allocated the nation's maritime resources among the several theaters and planned operations, now traveling to San Francisco to confer with Nimitz on the Pacific, now to London to see Stark on the African and continental invasions. As a member of the Joint (U.S.) Chiefs of Staff and the Combined (Anglo-American) Chiefs of Staff and as a participant in the great international conferences, he helped to plot global strategy. While accepting the primacy of the European theater, King never let his American and Allied colleagues forget that there was a war in progress against Japan. Indeed, his persistence elicited the exasperated remark from Sir John Dill that "King's war is against Japan."

The volume is a notable contribution to the history of the war and deserves a prominent place alongside the accounts by the other principal participants, Eisenhower, Stilwell, Bradley, Halsey, Leahy, and Clay. The amount of information on every aspect of the war — plans, operations, and logistics — is overwhelming. The European and Pacific phases are neatly interwoven. There are penetrating observations on leading personalities (of both world wars). The discussions that led to the major policy decisions are treated extensively. The book nevertheless has limitations. The style is rarely graceful and frequently labored. Words and phrases are often ill-chosen. Attempts to interject humorous situations appear superimposed and strained. The first half contains too much unnecessary dull routine and trivia; the second part lacks breadth and sweep. King tends to a dry recital of events and seems to be underplaying his own personal contribution. He is too much the author and narrator and too little the actor in the drama. Absent are his well-known and volatile reactions to men and situations. He leans on a quotation from Stilwell's diary for the single indication of his aroused temper. He lets the General describe for the reader a conference on China affairs where "King got good and sore. King almost climbed over the table at Brooke."

These deficiencies unquestionably flow from the Admiral's personality and temperament. The book, although written in collaboration, is King's own. Like the ships he commanded, it is taut but not happy. Like the man himself, it is unbending, restrained, and inflexible. But like the man himself, it is upright, sincere, and honest.

University of California, Berkeley ARMIN RAPPAPORT

History of Marine Corps Aviation in World War II. By Robert Sherrod. (Washington: Combat Forces Press, 1952. xiv + 496 pp. Illustrations, appendixes, and index. $6.50.)

The author states in his preface that "This is not an official history," but the reviewer believes that the book will be so considered. Its publication was financed by profits of Post Exchanges, and it was written for the men (and the handful of women) who served in Marine Corps aviation in World War II. More important, it was written after broad and solid research and it is based upon official documents and official or semiofficial books.

The book covers the whole field of Marine aviation in World War II, from high level decisions, through the activities of small units, to numerous episodes involving individuals. The first two chapters are background, telling the story of Marine aviation from 1912 (when the first Marine pilot, Lieutenant Alfred A. Cunningham, soloed) to Pearl Harbor. The third and fourth chapters deal with the travail of the handful of pilots who fought in the defense of Wake and the few who flew in the Battle of Midway. The next half dozen chapters are concerned with the Solomons. For the early defense of the Guadalcanal beachhead most of the air power available to the Allies consisted of a few squadrons of Marine aviation; these, with slowly increasing help from the Army Air Forces and naval aviation enabled the embattled ground troops to stop the Japanese. The author indicates that by the end of the Solomons campaign the cream of the enemy's naval air force had been wiped out and that the Marines deserve the greater part of the credit for this vitally important accomplishment. But the records show that the Japanese front-line naval aviation was not smashed until Rabaul had been neutralized and that the credit has to be divided about equally among the air forces of the several services.

The Marine flyers felt that their principal *raison d'etre* was to render close support, not to fly defensive patrols or long-range offensive missions, but it was not until the drive on Manila that they had the opportunity to engage in real close support. But one must question the author's handling of the story at this point, for he strongly implies that in the campaign to conquer Luzon the Marines introduced a new theory and practice of close support. Actually, the methods which they employed were already being used by the Army Air Forces in Italy and France.

The able way in which the Marines handled close support on Luzon evidently failed to impress the right people. For after the conclusion of the Philippines campaign, the flyers, operating from the carrier *Essex*, were used against the Chinese and Japanese coasts, and even at Okinawa, where Marine aviation was more highly concentrated than at any time since the Solomons, the navy supported the ground troops while the Marines flew patrols.

In the process of producing an interesting, well-written, and fully documented book the author has pointed out a number of errors in earlier accounts of the war in the Pacific. At least one of these, the message from Wake Island to "send us more Japs," is probably too much a part of the American tradition ever to be corrected.

The book contains 144 photographs, some of them captured Japanese pictures. The maps are satisfactory and the index is good. There are nine interesting appendixes, ranging from the names of the Medal of Honor winners among the Marine flyers to a short sketch of each Marine Aviation unit. These, together with the copious details which fill the book, will save hours of research for many a writer.

All in all, the *History of Marine Corps Aviation in World War II* is a welcome and most useful addition to the growing library of books on the last war.

Air University ALBERT F. SIMPSON

Operation Overlord; Design and Reality, The Allied Invasion of Western Europe. By Albert Norman. Foreword by Walter Bedell Smith. (Harrisburg: The Military Service Publishing Company, 1952. xiv + 230 pp. Maps, photographs, appendixes, bibliography, and index. $3.75.)

As the title promises, this is another of the many books now being published on various specific phases of World War II. However, Mr. Norman has distinguished himself as an author by bringing together three factors which make his book pleasant reading—good writing, scholarship, and brevity. Also refreshing is the fact that the author never mentions himself, even though he was a staff historian with General Bradley.

This work is a history of the years of planning and preparation for the invasion of Western Europe and of the staging of that invasion from England in the summer of 1944. The author has his topic well organized into the four specific problems which confronted the developers of the Overlord plan:

the strategic problem, organization for the invasion, the design, and the reality of the invasion.

The reader will come to respect the problems which confronted the Allies in their planning to invade Europe, and will also gain greater respect for that "nasty piece of water," the English Channel. The chief benefit of the book, however, is that one can now get a detailed description of the planning which went into this most spectacular of military events — "D-Day."

Mr. Norman weakens his book appreciably by leaving out many specific details which should be included in a monograph of this type — especially specific naval losses during the invasion and the period immediately following the landings. The author has also committed an error of fact when he states that the Eighth Air Force did not bomb at St. Lo on July 24 due to bad weather. This particular reader knows positively that units of the Eighth Air Force did bomb the St. Lo area on both July 24 and 25.

The book is a richer than normal contribution to the growing field of World War II historiography; and, thank goodness, succinct.

Stetson University JOHN JOHNS

The American Approach to Foreign Policy. By Dexter Perkins. (Cambridge: Harvard University Press, 1952. 203 pp. Bibliographical note and index. $3.75.)

While it would hardly be correct to say that there has been a plethora of monographs on American diplomatic history in recent years, those which have appeared have tended to concentrate on limited eras or selected aspects. In the process the fact that foreign policy has been a continual and a continuing thing has been obscured. It becomes useful on occasion, therefore, to take a sweeping backward glance through the diplomatic history of the United States. Nor is it to be regretted when an historical scholar of considerable repute dares to project that past into the future. Dexter Perkins has done both, and in a way that is rewarding to the general reader and to his colleagues as well.

The volume is a collection of essays which Professor Perkins prepared under the auspices of the Gottesman Foundation for delivery at the University of Uppsala, Sweden, in 1949. In their essence, the tracts seek to interpret for a foreign audience the broad motivations and fundamental principles of American foreign policy.

That this undertaking was especially timely at a moment when, in the propaganda war between East and West, those policies were being challenged and deliberately distorted, adds to their importance. The end product serves as a healthy reminder to our own countrymen, moreover, that the roots of American foreign policies are embedded deep in rich soil, a fact to strengthen one's faith in the instruments at hand for waging the psychological battle for men's minds.

Students of diplomatic history will find little that is new in Professor Perkins' suggestions of the fortuitous attributes of American expansionism; in his minimizing of the sinister forces of imperialism, especially as embodied in the designs of the commercial interests, businessmen, and bankers; or in a reminder that there has been "a highly moralistic flavor" to our diplomacy, along with a traditional idealism not always observable in the machinations of European governments. But the lectures were not intended to represent basic new research; rather, they stand as an interpretative account of the American story by one of its keenest students.

In bringing into the focus of historical perspective the present United States-U.S.S.R. rivalries, as is done in the closing chapters, Professor Perkins exercises a privilege which some of his professional colleagues will call into question, but which in the judgment of the reviewer should be applauded. Admitting that "not all the elements of a democratic foreign policy are favorable to the wise handling" of the Soviet threat, the author nevertheless leaves an impression that the negative factors may be outweighed by those on the more positive side. American policy, resulting as it almost always has from what the public has willed, thus records that the people have usually come up with the right answers.

Inescapably it is this latter section of the book which will evoke some disagreement, for each of us has become in his own mind Mr. Secretary of State. Within such a context it may be permissible to suggest that the least satisfying passages are those which detail a "rhythm theory" of American foreign policy, and particularly those which profess to see the broad outlines of the future reflected in the business cycles of the past. But these do not seriously detract from the stature of the book.

University of Wyoming GALE W. MCGEE

The American Record in the Far East, 1945-1951. By Kenneth Scott Latourette. (New York: The Macmillan Company, 1952. 208 pp. Bibliography and index. $3.00.)

The modest author of this little volume says in his introduction that he is only trying to provide a useful elementary summary of recent developments in an important field. He grants that many will not accept his conclusions, and admits that what is written now will be rewritten in the years to come.

The United States has been moving westward for three centuries, says Professor Latourette, and has been developing an interest in more of Asia each generation. Granting economic factors to be important, he considers them less significant than ideas. The present conflict he sees as one between communism and an American ideology based largely on Puritan protestantism.

Despite American errors and weakness, the author feels that the United States has achieved much in India and Southeast Asia since World War II. The American republic faced one of the greatest tests in its history in the occupation of Japan, and came out (he thinks) fairly well. In the Philippines, too, praise must accompany admission of blunders. China, however, provided the greatest defeat in American history. Professor Latourette finds fault with the Joseph Stilwell appointment; says Americans badly misjudged the Chinese Communists; hints that Truman erred in the George C. Marshall mission; and feels that Roosevelt should have pursued a different line at Yalta. But, he says, despite errors, the United States did not wreck the Chinese Nationalists; they wrecked themselves. We helped Chiang. Had we helped him more, he would still have lost. In Korea, too, Professor Latourette notes American shortcomings, but finds little wrong with the major decisions of American policymakers from the beginning of the occupation to the MacArthur removal. Everything considered, the author sees a continuing, and growing, American interest in Asia. He does not believe that American democracy can easily be introduced into the Orient, and appreciates the magnitude of the tasks ahead; yet he is reasonably optimistic about the future.

As Professor Latourette says, some will challenge his conclusions. The reviewer feels that at several points he underestimates economic factors, as in his historical section on the Open Door; that at several points he almost completely overlooks vital strategic factors; that he is not sufficiently critical of American occupation policy in Korea; and so on. The book's major fault, however, is one of coverage. American policies are described; but little is said as to why these policies were pursued. There is only passing mention of party politics. There is no mention at all of Dewey, who tried to make China an issue in 1948; no mention of Judd, or Owen Lattimore, or Henry Wallace, or Luce, or McCarthy, or Kohlbergy; no mention of the Institute of Pacific Relations, or the China Lobby. There is almost nothing on the view of American military men as to the strategic importance of the Far East, or on West Coast or business or other attitudes and influences vital to the central problem. The book is useful to the general reader and the specialist; but, as Professor Latourette says, the major job of analysis and judgment lies ahead.

University of Wisconsin FRED HARVEY HARRINGTON

The DP Story; The Final Report of the United States Displaced Persons Commission. (Washington: United States Government Printing Office, 1952. xi + 376 pp. Appendixes and tables. $1.00.)

Late in 1952 the McCarran-Walter Law became effective. Current press reports point to 500,000 refugees in Hong Kong, 880,000 dispossessed Arabs, and some 700,000 surplus persons in Puerto Rico. The metropolitan press has been featuring the Lanzas, Lucheses, and Luchianos among criminals in high places. With such a background the final report of the activities of the Displaced Persons Commission for the years from 1948 to 1952 should find a ready market.

The story of selecting, examining, and resettling some 400,000 Europeans is told in great detail. Due credit is given to several other governmental and some twenty nongovernmental agencies as also to the International Refugee Organization for important aid in the resettlement. The report is required reading for the expert but it is not to be expected that the average citizen will go through the details to get his information.

The Commission saw fit to use the report for propaganda in line with the veto of the McCarran Bill. The argument is that "immigration without restriction is in the noblest tradition and the highest self-interest of the United States" and that the dispossessed and surplus population of Europe should be admitted. In view of the fact that over nine tenths of the 400,000 were resettled in urban areas, it might well surprise students of Jefferson to find him quoted as in favor of the thesis of the Commission. Jefferson, Madison, and Frederick Jackson Turner seemed to sense a relation between free land and free men. Jefferson definitely opposed piling men up in large cities.

The reader might get the impression that emigration is the solution for the problem of surplus populations. If he has been exposed to the writings of Gini, Kuczynski, Kitaoka, Virtanen, Willcox, Mather, Singh, Ghosh, Carr-Saunders, Penrose, Latzky, Orr, Thompson, Bennett, Andrews, Vogt, Bland, Osborn, Burch and Pendell, Pearson and Harper, plus the work of the various research agencies, this simple solution will not be convincing. It would seem to require some thinking rather than thumbing through the traditions to solve the problem of population and resources. It may well be that those who insist on breeding more than they can feed are simply preparing the soil for dictators. Any student of the population statistics of Europe for the last half century might be tempted to reach that conclusion.

Finally, the Commission seems to suggest that the United States would be aiding in the making of a better world by taking the more desirable persons of the surplus population out of Europe and leaving the less desirable there. My acquaintances in Europe have not been enthusiastically in favor of that policy just as many Americans are not in favor of importing more immigrants of the Mafia type.

Western Reserve University JACOB C. MEYER

Graveyard of the Atlantic; Shipwrecks of the North Carolina Coast. By David Stick. (Chapel Hill: The University of North Carolina Press, 1952. ix + 276 pp. End maps, illustrations, references, and index. $5.00.)

Off the Outer Banks of North Carolina the northern and southern winds and waters meet; here a long sweeping series of shoal-infested bights and capes and inlets, in time of storm, have wrought havoc to an untold number of coastwise and transatlantic craft and have earned the Outer Banks its grim nickname.

The present study is a factual narrative account of some six hundred shipwrecks in this area from 1526 to the present. Only vessels generally over fifty tons and definitely known to have been total wrecks are listed. Inadequate accounts, or lack of any records, or confusion as to dates, places, and circumstances necessitated the elimination of "a major share of the thousands of shipwreck accounts examined." Major sources used were newspaper accounts, official records, and personal interviews.

For the general reader at least, a recital of wreck after wreck may grow a little monotonous. There is obviously something of a pattern in shipwrecks: vessels disabled, crews in mortal danger, and attempted rescues, heroic but often futile. In reality, however, shipwrecks are unique with plenty of drama. There are stories of childbirth in a lifeboat, of a dog that served as rescuer by taking the line ashore, of Dunbar Davis who worked around the clock to save five crews off Cape Fear in 1893, and of the great hurricane of 1899 which beached nine ships in two days. Some of the worst wrecks brought relief in their wake. Following the *Home* disaster of 1837 when 90 lives were lost, Congress passed legislation requiring seagoing ships to carry life belts for all passengers and crew. The loss of 103 lives on the *Huron* in 1877 and and of 85 on the *Metropolis* a few weeks later resulted in the establishment of efficient coastal lifesaving service.

We learn in two or three pages that "the past history and present life of the entire coast of North Carolina are closely integrated with shipwrecks." Stranded cargoes have brought wealth to the finders, and houses wholly or in part built from salvaged lumber may be found "in almost every coastal community." Descendants of shipwrecked mariners populate "entire villages today," and the major income of many coastal families is derived from services rendered, "past and present," as guardians of the shore.

David Stick, a resident of the Outer Banks, has done a careful research job; he has captured the spirit of the hazardous coast and has told his story well. Particular mention should be made of the many fine pen-and-ink drawings by the author's father. The publishers are to be commended for fine workmanship but the price seems high.

University of Oklahoma WILLIAM E. LIVEZEY

The Chattanooga Country, 1540-1951; From Tomahawks to TVA. By Gilbert E. Govan and James W. Livingood. (New York: E. P. Dutton and Company, 1952. 509 pp. Bibliography and index. $5.00.)

The Chattanooga Country is a worthy addition to the increasing list of good local histories which are replacing the studies formerly done by genealogists and amateurs. The authors have achieved their goal, "to examine the many experiences of the people of the Chattanooga region in the light of local, state and national events and to see how they were influenced by or contributed to the greater stream of history" (p. 7). The bibliography reveals the types of fine sources available to the local historian who has the will and the patience to consult them. Rarely does the reader feel burdened with minutiae and never does he encounter a list of local celebrities whose names were included merely to boost sales.

The Chattanooga country is admirably suited for study as a "microcosm of America." It is a land of scenic grandeur and rich mineral deposits, the topography of which has made it a crossroads of river and rail transportation. The colorful Cherokee Indians dominated the region until the seaboard colonists seeking elbowroom found it a natural gateway to the West. It was a flaming frontier in the Revolutionary era and the scene of some of the most crucial campaigns of the Civil War. Its human and natural resources destined it to be a manufacturing center. The steps of the earlier Industrial Revolution were repeated in the development of the chenille bedspread industry. A long history of the growth of heavy industry has culminated in the establishment of TVA and the Oak Ridge project.

The authors have successfully avoided the disconnected presentation found in some local histories by emphasizing certain themes which have recurred in the history of Chattanooga. For instance, much of the development of the city has been the result of pressures from the outside. This has been true from the international intrigues of colonial days down to TVA. Another traceable theme has been the continuing community effort to weld unity out of the various factions within the area, particularly Confederate and federal elements. The efforts seemed to receive national acclaim with the appointment of a Chattanoogan, D. M. Key, to a cabinet post as a part of the Compromise of 1876. Still another theme has been the influence of federal aid on the development of the region. It began with the first $200, appropriated for a survey of Muscle Shoals (at the insistence of John C. Calhoun in spite of the opposition cries of violation of state rights), and has finally reached the tremendous outlays for TVA.

The contributions of Chattanooga to life in America have been many, including such unique ones as Tom Thumb Golf and the great industry concerned with the bottling of Coca-Cola. Among the famous Americans with

Chattanooga backgrounds was Adolph Ochs, who, even as editor of the New York *Times*, never lost interest in his former community.

One volume can never include all that the curious desire to know concerning a region, and the authors must decide the inclusions and omissions. In this volume the authors have at times chosen to include sensational episodes occurring in the surrounding country while omitting serious discussion of the development of basic social institutions in the heart of the community. The Scottsboro case, the Dayton trial, the settlement at Rugby, and the snake-handlers of Dolly Pond were sensational news items in their day. But some discussion of the development of the instruments of law and order, a résumé of the growth of educational institutions (including some very fine preparatory schools as well as the University), a more adequate analysis of cultural opportunities in the city, and an interpretation of the growth of substantial religious bodies in Chattanooga would have been equally as valuable in a serious history. These few omissions do not materially detract, however, from the value of this splendid volume.

Nashville, Tennessee BLANCHE HENRY CLARK WEAVER

Smoky Mountain Country. By North Callahan. Edited by Erskine Caldwell. *American Folkways Series*. (New York: Duell, Sloan & Pearce, 1952. xii + 257 pp. End maps and index. $4.00.)

North Callahan is a native of the Smoky Mountain region of Tennessee who is now a New York journalist. In these two capacities he writes about the lives and folk customs of a people who until very recently were untouched by twentieth-century developments. He also describes the natural grandeur of the mountains along with the opportunities they afford for various types of recreation, including wild boar hunting, and gives much useful information regarding such modern tourist meccas as Gatlinburg, the Tennessee Valley Authority, and the atomic energy city of Oak Ridge. To the extent that he confines himself to contemporary description and reminiscences of his own experiences, Mr. Callahan writes with the clarity and skill that is usually characteristic of his profession.

Unfortunately the same cannot be said of his excursions into Smoky Mountain history. Here occur numerous inaccuracies which betray the scanty use of sources and carelessness in handling those that were used. Examples of this are the bland observation that John Sevier "has been largely neglected by historians" (p. 5); a meaningless explanation of the causes that led to the establishment of the State of Franklin (p. 22); and the statement that Sevier defeated Andrew Jackson for governor of Tennessee in 1803 (p. 22). If "100,000 people" (p. 22) were in the Watauga region in 1784, it would be interesting to know what led to such a reduction of this number, since there were only 87,775 in the entire state when it was admitted to the Union in

1796. Similarly intriguing is the statement that "the first railroad to pass through East Tennessee began to operate in 1889" (p. 124).

Equally nebulous assertions and concepts appear with reference to geography. That the battle of King's Mountain was fought in North Carolina (p. 20) represents the same type of loose expression as that the height of Clingman's Dome "is exceeded east of the Rockies only by Mount Mitchell" (p. 215). It is questionable as to whether the Smokies are broad enough to include the Dayton monkey trial (pp. 141-57), and they are certainly not sufficiently elastic to embrace James K. Polk and Alvin C. York of Middle Tennessee (pp. 247, 104-105); the Grand Ole Opry, universally associated with Nashville (pp. 138-40); and Eddie Arnold, the singing plowboy from Henderson, deep in West Tennessee (pp. 134-35).

This is the twenty-fourth volume in the *American Folkways Series*. Its value was not improved by the author's efforts to write also in the field of American history.

University of North Carolina JAMES W. PATTON

The History of American Epidemiology. By C.-E. A. Winslow, Wilson G. Smillie, James A. Doull, John E. Gordon. Edited by Franklin H. Top. (St. Louis: The C. V. Mosby Company, 1952. 190 pp. References and index. $4.75.)

The title *American Epidemiology* is misleading since developments in the continental United States only are discussed. The volume comprises four essays delivered before the Epidemiology section of the American Public Health Association in October, 1949. The initial paper covering the colonial era and the first years of the republic is by Dr. C.-E. A. Winslow of the Yale University School of Medicine. Dr. Wilson G. Smillie of the Cornell University Medical College discusses the years 1800-1875 in the United States, while Dr. James A. Doull of the American Leprosy Foundation covers what he terms "The Bacteriological Era (1876-1920)." The final essay by Dr. John E. Gordon of the School of Public Health, Harvard University, sketches epidemiology after 1920.

Epidemics have been studied since the time of Hippocrates twenty-four centuries ago but only during the past century has the subject become one for specialization. Epidemiology in its short span as a distinct discipline has contributed immeasurably to the understanding of disease.

These essays are interesting and, though incomplete, supply information not previously available under one cover. In the discussion of yellow fever which struck Philadelphia in 1793, there is no mention of Dr. Charles Caldwell whose exertions then were so meritorious. He antedated Benjamin Rush and suggested to him that the disease was not contagious. The ravages of cholera and especially of malaria with their influence upon the birth and death of towns in the Mississippi Valley would seem to have called for specific treatment. To assert arbitrarily that the year 1920 marks "the close of the Bacteriological Era" (p. 75) will be questioned. The final essay clearly indicates that bacteriology continues as an important field of investigation.

The "Index of Persons" and the "Subject Index" are to be commended for their completeness.

University of Louisville EMMET FIELD HORINE

Cavalcade of the American Novel; From the Birth of the Nation to the Middle of the Twentieth Century. By Edward Wagenknecht. (New York: Henry Holt and Company, 1952. xv + 575 pp. Appendix, bibliography, index of names, and index of titles. $6.50.)

Companion piece to his *Cavalcade of the English Novel*, Professor Wagenknecht's *Cavalcade of the American Novel* displays a good many of the qualities of its predecessor. It is a book for the scholar and the specialist rather than for the general reader. It is, moreover, rather a cavalcade of American novelists than a searching survey of the development of fictional art; indeed, it is difficult upon finishing the last chapter ("Fiction of the 'Forties and After") to see precisely, at least from this study, what artistic qualities differentiate the writers of this decade from the writers contemporary with Herman Melville.

Of course Mr. Wagenknecht does not neglect the art of fiction — his discussion of Henry James is proof that he does not — yet the book has more to do with writers than with what they write. Each major figure is viewed in a preliminary paragraph, followed by a brief biographical sketch; after that, the author categorizes the novels by types, or chronologically, and then discusses the leading works. Mr. Wagenknecht is nothing if not thorough; each such discussion of a major figure carries with it a series of footnotes almost invariably referring to some scholarly article on this or that special phase of the topic. There is a kind of plethora of information in the book, since, in addition to these scholarly flourishes, an immense bibliography occupies pages 497-555; and pages 465-96 constitute shorter discussions of "novelists not considered in the text."

If Mr. Wagenknecht is thus rather a historian than a critic, his aesthetic position is nevertheless discernible. He is a not illiberal conservative. If he takes a writer like Elsie Singmaster far more seriously than do most discussions of the American novel, he is nevertheless open-minded about Faulkner and excellent on a book like *Jurgen*. Nevertheless, his heart is with the older writers — Henry James, Willa Cather, Ellen Glasgow.

The unity of the book is somewhat marred by the fact that separate chapters have, in many instances, been published as individual articles. Consequently the point of view is not consistently maintained. It is amusing to note that Mr. Wagenknecht's aversion to the American entry into World War I pops up (like King Charles's head in *David Copperfield*) here and there throughout the work.

I suspect the book will be more useful as a work of reference and of encyclopedic information than as an aesthetic guide to great and lesser art.

Harvard University HOWARD MUMFORD JONES

Transatlantic Exchanges; Cross-Currents of Anglo-American Opinion in the Nineteenth Century. Selected and introduced by Yvonne ffrench. (New York: Library Publishers, 1952. 255 pp. Illustrations and index of authors. $3.75.)

Of the making of books based on travelers' reports on America there seems to be no end, but it was a happy thought to balance accounts of English travelers in the United States with comments of American visitors to England. The brief selections begin with Paine on "Monarchical versus Republican Government," and end with William Dean Howells paying tribute to London: "One feels that New York shall be; but London *is*," he wrote in 1904. Despite the occasional sour note struck by the visitor to Britain it is quite right to say, as does the author, that "the American comes to England searching reverently for his past."

In his less reverent moments he was contemptuous of monarchy, critical of England's heavy taxation, scornful of her class stratification — but always charmed by her countryside. The visiting Englishmen agreed on American hospitality and friendliness, but they found incongruous boasts of liberty and cries of slaves, while American journalism was dismissed as vulgar and corrupt. And as for scenery, Niagara seemed to balance England's landscape.

All the familiar names are here — Trollope, Martineau, Dickens, and Thackeray; similarly the oft-quoted Emerson, Hawthorne, and Henry James. Hawthorne was frequently caustic: "Every Englishman runs to the *Times* with his little grievance as a child runs to his mother." And again: "Nothing seems to touch the English nearer than this question of nautical superiority; and if we wish to hit them to the quick we must hit them there."

In a disarming introduction Miss ffrench summarizes the comments of her travelers, some of whom (if memory serves me right) have had part of their venom extracted. It is to be regretted that selections were not made from a wider variety of observers; literary figures are overrepresented here. True, they often had good insights, but whole areas of activity are left untouched in these snippets. Nothing is included indicating what English workingmen thought of America, nor is there comment from farmers, businessmen, or politicians from either country. Such materials are available and might well have been quoted. It is a pity that this well-meaning volume gives us too much of the familiar, for the crosscurrents of Anglo-American opinion in the nineteenth century were much deeper and more significant than herein revealed.

City College, New York MICHAEL KRAUS

Makers of Modern Journalism. By Kenneth Stewart and John Tebbel. (New York: Prentice-Hall, Inc., 1952. x + 514 pp. Illustrations, bibliography, and index. $6.65.)

This book, the authors tell us in a foreword, "is a history of American journalism told in terms of men and motives." A great many men of the nineteenth-century era of personal journalism and of the twentieth-century era of syndicates and the monopolistic press are introduced to the reader by means of rather brief, personal sketches. While there is little new given in the way of interpretation, some of these characterizations, particularly those of the nineteenth century, are well written and concisely drawn. In the case of such colorful figures as E. W. Scripps, Henry Watterson, and Joseph Patterson, the reader can feel that he has become properly acquainted with some of the editors who have, in the words of the authors, demonstrated "a freedom of thought and action unsurpassed anywhere else in the world."

It is also to the credit of Professors Stewart and Tebbel that they have found room to give some attention not only to the Bennetts, Greeleys, and Hearsts, but also to some of the lesser known but extremely interesting figures of America's provincial press, such as Joseph Dennie of New Hampshire, Ed Howe of Kansas, and those two exploding journalistic skyrockets who luridly lighted the skies over Denver, Fred G. Bonfils and Harry H. Tammen.

But in spite of the great number of men who make their appearance in this book, not only journalists but in the most recent period radio and TV news commentators, there are some rather surprising omissions. It is not to be expected, of course, that a book as limited in size as this can deal adequately with all major journalistic achievements in a period from 1690 to 1951. But it is difficult for the reviewer to understand on what basis the selection was made. Certainly Samuel Bowles and his Springfield *Republican* should at least rate some discussion in a book that devotes half of a chapter to Fremont Older. Notice is taken of the Kiplinger *Washington Letter* but not of the *Wall Street Journal.* And if the authors can justify devoting considerable space to the *Reader's Digest* on the grounds that it "exerts an impact on public opinion," it is difficult to understand how the golden age of American periodicals when such magazines as the *Outlook*, *Colliers'*, and the *American Magazine* gave direction to the Progressive era can be completely ignored.

Many of the more significant developments of modern journalism are presented but because of the biographical form of this book, these problems are always related to a particular individual. A defense of the monopolistic press, for instance, is given in a chapter on the Cowles family of Des Moines and Minneapolis. Such a personalized presentation could easily give the reader the impression that only the professional journalists and not such outside forces as big business, advertising agencies, and "100 per cent American" patriotic organizations have been "the makers of modern journalism."

The authors seem convinced that "the newspapers of America began as the voice of revolution and in little more than two centuries they have accomplished the full swing from radical revolt to solid conservatism." While we do stand in some danger of a one-party press, liberalism is not quite as moribund as this statement would indicate. For Professors Stewart and Tebbel to maintain that "Greeley became perhaps the only editor in American journalism who ever made liberalism pay," is to disregard their own accounts of E. W. Scripps, Joseph Pulitzer, and more recently Marshall Field. One must also ignore, as they do, James A. Wechsler of the New York *Post* and those two untiring voices of liberalism, the *Nation* and the *New Republic*.

This book is undocumented as to source material used, but it does contain a bibliography for each chapter which should be useful to the reader who wants to know more about American journalism than he can learn in these lively and well-written sketches of individual journalists.

Grinnell College JOSEPH F. WALL

America in Crisis; Fourteen Crucial Episodes in American History. Edited by Daniel Aaron. (New York: Alfred A. Knopf, 1952. xiv + 363 pp. Bibliography. $4.00.)

When the values that some men live by are threatened by the values that other men live by, there is bound to be a social crisis. Living through a crisis of this kind is an extremely painful experience, as our uneasy, insecure generation knows only too well. The experience is painful because it demands, among other things, our best creative thought and a critical appraisal of our whole system of values. This is what the present world crisis demands of us.

In meeting such a crisis it is wise to look back before looking ahead. Or so thought a committee of the Bennington College faculty when it picked the theme "American Response to Crisis" for an experimental course offered during the winter of 1950-1951. The result was a series of fourteen public lectures, each given by a competent visiting scholar, upon some crucial episode in American history. It was hoped that these episodes would reveal "how American values have manifested themselves in moments of crisis."

The problem of selection was a difficult one — most readers will think of some crisis that should not have been overlooked — but in the main the choices were logical. Only the most narrow political historian will object to their range, for they include crises in religion, education, art, agriculture, banking, labor relations, sectional relations, and foreign policy. In their published form the equality of these lectures is uneven. The best of them will be read with profit by student and teacher alike; some will appeal to one but not to the other; and a few, unfortunately, will appeal to neither. Some contributors managed always to keep the central theme in clear focus. Others, apparently forgetting that they were not reading papers at a professional meeting, lost themselves in a jumble of detail.

How does a study of these past crises help us "to meet and to surmount the present one"? Perhaps it may help a little just to be reminded that other generations had their crises, each of which seemed as cataclysmic to those who faced it as the one we face today. But, contrary to the smugly provincial claim on the dust jacket, these crises were no more "peculiarly American" than were the responses they called forth. People everywhere have encountered comparable situations and have responded in comparable ways. These essays deal with human behavior, not with "peculiarly American" behavior.

The deepest lesson to be learned from this book is that there never was a single uniform American response to a crisis situation. This altogether healthy diversity of response was inevitable so long as there was freedom of thought and freedom of expression. Those who would make a fetish of "bipartisanship" in time of crisis — even international crisis — might well be concerned about the cost, which is intellectual stagnation. The cheap political exploitation of a world crisis during a national election is deplorable. But muzzling the critical and creative thought which a great crisis itself generates could be fatal. These essays seem to establish this point rather conclusively.

University of California, Berkeley KENNETH M. STAMPP

Science and Religion in American Thought; The Impact of Naturalism. By Edward A. White. (Stanford: Stanford University Press, 1952. viii + 117 pp. $2.50.)

This little book is a significant contribution to a major enterprise — the revival of a specifically Christian interpretation of history. Since most of us are trained in a historical tradition dominated by liberalism and progress, it comes as a healthy shock to read an account of the conflict of science and religion written frankly from the standpoint of the latter, and presenting the victories of the former not as milestones of progress but as steps into a blind alley.

Mr. White's assumptions are both explicit and implicit; they include a transcendent God, criteria of good and evil independent of history, and the reality of a realm of human freedom outside the realm of natural law. It is no surprise that the name of Niebuhr occasionally crops up.

The story starts with the confident, largely pre-evolutionary positivism of John W. Draper, whose views, as Mr. White presents them, were little different from those of an eighteenth-century Deist. Next come the spokesmen of evolution, Andrew D. White and John Fiske. To them God was immanent in, not to say identical with, the process of evolution. This process held the sure key not only to the conflict of science and religion but also to the problems of American society.

Mr. White's most trenchant chapter, one of his shortest, deals with William James as the great watershed. James's thorough and imaginative empiricism denied exclusive validity to the realm of science and treated both science and religion as attempts to set up relations among objects of thought. The area of reconciliation was no longer evolutionary science, which to James might or might not confirm theistic assumptions, but rather the human personality, where experience and need furnished a sounder basis for religious truth. A generally convincing presentation of James is marred by one sentence (p. 53), which surely goes too far in placing him "in the tradition of that Christian mysticism which took its inspiration from Augustine" because he emphasized "the transcendent reality of inner human experience." Would it not be fairer to say that James was respectful toward this tradition rather than a part of it, and to omit the word "transcendent"?

In by far his longest chapter, Mr. White describes the unsystematic and not very compelling views of David Starr Jordan, who evidently combined the positivism of Draper and Fiske with some degree of the open-mindedness and respect for personality of James. Jordan makes a satisfactory representative of his optimistic day, but one doubts whether any but a loyal Stanford man would give him as much space in this company.

Inevitably, John Dewey becomes the target for Mr. White's sharpest criticism. In the first place, Dewey's assumption that the historic conflict will be resolved by the application of scientific method to the realm of values seems to Mr. White to beg the question: either there is a realm not amenable to such methods or religion, properly defined, has no meaning. Secondly, when Dewey claims that cooperation with nature will end man's anxieties he crassly ignores evil. Finally, religion, defined by Dewey as faith in inclusive ideal ends, is left with the sole function of integrating human personality for participation in social action. This, to Mr. White, again raises rather than answers a question: integration and action to what purpose? This question can be answered, the author insists, only from a standpoint transcending the self and nature.

The book's weakest chapter deals with the conflict between fundamentalism and modernism in the 1920's. At the chapter's outset Mr. White seems to champion the fundamentalists and says flatly that this "was not a fight for obscurantism." In a sentence which almost seems to sanction the famous anti-evolution laws, Mr. White states that the central issues for the fundamentalists were "man's moral nature and his power through the democratic process to control teachings which might corrupt it."

In the first place, it is not necessary to link these two issues. A case for intellectual freedom can obviously be made as well on a neo-orthodox basis as on a liberal one. In the second place, Mr. White's own treatment of fundamentalist spokesmen makes their obscurantist attitudes and methods abundantly clear. The error is one of historical interpretation: these foes of modernism were not representatives of the great tradition of Protestant theology Mr. White admires, but representatives of popular revivalism, a camp as filled with facile optimism and as lacking in profundity as that of its social-gospel opponents. This chapter would have been more palatable to the reviewer if Mr. White had confined his defense of the fundamentalists to a statement that some valid objections to modernism lay beneath their evident ignorance and fanaticism.

The question raised by history written from this standpoint is whether and in what sense it is amenable to historical criticism from those who do not fully share its central assumptions. Mr. White, who unlike many Christian apologists is as modest as he is intelligent, would be the first to admit that his book hardly provides an answer to that question. It is largely a series of essays, it makes little use of secondary works in an area where good ones exist, and it fails to relate its subject to an extensive social or intellectual context. It is, however, an attractive performance; it will stimulate those who have studied this material in other sources. Above all, it has the freshness that can come only from deep sincerity.

University of California, Berkeley HENRY F. MAY

Religion in the Development of American Culture, 1765-1840. By William Warren Sweet. (New York: Charles Scribner's Sons, 1952. xiv + 338 pp. Bibliography and index. $3.50.)

This is the second volume of a history of religion in America; the first was published ten years ago. "The central theme in this volume," Professor Sweet writes, "is the part played by organized religion in the transit of civilization westward." This theme is developed in nine chapters which deal with such subjects as the effect of the Revolution on religion, expansion westward, the church colleges, "The revolt against Calvinism," the growth of missions, and the origin and development of the utopian religious communities. Although the emphasis of Professor Sweet here, as elsewhere, is upon the denominational churches, his analysis of the doctrinal differences which separated the more liberal protestantism of the early nineteenth century from conservative congregationalism and presbyterianism gives proper attention to matters of creed and dogma.

Professor Sweet's many volumes on the history of religion on the American frontier give particular authority to his treatment of this subject in the present volume. The author points out that the followers of Frederick Jackson Turner have given undue emphasis to the economic motive in the development of the West. He suggests that the West would have reverted to the barbarism characteristic of all migratory peoples had not the rigors of frontier life been tempered by religious values. The frontiersman was not opposed to religion, and when its opportunities were made available to him he usually took full advantage of them. Revivalism and the camp meeting, although characteristic of the frontier, were not the only means utilized by the churches to spiritualize the West. The historian must resist the temptation to overidealize the frontier and be prepared to acknowledge, Professor Sweet asserts, that "the churches were an important — if not the most important — factor in maintaining decency and order in the average frontier community."

In one of the most illuminating chapters in the book, the author undertakes to appraise the influence exercised by religion in laying the foundations of American culture. Here he defines religion broadly as "the ultimate passion which determines men's attitudes," and he concludes that religion is one of the fundamental forces responsible for producing the "enlightenment and discipline" that come from mental and moral training. The chief instrument for the extension of religious influence in America was the church college, which until the latter decades of the nineteenth century dominated the higher educational scene. The American college, Professor Sweet points out, was founded as a frontier institution by churches that were determined to provide the means of education in the wilderness. Their purpose was explicitly to be the spread of Christianity through the training of ministers and not, said Bishop Philander Chase regarding Kenyon College, "the spread of mere secular knowledge or even general Christianity." To the many general colleges were added institutions organized specifically for training in theology. The central influences exerted by the colleges were intensified by the development of American religious journalism, by the circulation between 1816 and 1838 of over two million Bibles and Testaments, and by the dissemination of sixteen million pieces of religious literature provided by the American Tract Society and the American Sunday School Union.

This book breaks new ground in drawing together for the first time the vital story of American religious development during the crucial years of Revolution and frontier advance. Its materials are drawn from Professor Sweet's own original researches as well as from those of a generation of students whom he has trained in his seminars at the University of Chicago and elsewhere. The book has full documentation throughout, and includes an eighteen-page bibliography of published works, manuscript collections, and unpublished dissertations.

Scripps College EDWARD A. WHITE

Socialism and American Life. 2 vols. Edited by Donald Drew Egbert and Stow Persons. Princeton *Studies in American Civilization*, No. 4. (Princeton: Princeton University Press, 1952. Vol. I: xiv + 776 pp. Index. Vol. II: Bibliographer: T. D. Seymour Bassett. xiv + 575 pp. Bibliography: Descriptive and Critical, and index. $10.00 each volume; $17.50 the set.)

These volumes grew out of two year-long student conferences undertaken at Princeton University by the Program in American Civilization. The Program secured the aid of a group of collaborators to serve as lecturers at the student conferences; on the basis of their lectures they prepared the essays in Volume I. To suggest adequately the character of this survey, it is necessary to list the chapters and their authors: the introductory "Terminology and Types of Socialism," Donald Drew Egbert and Stow Persons; "Socialism in European History to 1848," E. Harris Harbison; "European Socialism since 1848," Harry W. Laidler; "The Religious Basis of Western Socialism," Albert T. Mollegen; "Christian Communitarianism in America," Stow Persons; "The Secular Utopian Socialists," T. D. Seymour Bassett; "The Background and Development of Marxian Socialism in the United States," Daniel Bell; "American Socialism and the Socialist Philosophy of History," David F. Bowers; "The Philosophical Basis of Marxian Socialism in the United States," Sidney Hook; "The Influence of Marxian Economics on American Thought and Practice," Paul M. Sweezy; "American Marxist Political Theory," Will Herberg; "Sociological Aspects of American Socialist Theory and Practice," Wilbert E. Moore; "The Psychology of American Socialism," George W. Hartmann; "American Writers on the Left," Willard Thorp; "Socialism and American Art," Donald Drew Egbert.

The editors in their preface to Volume I review their study and note that conservative critics will no doubt object to the book because it teaches socialism; this I doubt. They note also that Marxists will probably object to the book on the grounds that only acceptable Marxists can understand and write about socialism; this probably represents a correct judgment. They observe, finally, that critics will note the lack of a "single unified point of view" and that the different chapters "vary in the adequacy of their presentation"; the reviewer agrees with these judgments. He does not quarrel with the conclusions that the subject of the "relation of socialism to the various aspects of American life and thought is too complex to be treated adequately by any one man or from any single standpoint." But in a single-volume survey of the subject one competent researcher and author, such as Stow Persons, could have presented a more balanced study. A great deal of needless repetition characterizes the publication and this might have been avoided if the book had been written by a single author.

Apparently the editors could not enforce the suggested page limitations, for, although most of the chapters run to between 20 and 40 pages, one author wrote a little book of 192 pages and another wrote one of 132 pages. These two chapters, partly because the authors wrote too much, proved to be the poorest in the book in my judgment. Daniel Bell, for example, might easily have brought his essay into the compass of 40 or 50 pages by keeping to the main story instead of wandering far afield into what might be regarded as background or collateral materials. He might have avoided, too, implying (p. 242) that the Homestead and Coeur d'Alene strikes occurred in 1893 instead of 1892, that Grover Cleveland instead of Benjamin Harrison broke the Coeur d'Alene strike by sending federal troops to Idaho (p. 242), that Populism was born at Chicago in 1893 (p. 243) instead of St. Louis and Omaha in 1892, that the Populists at their convention wore "garish" costumes (p. 243) instead of the sober garb reported by almost all the observers present, or that the Bishop Creek of Gaylord Wilshire's mining ventures was in Colorado (p. 299) instead of California.

Volume II in many respects constitutes the more valuable part of the study. Although there are some omissions and errors they do not seriously mar the usefulness of the bibliography. The bibliographer and editors interpreted socialism broadly and sought to cast their study against the background of the ideals and institutions of nonsocialist America. The listings include books, serials, pamphlets, articles, and manuscripts. Each of the major parts is subdivided into a section on general reading and one on special topics. Each part and section is preceded by a preliminary essay in which the authors sought to introduce the subject matter of the listings. Many of the titles bear evaluations as well as descriptions, an aspect of the work which will produce controversy, but, nevertheless, which adds to the usefulness of the bibliography.

The two volumes reveal some of the successes and weaknesses inherent in planned cooperative research. Volume I suffers from too many authors; Volume II gains immeasurably from the combined operations of many scholars and students. It should be observed, also, that the entire project indicates some paradoxical features of the development of socialism in America. Several authors suggest reasons why socialism has not been very successful in the United States (Hook and Sweezy, for example); yet the study seems written on the assumption that socialism has had an enormous influence on the development of the United States. This is a value judgment, of course, and admits of variable interpretation. The tendency is all too strong in the reviewer's estimation to allege that liberal, progressive, and even some radical developments in American history are directly or indirectly the result of socialism. This tendency overlooks the strong, native, nonsocialist radicalism that has characterized American society since the colonial period.

Stanford University GEORGE HARMON KNOLES

Equality by Statute; Legal Controls Over Group Discrimination. By Morroe Berger. Foreword by Robert M. MacIver. (New York: Columbia University Press, 1952. xii + 238 pp. Bibliography, list of cases, and index. $3.25.)

In this little volume a Princeton University sociologist examines successively two contrasting methods of using law to prevent discrimination against minority groups. He devotes over half of his text to the generally familiar story of civil rights issues before the federal courts between the 1870's and 1950, for the purpose of assessing the amount of protection afforded to Negroes, west coast Japanese during World War II, and Jehovah's Witnesses by the Fifth Amendment and especially by the three much litigated phrases in the first section of the Fourteenth Amendment. Here, constitutional amendments, congressional enforcement acts, court cases, and judicial interpretations are the principal means whereby the reformative function of the laws is to be made operative. The burden of bringing suit is thrown upon the person — often poor in purse and unskilled in law — who believes that he has a just cause for complaint. Except during the last fifteen years, the United States Supreme Court has usually upheld the "social caste lines" between whites and Negroes, using its "separate but equal public facilities" doctrine to sanction much that is discriminatory in fact. The several segregated-school cases now before the Supreme Court lend a special timeliness to this portion of the volume.

In his fourth chapter the author turns to the Ives-Quinn Law of New York (1945 ff.) as an illustration of a different and more effective statutory device for eliminating discrimination. By this measure ample authority is conferred upon a small Commission to educate, investigate, conciliate, hold public hearings, issue cease and desist orders, and seek court decrees (in that ascending order of severity), so as to prevent employers, employment agencies, and labor unions from discriminating in employment against any person because of his race, religious creed, color, or national origin. Although the Commission has exercised its power cautiously, and has been criticized for being nonaggressive, slow in reaching decisions, and overly tender toward defendants, it has demonstrated that law can help to overcome discrimination in economic pursuits against members of minority groups. In a final chapter Professor Berger levies upon sociology, social psychology, and psychoanalysis to reinforce this judgment. Empirical studies seem to show that when discrimination is abolished, the prejudice of which it was an evidence tends also to disappear.

Even though he advances these conclusions without qualification, he frankly recognizes the limitations of his study. The Commission barred him from its files, obliging him to rely for data upon the speeches of its members, its press releases and annual reports, and upon his own interviews and questionnaires. Employment data in New York between 1945 and 1950 were obviously affected by many factors besides the Ives-Quinn Law, making its particular influence virtually impossible to isolate. This statute, moreover, and similar laws of other states have been in force too brief a time to justify a conviction that they are a complete success. For the most part they have been applied in urban, industrial areas where relationships between employer and employee, and between worker and worker, are more impersonal than in the countryside. The acid test of their efficacy in eliminating discrimination and prejudice must await a depression period when the labor market is overcrowded.

This careful study, however, suggests that a law designed to assure a minority group of its civil liberties should be channeled through an administrative commission and not be dependent for its enforcement upon unsystematic and occasional appeals to the judiciary by persons whose rights have allegedly been denied. Challenging, also, is Professor Berger's assurance that these liberties will be encroached upon less often if legislators have the vision and courage to enact statutes embodying American democratic ideals rather than the prejudices of their constituents.

University of Chicago WILLIAM T. HUTCHINSON

American History and American Historians; A Review of Recent Contributions to the Interpretation of the History of the United States. By H. Hale Bellot. (Norman: University of Oklahoma Press, 1952. x + 336 pp. Maps, bibliographical note, bibliography, and index. $4.00.)

There is greater significance in the fact that this book came to be written than in its actual content. The author became the first Englishman to hold a chair of American history in Great Britain and he was equipped with the broadening experience of historical training and work at Oxford, London, and in the provinces, in addition to practical knowledge of international economic problems. Following graduation from Lincoln College, Oxford, and a three-year tour of duty in His Majesty's Customs and Excise Office, he became identified with history as such through a novitiate in this field at University College, London. Three years as reader in modern history at the University of Manchester preceded his establishment, beginning in 1930, as Commonwealth Fund Professor of American History in the University of London. From that vantage point he has ever since been developing British knowledge of United States history. A slender volume, *Study of American History*, appeared in 1932 and six years later he delivered at the University of Birmingham a course of lectures on "Recent Advances in the Interpretation of American History," which he reworked into this volume.

Mr. Bellot's influence is noteworthy among those factors moving British historians to a greater interest in, and knowledge of, American backgrounds. The need for development of this interest is keenly felt by any American visitor who observes the place of historical study in British education, and the United States has cause to appreciate the recently established Anglo-American interchange of scholarly services. Further rapprochement has been achieved by the research activities in America of British professors as widely diversified as T. S. Ashton of the London School of Economics, Dennis Brogan of Cambridge, W. K. Hancock, formerly of Oxford, and John Hawgood of Birmingham.

Mr. Bellot contends, and rightly, that the work and influence of the Middle Western School of American historians, 1890-1940, has radically altered the outlook of American historiography. He develops this theme in his opening chapter, devoting the remaining six chapters to a survey of United States history from colonial times to the outbreak of the World War II, in the light of this historiography. Bibliographical notes following each chapter, plus a list of works cited, comprise nearly one third of the book. Seven black and white accordion maps, portraying the successive frontiers, enable readers to follow them on the right without each time flipping the pages of the text. A twelve-and-one-half-page index completes the equipment. The book should facilitate British exploration of American history, especially if it encourages amplification of British library facilities, still rather weak in American history.

American historians are, or should be, familiar with most of the material in this book, but it is useful to be reminded of these things by a foreigner of acute observation and broad outlook. He offers many penetrating comments. An understanding of American history since 1877 is presently best had, he says, from "a group of studies of social ideas and their gradual embodiment in new political machinery" (p. 239). He notes the slowness with which Americans have become conscious of new challenges "to the omnicompetence of the nation.... The solution of the problem of yesterday engages the public mind of today while the problem of today treads unnoticed upon its heel" (p. 214). He stresses our need to explore better the history of domestic power politics, wherein interior groups have such strength that it "may make or mar the fortunes of communities and frustrates the policy of the state whether at home or abroad" (p. 254).

Historians will, of course, reject some of Mr. Bellot's views. Some, he notes, have other candidates than his own selection for "the most notable contribution to the understanding of the West" (p. 35). Some may not agree that "most of the American history that was published before 1910 has been outmoded" (p. v.)—if one includes the political field. Some may wonder at omissions from the "List of Works Cited" of certain titles by Merle Curti, Lawrence Gipson, and others (pp. 293-324). Many may wish that the author were less addicted to very long sentences and paragraphs two and three pages in length.

But these are minor points. Most readers will, I think, do Mr. Bellot the honor to wish that he had given us more of this fare and had chosen 1950, rather than 1940, as his terminal date.

Philadelphia, Pennsylvania JEANNETTE P. NICHOLS

A Catalogue of Manuscripts in the Collection of Western Americana Founded by William Robertson Coe, Yale University Library. Compiled by Mary C. Withington. Introduction by James T. Babb. (New Haven: Yale University Press, 1952. x + 398 pp. Illustrations and index. $10.00.)

The Coe Collection, according to Henry Wagner, is "the finest collection of Western material in existence, and the finest undoubtedly that will ever be formed." This catalogue provides the first opportunity that many Westerners have had to gauge this and other western collections at the Yale University Library. They will agree that no one is likely to be able to match what Mr. Coe and his agent, Edward Eberstadt, have purchased. There is a heavy concentration of materials that few families are willing to part with except for high prices: over one fourth of the items listed are journals, letters, and other papers pertaining to journeys to the Far West, particularly gold-rush diaries. There are paintings, as those of George Catlin and Alfred Jacob Miller, and there are maps, as those of the Lewis and Clark expedition.

Westerners are likely to be impressed also by the many items that supplement larger series at other libraries. The generosity of Mr. Coe and of Yale University, who readily permit copying and microfilming, make such holdings more usable than they otherwise would be. The larger series at Yale include the papers of Governor Andrew J. Faulk of Dakota (No. 195), H. Miles Moore of Kansas (No. 352), Silas Reed, surveyor and army surgeon (No. 399), James J. Strang (No. 447), and Granville and James Stuart (Nos. 448-54), and journals of various members of the Wilkes expedition (Nos. 35, 101, 132, 133, 161, 162, 166-69, 260, 480). The Mormon items are outstanding. Business record series are few and relatively small (for example, Nos. 253, 280, 343, 345). Some items were published before Mr. Coe acquired them, as the journal of Russell Osborne (No. 411), the papers of Governor John W. Geary of Kansas (No. 212), and the autobiography of Isaac J. Wistar (No. 532). Some are described as varying from the published versions (Nos. 37, 156, 376, 378).

The catalogue is conveniently indexed. It follows closely the style of Edward Eberstadt's catalogues. Perhaps the main addition that might have been made is a listing of related collections in other libraries, but that would be a good deal to ask. Everyone who works in the history of the trans-Missouri West will have frequent occasion to refer to this volume, and to appreciate Mr. Coe's generosity and perseverance.

University of Oregon EARL POMEROY

Historical News and Comments

Association Activities

The headquarters of the annual meeting of the Mississippi Valley Historical Association in Lexington, Kentucky, May 7-9, will be in the Lafayette Hotel. Arrangements have been made to hold all of the sessions either in the Lafayette Hotel or in the Phoenix Hotel, less than a block away from the Lafayette.

The program committee has attempted to schedule sessions which will elicit broad discussions and avoid "inch-by-inch" history. Scheduled sessions include the Genesis and Nature of Recent American Conservatism; What was Right and Wrong with Civil War Leadership; The Limits of Intellectual History; Negro Ideologies; Middlewestern Nineteenth-Century Medicine; Civil Liberties in the Young Republic; John C. Calhoun; A Review Session, American Historical Writing: the Best of the Past Fifty Years; The Bases of Recent American Foreign Policy; Western Institutions; Organized Labor in American History; Economic Mobilization for War; Colonial Currency, a Reappraisal; American Foreign Policy During the Nineteen Twenties; and The New England Renascence. The presidential address, to be given by James L. Sellers, will be entitled "Before We Were Members." Joint sessions will be held with the Agricultural History Society, the Lexington Group, the American Studies Association, the Southern Historical Association, the American Folklore Society, Phi Alpha Theta, and the Teachers Section of the Association.

Personals

Arthur P. Whitaker, professor of history at the University of Pennsylvania, gave the Commonwealth Lectures at University College, London, January 26 to February 19, 1953. The title of the lectures was "The Western Hemisphere Idea and Pan Americanism, 1800-1950."

Clemson College announces the following promotions: C. Waldron Bolen and Ernest M. Lander, Jr., to professor of history and government, and Jack K. Williams to associate professor of history and government.

William D. Houlette, assistant professor of history at Drake University, has been appointed by Governor William S. Beardsley for a two-year term as a member of the Board of Curators of the State Historical Society of Iowa.

Albert Parker of the University of Oklahoma has been appointed assistant professor of history at the University of Wichita.

Fulmer Mood, professor of history at the University of Texas, delivered a series of three lectures on the theme of "The Structures of American Historiography" in December at the University of Kansas.

At the University of Oregon, Gordon Wright has returned from a term at the National War College. Quirinus Breen is at the University of Florence on a Fulbright research grant and is replaced by Liutpold Wallach, formerly of Hamilton College.

Gaston Litton, professor of history and university archivist at the University of Oklahoma, will be on leave of absence during 1953 to serve as consultant to the University of Parana, Brazil, under the auspices of the United States Department of State. Percy Buchanan, professor of history and director of Asiatic Affairs, will conduct twenty midwestern university students on a tour of the Far East during the summer months under the auspices of the Southwestern Student Christian Associations. The group will visit Japan, Formosa, Hongkong, the Philippines, Thailand, Singapore, Java, and Bali. Roy Gittinger, Regents Professor Emeritus, was honored on February 5 at the dedication of the new social sciences classroom building named in his honor, Gittinger Hall.

Ross H. McLean, professor of history at Emory University, has been granted a leave of absence for the spring term to engage in research.

At the annual meeting in Washington in December, Herbert Heaton of the department of history, University of Minnesota, was elected to a four-year term on the national council of the American Historical Association. He has recently received a summer research appointment from the Graduate School of the University of Minnesota, and plans to spend the coming summer in England doing research in Anglo-American trade, 1770-1850. Rodney C. Loehr, who has been on leave in Germany for the past two years, is expected to return to the University in July and will resume his teaching duties in the second summer session.

Chester McA. Destler of the department of history, Connecticut College, is visiting professor of history and visiting professor of industrial relations at Cornell University, spring term, 1953.

E. Merton Coulter, chairman of the history department, University of Georgia, has accepted a State Department appointment at the University of

Jerusalem for the first six months of 1953. Horace Montgomery, professor of history, has been named acting chairman of the history department. Robert S. Cotterill, professor emeritus at Florida State University, is visiting professor at the University of Georgia during the winter and spring terms of 1953.

Arthur P. Scott, Professor Emeritus of Modern History at the University of Chicago, will teach during the spring semester at Lincoln Memorial University, Harrogate, Tennessee. Richard J. Storr has been appointed assistant professor in the department of history. Louis Gottschalk was elected president of the American Historical Association at its December meeting. Donald F. Lach, assistant professor, is on leave until April 1, 1953, and is in Europe doing research.

James L. Godfrey, professor of history at the University of North Carolina, will be visiting professor at the 1953 summer session of the University of Missouri. Loren C. McKinney, professor of history, was elected to the board of editors of the *American Historical Review* at the December, 1952, meeting of the American Historical Association. The department reports the following promotions: Frank W. Klingberg, James E. King, and C. O. Cathey to associate professors, and George V. Taylor to assistant professor. James R. Caldwell, Jr., has been appointed assistant professor of social science. Mitchell B. Garrett, professor of history at the University since 1927, retired in June, 1952, and is now living in Canton, New York.

Ray Allen Billington will be on leave from Northwestern University to serve as Harmsworth Professor of American History at Oxford University during the year 1953-1954.

H. Bailey Carroll, professor of history at the University of Texas and director of the Texas State Historical Association, has been appointed chairman of a national committee to plan historical observances marking the 1957-1958 centennial of the overland mail service. The committee, chosen by the American Association for State and Local History, includes William J. Petersen of the Iowa Historical Society and Louis C. Jones of the New York State Historical Association.

Malcolm Lester of Mercer College will teach in the summer session of the University of Virginia. Richard Harwell of Emory University Library was appointed to the University of Virginia Library staff for the months of January and February as visiting consultant in bibliography and worked on problems connected with Confederate bibliography.

Paul H. Giddens, chairman of the department of history and political science at Allegheny College since 1938, has been elected president of Hamline University. Paul B. Cares has been appointed acting chairman of the Allegheny department. O. T. Driggs has been appointed assistant professor of history.

Thomas P. Martin is visiting professor of American history and consultant on manuscripts at Indiana University for 1952-1953.

Alan P. Stuckey has been appointed associate professor of history and political science at the University of Tampa.

John Hope Franklin of Howard University is visiting professor at the University of Wisconsin during the spring semester.

C. Herbert Laub, chairman of the department of history at the University of Tampa, died on November 19, 1952. He received his bachelor's degree from DePauw University in 1921 and his master's and doctor's degrees from the University of Wisconsin in 1922 and 1929. He had taught at the University of Tampa since 1933 and was a member of the Mississippi Valley Historical Association.

Grants and Awards

A. B. Bender, professor of history at Harris Teachers College, has received a grant from the American Philosophical Society toward a research study of "Philip St. George Cooke and the American West."

Edward Everett Dale, research professor emeritus at the University of Oklahoma, has accepted a Fulbright appointment to lecture at Melbourne and other universities in Australia during the period February to December, 1953.

Clarence L. Ver Steeg, of Northwestern University, was awarded the Albert J. Beveridge Prize for 1952 by the American Historical Association for his manuscript "Robert Morris: Revolutionary Financier." The prize carries an award of $1,000 and publication of the volume by the Association. Franklin D. Scott, now on leave of absence from Northwestern University to carry on work for the Social Science Research Council in Sweden, was named a Knight of the Order of the North Star by King Gustav VI of Sweden.

Edward Younger, Alan Hutchinson, Thomas P. Abernethy, and Julian Bishko of the University of Virginia have received grants from the Institute for Research in the Social Sciences.

Four special awards voted by the American Association for State and Local History at its recent convention went to Wisconsin organizations. *The History of La Crosse*, written by Albert H. Sanford, Harry J. Hirschheimer, and Robert Fries, and sponsored by the La Crosse County Historical Society, received a citation as one of the books making the greatest scholarly contribution to state and local history. *Grand Portage*, written by Walter O'Meara, was given an award as a popular history that made a great contribution to popular knowledge of the area. The Brown County Historical Society, Green Bay, was cited for its outstanding work as a county historical society. And the Milwaukee *Journal* received recognition for the continuing excellence and strength of its editorial support and news coverage of historical movements and events.

Historical Activities

The Abraham Lincoln Association which has carried on research and publication in the life of Lincoln for twenty-eight years ceased operations at the close of 1952. Its files of nearly 5,000 photostats of Lincoln documents and other materials have been transferred to the Illinois State Historical Library.

The National Historical Publications Commission announces the formal establishment of a project for the publication of the papers of John C. Calhoun by the University of South Carolina in cooperation with Clemson College and the Commission. Robert L. Meriwether, professor of history at the University of South Carolina and director of the South Caroliniana Library, has been named editor. Professor C. L. Epting of Clemson College is chairman of the Publications Committee, and J. H. Easterby of the Historical Commission of South Carolina is its secretary. Persons having information about Calhoun papers that are not readily available in well-known depositories, especially papers in private possession, are urged to communicate with the editor.

The American Studies Association held a conference on "Europe's View of America Today" in the Whittall Pavilion of the Library of Congress in December. Papers and discussions during the first three sessions covered "American Studies Programs in Europe," "Contemporary Western European Attitudes Towards the United States," and "Contemporary America as Seen by European Scholars." The final meeting was devoted to the Fulbright and Smith-Mundt programs and a summary of the findings of the conference. Two new officers of the American Studies Association were elected at a meeting of its Council. Charles Barker of Johns Hopkins University was elected president, and Stanley Pargellis of the Newberry Library, vice-president.

Robert Land of the Library of Congress continues as secretary-treasurer for the second of a two-year term.

The thirty-fourth annual Indiana History Conference met December 5 and 6, 1952, at Indianapolis. A showing of news reels taken by Harry Coburn in Indianapolis, 1910-1927, included the first 500-mile automobile race and scenes of World War I. At a session of the Economic and Business History Group, Herschel Hollopeter of the State Chamber of Commerce presiding, the following papers were presented: Kathryn Troxel, "Eighteenth Century Business and Economic History Materials at Indiana University"; Stephen G. Savage, "James Howard of Jeffersonville, Master Builder of Steamboats"; Thomas Wells Meloan, "Development of the House Trailer Industry in Indiana"; and a panel discussion by John D. Barnhart, Joseph A. Batchelor, Thomas P. Martin, Bernard Olsen, and L. L. Waters on "Those Old Records: Dead Today, Alive Tomorrow." Other papers and addresses presented at the Conference were: Walter O. Foster, "Interpretations of World War II: Tansill et al. vs. Langer et al."; Willard H. Smith, "Schuyler Colfax, A Reappraisal"; Robert L. Kincaid, "The Wilderness Road in the Development of the Northwest"; Marvin F. Kivett, "Excavations in the Missouri Valley"; and James W. Clarke, "Winston Churchill, Man of the Half-Century."

The North Carolina State Literary and Historical Association held its fifty-second annual session in Raleigh on December 5. George W. McCoy of Asheville read a paper on "Asheville and Thomas Wolfe"; Kermit Hunter of Chapel Hill spoke on "The Outdoor Historical Drama"; and LeGette Blythe of Huntersville gave a review of North Carolina nonfiction books of the year. J. G. de Roulhac Hamilton, speaker at the luncheon meeting, presented an address on "George Patterson, North Carolinian by Adoption." Frontis W. Johnston of Davidson College presented the presidential address, "Zebulon B. Vance — A Personality Sketch," and J. Donald Adams of New York spoke on "The Writer's Responsibility." At the business meeting which preceded the Association's morning meeting Frontis W. Johnston was re-elected president, Alice B. Keith of Raleigh, Burnham S. Colburn of Asheville, and Gertrude Weil of Goldsboro were re-elected vice-presidents, and Christopher Crittenden was re-elected secretary-treasurer.

The Business Historical Society has announced a Business History Fellowship for the academic year 1953-1954. The Fellowship carries a stipend of $4,000 and enables an advanced student in history to spend a year of study and research at the Harvard Graduate School of Business Administration. Requests for application blanks should be addressed to Professor

Thomas R. Navin, Executive Secretary, Business Historical Society, Boston 63, Massachusetts. Applications should be filed by April 1, 1953.

The State Historical Society of Missouri held its annual meeting at the University of Missouri Library on November 28, 1952. The luncheon meeting featured an address by Elmer Ellis, dean of the college of arts and sciences at the University of Missouri, on "An American Historian in Europe."

The annual meeting of the Pacific Coast Branch of the American Historical Association was held on December 28-30 at the University of British Columbia, Vancouver, Canada. W. Stull Holt of the University of Washington delivered the presidential address on "Some Significances of the Urban Movement in American History." Among the papers read at the various sessions were the following: "Chamberlain's Mission to Washington, 1887-1888," by Frederick D. Schneider, Stanford University; "The Kansas-Nebraska Act and the Pacific Northwest," by Robert W. Johannsen, University of Washington; "Petticoats at the Polls: Woman Suffrage in Territorial Wyoming," by T. A. Larson, University of Wyoming; "National Influences in the Development of a Western State: Montana," by Merrill G. Burlingame, Montana State College; "The Changing Relations of Canada and the United States Since the Second World War," by F. H. Soward, University of British Columbia; "The Sutler at Fort Bridger," by William Newell Davis, University of California at Berkeley; "George Chaffey, International Engineer," by Frederick Kershner, Ohio University; "Military and Naval Aspects of the Japanese-American Crisis of 1913," by E. Howard Brooks, Stanford University; "The Founding of a Colonial College," by Beverly McAnear, Stanford University; "The Pattern of Town-School Education in Colonial Massachusetts," by Norwood Cole, Skagit Valley Junior College; "Thomas Prince, Puritan Savant in the Age of Rationalism," by John van de Wetering, University of Washington; "The Klondike Gold Rush," by Stuart R. Tompkins, University of Oklahoma; "The Origins of the Parity Formula for Agricultural Prices, 1919-1923," by James H. Shideler, University of California at Davis; "Henry Ford and the Agricultural Depression of 1920-21; A Study in Agrarian Psychology," by Reynold M. Wik, Mills College; "The Farmers and the Supreme Court Issue of 1937: A Study of Public Opinion," by E. Kimbark MacColl, University of California at Los Angeles; "John Nobili, S.J., Founder of California's Santa Clara College: The New Caledonia Years, 1845-1849," by John B. McGloin, S.J., University of San Francisco; "The Church of England in the Old Oregon Country," by Thomas E. Jessett (Historiographer, Diocese of Olympia), Seattle, Washington; and "The United Church of Canada in British Columbia," by John Goodfellow, Princeton, British Columbia.

The eighth annual competition for the Albert J. Beveridge Award (formerly entitled the Albert J. Beveridge Memorial Fellowship) of the American Historical Association for the best original manuscript in American history will close on May 1, 1953. Established in 1945, the award has a cash value of $1,000 and also provides for free publication in the Beveridge series. Honorable mention may also be awarded to one or more additional manuscripts, and carries with it free publication in the Beveridge series. "American history" is interpreted as including the history of the United States, Canada, and Latin America. All correspondence, including requests for further information and forms of application, should be addressed to Dorothy Burne Goebel, Department of History, Hunter College, 695 Park Avenue, New York 21, N. Y.

Directory of Contributors

Lewis E. Atherton is professor of history at the University of Missouri.

Chester McArthur Destler is Charles J. MacCurdy Professor of American History at Connecticut College.

Earl Pomeroy is associate professor of history at the University of Oregon.

Donald F. Warner is associate professor of history at Macalester College.

Gilman M. Ostrander is a teaching assistant in history at the University of California, Berkeley.

Beverly McAnear is a visiting member of the history staff at Stanford University.

Index

AARON, DANIEL (ed.), *America in Crisis; Fourteen Crucial Episodes in American History*, revd., 802-803
Abbott, John S. C., hist., 4-5
Abolition, and Fourteenth Amendment, book on, revd., 136-37; and millenarianism, 451; and John Brown, note on, 713-26; book on, revd., 765-66
Abraham, Mohawk sachem, 737
Abraham Lincoln, by Albert J. Beveridge, cited, 301
Abraham Lincoln; A Biography, by Benjamin P. Thomas, revd., 564-65
Abraham Lincoln, The War Years, by Carl Sandburg, cited, 301
Abstinence Union, Catholic, book on, revd., 138-39
Adams, Brooks, biog. of, revd., 144-45
Adams, Charles F., Jr., quoted, 646, 661; cited, 667
Adams, George W., *Doctors in Blue; The Medical History of the Union Army in the Civil War*, revd., 565-66
Adams, Henry, cited, 10-12, 23, 259; book on, revd., 569-70
Adams, Herbert B., cited, 12, 673
Adams, John, and the cold war with France, papers on, summarized, 282
Adams, Ramon F., *Come An' Get It; The Story of the Old Cowboy Cook*, noted, 607
Addams, Jane, 486, 499, 503, 666
Addresses and State Papers of James Stephen Hogg, ed. by Robert C. Cotner, revd., 573-74
Admiral of the Ocean Sea, by Samuel E. Morison, 301
Advent Christian Church, 455
Africa, U. S. diplomatic papers on, book on, revd., 354-56
Age of Jackson, by Arthur M. Schlesinger, Jr., cited, 20, 300, 685 n.
Agnew, Theodore L., revs., 109-10
Agricultural History of the Genesee Valley, 1790-1860, by Neil A. McNall, revd., 554-55
Agricultural History Society, 283
Agricultural War Relations, records of bureau of, noted, 607
Agriculture, Alabama, paper on, by Glenn N. Sisk, summarized, 283-84
Alabama claims, 700
Alabama Territory, papers of, revd., 761-62
Alarm, 454
Alaskan Gold Mine, The Story of No. 9 Above, by Leland H. Carlson, revd., 146
Albany, N. Y., imprisonment for debt in, 91-92
Albany Congress, doc. on, 727-46
Alberta, ranching in, 71-72
Alcott, Bronson, 717; quoted, 722
Alden, John R., revs., 325, 754-55
Aldrich, Nelson W., 489
Alien acts, book on, revd., 548-52
Allen, Fred, 231
Allen, John M., biog. of, revd., 343-44
Allen, Johnny, minstrel man, 213
Allen, Rev. John, 252; quoted, 250-51
Allen, Robert, merchant, quoted, 629
Allen, William, sen., 31 n.
Allen, William B., and the Perry expedition, book on, revd., 336
Altgeld, John P., gov., 644
America in Crisis; Fourteen Crucial Episodes in American History, ed. by Daniel Aaron, revd., 802-803
American Approach to Foreign Policy, by Dexter Perkins, revd., 791-92
American Bar Association, 664-65
American Beginnings; Highlights and Sidelights of the Birth of the New World, by Jarvis M. Morse, revd., 749-50
American biography, guide to, noted, 180-81
American businessmen, opposition to social control during "Gilded Age," art. on, 641-72
American Colonies in the Eighteenth Century, by Herbert L. Osgood, 299
American Conservatism in the Age of Enterprise; A Study of William Graham Sumner, Stephen J. Field, and Andrew Carnegie, by Robert G. McCloskey, revd., 348-49
American Crisis Diplomacy, The Quest for Collective Security, 1918-1952, by Richard W. Van Alstyne, revd., 155-56
American culture, and religion, book on, revd., 805-806
American Democracy and the World War, by Frederic L. Paxson, cited, 689

American Diaries of Richard Cobden, ed. by Elizabeth H. Cawley, revd., 762-63
American Diplomacy, 1900-1950, by George F. Kennan, revd., 154-55
American Economic Association, and immigration, 79-80
American Federation of Labor, and immigration restriction, 80-81
American foreign policy, book on, noted, 181; in the Far East, paper on, summarized, 285; and progressivism, art. on, 483-504
American historical literature, democratic theme in, art. on, 3-28
American historiography, historians' preferred works, art. on, 289-302
American history, manuscript collections, guides to, noted, 180
American History and American Historians; A Review of Recent Contributions to the Interpretation of the History of the United States, by H. Hale Bellot, revd., 810-12
American investments, in Mexico, paper on, by David M. Pletcher, summarized, 282-83
American literature, George Washington in, book on, revd., 542-43
American Mind, by Henry S. Commager, 300
American Negro Slavery, by Ulrich B. Phillips, noted, 180
American neutrality, and Germany in World War II, book on, revd., 157-58
American novel, book on, revd., 799-800
American Protective Association, and immigration, 84, 86
American Record in the Far East, 1945-1951, by Kenneth S. Latourette, revd., 792-93
American regionalism, book on, revd., 112-15
American Revolution, books on, revd., 104-105, 321-27, 540-42, 753-57; noted, 181; paper on, summarized, 278
American Revolution Considered as a Social Movement, by J. Franklin Jameson, 293, 299
American Socialist Congress, 499
American stage, immigrant theme on the, art. on, 211-32
American Studies Association, 276
American theater, book on, revd., 585-86
American traditions, and the Four-Power Treaty of the Washington Conference, 306
"Amos and Andy," 212
Anarchism, and immigration restriction, 85
Anderson, Fannie, *Doctors Under Three Flags*, revd., 118
Anderson, John M. (ed.), *Calhoun: Basic Documents*, revd., 558
Anderson, Joseph, merchant, 627
Anderson, Oscar E., Jr., revs., 368-69
Anderson, Thornton, *Brooks Adams, Constructive Conservative*, revd., 144-45
Andrew Jackson, by Marquis James, 301
Andrews, Charles M., 10; *The Colonial Period of American History*, 299
Angle, Paul M., 275
Anglo-American opinion, book on, revd., 800-801
Anglo-Japanese Alliance, 304, 308
Anglo-Saxon heritage, in historical writing, 5-7
Annals of Albany, quoted, 91-92
Annexationists, and Canadian Northwest, 66-67; United States and the Riel Rebellion, art. on, 693-712
Annual meeting, Mississippi Valley Historical Association, report on, 275-88
Anti-Semitic literature, and immigration restriction, 86
Antislavery Origins of the Fourteenth Amendment, by Jacobus tenBroek, revd., 136-37
Apocalypse, and millenarianism, 444
Aptheker, Herbert (ed.), *A Documentary History of the Negro People in the United States*, revd., 111-12
Archbold, John D., industrialist, 642
Archibald, A. G., Manitoba lt. gov., 68; quoted, 67
Architecture, ante-bellum Georgia, book on, revd., 764-65
Architecture and Town Planning in Colonial Connecticut, by Anthony N. B. Garvan, revd., 751-52
Armament manufacture and troop training, relative priority of, paper on, summarized, 279
Armour, Philip D., 642, 671-72
Armour elevators, 667-69
Armour Meat Packing Company, 664
Armstrong, Francis, quoted, 101
Armstrong, Samuel C., 49-50, 60
Army, at Valley Forge, book on, revd., 754-55
Army Air Forces, World War II in Southwest Pacific, book on, revd., 160-61
Army Air Forces in World War II. Europe: Argument to V-E Day January 1944 to May 1945, Vol. III, ed. by Wesley F. Craven and James L. Cate, revd., 158-59
"Army's Mahan," 279
Art and Technics, by Lewis Mumford, noted, 607
Arthur, Chester A., and federal aid to education, 48
Asiatic immigration, 499-500
Aspinwall, William, *A Brief Description of the Fifth Monarchy, or Kingdome That Shortly Is to Come into the World*, cited, 445-46

Association of Nations, 303
Athearn, Robert G., paper on British travelers in Rocky Mountain area, summarized, 286
Atherton, Lewis E., "Mercantile Education in the Ante-Bellum South," 623-40
Atkinson, Theodore, 728-29; Albany Congress diary of, 729-39
Atlantic Migration, by Marcus L. Hansen, 300
Auctioneer, a play, 228
Audubon, John J., expedition of, book on, revd., 127-28
Austin, Rev. David, quoted, 450
Autobiography of William Allen White, 301
Aviation, Marine Corps, book on, revd., 789-90

BACHE, SÖREN, diary of, revd., 558-59
Back Door to War; The Roosevelt Foreign Policy, 1933-1941, by Charles C. Tansill, revd., 580-81
Bacon, Rev. Leonard W., 51-53
Baegert, Johann J., S.J., *Observations in Lower California*, revd., 318-20
Baird, Absalom, gen., 524
Baker, Carlos, *Hemingway, The Writer as Artist*, noted, 609
Baker, E. M., maj., 519 n.
Baker, I. G. and Company, St. Louis, 70
Baker, William T., pres. Chicago Board of Trade, 668-69
Baker and Farron, actors, 225
Baltimore, mercantile houses, 624
Balzar, Frederick B., gov., 680
Bancroft, George, cited, 9-10, 14, 16
Banks, Nathaniel P., gen., 700 n.
Banyar, Goldsbrow, Albany Congress secretary, 731 n.
Baptists, and premillennialism, 457
Bar Harbor, book on, revd., 773-74
Barbarians in Our Midst; A History of Chicago Crime and Politics, by Virgil W. Peterson, revd., 775-77
Barber, John, hist., 4
Barbour, James, sen., quoted, 89
Barnes, Abraham, Albany Congress delegate, 732
Barnes, Harry E., cited, 91
Barnes, James A., revs., 119-21, 566-67
Barney, Hiram, pol., 469
Barnhart, John D. (ed.), *Henry Hamilton and George Rogers Clark in the American Revolution with the Unpublished Journal of Lieut. Gov. Henry Hamilton*, revd., 323-24
Barrett, Richmond, *Good Old Summer Days; Newport, Narragansett Pier, Saratoga, Long Branch, Bar Harbor*, revd., 773-74
Bartlett, Ruhl, revs., 580-81
Bartow, Edith M., *News and These United States*, revd., 586-87
Bauer, Elizabeth K., *Commentaries on the Constitution, 1790-1860*, revd., 757-58
Baumann, Carl L. (co-ed. and trans.), *Observations in Lower California*, by John J. Baegert, S.J., revd., 318-20
Bayard, James A., rep., quoted, 95
Beale, Howard K., cited, 20 n.; quoted, 273 n.
Bean, Walton, revs., 147-48; *Boss Ruef's San Francisco; The Story of the Union Labor Party, Big Business, and the Graft Prosecution*, revd., 349-50; cited, 690 n.
Beard, Charles A., 14, 16, 18-19, 24-25, 257, 299, 682, 685; quoted, 676
Beard, Mary R., 19, 299, 682, 685
Becker, Carl, 24; *The Declaration of Independence*, 299
Becker, George, railroad official, 699; quoted, 69
Begg, Alexander, 71
Behind the Wall Street Curtain, by Edward Dies, revd., 583-84
Behold Virginia: The Fifth Crown. Being the Trials, Adventures & Disasters of the First Families of Virginia, the rise of the Grandees, & the eventual Triumph of the Common & Uncommon Sort in the Revolution, by George F. Willison, revd., 316-17
Belasco, David, theatrical producer, 228
Bell, John, 425
Bell, Samuel, sen., quoted, 96
Bell, W. R., farmer, 73
Bell, Whitfield J., paper on college science textbooks, summarized, 287
Bellamy, Francis R., *The Private Life of George Washington*, revd., 320-21
Bellamy, Joseph, theologian, 448, 450
Bell-Kelso farm, Minn., 73
Bellot, H. Hale, *American History and American Historians; A Review of Recent Contributions to the Interpretation of the History of the United States*, revd., 810-12
Bellows, Rev. Henry W., quoted, 478
Belmont, August, pol., 507
Bemis, Edward W., econ., 81; praised by Rutherford B. Hayes, 47
Bemis, Samuel F., quoted, 273 n.; *John Quincy Adams*, 301
Bender, Averam B., *The March of Empire; Frontier Defense in the Southwest, 1848-1860*, revd., 561-62; revs., 772-73
Benjamin Franklin, by Carl Van Doren, 301
Benjamin Harrison, Hoosier Warrior, 1833-1865, by Harry J. Sievers, revd., 766-67
Bennett, Edward E., revs., 553-54

Bent and Leon, actors, 228
Benteen, Frederick W., capt., 529
Benteen, Mrs. Frederick W., 521
Benton, Elbert H., quoted, 30; cited, 32, 35
Benton, Mont., 70-71
Benton, Thomas H., sen., quoted, 638
Berger, Morroe, *Equality by Statute; Legal Controls Over Group Discrimination*, revd., 809-10
Berger, Victor, pol., 499
Berlin, Irving, 229
Bernard, Sam, actor, 224
Berthoff, Rowland T., paper on contributions of English immigrants, summarized, 283
Bestor, Arthur E., Jr., revs., 112-15, 333-34; cited, 452
Bettersworth, John K., revs., 767-68
Beveridge, Albert J., 485, 488-89; *Abraham Lincoln*, 301; quoted, 484
Bibliography, international, historical sciences, book on, revd., 367-68
"Big Four" Meat Packers, 644
Bill, Alfred H., *Valley Forge; The Making of an Army*, revd., 754-55
Billington, Ray A., communication on John W. Powell, 164; "Guides to American History Manuscript Collections in Libraries of the United States," noted, 180; revs., 557
Bingham, Harold J., revs., 768-69
Binkley, Wilfred E., hist., cited, 31
Binkley, William C., *The Texas Revolution*, revd., 557
Biography, American, guide to, noted, 180
Biography, and James Parton, book on, revd., 364-65
Birmingham, influence of Louisville and Nashville Railroad on coal and iron industry of, paper on, summarized, 277-78
Bjork, Kenneth, revs., 747-49
Black, Robert C., III, *The Railroads of the Confederacy*, revd., 768-69
Black Republicans, 29
Blackstone, Sir William, 248-49
Blair, Henry W., sen., 48-49
Blakeslee, George, cited, 22
Bland, Sister Joan, *Hibernian Crusade, The Story of the Catholic Total Abstinence Union of America*, revd., 138-39
Blegen, Theodore C. (ed.), *Norwegian-American Studies and Records*, revd., 568-69
Bloodstoppers & Bearwalkers, by Richard M. Dorson, noted, 606
Bluejackets with Perry in Japan; A Day-by-Day Account Kept by Master's Mate John R. C. Lewis and Cabin Boy William B. Allen, ed. by Henry F. Graff, revd., 336
Blum, John M., 284
Blumenthal, Walter H., *Women Camp Followers of the American Revolution*, revd., 540-41
Bode, Carl, 276; revs., 770-72
Bolton, Herbert E., *Rim of Christendom*, 301
"Bonanza farming," 73
Bonaparte, Charles J., lawyer, quoted, 488
Bonaparte, Napoleon, and Virginia, book on, revd., 327-29
Booth, Bradford A. (co-ed.), *North America*, by Anthony Trollope, revd., 344-45
"*Boots and Saddles*," by Elizabeth B. Custer, 520 n.
Borah, William E., sen., 313, 489, 491-93
Borome, Joseph A., *Charles Coffin Jewett*, noted, 181
Boss Ruef's San Francisco; The Story of the Union Labor Party, Big Business, and the Graft Prosecution, by Walton Bean, revd., 349-50
Boston, imprisonment for debt in, 89, 91, 100
Boston financiers, and Michigan copper, book on, revd., 128-29
Boston Prison Discipline Society, 91, 100
Boston Y.M.C.A. and Community Need; A Century's Evolution, 1851-1951, by William B. Whiteside, revd., 130-31
Bostwick, Jabez A., industrialist, 642
Boucicault, Dion, playwright, 215, 217
Boulder, Colo., municipal government, paper on, summarized, 286
Bouquet, Henry, papers of, revd., 538-40
Bourne, Jonathan, sen., 489, 492
Bowen, Ephraim, 236 n.
Bowers, Claude G., *Jefferson and Hamilton*, 301
Boyce, Gray C., revs., 367-68
Boyce, James P., theologian, 52-53
Boyle, Patrick C., journ., 653
Brace, Charles L., auth., 461, 464
Bradbury and Evans, publ., 474
Braden, Charles, lt., 522, 529, 534
Braden, Charles S., *These Also Believe*, cited, 456 n.
Bradley, Harold W., 285
Braham, David, songwriter, 222
Brandegee amendment, 313
Brandenburg, M. M. (co-ed. and trans.), *Observations in Lower California*, by Johann J. Baegert, S.J., revd., 318-20
Brandon, Edgar E. (comp. and ed.), *Lafayette, Guest of the Nation; A Contemporary Account of the Triumphal Tour of General Lafayette Through the United States in 1824-1825 as Reported by the Local Newspapers*, Vol. I, revd., 123-24
Breckinridge, John C., 419-23, 434-37, 439
Brian O'Linn, a play, 218-19
Brice, Fannie, 229

Bridge, James H., *The Carnegie Millions and the Men Who Made Them; Being the Inside History of the Carnegie Steel Company*, quoted, 649-50
Brief Description of the Fifth Monarchy, or Kingdome That Shortly Is to Come into the World, by William Aspinwall, cited, 445
Briggs, Harold E., revs., 137-38
Brimlow, George F., *Harney County, Oregon, and Its Range Land*, revd., 370-71
Bristow, Joseph L., sen., 487, 492-93
British Commonwealth, and the United States, diplomatic papers, revd., 354-56
British Empire before the American Revolution, by Lawrence H. Gipson, 300
British North-West, United States and the Riel Rebellion, art. on, 693-712
British travelers, Rocky Mountain area, paper on, summarized, 286
Brooks, Phillips, theologian, 52
Brooks, Preston, rep., 714
Brooks, Robert P., *Georgia Studies*, ed. by Gregor Sebba, noted, 606
Brooks Adams, Constructive Conservative, by Thornton Anderson, revd., 144-45
Brough, John, gov., election of 1863, pp. 32, 34, 36, 39, 43 n., 44
Brougham, John, playwright, 215, 217-18, 220
Brown, Dee (co-auth.), *Trail Driving Days*, revd., 346
Brown, George, lawyer, 252-53
Brown, Gerald S. (co-auth.), *Canada and the United States; Some Aspects of Their Historical Relations*, revd., 353-54
Brown, Ira V., "Watchers for the Second Coming: The Millenarian Tradition in America," 441-58
Brown, John, note on, 713-26
Brown, Richard C., paper on Gen. Emory Upton and military thought, summarized, 279
Brown County, Ohio, and the election of 1863, p. 35
Brownson, Orestes A., quoted, 213
Brush, Daniel S., lt., 534
Bryan, William A., *George Washington in American Literature, 1775-1865*, revd., 542-43
Bryan, William J., 485-87, 502, 517
Bryant, Dan, minstrel man, 212-13
Bryant, William C., 461, 642
Buchanan, James, 420, 431
Buchanan, Lamont, *A Pictorial History of the Confederacy*, revd., 342-43
Buck, Paul H., *The Road to Reunion*, 300
"Bucket shops," 667-68
"Bugaboo of Trusts," by Andrew Carnegie, quoted, 648
Bullard, F. Lauriston, *Lincoln in Marble and Bronze*, noted, 606
Burgess, A. M., Canadian official, quoted, 73-74
Burke, Charlie, actor, 228
Burlingame, Merrill G., revs., 562
Burton, Theodore, rep., 489
Bush, Frank, actor, 227
Business history, essays on entrepreneurs, revd., 116-17; papers on, summarized, 281-82
Business in the Gilded Age; The Conservatives' Balance Sheet, by Edward C. Kirkland, revd., 566-67
Business training, in ante-bellum South, art. on, 623-40
Businessmen, opposition to social control during the "Gilded Age," art. on, 641-72
"Butte: A Phase in the Westward Movement of Capital," by K. Ross Toole, summarized, 286
Butterfield, Herbert, *History and Human Relations*, noted, 182
Butterfield, L. H. (ed.), *Letters of Benjamin Rush*, revd., 325-27

Cabot, James E., biographer, cited, 713
Caldwell, Edward, *A Tour Through Part of Virginia, in the Summer of 1808. Also, Some Account of the Islands of the Azores*, ed. by William M. E. Rachal, noted, 181
Calendar of the Speeches and Other Published Statements of Franklin D. Roosevelt: 1910-1920, comp. by Robert L. Jacoby, noted, 608
Calhoun, James, lt., 522, 534
Calhoun, John C., 280; book on, revd., 124-26
Calhoun, Mrs. James, 521
Calhoun: Basic Documents, ed. by John M. Anderson, revd., 558
California, gold rush, book on, revd., 130; recollections of a pioneer, book on, noted, 182; papers of Thomas O. Larkin, revd., 330-31; letters of R. R. Taylor, revd., 333
California Emigrant Letters, ed. by Walker D. Wyman, revd., 763-64
California Progressives, by George E. Mowry, revd., 350-51
Calkin, Homer L. (co-comp.), *Records of the National Recovery Administration*, noted, 608
Callahan, North, *Smoky Mountain Country*, revd., 797-98
Campbell, David, merchant, 628-29
Campbell, Hardy W., farmer, 73
Campbell, William M., lobbyist, 514
Canada, American economic control in western, 70-71; immigration from United States to, 74; Riel Rebellion and the United States, art. on, 693-712

Canada and the United States; Some Aspects of Their Historical Relations, by Hugh L. Keenleyside and Gerald S. Brown, revd., 353-54
Canadian-American regionalism, Great Plains, art. on, 61-76
Canadian Library Association (publ.), *Catalogue of Canadian Newspapers on Microfilm,* noted, 180
Canadian newspapers, on microfilm, catalogue, noted, 180
Canadian Pacific Railway, 68-69, 71
Canby, Henry S., *Thoreau,* cited, 716 n.
Cannon, Anthony (Tony Hart), actor, 221-23
Cantor, Eddie, 224, 229, 231
Cape Horn to the Pacific; The Rise and Decline of an Ocean Highway, by Raymond A. Rydell, revd., 332-33
Capper, Arthur, sen., 307
Cappon, Lester J., revs., 327-29
Care, Henry, political writer, 247-49, 252
Carey, Henry C., sociologist, biog. of, revd., 126-27
Carey, John M., atty., 664
Caribbean Commission; Background of Cooperation in the West Indies, by Bernard L. Poole, revd., 156-57
Carlson, Leland H., *An Alaskan Gold Mine, The Story of No. 9 Above,* revd., 146
Carlton, Frank T., 91
Carman, Henry J., quoted, 90
Carncross' Minstrels, 213
Carnegie, Andrew, 486, 647; and American conservatism, book on, revd., 348-49; quoted, 648-49
Carnegie Millions and the Men Who Made Them; Being the Inside History of the Carnegie Steel Company, by James H. Bridge, quoted, 649-50
Carosso, Vincent P., revs., 116-17
Carr, Robert, 246
Carroll, H. Bailey, *The Texas Santa Fe Trail,* revd., 560-61
Carson, William G. B., revs., 117-18
Carter, Clarence E., *Historical Editing,* noted, 608; (ed. and comp.), *The Territorial Papers of the United States,* Vol. XVIII, *The Territory of Alabama, 1817-1819,* revd., 761-62
Carter, James C., atty., 664
Carter, John, publ., 244, 247-49
Case, Shirley J., *The Millennial Hope; A Phase of War-Time Thinking,* cited, 442 n.
Cassatt, Alexander, railroad official, 666
Casseday, Ben, "Dignity of the Mercantile Profession," cited, 634
Catalogue of Canadian Newspapers on Microfilm, pub. by Canadian Library Association, noted, 180
Catalogue of Manuscripts in the Collection of Western Americana Founded by William Robertson Coe, Yale University Library, comp. by Mary C. Withington, revd., 812
Cate, James L. (co-ed.), *Europe: Argument to V-E Day January 1944 to May 1945,* Vol. III, *The Army Air Forces in World War II,* revd., 158-59
Cathedrals in the Wilderness, by J. Herman Schauinger, revd., 545-46
Catholic Church, 698, 710; in the wilderness, book on, revd., 545-46
Catholic Total Abstinence Union of America, book on, revd., 138-39
Catholic University of America, 83
Catholics, German, and Ohio election of 1863, p. 43
Cattle Kingdom, and northern Great Plains, 71-72
Caughey, John W., revs., 130, 330-31; "Historians' Choice: Results of a Poll on Recently Published American History and Biography," 289-302
Cavalcade of the American Novel; From the Birth of the Nation to the Middle of the Twentieth Century, by Edward Wagenknecht, revd., 799-800
Cavalier in the Wilderness; The Story of the Explorer and Trader Louis Juchereau de St. Denis, by Ross Phares, revd., 536-37
Cavanaugh, Helen M., *Funk of Funk's Grove: Farmer, Legislator, and Cattle King of the Old Northwest, 1797-1865,* revd., 556-57
Cawley, Elizabeth H. (ed.), *The American Diaries of Richard Cobden,* revd., 762-63
Centaur, British ship, 236
Central and Southern Pacific Railroad, 661
Central Elevator Company, 668
Central Pacific Railroad, 662
Chaddock, Robert E., cited, 38 n.
Chafee, Zechariah, *Free Speech in the United States,* 300
Chambers, John, N. Y. councilman, 731 n.
Chandler, Charles F., prof., 671
Chandler, John, Mass. delegate at Albany Congress, 731 n.
Chandler, Zachariah, sen., 696; quoted, 709
Chanfrau, F. S. (Mr. and Mrs.), actors, 215-16
Channing, Edward, 8-9, 673-74; *History of the United States,* art. on, 257-74
Channing, William E., quoted, 723
Charles II, 246
Charles Coffin Jewett, by Joseph A. Borome, noted, 181
Charles Waddell Chesnutt, Pioneer of the Color Line, by Helen M. Chesnutt, revd., 572-73

Charleston, St. Michael's, book on, revd., 537-38; mercantile houses, 624
Charleston Mercantile Library Association, 638
Chattanooga Country, 1540-1941; From Tomahawks to TVA, by Gilbert E. Govan and James W. Livingood, revd., 796-97
Chesapeake and Ohio Railroad, 662; paper on, summarized, 276
Chesapeake Bay, wars in, 1600-1677, book on, revd., 103-104
Chesnutt, Charles W., biog. of, revd., 572-73
Chesnutt, Helen M., *Charles Waddell Chesnutt, Pioneer of the Color Line*, revd., 572-73
Chester, Giraud, *Embattled Maiden; The Life of Anna Dickinson*, revd., 135-36
Chicago, and northern Great Plains, 66, 71; Swedish theater in, book on, revd., 137-38; crime and politics in, book on, revd., 775-77
Chicago and Northwestern Railroad, 668
Chicago Board of Trade, 667-69
Chicago, Burlington, & Quincy, 668
Chicago *Daily Democratic Press*, quoted, 66
Chicago Union-Stock-Yards Company, 644
Child labor, 484
Children of the Ghetto, a play by Israel Zangwill, 228
Chinard, Gilbert, *Thomas Jefferson*, 301
Chinatown Charlie, the Opium Fiend, a play by Owen Davis, 231
Chinese characters, on the American stage, 231
Chinese Exclusion Act, 500
Chronicle of Old Muskego; The Diary of Sören Bache, 1839-1847, trans. and ed. by Clarence A. Clausen and Andreas Elviken, revd., 558-59
Chronological pattern, and historians' preferred works, 294
Church, William C., col., paper on, summarized, 279
Churchill, Winston S., *Closing the Ring*, revd., 582-83
Cincinnati, and the election of 1863, p. 40
Cincinnati *Catholic Telegraph*, 43 n.
Cincinnati *Enquirer*, 33 n.
"Civil Disobedience," by Henry D. Thoreau, quoted, 716-18
Civil liberties, and the Ohio election of 1863, p. 37
Civil War, books on, revd., 337-41, 565-66, 770; Washington Territory and the Secession Crisis, art. on, 415-40; books on, noted, 608-609
Civil War and Reconstruction, by James G. Randall, 300
Claiborne, William, merchant venturer, biog. of, revd., 103-104
Clapp, Moses E., sen., 488-89, 492-93
Clark, George R., and the American Revolution, book on, revd., 323-24
Clark, Thomas D., revs., 545-46
Clark, Walter, chief justice, 9
Clausen, Clarence A. (co-ed. and trans.), *A Chronicle of Old Muskego; The Diary of Sören Bache, 1839-1847*, revd., 558-59
Claussen, Martin P., revs., 150-53
Cleveland, Frederick A., hist., 13-14
Cleveland, Grover, 486, 663; and immigrant restriction, 77; and patronage, note on, 505-18
Cleveland *Plain Dealer*, 33 n.
Climate, paper on, summarized, 278
Climatological and Hydrological Records of the Weather Bureau, comp. by Harold T. Pinkett, Helen T. Finneran, and Katherine H. Davidson, noted, 607-608
Clinton, George, gov., 737
Closing the Ring, by Winston S. Churchill, revd., 582-83
Coal and iron industry, influence of Louisville and Nashville Railroad on Birmingham, paper on, summarized, 277-78
Cobden, Richard, diaries of, revd., 762-63
Cochran, Thomas C., 281; paper on railroads, summarized, 276; revs., 359-60; quoted, 645
Cockburn, Sir A. J. E., atty. gen., 254
Coddington, Edwin B., revs., 339-40
Coe, William R., catalogue of manuscript collections, revd., 812
Coffee, John, gen., as merchant, 628
Coke, Edward, quoted, 254
Cold war, in historical writing, 28; with France, paper on, summarized, 282
Cole, Allan B., revs., 336
Cole, Arthur C., and southern Whigs, 280
Cole, George E., pol., 438-39
Cole, John, lawyer, 252-53
Collective security, book on, revd., 155-56
"Colleen Bawn," a play by Dion Boucicault, 217
College textbooks, scientific subjects, paper on, summarized, 287
Colonial Merchants and the American Revolution, by Arthur M. Schlesinger, 16
Colonial Period of American History, by Charles M. Andrews, 299
Colonial Records of South Carolina: The Journal of the Commons House of Assembly, September 12, 1739-March 26, 1741, ed. by J. H. Easterby, revd., 317-18
Colonial South Carolina; Two Contemporary Descriptions by Governor James Glen and Doctor George Milligen-

Johnston, ed. by Chapman J. Milling, revd., 750-51
Colonies, Edward Channing on, 264-66; book on, revd., 749-50; architecture and town planning in, book on, revd., 751-52; politics in Virginia, book on, revd., 752-53
Colored Men's National Progressive Association, 499
Colquitt, Alfred H., gov., 52-53
Colter, John, book on, revd., 552-53
Colton, David, railroad official, 661
Columbus (Ohio) *Crisis*, 30 n., 33 n.
Columbus *Ohio Statesman*, 33 n.
Comanches: Lords of the South Plains, by Ernest Wallace and E. Adamson Hoebel, noted, 607
Combinations: Their Uses and Abuses, With a History of the Standard Oil Trust, by Samuel C. T. Dodd, cited, 650
Come An' Get It; The Story of the Old Cowboy Cook, by Ramon F. Adams, noted, 607
Coming of the Civil War, by Avery O. Craven, 300
Commager, Henry S. (co-auth.), *The Growth of the American Republic*, 299, 686 n.; *The American Mind*, 300
Commentaries, by Sir William Blackstone, 248-49
Commentaries on the Constitution, 1790-1860, by Elizabeth K. Bauer, revd., 757-58
Commerce, in northern Great Plains, 70-71; colonial, Edward Channing on, 264
Commercial education, in the ante-bellum South, art. on, 623-39
Commission of Oyer and Terminer, and the *Gaspee* affair, 241-42
Communist party, and the Negro, book on, revd., 589
Cone, Carl B., *Torchbearer of Freedom; The Influence of Richard Price on Eighteenth Century Thought*, noted, 181
Confederacy, pictorial history of, book on, revd., 342-43; books on, revd., 767-69
Confederate States, soldiers, book on, noted, 180; ordnance, and Josiah Gorgas, book on, revd., 341-42
Conkling, Roscoe M., 664
Connecticut, imprisonment for debt in, 93; colonial, book on, revd., 751-52
Conquered Press, by William J. Coughlin, noted, 609
Conscripted City; Norfolk in World War II, by Marvin W. Schlegel, revd., 581-82
Conscription, military, papers on, summarized, 279
Conservation, federal, papers on, summarized, 284
Conservatism, in historical writing, 3
Constitution, historians' treatment of, 4-5; and the *Gaspee* affair, art. on, 233-56; book on, revd., 757-58
Continental army, book on, revd., 541-42
Cooke, Jay, 68-69, 696-99, 708-709
Cooke, Philip St. G., lt., military escort on Santa Fe Trail, book on, revd., 331-32
Cooley, Thomas M., 664
Coolidge, Calvin, 679
Coolidge, John, revs., 751-52
Copper mining, Michigan, book on, revd., 128-29
Copperheads, southern Ohio, election of 1863, pp. 29-44
Cordelia's Aspirations, a play by Edward Harrigan, 222
Corey, Albert B. (co-ed.), *The Papers of Sir William Johnson*, revd., 105-106
Cornell, Alonzo B., gov., 52
Corry, William M., pol., 38 n.
Corwin, Edward S., hist., 691 n.
Cotner, Robert C. (ed.), *Addresses and State Papers of James Stephen Hogg*, revd., 573-74
Cotterill, R. S., revs., 761-62
Cotton, John, and millenarianism, 445
Cotton gin, paper on, summarized, 283
Cotton Kingdom, by Frederick L. Olmsted, cited, 460, 480-82
Coughlin, William J., *Conquered Press*, noted, 609
Coulter, E. M., revs., 121-22
Cowboy cook, book on, noted, 607
Cox, Samuel S., Ohio rep., 32
Cramer, C. H., revs., 782
Crane, W. Murray, sen., 489
Craven, Avery, *The Coming of the Civil War*, 300; *Edmund Ruffin*, 301; revs., 337-39
Craven, Wesley F. (co-ed.), *Europe: Argument to V-E Day January 1944 to May 1945*, Vol. III, *The Army Air Forces in World War II*, revd., 158-59
Crawford County, Ohio, and the election of 1863, p. 43 n.
Craycroft, William T., lt., 522
"Creation of the Territory of Idaho," by Merle W. Wells, cited, 424 n.
Creel, George, 691 n.
Crime, in Chicago, book on, revd., 775-77
Criminal law, and the critics of John Adams' administration, paper on, summarized, 282
Crises, in American history, book on, revd., 802-803
Crisis in Freedom; The Alien and Sedition Acts, by John C. Miller, revd., 548-52
Crittenden compromise, 432
Croker, Richard, pol., 670

Croly, Herbert, 484, 503-504; *The Promise of American Life*, quoted, 501-502
Cross, Whitney R., paper on W. J. McGee, summarized, 284; quoted, 454
Cross-Channel Attack, United States Army in World War II: The European Theater of Operations, by Gordon A. Harrison, revd., 161-62
Crown Law, by Sir Michael Foster, 248
Croy, Homer, *He Hanged Them High; An Authentic Account of the Fanatical Judge Who Hanged Eighty-Eight Men*, revd., 774-75
Culbertson, Thaddeus A., *Journal of an Expedition to the Mauvaises Terres and the Upper Missouri in 1850*, ed. by John F. McDermott, revd., 562
Cullom Committee, 650, 663-64
Cummins, Albert B., sen., 491-93
Cummins, Cedric, revs., 575-76
Current, Richard N., 286; revs., 346-47, 558
Curry, Jabez L. M., educator, 51, 53, 56-60
Curti, Merle, 280; "The Democratic Theme in American Historical Literature," 3-28; *The Growth of American Thought*, 300
Curtis, George W., author, 461, 468, 476-77; quoted, 478
Custer, Elizabeth B., 521; "*Boots and Saddles*," cited, 520 n.
Custer, George A., legend of, book on, revd., 347-48; expedition to Yellowstone River, doc. on, 519-34
Custer, Thomas W., lt., 529, 534
Cuyler, Cornelius, col., 733 n.
Cypress Hills, 72

Daffer, James, cited, 11 n.
Dale, Edward E., revs., 346
Daly, Augustin, playwright, 230
Dana, Charles A., journ., 468, 474
Dandy, G. B., capt., 528 n.
Dangerfield, George, *The Era of Good Feelings*, revd., 760-61
Danhof, Clarence H., revs., 554-55
Daniels, Josephus, letters to and from Franklin D. Roosevelt, revd., 578-79
Dante, Harris L., paper on Reconstruction politics in Illinois, summarized, 280
Dargan, Marion, *Guide to American Biography*, Pt. II, noted, 180
"Dark Day," 448
Dartmouth, Lord, 250; quoted, 242-44
Darwin, Charles, quoted, 478
Darwinian theory, in historical writing, 10-11; influence on Edward Channing, 259
Davenport, John, theologian, quoted, 446-47
David, Henry, 283
David Thompson's Journals Relating to Montana and Adjacent Regions, 1808-1812, ed. by M. Catherine White, revd., 553-54
Davidson, Katherine H. (co-comp.), *Climatological and Hydrological Records of the Weather Bureau*, noted, 607-608
Davies, Wallace E., revs., 130-31
Davis, John W., 679
Davis, Owen, playwright, 231
Day, Donald (comp.), *Franklin D. Roosevelt's Own Story, Told in his own words from his private and public papers*, revd., 150-53
Day in New York, a play, 220
Day of Doom, by Michael Wigglesworth, quoted, 447
Dearing, Fred M., asst. secy. of state, 310
Debo, Angie, *Prairie City*, 297
De Bow, James D. B., cited, 634-35; quoted, 636
De Bow's Review, 633
Debt, imprisonment for, note on, 89-102
Declaration of Independence, by Carl Becker, 299
DeConde, Alexander, paper on William Vans Murray, summarized, 282
Defects of the Interstate Commerce Law. An Address . . . at a Meeting of the Washington Economic Society, in Washington, D. C., February 3, 1905, by Alpheus B. Stickney, quoted, 643
Defiance County, Ohio, and the election of 1863, p. 35 n.
De Lancey, James, lt. gov., 727-40
Democracy and Social Growth in America, by Bernard Moses, cited, 13
Democracy in American Life, by Avery Craven, cited, 21
Democracy's Norris, by Alfred Lief, quoted, 483
Democratic party, and Ohio election of 1863, pp. 29-44; presidential nomination of 1844, book on, revd., 335; in Washington Territory, 416-24, 434-39; patronage in Minnesota during Cleveland administration, note on, 505-18
Democratic press, in Washington Territory, 426-27
"Democratic Theme in American Historical Literature," by Merle Curti, 3-28
Denby, Edwin, secy. of navy, quoted, 304 n.
Dennett, Raymond (co-ed.), *Documents on American Foreign Relations*, Vol. XII, *January 1-December 31, 1950*, revd., 356-57
Dennett, Tyler, *John Hay*, 301
Dennison, A. P., Indian agent, 419 n.
Denny, Cecil E., capt., quoted, 70
DeNovo, John A., "Edward Channing's 'Great Work' Twenty Years After," 257-74

De Pew, Chauncey, lawyer, quoted, 660
De Rudio, Charles C., lt., 521, 527, 529-30
d'Estaing, Count, and the siege of Savannah, book on, revd., 325
Destler, Chester McA., paper on business history, summarized, 281-82; revs., 348-49; "The Opposition of American Businessmen to Social Control During the 'Gilded Age,'" 641-72
Detroit, physicians, book on, revd., 118
DeWeerd, H. A., revs., 161-62
Dewey, John, 277, 500
Diaz, Profirio, 502
Dick, Everett N., *The Sod-House Frontier*, 300; cited, 455 n.
Dickerson, Oliver M., *The Navigation Acts and the American Revolution*, revd., 104-105; revs., 323
Dickinson, Anna, biog. of, revd., 135-36
Dictionary, Practical, Theoretical, and Historical, of Commerce and Commercial Navigation, by John R. McCulloch, cited, 633 n.
Didsbury (Canada) *Pioneer*, quoted, 75 n.
Dies, Edward, *Behind the Wall Street Curtain*, revd., 583-84
Dillon, Mary E., *Wendell Willkie, 1892-1944*, revd., 785-86
Diplomatic history, books on, revd., 153-56; Far East, paper on, summarized, 285; Senate defense of the Four-Power Treaty of the Washington Conference, note on, 303-14
Discovery, of America, books on, revd., 535, 747-49
Discrimination, legal aspects of, book on, revd., 809-10
Displaced persons, book on, revd., 793-94
Disquisition on Imprisonment for Debt, As the Practice Exists in the State of New York, by Joseph D. Fay, quoted, 96-98
Disruption of American Democracy, by Roy F. Nichols, cited, 421 n.
District of Columbia, library facilities in, book on, noted, 183
Divine Plan of the Ages, by Charles T. Russell, cited, 455
Dix & Edwards, publ., 467-68, 470, 474, 476-77
Dixon, Joseph M., sen., 489, 499
Dobie, J. Frank, *The Longhorns*, 297
Doctors in Blue; The Medical History of the Union Army in the Civil War, by George W. Adams, revd., 565-66
Doctors Under Three Flags, by Fannie Anderson, revd., 118
Documentary History of the Negro People in the United States, ed. by Herbert Aptheker, revd., 111-12
Documents on American Foreign Relations, Vol. XII, *January 1-December 31, 1950*, ed. by Raymond Dennett and Robert K. Turner, revd., 356-57
Dodd, Samuel C. T., atty., cited, 645, 647, 650-51, 654-55, 658; quoted, 651-53, 656-57
Dodd, William E., quoted, 9; cited, 15-18
Dodge, William E., merchant, 52-53
Dodson, Leonidas, revs., 321-22, 749-50
Dodson, Sir John, advocate gen., 254
Dolbear, J. W., teacher, 637-39
Dolbear, Rufus, teacher, 637-39
Dolbear Commercial College, 639
Dollar Diplomacy, 484, 490-92
Dolliver, Jonathan P., sen., 488
Dominican Republic, 488
Donaldson, Arthur, actor, 230
Donnelly, Ignatius, and Cleveland administration patronage, note on, 505-18; quoted, 704
Donnelly, Mrs. Katherine, quoted, 507, 512-13
Doran, Michael, pol., 506, 508-509, 514-17
Dorfman, Joseph, *The Economic Mind in American Civilization*, 300; *Thorstein Veblen and His America*, 301
Dorsey, Emmett E., revs., 589
Dorson, Richard M., *Bloodstoppers & Bearwalkers*, noted, 606
Doster, James F., 278
Douglas, Stephen A., 420, 422, 434-37, 439
Douglass, Elisha P., revs., 541-42
Doull, James A. (co-auth.), *The History of American Epidemiology*, revd., 798-99
Downes, Randolph C., revs., 315-16
DP Story; The Final Report of the United States Displaced Persons Commission, revd., 793-94
Drama, immigrant theme in American, art. on, 211-32
"Drang Nach Norden: The United States and the Riel Rebellion," by Donald F. Warner, 693-712
Dred Scott case, effect in Washington Territory, 422
Drew, John, actor, 215-16
Dry farming, in northern Great Plains, 72-73
Dudingston, William, comdr. of the *Gaspee*, 233-36, 239, 241
Due Process of Law, 1932-1949; The Supreme Court's Use of a Constitutional Tool, by Virginia Wood, noted, 181-82
Duke University, papers and addresses of William P. Few, revd., 365-66
Dutch characters, on the American stage, 213, 223-25, 227
Dwight, Rev. Louis, 100
Dwight, Timothy, educator, quoted, 449-50
Dye, Job F., *Recollections of a Pioneer*,

1830-1852: Rocky Mountains, New Mexico, California, noted, 182
Dyer, Brainerd, revs., 335

Early Histories of St. Louis, ed. by John F. McDermott, revd., 544-45
Easterby, J. H. (ed.), *The Colonial Records of South Carolina: The Journal of the Commons House of Assembly, September 12, 1739-March 26, 1741,* revd., 317-18
Eastern Trunk Line Pool, 661
Easum, Chester V., revs., 563-64, 584-85
Ebey, Winfield S., pol., 422, 424; quoted, 421
Ecological sciences, significance to historians, papers on, summarized, 278
Economic distress, and immigration restriction, 87
Economic history, Michigan copper mining, book on, revd., 128-29
Economic History Association, 281
Economic History of the United States, Vol. IV, *The Transportation Revolution, 1815-1860,* by George R. Taylor, revd., 119-21
Economic Interpretation of the Constitution, by Charles A. Beard, cited, 16
Economic Mind in American Civilization, by Joseph Dorfman, 300
Economic mobilization, prior to Pearl Harbor, paper on, summarized, 279
Edmonds, Walter D., *They Fought With What They Had; The Story of the Army Air Forces in the Southwest Pacific, 1941-1942,* revd., 160-61
Edmund Ruffin, by Avery O. Craven, 301
Edmunds, George F., sen., 52
Edson, Cyrus, M.D., 671
Education, Rutherford B. Hayes and, art. on, 45-60; wartime, records of Senate committee, noted, 608; mercantile, in the ante-bellum South, art. on, 623-40
"Edward Channing's 'Great Work' Twenty Years After," by John A. DeNovo, 257-74
Edwards, Arthur T., publ., 468-69
Edwards, Jonathan, 448
Egbert, Donald D. (co-ed.), *Socialism and American Life,* revd., 807-808
Ekirch, Arthur A., cited, 20 n.; paper on War Department doctrine of conscription, summarized, 279
Elevators, grain, and opposition of American businessmen to social control, 667-70
Elihu Root, by Philip C. Jessup, 301
Elviken, Andreas (co-ed. and trans.), *A Chronicle of Old Muskego; The Diary of Sören Bache, 1839-1847,* revd., 558-59
Emancipation of Negroes, attitude toward, in Washington Territory, 432
Embattled Maiden; The Life of Anna Dickinson, by Giraud Chester, revd., 135-36
Emerson, Elizabeth H., *Walter C. Woodward, Friend on the Frontier; A Biography,* revd., 780-81
Emerson, Ralph W., 468, 713-26
"Emerson, Thoreau, and John Brown," by Gilman M. Ostrander, 713-26
Emerson, William, judge, 469, 477
Emigrant letters, from California, book on, revd., 763-64
Emigrant Train, or Go West, a play, 225
Emigration to America, a play by Joseph Lateiner, 228
Emmett, Joseph K., actor, 224
Emory College, Atticus G. Haygood, president of, 53, 55-56
"End of the World," by Perry Miller, cited, 445 n.
English, culture and the Canadian northern Great Plains, 76; characters on the American stage, 229-30; background of the American Revolution, paper on, summarized, 278; immigrants, contribution of, paper on, summarized, 283
English Discovery of America to 1585, by Franklin T. McCann, revd., 535
English Liberties, or, The free-born Subject's Inheritance, by Henry Care, 247-49
Entrepreneurship, book on, revd., 116-17
Environment, and historical writing, 12-13; and occupation of the Great Plains, papers on, summarized, 278
Epidemics, book on, revd., 798-99
Epochs of American history, influence on historians' choice of preferred works, 296
Equality by Statute; Legal Controls Over Group Discrimination, by Morroe Berger, revd., 809-10
Era of Good Feelings, by George Dangerfield, revd., 760-61
Erie Railroad, 660
Ersatz in the Confederacy, by Mary E. Massey, revd., 767-68
Erwin Frink Smith; A Story of North American Plant Pathology, by Andrew D. Rodgers, III, revd., 570-71
Essays Honoring Lawrence C. Wroth, ed. by Frederick R. Goff *et al.,* revd., 571-72
Europe, diplomatic papers, revd., 354-56
European politics, influence on farmers of northern Great Plains, 75
Evans, Elwood, pol., quoted, 423
Evarts, William M., sen., 50, 663 n., 665
Eve of Conflict: Stephen A. Douglas and the Needless War, by George F. Milton, 301
Evolution, and historical writing, 10-14; and Edward Channing, 259

"Evolution of Democracy," by Charles A. Beard, cited, 14
Ewan, Joseph, revs., 570-71
Expansionists, United States and the Riel Rebellion, art. on, 693-712
"Expedition to the Yellowstone River in 1873: Letters of a Young Cavalry Officer," ed. by George Frederick Howe, 519-34
Ezra Pound and The Cantos, by Harold H. Watts, noted, 609

FAHRNEY, RALPH R., quoted, 258, 270-71
Fairbank, N. K., 671
Fairfield County, Ohio, and the election of 1863, p. 35
Far Corner, A Personal View of the Pacific Northwest, by Stewart H. Holbrook, revd., 574-75
Far East, and the United States, books on, revd., 357, 792-93
Farmer, legal status of tenant in Southeast, book on, noted, 183
Farmers' Alliance, 74, 517
Farmers' Union, 74
Farming, northern Great Plains, 72-75
Fay, Joseph D., *A Disquisition on Imprisonment for Debt, As the Practice Exists in the State of New-York*, quoted, 96-98
Federal aid to education, Rutherford B. Hayes and, 48
Federal conservation, papers on, summarized, 284
Fenner, Arthur, court clerk, 253
Ferguson, E. James, revs., 123-24
Ferrell, Robert H., *Peace in Their Time, The Origins of the Kellogg-Briand Pact*, revd., 577-78
Few, William P., papers and addresses of, revd., 365-66
ffrench, Yvonne (comp.), *Transatlantic Exchanges; Cross-Currents of Anglo-American Opinion in the Nineteenth Century*, revd., 800-801
Field, Dudley, lawyer, 469
Field, Stephen J., and American conservatism, book on, revd., 348-49
Fields, Lew, actor, 225-26
Fifth Monarchy Men, 444
Fifty Years of the South Atlantic Quarterly, by William B. Hamilton, revd., 366-67
Filler, Louis, revs., 135-36
Fine, Sidney, revs., 782-85
Fink, Albert, railway official, 659-64
Finneran, Helen T. (co-comp.), *Climatological and Hydrological Records of the Weather Bureau*, noted, 607-608
Finnish immigrants, contributions of, paper on, summarized, 283
First Born, a play by Francis Powers, 231
First Military Escort on the Santa Fe Trail, 1829; From the Journal and Reports of Major Bennet Riley and Lieutenant Philip St. George Cooke, by Otis E. Young, revd., 331-32
Fischer, John, *Master Plan U. S. A.; An Informal Report on America's Foreign Policy and the Men Who Make It*, noted, 181
Fish, Carl R., cited, 17 n., 273; quoted, 259, 267
Fish, Hamilton, cited, 696, 702, 705-706
Fishbein, Meyer H. (co-comp.), *Records of the National Recovery Administration*, noted, 608
Fiske, John, cited, 12, 259
Fiske, Mary, actress, 225
Fite, Gilbert C., revs., 115-16; *Mount Rushmore*, revd., 575-76
Fleet Admiral King; A Naval Record, by Ernest J. King and Walter M. Whitehill, revd., 788-89
Fleischmann, James J. (co-comp.), *Records of the Price Decontrol Board*, noted, 608
Flint, Charles R., Jr., promoter, cited, 645, 654, 658
Florence, W. J., actor, 215-18
Flower, Milton E., *James Parton, The Father of Modern Biography*, revd., 364-65
Flowering of New England, by Van Wyck Brooks, 300
Folklore, Texas, book on, noted, 182
Forbes, John M., businessman, 482
Forbes, Kathryn, playwright, 230
Forbes expedition, book on, revd., 538-40
Force, Peter, publ., 729
Ford, Guy S., 691 n.
Ford, Henry, book on, revd., 782
Ford, Nick A., "Henry David Thoreau, Abolitionist," cited, 716 n.
Foreign affairs, West Indies, book on, revd., 156-57; World War II, book on, revd., 157-58; book on, noted, 181; Canada, book on, revd., 353-54; documents on, revd., 356-57; Far East, books on, revd., 357, 792-93; policy, book on, revd., 791-92
Foreign policy, in the Far East, paper on, summarized, 285; Senate defense of the Four-Power Treaty of the Washington Conference, noted, 303-14; and progressivism, art. on, 483-504; of Franklin D. Roosevelt, book on, revd., 580-81
Foreign Relations of the United States: Diplomatic Papers, 1934, Vol. I, *General, The British Commonwealth*; Vol. II, *Europe, Near East, Africa*, revd., 354-56
Foreign sources, use of, and Edward Channing, 268
Foreign-born Americans, portrayed in American comedy, 211-12

Foreigners in the Union Army and Navy, by Ella Lonn, revd., 339-40
Forsyth, George A., maj., 526 n.
Fort Garry, 694, 698, 701-702, 707
Fort Lincoln, 530
Fort Macleod (Alberta) *Gazette*, quoted, 62, 71 n.
Fort Rice, 526-27
"Forty-fifth Annual Meeting of the Mississippi Valley Historical Association," by Thomas LeDuc, 275-88
Forty-Niners, by Archer B. Hulbert, cited, 687
Foster, Sir Michael, 248
Four-Power Treaty of the Washington Conference, Senate defense of, note on, 303-14
Fourteenth Amendment, antislavery origins of, book on, revd., 136-37
Fox, Dixon R., quoted, 271, 452
France, in American Revolution, book on, revd., 755-57
France, Joseph I., sen., 313
Frankfurter, Felix, quoted, 502-503
Franklin, Benjamin, 730 n., 734, 736, 744
Franklin, John H., cited, 21
Franklin County, Ohio, and the election of 1863, pp. 35, 42 n., 43 n.
Franklin D. Roosevelt's Own Story, Told in his own words from his private and public papers, comp. by Donald Day, revd., 150-53
"Frederic L. Paxson and His Approach to History," by Earl Pomeroy, 673-92
"Frederick Law Olmsted in the 'Literary Republic'," by Laura W. Roper, 459-82
Free Methodists, and premillennialism, 457
Free Speech in the United States, by Zechariah Chafee, 300
Freedley, Edwin T., *A Practical Treatise on Business*, quoted, 632
Freedom's Ferment, by Alice F. Tyler, cited, 20
Freeman, Douglas S., *George Washington: A Biography*, Vol. III, *Planter and Patriot*, Vol. IV, *Leader of the Revolution*, revd., 107-109; Vol. V, *Victory with the Help of France*, revd., 755-57; *Lee's Lieutenants*, *R. E. Lee*, *Young Washington*, 301
Freidel, Frank, revs., 350-51
French, Thomas H., capt., 534
French characters, on the American stage, 229, 231
French Revolution, and millennial speculation, 448
Frontier, in northern Great Plains, 76; and Edward Channing, 266-67; Washington Territory and the secession crisis, art. on, 415-40; defense of, book on, revd., 561-62; and Frederic L. Paxson, 686-87; and railroads, book on, revd., 772-73
Frontier in American History, by Frederick J. Turner, 299
Frontiersman, portrayed in American comedy, 211
Froom, Le Roy E., *The Prophetic Faith of Our Fathers; The Historical Development of Prophetic Interpretation*, cited, 446 n.
Fuchs, James R. (co-comp.), *Records of the Petroleum Administration for War*, noted, 607
Fundamentalism, art. on Millenarian tradition in America, 441-58
Funk of Funk's Grove: Farmer, Legislator, and Cattle King of the Old Northwest, 1797-1865, by Helen M. Cavanaugh, revd., 556-57
Furman, Bess, *White House Profile, A Social History of the White House, Its Occupants and Its Festivities*, revd., 368-69

Gabriel, Ralph, cited, 20
Gaines, Edmund P., gen., 638
Gallia County, Ohio, and the election of 1863, p. 36
Galvez, Bernardo de, *Instructions for Governing the Interior Provinces of New Spain, 1786*, trans. and ed. by Donald E. Worcester, revd., 546-48
Gara, Larry, paper on the underground railroad, summarized, 286
Gardiner, Clinton H., 283
Garfield, James R., 496
Garfielde, Selucius, pol., 436-37
Garrett, Garet, *The Wild Wheel*, revd., 782
Garvan, Anthony N. B., *Architecture and Town Planning in Colonial Connecticut*, revd., 751-52
Gary, Elbert H., promoter, 645, 647
Gary, Elbridge, judge, 668
"*Gaspee* Affair: A Study of Its Constitutional Significance," by William R. Leslie, 233-56
Gatchel, Samuel, theologian, quoted, 448
Gates, Charles M., revs., 369-70
Gates, Paul W., revs., 131-32; on National Historical Publications Commission, 284
Gates, Rev. Frederick T., 657
Gates, William B., Jr., *Michigan Copper and Boston Dollars; An Economic History of the Michigan Copper Mining Industry*, revd., 128-29
Gay, Edwin F., biog. of, revd., 779-80
Gaynor, William J., biog. of, revd., 147
Geiger, George R., paper on the meaning of pragmatism, summarized, 276-77
Genesee Valley, agricultural history, book on, revd., 554-55

Gentlemen Freeholders; Political Practices in Washington's Virginia, by Charles S. Sydnor, revd., 752-53
Gentry, Claude, *Private John Allen, Gentleman — Statesman — Sage — Prophet*, revd., 343-44
Geographical determinism, 278
Geography, and Edward Channing, 269
George, Henry, praised by Rutherford B. Hayes, 46; and immigration, 87
George Washington: A Biography, by Douglas S. Freeman, Vol. III, *Planter and Patriot*, Vol. IV, *Leader of the Revolution*, revd., 107-109; Vol. V, *Victory with the Help of France*, revd., 755-57
George Washington and American Independence, by Curtis P. Nettels, revd., 321-22
George Washington in American Literature, 1775-1865, by William A. Bryan, revd., 542-43
Georgia, Negro colleges, book on, revd., 360-61; ante-bellum architecture, book on, revd., 764-65
Georgia Studies, by Robert P. Brooks, ed. by Gregor Sebba, noted, 606
German, Catholics and Ohio election of 1863, p. 43; immigration, theme on the American stage, 224-27; in Texas, 466; Forty-Eighters, book on, revd., 563-64
Germany and American Neutrality, 1939-1941, by H. L. Trefousse, revd., 157-58
Germer, Adolph, labor official, 499
Gholson, Richard D., gov., 423
Gibbon, Edward, 442
Gibson, Francis M., lt., 529
Gibson, Mrs. Francis M., 521
Gibson, Randall L., sen., 51 n.
Gilded Age, book on, revd., 566-67; opposition of American businessmen to social control during, art. on, 641-72
Gilder, Richard W., journ., 482
Gilman, Daniel C., educator, 51, 53-54; quoted, 56
Gilmore, Barney, singer and dancer, 215
Ginger, Ray, paper on the meaning of pragmatism, summarized, 276
Gipson, Lawrence H., *The British Empire before the American Revolution*, 300
Gladden, Rev. Washington, 658
Glen, James, royal gov., book on, revd., 750-51
Godfrey, Edward S., lt., 529, 534
Godfrey, Mrs. Edward S., 521
Godwin, Parke, author, 461, 468
Goff, Frederick R. *et al.* (eds.), *Essays Honoring Lawrence C. Wroth*, revd., 571-72
Gold mine, Alaska, book on, revd., 146
Gold rush, California, book on, revd., 130
Golden Age of the New Orleans Theater, by John S. Kendall, revd., 117-18
Goldman, Eric, cited, 14; revs., 583-84
Gondos, Victor, Jr. (co-comp.), *Records of the Price Decontrol Board*, noted, 608
Good Old Summer Days; Newport, Narragansett Pier, Saratoga, Long Branch, Bar Harbor, by Richmond Barrett, revd., 773-74
Goodloe, Daniel R., abolitionist, 479-80
Goodman, Samuel, railway agent, 659
Goodykoontz, Colin B., revs., 127-28, 560-61
Gordon, Cliff, actor, 225
Gordon, John E. (co-auth.), *The History of American Epidemiology*, revd., 798-99
Gorgas, Josiah, and Confederate ordnance, book on, revd., 341-42
Gorki, Maxim, quoted, 274
"Gospel of Wealth," 658
Gottschalk, Louis M., *Lafayette*, 301
Gould, Jay, 642, 647, 661, 663, 667
Govan, Gilbert E. (co-auth.), *The Chattanooga Country, 1540-1941; From Tomahawks to TVA*, revd., 796-97
Graebner, Norman A., revs., 155-56, 760-61
Graff, Henry F. (ed.), *Bluejackets with Perry in Japan; A Day-by-Day Account Kept by Master's Mate John R. C. Lewis and Cabin Boy William B. Allen*, revd., 336
Graham, Howard J., revs., 136-37
Graham, Hugh, merchant, 626 n.
Grain elevators, and opposition of American businessmen to social control, 667-70
Grain Growers' Guide (Winnipeg), quoted, 75
Grangers, in Minnesota, 507
Grant, Ulysses S., 696, 705
Grantham, Dewey W., Jr., revs., 573-74
Gras, N. S. B., and business historians, 281
Grasty, William C., merchant, 625
Graustein, Jeannette E. (ed.), *Nuttall's Travels into the Old Northwest; An Unpublished 1810 Diary*, revd., 329-30
Graveyard of the Atlantic; Shipwrecks of the North Carolina Coast, by David Stick, revd., 795
Gray, Asa, botanist, 468; quoted, 471
Gray, Wood, hist., 31 n., 35 n., 38 n., 42; quoted, 40 n.
Great Awakening, 448-49
Great Northern Railroad, paper on, summarized, 276
Great Plains, by Walter P. Webb, 299, 688
Great Plains, northern, art. on, 61-76;

prehistoric peoples of, paper on, summarized, 285
Green, Arnold W., *Henry Charles Carey, Nineteenth-Century Sociologist*, revd., 126-27
Green, Fletcher M., 284; revs., 107-109, 755-57
Green, Samuel A., 51 n.
Greenbackers, 15
Greene, Evarts B., 273
Greer, Thomas H., revs., 128-29, 786-87
Griffin, Russell A., revs., 344-45
Gronna, Asle J., sen., 493
Grover Cleveland, by Allan Nevins, 301
Growth of American Thought, by Merle Curti, 300
Growth of the American Republic, by Samuel E. Morison and Henry S. Commager, 299, 686 n.
Guam, American strategy in, book on, revd., 153-54; fortification of, 308
Guide to American Biography, Pt. II, by Marion Dargan, noted, 180
Guide to the History of Science, comp. by George Sarton, noted, 606-607
Guide to the Illinois Central Archives in the Newberry Library, 1851-1906, comp. by Carolyn C. Mohr, revd., 131-32
Guide to the Indian Tribes of Oklahoma, by Muriel H. Wright, revd., 132-33
"Guides to American History Manuscript Collections in Libraries of the United States," comp. by Ray A. Billington, noted, 180
Gunderson, Robert G., "Thurlow Weed's Network: Whig Party Organization in 1840," summarized, 281
Gunton, George, journ., 652-53, 657-58

HAFEN, LEROY R., 286; revs., 333
Hale, Eugene, sen., 489
Hale, Nathaniel C., *Virginia Venturer, A Historical Biography of William Claiborne, 1600-1677; The Story of the Merchant Venturers who Founded Virginia, and The War in the Chesapeake*, revd., 103-104
Hale, Owen, capt., 522, 529, 534
Halifax, Earl of, 728-29
Hall, Prescott F., cited, 83 n.
Hamer, Philip M., on National Historical Publications Commission, 284
Hamilton, Henry, journal of, revd., 323-24
Hamilton, Holman, *Zachary Taylor: Soldier of the Republic*, noted, 608
Hamilton, Milton W. (co-ed.), *The Papers of Sir William Johnson*, revd., 105-106
Hamilton, R. A., merchant, 629-30
Hamilton, William B., *Fifty Years of the South Atlantic Quarterly*, revd., 366-67
Hamilton County, Ohio, and the election of 1863, pp. 40-41
Hamilton Fish, by Allan Nevins, 301
Hammond, George P. (ed.), *The Larkin Papers; Personal, Business, and Official Correspondence of Thomas Oliver Larkin, Merchant and United States Consul in California*, revd., 330-31; revs., 536-37
Hampshire County, Mass., and imprisonment for debt in, 94
Handlin, Oscar, revs., 144-45; *The Uprooted; The Epic Story of the Great Migrations that Made the American People*, revd., 584-85
Hands Off, by Dexter Perkins, 297
Hannah, a Providence packet, 236
Hansen, Marcus L., *The Atlantic Migration*, 300
Harding, Warren G., 303, 494; quoted, 307 n., 309 n.
Harmon, George D., *Political Aspects of Slavery and the Civil War*, noted, 608-609; revs., 758-59
Harmony Society, 452-53
Harney County, Oregon, and Its Range Land, by George F. Brimlow, revd., 370-71
Harp Without a Crown, or *Mountcashel's Fair Daughter*, a play by William Kelly, 220
Harper, George W. F., merchant, 630
Harpers Ferry, 718, 724-25
Harrigan, Edward, actor and playwright, 221-23, 230, 232
Harriman, Edward H., 490
Harrington, Fred H., paper on American policy in the Far East, summarized, 285; revs., 792-93
Harris, Burton, *John Colter; His Years in the Rockies*, revd., 552-53
Harris, Charles W., lawyer, quoted, 631-32
Harris, Edward, journal of, revd., 127-28
Harris, T. H., teacher, 637
Harrison, Benjamin, book on, revd., 766-67
Harrison, Fairfax, quoted, 93-94
Harrison, Gordon A., *Cross-Channel Attack. United States Army in World War II: The European Theater of Operations*, revd., 161-62
Harrison, Mary R., *Lost America; The Story of Iron-Age Civilization Prior to Columbus*, 315-16
Harry Burns Hutchins and the University of Michigan, by Shirley W. Smith, revd., 147-48
Hart, Albert B., *National Ideals Historically Traced*, cited, 15
Hart, Mrs. Verling K., 521
Hart, Tony (Anthony Cannon), actor, 221-23

Hart, Verling K., capt., 529, 534
Harvey, Matthew, gov., quoted, 99
Hawkins, Dexter, lawyer, quoted, 423
Hawley, Joseph R., gen., 52
Hay, John, quoted, 683
Hayes, Rutherford B., as educator, art. on, 45-60; and immigration, 84
Haygood, Atticus G., bishop, 51, 53-57, 60; quoted, 53, 55
Haymarket riot, and immigration, 85
Hayne, Robert Y., quoted, 95
Hays, Samuel P., paper on river planning, summarized, 284
He Hanged Them High; An Authentic Account of the Fanatical Judge Who Hanged Eighty-Eight Men, by Homer Croy, revd., 774-75
Healer of Los Olmos, ed. by Wilson M. Hudson, noted, 182
Health, wartime, records of Senate committee, noted, 608
Heard, Alexander, *A Two-Party South?*, revd., 587-88
Heaton, Herbert, *A Scholar in Action: Edwin F. Gay*, revd., 779-80
Heavens on Earth; Utopian Communities in America, 1680-1880, by Mark Holloway, revd., 333-34
Hebrew characters, on the American stage, 231
Hecht, Arthur (co-comp.), *Records of the Bureau of the First Assistant Postmaster General, 1789-1942*, noted, 607
Helper, Hinton R., *The Impending Crisis of the South*, cited, 478
Helton, H. Stephen (comp.), *Records of the Office of Inter-American Affairs*, noted, 608
Hemingway, The Writer as Artist, by Carlos Baker, noted, 609
Hendrick, Mohawk sachem, 735, 737, 742
Henry, Anson G., quoted, 418
Henry Adams: Scientific Historian, by William H. Jordy, revd., 569-70
Henry Charles Carey, Nineteenth-Century Sociologist, by Arnold W. Green, revd., 126-27
Henry Clay, by Bernard Mayo, 301
"Henry David Thoreau, Abolitionist," by Nick A. Ford, cited, 716 n.
Henry Hamilton and George Rogers Clark in the American Revolution with the Unpublished Journal of Lieut. Gov. Henry Hamilton, ed. by John D. Barnhart, revd., 323-24
Hensinger, John, D.V.M., 532
Hepburn Committee, 659, 661
Herchmer, L. W., Canadian Indian Commissioner, quoted, 65
Hermit Philosopher of Liendo, by I. K. Stephens, revd., 143-44
Hershberger, Guy F., *The Mennonite Church in the Second World War*, revd., 353
Hertell, Thomas, *Remarks on the Law of Imprisonment for Debt; Showing Its Unconstitutionality, and Its Demoralizing Influence on the Community*, 96; quoted, 97-98, 102
Hesseltine, William B., quoted, 41 n.
Hewes, Leslie, revs., 132-33
Hewitt, Abram S., rep., 80
Heyburn, Weldon B., sen., quoted, 489
Hibernian Crusade, The Story of the Catholic Total Abstinence Union of America, by Sister Joan Bland, revd., 138-39
Hicks, John D., *The Populist Revolt*, 299
Higginbotham, Sanford W., *The Keystone in the Democratic Arch: Pennsylvania Politics, 1800-1816*, revd., 758-59
Higginson, Thomas W., author, 723 n.
Higham, John, "Origins of Immigration Restriction, 1882-1897: A Social Analysis," 77-88; revs., 357-58
Highland County, Ohio, election of 1863, pp. 39-40
Hildreth, Richard, 6-7, 14
Hill, "Gus," actor, 229
Hill, James J., 663; and Cleveland administration patronage, note on, 505-18
Hill, Lawrence F., revs., 156-57
Hill, Nathaniel P., sen., 663
Hills of Erin, or Ireland's Last Struggle, a play, 220
Hillsborough, Earl of, secy. of state for colonies, 237-39
Himes, Rev. Joshua V., 454
Hindle, Brook, paper on history of science in the college curriculum, summarized, 287
"Historians' Choice: Results of a Poll on Recently Published American History and Biography," by John W. Caughey, 289-302
Historical collections, South Dakota, book on, revd., 115-16
Historical Editing, by Clarence E. Carter, noted, 608
Historical figures, their place in American history, Edward Channing and, 261-62
Historical method, and Edward Channing, 268-69
Historical research, influence of Edward Channing, 264
"Historical Retrospect," A. H. A. presidential address by Edward Channing, quoted, 260-61
Historical Scholarship in the United States, 1876-1901; As Revealed in the Correspondence of Herbert B. Adams, by W. Stull Holt, cited, 12 n.

Historical sciences, international bibliography, book on, revd., 367-68
Historiography, American, art. on, 3-28; Edward Channing, art. on, 257-74; historians' preferred works in American history, art. on, 289-302; Frederic L. Paxson, art. on, 673-92; book on, revd., 810-12
History and Human Relations, by Herbert Butterfield, noted, 182
History of American Epidemiology, by C.-E. A. Winslow, Wilson G. Smillie, James A. Doull, John E. Gordon, ed. by Franklin H. Top, revd., 798-99
History of Marine Corps Aviation in World War II, by Robert Sherrod, revd., 789-90
History of science, in college curriculum, paper on, by Brook Hindle, summarized, 287
History of the American Frontier, by Frederic L. Paxson, cited, 688-89, 674 n.
History of the American Theatre, 1700-1950, by Glenn Hughes, revd., 585-86
History of the State of Ohio, ed. by Carl Wittke, cited, 31 n.
History of the United States, by Edward Channing, 299; art. on, 257-74
History of the United States From Hayes to McKinley, by James F. Rhodes, cited, 684
History of the United States of America, by Richard Hildreth, cited, 6
History of the United States of America under the Constitution, by James F. Rhodes, cited, 7-8
History of the United States Since the Civil War, by Ellis P. Oberholtzer, cited, 684-85
Hitchcock, Daniel, lawyer, 252-53
Hitt, Homer L. (co-auth.), *The People of Louisiana*, noted, 183
Hoar, George F., sen., 52, 663 n.
Hodgson, Benjamin H., lt., 522, 534
Hoebel, E. Adamson (co-auth.), *The Comanches: Lords of the South Plains*, noted, 607
Hogg, James S., addresses and papers of, revd., 573-74
Holbrook, Stewart H., *Far Corner, A Personal View of the Pacific Northwest*, revd., 574-75
Holley, Irving B., paper on economic mobilization prior to Pearl Harbor, summarized, 279
Holloway, Mark, *Heavens on Earth; Utopian Communities in America, 1680-1880*, revd., 333-34
Holmes, Oliver W., archivist, 284
Holmes County, Ohio, and the election of 1863, pp. 37, 43 n.
Holt, W. Stull, *Historical Scholarship in the United States, 1876-1901; As Revealed in the Correspondence of Herbert B. Adams*, cited, 12 n.
Holverstott, Lyle J. (co-comp.), *Records of the United States Mint at Philadelphia*, noted, 608
Home in the Woods, comp. by Howard Johnson, noted, 181
Hooker, Richard J., revs., 750-51
Hoover, Herbert, 494; memoirs of, revd., 782-85
Hopkins, Mark, educator, quoted, 451
Hopkins, Samuel, theologian, 448
Hopkins, Stephen, chief justice of R. I., 243, 732, 734
Horine, Emmet F., revs., 798-99
Howard, Jacob M., sen., 696
Howard, Martin, Jr., 732, 734
Howard, Victor, cited, 39 n.
Howe, George F. (ed.), "Expedition to the Yellowstone River in 1873: Letters of a Young Cavalry Officer," 519-34
Howe, Mark A. DeW., cited, 7 n.
Howe, Samuel G., reformer, 723 n.
Howells, William D., 223; book on, revd., 770-72
Howells & Italy, by James L. Woodress, Jr., revd., 770-72
Hoyt, Charles H., playwright, 231
Hubbard, John R., revs., 582-83
Hubbart, Henry C., cited, 31 n., 37 n., 38 n.; quoted, 31
Hudson, Wilson M. (ed.), *The Healer of Los Olmos*, noted, 182
Hudson River Railroad, 659
Hudson's Bay Company, 66, 693-95, 700
Hughes, Charles E., 495-96, 679; quoted, 310 n.
Hughes, Glenn, *A History of the American Theater, 1700-1950*, revd., 585-86
Huit, Ephraim, theologian, 445
Hulbert, Archer B., *Forty-Niners*, cited, 687
Hult, Ruby E., *Steamboats in the Timber*, revd., 346-47
Human relations, and history, book on, noted, 182
Humanitarianism, Rutherford B. Hayes, 60; and immigration restriction, 79
Hundley, Daniel R., *Social Relations in Our Southern States*, quoted, 475-76, 627-28
Hunter, Louis, 279
Huntington, Collis P., railroad executive, 647, 661
Hunt's Merchants' Magazine, 633-34
Hurlbert, William H., journ., 473
Hurley, Sister Helen A., *On Good Ground; The Story of the Sisters of St. Joseph in St. Paul*, revd., 129
Hutchins, Harry B., and the University of Michigan, book on, revd., 147-48

Hutchinson, Thomas, royal gov., 251, 731 n., 734, 739
Hutchinson, William T., revs., 809-10
Hutton, Laurence, quoted, 217
Hydrographic Office, records of, noted, 608

Ickes, Harold, 498
"Ignatius Donnelly, James J. Hill, and Cleveland Administration Patronage," by Horace S. Merrill, 505-18
Illinois, support for Civil War in, 30; Reconstruction politics in, paper on, summarized, 280
Illinois Board of Warehouse and Railroad Commissioners, 669-70
Illinois Central Railroad, 668; guide to archives of, revd., 131-32; paper on, summarized, 286
Illinois Manufacturers' Association, 665
"Immigrant Theme on the American Stage," by Carl Wittke, 211-32
Immigration, Canadian, from U. S., 74; restriction of from 1882 to 1897, note on, 77-88; papers on, summarized, 283
Impending Crisis of the South, by Hinton R. Helper, cited, 478
Imperial school, and Edward Channing, 265
Imperialism, and progressivism, art. on, 483-504
Impressions Respecting New Orleans, Diary & Sketches, 1818-1820, by Benjamin H. B. Latrobe, ed. by Samuel Wilson, Jr., revd., 121-22
"Imprisonment For Debt in America: Fact and Fiction," by Edwin T. Randall, 89-102
Indiana, support for Civil War in, 30
Indians, in northern Great Plains, 64-65; in Oklahoma, book on, revd., 132-33; in New Spain, book on, revd., 536; Albany Congress, doc. on, 727-46
Industrial education, and Rutherford B. Hayes, 49-50
Industrial revolution, in the South, papers on, summarized, 277-78
Industrialization, Edward Channing on, 266-67
Instructions for Governing the Interior Provinces of New Spain, 1786, by Bernardo de Galvez, trans. and ed. by Donald E. Worcester, revd., 546-47
Intellectual history, American, book on, revd., 133-35
Inter-American Affairs, records of office of, noted, 608
International Bibliography of Historical Sciences, ed. by Jirina Sztachova and Adolf Sztacho, revd., 367-68
Interstate Commerce Act, 666
Interstate Commerce Commission, 652, 663-65
Inter-Varsity Christian Fellowship, 457 n.
Iowa, Reconstruction politics in, paper on, summarized, 279-80
Ireland and America, a play, 219-20
Irish Assurance and Yankee Modesty, a play, 219
Irish characters, on the American stage, 212-23; songs, 216
Irish Emigrant, a play by John Brougham, 218
Irish Yankee; or the Birthday of Freedom, a play by John Brougham, 220
Iron and coal industry, influence of Louisville and Nashville Railroad on Birmingham, paper on, summarized, 277-78
Iron-Age, in America, book on, revd., 315-16
Irony of American History, by Reinhold Niebuhr, revd., 357-58
Irvine, A. G., Canadian police commissioner, quoted, 65, 70
Isabella, Queen, 262
Isolationism, in northern Great Plains, 75; midwestern, papers on, summarized, 277
Italian characters, on the American stage, 230-31
Italy, and William D. Howells, book on, revd., 770-72
Iturbide of Mexico, by William S. Robertson, revd., 122-23
Iverson, Alfred, sen., 430

Jackson, Alice F. (co-auth.), *Three Hundred Years American; The Epic of a Family from seventeenth-century New England to twentieth-century Midwest*, revd., 109-10
Jackson, Andrew, as merchant, 628; quoted, 638
Jackson, Bettina (co-auth.), *Three Hundred Years American; The Epic of a Family from seventeenth-century New England to twentieth-century Midwest*, revd., 109-10
Jackson, H. Nelson, M.D., pol., quoted, 493-94
Jacksonian contributions, historians' treatment of, 4-5
"Jacksonian Riddle: New Jersey," by Richard P. McCormick, summarized, 280
Jacobs, Wilbur R., paper on Frederick J. Turner as a teacher, summarized, 287-88
Jacoby, Robert L. (co-comp.), *A Calendar of the Speeches and Other Published Statements of Franklin D. Roosevelt: 1910-1920*, noted, 608
James, Edmund, cited, 79
James, Marquis, *Andrew Jackson*, 301
James Parton, The Father of Modern

Biography, by Milton E. Flower, revd., 364-65
Jameson, J. Franklin, *The American Revolution Considered as a Social Movement*, 293, 299
Japan, and the Four-Power Treaty of the Washington Conference, 307
Jefferson, Thomas, quoted, 93
Jefferson, by Dumas Malone, 297
Jefferson and Hamilton, by Claude G. Bowers, 301
Jefferson and His Time, by Dumas Malone, 301
Jehovah's Witnesses, 455-56
Jensen, Merrill (ed.), *Regionalism in America*, revd., 112-15; revs., 540-41
Jessel, George, actor, 229
Jessup, Philip C., *Elihu Root*, 301
Jesup, Morris K., philanthropist, 49, 52-56
Jewett, Charles C., biog. of, noted, 181
Jewett, Hugh J., pol., 33
Jewish, characters on the American stage, 227-29, 231-32; trade unions, paper on, summarized, 283
Joachim of Flores, 443
Johannsen, Robert W., "The Secession Crisis and the Frontier: Washington Territory, 1860-1861," pp. 415-40
John Brown, The Making of a Martyr, by Robert P. Warren, quoted, 722
John C. Calhoun, by Charles M. Wiltse, 301
John Colter; His Years in the Rockies, by Burton Harris, revd., 552-53
John Hay, by Tyler Dennett, 301
John Jacob Astor, by Kenneth W. Porter, 301
John Quincy Adams, by Samuel F. Bemis, 301
Johns, John, revs., 790-91
Johnson, Hiram W., sen., 313, 496; quoted, 307-308
Johnson, Howard (comp.), *A Home in the Woods*, noted, 181
Johnson, Luke G., 54 n.
Johnson, Oliver, reminiscences of Marion County, Ind., book on, noted, 181
Johnson, Richard M., sen., quoted, 89; cited, 92
Johnson, Samuel D., playwright, 215
Johnson, Sir William, papers of, revd., 105-106
Johnson, Walter, 285; revs., 351-52
Johnson, Walter A., pol., 493
Johnson, William, col., 731 n., 732, 737, 739-40, 742, 743 n.
Jones, Howard M., revs., 799-800
Jones, Hugh, author, quoted, 93
Jones, James H., lt., 529, 534
Jones, Stanley L., paper on John Wentworth, summarized, 286
Jordy, William H., *Henry Adams: Scientific Historian*, revd., 569-70
Journal of an Expedition to the Mauvaises Terres and the Upper Missouri in 1850, by Thaddeus A. Culbertson, ed. by John F. McDermott, revd., 562
Journalism, book on, revd., 801-802
Journey in the Back Country, by Frederick L. Olmsted, cited, 459, 477-80
Journey in the Seaboard Slave States, by Frederick L. Olmsted, cited, 459, 468-73
Journey through Texas, by Frederick L. Olmsted, cited, 459, 473-76
Joyner, Fred B., revs., 336-37

KAHN, HERMAN, 277
Kansas, and John Brown, 713-19
Kansas issue, and Washington Territory, 420
Kapp, Friedrich, quoted, 478
Katy Railroad and the Last Frontier, by V. V. Masterson, revd., 772-73
Keeler, Robert, British naval officer, 235 n.
Keenleyside, Hugh L. (co-auth.), *Canada and the United States; Some Aspects of Their Historical Relations*, revd., 353-54
Kees, John W., journ., 37 n.
Keith, Jean E., paper on influence of Louisville and Nashville Railroad on the Birmingham coal and iron industry, 277-78
Kelley, Florence, reformer, 644
Kellog, Ira N., Jr. (co-comp.), *Records of the War Refugee Board*, noted, 608
Kellogg, Martin, 736 n.
Kellogg-Briand Pact, book on, revd., 577-78
Kelly, John T., comedian, 215
Kelly, Patrick H., pol., 506, 508-10, 512-13, 514-17; quoted, 513
Kelly, William, playwright, 220
Kelly and Ryan, vaudeville team, 221
Kelvin, Lord William T., influence on Henry Adams, 11-12
Kemble, John H., revs., 763-64
Kendall, John S., *The Golden Age of the New Orleans Theater*, revd., 117-18
Kennan, George F., *American Diplomacy, 1900-1950*, revd., 154-55
Kent, Donald H. (co-ed.), *The Papers of Henry Bouquet*, Vol. II, *The Forbes Expedition*, revd., 538-40
"Kentucky Resolutions of 1798," by Edward Channing, cited, 269
Kenyon, Cecelia M., revs., 124-26
Ketchum, Hiram H., lt., 534
Keystone in the Democratic Arch: Pennsylvania Politics, 1800-1816, by Sanford W. Higginbotham, revd., 758-59
Kilpatrick, Carroll (ed.), *Roosevelt and*

Daniels, A Friendship in Politics, revd., 578-79
King, Ernest J. (co-auth.), *Fleet Admiral King; A Naval Record*, revd., 788-89
King Lager, or Ye Sons of Malt, a play, 224
King's Friends, 278
Kirkland, Edward C., *Business in the Gilded Age; The Conservatives' Balance Sheet*, revd., 566-67; revs., 779-80
Kirwan, A. D., revs., 140-41
Knight, Edgar W., revs., 360-61
Knights of Labor, and immigration restriction, 80; and Piedmont textile industry, 277
Knoles, George H., revs., 807-808
Knollenberg, Bernhard, 278
Knox, Philander C., 490
Kolehmainen, John I., paper on contributions of Finnish immigrants, summarized, 283
Kraus, Michael, revs., 800-801
Kuhlman, Charles, *Legend into History; The Custer Mystery; An Analytical Study of the Battle of the Little Big Horn*, revd., 347-48
Kull, Irving S. (co-auth.), *A Short Chronology of American History, 1492-1950*, noted, 183
Kull, Nell W. (co-auth.), *A Short Chronology of American History, 1492-1950*, noted, 183
Kwiat, Joseph J., revs., 543-44

Labor, Rutherford B. Hayes's attitude toward, 47
Labor unions, and immigration restrictions, 80-81, 84-87
Lafayette, by Louis M. Gottschalk, 301
Lafayette, Guest of the Nation; A Contemporary Account of the Triumphal Tour of General Lafayette Through the United States in 1824-1825 as Reported by the Local Newspapers, Vol. I, comp. and ed. by Edgar E. Brandon, revd., 123-24
La Follette, Robert M., sen., 313, 488, 493, 679
Lake Coeur d'Alene, book on, revd., 346-47
Lake Shore and Michigan Southern Railway Company, 643
Lamar, Lucius Q. C., sen., 513
Lambert, John, auth., cited, 90
Lamerick, John K., gen., 419 n.
Lamont, Daniel S., secy. of war, 516
Land, Aubrey, revs., 104-105
Lander, Edward, pol., 436-37 n.
Lane, Joseph, sen., 419-20, 426 n., 439; quoted, 419 n.
Lang, Elfrieda, revs., 329-30
Lansing, Jacob J., 730 n.
Larkin, Thomas O., papers of, revd., 330-31
Larkin Papers; Personal, Business and Official Correspondence of Thomas Oliver Larkin, Merchant and United States Consul in California, ed. by George P. Hammond, revd., 330-31
Larned, Charles W., lt., expedition to Yellowstone River, letters of, 519-34
Larned, Paul, maj., 520
Lasswell, Harold D. (co-ed.), *The Policy Sciences; Recent Developments in Scope and Method*, revd., 359-60
Last American Frontier, by Frederic L. Paxson, 674 n.
Last of the Hogans, a play, 223
Lateiner, Joseph, playwright, 228
Latourette, Kenneth S., *The American Record in the Far East, 1945-1951*, revd., 792-93
Latrobe, Benjamin H. B., diary of, revd., 121-22
Latter Day Saints, 453
Lawrence, Alexander A., *Storm Over Savannah; The Story of Count d'Estaing and the Siege of the Town in 1779*, revd., 325
Lawrence County, Ohio, and the election of 1863, p. 36
Leaders of Men by Woodrow Wilson, ed. by T. H. Vail Motter, noted, 182
League of Nations, 303-304
Leavitt, Michael B., actor and producer, cited, 221
LeDuc, Thomas, "The Forty-fifth Annual Meeting of the Mississippi Valley Historical Association," 275-88; revs., 361-63
Lee, "Mother Ann," 452
Leech, John, journ., 474
Lee's Lieutenants, by Douglas S. Freeman, 301
Legal Status of the Tenant Farmer in the Southeast, by Charles S. Mangrum, noted, 183
Legend into History: The Custer Mystery; An Analytical Study of the Battle of the Little Big Horn, by Charles Kuhlman, revd., 347-48
Leighton, Richard M., paper on relative priority of troop training and armament manufacture, summarized, 279
Lemon, Mark, journ., 474
Lenroot, Irvin, sen., 305-306, 312
Leonard, Autumn L. (co-ed.), *The Papers of Henry Bouquet*, Vol. II, *The Forbes Expedition*, revd., 538-40
Leopold, Richard W., revs., 157-58, 354-56, 577-78
Lerner, Daniel (co-ed.), *The Policy Sciences; Recent Developments in Scope and Method*, revd., 359-60
Leslie, William R., "The *Gaspee* Affair:

A Study of Its Constitutional Significance," 233-56; revs., 757-58
Letters from America, 1773 to 1780; Being the letters of a Scots officer, Sir James Murray, to his home during the War of American Independence, ed. by Eric Robson, revd., 323
Letters of Benjamin Rush, ed. by L. H. Butterfield, revd., 325-27
Letters of Theodore Roosevelt, ed. by Elting E. Morison, Vols. V and VI, revd., 777-79
Leuchtenburg, William E., "Progressivism and Imperialism: The Progressive Movement and American Foreign Policy, 1898-1916," pp. 483-504
Lewis, John R. C., log of the Perry expedition, book on, revd., 336
Lexington Group, 275-76
Liberalism, in historical writing, 3
Library and Reference Facilities in the Area of the District of Columbia, issued by Library of Congress, noted, 183
Licking County, Ohio, and the election of 1863, p. 35
Lief, Alfred, *Democracy's Norris*, quoted, 483
Life and Labor in the Old South, by Ulrich B. Phillips, 299
Life and Times of Stephen Girard, by John B. McMaster, cited, 684
Life of Billy Yank, The Common Soldier of the Union, by Bell I. Wiley, revd., 340-41
Life of Johnny Reb, by Bell I. Wiley, noted, 180
Lincoln, Abraham, 437, 683; and election of 1860, p. 422; biog. of, revd., 564-65; and John Brown myth, 726
Lincoln, Robert Todd, 683
Lincoln, by J. G. Randall, 297
Lincoln and His Generals, by T. Harry Williams, revd., 337-39
Lincoln in Marble and Bronze, by F. Lauriston Bullard, noted, 606
Lincoln the President, by James G. Randall, 301
Link, Arthur S., paper on midwestern isolationism, summarized, 277
Linton, William A., rep., 84
Linzee, John, capt. of H. M. S. *Beaver*, 238
Lipscombe, Rev. Andrew A., quoted, 464
Literary Criticism of "Young America," by John Stafford, noted, 607
"Literary Republic," and Frederick L. Olmsted, art. on, 459-82
Little Big Horn, battle of, book on, revd., 347-48
Livezey, William E., revs., 795
Livingood, James (co-auth.), *The Chattanooga Country, 1540-1951; From Tomahawks to TVA*, revd., 796-97
Lloyd, Henry D., 486, 642, 653
Lloyd, James, sen., 100
Lodge, Henry C., 309, 491, 496, 498; quoted, 305-308, 312
Logan, John A., sen., 663 n.
Long, Alexander, rep., 31-32, 38 n.
Long, J. C., *Bryan, The Great Commoner*, cited, 677-78
Long Branch, book on, revd., 773-74
Longfellow, Henry W., 468
Longhorns, by J. Frank Dobie, cited, 297
Lonn, Ella, *Foreigners in the Union Army and Navy*, revd., 339-40; revs., 341-42
Lossing, Benson, hist., 4-5
Lost America; The Story of Iron-Age Civilization Prior to Columbus, by Arlington H. Mallery and Mary R. Harrison, revd., 315-16
Lost Discovery; Uncovering the Track of the Vikings in America, by Frederick J. Pohl, revd., 747-49
Louisiana, population study, book on, noted, 183; University of, 634-35
Louisiana Purchase, significance of, Edward Channing on, 260
Louisville and Nashville Railroad, influence on Birmingham coal and iron industry, paper on, summarized, 277-78
Lowell, James R., 468; quoted, 481
Lowitt, Richard, revs., 785-86
Loyalty purges, 7, 28
Ludlum, David M., *Social Ferment in Vermont*, cited, 454-55
Lynch, Anne C., author, 461

McAnear, Beverly, "Personal Accounts of the Albany Congress of 1754," 727-46
MacArthur, Douglas, and the press, book on, noted, 609
McCann, Franklin T., *English Discovery of America*, revd., 535
McCloskey, Robert G., *American Conservatism in the Age of Enterprise; A Study of William Graham Sumner, Stephen J. Field, and Andrew Carnegie*, revd., 348-49
McCormick, Medill, sen., 310
McCormick, Richard P., "The Jacksonian Riddle: New Jersey," summarized, 280
McCormick, Robert, publ., 43
McCornack, Richard B., paper on Pan-Americanism during the French occupation of Mexico, summarized, 282
McCulloch, John R., *A Dictionary, Practical, Theoretical, and Historical, of Commerce and Commercial Navigation*, cited, 633 n.
McCumber, Fordney, sen., 307
McDermott, John F. (ed.), *Up the Missouri with Audubon; The Journal of Edward Harris*, revd., 127-28; (ed.), *The Early Histories of St. Louis*, revd.,

544-45; *Journal of An Expedition to the Mauvaises Terres and the Upper Missouri*, by Thaddeus A. Culbertson, revd., 562.
Macdonald, Sir John A., 704, 707 n., 711-12
McDougall, Thomas M., lt., 534
McDougall, William, lt. gov., 695-96, 701-702
McFadden, Obadiah B., chief justice, quoted, 430
McGee, Gale W., revs., 791-92
McGee, W. J., paper on, summarized, 284
McGill, Henry M., gov., 438
MacIntosh, Donald, lt., 523, 529, 534
MacIntosh, Mrs. Donald, 521
Mackay, Angus, 73
McKelvey, Blake, revs., 147, 581-82
McLaughlin, Andrew C., 17-19
McMaster, John B., cited, 14-16, 454, 675, 684-85, 687; quoted, 89-90
McMillan, Malcolm C., paper on the cotton gin, summarized, 283
McNall, Neil A., *An Agricultural History of the Genesee Valley, 1790-1860*, revd., 554-55
McNeil, Floyd A., revs., 544-45
McNiece, Jean (co-comp.), *Records of the United States Mint at Philadelphia*, noted, 608
McReynolds, Edwin C., revs., 561-62
Mcvane, S. M., cited, 22
MacVeagh, Wayne, atty., 658
Mademoisselle Celeste, 631
Mahan, Alfred T., capt., 502-503
Main Currents in American Thought, by Vernon L. Parrington, 19-20, 299
Maine, imprisonment for debt in, 99
Makers of Modern Journalism, by Kenneth Stewart and John Tebbel, revd., 801-802
Malin, James C., 278; cited, 716 n.
Mallery, Arlington H. (co-auth.), *Lost America; The Story of Iron-Age Civilization Prior to Columbus*, revd., 315-16
Malmros, Oscar, gen., 698-99, 701, 703, 705, 707; quoted, 69, 702, 708
Malone, Dumas, *Jefferson*, 297; *Jefferson and His Time*, 301
"Mama's Bank Account," a play by Kathryn Forbes, 230
Mangrum, Charles S., *The Legal Status of the Tenant Farmer in the Southeast*, noted, 183
Manifest Destiny, and Riel Rebellion, art. on, 693-712
Manitoba, 69, 697, 700, 703-706, 710-11
Mann, Lewis, actor, 224
Manning, Clarence A., *The Siberian Fiasco*, noted, 607
Manning, Thomas G., communication on John W. Powell, 163-64
Mansfield, Lord, quoted, 254
Manuscript collections, American history, guides to, noted, 180; western Americana, catalogue of, revd., 812
Marbut, Frederick B., revs., 586-87
March of Empire; Frontier Defense in the Southwest, 1848-1860, by Averam B. Bender, revd., 561-62
Marchant, Henry, colonial pol., 238
Marchman, Watt P., revs., 118-19
Marcosson, Isaac F., *"Marse Henry," A Biography of Henry Watterson*, revd., 140-41
Marine Corps, aviation, book on, revd., 789-90
Marion County, Ind., reminiscences of Oliver Johnson, book on, noted, 181
Maritime History of Massachusetts, by Samuel E. Morison, 299
Marryat, Frank, *Mountains and Molehills, or Recollections of a Burnt Journal*, revd., 130
"Marse Henry," A Biography of Henry Watterson, by Isaac F. Marcosson, revd., 140-41
Marshall, William, gov., 708-709
Marshall Islands, 308
Martin, Helen R., auth., 223
Mason Brothers, publ., 477, 479-80, 482
Massey, Mary E., *Ersatz in the Confederacy*, revd., 767-68
Master Plan U. S. A.; An Informal Report on America's Foreign Policy and the Men Who Make It, by John Fischer, noted, 181
Masterson, V. V., *The Katy Railroad and the Last Frontier*, revd., 772-73
Mather, Cotton, quoted, 446
Mather, Increase, *A Discourse Concerning Faith and Fervency in Prayer, and the Glorious Kingdom of the Lord Jesus Christ, on Earth, Now Approaching*, quoted, 446; *The Mystery of Israel's Salvation*, cited, 446
Mathey, Edward G., lt., 534
Mattes, Merrill J., revs., 331-32, 552-53
Matthews, Charles B., 645
Mauvaises Terres, book on, revd., 562
Mavor, James, quoted, 72 n.
Mawney, John, 236 n.
Maxwell, Robert S., revs., 777-79
May, Henry F., revs., 803-805
Mayer, George H., *The Political Career of Floyd B. Olson*, revd., 149-50
Mayhew, Henry, journ., 474
Mayo, Bernard, *Henry Clay*, 301
Meat inspection, 484
Meat packers, "Big Four," 644; and opposition to social control, 670-72
Medary, Samuel, journ., 31, 32, 34 n.; quoted, 30 n.

Medical history, Union army, book on, revd., 565-66
Medley, Joseph, N. C. sheriff, quoted, 99
Meilicke, Emil J., Minn. state sen., 73
Memoirs of Herbert Hoover, 2 vols., revd., 782-85
Men in Business; Essays in the History of Entrepreneurship, ed. by William Miller, revd., 116-17
Mencken, Henry L., cited, 224
Mennonite Church in the Second World War, by Guy F. Hershberger, revd., 353
"Mercantile Education in the Ante-Bellum South," by Lewis E. Atherton, 623-40
Mercer County, Ohio, and the election of 1863, p. 43
"Merchant of the Past and the Present," by John Tyler, cited, 633-34
Merrill, Horace S., "Ignatius Donnelly, James J. Hill, and Cleveland Administration Patronage," 505-18
Metcalf, R. B., Indian agent, 419 n.
Métis, 695-96, 705, 710-11
Metzger, Charles H., revs., 753-54
Mexico, 493; Iturbide, biog. of, revd., 122-23; papers on, summarized, 282
Meyer, Jacob C., revs., 353, 793-94
Michigan, University of, and Harry B. Hutchins, book on, revd., 147-48
Michigan Copper and Boston Dollars; An Economic History of the Michigan Copper Mining Industry, by William B. Gates, Jr., revd., 128-29
Micronesia, American strategy in, 153-54
Middle period, party politics in the, papers on, summarized, 280
Middleton & McMaster, bookdealers, 475
Midnight Cry, 454
Midwestern isolationism, papers on, by Arthur S. Link and Jeannette P. Nichols, summarized, 277
Mifflin, Thomas, book on, revd., 753-54
Military conscription, papers on, summarized, 279
Military history, recent, papers on, summarized, 279
Military mind, in America, papers on, summarized, 278-79
Mill, John S., cited, 481
Millenarian tradition in America, art. on, 441-58
Millennial Harp, 454
Millennial Hope; A Phase of War-Time Thinking, by Shirley J. Case, cited, 442 n.
Millennium and Utopia: A Study in the Background of the Idea of Progress, by Ernest L. Tuveson, cited, 444 n.
Miller, John C., cited, 234 n.; *Crisis in Freedom; The Alien and Sedition Acts*, revd., 548-52
Miller, Perry, 24, 445 n.; *The New England Mind*, 300
Miller, William (ed.), *Men in Business; Essays in the History of Entrepreneurship*, revd., 116-17
Miller, William, millennialist, 441, 453-55, 457
Miller, William W., supt. Indian Affairs, quoted, 423-24
Miller and Curtis, publ., 476-77
Milligen-Johnston, George, M.D., book on, revd., 750-51
Milling, Chapman J. (ed.), *Colonial South Carolina; Two Contemporary Descriptions by Governor James Glen and Doctor George Milligen-Johnston*, revd., 750-51
Milton, George F., *Eve of Conflict: Stephen A. Douglas and the Needless War*, 301
Mining, California, book on, revd., 130
Minnesota, Democratic patronage in, note on, 505-18
Minnesota Railroad Act of 1871, p. 643
Minnesota Rate Case, 665
Minot, George R., quoted, 94
Minstrel show, and the Negro, 212
Mississippi Valley Historical Association, presidential address, 3-28; annual meeting, 275-88; report of the secretary-treasurer, 390-402
Mogul Steamship Company *v.* McGregor, 655
Mohr, Carolyn C. (comp.), *Guide to the Illinois Central Archives in the Newberry Library, 1851-1906*, revd., 131-32
Monck, Lord, 695 n.
Monroe, James, 262
Monroe County, Ohio, and the election of 1863, p. 35
Monroe Doctrine, 490, 492
Montagu, John, British admiral, and the *Gaspee* affair, 235, 243-44; quoted, 237
Montana, journals of David Thompson, revd., 553-54
Montana Stock Growers' Association, 71
Montgomery, Edmund D., biog. of, revd., 143-44
Montross, Lynn, *Rag, Tag and Bobtail; The Story of the Continental Army, 1775-1783*, revd., 541-42
Mooney, Chase C., revs., 343-44
Moore, Eva G., Edward Channing's secretary, 270
Moore, John B., cited, 22, 82 n.; quoted, 487
Moore, W. H., judge, 645
Morgan, J. Pierpont, 647, 664, 666
Morgan, Murray, *Skid Road; An Informal Portrait of Seattle*, revd., 369-70
Morison, Elting E. (ed.), *The Letters of Theodore Roosevelt*, revd., 777-79
Morison, Samuel E., cited, 273, 686; (co-

auth.), *The Growth of the American Republic*, 299; *The Maritime History of Massachusetts*, 299; *Admiral of the Ocean Sea*, 301
Mormonism, 453
Morris, D. L., minstrel man, 213
Morris, Joe A. (co-ed.), *The Private Papers of Senator Vandenberg*, revd., 351-52
Morrow, William M., pol., quoted, 421
Morse, Jarvis M., *American Beginnings; Highlights and Sidelights of the Birth of the New World*, revd., 749-50
Morse, John T., Jr., quoted, 714
Morse, Rev. Jedidiah, quoted, 450
Morton, Arthur S., quoted, 73 n.; cited, 707 n.
Morton, Richard L., revs., 103-104, 316-17
Morton, W. L., quoted, 63
"Mose and Jake" plays, 214
Moses, Bernard, *Democracy and Social Growth in America*, cited, 13
Mott, Frank L., revs., 366-67
Mott, Lucretia, diary of, noted, 608
Motter, T. H. Vail (ed.), *Leaders of Men by Woodrow Wilson*, noted, 182
Mount Rushmore, by Gilbert C. Fite, revd., 575-76
Mountains and Molehills, or Recollections of a Burnt Journal, by Frank Marryat, revd., 130
Mowry, George E., 278-79; *The California Progressives*, book on, revd., 350-51
"Mulligan Series," plays by Edward Harrigan, 221-22
Mumford, Lewis, *Art and Technics*, noted, 607
Municipal government, Boulder, Colo., paper on, summarized, 286
Munsell, Joel, quoted, 728
Munsey, Frank, journ., quoted, 491
Munson, J. H., quoted, 434 n.
Murdock, Kenneth, quoted, 446
Murdock, Victor, pol., quoted, 494
Murphy, Joseph, minstrel man, 213
Murray, Joseph, lawyer, 731 n.
Murray, Pauli (comp.), *States' Laws on Race and Color*, noted, 183
Murray, Sir James, letters of, book on, revd., 323
Murray, William Vans, paper on, summarized, 282
Murrell, William, merchant, 624, 631
Muskego (Wis.), diary of Sören Bache, revd., 558-59
Mysteries of Ohio's Underground Railroads, by Wilbur H. Siebert, revd., 336-37
Mystery of Israel's Salvation, by Increase Mather, cited, 446

Naeseth, Henriette C. K., *The Swedish Theatre of Chicago, 1868-1950*, revd., 137-38
Narragansett Pier, book on, revd., 773-74
Nashville, University of, 50-51
National Anti-Trust Conference, 657
National Historical Publications Commission, papers on, summarized, 284
National histories, and historians' preferred works, 294
National Ideals Historically Traced, by Albert B. Hart, cited, 15
"National Issues and Local Politics in Washington Territory, 1857-1861," by Robert W. Johannsen, cited, 416 n.
National Prison Reform Association, 58
National Recovery Administration, records of, noted, 608
National Republicans, 280
National Road, in Ohio, and election of 1863, pp. 34-35, 41
Nationalism, and the northern Great Plains, 63-64
Nativism, and immigration restriction, 1882-1897, note on, 77-88
Natural rights philosophy, and James Schouler, 7; and George Bancroft, 9
Naturalism, in American thought, book on, revd., 803-805
Navigation Acts and the American Revolution, by Oliver M. Dickerson, revd., 104-105
Navin, Thomas R., paper on business history, summarized, 281
Navy, 488-89; book on, revd., 788-89
Nazarenes, and premillennialism, 457
Near East, diplomatic papers, revd., 354-56
Negro, in Ohio, 40; education and Rutherford B. Hayes, 47-50; documentary history of, book on, revd., 111-12; slavery, book on, noted, 180; portrayed in American comedy, 211-12; colleges in Georgia, book on, revd., 360-61; in Washington Territory, 426 n.; attitude of Frederick L. Olmsted toward, 461-66; and progressivism, 498-99; and John Brown, note on, 713-26
Negro and the Communist Party, by Wilson Record, revd., 589
Nelson, William, legal writer, 247
Nettels, Curtis P., 20; English background of the American Revolution, paper on, summarized, 278; *George Washington and American Independence*, revd., 321-22
Nettleton, A. B., railway official, quoted, 68-69
Nevins, Allan, 650; *Ordeal of the Union*, 300; *Grover Cleveland*, 301; *Hamilton Fish*, 301
New Deal, and historical writing, 20-25
New England Emigrant Aid Society, 476

New England Mind, by Perry Miller, 300
New England point of view, and Edward Channing, 271
New Harmony, 453
New Mexico, recollections of a pioneer, book on, noted, 182
New Nation, by Frederic L. Paxson, 674 n.
New Orleans, theater, book on, revd., 117-18; sketches of, book on, revd., 121-22; commercial education in, 634-39
New South, origins of, book on, revd., 141-42
New Spain, book on, revd., 536; and Bernardo de Galvez, book on, revd., 546-48
New Viewpoints in American History, by Arthur M. Schlesinger, 299
New York, 629-30; imprisonment for debt in, 90, 96-98, 100; biog. of William J. Gaynor, revd., 147
New York Central, 659-61
New York Chamber of Commerce, 660
New York *Times*, and Frederick L. Olmsted, 461-66
New York *Tribune*, and northern Great Plains, quoted, 68
Newberry Library, Illinois Central Archives in, guide to, revd., 131-32
Newcomb, Rexford, revs., 764-65
Newnan, J. C., teacher, 636
Newport, book on, revd., 773-74
Newport *Mercury*, and the *Gaspee* affair, quoted, 235, 243 n.
News and These United States, by Edith M. Bartow, revd., 586-87
Newton, Sir Isaac, *Observations upon the Prophecies of Daniel and the Apocalypse*, cited, 444
Nichols, Jeannette P., paper on midwestern isolationism, summarized, 277; revs., 810-12
Nichols, Roy F., *The Disruption of American Democracy*, cited, 421 n.
Niebuhr, Reinhold, *The Irony of American History*, revd., 357-58
Nivert, Frank J. (co-comp.), *Records of the Bureau of the First Assistant Postmaster General, 1789-1942*, noted, 607
Nixon, H. C., paper on industrial revolution in the South, summarized, 277
Noble County, Ohio, and the election of 1863, p. 37
Nonpartisan League, in northern Great Plains, 63, 74
Norfolk, in World War II, book on, revd., 581-82
Norman, Albert, *Operation Overlord; Design and Reality, The Allied Invasion of Western Europe*, revd., 790-91
Norris, George, sen., 483, 487, 493; quoted, 488, 498
Norris, Isaac, merchant, 730 n., 732, 744
North America, by Anthony Trollope, ed. by Donald Smalley and Bradford A. Booth, revd., 344-45
North Carolina, imprisonment for debt in, 99; shipwrecks on coast of, book on, revd., 795
"Northern Great Plains: A Study in Canadian-American Regionalism," by Paul F. Sharp, 61-76
Northern Pacific Railroad, 68-69, 519, 662, 696-97, 700
Northern Railroads in the Civil War, 1861-1865, by Thomas Weber, revd., 770
Northern Securities case, 490
Northwest Mounted Police, Canada, 64, 70
Northwestern University, pictorial history of, noted, 182
Norton, Charles E., journ., quoted, 459, 478
Norwegian-American Studies and Records, Vols. XVI-XVII, ed. by Theodore C. Blegen, revd., 568-69
Nott, Eliphalet, quoted, 451-52
Novel, American, book on, revd., 799-800
Nowell, Charles E., revs., 535
Noyes, John H., reformer, 452
Nursing in Ohio; A History, by James H. Rodabaugh and Mary J. Rodabaugh, revd., 118-19
Nuttall's Travels into the Old Northwest; An Unpublished 1810 Diary, ed. by Jeannette E. Graustein, revd., 329-30

Oberholtzer, Ellis P., *A History of the United States Since the Civil War*, 684-85
Observations in Lower California, by Johann J. Baegert, S.J., trans. and ed. by M. M. Brandenburg and Carl L. Baumann, revd., 318-20
Observations upon the Prophecies of Daniel and the Apocalypse, by Sir Isaac Newton, cited, 444
O'Donoghue, W. E. B., annexationist, 699, 702-703, 707
O'Flannigan and the Fairies, or a Midsummer Night's Dream, not Shakespeare's, 214
Ogilvie, Rev. John, 733 n., 736, 739
Ohio, southern, and the Union, art. on, 29-44; nursing, book on, revd., 118-19; underground railroads in, book on, revd., 336-37
Ohio Valley, and Copperheadism, 30-31
Oklahoma, Indians, book on, revd., 132-33
Old Dominion and Napoleon Bonaparte; A Study in American Opinion, by Joseph I. Shulim, revd., 327-29
Old-Fashioned Revival Hour, 457
Old Northwest, and copperheadism, 29; diary of Thomas Nuttall, revd., 329-30

Old Regime in Canada, by Francis Parkman, cited, 5
Olds, Edson B., rep., 37 n.
Olmsted, Frederick L., art. on, 459-82
Olmsted, John, 469
Olmsted, John H., M.D., 463, 470; quoted, 467-68
Olson, Floyd B., political career, biog. of, revd., 149-50
Olympia, Wash., 419
"Olympia clique," 416
Olympia *Pioneer and Democrat*, quoted, 418, 426, 438
On Freedom's Altar; The Martyr Complex in the Abolition Movement, by Hazel C. Wolf, revd., 765-66
On Good Ground; The Story of the Sisters of St. Joseph in St. Paul, by Sister Helen A. Hurley, revd., 129
Oneida Perfectionists, 452
Open door, and the Anglo-Japanese Alliance, 304
Operation Overlord; Design and Reality, The Allied Invasion of Western Europe, by Albert Norman, revd., 790-91
Oppenheim, Lassa F. L., lawyer, 311
"Opposition of American Businessmen to Social Control During the 'Gilded Age,'" by Chester McA. Destler, 641-72
Oration on the Beauties of Liberty, or the Essential Rights of the Americans, by John Allen, cited, 250-51
Ordeal of the Union, by Allan Nevins, 300
Order of Railway Conductors, and immigration, 85
Oregon, range land of Harney County, book on, revd., 370-71; territory, and slavery, 417 n.
Oriental immigration, 499-500
"Origins of Immigration Restriction, 1882-1897: A Social Analysis," by John Higham, 77-88
Origins of the New South, 1877-1913. A History of the South, Vol. IX, by C. Vann Woodward, revd., 141-42
Orr, Gustavus J., educator, 53
Osborne, Sir Danvers, gov., 729
Osgood, Herbert L., *The American Colonies in the Eighteenth Century*, 299
Osterweis, Rollin G., revs., 773-74
Ostrander, Gilman M., "Emerson, Thoreau, and John Brown," 713-26
Our American Cousin, a play, 229
Owen, Robert, 453
Owsley, Frank L., revs., 587-88
Oxford History of the United States, by Samuel E. Morison, cited, 686
Oxford University, 253-54

Pacific Northwest, and secession crisis, art. on, 415-40
Pacific Outpost; American Strategy in Guam and Micronesia, by Earl S. Pomeroy, revd., 153-54
Pacific Republic, 427-29
Paine, Mrs. Clarence S., "Report of the Secretary-Treasurer for the Year 1951-1952," pp. 390-402
Palmer, I. S., Madison Co., N. Y., sheriff, 101
Pan-Americanism, during the French occupation of Mexico, paper on, summarized, 282
Panic of 1837, and Edward Channing, 264
Panic of 1857, reflected in the *Poor of New York*, a play by Dion Boucicault, 217
Papers and Addresses of William Preston Few, Late President of Duke University, ed. by Robert H. Woody, revd., 365-66
Papers of Henry Bouquet, Vol. II, *The Forbes Expedition*, ed. by S. K. Stevens, Donald H. Kent, and Autumn L. Leonard, revd., 538-40
Papers of Sir William Johnson, by Milton W. Hamilton and Albert B. Corey, revd., 105-106
Parable of the Ten Virgins Opened and Applied, by Thomas Shepard, cited, 445
"Parchment Peace: The Senate Defense of the Four-Power Treaty of the Washington Conference," by J. Chal Vinson, 303-14
Pargellis, Stanley, revs., 571-72
Park Belt, 72
Parker, Isaac C., judge, book on, revd., 774-75
Parker, Theodore, theologian, 6, 723 n.
Parker, Thomas, *The Visions and Prophecies of Daniel Expounded*, cited, 445
Parkman, Francis, 5-6
Parrington, Vernon L., *Main Currents in American Thought*, 19-20, 299
Parton, James, 4; biog. of, revd., 364-65
Partridge, Oliver, 731 n.
Party politics, in the middle period, papers on, summarized, 280
Pascal, Leo (co-comp.), *Records of the National Recovery Administration*, noted, 608
Paschal, George, merchant, 626-27
Patriotism, in historical writing, 4-5
Patronage, in Washington Territory, 416, 439
Patton, James W., revs., 797-98
Paxson, Frederic L., cited, 22-23; art. on, 673-92
Payne, Henry B., sen., 663
Payne-Aldrich tariff, 485, 489-90
Peabody, George, 50
Peabody, George, Fund, 49-51, 53, 57-59
Peabody Normal College, 50-51

Peace Democrats, Ohio, election of 1863, pp. 29-44
Peace in Their Time; The Origins of the Kellogg-Briand Pact, by Robert H. Ferrell, revd., 577-78
Peale, Charles W., book on, revd., 543-44
Pearl, Jack, actor, 227
"Peculiar Legislation," by Samuel C. T. Dodd, quoted, 656-57
Peel, Sir Robert, 460
Pelzer Award essay, 415-40
Pembina, 698
Pendleton, George H., rep., 31-32
Penn, John, lt. gov., 730 n.
Penn, Thomas, Pa. prop., 728
Penn, William, 262
Pennsylvania, politics in, book on, revd., 758-59
Pennsylvania Railroad, 662
People of Louisiana, by T. Lynn Smith and Homer L. Hitt, noted, 183
Perdicaris case, 493
Perkerson, Medora F., *White Columns in Georgia*, revd., 764-65
Perkins, Dexter, revs., 154-55; *Hands Off*, 297; *The American Approach to Foreign Policy*, revd., 791-92
Perkins, George W., banker, 488, 498
Perrigo, Lynn I., paper on municipal government in Boulder, Colo., summarized, 286
Perros, George P. (comp.), *Records of the Senate Committee on Education and Labor: Subcommittee on Wartime Health and Education*, noted, 608
Perry, George S., *The Story of Texas A. and M.*, revd., 363-64
Perry, Matthew, expedition, book on, revd., 336
Perry, Ralph B., 24; *The Thought and Character of William James*, 301
Perry County, Ohio, and the election of 1863, p. 35
"Personal Accounts of the Albany Congress of 1754," ed. by Beverly McAnear, 727-46
Personal liberty laws, 430
Persons, Stow S., 284; (co-ed.), *Socialism and American Life*, revd., 807-808
Peters, Richard, provincial secy., 728, 730 n., 732-34, 739
Peterson, Virgil W., *Barbarians in Our Midst; A History of Chicago Crime and Politics*, revd., 775-77
Petroleum Administration for War, records of, noted, 607
Pettigrew, Richard, sen., 487-88
Phares, Ross, *Cavalier in the Wilderness; The Story of the Explorer and Trader Louis Juchereau de St. Denis*, revd., 536-37
Philippines, fortification of, 308
Phillips, Edward H., paper on the tariff, summarized, 283
Phillips, Sampson & Company, publ., 477
Phillips, Ulrich B., *American Negro Slavery*, noted, 180; and southern Whigs, 280; *Life and Labor in the Old South*, 299
Phillips, Wendell, reformer, cited, 713
Phipps, Lawrence, sen., quoted, 305; cited, 307
Physicians, Detroit, book on, revd., 118
Physiography, paper on, summarized, 278
Pickaway County, Ohio, and the election of 1863, p. 35
Pickering, William, gov. Washington Territory, quoted, 430 n.
Pictorial History of Northwestern University, ed. by Franklin D. Scott *et al.*, noted, 182
Pictorial History of the Confederacy, by Lamont Buchanan, revd., 342-43
Piedmont, textile business in, paper on, summarized, 277
Pierce, Franklin, 420
Pierson, George W., *Yale College, An Educational History, 1871-1921*, Vol. I, *Yale: College and University, 1871-1937*, revd., 361-63
Pigeon, Frederic, merchant, 636
Piles amendment, 489
Pilgrim, James, playwright, 215, 218
Pinchot, Gifford, 487; quoted, 496
Pingree, Hazen S., gov., 486
Pinkett, Harold T. (co-comp.), *Climatological and Hydrological Records of the Weather Bureau*, noted, 607-608; (comp.), *Records of the Office for Agricultural War Relations*, noted, 607
Pitkin, William, colonial gov., 730, 734
Platt, Thomas C., sen., 489
Platt amendment, 488
"Plea for Captain John Brown," by Henry D. Thoreau, cited, 724
Pletcher, David M., paper on American investments in Mexico, summarized, 282-83
Pleuro-Pneumonia Bill, 671
Ploughshares Into Swords: Josiah Gorgas and Confederate Ordnance, by Frank E. Vandiver, revd., 341-42
Pohl, Frederick J., *The Lost Discovery; Uncovering the Track of the Vikings in America*, revd., 747-49
Poindexter, Miles, sen., 493
Policy Sciences; Recent Developments in Scope and Method, ed. by Daniel Lerner and Harold D. Lasswell, revd., 359-60
Political Aspects of Slavery and the Civil War, by George D. Harmon, noted, 608-609

Political biographies, and historians' preferred works, 294
Political Career of Floyd B. Olson, by George H. Mayer, revd., 149-50
"Political Economy of Seventy-Three Million Dollars," by Henry D. Lloyd, cited, 642
Political Theory of John C. Calhoun, by August O. Spain, revd., 124-26
Politics, in Washington Territory, and the secession crisis, art. on, 415-40; in Virginia, book on, revd., 752-53; in revolutionary period, book on, revd., 753-54; in Pennsylvania, book on, revd., 758-59; in Chicago, book on, revd., 775-77
Poll, on historians' preferred works in American history and biography, art. on, 289-302
Pomeroy, Earl S., 285-86; *Pacific Outpost; American Strategy in Guam and Micronesia*, revd., 153-54; "Frederic L. Paxson and His Approach to History," 673-92; revs., 812
Poole, Bernard L., *The Caribbean Commission; Background of Cooperation in the West Indies*, revd., 156-57
Poor of New York, a play, by Dion Boucicault, 217
Popular histories, and historians' perferred works, 293
Populist Revolt, by John D. Hicks, 299
Port Townsend *North-West*, quoted, 427-28
Port Townsend *Register*, quoted, 418, 427
Porter, George H., cited, 31 n., 33 n., 35 n.
Porter, James D., gov., 51 n.
Porter, Kenneth W., *John Jacob Astor*, 301
Portraits and Miniatures by Charles Willson Peale, by Charles C. Sellers, revd., 543-44
Posey, Walter B., revs., 537-38
Postell, W. D., revs., 118
Postmaster General, records of First Assistant, noted, 607
Postmillennialists, 441, 447
Postwar Years, by Frederic L. Paxson, quoted, 676 n.
Pottawatomie Creek, 713-15
"Potter Law," Wis., 646
Pound, Ezra, and *The Cantos*, book on, noted, 609
Powell, J. H., revs., 325-27
Powell, John W., explorer, communications on, 163-64
Powell, Philip W., *Soldiers, Indians and Silver; The Northwest Advance of New Spain, 1550-1600*, revd., 536
Power, Tyrone, actor, 214
Powers, Francis, playwright, 231
Pownall, John, board of trade secy., 240, 242, 255
Pownall, Thomas, colonial gov., 728-29; letter on Albany Congress, 740-46
Practical Treatise on Business, by Edwin T. Freedley, quoted, 632
Pragmatism, in historical writing, 16; papers on the meaning of, summarized, 276-77
Prairie City, by Angie Debo, 297
Pratt, Julius W., revs., 153-54
"Prehistoric Peoples of the Great Plains," by Waldo R. Wedel, summarized, 285
Premillennialists, 441
Presbyterians, and premillennialism, 457
"Present Legal Status of Trusts," by Samuel C. T. Dodd, cited, 655
Present State of Europe Compared with the Antient Prophecies, by Joseph Priestley, quoted, 448-49
Presentism, in historical writing, 3-5, 9, 15-16, 18-19, 21, 26
Presidential address, Mississippi Valley Historical Association, 3-28
Presidential Succession, by Ruth C. Silva, noted, 181
Press, and Douglas MacArthur, book on, noted, 609
Price, Richard, biog. of, noted, 181
Price Decontrol Board, records of, noted, 608
Priestley, Joseph, *The Present State of Europe Compared with the Antient Prophecies*, quoted, 448-49
Pringle, Henry F., *Theodore Roosevelt*, 301
Private John Allen, Gentleman — Statesman — Sage — Prophet, by Claude Gentry, revd., 343-44
Private Life of George Washington, by Francis R. Bellamy, revd., 320-21
Private Papers of Senator Vandenberg, ed. by Arthur H. Vandenberg, Jr., and Joe A. Morris, revd., 351-52
Privy Council, and the *Gaspee* affair, 238-40
Progressive movement, California, book on, revd., 350-51
Progressivism, in historical writing, 16
"Progressivism and Imperialism: The Progressive Movement and American Foreign Policy, 1898-1916," by William E. Leuchtenburg, 483-504
Promise of American Life, by Herbert Croly, quoted, 501-502
Prophetic Faith of Our Fathers; The Historical Development of Prophetic Interpretation, by LeRoy E. Froom, cited, 446 n.
Protestantism, postmillennialism in, 447
Providence, R. I., imprisonment for debt in, 91
Providence *Gazette*, and the *Gaspee* affair, quoted, 236, 244 n., 245

Provincialism, influence on historians' choice of preferred works, 296
Pry, George L., cited, 43 n.
Pugh, George E., sen., 31-32
Pulitzer awards, 297-98
Purcell, John B., archbishop, 43 n.
Puritans, and millenarianism, 444-45
Putnam, George P., publ., 461, 467, 479

QUAKERS, book on, revd., 780-81
Qualey, Carlton C., revs., 129, 558-59
Qu'Appelle Valley, 73

R. E. Lee, by Douglas S. Freeman, 301
Rachal, William M. E. (ed.), *A Tour Through Part of Virginia, in the Summer of 1808. Also, Some Account of the Islands of the Azores*, by Edward Caldwell, noted, 181
Racial laws, in states, compilation of, noted, 183
Rae, John B., paper on Great Northern Railroad, summarized, 276
Rag, Tag and Bobtail; The Story of the Continental Army, by Lynn Montross, 541-42
Railroads, guide to Illinois Central Archives, revd., 131-32; papers on history of, summarized, 275-76; paper on Illinois Central, summarized, 286; and opposition to social control, 659-68; northern, in Civil War, book on, revd., 770
Railroads of the Confederacy, by Robert C. Black, III, revd., 768-69
Ramsey, Alexander, sen., 69, 696-97, 700, 705, 709
Ranching, northern Great Plains, 71-72
Randall, Edwin T., "Imprisonment For Debt in America: Fact and Fiction," 89-102
Randall, James G., *Lincoln*, 297; *The Civil War and Reconstruction*, 300; *Lincoln the President*, 301
Randall, Samuel J., rep. 513
Range, Willard, *The Rise and Progress of Negro Colleges in Georgia, 1865-1949*, revd., 360-61
Range land, Harney County, Oregon, book on, revd., 370-71
Ranney, Rufus P., pol., 38 n.
Ransome, John W., actor, 225
Raoul, W. G., railway official, 664; quoted, 663
Rapp, George, religious leader, 452-53
Rappaport, Armin, revs., 788-89
Raymond, Henry J., journ., 461-63, 474
Reagan Bill, 661
Recent History of the United States, by Frederic L. Paxson, cited, 674 n.
Reciprocity Treaty of 1854, p. 700
Recollections of a Pioneer, 1830-1852: Rocky Mountains, New Mexico, California, ed. by Job F. Dye, noted, 182
Reconstruction politics, in Iowa, paper on, summarized, 279-80; in Illinois, paper on, summarized, 280
Record, Wilson, *The Negro and the Communist Party*, revd., 589
Records of the Bureau of the First Assistant Postmaster General, 1789-1942, comp. by Frank J. Nivert and Arthur Hecht, noted, 607
Records of the Hydrographic Office, comp. by Walter W. Weinstein, noted, 608
Records of the National Recovery Administration, comp. by Homer L. Calkin, Meyer H. Fishbein, and Leo Pascal, noted, 608
Records of the Office for Agricultural War Relations, comp. by Harold T. Pinkett, noted, 607
Records of the Office of Inter-American Affairs, comp. by H. Stephen Helton, noted, 608
Records of the Petroleum Administration for War, comp. by James R. Fuchs and Albert Whimpey, noted, 607
Records of the Price Decontrol Board, comp. by James J. Fleischmann and Victor Gondos, Jr., noted, 608
Records of the Senate Committee on Education and Labor: Subcommittee on Wartime Health and Education, comp. by George P. Perros, noted, 608
Records of the United States Mint at Philadelphia, comp. by Lyle J. Holverstott and Jean McNiece, noted, 608
Records of the War Refugee Board, comp. by Henry T. Vlasek and Ira N. Kellog, Jr., noted, 608
Red River area, 697, 701-706
Redpath, James, journ., 726
Reed, Thomas B., rep., 486
Reform, opposition of American businessmen to social control, art. on, 641-72
Refugees of Revolution; The German Forty-Eighters in America, by Carl Wittke, revd., 563-64
"Refuse Ideas and their Disposal," by Dixon R. Fox, quoted, 452
Regional study, northern Great Plains, art. on, 61-76
Regionalism in America, ed. by Merrill Jensen, revd., 112-15
Reid, Whitelaw, journ., cited, 31 n.
Reilly and the 400, a play by Edward Harrigan, 223
Relativism, in historical writing, 3-4, 18, 21-22, 24, 26
Religion, millenarian tradition in America, art. on, 441-58; and American thought, book on, revd., 803-805
Religion in the Development of American

Culture, 1765-1840, by William W. Sweet, revd., 805-806
Remarks on the Law of Imprisonment for Debt; Showing its Unconstitutionality, and Its Demoralizing Influence on the Community, by Thomas Herttell, quoted, 96-98
"Report of the Secretary-Treasurer for the Year 1951-1952," by Mrs. Clarence S. Paine, 390-402
Republican party, in Ohio election of 1863, p. 30; in Iowa, 279; in Washington Territory, 416, 421-22, 432-39
Revivalism, 451
Reynolds, John, sheriff, Campbell County, Va., quoted, 93-94
Rhode Island, and the *Gaspee* affair, art. on, 233-56
Rhodes, James F., cited, 7-8, 674 n., 678, 684; quoted, 85 n., 684 n.
Richardson, Rupert N., revs., 143-44
Riddle, Donald W., revs., 564-65
Riegel, Robert E., revs., 770
Riel, Louis, 69, 696, 698, 701-704, 706-10
Riel Rebellion, and the United States, art. on, 693-712
Rift in the Democracy, by James C. N. Paul, revd., 335
Riis, Jacob, cited, 80 n.; quoted, 487, 497
Riley, Bennet, maj., military escort on Santa Fe Trail, book on, revd., 331-32
Rim of Christendom, by Herbert E. Bolton, cited, 301
Riparian rights, and northern Great Plains, 76
Ripley, George, reformer, 461, 470
Rischin, Moses, paper on contributions of Jewish trade unions, summarized, 283
Rise and Progress of Negro Colleges in Georgia, 1865-1949, by Willard Range, revd., 360-61
Rise of American Civilization, by Charles A. and Mary R. Beard, cited, 19, 299, 685
Ritchie *v.* The People of Illinois, 665
River planning, paper on, by Samuel P. Hays, 284
Road to Reunion, by Paul H. Buck, 300
Robbins, Roy M., revs., 370-71
Roberts, David, revs., 762-63
Robertson, Agnes, actress, 217
Robertson, William S., *Iturbide of Mexico,* revd., 122-23
Robins, Raymond, pol., 495; quoted, 496-97
Robinson, Henry, maj., 703
Robson, Eric (ed.), *Letters from America, 1773 to 1780; Being the letters of a Scots officer, Sir James Murray, to his home during the War of American Independence,* revd., 323
Rockefeller, John D., 642, 657; quoted, 650
Rocky Mountains, recollections of a pioneer in, book on, noted, 182; British travelers in, paper on, summarized, 286; urban development in, papers on, summarized, 286
Rodabaugh, James H. (co-auth.), *Nursing in Ohio; A History,* revd., 118-19; revs., 323-24
Rodabaugh, Mary J. (co-auth.), *Nursing in Ohio; A History,* revd., 118-19
Rodgers, Andrew D., III, *Erwin Frink Smith; A Story of North American Plant Pathology,* revd., 570-71
Rolette, Joseph (Joe), Jr., promoter, 698
Rolph, William K., revs., 353-54
Roman Catholic Church, 698, 710; and immigration, 78, 83-84
Roosevelt, Franklin D., letters of, revd., 150-53; foreign policy, book on, revd., 580-81; calendar of speeches, noted, 608; book on, revd., 786-87
Roosevelt, Theodore, 308 n., 483, 487, 490-91, 495-96, 498-99, 501, 645, 666; quoted, 491-93, 497; letters of, revd., 777-79
Roosevelt and Daniels, A Friendship in Politics, ed. by Carroll Kilpatrick, revd., 578-79
Roosevelt and Hopkins, by Robert E. Sherwood, 301
Root, Elihu, 491
Roots of American Civilization, by Curtis Nettles, cited, 20
Roper, Laura W., "Frederick Law Olmsted in the 'Literary Republic,'" 459-82
Roppolo, Joseph P., revs., 585-86
Rose, Julian, actor, 228
Roseboom, Eugene H., "Southern Ohio and the Union in 1863," pp. 29-44; revs., 340-41
Rosenman, Samuel I., *Working with Roosevelt,* revd., 786-87
Ross, Earle D., revs., 149-50
Rosser, Thomas L., engineer, 520 n.
Rossman, Kenneth R., *Thomas Mifflin and the Politics of the American Revolution,* revd., 753-54
Royall Young and Company, 625
Ruef, Abraham, labor leader, book on, revd., 349-50
Rush, Benjamin, letters of, revd., 325-27
Rushmore, Mount, book on, revd., 575-76
Russell, Charles T., *The Divine Plan of the Ages,* 455
Russell Brothers, actors, 215
Rutherford, "Judge" Joseph F., 455
"Rutherford B. Hayes, Educator," by Henry L. Swint, 45-60
Rutter, James H., railway official, 659
Rydell, Raymond A., *Cape Horn to the Pacific; The Rise and Decline of an Ocean Highway,* revd., 332-33

SAFETY VALVE THEORY, and immigration restriction, 87
Sage, Leland L., paper on Reconstruction politics in Iowa, summarized, 279-80
Sage, Walter N., revs., 146
St. Denis, Louis Juchereau de, book on, revd., 536-37
St. John, S. T., Canadian pioneer leader, quoted, 62 n.
St. Joseph, Sisters of, in St. Paul, book on, revd., 129
St. Louis, early history, book on, revd., 544-45
St. Michael's, Charleston, 1751-1951, by George W. Williams, revd., 537-38
St. Paul, 694; and the northern Great Plains, 66-69, 71; Sisters of St. Joseph in, book on, revd., 129; Democratic organization in, 508
St. Paul *Advertiser*, quoted, 66-67
St. Paul & Pacific Railroad, 697
Salem, Mass., imprisonment for debt in, 91
Sampson Low, Son & Company, publ., 479
Sanborn, Franklin B., reformer, 723 n., 726; quoted, 718-19, 721
Sandburg, Carl, *Abraham Lincoln, The War Years*, 301
San Francisco, and the Union Labor party, book on, revd., 349-50
Santa Fe Trail, books on, revd., 331-32, 560-61
Saratoga, book on, revd., 773-74
Sarton, George (comp.), *Guide to the History of Science*, noted, 606-607
Saskatchewan, and the northern Great Plains, 67; ranching in, 71
Saskatchewan Valley Land Company, 73
Savannah, book on, revd., 325
Savannah *Republican*, quoted, 463
Savelle, Max, revs., 548-52
Scanlan, "Billy," singer, 216
Schauinger, J. Herman, *Cathedrals in the Wilderness*, revd., 545-46; revs., 766-67
Schevill, Ferdinand, revs., 569-70
Schlegel, Marvin W., *Conscripted City; Norfolk in World War II*, revd., 581-82
Schlesinger, Arthur M., cited, 16, 24; presidential ratings, 289; *New Viewpoints in American History*, 299
Schlesinger, Arthur M., Jr., cited, 20, 685 n.; *The Age of Jackson*, 300
Schmitt, Martin F. (co-auth.), *Trail Driving Days*, revd., 346
Schmitz, Joseph W., *Society of Mary in Texas*, noted, 182
Scholar in Action; Edwin F. Gay, by Herbert Heaton, revd., 779-80
Scholes, Walter V., paper on liberalism in the Reform period of Mexico, summarized, 282; revs., 536
Schouler, James, cited, 6-9
Schurz, Carl, 486
Schuyler, Philip, col., 733
Science, evolution and historical writing, 10-14; guide to history of, noted, 606-607
Science and Religion in American Thought; The Impact of Naturalism, by Edward A. White, revd., 803-805
Scioto County, Ohio, and the election of 1863, p. 36
Scofield, Shurmer & Teagle, 643
Scott, Alfred H., annexationist, 706, 708-709
Scott, Franklin D. (gen. ed.), *A Pictorial History of Northwestern University*, noted, 182
Scott, Thomas, Ontario Orangeman, 710 n.
Scripps, John L., quoted, 66
Sears, Barnas, theologian, 50-51, 57
Sears, Louis M., revs., 320-21
Seattle, book on, revd., 369-70
Sebba, Gregor (ed.), *Georgia Studies*, by Robert P. Brooks, noted, 606
"Secession Crisis and the Frontier: Washington Territory, 1860-1861," by Robert W. Johannsen, 415-40
Sectional conflicts, Edward Channing on, 267; in Washington Territory, art. on, 415-40
Sedition acts, book on, revd., 548-52
Seeing the Elephant; Letters of R. R. Taylor, Forty-Niner, ed. by John W. Caughey, revd., 333
Sellers, Charles C., *Portraits and Miniatures by Charles Willson Peale*, revd., 543-44
Sellers, Charles G., Jr., "Who Were the Southern Whigs?", summarized, 280-81
Sellers, James L., 280
Senate, defense of the Four-Power Treaty of the Washington Conference, note on, 303-14
Sessions, Darius, dep. gov. of R. I., 243 n.; quoted, 236-37
Seventh-Day Adventist, 455
Seymour, Horatio, 507
Shaker Society, 452
Shandy Maguire, a play by James Pilgrim, 218
Shannon, David, 283
Shannon, Fred A., 279
Sharp, Paul F., "The Northern Great Plains: A Study in Canadian-American Regionalism," 61-76
Shaughraun, a play by Dion Boucicault, 217
Shaw, Francis G., 477
Shaw, John B., quoted, 742 n.
Shaw, Thomas, 73
Shay's Rebellion, historians' treatment of, 4; and imprisonment for debt, 94
Shepard, Thomas, *The Parable of the Ten Virgins Opened and Applied*, cited, 445

Sherburne, Henry, Jr., 730 n., 738
Sheridan, Philip H., gen., 526
Sherman Anti-Trust Act, 648-50, 655, 665
Sherrod, Robert, *History of Marine Corps Aviation in World War II*, revd., 789-90
Sherwood, Joseph, 238
Sherwood, Robert E., *Roosevelt and Hopkins*, 301
Shideler, James H., revs., 349-50
Shiels, W. Eugene, S.J., 282
Shipwrecks, book on, revd., 795
Shirley, William, gov., 727
Short Chronology of American History, 1492-1950, by Irving S. and Nell W. Kull, noted, 183
Shortridge, Samuel, sen., quoted, 305
Shryock, Richard H., 287
Shugg, Roger W., revs., 141-42
Shulim, Joseph I., *The Old Dominion and Napoleon Bonaparte; A Study in American Opinion*, revd., 327-29
Siberian Fiasco, by Clarence A. Manning, noted, 607
Siebert, Wilbur H., *The Mysteries of Ohio's Underground Railroads*, revd., 336-37
Sievers, Harry J., *Benjamin Harrison, Hoosier Warrior, 1833-1865*, revd., 766-67
Signs of the Times, cited, 454
Silva, Ruth C., *Presidential Succession*, noted, 181
Silver, in New Spain, book on, revd., 536
Simkins, Francis B., revs., 572-73
Simmons, E. C., merchant, 664
Simms, Henry H., revs., 342-43
Simpson, Albert F., revs., 789-90
Singmaster, Elsie, auth., 223
Sioux Indians, 532-34
Sisk, Glenn N., paper on Alabama agriculture, summarized, 283-84
Sisters of St. Joseph, in St. Paul, book on, revd., 129
Sitterson, J. Carlyle, revs., 578-79
Sitting Bull, 519 n.
Six Nations, doc. on Albany Congress, 727-46
Skid Road; An Informal Portrait of Seattle, by Murray Morgan, revd., 369-70
Slater, John F., Fund, 49-60
Slater, William A., 52, 54 n.
Slavery, attitude toward, in Washington Territory, 416-17, 428, 432, 437; and Frederick L. Olmsted, 461-67; and the Civil War, book on, noted, 608-609
Slavery and "The Woman Question," by Lucretia Mott, ed. by Frederick B. Tolles, noted, 608
Slavic characters, absence of, on American stage, 232
Smalley, Donald (co-ed.), *North America*, by Anthony Trollope, revd., 344-45
Smelser, Marshall, paper on cold war with France, 282
Smillie, Wilson G. (co-auth.), *The History of American Epidemiology*, revd., 798-99
Smith, Charles E., revs., 158-59
Smith, Donald A., Canadian official, 706
Smith, Erwin F., biog. of, revd., 570-71
Smith, Ethan, *Dissertation on the Prophecies relative to Antichrist and the Last Times*, quoted, 450-51
Smith, Gerrit, reformer, 723 n.
Smith, Henry N., revs., 542-43
Smith, James M., paper on criminal law and the critics of John Adams' administration, summarized, 282
Smith, Joseph, 453
Smith, Joseph P., cited, 32 n.
Smith, Mortimer, *William Jay Gaynor, Mayor of New York*, revd., 147
Smith, Shirley W., *Harry Burns Hutchins and the University of Michigan*, revd., 147-48
Smith, T. Lynn (co-auth.), *The People of Louisiana*, noted, 183
Smith, Theodore C., quoted, 682
Smith, W. E., revs., 364-65
Smith, William, sen., quoted, 95, 98
Smith, William, Sr., lawyer, 731 n., 734
Smoky Mountain Country, by North Callahan, revd., 797-98
Smyth, Frederick, commissioner in the *Gaspee* investigation, quoted, 250
Smyth *v.* Ames, 665
Social control, opposition of American businessmen to, in "Gilded Age," art. on, 641-72
Social Darwinism, 647-50
Social Ferment in Vermont, by David M. Ludlum, cited, 454-55
Social history, origins of immigration restriction, note on, 77-88; New Orleans, book on, revd., 121-22; book on, revd., 133-35
Social Relations in Our Southern States, by Daniel R. Hundley, quoted, 475-76
Social sciences, applied, book on, revd., 359-60
Socialism and American Life, ed. by Donald D. Egbert and Stow Persons, revd., 807-808
Society and Thought in Modern America: A Social and Intellectual History of the American People from 1865, by Harvey Wish, revd., 133-35
Society of Equity, 74
Society of Friends, biog. of Walter C. Woodward, revd., 780-81
Society of Mary in Texas, by Joseph W. Schmitz, noted, 182
Sociology, biog. of Henry C. Carey, revd., 126-27

Sod-House Frontier, by Everett N. Dick, 300
Soils, paper on, summarized, 278
Soldier vote, Ohio election of 1863, pp. 33-34
Soldiers, Indians and Silver; The Northward Advance of New Spain, 1550-1600, by Philip W. Powell, revd., 536
Sons of the American Revolution, and immigration, 86
Sothern, Edward A., actor, 229
South, trade with Ohio, 40; origins of the New, book on, revd., 141-42; industrial revolution in, papers on, summarized, 277-78; and Frederick L. Olmsted, art. on, 459-82; book on, revd., 587-88; mercantile education in ante-bellum, art. on, 623-40
South Atlantic Quarterly, history of, revd., 366-67
South Carolina, Commons House of Assembly journal, revd., 317-18
South Dakota Historical Collections and Report, comp. by the State Historical Society, Vol. XXV, 1950, revd., 115-16
South Western Stock Association, 71
Southern Commercial College, 639
Southern education, Rutherford B. Hayes on, 47-49
Southern Literary Messenger, quoted, 472
"Southern Ohio and the Union in 1863," by Eugene H. Roseboom, 29-44
Southwest, frontier defense, book on, revd., 561-62
Southwick, Solomon, publ., 244
Spain, August O., *The Political Theory of John C. Calhoun*, revd., 124-26
Spanish-American War, 497
Spencer, Herbert, 649
Spenser, Seldon P., sen., quoted, 311
Spooner, John C., sen., 663 n.
Sproat, Gilbert M., Indian commissioner, quoted, 64
Squatter Sovereignty, a play by Edward Harrigan, 222
Stafford, John, *The Literary Criticism of "Young America,"* noted, 607
Stampp, Kenneth M., cited, 21, 280, 415 n.; revs., 802-803
Standard Oil Co., 643-44, 646, 648-59
Stanford, Leland, sen., 663 n.; quoted, 661
Stanley, David S., gen., 525-26, 529-30, 533
Stanton, Elizabeth C., quoted, 486
Staples, William R., hist., quoted, 237
Starr, Chester G., Jr., revs., 576-77
State of Ohio *v.* Standard Oil Company, cited, 654
States' Laws on Race and Color, comp. by Pauli Murray, noted, 183
Statistics, use of, and Edward Channing, 268
Steamboats in the Timber, by Ruby E. Hult, revd., 346-47
Stearns, George L., Free-Soiler, 723 n.
Stearns, Raymond P., revs., 105-106
Steinberger, Justus, steamship agent, 419 n.
Stephens, I. K., *The Hermit Philosopher of Liendo*, revd., 143-44
Stephenson, Wendell H., 16
Steps in the Development of American Democracy, by Andrew C. McLaughlin, cited, 17-18
Sterne, Simon, reformer, 642
Stevens, Arent, interpreter, 731 n.
Stevens, Isaac I., gov., 419-21, 423-24, 431, 439; quoted, 425, 431 n., 433, 435
Stevens, S. K. (co-ed.), *The Papers of Henry Bouquet*, Vol. II, *The Forbes Expedition*, revd., 538-40
Stewart, John A., banker, 52-53
Stewart, Kenneth (co-auth.), *Makers of Modern Journalism*, revd., 801-802
Stick, David, *Graveyard of the Atlantic; Shipwrecks on the North Carolina Coast*, revd., 795
Stickney, Alpheus B., 666-67; quoted, 643
Still, Bayrd, revs., 365-66
Stipp, John L., cited, 31 n.
Storekeepers, training of, in ante-bellum South, art. on, 623-40
Storey, William W., sculptor, 474
Storm Over Savannah; The Story of Count d'Estaing and the Siege of the Town in 1779, by Alexander A. Lawrence, revd., 325
Story, Joseph, justice, 251
Story of Texas A. and M., by George S. Perry, revd., 363-64
Stout, Lansing, rep., 419 n.
Stover, John F., paper on Illinois Central Railroad, summarized, 286
Stowe, Harriet B., 461, 468, 471
Straight, Willard D., diplomat, 490
Strait, Horace B., rep., 507
Straus, Oscar, lawyer, 487
Strikes, and immigration restriction, 84-85
Strong, Josiah, reformer, 80
Strong, William, justice, 52
"Struggle for Democracy in the United States," by William E. Dodd, cited, 17
Stuart, Alexander H. H., rep., 50
Sturgis, Samuel D., gen., 524
Stutsman, Enos, col., 698, 701-703
Sumner, Charles, 715, 721; quoted, 481
Sumner, Helen L., quoted, 91
Sumner, William G., and American conservatism, book on, revd., 348-49; cited, 651
Supreme Court, and immigration restriction, 79; and due process of law, book on, noted, 181-82
Supreme Court in United States History, by Charles Warren, 299

Sutton, Robert M., revs., *556-57*
Swedish characters, on the American stage, 230
Swedish Theatre of Chicago, 1868-1950, by Henriette C. K. Naeseth, revd., 137-38
Sweet, William W., *Religion in the Development of American Culture, 1765-1840*, revd., 805-806
Swint, Henry L., "Rutherford B. Hayes, Educator," 45-60
Sydnor, Charles S., *Gentlemen Freeholders; Political Practices in Washington's Virginia*, revd., 752-53
Sztacho, Adolf (co-ed.), *International Bibliography of Historical Sciences*, revd., 367-68
Sztachova, Jirina (co-ed.), *International Bibliography of Historical Sciences*, revd., 367-68

Taft, William H., 490-92, 499
Tanner, John R., gov., 669
Tansill, Charles C., *Back Door to War; The Roosevelt Foreign Policy, 1933-1941*, revd., 580-81
Tariff, paper on, by Edward H. Phillips, summarized, 283
Tasker, Benjamin, Jr., 728, 732, 734
Taylor, Bayard, journ., 461
Taylor, George R., *The Economic History of the United States*, Vol. IV, *The Transportation Revolution, 1815-1860*, revd., 119-21; revs., 332-33
Taylor, James W., consular officer, quoted, 67-68, 701; cited, 69, 699-700 n.
Taylor, R. R., letters of, revd., 333
Taylor, Tom, journ., 474
Taylor, William, merchant, 624
Tea Act, 247
Tebbel, John (co-auth.), *Makers of Modern Journalism*, revd., 801-802
Technics, and art, book on, noted, 607
Teeters, Negley K., cited, 91
Teller, Henry M., sen., 488, 663 n.
Temperance crusade, 451; on the stage, 214
"Ten Years of the Standard Oil Trust," by Samuel C. T. Dodd, cited, 651
tenBroek, Jacobus, *The Antislavery Origins of the Fourteenth Amendment*, revd., 136-37
Territorial Papers of the United States, Vol. XVIII, *The Territory of Alabama, 1817-1819*, comp. and ed. by Clarence E. Carter, revd., 761-62
Terry, Alfred H., gen., *524, 526, 528*
Texas, folklore, book on, noted, 182; Society of Mary in, book on, noted, 182; and Frederick L. Olmsted, 466
Texas A. and M., history of, revd., 363-64
Texas and Pacific Railroad, 661; paper on, summarized, 276
Texas Revolution, by William C. Binkley, revd., *557*
Texas Santa Fe Trail, by H. Bailey Carroll, revd., 560-61
Textbooks, scientific subjects, paper on, summarized, 287
Textile business, Piedmont area, paper on, summarized, 277
Thackeray, William M., 474
Thatcher, Peter O., judge, 100
Theater, New Orleans, book on, revd., 117-18; Swedish, in Chicago, book on, revd., 137-38; immigrant theme in the, art. on, 211-32; history of, revd., *585-86*
Theodore Roosevelt, by Henry F. Pringle, 301
These Also Believe, by Charles S. Braden, cited, 456 n.
They Fought With What They Had; The Story of the Army Air Forces in the Southwest Pacific, 1941-1942, by Walter D. Edmonds, revd., 160-61
Third Plenary Council of Roman Catholic Church, and immigration, 83
Thomas, Benjamin P., *Abraham Lincoln; A Biography*, revd., 564-65.
Thomas, L. G., quoted, 72
Thomas Jefferson, by Gilbert Chinard, 301
Thomas Mifflin and the Politics of the American Revolution, by Kenneth R. Rossman, revd., *753-54*
Thompson, David, journals of, revd., *553-54*
Thompson, William, capt., *522*
Thoreau, by Henry S. Canby, cited, 716 n.
Thoreau, Henry D., and John Brown, note on, 713-26
Thornton, Edward, diplomat, quoted, 709; cited, 710
Thorp, James, paper on soils and physiography, summarized, 278
Thorstein Veblen and His America, by Joseph Dorfman, 301
Thought and Character of William James, by Ralph B. Perry, 301
Three Hundred Years American; The Epic of A Family from seventeenth-century New England to twentieth-century Midwest, by Alice F. and Bettina Jackson, revd., 109-10
"Thurlow Weed's Network: Whig Party Organization in 1840," by Robert G. Gunderson, summarized, 281
Thurman, Allen G., pol., 31 n.
Tidewater Petroleum Company, 658
Tilden, Samuel J., 507-508
Tilford, Joseph G., maj., 521
Tilton, James, surveyor gen., Washington Territory, 417
Timayenis, Telemachus T., auth., cited, 86 n.
Tokugawa, Prince Iyesato, quoted, 307

Tolles, Frederick B. (ed.), *Slavery and "The Woman Question,"* by Lucretia Mott, noted, 608; revs., 780-81
Tom Watson, Agrarian Rebel, by C. Vann Woodward, 301
Toole, K. Ross, "Butte: A Phase in the Westward Movement of Capital," summarized, 286
Top, Franklin H. (ed.), *The History of American Epidemiology,* revd., 798-99
Torchbearer of Freedom; The Influence of Richard Price on Eighteenth Century Thought, by Carl B. Cone, noted, 181
Totalitarianism, influence on American historical writing, 21-22
Tour Through Part of Virginia, in the Summer of 1808. Also, Some Account of the Islands of the Azores, by Edward Caldwell, ed. by William M. E. Rachal, noted, 181
Townshend Acts, 233
Trade unions, contributions of Jewish, paper on, summarized, 283
Trail Driving Days, by Dee Brown and Martin F. Schmitt, revd., 346
Transappalachia, Edward Channing on, 267
Transatlantic Exchanges; Cross-Currents of Anglo-American Opinion in the Nineteenth Century, comp. by Yvonne ffrench, revd., 800-801
Transcendentalists, and John Brown, 717
Transportation Revolution, 1815-1860. The Economic History of the United States, Vol. IV, by George R. Taylor, revd., 119-21
Traxler, Ralph N., paper on Texas and Pacific Railroad, summarized, 276
Trefousse, H. L., *Germany and American Neutrality, 1939-1941,* revd., 157-58
Trescott, Samuel C., pvt., quoted, 34
Trewartha, Glenn T., paper on climate, summarized, 278
Trexler, H. A., revs., 363-64
Trip to Chinatown, a play by Charles H. Hoyt, 231
Trollope, Anthony, *North America,* ed. by Donald Smalley and Bradford A. Booth, revd., 344-45
Troop training and armament manufacture, relative priority of, paper on, summarized, 279
Troy, N. Y., imprisonment for debt in, 100
Trust: Its Book, by Charles R. Flint, Jr., cited, 654
Trusts, by Samuel C. T. Dodd, cited, 654
Trusts, opposition to social control, art. on, 641-72
Tucker, George, *The History of the United States, From Their Colonization to the End of the Twenty-Sixth Congress, in 1841,* quoted, 6 n.
Tucker, John R., 664
Tuley, M. F., judge, 668
Turner, Charles W., paper on Chesapeake and Ohio railroad, summarized, 276
Turner, Frederick J., cited, 10-13, 25, 27, 257, 673, 686-87; contrasted with Edward Channing, 267; as a teacher, paper on, summarized, 287-88; *The Frontier in American History,* 299
Turner, Robert K. (co-ed.), *Documents on American Foreign Relations,* Vol. XII, *January 1-December 31, 1950,* revd., 356-57
Tuveson, Ernest L., *Millennium and Utopia: A Study in the Background of the Idea of Progress,* cited, 444 n.
Two Bears, 526
Two-Party South?, by Alexander Heard, revd., 587-88
Tyler, Alice F., *Freedom's Ferment,* cited, 20
Tyler, John, "The Merchant of the Past and the Present," cited, 633-34

Under the Gaslight, a play by Augustin Daly, 230
Underground railroad, paper on, summarized, 286; book on, revd., 336-37
Underwood, Oscar W., sen., quoted, 306-307, 308, 310, 312-13
Union army, foreigners in, book on, revd., 339-40; medical history of, book on, revd., 565-66
Union Labor party, and San Francisco, book on, revd., 349-50
Union Pacific Railroad, 65, 662
Union navy, foreigners in, book on, revd., 339-40
Union soldiers, book on, revd., 340-41
Unionist sentiment, 261, 499; in Ohio in 1863, pp. 29-44; in Washington Territory, 429-30
United Society of Believers in Christ's Second Appearing, 452
United States, and the Riel Rebellion, art. on, 693-712
United States and the Far East, 1945-1951, by Harold M. Vinacke, revd., 357
United States Army in the World War, 1917-1919, Vols. V-X, ed. by Historical Division, Department of the Army, revd., 576-77
United States Displaced Persons Commission, report of, revd., 793-94
United States Mint, records of, noted, 608
United States Pipe Line, 658-59
United States Since 1865, by Louis M. Hacker and Benjamin B. Kendrick, 683 n.
Universal education, and Rutherford B. Hayes, 45-47

University press publications, and historians' preferred works, 293
"Unseen Hand," and the writings of Edward Channing, 259
Unsworth, J. H., song writer, 213
Untermann, Ernest, pol., quoted, 499
Up the Missouri with Audubon; The Journal of Edward Harris, ed. by John F. McDermott, revd., 127-28
Upper Missouri, book on, revd., 562
Uprooted; The Epic Story of the Great Migrations that Made the American People, by Oscar Handlin, revd., 584-85
Upton, Emory, gen., and military thought, paper on, summarized, 279
Urban development, Rocky Mountain area, papers on, summarized, 286
Urban reform, and immigration restriction, 78-80
Utilitarianism, in historical writing, 4
Utopian communities, book on, revd., 333-34; and millenarianism, 451

Vallandigham, Clement L., 31-44
Valley Forge; The Making of an Army, by Alfred H. Bill, revd., 754-55
Van Alstyne, Richard W., 277; *American Crisis Diplomacy, The Quest for Collective Security, 1918-1952*, revd., 155-56; revs., 357
Van Buren, Martin, 638
Vandenberg, Arthur S., papers of, revd., 351-52
Vandenberg, Arthur S., Jr. (co-ed.), *The Private Papers of Senator Vandenberg*, revd., 351-52
Vanderbilt, Cornelius, 647
Vanderbilt, William H., 661, 667; quoted, 659
Vandiver, Frank E., *Ploughshares Into Swords: Josiah Gorgas and Confederate Ordnance*, revd., 341-42
Van Doren, Carl, *Benjamin Franklin*, 301
Van Sweringen brothers, 276
Van Wyck, Charles H., sen., 663
Varnum, Charles A., lt., 534
Venerable, W. A. D., Negro leader, 499
Vest Committee, 644, 671
Vetake, Henry, prof., 633 n.
Victory with the Help of France, Vol. V, *George Washington; A Biography*, by Douglas S. Freeman, revd., 755-57
Vikings, book on, revd., 747-49
Vilas, William F., postmaster gen., quoted, 505 n., 510-14
Vinacke, Harold M., *United States and the Far East, 1945-1951*, revd., 357
Vinson, J. Chal, "The Parchment Peace: The Senate Defense of the Four-Power Treaty of the Washington Conference," 303-14; revs., 356-57
Virginia, imprisonment for debt in, 93; travel account, noted, 181; colonial, book on, revd., 316-17; and Napoleon Bonaparte, book on, revd., 327-29; politics in, book on, revd., 752-53
Virginia Military Tract, Ohio, and the election of 1863, pp. 38-39
Virginia Venturer, A Historical Biography of William Claiborne, 1600-1677; The Story of The Merchant Venturers who Founded Virginia, and The War in the Chesapeake, by Nathaniel C. Hale, revd., 103-104
Visions and Prophecies of Daniel Expounded, by Thomas Parker, cited, 445
Vlasek, Henry T. (co-comp.), *Records of the War Refugee Board*, noted, 608
Volwiler, A. T., revs., 538-40
von Holst, Hermann E., 257
von Ranke, Leopold, cited, 10

Wachman, Marvin, revs., 133-35
Wade, Benjamin F., sen., 430
Wagenknecht, Edward, *Cavalcade of the American Novel; From the Birth of the Nation to the Middle of the Twentieth Century*, revd., 799-800
Waite, Morrison R., chief justice, 50-53
Walker, Beverly B., merchant apprentice, 625
Walks and Talks of an American Farmer in England, by Frederick L. Olmsted, quoted, 460 n.; cited, 460-61
Wall, Bennett H., 282
Wall, Joseph F., revs., 801-802
Wall Street, book on, revd., 583-84
Wallace, Ernest (co-auth.), *The Comanches: Lords of the South Plains*, noted, 607
Wallace, George D., lt., 523, 529, 534
Wallace, William H., territorial gov., 437
Walter C. Woodward, Friend on the Frontier; A Biography, by Elizabeth H. Emerson, revd., 780-81
Wanton, Joseph, gov., and the *Gaspee* affair, 234, 237-38, 250; quoted 237, 242
"War Against Wealth," by Samuel C. T. Dodd, cited, 653
War department, and conscription, paper on, summarized, 279
War Refugee Board, records of, noted, 608
Warfield, David, actor, 228
Warner, Donald F., "Drang Nach Norden: The United States and the Riel Rebellion," 693-712
Warner, Landon, revs., 775-77
Warren, Charles, *The Supreme Court in United States History*, 299
Warren, Harris G., revs., 122-23
Warren, Robert P., cited, 721; quoted, 722
Washburn, William D., pol., 510
Washington, George, biogs. of, revd., 107-109, 320-21; and American independ-

ence, book on, revd., 321-22; in American literature, book on, revd., 542-43; and Ft. Necessity, 744
Washington Conference, Senate defense of the Four-Power Treaty, note on, 303-14
Washington Territory, and the secession crisis, art. on, 415-40
"Watchers for the Second Coming: The Millenarian Tradition in America," by Ira V. Brown, 441-58
Watchtower, quoted, 456
Watson, Richard L., Jr., revs., 160-61
Watterson, Henry, biog. of, revd., 140-41
Watts, Harold H., *Ezra Pound and The Cantos*, noted, 609
We Who Built America, by Carl F. Wittke, 300
Wealth, distribution of, and Rutherford B. Hayes, 46-47
Wealth Against Commonwealth, by Henry D. Lloyd, cited, 653
Weare, Meshech, colonial pol., 730 n., 735
Weather Bureau, records of, noted, 607-608
Weaver, Blanche H. C., revs., 796-97
Webb, Walter P., *The Great Plains*, 299, 688
Weber, Joseph, actor, 225-26
Wedel, Waldo R., "Prehistoric Peoples of the Great Plains," summarized, 285
Weed, Thurlow, paper on, summarized, 281
Weems, Mason L., 269
Weinstein, Walter W. (comp.), *Records of the Hydrographic Office*, noted, 608
Weisenburger, Francis P., cited, 31 n., 35 n.; revs., 568-69
Weiser, Johann C., Indian agent, 743
Welch, Ben, actor, 228
Welch, Joe, actor, 228
Welcker, Charles F., merchant, 625 n.
Welles, Samuel, 731 n., 732, 736
Wells, Merle W., "The Creation of the Territory of Idaho," cited, 424 n.
Wendell, Jacob, merchant, 730
Wendell Willkie, 1892-1944, by Mary E. Dillon, revd., 785-86
Wentworth, Benning, gov., 730, 737
Wentworth, E. N., 283
Wentworth, John, paper on, summarized, 286
Wertenbaker, Thomas J., 16
West Indies, Caribbean Commission, book on, revd., 156-57
Western Americana, manuscripts collection, catalogue of, revd., 812
Western history, books on, revd., 346-47; and Frederic L. Paxson, 686-87
Western Reserve, election of 1863, pp. 36, 37, 41
Western Union, 648
"What the Social Classes Owe to Each Other," by William G. Sumner, cited, 651
Wheelock, Joseph A., editor, 697; quoted, 708-10
Whig party, 280-81; in Washington Territory, 416
Whimpey, Albert (co-comp.), *Records of the Petroleum Administration for War*, noted, 607
Whipple, Henry B., bishop, 51 n.
Whisky Trust, 655
Whitby, Daniel, *Paraphrase and Commentary on the New Testament*, cited, 447-48
White, Edward A., *Science and Religion in American Thought; The Impact of Naturalism*, revd., 803-805; revs., 805-806
White, M. Catherine (ed.), *David Thompson's Journals Relating to Montana and Adjacent Regions, 1808-1812*, revd., 553-54
White, Maunsel, cotton factor, 635
White, William A., 498; *Autobiography*, 301; quoted, 486, 500 n.
White Columns in Georgia, by Medora F. Perkerson, revd., 764-65
White House Profile; A Social History of the White House, Its Occupants and Its Festivities, by Bess Furman, revd., 368-69
Whitehill, Walter M. (co-auth.), *Fleet Admiral King; A Naval Record*, revd., 788-89
Whiteside, William B., *The Boston Y.M.C.A. and Community Need; A Century's Evolution, 1851-1951*, revd., 130-31
Whitlock, Brand, diplomat, quoted, 489-90
Whittier, John G., 471
"Who Were the Southern Whigs?" by Charles G. Sellers, Jr., summarized, 280-81
Whoop-up Trail, 70
Wibird, Richard, colonial pol., 730 n., 738
Wigglesworth, Michael, *The Day of Doom*, quoted, 447
Wild Wheel, by Garet Garrett, revd., 782
Wiley, Bell I., *The Life of Johnny Reb*, noted, 180; *The Life of Billy Yank, The Common Soldier of the Union*, revd., 340-41
William Jay Gaynor, Mayor of New York, by Mortimer Smith, revd., 147
Williams, Barney, actor, 215-16, 218-19
Williams, Elisha, clergyman, 730 n., 732, 733 n.
Williams, George W., *St. Michael's, Charleston, 1751-1951*, revd., 537-38
Williams, Gus, actor, 224-25

Williams, T. Harry, 286; *Lincoln and His Generals*, revd., 337-39
Williamson, Gustavus G., paper on textile business in the Piedmont, summarized, 277
Williamson, Harold F., 282
Willis, Frank, sen., quoted, 311-12
Willison, George F., *Behold Virginia: The Fifth Crown. Being the Trials, Adventures & Disasters of the First Families of Virginia, the rise of the Grandees, & the eventual Triumph of the Common & Uncommon Sort in the Revolution*, 316-17
Willkie, Wendell, biog. of, revd., 785-86
Wills, William H., journ., 474
Wilson, Lizzie, actress, 225
Wilson, Russell, Saskatoon mayor, quoted, 74 n.
Wilson, Samuel, Jr. (ed.), *Impressions Respecting New Orleans. Diary & Sketches, 1818-1820*, by Benjamin H. B. Latrobe, revd., 121-22
Wilson, Woodrow, 485, 492-93, 496, 499-500, 679, 690 n.; as historian, 8-9; *Leaders of Men*, noted, 182
Wiltse, Charles M., *John C. Calhoun*, 301
Winnipeg, and the northern Great Plains, 71; and the Riel Rebellion, 698, 709
Winship, George P., quoted, 270
Winslow, C.-E. A. (co-auth.), *The History of American Epidemiology*, revd., 798-99
Winsor, Justin, influence on Edward Channing, 269
Winther, Oscar O., revs., 574-75
Winthrop, Robert C., sen., 50, 57
Wish, Harvey, 283; revs., 111-12; *Society and Thought in America*, Vol. II, *Society and Thought in Modern America: A Social and Intellectual History of the American People from 1865*, revd., 133-35
Withington, Mary C. (comp.), *A Catalogue of Manuscripts in the Collection of Western Americana Founded by William Roberston Coe, Yale University Library*, revd., 812
Wittke, Carl F., cited, 23-25, 31 n.; revs., 138-39; "The Immigrant Theme on the American Stage," 211-32; *We Who Built America*, 300; *Refugees of Revolution; The German Forty-Eighters in America*, revd., 563-64
Wolcott, Roger, Jr., 730 n.
Wolcott, Roger, Sr., colonial gov., 730 n.
Wolf, Hazel C., *On Freedom's Altar; The Martyr Complex in the Abolition Movement*, revd., 765-66
Women Camp Followers of the American Revolution, by Walter H. Blumenthal, revd., 540-41
Wood, Sir W. P., solicitor gen., 254
Wood, Virginia, *Due Process of Law, 1932-1949; The Supreme Court's Use of A Constitutional Tool*, noted, 181-82
Woodbury, Levi, sen., quoted, 99
Woodress, James L., Jr., *Howells & Italy*, revd., 770-72
Woodward, C. Vann, *A History of the South, 1877-1913*, Vol. IX, *Origins of the New South*, revd., 141-42; *Tom Watson, Agrarian Rebel*, 301
Woodward, Walter C., biog. of, 780-81
Woody, Robert H. (ed.), *The Papers and Addresses of William Preston Few, Late President of Duke University*, revd., 365-66
Woolsey, Theodore D., educator, 51-52
Worcester, Donald E. (trans. and ed.), *Instructions for Governing the Interior Provinces of New Spain, 1786*, by Bernardo de Galvez, revd., 546-48
Working with Roosevelt, by Samuel I. Rosenman, revd., 786-87
Works, John D., sen., 492-93
World peace, and the Washington Conference, 303
World War I, paper on midwestern isolationism in, summarized, 277; books on, revd., 576-77
World War II, books on, revd., 157-58, 789-91; Army Air Forces in, books on, revd., 158-61; cross-channel attack, book on, revd., 161-62; paper on midwestern isolation in, summarized, 277; Mennonite Church in, book on, revd., 353; Norfolk in, book on, revd., 581-82
Worley, Ted R., revs., 774-75
Wormeley, Katherine P., auth., 461
Worthington, John, col., 730 n., 731 n., 734
Wraxall, Peter, Indian agent, 731 n., 734
Wright, Muriel H., *A Guide to the Indian Tribes of Oklahoma*, revd., 132-33
Wright, Quincy, pol. sci., cited, 22
Writings on American History, published by National Historical Publications Commission, cited, 284
Wroth, Lawrence C., essays honoring, revd., 571-72
Wyllie, Irvin G., revs., 126-27
Wyman, Walker D., revs., 347-48; (ed.), *California Emigrant Letters*, revd., 763-64

Xenophobia, 84

Y.M.C.A., in Boston, book on, revd., 130-31
Yale College, An Educational History, 1871-1921, Vol. I, *Yale: College and University, 1871-1937*, by George W. Pierson, revd., 361-63
Yates, George W., capt., 523, 531, 534

Yates, Mrs. George W., 521-22
Yeamans, Annie, actress, 222-23
Yeamans, Jennie, actress, 222
Yellowstone River, expedition to, doc. on, 519-34
Yerkes, Charles T., grain speculator, 669-70
Young, James H., revs., 765-66
Young, Otis E., *The First Military Escort on the Santa Fe Trail, 1829; From the Journal and Reports of Major Bennet Riley and Lieutenant Philip St. George Cooke*, revd., 331-32
Young Washington, by Douglas S. Freeman, 301

Zachary Taylor: Soldier of the Republic, by Holman Hamilton, noted, 608
Zangwill, Israel, playwright, 228
Zion's Watch Tower Society, 455